"AN INDEX
TO BOOK REVIEWS
IN THE HUMANITIES"

VOLUME 25
1984

PHILLIP THOMSON
WILLIAMSTON, MICHIGAN

This volume of the Index contains data collected up to 31 December 1984.

This is an index to book reviews in humanities periodicals. Beginning with volume 12 of this Index (dated 1971), the former policy of selectively indexing reviews of books in certain subject categories only was dropped in favor of a policy of indexing all reviews in the periodicals indexed, with the one exception of children's books — the reviews of which will not be indexed.

The form of the entries used is as follows:

Author. Title.
Reviewer. Identifying Legend.

The author's name used is the name that appears on the title-page of the book being reviewed, as well as we are able to determine, even though this name is known to be a pseudonym. The title only is shown; subtitles are included only where they are necessary to identify a book in a series. The identifying legend consists of the periodical, each of which has a code number, and the date and page number of the periodical where the review is to be found. PMLA abbreviations are also shown (when a periodical has such an abbreviation, but such abbreviations are limited to four letters) immediately following the code number of the periodical. To learn the name of the periodical in which the review appears, it is necessary to refer the code number to the numerically-arranged list of periodicals beginning on page iii. This list also shows the volume and number of the periodical issues indexed in this volume.

Reviews are indexed as they appear and no attempt is made to hold the title until all the reviews are published. For this reason it is necessary to refer to previous and subsequent volumes of this Index to be sure that the complete roster of reviews of any title is seen. As an aid to the user, an asterisk (*) has been added immediately following any title that was also indexed in Volume 24 (1983) of this Index.

Authors with hyphenated surnames are indexed under the name before the hyphen, and the name following the hyphen is not cross-indexed. Authors with more than one surname, but where the names are not hyphenated, are indexed under the first of the names and the last name is cross-indexed. When alphabetizing surnames containing umlauts, the umlauts are ignored. Editors are always shown in the author-title entry, and they are cross-indexed (except where the editor's surname is the same as that of the author). Translators are shown only when they are necessary to identify the book being reviewed (as in the classics), and they are not cross-indexed unless the book being reviewed has no author or editor. Certain reference works and anonymous works that are known primarily by their title are indexed under that title and their editors are cross-indexed.

A list of abbreviations used is shown on page ii.

ABBREVIATIONS

Anon.........Anonymous
Apr..........April
Aug..........August
Bk...........Book
Comp(s)......Compiler(s)
Cont.........Continued
Dec..........December
Ed(s)........Editor(s) [or] Edition(s)
Fasc.........Fascicule
Feb..........February
Jan..........January
Jul..........July
Jun..........June
Mar..........March
No...........Number
Nov..........November
Oct..........October
Prev.........Previous volume of this Index
Pt...........Part
Rev..........Revised
Sep..........September
Ser..........Series
Supp.........Supplement
Trans........Translator(s)
Vol..........Volume
* (asterisk)....This title was also shown
                in the volume of this Index
                immediately preceding this
                one

The periodicals in which the reviews appear are identified in this Index by a number. To supplement this number, and to promote ready identification, PMLA abbreviations are also given following this number. Every attempt will be made to index those issues shown here as "missing" in a later volume of this Index.

The following is a list of the periodicals indexed in volume 25:

89(BJA) – The British Journal of Aesthetics. Oxford.
　　Winter83 thru Autumn83 (vol 23 complete)
90 – Burlington Magazine. London.
　　Jan83 thru Dec83 (vol 125 complete)
95(CLAJ) – CLA Journal. Atlanta.
　　Sep83 thru Jun84 (vol 27 complete)
97(CQ) – The Cambridge Quarterly. Cambridge.
　　Vol 12 complete
98 – Critique. Paris.
　　Jan-Feb83 thru Dec83 (vol 39 complete)
99 – Canadian Forum. Toronto.
　　Apr83 thru Mar84 (vol 63 complete)
102(CanL) – Canadian Literature. Vancouver.
　　Winter82 thru Autumn83 (no 95-98)
104(CASS) – Canadian-American Slavic Studies/Revue canadienne-américaine d'études slaves. Irvine.
　　Spring83 thru Winter83 (vol 17 complete)
105 – Canadian Poetry. London, Ont.
　　Spring/Summer83 and Fall/Winter83 (no 12 and 13)
106 – The Canadian Review of American Studies. Winnipeg.
　　Spring83 thru Winter83 (vol 14 complete)
107(CRCL) – Canadian Review of Comparative Literature/Revue Canadienne de Littérature Comparée. South Edmonton.
　　Mar83 thru Dec83 (vol 10 complete)
108 – Canadian Theatre Review. Downsview.
　　Spring83 and Fall83 (no 37 and 38)
110 – Carolina Quarterly. Chapel Hill.
　　Fall83 thru Spring84 (vol 36 complete)
111 – Cauda Pavonis. Pullman.
　　Spring83 thru Fall84 (vols 2 and 3 complete)
112 – Celtica. Dublin.
　　Vol 15
114(ChiR) – Chicago Review. Chicago.
　　Summer83 and Spring84 (vol 34 no 1 and 2) [Summer83 (vol 33 no 4) done in prev should have been dated Spring83]
116 – Chinese Literature: Essays, Articles, Reviews. Madison.
　　Jan82 and Jul82 (vol 4 complete)
121(CJ) – Classical Journal. Greenville.
　　Oct/Nov83 thru Apr/May84 (vol 79 complete)
122 – Classical Philology. Chicago.
　　Jan83 thru Oct83 (vol 78 complete)
123 – Classical Review. London.
　　Vol 33 complete
124 – Classical World. Pittsburgh.
　　Sep/Oct83 thru Jul/Aug84 (vol 77 complete)
125 – Clio. Ft. Wayne.
　　Fall82 thru Summer83 (vol 12 complete)
127 – Art Journal. New York.
　　Spring83 thru Winter83 (vol 43 complete)
128(CE) – College English. Champaign.
　　Jan83 thru Dec83 (vol 45 complete)

129 – Commentary. New York.
　　Jan84 thru Dec84 (vols 77 and 78 complete)
130 – Comparative Drama. Kalamazoo.
　　Spring83 thru Winter83/84 (vol 17 complete)
131(CL) – Comparative Literature. Eugene.
　　Winter83 thru Fall83 (vol 35 complete)
133 – Colloquia Germanica. Bern.
　　Band 16 Heft 1 and Band 16 Heft 2/3
134(CP) – Concerning Poetry. Bellingham.
　　Spring83 and Fall83 (vol 16 complete)
135 – Connoisseur. New York.
　　Oct82 and Dec82, Jan83 thru Dec83 (no 848 and 850, no 851-862)
136 – Conradiana. Lubbock.
　　Vols 15 and 16 complete
137 – CV/II: Contemporary Verse Two. Winnipeg.
　　Nov82 thru Jan84 (vol 7 complete)
139 – American Craft. New York.
　　Dec82/Jan83 and Feb/Mar83 thru Dec83/Jan84 (vol 42 no 6 and vol 43 complete)
141 – Criticism. Detroit.
　　Winter83 thru Fall83 (vol 25 complete)
142 – Philosophy and Social Criticism. Chestnut Hill.
　　Spring82 thru Fall-Winter82 (vol 9 complete)
145(Crit) – Critique. Washington.
　　Vol 24 no 3, vol 24 no 4 and Fall83 thru Summer84 (vol 25 complete)
148 – Critical Quarterly. Manchester.
　　Spring83 thru Winter83 (vol 25 complete)
149(CLS) – Comparative Literature Studies. Champaign.
　　Spring83 thru Winter83 (vol 20 complete)
150(DR) – Dalhousie Review. Halifax.
　　Spring83 thru Winter83/84 (vol 63 complete)
151 – Dance Magazine. New York.
　　Feb81 thru Jun81, Jul82 thru Dec82 and Jan83 thru Jun83 (vol 55 no 2-6, vol 56 no 7-12, vol 57 no 1-6)
152(UDQ) – The Denver Quarterly. Denver.
　　Spring83 thru Winter84 (vol 18 complete)
153 – Diacritics. Baltimore.
　　Spring83 thru Winter83 (vol 13 complete)
154 – Dialogue. Waterloo.
　　Mar83 thru Dec83 (vol 22 complete)
155 – The Dickensian. London.
　　Spring83 thru Autumn83 (vol 79 complete)
156(JDSh) – Deutsche Shakespeare-Gesellschaft West Jahrbuch. Bochum.
　　Jahrbuch 83
157 – Drama/The Quarterly Theatre Review. London.
　　Spring83 thru Winter83 (no 147-150)
161(DUJ) – Durham University Journal.
　　Dec82 and Jun83 (vol 75 complete)

165(EAL) - Early American Literature.
Chapel Hill.
Fall83 thru Fall84 (vol 18 no 2
and 3, vol 19 no 1 and 2)
167 - Erkenntnis. Dordrecht.
May83 thru Nov83 (vols 19 and
20 complete)
168(ECW) - Essays on Canadian Writing.
Downsview.
Summer83 and Winter83/84 (no 26
and 27)
172(Edda) - Edda. Oslo.
1983/1 thru 1983/6 (vol 83 complete)
173(ECS) - Eighteenth-Century Studies.
Northfield.
Fall83 thru Spring84 (vol 17 no
1-3)
174(Éire) - Éire-Ireland. St. Paul.
Spring83 thru Winter83 (vol 18
complete)
175 - English. Oxford.
Spring83 thru Autumn83 (vol 32
complete)
176 - Encounter. London.
Jan84 thru Dec84 (vols 62 and 63
complete)
177(ELT) - English Literature in Transition. Tempe.
Vol 26 complete
178 - English Studies in Canada. Edmonton.
Mar83 thru Dec83 (vol 9 complete)
179(ES) - English Studies. Lisse.
Feb83 thru Dec83 (vol 64 complete)
181 - Epoch. Ithaca.
Fall-Winter83 thru Summer-Fall84
(Vol 33 complete)
183(ESQ) - ESQ: A Journal of the American
Renaissance. Pullman.
Vol 29 complete
184(EIC) - Essays in Criticism. Oxford.
Jan83 thru Oct83 (vol 33 complete)
185 - Ethics. Chicago.
Oct83 thru Jul84 (vol 94 complete)
186(ETC.) - ETC. San Francisco.
Spring83 thru Winter83 (vol 40
complete)
187 - Ethnomusicology. Ann Arbor.
Jan84 thru Sep84 (vol 28 complete)
188(ECr) - L'Esprit Créateur. Baton Rouge.
Spring83 thru Winter83 (vol 23 complete)
189(EA) - Etudes Anglaises. Paris.
Jan-Mar83 thru Oct-Dec84 (vols 36
and 37 complete)
191(ELN) - English Language Notes. Boulder.
Sep83 thru Jun84 (vol 21 complete)
192(EP) - Les Études Philosophiques. Paris.
Jan-Mar83 thru Oct-Dec83
193(ELit) - Études Littéraires. Québec.
Apr83 thru Dec83 (vol 16 complete)
196 - Fabula. Berlin.
Band 24 complete
198 - The Fiddlehead. Fredericton.
Jan83 thru Jan84 (no 135-138)
199 - Field. Oberlin.
Fall83 and Spring84 (no 29 and 30)
200 - Films in Review. New York.
Jan83 thru Dec83 (vol 34 complete)
203 - Folklore. London.
Vol 94 complete

204(FdL) - Forum der Letteren. Den Haag.
Mar82 thru Dec83 (vols 23 and 24
complete)
205(ForL) - Forum Linguisticum. Lake
Bluff.
Aug81 thru Apr82 (vol 6 complete)
207(FR) - French Review. Champaign.
Oct83 thru May84 (vol 57 complete)
208(FS) - French Studies. London.
Jan83 thru Oct83 (vol 37 complete)
209(FM) - Le Français Moderne. Paris.
Jan83 thru Oct83 (vol 51 complete)
210(FrF) - French Forum. Lexington.
Jan83 thru Sep83 (vol 8 complete)
214 - Gambit. London.
Vol 10 no 39/40 (no reviews indexed)
215(GL) - General Linguistics. University Park.
Spring83 thru Vol 23 no 4 (vol 23
complete)
219(GaR) - Georgia Review. Athens.
Spring83 thru Winter83 (vol 37 complete)
220(GL&L) - German Life and Letters.
Oxford.
Oct83 thru Jul84 (vol 37 complete)
221(GQ) - German Quarterly. Cherry Hill.
Jan83 thru Nov83 (vol 56 complete)
222(GR) - Germanic Review. Washington.
Winter83 thru Fall83 (vol 58 complete)
224(GRM) - Germanisch-Romanische Monats-
schrift. Heidelberg.
Band 33 Heft 1-3
228(GSLI) - Giornale storico della letteratura italiana. Torino.
Vol 160 complete
231 - Harper's Magazine. New York.
Jan84 thru Dec84 (vols 268 and 269
complete)
234 - The Hemingway Review. Ada.
Fall83 and Spring84 (vol 3 complete)
236 - The Hiram Poetry Review. Hiram.
Spring-Summer83 and Fall-Winter83
(no 34 and 35)
238 - Hispania. University.
Mar83 thru Dec83 (vol 66 complete)
240(HR) - Hispanic Review. Philadelphia.
Winter83 thru Autumn83 (vol 51 complete)
241 - Hispanófila. Chapel Hill.
Jan83 thru Sep83 (no 77-79)
244(HJAS) - Harvard Journal of Asiatic
Studies. Cambridge.
Jun83 and Dec83 (vol 43 complete)
249(HudR) - Hudson Review. New York.
Spring83 thru Winter83/84 (vol 36
complete)
250(HLQ) - The Huntington Library Quarterly. San Marino.
Winter83 thru Autumn83 (vol 46
complete)
256 - Humanities in Society. Los Angeles.
Winter83 thru Fall83 (vol 6 complete) (no reviews indexed)
257(IRAL) - IRAL: International Review of
Applied Linguistics in Language Teaching. Heidelberg.
Feb83 thru Nov83 (vol 21 complete)

258 - International Philosophical Quarterly. New York and Namur.
    Mar83 thru Dec83 (vol 23 complete)
259(IIJ) - Indo-Iranian Journal. Dordrecht.
    Jan83 thru Dec83 (vols 25 and 26
    complete)
260(IF) - Indogermanische Forschungen.
  Berlin.
    Band 87 and Band 88
261 - Indian Linguistics. Pune.
    Mar-Dec81 (vol 42)
262 - Inquiry. Oslo.
    Mar83 thru Dec83 (vol 26 complete)
263(RIB) - Revista Interamericana de Bibli-
  ografía/Inter-American Review of Bibliography. Washington.
    Vol 33 complete
268(IFR) - The International Fiction
  Review. Fredericton.
    Winter84 and Summer84 (vol 11 com-
    plete)
269(IJAL) - International Journal of American Linguistics. Chicago.
    Jan83 thru Oct83 (vol 49 complete)
271 - The Iowa Review. Iowa City.
    Vol 13 no 3/4
272(IUR) - Irish University Review. Dublin.
    Spring83 and Autumn83 (vol 13
    complete)
273(IC) - Islamic Culture. Hyderabad.
    Jan83 thru Oct83 (vol 57 complete)
276 - Italica. New York.
    Spring83 thru Winter83 (vol 60 com-
    plete)
278(IS) - Italian Studies. Hull.
    Vol 38
279 - International Journal of Slavic Linguistics and Poetics. Columbus.
    Vol 25 and 26, vol 27, vol 28
283 - Jabberwocky - The Journal of the
  Lewis Carroll Society. Burton-on-
  Trent.
    Summer81 and Autumn81, Summer82
    and Autumn82, Winter82/83 and
    Spring83 (vol 10 no 3 and 4, vol
    11 no 3 and 4, vol 12 no 1 and 2)
284 - The Henry James Review. Baton
  Rouge.
    Fall83 and Winter84 (vol 5 no 1
    and 2)
285(JapQ) - Japan Quarterly. Tokyo.
    Jan-Mar83 thru Oct-Dec83 (vol 30
    complete)
287 - Jewish Frontier. New York.
    Jan/Feb83 thru Dec83 (vol 50 com-
    plete)
289 - The Journal of Aesthetic Education.
  Urbana.
    Spring83 thru Winter83 (vol 17
    complete)
290(JAAC) - Journal of Aesthetics and
  Art Criticism. Greenvale.
    Fall83 thru Summer84 (vol 42 com-
    plete)
292(JAF) - Journal of American Folklore.
  Washington.
    Jan-Mar83 thru Oct-Dec83 (vol 96
    complete)
293(JASt) - Journal of Asian Studies. Ann
  Arbor.
    Nov82 thru Aug83 (vol 42 complete)

294 - Journal of Arabic Literature. Leiden.
    Vol 14
295(JML) - Journal of Modern Literature.
  Philadelphia.
    Mar83 thru Nov83 (vol 10 complete)
297(JL) - Journal of Linguistics. Cambridge.
    Mar83 and Sep83 (vol 19 complete)
298 - Journal of Canadian Studies/Revue
  d'études canadiennes. Peterborough.
    Spring83 thru Winter83/84 (vol 18
    complete)
300 - Journal of English Linguistics. Bellingham.
    Mar83 (vol 16)
301(JEGP) - Journal of English and Germanic
  Philology. Champaign.
    Jan83 thru Oct83 (vol 82 complete)
302 - Journal of Oriental Studies. Hong
  Kong.
    Vol 19 complete [entries in this
    periodical wholly in Chinese are
    not indexed]
303(JoHS) - Journal of Hellenic Studies.
  London.
    Vol 103
304(JHP) - Journal of Hispanic Philology.
  Tallahassee.
    Spring83 and Fall83 (vol 7 no 3,
    vol 8 no 1)
305(JIL) - The Journal of Irish Literature.
  Newark.
    Jan83 thru Sep83 (vol 12 complete)
307 - Journal of Literary Semantics. Heidelberg.
    Oct80, Oct82, Apr83 and Oct83 (vol
    9 no 2, vol 11 no 2, vol 12 com-
    plete)
308 - Journal of Music Theory. New Haven.
    Spring83 and Fall83 (vol 27 com-
    plete)
311(JP) - Journal of Philosophy. New York.
    Jan83 thru Dec83 (vol 80 complete)
313 - Journal of Roman Studies. London.
    Vol 73
314 - Journal of South Asian Literature.
  East Lansing.
    Winter-Spring83 and Summer-Fall83
    (vol 18 complete)
316 - Journal of Symbolic Logic. Pasadena.
    Mar83 thru Dec83 (vol 48 complete)
317 - Journal of the American Musicologi-
  cal Society. Philadelphia.
    Spring83 thru Fall83 (vol 36 com-
    plete)
318(JAOS) - Journal of the American
  Oriental Society. New Haven.
    Jan-Mar82 thru Oct-Dec82 (vol 102
    complete)
319 - Journal of the History of Philosophy.
  San Diego.
    Jan84 thru Oct84 (vol 22 complete)
320(CJL) - Canadian Journal of Linguistics.
  Ottawa.
    Spring83 and Fall83 (vol 28 com-
    plete)
321 - The Journal of Value Inquiry. The
  Hague.
    Vol 17 complete
322(JHI) - Journal of the History of Ideas.
  Philadelphia.
    Jan-Mar83 thru Oct-Dec83 (vol 44
    complete)

432(NEQ) – New England Quarterly. Boston.
Mar83 thru Dec83 (vol 56 complete)
434 – New England Review and Bread Loaf
Quarterly. Hanover.
Autumn83 thru Summer84 (vol 6
complete)
435 – New Orleans Review. New Orleans.
Spring83 thru Winter83 (vol 10
complete)
436(NewL) – New Letters. Kansas City.
Fall83 thru Summer84 (vol 50 complete)
439(NM) – Neuphilologische Mitteilungen.
Helsinki.
1983/1 thru 1983/4 (vol 84 complete)
441 – New York Times Book Review. New
York.
1Jan84 thru 30Dec84 (vol 89 complete)
442(NY) – New Yorker. New York.
2Jan84 thru 31Dec84 (vol 59 no 46-
52, vol 60 no 1-46) (vol 60 begins
with 20Feb84 issue)
445(NCF) – Nineteenth-Century Fiction.
Berkeley.
Jun83 thru Mar84 (vol 38 complete)
446(NCFS) – Nineteenth-Century French
Studies. Fredonia.
Fall-Winter83/84 and Spring84 (vol
12 no 1/2 and 3)
447(N&Q) – Notes and Queries. London.
Feb82 thru Dec82 (vol 29 complete)
448 – Northwest Review. Eugene.
Vol 21 complete
449 – Noûs. Bloomington.
Mar83 thru Nov83 (vol 17 complete)
450(NRF) – La Nouvelle Revue Française.
Paris.
Jan83 thru Dec83 (vols 61 and 62
complete)
451 – 19th Century Music. Berkeley.
Summer83 thru Apr84 (vol 7 complete)
453(NYRB) – The New York Review of Books.
New York.
19Jan84 thru 20Dec84 (vol 30 no
21/22 and vol 31 no 1-20)
454 – Novel. Providence.
Fall83 thru Spring84 (vol 17 complete)
457(NRFH) – Nueva Revista de Filología
Hispánica. Mexico City.
Tomo31núm1 and Tomo31núm2
460(OhR) – The Ohio Review. Athens.
No 32
461 – The Ontario Review. Princeton.
Spring/Summer83 and Fall/Winter83/
84 (no 18 and 19)
462(OL) – Orbis Litterarum. Copenhagen.
Vols 37 and 38 complete
463 – Oriental Art. Richmond.
Spring83 thru Winter83/84 (vol 29
complete)
468 – Paideuma. Orono.
Spring83 and Fall/Winter83 (vol 12
complete)
469 – Parabola. New York.
Vol 9 complete
471 – Pantheon. München.
Jan/Feb/Mar83 thru Oct/Nov/Dec83
(vol 41 complete)

472 – Parnassus: Poetry in Review. New
York.
Fall/Winter83&Spring/Summer84 (vol
11 no 2)
473(PR) – Partisan Review. Boston.
1/1983 thru 4/1983 (vol 50 complete)
474(PIL) – Papers in Linguistics. Edmonton.
Vol 15 no 1/4
475 – Papers on French Seventeenth Century
Literature. Seattle and Tübingen.
Vol 10 no 18 and 19
477(PLL) – Papers on Language and Literature. Edwardsville.
Winter83 thru Fall83 (vol 19 complete)
478 – Philosophy and Literature. Baltimore.
Apr83 and Oct83 (vol 7 complete)
479(PhQ) – Philosophical Quarterly.
Oxford.
Jan83 thru Oct83 (vol 33 complete)
480(P&R) – Philosophy and Rhetoric. University Park.
Vol 16 complete
481(PQ) – Philological Quarterly. Iowa
City.
Winter83 thru Fall83 (vol 62 complete)
482(PhR) – Philosophical Review. Ithaca.
Jan83 thru Oct83 (vol 92 complete)
483 – Philosophy. Cambridge.
Oct81 and Jan83 thru Oct83 (vol 56
no 218 and vol 58 complete)
484(PPR) – Philosophy and Phenomenological
Research. Providence.
Sep83 thru Jun84 (vol 44 complete)
485(PE&W) – Philosophy East and West.
Honolulu.
Jan83 thru Oct83 (vol 33 complete)
486 – Philosophy of Science. East Lansing.
Mar83 thru Dec83 (vol 50 complete)
487 – Phoenix. Toronto.
Spring83 thru Winter83 (vol 37 complete)
488 – Philosophy of the Social Sciences.
Waterloo.
Mar83 thru Dec83 (vol 13 complete)
489(PJGG) – Philosophisches Jahrbuch.
Freiburg.
Band 90 complete
491 – Poetry. Chicago.
Apr83 thru Mar84 (vols 142 and
143 complete)
493 – Poetry Review. London.
Mar83 thru Sep83 (vol 73 no 1-3)
494 – Poetics Today. Jerusalem.
Vol 4 no 2-4 (vol 4 no 1 missing)
495(PoeS) – Poe Studies. Pullman.
Jun83 and Dec83 (vol 16 complete)
497(PolR) – Polish Review. New York.
Vol 28 complete
498 – Popular Music and Society. Bowling
Green.
Vol 9 no 1 and 2
500 – Post Script. Jacksonville.
Fall83 thru Spring/Summer84 (vol 3
complete)
502(PrS) – Prairie Schooner. Lincoln.
Spring83 thru Winter83 (vol 57
complete)

503 - The Private Library. Pinner.
  Spring83 thru Autumn83 (vol 6
  no 1-3)
505 - Progressive Architecture. New York.
  Jan83 thru Dec83 (vol 64 complete)
506(PSt) - Prose Studies. London.
  May83 thru Dec83 (vol 6 complete)
513 - Perspectives of New Music. Seattle.
  Fall-Winter81/Spring-Summer82 and
  Fall-Winter82/Spring-Summer83 (vol
  20 no 1/2 and vol 21 no 1/2)
517(PBSA) - Papers of the Bibliographical
  Society of America. New York.
  Oct-Dec80 (vol 74 no 4) and Vol
  77 complete
518 - Philosophical Books. Oxford.
  Jan83 thru Oct83 (vol 24 complete)
519(PhS) - Philosophical Studies. Dordrecht.
  Jan83 thru Nov83 (vols 43 and 44
  complete)
520 - Phronesis. Assen.
  Vol 28 complete
526 - Quarry. Kingston.
  Winter83 thru Autumn83 (vol 32 complete)
529(QQ) - Queen's Quarterly. Kingston.
  Spring83 thru Winter83 (vol 90
  complete)
535(RHL) - Revue d'Histoire Littéraire de
  la France. Paris.
  Jan-Feb83 thru Sep-Dec83 (vol 83
  complete)
537 - Revue de Musicologie. Paris.
  Vol 69 complete
539 - Renaissance and Reformation/Renais-
  sance et Réforme. Mississauga.
  Nov83 thru Aug84 (vol 7 no 4, vol
  8 no 1-3)
540(RIPh) - Revue Internationale de Philosophie. Wetteren.
  Vol 37 complete
541(RES) - Review of English Studies. London.
  Feb83 thru Nov83 (vol 34 complete)
542 - Revue Philosophique de la France et
  de l'Étranger. Paris.
  Jan-Mar83 thru Oct-Dec83 (vol 173
  complete)
543 - Review of Metaphysics. Washington.
  Sep82 thru Jun83 (vol 36 complete)
545(RPh) - Romance Philology. Berkeley.
  Aug82 thru May83 (vol 36 complete)
546(RR) - Romanic Review. New York.
  Jan83 thru Nov83 (vol 74 complete)
547(RF) - Romanische Forschungen. Frankfurt am Main.
  Band 95 complete
549(RLC) - Revue de Littérature Comparée.
  Paris.
  Jan-Mar83 thru Oct-Dec83 (vol 57
  complete)
550(RusR) - Russian Review. Stanford.
  Jan83 thru Oct83 (vol 42 complete)
551(RenQ) - Renaissance Quarterly. New
  York.
  Spring83 thru Winter83 (vol 36
  complete)
552(REH) - Revista de estudios hispánicos.
  University.
  Jan83 thru Oct83 (vol 17 complete)

553(RLiR) - Revue de Linguistique Romane.
  Strasbourg.
  Jan-Jun83 and Jul-Sep83 (vol 47
  complete)
554 - Romania. Paris.
  Vol 103 complete
555 - Revue de Philologie. Paris.
  Vol 57 complete
556 - Russell. Hamilton.
  Summer83 and Winter83/84 (vol 3
  complete)
558(RLJ) - Russian Language Journal. East
  Lansing.
  Winter-Spring83 and Fall83 (vol
  37 complete)
559 - Russian Linguistics. Dordrecht.
  Vol 7 complete
560 - Salmagundi. Saratoga Springs.
  Spring-Summer83 and Fall83 (no 60
  and 61)
561(SFS) - Science-Fiction Studies.
  Montréal.
  Mar83 thru Nov83 (vol 10 complete)
562(Scan) - Scandinavica. Norwich.
  May82 thru Nov83 (vols 21 and 22
  complete)
563(SS) - Scandinavian Studies. Lawrence.
  Winter83 thru Autumn83 (vol 55
  complete)
564 - Seminar. Toronto.
  Feb83 thru Nov83 (vol 19 complete)
565 - Stand Magazine. Newcastle upon
  Tyne.
  Vol 24 complete
566 - The Scriblerian. Philadelphia.
  Autumn83 and Spring84 (vol 16
  complete)
567 - Semiotica. Amsterdam.
  Vols 42-45 complete
568(SCN) - Seventeenth-Century News.
  University Park.
  Spring-Summer82 thru Winter83 (vol
  41 complete)
569(SR) - Sewanee Review. Sewanee.
  Winter83 thru Fall83 (vol 91 complete)
570(SQ) - Shakespeare Quarterly. Washington.
  Spring83 thru Winter83 (vol 34 complete)
571(ScLJ) - Scottish Literary Journal.
  Aberdeen.
  May83 and Dec83 (vol 10 complete
  plus supps 18 and 19)
572 - Shaw: The Annual of Bernard Shaw
  Studies. University Park.
  Vol 4
573(SSF) - Studies in Short Fiction. New-
  berry.
  Winter83 thru Fall83 (vol 20 complete)
574(SEEJ) - Slavic and East European
  Journal. Tucson.
  Spring83 thru Winter83 (vol 27
  complete)
575(SEER) - Slavonic and East European
  Review. London.
  Jan83 thru Oct83 (vol 61 complete)
576 - Journal of the Society of Architectural Historians. Philadelphia.
  Mar83 thru Dec83 (vol 42 complete)

577(SHR) - Southern Humanities Review.
Auburn.
Winter83 thru Fall83 (vol 17 complete)
578 - Southern Literary Journal. Chapel
Hill.
Spring84 and Fall84 (vol 16 no 2,
vol 17 no 1)
579(SAQ) - South Atlantic Quarterly. Durham.
Winter83 thru Autumn83 (vol 82
complete)
580(SCR) - The South Carolina Review.
Clemson.
Fall83 and Spring84 (vol 16 complete)
581 - Southerly. Marrickville.
Mar83 thru Dec83 (vol 43 complete)
582(SFQ) - Southern Folklore Quarterly.
Gainesville.
Vol 44
583 - Southern Speech Communication Journal. Tampa.
Fall83 thru Summer84 (vol 49 complete)
584(SWR) - Southwest Review. Dallas.
Winter83 thru Autumn83 (vol 68 complete)
585(SoQ) - The Southern Quarterly. Hattiesburg.
Fall82 thru Summer83 (vol 21 complete)
587(SAF) - Studies in American Fiction.
Boston.
Spring83 and Autumn83 (vol 11 complete)
588(SSL) - Studies in Scottish Literature.
Columbia.
Vol 18
589 - Speculum. Cambridge.
Jan83 thru Oct83 (vol 58 complete)
590 - Studies in the Humanities. Indiana.
Dec83 and Jun84 (vol 10 no 2 and
vol 11 no 1)
591(SIR) - Studies in Romanticism. Boston.
Spring83 thru Winter83 (vol 22 complete)
592 - Studio International. London.
Jan-Feb83 thru vol 196 no 1003
(vol 196 complete)
593 - Symposium. Washington.
Spring83 thru Winter83/84 (vol 37
complete)
594 - Studies in the Novel. Denton.
Spring83 thru Winter83 (vol 15
complete)
595(ScS) - Scottish Studies. Edinburgh.
Vol 26
596(SL) - Studia Linguistica. Lund.
Vol 37 complete
597(SN) - Studia Neophilologica. Stockholm.
Vol 55 complete
598(SoR) - The Southern Review. Baton
Rouge.
Winter84 thru Autumn84 (vol 20 complete)
599 - Style. De Kalb.
Winter83 thru Summer/Fall83 (vol
17 complete)
600 - Simiolus. Utrecht.
Vol 13 complete

602 - Sprachkunst. Vienna.
Vol 14 (no reviews indexed)
603 - Studies in Language. Amsterdam.
Vol 7 complete
604 - Spenser Newsletter. Albany.
Winter83 thru Fall83 (vol 14 complete)
605(SC) - Stendhal Club. Grenoble.
15Oct83 thru 15Jul84 (vol 26 complete)
606 - Synthese. Dordrecht.
Jan83 thru Dec83 (vols 54-57 complete)
607 - Tempo. London.
Mar83 thru Dec83 (no 144-147)
608 - TESOL Quarterly. Washington.
Mar84 thru Dec84 (vol 18 complete)
609 - Theater. New Haven.
Fall/Winter81 and Winter83 thru
Summer/Fall83 (vol 13 no 1, vol
15 complete)
610 - Theatre Research International.
Oxford.
Winter81/82 thru Autumn83 (vols
7 and 8 complete)
611(TN) - Theatre Notebook. London.
Vol 37 complete
612(ThS) - Theatre Survey. Albany.
May/Nov83 (vol 24 no 1/2)
613 - Thought. Bronx.
Mar83 thru Dec83 (vol 58 complete)
614 - The Textile Booklist. Lopez Island.
Winter84 thru Fall84 (vol 9 complete)
615(TJ) - Theatre Journal. Baltimore.
May82, Oct82 and Mar83 thru Dec83
(vol 34 no 2 and 3, vol 35 complete) [Mar82 and Dec82 issues
missing]
617(TLS) - Times Literary Supplement.
London.
6Jan84 thru 28Dec84 (no 4214-4265)
619 - Transactions of the Charles S.
Peirce Society.
Winter83 thru Fall83 (vol 19 complete)
627(UTQ) - University of Toronto Quarterly.
Toronto.
Fall82 thru Summer83 (vol 52 complete) [in Summer issue, only the
"Humanities" section is indexed]
636(VP) - Victorian Poetry. Morgantown.
Spring83 thru Winter83 (vol 21 complete)
637(VS) - Victorian Studies. Bloomington.
Autumn82 thru Summer83 (vol 26
complete)
639(VQR) - Virginia Quarterly Review.
Charlottesville.
Winter83 thru Autumn83 (vol 59
complete)
646 - Walt Whitman Quarterly Review.
Iowa City.
Jun83 thru Mar84 (vol 1 complete)
648(WCR) - West Coast Review. Burnaby.
Jun83 thru Apr84 (vol 18 complete)
649(WAL) - Western American Literature.
Logan.
May83 thru Feb84 (vol 18 complete)
650(WF) - Western Folklore. Glendale.
Jan83 thru Oct83 (vol 42 complete)

651(WHR) - Western Humanities Review.
Salt Lake City.
Spring83 thru Winter83 (vol 37
complete)
654(WB) - Weimarer Beiträge. Berlin.
1/1982 thru 12/1983 (vols 28 and
29 complete)
656(WMQ) - William and Mary Quarterly.
Williamsburg.
Jan83 thru Oct83 (vol 40 complete)
658 - Winterthur Portfolio. Chicago.
Spring83 thru Winter83 (vol 18
complete)
659(ConL) - Contemporary Literature.
Madison.
Spring84 thru Winter84 (vol 25 complete)
660(Word) - Word. Elmont.
Apr83 thru Dec83 (vol 34 complete)
661(WC) - The Wordsworth Circle. Philadelphia.
Winter83 thru Autumn83 (vol 14 complete)
676(YR) - Yale Review. New Haven.
Autumn83 thru Summer84 (vol 73
complete)
677(YES) - The Yearbook of English Studies.
London.
Vol 13
678(YCGL) - Yearbook of Comparative and
General Literature. Bloomington.
No 31
679 - Zeitschrift für allgemeine Wissenschaftstheorie. Wiesbaden.
Band 14 complete
680(ZDP) - Zeitschrift für deutsche Philologie. Berlin.
Band 102 complete
682(ZPSK) - Zeitschrift für Phonetik,
Sprachwissenschaft und Kommunikations-
forschung. Berlin.
Band 36 complete
683 - Zeitschrift für Kunstgeschichte.
München.
Band 46 complete
684(ZDA) - Zeitschrift für deutsches Alter-
tum und deutsche Literatur [Anzeiger
section]. Wiesbaden.
Band 112 complete
685(ZDL) - Zeitschrift für Dialektologie
und Linguistik. Wiesbaden.
1/1983 thru 3/1983 (vol 50 complete)
687 - Zeitschrift für Philosophische Forschung. Meisenheim/Glan.
Jan-Mar83 thru Oct-Dec83 (Band
37 complete)
688(ZSP) - Zeitschrift für slavische
Philologie. Heidelberg.
Band 43 Heft 2
701(SinN) - Sin Nombre. San Juan.
Oct-Dec82 thru Jul-Sep83 (vol 13
complete)
702 - Shakespeare Studies. New York.
Vol 16

Each year we are unable (for one reason
or another) to index the reviews appearing
in all of the periodicals scanned. The
following is a list of the periodicals
whose reviews were not included in this
volume of the Index. Every attempt will
be made to index these reviews in the next
volume of the Index:

73 - Art Magazine. Toronto.
113 - Centrum. Minneapolis.
180(ESA) - English Studies in Africa.
Johannesburg.
255(HAB) - Humanities Association Review/
La Revue de l'Association des Humani-
tés. Kingston.
277(ITL) - ITL, a Review of Applied Linguistics. Leuven.
296(JCF) - Journal of Canadian Fiction.
Guelph.
299 - Journal of Beckett Studies. London.
326 - Journal of the William Morris Society. London.
360(LP) - Lingua Posnaniensis. Poznań.
376 - Malahat Review. Victoria.
379(MedR) - Medioevo romanzo. Bologna.
380 - Master Drawings. New York.
384 - Merkur. Stuttgart.
403(MLS) - Modern Language Studies. New
York.
404 - Modern Haiku. Madison.
459 - Obsidian. Detroit.
476 - Performing Arts Review. Washington.
492 - Poetics. Amsterdam.
496 - Poet Lore. Washington.
504 - Praxis. Los Angeles.
507 - Print. New York.
538(RAL) - Research in African Literatures.
Austin.
586(SoRA) - Southern Review. Adelaide.
601(SuF) - Sinn und Form. Berlin.
628(UWR) - University of Windsor Review.
Windsor.
675(YER) - Yeats Eliot Review. Edmonton.
700 - Shenandoah. Lexington.
703 - Sulfur. Los Angeles.

Adcock, F. Selected Poems.*
    C. Boyle, 364:Dec83/Jan84-120
    J. Mole, 176:Mar84-48
    C. Rawson, 493:Sep83-58
Addis, P.K. Through a Women's I.
    D.W. Meredith, 87(BB):Sep83-195
Addison, J. The Freeholder.* (J. Leheny,
    ed)
    O. Smith, 447(N&Q):Feb82-80
Addison, J. and R. Steele. Selections
    from "The Tatler" and "The Spectator" of
    Steele and Addison.* (A. Ross, ed)
    A. Bony, 189(EA):Apr-Jun84-194
Addison, W. Local Styles of the English
    Parish Church.
    D. Guinness, 576:Dec83-390
Adelson, D. Operation Susannah.
    S. Bray, 390:Oct83-63
Adelson, L. and A. Tracht. Aymara Weav-
    ings.
    B. Femenias, 614:Winter84-16
Adgar. Le Gracial. (P. Kunstmann, ed)
    F. Collins, 627(UTQ):Summer83-453
Adi-Rubin, M. Israeli Yemenite Embroidery.
    P. Bach, 614:Spring84-24
Adler, A. Am Stillen Herd...
    F. Betz, 221(GQ):Jan83-117
Adler, B. and T. Chastain. The Revenge of
    the Robbins Family.
    J. Kaufman, 441:2Sep84-14
Adler, E. and R. Needlepoint.
    P. Bach, 614:Summer84-23
Adler, R. Pitch Dark.*
    J. Epstein, 129:Jun84-62
    M. Hofmann, 617(TLS):20Jul84-817
    J. Mellors, 362:23Aug84-27
    R. Shattuck, 453(NYRB):15Mar84-3
    S. Simmons, 231:Feb84-76
Adler, S. The Study of Orchestration.
    P. Standford, 415:Jun83-361
Adler, W. Corpus Rubenianum Ludwig Bur-
    chard. (Pt 18, Vol 1)
    G. Martin, 90:Mar83-165
Adler, W. Random Hearts.
    M. Berkley, 441:6May84-26
Admoni, W.G. Zur Ausbildung der Norm der
    deutschen Literatursprache im Bereich
    des neuhochdeutschen Satzgefüges (1470-
    1730).
    J. Scharnhorst, 682(ZPSK):Band36Heft4-
    463
Adomeit, R.E. Three Centuries of Thumb
    Bibles.
    G. Dawson, 517(PBSA):Vol77No1-108
Adorni, S. and K. Primorac. English Gram-
    mar for Students of Italian.
    T. Boli, 276:Autumn83-296
Adorno, T. In Search of Wagner.*
    J. Deathridge, 451:Summer83-81
Adorno, T. and others. The Positivist
    Dispute in German Sociology.
    E. Gellner, 84:Jun83-173
Adorno, T.W. Against Epistemology.
    A. Reix, 542:Oct-Dec83-490
Adorno, T.W. Prisms.*
    R.C. Holub, 221(GQ):Mar83-285
Adrados, F.R. Historia de la fábula greco-
    latina. (Vol 1)
    J. Henderson, 303(JoHS):Vol 103-188
Adrados, F.R., ed and trans. Líricos
    griegos, Elegiacos y Yambógrafos arca-
                                  [continued]

[continuing]
icos (siglos VII-V a.C.).
    D. Arnould, 555:Vol57fasc1-119
    S.R. Slings, 394:Vol36fasc3/4-393
Adrados, F.R. El mundo de la lírica griega
    antiqua.*
    A.M. Bowie, 303(JoHS):Vol 103-183
    S.R. Slings, 394:Vol36fasc3/4-393
Adrados, F.R. Orígenes de la lírica
    griega.
    S.R. Slings, 394:Vol36fasc3/4-393
Adrados, F.R. Sprache und Bedeutung.
    G.F. Meier, 682(ZPSK):Band36Heft4-465
Adriani, G. Cézanne Watercolors.
    P-L. Adams, 61:Mar84-133
Aebersold, D. Céline, un démystificateur
    mythomane.
    L. Davis, 208(FS):Oct83-484
Aers, D. Chaucer, Langland, and the Cre-
    ative Imagination.*
    P.M. Kean, 402(MLR):Apr83-424
    B. Nolan, 589:Jan83-139
    A.V.C. Schmidt, 184(EIC):Jul83-238
Aers, D., J. Cook and D. Punter. Romanti-
    cism and Ideology.*
    C. Clausen, 569(SR):Fall83-672
    T.M. Kelley, 661(WC):Summer83-127
Aers, D., B. Hodge and G. Kress. Litera-
    ture, Language and Society in England,
    1580-1680.*
    G. Hammond, 148:Autumn83-79
    R. Helgerson, 131(CL):Fall83-362
    R. Howell, Jr., 366:Autumn83-265
Aeschylus. L'Agamemnon d'Eschyle. (Vol 1)
    (J. Bollack and P. Judet de la Combe,
    eds)
    A.F. Garvie, 303(JoHS):Vol 103-162
Aeschylus. The Oresteia.* (T. Harrison,
    trans)
    J. Fontenrose, 124:Sep-Oct83-53
Aeschylus - see under Johansen, H.F. and
    E.W. Whittle
Affron, C. Cinema and Sentiment.
    M.A. Anderegg, 385(MQR):Spring84-281
    C. Eidsvik, 141:Summer83-288
Agassi, J. Science and Society.*
    R.N.D. Martin, 486:Jun83-345
Agassi, J.B. Women on the Job.
    M.P. Maxwell, 488:Dec83-532
Agazzi, E., ed. Modern Logic — a Survey.
    R.R. Rockingham Gill, 393(Mind):Apr83-
    286
Ageyev, M. Novel with Cocaine.
    H. Benedict, 441:25Nov84-26
Aggarwal, N.K., comp. English in South
    Asia.
    C.L. Nelson, 350:Jun84-459
Agosín, M. Conchalí.
    A. Natella, Jr., 701(SinN):Jul-Sep83-
    91
El-Agraa, A.M., ed. Britain Within the
    European Community.
    E. Roll, 617(TLS):27Jan84-79
Agrawala, P.K. Śrīvatsa.
    C.R. Bolon, 57:Vol44No4-330
Agresti, M.S. Literatura y realidades.
    M.I. Lichtblau, 263(RIB):Vol33No1-33
Agresto, J. and P. Riesenberg, eds. The
    Humanist as Citizen.
    J.S. Allen, 569(SR):Summer83-426
Aguilar Fernández, R.M. La Noción del
    Alma Personal en Plutarco.
    D.A. Russell, 123:Vol33No2-316

3

Aguilar Piñal, F. Bibliografía de autores
españolas del siglo XVIII. Índice de
las poesías publicadas en los periódicos
españolas del siglo XVIII.
I.L. McClelland, 86(BHS):Apr83-154
Aguinaga, C.B., J. Rodríguez Puertolas
and I.M. Závala - see under Blanco
Aguinaga, C., J. Rodríguez Puertolas and
I.M. Závala
Aguirre, J.M. - see Zayas, A.
Agulhon, M. Marianne into Battle.*
A. Rifkin, 59:Sep83-368
Agulhon, M. The Republican Experiment,
1848-1852.
R.N. Gildea, 617(TLS):2Mar84-229
Ahearn, B. Zukofsky's "A."
N. Wheale, 617(TLS):20Jul84-806
Ahearn, E.J. Rimbaud.
C. Scott, 617(TLS):29Jun84-730
Ahern, E.M. and H. Gates, eds. The Anthro-
pology of Taiwanese Society.
E. Cooper, 293(JASt):Nov82-119
Ahern, T. Hecatombs of Lake.
W. Ferguson, 441:5Aug84-18
Ahern, T. - see Joyce, J.
Ahlgrimm, I. and B. Billeter - see Hartung,
P.C.
Ahlmo-Nilsson, B., S. Göransson and H-E.
Johannesson, eds. Perspektiv på prosa.
K. Petherick, 562(Scan):May83-94
Ahlqvist, A., ed. Papers from the 5th
International Conference on Historical
Linguistics.
M.E. Winters, 350:Dec84-984
Ahmad, S. The Third Notch and Other
Stories.
M.H. Salleh, 293(JASt):Aug83-1008
Aichinger, I. Selected Poetry and Prose.
(A.H. Chappel, ed and trans)
S. Friebert, 199:Spring84-64
Aichinger, P. - see de Lorimier, C-N-G.
Aid, F.M., M.C. Resnick and B. Saciuk, eds.
1975 Colloquium on Hispanic Linguistics.
R. de Gorog, 545(RPh):Nov82-242
Aidala, T.R. and C. Bruce. Hearst Castle:
San Simeon.
L.G. Bowman, 658:Summer/Autumn83-225
Aiello, L. The Prentice-Hall Concise Book
of the Origins of Man.
529(QQ):Spring83-282
Aigner Foresti, L. Der Ostalpenraum und
Italien.
L. Bonfante, 24:Fall83-312
Aiken, J. Mansfield Revisited.
L. Duguid, 617(TLS):26Oct84-1224
Aikman, L. Rider With Destiny.
J.K. Davison, 441:15Jan84-19
Ailman, H.B. Pioneering in Territorial
Silver City. (H.J. Lundwell, ed)
L. Milazzo, 584(SWR):Summer83-vi
Aird, C. Harm's Way.
T.J.B., 617(TLS):16Nov84-1301
Aitchison, J. Language Change.*
D. Denison, 297(JL):Sep83-503
Aitken, A.J. and T. McArthur. Languages
of Scotland.*
G. Melchers, 597(SN):Vol55No2-199
Aitmatov, C. The Day Lasts More Than a
Hundred Years.*
442(NY):23Apr84-129
Aïtmatov, T. Une journée plus longue
qu'un siècle.
J-L.G., 450(NRF):Apr83-145

Aitzetmüller, R. Altbulgarische Grammatik
als Einführung in die slavische Sprach-
wissenschaft.
J. Udolph, 260(IF):Band87-364
Akers, C.W. The Divine Politician.
R.D. Brown, 656(WMQ):Apr83-321
J.A. Schutz, 432(NEQ):Jun83-297
Akhmadi, H. - see under Heri Akhmadi
Akhmatova, A. Poems. (L. Coffin, trans)
J. Bayley, 453(NYRB):19Jan84-21
H. Gifford, 617(TLS):9Mar84-250
D. McDuff, 472:Fall/Winter83Spring/
Summer84-51
Akhmedov, I. In and Out of Stalin's GRU.
J.M. Elukin, 441:30Sep84-29
"Akicita."
R.L. Shep, 614:Fall84-12
Akillian, M. The Eating of Names.
J. Silkin, 617(TLS):31Aug84-962
Akmajian, A. and F. Heny. An Introduction
to the Principles of Transformational
Syntax.
J. Casagrande, 205(ForL):Aug81-92
Akrigg, G.P.V. - see King James VI and I
Aksyonov, V. The Burn.
J. Bayley, 453(NYRB):22Nov84-28
G. Hosking, 617(TLS):2Nov84-1238
A. Shub, 441:25Nov84-12
Aksyonov, V. The Island of Crimea.*
J. Bayley, 453(NYRB):22Nov84-28
"Akten zur deutschen auswärtigen Politik,
1918-1945." (Ser B, Vols 16 and 17)
F.L. Carsten, 575(SEER):Jul83-459
Alan of Lille. The Plaint of Nature.*
(J.J. Sheridan, ed and trans)
G. Constable, 543:Jun83-913
Alanen, L. Studies in Cartesian Episte-
mology and Philosophy of Mind.
J-M. Beyssade, 542:Oct-Dec83-465
Alarcón, C.S. - see under Saco Alarcón, C.
de Alarcón, P.A. El sombrero de tres
picos. (L. Bonet, ed)
C. De Coster, 240(HR):Autumn83-472
Alarcos Llorach, E. Anatomía de "La lucha
por la vida."
J. Matas, 240(HR):Autumn83-475
Alas, L. Clarín político. (Vol 1) (Y.
Lissorgues, ed)
N.M. Valis, 240(HR):Summer83-336
Alas, L. His Only Son. (J. Jones, ed and
trans)
M-E. Bravo, 552(REH):Jan83-147
Alas, L. La Regenta. (J. Rutherford,
trans)
J. Bayley, 362:8Mar84-21
R. Carr, 617(TLS):1Jun84-607
R.P. Mills, 441:25Mar84-20
Alas, L. La Regenta. (G. Sobejano, ed)
R.B. Klein, 238:Sep83-434
J. Rutherford, 86(BHS):Jan83-89
N.M. Valis, 240(HR):Winter83-110
Alas, L. Su único hijo.* (C. Richmond,
ed)
R.M. Jackson, 238:May83-296
Albano Leoni, F., ed. Tre glossari longo-
bardo-latini.
N. Wagner, 684(ZDA):Band112Heft1-5
Alber, C.J. - see Semanov, V.I.
Alberoni, F. Le choc amoureux.
L. Paquet, 193(ELit):Dec83-473
Alberoni, F. Falling in Love.
E. Segal, 441:12Feb84-15

Alberti, R. Antología poética. (N. Cala-
mai, ed)
  M. Junquera, 552(REH):May83-313
Albi, J. Joan de Joanes y sus círculos
artísticos.
  D. Angulo Íñiguez, 48:Jan-Mar79-90
Alblas, J.B.H. and R. Todd, eds. From Cax-
ton to Beckett.
  H. Wilcox, 447(N&Q):Apr82-172
de Albornoz, A., ed. Juan Ramón Jiménez.
  D. Harris, 86(BHS):Jan83-90
  J.C. Wilcox, 240(HR):Autumn83-476
de Albornoz, A. - see Jiménez, J.R.
Albrecht, M. Kants Antinomie der prakti-
schen Vernunft.*
  A. Winter, 342:Band74Heft3-364
Albrecht von Eyb. Ob einem manne sey
zunemen ein eelichs weyb oder nicht.
  M. Dallapiazza, 684(ZDA):112Heft3-135
Albright, D. Representation and the Imag-
ination.*
  M.C., 189(EA):Apr-Jun84-234
  P. Lawley, 402(MLR):Jul83-660
Alcaide, V.N. - see under Nieto Alcaide, V.
Alcock, N.W. Cruck Construction.
  R. Brunskill, 44:Vol26-105
  L.T. Courtenay, 576:May83-199
Alcover, M. Poullain de La Barre.*
  J. Barchilon, 207(FR):Oct83-107
"Alcuin: The Bishops, Kings, and Saints of
York." (P. Godman, ed)
  H. Mayr-Harting, 617(TLS):29Jun84-720
Alden, J., with D.C. Landis, eds. Euro-
pean Americana.* (Vol 1)
  H.P. Williams, 70:Mar-Apr82-126
Alden, J. and D.C. Landis, eds. European
Americana.* (Vol 2)
  D.B. Quinn, 551(RenQ):Winter83-586
Alden, J.R. Stephen Sayre.
  D.J.R. Bruckner, 441:8Jan84-19
Alden, J.R. George Washington.
  P. Anderson, 441:5Aug84-9
  M. Cunliffe, 453(NYRB):11Oct84-47
Alden, M.J. Bronze Age Population Fluctua-
tions in the Argolid from the Evidence
of Mycenaean Tombs.
  S. Hood, 123:Vol33No2-354
  C. Runnels, 487:Summer83-178
Alderson, B. - see Darton, F.J.H.
Alderson, J. Law and Disorder.
  L. Taylor, 617(TLS):21Sep84-1046
Aldgate, A. Cinema and History.
  M.T. Isenberg, 488:Mar83-118
Aldington, R. and L. Durrell. Literary
Lifelines.* (I.S. MacNiven and H.T.
Moore, eds)
  C. Guillemard, 189(EA):Jan-Mar84-109
Aldiss, B. Seasons in Flight.
  D. Montrose, 617(TLS):23Nov84-1358
Aldiss, B. This World and Nearer Ones.*
  C. Fredericks, 561(SFS):Nov83-346
Aldiss, B.W. Helliconia Summer.* Hellico-
nia Spring.
  G. Jonas, 441:26Feb84-31
Aldridge, A.O. Early American Literature.
  R. Asselineau, 189(EA):Jul-Sep84-351
  R.A. Bosco, 432(NEQ):Dec83-588
  N.S. Grabo, 27(AL):Oct83-453
  R.H. Pearce, 165(EAL):Fall84-217
Aldridge, J.W. The American Novel and the
Way We Live Now.*
  R.F. Lucid, 385(MQR):Spring84-289
                              [continued]

[continuing]
  T. Schaub, 27(AL):Oct83-452
  J.J. Waldmeir, 395(MFS):Winter83-750
  295(JML):Nov83-411
Aldridge, M.V. English Quantifiers.*
  Masatake Muraki, 474(PIL):Vol 25No1/4-
  311
Aldwell, E. and C. Schachter. Harmony and
Voice Leading.
  D.L. Brodbeck, 513:Fall-Winter82/
  Spring-Summer83-425
Aldyne, N. Slate.
  N. Callendar, 441:22Jul84-32
Alegría, C. Flowers from the Volcano
(Flores del Volcán).
  C. Wright, 448:Vol21No2/3-175
Alegría, F., ed. Chilean Writers in
Exile.*
  R.L. Acevedo, 238:May83-303
Aleichem, S. In the Storm.
  G. Schulman, 441:22Jul84-16
  442(NY):30Apr84-117
Aleixandre, V. The Crackling Sun.
  A. Byrum, 238:May83-297
  G. Castresana, 552(REH):Oct83-460
Alekseyev, M.P. Russko-angliyskiye litera-
turnyye svyazi (XVIII vek — pervaya
polovina XIX veka).
  A.G. Cross, 575(SEER):Jul83-418
Aler, J. and C. van Praag, eds. Frauen
über Frauen.
  E. Frederiksen, 133:Band16Heft1-77
Aleramo, S. A Woman.
  M.J. Ciccarello, 276:Autumn83-291
Alexander, C.C. Ty Cobb.
  J. Brosnan, 441:8Apr84-13
Alexander, D. and W.L. Strauss, eds. The
German Single-Leaf Woodcut 1600-1700.
  W. Harms, 196:Band24Heft1/2-125
  M. Schilling, 224(GRM):Band33Heft1-111
Alexander D.G. Atlantic Canada and Con-
federation. (E.W. Sager, L.R. Fischer
and S.O. Pierson, eds)
  D. Frank, 99:Dec83-32
Alexander, F. Red Deer.
  G. Johnson, 461:Spring/Summer83-96
Alexander, G.M. The Prelude to the Truman
Doctrine.*
  C.M. Woodhouse, 453(NYRB):11Oct84-51
Alexander, J.C. Theoretical Logic in
Sociology. (Vol 3)
  G. Marshall, 617(TLS):18May84-560
Alexander, J.W. Ranulf of Chester.
  M.T. Clanchy, 617(TLS):13Apr84-408
Alexander, M. The Poetic Achievement of
Ezra Pound.*
  A.W. Litz, 405(MP):Nov83-214
Alexander, M. The Poetic Self.
  C. Clausen, 569(SR):Fall83-672
  G.M. White, 646:Mar84-36
Alexander, M. and others. Thuburbo Majus.
  K.M.D. Dunbabin, 124:May-Jun84-327
Alexander, M. and S. Anand. Queen Vic-
toria's Maharajah.
  G.R.G. Hambly, 637(VS):Winter83-228
Alexander, P. Roy Campbell.*
  P. Le Bon, 189(EA):Apr-Jun84-221
Alexander, P. - see Campbell, R.
Alexander, P. and R. Gill, eds. Utopias.
  J.N. Gray, 617(TLS):13Jul84-776
Alexander, R.J., ed. Political Parties of
the Americas.
  R.H. Dix, 263(RIB):Vol33No3-395

Allerhand, J. Das Judentum in der Aufklä-
rung.
   A. Springer, 173(ECS):Fall83-117
Allerton, D.J. Essentials of Grammatical
Theory.*
   A.A. Hill, 599:Winter83-86
Allerton, D.J. Valency and the English
Verb.
   R. Hudson, 361:Oct/Nov83-283
   R.W. Langacker, 350:Sep84-607
Alleyne, M.C. Comparative Afro-American.*
   M. Görlach, 260(IF):Band88-382
Allingham, W. Laurence Bloomfield in
Ireland.
   R. Tracy, 445(NCF):Dec83-354
Allison, A.W. and others, eds. The Norton
Anthology of Poetry. (3rd ed)
   D. Bromwich, 617(TLS):17Aug84-911
Allison, G. Life: Still.
   H. Kirkwood, 526:Summer83-76
Allman, T.D. Unmanifest Destiny.
   T.G. Ash, 441:7Oct84-13
Allmand, C.T. Lancastrian Normandy, 1415-
1450.
   P.S. Lewis, 617(TLS):2Mar84-229
Allott, M., ed. Essays on Shelley.
   W. Keach, 340(KSJ):Vol32-220
Alloway, L. Network.
   R. Baranik, 62:Summer84-81
Allshouse, R.H. - see Prokudin-Gorskii,
S.M.
Allswang, J.M. Bosses, Machines and
Urban Voters.
   K. Cassidy, 106:Spring83-97
Alluntis, F. and A.B. Wolter - see Scotus,
J.D.
Almansi, G. and S. Henderson. Harold
Pinter.
   R. Strang, 610:Autumn83-276
Almeder, R. The Philosophy of Charles S.
Peirce.*
   V.G. Potter, 258:Jun83-205
   G.L. Stephens, 449:Nov83-707
de Almeida, H. Byron and Joyce through
Homer.*
   L.A. Marchand, 340(KSJ):Vol32-218
Almeida, J., S.C. Mohler and R.H. Stinson.
Descubrir y crear. (2nd ed)
   S.A. Williams, 399(MLJ):Spring83-94
de Almela, D.R. - see under Rodríguez de
Almela, D.
Almendros, N. A Man With a Camera.
   G. Mast, 441:30Sep84-29
Alonso Hernández, J.L. and others.
Spaanse Letterkunde.
   D. te Riele, 204(FdL):Jun83-144
Alonso-Núñez, J.M. The Ages of Rome.
   M. Griffin, 123:Vol33No2-351
Alperovitz, G. and J. Faux. Rebuilding
America.
   R. Lekachman, 441:20May84-19
Alpers, H.J., W. Fuchs and R.M. Hahn, eds.
Reclams Science Fiction.*
   M. Nagl, 196:Band24Heft3/4-287
Alpers, K. Das attizistische Lexikon des
Oros.
   M.D. MacLeod, 303(JoHS):Vol 103-183
   M.L. West, 123:Vol33No1-20
Alpers, P. The Singer of the "Eclogues."*
   R. Coleman, 131(CL):Spring83-175
Alpers, S. The Art of Describing.*
   J. Ferguson, 324:Jun84-475

Alquié, F. Le rationalisme de Spinoza.*
   G. Brykman, 542:Oct-Dec83-469
   J. Rivelaygue, 542:Jan-Mar83-100
Alsdorf, L. - see Trenckner, V.
Alsop, J. The Rare Art Traditions.*
   P. Burke, 90:Nov83-707
   E.H. Gombrich, 592:Aug83-22
   S. Holo, 55:Nov83-54
   E.V. Thaw, 31(ASch):Autumn83-550
Alsop, S.M. The Congress Dances.
   H. Goodman, 441:22Jul84-21
Alston, R.C. and M.J. Crump, eds. Eigh-
teenth Century Short Title Catalogue.
   O.M. Brack, Jr., 617(TLS):14Sep84-1035
Alter, R. The Art of Biblical Narrative.*
   M.W. Bloomfield, 473(PR):4/1983-633
   E. Jacobs, 577(SHR):Spring83-184
Althaus, H.P., H. Henne and H.E. Weigand,
eds. Lexikon der germanistischen Lin-
guistik.* (2nd ed)
   A. Greule, 260(IF):Band88-350
   D. Nehls, 257(IRAL):Feb83-69
   P. Suchland, 682(ZPSK):Band36Heft4-481
Alther, L. Other Women.
   N. Evans, 441:11Nov84-26
Altieri, C. Act and Quality.*
   J.M. Ellis, 131(CL):Fall83-376
   C. Molesworth, 301(JEGP):Jan83-124
Altieri, C. Enlarging the Temple.
   R. Kroetsch, 106:Summer83-219
Altman, J.G. Epistolarity.*
   T. Castle, 566:Spring84-168
   J.G. Kennedy, 188(ECr):Fall83-109
   J.R. Loy, 210(FrF):Sep83-278
   D.C. Spinelli, 207(FR):Mar84-545
Altmann, A. Freiheit im Spiegel des
rationalen Gesetzes bei Kant.
   W. Steinbeck, 342:Band74Heft4-510
Altmann, A. - see Mendelssohn, M.
Altmann, G. Statistik für Linguisten.
   S.M. Embleton, 660(Word):Aug83-129
Altmann, G. and W. Lehfeldt. Einführung
in die quantitative Phonologie.
   L.D. Stephens, 350:Sep84-651
Altmann, H. Die Gradpartikeln im Deut-
schen.
   U. Schwartz, 260(IF):Band87-359
Altshuler, D., ed. The Precious Legacy.
   L. Wieseltier, 441:15Jan84-9
Álvarez, J.P. - see under Pimentel Álvarez,
J.
Álvarez Pinedo, F. and J.M. Ramírez Mar-
tínez. Fray Bernardo de Fresneda y la
capilla mayor de la iglesia de San Fran-
cisco en Santo Domingo de la Calzada.
   M. Estella, 48:Oct-Dec80-505
Alvaro Ríos, A. The Iguana Killer.
   J. Daynard, 441:23Dec84-16
Alver, B.G. and others. Botare.
   C-H. Tillhagen, 64(Arv):Vol37-195
Alvis, J. and T.G. West, eds. Shakespeare
as Political Thinker.*
   M. Evans, 551(RenQ):Summer83-297
Alyn, M. The Sound of Anthems.
   P. Craig, 617(TLS):6Apr84-368
Amabile, G. Ideas of Shelter.
   C. MacCulloch, 526:Winter83-74
Amacher, R.E. and V. Lange, eds. New Per-
spectives in German Literary Criticism.*
   B. Sorg, 52:Band17Heft1-82
al-'Amad, H. Al-'Amthāl al-sha'biyyah
al-'urduniyyah.
   S.L. Khayyat, 196:Band24Heft3/4-301

Amado, J. Jubiaba. Sea of Death.
I. Stern, 441:28Oct84-16
Amalrik, A. Notes of a Revolutionary.*
V. Krasnov, 550(RusR):Jul83-341
A. Leong, 574(SEEJ):Fall83-393
L. Lipson, 676(YR):Winter84-280
W. Maxwell, 442(NY):26Mar84-120
Amal'rik, A. Zapiski dissidenta.
V. Krasnov, 550(RusR):Jul83-341
Amann, R. and J.M. Cooper, eds. Indus-
trial Innovation in the Soviet Union.*
M.R. Beissinger, 550(RusR):Jul83-335
M. McCauley, 575(SEER):Jul83-466
Amastae, J. and L. Elías-Olivares, eds.
Spanish in the United States.
F. Peñalosa, 350:Mar84-152
Ambrose, A. - see Wittgenstein, L.
Ambrose, S.E. Eisenhower. (Vol 2)
R.J. Donovan, 441:9Sep84-1
Amburger, E. Fremde und Einheimische im
Wirtschafts- und Kulturleben des Neuzeit-
lichen Russlands. (K. Zernack, ed)
R.P. Bartlett, 575(SEER):Oct83-619
Ambuter, C. The Open Canvas.
P. Bach, 614:Summer84-24
"Les Américains et les autres."
R.A. Day, 189(EA):Oct-Dec84-486
"The American Heritage Dictionary."* (2nd
college ed)
T.C. Holyoke, 42(AR):Winter83-116
Ameriks, K. Kant's Theory of Mind.
P. Kitcher, 482(PhR):Apr83-285
G. Stock, 518:Jan83-24
M.C. Washburn, 319:Apr84-245
D. Whewell, 83:Autumn83-197
Ameringer, C.D. Democracy in Costa Rica.
K.J. Grieb, 263(RIB):Vol133No3-396
"Amérique; Les années noires."
F. Brunet, 98:Dec83-941
Ames, R.T. The Art of Rulership.*
A.C.Y., 185:Apr84-559
Ames-Lewis, F. Drawing in Early Renais-
sance Italy.*
M. Kemp, 59:Mar83-107
Ames-Lewis, F. and J. Wright. Drawing in
the Italian Renaissance Workshop.
F. Russell, 39:Oct83-353
"Ami and Amile." (S. Danon and S.N. Rosen-
berg, trans)
G. Ashby-Beach, 545(RPh):Feb83-504
Amichai, Y. Great Tranquillity.* Time.
Love Poems.
N. Stiller, 472:Fall/Winter83Spring/
Summer84-155
Amies, H. Still Here.
A. Scott-James, 617(TLS):11May84-521
Amini, M. Oriental Rugs.
G. Wills, 39:Feb83-147
Amirthanayagam, G., ed. Asian and Western
Writers in Dialogue.
A.H. Qureshi, 107(CRCL):Jun83-298
Amis, K. Stanley and the Women.
R. Davies, 362:24May84-23
J. Lasdun, 176:Sep/Oct84-49
J.K.L. Walker, 617(TLS):25May84-571
Amis, M. Money.
A. Huth, 362:27Sep84-32
E. Korn, 617(TLS):5Oct84-1119
Ammons, A.R. Lake Effect Country.*
H. Beaver, 472:Fall/Winter83Spring/
Summer84-349
J.F. Cotter, 249(HudR):Winter83/84-723
[continued]

[continuing]
P. Mesic, 491:Feb84-303
639(VQR):Autumn83-133
Ammons, A.R. Worldly Hopes.*
J.F. Cotter, 249(HudR):Winter83/84-723
D. Lehman, 617(TLS):25May84-573
Amoroso, V. François Mauriac en Italie.
A. Séailles, 535(RHL):May/Jun83-488
Amory, M. - see Waugh, E.
Amos, A.C. Linguistic Means of Determin-
ing the Dates of Old English Literary
Texts.*
C. Sisam, 382(MAE):1983/1-138
C-D. Wetzel, 38:Band101Heft3/4-487
Amossy, R. Les jeux de l'allusion litté-
raire dans "Un Beau Ténébreux" de Julien
Gracq.*
M. Monballin, 356(LR):Nov83-361
M. Murat, 535(RHL):Sep/Dec83-969
A. Whiteside, 627(UTQ):Spring83-310
Amossy, R. Parcours symboliques chez
Julien Gracq.*
G. Cesbron, 535(RHL):Mar/Apr83-308
M. Davies, 402(MLR):Oct83-933
M. Monballin, 356(LR):Aug83-247
Amossy, R. and E. Rosen. Les Discours du
cliché.
J.T. Day, 494:Vol14No2-367
E.F. Gray, 395(MFS):Summer83-300
B. Tritsmans, 446(NCFS):Fall-
Winter83/84-215
"Amours et phobies."
V.D.L., 605(SC):15Jul84-377
Ampleman, G. and others. Pratiques de con-
scientisation.
M. Laroche, 193(ELit):Aug83-300
Amprimoz, A. Changements de tons.
M.E. Kidd, 102(CanL):Spring83-141
Amprimoz, A.L. Odes for Sterilized
Streets.
R. Hatch, 102(CanL):Winter82-144
Amprimoz, A.L. Other Realities.*
L. Hutchman, 137:Sep83-15
Anacreontea. Anacreónticas. (M. Brioso
Sánchez, ed and trans)
D. Arnould, 555:Vol157fasc2-315
M. Campbell, 303(JoHS):Vol 103-188
M.L. West, 123:Vol133No2-310
Anagnostakis, M. The Target.
M.B. Raizis, 678(YCGL):No31-151
Anand, V. The Disputed Crown.
639(VQR):Summer83-92
Anand, V. To a Native Shore.
B. Thompson, 441:22Jan84-17
Anania, M. The Red Menace.
M. Tucker, 441:14Oct84-26
Anawalt, P.R. Indian Clothing before
Cortés.*
C. Tate, 2(AfrA):Aug83-84
Anaxagoras. The Fragments of Anaxagoras.*
(D. Sider, ed)
C.A. Huffman, 121(CJ):Oct/Nov83-68
Anaya, R.A. The Silence of the Llano.
P. Skenazy, 649(WAL):Feb84-351
Anbeek, T. and J.J. Kloek. Literatuur in
verandering.
B. Luger, 204(FdL):Sep82-233
Anbeek van der Meijden, A.G.H. "In puinho-
pen voel ik mij prettig, ergens anders
hoor ik niet thuis."
S. Levie, 204(FdL):Dec83-309

Anderes, F. and A. Agranoff. Ice Palaces.
    R. Banham, 617(TLS):17Feb84-171
    P. Goldberger, 441:2Dec84-18
Anders, E. Boss Rule in South Texas.
    L. Milazzo, 584(SWR):Winter84-v
Andersch, A. Der Vater eines Mörders.
    U. Reinhold, 654(WB):2/1982-141
Andersen, F.G., O. Holzapfel and T. Pet-
    titt. The Ballad as Narrative.
    H. Shields, 595(ScS):Vol26-61
Andersen, H.C. Tales and Stories by Hans
    Christian Andersen.* (P.L. Conroy and
    S.H. Rossel, ed and trans)
    U. Palmenfelt, 64(Arv):Vol37-185
Andersen, L.P. - see under Praestgaard
    Andersen, L.
Andersen, R.W., ed. New Dimensions in
    Second Language Acquisition Research.
    S.M. Embleton, 320(CJL):Fall83-185
Anderson, D., ed. The Kindness that Kills.
    K. Leech, 617(TLS):19Oct84-1199
Anderson, D.R. American Flower Painting.
    M.S. Young, 39:Sep83-272
Anderson, G. Eros Sophistes.
    J.J. Winkler, 487:Spring83-88
Anderson, G.D. Fascists, Communists, and
    the National Government.
    A.P. Cappon, 436(NewL):Summer84-101
Anderson, G.K., ed and trans. The Saga of
    the Völsungs.
    T.M. Andersson, 589:Jul83-841
    P. Schach, 221(GQ):Mar83-304
Anderson, G.W., ed. Tradition and Inter-
    pretation.
    H.M. Orlinsky, 318(JAOS):Oct-Dec82-656
Anderson, J. Jean Anderson Cooks.
    W. and C. Cowen, 639(VQR):Spring83-65
Anderson, J. Education and Inquiry.*
    (D.Z. Phillips, ed)
    A.G.N. Flew, 518:Jan83-33
Anderson, J., ed. Language Form and Lin-
    guistic Variation.*
    F. Chevillet, 189(EA):Apr-Jun84-179
Anderson, J. The Milky Way.*
    P. Mesic, 491:Feb84-297
    P. Stitt, 441:15Apr84-31
Anderson, J. Sir Walter Scott and History.
    T. Crawford, 571(ScLJ):Winter83-51
    T. Dale, 588(SSL):Vol 18-272
Anderson, J. This Was Harlem, 1900-1950.
    O. Handlin, 31(ASch):Spring83-265
Anderson, J. Tirra Lirra by the River.
    H. Waugh, 441:19Feb84-24
Anderson, J. Unforbidden Sweets.
    W. and C. Cowen, 639(VQR):Spring83-70
Anderson, J.H. Biographical Truth.
    J. Briggs, 617(TLS):20Jul84-805
Anderson, J.I. William Howard Taft.
    S.I. Bellman, 584(SWR):Winter83-96
Anderson, J.J., ed. Records of Early
    English Drama: Newcastle-Upon-Tyne.
    C. Gauvin, 189(EA):Oct-Dec84-459
Anderson, L. To Stay Alive.
    P. Craig, 617(TLS):29Jun84-736
Anderson, L. United States.
    S. Laschever, 441:12Aug84-20
Anderson, M.L. Windthorst.
    J. Doerr, 150(DR):Summer83-341
    K.P. Fischer, 396(ModA):Spring83-220
    T.S. Hamerow, 221(GQ):Mar83-354
Anderson, M.S. Historians and Eighteenth-
    Century Europe, 1715-1789.*
    T.F. Sheppard, 656(WMQ):Jan83-137

Anderson, P. In the Tracks of Historical
    Materialism.
    S. Avineri, 441:27May84-19
    M. Jay, 617(TLS):5Oct84-1132
    A. Ryan, 362:2Feb84-25
Anderson, P. Lords of the Earth.
    C.R. Larson, 441:13May84-22
Anderson, R.S. and others, eds. Science,
    Politics, and the Agricultural Revolu-
    tion in Asia.
    J.E. Nickum, 293(JASt):Aug83-893
Anderson, S. Selected Letters. (C.E. Mod-
    lin, ed)
    R. Carver, 441:22Apr84-6
Anderson, T.P. Politics in Central
    America.
    E.A. Baloyra, 263(RIB):Vol33No2-248
Anderson, W. Dante the Maker.*
    T.G. Bergin, 569(SR):Spring83-261
Anderson, W. The Waking Dream.
    L. Mackinnon, 617(TLS):23Mar84-312
Andersson, B-M. Emaux Limousins en Suède.
    F. Lindahl, 341:Vol152No1-44
Andersson, T.M. The Legend of Brynhild.*
    R.J. Glendinning, 131(CL):Spring83-177
    H.M. Heinrichs, 301(JEGP):Jan83-118
    S-B. Jansson, 64(Arv):Vol37-175
    L.S., 382(MAE):1983/2-336
Andics, E., ed. A nagybirtokos arisztokrá-
    cia ellenforadalmi szerepe 1848-49-ben.
    (Vol 1)
    L. Péter, 575(SEER):Oct83-623
de Andrade, C.D. - see under Drummond de
    Andrade, C.
André, J. L'alimentation et la cuisine
    à Rome.
    P. Flobert, 555:Vol57fasc2-364
André, J. - see Saint Isidore of Seville
André, P. Schumann.
    A. Suied, 98:Dec83-1007
André, R. Homemakers.
    A.C. Fellman, 106:Fall83-297
Andrew, C. and D. Dilks, eds. The Missing
    Dimension.
    Z. Steiner, 617(TLS):12Oct84-1162
Andrew, E. Closing the Iron Cage.
    J.H., 185:Oct83-162
Andrew, J. Russian Writers and Society in
    the Second Half of the Nineteenth Cen-
    tury.
    R. Freeborn, 575(SEER):Apr83-264
    P.R. Hart, 395(MFS):Winter83-801
    N.V. Riasanovsky, 550(RusR):Jan83-122
    F. Wigzell, 402(MLR):Oct83-998
Andrew, M. The Gawain Poet.
    J. Ruud, 125:Spring83-308
Andrew, M. and R. Waldron, eds. The
    Poems of the "Pearl" Manuscript.*
    R.J. Blanch, 72:Band220Heft1-151
Andrews, B. and C. Bernstein, eds. The
    L=A=N=G=U=A=G=E Book.
    M. Perloff, 29:May/Jun84-15
Andrews, B.G. and W.H. Wilde. Australian
    Literature to 1900.
    A. Lawson, 402(MLR):Jul83-692
Andrews, J.S. A Study of German Hymns in
    Current English Hymnals.
    N. Temperley, 415:Sep83-575
Andrews, K. The Flight of Ikaros.
    617(TLS):28Dec84-1511
Andrews, W.L. The Literary Career of
    Charles W. Chesnutt.*
    R. Gray, 447(N&Q):Aug82-379

Andrews, W.L., ed. Literary Romanticism in America.*
A.M. Woodlief, 577(SHR):Fall83-373
Andries, L. and others. La Bibliothèque Bleue nel Seicento o della Letteratura per il popolo.
A. Filippi, 475:Vol 10No18-296
Andrieu, R. Stendhal ou le bal masqué.
V.D.L., 605(SC):15Jan84-199
Andrzejewski, J. Ashes and Diamonds.
B.T. Lupack, 497(PolR):Vol28No2-108
Angel, M.D. La America.
B. Levine, 287:Nov83-25
Angeles, P.A. A Dictionary of Philosophy.
483:Oct81-593
Angelet, C. Symbolisme et invention formelle dans les premiers écrits d'André Gide (Le Traité du Narcisse, Le Voyage d'Urien, Paludes).
P. Cola, 356(LR):Feb-May83-147
Angelou, M. I Know Why The Caged Bird Sings.
J. O'Faolain, 617(TLS):17Feb84-157
Angenot, M. La Parole Pamphlétaire.
G. Seidel, 402(MLR):Oct83-939
Angioni, M.L. - see under Lörinczi Angioni, M.
Ankersmit, F.R. Narrative Logic.
M. Zaalberg, 204(FdL):Dec82-303
Anna, T.E. Spain and the Loss of America.*
M. Rodríguez, 263(RIB):Vol33No3-397
Annan, N. Leslie Stephen.
S. Collini, 617(TLS):5Oct84-1113
D. Donoghue, 441:30Dec84-8
P.N. Furbank, 362:1Nov84-28
Annas, J. An Introduction to Plato's "Republic."*
M.M. Mackenzie, 303(JoHS):Vol 103-170
R.F. Stalley, 123:Vol33No1-55
F.C. White, 63:Sep83-321
Anpilogova, B.G. and others. Slovar'.
L. Pacira, 558(RLJ):Winter-Spring83-231
Anscombe, G.E.M. Collected Philosophical Papers.*
R. Gaita, 63:Mar83-96
A.R. White, 479(PhQ):Apr83-192
Anscombe, I. Omega and After.*
V. Powell, 39:May83-415
Anselmi, G.M. Umanisti, storici e traduttori.
R.G. Witt, 551(RenQ):Summer83-233
Anson, R.S. Exile.
J.A. Lukas, 441:1Jul84-7
S.C. Munson, 129:Oct84-72
442(NY):20Aug84-93
Anstett, J-J. - see Schlegel, F.
Anstey, S. - see Thomas, R.S.
Antès, S. - see Corippus, F.C.
Anthony, J.R. La Musique en France à l'époque baroque.
M. Roche, 537:Vol169No2-234
Anthony, J.R. - see Delalande, M-R.
Anthony, P.D. John Ruskin's Labour.
J. Harris, 617(TLS):31Aug84-963
Antoine, G. Vis-à-vis ou le double regard critique.
D. Bouverot, 209(FM):Oct83-368
Antoine de la Sale. Le Reconfort de Madame de Fresne. (I. Hill, ed)
J.M. Ferrier, 208(FS):Jul83-331

Anton, J.P., ed. Science and the Sciences in Plato.*
G. Anagnostopoulos, 262:Jun83-237
C. Griswold, 543:Sep82-441
Antonov-Ovseyenko, A. Portrait of a Tyrant. [in Russian]
M. Heller, 390:Jun/Jul83-49
Antonov-Ovseyenko, A. The Time of Stalin.*
T.J. Uldriks, 550(RusR):Jul83-333
Antunes, A.L. South of Nowhere.*
P. Lewis, 364:Feb84-101
Anz, T. and J. Vogl, eds. Die Dichter und der Krieg.
G.P. Knapp, 221(GQ):Nov83-677
Anzelewsky, F. Dürer.
J. Rowlands, 39:Jul83-112
Apel, F. Die Zaubergärten der Phantasie.
J. Zipes, 406:Fall83-327
Apel, K-O. Charles S. Peirce.*
R.H., 543:Sep82-155
C.R. Hausman, 480(P&R):Vol 16No4-267
V.G. Potter, 258:Jun83-205
Apollinaire, G. Le Poète Assassiné. (R. Padgett, trans)
J. Updike, 442(NY):9Jul84-89
Apollonius of Rhodes. Apollonios de Rhodes, "Argonautiques."* (Vol 3) (F. Vian, ed; E. Delage and F. Vian, trans)
N. Hopkinson, 303(JoHS):Vol 103-179
Apostolidès, J-M. Le Roi-machine.*
R. Albanese, Jr., 188(ECr):Fall83-107
B. Magné, 535(RHL):Mar/Apr83-274
O. Ranum, 400(MLN):May83-745
J. Thomas, 547(RF):Band95Heft4-492
Appadurai, A. Worship and Conflict under Colonial Rule.
L.A. Babb, 293(JASt):Nov82-177
Appelfeld, A. The Age of Wonders.*
W. Bargad, 390:Mar83-61
Appelfeld, A. The Retreat.
J. Lind, 441:20May84-38
442(NY):4Jun84-13
Appelfeld, A. Tzili.*
J-A. Mort, 287:Oct83-21
Appiah-Kubi, K. Man Cures, God Heals.
D.M. Warren, 69:Vol53No3-92
Apple, M. Free Agents.
W. Kotzwinkle, 441:17Jun84-11
Apple, M.W. Education and Power.
L.B.G., 185:Jan84-379
Applebaum, S. Jews and Greeks in Ancient Cyrene.
J. Linderski, 318(JAOS):Jan-Mar82-210
Applewhite, J. Foreseeing the Journey.
J.F. Cotter, 249(HudR):Winter83/84-713
639(VQR):Autumn83-133
Appleyard, B. The Culture Club.
P. Kemp, 362:29Mar84-27
Apter, D.E. and N. Sawa. Against the State.
D. Kondo, 441:16Sep84-13
Apter, T.E. Fantasy Literature.
C.C. Smith, 395(MFS):Summer83-350
Ara, A. and C. Magris. Trieste.
M-A. Lescourret, 98:Aug-Sep83-734
Arac, J., W. Godzich and W. Martin, eds. The Yale Critics.
V. Leitch, 400(MLN):Dec83-1305
Aragon, L. and J. Cocteau. Conversations on the Dresden Gallery.*
M. Yorke, 324:Jan84-139

Arana, J. Ciencia y metafísica en el Kant precrítico (1746-1764).
N. Demé, 542:Jan-Mar83-128
Arancón, A.M.M. - see under Martínez Arancón, A.M.
Arant, P.M. Russian for Reading.*
J.M. Kirkwood, 575(SEER):Jul83-474
Arata, L.O. The Festive Play of Fernando Arrabal.
G. Edwards, 402(MLR):Oct83-950
M. Esslin, 615(TJ):May83-266
M.T. Halsey, 593:Winter83/84-321
P.L. Podol, 238:Mar83-134
J.M. Polo de Bernabé, 238:Dec83-640
D. Whitton, 610:Spring83-73
Araya, G. De Garcilaso a García Lorca.
A. Gier, 553(RLiR):Jul-Dec83-456
Arbeitman, Y.L. and A.R. Bomhard, eds. Bono homini donum.
L. Zgusta, 350:Mar84-182
Arboleda, J.R. Historia de los templos de España de Gustavo Adolfo Bécquer.
E.B. Hastings, 552(REH):Oct83-443
Arbukov, A. Selected Plays of Aleksei Arbukov.
D. Devlin, 157:Autumn83-31
"Diane Arbus: Magazine Work." (D. Arbus and M. Israel, eds)
A. Grundberg, 441:2Dec84-16
H. Hinson, 61:Nov84-129
Arcana, J. Every Mother's Son.
42(AR):Fall83-505
Arce, J. La poesía del siglo ilustrado.*
J.H.R. Polt, 173(ECS):Fall83-96
Archambault, G. Le Voyageur distrait.
P. Merivale, 102(CanL):Spring83-147
Archbold, G.J.D.E. A Concordance to the "History" of Ammianus Marcellinus.
G. Sabbah, 487:Winter83-361
Archer, J. First Among Equals.
M.S. Kaplan, 441:16Sep84-30
"Architectures en France, Modernité/Postmodernité."
A. Alofsin, 576:Mar83-82
"Archives de philosophie du droit." (Vol 27)
J-L. Gardies, 542:Jul-Sep83-337
"Archizō ta Ellēnika (Beginner's Level)."
J.E. Rexine, 399(MLJ):Autumn83-294
Arcos, A.G. - see under Gomez Arcos, A.
Ardagh, J. France in the 1980's.*
P.P. Clark, 207(FR):Apr84-746
M.A. Garnett, 207(FR):Dec83-281
J.G. Weightman, 208(FS):Jul83-374
Ardagh, J. Rural France.
N. Roberts, 617(TLS):10Feb84-148
Arden, H. The Fools' Plays.*
A. Hindley, 208(FS):Oct83-445
Ardizzone, E. Indian Diary 1952-53.
A. Motion, 617(TLS):22Jun84-692
Ardley, G. The Common Sense Philosophy of James Oswald (1703-93).*
J.B., 543:Sep82-157
P. Hutchings, 63:Jun83-222
Ardouin, P. Maurice Scève.
Y. Bellenger, 535(RHL):Sep/Dec83-910
Arellano, I. - see Calderón de la Barca, P.
Arendt, H. Lectures on Kant's Political Philosophy.* (R. Beiner, ed)
S.B. Smith, 185:Apr84-531
Arendt, H. La vie de l'esprit.* (Vol 1)
R. Schürmann, 192(EP):Jul-Sep83-357

Arens, A., ed. Friedrich Spee von Langenfeld.
G.R. Dimler, 221(GQ):Mar83-310
Arens, W. and R. Schöwerling, eds. Mittelenglische Lyrik.
H. Sauer, 72:Band219Heft2-436
Areopagite, P-D. - see under Pseudo-Dionysius Areopagite
Argyle, G. German Elements in the Fiction of George Eliot, Gissing and Meredith.*
W.E. Davis, 395(MFS):Winter83-763
Arias, F.F. - see under Franco Arias, F.
Arias de Cossío, A.M. José Gutiérrez de la Vega.
D. Angulo Íñiguez, 48:Jan-Mar79-101
Arias Muñoz, A. La radicalidad de la fenomenología husserliana.
A. Reix, 542:Oct-Dec83-490
Aris, M. View of Medieval Bhutan.
60:Jul-Aug83-118
Aris, M. and A.S.S. Kyi, eds. Tibetan Studies in Honour of Hugh Richardson.
J.W. de Jong, 259(IIJ):Apr83-217
Aris, R., H.T. Davis and R.H. Stuewer, eds. Springs of Scientific Creativity.
J.B. Brackenridge, 617(TLS):27Jan84-82
Aristophanes. The Comedies. (Vol 1: Acharnians.) (A.H. Sommerstein, ed and trans)
L.P.E. Parker, 123:Vol33No1-10
R.G. Ussher, 303(JoHS):Vol 103-168
Aristophanes. The Comedies. (Vol 2: Knights.) (A.H. Sommerstein, ed and trans)
D.M. Lewis, 123:Vol33No2-175
Aristophanes. The Comedies. (Vol 3: Clouds.) (A.H. Sommerstein, ed and trans)
D.M. MacDowell, 123:Vol33No2-173
Aristophanes. Four Plays of Aristophanes. (J.H. Mantinband, trans)
J.A. Hanson, 124:Sep-Oct83-47
Aristotle. Aristote, "Météorologiques." (Vols 1 and 2) (P. Louis, ed and trans)
R.W., 555:Vol57fasc2-307
Aristotle. Aristotle's "De Motu Animalium."* (M.C. Nussbaum, ed and trans)
J. Bogen, 606:Jun83-373
Aristotle. Aristotle's "Eudemian Ethics."* (Bks 1, 2 and 8) (M. Woods, ed and trans)
P. Louis, 555:Vol57fasc2-305
D.B. Robinson, 518:Oct83-215
C.J. Rowe, 123:Vol33No1-60
Aristotle. De Generatione et Corruptione. (C.J.F. Williams, ed and trans)
D.W. Hamlyn, 518:Apr83-74
J.G. Lennox, 319:Oct84-472
Aristotle. The Politics.* (T.A. Sinclair, trans; rev by T.J. Saunders)
F.D. Harvey, 123:Vol33No2-238
Arkush, R.D. Fei Xiaotung and Sociology in Revolutionary China.
E. Lubot, 293(JASt):Aug83-898
Arland, M. Lumière du soir.
G. Auclair, 450(NRF):Oct83-116
Arlen, M.J. Say Goodbye to Sam.
I. Gold, 441:21Oct84-12
442(NY):19Nov84-190
Arlott, J. A Word From Arlott. (D.R. Allen, ed)
A.L. Le Quesne, 617(TLS):4May84-493
Armand, O., ed. Toward an Image of Latin American Poetry.
R.O. Salmon, 238:Dec83-644

de Armas, A.R. - see under Rumeu de Armas, A.

de Armas, F.A., D.M. Gitlitz and J.A. Madrigal, eds. Critical Perspectives on Calderón de la Barca.*
   J.H. Parker, 238:May83-295
   A.K.G. Paterson, 86(BHS):Jan83-69

Armengol, P.O. - see under Ortiz Armengol, P.

Armes, R. The Films of Alain Robbe-Grillet.
   C.J. Murphy, 207(FR):Mar84-568
   K. Reader, 208(FS):Jul83-368

Armistead, J.M. Nathaniel Lee.
   D. Hopkins, 447(N&Q):Dec82-552

Armistead, S.G. El Romancero judeo-español en el Archivo Menéndez Pidal.
   B. Mariscal de Rhett, 457(NRFH): Tomo31núm2-310

Armistead, S.G., D. Catalán and A. Sánchez Romeralo, eds. El Romancero hoy.
   M.E. Barrick, 240(HR):Winter83-89

Armistead, S.G. and J.H. Silverman - see Benardete, M.J.

Armour, L. The Idea of Canada and the Crisis of Community.*
   G.W., 102(CanL):Spring83-156

Armour, L. and E. Trott. The Faces of Reason.*
   D. Braybrooke, 529(QQ):Autumn83-688
   T.A. Goudge, 154:Jun83-339

Armour, P. The Door of Purgatory.
   D. Robey, 617(TLS):25May84-596

Arms, G. and others - see Howells, W.D.

Armstrong, D. and N. Malcolm. Consciousness and Causality.
   T. Baldwin, 176:Nov84-62

Armstrong, D.M. The Nature of Mind and other Essays.*
   W.G. Lycan, 482(PhR):Jul83-471

Armstrong, D.M. What is a Law of Nature?
   D.H. Mellor, 617(TLS):19Oct84-1197

Armstrong, I. Language as Living Form in Nineteenth-Century Poetry.
   G. Woodcock, 569(SR):Fall83-664

Armstrong, L. Castle Mountain.
   I. Sowton, 102(CanL):Summer83-124

Armstrong, L. Renaissance Miniature Painters and Classical Imagery.*
   C.H. Clough, 324:Oct84-742
   M.D. Feld, 517(PBSA):Vol77No3-391
   C. Lloyd, 278(IS):Vol38-100
   M. Lowry, 90:Jan83-37
   M.B. McNamme, 377:Nov83-185
   D. Pincus, 551(RenQ):Spring83-102
   T. Tolley, 59:Sep83-391

Armstrong, P.B. The Phenomenology of Henry James.
   M. Seymour, 617(TLS):25May84-594

Armstrong, R.D. Nevada Printing History.
   R.W. Ryan, 87(BB):Dec83-257

Armstrong, R.P. The Powers of Presence.*
   S.J. Bronner, 292(JAF):Jul-Sep83-348
   C.R. Farrer, 650(WF):Jul83-228

Arnaldi, G. and M. Pastore Stocchi, eds. Storia della cultura veneta. (Vol 3)
   M. Pozzi, 228(GSLI):Vol 160fasc510-296

Arnason, D. and M. Olito, eds. The Icelanders.
   D. Brydon, 102(CanL):Winter82-168

Árnason, K. Quality in Historical Phonology.*
   E. Haugen, 562(Scan):May83-72

Arnaud, N. and H. Bordillon - see Jarry, A.

Arnaud, P. and J. Raimond. Le Préromantisme anglais.
   J. Pittock, 402(MLR):Oct83-902

Arnaut Daniel. The Poetry of Arnaut Daniel.* (J.J. Wilhelm, ed and trans)
   E.A. Hanawalt, 589:Oct83-1026

Arndt, H.W. - see Descartes, R.

Arnell, P. and T. Bickford, eds. Robert A.M. Stern.
   W.C. Miller, 505:Feb83-145

Arnell, P. and T. Bickford, eds. A Tower for Louisville.*
   W. Morgan, 505:May83-229

Arnheim, M. Is Christianity True?
   A.J. Ayer, 362:10May84-26

Arnheim, R. The Power of the Center.*
   N. Bryson, 90:Jun83-373
   P. Meeson, 89(BJA):Summer83-262
   H.P. Raleigh, 289:Spring83-111

Arnobius. Arnobe, "Contre les Gentils." (Bk 1) (H. Le Bonniec, ed and trans)
   M. Reydellet, 555:Vol157fasc1-173

Arnold, A., ed. Sherlock Holmes auf der Hintertreppe.
   W. Slaymaker, 221(GQ):Jan83-115

Arnold, A.J. Modernism and Negritude.
   F.R. Smith, 402(MLR):Apr83-465

Arnold, B. Margaret Thatcher.
   V. Bogdanor, 617(TLS):17Aug84-912

Arnold, D. Bach.
   H. Cole, 362:20Sep84-28

Arnold, D. Monteverdi Church Music.
   D. Stevens, 415:Apr83-236

Arnold, D., general ed. The New Oxford Companion to Music.*
   H. Cole, 362:5Jan84-24

Arnold, E. In America.*
   R. Coonan, 617(TLS):20Jul84-821

Arnold, H.L., ed. Georg Büchner III.
   D.G. Richards, 221(GQ):Mar83-320

Arnold, H.L., ed. Hubert Fichte.
   A. Stephan, 221(GQ):Nov83-711

Arnold, K. Niklashausen 1476.
   R.F.M. Byrn, 402(MLR):Oct83-967

Arnott, W.G. - see "Menander"

Arnould, D. Guerre et paix dans la poésie grecque de Callinos à Pindare.
   P. Demont, 555:Vol157fasc1-120

Arnstein, W.L. Protestant Versus Catholic in Mid-Victorian England.
   J.L. Altholz, 637(VS):Spring83-363

Arntz, M.L., ed. Richard Rolle and "þe Holy Boke Gratia Dei."
   S.J. Ogilvie-Thomson, 382(MAE):1983/2-316

Arntzen, E. and R. Rainwater. Guide to the Literature of Art History.*
   A. Ross, 54:Mar83-169

Arntzen, H. Musil-Kommentar sämtlicher zu Lebzeiten erschienener Schriften ausser den Roman "Der Mann ohne Eigenschaften."
   U. Karthaus, 224(GRM):Band33Heft3-361

Aron, R. Mémoires.* Le spectateur engagé.
   F. George, 98:Nov83-837

Aron, R., with J-L. Missiska and D. Wolton. The Committed Observer.*
   442(NY):9Apr84-145

Aronoff, M. and M-L. Kean, eds. Juncture.
   A.H. Sommerstein, 297(JL):Mar83-227

Arons, S. Compelling Belief.
   W.H., 185:Jan84-379

12

Aspland, C.W. A Medieval French Reader.
  P. Ménard, 545(RPh):Feb83-494
Aspley, K., D. Bellos and P. Sharratt, eds.
  Myth and Legend in French Literature.
  A.E. Pilkington, 208(FS):Jul83-370
Asquith, H.H. H.H. Asquith: Letters to
  Venetia Stanley.* (M. and E. Brock, eds)
  J.A. Stein, 31(ASch):Autumn83-552
  P. Williamson, 161(DUJ):Jun83-101
  639(VQR):Summer83-81
Asquith, S. Children and Justice.*
  H.C., 185:Jul84-741
Asselineau, R. The Transcendentalist Con-
  stant in American Literature.*
  L. Ziff, 677(YES):Vol 13-342
de Assis, J.M.M. - see under Machado de
  Assis, J.M.
Aster, E. Personalbibliographie von
  Gustav Meyrink.
  J.B. Berlin, 221(GQ):Mar83-331
Aster, H. - see Layton, I.
Astolfi, D.M., ed. Teaching the Ancient
  World.
  E.M.A. Kovach, 124:Jul-Aug84-385
Åström, P. and S.A. Eriksson. Finger-
  prints and Archaeology.
  J-C. Margueron, 318(JAOS):Oct-Dec82-
  666
Asturias, M.A. Viajes, ensayos y fan-
  tasías. (R.J. Callan, ed)
  J.J. Himelblau, 238:Dec83-650
Athanassiadi-Fowden, P. Julian and Hel-
  lenism.
  J. Bouffartique, 555:Vol57fasc1-139
  G.W. Bowersock, 123:Vol33No1-81
Atil, E. Kalila wa Dimna.
  J.S. Cowen, 463:Spring83-70
Atiyah, P.S. Law and Modern Society.
  L. Scarman, 617(TLS):10Feb84-145
Atiyah, P.S. Promises, Morals and Law.*
  J.P.W. Cartwright, 479(PhQ):Jul83-315
  J. Cottingham, 393(Mind):Jul83-474
Atkins, E.W. The Elgar-Atkins Friendship.
  D. Mitchell, 617(TLS):14Sep84-1011
Atkins, G.D. The Faith of John Dryden.*
  J.H. O'Neill, 161(DUJ):Jun83-131
Atkins, G.D. Reading Deconstruction/
  Deconstructive Reading.
  C. Norris, 617(TLS):27Apr84-470
Atkins, S. - see Heine, H.
Atkinson, A.B. Social Justice and Public
  Policy.
  R.E. Goodin, 185:Apr84-541
Atkinson, B. Sean O'Casey.* (R.G. Lowery,
  ed)
  B. Dolan, 305(JIL):May83-114
  C. Murray, 272(IUR):Spring83-128
Atkinson, C.W. Mystic and Pilgrim.
  639(VQR):Autumn83-125
Atkinson, F. Dictionary of Literary
  Pseudonyms. (3rd ed)
  K.B. Harder, 424:Mar83-71
Atkinson, J.E. A Commentary on Q. Curtius
  Rufus' "Historiae Alexandri Magni"
  Books 3 and 4.*
  E.N. Borza, 121(CJ):Dec83/Jan84-162
  A.B. Bosworth, 122:Apr83-150
  E.E. Rice, 123:Vol33No1-39
Atkinson, M. Our Masters' Voices.
  P. Whitehead, 617(TLS):9Nov84-1275
Atkinson, M., D. Kilby and I. Roca. Found-
  ations of General Linguistics.
  J.S. Ryan, 67:May83-158

Atlan, J. Eloges des rites et des jeux.
  M. Adam, 542:Oct-Dec83-443
Attebery, B. The Fantasy Tradition in
  American Literature.*
  M. Bickman, 495(PoeS):Dec83-46
Attenborough, D. The Living Planet.
  T. Halliday, 617(TLS):28Sep84-1100
Attenborough, R. In Search of Gandhi.*
  G.W. Jones, 584(SWR):Spring83-203
Atterbury, P., ed. The History of Porce-
  lain.
  G. Wills, 39:Nov83-455
Attman, A. The Bullion Flow between
  Europe and the East, 1000-1750.*
  T.S. Noonan, 575(SEER):Jul83-447
Attridge, D. The Rhythms of English
  Poetry.*
  A. Easthope, 349:Spring83-244
  B. Hayes, 350:Dec84-914
Attuel, J. Le style de Stendhal.
  F. Deloffre, 209(FM):Oct83-371
  J-L. Seylaz, 535(RHL):Mar/Apr83-292
Atwood, M. Bluebeard's Egg.
  M. Redekop, 99:Jan84-30
Atwood, M. Bodily Harm.*
  C. Blaise, 102(CanL):Winter82-110
  I.D. Carrington, 168(ECW):Summer83-45
Atwood, M. Dancing Girls.*
  P. Craig, 617(TLS):21Sep84-1066
  D. Flower, 249(HudR):Summer83-364
  639(VQR):Spring83-57
Atwood, M. Murder in the Dark.
  J. Crace, 617(TLS):23Mar84-311
  K. Mezei, 648(WCR):Oct83-51
  B. Wineapple, 150(DR):Summer83-360
Atwood, M., ed. The New Oxford Book of
  Canadian Verse in English.
  M. Abley, 617(TLS):27Apr84-460
  A. Appenzell, 102(CanL):Summer83-108
  W.J. Keith, 105:Spring/Summer83-77
Atwood, M. Second Words.*
  S. Solecki, 529(QQ):Winter83-1026
Atwood, M. True Stories.*
  E. Larrissy, 493:Mar83-61
  L. Weir, 102(CanL):Winter82-112
Atwood, W.G. The Lioness and the Little
  One.*
  C. Robinson, 447(N&Q):Aug82-380
Atzeni, E. and others. Ichnussa.
  D. Ridgway, 617(TLS):5Oct84-1131
Aubert, J. - see Joyce, J.
Aubert, J-F. Exposé des institutions
  politiques de la Suisse à partir de
  quelques affaires controversées.
  C.J. Hughes, 617(TLS):7Dec84-1425
Auboyer, J. Buddha.
  C. Zaleski, 469:Vol9No3-108
Aubreton, R., with F. Buffière, eds and
  trans. Anthologie grecque.* (Pt 2,
  Vol 13)
  R.C. McCail, 303(JoHS):Vol 103-187
Auburger, L. Funktionale Sprachvarianten.
  B.J. Koekkoek, 221(GQ):May83-490
Auburger, L. and H. Kloss, eds. Deutsch
  als Muttersprache in Kanada. Deutsch
  als Muttersprache in den Vereinigten
  Staaten. (Pt 1)
  J. Eichhoff, 685(ZDL):2/1983-247
Auchincloss, L. The Book Class.
  A. McCarthy, 441:12Aug84-12
Auchincloss, L. Exit Lady Masham.
  S. Altinel, 617(TLS):3Aug84-875
  C. Ricks, 441:1Jan84-24

14

Bader, W. Grundprobleme der Literatur-
theorie Lucien Goldmanns.
   R. Theis, 72:Band219Heft2-401
Badger, A.J. North Carolina and the New
Deal.
   M. Billington, 9(AlaR):Jul83-237
Badham, P. and L. Immortality or Extinc-
tion.
   A. Flew, 483:Jul83-407
Badinter, E. Emilie, Emilie.
   C. Slawy-Sutton, 207(FR):Mar84-579
Badinter, E. L'amour en plus.
   M. Jeay, 539:May84-125
"Leo Baeck Institute: Year Book XXVI."
(A. Paucker, ed)
   F.L. Carsten, 575(SEER):Apr83-287
Baehr, R. - see von Richthofen, E.
Baender, P. - see Twain, M.
Baer, F.E. Sources and Analogues of the
Uncle Remus Tales.
   R. Wehse, 196:Band24Heft3/4-289
Bagdikian, B.H. The Media Monopoly.*
   J. Beerman, 42(AR):Fall83-503
Baghio'o, J-L. The Blue Flame-Tree.
   P.L. Bowles, 617(TLS):11May84-529
Bagley, D. Night of Error.
   T.J. Binyon, 617(TLS):30Nov84-1391
Baguley, D. Bibliographie de la critique
sur Émile Zola, 1971-1980.*
   J. Allard, 627(UTQ):Summer83-461
   E.F. Gray, 395(MFS):Summer83-300
Bahm, A.J. The Philosopher's World Model.
   W. Gerber, 543:Mar83-687
Bahmet, A., G. Luznycky and L. Rudnytsky,
eds. Dictionary of Ukrainian Synonyms.
(Vol 1)
   T.E. Bird, 574(SEEJ):Fall83-405
Bahr, E., ed. Erläuterungen und Dokumente
zu J.W. Goethe, "Wilhelm Meisters Lehr-
jahre."
   H.R. Vaget, 221(GQ):May83-502
Bahr, E. Nelly Sachs.*
   K. Weissenberger, 133:Band16Heft2/3-
280
Bahr, E. - see von Goethe, J.W.
Bahr, E., E.P. Harris and L.G. Lyon, eds.
Humanität und Dialog.
   E.W. Herd, 564:Sep83-217
Bahri, H. Learner's Hindi-English Diction-
ary.
   M. Gatzlaff, 682(ZPSK):Band36Heft2-240
Bahuchet, S., ed. Pygmées de Centrafrique.
   N. Kazadi, 69:Vol53No1-92
Baigent, B. Ancestral Dreams.
   D. O'Rourke, 102(CanL):Winter82-130
Bail, M. Ian Fairweather.
   D. Miller, 364:Aug/Sep83-105
Bailey, A. Along the Edge of the Forest.*
   C. Booker, 617(TLS):22Jun84-702
Bailey, A. Miramichi Lightning.*
   G. Hamel, 198:Jan83-101
Bailey, A.M. and J.R. Llobera, eds. The
Asiatic Mode of Production.
   S. Weigelin-Schwiedrzik, 293(JASt):
Aug83-899
Bailey, D. Making Up.
   P. Morley, 102(CanL):Summer83-101
   K. Tudor, 198:Jan84-81
Bailey, D. and M. Harrison. Black and
White Memories.
   M. Jordan, 617(TLS):20Jul84-821
Bailey, D.R.S. - see under Shackleton
Bailey, D.R.

Bailey, F.G. The Tactical Uses of Pas-
sion.*
   I.S., 185:Apr84-551
Bailey, G. The Mythology of Brahmā.
   W.D. O'Flaherty, 617(TLS):23Nov84-1357
Bailey, H. All the Days of My Life.
   K.C. O'Brien, 362:29Nov84-25
Bailey, K.M., M.H. Long and S. Peck, eds.
Second Language Acquisition Studies.
   C. Chaudron, 608:Mar84-129
Bailey, R.W. and M. Görlach, eds. English
as a World Language.
   J. Holm, 660(Word):Apr83-42
   J.S. Ryan, 67:May83-162
   E.W. Schneider, 685(ZDL):3/1983-393
Bailey, R.W., L. Matejka and P. Steiner,
eds. The Sign.
   B. Malmberg, 567:Vol144No3/4-363
Bailey, V., ed. Policing and Punishment
in Nineteenth Century Britain.
   J.E. Thomas, 637(VS):Autumn82-109
Bailly-Herzberg, J. - see Pissarro, C.
Bain, D. Masters, Servants and Orders
in Greek Tragedy.
   M. Anderson, 610:Summer83-157
   E.M. Craik, 303(JoHS):Vol 103-185
   J. Diggle, 123:Vol33No1-127
   D.J. Mastronarde, 487:Spring83-84
Bain, D.H. Sitting in Darkness.
   S. Lohr, 441:23Sep84-11
Bainbridge, B. English Journey.
   B. Nightingale, 441:23Sep84-24
   J. Raban, 453(NYRB):25Oct84-46
Bainbridge, B. Watson's Apology.
   R. Blythe, 362:25Oct84-23
   J. Symons, 617(TLS):5Oct84-1118
Baines, B. Fashion Revivals: From the
Elizabethan Age to the Present Day.*
   R.L. Shep, 614:Fall84-17
Baird, I.F., ed. Scotish Feilde and Flod-
den Feilde.
   H. Kelliher, 354:Dec83-414
Baird, J.D. and C. Ryskamp - see Cowper, W.
Baird, T. Villa Aphrodite.
   R. Robinson, 441:25Nov84-27
   442(NY):31Dec84-70
Bakelants, L. and R. Hoven. Bibliographie
des oeuvres de Nicolas Clénard, 1529-
1700.
   A. Anninger, 517(PBSA):Vol77No3-404
Bakema, J.B. Thoughts on Architecture.
   P.B., 46:Feb83-71
Baker, C. The Echoing Green.
   S. French, 617(TLS):17Aug84-925
Baker, C. - see Hemingway, E.
Baker, C.L. and J.J. McCarthy, eds. The
Logical Problem of Language Acquisition.
   P.W. Culicover, 350:Mar84-115
Baker, D.C., J.L. Murphy and L.B. Hall,
Jr., eds. Late Medieval Religious Plays
of Bodleian MSS Digby 133 and E Museo
160.
   B. Cottle, 301(JEGP):Jul83-439
   S. Spector, 589:Jul83-727
   M. Twycross, 175:Autumn83-251
Baker, G.P. and P.M.S. Hacker. Wittgen-
stein.*
   C. Imbert, 540(RIPh):Vol137fasc1/2-205
   B. Stroud, 482(PhR):Apr83-282
Baker, J. Full Circle.
   E. Forbes, 415:Apr83-239

Baker, J. Time and Mind in Wordsworth's
Poetry.*
    W.J.B. Owen, 541(RES):Aug83-346
    R. Sharrock, 191(ELN):Jun84-76
Baker, J.S. Japanese Art.
    R.L. Shep, 614:Fal184-19
Baker, J.W. Heinrich Bullinger and the
Covenant.
    J.S. Preus, 125:Fal182-101
Baker, L. Brandeis and Frankfurter.
    L.M. Friedman, 441:24Jun84-18
Baker, N.L. A Research Guide for Under-
graduate Students.
    D. Mann, 365:Summer/Fal183-137
Baker, P. and C. Corne. Isle de France
Creole.
    R.W. Andersen, 350:Dec84-945
Baker, R. Growing Up.
    C. Hitchens, 617(TLS):6Apr84-361
Baker, R.L. Hoosier Folk Legends.
    L.S. Person, Jr., 650(WF):Oct83-314
Baker, S.E. Georges Feydeau and the
Aesthetics of Farce.*
    W.D. Howarth, 610:Summer83-172
    N. Shapiro, 397(MD):Sep83-394
Baker, S.R. Collaboration et originalité
chez La Rochefoucauld.*
    B. Croquette, 535(RHL):May/Jun83-469
    L.K. Horowitz, 546(RR):Jan83-84
    J. Lafond, 475:Vol 10No18-294
    O. de Mourgues, 208(FS):Apr83-212
    H. Mydlarski, 345(KRQ):Vol130No2-219
Baker, W. Backward.
    W. Least Heat Moon, 441:3Jun84-34
Baker, W. - see Eliot, G.
Baker, W.J. Beyond Port and Prejudice.
    R.N. Bérard, 150(DR):Summer83-370
Bakere, J.A. The Cornish Ordinalia.
    B. Ó Cuív, 112:Vol 15-179
Bakhash, S. The Reign of the Ayatollahs.
    M. Zonis, 441:21Oct84-26
Bakhtin, M.M. The Dialogic Imagination.*
(M. Holquist, ed)
    D. Carroll, 153:Summer83-65
    J. Fizer, 478:Oct83-270
    P.W. Nutting, 221(GQ):May83-458
    D.E. Rivas, 577(SHR):Spring83-189
    H. White, 473(PR):2/1983-307
Bakir, G. Sophilos.*
    D.C. Kurtz, 303(JoHS):Vol 103-223
Bakker, B.H. - see Zola, É.
Bakker, B.H., with C. Becker - see Zola, É.
Bakker, J. and D.R.M. Wilkinson, eds.
From Cooper to Philip Roth.
    K. Carabine, 402(MLR):Jul83-689
Bal, W. Dialectologie en Wallonie.
    P. Rézeau, 553(RLiR):Jul-Dec83-483
Bal, W. and J. Germain, comps. Guide bib-
liographique de linguistique romane.
    Y.M., 545(RPh):Nov82-319
Balaban, J. Blue Mountain.*
    W.D. Ehrhart, 639(VQR):Summer83-553
Baladié, R. Le Péloponnèse de Strabon.*
    P. Pédech, 555:Vol157fasc1-133
Balakian, A., ed. The Symbolist Movement
in the Literature of European Languages.
    A.G. Engstrom, 207(FR):May84-881
Balakian, P. Father Fisheye.
    W. Zander, 363(LitR):Winter84-272
Balard, M., ed. Gênes et l'Outre-Mer.*
(Vol 2)
    J.W. Barker, 589:Oct83-1106

Balawyder, A. The Maple Leaf and the
White Eagle.*
    M.B. Biskupski, 497(PolR):Vol28No1-114
Balázs, É.H., ed. Beförderer der Aufklä-
rung in Mittel- und Osteuropa.
    J.M. Tudor, 83:Spring83-127
Balbus, I.D. Marxism and Domination.*
    P.S.M., 185:Apr84-552
Balcerzan, E., ed. Pisarze polscy o
sztuce przekładu, 1440-1974.
    C. Kasparek, 497(PolR):Vol28No2-83
Baldick, C. The Social Mission of English
Criticism 1848-1932.
    J. Lucas, 617(TLS):13Jan84-29
Baldinger, K. Dictionnaire étymologique
de l'ancien français, G4.
    G. Roques, 553(RLiR):Jul-Dec83-457
Baldinger, K. Dictionnaire onomasiolog-
ique de l'ancien occitan.* (fasc 1)
(rev by I. Popelar)
    G.F. Meier, 682(ZPSK):Band36Heft3-349
Baldinger, K. Semantic Theory. (R.
Wright, ed)
    D. Geeraerts, 361:Jun/Jul83-231
    L. Hermodsson, 597(SN):Vol55No1-89
Baldini, G. The Story of Giuseppe Verdi.
(F. d'Amico, ed; R. Parker, ed and trans
of English edition)
    D. Rosen, 415:Jun83-353
Baldini Moscadi, L. and others. Cultura e
ideologia da Cicerone a Seneca.
    M. Griffin, 123:Vol33No1-138
Baldwin, A.P. The Theme of Government in
"Piers Plowman."
    C. Brewer, 447(N&Q):Oct82-425
    C. Clark, 179(ES):Apr83-189
    R.A. Peck, 589:Oct83-1106
    J. Simpson, 382(MAE):1983/2-317
de Baleine, P. Le Petit Train de la
Brousse.
    H. Cronel, 450(NRF):Apr83-139
Balentine, S.E. The Hidden God.
    A. Phillips, 617(TLS):24Feb84-199
Balinski, M.L. and H.P. Young. Fair Rep-
resentation.
    N.R.M., 185:Jan84-363
Ball, G.W. The Past Has Another Pattern.*
    T.E. Vadney, 529(QQ):Winter83-983
    639(VQR):Winter83-10
Ball, H. Der Künstler und die Zeitkrank-
heit. (H.B. Schlichting, ed)
    R. Cardinal, 617(TLS):7Dec84-1428
Ball, R.J. - see Highet, G.
Ball, W. and T. Martin. Rare Afro-
Americana.
    P. Lapsansky, 517(PBSA):Vol77No1-91
Balland, A. Fouilles de Xanthos.* (Vol 7)
    C.P. Jones, 487:Spring83-71
    A.G. Woodhead, 303(JoHS):Vol 103-228
Ballard, A.B. One More Day's Journey.
    D.L. Lewis, 441:12Aug84-14
Ballard, J.G. Empire of the Sun.
    J.C. Batchelor, 441:11Nov84-11
    D.J. Enright, 453(NYRB):22Nov84-45
    R. Jones, 362:20Sep84-27
    P. Kemp, 617(TLS):14Sep84-1018
    442(NY):26Nov84-148
Ballesta, J.C. - see under Cano Ballesta,
J.
Ballhatchet, K. and J. Harrison, eds. The
City in South Asia.
    V.T. Oldenburg, 293(JASt):May83-692

Balliett, W. Jelly Roll, Jabbo and Fats.
C. Fox, 617(TLS):4May84-490
Ballin, M., ed. D.H. Lawrence's "Women in Love."
M.L. Ross, 627(UTQ):Summer83-438
Ballingall, J. A Taste of China.
D. Davin, 617(TLS):26Oct84-1206
Ballmer, T. and W. Brennenstuhl. Speech Act Classification.*
E. Adegbija, 215(GL):Vol23No3-216
Balmary, M. Psychoanalyzing Psychoanalysis.
S. Marcus, 473(PR):2/1983-291
639(VQR):Spring83-64
Balmuth, M.S. and R.J. Rowland, Jr., eds. Studies in Sardinian Archaeology.
D. Ridgway, 617(TLS):5Oct84-1131
Baloyra, E.A. El Salvador in Transition.
R.H. McDonald, 263:Vol33No2-249
Balpinar, B. and U. Hirsch. Flatweaves/Flachgewebe.
P. Bach, 614:Winter84-17
Baltes, M. Die Weltentstehung des platonischen Timaios nach den antiken Interpreten. (Vol 2)
D. O'Meara, 543:Jun83-914
J. Whittaker, 303(JoHS):Vol 103-182
de Balzac, H. Béatrix. (M. Fargeaud, ed)
C. Smethurst, 208(FS):Oct83-473
"Balzac, l'invention du roman."
C. Massol-Bédoin, 535(RHL):Sep/Dec83-945
Bambeck, M. Studien zu Dantes "Paradiso."*
G. Costa, 545(RPh):Nov82-340
Bamber, L. Comic Women, Tragic Men.*
I. Leimberg, 156(JDSh):Jahrbuch 1983-242
W.A. Rebhorn, 551(RenQ):Autumn83-471
Bamborschke, U., ed. Der altčechische Tandariuš nach den 3 überlieferten Handschriften mit Einleitung und Wortregister.
W. Baumann, 684(ZDA):Band112Heft3-131
Bamert, A. Africa, Tribal Art of Forest and Savanna.
M. Gilbert, 69:Vol53No3-99
Bamforth, I. The Modern Copernicus.
N. Corcoran, 617(TLS):7Sep84-1004
Bammel, E. and C.F.D. Moule, eds. Jesus and the Politics of His Day.
J.L. Houlden, 617(TLS):6Jul84-765
Bammer, A. Wohnen im Vergänglichen.
W. Müller-Wiener, 43:Band13Heft1-85
Bammesberger, A. Beiträge zu einem etymologischen Wörterbuch des Altenglischen.
E.G. Stanley, 447(N&Q):Apr82-150
Bammesberger, A. A Handbook of Irish. (Vol 1)
R.A. Fowkes, 660(Word):Dec83-230
Ban, S.H., P.Y. Moon and D.H. Perkins. Rural Development.
K. Moskowitz, 293(JASt):Nov82-63
D.I. Steinberg, 293(JASt):Nov82-91
Banchieri, A. Conclusions for Playing the Organ (1609).
P. Williams, 410(M&L):Jul/Oct83-286
Bander, R.G. Sentence Making.
J.J. Kohn, 399(MLJ):Spring83-101
Bandle, O., W. Baumgartner and J. Glauser, eds. Strindbergs Dramen im Lichte neuerer Methodendiskussionen.
E. Sprinchorn, 563(SS):Autumn83-388
T. Stenström, 562(Scan):Nov82-195

Banfield, A. Unspeakable Sentences.
M. Rapisarda, 395(MFS):Summer83-362
Banfield, E.C. The Democratic Muse.
C.E. Finn, Jr., 129:Sep84-77
R.W. Lyman, 441:25Mar84-14
Bange, E. An den Grenzen der Sprache.
M. Kesting, 547(RF):Band95Heft4-497
Bangerter, L.A. The Bourgeois Proletarian.
K-H. Schoeps, 301(JEGP):Oct83-609
Bank, S.P. and M.D. Kahn. The Sibling Bond.
E. Bermann, 385(MQR):Winter84-119
Banks, A., ed. First-Person America.
D.D. Fanelli, 658:Spring83-114
Banks, I. The Wasp Factory.
P. Craig, 617(TLS):16Mar84-287
Banks, J. Vertue Betray'd: Or, Anna Bullen. (D. Dreher, ed)
M-M.M., 189(EA):Oct-Dec84-490
Banks, J.A. Victorian Values.
A. McLaren, 637(VS):Winter83-234
Banks, L.R. The Warning Bell.
T. Fitton, 617(TLS):24Aug84-953
Banks, M.A. Understanding Science Fiction.
C.B. Hunter, 561(SFS):Mar83-113
Banks, O. The Caravaggio Obsession.
442(NY):23Apr84-135
Banks, R. The Relation of My Imprisonment.
D. Bair, 441:1Apr84-8
Bann, S. The Clothing of Clio.
E. Weber, 617(TLS):28Sep84-1072
al-Bannā, Ḥ. Five Tracts of Ḥasan al-Bannā' (1906-1949). (C. Wendell, ed and trans)
U. Abd-Allāh, 318(JAOS):Jul-Sep82-564
Banner, L.W. American Beauty.*
M. Secrest, 364:Oct83-69
Banner, W.A. Moral Norms and Moral Order.
W. Gerber, 543:Mar83-688
Bannerji, H. A Separate Sky.
I. Davies, 99:Apr83-33
Banning, K., ed. A Catalogue of Wall-Paintings in the Churches of Medieval Denmark, 1100-1600, Scania, Halland, Blekinge.
M.H. Caviness, 589:Jan83-142
Banninster, D. The Summer Boy.
J. Melmoth, 617(TLS):7Sep84-1005
Banting, K.G. The Welfare State and Canadian Federalism.
G. Teeple, 529(QQ):Autumn83-866
Banting, P. Running Into the Open.
D. Daymond, 102(CanL):Summer83-140
Banville, J. Birchwood.
P. Craig, 617(TLS):21Sep84-1066
Banville, J. The Newton Letter.
P. Lewis, 565:Vol24No1-58
Baragwanath, A.K. Currier & Ives.
M.S. Young, 39:Nov83-456
Baraka, A. - see under Jones, L./A. Baraka
Barakat, R.A. A Contextual Study of Arabic Proverbs.
W. Mieder, 196:Band24Heft1/2-127
Baratin, M. and F. Desbordes, with others. L'analyse linguistique dans l'antiquité classique. (Vol 1)
T. Hébert, 555:Vol57fasc1-148
C. de Lamberterie, 542:Jan-Mar83-75

Barba, K. Deutsche Dialekte in Rumänien.
 K. Rein, 72:Band220Heft2-380
Barbarić, S. Zur grammatischen Terminologie von Justus Georg Schottelius und Kaspar Stieler.
 W.G. Marigold, 221(GQ):Nov83-644
Barbarski, K. Polish Armour 1939-45.
 W.M. Drzewieniecki, 497(PolR):Vol28No3-103
Barbellion, W.N.P. The Journal of a Disappointed Man [and] A Last Diary.
 B. Aldiss, 617(TLS):18May84-547
Barber, B.R. Strong Democracy.
 J.L. Auspitz, 441:25Nov84-34
Barber, F. and R. Hyde. London As it Might Have Been.
 V. Powell, 39:May83-415
Barber, G. - see Contat, N.
Barber, G. and B. Fabian, eds. Buch und Buchhandel in Europa im achtzehnten Jahrhundert.
 J. Flood, M. Jannetta and D. Shaw, 354:Jun83-185
 D. Paisey, 78(BC):Winter83-484
Barber, J. Soviet Historians in Crisis, 1928-1932.
 L.E. Holmes, 125:Winter83-192
 J. Keep, 575(SEER):Apr83-295
Barber, R. The Knight and Chivalry.
 L.D. Benson, 589:Apr83-546
Barber, R. The Pastons.
 S.M., 617(TLS):18May84-562
Barber, R. - see "Arthurian Literature"
Bàrberi Squarotti, G. Il romanzo contro la storia.
 C. Godt, 400(MLN):Jan83-118
"Barbey d'Aurevilly, 11."
 P. Pelckmans, 535(RHL):Mar/Apr83-302
Barbour, R. Greek Literary Hands (A.D. 400-1600).*
 J. Irigoin, 303(JoHS):Vol 103-230
de la Barca, P.C. - see under Calderón de la Barca, P.
Barceló, P.A. Roms auswärtige Bezeichnungen Constantinischen Dynastie (306-363).
 A. Chastagnol, 555:Vol57fasc2-360
 B.H. Warmington, 123:Vol33No2-277
Barchilon, J. and P. Flinders. Charles Perrault.*
 S.R. Baker, 207(FR):Dec83-248
 J.L. Logan, 210(FrF):May83-162
 V. Mylne, 402(MLR):Jan83-185
Bareham, T., ed. Anthony Trollope.*
 F.W. Bradbrook, 447(N&Q):Jun82-252
 S.M. Smith, 541(RES):May83-238
 J.P. Vernier, 677(YES):Vol 13-334
Barenholz, B. and I. McClintock. American Antique Toys.
 V. Powell, 39:Apr83-338
Barentsen, A.A., B.M. Groen and R. Sprenger - see "Studies in Slavic and General Linguistics"
Barentsen, A.A., R. Sprenger and M.G.M. Tielemans, eds. South Slavic and Balkan Linguistics.
 E. Battistella, 350:Mar84-193
Barfoot, C.C. The Thread of Connection.*
 M.A. Doody, 445(NCF):Sep83-220
 D. Mehl, 72:Band219Heft2-478
Barga, C. Los pasos contados. (Vol 1)
 J.W. Zdenek, 552(REH):May83-293

Barga, C. Los pasos contados. (Vols 3 and 4)
 J.A. Feustle, Jr., 552(REH):Oct83-442
Bargainnier, E.F. The Gentle Art of Murder.
 P. Wolfe, 395(MFS):Autumn83-389
Bargainnier, E.F., ed. 10 Women of Mystery.
 P. Wolfe, 395(MFS):Autumn83-389
Barich, B. Traveling Light.
 J. Elukin, 441:5Feb84-19
Barickman, R., S. MacDonald and M. Stark. Corrupt Relations.*
 J.R. Reed, 445(NCF):Sep83-226
Barilier, E. La Créature.
 J.H. Mole, 617(TLS):7Dec84-1430
Barish, J. The Antitheatrical Prejudice.*
 R. Davies, 627(UTQ):Winter82/83-214
 G.E. Wellwarth, 405(MP):Feb84-329
Bark, R. Strindbergs drömspelsteknik — i drama och teater.
 J.E. Bellquist, 563(SS):Autumn83-394
 E. Törnqvist, 562(Scan):Nov83-226
Barkan, L. - see "Renaissance Drama X"
Barker, A., ed. Greek Musical Writings. (Vol 1)
 E.K. Borthwick, 617(TLS):19Oct84-1183
Barker, A.L. Life Stories.
 C. Larrière, 189(EA):Apr-Sep83-351
Barker, A.L. Relative Successes.
 K.C. O'Brien, 362:4Oct84-28
 D. Profumo, 617(TLS):3Aug84-864
Barker, A.W., ed. Dear Robertson.
 C. Munro, 71(ALS):Oct83-286
Barker, E. The British between the Superpowers, 1945-50.
 V. Rothwell, 617(TLS):16Mar84-264
Barker, E. The Making of a Moonie.
 A. Burgess, 617(TLS):9Nov84-1273
Barker, F. and others, eds. 1642.
 I. Roots, 366:Spring83-114
Barker, G. Anno Domini.
 D. Dunn, 364:Aug/Sep83-109
 D. O'Driscoll, 493:Sep83-66
Barker, G. Landscape and Society.
 T.W. Potter, 313:Vol73-222
Barker, H. Victory.
 B. Nelson, 391:May83-52
Barker, J. The Superhistorians.
 639(VQR):Winter83-8
Barker, N. and J. Collins. A Sequel to An Enquiry into the Nature of Certain Nineteenth Century Pamphlets by John Carter and Graham Pollard.
 T.A.J. Burnett, 617(TLS):16Mar84-286
 K.K. Leab, 441:4Mar84-27
Barker, N. and J. Collins - see Carter, J. and G. Pollard
Barker, P. Blow Your House Down.
 J. Lasdun, 176:Sep/Oct84-50
 K. Pollitt, 441:21Oct84-7
 J. Rogers, 617(TLS):13Jul84-790
 M. Wandor, 362:12Jul84-28
Barker, P. Union Street.*
 P. Lewis, 565:Vol24No1-58
Barker, P. and C.G. Shugart, eds. After Einstein.
 J. Largeault, 542:Jul-Sep83-345
Barkin, D. and B. Suarez. El fin de autosuficiencia alimentaria.
 S.E. Sanderson, 263(RIB):Vol33No4-562

Barkin, F., E.A. Brandt and J. Ornstein-
Galicia, eds. Bilingualism and Language
Contact.
N.C. Dorian, 660(Word):Dec83-233
J. Edwards, 399(MLJ):Autumn83-279
Barlow, F. The Norman Conquest and Beyond.
M.T. Clanchy, 617(TLS):13Apr84-408
Barlow, F. William Rufus.
R.H.C. Davis, 617(TLS):13Jan84-36
Barmé, G., ed. Lazy Dragon.
J.S.M. Lau, 116:Jul82-296
Barnach-Calbó, E. La lengua española en
Estados Unidos.
T.R. Arrington, 238:Sep83-449
Barnard, M. Assault on Mount Helicon.
M. Cowley, 441:6May84-29
Barnard, R. Corpse in a Gilded Cage.
P-L. Adams, 61:Dec84-146
N. Callendar, 441:2Dec84-62
Barnard, R. A Little Local Murder.*
639(VQR):Autumn83-127
Barnard, R. School for Murder.
P-L. Adams, 61:Apr84-148
N. Callendar, 441:25Mar84-24
Barnes, A., with K. Harding and C. Gibbs.
Tough Annie.
D. Gittins, 637(VS):Summer83-431
Barnes, B. T.S. Kuhn and Social Science.
J. Forge, 63:Dec83-444
Barnes, C. Nureyev.
R. Philp, 151:Feb83-79
Barnes, C.F., Jr. Villard de Honnecourt,
the Artist and his Drawings.
F. Bucher, 576:Oct83-299
Barnes, H.E. Sartre and Flaubert.*
D. Cosper, 478:Apr83-122
T.R. Flynn, 319:Jan84-133
W. Fowlie, 569(SR):Winter83-x
J.H. McMahon, 207(FR):Dec83-255
Barnes, J. The American Book of the Dead.*
W. Harmon, 569(SR):Summer83-457
G. Johnson, 461:Spring/Summer83-96
639(VQR):Summer83-97
Barnes, J. Flaubert's Parrot.
D. Coward, 617(TLS):5Oct84-1117
D. May, 362:18Oct84-31
Barnes, J. The Presocratic Philosophers.*
A.W.H. Adkins, 122:Jan83-68
Barnes, J. and others, eds. Science and
Speculation.
R. Joly, 540(RIPh):Vol37fasc3-362
Barnes, J.A. Who Should Know What?
A. Kuper, 488:Dec83-530
Barnes, J.J. and P.P. Hitler's "Mein
Kampf" in Britain and America.
M.L. Turner, 517(PBSA):Vol77No3-373
Barnes, L. Dead Heat.
N. Callendar, 441:25Mar84-24
Barnes, T.D. Constantine and Eusebius.*
The New Empire of Diocletian and Con-
stantine.
A. Cameron, 313:Vol73-184
J. Rougé, 487:Spring83-75
B.H. Warmington, 123:Vol33No2-278
Barnet, C., with S. Dance. Those Swinging
Years.
I. Gitler, 441:29Jul84-16
Barnet, R.J. The Alliance.*
S.C. Munson, 129:Apr84-71
Barnet, R.J. Allies.
I. Nish, 617(TLS):1Jun84-604

Barnetová, V. and others. Russkaja gram-
matika.
T. Pettersson, 559:Vol7No1-63
Barnett, A.D. China's Economy in Global
Perspective.
S.I. Levine, 293(JASt):Aug83-901
Barnett, L.K. Swift's Poetic Worlds.*
P. Danchin, 189(EA):Apr-Jun84-202
R. Quintana, 402(MLR):Apr83-428
Barnett, R.D. Ancient Ivories in the
Middle East.
M. Vickers, 90:May83-303
Barnett, U. A Vision of Order.
C. Hope, 617(TLS):2Nov84-1240
Barnett, V.E. Kandinsky at the Guggenheim.
J. Willett, 617(TLS):8Jun84-630
Barney, S.A. Allegories of History, Alle-
gories of Love.*
G. Clifford, 599:Winter83-68
L.S. Lerner, 545(RPh):May83-596
Barnhart, C.L. and others, eds. The
Second Barnhart Dictionary of New
English.*
W.K. Evans, 35(AS):Fall83-255
Barnickel, K-D. Sprachliche Varianten des
Englischen.
E.W. Schneider, 38:Band101Heft1/2-192
Barns, J.W.B., G.M. Browne and J.C. Shel-
ton, eds. Nag Hammadi Codices: Greek
and Coptic Papyri from the Cartonnage of
the Covers.
B. Layton, 318(JAOS):Apr-Jun82-397
Barnstone, W. - see Borges, J.L.
Barnum, P.T. Selected Letters of P.T.
Barnum.* (A.H. Saxon, ed)
D.B. Wilmeth, 612(ThS):May/Nov83-165
Barnwell, H.T. The Tragic Drama of Cor-
neille and Racine.*
C. Fettes, 157:Spring83-50
G. Gerhardi, 547(RF):Band95Heft3-347
G. May, 400(MLN):Dec83-1369
J. Scherer, 610:Autumn83-258
Barnwell, J. Love of Order.
639(VQR):Winter83-9
Baroli, M. La Vie quotidienne en Berry au
temps de George Sand.
M.G. Paulson, 207(FR):Mar84-577
Baron, C. - see Neville, G.H.
Baron, D.E. Grammar and Good Taste.
R.C. Bambas, 191(ELN):Jun84-71
J.H. Fisher, 27(AL):Dec83-671
Baron, F. Faustus.
H.G. Haile, 221(GQ):May83-496
"Baroque." (No 9 and 10)
H. Lafay, 535(RHL):May/Jun83-467
Barr, A. and P. Levy. The Official Foodie
Handbook.
K. Visick, 617(TLS):21Dec84-1486
Barr, J. Holy Scripture.
D. Nineham, 617(TLS):20Apr84-441
Barr, M.S., ed. Future Females.
L. Leith, 561(SFS):Jul83-247
Barr, W. - see Claudian
Barr-Sharrar, B. and E.N. Borza, eds. Mac-
edonia and Greece in Late Classical and
Early Hellenistic Times.
A.R. Burn, 303(JoHS):Vol 103-208
Barrabini, V. L'Odissea a Trapani.
P.V. Jones, 123:Vol33No1-126
Barragán, M.G.G. - see under García Barra-
gán, M.G.

de Barral, B.M. La Música Teúrgico-
Mágica de los Indios Guaraos.
    D.A. Olsen, 187:Sep84-561
Barratt, G. Russia in Pacific Waters:
1715-1825.
    G.W., 102(CanL):Spring83-189
Barratt, P. M. Annaei Lucani Belli
Civilis Liber V, A Commentary.
    P.H. Schrijvers, 394:Vol36fasc3/4-431
Barreau, J-C. Les Innocents de Pigalle.
    B. Knapp, 207(FR):Apr84-731
Barrell, J. The Dark Side of the Land-
scape.*
    J. Wordsworth, 541(RES):Feb83-83
Barrera Vásquez, A. and others, comps.
Diccionario Maya Cordemex.
    T. Kaufman, 269(IJAL):Apr83-208
Barrère, J-B. Claudel.*
    J-N. Segrestaa, 535(RHL):Jul/Aug83-660
Barreto-Rivera, R. Voices Noises.
    P. Monk, 150(DR):Spring83-179
Barrett, H. Daring To Be.
    W.S. Howell, 583:Spring84-336
Barrett, W. The Truants.*
    G.B. Bullert, 396(ModA):Winter83-85
Barricelli, J-P. and J. Gibaldi, eds.
Interrelations of Literature.
    S. Soupel, 189(EA):Oct-Dec84-448
Barrickman, R., S. MacDonald and M. Spark.
Corrupt Relations.
    J. Blondel, 189(EA):Jul-Sep84-339
Barrier, B. Les activités du solitaire en
Chartreuse d'après ses plus anciens
témoins.
    R.B. Marks, 589:Oct83-1107
Barringer, F. Flight from Sorrow.
    G.A. De Candido, 441:4Mar84-22
Barrionuevo, C.R. - see under Ruiz Barrio-
nuevo, C.
Barris, C. Confessions of a Dangerous
Mind.
    D. Henstell, 441:27May84-16
Barron, J. An Introduction to Greek Sculp-
ture.
    H. Plommer, 123:Vol33No1-91
Barron, J. KGB Today.
    I. Elliot, 617(TLS):26Oct84-1207
    E.J. Epstein, 129:Mar84-76
Barron, W.R.J. "Trawthe" and Treason.*
    J.A. Burrow, 447(N&Q):Feb82-66
    P.J.C. Field, 382(MAE):1983/1-136
    P. Gradon, 541(RES):Aug83-323
    E.D. Kennedy, 38:Band101Heft1/2-229
    E. Wilson, 402(MLR):Apr83-423
Barros, J. Britain, Greece and the
Politics of Sanctions.
    R. Clogg, 617(TLS):15Jun84-679
Barrow, A., ed. The Gossip Family Hand-
book. International Gossip.
    A. Forbes, 617(TLS):6Jan84-7
Barrow, G.W.S. Kingship and Unity.
    R. Nicholson, 589:Jan83-145
Barrow, R. Happiness.
    E.J. Bond, 529(QQ):Summer83-565
Barrow, R. Injustice, Inequality and
Ethics.
    B. Cohen, 479(PhQ):Jul83-309
    J.D., 185:Oct83-159
Barrows, S. Distorting Mirrors.*
    E.F. Gray, 395(MFS):Summer83-300

Barrutia, R. and T.D. Terrell. Fonética y
fonología españolas.
    T.R. Arrington, 238:Sep83-450
    J.P. Lantolf, 399(MLJ):Summer83-203
Barry, J. George Sand ou le scandale de
la liberté.
    J. Aeply, 450(NRF):Apr83-111
Barry, S. The Water-Colourist.
    D. Profumo, 617(TLS):28Sep84-1105
Barry, W. The Wheel.
    P. Stitt, 491:Oct83-39
Barsky, O. and others. Políticas agrarias,
colonización y desarrollo rural en Ecua-
dor.
    C.E. Aramburu, 263(RIB):Vol33No2-250
Barsotti, A. Pier Maria Rosso di San
Secondo.
    G. Marrone-Puglia, 276:Spring83-79
Barss, P. Older Ways.
    G.L. Pocius, 658:Spring83-109
Barstow, S. A Brother's Tale.
    M. Théry, 189(EA):Apr-Sep83-350
Barstow, S. The Glad Eye and Other
Stories.
    J. Melmoth, 617(TLS):18May84-546
Bart, B.F. and R.F. Cook. The Legendary
Sources of Flaubert's Saint Julien.
    H. Redman, Jr., 546(RR):Mar83-248
Barth, A. The Rights of Free Men. (J.E.
Clayton, ed)
    N.A. Cherniss, 441:1Apr84-23
Barth, E.M. and J.L. Martens, eds. Argu-
mentation.
    J.L. Subbiondo, 350:Sep84-688
Barth, J. The Friday Book.
    W. Kendrick, 441:18Nov84-16
Barth, J. Sabbatical.*
    S. Pinsker, 577(SHR):Summer83-272
    P. Stevick, 473(PR):3/1983-469
Barthel, D.L. Amana.
    D. Manuel, 441:2Sep84-15
Barthel, M. The Jesuits.
    B. Dubivsky, 441:22Jul84-21
Barthélemy-Madaule, M. Lamarck the Myth-
ical Precursor.
    M. Ruse, 529(QQ):Autumn83-885
Barthelme, F. Second Marriage.
    R. Loewinsohn, 441:30Sep84-1
    442(NY):12Nov84-192
Barthes, R. A Barthes Reader.* (S. Son-
tag, ed)
    J. Parini, 249(HudR):Summer83-411
    42(AR):Winter83-120
Barthes, R. Camera Lucida.*
    C. Norris, 148:Spring83-88
    A.P., 617(TLS):12Oct84-1171
Barthes, R. Empire of Signs.*
    C. Fawcett, 46:Aug83-73
    J.B. Gordon, 560:Fall83-99
Barthes, R. L'obvie et l'obtus.
    A. Lavers, 208(FS):Oct83-487
Barthes, R. The Responsibility of Forms.
    M. Thiébaux, 441:23Dec84-17
Barthes, R. and L. Bersani. Littérature
et réalité.
    D. Hollier, 98:Apr83-271
Bartlett, A. Drawing and Painting the
Landscape.
    C. Ashwin, 592:Apr/May83-26
Bartlett, B. Cattail Week.
    D. Daymond, 102(CanL):Summer83-140
Bartlett, E. Strange Territory.
    J. Mole, 176:Jun84-58

Bartlett, L., ed. The Beats.
R. Weinreich, 649(WAL):Aug83-160
Bartlett, L. - see Everson, W.
Bartley, J. Invocations.
T. Marshall, 529(QQ):Winter83-1152
Bartley, W.W. 3d - see Popper, K.R.
Bartolozzi, B. New Sounds for Woodwind.
(2nd ed) (R.S. Brindle, ed and trans)
N. O'Loughlin, 415:Mar83-172
Barton, A. Ben Jonson, Dramatist.
I. Donaldson, 617(TLS):7Dec84-1417
H. Levin, 453(NYRB):20Dec84-61
Barton, J. Playing Shakespeare.
S. Wells, 617(TLS):12Oct84-1160
Barton, M. and A. Jacobs - see "British
Music Yearbook 1983"
Bartsch, A. The Illustrated Bartsch.
(Vols 7-11 thru 7-13, 8-14 thru 8-17,
13-24 and 13-25)
D. Landau, 90:Mar83-169
Bartsch, R. and T. Vennemann. Grundzüge
der Sprachtheorie.*
G. Hammarström, 67:Nov83-330
K.H. Schmidt, 685(ZDL):3/1983-373
Bartstra, G-J. Contributions to the Study
of the Palaeolithic Patjitan Culture,
Java, Indonesia. (Pt 1)
K.L. Hutterer, 318(JAOS):Jul-Sep82-582
Baruchello, G. and H. Martin. How to
Imagine.
D. Hall, 441:15Apr84-20
Barwick, G. Sir John Did His Duty.
D. Markwell, 617(TLS):20Apr84-439
Barwick, S. A Century of Style.
P. Bach, 614:Fall84-13
de Bary, W.T. Neo-Confucian Orthodoxy
and the Learning of the Mind-and-Heart.
D.S. Nivison, 293(JASt):Aug83-910
Barzel, B. Mystique de l'ineffable dans
l'hindouisme et le christianisme.
A. Reix, 542:Jan-Mar83-77
Barzini, L. The Europeans.* (British
title: The Impossible Europeans.)
639(VQR):Autumn83-131
Barzun, J. A Stroll With William James.*
R. Dinnage, 617(TLS):17Feb84-158
G. Pool, 344:Winter84-134
Bascetta, C., ed. Sport e giuochi.
A. Jacobs, 70:Mar-Apr81-130
Basham, A.L., ed. A Cultural History of
India.
H. Tinker, 617(TLS):24Aug84-934
Bashan, E. and R. Attal, eds. A History
of the Jews in North Africa. (Vol 2)
M. Brett, 69:Vol53No4-93
Baskiyar, D.D. The Inextinguishable Flame.
M. O'Neill, 161(DUJ):Jun83-135
Basmajian, S. Surplus Waste and Other
Poems.
B. Pell, 102(CanL):Summer83-112
Bass, A. - see Derrida, J.
Bass, E.E. Aldous Huxley.
P. Miles, 354:Mar83-77
Bass, R. The Emerald Illusion.
J. Kaufman, 441:19Feb84-22
Bassnett-McGuire, S. Translation Studies.*
M. Griffith, 447(N&Q):Feb82-63
D.H., 355(LSoc):Mar83-133
J. Kornelius, 38:Band101Heft1/2-200
Basso, I.D. - see under Dardano Basso, I.
Bastet, F.L. and M. de Vos. Il terzo
stile pompeiano.
R. Higgins, 39:Jan83-71

Bastian, F. Defoe's Early Life.*
T.R. Knox, 568(SCN):Spring/Summer83-13
Bastian, U. Die "Kinder- und Hausmärchen"
der Brüder Grimm in der literaturpäda-
gogischen Diskussion des 19. und 20.
Jahrhunderts.
O.F. Gmelin, 196:Band24Heft1/2-129
G. Opie, 402(MLR):Oct83-982
Bastin, J. and P. Rohatgi. Prints of
Southeast Asia in the India Office
Library.
V. Powell, 39:Feb83-151
Bastin, M-L. La Sculpture Tshokwe.
D.J. Crowley, 2(AfrA):Aug83-11
Bastos, A.R. - see under Roa Bastos, A.
Bastos, J.B. Analise de duas experiencias
de universidade aberta: Londres e Quebec.
T.F. Carvalhal, 193(ELit):Aug83-296
Bataille, G. L'Abbé C.*
M. Véron, 441:26Feb84-24
Batchelor, J. The Edwardian Novelists.
T.E.M. Boll, 177(ELT):Vol26No1-55
R.H. Costa, 395(MFS):Summer83-266
J. Hawthorn, 136:Vol 15No1-22
T.C. Moser, 569(SR):Spring83-282
Batchelor, J. - see Conrad, J.
Bates, D. The Fashoda Incident of 1898.
M. Crowder, 617(TLS):16Mar84-273
Bates, H.E. My Uncle Silas.
P. Craig, 617(TLS):28Dec84-1506
Bateson, M.C. With a Daughter's Eye.
M. Sahlins, 441:26Aug84-1
S. Toulmin, 453(NYRB):6Dec84-3
442(NY):15Oct84-179
Baticle, Y.R. Clés et codes du cinéma.
(2nd ed)
C.P. James, 207(FR):Feb84-441
Bátori, I., J. Krause and H.D. Lutz, eds.
Linguistische Datenverarbeitung.
M. Johnson, 350:Jun84-470
G.F. Meier, 682(ZPSK):Band36Heft6-748
Bätschmann, O. Dialektik der Malerei von
Nicolas Poussin.*
E. Cropper, 54:Dec83-700
Battcock, G., ed. Breaking the Sound
Barrier.
T.J. O'Grady, 414(MusQ):Winter83-138
Battesti-Pelegrin, J. - see de Stúñiga, L.
Battin, M.P. Ethical Issues in Suicide.
S.E. Marshall, 479(PhQ):Jul83-308
Battiscombe, G. The Spencers of Althorp.
D. Cannadine, 617(TLS):2Nov84-1254
Battisti, E. Filippo Brunelleschi.*
B.L. Brown, 90:Feb83-98
Battle, L. Southern Women.
M. Berkley, 441:16Sep84-30
Battus. Opperlandse taal- & letterkunde.
R. Doeve, 204(FdL):Sep82-234
Bauchhenss, G. and P. Noelke. Die Iupiter-
säulen in den germanischen Provinzen.
D.E.E. and F.S. Kleiner, 576:Mar83-74
Baude, M. and M-M. Münch, eds. Romantisme
et religion.*
M. Evdokimov, 549(RLC):Apr-Jun83-233
Baudelaire, C. Die Blumen des Bösen.
(W.R. Berger, ed and trans)
J. von Stackelberg, 52:Band18Heft1-105
Baudelaire, C. Les Fleurs du Mal.* (R.
Howard, trans)
R. Feld, 472:Fall/Winter83Spring/
Summer84-39
L. Stall, 598(SoR):Winter84-232
[continued]

23

Baudelaire, C. Les Fleurs du Mal. (R. Howard, trans) [continuing]
P.T. Starr, 400(MLN):Dec83-1355
639(VQR):Winter83-26
Baudemont, S. L'Histoire et la légende dans l'école élémentaire victorienne (1862-1917).
I. Campbell, 189(EA):Jan-Mar83-89
Baudet, J-L. - see Zweig, S.
Bauer, C., ed. Graded French Reader, Deuxième Etape.* (2nd ed)
B.G. Hirsch, 399(MLJ):Summer83-191
Bauer, E., ed. Heinrich Hallers Übersetzung der "Imitatio Christi."
H. Kolb, 72:Band220Heft1-138
Bauer, H. and others. Corpus der barocken Deckenmalerei in Deutschland. (Vol 2)
A. Laing, 90:Dec83-768
Bauer, L. and others. American English Pronunciation.*
F.W. Gester, 72:Band220Heft2-387
Bauer, P.T. Reality and Rhetoric.
N. Macrae, 441:26Feb84-29
M. Novak, 129:Sep84-66
D. Rimmer, 617(TLS):9Mar84-236
J. Wood, 176:Dec84-42
Bauerle, R.H., ed. The James Joyce Songbook.*
S. Benstock, 395(MFS):Summer83-284
295(JML):Nov83-507
de Bauffremont, A. Journal de campagne dans les pays barbaresques (1766). (M. Chirac, ed)
R. Lebègue, 535(RHL):Jan/Feb83-127
Baum, G. The Priority of Labour.
R. Hutchinson, 99:May83-30
Baum, R. "Dependenzgrammatik."
R. Emons, 38:Band101Heft1/2-162
G.F. Meier, 682(ZPSK):Band36Heft4-469
Bauman, R. Let Your Words Be Few.
C. Hill, 617(TLS):6Apr84-364
Bauman, Z. Hermeneutics and Social Science.
L.M. Hinman, 484(PPR):Dec83-281
Baumann, G. Robert Musil: Ein Entwurf.
J. Strelka, 133:Band16Heft2/3-267
R. Whitinger, 564:Sep83-228
Baumer, R.V.M. and J.R. Brandon, eds. Sanskrit Drama in Performance.
K. Hansen, 293(JASt):Nov82-179
Baumgart, W. The Peace of Paris.
N.G.O. Pereira, 550(RusR):Jan83-108
Baumgarten, M. City Scriptures.
S.S. Pinsker, 395(MFS):Summer83-373
W.P. Randel, 27(AL):Mar83-117
Baumgartner, A.J. Untersuchungen zur Anthologie des Codex Salmasienus.*
J. Soubiran, 555:Vol57fasc2-344
Baumgartner, E. - see "La Quête du Saint Graal"
Baumgartner, W. Triumph des Irrealismus.*
M. Brøndsted, 462(OL):Vol137No2-196
Baur, G.W. Bibliographie zur Mundartforschung in Baden-Württemberg, Vorarlberg und Liechtenstein.
D. Stellmacher, 685(ZDL):1/1983-96
Baurmann, J. Textrezeption und Schule.
W. Schmidt, 682(ZPSK):Band36Heft4-458
Baurmeister, U. and others, eds. Bibliothèque Nationale: Catalogue des incunables. (Vol 2, fasc 1)
B.M. Rosenthal, 517(PBSA):Vol77No1-114

Baurmeister, U. and others, eds. Bibliothèque Nationale: Catalogue des incunables. (Vol 2, fasc 2)
B.M. Rosenthal, 517(PBSA):Vol77No3-410
Bausch, R. The Last Good Time.
N. Forbes, 441:23Dec84-25
Bausch, R. The Lives of Riley Chance.
C. Verderese, 441:13May84-22
Bauschatz, P.C. The Well and the Tree.
A. Liberman, 222(GR):Fall83-158
Baviskar, B.S. The Politics of Development.
J. Das Gupta, 293(JASt):Nov82-105
Baxandall, M. The Limewood Sculptors of Renaissance Germany.*
C. Lowenthal, 551(RenQ):Summer83-257
Baxter, J. Shakespeare's Poetic Styles.*
M. Coyle, 447(N&Q):Feb82-72
L.C. Knights, 402(MLR):Jan83-137
J. Reibetanz, 178:Sep83-371
Baxter, J.K. Collected Plays. (H. McNaughton, ed)
T. James, 617(TLS):10Feb84-149
Baxter, J.K. Selected Poems. (J.E. Weir, ed)
C. Boyle, 364:Nov83-84
R. Garfitt, 617(TLS):20Jul84-819
Baxter, M.G. One and Inseparable.
M. Kammen, 441:23Dec84-10
Baxter, S.B., ed. England's Rise to Greatness, 1660-1763.*
639(VQR):Summer83-86
Bayard, J. Works of Splendour and Imagination.
M. Rosenthal, 59:Jun83-242
Bayard, P. Symptôme de Stendhal.
F.W. Saunders, 208(FS):Oct83-471
Bayer, R., A.L. Caplan and N. Daniels, eds. In Search of Equity.
T.D., 185:Jul84-743
Bayer, W. Switch.
N. Callendar, 441:19Aug84-20
Bayer-Berenbaum, L. The Gothic Imagination.
N. Homad-Sultan, 549(RLC):Jan-Mar83-118
Bayley, J. Selected Essays.
B. Bergonzi, 176:Jul/Aug84-48
P.N. Furbank, 362:26Apr84-28
G. Steiner, 617(TLS):20Apr84-423
Bayley, J. Shakespeare and Tragedy.*
L.S. Champion, 179(ES):Jun83-276
E.A.J. Honigmann, 447(N&Q):Dec82-540
L.R. Leavis, 396(ModA):Summer/Fall83-341
C.J. Sugnet, 481(PQ):Winter83-112
Bayley, P. French Pulpit Oratory, 1598-1650.*
P. Zoberman, 546(RR):May83-375
Bayley, P. and D.G. Coleman, eds. The Equilibrium of Wit.
Q.M. Hope, 210(FrF):Sep83-275
J. Moravcevich, 207(FR):Feb84-392
P.A. Wadsworth, 475:Vol 10No19-874
Bayley, S. Harley Earl and the Dream Machine.
H. Mitgang, 441:1Jan84-20
Baylon, C. and P. Fabre. Les noms de lieux et de personnes.
R. Arveiller, 209(FM):Jul83-281
J-P. Chambon, 553(RLiR):Jul-Dec83-496
H.J. Siskin, 207(FR):Mar84-581

Baylon, C. and P. Fabre. La Sémantique avec des travaux pratiques d'application et leurs corrigés.*
  G. Price, 208(FS):Oct83-501

Bazlen, R. Note senza testo.
  P. Lombardo, 98:Aug-Sep83-653

Bazlen, R. Scritti.
  M. d'Amico, 617(TLS):7Sep84-986

Beach, E. Dance of the Dialectic.
  S.H. Lee, 543:Dec82-442

Beach, M.C. The Imperial Image.
  U. Roberts, 60:Jan-Feb83-139

Beadle, R., ed. The York Plays.*
  D.C. Baker, 401(MLQ):Jun83-207
  C. Gauvin, 189(EA):Oct-Dec84-460

Beal, G.W.J. and others. Jim Dine.
  A. Barnet, 441:24Jun84-22

Beal, P., comp. Index of English Literary Manuscripts.* (Vol 1, Pts 1 and 2)
  S.H. Garrison, 70:May-Jun81-161

Beale, P. - see Partridge, E.

Bealer, G. Quality and Concept.*
  G. Stahl, 542:Jul-Sep83-347

Beam, C.R. Pennsylvania German Dictionary: English to Pennsylvania Dutch.
  R. Ambacher, 399(MLJ):Autumn83-292

Bean, M.C. The Development of Word Order Patterns in Old English.
  E. Battistella, 350:Jun84-455

Bean, P. Punishment.*
  S.L. Mendus, 518:Jan83-36
  J. Narveson, 483:Jul83-405

Bear, J. Computer Wimp.
  J. Hackney, 617(TLS):14Dec84-1443

Beard, G. International Modern Glass.
  G. Wills, 39:Mar83-263

Beard, G. Stucco and Decorative Plasterwork in Europe.*
  N. Powell, 39:Oct83-352

Beard, G. The Work of Christopher Wren.
  J. Lees-Milne, 39:Jan83-72

Beard, J. Beard on Pasta.*
  W. and C. Cowen, 639(VQR):Autumn83-138
  42(AR):Summer83-379

Beard, R. The Indo-European Lexicon.*
  R.A. Fowkes, 660(Word):Aug83-138

Beardmore, G. Civilians at War.
  C. Townshend, 617(TLS):9Nov84-1278

Beardsley, D. Kissing the Body of My Lord.
  A. Mitcham, 102(CanL):Autumn83-112

Beardsley, M.C. The Aesthetic Point of View. (M.J. Wreen and D.M. Callen, eds)
  J.R., 185:Jan84-364
  A. Silvers, 290(JAAC):Winter83-213

Beardsmore, H.B. Bilingualism.
  V. Arizpe, 399(MLJ):Autumn83-280
  S. Romaine, 353:Vol20No3/4-359

Beasley, J.C. Novels of the 1740s.
  P-G. Boucé, 189(EA):Oct-Dec84-468
  D.S. Durant, 70:Mar-Apr83-125
  M. Moseley, 569(SR):Spring83-xl
  D. Nokes, 566:Spring84-166

Beason, R.G. Hanging On.
  R. Elman, 441:20May84-30

Beaton, R. Folk Poetry of Modern Greece.*
  S.G. Armistead, 131(CL):Winter83-89
  M. Herzfeld, 292(JAF):Jan-Mar83-96

Beatrice, P.F. and others, eds. Cento anni bibliografia ambrosiana (1874-1974).
  P. Petitmengin, 555:Vol57fasc1-177

Beattie, A. The Burning House.*
  D. Flower, 249(HudR):Summer83-359
  S. Pinsker, 573(SSF):Spring-Summer83-144
  639(VQR):Spring83-57

Beattie, H.J. Land and Lineage in China.
  E. Wickberg, 318(JAOS):Jul-Sep82-577

Beattie, J. James Beattie, "The Minstrel." (P. Morère, ed)
  J.H. Pittock, 571(ScLJ):Winter83-50
  G.R. Roy, 189(EA):Jul-Sep84-335

Beattie, S. The New Sculpture.*
  J.M. Crook, 617(TLS):17Feb84-171
  R. Jefferies, 324:Oct84-747

Beauchamp, T.L. and J.F. Childress, eds. Principles of Biomedical Ethics. (2nd ed)
  T.D., 185:Jul84-744

Beauchamp, T.L. and A. Rosenberg. Hume and the Problem of Causation.*
  B. Berofsky, 311(JP):Aug83-478
  D.H. Sanford, 449:Sep83-502

de Beaugrande, R. Text, Discourse, and Process.*
  J.P. Thorne, 541(RES):May83-199

de Beaugrande, R. - see Schmidt, S.J.

de Beaugrande, R-A. and W.U. Dressler. Introduction to Text Linguistics.* (German title: Einführung in die Textlinguistik.)
  C. McAfee, 506(PSt):Sep83-178

de Beaujoyeulx, B. Le Balet comique, 1581.
  P. Ford, 208(FS):Apr83-209

Beaulieu, J. J'ai beaucoup changé depuis...
  J. Moss, 102(CanL):Spring83-143

Beaulieu, M. Visages.
  S. Lawall, 207(FR):Oct83-130

Beauman, S. The Royal Shakespeare Company.
  G. Giesekam, 610:Autumn83-274
  J. Griffin, 157:Spring83-51

Beaumont, C. - see Thompson, R.

Beaumont, F. and J. Fletcher. The Dramatic Works in the Beaumont and Fletcher Canon.* (Vol 4) (F. Bowers, ed)
  J. Gerritsen, 541(RES):May83-212

Beaumont, F. and J. Fletcher. The Dramatic Works in the Beaumont and Fletcher Canon. (Vol 5) (F. Bowers, general ed)
  L. Scragg, 148:Autumn83-87

Beausoleil, C. Le Surface du paysage.
  D.F. Rogers, 102(CanL):Summer83-160

de Beauvoir, S. Adieux.
  D. Johnson, 441:6May84-11
  R. Sennett, 61:May84-116
  M. Warnock, 362:21Jun84-23
  442(NY):21May84-133

de Beauvoir, S. Quand prime le spirituel.
  A. Cismaru, 77:Spring83-170

de Beauvoir, S. When Things of the Spirit Come First.*
  P. Lewis, 565:Vol24No1-58

de Beauvoir, S. - see Sartre, J-P.

Bebek, B. The Third City.*
  D.J.G., 185:Apr84-554

Bec, P. La Lyrique française au moyen âge (XIIe-XIIIe siècles).*
  E.W. Poe, 545(RPh):Nov82-298

Béchade, H.D. Les Romans comiques de Charles Sorel.*
  Y. Galet, 209(FM):Jul83-276
  R.G. Hodgson, 402(MLR):Jan83-183
  G. Molinié, 535(RHL):Mar/Apr83-269

Bechert, H., ed. Die Sprache der ältesten buddhistischen Überlieferung.*
  O. von Hinüber, 260(IF):Band88-307
Bechert, H. and H. Braun. Pāli Nīti Texts of Burma.
  J.W. de Jong, 259(IIJ):Mar83-150
Beck, B.E.F. The Three Twins.
  C.S. Littleton, 292(JAF):Oct-Dec83-492
Beck, E.T., ed. Nice Jewish Girls.
  S. Bronznick, 287:Mar83-29
Beck, J., ed. Le Concil de Basle (1434).*
  J.C. Laidlaw, 382(MAE):1983/2-328
  N. Mann, 208(FS):Apr83-203
  G.A. Runnalls, 545(RPh):Nov82-312
Beck, J.M. Joseph Howe. (Vol 1)
  J. Fingard, 150(DR):Winter83/84-689
Beck, L.W. Essays on Kant and Hume.*
  R. Malter, 342:Band74Heft2-225
Becker, C., ed. Les Soirées de Médan.
  D. Baguley, 535(RHL):Jul/Aug83-656
Becker, D.G. The New Bourgeoisie and the Limits of Dependency.
  R. Thorp, 617(TLS):10Feb84-142
Becker, G.S. A Treatise on the Family.
  M. Wallerstein, 185:Oct83-152
Becker, H.S. Art Worlds.*
  T.J. Diffey, 89(BJA):Autumn83-367
  D. Kuspit, 62:Apr84-73
Becker, J. The PLO.
  C.C. O'Brien, 362:26Apr84-29
  D. Pipes, 129:Nov84-67
  D. Pryce-Jones, 176:Jun84-61
  M. Yapp, 617(TLS):11May84-514
Becker, J. Sleeping Days.
  P. Lewis, 565:Vol124No3-36
Becker, L.C. Property Rights.
  S.A.C., 543:Sep82-159
Becker, M.G., R.J. Dilligan and T.K. Bender, eds. A Concordance to the Poems of John Keats.
  C. Dunbar, 340(KSJ):Vol132-225
  H. Kelliher, 354:Jun83-192
Becker, R.H. - see Wagner, H.R. and C.L. Camp
Becker, R.P., ed. German Humanism and Reformation.
  E. Bernstein, 221(GQ):Nov83-638
Becker, R.P. A War of Fools.*
  W. Frey, 684(ZDA):Band112Heft1-47
Becker-Cantarino, B., ed. Die Frau von der Reformation zur Romantik.
  S.L. Cocalis, 221(GQ):Mar83-356
Beckett, B.A. The Reception of Pablo Neruda's Works in the German Democratic Republic.
  M. Gerber, 221(GQ):Nov83-701
Beckett, S. A Samuel Beckett Reader. (J. Calder, ed)
  V. Cunningham, 617(TLS):10Feb84-135
Beckett, S. Catastrophe et autres dramaticules.
  C. Dis, 450(NRF):Jan83-107
  B.L. Knapp, 207(FR):Oct83-131
Beckett, S. Collected Poems 1930-1978.
  A. Jenkins, 176:Jul/Aug84-52
Beckett, S. Collected Shorter Plays.
  A.J., 617(TLS):20Apr84-443
  A. Jenkins, 176:Jul/Aug84-54
Beckett, S. Disjecta. (R. Cohn, ed)
  V. Cunningham, 617(TLS):10Feb84-135
  A. Jenkins, 176:Jul/Aug84-51
Beckett, S. Ill Seen Ill Said.
  42(AR):Spring83-252

Beckett, S. Three Occasional Pieces.
  D. Devlin, 157:Autumn83-31
Beckett, S. Worstward Ho.*
  V. Cunningham, 617(TLS):10Feb84-135
  442(NY):26Mar84-133
Beckwith, C. and M. van Offelen. Nomads of the Niger.*
  R.L. Shep, 614:Spring84-25
Bécquer, G.A. Leyendas. (J. Campos, ed)
  D. Keown, 86(BHS):Jan83-90
Bedard, B. Hour of the Beast and Other Stories.
  G. Weaver, 344:Fall84-107
Beddow, M. The Fiction of Humanity.
  R. Nicholls, 131(CL):Summer83-300
Bédé, J-A. and W.B. Edgerton, eds. Columbia Dictionary of Modern European Literature.* (2nd ed)
  D.M. Bethea, 574(SEEJ):Spring83-109
  H. McCarthy, 70:Sep/Oct81-28
  A. Thorlby, 678(YCGL):No31-161
Bedford, S. A Legacy. A Favourite of The Gods. A Compass Error.
  L. Marcus, 617(TLS):1Jun84-623
Bedford, S. A Visit to Don Otavio.
  S.O., 617(TLS):22Jun84-711
Beechey, W. The Rich Mrs. Robinson.
  J. Burnett, 617(TLS):30Mar84-331
Beeching, J. The Galleys at Lepanto.*
  639(VQR):Autumn83-118
Beer, B.L. Rebellion and Riot.*
  G.R. Elton, 551(RenQ):Autumn83-427
de Beer, E.S. - see Locke, J.
Beer, G. Darwin's Plots.
  J. Durant, 617(TLS):31Aug84-965
  D. Joravsky, 453(NYRB):25Oct84-43
  G. Levine, 454:Winter84-188
Beer, J. Musicalische Discurse.
  G.J. Buelow, 410(M&L):Jul/Oct83-261
Beer, J. Wordsworth in Time.
  M. Isnard, 189(EA):Jan-Mar83-84
Beer, J.M.A. Narrative Conventions of Truth in the Middle Ages.
  N.J. Lacy, 207(FR):Oct83-103
  P.S. Noble, 382(MAE):1983/2-320
  R. Pensom, 208(FS):Oct83-442
Beer, P. The Lie of the Land.*
  B. Jones, 364:Jul83-78
  M. O'Neill, 493:Jun83-58
Beer, S.H. Britain Against Itself.
  639(VQR):Spring83-60
Beeston, A.F.L. and others, eds. Arabic Literature to the End of the Umayyad Period.
  P. Avery, 617(TLS):7Sep84-1001
Beeston, A.F.L. and others. Sabaic Dictionary.
  P. Swiggers, 350:Sep84-672
Beetz, K.H. Algernon Charles Swinburne: A Bibliography of Secondary Works, 1861-1980.*
  A.H. Harrison, 405(MP):Aug83-89
Beetz, M. Rhetorische Logik.
  F. Gaede, 406:Winter83-430
Beevor, A. The Faustian Pact.*
  N. Callendar, 441:28Oct84-39
  M. Laski, 362:9Feb84-26
Beg, M.A.J. Arabic Loan-Words in Malay.
  Tham Seong Chee, 302:Vol 19No2-230
Beg, M.A.J. Persian and Turkish Loan-Words in Malay.
  J.U. Wolff, 350:Sep84-680

Beggiato, F., ed. Le lettere di Abelardo ed Eloisa nella traduzione di Jean de Meun.
E. Hicks, 554:Vol 103No2/3-384
Béhague, G. Music in Latin America.
S. Collier, 410(M&L):Jan/Apr83-89
Behal, V.J. Möbel des Jugendstils.
S. Jervis, 90:May83-305
Béhar, H. Jarry dramaturge.
K.S. Beaumont, 208(FS):Apr83-244
Behbehani, H.S.H. China's Foreign Policy in the Arab World, 1955-75.
R.M. Lorantas, 293(JASt):Aug83-902
Behler, E. - see Schlegel, F.
Behler, E. and others - see Schlegel, F.
Behler, E. and U. Struc-Oppenberg - see Schlegel, F.
Behlmer, G.K. Child Abuse and Moral Reform in England, 1870-1908.
B. Wasserstein, 617(TLS):20Jan84-67
Behn, N. Seven Silent Men.
R.P. Mills, 441:15Jul84-18
Behrens, F.R. Werkausgabe. (Vol 1) (G. Rühm, ed)
J. Rieckmann, 221(GQ):Jan83-151
Behrens, L. Zur funktionalen Motivation der Wortstellung.
J. Haiman, 350:Sep84-671
Behrens, R. Problematische Rhetorik.
G. Le Coat, 475:Vol 10No18-301
Beichman, J. Masaoka Shiki.
J.R. Morita, 407(MN):Autumn83-324
Ōoka Makoto, 285(JapQ):Jul-Sep83-314
Beidelman, T.O. Colonial Evangelism.
J. Murray, 69:Vol53No3-89
Beier, U. Yoruba Beaded Crowns.*
J.M. Borgatti, 2(AfrA):Nov82-88
Beiner, R. Political Judgment.
M.J. Sandel, 441:19Aug84-16
J. Waldron, 617(TLS):27Apr84-469
Beiner, R. - see Arendt, H.
Beissel, H. and F. Lach. Cantos North.
L. Welch, 198:Jun83-91
G. Woodcock, 102(CanL):Summer83-163
Beitel, W. and J. Noetzold. Deutsch-sowjetische Wirtschaftsbeziehungen in der Zeit der Weimarer Republik.
P.R. Gregory, 550(RusR):Oct83-435
"Beiträge aus der Thesaurus-Arbeit."
J.E.G. Zetzel, 122:Oct83-360
Bejarano Díaz, H. - see Restrepo, F.
Bekker-Nielsen, H. and others, eds. Hagiography and Medieval Literature.
J.M. Jochens, 563(SS):Summer83-258
Bekker-Nielsen, H. and others, eds. Medieval Narrative.
D.M. Mennie, 562(Scan):May82-95
Belamich, A. - see Lorca, F.G.
Belanger, T., ed. Proceedings of the Fine Printing Conference at Columbia University, 19-22 May 1982.
N. Barker, 617(TLS):20Jan84-71
Belay, M. La mort dans le théâtre de Gabriel Marcel.*
A. Reix, 192(EP):Apr-Jun83-225
Beletskaja, E. and Z. Pokrovskaja. Domenico Gilardi.
V. Antonow, 43:Band13Heft1-83
Bélil, M. Greenwich.*
J.A. Yeager, 207(FR):Mar84-583

Belkin, J.S. and E.R. Caley. Eucharius Rösslin the Younger: On Minerals and Mineral Products.
B.D. Haage, 680(ZDP):Band102Heft3-464
Belknap, M.R., ed. American Political Trials.
W.F. Pratt, Jr., 579(SAQ):Summer83-321
Bell, A. Sydney Smith.
P. Rogers, 402(MLR):Jan83-159
Bell, A.O., with A. McNeillie - see Woolf, V.
Bell, D. Frege's Theory of Judgement.
C. Thiel, 53(AGP):Band65Heft1-105
Bell, D. Spinoza in Germany from 1670 to the Age of Goethe.
E. Ronchetti, 617(TLS):16Nov84-1308
Bell, D. and I. Kristol, eds. The Crisis in Economic Theory.
F. Petrella, 396(ModA):Spring83-209
Bell, G. Shadows on the Sand.
D. Bates, 617(TLS):6Jul84-748
Bell, I.F.A. Critic as Scientist.*
A.W. Litz, 405(MP):Nov83-214
Bell, J. Policy Arguments in Judicial Decisions.
W. Twining, 617(TLS):30Mar84-351
Bell, M. Drawn by Stones, by Earth, by Things that Have Been in the Fire.
H. Beaver, 441:11Nov84-14
Bell, M., ed. 1900-1930, the Context of English Literature.*
R.G. Cox, 447(N&Q):Oct82-476
Bell, M. Old Snow Just Melting.
D. Baker, 434:Winter83-332
Bell, M. The Sentiment of Reality.*
295(JML):Nov83-412
Bell, M. These Green-Going-to-Yellow.*
D. Baker, 434:Winter83-334
Bell, M. 3d. Morgantina Studies. (Vol 1)
C.E. Vafopoulou-Richardson, 123: Vol33No2-361
Bell, M.D. The Development of American Romance.*
E.H. Redekop, 106:Winter83-415
Bell, M.S. The Washington Square Ensemble.*
42(AR):Spring83-249
Bell, N.K., ed. Who Decides?
B.B., 185:Oct83-181
Bell, V.M. Robert Lowell.*
J. Cantor, 432(NEQ):Dec83-606
A. Gelpi, 27(AL):Oct83-481
L. Keller, 659(ConL):Summer84-242
Bellamy, B.E. Private Presses and Publishing in England since 1945.
W.G. Hammond, 517(PBSA):Vol77No1-112
Bellamy, F. Caribbean Island Hopping.
B.F. Carruthers, 37:Nov-Dec83-61
Bellamy, G. The Sinner's Congregation.
442(NY):1Oct84-133
Bellamy, J.D., ed. American Poetry Observed.
S. Moss, 441:30Sep84-16
Bellanger, L. L'expression écrite.
F. Helgorsky, 209(FM):Apr83-183
du Bellay, J. La Monomachie de David et de Goliath.* (E. Caldarini, ed)
W.J. Beck, 207(FR):Apr84-709
Y. Bellenger, 535(RHL):Sep/Dec83-911
du Bellay, J. Oeuvres poétiques. (Vol 1) (H. Chamard, ed; newly ed by Y. Bellenger)
M. Simonin, 535(RHL):Sep/Dec83-909

Benjamin, R. Naked at Forty.
  R.P. Mills, 441:24Jun84-22
Benjamin, W. Charles Baudelaire.
  R. Rochlitz, 98:Apr83-287
  A. Suied, 450(NRF):Apr83-130
Benjamin, W. Das Passagen-Werk.* (R.
  Tiedemann, ed)
  R. Rochlitz, 98:Apr83-287
Benkovitz, M.J. A Bibliography of Ronald
  Firbank. (2nd ed)
  E. James, 354:Dec83-438
Benn, S.I. and G.F. Gaus, eds. Public and
  Private in Social Life.
  N. MacCormick, 617(TLS):20Jan84-58
Bennett, A. The Journals.
  A.S.B., 617(TLS):16Nov84-1323
Bennett, B. Death, Too, For The-Heavy-
  Runner.
  C.L. Rawlins, 649(WAL):Aug83-171
Bennett, B. Modern Drama and German Clas-
  sicism.*
  O.W. Johnston, 400(MLN):Apr83-502
Bennett, B. and K. Upton. The Joys of
  Cocktails and Hors d'Oeuvre.
  M. Burros, 441:2Dec84-14
Bennett, B.A. and D.G. Wilkins. Donatello.
  S. Gardiner, 362:17May84-26
Bennett, B.T. - see Shelley, M.W.
Bennett, D. Margot.
  J.A. Turner, 617(TLS):27Jul84-850
Bennett, G., comp. The Kent Bibliography.
  (W. Bergess and C. Earl, eds)
  R.J. Goulden, 354:Sep83-297
Bennett, I. Oriental Rugs. (Vol 1)
  G. Wills, 39:Feb83-147
Bennett, J. A Study of Spinoza's Ethics.
  S. Hampshire, 617(TLS):16Nov84-1308
Bennett, J., with S. Goodwin. Godfrey.
  J.W. Lambert, 157:Winter83-36
Bennett, J.A.W. The Humane Medievalist.*
  (P. Boitani, ed) Poetry of the Passion.*
  A.V.C.S., 382(MAE):1983/1-115
Bennett, L. Dangerous Wives and Sacred
  Sisters.
  C. von Fürer-Haimendorf, 617(TLS):
  16Nov84-1316
Bennett, T. Formalism and Marxism.*
  D. Bellos, 307:Oct80-121
  J.W. Davidson, 477(PLL):Winter83-93
  D.E. Rivas, 577(SHR):Spring83-189
Bennett, W.H. An Introduction to the
  Gothic Language.
  M. Durrell, 402(MLR):Jan83-217
  R.D. Fulk, 481(PQ):Spring83-276
Bennett, W.L. and M.S. Feldman. Recon-
  structing Reality in the Courtroom.
  S.U. Philips, 355(LSoc):Dec83-514
Benoist, J-M. Le Devoir d'opposition.
  J. Paulhan, 207(FR):May84-892
Benoit, J. Gisèle et le serpent.
  P. Collet, 102(CanL):Summer83-133
Bénouis, M.K. Le Français économique et
  commercial.*
  W. Greenberg, 399(MLJ):Summer83-188
Benrekassa, G. Le concentrique et l'excen-
  trique.*
  D. Fletcher, 208(FS):Jul83-344
Bensley, C. Moving In.
  J. Mole, 176:Dec84-61
Benson, C.D. The History of Troy in
  Middle English Literature.*
  E.D. Kennedy, 38:Band101Heft3/4-503

Benson, E.F. Queen Lucia.
  P-L. Adams, 61:May84-123
Benson, J.J. The True Adventures of John
  Steinbeck, Writer.
  T.R. Edwards, 453(NYRB):16Feb84-25
  S. Fender, 617(TLS):13Apr84-391
  K. Starr, 441:22Jan84-1
  442(NY):6Feb84-127
Benson, L.D. and J. Leyerle, eds. Chival-
  ric Literature.*
  R.F. Green, 589:Oct83-1027
Benson, M. - see Fugard, A.
Benson, R.G. Medieval Body Language.*
  R.T. Davies, 447(N&Q):Apr82-157
Benstock, B., ed. Essays on Detective Fic-
  tion.
  R. Hill, 617(TLS):26Oct84-1225
Benstock, B., ed. Pomes for James Joyce.
  W. Potts, 305(JIL):Sep83-83
Benstock, B., ed. The Seventh of Joyce.*
  M.P. Gillespie, 594:Winter83-364
  W. Potts, 305(JIL):Sep83-83
Benstock, S. and B. Who's He When He's at
  Home.*
  R. Mason, 447(N&Q):Oct82-469
  R.D. Newman, 577(SHR):Fall83-391
Bent, I., ed. Source Materials and the
  Interpretation of Music.
  J. Haar, 415:Nov83-682
  D. Stevens, 410(M&L):Jul/Oct83-229
Bente, M., ed. Musik: Edition, Interpreta-
  tion.
  A.H. King, 410(M&L):Jan/Apr83-76
Bentham, J. An Introduction to the Prin-
  ciples of Morals and Legislation. (J.H.
  Burns and H.L.A. Hart, eds)
  C. Silver, 185:Jan84-355
Bentinck-Smith, W., ed. The Harvard Book.
  (rev)
  M. Freiberg, 432(NEQ):Mar83-153
Bentley, E. The Brecht Commentaries, 1943-
  1980.*
  S. Mews, 400(MLN):Apr83-505
Bentley, G.E. The Profession of Player in
  Shakespeare's Time 1590-1642.
  J. Hankey, 617(TLS):10Aug84-884
Bentley, M. Politics Without Democracy
  1815-1914.
  N. Gash, 617(TLS):9Nov84-1292
Benton, G., ed. Wild Lilies, Poisonous
  Weeds.
  T.B. Gold, 293(JASt):Aug83-904
Bentzinger, R., ed. "Die Wahrheit muss
  ans Licht!"
  I. Spriewald, 654(WB):11/1983-2016
Benvenga, N. Kingdom on the Rhine.*
  R. Anderson, 415:Jun83-362
Benveniste, A. Throw Out the Life Line
  Lay Out the Corse.
  J. Silkin, 617(TLS):31Aug84-962
Benvenuti, S. and G. Rizzoni. The Who-
  dunit.
  P. Wolfe, 395(MFS):Autumn83-389
Benz, W., ed. Die Bundesrepublik Deutsch-
  land.
  W. Laqueur, 617(TLS):17Aug84-921
Benzie, W. Dr. F.J. Furnivall.
  R.B. Martin, 617(TLS):13Jan84-27
Benzing, J. Die Buchdrucker des 16. und
  17. Jahrhunderts im deutschen Sprach-
  gebiet. (2nd ed)
  J.E. Walsh, 517(PBSA):Vol77No3-407
"Beowulf" - see also "A Readable 'Beowulf'"

de Berceo, G. El Libro de Alixandre.
(D.A. Nelson, ed)
 R.S. Willis, 240(HR):Winter83-63
de Berceo, G. "El Sacrificio de la Misa,"
"La Vida de Santa Oria," "El Martirio
de San Lorenzo" by Gonzalo de Berceo.
(B. Dutton, ed)
 E. Drayson, 382(MAE):1983/2-332
Beregovski, M. Old Jewish Folk Music. (M.
Slobin, ed and trans)
 G.H. Haskell, 650(WF):Oct83-301
Berend, I.T. and G. Ránki. The European
Periphery and Industrialization, 1780-
1914.
 F.W. Carter, 575(SEER):Oct83-620
Berenson, F.M. Understanding Persons.*
 M. Hughes, 483:Jan83-126
 L.A. Reid, 393(Mind):Jul83-452
Berenson, M. Mary Berenson: A Self-
Portrait from her Letters and Diaries.*
(B. Strachey and J. Samuels, eds)
 P-L. Adams, 61:Jul84-116
 J. Gross, 441:22Apr84-8
 S. Spender, 453(NYRB):8Nov84-32
 442(NY):7May84-159
Beresford-Howe, C. The Marriage Bed.*
 D. Duffy, 529(QQ):Spring83-241
Berg, C. Jean de Boschère ou le mouvement
de l'attente.
 Y-A. Favre, 535(RHL):May/Jun83-483
Berg, J. - see Bolzano, B.
Berg, J. and others. Sozialgeschichte der
deutschen Literatur von 1918 bis zur
Gegenwart.
 H.A. Pausch, 107(CRCL):Jun83-276
Berg, M., P. Hudson and M. Sonenscher, eds.
Manufacture in Town and Country before
the Factory.
 D.C. Coleman, 617(TLS):11May84-532
Berg, R.E. and D.G. Stork. The Physics of
Sound.
 C. Taylor, 415:Jun83-361
Berg, S. With Akhmatova at the Black
Gates.*
 G. Simon, 448:Vol21No2/3-184
Berg, W.J., M. Grimaud and G. Moskos.
Saint/Oedipus.*
 U. Schulz-Buschhaus, 547(RF):Band95
 Heft3-362
Berg-Pan, R. Bertolt Brecht and China.
 A. Hsia, 107(CRCL):Mar83-122
Bergad, L.W. Coffee and the Growth of
Agrarian Capitalism in Nineteenth-Cen-
tury Puerto Rico.
 V. Bulmer-Thomas, 617(TLS):27Jan84-79
Bergamín, J. Poesías casi completas.
 G. Navajas, 552(REH):Oct83-429
Bergé, C. Secrets, Gossip and Slander.
 J. Haskins, 441:1Jul84-20
Bergé, M. Les Arabes.
 H.L. Bodman, Jr., 318(JAOS):Jan-Mar82-
 212
Berger, C. Knock Wood.
 G. Mallet, 441:8Apr84-11
Berger, B. and P.L. The War Over the
Family.*
 P. Laslett, 617(TLS):13Jan84-39
 A.S., 185:Apr84-570
Berger, C.R. and J.J. Bradac. Language
and Social Knowledge.
 A. Cicourel, 350:Dec84-959

Berger, D., ed and trans. The Jewish-
Christian Debate in the High Middle Ages.
 J. Cohen, 318(JAOS):Apr-Jun82-401
Berger, G.M. - see Mutsu Munemitsu
Berger, J. And Our Faces, My Heart, Brief
as Photos.
 P. Schjeldahl, 441:13May84-18
Berger, K. Japonismus in der westlichen
Malerei, 1860-1920.
 H. Adams, 54:Sep83-495
 T. Watanabe, 59:Sep83-384
Berger, K. Theories of Chromatic and
Enharmonic Music in Late 16th Century
Italy.*
 D.S., 412:Aug-Nov82-265
Berger, M., E. Berger and J. Patrick.
Benny Carter.
 F. Hoffmann, 498:Vol9No2-88
Berger, P. Deadly Kisses.
 M. Levin, 441:9Dec84-26
Berger, P.L., ed. The Other Side of God.
 C. Davis, 529(QQ):Autumn83-912
Berger, R. Littérature et société arra-
geoises au XIIIe siècle.
 L.B. Richardson, 589:Jul83-728
Berger, T. Arthur Rex.
 J. Ruud, 145(Crit):Winter84-92
Berger, T. The Feud.*
 J. Clute, 617(TLS):10Feb84-136
Berger, T.R. Fragile Freedoms.*
 E.Z. Friedenberg, 529(QQ):Autumn83-861
Berger, W.R. - see Baudelaire, C.
de Bergerac, C. - see under de Cyrano de
Bergerac, S.
Bergeron, L. The Québécois Dictionary.
 T.R. Wooldridge, 627(UTQ):Summer83-535
Bergeron, P.H. Antebellum Politics in
Tennessee.
 639(VQR):Summer83-84
Berges, R. The Collector's Cabinet.
 G. Wills, 39:Jul83-113
Bergess, W., ed. The Kent Bibliography
Supplement.
 R.J. Goulden, 354:Sep83-297
Bergess, W. and C. Earl - see Bennett, G.
Berggren, E. and K., with others. San
Giovenale. (Vol 2, fasc 2)
 D. Ridgway, 123:Vol33No2-364
Berghahn, K.L. - see Lessing, G.E.
Berghahn, K.L. and B. Pinkerneil. Am
Beispiel "Wilhelm Meister."*
 H.R. Vaget, 221(GQ):May83-502
Berghahn, M. German-Jewish Refugees in
England.
 B. Wasserstein, 617(TLS):10Aug84-896
Berghahn, V.R. Modern Germany.
 I. Deak, 453(NYRB):31May84-37
 639(VQR):Autumn83-121
Bergier, J-F. Histoire économique de la
Suisse.
 P.K. O'Brien, 617(TLS):7Dec84-1400
Bergin, T.G. Boccaccio.*
 A.K. Cassell, 589:Apr83-434
 J. Markulin, 577(SHR):Spring83-186
 L. Nelson, Jr., 276:Summer83-154
Berglund, S. Paradoxes of Political
Parties.
 R.F. Tomasson, 563(SS):Summer83-249
Bergman, H.E. and S.E. Szmuk. A Catalogue
of comedias sueltas in the New York
Public Library.*
 D.W. Cruickshank, 86(BHS):Jan83-67

Bergman, I. Fanny et Alexandre.
 A. Suied, 98:Jun-Jul83-581
Bergman, J. Vera Zasulich.*
 B.E. Clements, 104(CASS):Summer83-277
Bergman, M. Hieronymus Bosch and Alchemy.
 R. Blair, 111:Spring83-1
Bergmann, F. Robert Grant.
 F.M. Blake, 26(ALR):Spring83-156
Bergmann, R., W. König and H. Stopp. Bib-
 liographie zur Namenforschung, Mundart-
 forschung und historischen Sprachwissen-
 schaft Bayerisch-Schwabens.*
 D. Stellmacher, 685(ZDL):1/1983-96
Bergmann, R., P. Pauly and M. Schlaefer.
 Einführung in die deutsche Sprachwissen-
 schaft.*
 M. Durrell, 402(MLR):Oct83-954
Bergquist, M.F. Ibero-Romance.
 R. Penny, 86(BHS):Jul83-253
 D.P. Seniff, 238:May83-310
Bergreen, L. James Agee.
 P. French, 441:8Jul84-1
 L. Rose, 18:Sep84-57
Berk, R.A. and others. Water Shortage.
 T.C. Holyoke, 42(AR):Winter83-117
Berke, B. Tragic Thought and the Grammar
 of Tragic Myth.*
 639(VQR):Spring83-44
Berkeley, E. and D.S. The Life and
 Travels of John Bartram.
 J. Seelye, 165(EAL):Spring84-90
Berkeley, G. De l'obéissance passive. (D.
 Deleule, ed and trans)
 G. Brykman, 542:Oct-Dec83-470
Berkeley, G. Viaggio in Italia. (T.E.
 Jessop and M. Firmiani, eds and trans)
 A. Blunt, 90:Feb83-102
Berkhout, C.T. and M.M. Gatch, eds. Anglo-
 Saxon Scholarship: The First Three
 Centuries.
 A. Cameron, 539:Aug84-226
 A. Lutz, 38:Band101Heft3/4-480
Berkowitz, G.M. David Garrick.
 I. Donaldson, 541(RES):Feb83-81
 C. Price, 447(N&Q):Dec82-556
Berkowitz, G.M. New Broadways.
 J. Schlueter, 397(MD):Sep83-399
Berkowitz, G.M. Sir John Vanbrugh and the
 End of Restoration Comedy.
 B. Corman, 173(ECS):Fall83-118
 L. Harris, 615(TJ):Mar83-133
 F. McCormick, 447(N&Q):Dec82-550
Berkvam, D.D. Enfance et maternité dans
 la littérature française des XIIe et
 XIIIe siècles.
 J-C. Aubailly, 547(RF):Band95Heft1/2-
 172
 S. Kay, 402(MLR):Apr83-446
Berland, A. Culture and Conduct in the
 Novels of Henry James.*
 A.W. Bellringer, 402(MLR):Jan83-167
Berlanga, J.L.V. - see under Villacañas
 Berlanga, J.L.
Berle, B.B. A Life in Two Worlds.
 M. Cantwell, 441:5Feb84-23
von Berlichingen, G. Götz von Berlich-
 ingen: Mein Fehd und Handlungen. (H.
 Ulmschneider, ed)
 D.L. Paisey, 221(GQ):Jan83-134
Berlin, E.A. Ragtime.*
 R.M. Raichelson, 292(JAF):Apr-Jun83-
 212
 [continued]

[continuing]
 J.R. Scotti, 513:Fall-Winter81/Spring-
 Summer82-560
Berlin, I. Concepts and Categories.
 H.M. Curtler, 396(ModA):Winter83-99
Berlin, I. Personal Impressions.* (H.
 Hardy, ed)
 M. Ellmann, 569(SR):Winter83-120
Berlin, I., with J.P. Reidy and L.S. Row-
 land, eds. Freedom.* (Series 2)
 E. Foner, 453(NYRB):1Mar84-37
Berlin, N. Eugene O'Neill.
 C. Edwards, 157:Autumn83-29
Berlin, N. The Secret Cause.
 J-M. Rabaté, 189(EA):Apr-Sep83-317
 J. Schlueter, 397(MD):Mar83-107
Berliner, R. and G. Egger. Ornamentale
 Vorlageblätter des 15.-19. Jahrhunderts.
 P. Vergo, 90:Jul83-431
 C-P. Warncke, 471:Jan/Feb/Mar83-86
Berlioz, H. Correspondance générale.
 (Vol 4) (P. Citron, Y. Gérard and H.
 Macdonald, eds)
 J. Warrack, 617(TLS):16Mar84-281
Berman, L. Planning a Tragedy.
 639(VQR):Winter83-23
Berman, M. All That Is Solid Melts into
 Air.*
 639(VQR):Summer83-100
Berman, R. Culture and Politics.
 C.E. Finn, Jr., 129:Sep84-77
Bermant, C. Dancing Bear.
 B. Morton, 617(TLS):16Nov84-1302
Bermel, A. Farce.
 J.D. Mason, 615(TJ):Dec83-565
 639(VQR):Autumn83-117
Bernadelli, G. La poesia a rovescio.
 M. Tilby, 208(FS):Jan83-97
Bernard, B. The Bible and Its Painters.
 J. Russell, 441:2Dec84-11
Bernard, I. - see de La Chaussée, P.C.N.
Bernard, J. Le sang et l'histoire.
 M.A. Sinaceur, 98:Nov83-886
Bernard, M. Truth and Consequences.
 J. Mellors, 364:Apr/May83-133
Bernard, S. and A. Guyaux - see Rimbaud, A.
Bernath, K., ed. Thomas von Aquin, I.
 B.M.B., 543:Sep82-160
Bernbaum, E. The Way to Shambhala.
 O. Lattimore, 293(JASt):Nov82-121
Bernd, C.A. German Poetic Realism.*
 W.P. Hanson, 402(MLR):Apr83-495
Bernen, R. The Hills.
 J. Domini, 441:12Feb84-20
 442(NY):6Feb84-125
Bernhard, T. Concrete.
 P. Brady, 617(TLS):28Sep84-1085
 J. Simon, 441:1Jul84-9
Bernhard, T. Le Souffle.
 V. Beauvois, 450(NRF):Dec83-117
Bernheimer, C. Flaubert and Kafka.
 R.T. Denommé, 207(FR):Mar84-558
 C. Koelb, 395(MFS):Summer83-297
 E.J. Talbot, 210(FrF):Sep83-281
Berni Canani, U. and others. L'analisi
 delle frequenze.
 O. Weijers, 361:Oct/Nov83-259
Berns, J.J. - see Schottelius, J.G.
Bernson, N.O. Knowledge.
 T.O. Buford, 543:Dec82-443
Bernstein, C. Islets/Irritations. Resis-
 tance.
 M. Perloff, 29:May/Jun84-15

31

Bernstein, J. Three Degrees Above Zero.
R. Williams, 441:14Oct84-15
Bernstein, L.S. The Offical Guide to
Wine Snobbery.
K. Jeffery, 617(TLS):17Feb84-175
Bernstein, R.J. Beyond Objectivism and
Relativism.
B. Barnes, 617(TLS):22Jun84-710
Bernstein, W. and R. Cawker. Contemporary
Canadian Architecture.
G. Kapelos, 627(UTQ):Summer83-550
Berque, A. Vivre l'espace au Japon.
G. Balandier, 98:Jan-Feb83-22
Berquet, G. and J-P. Collinet - see
Conrart, V.
Berrendonner, A. Eléments de pragmatique
linguistique.
P. Engel, 542:Jul-Sep83-348
Berrendonner, A. L'éternel grammairien.
R. Martin, 553(RLiR):Jan-Jun83-176
Berriault, G. The Lights of Earth.
E. Spencer, 441:8Apr84-9
Berry, C.R. The Reform in Oaxaca, 1856-
76.*
J. Fisher, 86(BHS):Apr83-163
Berry, D. The Creative Vision of Guil-
laume Apollinaire.
D.E. Rivas, 210(FrF):Sep83-284
Berry, J. Lucy's Letters and Loving.
S. Brown, 493:Jun83-67
Berry, M.E. Hideyoshi.
Asao Naohiro, 285(JapQ):Oct-Dec83-437
H. Bolitho, 407(MN):Winter83-451
M.B. Jansen, 244(HJAS):Dec83-671
C. Totman, 293(JASt):Aug83-951
Berry, M.F. and J.W. Blassingame. Long
Memory.
D.L. Lewis, 579(SAQ):Autumn83-437
Berry, R. Changing Styles in Shakespeare.*
G. Lloyd Evans, 611(TN):Vol137No1-38
Berry, R. Shakespearean Structures.
E.A.J. Honigmann, 570(SQ):Summer83-248
R.S. White, 447(N&Q):Dec82-542
Berry, W. Standing by Words.*
G. Davenport, 344:Summer84-108
J. Parini, 434:Summer84-630
Berry, W. The Wheel.*
W. Prunty, 598(SoR):Autumn84-958
639(VQR):Spring83-62
Berryman, P. The Religious Roots of Rebel-
lion.
A. Angell, 617(TLS):12Oct84-1151
Bersani, L. Baudelaire et Freud.
D. Hollier, 98:Apr83-271
Bersani, L. The Death of Stéphane Mal-
larmé.*
R. Cardinal, 529(QQ):Autumn83-895
G. Craig, 402(MLR):Apr83-459
J.M. Dornbush, 401(MLQ):Dec82-410
D. Hollier, 98:Apr83-271
Berschin, W. Griechisch-lateinisches
Mittelalter von Hieronymus zu Nikolaus
von Kues.*
P.O. Kristeller, 589:Jan83-147
M. Winterbottom, 382(MAE):1983/2-318
Berschin, W. and R. Düchting, eds. Late-
inische Dichtungen des X. und XI. Jahr-
hunderts.
P. Stotz, 547(RF):Band95Heft1/2-156
J. Ziolkowski, 589:Jan83-149
Bersier, G. Wunschbild und Wirklichkeit.
E.E. Reed, 221(GQ):Nov83-649

Berssenbrugge, M-M. Summits Move With the
Tide.
G.S.S. Chandra, 436(NewL):Summer84-114
Berst, C.A. - see "Shaw: The Annual of Ber-
nard Shaw Studies"
Bertaud, M. La Jalousie dans la Littéra-
ture au Temps de Louis XIII.*
N. Aronson, 207(FR):Dec83-245
C. Morlet-Chantalat, 535(RHL):
Jul/Aug83-628
D.A. Watts, 402(MLR):Jan83-181
Bertelli, I. La poesia di Guido Guiniz-
zelli e la poetica del "Dolce stil
nuovo."
M. Marti, 228(GSLI):Vol 160fasc511-448
Berteloot, A. and H-L. Worm, eds and trans.
Van den vos Reynaerde: Reinart Fuchs.
D. Blamires, 402(MLR):Oct83-961
Berthaud, M. La Jalousie dans la littéra-
ture au temps de Louis XIII.
R.W. Tobin, 210(FrF):May83-183
Berthier, P. Stendhal et la sainte fam-
ille.
J-J. Hamm, 605(SC):15Jul84-382
Berthold, D. and K.M. Price - see Whitman,
T.J.
Bertholf, R.J. and A.S. Levitt, eds.
William Blake and the Moderns.
G. Bornstein, 661(WC):Summer83-162
P. Mann, 88:Spring84-169
W. Weathers, 329(JJQ):Winter84-192
de Bertier de Sauvigny, G. La France et
les Français vus par les voyageurs
américains, 1814-1848.
J-M. Guieu, 207(FR):Oct83-124
de Bertier de Sauvigny, G. and D.H. Pink-
ney. History of France.
D.T. Stephens, 207(FR):Dec83-280
Bertin-Maghit, J-P. Le Cinéma sous Vichy.
E.B. Turk, 207(FR):Feb84-442
Bertini, G.M. and M. Assunta Pellazza.
Ensayo de literatura espiritual com-
parada hispano-italiana.
C.P. Thompson, 86(BHS):Jan83-65
Bertini, M.B. - see under Bongiovanni
Bertini, M.
Bertòla, A.D. Diari del viaggio in Sviz-
zera e in Germania (1787). (M. and A.
Stäuble, eds)
E. Bogani, 228(GSLI):Vol 160fasc511-
458
Berton, P. Flames Across the Border.
L.D. Cress, 432(NEQ):Mar83-134
Berton, P., P.F. Langer and G.O. Totten -
see Nobori Shomu and Akamatsu Katsumaro
Bertoni, G., ed. Il canzoniere provenzale
estense. (Pt 1)
J. Monfrin, 554:Vol 103No2/3-397
Bertram, P. White Spaces in Shakespeare.*
M. Grivelet, 189(EA):Jan-Mar84-92
D.F. McKenzie, 354:Mar83-72
S. Orgel, 551(RenQ):Summer83-302
Bertrand, A. Gaspard de la Nuit.* (M.
Milner, ed)
K. Slott, 446(NCFS):Fall-Winter83/84-
231
Bertsch, G.K. Power and Policy in Com-
munist Systems. (2nd ed)
R.J. Osborn, 550(RusR):Jan83-117
Bertz, S. Der Dubliner Stadtdialekt. (Pt
1)
H. Bluhme, 685(ZDL):3/1983-401

Bickerton, D. Roots of Language.*
  R.R. Butters, 579(SAQ):Autumn83-456
  R.B. Le Page, 297(JL):Mar83-258
  J.M. Meisel, 361:Oct/Nov83-231
Bickley, R.B., Jr., ed. Critical Essays
  on Joel Chandler Harris.
  B. Hitchcock, 577(SHR):Fall83-388
  C. Werner, 392:Winter82/83-74
Bickman, M. The Unsounded Centre.*
  W.L. Andrews, 587(SAF):Spring83-125
Bicknell, P. Beauty, Horror, and Immen-
  sity.*
  M. Rosenthal, 59:Jun83-242
Bicknell, P., ed. The Illustrated Words-
  worth's Guide To The Lakes.
  J. Keates, 617(TLS):22Jun84-690
Bidart, F. The Sacrifice.*
  P. Stitt, 219(GaR):Winter83-894
  D. Young, 199:Spring84-83
Biddle, G. and O.S. Nock. The Railway Her-
  itage of Britain.
  D. Luckhurst, 324:Jun84-474
Bidler, R.M. - see de Hauteville, P.
Bidwell, B. and L. Heffer. The Joycean
  Way.
  B. Benstock, 395(MFS):Summer83-281
  639(VQR):Winter83-14
Bieber, K. Simone de Beauvoir.
  L. Czyba, 535(RHL):May/Jun83-489
Bieber, M. Ancient Copies.
  S. Howard, 121(CJ):Oct/Nov83-75
Bielenstein, H. The Bureaucracy of Han
  Times.
  M. Loewe, 244(HJAS):Dec83-676
Bieler, A. and others. Perspectives de
  France. (3rd ed)
  J.T. Mitchell, 399(MLJ):Autumn83-283
Bieler, M. Der Bär.
  M. Hulse, 617(TLS):5Oct84-1136
Biemel, W. and others. Qu'est-ce que
  l'homme?
  A. Reix, 542:Jul-Sep83-374
Bien, H., with G. Sokoll, eds. Die nord-
  ischen Literaturen als Gegenstand der
  Literaturgeschichtsschreibung.
  F. Paul, 562(Scan):Nov83-234
  G. Wenzel, 654(WB):12/1982-172
Bienek, H. The First Polka.
  N. Ascherson, 453(NYRB):26Apr84-7
  J. Kott, 441:8Apr84-26
Bierbach, C. Sprache als "Fait social."
  G. Van der Elst, 685(ZDL):2/1983-214
Bierbach, M. Die Verbindung von Verbal-
  und Nominalelement im Französischen.
  R. Martin, 553(RLiR):Jul-Dec83-476
Bierhorst, J., ed. The Sacred Path.
  T. Buckley, 469:Vol9No2-123
Bierhorst, J. - see "Spirit Child"
Biès, J. Passeports pour des temps nou-
  veaux.
  M. Adam, 542:Jan-Mar83-56
Biesantz, H. and A. Klingborg. The Goethe-
  anum.
  P.B. Jones, 46:May81-318
Bigalke, R. Dizionario dialettale della
  Basilicata con un breve saggio della
  fonetica.
  T. Stehl, 72:Band220Heft1-206
Biggs, B. The Complete English-Maori Dic-
  tionary.
  J. Verschueren, 350:Mar84-197

Bigsby, C.W.E., ed. Contemporary English
  Drama.*
  G. Bas, 189(EA):Apr-Sep83-337
Bigsby, C.W.E. A Critical Introduction to
  Twentieth-Century American Drama. (Vol
  1)
  P.L. Hays, 610:Autumn83-265
Bigsby, C.W.E. Joe Orton.
  G. Bas, 189(EA):Apr-Sep83-342
  B. Cardullo, 609:Summer/Fall84-74
Bihari, A. Magyar Hiedelemmonda Katalógus.
  W.D. Hand, 650(WF):Jan83-63
Bilan, R.P. The Literary Criticism of F.R.
  Leavis.*
  W. Baker, 477(PLL):Fall83-461
Bilik, D.S. Immigrant-Survivors.*
  R. Adolph, 106:Winter83-481
Bilke, M. Zeitgenossen der "Fackel."
  F. Achberger, 406:Winter83-419
Billanovich, G. La tradizione del testo
  di Livio e le origini dell'umanesimo.
  (Vol 1, Pt 1 and Vol 2)
  F. Chiappelli, 589:Jul83-731
  P.O. Kristeller, 551(RenQ):Spring83-78
Billick, D.J. José de Espronceda.
  R.A. Cardwell, 86(BHS):Apr83-155
Billington, D.P. The Tower and the Bridge.
  P. Goldberger, 441:26Feb84-23
Billington, J.H. Fire in the Minds of
  Men.*
  H. Seton-Watson, 575(SEER):Apr83-282
Billington, M. Alan Ayckbourn.
  J. Spurling, 176:Jan84-54
Billington, M. The Guinness Book of Thea-
  tre Facts and Feats.
  G. Playfair, 157:Summer83-28
Bílý, M. Intrasentential Pronominaliza-
  tion and Functional Sentence Perspec-
  tive.
  B. Comrie, 350:Sep84-670
Binchy, M. London Transports.
  H. Harris, 617(TLS):30Mar84-354
Binder, A. and H. Richartz - see Campe,
  J.H.
Binder, H. - see Crane, S.
Binding, P. Harmonica's Bridegroom.
  C. Hawtree, 617(TLS):1Jun84-622
  J. Mantle, 362:21Jun84-27
Binding, T.J., ed. Firebird 1.*
  P. Lewis, 565:Vol24No1-58
Bindman, D. William Blake: His Art and
  Times.*
  D. Fuller, 83:Autumn83-207
  E. Larrissy, 59:Dec83-478
Binford, L.R. In Pursuit of the Past.
  G. Daniel, 617(TLS):30Mar84-352
Bingham, A.J. and V.W. Topazio, eds. En-
  lightenment Studies in Honour of Lester
  G. Crocker.*
  J.H. Brumfitt, 208(FS):Jul83-345
  J. Chouillet, 549(RLC):Jan-Mar83-116
Bingham, J. and G. Scholt. Fifteen Cen-
  turies of Children's Literature.
  S.A. Grider, 292(JAF):Apr-Jun83-240
Binnersly, T. and J. Miller, eds. Play-
  makers.
  J. Doolittle, 108:Fall83-134
Binney, M. Sir Robert Taylor.
  K. Downes, 617(TLS):28Sep84-1103
Binney, M. and E. Milne, eds. Vanishing
  Houses of England.
  C.G.R. Buxton, 324:Apr84-347

34

Binni, W. Saggi alfieriani.
A. di Benedetto, 228(GSLI):Vol 160
fasc510-312
Binnie, P. - see Peele, G.
Binyon, H. Eric Ravilious.*
B. Crutchley, 324:Nov84-816
C. de Beaurepaire, 364:Feb84-110
Binyon, M. Life in Russia.
V. Conolly, 617(TLS):3Feb84-100
C.R. Whitney, 441:15Apr84-30
Binyon, T.J. Swan Song.*
N. Callendar, 441:28Oct84-39
Birch, C. and J.B. Cobb, Jr. The Libera-
tion of Life.
H. Kamminga, 84:Dec83-393
Bircher, M. and B. Weber, with B. von
Waldkirch. Salomon Gessner.
D.W. Dörrbecker, 90:Dec83-767
Bird, D.T., comp. A Catalogue of Six-
teenth-Century Medical Books in Edin-
burgh Libraries.
E. Brodman, 517(PBSA):Vol77No2-245
B. Hillyard, 354:Dec83-420
D. McKitterick, 78(BC):Spring83-110
70:May-Jun83-162
Bird, I.L. A Lady's Life in the Rocky
Mountains.
D. Roberts, 135:Aug83-112
Bird, J. Percy Grainger.
R. Falck, 529(QQ):Winter83-1146
Bird, M. and T. Kobayashi. A Splendid
Harvest.
S.T. Swank, 658:Spring83-107
Birely, R. Religion and Politics in the
Age of the Counterreformation.
J.A. Vann, 551(RenQ):Summer83-275
Birkett, M.E. Lamartine and the Poetics
of Landscape.
S. Nash, 210(FrF):Sep83-279
Birley, A.R. The "Fasti" of Roman Britain.
E. Champlin, 24:Fall83-310
Birley, A.R. - see Syme, R.
Birmelin, B.T. The Superintendent.
R. Elman, 441:6May84-26
Birmingham, D. Central Africa to 1870.
J. Vansina, 69:Vol53No1-93
Birmingham, D. and P.M. Martin, eds. His-
tory of Central Africa.
R. Gray, 617(TLS):6Jul84-764
Birmingham, S. "The Rest of Us."
S. Zion, 441:14Oct84-14
"Lisa Birnbach's College Book."
J. Kaufman, 441:28Oct84-27
Birnbaum, H. Essays in Early Slavic Civ-
ilization/Studien zur Frühkultur der
Slaven.
H.G. Lunt, 550(RusR):Apr83-219
M. Ziolkowski, 574(SEEJ):Fall83-379
Birnbaum, P. - see "Rabbits, Crabs, Etc."
Birnbaum, S., ed. The Caribbean, Bermuda
and the Bahamas 1983.
B.F. Carruthers, 37:Nov-Dec83-61
Birnbaum, S.A. Yiddish.*
W. Röll, 680(ZDP):Band102Heft3-466
Birney, E. Spreading Time.* (Bk 1)
L. McLeod, 49:Jan83-83
Biro, A. and R. Passeron. Dictionnaire
général du surréalisme et de ses envi-
rons.
B.L. Knapp, 207(FR):Apr84-723
Biro, J. and R.W. Shahan, eds. Mind,
Brain and Function.
R.V.G., 185:Oct83-169

Birrell, A. - see "Yü-t'ai hsin-yung (New
Songs from a Jade Terrace)"
Birrell, G. The Boundless Present.
C.L. Nollendorfs, 406:Spring83-78
Bisanz, A.J. and R. Trousson, eds. Ele-
mente der Literatur.
F. Jost, 107(CRCL):Jun83-244
Bischoff, B. Mittelalterliche Studien III.
Die südostdeutschen Schreibschulen und
Bibliotheken in der Karolingerzeit II.
W. Berschin, 684(ZDA):Band112Heft1-8
Bischoff, K. Germ. "*hlaiw-" "Grabhügel,
Grab, Hügel" im Deutschen.
W. Sanders, 685(ZDL):1/1983-66
Bishop, E. The Collected Prose. (R.
Giroux, ed)
D.J. Enright, 362:15Mar84-26
D. Kalstone, 441:15Jan84-1
L. Sage, 617(TLS):27Apr84-461
H. Vendler, 453(NYRB):16Feb84-3
Bishop, E. The Complete Poems 1927-1979.*
B. Costello, 491:Jul83-231
C. Doreski, 363(LitR):Winter84-262
A. Hollinghurst, 493:Jun83-73
M. Kinzie, 344:Winter84-111
639(VQR):Summer83-97
Bishop, I. Chaucer's "Troilus and Cri-
seyde."
S.A. Barney, 589:Jul83-843
B. Windeatt, 382(MAE):1983/1-132
Bishop, J.P. and A. Tate. The Republic of
Letters in America.* (T.D. Young and
J.J. Hindle, eds)
A. Gelpi, 405(MP):May84-447
T. Nieman, 31(ASch):Winter82/83-141
V. Strandberg, 579(SAQ):Summer83-333
Bishop, R. and P. Coblentz. American Deco-
rative Arts.
K.E. Johnson, 658:Winter83-301
J.V. Turano, 16:Spring83-76
Bisicchia, A. Invito alla lettura di Pier
Maria Rosso di San Secondo.
G. Marrone-Puglia, 276:Spring83-79
Biskind, P. Seeing is Believing.
R. Ebert, 441:15Jan84-12
Bissell, C. The Young Vincent Massey.*
A.B. McKillop, 627(UTQ):Summer83-479
Bissell, R.W. Orazio Gentileschi and the
Poetic Tradition in Caravaggesque Paint-
ing.
S. Pepper, 90:Nov83-699
Bissett, B. Beyond Even Faithful Legends.
G. Boire, 102(CanL):Summer83-166
Bissonette, D., L. Munger and M. Vallee.
Le Fleuve au coeur.*
R. Usmiani, 102(CanL):Winter82-157
Bittrich, B. Marie von Ebner-Eschenbach:
Unsühnbar.
J.P. Strelka, 564:Sep83-220
Björk, L. - see Hardy, T.
Björklund, K. Riki och Den förtrollade
vägen.
T. Lundell, 563(SS):Autumn83-396
Björkvall, G., G. Iversen and R. Jonsson,
eds. Corpus Troporum III.
M. Huglo, 537:Vol169No2-228
Bjørnflaten, J.I. Marr og språkviten-
skapen i Sovjetunionen.
R. Hammarberg, 350:Jun84-449
Bjornson, R. The Picaresque Hero in
European Fiction.
D. Lynch, 241:May83-85

Bjørnvig, T. The Pact.
R. Harris, 617(TLS):11May84-521
Bjurström, P. French Drawings: Eighteenth
Century.
P. Reuterswärd, 341:Vol52No3-138
de Blacha, N.M.G. - see under Girbal de
Blacha, N.M.
Black, D. Murder at the Met.
M.S. Kaplan, 441:21Oct84-18
Black, E. The Transfer Agreement.
R.S. Levy, 129:Sep84-68
A.J. Sherman, 441:10Jun84-26
Black, E.R. Politics and the News.
W.O. Gilsdorf, 529(QQ):Winter83-1161
Black, J.L. Citizens for the Fatherland.
R.L. Nichols, 173(ECS):Fall83-82
Black, K. - see Matejić, M. and others
Black, M. Poetic Drama as Mirror of the
Will.
K.W. Benston, 402(MLR):Apr83-409
Black, M. The Prevalence of Humbug and
Other Essays.*
T.M.R., 185:Jul84-727
Black, M. Selected Writings of the Late
Sir Misha Black, OBE RDI. (A. Blake, ed)
S. Rose, 324:May84-408
Black, M. and J.S. Reed, eds. Perspec-
tives on the American South.*
C.P. Roland, 579(SAQ):Spring83-223
Black, M.H. Cambridge University Press
1584-1984.
J. Sutherland, 617(TLS):15Jun84-661
Black Elk. The Sixth Grandfather. (R.J.
De Mallie, ed)
P.J. Powell, 469:Vol9No3-101
Blackall, E.A. The Novels of the German
Romantics.*
H. Steinecke, 680(ZDP):Band102Heft4-
616
Blackbourn, D. Class, Religion and Local
Politics in Wilhelmine Germany.
J. Doerr, 150(DR):Summer83-341
Blackburn, E. In and Out the Windows.
D. Gittins, 637(VS):Summer83-431
Blackburn, S. Spreading the Word.
C. McGinn, 617(TLS):2Mar84-217
Blackmur, R.P. Studies in Henry James.*
(V.A. Makowsky, ed)
295(JML):Nov83-501
Blackwell, K. and others - see Russell, B.
Blackwell, M.J., ed. Structures of Influ-
ence.
F. Paul, 301(JEGP):Apr83-306
O. Reinert, 678(YCGL):No31-155
M. Robinson, 562(Scan):Nov82-197
Blackwood, C. Corrigan.
P. Craig, 617(TLS):19Oct84-1179
J. Mellors, 362:8Nov84-28
Blackwood, C. Good Night Sweet Ladies.*
J. Mellors, 362:19Jan84-26
I. Thomson, 364:Dec83/Jan84-151
Blackwood, C. On the Perimeter.
M. Ruthven, 617(TLS):21Sep84-1048
Blades, J. Percussion Instruments and
Their History.
A.J.G.H., 617(TLS):20Jul84-822
Blaga, L. Trilogia Cunoasterii. (D.
Blaga, ed)
V. Nemoianu, 617(TLS):24Aug84-938
Blaikie, P., J. Cameron and D. Seddon.
Nepal in Crisis.
J. Das Gupta, 293(JASt):Nov82-105

Blaikie, W.B. Origins of the "Forty-Five."
F.J. Lynn, 83:Spring83-111
Blair, C., ed. Pollard's History of Fire-
arms.
G.M. Wilson, 617(TLS):20Jul84-820
Blair, D.S. African Literature in French.
L. Yoder, 207(FR):Feb84-385
Blair, P.H. Anglo-Saxon Northumbria. (M.
Lapidge and P.H. Blair, eds)
C.P. Wormald, 617(TLS):31Aug84-975
Blais, M-C. Visions d'Anna ou le vertige.
P.G. Lewis, 207(FR):Oct83-132
Blake, A. - see Black, M.
Blake, C.F. Ethnic Groups and Social
Change in a Chinese Market Town.
J. Omohundro, 293(JASt):Nov82-122
Blake, E.O., ed. The Cartulary of the
Priory of St. Denys near Southampton.
W.T. Reedy, 589:Jul83-733
Blake, K. Love and the Woman Question
in Victorian Literature.
K. Flint, 617(TLS):27Apr84-472
Blake, N. and K. Pole, eds. Dangers of
Deterrence.
T. Garden, 176:Apr84-58
Blake, N.F. - see Chaucer, G.
Blake, P. - see Hayward, M.
Blake, R. Disraeli's Grand Tour.*
S. Pickering, 569(SR):Winter83-xv
Blake, W. William Blake, Selected Poems.*
(P.H. Butter, ed)
F.P., 189(EA):Jul-Sep84-363
Blake, W. The Complete Poetry and Prose
of William Blake. (rev) (D.V. Erdman,
ed)
42(AR):Winter83-124
Blakely, R. La Grande Illusion de Jean
Renoir.* Pépé le Moko de Julien
Duvivier.
M.G. Hydak, 399(MLJ):Autumn83-284
Blakemore, F. Japanese Design Through
Textile Patterns.
R.L. Shep, 614:Summer84-18
Blakiston, G. Woburn and the Russells.
K. Willis, 556:Summer83-49
Blamires, H., ed. A Guide to Twentieth-
Century Literature in English.
N. Berry, 617(TLS):11May84-526
Blamires, H. Twentieth-Century English
Literature.
L. Bonnerot, 189(EA):Jul-Sep84-344
Blampain, D. La Littérature de jeunesse,
pour un autre usage.*
H. Godin, 208(FS):Oct83-492
Blanch, J.M.L. - see under Lope Blanch,
J.M.
Blanch, L. Pierre Loti.*
J. Mellors, 364:Dec83/Jan84-125
Blanchard, M.E. Description.
T. Bahti, 131(CL):Winter83-87
Blanchard, M-E. Saint-Just & Cie.*
L. Hunt, 173(ECS):Fall83-99
Blanchard, R.G. The First Editions of
John Buchan.
A.J. Tucher, 517(PBSA):Vol77No1-97
Blanchot, M. La Bête de Lascaux.
J. Laurans, 450(NRF):May83-121
Blanck, J., comp. Bibliography of Ameri-
can Literature. (Vol 7) (V.L. Smyers
and M. Winship, eds)
27(AL):Dec83-679

Blanco Aguinaga, C., J. Rodríguez Puérto-
las and I.M. Závala. Historia social de
la Literatura Española (en Lengua Cas-
tellana).*
  C. Zamora, 701(SinN):Oct–Dec82–77
Blanke, R. Prussian Poland in the German
Empire (1871–1900).
  R.F. Leslie, 575(SEER):Jul83–455
Blanning, T.C.W. The French Revolution in
Germany.
  C. Lucas, 617(TLS):16Nov84–1320
Blanshard, B. Four Reasonable Men.
  A. Quinton, 441:15Jul84–20
Blaser, R. – see Bowering, G.
Blashford-Snell, J. Mysteries.
  R. Hanbury-Tenison, 617(TLS):22Jun84–
694
Blass, F. and A. Debrunner. Grammatica
del greco del Nuovo Testamento. (new ed
by F. Rehkopf; Italian ed by G. Pisi)
  É. des Places, 555:Vol57fasc2–323
Blasucci, S. Il problema dell' intuizione
in Cartesio, Kant e Bergson.
  M. Adam, 542:Jan–Mar83–102
Blau, E. Ruskinian Gothic.*
  K.O. Garrigan, 576:Mar83–78
Blau, J. A Grammar of Biblical Hebrew.
  B. Grossfeld, 318(JAOS):Jan–Mar82–187
Blaug, M. The Methodology of Economics.
  I.C. Jarvie, 84:Sep83–289
Blaukopf, H. – see Mahler, G. and R.
Strauss
Blaukopf, K. Musik im Wandel der Gesell-
schaft.
  M. Bolling, 187:May84–334
Blavier, A. Les Fous littéraires.*
  A. Calame, 450(NRF):Apr83–120
  W.F. Motte, Jr., 207(FR):May84–864
Blazer, S. ricochet.
  639(VQR):Autumn83–135
Blázquez Martínez, J.M., ed. Produccion y
comercio del aceite en la antigüedad.
  N. Purcell, 313:Vol73–246
Blecua, J.M. – see de Vega Carpio, L.
Bleiberg, G., ed. La vida de Lazarillo de
Tormes, y de sus fortunas y adversidades.
  R. Geraldi, 552(REH):May83–296
Bleich, D. Subjective Criticism.
  D.H. Hirsch, 569(SR):Summer83–417
  E.F. Timpe, 221(GQ):May83–458
Bleicher, J. Contemporary Hermeneutics.*
  R. Bubner, 482(PhR):Jul83–480
  R.J. Schoeck, 125:Spring83–301
Bleicher, J. The Hermeneutic Imagination.
  J.J., 185:Apr84–553
Bleicken, J. Zum Regierungsstil des
römischen Kaisers.
  J. Crook, 123:Vol33No2–275
Bleier, R. Science and Gender.
  S.J. Gould, 441:12Aug84–7
Bleiler, E.F. Science Fiction Writers.
  C. Elkins, 561(SFS):Mar83–101
Bleiler, E.F. – see Doyle, A.C.
Bleser, C., ed. The Hammonds of Red-
cliffe.*
  E. Current-Garcia, 577(SHR):Fall83–371
  F. Hobson, 392:Fall83–585
  A.F. Scott, 579(SAQ):Summer83–344
Blessin, S. Die Romane Goethes.
  H.R. Vaget, 221(GQ):May83–502
Blessington, F.C. "Paradise Lost" and the
Classical Epic.*
  D. Hopkins, 447(N&Q):Apr82–173

Blinken, M. Stories.
  R. Elman, 441:18Mar84–18
Blinn, H., ed. Shakespeare-Rezeption.
  W. Bies, 52:Band18Heft3–328
Blishen, E. Donkey Work.*
  442(NY):23Apr84–131
Bliss, A. A Handbook of Dyes from Natural
Materials.
  S.F. Bill, 614:Summer84–17
Bliss, A. Spoken English in Ireland,
1600–1740.*
  M. Görlach, 72:Band219Heft1–182
  B. Ó Cuív, 112:Vol 15–170
Bliss, M. The Discovery of Insulin.
  J. Austoker, 617(TLS):16Mar84–284
Blitz, M. Heidegger's "Being and Time"
and the Possibility of Political Philos-
ophy.*
  M. Gelven, 529(QQ):Spring83–253
Bloch, A., ed. The Real Poland.
  Z. Gołąb, 497(PolR):Vol28No3–77
Bloch, M. Operation Willi.
  F. Donaldson, 617(TLS):14Dec84–1440
Bloch, M. Les Rois thaumaturges.* (new
ed)
  G. Sartoris, 450(NRF):Sep83–142
Bloch, R.H. Etymologies and Genealogies.
  N. Mann, 617(TLS):9Mar84–256
Bloch, R.H. Medieval French Literature
and Law.
  G. Armstrong, 545(RPh):Feb83–496
Bloch, S. and P. Reddaway. Soviet Psychi-
atric Abuse.
  B.A. Farrell, 176:Nov84–57
  J.K. Wing, 617(TLS):31Aug84–976
Block, A.F. The Early French Parody Noël.*
  F. Dobbins, 415:Dec83–748
Block, H. Herblock Through the Looking
Glass.
  C. Trueheart, 441:4Nov84–25
  442(NY):12Nov84–192
Block, I., ed. Perspectives on the Philos-
ophy of Wittgenstein.*
  D. Bell, 556:Summer83–66
Block, J.F. The Uses of Gothic.
  R. Harbison, 617(TLS):15Jun84–653
Block, L. The Buglar Who Painted Like
Mondrian.*
  T.J. Binyon, 617(TLS):21Sep84–1064
  M. Laski, 362:19Jul84–27
  442(NY):2Jan84–91
Block, L. Eight Million Ways to Die.
  T.J. Binyon, 617(TLS):27Jan84–93
Block, L. The Topless Tulip Caper.
  T.J. Binyon, 617(TLS):30Nov84–1391
Block, N., ed. Readings in the Philosophy
of Psychology. (Vol 2)
  R. Quinton, 486:Mar83–175
Blockley, R.C. The Fragmentary Classicis-
ing Historians of the Later Roman Empire.
  A. Cameron, 123:Vol33No1–18
  B. Croke, 487:Summer83–175
Blodgett, E.D. Beast Gate.
  R. Donovan, 137:Nov82–19
  R.A. Swanson, 168(ECW):Summer83–92
Blogie, J. Répertoire des catalogues de
ventes de livres imprimés. (Vol 1)
  G. Austin, 517(PBSA):Vol77No4–508
Blok, A. Selected Poems.*
  G. Clark, 399(MLJ):Spring83–91
Blok, A. The Twelve, and the Scythians.
  D. McDuff, 565:Vol24No3–67

Blom, F.J.M. Christoph and Andreas Arnold
and England.*
   D.L. Paisey, 78(BC):Autumn83-354
Blom, J.M. The Post-Tridentine English
Primer.
   R.K. Browne, 354:Jun83-182
   W.J. Grisbrooke, 447(N&Q):Oct82-431
Blomeyer, G.R. and B. Tietze, with E. Nord.
Ko-operatives Bauen.
   W. Segal, 46:Dec83-5
Blondel, É. Nietzsche.
   J. Figl, 687:Jul-Sep83-459
Blondin, A. Ma vie entre les lignes.
   W. de Spens, 450(NRF):Jan83-112
Bloom, A.H. The Linguistic Shaping of
Thought.
   D. Birdsong and T. Odlin, 351(LL):
      Sep83-401
   B.A. Elman, 293(JASt):May83-611
Bloom, E.A. and L.D., eds. Addison and
Steele: The Critical Heritage.*
   D.C. Mell, Jr., 677(YES):Vol 13-322
Bloom, E.A., with L.D. Bloom - see
Burney, F.
Bloom, H. Agon.*
   S.G. Axelrod, 405(MP):Feb84-290
   R. Jarvis, 153:Fall83-44
   A.N. Jeffares, 651(WHR):Autumn83-279
Bloom, H. The Breaking of the Vessels.*
   S.G. Axelrod, 405(MP):Feb84-290
Bloom, H. Poetry and Repression.*
   R. Jarvis, 153:Fall83-44
Bloom, H. - see Stone, A.
Bloom, H. and others. Deconstruction and
Criticism.*
   B. Cowan, 543:Mar83-690
   P. Hobsbaum, 402(MLR):Apr83-386
Bloomfield, M.W., ed. Allegory, Myth, and
Symbol.
   P. Rollinson, 604:Winter83-1
Blosen, H., ed. Das Wiener Osterspiel.
   R. Bergmann, 684(ZDA):Band12Heft1-39
Blosen, H. and H. Pors, comps. Rollen-
register zu Adalbert von Kellers Samm-
lung.
   J.E. Tailby, 402(MLR):Oct83-969
Blotnick, S. The Corporate Steeplechase.
   A. Cox, 441:2Sep84-15
Blount, R., Jr. What Men Don't Tell Women.
   D. Greenburg, 441:13May84-12
Bludau, B. Frankreich im Werk Nietzsches.*
   F.R. Love, 221(GQ):Jan83-149
Blue, W.R. The Development of Imagery in
Calderón's "Comedias."
   F.A. de Armas, 304(JHP):Fall83-78
"The Blue Cliff Record." (T. and J.C.
Cleary, trans)
   S.B. Park, 318(JAOS):Apr-Jun82-424
Blue Cloud, P. Elderberry Flute Song.
   C.L. Rawlins, 649(WAL):May83-67
Blum, A. and P. McHugh, eds. Friends,
Enemies, and Strangers.
   A. Walker, 488:Mar83-73
Blum, A.F. Socrates.
   A. Walker, 488:Mar83-73
Blum, L.A. Friendship, Altruism and Moral-
ity.*
   R.P. Blum, 484(PPR):Sep83-121
   P. Helm, 393(Mind):Apr83-312
   L. Thomas, 482(PhR):Jan83-135
Blumberg, R.L. India's Educated Women.
   A. Bandarage, 293(JASt):May83-694

Blume, B. Existenz und Dichtung.*
   B.L. Bradley, 133:Band16Heft2/3-265
Blume, J. Smart Women.
   L.B. Francke, 441:19Feb84-27
   K.C. O'Brien, 362:16Aug84-26
Blumenberg, H. Arbeit am Mythos.
   A.B. Neschke, 687:Jul-Sep83-448
Blumenson, M. Mark Clark.
   M. Carver, 441:12Aug84-16
Blumenthal, H.J. and A.C. Lloyd, eds.
Soul and the Structure of Being in Late
Neoplatonism.
   A. Reix, 542:Oct-Dec83-457
Blumenthal, H.J. and R.A. Markus, eds.
Neoplatonism and Early Christian Thought.
   S. Gersh, 589:Apr83-547
Blumenthal, M. Days We Would Rather Know.
   A. Brumer, 441:23Sep84-14
Blumenthal, P. La syntaxe du message.*
   K-H. Körner, 72:Band220Heft1-198
Blumenthal, U-R. Der Investiturstreit.
   J. Gilchrist, 589:Oct83-1028
Blunden, C. and M. Elvin. Cultural Atlas
of China.
   J. Rawson, 617(TLS):18May84-554
Blunt, A. Guide to Baroque Rome.
   K. Downes, 90:Jan83-40
Blunt, W. Married to a Single Life.
   T. Rothon, 617(TLS):3Feb84-107
Blustein, J. Parents and Children.
   H. Cohen, 185:Jan84-345
Bly, P. Pérez Galdós: La de Bringas.
   J. Lowe, 86(BHS):Apr83-158
   J. Whiston, 402(MLR):Oct83-947
Blyth, A., ed. Opera on Record, 2.
   M. Tanner, 617(TLS):10Feb84-133
Blyth, A. Remembering Britten.
   J.B., 412:May82-152
Blythe, A.E. The Ballad of Alice Moon-
child — and Others.
   F.W. Kaye, 649(WAL):Nov83-271
Blythe, R. Characters and Their Land-
scapes.*
   N. Delbanco, 441:29Jan84-27
   J. Updike, 442(NY):27Feb84-129
Bø, O. and others, eds. Norske Segner.
   B. af Klintberg, 64(Arv):Vol137-186
Boaistuau, P. Bref discours de l'excel-
lence et dignité de l'homme (1558).
   A. Buck, 72:Band220Heft2-451
Boaistuau, P. Le Théâtre du Monde (1558).
(M. Simonin, ed)
   P. Cherchi, 405(MP):Aug83-63
   F. Lestringant, 535(RHL):Jul/Aug83-622
Boardman, J. and others, eds. The Cam-
bridge Ancient History. (Vol 3, Pt 1)
(2nd ed)
   A.R. Burn, 123:Vol33No2-249
Boardman, J. and N.G.L. Hammond, eds. The
Cambridge Ancient History. (Vol 3, Pt 3)
(2nd ed)
   A.R. Burn, 123:Vol33No2-249
   H.D. Westlake, 303(JoHS):Vol 103-202
Boardman, M. Defoe and the Uses of Narra-
tive.
   P.R. Backscheider, 566:Spring84-161
   A.M. Duckworth, 594:Winter83-378
Boardman, P. The Shining Mountain.
   C. Wren, 441:1Apr84-24
Boase, R. The Troubadour Revival.
   R.R. Langbehn, 457(NRFH):Tomo31núm1-
      133
   C. Stern, 545(RPh):May83-643

Boatright, M.C. Tall Tales from Texas Cow Camps.
F.E. Abernethy, 584(SWR):Autumn83-398
L. Milazzo, 584(SWR):Spring83-vii
Bobbitt, P. Constitutional Fate.
A.A. Morris, 185:Apr84-501
Bobes, M.D. and others. Crítica Semiológica. (2nd ed)
C. González, 241:May83-90
Bobrowski, J. Shadow Lands.
J. Adler, 617(TLS):28Sep84-1094
D. Davis, 362:6Dec84-33
Bobunova, A.N. and V.K. Morozov. Russian for Businessmen.*
G.F. Holliday, 558(RLJ):Fall83-215
Bocca, G. Best Seller.
F. Milley, 395(MFS):Summer83-324
Boccaccio, G. Chaucer's Boccaccio. (N.R. Havely, ed and trans)
G.H. McWilliam, 402(MLR):Jan83-133
Boccaccio, G. Decameron. (C.S. Singleton, ed)
R.M. Adams, 453(NYRB):12Apr84-13
Bochmann, K. Der politisch-soziale Wortschatz des Rumänischen von 1821 bis 1850.*
K. Heitmann, 72:Band219Heft1-238
Bock, A.E. Mikio Naruse.
J. Kirkup, 617(TLS):25May84-581
Bock, C.C. Henri Matisse and Neo-impressionism.
N. Watkins, 90:Jan83-42
Bock, H. and A. Wertheim, eds. Essays on Contemporary American Drama.
D.L. Rinear, 397(MD):Sep83-384
Bock, H. and A. Wertheim, eds. Essays on Contemporary British Drama.
K. Morrison, 397(MD):Sep83-382
Bock, H-M., ed. Cinegraph.
S.S. Prawer, 617(TLS):28Sep84-1087
Bock, S. Literatur — Gesellschaft — Nation.*
R.C. Reimer, 406:Winter83-458
Bocuse, P. Paul Bocuse in Your Kitchen.
W. and C. Cowen, 639(VQR):Spring83-68
Bodde, D. Essays on Chinese Civilization. (C. Le Blanc and D. Borei, eds)
D. Grafflin, 293(JASt):Feb83-377
Boddy, M. and C. Fudge, eds. Local Socialism?
A. Sofer, 617(TLS):31Aug84-960
Boden, M.A. Minds and Mechanism.*
C. Mitchell, 529(QQ):Winter83-1061
Boden, M.A. Piaget.
F. Berenson, 483:Oct81-589
Bodenheimer, E. Philosophy of Responsibility.
F. Schoeman, 482(PhR):Jan83-140
Bodéüs, R. Le philosophie et la Cité.
J. Brun, 192(EP):Jul-Sep83-365
Y. Lafrance, 154:Dec83-703
Bodin, J. Selected Writings on Philosophy, Religion and Politics. (P.L. Rose, ed)
C. Baxter, 208(FS):Jan83-74
Bodoni, V. The Hands of the South.
W.S. Di Piero, 472:Fall/Winter83Spring/Summer84-169
Body, J. - see Giraudoux, J.
Boehme, J. The Key of Jacob Boehme.
J. Godwin, 111:Spring84-6
Boekholt, A. Puppets and Masks.
A. Cornish, 157:Summer83-31

de Boer, S.P., E.J. Driessen and H.L. Verhaar, eds. Biographical Dictionary of Dissidents in the Soviet Union, 1956-1975.
J. Rubinstein, 550(RusR):Jul83-338
Boeri, D. People of the Ice Whale.
W. Turner, 441:12Aug84-25
Boerner, W. Das "Cymbalum Mundi" des Bonaventure Des Périers.
P.A. Chilton, 546(RR):Nov83-496
G. Demerson, 547(RF):Band95Heft1/2-185
Boethius. Boethian Number Theory. (M. Masi, ed and trans)
J.F. Daly, 377:Nov83-183
Boewe, C. Fitzpatrick's Rafinesque.
J. Ewan, 517(PBSA):Vol77No3-388
Boewe, C. - see Fitzpatrick, T.J.
Bogaards, P. Moderne vreemde talen op school.
V.J. van Heuven, 204(FdL):Jun83-146
Bogan, J. and F. Goss, eds. Sparks of Fire.
G.S.S. Chandra, 436(NewL):Fall83-121
Bogarde, D. West of Sunset.
M. Bell, 441:2Sep84-14
J. Mellors, 362:5Apr84-28
442(NY):22Oct84-159
Bogardus, R.F. and F. Hobson, eds. Literature at the Barricades.
C.C. Nash, 219(GaR):Spring83-224
Bogdal, K-M. Heinrich von Kleist: "Michael Kohlhaas."
W. Wittkowski, 221(GQ):Jan83-144
Bogdan, R. and S.J. Taylor. Inside Out.
G.R. Lowe, 529(QQ):Summer83-295
Bogdanor, V., ed. Parties and Democracy in Britain and America.
H.G. Nicholas, 617(TLS):19Oct84-1177
Bogdanov, A. Red Star. (L. Graham and R. Stites, eds and trans)
W. Miller, Jr., 441:8Jul84-11
A. Myers, 617(TLS):2Nov84-1258
442(NY):9Jul84-94
Bogdanovich, P. The Killing of the Unicorn.
S. Gold, 441:23Sep84-29
Boggis, D. The Woman They Sent to Fight.
M. Laski, 362:9Feb84-26
Boghardt, C., M. Boghardt and R. Schmid. Die Zeitgenössischen Drucke von Klopstocks Werken.*
H. Siefken, 78(BC):Summer83-230
Bogin, G. In a Surf of Strangers.
L.G. Harvey, 436(NewL):Fall83-119
Boglioni, P., ed. La Culture populaire au moyen âge.*
P. Bourgain, 554:Vol 103No1-135
L.M. Paterson, 382(MAE):1983/1-157
Bogojavlensky, M. Russian Review Grammar.
A.K. Donchenko, 574(SEEJ):Spring83-130
M.K. Frank, 399(MLJ):Spring83-93
Bohm, D. Wholeness and the Implicate Order.*
H.J. Robinson, 529(QQ):Autumn83-903
Bohnen, K., ed. Nationalsozialismus und Literatur.
S.G. Payne, 406:Fall83-323
Bohner, C.H. Robert Penn Warren. (rev)
M.K. Spears, 569(SR):Fall83-655
Bohtz, C.H. Das Demeter-Heiligtum.
J.J. Coulton, 123:Vol33No2-359
Boirel, R. Le mécanisme.
J. Largeault, 542:Jul-Sep83-351

Boissel, J. Gobineau (1816-1882).*
  P. Brunel, 535(RHL):Jul/Aug83-653
Boitani, P., ed. Chaucer and the Italian
  Trecento.
  A. Bruten, 617(TLS):6Jan84-20
Boitani, P. English Medieval Narrative in
  the Thirteenth and Fourteenth Centuries.
  N.F. Blake, 179(ES):Feb83-77
  D. Pearsall, 38:Band101Heft3/4-501
Boitani, P. - see Bennett, J.A.W.
Bok, D. Beyond the Ivory Tower.
  S. Pickering, 569(SR):Summer83-434
  639(VQR):Winter83-23
Bok, S. Secrets.*
  T. Baldwin, 176:Nov84-64
  M. Midgley, 617(TLS):6Apr84-363
  K.L. Scheppele, 185:Apr84-538
  M. Warnock, 362:26Apr84-26
Boker, C. Joris Ivens, Film-Maker.
  M. Keller, 127:Fall83-284
Böker-Heil, N., H. Heckmann and I. Kinder-
  mann, eds. Das Tenorlied. (Vol 2)
  C. Meyer, 537:Vol69No1-108
Bokser, B.M. Post Mishnaic Judaism in
  Transition.
  M. Chernick, 318(JAOS):Oct-Dec82-665
Bol, L.J. and G.S. Keyes. Netherlandish
  Paintings and Drawings from the Collec-
  tion of F.C. Butôt.
  E. Young, 39:Feb83-150
Bol, P.C. Grossplastik aus Bronze in
  Olympia.
  C.A. Picón, 123:Vol33No1-102
"Un Bol de Nids d'Hirondelles ne fait
  pas le Printemps de Pékin" - see under
  "Un . . . "
Boland, E. Night Feed.
  M. Harmon, 272(IUR):Spring83-114
  M. O'Neill, 617(TLS):11May84-516
  V. Young, 249(HudR):Summer83-408
Bold, A., ed. The Sexual Dimension in
  Literature.
  J.V. Price, 189(EA):Jul-Sep84-314
  295(JML):Nov83-369
Bold, A., ed. Smollett.*
  D. Brooks-Davies, 148:Spring83-83
  S. Soupel, 189(EA):Apr-Jun84-207
Bold, A. - see MacDiarmid, H.
Bolduc, Y. Alain Grandbois.
  C. Cloutier-Wojciechowska, 627(UTQ):
  Summer83-525
Boldy, S. The Novels of Julio Cortázar.*
  W.B. Berg, 72:Band220Heft2-464
Bolens, L. Agronomes andalous du moyen-
  âge.
  W.H. Te Brake, 589:Jul83-736
Bolger, D. No Waiting America.
  M. Harmon, 272(IUR):Spring83-114
"Lord Bolingbroke: Contributions to the
  'Craftsman'."* (S. Varey, ed)
  D. Fletcher, 83:Autumn83-275
  W.H., 148:Autumn83-90
Bolinger, D. Language — the Loaded
  Weapon.*
  M.M. Bryant, 660(Word):Apr83-37
  T. Taylor and C. Hutton, 541(RES):
  Aug83-318
  J.P. Thorne, 297(JL):Mar83-245
Bolkestein, A.M. Problems in the Descrip-
  tion of Modal Verbs.
  E. Tucker, 123:Vol33No1-145
Böll, H. And Never Said a Word.
  P. Lewis, 565:Vol24No3-36

Böll, H. Irish Journal.* (French title:
  Journal irlandais.)
  P. Lewis, 565:Vol24No3-36
Böll, H. What's To Become of the Boy?
  P-L. Adams, 61:Nov84-148
  G.A. Craig, 441:7Oct84-3
  442(NY):12Nov84-195
Boll-Johansen, H. and L.W. Petersen, eds.
  Moderne italiensk litteratur.
  D. von der Fehr, 172(Edda):1983/3-190
Bollacher, M. Lessing: Vernunft und Ge-
  schichte.
  R. Schrader, 406:Fall83-339
Bollack, J. and P. Judet de la Combe - see
  Aeschylus
Boller, P.F., Jr. Presidential Campaigns.
  G.E. Reedy, 441:15Jul84-11
  442(NY):30Apr84-122
Bollino, F. Teoria e sistema delle belle
  arti.*
  N. Suckling, 208(FS):Apr83-222
Bollvåg, M.A. Kjaerlighetsbegrepet i
  Sigurd Hoels forfatterskap.*
  S. Lyngstad, 563(SS):Winter83-88
Bolsterli, M.J. - see Jackson, N.S.
Bolter, J.D. Turing's Man.
  A.J. Ayer, 453(NYRB):1Mar84-15
  P. Delany, 441:18Mar84-13
  A. Hodgkin, 617(TLS):14Dec84-1454
Bolton, S.C. Southern Anglicanism.
  W.H. Kenney 3d, 656(WMQ):Jul83-473
Bolton, W.F. The Language of 1984.
  R. Harris, 617(TLS):3Aug84-859
  M., 176:Dec84-26
  T. Nieman, 441:2Sep84-15
Bolton, W.F. A Living Language.
  J. Algeo, 660(Word):Dec83-235
  S. Lerer, 405(MP):Feb84-330
Bolz, N.W., ed. Wer hat Angst vor der
  Philosophie?
  R. Schrastetter, 489(PJGG):Band90Heft2-
  414
Bolzano, B. Philosophische Tagebücher,
  1811-1817. (Pt 1) (J. Berg, ed)
  I. Angelelli, 319:Apr84-249
Bomar, G.W. Texas Weather.
  L. Milazzo, 584(SWR):Autumn83-viii
Bombal, M.L. New Islands.*
  J. Mellors, 362:2Feb84-28
Bommelaer, J-F. Lysandre de Sparte.
  G.L. Cawkwell, 123:Vol33No1-73
Bon, F. Sortie d'usine.
  M.G. Rose, 207(FR):Dec83-264
Bonaccorso, G. and others - see Flaubert,
  G.
Bonacich, E. and J. Modell. The Economic
  Basis of Ethnic Solidarity.
  J.T. Omohundro, 293(JASt):Nov82-159
Bonafede, C.W. Norge i Italia/La Norvegia
  in Italia.
  I.M. Gabrieli, 562(Scan):May83-99
Bonaparte, F. The Triptych and the Cross.
  H. Foltinek, 402(MLR):Jul83-696
Bond, B. War and Society in Europe 1870-
  1970.
  E.M. Spiers, 617(TLS):9Mar84-245
Bond, D.J. The Fiction of André Pieyre de
  Mandiargues.
  A. Thiher, 395(MFS):Winter83-798
Bond, D.J. The Temptation of Despair.*
  R. Lecker, 395(MFS):Summer83-318
Bond, E. Restoration.
  G.E.H. Hughes, 148:Winter83-77

Bond, E.J. Reason and Value.
  B. Mayo, 518:Jul83-186
Bond, G.W. Euripides, "Heracles."*
  [shown in prev under Euripides]
  D. Bain, 123:Vol33No1-7
Bonenfant, C. and R., eds. Petite Antholo-
  gie du Noroît.
  A.L. Amprimoz, 102(CanL):Autumn83-110
Bonet, L. Gabriel Ferrater.
  A. Terry, 617(TLS):24Feb84-201
Bonet, L. - see de Alarcón, P.A.
Bonet, L. - see de Pereda, J.M.
Bonet Correa, A. and others. Bibliografía
  de Arquitectura, Ingeniería y Urbanismo
  en España (1498-1880).*
  F. Marías, 48:Oct-Dec80-503
Bonfante, G. and L. The Etruscan Language.
  D. Ridgway, 617(TLS):24Feb84-196
Bonfante, L. Out of Etruria.
  T.W. Potter, 123:Vol33No1-151
Bonfield, L. Marriage Settlements, 1601-
  1740.*
  L. Stone, 453(NYRB):29Mar84-42
Bongard-Levin, G.M. Drevneindijskaja
  Civilizacija.
  E. Gerow, 318(JAOS):Jan-Mar82-225
Bongiovanni Bertini, M. Guida a Proust.
  A. Eissen, 535(RHL):Sep/Dec83-960
Bonham-Carter, V. Authors by Profession.
  (Vol 2)
  D.J. Enright, 617(TLS):11May84-526
  J. Sutherland, 362:24May84-25
Bonheim, H. The Narrative Modes.
  A.B., 189(EA):Apr-Jun84-231
  F. Gado, 573(SSF):Spring-Summer83-152
  W.N., 102(CanL):Winter82-175
Bonnard, H. Code du français courant.
  J. Pohl, 209(FM):Oct83-361
  V.L. Remillard, 399(MLJ):Summer83-189
Bonnard, H. Procédés annexes d'expression.
  J-M. Klinkenberg, 209(FM):Oct83-365
  V.L. Remillard, 399(MLJ):Summer83-189
Bonnard, H. and R. Arveiller. Exercices
  de langue française.
  J. Chaurand, 209(FM):Oct83-367
  V.L. Remillard, 399(MLJ):Summer83-189
Bonneff, M. and others. Pantjasila.
  D.S. Lev, 293(JASt):May83-713
Bonnefoy, Y. Entretiens sur la poésie.*
  M. Bishop, 207(FR):Feb84-404
Bonnell, F.W. and F.C. Conrad Aiken.
  W. McBrien, 617(TLS):4May84-504
Bonnell, P. and F. Sedwick. Conversation
  in German. (3rd ed)
  J.L. Fox, 399(MLJ):Spring83-79
Bonner, R. Weakness and Deceit.
  C. Dickey, 453(NYRB):14Jun84-25
  A.F. Lowenthal, 441:27May84-6
  442(NY):30Jul84-87
Bonnerjee, G. and J. Dictionary of
  Foreign Words in Bengali.
  R.P. Das, 259(IIJ):Apr83-215
Bonnet, C. L'enfant et le symbolique.
  G. Mounin, 567:Vol45No3/4-371
Bonnet, G. La France et l'intolérance:
  de la Révolution de 1789 à la fin de la
  IVe République.
  J. Paulhan, 207(FR):May84-892
Bonnet, G. La France et l'intolérance:
  des sources à la Révolution de 1789.
  J. Paulhan, 207(FR):May84-892
Bonnet, H., with B. Brun - see Proust, M.

Bonneville, J-P. Marc-Aurèle Fortin en
  Gaspésie.
  W.N., 102(CanL):Winter82-176
Bonney, R. The King's Debts.*
  J. Lough, 208(FS):Oct83-457
Bonney, W.W. Thorns and Arabesques.*
  C.R. La Bossière, 107(CRCL):Mar83-116
Bontemps, A. and L. Hughes. Arna Bontemps
  — Langston Hughes: Letters 1925-1967.
  (C.H. Nichols, ed)
  M.K. Mootry-Ikerionwu, 95(CLAJ):Dec83-
  226
  D.T. Turner, 27(AL):Oct83-473
Bonvouloir-Bayol, T. Les Soeurs d'Io.
  K. Mezei, 102(CanL):Summer83-128
Bony, J. French Gothic Architecture of
  the 12th and 13th Centuries.
  R. Mark, 441:15Jan84-24
  W. Sauerländer, 453(NYRB):8Nov84-43
  C. Wilson, 617(TLS):16Nov84-1319
Boockmann, H. Der Deutsche Orden.
  U. Arnold, 684(ZDA):Band112Heft1-27
  I. Sterns, 589:Jan83-254
Boodberg, P.A. Selected Works of Peter A.
  Boodberg. (A.P. Cohen, comp)
  A.E. Dien, 318(JAOS):Apr-Jun82-422
Booij, G.E. Generatieve fonologie van het
  Nederlands.
  J.G. Kooij, 204(FdL):Jun82-150
"The Book of Lech Walesa."
  W. Stelmaszynski, 99:Oct83-27
"Book Review Index: A Master Cumulation,
  1969-1979." (G.C. Tarbert, ed)
  A. Cooper, 402(MLR):Jul83-665
Boon, K. L'Epoque de Lucas de Leyde et
  Pierre Bruegel.
  C. White, 39:Feb83-146
Boone, E.H. - see "The Codex Magliabech-
  iano"
Boorstin, D.J. The Discoverers.*
  J. Bernstein, 442(NY):12Mar84-157
  K. Thomas, 453(NYRB):10May84-20
Booth, E. Aristotelian Aporetic Ontology
  in Islamic and Christian Thinkers.
  J. Marenbon, 617(TLS):17Feb84-173
Booth, G. Omnibooth.
  P-L. Adams, 61:Nov84-149
Booth, J. Writers and Politics in Nigeria.
  M. Corner, 69:Vol153No2-76
Booth, M.R. Prefaces to English Nine-
  teenth-Century Theatre.*
  P.A. Dale, 149(CLS):Winter83-448
Booth, M.R. Victorian Spectacular Theatre
  1850-1910.*
  R.A. Cave, 611(TN):Vol37No3-138
Booth, M.R., ed. Victorian Theatrical
  Trades.
  D. Mayer, 611(TN):Vol37No1-46
Booth, M.W. The Experience of Song.*
  N.A. Brittin, 577(SHR):Spring83-197
  F.G., 189(EA):Jan-Mar83-108
Booth, S. Dance with the Devil.
  R. Palmer, 441:11Nov84-34
  J. Wolcott, 453(NYRB):22Nov84-15
Booth, S. "King Lear," "Macbeth," Indefin-
  ition, and Tragedy.
  G. Bradshaw, 617(TLS):27Jan84-90
Booth, W.C. Critical Understanding.*
  J. Phelan, 153:Summer83-39
  J. Preston, 402(MLR):Jul83-631
  M. Steinmann, Jr., 599:Winter83-41
  M.J. Valdés, 107(CRCL):Jun83-220

Booty, J.E., ed. The Godly Kingdom of
Tudor England.
J.N. King, 551(RenQ):Summer83-271
Booty, J.E. - see Hooker, R.
Boozer, J.S. - see Otto, R.
Borchert, J. Alley Life in Washington.
J.N. Ingham, 106:Summer83-175
J.M. Vlach, 292(JAF):Jan-Mar83-88
Borchmeyer, D. Dienst und Herrschaft.*
G.C. Avery, 406:Winter83-448
K. Wagner, 224(GRM):Band33Heft3-352
Borchmeyer, D. Die Weimarer Klassik.
T.J. Reed, 402(MLR):Jul83-757
Bordes, P. Le Serment du Jeu de Paume de
Jacques-Louis David.
F. Haskell, 453(NYRB):20Dec84-25
Bordillon, H. - see Jarry, A.
Bordinat, P. and S.B. Blaydes. William
Davenant.
W.J. Burling, 568(SCN):Spring/Summer83-
9
Bordman, G. American Musical Comedy.
J. Lahr, 157:Winter83-36
Bordow, J. The Ultimate Loss.
639(VQR):Summer83-100
Borel, J.P. and P. Rollell. La narrativa
más transparente.
S. Boldy, 86(BHS):Apr83-166
Borello, E. La teoria dei linguaggi
formali in Noam Chomsky.
G. Tonfoni, 260(IF):Band88-292
Borg, A.J. A Study of Aspect in Maltese.
B. Comrie, 350:Jun84-462
Borg, D. and W. Heinrichs, eds. Uncertain
Years.
K.S. Chern, 293(JASt):Nov82-124
Borgeaud, P. Recherches sur le dieu Pan.
S. Saïd, 555:Vol57fasc1-115
Borgen, A. Deg.
J. Garton, 562(Scan):May82-104
Borgen, J. Lillelord.
J. Garton, 562(Scan):May83-93
Borges, J.L. Borges at Eighty.* (W. Barn-
stone, ed)
G. Guinness, 395(MFS):Summer83-315
Borgström, B-E. The Patron and the Panca.
R. Burghart, 293(JASt):May83-695
Borinski, L. and C. Uhlig. Literatur der
Renaissance.
H.M. Klein, 72:Band219Heft2-439
Borish, E. Literary Lodgings.
J.K.L. Walker, 617(TLS):14Dec84-1439
Borkenau, F. End and Beginning.* (R.
Lowenthal, ed)
G. Woodcock, 529(QQ):Summer83-305
Borkowski, Z. Inscriptions des factions à
Alexandrie.
W. Liebeschuetz, 313:Vol73-247
Born, K. Skulpturen aus Kamerun.
C.M. Geary, 2(AfrA):Feb83-8
Bornkamm, H. Luther in Mid-Career 1521-
1530.* (German title: Martin Luther in
der Mitte seines Lebens.)
R. Scribner, 617(TLS):25May84-599
Bornmann, F. and M. Carpitella - see
Nietzsche, F.
Bornstein, D., ed. Ideals for Women in
the Works of Christine de Pizan.
D. Fraioli, 589:Apr83-437
Bornstein, D. The Lady in the Tower.
B. Ward, 617(TLS):31Aug84-975
de Boron, R. - see under Robert de Boron

Borowitz, A. The Woman Who Murdered Black
Satin. A Gallery of Sinister Perspec-
tives.
L. Taylor, 155:Spring83-51
Borque, J.M.D. - see under Díez Borque,
J.M.
Borrás, A.A., ed. The Theater and His-
panic Life.
S.E. Torres, 238:Dec83-632
Borrás Gualis, G.M. Arte mudéjar aragonés.
J.E. Arias Anglés, 48:Jan-Mar79-100
Borrie, G. The Development of Consumer
Law and Policy.
D. Pannick, 362:17May84-27
Borrow, G. George Borrow: Letters to John
Hasfeld. (A.M. Fraser, ed)
R. Fréchet, 189(EA):Oct-Dec84-471
Borsche, T. Sprachansichten.
B. Bitsch, 687:Apr-Jun83-323
Borson, R. Rain.* In the Smoky Light of
the Fields.
S.D. Harasym, 137:Nov82-22
Borson, R. A Sad Device.
M.T. Lane, 198:Jun83-75
B. Whitman, 529(QQ):Autumn83-876
Borsook, E. The Mural Painters of Tuscany
from Cimabue to Andrea del Sarto.* (2nd
ed)
R. Goffen, 551(RenQ):Autumn83-413
Borsook, E. and J. Offerhaus. Francesco
Sassetti and Ghirlandaio at Santa Trin-
ita, Florence.*
D.A. Covi, 54:Mar83-151
R. Goffen, 551(RenQ):Autumn83-413
Borst, R.R. Henry David Thoreau.*
J.C. Broderick, 365:Summer/Fall83-119
Bortner, M.A. Inside a Juvenile Court.
J.M.G., 185:Jul84-742
Borton, L. Sensing the Enemy.
H. Kamm, 441:29Apr84-19
Bos, H.J. and others, eds. Studies on
Christian Huygens.
A. Elzinga, 84:Sep83-295
Bosco, D. Metamorfosi del "libertinage."
F. Waquet, 535(RHL):May/Jun83-471
Bosco, M. Portrait de Zeus peint par
Minerve.
C-L. Rogers, 102(CanL):Autumn83-69
Bosco, R.A. and G.M. Johnson - see Emerson,
R.W.
Bose, N.S. Racism, Struggle for Equality
and Indian Nationalism.
R.A. Huttenback, 293(JASt):Nov82-182
Bosha, F.J. Faulkner's "Soldiers' Pay."
M. Yonce, 392:Summer83-506
Bosley, K., general ed. Poetry of Asia.
J.D. Yohannan, 318(JAOS):Jan-Mar82-152
Boslough, J. Stephen Hawking's Universe.
T. Ferris, 441:2Dec84-76
Bossong, G. Probleme der Übersetzung wis-
senschaftlicher Werke aus dem Arabischen
in das Altspanische zur Zeit Alfons des
Weisen.*
H-J. Niederehe, 457(NRFH):Tomo31núm2-
305
Bossus, F. Une Affaire sociale.
J.J. Herlan, 207(FR):Oct83-133
Boswell, J. Mr. Boswell Dines with Profes-
sor Kant.
R. Malter, 342:Band74Heft3-355

Boswell, J. Boswell: The Applause of the Jury, 1782-1785.* (I.S. Lustig and F.A. Pottle, eds)
C.J. Rawson, 569(SR):Spring83-269
I. Ross, 588(SSL):Vol 18-303
Boswell, T. Why Time Begins on Opening Day.
L.S. Ritter, 441:3Jun84-9
Boswinkel, E. and P.W. Pestman. Textes grecs, démotiques et bilingues (P.L. Bat. 19).
J.H. Johnson, 318(JAOS):Apr-Jun82-396
G. Mussies, 394:Vol36fasc1/2-224
Bosworth, A.B. A Historical Commentary on Arrian's History of Alexander.* (Vol 1)
A.R. Burn, 303(JoHS):Vol 103-206
P.A. Stadter, 121(CJ):Dec83/Jan84-160
Bosworth, P. Diane Arbus.
G. Glueck, 441:24Jun84-10
H. Hinson, 61:Nov84-129
J. Lieberson, 453(NYRB):16Aug84-9
Bosworth, S. Almost Innocent.
D.G. Myers, 441:30Dec84-16
Botha, R.P. The Conduct of Linguistic Inquiry.*
G. Mallinson, 307:Oct83-67
Bothwell, R., I. Drummond and J. English. Canada Since 1945.
P. Pénigault-Duhet, 189(EA):Jan-Mar84-111
Botkin, J., D. Dimancescu and R. Stata. The Innovators.
B. Harvey, 441:18Nov84-33
Botkin, J.W., M. Elmandjra and M. Malitza. No Limits to Learning.
G.L. Ervin, 399(MLJ):Autumn83-271
Botoman, R.C., D.E. Corbin and E.G. Walters. Îmi place limba română.
D. Deletant, 575(SEER):Oct83-636
Botsch, R.E. We Shall Not Overcome.*
W.I. Hair, 9(AlaR):Jan83-71
Böttcher, J. Gutes Deutsch kann jeder lernen.
J. Göschel, 685(ZDL):3/1983-406
Bottoms, D. In a U-Haul North of Damascus.
D. Baker, 434:Winter83-344
M. Cass, 598(SoR):Summer84-743
P. Mesic, 491:Feb84-296
Bottrall, R. Against a Setting Sun.
D. Davis, 362:19Jul84-25
G. Szirtes, 617(TLS):22Jun84-705
Boucé, P-G., ed. Sexuality in Eighteenth-Century Britain.*
D. Coward, 83:Autumn83-286
M. Roberts, 148:Winter83-83
L. Stone, 453(NYRB):29Mar84-42
Boucher, S. Recherches sur les bronzes figurés de Gaule pré-romaine et romaine.
M. Henig, 123:Vol33No1-152
Bouchier, D. The Feminist Challenge.
M. Midgley, 617(TLS):28Sep84-1080
Boucourechliev, A. Igor Stravinsky.
A. Suied, 450(NRF):Jan83-142
Boudard, A. Les Enfants de choeur.
R.J. Golsan, 207(FR):Dec83-265
de Bougainville, L.A. Voyage autour du Monde par la frégate "La Boudeuse" et la flûte "L'Etoile" en 1766, 1767, 1768 et 1769. (J. Proust, ed)
J. Lough, 83:Spring83-120

Président Bouhier. Correspondance littéraire du Président Bouhier. (No 5-8) (H. Duranton and others, eds)
J. Lough, 208(FS):Jul83-337
Bouhier, J., ed. Les Poètes de l'École de Rochefort.
G. Cesbron, 356(LR):Nov83-362
Bouhours, D. The Art of Criticism (1705).
566:Autumn83-65
Boulay, C. Benedetto Croce jusqu'en 1911.
A. Reix, 542:Oct-Dec83-491
du Boulay, S. Cicely Saunders.
A. Webster, 617(TLS):23Nov84-1356
Boulby, M. Karl Philipp Moritz.
A.R. Schmitt, 406:Summer83-208
Boulet, R.H. The Tranquility and the Turbulence.
M. Bell, 529(QQ):Autumn83-860
Boulez, P. Pierre Boulez: Conversations with Célestin Deliège.
A.W., 412:Feb82-68
Boulez, P. Points de repère.
M. Cooper, 208(FS):Oct83-487
Boulger, J.D. The Calvinist Temper in English Poetry.*
V. Newey, 402(MLR):Apr83-427
D. Norbrook, 447(N&Q):Oct82-440
J.H. Ottenhoff, 568(SCN):Fall83-45
D.M. Welch, 88:Winter83/84-117
Boult, A. Boult on Music.
J.N. Moore, 617(TLS):20Jan84-56
Boulton, J.T. - see Lawrence, D.H.
Boulton, M. The Anatomy of Literary Studies.
B. Martin, 447(N&Q):Dec82-566
Boumelha, P. Thomas Hardy and Women.
P.J. Casagrande, 268(IFR):Winter84-64
K. Flint, 175:Spring83-81
J. Halperin, 395(MFS):Summer83-274
A.C. Patterson, 177(ELT):Vol26No3-214
R.C. Schweik, 445(NCF):Jun83-117
J.E. Thomas, 637(VS):Spring83-360
295(JML):Nov83-489
Bounemeur, A. Les Bandits de l'Atlas.*
L. Kovacs, 450(NRF):Oct83-129
Bounni, A. and J. Teixidor. Inventaire des inscriptions de Palmyre. (fasc 12)
J. Naveh, 318(JAOS):Jan-Mar82-184
Bouraoui, H. The Critical Strategy.
M. Bishop, 150(DR):Winter83/84-695
S.G. Kellman, 395(MFS):Winter83-812
Bouraoui, H. Vers et l'Envers.
L. Welch, 198:Oct83-98
Bouras, C. Nea Moni on Chios.
R. Ousterhout, 576:Oct83-298
Bourcier, G. An Introduction to the History of the English Language.*
F. Chevillet, 189(EA):Apr-Jun84-176
Bourcier, G. L'Explication grammaticale anglaise.
R. Ball, 189(EA):Apr-Jun84-181
Bourdieu, P. Leçon sur la leçon.
G. Auclair, 450(NRF):Apr83-137
Bourg, J., P. Dupont and P. Geneste - see de Quevedo, F.
Bourgeade, P. Les Serpents.*
A. Clerval, 450(NRF):Apr83-123
Bourgeault, C. - see Smoldon, W.L.
Bourgeois, R. - see Constant, B.
Bourlet, C., C. Doutrelepont and S. Luisignan. Ordinateur et études médiévales. (Vol 1)
N. Hinton, 377:Nov83-184

Boxer, C.R., with J.C. Aldridge, eds.
Descriptive List of the State Papers
Portugal, 1661-1780, in the Public
Record Office, London. (Vol 3)
R. Ollard, 617(TLS):13Jul84-785
Boxill, A. V.S. Naipaul's Fiction.
J. Healey, 268(IFR):Summer84-125
Boycott, R. A Nice Girl Like Me.
C. Moorehead, 617(TLS):11May84-521
C. Sigal, 362:3May84-25
Boyd, B.M. The Redneck Way of Knowledge.
J.D. Houston, 649(WAL):May83-72
Boyd, J.R. and M.A. Before Book One.
M. Martin, 399(MLJ):Summer83-183
Boyd, M. Bach.
H. Cole, 362:20Sep84-28
S. Daw, 617(TLS):18May84-542
Boyd, M. Sew and Save Source Book.
J. Zarbaugh, 614:Summer84-28
Boyd, W. An Ice-Cream War.*
639(VQR):Autumn83-128
Boyd, W. On the Yankee Station.
B. McCabe, 441:5Aug84-12
442(NY):15Oct84-177
Boyd, W. Stars and Bars.
A. Huth, 362:27Sep84-32
D. Montrose, 617(TLS):21Sep84-1065
Boyd Whyte, I. Bruno Taut and the Archi-
tecture of Activism.*
A. Forty, 59:Sep83-389
M. Swenarton, 46:Mar83-74
Boyde, P. Dante, Philomythes and Philoso-
pher.*
R.B. Backhouse, 67:May83-149
R. Kirkpatrick, 382(MAE):1983/1-173
J.L. Miller, 589:Jan83-150
Boyer, E.L. High School.
A. Hacker, 453(NYRB):12Apr84-35
T.S. Healy, 441:13May84-14
Boyer, P. Urban Masses and Moral Order in
America, 1820-1920.
K. Cassidy, 106:Spring83-97
Boyer, R. Éléments de grammaire de
l'islandais ancien.
C.D.M. Cossar, 402(MLR):Oct83-994
Boyer, R. The Penny Ferry.
N. Callendar, 441:14Oct84-46
Boyer, R. Yggdrasill.
A. Reix, 542:Jan-Mar83-78
Boyers, R. F.R. Leavis.
W. Baker, 477(PLL):Fall83-461
Boylan, C. Last Resorts.
J. Mellors, 362:8Nov84-28
L. Taylor, 617(TLS):2Nov84-1239
Boylan, C. A Nail on the Head.*
J. Mellors, 362:19Jan84-26
D. Taylor, 364:Jul83-94
Boyle, A.J. and others. Virgil's Ascraean
Song.
P.F. Hovingh, 394:Vol36fasc3/4-427
Boyle, J. The Pain of Confinement.
D. Widgery, 362:16Aug84-25
Boyle, T. The Cold Stove League.
N. Callendar, 441:17Jun84-22
Boyle, T.C. Budding Prospects.
J. Clute, 617(TLS):14Sep84-1020
M. Gorra, 441:1Jul84-18
Bozoky, E., ed and trans. Le Livre Secret
des Cathares: Interrogatio Iohannis.
S. Runciman, 382(MAE):1983/2-360
Brabazon, J. Dorothy L. Sayers.*
P. Wolfe, 395(MFS):Autumn83-389

Bracken, P. The Command and Control of
Nuclear Forces.*
P. Towle, 617(TLS):9Mar84-241
Brackert, H., ed. Und wenn sie nicht
gestorben sind ... *
J. Zipes, 406:Fall83-327
Bradbrook, M.C. The Collected Papers of
Muriel Bradbrook. (Vol 2)
639(VQR):Autumn83-124
Bradbury, M. The Modern American Novel.
42(AR):Fall83-508
Bradbury, M. Rates of Exchange.*
C. Hawtree, 364:Apr/May83-130
Bradby, D., L. James and B. Sharratt, eds.
Performance and Politics in Popular
Drama.*
M. Page, 397(MD):Mar83-111
Braddon, M.E. Aurora Floyd.
P. Craig, 617(TLS):21Sep84-1066
Brademann, K. Die Bezeichnungen für den
Begriff des "Erinnerns" im Alt- und
Mittelfranzösischen.*
M. Offord, 208(FS):Jan83-69
Bradfield, V.J., ed. Information Sources
in Architecture.
J.S. Curl, 324:Aug84-642
Bradford, M.E. A Worthy Company.
M. Bordelon, 396(ModA):Winter83-93
Bradford, S. Princess Grace.
J. Barthel, 441:27May84-13
E. Sirkin, 18:Jul-Aug84-43
E.S. Turner, 617(TLS):8Jun84-633
Bradley, A. and T. Smith, eds. Australian
Art and Architecture.*
G. Herbert, 576:Dec83-395
Bradley, B. James Joyce's Schooldays.
J. Coolahan, 272(IUR):Autumn83-270
M.P. Gillespie, 594:Winter83-364
W. Potts, 305(JIL):Sep83-83
Bradley, B.L. Rainer Maria Rilkes "Der
Neuen Gedichte anderer Teil."
H.M.K. Riley, 221(GQ):Jan83-156
Bradley, I. - see Gilbert, W.S. and A.S.
Sullivan
Bradley, M.Z. The Mists of Avalon.*
J.S. Beerman, 42(AR):Summer83-370
Bradley, R.L. Narrator and Audience.
D.H. Green, 402(MLR):Jul83-743
Bradley, S.A.J., ed and trans. Anglo-
Saxon Poetry.*
A. Crépin, 189(EA):Jul-Sep84-318
G.R. Owen, 148:Spring83-85
Bradner, J.H. Mammoth Vehicles of the
World.
529(QQ):Spring83-282
Bradstock, M. and others, eds. Edge City
on Two Different Plans.
B. Roberts, 381:Dec83-486
Brady, F. James Boswell: The Later Years
1769-1795.
P. Johnson, 362:22Nov84-26
K. Walker, 617(TLS):16Nov84-1306
Brady, J. The Unmaking of a Dancer.
M. Ellmann, 569(SR):Winter83-120
R. Philp, 151:Oct82-96
Brady, K. The Short Stories of Thomas
Hardy.
J. Halperin, 395(MFS):Summer83-274
R.C. Schweik, 445(NCF):Jun83-117
Brady, K. Ida Tarbell.
A. Whitman, 441:14Oct84-27

45

Braekman, W.L., ed. Christiaen zan Vaeren-
brakens "Conste van musike oft vanden
Sanghe."
   R. Leppert, 589:Apr83-548
Braemme, E. Soya's sociale budskab, fire
sceniske debatstykker og deres mod-
tagelse hos presse og publikum.
   F. Hugus, 563(SS):Spring83-198
Braestrup, P., ed. Vietnam as History.
   R.H. Ullman, 441:1Jul84-22
Braet, H., ed and trans. Deux Lais féer-
iques bretons.*
   D. Robertson, 545(RPh):Feb83-502
Bragg, M. Laurence Olivier.
   C. Brown, 617(TLS):7Dec84-1418
Brague, R. Du temps chez Platon et Aris-
tote.
   Y. Lafrance, 154:Jun83-356
Braham, A. The Architecture of the French
Enlightenment.
   C. Tadgell, 576:Oct83-302
Braham, R.L., ed. Social Justice.
   J.H.C., 185:Apr84-547
Brahmanand - see Narayan, J.
Brahms, J. Johannes Brahms: Alto Rhapsody,
Opus 53. (W. Frisch, ed)
   E. Sams, 617(TLS):26Oct84-1226
Brain, J.B. Christian Indians in Natal
1860-1911.
   C. Hope, 617(TLS):16Mar84-269
Brain, R. Art and Society in Africa.*
   M. Gilbert, 69:Vol53No3-99
Braine, J. One and Last Love.
   M. Théry, 189(EA):Apr-Sep83-354
Braine, J. The Two of Us.
   P. Kemp, 617(TLS):9Mar84-251
Brainerd, B., ed. Historical Linguistics.
   A.J. Naro, 350:Dec84-929
Brakhage, S. Brakhage Scrapbook. (R.A.
Haller, ed)
   T. Lyman, 42(AR):Spring83-248
Branca, V. and others, eds. Il Rinas-
cimento.
   M. Pozzi, 228(GSLI):Vol 160fasc511-429
Brancazio, P.J. Sport Science.
   442(NY):4Jun84-135
Branch, E.M. and R.H. Hirst, with H.E.
Smith - see Twain, M.
Brandauer, F.P. Tung Yüeh.*
   K. Carlitz, 318(JAOS):Jan-Mar82-141
   R.E. Hegel, 116:Jan82-140
von Brandenstein, C.G. Names and Sub-
stances of the Australian Subsection
System.
   J. Heath, 350:Jun84-466
Brandmeyer, R. Biedermeierroman und Krise
der ständischen Ordnung.
   E. Gallati, 133:Band16Heft2/3-252
   J.L. Sammons, 301(JEGP):Apr83-295
Brandon, J.R., ed. Chūshingura.
   L.C. Pronko, 407(MN):Spring83-109
   D. Waterhouse, 187:Sep84-576
Brandon, J.R., W.P. Malm and D.H. Shively.
Studies in Kabuki.
   S.L. Leiter, 318(JAOS):Jan-Mar82-140
Brandreth, G. John Gielgud.
   C. Brown, 617(TLS):7Dec84-1418
Brandreth, G. Great Theatrical Disasters.
   G. Playfair, 157:Summer83-28
Brandt, B. London in the Thirties.
   S. Laschever, 441:28Oct84-26
"Bill Brandt: Portraits."
   M. Amaya, 592:Jul83-58

Brandt, G.W., ed. British Television
Drama.*
   J. Caughie, 610:Spring82-138
Brandt, H. and M. Beyer, eds. Ansichten
der deutschen Klassik.
   W. Albrecht, 654(WB):10/1982-174
Brandt, P., T. Hofmann and R. Zilkenat.
Preussen. (Vol 3)
   I.K. Rogoff, 59:Jun83-250
Brandys, K. A Warsaw Diary 1978-1981.
   N. Ascherson, 453(NYRB):26Apr84-7
   T.G. Ash, 617(TLS):28Sep84-1098
   C. Gati, 441:11Mar84-9
   Z. Tomin, 362:9Aug84-26
   442(NY):2Apr84-133
Brann, N.L. The Abbot Trithemius (1462-
1516).*
   F. Baron, 551(RenQ):Summer83-235
Brannigan, A. The Social Basis of Scien-
tific Discoveries.
   M. Ruse, 529(QQ):Spring83-267
   K.S., 185:Apr84-553
Brantley, R.E. Locke, Wesley, and the
Method of English Romanticism.
   R. Trickett, 617(TLS):21Dec84-1467
Brasch, W.M. Black English and the Mass
Media.*
   G.W. Beattie, 353:Vol20No3/4-354
   R.R. Butters, 579(SAQ):Winter83-106
   B. Jackson, 292(JAF):Oct-Dec83-485
Brasch, W.M. Columbia County Place Names.
   M.R. Miller, 35(AS):Winter83-365
   R.M. Rennick, 424:Mar83-68
Brasil, E. and W.J. Smith, eds. Brazilian
Poetry 1950-1980.
   J. Gledson, 617(TLS):27Apr84-461
Brassaï. The Artists of My Life.*
   M. Amaya, 592:Jul83-58
   A. Berman, 55:Summer83-28
Brassel, R. and others, eds. Zauberformel:
Fauler Zauber?
   C.J. Hughes, 617(TLS):7Dec84-1425
Lady Brassey. A Voyage in the Sunbeam.
   L.D., 617(TLS):22Jun84-711
Braswell, L.N. Western Manuscripts from
Classical Antiquity to the Renaissance.*
   G. Warkentin, 627(UTQ):Summer83-403
Braswell, M.F. The Medieval Sinner.
   C.R. Sleeth, 617(TLS):13Apr84-408
Bratchell, D.F. - see Greene, R.
Brathwaite, E.K. Third World Poems.
   S. Brown, 493:Jun83-67
Bratton, J.S. The Impact of Victorian
Children's Fiction.*
   M. Burgan, 637(VS):Spring83-352
   A. Kertzer, 49:Apr83-86
Brauch, E. Übersetzung, Paraphrase und
Plagiat.
   M. Kruse, 72:Band219Heft2-465
Braude, B. and B. Coste. Engagements.
   A.S. Bates, 399(MLJ):Summer83-192
Braudel, F. Civilization and Capitalism
15th-18th Century. (Vol 1: The Struc-
ture of Everyday Life.)
   J.A. Leith, 529(QQ):Summer83-549
Braudel, F. Civilization and Capitalism,
15th-18th Century.* (Vol 2: The Wheels
of Commerce.)
   639(VQR):Autumn83-120

Braudel, F. Civilization and Capitalism, 15th-18th Century. (Vol 3: The Perspective of the World.)
N. Bliven, 442(NY):26Nov84-145
A. Calder, 362:28Jun84-23
K. Thomas, 453(NYRB):22Nov84-41
E.R. Wolf, 441:4Nov84-11
Braudel, F. On History.
G. McLennan, 366:Spring83-107
Braun, E. The Director and the Stage.
J. McGrath, 610:Autumn83-264
Braun, E. The Theatre of Meyerhold.
A. Parkin, 397(MD):Dec83-576
Braun, K. and T.E. Haevernick. Das Kabirenheiligtum bei Theben. (Vol 4)
J. Boardman, 123:Vol33No1-149
Braun, T. Disraeli the Novelist.
C. Dahl, 191(ELN):Sep83-66
J. Halperin, 125:Winter83-190
S. Monod, 189(EA):Oct-Dec83-476
R. O'Kell, 637(VS):Spring83-347
Braun, V. Stücke.
J. Hilton, 617(TLS):27Apr84-471
Brauneck, M., ed. Weltliteratur im 20. Jahrhundert.
E. Kaufmann, 654(WB):6/1983-1139
Braunmuller, A.R., ed. A Seventeenth-Century Letter-Book.
S. Schoenbaum, 617(TLS):26Oct84-1220
Brautigan, R. So The Wind Won't Blow It All Away.*
D. Durrant, 364:Jun83-102
A. Ronald, 649(WAL):Aug83-164
Brawley, E. The Alamo Tree.
D.G. Myers, 441:26Aug84-16
Bray, M. Universal Primary Education in Nigeria.
R.F. Stock, 69:Vol53No3-104
de Bray, R.G.A. Guide to the Slavonic Languages.* (Vols 1-3) (3rd ed)
W.W. Derbyshire, 558(RLJ):Fall83-217
Brazeau, P. Parts of a World.*
C. Berger, 676(YR):Winter84-290
Brecht, B. Briefe.* (G. Glaeser, ed)
J. Fuegi, 221(GQ):Mar83-337
Brecht, B. Das grosse Brecht-Liederbuch. (F. Hennenberg, ed)
J. Willett, 617(TLS):5Oct84-1137
Brecht, B. Leben des Galilei. (2nd ed) (H.F. Brookes and C.E. Fraenkel, eds)
M.C. Crichton, 221(GQ):Mar83-337
Brecht, B. Mr. Puntila and his Man Matti.
D. Constantine, 161(DUJ):Dec82-118
Brecht, B. Short Stories, 1921-1946.* (J. Willett and R. Manheim, eds)
W.G. Regier, 502(PrS):Winter83-93
"Brecht 80."
R. Karachouli, 654(WB):9/1982-186
D.S. Lloyd, 221(GQ):Mar83-338
"The Brecht Yearbook." (Vol 11: Beyond Brecht.) (J. Fuegi, G. Bahr and J. Willett, eds)
P. Brady, 617(TLS):23Mar84-309
Bredin, J-D. L'Affaire.
D. Coward, 617(TLS):27Apr84-478
Brednich, R.W. The Bible and the Plough.
V. Peters, 196:Band24Heft1/2-131
van Bree, C. Hebben-constructies en datiefconstructies binnen het Nederlandse taalgebied.
H. Bloemhoff, 204(FdL):Dec82-294

Breen, D.H. The Canadian Prairie West and the Ranching Frontier 1874-1924.
R. McLeod, 529(QQ):Winter83-1228
Breen, J. Vicar's Roses.
T.J. Binyon, 617(TLS):18May84-557
Breen, J.L. The Gathering Place.
N. Callendar, 441:20May84-39
de Breffny, B., general ed. Ireland.
C. McAll, 617(TLS):20Apr84-440
Bréguet, E. - see Cicero
Breisach, E. Historiography.
J.P. Kenyon, 617(TLS):2Mar84-222
Breivik, L.E. Existential "There."
R.A. Jacobs, 350:Sep84-663
von Bremen, T. Lord Byron als Erfolgsautor.
G. Blaicher, 38:Band101Heft3/4-527
Bremner, G. Order and Chance.
C. Blum, 617(TLS):16Mar84-285
D. Fletcher, 83:Autumn83-273
Brendel, A. Musical Thoughts and Afterthoughts. (2nd ed)
C. Ehrlich, 415:May83-301
Brendel, O.J. The Visible Idea.*
R. Higgins, 39:Jan83-71
Brendon, P. Winston Churchill.
C.M. Woodhouse, 617(TLS):13Apr84-394
Brenman-Gibson, M. Clifford Odets.*
M.J. Mendelsohn, 397(MD):Jun83-239
Brennan, M. The Stars and the Stones.
A. Burl, 617(TLS):30Mar84-352
Brennan, P. Zarkeen.
J. Parks, 526:Autumn83-94
Brenner, J. Tableau de la vie littéraire en France d'avantguerre à nos jours.
D. Boak, 67:May83-135
Brenni, V.J. The Bibliographic Control of American Literature 1920-1975.
J. Myerson, 517(PBSA):Oct-Dec80-412
Brentano, C. Anna Katharina Emmerick-Biographie. (J. Mathes, ed)
H.M.K. Riley, 133:Band16Heft1-70
Brentano, C. Sämtliche Werke und Briefe. (Vols 6-9 ed by H. Rölleke; Vol 14 ed by G. Mayer and W. Schmitz; Vol 16 ed by W. Bellmann; Vol 26 ed by B. Gajek; Vol 28 ed by J. Mathes)
H-G. Werner, 680(ZDP):Band102Heft2-285
Brentano, F. The Theory of Categories.*
R. Hanna, 543:Dec82-444
Brereton, G.E. and J.M. Ferrier - see "Le Menagier de Paris"
Breton, A. Poems of André Breton. (J-P. Cauvin and M.A. Caws, ed and trans)
R. Cardinal, 617(TLS):27Apr84-450
M. Perloff, 29:Jan/Feb84-40
Bretone, M. Tecniche e ideologie dei giuristi romani.
C. Cantègrit-Moatti, 555:Vol57fasc2-366
Brett, B. White Monster.
L.R. Ricou, 102(CanL):Summer83-118
Brett, P. - see Britten, B.
Brett, S., ed. The Faber Book of Parodies.
K. Amis, 617(TLS):8Jun84-640
I. Hislop, 362:24May84-27
Brett, S. Not Dead, Only Resting.
T.J.B., 617(TLS):28Sep84-1082
Brettschneider, W. Zorn und Trauer. (2nd ed)
K. Kändler, 654(WB):8/1983-1490

Bretz, M.L. La evolución novelística de
Pío Baroja.*
  D.F. Brown, 345(KRQ):Vol30No1-107
  R. Di Franco, 552(REH):Jan83-150
Breuer, H. Vorgeschichte des Fort-
schritts.*
  D. Daphinoff, 570(SQ):Spring83-117
  G. Schmitz, 38:Band101Heft3/4-517
Breuer, H-P. and D.F. Howard - see Butler,
S.
du Breuil, P. Le zoroastrisme.
  A. Reix, 542:Jan-Mar83-79
Breva-Claramonte, M. Sanctius' Theory of
Language.
  J.L. Subbiondo, 350:Dec84-985
Brew, K. African Panorama.
  G.S.S. Chandra, 436(NewL):Summer84-114
Brewer, D. Symbolic Stories.*
  W.R.J. Barron, 541(RES):May83-245
  J. Preston, 402(MLR):Apr83-390
Brewer, J. and J. Styles, eds. An Ungov-
ernable People.
  S. Staves, 173(ECS):Fall83-102
Brewer, K. To Remember What Is Lost.
  C.L. Rawlins, 649(WAL):Feb84-376
Brewster, E. Digging In.
  C. MacMillan, 198:Oct83-87
Brewster, E. Junction.
  J. Parks, 526:Autumn83-94
Brewster, E. The Way Home.
  H. Kirkwood, 526:Summer83-76
  C. MacMillan, 198:Oct83-87
  P. Monk, 150(DR):Spring83-179
Breyer, B.J.S. - see Trollope, A.
Breyer, P. Grammar Work.
  J.M. Hendrickson, 399(MLJ):Summer83-
186
Breymayer, R. and F. Häussermann - see
Oetinger, F.C.
Breytenbach, B. In Africa Even the Flies
Are Happy.
  T. Des Pres, 472:Fall/Winter83Spring/
Summer84-83
Breytenbach, B. Mouroir.
  N. Ascherson, 453(NYRB):25Oct84-23
  N. Gordimer, 61:Jul84-114
  J. Mellors, 362:24May84-28
  442(NY):16Jul84-91
Breytenbach, B. The True Confessions of
an Albino Terrorist.
  R. Jones, 362:15Nov84-30
Bricktop, with J. Haskins. Bricktop.
  S. Gold, 441:4Mar84-23
Bridenbaugh, C. - see Pynchon, J.
Bridger, F., ed. The Cross and the Bomb.
  D. Martin, 617(TLS):24Feb84-182
Bridges, R. The Selected Letters of
Robert Bridges. (Vol 1) (D.E. Stanford,
ed)
  F. Spalding, 362:10May84-30
Bridgman, R. Dark Thoreau.*
  G.V. Boudreau, 651(WHR):Spring83-93
  W.G. Heath, 106:Winter83-447
Brière, E.A., J. Frommer and B.R. Woshin-
sky. La France et la francophonie.
  J.A. Reiter, 207(FR):Oct83-148
Brierley, D. Blood Group O.
  R. Smith, 441:12Aug84-20
  442(NY):22Oct84-163
Brierley, D. Cold War.
  N. Callendar, 441:11Mar84-21
  442(NY):30Apr84-124

Briganti, G. Pietro da Cortona o della
pittura barocca.
  A. Blunt, 90:Apr83-230
Briggs, A. A Social History of England.*
  R.K. Webb, 441:1Apr84-9
  P. Whitehead, 362:19Jan84-25
  442(NY):18Jun84-116
Briggs, A.D.P. Alexander Pushkin.
  A. Klimoff, 550(RusR):Jul83-342
Briggs, C.J. The Wood Carvers of Córdova,
New Mexico.
  C.R. Farrer, 292(JAF):Apr-Jun83-218
Briggs, D.C. and M. Alisky. Historical
Dictionary of Mexico.
  J. Fisher, 86(BHS):Jan83-92
Briggs, G. and F. Taylor. The Cambridge
Photographic Atlas of the Planets.
  42(AR):Winter83-124
Bright, M. Cities Built to Music.
  P.S. Byard, 441:7Oct84-23
Bright, P. Dr. Richard Bright, 1789-1858.*
  P-L. Adams, 61:Jun84-124
Bright, W., ed. Discovered Tongues.
  L. Menn, 350:Sep84-690
Brigneau, F. Mon village à l'heure social-
iste.
  J. Paulhan, 207(FR):May84-892
Brigstocke, H. - see Buchahan, W.
Brillante, C., M. Cantilena and C.O.
Pavese, eds. I poemi epici rapsodici
non omerici e la tradizione orale.
  P.V. Jones, 123:Vol33No1-123
  W. McLeod, 487:Winter83-347
Brilliant, R. Visual Narratives.
  M. Henig, 617(TLS):15Jun84-671
Brillon, Y. Ethnocriminologie de
l'Afrique noire.
  J. Vanderlinden, 69:Vol153No4-101
Brindle, R.S. - see Bartolozzi, B.
Bringhurst, R. The Beauty of the Weapons.
  S. Hamill, 649(WAL):Aug83-187
Brink, A. A Chain of Voices.*
  W.N., 102(CanL):Summer83-191
Brink, A. Mapmakers.*
  M. Thorpe, 99:Dec83-32
Brink, A. The Wall of the Plague.
  J. Crace, 617(TLS):5Oct84-1140
  R. Jones, 362:20Sep84-27
Brink, A. Writing in a State of Siege.
  442(NY):9Apr84-144
Brink, C.O. Horace on Poetry.*
  N. Rudd, 487:Autumn83-278
  D.A. Russell, 123:Vol133No2-198
Brinkhus, G. Eine bayerische Fürsten-
spiegelkompilation des 15. Jahrhunderts.
  T. Struve, 684(ZDA):Band112Heft1-41
Brinkmann, H. Mittelalterliche Herme-
neutik.*
  H. Freytag, 680(ZDP):Band102Heft3-444
Brinkmann, R. Expressionismus.*
  A. Otten, 406:Spring83-85
Brinkmann, R., ed. Romantik in Deutsch-
land.
  R. Immerwahr, 406:Fall83-345
Brinnin, J.M. Sextet.*
  M. Ellmann, 569(SR):Winter83-120
  W. Harmon, 577(SHR):Fall83-381
Brinton, D. and R. Newman. Getting Along.
  D.E. Eskey, 399(MLJ):Summer83-185
Brioso Sánchez, M. - see Anacreontea

48

Brown, G.M. Time in a Red Coat. Three
Plays.
D. Profumo, 617(TLS):15Jun84-676
Brown, G.M. Voyages.
C. Boyle, 364:Dec83/Jan84-120
D. Dunn, 617(TLS):20Jan84-54
Brown, H.I. Perception, Theory and Commit-
ment.
H. Siegel, 606:Jul83-61
Brown, H.M., ed. A Florentine Chansonnier
from the Time of Lorenzo the Magnificent.
D. Fallows, 617(TLS):27Apr84-474
Brown, H.M. - see Peri, J.
Brown, H.P. The Origins of Trade Union
Power.
H. Clegg, 617(TLS):20Jan84-58
Brown, J. Gardens of a Golden Afternoon.
P. Davey, 46:Sep83-68
P.F. Norton, 576:Dec83-390
Brown, J. and J.H. Elliott. A Palace for
a King.* (Spanish title: Un Palacio
para el Rey.)
M-A. Börger-Reese, 240(HR):Autumn83-
465
Brown, J.C. In the Shadow of Florence.
D.V. Kent, 551(RenQ):Autumn83-403
A. Molho, 589:Jul83-738
Brown, J.L. Valery Larbaud.*
S. Jeune, 535(RHL):Jul/Aug83-659
Brown, J.M. Dickens.*
M. Shelden, 637(VS):Summer83-459
Brown, J.R. Discovering Shakespeare.*
T.L. Berger, 579(SAQ):Winter83-110
Brown, J.R. A Short Guide to Modern
British Drama.
J. Spurling, 176:Jan84-52
Brown, J.S., Jr., ed. Up Before Daylight.
V.V. Hamilton, 9(AlaR):Jul83-220
Brown, K. Anastasio Pantaleón de Ribera
(1600-1629).
M. Lunenfeld, 552(REH):Jan83-156
Brown, K.D. The English Labour Movement
1700-1951.
C. Ó Gráda, 272(IUR):Spring83-119
Brown, M. Marked to Die.
T. Rutkowski, 441:6May84-27
Brown, M.E. Burns and Tradition.
E. Letley, 617(TLS):12Oct84-1170
Brown, M.E. Double Lyric.*
S. Holmes, 565:Vol24No3-18
Brown, M.E. and P.S. Smith. Ballad and
Folksong.
N. Philip, 203:Vol194No1-130
Brown, M.J.E. Schubert.*
L. Salter, 415:May83-298
Brown, N. Sexuality and Feminism in
Shelley.
A. Leighton, 339(KSMB):No34-86
Brown, N.A.H. The Milanese Architecture
of Galeazzo Alessi.
B.B., 90:Jun83-374
Brown, N.D. Hood, Bonnet, and Little
Brown Jug.
R. Dugger, 441:13May84-23
Brown, N.D. - see Petty, E.P.
Brown, P. The Cult of Saints.
J.M. McCulloh, 589:Jan83-152
A. Murray, 313:Vol73-191
Brown, P. Religion and Society in the Age
of St. Augustine. The World of Late
Antiquity. Society and the Holy in Late
Antiquity. The Making of Late Antiquity.
A. Murray, 313:Vol73-191

Brown, P. and S. Gaines. The Love You
Make.*
C. Hawtree, 364:Dec83/Jan84-149
F. Spiegl, 362:9Feb84-25
Brown, P. and K. Schweizer - see Caven-
dish, W.
Brown, P.G. and H. Shue, eds. The Border
That Joins.
A.R.Z., 185:Apr84-568
Brown, R. Civil Wars.
R. Kaveney, 617(TLS):14Sep84-1019
L.S. Schwartz, 441:6May84-15
442(NY):14May84-149
Brown, R. The Nature of Social Laws.
A. Ryan, 617(TLS):23Nov84-1335
Brown, R.L. Moving to the Country.
D. Cole, 441:1Jan84-20
Brown, R.L. Music, Printed and Manuscript
in the James Weldon Johnson Memorial Col-
lection of Negro Arts and Letters.
M.F., 189(EA):Apr-Jun84-237
Brown, R.M. Southern Discomfort.
G. Davenport, 569(SR):Summer83-439
Brown, R.M. Elie Wiesel.
E. Pfefferkorn, 390:Nov83-57
Brown, S., ed. Caribbean Poetry Now.
D. Constantine, 176:Sep/Oct84-43
Brown, S.A. The Collected Poems of Ster-
ling A. Brown.* (M.S. Harper, ed)
S.W. Allen, 418(MR):Autumn83-649
Brown, S.C. Wines and Beers of Old New
England.
P. Buitenhuis, 106:Winter83-475
Brown, T. Devon Ghosts.
A. Blaen, 203:Vol194No2-265
Brown, T. Life as a Party.*
A. Forbes, 617(TLS):6Jan84-7
Brown, V.P. and L. Owens. Toting the Lead
Row.
C.L. Perdue, Jr., 292(JAF):Oct-Dec83-
474
Browne, E.M., with H. Browne. Two in One.*
C.H. Smith, 397(MD):Mar83-120
Browne, N. The Rhetoric of Filmic Narra-
tion.
M. Keller, 127:Fall83-284
Browne, T. Pseudodoxia Epidemica. (R.
Robbins, ed)
T.N. Corns, 506(PSt):Sep83-191
A. Favre, 189(EA):Oct-Dec83-466
Browning, I. Palmyra.
H.J.W. Drijvers, 318(JAOS):Jul-Sep82-
539
Browning, R. Oxford Poetical Works of
Robert Browning. (Vol 1) (I. Jack and
M. Smith, eds)
M. Dodsworth, 175:Summer83-192
Browning, R. The Poems.* (J. Pettigrew
and T.J. Collins, eds)
E. Cook, 627(UTQ):Summer83-425
Browning, R. Political and Constitutional
Ideas of the Court Whigs.*
E.A. Reitan, 173(ECS):Spring84-348
639(VQR):Spring84-55
"Browning Institute Studies." (Vol 7)
(W.S. Peterson, ed)
J. Woolford, 541(RES):Feb83-91
Brownjohn, A. Collected Poems 1952-83.
D. Davis, 362:14Jun84-26
D. Dunn, 364:Mar84-92
J. Mole, 176:Mar84-47
W. Scammell, 617(TLS):17Feb84-168

51

Brownlee, M.S. The Poetics of Literary
Theory.*
  J.S. Chittenden, 238:May83-295
  D. McGrady, 240(HR):Summer83-329
Brownlee, W.H. The Midrash Pesher of
Habakkuk.
  I. Rabinowitz, 318(JAOS):Jan-Mar82-191
Brownlow, K. "Napoleon:" Abel Gance's
Classic Film.*
  A. Brownjohn, 176:Jan84-64
  J.M. Welsh, 18:Dec83-67
Brownmiller, S. Femininity.
  C. Gilligan, 441:15Jan84-7
Brownstein, R.M. Becoming a Heroine.*
  D. Kaplan, 454:Fall83-81
  D. Robinson, 594:Winter83-384
Broyles, Y.J. The German Response to
Latin American Literature and the Recep-
tion of Jorge Luis Borges and Pablo
Neruda.
  U. Schulz-Buschhaus, 547(RF):Band95
    Heft1/2-235
Bruccoli, M.J. James Gould Cozzens.*
  42(AR):Fall83-508
  517(PBSA):Vol77No4-520
Bruccoli, M.J. F. Scott Fitzgerald: A
Descriptive Bibliography. Supplement
to F. Scott Fitzgerald: A Descriptive
Bibliography.
  P.B. Eppard, 517(PBSA):Vol77No1-99
Bruccoli, M.J. Ross Macdonald.
  T.J. Binyon, 441:1Apr84-20
  442(NY):30Apr84-122
Bruccoli, M.J. and M.M. Duggan - see
Fitzgerald, F.S.
Bruce-Gardyne, J. Mrs. Thatcher's First
Administration.
  J.E.S. Hayward, 617(TLS):28Dec84-1504
Bruce-Mitford, R. and others. The Sutton
Hoo Ship Burial. (Vol 3) (A.C. Evans,
ed)
  J. Graham-Campbell, 617(TLS):1Jun84-
    608
Bruchac, J. Translator's Son. Remember-
ing the Dawn.
  G.S.S. Chandra, 436(NewL):Summer84-114
Bruchey, S.W., ed. Small Business in Amer-
ican Life.
  J.W. Tyler, 658:Summer/Autumn83-217
Bruchis, M. One Step Backwards, Two Steps
Forward.
  D. Deletant, 617(TLS):13Jul84-777
  S.M. Horak, 104(CASS):Winter83-567
Bruck, P. and W. Karrer, eds. The Afro-
American Novel since 1960.
  C. Werner, 395(MFS):Summer83-319
Bruckner, D.J.R., S. Chwast and S. Heller.
Art Against War.
  A. Barnet, 441:10Jun84-24
Bruckner, M.T. Narrative Invention in
Twelfth-Century French Romance.*
  L. Brind'Amour, 188(ECr):Spring83-103
Bruézière, M. Pages d'auteurs contempor-
ains.
  R. Danner, 207(FR):Dec83-261
Brüggemann, T. and H-H. Ewers, eds. Hand-
buch zur Kinder- und Jungendliteratur,
von 1750 bis 1800.
  H. ten Doornkaat, 196:Band24Heft3/4-
    290
  D.C.G. Lorenz, 221(GQ):Nov83-651
  W. Neuber, 680(ZDP):Band102Heft2-315

Bruggen, C. Crumbs Under the Skin.
  P. Craig, 617(TLS):13Jul84-790
Bruhn, K. and A. Wezler, eds. Studien zum
Jainismus und Buddhismus.
  J.W. de Jong, 259(IIJ):Mar83-145
Bruhn, P. Russika und Sowjetika unter den
deutschsprachigen Hochschulschriften
(1973-1975).
  G. Walker, 575(SEER):Apr83-318
Bruhn, P. and H. Glade. Heinrich Böll in
der Sowjetunion (1952-1979).*
  G. Guntermann, 52:Band17Heft1-102
  N. Riedel, 133:Band16Heft1-85
Brulotte, G. Le Surveillant.
  C.A. Demharter, 207(FR):Apr84-731
Brumbaugh, R.S. Whitehead, Process Philos-
ophy, and Education.
  E.M. Kraus, 619:Summer83-323
Brumberg, A., ed. Poland.*
  A.J. Matejko, 497(PolR):Vol28No4-113
Brumble, H.D. 3d. An Annotated Bibliog-
raphy of American Indian and Eskimo
Autobiographies.*
  R. Maud, 106:Spring83-71
  C. Mishler, 292(JAF):Oct-Dec83-494
Brumm, U. Geschichte und Wildnis in der
amerikanischen Literatur.*
  A.P. Frank, 38:Band101Heft3/4-533
Brummack, J., ed. Heinrich Heine: Epoche —
Werk — Wirkung.* [shown in prev under
Heine, H.]
  R.C. Holub, 406:Winter83-445
Brunel, J. - see Rapin, N.
Bruner, E. and J. Becker, eds. Art, Rit-
ual and Society in Indonesia.
  M. Adams, 293(JASt):May83-713
Bruner, J. Child's Talk.
  J. Greene, 617(TLS):13Jul84-779
Bruner, J. In Search of Mind.
  J. Greene, 617(TLS):13Jul84-779
  H. Gruber, 441:8Jan84-6
Brunet, E. Le vocabulaire de Proust.
  G. Straka, 553(RLiR):Jan-Jun83-207
Brunet, É. Le Vocabulaire français de
1789 à nos jours.*
  R. Posner, 208(FS):Jan83-119
Bruneteau, C. and B. Cotteret - see
Mercier, L-S.
Bruni, A. - see Parini, G.
Bruni, F., ed. Libru di li vitii et di li
virtuti.
  C. Kleinhenz, 545(RPh):Feb83-481
Bruni, R.L. and D.W. Evans. A Catalogue
of Italian Books, 1601-1700, in Exeter
Libraries.
  U.L., 278(IS):Vol138-110
Brunius, T. and B-E. Benktson. Violet
Tengberg.
  J.P. Hodin, 89(BJA):Summer83-266
Brunkhorst, M. Tradition und Transforma-
tion.*
  L. Löb, 402(MLR):Oct83-901
Brunner, C.J. Sasanian Stamp Seals in the
Metropolitan Museum of Art.
  D.S. Flattery, 318(JAOS):Jan-Mar82-196
Brunold, P., with K. Gilbert and D.
Moroney - see Couperin, F.
Bruns, G.L. Inventions.
  A. Bony, 189(EA):Apr-Jun84-172
  C.S. Brown, 131(CL):Summer83-280
  R. Buchanan, 290(JAAC):Spring84-342
  T. Eagleton, 366:Autumn83-260

[continued]

Bruns, G.L. Inventions. [continuing]
  W.J. Kennedy, 221(GQ):Nov83-624
  M. Rapisarda, 395(MFS):Summer83-362
  639(VQR):Winter83-16
Brunt, P.A. - see Arrian
Brunton, P. The Notebooks of Paul Brunton:
  Perspectives.
  T. Cochran, 469:Vol9No4-116
Brunvand, J.H. The Vanishing Hitchhiker.*
  B. af Klintberg, 64(Arv):Vol37-188
  J.L. Langlois, 292(JAF):Jul-Sep83-356
Brushwood, J.S. Genteel Barbarism.*
  S. Boldy, 402(MLR):Oct83-951
  J.M. Kirk, 268(IFR):Winter84-57
  D.C. Scroggins, 238:May83-301
  D.L. Shaw, 86(BHS):Jul83-264
Bruss, E.W. Beautiful Theories.*
  W.V. Harris, 401(MLQ):Jun83-217
  D.T. O'Hara, 659(ConL):Summer84-250
Bruss, P. Victims.*
  D.J. Cahill, 594:Fall83-278
  A.H. Carter 3d, 573(SSF):Winter83-70
Bruter, C.P. Les architectures du feu.
  J-L. Gardies, 542:Jul-Sep83-353
de Bruyn, L. Woman and the Devil in Six-
  teenth-Century Literature.*
  A.A. MacDonald, 179(ES):Feb83-93
Bryan, C.D.B. Beautiful Women, Ugly
  Scenes.*
  W.H. Pritchard, 249(HudR):Winter83/84-
  745
Bryan, S. Salt Air.*
  D. Stuart, 598(SoR):Autumn84-969
Bryant, D. Lyric Poets of the Southern
  T'ang.
  S. Owen, 244(HJAS):Dec83-711
Bryce, G.E. A Legacy of Wisdom.
  R.J. Williams, 318(JAOS):Oct-Dec82-659
Bryce, I. You Only Live Once.
  M. Amory, 617(TLS):28Sep84-1076
  D.J. Enright, 362:30Aug84-26
Bryer, J.R., ed. The Short Stories of F.
  Scott Fitzgerald.
  J.M. Flora, 573(SSF):Fall83-334
  R. Nelson, 268(IFR):Winter84-55
  L. Thornton, 651(WHR):Summer83-183
Bryer, J.R. - see O'Neill, E.
Bryson, N. Vision and Painting.*
  B. Scott, 39:Oct83-354
Bryson, N. Word and Image.*
  A. Brookner, 90:Dec83-762
  C. Duncan, 59:Jun83-246
  D. Fletcher, 83:Spring83-121
  J. Undank, 400(MLN):May83-811
Brzezinski, Z. Power and Principle.*
  E. Kedourie, 176:Nov84-15
  42(AR):Summer83-377
Bubner, R. Modern German Philosophy.
  D. Dahlstrom, 543:Mar83-692
  W.V. Doniela, 63:Mar83-104
  M.J. Inwood, 393(Mind):Oct83-607
  G.J. Stack, 484(PPR):Mar84-428
Bucco, M. René Wellek.
  J.P. Strelka, 131(CL):Summer83-279
Bucer, M. Correspondance de Martin Bucer.
  (Vol 1) (J. Rott, ed) Martini Buceri
  Opera Latina. (Vol 1) (C. Augustijn,
  P. Fraenkel and M. Lienhard, eds)
  J.M. Kittleson, 539:Nov83-301
Buch, H.C. Die Hochzeit von Port-au-
  Prince.
  J.J. White, 617(TLS):20Jul84-816

"Buch und Sammler."*
  D. Gutzen, 52:Band17Heft2-210
Buchan, J. The Best Short Stories of John
  Buchan. (Vol 2) (D. Daniell, ed)
  J.R. Cox, 177(ELT):Vol26No4-329
Buchan, J. Memory Hold-the-Door.
  A.S.B., 617(TLS):12Oct84-1171
Buchan, J. A Parish of Rich Women.
  P. Keegan, 617(TLS):27Jul84-848
  J. Mantle, 362:26Jul84-28
Buchan, J. Thatched Village.
  S. Mills, 617(TLS):13Jul84-780
Buchan, W. John Buchan.*
  J.R. Cox, 177(ELT):Vol26No4-329
Buchan, W. - see Masefield, J.
Buchanan, B. Early Near Eastern Seals in
  the Yale Babylonian Collection.
  P. Amiet, 318(JAOS):Jul-Sep82-533
Buchanan, G. Adjacent Columns.
  M. O'Neill, 617(TLS):11May84-516
Buchanan, K., C.P. Fitz Gerald and C.A.
  Ronan. China.
  R. Demeritt, 293(JASt):Aug83-907
Buchanan, T. Photographing Historic Build-
  ings.
  J. Wall, 324:Apr84-346
Buchanan, W. William Buchanan and the
  19th Century Art Trade. (H. Brigstocke,
  ed)
  J. Ingamells, 90:Jul83-434
Buchholz, A., ed. Soviet and East Euro-
  pean Studies in the International
  Framework.
  A.H. Kassof, 550(RusR):Apr83-221
Buchholz, P. Vorzeitkunde.*
  J.M. Stitt, 292(JAF):Jan-Mar83-93
"Georg Büchner Jahrbuch 1, 1981." (T.M.
  Mayer, ed)
  J.H. Petersen, 564:Nov83-299
Buchner, H., W.G. Jacobs and A. Pieper -
  see Schelling, F.W.J.
Buchner, H. and J. Jantzen - see Schelling,
  F.W.J.
Buchner, H. and O. Pöggeler - see Hegel,
  G.W.F.
Buchthal, H. Art in the Mediterranean
  World, A.D. 100 to 1400.
  R. Cormack, 90:Oct83-623
Buck, A., ed. Die Rezeption der Antike.
  J.C. King, 221(GQ):Mar83-308
Buck, A. and others, eds. Europäische
  Hofkultur im 16. und 17. Jahrhundert.
  J. Hardin, 301(JEGP):Oct83-596
Buck, G. The History of King Richard the
  Third.* (A.N. Kincaid, ed)
  M.J.C. Lowry, 677(YES):Vol 13-314
Buck, J.J. The Only Place to Be.
  639(VQR):Winter83-20
Buck, P. American Science and Modern
  China 1876-1936.*
  C. Partington, 302:Vol 19No2-257
Buck, R.J. A History of Boeotia.*
  G.J.M.J. te Riele, 394:Vol36fasc1/2-
  230
Buckland, T., ed. Traditional Dance.
  (Vol 1)
  S. Billington, 203:Vol94No2-260
Buckler, J. The Theban Hegemony, 371-
  362 B.C.*
  L.A. Tritle, 122:Oct83-344
Buckler, W.E. Matthew Arnold's Prose.
  C. Baldick, 617(TLS):6Apr84-370

Buckler, W.E. The Poetry of Thomas Hardy.*
    N. Page, 150(DR):Autumn83-542
Buckley, J.H. The Turning Key.
    J. Sturrock, 617(TLS):16Nov84-1307
    J. Sullivan, 441:27May84-17
Buckley, R. Occupation Diplomacy.*
    H. Masahiro, 407(MN):Autumn83-349
    B-A. Shillony, 293(JASt):Aug83-971
    Sodei Rinjirō, 285(JapQ):Oct-Dec83-431
Buckley, T. Violent Neighbors.
    C. Dickey, 453(NYRB):14Jun84-25
    M. Kramer, 441:6May84-20
    442(NY):14May84-150
Buckley, V. Cutting Green Hay.
    T. Coady, 381:Sep83-349
Buckley, W.F., Jr. The Story of Henri Tod.
    R. Grenier, 617(TLS):27Jul84-849
    M. Malone, 441:5Feb84-22
Budd, L.J., ed. Critical Essays on Mark
    Twain, 1867-1910.
    S. Brodwin, 26(ALR):Spring83-132
    J.S. Tuckey, 445(NCF):Sep83-247
Budd, L.J. Our Mark Twain.
    H. Beaver, 617(TLS):15Jun84-657
    L. Leary, 578:Spring84-107
Budd, L.J., E.H. Cady and C.L. Anderson,
    eds. Towards a New American Literary
    History.*
    D. Tallack, 541(RES):Feb83-114
Buddecke, W. and H. Fuhrmann. Das deutsch-
    sprachige Drama seit 1945.*
    J.J. White, 402(MLR):Oct83-993
Budden, J. The Operas of Verdi. (Vol 2)
    D. Rosen, 415:Jun83-353
Budden, J. The Operas of Verdi.* (Vol 3)
    D. Rosen, 415:Jun83-353
    P. Weiss, 414(MusQ):Winter83-130
Buddensieg, T., with H. Rogge. Industrie-
    kultur.
    D.J.R. Bruckner, 441:27May84-16
Budé, A.W.A.M. De Hypotheseis der Griekse
    tragedies en komedies.
    D. Holwerda, 394:Vol136fascl/2-173
Buechner, F. A Room Called Remember.
    A. Shapiro, 441:11Mar84-19
Buel, J.D. and R. Buel, Jr. The Way of
    Duty.
    P. Maier, 441:5Feb84-19
Bugayeva, K.N. Vospominaniya o Belom.
    (J.E. Malmstad, ed)
    O.M. Cooke, 575(SEER):Oct83-602
Bugialli, G. Giuliano Bugialli's Foods of
    Italy.
    M. Burros, 441:2Dec84-14
Bühnemann, G. Der allwissende Buddha.
    J.W. de Jong, 259(IIJ):Mar83-155
Bühnemann, G. - see Ratnakīrti
Buisseret, D. Henry IV.
    R.J. Knecht, 617(TLS):28Sep84-1092
Bujold, R-G. Le p'tit ministre-les-pommes.
    R.G. Hodgson, 102(CanL):Winter82-153
Bujold, R-G. La Sang-mêlée d'arrière-pays.
    M. Greenstein, 102(CanL):Autumn83-92
    J.A. Yeager, 207(FR):May84-904
Bukdahl, E.M. Diderot, critique d'art.*
    (Vol 1)
    E. Sundler, 341:Vol52No2-89
Bukdahl, E.M. Diderot, critique d'art.
    (Vol 2)
    J. Chouillet, 208(FS):Oct83-460
    B. Scott, 39:Jan83-69
    E. Sundler, 341:Vol52No2-89

Bukowski, C. Hot Water Music.
    D. Montrose, 617(TLS):4May84-486
Bulciolu, M.T. L'école saint-simonienne
    et la femme.*
    N. Mozet, 535(RHL):Sep/Dec83-942
    A. Reix, 542:Jan-Mar83-131
Bulgakov, M. Molière. (adaptation by D.
    Hughes)
    D. Devlin, 157:Winter83-38
Bulgakov, M.A. Sobranie sočinenij.
    (Vol 1) (E. Proffer, ed)
    L. Tikos, 574(SEEJ):Winter83-493
Bulhof, I.N. Wilhelm Dilthey.*
    A. Donoso, 543:Jun83-915
    H.N. Tuttle, 125:Fall82-99
Bull, D. Classic Ground.
    M. Rosenthal, 59:Jun83-242
Bullard, L.F. and B.J. Shiell. Chintz
    Quilts.
    S.J. Garoutte, 614:Summer84-12
Bullen, R.J., H.P. von Strandmann and A.B.
    Polonsky, eds. Ideas into Politics.
    M. Howard, 617(TLS):5Oct84-1114
"Bulletin de la Commission Royale de Topo-
    nymie et Dialectologie." (No 51) Bulle-
    tin de la Commission Royale de Toponymie
    et Dialectologie." (No 52)
    H.J. Wolf, 547(RF):Band95Heft4-485
Bulliet, R. The Gulf Scenario.
    R. Smith, 441:11Mar84-18
Bullock, A. Ernest Bevin: Foreign Secre-
    tary, 1945-1951.*
    S. Koss, 441:6May84-13
    D. Marquand, 176:Apr84-43
Bullock, A. - see Ginzburg, N.
Bullock, C. and D. Peck, comps. Guide to
    Marxist Literary Criticism.*
    J. Steele, 178:Dec83-527
    M. Wilding, 402(MLR):Jul83-632
Bullock, M. Lines in the Dark Wood.
    L. Lemire-Tostevin, 102(CanL):Summer83-
    168
Bullough, W.A. The Blind Boss and His
    City.
    K. Cassidy, 106:Spring83-97
Bulmahn, H. Adolf Glassbrenner.*
    W.E. Yates, 221(GQ):Nov83-662
Bulman, J.C. and J.M. Nosworthy, eds.
    Timon.
    M. Hattaway, 541(RES):May83-215
Bumke, J. The Concept of Knighthood in
    the Middle Ages.
    M. Keen, 382(MAE):1983/1-119
Bumke, J. Mäzene im Mittelalter.*
    I. Bennewitz-Behr, 680(ZDP):Band102
    Heft1-125
Bump, J. Gerard Manley Hopkins.*
    H.W. Fulweiler, 636(VP):Spring83-92
Bumsted, J.M. The People's Clearance
    1770-1815.*
    M. Gray, 83:Autumn83-247
Bundtzen, L.K. Plath's Incarnations.
    D.W. Hartnett, 617(TLS):9Nov84-1290
    L.W. Wagner, 659(ConL):Winter84-509
Bungarten, T., ed. Wissenschaftssprache.
    A. Sandor, 221(GQ):May83-466
Bunge, M. The Mind-Body Problem.*
    J.J. Furlong, 543:Mar83-694
    M.E. Levin, 449:May83-316
Bunn, J. The Dimensionality of Signs,
    Tools, Models.
    R.E. Innis, 258:Mar83-105

Bunnens, G. L'expansion phénicienne en
Méditerranée.*
   J. Teixidor, 318(JAOS):Jan-Mar82-199
Bünting, K-D. and H. Bergenholtz. Einfüh-
rung in die Syntax.
   H. Eilers, 685(ZDL):2/1983-232
Buñuel, L., with J-C. Carrière. My Last
Sigh.* (French title: Mon Dernier
Soupir; British title: My Last Breath.)
   J. Paulhan, 207(FR):Apr84-741
   R.S. Short, 617(TLS):27Jan84-87
Bunyan, J. The Miscellaneous Works of
John Bunyan.* (Vol 1) (T.L. Underwood,
ed)
   J.B.H. Alblas, 179(ES):Apr83-190
   J. Richetti, 402(MLR):Jan83-143
   O.C. Watkins, 161(DUJ):Jun83-129
Bunyan, J. The Miscellaneous Works of
John Bunyan. (Vol 8) (R.L. Greaves, ed)
   O.C. Watkins, 161(DUJ):Jun83-129
Bunyan, J. The Miscellaneous Works of
John Bunyan.* (Vol 9) (R.L. Greaves,
ed)
   E. Bourcier, 189(EA):Oct-Dec83-465
   N.H. Keeble, 447(N&Q):Dec82-549
Bunyan, J. The Poems.* (G. Midgley, ed)
   J.B.H. Alblas, 179(ES):Apr83-190
Bura, L., ed. Szatmári Népballadák.
   L. Kürti, 187:May84-346
Burawoy, M. and T. Skocpol, eds. Marxist
Inquiries.*
   W.H.S., 185:Apr84-563
Burbank, R. Twentieth Century Music.
   R. Christiansen, 617(TLS):26Oct84-1226
Burbidge, J. On Hegel's Logic.
   Q. Lauer, 258:Mar83-95
Burbridge, J.R. Les Petites dames de mode.
   R.L. Shep, 614:Fall84-22
Burchfield, R.W. - see "A Supplement to
the Oxford English Dictionary"
Burckhardt, J. The Architecture of the
Italian Renaissance. (P. Murray, ed)
Die Kunst der Betrachtung.
   J. Rykwert, 617(TLS):7Dec84-1427
Burdett, D.L. Hix Nix Stix Pix.
   N. Shack, 617(TLS):1Jun84-622
   B.F. Williamson, 441:8Apr84-20
Burford, E.J., ed. Bawdy Verse.*
   P-G.B., 189(EA):Apr-Jun84-232
Burg, B.R. Richard Mather.
   M. Kramer, 165(EAL):Winter83/84-292
   C. Rainwater, 568(SCN):Fall83-56
Burger, R. Plato's "Phaedrus."*
   G.J. de Vries, 394:Vol36fasc1/2-189
Burgess, A. Enderby's Dark Lady.
   P-L. Adams, 61:May84-122
   D.A.N. Jones, 362:5Apr84-24
   W. Kerr, 441:22Apr84-10
   M. Wood, 617(TLS):30Mar84-328
Burgess, A. - see "Richard Strauss: 'Der
Rosenkavalier'"
Burgin, D. and K. O'Connor - see Chukovsky,
K.
Bürgin, H. and H-O. Mayer. Die Briefe
Thomas Manns: Regesten und Register.
(Vol 1) (Y. Schmidlin and others, eds)
   H. Matter, 654(WB):5/1983-953
Bürgin, H. and H-O. Mayer. Die Briefe
Thomas Manns: Regesten und Register.
(Vol 2) (Y. Schmidlin and others, eds)
   W. Grothe, 597(SN):Vol55No2-215
   A.D. Latta, 406:Fall83-347
                              [continued]

[continuing]
   H. Matter, 654(WB):5/1983-953
   O. Seidlin, 400(MLN):Apr83-507
Burgin, V., ed. Thinking Photography.
   R. Ginsberg, 290(JAAC):Fall83-101
Burgis, N. - see Dickens, C.
Burgos-Debray, E. - see Menchú, R.
Burgschmidt, E. and D. Götz. Kontrastive
Linguistik Deutsch/Englisch.
   C.V.J. Russ, 685(ZDL):3/1983-400
Burk, B. Elemente idyllischen Lebens.
   G. Hillen, 221(GQ):Nov83-650
Burke, D. Notes on Literary Structure.
   P. Lamarque, 89(BJA):Spring83-186
Burke, E. The Writings and Speeches of
Edmund Burke. (Vol 2 ed by P. Langford;
Vol 5 ed by P.J. Marshall)
   J. Cannon, 83:Autumn83-239
Burke, J. and I. Pleeth. Musical Land-
scapes.
   L. Foreman, 607:Jun83-46
Burke, J.J., Jr. and D. Kay, eds. The
Unknown Samuel Johnson.
   J. Gray, 150(DR):Spring83-188
Burke, M. The Commissar's Report.
   H. Mitgang, 441:29Apr84-32
Burke, M. Outrageous Good Fortune.
   L.S. Ritter, 441:18Nov84-18
Burke, P. Montaigne.*
   S.J. Holyoake, 402(MLR):Oct83-921
Burkert, W. Homo Necans.
   R. Parker, 617(TLS):15Jun84-654
Burkert, W. Structure and History in
Greek Mythology and Ritual.*
   G. Beckman, 318(JAOS):Jan-Mar82-207
Burkhard, M. and G. Labroisse, eds. Zur
Literatur der deutschsprachigen Schweiz.*
   R. Hargreaves, 447(N&Q):Feb82-90
   C. Siegrist, 406:Summer83-203
Burkhardt, F.H., F. Bowers and I.K. Skrup-
skelis - see James, W.
Burkhardt, H. Logik und Semiotik in der
Philosophie von Leibniz.*
   J-L. Gardies, 542:Jan-Mar83-102
Burkholder, M.A. Politics of a Colonial
Career.
   J. Fisher, 86(BHS):Jan83-83
Burkholder, M.A. and D.S. Chandler, comps.
Biographical Dictionary of Audiencia
Ministers in the Americas, 1687-1821.
   T.E. Anna, 263(RIB):Vol33No4-583
Burn, G. "Somebody's husband, somebody's
son."
   A. Rusbridger, 617(TLS):22Jun84-686
Burne-Jones, E.C. Burne-Jones Talking,
His Conversations 1895-1898.* (M. Lago,
ed)
   M. Case, 177(ELT):Vol26No2-146
   V. Powell, 39:Jun83-514
Burner, D. and T.R. West. The Torch is
Passed.
   W. Karp, 441:9Sep84-18
Burnett, A. Milton's Style.*
   D. Griffin, 551(RenQ):Autumn83-482
   R.H. Sundell, 568(SCN):Fall83-34
   S. Wintle, 175:Summer83-160
Burnett, A.P. Three Archaic Poets.
   M.L. West, 617(TLS):13Jan84-30
Burnett, L., ed. F.M. Dostoevsky (1821-
1881).
   C. Pike, 402(MLR):Oct83-995

55

Burnett, T.A.J. The Rise and Fall of a Regency Dandy.*
  T.K. Bender, 577(SHR):Fall83-390
  M. Butler, 339(KSMB):No34-80
Burnett, V. Skiamachia.
  T. Goldie, 102(CanL):Summer83-104
Burnett, W.R. The Asphalt Jungle.
  N. Callendar, 441:24Jun84-41
Burney, A.C. Tempi Moderni.
  D. Marx-Scouras, 399(MLJ):Spring83-83
  J. Vizmuller-Zocco, 276:Autumn83-295
Burney, F. Evelina. (E.A. Bloom, with L.D. Bloom, eds)
  M. O'Neill, 83:Spring83-85
Burney, F. The Journals and Letters of Fanny Burney (Madame d'Arblay). (Vol 8) (P. Hughes, with J. Hemlow, eds)
  R.L. Brett, 541(RES):May83-249
Burnham, D.K. The Comfortable Arts.
  M. McAlpine, 102(CanL):Winter82-169
Burnier, A. and others. De vrouw als auteur.
  A. Vink, 204(FdL):Dec82-310
Burnikel, W. Untersuchungen zur Struktur des Witzepigramms bei Lukillios und Martial.
  P. Howell, 123:Vol33No1-34
Burnley, D. A Guide to Chaucer's Language.
  B. O'Donoghue, 617(TLS):18May84-555
  B. Windeatt, 176:Jul/Aug84-55
Burnley, J.D. Chaucer's Language and the Philosophers' Tradition.*
  D. Staines, 597(SN):Vol55No2-206
Burns, A. Nature and Culture in D.H. Lawrence.*
  J. Worthen, 447(N&Q):Oct82-469
Burns, C.A. Henry Céard et le Naturalisme.
  M.G. Lerner, 356(LR):Feb-May83-145
  P.M. Wetherill, 208(FS):Oct83-478
Burns, F. Heigh for Cotswold!
  J. Eltenton, 203:Vol194No2-265
Burns, J.H. and H.L.A. Hart - see Bentham, J.
Burns, J.M. The Power to Lead.
  T. Noah, 441:29Apr84-44
  442(NY):25Jun84-109
Burns, J.M. The Vineyard of Liberty.
  A. Brinkley, 432(NEQ):Mar83-140
Burns, O.A. Cold Sassy Tree.
  J. Berry, 441:11Nov84-32
  442(NY):31Dec84-70
Burns, R. The Quest for Modernity.
  F. Achberger, 221(GQ):May83-524
Burns, R. Roots/Routes.
  M. Hulse, 617(TLS):12Oct84-1169
Burns, R. Strip Search.
  N. Callendar, 441:13May84-35
Burns, R.I. Muslims, Christians, and Jews in the Crusader Kingdom of Valencia.
  D.J.R. Bruckner, 441:29Jul84-21
  D.W. Lomax, 617(TLS):4May84-491
Burns, R.M. The Great Debate on Miracles from Joseph Glanvill to David Hume.*
  J. Noxon, 319:Apr84-239
Burns, W. Journey Through the Dark Woods.
  J.H. Adler, 395(MFS):Winter83-822
Burnyeat, M. and others. Notes on Book Zeta of Aristotle's "Metaphysics."*
  T.H. Irwin, 123:Vol33No2-234
Buroker, J.V. Space and Incongruence.*
  H. Duncan, 486:Jun83-346
  R. Meerbote, 53(AGP):Band65Heft2-201
  L. Sklar, 449:May83-321

Burr, A. Political Correspondence and Public Papers of Aaron Burr. (M-J. Kline, with J.W. Ryan, eds)
  R.A. Ryerson, 441:12Feb84-30
  G.S. Wood, 453(NYRB):2Feb84-23
  E. Wright, 617(TLS):28Sep84-1078
Burr, E.E. The Journal of Esther Edwards Burr: 1754-1757. (C.F. Karlsen and L. Crumpacker, eds)
  M. Peters, 441:27May84-17
Burroughs, W. Port of Saints.
  J. Lasdun, 176:May84-61
Burroughs, W.S. Letters to Allen Ginsburg, 1953-1957.
  J.Z. Guzlowski, 395(MFS):Winter83-737
  L. Sante, 453(NYRB):10May84-12
Burroughs, W.S. Naked Lunch: The Twenty-Fifth Anniversary Edition.
  L. Sante, 453(NYRB):10May84-12
Burroughs, W.S. The Place of Dead Roads.
  A. Hollinghurst, 617(TLS):4May84-486
  P. Meisel, 441:19Feb84-8
  L. Sante, 453(NYRB):10May84-12
Burrow, J.A. Essays on Medieval Literature.
  D. Fox, 617(TLS):6Jul84-759
Burrow, J.A. Medieval Writers and their Work.*
  F.C., 189(EA):Apr-Jun84-232
  T. Davenport, 175:Summer83-155
Burrow, J.W. A Liberal Descent.*
  R.C. Richardson, 366:Spring83-125
  R.N. Soffer, 637(VS):Winter83-236
Burrowes, J. Jamesie's People.
  B. McCabe, 617(TLS):14Dec84-1457
Bursill-Hall, G.L. A Census of Medieval Latin Grammatical Manuscripts.
  N. Kretzmann, 221(GQ):May83-494
  R. Pfister, 547(RF):Band95Heft3-306
  W. Wegstein, 684(ZDA):Band112Heft2-71
Bursk, C. Little Harbor.
  G. Johnson, 461:Spring/Summer83-96
Burstein, S.M. The Babyloniaca of Berossus.
  G.H. Oller, 318(JAOS):Jan-Mar82-165
Burstow, C.A. The Songs of Bathsheba.*
  R. Hatch, 102(CanL):Winter82-144
Burt, J.R. From Phonology to Philology.
  S.N. Dworkin, 545(RPh):Aug82-105
  R.J. Steiner, 552(REH):Oct83-459
  R.L. Surles, 399(MLJ):Spring83-99
Burton, A. The Waterways of Britain.
  H. Carpenter, 617(TLS):29Jun84-722
Burton, D. Dialogue and Discourse.*
  S. Bassnett-McGuire, 307:Apr83-100
  P.N. Campbell, 615(TJ):May82-283
  P. Johnson, 677(YES):Vol 13-364
Burton, R.W.B. The Chorus in Sophocles' Tragedies.*
  M. McCall, 121(CJ):Oct/Nov83-65
  A.M. van Erp Taalman Kip, 394:Vol136 fasc3/4-401
Buruma, I. Behind the Mask.
  D. Kondo, 441:16Sep84-13
Buruma, I. A Japanese Mirror.
  J. Kirkup, 617(TLS):9Mar84-240
  P. Windsor, 362:9Feb84-27
Burzle, J.A. - see "Yearbook of German-American Studies, 16"
Busa, R., ed. Global Linguistic Statistical Methods to Locate Style Identities.
  O. Weijers, 361:Oct/Nov83-259

Byatt, A.S. The Game.
  P. Craig, 617(TLS):9Mar84-259
Bye, A.E. Art into Landscape, Landscape
  into Art.
  505:Aug83-130
Byl, S. Recherches sur les grands traités
  biologiques d'Aristote.
  P. Louis, 555:Vol57fasc1-131
Bylinsky, G. Life in Darwin's Universe.
  A. Crowder, 529(QQ):Spring83-265
Bynner, W. The Works of Witter Bynner.*
  (Vols 1-5) (J. Kraft, general ed)
  D.E. Stanford, 249(HudR):Summer83-389
Bynon, T. Historical Linguistics. (Ger-
  man title: Historische Linguistik.)
  M. Görlach, 72:Band220Heft2-384
  W.P. Lehmann, 133:Band16Heft2/3-217
  K.H. Schmidt, 685(ZDL):3/1983-376
Bynum, D.E. The Daemon in the Wood.*
  D. Ben-Amos, 131(CL):Spring83-173
Bynum, W.F., E.J. Brown and R. Porter, eds.
  Dictionary of the History of Science.
  E. Block, 651(WHR):Summer83-186
Byrd, M. Fly Away, Jill.
  M. Laski, 362:25Oct84-29
Byrne, J.S. Renaissance Ornament Prints
  and Drawings.
  H. Barkley, 90:Jan83-39
Byrne, M.S., ed. The Lisle Letters.*
  J. Thirsk, 366:Autumn83-262
Byrnes, J.F. The Virgin of Chartres.*
  R.W. Harvey, 106:Winter83-467
Byrnes, T., ed. Matinees Daily.
  M.G. Osachoff, 102(CanL):Winter82-165
Lord Byron. Byron's Letters and Journals.*
  (Vols 1-6) (L.A. Marchand, ed)
  J. Buxton, 339(KSMB):No34-73
Lord Byron. Byron's Letters and Journals.*
  (Vols 7-9) (L.A. Marchand, ed)
  J. Buxton, 339(KSMB):No34-73
  J. Clubbe, 579(SAQ):Summer83-314
Lord Byron. Byron's Letters and Journals.*
  (Vol 10) (L.A. Marchand, ed)
  J. Buxton, 339(KSMB):No34-73
  J. Clubbe, 579(SAQ):Summer83-314
  W.S. Di Piero, 569(SR):Fall83-681
Lord Byron. Byron's Letters and Journals.*
  (Vol 11) (L.A. Marchand, ed)
  J. Buxton, 339(KSMB):No34-73
  J. Clubbe, 579(SAQ):Summer83-314
  W.S. Di Piero, 569(SR):Fall83-681
  C.W. Hagelman, Jr., 340(KSJ):Vol32-212
  J. Perrins, 506(PSt):Dec83-290
Lord Byron. The Complete Poetical Works.*
  (Vol 1) (J.J. McGann, ed)
  J.D. Bone, 402(MLR):Jan83-154
  A. Elliott, 541(RES):May83-232
  D.H. Reiman, 339(KSMB):No34-66
Lord Byron. The Complete Poetical Works.*
  (Vol 2) (J.J. McGann, ed)
  J.D. Bone, 402(MLR):Jan83-154
  S. Curran, 340(KSJ):Vol32-207
  A. Elliott, 541(RES):May83-232
  D.H. Reiman, 339(KSMB):No34-66
Lord Byron. The Complete Poetical Works.*
  (Vol 3) (J.J. McGann, ed)
  C. Bergerolle, 189(EA):Jan-Mar83-87
  J.D. Bone, 402(MLR):Jan83-154
  S. Curran, 340(KSJ):Vol32-207
  D.H. Reiman, 339(KSMB):No34-66

Lord Byron. Selected Letters and Journals.
  (L.A. Marchand, ed)
  J. Buxton, 339(KSMB):No34-73
  W.S. Di Piero, 569(SR):Fall83-681
Byron, H.J. Plays by H.J. Byron. (J.
  Davis, ed)
  J. Hankey, 617(TLS):20Jul84-823
Byron, R. The Road to Oxiana.
  V. Young, 31(ASch):Winter82/83-138

de Caballero, G.C., V.M. Franco Pellotier
  and H. Muñoz Cruz - see under Coronado
de Caballero, G., V.M. Franco Pellotier
  and H. Muñoz Cruz
Cabrera, R. and P.F. Meyers. Classic Tai-
  loring Techniques.
  P. Bach, 614:Spring84-21
Cabrera Infante, G. Infante's Inferno.
  J. Butt, 617(TLS):12Oct84-1166
  A. Josephs, 441:6May84-33
  M. Wood, 453(NYRB):28Jun84-21
Cachin, F., C.L. Moffett and J.W. Bareau.
  Exposition Manet.
  E. Darragon, 98:May83-432
de Cadalso, J. Escritos autobiográficos y
  epistolario.* (N. Glendinning and N.
  Harrison, eds)
  S. Herpoel, 356(LR):Nov83-356
Cadbury, W. and L. Poague. Film Criticism.
  D.M. Callen, 289:Fall83-115
Cadina, O.M. - see under Muñoz Cadina, O.
Cadora, F.J. Interdialectical Lexical Com-
  patibility in Arabic.
  A.S. Kaye, 318(JAOS):Jan-Mar82-218
Cadsby, H. Traditions.
  C. Hlus, 137:Sep83-18
  P.K. Smith, 102(CanL):Summer83-138
Cady, E.H. - see Howells, W.D.
Caesar, M. and P. Hainsworth, eds. Writ-
  ers and Society in Contemporary Italy.
  J.R. Woodhouse, 617(TLS):25May84-596
Cage, J. Themes and Variations.*
  R.M. Radano, 513:Fall-Winter82/Spring-
  Summer83-417
Cagin, S. and P. Dray. Hollywood Films of
  the Seventies.
  N. Sayre, 441:1Apr84-16
"Cahiers Jean Paulhan." (Vol 2)
  P-L. Rey, 450(NRF):Feb83-124
"Cahiers Roucher-André Chénier." (No 1)
  J. Biard-Millérioux, 535(RHL):
  Mar/Apr83-283
"Cahiers Saint-John Perse." (Vol 6)
  D. Leuwers, 450(NRF):Dec83-100
Cahill, J., comp. An Index of Early Chi-
  nese Painters and Paintings: T'ang, Sung,
  and Yüan.*
  A.C. Soper, 57:Vol144No4-325
Cahill, J. Parting at the Shore.
  Ju-hsi Chou, 463:Autumn83-291
Cahn, R. Der diegetische Romancier im
  Werk von André Gide.
  R. Theis, 547(RF):Band95Heft1/2-209
Cahn, S. The Songwriter's Rhyming Diction-
  ary.
  G. Ewart, 617(TLS):16Nov84-1318
Cahn, W. Romanesque Bible Illumination.*
  L. Antonsen, 469:Vol9No1-104
  C. Nordenfalk, 341:Vol152No3-132
Cahné, P-A. Un autre Descartes.*
  J-M. Beyssade, 542:Jan-Mar83-107

Caillois, R. La Nécessité d'Esprit.
P. Collier, 402(MLR):Jan83-195
Caimi, M.P.M. Kants Lehre von der Empfindung in der Kritik der reinen Vernunft.
W. Steinbeck, 342:Band74Heft3-357
Cain, T.G.S., ed. Jacobean and Caroline Poetry.
D.L. Russell, 568(SCN):Spring/Summer83-8
Caird, G.B. The Language and Imagery of the Bible.
E.L. Greenstein, 318(JAOS):Oct-Dec82-657
Cairncross, A. and B. Eichengreen. Sterling in Decline.
S. Strange, 617(TLS):24Feb84-188
Cairncross, J. La Fontaine Fables and Other Poems.
Z. Youssef, 475:Vol 10No19-886
Cairns, A. Strained Relations.
N. Callendar, 441:8Jan84-27
Calabresi, G. A Common Law for the Age of Statutes.
B.R. Gross, 185:Oct83-156
Calabresi, G. and P. Bobbitt. Tragic Choices.
B. Barry, 185:Jan84-303
Calabrò, G., ed. La Rosa Necessaria.
D. Keown, 86(BHS):Jan83-90
de Calahorra, D.O. - see under Ortúñez de Calahorra, D.
Calamai, N. - see Alberti, R.
Calame, A. - see Regnard, J-F.
Calboli Montefusco, L. Consulti Fortunatiani Ars Rhetorica.
D.M. Schenkeveld, 394:Vol36fasc1/2-207
Calcraft, R.P. The Sonnets of Luis de Góngora.*
P. Waley, 86(BHS):Jan83-89
Caldarini, E. - see du Bellay, J.
Calder, A. and D. Sheridan, eds. Speak for Yourself.
T. Parker, 617(TLS):23Mar84-298
Calder, B.J. The Impact of Intervention.
R.D. Crassweller, 441:14Oct84-27
L. Whitehead, 617(TLS):27Jul84-827
Calder, D.G. Cynewulf.
J.J. Campbell, 589:Jan83-154
J.P. Hermann, 301(JEGP):Jul83-432
Calder, J. Robert Louis Stevenson: A Life Study.*
E.F. Block, Jr., 577(SHR):Winter83-84
Calder, J., ed. Stevenson and Victorian Scotland.*
E.F. Block, Jr., 577(SHR):Winter83-84
H-P. Breuer, 395(MFS):Summer83-263
P. Hinchcliffe, 637(VS):Winter83-238
D. Low, 588(SSL):Vol 18-299
Calder, J. - see Beckett, S.
Calder, N. The Comet is Coming!
R.N. Henriksen, 529(QQ):Autumn83-851
Calderón de la Barca, P. Celos aún del aire matan.* (M.D. Stroud, ed and trans)
A.K.G. Paterson, 402(MLR):Jul83-736
J.E. Varey, 86(BHS):Apr83-153
Calderón de la Barca, P. No hay burlas con el amor. (I. Arellano, ed)
F. Lautre, 552(REH):May83-295
A. Valbuena-Briones, 240(HR):Autumn83-468
Calderón de la Barca, P. El Príncipe constante. (A. Porqueras Mayo, ed)
D. Briesemeister, 72:Band219Heft2-472

Calderón Quijano, J.A. and others. Cartografía marítima y militar de Cádiz, 1513-1878.
C. Pemán, 48:Jan-Mar79-93
Calderwood, J.L. Metadrama in Shakespeare's Henriad.*
D. Hamblock, 38:Band101Heft3/4-520
Caldicott, C.E.J. - see Guérin du Bouscal, D.
Caldicott, H. Missile Envy.
T. Branch, 441:29Jul84-13
Caldwell, E. Stories of Life North and South.* (E.C. Lathem, ed)
R.J. Kelly, 584(SWR):Autumn83-407
Caldwell, J. The Deer at the River.
442(NY):4Jun84-133
Caldwell, P. The Puritan Conversion Narrative.
S. Fender, 617(TLS):25May84-594
E.S. Morgan, 453(NYRB):31May84-33
D.B. Shea, 165(EAL):Fall84-218
Calet, H. Le Bouquet.
C. Dis, 450(NRF):Nov83-141
Calhoun, T.O. Henry Vaughan.*
R. Ellrodt, 189(EA):Jan-Mar84-94
Callaghan, B. The Black Queen Stories.
R.P. Knowles, 198:Oct83-94
Callaghan, J. Yorkshire's Pride.
A.L. Le Quesne, 617(TLS):4May84-493
Callaghan, M. A Time for Judas.
D.J. Dooley, 99:Oct83-24
442(NY):4Jun84-132
Callahan, D. and H.T. Engelhardt, Jr., eds. The Roots of Ethics.
B. Barry, 185:Oct83-138
Callahan, D. and B. Jennings, eds. Ethics, the Social Sciences and Policy Analysis.
S.S., 185:Jul84-737
Callan, E. Auden.*
H. Haughton, 617(TLS):27Apr84-457
M. Hennessy, 659(ConL):Fall84-368
295(JML):Nov83-430
Callan, H. and S. Ardener, eds. The Incorporated Wife.
C. Driver, 617(TLS):9Nov84-1291
Callan, R.J. - see Asturias, M.A.
Callaway, K. Heart of the Garfish.
W.H. Pritchard, 491:Jan84-228
Callesen, G., H. Caspersen and K. Knudsen. "Fremad og aldrig glemme."
J. Logue, 563(SS):Autumn83-391
Callinicos, A. Marxism and Philosophy.
W.H.S., 185:Apr84-556
Callot, E. La philosophie instituée.
M. Adam, 542:Oct-Dec83-444
Calloud, J. and F. Genuyt. La première épître de Pierre.
L. Milot, 193(ELit):Apr83-171
Callow, P. Cave Light.
R. Pybus, 565:Vol24No2-73
Callow, S. Being an Actor.
C. Brown, 617(TLS):7Dec84-1418
Calo, J.L. - see under Lopez Calo, J.
Calvesi, M. and E. Coen. Boccioni.
J. Golding, 617(TLS):23Mar84-291
Calvet, C. Has Corinne Been a Good Girl?
K. Turan, 18:Dec83-62
Calvino, I. Adam, One Afternoon and Other Stories.*
J.R.B., 148:Autumn83-91

Calvino, I. Difficult Loves.
  M. Atwood, 441:7Oct84-13
  R. Towers, 453(NYRB):6Dec84-33
  U. Varnai, 617(TLS):29Jun84-716
Calvino, I. Marcovaldo.*
  F. Ferrucci, 441:22Jan84-8
  J. Lasdun, 176:Jan84-70
  J. Updike, 442(NY):10Sep84-136
Calvino, I. Palomar.
  U. Varnai, 617(TLS):29Jun84-716
Calvocoressi, M.D. Mussorgsky. (rev by
  G. Abraham)
  A.F.L.T., 412:Feb82-66
Calvocoressi, P. Top Secret Ultra.
  R.A. Woytak and C. Kasparek, 497(PolR):
  Vol28No2-98
Camacho, A. Societies and Social Decision
  Functions.
  R. Hardin, 185:Jan84-335
Cambon, G. Ugo Fascolo, Poet of Exile.*
  E. Hatzantonis, 131(CL):Fall83-389
  G.L. Lucente, 400(MLN):Jan83-148
  S. Orlando, 228(GSLI):Vol 160fasc511-
  462
Cambon, G. Eugenio Montale's Poetry.
  295(JML):Nov83-537
Cambrensis, G. - see under Geraldus
  Cambrensis
Camden, A. Blow by Blow.
  W. Waterhouse, 415:Mar83-171
Camenzind-Herzog, E. Robert Walser —
  "eine Art verlorener Sohn."
  R.E. Lorbe, 221(GQ):Nov83-693
Camerino, G.A. Italo Svevo.
  B. Maier, 228(GSLI):Vol 160fasc512-619
  E. Saccone, 400(MLN):Jan83-160
Cameron, A. Daughters of Copper Woman.
  P. Dale, 648(WCR):Oct83-59
Cameron, D.K. The Cornkister Days.
  B. Urquhart, 617(TLS):28Dec84-1499
Cameron, E. Hugh MacLennan.*
  R. Hyman, 627(UTQ):Summer83-489
  R. Lecker, 395(MFS):Summer83-318
  L. Surette, 178:Jun83-245
Cameron, I. Mountains of the Gods.
  C. Thubron, 617(TLS):22Jun84-684
Cameron, K., ed. Montaigne and His Age.*
  G. Nakam, 535(RHL):Sep/Dec83-913
Cameron, K. - see Meigret, L.
Cameron, R. and P. Salinger. Above Paris.
  G. Plimpton, 441:2Dec84-12
Cameron, S. Lyric Time.
  L.Y. Gossett, 569(SR):Summer83-445
  D.L. Higdon, 599:Winter83-65
Camic, C. Experience and Enlightenment.
  N. Phillipson, 617(TLS):13Apr84-398
  F. Spencer, 441:19Feb84-23
Camilleri, J. Chinese Foreign Policy.
  D.E. Waterfall, 529(QQ):Spring83-214
Cammann, A. Turmberg-Geschichten.
  U. Tolksdorf, 196:Band24Heft1/2-132
Cammann, A. and A. Karasek, eds. Volkser-
  zählung der Karpatendeutschen: Slowakei.
  (Pts 1 and 2)
  E. Moser-Rath, 196:Band24Heft1/2-133
Camoin, F. The End of the World is Los
  Angeles.
  D. Grumbach, 219(GaR):Winter83-889
  P. Lewis, 565:Vol24No1-58
Camoin, F. Why Men Are Afraid of Women.
  G. Weaver, 344:Fall84-107

de Camp, L.S., C.C. de Camp and J.W.
  Griffin. Dark Valley Destiny.
  P-L. Adams, 61:Jan84-100
Camp, R.A., comp. Mexican Political
  Biographies, 1935-1981. (2nd ed)
  E.V. Niemeyer, Jr., 263(RIB):Vol33No3-
  398
Campanella, T. La città del sole: dialogo
  poetico/The City of the Sun: A Poetical
  Dialogue.* (D.J. Donno, ed and trans)
  A. Bullock, 276:Summer83-174
  C. Trinkaus, 551(RenQ):Spring83-128
Campbell, A. The Girls in the Gang.
  A. Carter, 617(TLS):14Dec84-1455
  E.L. Sturz, 441:9Dec84-20
Campbell, A.V. Moderated Love.
  J. Mathers, 617(TLS):23Nov84-1356
Campbell, D.A. The Golden Lyre.*
  A.M. Bowie, 123:Vol33No2-169
  R.A. Hornsby, 124:May-Jun84-321
Campbell, D.A. - see "Greek Lyric"
Campbell, E.D.C., Jr. The Celluloid
  South.*
  F. Chappell, 577(SHR):Spring83-193
  W. French, 585(SoQ):Winter83-79
Campbell, G. First Poems.
  M.F., 189(EA):Apr-Jun84-237
Campbell, H.H. and C.E. Modlin, eds. Sher-
  wood Anderson.
  T.J. Matheson, 106:Fall83-321
Campbell, I. The Kailyard.*
  D. Low, 588(SSL):Vol 18-299
Campbell, I. - see Gibbon, L.G.
Campbell, J. Invisible Country.
  A. Smith, 617(TLS):13Apr84-398
Campbell, J., ed. New Edinburgh Review
  Anthology.
  C. Craig, 571(ScLJ):Winter83-73
Campbell, J. F.E. Smith, First Earl of
  Birkenhead.*
  P. Johnson, 176:Mar84-41
  A. Watkins, 362:23Feb84-25
Campbell, J. The Way of the Animal Powers.
  D. Leeming, 469:Vol9No1-90
  W. Sargeant, 442(NY):13Feb84-126
Campbell, J.B. The Emperor and the Roman
  Army: 31 BC — AD 235.
  A. Birley, 617(TLS):23Nov84-1332
Campbell, J.L., ed and trans. Hebridean
  Folksongs. (Vols 1 and 2)
  M. Macleod, 595(ScS):Vol26-62
Campbell, J.L., ed and trans. Hebridean
  Folksongs.* (Vol 3)
  V. Blankenhorn, 112:Vol 15-181
  M. MacLeod, 203:Vol194No1-126
  M. Macleod, 595(ScS):Vol26-62
Campbell, L. and M. Mithun, eds. The Lan-
  guages of Native America.
  J. van Eijk, 361:Feb/Mar83-275
Campbell, M. A Commentary on Quintus
  Smyrnaeus, Posthomerica XII.
  M.L. West, 123:Vol33No1-129
Campbell, M. Echoes and Imitations of
  Early Epic in Apollonius Rhodius.
  M.L. West, 123:Vol33No1-129
Campbell, P., ed. A House in Town.
  H. Colvin, 617(TLS):31Aug84-967
Campbell, P.J. Passing the Hat.
  E.K., 187:Jan84-160
Campbell, R. Cinema Strikes Back.
  M. Keller, 127:Fall83-284

Campbell, R. Selected Poems. (P. Alexander, ed)
D. McDuff, 565:Vol24No3-67
V. Young, 249(HudR):Summer83-400
Campbell, R.H. and A.S. Skinner. Adam Smith.
M. Jack, 173(ECS):Spring84-378
Campbell, T. The Left and Rights.
G.W.P., 185:Jan84-362
Campbell, T. Seven Theories of Human Society.
K.E.S., 185:Oct83-168
Campe, J.H. Robinson der Jüngere, zur angenehmen und nützlichen Unterhaltung für Kinder.* (A. Binder and H. Richartz, eds)
D. Koester, 221(GQ):Jan83-135
Campoamor, A. and F. Solana - see Jiménez, J.R.
Campos, J. Introducción a Pío Baroja.
E.I. Fox, 240(HR):Summer83-343
Campos, J. - see Bécquer, G.A.
Campos-De Metro, J. The Slugger Heart and Other Stories.
A. Shapiro, 441:22Apr84-14
Camps, G. Berbères.
L. Galand, 555:Vol157fasc2-362
Camps, W.A. An Introduction to Homer.
F.M. Combellack, 122:Apr83-169
Camron, K. Let's Fit the Bodice.
G. Brown, 614:Fall84-19
Camus, A. Selected Political Writings. (J.H. King, ed)
I.H. Walker, 402(MLR):Apr83-464
Cañada Castillo, P. and others - see Rodríguez Moñino, A.R.
Cañal, V.L. - see Lleó Cañal, V.
Canani, U.B. and others - see under Berni Canani, U. and others
Candaux, J-D. and others - see de Charrière, I.
Candelaria, F. - see Cooperman, S.
Candinas, T. Romontsch sursilvan.
M. Ulleland, 597(SN):Vol55No2-243
J. Van Eerde, 399(MLJ):Summer83-199
Candrakīrti. Lucid Exposition of the Middle Way. (M. Sprung, with T.R.V. Murti and U.S. Vyas, trans)
E. Steinkellner, 318(JAOS):Apr-Jun82-411
Candy, E. Words for Murder Perhaps.
N. Callendar, 441:4Mar84-19
Canetti, E. The Human Province.
S.I. Gurney, 396(ModA):Summer/Fall83-355
Canetti, E. The Tongue Set Free.
W.A. Strauss, 651(WHR):Spring83-75
Canetti, E. The Torch in My Ear.
J-A. Mort, 287:Apr83-25
295(JML):Nov83-362
Canfield, D.L. Spanish Pronunciation in the Americas.*
R. Penny, 402(MLR):Jul83-729
P. Quijas Corzo, 457(NRFH):Tomo31núm2-331
Canfield, J.V. Wittgenstein.
T.E. Burke, 393(Mind):Oct83-633
H.O. Mounce, 483:Jan83-124
Canfora, L. Studi sull'"Athenaion politeia" pseudosenofontea.
M. Nouhaud, 555:Vol157fasc1-128

Canger, U. Five Studies Inspired by Nahuatl Verbs in "-oa."
K. Dakin, 269(IJAL):Jan83-102
Canh, N.V., with E. Cooper. Vietnam under Communism, 1975-1982.
R.B. Smith, 617(TLS):2Nov84-1253
Canning, J., ed. 100 Great Nineteenth-Century Lives.
A.O.J. Cockshut, 617(TLS):13Jan84-28
Cannon-Geary, I.S. The Bourgeoisie Looks at Itself.
D. Blamires, 402(MLR):Apr83-489
Cano Ballesta, J. Literatura y tecnología.*
G. Gullón, 240(HR):Summer83-341
Cano Gonzáles, A.M. El habla de Somiedo (Occidente de Asturias).
H. Meier, 72:Band220Heft2-434
"Cantar de Mío Cid/Chanson de mon Cid."* (J. Horrent, ed and trans)
H. Klüppelholz, 356(LR):Nov83-352
Cantarutti, G. La fortuna critica dell'-aforismo nell'area tedesca.
R. Scalmana-Roos, 52:Band17Heft2-213
R.R. Wuthenow, 133:Band16Heft2/3-247
Cantilena, M. Ricerche sulla dizione epica 1.
R. Janko, 487:Autumn83-271
Cantor, G.N. and M.J.S. Hodge, eds. Conceptions of Ether.*
J. Watling, 393(Mind):Jul83-467
Cantor, P.A. Creature and Creator.
I. McGilchrist, 617(TLS):3Aug84-862
Cantrill, H. The Invasion from Mars.
G.S., 617(TLS):18May84-562
Capek, K. The Gardener's Year.
J. Updike, 441:2Dec84-9
Capizzi, A. Eraclito e la sua leggenda.
C. Emlyn-Jones, 303(JoHS):Vol 103-161
Caplan, A.L. and D. Callahan, eds. Ethics in Hard Times.
B. Barry, 185:Oct83-138
G. Geiger, 42(AR):Winter83-116
Caplan, L. The Insanity Defense and the Trial of John W. Hinckley, Jr.
S.M. Halpern, 441:4Nov84-25
Caplan, M., ed. "Variety" International Showbusiness Reference.
J. Fowler, 611(TN):Vol37No1-39
Caplan, R. By Design.
P. Bach, 614:Spring84-20
Caplan, U. Like One That Dreamed.*
E.S. Fisher, 627(UTQ):Summer83-492
R. Lemm, 150(DR):Spring83-192
T. Marshall, 529(QQ):Spring83-221
Caplin, L.E., ed. The Business of Art.
639(VQR):Winter83-29
Caplow, T., H.M. Bahr and B.A. Chadwick. All Faithful People.
R. Towler, 617(TLS):6Jul84-765
G. Weales, 453(NYRB):26Apr84-43
Capote, T. Music for Chameleons.* (French title: Musique pour Caméléons.)
P. Mauriès, 98:May83-415
Cappelletti, A.J. Ensayos sobre los atomistas griegos.
Z. Kouřím, 542:Jan-Mar83-79
Cappon, A.P. Aspects of Wordsworth and Whitehead.
R.C. Jones, 436(NewL):Summer84-118
Capra, F. and C. Spretnak. Green Politics.
J. Dunn, 362:18Oct84-30

Carpenter, H. and M. Prichard. The Oxford Companion to Children's Literature.
  H. Brogan, 617(TLS):4May84-505
  E. Welty, 441:19Aug84-3
Carpenter, J.D. Swimming at Twelve Mile.
  P. Mitcham, 102(CanL):Summer83-144
Carpenter, K. Vom Penny Dreadful zum Comic.
  R.W. Brednich, 196:Band24Heft1/2-135
Carpentier, A. Du pain des oiseaux.
  P.G. Lewis, 207(FR):May84-905
Carpio, L.D. - see under de Vega Carpio, L.
Carr, A.D. Llywelyn ap Gruffydd.
  J. Rowland, 112:Vol 15-178
Carr, D.J., ed. Sydney Parkinson.
  H. Carter, 617(TLS):2Nov84-1263
Carr, E.H. The Comintern and the Spanish Civil War. (T. Deutscher, ed)
  T. Jacoby, 441:25Nov84-44
Carr, E.H. The Twilight of Comintern, 1930-1935.*
  F.L. Carsten, 575(SEER):Oct83-629
Carr, F. Mozart and Constanze.
  A. Hutchings, 617(TLS):20Jan84-56
  R. Roberts, 441:2Sep84-15
Carr, J.L. A Month in the Country.
  T. Gibbs, 442(NY):9Apr84-138
  M. Panter-Downes, 442(NY):7May84-152
  M. Wood, 453(NYRB):16Aug84-47
Carr, R. Puerto Rico.
  J. Heine, 441:22Jul84-9
  G.K. Lewis, 617(TLS):21Sep84-1049
  R.M. Morse, 453(NYRB):6Dec84-17
Carr, V.S. Dos Passos.
  K.S. Lynn, 441:23Sep84-3
  442(NY):1Oct84-134
Carrasco, D. Quetzalcoatl and the Irony of Empire.*
  M. Leon-Portilla, 263(RIB):Vol33No3-399
le Carré, J. The Little Drummer Girl.*
  S.G. Kellman, 219(GaR):Winter83-905
  P. Wolfe, 502(PrS):Fall83-90
  639(VQR):Summer83-91
Carre, O., ed. L'Islam et l'état dans le monde d'aujourd'hui.*
  I. Mehdi, 273(IC):Oct83-311
Carrell, S.L. Le Soliloque de la passion féminine ou le dialogue illusoire.*
  R.C. Rosbottom, 207(FR):May84-876
Carreño, A. La dialéctica de la identidad en la poesía contemporánea.
  G.G. MacCurdy, 238:Dec83-640
  E.M. Santi, 400(MLN):Mar83-315
Carreño, J. and D. Larson. Spanish, Practical Communication for Health Professionals.
  H. Cannon, 238:Sep83-452
Carrère d'Encausse, H. Confiscated Power.*
  639(VQR):Summer83-94
Carrère d'Encausse, H. A History of Soviet Russia, 1917-1953.
  M. McCauley, 575(SEER):Apr83-291
Carretta, V. The Snarling Muse.
  I. Donaldson, 617(TLS):2Nov84-1241
Carrier, R. La Dame qui avait des chaînes aux chevilles.
  P. Merivale, 102(CanL):Spring83-147
Carrigan, A. Salvador Witness.
  S. Schlesinger, 441:30Dec84-6
Carrithers, M. The Buddha.
  R. Blythe, 362:16Feb84-24

Carrithers, M. The Forest Monks of Sri Lanka.
  E. Rice, 469:Vol9No2-125
Carroll, D. The Subject in Question.
  V. Aarons, 395(MFS):Summer83-360
Carroll, F.M. American Opinion and the Irish Question 1910-1923.
  J.A. Ward, 174(Éire):Fall83-154
Carroll, J., ed. Intruders in the Bush.
  A. Seymour, 364:Apr/May83-140
Carroll, J. The Life and Times of Greg Clark.
  M. Whitaker, 102(CanL):Spring83-132
Carroll, J. Prince of Peace.
  W. Schott, 441:4Nov84-44
Carroll, J. Sceptical Sociology.
  R.R. Sullivan, 488:Jun83-253
Carroll, J., B. Hargrove and A. Lummis. Women of the Cloth.
  639(VQR):Autumn83-130
Carroll, L. Alice's Adventure in Wonderland.* [The Pennyroyal Alice.] (S.H. Goodacre, ed)
  M. Burstein, 283:Summer82-84
  J. Espey, 445(NCF):Sep83-238
Carroll, L. The Selected Letters of Lewis Carroll. (M.N. Cohen, ed)
  J. Hepburn, 569(SR):Summer83-503
Carruth, H. If You Call This Cry A Song.
  J.D. McClatchy, 441:22Jan84-12
Carruth, H. The Sleeping Beauty.*
  R. Mitchell, 460(OhR):No32-128
Carruth, H. Working Papers.* (J. Weissman, ed)
  R.A., 189(EA):Apr-Jun84-239
  J. Parini, 434:Summer84-630
  J.A. Porter, 579(SAQ):Summer83-330
Carsaniga, G. Italiano Espresso.
  A. Seldis, 399(MLJ):Spring83-83
Carson, N. Arthur Miller.*
  J.N. Harris, 610:Autumn83-270
  J.J. Martine, 397(MD):Sep83-388
Carsten, F.L. Britain and the Weimar Republic.
  P. Kennedy, 617(TLS):21Sep84-1051
Carsten, F.L. The Rise of Fascism. (2nd ed)
  U-K. Ketelsen, 221(GQ):Mar83-352
Carswell, J. The Exile.*
  K. Fitzlyon, 364:Nov83-102
  A.S. Grossman, 129:Sep84-74
Carter, A. Nights at the Circus.
  A. Mars-Jones, 617(TLS):28Sep84-1083
  J. Mellors, 362:11Oct84-30
Carter, A.B. Directed Energy Missile Defense in Space.
  M.R. Gordon, 441:16Sep84-22
Carter, A.B. and D.N. Schwartz, eds. Ballistic Missile Defense.
  M. Bundy, 441:11Mar84-3
Carter, B. A Black Fox Running.
  J.W. Blench, 161(DUJ):Jun83-142
Carter, G.M. and P. O'Meara, eds. Southern Africa.*
  W.M. Freund, 69:Vol53No4-94
Carter, J. Keeping Faith.*
  E. Kedourie, 176:Nov84-15
Carter, J. and P.H. Muir, eds. Printing and the Mind of Man. (2nd ed)
  G. Naylor, 617(TLS):8Jun84-647

Castle, T. Clarissa's Ciphers.
  J.A. Dussinger, 173(ECS):Spring84-350
  I. Grundy, 566:Spring84-153
  S. Soupel, 189(EA):Jul-Sep84-329
  W.B. Warner, 153:Winter83-12
  L.E. Warren, 301(JEGP):Oct83-562
Casto, R.C. The Arrivals.
  B. Pell, 102(CanL):Summer83-112
Castor, G. and T. Cave, eds. Neo-Latin
  and the Vernacular in Renaissance France.
  A. Levi, 617(TLS):10Aug84-890
de Castro, Á.G. - see under Gómez de
  Castro, Á.
de Castro, G. Las hazañas del Cid. (J.
  Weiger, ed)
  F. Menchacatorre, 238:Mar83-130
Catach, N. L'Orthographe française.*
  P. Rickard, 208(FS):Jul83-376
Catach, N., D. Duprez and M. Legris.
  L'Enseignemen de l'orthographe.
  P. Rickard, 208(FS):Jul83-376
Catalán, D., ed. Gran crónica de Alfonso
  XI.
  H-J. Niederehe, 457(NRFH):Tomo31núm1-
  118
Catalán, D. - see Menéndez Pidal, R.
Catalano, G. The Years of Hope.
  U. Hoff, 39:Oct83-352
Catan, J.R. - see Owens, J.
Cate, G.A. - see Carlyle, T. and J. Ruskin
Cather, W. Shadows on the Rock.
  P. Craig, 617(TLS):28Dec84-1506
Catlow, L., ed and trans. Pervigilium
  Veneris.*
  P. Godman, 123:Vol33No2-209
Cattaneo, C. Scritti letterari. (P.
  Treves, ed)
  F. Focher, 228(GSLI):Vol 160fasc511-
  468
Catullus. The Poems of Catullus. (P.
  Wigham, ed and trans)
  E.S. de Angeli, 124:Jul-Aug84-384
"Catullus."* (G.P. Goold, ed and trans)
  M.B. Skinner, 124:Jul-Aug84-375
Caunitz, W.J. One Police Plaza.
  M. Bell, 441:4Mar84-22
Caute, D. Under the Skin.*
  C. Hope, 364:Jun83-86
Cauvin, J-P. and M.A. Caws - see Breton, A.
Cavalca Schiroli, M.G. - see Seneca
Cavaliero, G. Elegy for St. Anne's and
  Other Poems.*
  A. Haberer, 189(EA):Jul-Sep84-349
Cavallari, H.M. Leopoldo Marechal.
  V.M. Valenzuela, 238:Mar84-441
Cavallini, G. La decima giornata del
  "Decameron."
  R.S. Dombroski, 276:Summer83-170
Cavanagh, B. Music of the Netsilik Eskimo.
  M. Desroches, 187:Sep84-559
Cave, K. - see Farington, J.
Cave, M., A. McAuley and J. Thornton, eds.
  New Trends in Soviet Economics.
  D.A. Dyker, 575(SEER):Jul83-468
Cave, R. The Private Press. (2nd ed)
  D. Chambers, 503:Autumn83-144
  70:May-Jun83-163
Cave, T.C. The Cornucopian Text.
  J.D. Lyons, 153:Fall83-33
Caveing, M. Zénon d'Elée.
  L. Brisson, 154:Sep83-495

Cavell, S. Pursuits of Happiness.*
  M.A. Anderegg, 385(MQR):Spring84-281
  F. Chappell, 577(SHR):Spring83-194
  R. Eldridge, 478:Apr83-140
  G. Mast, 289:Spring83-120
  S.J. Whitfield, 639(VQR):Winter83-140
Cavendish, G. Metrical Visions.* (A.S.G.
  Edwards, ed)
  D. Pearsall, 677(YES):Vol 13-302
Cavendish, W. (Lord Devonshire) The
  Devonshire Diary. (P. Brown and K.
  Schweizer, eds)
  J. Black, 83:Autumn83-249
Caws, M.A. The Eye in the Text.*
  M. Cranston, 207(FR):Feb84-388
  M-M. Martinet, 189(EA):Apr-Jun84-173
  D. Summers, 127:Winter83-413
Caws, M.A. A Metapoetics of the Passage.
  A.D. Ketchum, 207(FR):Mar84-563
Caws, P. Sartre.*
  A. MacIntyre, 311(JP):Dec83-813
Cazaux, Y. - see Palma-Cayet, P-V.
Cazden, N., H. Haufrecht and N. Studer.
  Folk Songs of the Catskills. Notes and
  Sources for Folk Songs of the Catskills.
  G. Chase, 414(MusQ):Spring83-266
Cazotte, J. Correspondance de Jacques
  Cazotte. (G. Décote, ed)
  J-L. Lecercle, 535(RHL):Jul/Aug83-645
Cazottes, G. - see Tirso de Molina
Cecchetti, D. Petrarca, Pietramala e
  Clamanges.
  N.M., 382(MAE):1983/2-335
Cecchetti, G. Giovanni Verga.
  N. Patruno, 276:Autumn83-286
Cecil, D., ed. Desmond MacCarthy.
  H. Lee, 617(TLS):8Jun84-628
Cecil, E. The Leisure of an Egyptian
  Official.
  M.F., 617(TLS):16Nov84-1323
Celan, P. Gesammelte Werke.
  G. Steiner, 617(TLS):28Sep84-1093
Céline, L-F. Journey to the End of the
  Night.
  B.L. Knapp, 399(MLJ):Autumn83-284
Celis, R., ed. Littérature et musique.
  J. Michon, 189(EA):Oct-Dec84-451
Cendrars, B. Gold.*
  D.J.R. Bruckner, 441:18Mar84-18
Cenerini, L. L'eclissi della fortuna.
  F. Waquet, 535(RHL):May/Jun84-469
"Centenario Belae Bartók."
  P.A. Autexier, 537:Vol169No2-246
Centerprise. The Island.
  D. Gittins, 637(VS):Summer83-431
Centore, F.F. Persons.
  J.W. Yolton, 488:Dec83-519
Cepeda, I.V. - see under Vilares Cepeda, I.
Ceplair, L. and S. Englund. The Inquisi-
  tion in Hollywood.
  G.D. Black, 488:Mar83-123
Cercignani, F. The Consonants of German.
  L.H. Hathaway, 301(JEGP):Oct83-590
Cercignani, F. Shakespeare's Works and
  Elizabethan Pronunciation.*
  G. Bourcier, 189(EA):Apr-Jun84-184
  F.H. Brengelman, 301(JEGP):Apr83-227
  A. Bruten, 191(ELN):Jun84-74
  B. Diensberg, 179(ES):Feb83-95
Cerf, C. and V. Navasky, eds. The Experts
  Speak.
  442(NY):19Nov84-192

Ceronetti, G.   Un Viaggio in Italia, 1981-
1983.
   F. Donini, 617(TLS):22Jun84-700
Cerquiglini, B.   La parole médiévale.
   M.T. Bruckner, 188(ECr):Spring83-105
   J. Simonin, 98:Apr83-355
Cerquiglini, J. - see Christine de Pisan
Cervantes, L.D.   Emplumada.*
   J. Addiego, 448:Vol21No1-147
de Cervantes Saavedra, M.   Poesías com-
pletas.   (Vol 2)   (V. Gaos, ed)
   J.F.G. Gornall, 402(MLR):Jan83-208
Césaire, A.   Aimé Césaire: The Collected
Poetry.   (C. Eshleman and A. Smith, eds
and trans)
   S. Gavronsky, 441:19Feb84-14
   M. Perloff, 29:Jan/Feb84-40
de Cesare, R.   Balzac e Manzoni.
   P. Cola, 356(LR):Nov83-357
Cesarini, R. and L. De Federicis.   Il
materiale e l'immaginario.   (Vol 7)
   J. Hösle, 52:Band18Heft3-332
"Česká literární věda 1971: Bohemistika."
"Česká literární věda 1972: Bohemisti-
ka."   (E. Macek, B. Mědílek and V.
Vladyková, eds of both)
   R.B. Pynsent, 575(SEER):Apr83-314
Cevasco, G.A.   John Gray.
   E. Gilcher, 177(ELT):Vol26No4-322
Chabot, C.B.   Freud on Schreber.*
   S. Weiland, 128(CE):Nov83-705
Chabot, D.   La Province lunaire.
   C.R. La Bossiere, 102(CanL):Autumn83-
80
   J.D. Wilson, 207(FR):Dec83-265
Chace, J.   Endless War.
   T.G. Ash, 441:7Oct84-13
Chadwick, H.   Boethius: the Consolations
of Music, Logic, Theology, and Philos-
ophy.
   G.H. Allard, 589:Jul83-742
   J. Dillon, 123:Vol33No1-117
   A. Hughes, 410(M&L):Jul/Oct83-267
   P. Wormald, 313:Vol73-243
Chafets, Z.   Double Vision.
   E. Abel, 441:4Nov84-15
Chahine, S.A.   Regards sur le théâtre
d'Arthur Adamov.
   D. Bradby, 402(MLR):Jan83-198
   R. Laubreaux, 535(RHL):May/Jun83-491
Chai-Anan Samudavanija.   The Thai Young
Turks.
   G.W. Fry, 293(JASt):Aug83-1010
Chailley, J.   La musique grecque antique.*
   J. Solomon, 122:Jul83-316
Chaillou, M.   Domestique chez Montaigne.*
   F. de Martinoir, 450(NRF):Feb83-127
Chalfant, E.   Both Sides of the Ocean.*
   E.N. Harbert, 432(NEQ):Sep83-472
   R.E. Spiller, 27(AL):May83-260
   295(JML):Nov83-426
   639(VQR):Spring83-50
"The Challenge of Peace: God's Promise and
Our Response."*
   D. Martin, 617(TLS):24Feb84-182
Chalmers, A.F.   What is this Thing Called
Science?   (2nd ed)
   F.J. Clendinnen, 63:Dec83-446
Chamard, H. - see du Bellay, J.
Chamberlain, J.S.   Ibsen.
   H.S. Naess, 563(SS):Summer83-268
   O. Reinert, 397(MD):Dec83-570

Chamberlain, M.   Fenwomen.
   D. Gittins, 637(VS):Summer83-431
Chamberlain, V.D.   When Stars Came Down to
Earth.
   M.J. Young, 292(JAF):Oct-Dec83-483
Chamberland, P.   L'Enfant doré.
   D.F. Rogers, 102(CanL):Summer83-161
Chambers, H.E.   Supernatural and Irratio-
nal Elements in the Works of Theodor
Fontane.
   U. Rainer, 680(ZDP):Band102Heft2-302
Chambers, J.K., ed.   The Languages of
Canada.*
   R. Darnell, 355(LSoc):Mar83-103
Chambers, J.K. and P. Trudgill.   Dialectol-
ogy.*
   P. Beade, 320(CJL):Spring83-80
Chambers, M. and others.   The Oxyrhynchus
Papyri.   (Vol 48)
   B. Kramer, 123:Vol33No2-300
Chambers, R.   Meaning and Meaningfulness.
   C. Filteau, 535(RHL):Sep/Dec83-975
Chambers, S.A., Jr.   Lynchburg.
   H.N. Cooledge, Jr., 576:Mar83-78
"Chambers Universal Learners' Dictionary."
(E.M. Kirkpatrick, ed)
   B. Cottle, 541(RES):May83-196
Chamoux, F.   La civilisation hellenistique.
   D. Knoepfler, 555:Vol157fasc1-109
Champagne, A.   Congressman Sam Rayburn.
   C.R. Herron, 441:12Aug84-21
Champe, F.W.   The Matachines Dance of the
Upper Rio Grande.
   L. Milazzo, 584(SWR):Autumn83-viii
Champion, L.S.   "King Lear."*
   E.H. Hageman, 702:Vol 16-329
Champion, L.S.   Perspective in Shake-
speare's English Histories.*
   M. Charney, 677(YES):Vol 13-310
   E. Jones, 541(RES):Nov83-495
   G.P. Jones, 627(UTQ):Fal182-106
Chan, A., R. Madsen and J. Unger.   Chen
Village.
   M. Goldman, 441:7Oct84-20
Chan, M.   Kao Shih.
   W.H. Nienhauser, Jr., 318(JAOS):
Jan-Mar82-149
Chan, M.   Music in the Theatre of Ben
Jonson.*
   C.R. Wilson, 541(RES):Nov83-504
Chan, M.K.   Historiography of the Chinese
Labor Movement.
   G.W. Berkley, 293(JASt):Nov82-126
Chand, M.   The Bonsai Tree.*
   J. Mellors, 364:Jun83-92
   M. Simpson, 441:8Jan84-18
Chandernagor, F.   The King's Way.*
(French title: L'Allée du Roi.)
   P-L. Adams, 61:Mar84-132
   A. Foote, 441:11Mar84-22
   442(NY):16Apr84-158
Chandler, D.P.   A History of Cambodia.
   A. Barnett, 617(TLS):14Sep84-1016
Chandler, R.   The Chandler Collection.
   T.J. Binyon, 617(TLS):6Jul84-762
Chandler, R.   Raymond Chandler Speaking.
(D. Gardiner and K.S. Walker, eds)
   T.J. Binyon, 617(TLS):6Jul84-762
Chandler, R.   Selected Letters of Raymond
Chandler.*   (F. MacShane, ed)
   T.J. Binyon, 617(TLS):6Jul84-762
   P. Wolfe, 395(MFS):Autumn83-389

Chandola, A. Situation to Sentence.
M.H. Klaiman, 361:Sep83-77
Chandos, J. Boys Together.
J. Rae, 362:26Apr84-24
M.J. Wiener, 441:21Oct84-22
A. Wooldridge, 617(TLS):4May84-492
Chandra, G.S.S. Heirloom.
A. Struthers, 436(NewL):Fall83-116
Chandra, P. On the Study of Indian Art.
S. Digby, 617(TLS):20Apr84-425
Chandrasekhar, S. Eddington.
B. Pippard, 617(TLS):17Feb84-174
Chaney, E. and N. Ritchie, eds. Oxford,
China and Italy.
J. Keates, 617(TLS):26Oct84-1212
Chang, C.S. The Japanese Auto Industry
and the U.S. Market.
H. Matsusaki, 293(JASt):Feb83-419
Chang, C-S. and J. Smythe. South China in
the Twelfth Century.
B.E. McKnight, 293(JASt):Feb83-378
Chang, H.C. Chinese Literature 3.
D.J. Enright, 617(TLS):16Mar84-268
Chang, K-C. Shang Civilization.*
Cheng Te-K'un, 302:Vol 19No2-254
Chang-Rodríguez, R. Violencia y subver-
sión en la prosa colonial hispanoameri-
cana, siglos XVI y XVII.
D. Turner, 238:Dec83-643
"Changing Course."
J. Le Moyne, 441:15Apr84-24
Channon, H. Chips. (R.R. James, ed)
L.D., 617(TLS):17Aug84-927
Chanteur, J. Platon, le désir et la cité.*
T.E. Marshall, 543:Jun83-917
Chantreau, A. Stendhal et Nantes.
V.D.L., 605(SC):15Apr84-287
Chao, D.W. Le Style du "Journal d'un curé
de campagne" de Georges Bernanos.
G. Montbertrand, 207(FR):Feb84-403
Chao, G.H. The Life and Times of Sir Kai
Ho Kai.
E. Sinn, 302:Vol 19No2-237
"Chapeau bas."*
L.E. Doucette, 108:Fall83-135
Chapel, J. Victorian Taste.
G. Reynolds, 39:Dec83-529
Chapman, C. Russell of The Times.
H. Brogan, 617(TLS):13Jul84-774
Chapman, R. The Language of English Lit-
erature.
G. Bourcier, 189(EA):Apr-Jun84-180
Chapman, R. The Treatment of Sounds in
Language and Literature.
A. Burgess, 617(TLS):28Dec84-1491
Chapman, R., I. Kinnes and K. Randsborg,
eds. The Archaeology of Death.
J.A. North, 313:Vol73-169
S.R.F. Price, 303(JoHS):Vol 103-195
Chapman, R.G. and C.T. Duval, eds.
Charles Darwin 1809-1882.
G. Beer, 617(TLS):10Feb84-132
Chapman, S.D. and S. Chassagne. European
Textile Printers in the Eighteenth
Century.
A.J. Budd, 83:Spring83-103
Chappel, A.H. - see Aichinger, I.
Chappell, F. Midquest.*
A.B. Mangum, 398(MPS):Vol 11No3-308
M. Williams, 651(WHR):Spring83-53
Chappell, F. Moments of Light.
G. Garrett, 569(SR):Winter83-112

Chappell, S.K. and A. Van Zanten. Barry
Byrne/John Lloyd Wright.
H. Searing, 576:May83-190
Chapple, F. Sparks Fly!
S. Jenkins, 617(TLS):16Nov84-1304
Chapple, G. and H.H. Schulte, eds. The
Turn of the Century.*
W. Paulsen, 564:Nov83-305
Char, S.V.D. - see under Desika Char, S.V.
du Chardin, P. Le Roman de la conscience
malheureuse.
F.C. St. Aubyn, 207(FR):Apr84-718
Charlebois, J. La Mour suivi de L'Amort.
A.L. Amprimoz, 102(CanL):Autumn83-110
Charles-Saget, A. L'architecture du divin.
Y. Lafrance, 154:Dec83-727
É. des Places, 555:Vol57fasc2-322
Charlesworth, J.H., ed. The Old Testament
Pseudepigrapha. (Vol 1)
H. Bloom, 453(NYRB):19Jan84-25
G. Vermes, 617(TLS):18May84-561
Charlton, M. The Eagle and the Small
Birds.
K. Kyle, 362:18Oct84-28
Charlton, P. John Stainer and the Musical
Life of Victorian Britain.
N. Temperley, 617(TLS):11May84-517
Charney, H. The Detective Novel of
Manners.
P. Wolfe, 395(MFS):Autumn83-389
Charney, M. Sexual Fiction.*
M.K. Flavell, 402(MLR):Apr83-418
Charpentier, F. Les Débuts de la tragé-
die héroïque.
J. Morel, 535(RHL):Sep/Dec83-918
Charpentier, F. - see du Guillet, P.
Charpentier, J-M. Le pidgin Bislama(n) et
le multilinguisme aux Nouvelles-Hébrides.
R. Clark, 355(LSoc):Vol83-539
Charrière, C. Le Baptême de l'ombre.
R.C. Lamont, 207(FR):Apr84-732
de Charrière, I. [Belle de Zuylen].
Oeuvres complètes. (Vols 3, 9 and 10)
(J-D. Candaux and others, eds)
K. Kloocke, 547(RF):Band95Heft4-493
Charron, D. - see Rotrou, J.
Charteris, L. Salvage for the Saint.
T.J. Binyon, 617(TLS):16Mar84-270
Charters, A., ed. The Beats.
27(AL):Dec83-681
Charters, S. Jelly Roll Morton's Last
Night at the Jungle Inn.
W. Balliett, 442(NY):21May84-102
Chartier, R. and others. La Ville clas-
sique de la Renaissance aux Révolutions.
H. Ballon, 576:Dec83-397
Charvet, J. A Critique of Freedom and
Equality.*
D.A. Lloyd Thomas, 479(PhQ):Jul83-301
Charyn, J. Pinocchio's Nose.*
R.L. Patten, 454:Fall83-67
Chase, C., ed. The Dating of "Beowulf."*
T.M. Andersson, 627(UTQ):Spring83-288
A.A. Lee, 178:Sep83-363
Chase, J. During the Reign of the Queen
of Persia.*
S. Altinel, 617(TLS):15Jun84-676
L. Franks, 461:Fall/Winter83/84-91
Chase, N. Locksley.
S. Altinel, 617(TLS):3Aug84-875
Chase, W.P. New York: The Wonder City.
J. Gross, 441:29Jan84-8

Chastel, A. L'Art italien.
  J. Clair, 450(NRF):Apr83-151
Chastel, A. The Sack of Rome, 1527.*
  C. Gould, 39:Oct83-354
Chastel, A. and others. The Renaissance.
  C.A. Patrides, 604:Spring-Summer83-30
Château, J. Les grandes psychologies dans
  l'Antiquité.
  A. Reix, 192(EP):Apr-Jun83-226
de Chateaubriand, F.R. Correspondance
  générale.* (Vol 3) (P. Riberette, ed)
  R. Lebègue, 535(RHL):Mar/Apr83-284
  C.A. Porter, 207(FR):May84-879
de Chateaubriand, F.R. Correspondance
  générale. (Vol 4) (P. Riberette, ed)
  G.D. Painter, 617(TLS):30Mar84-324
Châteaureynaud, G-O. La Faculté des
  songes.
  S. Smith, 207(FR):Oct83-134
Châtelet, A. Early Dutch Painting.*
  R.G. Calkins, 54:Sep83-508
Chatham, J.R. and C.C. McClendon, with
  others. Dissertations in Hispanic Lan-
  guages and Literatures. (Vol 2)
  D. Briesemeister, 547(RF):Band95
  Heft1/2-222
  A.J. Cardenas, 238:Mar83-130
Chatham, J.R. and S.M. Scales, with others.
  Western European Dissertations on the
  Hispanic and Luso-Brazilian Languages
  and Literatures.
  H.F. Williams, 304(JHP):Fall83-67
Chatman, S., U. Eco and J-M. Klinkenberg,
  eds. A Semiotic Landscape.*
  L. Orr, 599:Winter83-56
Chatten, E.N. Samuel Foote.
  M. Jones, 447(N&Q):Feb82-84
Chatterji, R. Unions, Politics and the
  State.
  J. Das Gupta, 293(JASt):Nov82-105
Chattopadhyaya, A. Atīśa and Tibet.
  D.S. Lopez, Jr., 293(JASt):May83-697
Chatwin, B. On the Black Hill.*
  D. Flower, 249(HudR):Summer83-369
  42(AR):Spring83-249
  639(VQR):Summer83-91
Châu, H.T. Grundkurs Vietnamesisch.
  G.F. Meier, 682(ZPSK):Band36Heft4-487
Chaucer, G. The Canterbury Tales.* (P.G.
  Ruggiers, ed)
  E.G. Stanley, 447(N&Q):Oct82-426
Chaucer, G. "The Canterbury Tales" by
  Geoffrey Chaucer. (N.F. Blake, ed)
  J. Kerling, 179(ES):Feb83-91
  C. von Nolcken, 541(RES):Feb83-56
  E.G. Stanley, 447(N&Q):Oct82-428
Chaucer, G. Geoffrey Chaucer: The
  Franklin's Tale. (G. Morgan, ed)
  N. Jacobs, 382(MAE):1983/1-126
Chaudenson, R. Textes créoles anciens (La
  Réunion et Ile Maurice).
  A. Hull, 207(FR):Oct83-146
Chaudhuri, S. Infirm Glory.
  R.D. Sell, 597(SN):Vol55No2-209
Chaudonneret, M-C. La Peinture Troubadour.
  J. Whiteley, 90:Oct83-629
Chaunu, P. Histoire et décadence.*
  A. Reix, 542:Jan-Mar83-56
Chaurette, N. Fêtes d'Automne.*
  J. Moss, 102(CanL):Autumn83-87

Chaurette, N. Provincetown Playhouse,
  juillet 1919, j'avais 19 ans.
  T.H. Brown, 207(FR):Apr84-734
  J. Moss, 102(CanL):Spring83-143
Chauvin, B., ed. Mélanges à la mémoire du
  Père Anselme Dimier. (Pt 3, Vols 5 and
  6)
  H. Grüger, 683:Band46Heft4-458
Cheauré, E. E.T.A. Hoffman: Inszenierung
  seiner Werke auf russischen Bühnen.
  E.W. Clowes, 574(SEEJ):Spring83-108
Cheauré, E. Abram Terc (Andrej Sinjav-
  skij).
  C. Barnes, 575(SEER):Jul83-440
Chęcinski, M. Poland.*
  W.W. Soroka, 497(PolR):Vol28No4-105
Checkland, O. and M. Lamb, eds. Health
  Care as Social History.
  R. Steele, 529(QQ):Winter83-1195
Checkland, S. and O. Industry and Ethos.
  T.M. Devine, 617(TLS):1Jun84-617
Chédin, O. Sur l'esthétique de Kant et la
  théorie critique de la représentation.
  A. Stanguennec, 542:Oct-Dec83-473
Cheever, J. Oh What a Paradise It Seems!
  R. Hadas, 473(PR):4/1983-622
  M. Pearson, 577(SHR):Summer83-283
Cheever, S. Home Before Dark.
  E. Hardwick, 453(NYRB):20Dec84-3
  J. Kaplan, 441:21Oct84-7
Chekhov, A. Chekhov: The Early Stories,
  1883-1888.* (P. Miles and H. Pitcher,
  eds and trans)
  V. Belenkaya, 573(SSF):Fall83-324
Chekhov, A. The Tales. (Vols 1 and 2)
  (C. Garnett, trans)
  S.S. Prawer, 617(TLS):17Aug84-926
Ch'en, C-Y. Hsün Yüeh and the Mind of
  Late Han China.*
  E.T. Ch'ien, 244(HJAS):Jun83-333
Ch'en, P.H-C. The Formation of the Early
  Meiji Legal Order.
  J.B. Leavell, 407(MN):Summer83-213
Cheney, M.G. Roger, Bishop of Worcester,
  1164-1179.*
  M.C. Buck, 382(MAE):1983/2-353
Cheng, C-Y. China's Economic Development.
  R.M. Field, 293(JASt):Aug83-908
Cheng Ch'ien. Pei-ch'ü Hsin-p'u.
  J.I. Crump, Jr., 116:Jul82-233
Cheng Sait Chia. Turned Clay.
  L. Welch, 198:Oct83-98
Cheng, V.J. Shakespeare and Joyce.
  R.M. Adams, 453(NYRB):31May84-42
Chern, K.S. Dilemma in China.*
  W. Lafeber, 302:Vol 19No2-259
Chernaik, W.L. The Poet's Time.*
  A. Phillips, 364:Jun83-100
  639(VQR):Autumn83-116
Chernow, B. The Drawings of Milton Avery.
  J. Russell, 441:2Dec84-12
Chernyonok, M. Losing Bet.
  M.C. Smith, 441:6May84-9
Cherrington, J. A Farming Year.
  S. Mills, 617(TLS):13Jul84-780
Cherry, B. and N. Pevsner. London 2:
  South.
  A. Hollinghurst, 617(TLS):6Jan84-8
  J. Meades, 46:Dec83-6
Cherry, K. The Lost Traveller's Dream.
  D. Stern, 441:22Apr84-14
Cherryh, C.J. Voyager in Night.
  G. Jonas, 441:25Nov84-20

Cherubim, D., ed. Fehlerlinguistik.
  A. Cutler, 353:Vol20No1/2-143
  U. Thilo, 260(IF):Band88-300
Cheshire, J. Variation in an English
  Dialect.
  T.C. Frazer, 350:Mar84-189
Chesi, G. The Last Africans.
  M. Gilbert, 69:Vol53No3-99
Chesney, E.A. The Countervoyage of Rabe-
  lais and Ariosto.*
  C.P. Brand, 131(CL):Spring83-179
  E.B. Weaver, 551(RenQ):Summer83-283
Chesnut, M. The Private Mary Chesnut.
  (C.V. Woodward and E. Muhlenfeld, eds)
  442(NY):31Dec84-71
"The Chester Mystery Cycle: A Reduced Fac-
  simile of Huntington Library MS. 2."*
  C. Clark, 179(ES):Feb83-93
  N. Davis, 447(N&Q):Feb82-68
Chesterton, G.K. Dickens.
  C. Jordis, 450(NRF):Feb83-150
Cheuse, A. Candace and Other Stories.
  G. Garrett, 569(SR):Winter83-112
Chevalier, J-C. Verbe et phrase.
  M. Dominicy, 209(FM):Jul83-260
Chevalier, J-C. and M. Gross, eds.
  Méthodes en grammaire française.
  F.M. Jenkins, 545(RPh):Aug82-108
Chevalier, J.M. Civilization and the
  Stolen Gift.
  P.L. Doughty, 263(RIB):Vol33No2-254
Chevalier, M. - see Doni, A.F.
Chevallier, R., ed. Colloque l'épopée
  gréco-latine et ses prolongements
  européens: Calliope II.
  C. Moussy, 555:Vol57fasc1-163
Chevrel, Y. Le Naturalisme.
  C. Bertrand-Jennings, 207(FR):Mar84-
  560
  A. Pagès, 446(NCFS):Fall-Winter83/84-
  242
Chevrette, A. Le Premier Homme.
  A.L. Amprimoz, 102(CanL):Summer83-126
Chevrier, J-F. Proust et la photographie.
  F. de Méredieu, 450(NRF):Jan83-149
Chi-keung, L., J.W. Cushman and Wang
  Gungwu - see under Leung Chi-keung, J.W.
  Cushman and Wang Gungwu
Chia, C.S. - see under Cheng Sait Chia
Chiampi, J.T. Shadowy Prefaces.*
  M. Davie, 402(MLR):Apr83-466
Chiari, A. Manzoni il credente.
  C. Godt, 400(MLN):Jan83-118
Chiarini, P. and W. Dietze, eds. Deutsche
  Klassik und Revolution.
  W. Stellmacher, 654(WB):3/1983-555
Ch'ien, C. - see under Cheng Ch'ien
Ch'ien Chung-shu. Fortress Besieged. (J.
  Kelly and N.K. Mao, trans)
  D.T. Hu, 116:Jan82-127
Chierici, S. and D. Citi. Il Piemonte, La
  Val d'Aosta, La Liguria.
  D.F. Glass, 54:Jun83-340
Chikafusa, K. - see under Kitabatake Chika-
  fusa
Child, L.M. Lydia Maria Child: Selected
  Letters, 1817-1880.* (M. Meltzer and
  P.G. Holland, eds)
  639(VQR):Summer83-79
Childers, T. The Nazi Voter.
  I. Deak, 453(NYRB):31May84-37
  J. Noakes, 617(TLS):21Sep84-1051

"Children's Clothes and Toys."
  M. Cowan, 614:Spring84-21
"Children's Literature." (Vol 8) (F.
  Butler, E. Francis and S. Pickering, Jr.,
  eds)
  G. Avery, 447(N&Q):Feb82-91
  P. Pénigault-Duhet, 189(EA):Jan-Mar83-
  68
"Children's Literature." (Vol 11)
  P. Pénigault-Duhet, 189(EA):Oct-Dec84-
  447
Childress, J.F. Moral Responsibility in
  Conflicts.*
  J.D., 185:Apr84-544
Childress, J.F. Who Should Decide?
  T.M.R., 185:Apr84-569
Childress, M. A World Made of Fire.
  V. Miner, 441:16Dec84-17
Childs, D. The GDR.
  T.G. Ash, 617(TLS):8Jun84-644
Childs, J. Armies and Warfare in Europe,
  1648-1789.*
  P. Dukes, 83:Autumn83-254
Chilton, J. Stomp Off, Let's Go!
  J. Stokes, 617(TLS):30Nov84-1389
Chin-hsiung, H. - see under Hsü Chin-
  hsiung
Ching, M.K.L., M.C. Haley and R.F. Luns-
  ford, eds. Linguistic Perspectives on
  Literature.
  E.C. Traugott, 599:Winter83-46
Chinnery, V. Oak Furniture, the British
  Tradition.
  R.F. Trent, 658:Summer/Autumn83-215
Chinoy, H.K. and L.W. Jenkins. Women in
  American Theatre.*
  G. Crane, 615(TJ):May82-273
Chirac, M. - see de Bauffremont, A.
Chirovsky, N.L. An Introduction to
  Ukrainian History.* (Vol 1)
  T.S. Noonan, 550(RusR):Apr83-238
Chisholm, A.H. and R. Tyers, eds. Food
  Security.
  J.E. Nickum, 293(JASt):Aug83-893
Chisholm, K. and J. Ferguson. Rome: The
  Augustan Age.*
  E.D. Hunt, 161(DUJ):Jun83-110
Chisholm, R.M. Brentano and Meinong
  Studies.
  T.M.R., 185:Jul84-731
Chisholm, R.M. The First Person.
  S.E. Boer, 482(PhR):Apr83-273
  D. Dahlstrom, 543:Mar84-695
  B. Harrison, 483:Jul83-403
  B.F. Scarlett, 63:Jun83-205
Chisholm, R.M. The Foundations of Know-
  ing.*
  P. Bell, 518:Jul83-168
Chissell, J. Clara Schumann.*
  H.C. Schonberg, 441:1Jan84-21
  442(NY):2Jan84-90
Chitnis, S. and P.G. Altbach, eds. The
  Indian Academic Profession.
  P.K-M. New, 293(JASt):Nov82-186
Chittick, W. The Sufi Path of Love.
  C.W. Ernst, 469:Vol9No1-122
Chiu, H. Agreements of the People's
  Republic of China.
  H. Warshawsky, 293(JASt):Aug83-909
Chocrón, I., comp. Nueva Crítica de
  Teatro Venezolano.*
  F. Dauster, 37:Jan-Feb83-62

Duc de Choiseul. Mémoires. (J-P. Guic-
ciardi and P. Bonnet, eds)
  J. Aeply, 450(NRF):Oct83-112
Chomsky, N. The Fateful Triangle.
  A. Margalit, 453(NYRB):28Jun84-9
Chomsky, N. Language and Responsibility.
  S. Richmond, 488:Mar83-109
  G. Smitherman, 355(LSoc):Sep83-349
Chomsky, N. Lectures on Government and
Binding.
  G. Tonfoni, 260(IF):Band88-289
  E. Williams, 350:Jun84-400
Chomsky, N. Radical Priorities. (C.P.
Otero, ed)
  D.H., 355(LSoc):Mar83-135
Chomsky, N. Rules and Representations.*
  J.R. Cameron, 393(Mind):Apr83-283
  S.D. Guttenplan, 483:Oct81-587
  S. Ohlander, 597(SN):Vol55No1-98
Chomsky, N. Some Concepts and Conse-
quences of the Theory of Government and
Binding.
  S. Carroll, 320(CJL):Fall83-175
  D.H., 355(LSoc):Sep83-418
  E. Williams, 350:Jun84-400
Chomsky, N. Towards a New Cold War.
  42(AR):Winter83-123
Chomsky, N., with R. Huybregts and H. van
Riemsdijk. On the Generative Enterprise.
  M-L. Kean, 350:Sep84-600
Chopin, F. Correspondance de Frédéric
Chopin (1810-1849). (B.É. Sydow, with
S. and D. Chainaye, eds and trans)
  H. Musielak, 537:Vol69No2-237
Choquette, G. Wednesday's Child.*
  D.R. Bartlett, 102(CanL):Summer83-122
"Choreography by George Balanchine."*
  S.A. Manning, 612(ThS):May/Nov83-162
Chouillet, J. and A-M. - see Diderot, D.
Chrétien de Troyes. Lancelot or The
Knight of the Cart.* (W.W. Kibler, ed
and trans)
  T. Hunt, 208(FS):Oct83-440
  D. Staines, 589:Jan83-257
Chrétien de Troyes. Perceval, the Story
of the Grail. (N. Bryant, trans)
  M-M. Dubois, 189(EA):Oct-Dec84-458
Chrisman, M.U. Lay Culture, Learned Cul-
ture.* Bibliography of Strasbourg
Imprints, 1480-1599.*
  T.A. Brady, Jr., 551(RenQ):Winter83-
606
Christensen, A.S. Lactantius the Histo-
rian.
  J. den Boeft, 394:Vol36fasc3/4-436
Christensen, C.C. Art and the Reformation
in Germany.*
  J.M. Stayer, 539:Feb84-54
Christensen, D.E. - see "Contemporary
German Philosophy"
Christensen, J. Coleridge's Blessed
Machine of Language.*
  A. Reed, 591(SIR):Winter83-623
  B. Ross, 529(QQ):Summer83-554
  M.F. Schulz, 301(JEGP):Oct83-566
Christensen, M. and C. Stauth. The Sweeps.
  J.J. O'Connor, 441:11Nov84-33
Christensen, T. Christus oder Jupiter.
  M. Beller, 52:Band18Heft1-92
Christian, W.A., Jr. Apparitions in Late
Medieval and Renaissance Spain.* Local
Religion in Sixteenth-Century Spain.*
  J.B. Owens, 539:Feb84-73

Christiansen, E. The Northern Crusades.*
  S. Jenks, 589:Jan83-245
Christiansen, E. - see Saxo Grammaticus
Christiansen, K. Gentile da Fabriano.
  M. Camille, 59:Dec83-501
  J. Gardner, 90:Jun83-364
  F. Russell, 39:Jan83-66
Christiansen, R. Prima Donna.
  M. Tanner, 617(TLS):16Nov84-1309
Christiansson, C. Soil Erosion and Sedi-
mentation in Semi-Arid Tanzania.
  P. Temple, 69:Vol153No1-98
Christie, I.R. Wars and Revolutions:
Britain, 1760-1815.
  639(VQR):Winter83-9
Christine de Pisan. The Book of The City
of Ladies.* (E.J. Richards, trans)
  D.D.R. Owen, 617(TLS):3Feb84-117
Christine de Pisan. Cent ballades d'amant
et de dame. (J. Cerquiglini, ed)
  G. Roques, 553(RLiR):Jan-Jun83-259
Christoff, P.K. K.S. Aksakov.*
  J.D. Morison, 575(SEER):Oct83-621
Christoph, S.R. Wolfram von Eschenbach's
Couples.
  M.E. Gibbs, 406:Winter83-437
  W. McConnell, 221(GQ):Jan83-131
  R.E. Wallbank, 402(MLR):Oct83-964
Christopher, G.B. Milton and the Science
of the Saints.*
  B. Berry, 141:Spring83-168
  B.K. Lewalski, 551(RenQ):Winter83-678
Christopher, N. On Tour with Rita.*
  J.D. McClatchy, 491:Dec83-167
Chryssafis, G. A Textual and Stylistic
Commentary on Theocritus' Idyll XXV.
  N. Hopkinson, 123:Vol33No1-130
Chu, P-C. V.K. Wellington Koo.
  T.E. Lautz, 293(JASt):May83-614
Chü-i, P. - see under Po Chü-i
"Chuang-tzu: The Seven Inner Chapters and
Other Writings from the Book Chuang-tzu."
  (A.C. Graham, trans)
  R.T. Ames, 293(JASt):May83-615
Chubb, J.E. Interest Groups and the
Bureaucracy.
  E.M.U., 185:Jul84-746
Chudodeev, Y.V., ed. Soviet Volunteers in
China, 1925-1945.
  S.I. Levine, 293(JASt):May83-644
Chukovskaia, L. Zapiski ob Anne Akhmato-
voi, 1952-1962. (Vol 2)
  R. Kemball, 550(RusR):Jan83-126
Chukovsky, K. Alexander Blok as Man and
Poet. (D. Burgin and K. O'Connor, eds
and trans)
  L. Vogel, 574(SEEJ):Winter83-490
Chukovsky, K.I. The Art of Translation
("A High Art"). (L.G. Leighton, ed and
trans)
  M. Glenny, 617(TLS):5Oct84-1134
  M.H. Heim, 441:11Nov84-24
Chun, B.D., W. Shaw and D-K. Choi. Tradi-
tional Korean Legal Attitudes.
  S.B. Young, 293(JASt):May83-682
Chun-ming, H. - see under Hwang Chun-ming
Chung, Y.Y. The Art of Oriental Embroid-
ery.
  A.L. Mayer, 614:Summer84-10
Chung-shu, C. - see under Ch'ien Chung-shu
Church, C.H. Europe in 1830.
  I. Collins, 617(TLS):18May84-556

Church, C.H. Revolution and Red Tape.
J.C. White, 173(ECS):Winter83/84-210
Churchill, K. Italy and English Literature 1764-1930.*
A. Rodway, 447(N&Q):Oct82-475
Churchill, W.S. and F.D. Roosevelt.
Churchill and Roosevelt: The Complete Correspondence. (W.F. Kimball, ed)
A. Horne, 441:21Oct84-11
A. Schlesinger, Jr., 61:Oct84-114
Churchland, P.M. Scientific Realism and the Plasticity of Mind.*
J.R. Brown, 258:Jun83-226
Chute, P. Eva's Music.
M. Simpson, 441:12Feb84-20
Chūya, N. - see under Nakahara Chūya
Chvany, C.V. and R.D. Brecht, eds. Morphosyntax in Slavic.
F.E. Knowles, 575(SEER):Apr83-261
Chvatík, K. Tschechoslowakischer Strukturalismus.
A. Měšťan, 688(ZSP):Band43Heft2-428
R. Wellek, 549(RLC):Oct-Dec83-513
Cianci, G. - see Lewis, W.
Ciardi, J. A Second Browser's Dictionary and Native's Guide to the Unknown American Language.
E. Korn, 617(TLS):6Apr84-382
42(AR):Summer83-379
Ciavarelli, M.E. El tema de la fuerza de la sangre.
D.W. Bleznick, 240(HR):Winter83-98
K.R. Scholberg, 552(REH):Oct83-472
Ciccone, S.D., I. Bonomi and A. Masini. La stampa periodica milanese della prima metà dell'Ottocento.
G. Lepschy, 617(TLS):16Nov84-1317
Cicero. Marco Tulio Cicerón: "Disputas tusculanas." (J. Pimentel Álvarez, ed and trans)
P. Cherchi, 122:Jul83-261
A.E. Douglas, 123:Vol33No2-213
Cicero. Cicéron, "La République," Tome 1. (Bk 1, Vol 2) (E. Bréguet, ed) M. Tullius Cicero, "De Legibus." (K. Ziegler, ed) (3rd ed rev by W. Görler)
A.E. Douglas, 123:Vol33No2-213
Cicero. M. Tulli Ciceronis Epistulae: "Epistulae ad Familares." (W.S. Watt, ed)
C. Natunewicz, 124:Jan-Feb84-199
Cicero. M. Tulli Ciceronis scripta quae manserunt omnia. (fasc 5: Orator) (R. Westman, ed)
J.G.F. Powell, 123:Vol33No1-38
Cicero. Epistulae ad Quintum fratrem et M. Brutum. (D.R. Shackleton Bailey, ed)
G.V. Sumner, 122:Oct83-358
Cicero. Select Letters. (D.R. Shackleton Bailey, ed)
G.V. Sumner, 122:Apr83-173
Cicero and Lucretius. Marco Tulio Cicerón: "Lelio; Sobre la amistad" (A.J. Cappelletti, trans) [together with] Tito Lucrecio Caro: "De la naturaleza de las cosas." (L. Alvarado, trans)
A. Reix, 542:Oct-Dec83-458
Čikobava, A. Iberiul-k'avk'asiuri enatmecnierebis šesavali.
T. Šaradzenidse, 682(ZPSK):Band36Heft1-94

Ciment, M. Kubrick.*
G. Kaufman, 362:19Apr84-26
M. Kernan, 18:Oct83-90
Ciment, M. and J. Schatzberg. Schatzberg.
J-L. Bourget, 98:Mar83-264
Cingria, C-A. Bois sec bois vert. Florides helvètes et autres textes.
D. Gascoyne, 617(TLS):7Dec84-1430
"Charles-Albert Cingria: 1883-1954."
D. Gascoyne, 617(TLS):7Dec84-1430
Cinzio, G.G. - see under Giraldi Cinzio, G.
Ciononi-Visani, M. and G. Gamulin. Giorgio Giulio Clovio.
B. Boucher, 39:Oct83-355
Cioran, E.M. Drawn and Quartered.
G. Steiner, 442(NY):16Apr84-152
Cipolla, G. - see Tasso, T.
Citino, D. The Appassionata Poems.*
C. Wasserburg, 385(MQR):Fall84-613
Citino, D. Last Rites and Other Poems.
C. Donley, 236:Fall-Winter83-41
W. Zander, 363(LitR):Winter84-272
Citroen, P., comp. Palet.
E. van Uitert, 600:Vol 13No3/4-238
Citron, P. - see Giono, J.
Citron, P., Y. Gérard and H. Macdonald - see Berlioz, H.
Cixous, H. Limonade tout était si infini.
I.M. Kohn, 207(FR):May84-906
Clabburn, P. Patchwork.
R.L. Shep, 614:Winter84-21
Clair, J. Considérations sur l'état des Beaux-Arts.
M. le Bot, 450(NRF):Jun83-136
Clairmont, R.E., ed. A Commentary on Seneca's "Apocolocyntosis diui Claudii" or "Glose in Librum de ludo Claudii Annei Senece."
J.B. Allen, 589:Jul83-844
Clampitt, A. The Kingfisher.*
D. Baker, 434:Winter83-336
D. Davis, 362:19Jul84-25
E. Grosholz, 249(HudR):Autumn83-582
J. Hollander, 676(YR):Autumn83-xiv
J.D. McClatchy, 491:Dec83-165
J. Mole, 176:Dec84-58
P.A. Olson, 502(PrS):Spring83-99
P. Stitt, 219(GaR):Summer83-428
639(VQR):Autumn83-132
Clare, A. In the Psychiatrist's Chair.
R. Ingrams, 362:28Jun84-27
R. Littlewood, 617(TLS):21Sep84-1046
Clare, G. Last Waltz in Vienna.*
G. Leviant, 390:Apr83-62
Clare, J. The Later Poems of John Clare. (E. Robinson and D. Powell, eds)
J. Lucas, 617(TLS):27Jul84-845
Clare, J. The Natural History Prose Writings of John Clare. (M. Grainger, ed)
J. Buxton, 617(TLS):11May84-519
Clare, J. The Oxford Authors: John Clare. (E. Robinson and D. Powell, eds)
W.W. Robson, 617(TLS):26Oct84-1221
Clare, J. The Rural Muse. (R.K.R. Thornton, ed) John Clare's Birds. (E. Robinson and R. Fitter, eds)
P.M.S. Dawson, 148:Summer83-90
Clarens, C. Crime Movies.
B.K. Grant, 106:Spring83-107
Clark, A. Psychological Models and Neural Mechanisms.*
J-M. Gabaude, 542:Jul-Sep83-333

Claus, H. The Theatre Director Otto
Brahm.
  J. Osborne, 610:Summer83-171
Clausen, C. The Place of Poetry.*
  C. Sanders, 289:Spring83-115
  K. Shevelow, 405(MP):Feb84-337
  K. Wilson, 529(QQ):Spring83-225
Clauss, M. Der magister officiorum in der
Spätantike (4.-6. Jahrhundert).
  E.D. Hunt, 123:Vol33No1-86
Clavell, J. The Children's Story.
  P. Nodelman, 102(CanL):Spring83-149
Claxton, A.O.D. Suffolk Dialect.
  F.C., 189(EA):Apr-Jun84-233
Clay, J.S. The Wrath of Athena.
  J. Griffin, 617(TLS):10Feb84-134
Clayman, D.L. Callimachus' "Iambi."
  E. Phinney, 122:Apr83-171
Clayre, A. The Heart of the Dragon.
  D. Pollard, 176:Apr84-56
Clayton, A. The Zanzibar Revolution and
its Aftermath.
  D. Petterson, 69:Vol53No4-98
Clayton, B., Jr. The Complete Book of
Pastry.
  W. and C. Cowen, 639(VQR):Spring83-69
Clayton, B., Jr. The Complete Book of
Soups and Stews.
  M. Burros, 441:2Dec84-14
Clayton, J.D. and G. Schaarschmidt, eds.
Poetica Slavica.*
  A. McMillin, 575(SEER):Apr83-313
  I. Nagurski, 497(PolR):Vol28No1-90
Clayton, J.E. - see Barth, A.
Clayton, J.J. Bodies of the Rich.
  D.H. Bell, 441:7Oct84-22
  G. Weaver, 344:Fall84-107
Clearman, M. Lambing Out and Other Stor-
ies.
  M.S. Trimble, 649(WAL):May83-85
Cleary, T. and J.C. - see "The Blue Cliff
Record"
Cleator, P.E. - see Mencken, H.L.
Clecak, P. America's Quest for the Ideal
Self.*
  C. Lasch, 453(NYRB):2Feb84-36
Clemens, P.G.E. The Atlantic Economy and
Colonial Maryland's Eastern Shore.
  R.R. Johnson, 173(ECS):Winter83/84-221
Clément, O. Sources.
  A. Reix, 542:Jan-Mar83-80
Clement, W. Hardrock Mining.
  V. Di Norcia, 529(QQ):Summer83-527
Clements, C.D. Medical Genetics Casebook.
  K.P.G., 185:Jan84-382
Clements, H. Alfred Russel Wallace.
  W. George, 617(TLS):2Nov84-1260
Clements, P. and J. Grindle, eds. The
Poetry of Thomas Hardy.*
  S. Hunter, 677(YES):Vol 13-337
  S. Trombley, 447(N&Q):Jun82-257
Clements, P. and I. Grundy, eds. Virginia
Woolf.
  J. Batchelor, 617(TLS):10Aug84-900
Clemoes, P., ed. Anglo-Saxon England.
(Vols 6, 7 and 11)
  M. Sjöström, 70:May-Jun83-161
Clemoes, P., ed. Anglo-Saxon England.*
(Vol 8)
  M. Sjöström, 70:May-Jun83-161
  E.G. Stanley, 72:Band219Heft2-420

Clemoes, P., ed. Anglo-Saxon England.*
(Vol 9)
  C. Gauvin, 189(EA):Jan-Mar84-86
  M. Sjöstrom, 70:May-Jun83-161
  E.G. Stanley, 72:Band219Heft2-420
Clemoes, P., ed. Anglo-Saxon England.
(Vol 10)
  C. Gauvin, 189(EA):Jan-Mar84-87
  M. Sjöström, 70:May-Jun83-161
Clerc, C., ed. Approaches to "Gravity's
Rainbow."*
  S.S. Ames, 268(IFR):Winter84-68
  B. Duyfhuizen, 395(MFS):Winter83-741
  T. Le Clair, 27(AL):Oct83-485
  42(AR):Summer83-371
de Clerck, W. Zuidnederlands Woordenboek.
  G. Janssens, 204(FdL):Dec82-301
Cliff, M. Abeng.
  F. Levy, 441:25Mar84-20
Cliff, W. America.
  D. Leuwers, 450(NRF):Jun83-121
Cliffe, J.T. The Puritan Gentry.
  N. Malcolm, 617(TLS):1Jun84-605
Clifford, T. Turner at Manchester.
  N.A., 90:Jun83-371
Clift, D. Quebec Nationalism in Crisis.
  R. Hudon, 529(QQ):Autumn83-872
Clifton, H. Comparative Lives.
  M. Harmon, 272(IUR):Spring83-114
Clifton, R. The Last Popular Rebellion.
  J.P. Kenyon, 617(TLS):17Aug84-913
Clifton, T. Music as Heard.
  A. Berleant, 290(JAAC):Spring84-345
Clifton-Taylor, A. and A.S. Ireson.
English Stone Building.
  J.M. Robinson, 39:Dec83-530
Clinton, C. The Plantation Mistress.*
  639(VQR):Summer83-86
Clogan, P.M., ed. Medievalia et Humanis-
tica. (New Ser, No 11)
  G. Josipovici, 402(MLR):Jul83-646
Clopper, L.M., ed. Records of Early
English Drama: Chester.*
  A.H. Nelson, 402(MLR):Jan83-131
de Closets, F. Toujours plus!
  H.B. Sutton, 207(FR):Oct83-122
Cloulas, I. La Vie quotidienne dans les
châteaux de la Loire au temps de la
Renaissance.
  M.G. Paulson, 207(FR):Apr84-753
Cloutier, G. Cette Profondeur parfois.
  E. Hamblet, 207(FR):Dec83-266
Clover, C.J. The Medieval Saga.*
  R.B. Bosse, 477(PLL):Summer83-331
  R.F. Green, 529(QQ):Winter83-1185
Clowes, F.W. Pol-Am.
  J.G.V. Maciora, 497(PolR):Vol28No1-116
Clowse, C.D. Measuring Charleston's Over-
seas Commerce, 1717-1767.
  P.V. Bergstrom, 656(WMQ):Oct83-633
Clubbe, J. - see Froude, J.A.
Clucas, L. The Trial of John Italos and
the Crisis of Intellectual Values in
Byzantium in the Eleventh Century.
  M. Arbagi, 589:Oct83-1110
Clutterbuck, R. Industrial Conflict and
Democracy.
  D. MacIntyre, 617(TLS):7Sep84-991
Clüver, C. Thornton Wilder und André Obey.
  M. Brunkhorst, 107(CRCL):Mar83-124
Cluysenaar, A. and S. Hewat. Double
Helix.*
  E. Larrissy, 493:Mar83-61

Clyne, M. Deutsch als Muttersprache in
Australien.
 J. Heath, 350:Mar84-192
 B.J. Koekkoek, 221(GQ):Jan83-128
Coale, S. Anthony Burgess.
 A.A. De Vitis, 395(MFS):Winter83-788
Coarelli, F. and others. L'area sacra di
Largo Argentina. (Vol 1)
 P. Flobert, 555:Vol57fasc2-366
Coates, C.A. John Cowper Powys in Search
of a Landscape.*
 R.L. Blackmore, 395(MFS):Winter83-777
 295(JML):Nov83-558
Cobb, C.H. La cultura y el pueblo, España
1930-1939.
 F.G. Sarría, 86(BHS):Jul83-261
Cobb, M.G. - see Debussy, C.
Cobb, R. Still Life.*
 J. Parks, 364:Dec83/Jan84-148
Cobban, H. The Palestinian Liberation
Organisation.
 M. Yapp, 617(TLS):11May84-514
Cobbett, W. Cobbett in Ireland. (D.
Knight, ed)
 C. MacCabe, 362:26Jul84-24
 C. Townshend, 617(TLS):19Oct84-1184
Coben, L.A. and D.C. Ferster. Japanese
Cloisonné.
 K. Bates, 139:Feb/Mar83-32
 U. Roberts, 60:Nov-Dec83-146
Coburn, K. Experience into Thought.*
 P. Morgan, 179(ES):Aug83-366
Coburn, K. - see Coleridge, S.T.
Cocchiara, G. The History of Folklore in
Europe.
 J. Harris, 221(GQ):Mar83-291
 J.W. Miller, 650(WF):Apr83-152
Cochran, R. and M. Luster. For Love and
For Money.
 T.C. Humphrey, 650(WF):Oct83-304
Cochran, S. and A.C.K. Hsieh, with J. Coch-
ran, eds and trans. One Day in China:
21 May, 1936.*
 D. Pollard, 176:Apr84-51
Cochran, T.B., W.M. Arkin and M.M. Hoenig.
Nuclear Weapons Databook. (Vol 1)
 M. Bundy, 441:11Mar84-3
Cochran, T.C. Frontiers of Change.
 T.M. Doerflinger, 656(WMQ):Apr83-302
 G. Kulik, 658:Spring83-101
Cochrane, D. and M. Schiralli, eds. Phi-
losophy of Education.
 B. Hendley, 154:Mar83-168
Cochrane, E. Historians and Historio-
graphy in the Italian Renaissance.*
 S. Epstein, 125:Winter83-183
 M. Phillips, 589:Apr83-440
Cockburn, A. The Threat.*
 M. Carver, 617(TLS):9Mar84-241
 639(VQR):Autumn83-132
Cockcroft, J.D. Mexico.
 A. Wald, 385(MQR):Spring84-308
Cockerell, M., P. Hennessy and D. Walker.
Sources Close to the Prime Minister.
 A. Rusbridger, 362:7Jun84-23
 N. Shrapnel, 617(TLS):15Jun84-655
Cockerill, A.W. Sons of the Brave.
 K. Jeffery, 617(TLS):26Oct84-1213
Cocking, J.M. Proust.*
 R. Gibson, 402(MLR):Jul83-718
 J. Grieve, 67:Nov83-320
 A.H. Pasco, 446(NCFS):Fall-Winter83/84-
  245 [continued]

[continuing]
 L.M. Porter, 395(MFS):Summer83-304
 J-Y. Tadié, 208(FS):Jan83-101
 295(JML):Nov83-558
Cocks, A.S. and C. Truman. The Thyssen-
Bornemisza Collection.
 C. le Corbeiller, 617(TLS):20Jul84-820
Cockshut, A.O.J. The Art of Autobiography
in 19th and 20th Century England.
 J. Sturrock, 617(TLS):16Nov84-1307
"The Codex Magliabechiano." (Vol 1 ed by
Z. Nuttall; Vol 2 ed and trans by E.H.
Boone)
 J.S. Henderson, 441:18Nov84-51
Cody, L. Stalker.
 M. Laski, 362:25Oct84-29
Cody, P. Continuous Line Quilting.
 B. King, 614:Fall84-13
Coe, M.D. Old Gods and Young Heroes.
 C. Tate, 2(AfrA):Feb83-86
Coe, S. and H. Metz. How to Commit Sui-
cide in South Africa.
 J. Lewis, 62:Apr84-72
Coekelberghs, D. and others. L'Eglise
Saint-Jean-Baptiste au Béguinage à
Bruxelles et son Mobilier.
 K. Downes, 90:Jan83-40
Coel, M. Chief Left Hand, Southern
Arapaho.
 C. Roberts, 649(WAL):May83-60
Coenen, D. and O. Holzapfel, comps.
Herder-Lexikon: Germanische und kelt-
ische Mythologie mit rund 1400 Stichwör-
tern sowie über 90 Abbildungen und Tab-
ellen.
 W. Bies, 196:Band24Heft3/4-303
Coetzee, J.M. Life and Times of Michael
K.*
 P-L. Adams, 61:Feb84-105
 N. Gordimer, 453(NYRB):2Feb84-3
 C. Hope, 364:Dec83/Jan84-139
 J. Lasdun, 176:Jan84-69
 442(NY):27Feb84-132
Coffey, B. Death of Hektor.
 M. O'Neill, 617(TLS):11May84-516
 A. Suberchicot, 272(IUR):Autumn83-259
Coffin, B. Overtones of Bel Canto.
 P. Howell, 353:Vol20No1/2-154
Cogan, M. The Human Thing.
 V. Hunter, 487:Spring83-66
Cogell, E.C. Ursula K. Le Guin.
 J.W. Bittner, 561(SFS):Nov83-350
Cogswell, F. Selected Poems.
 J. Bell, 526:Autumn83-90
Cohan, T. Opium.
 M. Buck, 441:19Aug84-18
Cohen, A. Angel Without Mercy.
 N. Callendar, 441:18Mar84-27
Cohen, A. Jewish Life under Islam.
 R.P. Lindner, 441:9Sep84-38
Cohen, A. Music in the French Royal
Academy of Sciences.*
 F. Getreau, 537:Vol69No1-116
 C. Verba, 308:Spring83-135
Cohen, A.A. Herbert Bayer: The Complete
Work.
 S. Bodine, 441:11Nov84-32
Cohen, A.P. - see Boodberg, P.A.
Cohen, B. Education and the Individual.
 J. Harris, 479(PhQ):Apr83-202
 J. White, 393(Mind):Jul83-472

Cohen, G.A. Karl Marx's Theory of History.*
    H. Klenner, 53(AGP):Band65Heftl-103
    D. Lecourt, 542:Apr-Jun83-245
    K. Nielsen, 154:Jun83-319
Cohen, G.B. The Politics of Ethnic Survival.
    F.L. Carsten, 575(SEER):Apr83-286
Cohen, H.F. Quantifying Music.
    B. Pippard, 617(TLS):21Dec84-1469
Cohen, I.H. Ideology and Unconsciousness.
    W.M., 185:Oct83-171
Cohen, J. The Friars and the Jews.
    D.J. Lasker, 589:Jul83-743
Cohen, J.M. A Samaritan Chronicle.
    S. Isser, 318(JAOS):Jul-Sep82-537
Cohen, K. Film and Fiction.*
    J. Preston, 402(MLR):Apr83-389
Cohen, L.H. The Revolutionary Histories.*
    M.M. Klein, 173(ECS):Fall83-114
Cohen, L.J. and M.B. Hesse, eds. Applications of Inductive Logic.
    J. Butterfield, 393(Mind):Jan83-145
    P. Horwich, 486:Mar83-167
Cohen, L.M. Chinese in the Post-Civil War South.
    P. Giddings, 441:14Oct84-27
Cohen, M. Café Le Dog.
    J. Kertzer, 99:Nov83-34
Cohen, M., ed. Ronald Dworkin and Contemporary Jurisprudence.
    D. Pannick, 362:12Jul84-26
    A.W.B. Simpson, 617(TLS):10Aug84-895
Cohen, M.N. - see Carroll, L.
Cohen, M.P. The Pathless Way.
    D.R. Wallace, 441:16Sep84-17
Cohen, N. Long Steel Rail.*
    B. Feintuch, 650(WF):Jan83-69
    I.M. Tribe, 292(JAF):Apr-Jun83-211
Cohen, N. The Prentice-Hall Concise Book of Genetics.
    529(QQ):Spring83-282
Cohen, P.A. and J.E. Schrecker, eds. Reform in Nineteenth Century China.
    S. Spector, 318(JAOS):Oct-Dec82-668
Cohen, S. Zap!
    W. Stockton, 441:24Jun84-16
Cohen, S.F., ed. An End to Silence.
    V. Krasnov, 550(RusR):Jul83-339
Cohen, S.J. Next Week, Swan Lake.
    A. Armelagos, 290(JAAC):Fall83-98
    T. Tobias, 151:May83-152
Cohen, S.T. The Truth about the Neutron Bomb.
    639(VQR):Summer83-95
Cohen, T. and P. Guyer, eds. Essays in Kant's Aesthetics.*
    R. Hanna, 543:Jun83-919
    E. Schaper, 89(BJA):Spring83-171
    J. Wieand, 342:Band74Heft2-233
Cohen, Y. Les Thèses québécoises sur les femmes 1921-1981.
    C. Verduyn, 298:Fall83-162
Cohn, R. Just Play.*
    A. Kennedy, 402(MLR):Apr83-442
    P. Murphy, 541(RES):Feb83-107
Cohn, R. New American Dramatists: 1960-1980.*
    P. Auslander, 615(TJ):May83-277
    C. Edwards, 157:Autumn83-29
    J.N. Harris, 610:Autumn83-270
    G. Weales, 397(MD):Dec83-583

Cohn, R. - see Beckett, S.
Cohn, R.G. Mallarmé: "Igitur."
    R. Cardinal, 529(QQ):Autumn83-895
    G. Craig, 208(FS):Jan83-96
Coke, T. Vice Chamberlain Coke's Theatrical Papers 1706-1715. (J. Milhous and R.D. Hume, eds)
    G. Barlow, 611(TN):Vol37No2-88
    P. Danchin, 612(ThS):May/Nov83-139
    W. Dean, 410(M&L):Jul/Oct83-269
    J.J. Stathis, 570(SQ):Winter83-508
    A. Toyne, 610:Summer83-164
Colas, D. Le léninisme.
    F. Guery, 542:Apr-Jun83-261
Coldewey, J.C. and B.P. Copenhaver - see Mewe, W.
Cole, B. The Renaissance Artist at Work.*
    F. Russell, 324:Aug84-643
Cole, H.C. The "All's Well" Story from Boccaccio to Shakespeare.*
    T.G. Bergin, 276:Summer83-171
    L.S. Champion, 179(ES):Jun83-276
    S. Snyder, 570(SQ):Winter83-492
    156(JDSh):Jahrbuch1983-266
Cole, H.M. Mbari.*
    P.M. Peek, 2(AfrA):Nov82-14
Cole, J.A. Prince of Spies.
    L. O Broin, 617(TLS):20Jul84-815
Cole, K.C. Sympathetic Vibrations.
    T. Ferris, 441:2Dec84-76
Cole, P., ed. Radical Pragmatics.
    T. Givón, 603:Vol7No1-151
    D.H. Hymes, 355(LSoc):Mar83-100
Cole, R., ed. Current Issues in Linguistic Theory.
    M. Atkinson, 307:Oct80-105
Cole, W.O. Sikhism and its Indian Context 1469-1708.
    C. Shackle, 617(TLS):13Jul84-786
Colecchia, F., ed. García Lorca.
    D.J. Billick, 238:Dec83-638
Colegate, I. Three Novels.
    442(NY):7May84-158
Coleiro, A. An Introduction to Vergil's Bucolics with a Critical Edition of the Text.
    R.E.H. Westendorp Boerma, 394:Vol136 fascl/2-213
Coleman, A. and A. Hammond, eds. Poetry and Drama, 1570-1700.
    C. Hill, 366:Autumn83-250
Coleman, F.M. Hobbes and America.
    S.H. Daniel, 543:Mar83-698
Coleman, J. Medieval Readers and Writers 1350-1400.*
    C.R. Young, 579(SAQ):Winter83-109
Coleman, J.S., T. Hoffer and S. Kilgore. High School Achievement.
    A. Hacker, 453(NYRB):12Apr84-35
Coleman, P., L. Shrubb and V. Smith, eds. Quadrant: Twenty-Five Years.
    J. Tulip, 71(ALS):May83-121
Coleman, W.E. - see Philippe de Mézières
Colenbrander, J. A Portrait of Fryn.
    V. Glendinning, 617(TLS):23Mar84-294
    A. Shapiro, 441:30Sep84-29
    F. Spalding, 362:22Mar84-24
Coleridge, N. Around The World In 78 Days.
    J. Ure, 617(TLS):5Oct84-1112
Coleridge, S.T. The Collected Works of Samuel Taylor Coleridge.* (Vol 7: Biographia Literaria, or Biographical
        [continued]

Colville, J. Strange Inheritance.
  T. Fitton, 617(TLS):13Apr84-394
Colvin, H. Unbuilt Oxford.*
  J. Glancey, 46:Dec83-5
  D. Piper, 453(NYRB):1Mar84-36
Colwin, L. The Lone Pilgrim.*
  G. Garrett, 569(SR):Winter83-112
Combaz, C. Constance D.
  A. Clerval, 450(NRF):Feb83-134
Combet-Farnoux, B. Mercure romain.
  M. Beard, 313:Vol73-215
Comeau, R.F. and N.J. Lamoureux. Echanges.
  R.J. Melpignano, 399(MLJ):Spring83-73
  O.W. Rolfe, 207(FR):Oct83-150
Comella, A. Materiali del Museo Archeo-
  logico Nazionale di Tarquinia IV.
  H. Nagy, 124:Mar-Apr84-259
Comito, T. The Idea of the Garden in the
  Renaissance.
  D.M. Friedman, 301(JEGP):Apr83-224
"Common Crisis North-South."
  T.C. Holyoke, 42(AR):Fall83-502
Comnena, A. Anonyme Metaphrase zu Anna
  Komnene, Alexias xi-xiii.
  D. Holton, 303(JoHS):Vol 103-232
Comotti, G. Storia della musica.* (Vol 1,
  Pt 1)
  J. Solomon, 122:Jul83-236
Compagnon, A. La Seconde Main.*
  J.B. Atkinson, 207(FR):Dec83-237
Compagnon, A. La Troisième République des
  lettres, de Flaubert à Proust.
  J. Grieve, 617(TLS):20Jan84-64
"Comparative Criticism." (Vol 2) (E.S.
  Shaffer, ed)
  C. Norris, 402(MLR):Apr83-375
"Comparative Criticism." (Vol 3) (E.S.
  Shaffer, ed)
  C. Norris, 402(MLR):Apr83-375
  D. Watson, 366:Spring83-106
"Comparative Criticism." (Vol 4) (E.S.
  Shaffer, ed)
  C. Sanders, 289:Fall83-117
Compton, C.J. Courting Poetry in Laos.
  T.E. Miller, 187:Jan84-156
  G. Wiersma, 293(JASt):May83-715
Compton, M.D. Ricardo Palma.*
  L.A. Daniel, 238:Sep83-446
Compton-Burnett, I. A God and His Gifts.
  W.H. Pritchard, 249(HudR):Winter83/84-
  747
"Computerized Manufacturing Automation:
  Employment, Education, and the Work-
  place."
  J. Fallows, 453(NYRB):27Sep84-11
Comrie, B. Language Universals and Lin-
  guistic Typology.*
  P. Coopmans, 297(JL):Sep83-455
  G. Mallinson, 307:Oct82-124
Comrie, B. The Languages of the Soviet
  Union.*
  D. Kilby, 297(JL):Mar83-214
  J. Nichols, 660(Word):Dec83-215
  B. Rigsby, 355(LSoc):Mar83-136
  R.A. Rothstein, 558(RLJ):Winter-
  Spring83-251
Conacher, D.J. Aeschylus' "Prometheus
  Bound."*
  N.P. Miller, 303(JoHS):Vol 103-164
  O. Taplin, 627(UTQ):Summer83-397
Conard, R.C. Heinrich Böll.
  E. Friedrichsmeyer, 221(GQ):May83-530

Conati, M., ed. Encounters With Verdi.
  P.G. Davis, 441:17Jun84-7
Concha, J. Vincente Huidobro.
  D. Bary, 240(HR):Autumn83-480
Conche, M. Le fondement de la morale.
  M. Adam, 542:Jan-Mar83-57
Concolorcorvo. El Lazarillo de ciegos
  caminantes. (A. Lorente Medina, ed)
  C. Freixas, 552(REH):Oct83-475
Conder, F. The Men Who Built Railways.
  (J. Simmons, ed)
  T. Coleman, 617(TLS):23Mar84-310
Condon, R. A Trembling Upon Rome.*
  S. Altinel, 617(TLS):3Aug84-875
Condon, V. Seven Royal Hymns of the
  Ramesside Period.
  V.L. Davis, 318(JAOS):Jan-Mar82-175
Cone, E.T. - see Sessions, R.
Cone, J.F. First Rival of the Metropoli-
  tan Opera.
  R. Christiansen, 617(TLS):10Feb84-133
Coney, M. The Celestial Steam Locomotive.
  G. Jonas, 441:15Jan84-29
Conforti, J.A. Samuel Hopkins and the New
  Divinity Movement.
  R.D. Birdsall, 656(WMQ):Jan83-148
Congdon, L. The Young Lukács.*
  295(JML):Nov83-529
Congdon, L.O.K. Caryatid Mirrors of
  Ancient Greece.
  C.A. Picón, 123:Vol33No1-97
Congreve, W. The Comedies of William Con-
  greve.* (A.G. Henderson, ed)
  F. McCormick, 566:Autumn83-63
Conklin, H.C. Ethnographic Atlas of
  Ifugao.
  R. Rosaldo, 293(JASt):Aug83-1011
Conlon, J.J. Walter Pater and the
  French Tradition.*
  F. Bassan, 207(FR):Mar84-558
Conlon, P.M. Ouvrages français relatifs à
  Jean-Jacques Rousseau, 1751-1799.*
  M. Carroll, 402(MLR):Jan83-190
  K. Kloocke, 547(RF):Band95Heft1/2-196
  J.S. Spink, 208(FS):Jan83-83
Conn, P. The Divided Mind.
  A. Trachtenberg, 441:19Feb84-12
Conn, S. The Divided Mind.
  C. Lasch, 617(TLS):25May84-574
Connell, C. They Gave Us Shakespeare.
  M. Grivelet, 189(EA):Jan-Mar84-93
Connell, E.S. Son of the Morning Star.
  P-L. Adams, 61:Oct84-126
Connell, T. and E. Van Heusden. The Span-
  ish Verb.
  T.R. Arrington, 399(MLJ):Summer83-205
Connellan, L. Shatterhouse.
  H. Carruth, 436(NewL):Summer84-111
Connelly, M.T. The Response to Prostitu-
  tion in the Progressive Era.
  P.G. Skidmore, 106:Winter83-437
Connelly, T.L. and B.L. Bellows. God and
  General Longstreet.
  639(VQR):Winter83-7
Conner, V.J. The National War Labor Board.
  639(VQR):Autumn83-118
Connerton, P. The Tragedy of Enlighten-
  ment.
  B. Agger, 488:Sep83-347
Conniff, M.L., ed. Latin American Popu-
  lism in Comparative Perspective.
  A. Ciria, 263(RIB):Vol33No1-35

Connolly, C. Cyril Connolly: Journal and
Memoir.* (D. Pryce-Jones, ed)
J. Updike, 442(NY):3Sep84-88
Connolly, C. The Selected Essays of Cyril
Connolly. (P. Quennell, ed)
H. Kramer, 441:29Feb84-3
V.S. Pritchett, 453(NYRB):15Mar84-6
J. Updike, 442(NY):3Sep84-92
Connolly, C. The Unquiet Grave.* Enemies
of Promise. The Rock Pool.
H. Kramer, 441:29Feb84-3
V.S. Pritchett, 453(NYRB):15Mar84-6
Connolly, J. Jerome K. Jerome.
C. Markgraf, 177(ELT):Vol26No3-202
Connolly, J.W. Ivan Bunin.
M. Greene, 575(SEER):Oct83-606
S. Kryzytski, 558(RLJ):Fall83-228
G.N. Slobin, 550(RusR):Jul83-343
Connolly, P., ed. Literature and the
Changing Ireland.
K.E. Marre, 395(MFS):Summer83-292
Connor, N. and others. Talitha Cumi.*
M. O'Neill, 493:Sep83-72
Connor, T. New and Selected Poems.*
W.H. Pritchard, 491:Jan84-228
639(VQR):Summer83-97
Connor, W.R. Thucydides.
R. Seager, 617(TLS):24Aug84-951
Conot, R.E. Justice At Nuremberg.*
W. Mommsen, 617(TLS):3Feb84-120
Conover, T. Rolling Nowhere.
B. Shulgasser, 441:4Mar84-23
442(NY):13Feb84-130
Conrad, G.R. and C.A. Brasseaux. A
Selected Bibliography of Scholarly Lit-
erature on Colonial Louisiana and New
France.
J.L. Pallister, 207(FR):Oct83-125
Conrad, G.W. and A.A. Demarest. Religion
and Empire.
J.H. Elliott, 453(NYRB):19Jul84-29
Conrad, J. The Collected Letters of
Joseph Conrad.* (Vol 1) (F.R. Karl
and L. Davies, eds)
M. Dodsworth, 175:Autumn83-297
P. Kemp, 362:15Mar84-24
R. O'Hanlon, 617(TLS):24Feb84-185
A. Phillips, 364:Dec83/Jan84-128
V.S. Pritchett, 442(NY):9Jan84-106
Conrad, J. Joseph Conrad.*
R.O. Evans, 569(SR):Winter83-ii
D. Hewitt, 541(RES):Aug83-365
C.J. Rawson, 402(MLR):Oct83-913
Conrad, J. Lord Jim. (J. Batchelor, ed)
The Secret Agent. (R. Tennant, ed)
Under Western Eyes. (J. Hawthorn, ed)
M. Dodsworth, 175:Autumn83-296
Conrad, J. Opere Varie. (U. Mursia, ed)
S. Monod, 189(EA):Jul-Sep84-345
Conrad, P. The Art of the City.
F.X. Clines, 441:29Apr84-16
S. Fender, 362:9Aug84-25
E. Mendelson, 617(TLS):21Sep84-1050
Conrad, P. Romantic Opera and Literary
Form.
C. Crawley, 529(QQ):Spring83-194
Conradi-Bleibtreu, E. Im Schatten des
Genius.
U. Rainer, 221(GQ):Nov83-653
Conrart, V. Lettres à Lorenzo Magalotti.
(G. Berquet and J-P. Collinet, eds)
D.C. Potts, 402(MLR):Jan83-184
P. Wolfe, 475:Vol 10No18-310

Conroy, J. The Disinherited.
D.C. Wixson, 436(NewL):Summer84-108
Conroy, J.F. A l'aventure!*
P. Silberman, 399(MLJ):Spring83-74
Conroy, P.L. and S.H. Rossel - see Ander-
sen, H.C.
Constant, B. L'affaire Regnault. (R.
Bourgeois, ed)
M. Schaettel, 356(LR):Aug83-242
Constantine, D. Early Greek Travellers
and the Hellenic Ideal.
W. St. Clair, 617(TLS):12Oct84-1148
Constantine, D. Watching for Dolphins.*
J. Mole, 176:Mar84-50
M. O'Neill, 493:Sep83-72
M.K. Spears, 598(SoR):Winter84-221
Constantine, K.C. The Man Who Liked Slow
Tomatoes.
T.J. Binyon, 617(TLS):13Jul84-790
Contamine, P. War in the Middle Ages.
R. Rogers, 617(TLS):19Oct84-1195
Contat, M. and M. Rybalka, with others -
see Sartre, J-P.
Contat, N. Anecdotes Typographiques.*
(G. Barber, ed)
N. Barker, 78(BC):Summer83-232
R. Birn, 517(PBSA):Vol77No1-78
Conte, G.B. Il genere e i suoi confini.
A.L. Johnson, 494:Vol4No2-363
"Contemporary German Philosophy." (Vol 1,
1982) (D.E. Christensen, ed)
M. Rosen, 617(TLS):27Apr84-484
de la Conterie, F. Noms de terrois vel-
laves d'après le compois de Châteauneuf-
les-Monestiers (1692).
J-P. Chambon, 553(RLiR):Jan-Jun83-248
Còntini, G. Le lettere malate di Svevo.
M. Anderson, 400(MLN):Jan83-157
Contoski, V. A Kansas Sequence.
V. Crummett, 436(NewL):Summer84-106
Contreras, H. and J. Klausenburger, eds.
Proceedings of the Tenth Anniversary Sym-
posium on Romance Linguistics.
W.J. Ashby, 350:Mar84-182
di Conversino, G. Giovanni di Conversino
da Ravenna: "Dragmalogia de Eligibili
Vite Genere." (H.L. Eaker, ed and trans)
T. Boli, 276:Summer83-175
J.H. Whitfield, 382(MAE):1983/1-170
Conway, A. The Principles of the most
Ancient and Modern Philosophy. (P.
Loptson, ed)
R.S. Woolhouse, 518:Apr83-76
Conyngham, W.J. The Modernization of
Soviet Industrial Management.
M.R. Beissinger, 550(RusR):Jul83-335
Conzemius, V. - see von Döllinger, I.
Cook, A. French Tragedy.*
F. Assaf, 475:Vol 10No18-322
J.W. Schweitzer, 345(KRQ):Vol130No4-441
J. Van Baelen, 130:Fall83-293
Cook, A.J. The Privileged Playgoers of
Shakespeare's London, 1576-1642.*
J.L. Barroll, 405(MP):May84-417
R. Berry, 529(QQ):Summer83-372
T.W. Craik, 161(DUJ):Dec82-106
J.L. Halio, 301(JEGP):Apr83-232
C. Hill, 366:Autumn83-250
P.N. Siegel, 191(ELN):Dec83-52
E.M. Waith, 702:Vol 16-335
Cook, A.S. Myth and Language.*
M.E. Workman, 292(JAF):Jan-Mar83-82

Cook, C. Dictionary of Historical Terms.
  R. Foster, 617(TLS):6Apr84-382
Cook, C. A Short History of the Liberal
  Party, 1900-84.
  J. Campbell, 617(TLS):9Nov84-1275
Cook, D. Charles de Gaulle.
  W. Lord, 441:22Jan84-11
  R.O. Paxton, 453(NYRB):26Apr84-16
  442(NY):27Feb84-134
Cook, D. Sunrising.
  D. Profumo, 617(TLS):2Mar84-216
Cook, E. and others, eds. Centre and Laby-
  rinth.
  D.S. Kastan, 617(TLS):17Feb84-163
Cook, F.D. How to Raise an Ox.
  S.F. Lombardo, 318(JAOS):Jan-Mar82-148
Cook, F.J. Maverick.
  T. Rutkowski, 441:30Sep84-29
Cook, G.M. Love from Backfields.
  R. Hatch, 102(CanL):Winter82-144
Cook, J. A Moral Response to Industrial-
  ism. (J.T. Cumbler, ed)
  R.D. Brown, 432(NEQ):Mar83-117
Cook, M., ed. Contes révolutionnaires.
  J. Lough, 83:Autumn83-262
Cook, M. Early Muslim Dogma.
  R.C. Martin, 589:Apr83-443
Cook, M. Muhammad.
  R. Blythe, 362:16Feb84-24
Cook, M.L. Monthly Murders.
  P. Wolfe, 395(MFS):Autumn83-389
Cook, O. The English Country House.
  M.F., 617(TLS):23Mar84-319
Cook, R.F. "Chanson d'Antioche," chanson
  de geste.*
  K. Busby, 547(RF):Band95Heft3-335
  T. Hunt, 402(MLR):Oct83-917
  D.D.R. Owen, 382(MAE):1983/2-322
Cook, T.H. Tabernacle.
  D. Myers, 441:4Mar84-22
Cooke, D. Vindications.*
  M. Kennedy, 410(M&L):Jan/Apr83-98
  J. Warrack, 415:Jan83-103
Cooke, T.D., ed. The Present State of
  Scholarship in Fourteenth-Century Litera-
  ture.
  N.J. Lacy, 207(FR):Dec83-241
Cookson, C. The Black Velvet Gown.
  M. Simpson, 441:8Apr84-25
Cookson, J.E. The Friends of Peace.
  M. Fitzpatrick, 83:Autumn83-240
Cooley, D., ed. Draft.*
  C. Levenson, 529(QQ):Spring83-246
  S. Morrissey, 137:Nov82-51
Cooley, J.K. Libyan Sandstorm.*
  639(VQR):Spring83-61
Cooley, J.R. Savages and Naturals.*
  J. Fetterley, 27(AL):May83-278
  C. Werner, 395(MFS):Summer83-319
Coolidge, C. Mine.
  M. Perloff, 29:May/Jun84-15
Coolidge, C. Research.
  M. Boruch, 271:Vol 13No3/4-251
Coomer, J. The Decatur Road.*
  I. Gold, 441:1Jan84-14
Cooms, H. and P., eds. John Skinner.
  G. Avery, 617(TLS):27Jul84-850
Cooney, E. All the Way Home.
  J. Grossman, 441:24Jun84-22
Cooney, J. The American Pope.
  W.V. Shannon, 441:28Oct84-11

Cooper, A.A. (Lord Shaftesbury). Complete
  Works, Selected Letters, and Posthumous
  Writings in English with Parallel German
  Translation.* (Pt 1, Vol 1) (G. Hemme-
  rich and W. Benda, eds and trans)
  A.O. Aldridge, 52:Band18Heft3-324
  J.B. Schneewind, 154:Jun83-366
  E. Vollrath, 489(PJGG):Band90Heft2-412
  R.B. Wolf, 405(MP):Feb84-311
Cooper, D. and D. A Durable Fire.* (A.
  Cooper, ed)
  M. Panter-Downes, 442(NY):17Dec84-152
Cooper, D.E. Authenticity and Learning.
  M. Tanner, 617(TLS):9Nov84-1277
Cooper, D.J. Brooks Range Passage.
  M. Lyon, 649(WAL):Nov83-258
Cooper, G. and C. Wortham - see "Everyman"
Cooper, H. Great Grandmother Goose.
  D. Gray, 382(MAE):1983/1-149
Cooper, H. The Structure of "The Canter-
  bury Tales."
  B. O'Donoghue, 617(TLS):18May84-555
  B. Windeatt, 176:Jul/Aug84-56
Cooper, H.A., ed. John Trumbull.
  A. Wilton, 90:Dec83-761
  M.S. Young, 39:Sep83-272
Cooper, H.R., Jr. Francè Prešeren.
  H. Leeming, 402(MLR):Jul83-765
Cooper, J., ed. Mackintosh Architecture.
  D. Watkin, 39:Feb83-144
Cooper, J. Opera Stitch. (Ser 1-6)
  J. Zarbaugh, 614:Summer84-25
Cooper, J. Scaffolding.
  M. O'Neill, 617(TLS):30Nov84-1393
Cooper, J.M., Jr. The Warrior and the
  Priest.*
  P. Marshall, 617(TLS):25May84-577
  R. Steel, 453(NYRB):16Feb84-30
Cooper, J.P. Land, Men and Beliefs. (G.E.
  Aylmer and J.S. Morrill, eds)
  J. Guy, 617(TLS):20Apr84-424
Cooper, P.L. Signs and Symptoms.
  B. Duyfhuizen, 27(AL):Dec83-664
  P.B. McElwain, 590:Dec83-99
  T. Schaub, 659(ConL):Summer84-260
  295(JML):Nov83-560
Cooper, R.L., ed. Language Spread.
  B.B. Kachru, 350:Dec84-961
Cooper, R.M. A Concordance to the English
  Poetry of Richard Crashaw.
  S. Hockey, 447(N&Q):Oct82-443
  P. Palmer, 677(YES):Vol 13-318
Cooper, W. Scenes From Later Life.*
  P. Craig, 617(TLS):21Sep84-1066
Cooper, W. Scenes from Married Life [and]
  Scenes from Later Life.* [one-vol ed]
  L. Graver, 441:26Aug84-12
  442(NY):3Sep84-94
Cooper, W. and E. Walker, eds. Sentence
  Processing.
  A. Houston, 355(LSoc):Jun83-281
Cooper, W.E. Speech Perception and Pro-
  duction.
  N. Harvey, 353:Vol20No7/8-561
Cooperman, S. Greco's Last Book.* (F.
  Candelaria, ed)
  F. Cogswell, 198:Jan83-129
Coote, S., ed. The Penguin Book of Homo-
  sexual Verse.*
  T. Warr, 493:Jun83-74
Coover, R. Spanking the Maid.
  D. Anderson, 381:Dec83-499

Cope, J. The Adversary Within.
  C. Hope, 364:Apr/May83-139
Cope, J.I. and G. Green, eds. Novel vs.
  Fiction.*
  H. Charney, 363(LitR):Winter84-279
  P. Lawley, 402(MLR):Jul83-660
  L. McCaffery, 659(ConL):Spring84-116
Copland, A. and V. Perlis. Copland: 1900
  through 1942.
  D. Henahan, 441:30Sep84-9
  W. Mellers, 617(TLS):2Nov84-1237
Copleston, F.C. On the History of Philos-
  ophy and Other Essays.*
  M.G. Vater, 543:Mar83-700
Corbett, G.G. Predicate Agreement in Rus-
  sian.
  W. Birkenmaier, 257(IRAL):Aug83-240
Corbin, H. Creative Imagination in the
  Ṣūfism of Ibn 'Arabī.
  S. Vahiduddin, 273(IC):Jul83-245
Corbin, H. The Man of Light in Iranian
  Sufism.
  H. Landolt, 318(JAOS):Jan-Mar82-213
Corcoran, N. The Song of Deeds.*
  A. Cazade, 189(EA):Oct-Dec84-474
  T. Stoneburner, 344:Fal184-119
Corder, S.P. Error Analysis and Interlan-
  guage.
  M.M. Azevedo, 399(MLJ):Spring83-85
  R. Sussex, 67:May83-159
Coren, A. Bumf.
  R. Boston, 617(TLS):21Dec84-1482
Coren, A., ed. Pick of Punch.
  N. Berry, 617(TLS):28Dec84-1505
Corfield, P.J. The Impact of English
  Towns, 1700-1800.
  L. Stone, 453(NYRB):29Mar84-42
  R. Wordie, 83:Spring83-101
Corippus, F.C. Corippe, "Éloge de l'emper-
  eur Justin II." (S. Antès, ed and trans)
  M. Reydellet, 555:Vol57fasc2-350
Corkett, A. Between Seasons.
  B. Whitman, 529(QQ):Autumn83-876
Cormier, R. and J.L. Pallister. Waiting
  for Death.*
  P. Murphy, 541(RES):Feb83-107
Corn, A. Notes From a Child of Paradise.
  P. Breslin, 441:22Jul84-15
Corn, W.M. Grant Wood.
  D. Bowen, 324:Jul84-554
  H. Herrera, 617(TLS):23Mar84-302
Cornea, L. Cartea străină veche în Bib-
  lioteca "Astra," sec. XVIII, catalog.
  354:Dec83-444
Cornebise, A.E. Typhus and Doughboys.
  M.B. Biskupski, 497(PolR):Vol28No4-117
Corneille, P. La Galerie du Palais ou
  l'Amie rivale.* (M.R. Margitić, ed)
  L. Picciola, 535(RHL):Sep/Dec83-919
Corneille, T. Ariadne. (O. Mandel, trans)
  R.J. Melpignano, 475:Vol 10No19-924
  J. Moravcevich, 207(FR):May84-874
Cornelisen, A. Any Four Women Could Rob
  The Bank of Italy.
  P-L. Adams, 61:Mar84-131
  H. Dudar, 441:12Feb84-22
  442(NY):26Mar84-134
Cornell, J. and A. Lightman, eds. Reveal-
  ing the Universe.
  42(AR):Fal183-507
Cornell, P. Den hemliga källan.
  Å. Fant, 341:Vol52No3-140

Cornell, T. and J. Matthews. Atlas of the
  Roman World.
  M.A.R. Colledge, 123:Vol33No2-270
Cornet, J. Art Royal Kuba.
  J. Vansina, 2(AfrA):May83-12
Cornfeld, B. and O. Edwards. Quintessence.
  442(NY):23Jan84-107
Cornman, J.W. Skepticism, Justification
  and Explanation.*
  E.E. Sleinis, 63:Mar83-117
Corns, T.N. The Development of Milton's
  Prose Style.*
  W.G. Riggs, 551(RenQ):Autumn83-479
Cornwell, B. Sharpe's Enemy.
  S. Altinel, 617(TLS):3Aug84-875
  W. Ferguson, 441:1Jul84-21
Cornwell, J. Earth to Earth.
  D. Leavitt, 441:25Nov84-15
Coronado de Caballero, G., V.M. Franco
  Pellotier and H. Muñoz Cruz. Bilingü-
  ismo y educación en el Valle del Mezqui-
  tal.
  K. Woolard, 355(LSoc):Jun83-282
Correa, A.B. and others - see under Bonet
Correa, A. and others
  "Charles Correa."
  J.M. Richards, 617(TLS):14Sep84-1029
Correa, G., ed. Antología de la poesía
  española (1900-1980).*
  A.P. Debicki, 240(HR):Winter83-113
Corri, A. The Search for Gainsborough.
  G. Reynolds, 617(TLS):21Dec84-1473
Corriente, F. Gramatica Arabe.
  A.S. Kaye, 318(JAOS):Oct-Dec82-669
Corrigan, R.W. The Making of Theatre.
  S.H. Smith, 615(TJ):Oct83-429
Corrigan, T. Coleridge, Language, and
  Criticism.*
  R. Modiano, 661(WC):Summer83-139
  K. Watson, 290(JAAC):Winter83-227
Corrington, J.W. The Southern Reporter.*
  W. Domnarski, 639(VQR):Summer83-523
  G. Garrett, 569(SR):Winter83-112
Corry, J.A. My Life and Work — A Happy
  Partnership.
  J.F. Leddy, 529(QQ):Spring83-200
Corsaro, F. Studi Rutiliani.
  J-P. Callu, 555:Vol57fasc1-172
  A-M. Palmer, 123:Vol33No1-134
Corsini, R.P. - see Loos, A.
Corsten, S. Die Kölnische Chronik von
  1499.
  L. Hellinga, 354:Jun83-180
Cortázar, J. A Certain Lucas.
  R. Coover, 441:20May84-15
  442(NY):18Jun84-113
Cortázar, J. A Change of Light and Other
  Stories.
  N. Rankin, 617(TLS):30Nov84-1392
Cortázar, J. We Love Glenda So Much and
  Other Tales.*
  G. Kearns, 249(HudR):Autumn83-558
  N. Rankin, 617(TLS):20Jan84-70
Cortazzi, H. - see Fraser, M.C.
Cortelazzo, M. I dialetti e la dialet-
  tologia in Italia (fino al 1800).*
  M. Contini, 553(RLiR):Jan-Jun83-181
Cortelazzo, M. - see Kahane, H. and R.,
  with L. Bremner
Corti, M. La Felicità mentale.
  Z.G. Barański, 617(TLS):10Feb84-146

Corwin, E.S. Corwin on the Constitution.
(R. Loss, ed)
639(VQR):Winter83-22
Cosbey, R.C. All in Together, Girls.
E. Fowke, 292(JAF):Jan-Mar83-110
Coser, L.A., C. Kadushin and W.W. Powell.
Books.*
D.L. Eder, 31(ASch):Spring83-268
Coseriu, E. Von Genebrardus bis Hervás.
K. Heitmann, 72:Band220Heft2-442
Cossé, L. Le Premier Pas d'amante.
F. de Martinoir, 450(NRF):Nov83-143
de Cossío, A.M.A. - see Arias de Cossío,
A.M.
Cosslett, T., ed. Science and Religion in
the Nineteenth Century.
M. Mason, 617(TLS):1Jun84-606
Cosslett, T. The "Scientific Movement"
and Victorian Literature.*
G. Levine, 445(NCF):Sep83-232
B.M., 148:Autumn83-91
Costa, D. Irenic Apocalypse.
S.J. Noakes, 589:Apr83-445
Costa-Zalessow, N. Scrittrici italiane
dal XIII al XX secolo.
F. Karlinger, 547(RF):Band95Heft1/2-
239
Costantini, H. The Gods, the Little Guys
and the Police.
L. Hunt, 441:29Apr84-34
442(NY):21May84-132
Costello, B. Marianne Moore.*
J.M. Reibetanz, 106:Winter83-497
Costello, D.P. Fellini's Road.
D. Lavery, 500:Winter84-85
Costich, J.F. The Poetry of Change.*
F.R. Smith, 208(FS):Jan83-106
"John Sell Cotman: 1782-1842."
A. Tennant, 59:Sep83-385
Cott, J. Conversations with Glenn Gould.
E. Hoffman, 441:4Nov84-20
Cott, J. Dylan.
J. Klemesrud, 441:18Nov84-33
J. Wolcott, 453(NYRB):22Nov84-15
Cotterell, A. The First Emperor of China.*
J. Rawson, 59:Jun83-217
Cottez, H. Dictionnaire des structures du
vocabulaire savant.*
G. Roques, 553(RLiR):Jul-Dec83-468
Cottino-Jones, M. and E.F. Tuttle, eds.
Boccaccio.
M. Marcus, 276:Summer83-165
Cotton, H. Documentary Letters of Recom-
mendation in Latin from the Roman Empire.
M. Winterbottom, 123:Vol133No2-330
Cotton, J. The Storyville Portraits.
J. Mole, 176:Jun84-60
Cottrell, A. How Safe is Nuclear Energy?
R. Wilson, 61:Aug84-104
Cottrell, R.D. Sexuality/Textuality.*
J. Brody, 131(CL):Winter83-70
M.B. McKinley, 546(RR):Jan83-105
R.L. Regosin, 210(FrF):Jan83-88
S. Rendall, 400(MLN):May83-815
Couani, A. Were all women sex mad?
E. Webby, 381:Mar83-34
Couch, A. Memoirs of a Twelfth Man.
S. Rae, 617(TLS):24Aug84-941
Coudrette. Le roman de Mélusine ou His-
toire de Lusignan. (E. Roach, ed)
G. Roques, 553(RLiR):Jan-Jun83-254
Coughlin, W.J. The Twelve Apostles.
A. Cheuse, 441:2Sep84-14

Coulloubaritsis, L. L'Avènement de la
science physique.*
J.P. Anton, 319:Jan84-116
Coulson, A. Tanzania.
J. Doherty, 69:Vol53No2-85
Coulson, J. Religion and Imagination "in
Aid of a Grammar of Assent."
W. Myers, 569(SR):Spring83-275
Coulson, J., N. Rankin and D. Thompson,
comps. The Pocket Oxford Russian Dic-
tionary.
N.J. Brown, 575(SEER):Apr83-311
G.F. Holliday, 399(MLJ):Spring83-92
F. Knowles, 402(MLR):Jul83-759
Coulthard, M. and M. Montgomery, eds.
Studies in Discourse Analysis.
C.J. Kramsch, 399(MLJ):Autumn83-298
M. Toolan, 307:Oct82-137
Countryman, E. A People in Revolution.*
M.M. Klein, 656(WMQ):Apr83-325
639(VQR):Winter83-7
Couper, A., ed. The Times Atlas of the
Oceans.
C. Vita-Finzi, 617(TLS):6Jan84-18
Couperin, F. Oeuvre complètes. (Vol 3)
(P. Brunold, with K. Gilbert and D.
Moroney, eds)
P. Prévost, 537:Vol69No2-254
Courdy, J-C. The Japanese.
D. Kondo, 441:16Sep84-13
Couric, E., ed. Women Lawyers.
D.L. Jacobs, 441:21Oct84-31
Courlander, H. The Crest and the Hide.
D.J. Cosentino, 2(AfrA):Feb83-84
Courlander, H. Hopi Voices.
T.D. Allen, 2(AfrA):May83-25
Courlander, H. and O. Sako. The Heart of
the Ngoni.
K. Drame, 2(AfrA):Feb83-86
Courter, G. River of Dreams.
R.P. Mills, 441:27May84-16
Courtney, C.P. A Bibliography of Editions
of the Writings of Benjamin Constant to
1833.*
B. Fink, 207(FR):Dec83-252
D. Gilson, 354:Jun83-193
D.K. Lowe, 208(FS):Jan83-88
D. Wood, 78(BC):Summer83-234
Courtney, E. A Commentary on the Satires
of Juvenal.*
R.A. La Fleur, 121(CJ):Feb/Mar84-257
M.D. Reeve, 123:Vol133No1-27
Courtney, W.F. Young Charles Lamb, 1775-
1802.*
J.I. Ades, 661(WC):Summer83-142
J.O. Hayden, 191(ELN):Mar84-69
Courtot, C. La voix pronominale.
A. Masson, 98:Apr83-360
Cousins, N. The Healing Heart.
B. Hepburn, 617(TLS):30Mar84-331
J. Rascoe, 441:1Jan84-10
Cousse, R. Le Bâton de la maréchale.
F.C. St. Aubyn, 207(FR):Oct83-135
Cousteau, J. and M. Richards. Jacques
Cousteau's Amazon Journey.
G. Plimpton, 441:2Dec84-14
Coustillas, P. - see Gissing, G.
Coutinho, A. Conceito de literatura
brasileira. Caminhos do pensamento
crítico.
M.O.L. McBride, 238:May83-307

Couve de Murville, M.N.L. and P. Jenkins.
Catholic Cambridge.
R. Incledon, 617(TLS):20Apr84-441
Couvreur, W. and others, eds. Studia
Germanica Gandensia XXI.
H.H. Meier, 179(ES):Feb83-89
Covell, J.C., with S. Yamada. Zen's Core.
F. Franck, 469:Vol9No3-96
Coven, B. American Women Dramatists of
the Twentieth Century.
S.B. Barnard, 87(BB):Sep83-196
Covino, M. Unfree Associations.
W. Zander, 363(LitR):Winter84-272
Cowan, B. Exiled Waters.
R.H. Brodhead, 445(NCF):Sep83-214
W.B. Dillingham, 569(SR):Fall83-lxxxvi
M.E. Grenander, 651(WHR):Summer83-174
Cowan, J.C. D.H. Lawrence. (Vol 1)
E.D., 189(EA):Jul-Sep84-366
295(JML):Nov83-520
Cowan, R.C. Hauptmann-Kommentar zum
nichtdramatischen Werk.
S. Hoefert, 221(GQ):May83-523
P. Skrine, 402(MLR):Oct83-987
Coward, D. Marguerite Duras: "Moderato
Cantabile."
L. Hill, 402(MLR):Oct83-936
H. Peyre, 207(FR):Oct83-114
Coward, H. and D.E. Larsen, eds. Ethical
Issues in the Allocation of Health Care
Resources.
D.T.O., 185:Jul84-743
Coward, H.G. Bhartṛhari.
W. Rau, 318(JAOS):Jan-Mar82-232
Coward, H.G. The Sphoṭa Theory of Lan-
guage.*
R. Rocher, 318(JAOS):Oct-Dec82-673
Coward, N. The Noël Coward Diaries. (G.
Payn and S. Morley, eds)
M. Goldstein, 569(SR):Summer83-501
A. Strachan, 157:Spring83-47
Coward, N. The Lyrics.
R. Davies, 617(TLS):13Jan84-33
Coward, N. A Withered Nosegay.
A.J.G.H., 617(TLS):20Apr84-443
Cowart, D. Thomas Pynchon.*
P. Balbert, 594:Fall83-265
S. Strehle, 599:Winter83-84
G.F. Waller, 106:Summer83-207
Cowart, D. and T.L. Wymer, eds. Twentieth
Century American Science-Fiction Writ-
ers.*
C. Elkins, 561(SFS):Mar83-101
Cowart, G. The Origins of Modern Musical
Criticism: French and Italian Music,
1600-1750.*
B. Norman, 207(FR):Dec83-283
Cowdrey, H.E.J. The Age of Abbot Desid-
erius.
G. Leff, 617(TLS):3Feb84-122
Cowie, P. Ingmar Bergman.*
A. Brownjohn, 176:Jan84-66
Cowles, V. The Great Marlborough and His
Duchess.
G.A. De Candido, 441:8Jan84-19
Cowley, M. The Dream of the Golden
Mountains.
R.F. Bogardus, 577(SHR):Winter83-88
Cowley, R.L.S. Marriage à-la-mode.
J. Riely, 90:Dec83-761
L. Stone, 453(NYRB):29Mar84-42
Cowper, R. The Tithonian Factor.
C. Greenland, 617(TLS):3Aug84-875

Cowper, W. The Letters and Prose Writ-
ings of William Cowper.* (Vol 1) (J.
King and C. Ryskamp, eds)
J.H. Pittock, 83:Autumn83-208
Cowper, W. The Letters and Prose Writ-
ings of William Cowper.* (Vol 2) (J.
King and C. Ryskamp, eds)
N. Dalrymple-Champneys, 447(N&Q):Dec82-
557
V. Newey, 506(PSt):May83-76
J.H. Pittock, 83:Autumn83-208
Cowper, W. The Letters and Prose Writings
of William Cowper.* (Vol 3) (J. King
and C. Ryskamp, eds)
W.H., 148:Autumn83-90
D.H. Reiman, 88:Summer83-26
S. Soupel, 189(EA):Jul-Sep84-332
506(PSt):Dec83-310
Cowper, W. The Letters and Prose Writings
of William Cowper. (Vol 4) (J. King and
Charles Ryskamp, eds)
P. Rogers, 617(TLS):11May84-519
Cowper, W. The Poems of William Cowper.*
(Vol 1) (J.D. Baird and C. Ryskamp, eds)
N. Dalrymple-Champneys, 447(N&Q):Feb82-
83
P. Danchin, 179(ES):Aug83-376
P. Drew, 402(MLR):Oct83-905
Cox, A. Adversary Politics and Land.
D.R. Denman, 617(TLS):10Aug84-896
Cox, A. Freedom of Expression.
F.B., 185:Oct83-160
Cox, A. and A. Rockingham Pottery and Por-
celain 1745-1842.
T. Hughes, 324:Jun84-476
T. Lockett, 617(TLS):6Jan84-23
Cox, C.B., ed. Conrad: "Heart of Dark-
ness," "Nostromo," and "Under Western
Eyes."
S. Monod, 189(EA):Oct-Dec83-486
Cox, C.B. and D.J. Palmer, eds. Shake-
speare's Wide and Universal Stage.
S. Wells, 617(TLS):30Nov84-1390
Cox, H. Religion in the Secular City.
J.M. Cameron, 453(NYRB):11Oct84-39
J.A. Coleman, 441:4Mar84-1
M. Tedeschi, 129:May84-77
442(NY):30Apr84-122
Cox, L.H., ed. William Faulkner: Biograph-
ical and Reference Guide.* William
Faulkner: Critical Collection.*
D. Fowler, 594:Winter83-385
Cox, M. Mysticism.
C. Thompson, 617(TLS):13Jan84-42
Cox, P. Biography in Late Antiquity.
H. Chadwick, 617(TLS):16Mar84-272
Cox, S.D. "The Stranger Within Thee."*
J. Sitter, 173(ECS):Winter83/84-189
Coy, H. FitzGerald as Printmaker.
C.A. Phillips, 529(QQ):Autumn83-858
Coyle, W. and W.M. Fowler, eds. The Amer-
ican Revolution.
B. Tucker, 106:Spring83-49
Crabtree, L.V. Sweet Hollow.
R. Hoffman, 441:4Mar84-22
Cracraft, J., ed. For God and Peter the
Great.
P. Bushkovitch, 550(RusR):Jan83-103
Craddock, P.B. Young Edward Gibbon.
M. Baridon, 83:Spring83-118
M. Baridon, 189(EA):Apr-Jun84-204
W.A. Speck, 366:Autumn83-272
639(VQR):Winter83-9

Craft, J.L. and R.E. Hustwit - see
Bouwsma, O.K.
Craft, R. A Stravinsky Scrapbook.
D. Hamilton, 441:5Aug84-11
Craft, R. - see Stravinsky, I.
Crafton, D. Before Mickey.
B. Tannenbaum, 127:Fall83-299
J.F. Weldon, 529(QQ):Autumn83-888
Craig, C. Yeats, Eliot, Pound and the
Politics of Poetry.*
M. Perloff, 659(ConL):Spring84-88
Craig, E.G. Craig on Theatre. (J.M. Wal-
ton, ed)
P. Holland, 617(TLS):10Feb84-149
Craig, E.G. Edward Gordon Craig: The Last
Eight Years. (E. Craig, ed)
P. Holland, 617(TLS):10Feb84-149
Craig, E.Q. Black Drama of the Federal
Theatre Era.*
L. Sanders, 106:Fall83-343
Craig, G.A. The End of Prussia.
P. Pulzer, 617(TLS):5Oct84-1115
Craig, G.A. The Germans.
P.J. Campana, 399(MLJ):Summer83-195
I. Deak, 453(NYRB):31May84-37
P. Schoonover, 221(GQ):Mar83-358
Craig, G.M. But This is Our War.*
S. Neuman, 102(CanL):Winter82-118
Craig, M. The Architecture of Ireland
from the Earliest Times to 1880.*
A.O. Crookshank, 46:May83-76
J.M. Robinson, 39:Aug83-195
Craig, S. and C. Schwarz. Down and Out.
D. Widgery, 362:31May84-23
Craig, W.L. The Cosmological Argument
from Plato to Leibniz.*
E. Stump, 543:Mar83-701
Craige, B.J. Literary Relativity.
V. Aarons, 395(MFS):Summer83-360
Craigie, J. and A. Law, eds. Minor Prose
Works of King James VI and I.
D. Fox, 617(TLS):17Aug84-924
Craik, T.W., ed. The Revels History of
Drama in English. (Vol 2)
G. Barlow, 610:Winter81/82-62
D. Mills, 541(RES):Nov83-481
Cramer, T. Die kleineren Liederdichter
des 14. und 15. Jahrhunderts. (Vol 3)
C. Petzsch, 72:Band220Heft2-379
Cramer, T., ed. Maeren-Dichtung.
F.H. Bäuml, 221(GQ):Mar83-306
Crane, E. The Archaeology of Beekeeping.
D. Galton, 617(TLS):20Jan84-69
Crane, J. Willa Cather.*
D. Stouck, 649(WAL):Nov83-240
J.L.W. West 3d, 517(PBSA):Vol77No4-501
295(JML):Nov83-449
Crane, S. The Red Badge of Courage.* (H.
Binder, ed)
R. Shulman, 26(ALR):Spring83-149
Craney, J. and E. Caldwell, eds. The
True Life Story of ...
E. Webby, 381:Mar83-34
Crankshaw, E. Putting up with the Rus-
sians 1947-1984.
G.A. Hosking, 617(TLS):27Jul84-828
Cranston, M. Jean-Jacques.*
A. Phillips, 364:Jul83-84
P. Robinson, 83:Autumn83-270
Cranston, M. Orion Resurgent.
H. Peyre, 207(FR):Dec83-256
Cranz, G. The Politics of Park Design.
J.M. Neil, 576:May83-193

Crase, D. The Revisionist.*
W.H. Pritchard, 560:Spring-Summer83-
176
R. Tillinghast, 569(SR):Summer83-473
Craton, M. Testing the Chains.*
D.B. Gaspar, 656(WMQ):Oct83-624
639(VQR):Summer83-84
Craven, W.G. Giovanni Pico della Miran-
dola "Symbol of His Age."
A. Buck, 72:Band220Heft1-229
Crawford, A. and others, eds. The Europa
Biographical Dictionary of British
Women.
V. Glendinning, 617(TLS):6Apr84-380
Crawford, A.F. and C.S. Ragsdale. Women
in Texas.
D.C. Grover, 649(WAL):Aug83-192
Crawford, F.D. Mixing Memory and Desire.
M. Magalaner, 395(MFS):Summer83-261
295(JML):Nov83-362
Crawford, M., ed. Sources for Ancient His-
tory.
R. Seager, 617(TLS):2Mar84-222
Crawford, M.H. and D. Whitehead, eds and
trans. Archaic and Classical Greece.
D.L. Stockton, 123:Vol33No2-345
Crawford, T. Walter Scott.
P. Garside, 571(ScLJ):Autumn83-15
Crawford, T. Society and the Lyric.*
A.H. MacLaine, 541(RES):Feb83-112
Crawford, W.B., ed. Reading Coleridge.
G. Little, 541(RES):Feb83-88
J.A. Michie, 447(N&Q):Jun82-244
P. Morgan, 179(ES):Aug83-366
Crawley, A. The House of War.
S. Altinel, 617(TLS):7Dec84-1420
Creal, M. The Man Who Sold Prayers.*
C. Kerr, 102(CanL):Spring83-120
Creamer, R.W. Stengel.
L.S. Ritter, 441:25Mar84-1
Crean, J.E., Jr., and others. Deutsche
Sprache und Landeskunde.
R.W. Dunbar, 399(MLJ):Spring83-76
Crean, S. and M. Rioux. Two Nations.
P. Smart, 99:Feb84-32
Creangă, I. Memories of My Boyhood [and]
Stories and Tales.
V. Nemoianu, 617(TLS):27Jan84-80
de Crébillon, P.J. Prosper Jolyot de
Crébillon: "Electre." (J. Dunkley, ed)
G. Saba, 475:Vol 10No19-898
Creed, D. Travellers in an Antique Land.
M. Simpson, 441:6May84-26
442(NY):2Apr84-132
Creel, B.L. The Religious Poetry of Jorge
de Montemayor.*
J. Crosbie, 402(MLR):Oct83-944
Creeley, R. The Collected Poems of
Robert Creeley 1945-1975.*
V. Crummett, 436(NewL):Summer84-105
J. Wilson, 271:Vol 13No3/4-233
639(VQR):Summer83-96
Creeley, R. The Collected Prose of Robert
Creeley.
M.L. Rosenthal, 441:23Sep84-34
Creeley, R. Mirrors.
A. Turner, 199:Spring84-75
Crehan, S. Blake in Context.
P. Hamilton, 617(TLS):15Jun84-674
Creider, C.A. Studies in Kalenjin Nominal
Tonology.
L.M. Hyman, 350:Sep84-674

Creighton, J.V. Joyce Carol Oates.
  G.F. Manning, 106:Summer83-225
Crémieux, F. and J. Estager. Sur le Parti
  1939-1940.
  D. Johnson, 617(TLS):9Mar84-237
Cremona, J. Buongiorno Italia!
  G. Jackson, 399(MLJ):Autumn83-296
Crépin, A., ed and trans. Poèmes héro-
  ïques vieil-anglais.
  P.R., 189(EA):Apr-Jun84-233
Cress, L.D. Citizens in Arms.
  T.P. Slaughter, 656(WMQ):Oct83-649
Crewe, J.V. Unredeemed Rhetoric.*
  K.E. Maus, 400(MLN):Dec83-1347
  639(VQR):Summer83-89
Crewe, Q. In Search of the Sahara.
  R. Whitney, 617(TLS):2Mar84-230
Crews, C.F. English Catholic Modernism.
  A. Vidler, 617(TLS):21Sep84-1052
Crichton, R. Falla.*
  R. Orledge, 410(M&L):Jan/Apr83-86
Crick, B. George Orwell.*
  S. Monod, 189(EA):Jan-Mar84-105
  A.G. Sandison, 506(PSt):Sep83-198
Crick, F. Life Itself.
  A. Crowder, 529(QQ):Spring83-265
Crick, M. Militant.
  H. Young, 617(TLS):22Jun84-685
"Criminal Law, The General Part: Liability
  and Defences." [Law Reform Commission
  of Canada]
  M.D. Bayles, 154:Sep83-553
Crist, J., with S. Sealy. Take 22.
  K. Turan, 441:16Dec84-21
Cristofolini, P. Il Cielo aperto di
  Pierre Cuppé.
  G. Menant-Artigas, 535(RHL):Jul/Aug83-
  636
Critchfield, R. Villages.
  D.H. Akenson, 529(QQ):Spring83-272
"Critique et création littéraires en
  France au XVIIe siècle."*
  R.G. Moyles, 107(CRCL):Sep83-418
Crittenden, A., ed. The Almanac of Invest-
  ments.
  K.W. Arenson, 441:21Oct84-50
Croad, S. London's Bridges.
  A. Hollinghurst, 617(TLS):6Jan84-8
Croall, J. Neill of Summerhill.*
  C.E. Finn, Jr., 441:26Feb84-33
Croce, A. Going to the Dance.
  M. Aloff, 151:Nov82-90
  J. Kavanagh, 31(ASch):Summer83-411
Croce, B. Poetry and Literature. (G.
  Gullace, ed and trans)
  L. Bolle, 356(LR):Aug83-221
  P.H. Gray, 583:Fall83-97
  C.A. Lyas, 518:Jan83-32
Crocker, L. Positive Liberty.*
  L.C. Becker, 482(PhR):Apr83-243
  D. Knowles, 393(Mind):Apr83-298
Croft, P.J. - see Sidney, R.
Croisille, J-M. Poésie et art figuré de
  Néron aux Flaviens.
  R.J. Ling, 123:Vol33No2-294
  A. Wallace-Hadrill, 313:Vol73-180
Croll, E. The Politics of Marriage in Con-
  temporary China.
  S.L. Greenblatt, 293(JASt):Nov82-127
Crone, P. Slaves on Horses.
  F.M. Donner, 318(JAOS):Apr-Jun82-367

Cronin, A. New and Selected Poems.*
  T. Eagleton, 565:Vol24No3-77
  M. Harmon, 272(IUR):Spring83-114
Cronin, A. Reductionist Poem.* 41 Sonnet-
  Poems 82. R.M.S. Titanic.
  M. Harmon, 272(IUR):Spring83-114
Cronin, K. Colonial Casualties.
  A. Markus, 381:Mar83-85
Cronin, R. Shelley's Poetic Thoughts.*
  T. Webb, 591(SIR):Winter83-639
Cronley, J. Cheap Shot.
  442(NY):3Sep84-97
Cronon, W. Changes in the Land.
  J. Demos, 441:20May84-3
Crook, D.P. Benjamin Kidd.
  S. Collini, 617(TLS):14Dec84-1435
de Croome, D.E. - see under Empaytaz de
  Croome, D.
Cros, L. Les Images retournées.
  R.J. Nelson, 207(FR):Dec83-276
Crosby, J. Men in Arms.*
  T.J. Binyon, 617(TLS):21Sep84-1064
Crosby, J.O. - see de Quevedo, F.
Crosland, M. Beyond the Lighthouse.*
  W.N., 102(CanL):Spring83-156
Cross, A. Death in a Tenured Position.
  M.A. Mikolajczak, 568(SCN):Fall83-57
Cross, A. Sweet Death, Kind Death.
  N. Callendar, 441:24Jun84-41
  442(NY):14May84-151
Crosskey, W.W. and W. Jeffrey, Jr. Poli-
  tics and the Constitution in the History
  of the United States.* (Vol 3)
  G. Anastaplo, 396(ModA):Summer/Fall83-
  365
Crossley-Holland, K. Time's Oriel.
  H. Lomas, 364:Feb84-83
  J. Mole, 176:Mar84-50
  S. Rae, 617(TLS):17Feb84-168
Crossley-Holland, P. Musical Instruments
  in Tibetan Legend and Folklore.
  D.A. Lentz, 187:Sep84-573
Crothers, E.J. Paragraph Structure Infer-
  ence.
  A. Houston, 355(LSoc):Sep83-419
Crouan, K. John Linnell.
  G. Reynolds, 39:Dec83-529
Crouch, H., Kam Hing Lee and M. Ong, eds.
  Malaysian Politics and the 1978 Election.
  R.S. Milne, 293(JASt):Feb83-452
Crouzet, M. Stendhal et le langage.*
  D.F. Bell, 400(MLN):May83-795
Crouzet, M. Stendhal et l'italianité.*
  P. Berthier, 535(RHL):Sep/Dec83-947
Crovetto, P.L., ed. Storia di una ini-
  quità.
  D.L. Shaw, 86(BHS):Jul83-265
Crow, C.M. Paul Valéry and the Poetry of
  Voice.
  U. Franklin, 207(FR):Feb84-402
  P. Gifford, 402(MLR):Jul83-720
  C.A. Hackett, 208(FS):Jan83-103
  L. Vines, 478:Apr83-125
Crozier, M. Strategies for Change.*
  J.M. Sherwood, 529(QQ):Spring83-88
Cruickshank, C. SOE in the Far East.
  M.R.D. Foot, 617(TLS):20Jan84-59
  D. Hunt, 362:12Jan84-25
Cruickshank, J. Variations on Catastrophe.
  F. Bassan, 207(FR):Feb84-424
  W.D. Redfern, 402(MLR):Oct83-931
  C. Slater, 208(FS):Oct83-490

Cruickshanks, E., ed. Ideology and Conspiracy.
  H.T. Dickinson, 566:Spring84-172
Crum, M., comp. Catalogue of the Mendelssohn Papers in the Bodleian Library, Oxford.* (Vol 1)
  M.J. Citron, 451:Summer83-85
Crummey, R.C. Aristocrats and Servitors.
  I. de Madariaga, 617(TLS):2Mar84-210
Crump, J.I. Chinese Theater in the Days of Kublai Khan.
  D.R. Johnson, 293(JASt):Feb83-380
  J.P. Seaton, 116:Jul82-297
Crump, M. and M. Harris, eds. Searching the Eighteenth Century.
  O.M. Brack, Jr., 617(TLS):14Sep84-1035
Crunden, R. Ministers of Reform.
  639(VQR):Winter83-9
van der Cruysse, D. La mort dans les "Memoires" de Saint-Simon.* [shown in prev under Van]
  J. Brody, 402(MLR):Jul83-710
  R. Favre, 535(RHL):May/Jun83-472
de la Cruz, J.I. - see under Inés de la Cruz, J.
de la Cruz, R. Sainetes. (J. Dowling, ed)
  D.C. Buck, 615(TJ):Oct83-428
de Cruz-Sáenz, M.S. - see under Schiavone de Cruz-Sáenz, M.
Cruz Santos, A. Cinco hombres en la historia de Colombia.
  J.L. Helguera, 263(RIB):Vol33No2-252
Crystal, D. A First Dictionary of Linguistics and Phonetics.*
  L.S. Evensen, 257(IRAL):Aug83-236
Crystal, D., ed. Linguistic Controversies.
  J.R. Hurford, 350:Jun84-409
Crystal, D. Who Cares About English Usage?
  R. Harris, 617(TLS):3Aug84-859
Csapodi-Gárdonyi, K. Europäische Buchmalerei.
  70:May-Jun83-163
Cua, A.S. The Unity of Knowledge and Action.
  J. Louton, 485(PE&W):Oct83-412
  R.C. Neville, 543:Mar83-703
Cubberley, P.V. The Suprasegmental Features in Slavonic Phonetic Typology.
  F.E. Knowles, 575(SEER):Apr83-260
"Cuckolds, Clerics, and Countrymen." (J. Du Val, trans)
  J-C. Seigneuret, 399(MLJ):Summer83-191
Cude, W. A Due Sense of Differences.*
  T.D. MacLulich, 168(ECW):Summer83-130
Cudjoe, S.R. Resistance and Caribbean Literature.*
  I. López Jiménez, 701(SinN):Jan-Mar83-87
Cudlip, D. Comprador.
  P. Anderson, 441:10Jun84-24
Cuénin, M. Roman et société sous Louis XIV: Mme. de Villedieu.*
  E. Berg, 188(ECr):Summer83-117
Cullen, P. and T.P. Roche, Jr. - see "Spenser Studies"
Culler, J. Barthes.*
  F. de Haan, 204(FdL):Dec83-313
  D. O'Hara, 290(JAAC):Spring84-323
Culler, J. On Deconstruction.*
  S. Haig, 207(FR):May84-891
  D. O'Hara, 290(JAAC):Spring84-323
  L. Waters, 400(MLN):Dec83-1301
  42(AR):Summer83-373

Culler, J. The Pursuit of Signs.*
  F. Baker, 208(FS):Jan83-112
  D. Boak, 67:May83-139
  P. Chilton, 307:Apr83-73
  J.W. Davidson, 477(PLL):Winter83-93
  D.H. Hirsch, 569(SR):Summer83-417
  J. Lothe, 172(Edda):1983/1-58
  T. Rajan, 529(QQ):Spring83-229
  S. Raval, 50(ArQ):Summer83-181
Cullingford, E. Yeats, Ireland and Fascism.*
  B. Tippett, 366:Spring83-127
Culver, C.M. and B. Gert. Philosophy in Medicine.*
  J. Harris, 479(PhQ):Jul83-307
Cumbler, J.T. - see Cook, J.
Cumming, R.D. Starting Point.*
  G. Shapiro, 319:Jan84-131
Cummings, A.L. The Framed Houses of Massachusetts Bay, 1625-1725.
  R. Brunskill, 44:Vol26-105
Cummins, P.W. Commercial French.*
  D.E. Rivas, 399(MLJ):Summer83-187
da Cunha, E. Los sertones.
  E. Suárez Galbán, 701(SinN):Oct-Dec82-81
Cunliffe, B. Danebury.
  D.W. Harding, 617(TLS):17Feb84-170
Cunningham, I.C. Greek Manuscripts in Scotland.
  P. Pattenden, 123:Vol33No1-155
Cunningham, J.S. - see Marlowe, C.
Cunningham, J.W. A Vanquished Hope.
  R.L. Nichols, 550(RusR):Apr83-240
Cunningham, M. The Fannie Farmer Baking Book.
  M. Burros, 441:2Dec84-14
Cunningham, M. Golden States.
  442(NY):30Apr84-118
Cunningham, M. and F. Schumer. Power Play.
  J. Cohn, 129:Oct84-76
  S. Lee, 441:27May84-7
Cunningham, V., ed. The Penguin Book of Spanish Civil War Verse.
  F. McCombie, 447(N&Q):Oct82-477
Cunningham, W. The Keyboard Music of John Bull.
  W. Mellers, 617(TLS):21Dec84-1469
Cunninghame Graham, R.B. The Scottish Sketches of R.B. Cunninghame Graham. (J. Walker, ed)
  N. Curme, 571(ScLJ):Autumn83-25
  E. Waterston, 627(UTQ):Summer83-443
Cuomo, M.M. Diaries of Mario M. Cuomo.
  M. Kempton, 453(NYRB):19Jul84-3
  W. Kennedy, 441:13May84-13
Curat, H. La locution verbale en français moderne.
  T.J. Cox, 207(FR):May84-919
Ćurčić, S. Gračanica.*
  D. Buckton, 39:Feb83-153
di Curcio, R.A. Art on Nantucket.
  J. Simpson, 55:Feb83-27
"Curial and Guelfa."* (P. Waley, trans)
  J.E. Keller, 86(BHS):Oct83-348
Curl, J.S. The Life and Work of Henry Roberts 1803-1876: Architect.*
  D. Linstrum, 324:May84-412
Curran, J. and V. Porter, eds. British Cinema History.
  A. Brownjohn, 176:Jan84-68

Daiches, D. God and the Poets.
  J. Eidus, 441:26Aug84-17
  C.H. Sisson, 617(TLS):21Dec84-1468
Daiches, D. Literature and Gentility in
  Scotland.
  D. Hewitt, 571(ScLJ):Winter83-36
Daiches, D. and J. Flower. Literary Land-
  scapes of the British Isles.
  E. Newman, 441:3Jun84-12
Dailey, J. Silver Wings, Santiago Blue.
  M. Berkley, 441:26Aug84-16
Daitz, S. The Pronunciation of Ancient
  Greek.
  D.H. Roberts, 124:Nov-Dec83-134
Daix, P. Cubists and Cubism.
  N. Miller, 42(AR):Winter83-115
Daix, P. La vie du peintre d'Edouard
  Manet.
  E. Darragon, 98:May83-432
Dal, E., with P. Skårup. The Ages of Man
  and the Months of the Year.
  J. Beck, 545(RPh):Nov82-337
Dalai Lama. Kindness, Clarity, and
  Insight. (J. Hopkins and E. Napper, ed)
  D.S. Lopez, Jr., 469:Vol9No4-101
Dalaï-Lama. Méditation sur l'esprit.
  A. Reix, 542:Jan-Mar83-58
Dalal, N.A. - see Jayavanta-Sūri
Dalby, L.C. Geisha.
  J. Burnham, 617(TLS):14Dec84-1455
  D. Richie, 441:5Feb84-8
Dalby, R. Bram Stoker.
  T.D. Smith, 617(TLS):27Jul84-856
Dale, P. Too Much of Water.
  L. Mackinnon, 617(TLS):27Jul84-838
Dale, S.F. Islamic Society on the South
  Asian Frontier.
  S.B. Freitag, 293(JASt):Feb83-432
van Dalen, D. - see Brouwer, L.E.J.
D'Alfonso, A. Black Tongue.
  J. Bell, 526:Autumn83-90
Dallaire, M. Regards sans l'eau.
  J. Viswanathan, 102(CanL):Autumn83-108
Dallapiccola, A.L., with S.Z-A. Lallemant,
  eds. The Stūpa.*
  E. Bender, 318(JAOS):Jul-Sep82-583
Dalla Valle, D. and A. Carriat - see
  Guérin de Bouscal, D.
Dallek, R. Ronald Reagan.
  N. Fountain, 362:5Jul84-25
  R.G. Kaiser, 453(NYRB):28Jun84-38
  M. Kondracke, 441:4Mar84-12
  R. Sherrill, 61:Mar84-127
  D.H. Wrong, 617(TLS):19Oct84-1175
Dallinger, N. Unforgettable Hollywood.
  M. Buckley, 200:Jun/Jul83-380
d'Allonnes, O.R. Musical Variations on
  Jewish Thought.
  E. Rothstein, 129:Dec84-74
Dalmonte, R. and others. Il gesto della
  forma.*
  M. Eckert, 308:Spring83-140
Dalton, D. and R. Cayen. James Dean.
  S. Gold, 441:4Nov84-13
Daly, M. Pure Lust.
  D. Wehr, 441:22Jul84-14
Daly, P.M. Literature in the Light of the
  Emblem.*
  P. Horden, 38:Band101Heft1/2-245
  D. Sulzer, 52:Band18Heft2-202
Daly, R.R. and P. Stiff. Selous Scouts.
  R. West, 617(TLS):16Mar84-269

d'Amboise, C. Leap Year.*
  R. Philp, 151:Feb83-78
Damiani, B.M. "La Diana" of Montemayor as
  Social and Religious Teaching. Monte-
  mayor's "Diana," Music, and the Visual
  Arts.
  D.H. Darst, 304(JHP):Fall83-75
Damiani, B.M. - see López de Ubeda, F.
d'Amico, F. - see Baldini, G.
Damisch, H. Fenêtre jaune cadmium.
  S. Bann, 617(TLS):14Dec84-1452
Damrosch, L., Jr. Symbol and Truth in
  Blake's Myth.*
  T.R. Frosch, 661(WC):Summer83-152
  N. Hilton, 173(ECS):Fall83-64
  E. Larrissy, 59:Dec83-478
  A. Lincoln, 541(RES):Aug83-345
Damsteegt, T. Epigraphical Hybrid San-
  skrit.*
  H.S. Ananthanarayana, 261:Mar-Dec81-
  138
Danchin, P. The Prologues and Epilogues
  of the Restoration 1660-1700.* (Pt 1)
  J. Jacquot, 610:Summer83-162
  J. Milhous, 611(TN):Vol37No2-89
  A.H. Scouten, 189(EA):Oct-Dec83-468
Dancy, J., ed. Papers on Language and
  Logic.
  M. Bell, 393(Mind):Jan83-140
Danek, J., ed. Vérité et Ethos.
  P. Bellemare, 154:Sep83-561
Danelski, D.J. Rights, Liberties, and
  Ideals.
  M.M. Kampelman, 390:Nov83-59
Daneš, F. and D. Viehweger, eds. Linguis-
  tica I.
  P. Paul, 361:Oct/Nov83-267
Daneš, F. and D. Viehweger. Satzseman-
  tische Komponenten und Relationen im
  Text.
  W. Koch, 596(SL):Vol137No1-101
Danesi, M., ed. Issues in Language.
  L. Pérez, 320(CJL):Fall83-192
Danforth, L.M. The Death Rituals of Rural
  Greece.*
  D.J. Constantelos, 124:Sep-Oct83-53
D'Angelo, E. and others. Contemporary
  East European Marxism. (Vol 2)
  G.W.P., 185:Jan84-371
Daniel, A. - see under Arnaut Daniel
Daniel, C. Lords, Ladies and Gentlemen.
  L. Heren, 441:1Jul84-19
Daniel, H. Double Agent.
  K. Gelder, 71(ALS):May83-139
Daniel, N. The Laughing Man.
  P. Smelt, 617(TLS):22Jun84-706
Daniel, N. Heroes and Saracens.
  D.D.R. Owen, 617(TLS):18May84-555
Daniell, D. - see Buchan, J.
Daniell, J.R. Colonial New Hampshire.
  J.A. Schutz, 656(WMQ):Jan83-139
Danielson, D.R. Milton's Good God.*
  C. Hill, 366:Autumn83-267
  R. Lejosne, 189(EA):Jul-Sep84-323
  B. Sherry, 67:Nov83-308
  639(VQR):Winter83-14
Danielson, H., ed and trans. Ādideśa:
  The Essence of Supreme Truth (Paramārtha-
  sāra).*
  V.A. van Bijlert, 485(PE&W):Jan83-99
Danielsson, B. and A. Gabrielson - see
  Gill, A.

Danly, R.L. In the Shade of Spring
Leaves.*
  S. Goldstein, 395(MFS):Summer83-379
  J.A. Walker, 293(JASt):Nov82-160
Danon, S. and S.N. Rosenberg - see "Ami
and Amile"
Dansereau, L-M. Chez Paul-Ette, bière,
vin, liqueur et nouveautés.
  R. Usmiani, 102(CanL):Winter82-157
Dansereau, L-M. Ma Maudite Main gauche
veut pus suivre.
  R. Usmiani, 102(CanL):Autumn83-82
Danson, L., ed. On "King Lear."
  J.Z. Kronenfeld, 539:Nov83-297
  G. Taylor, 570(SQ):Autumn83-367
Dante Alighieri. Dante's "Purgatory."*
(M. Musa, ed and trans)
  T.G. Bergin, 569(SR):Spring83-261
  V. Moleta, 382(MAE):1983/2-333
  M.U. Sowell, 589:Apr83-448
Dante Alighieri. Dante's Rime. (P.S.
Diehl, trans) Dante, "The Divine
Comedy."* (C.H. Sisson, trans)
  T.G. Bergin, 569(SR):Spring83-261
Dante Alighieri. Inferno.* (A. Mandel-
baum, trans)
  M.D. Lammon, 436(NewL):Fall83-111
Dante Alighieri. Paradiso. (A. Mandel-
baum, ed and trans)
  D.S. Carne-Ross, 453(NYRB):20Dec84-9
Dante Alighieri. Purgatorio.* (A. Mandel-
baum, trans)
  T.G. Bergin, 569(SR):Spring83-261
  A.R.C. Duncan, 529(QQ):Winter83-1218
Danto, A.C. The Transfiguration of the
Commonplace.*
  W. Quinn, 482(PhR):Jul83-481
Daoudi, M.S. and M.S. Dajani. Economic
Sanctions.
  P. Oppenheimer, 617(TLS):27Jan84-79
Daoust, Y. Roger Planchon.*
  B.L. Knapp, 615(TJ):Oct82-412
  N. Lane, 207(FR):Dec83-259
  F.H. Londré, 130:Fall83-287
Daphinoff, D. - see Echlin, E.
Darby, E. and N. Smith. The Cult of the
Prince Consort.*
  D. Cannadine, 453(NYRB):8Nov84-22
  T. Russell-Cobb, 324:Feb84-212
Darby, M. and others. The Victoria and
Albert Museum.
  R.L. Shep, 614:Winter84-23
Darby, T. The Feast.*
  H.S. Harris, 627(UTQ):Summer83-563
Dardano Basso, I. L'ancora e gli specchi.
  R.G. Zardini Lana, 475:Vol 10No18-328
d'Ardenne, S.R.T.O. and E.J. Dobson, eds.
Seinte Katerine.
  B. Cottle, 301(JEGP):Apr83-222
  A.S.G. Edwards, 589:Jan83-161
Dardigna, A-M. Les châteaux d'Éros ou
l'infortune du sexe des femmes.
  193(ELit):Dec83-474
Dardigna, A-M. La Presse "féminine."
  C-M. Gagnon, 193(ELit):Dec83-471
Dardis, T. Harold Lloyd.*
  R. Goff, 453(NYRB):1Mar84-23
  L. Silvian, 200:Nov83-574
de Dargies, G. - see under Gautier de
Dargies
Darling, M.E., ed. A.J.M. Smith.
  T. Goldie, 102(CanL):Spring83-153
  B. Whiteman, 168(ECW):Winter83/84-81

Darlington, B. - see Wordsworth, W. and M.
Darmon, P. Mythologie de la femme dans
l'Ancienne France.
  J. Aeply, 450(NRF):Jul/Aug83-237
Darms, G. Schwäher und Schwager, Hahn und
Huhn.
  A. Greule, 260(IF):Band87-342
D'Arms, J.H. Commerce and Social Standing
in Ancient Rome.
  J. Briscoe, 123:Vol33No1-79
Darnton, R. The Great Cat Massacre.
  P-L. Adams, 61:Feb84-104
  M. Gallant, 441:12Feb84-12
Darnton, R. The Literary Underground of
the Old Regime.
  J. McLelland, 400(MLN):Dec83-1365
Darracott, J. The World of Charles
Ricketts.
  M. Henderson, 611(TN):Vol137No1-37
Darragh, T. on the corner to off the
corner.
  M. Perloff, 29:May/Jun84-15
Darras, J. Conrad and the West.*
  J.J. Conlon, 177(ELT):Vol26No2-149
  R.O. Evans, 569(SR):Spring83-291
  D.L. Higdon, 395(MFS):Winter83-766
  295(JML):Nov83-453
Darton, F.J.H. Children's Books in En-
gland.* (3rd ed rev by B. Alderson)
  L.G.E. Bell, 503:Spring83-47
  P. Pénigault-Duhet, 189(EA):Oct-Dec84-
  447
Daruwalla, K.N., ed. Two Decades of
Indian Poetry, 1960-1980.*
  S.N. Vikram Raj Urs, 49:Oct83-88
Darwin, E. The Letters of Erasmus Darwin.*
(D. King-Hele, ed)
  P. Rogers, 83:Spring83-80
Das, J.P. Puri Paintings — The Chitrakâra
and His Work.
  E. Fischer, 57:Vol44No2/3-236
Dash, I.G. Wooing, Wedding, and Power.
  R.K. Bank, 615(TJ):Mar83-129
  M.G. Free, 702:Vol 16-340
  I. Leimberg, 156(JDSh):Jahrbuch
  1983-242
  C. Lewis, 639(VQR):Winter83-155
  M.B. Rose, 405(MP):Feb84-308
Dash, J.M. Literature and Ideology in
Haïti, 1915-1961.
  L-F. Hoffmann, 535(RHL):Mar/Apr83-315
  C. Zimra, 207(FR):Dec83-240
Da Silva, Z.S. On with Spanish. (3rd ed)
  C.M. Cherry, 399(MLJ):Summer83-210
Daspre, A. - see du Gard, R.M.
Dathorne, O.R. Dark Ancestor.*
  R. Hemenway, 395(MFS):Winter83-746
d'Aubigné, A. Histoire universelle. (Vol
1) (A. Thierry, ed)
  R. Zuber, 535(RHL):Jan/Feb83-119
Dauge, Y-A. Le Barbare.
  P. Jal, 555:Vol57fasc2-354
Daumal, R. René Daumal / ou / le retour à
soi /.*
  M. Picard, 535(RHL):Sep/Dec83-963
Daunton, M.J. House and Home in the Vic-
torian City.
  D. Bowen, 324:Oct84-744
  P.J. Waller, 617(TLS):20Jan84-67
Dauster, F. and L.F. Lyday, eds. En un
acto. (2nd ed)
  J.E. Bixler, 352(LATR):Fall83-93

Dautel, K. Zur Theorie des literarischen Erbes in der "entwickelten sozialistischen Gesellschaft" der DDR.
   P. Hutchinson, 402(MLR):Jan83-248
Davenport, M. and others, eds. Current Topics in English Historical Linguistics.
   S.M. Embleton, 350:Sep84-662
Davenport, W.A. Fifteenth-Century English Drama.
   M. Twycross, 175:Autumn83-251
Davey, F. The Arches. (B.P. Nichol, ed)
   G. Boire, 102(CanL):Summer83-166
Davey, F. Capitalistic Affection!
   P. Stuewe, 529(QQ):Winter83-1034
Davey, F. Louis Dudek and Raymond Souster.*
   T. Goldie, 168(ECW):Winter83/84-86
   T. Marshall, 178:Mar83-122
Daviau, D-M. Histoires Entre Quatres Murs.
   M. Greenstein, 102(CanL):Autumn83-92
Daviault, A., ed and trans. "Comoedia Togata," Fragments.*
   W.S. Anderson, 124:Sep-Oct83-51
   H. Zehnacker, 555:Vol57fasc1-156
David, C. - see Kafka, F.
David, D. Fictions of Resolution in Three Victorian Novels.*
   E. Hollahan, 594:Summer83-147
   R. Mason, 447(N&Q):Aug82-367
David, E. An Omelette and a Glass of Wine.
   J. Grigson, 617(TLS):21Dec84-1486
David, J. and R. Lecker, eds. Canadian Poetry.
   W.J. Keith, 105:Spring/Summer83-77
David, L. and I. The Shirley Temple Story.
   C. Brown, 617(TLS):28Dec84-1507
David, M. La psicoanalisi nella cultura italiana.
   J. Nobécourt, 98:Aug-Sep83-623
Davidson, A.A. Early American Modernist Painting, 1910-1935.*
   M.S. Young, 39:Aug83-196
Davidson, A.E. Mordecai Richler.
   A. Mitcham, 268(IFR):Summer84-133
Davidson, A.E. and C.N., eds. The Art of Margaret Atwood.*
   M. Taylor, 105:Spring/Summer83-91
Davidson, C., ed. The Drama of the Middle Ages.
   C. Gauvin, 189(EA):Oct-Dec84-458
Davidson, C., ed. Minority Vote Dilution.
   W. Kaminer, 441:14Oct84-27
Davidson, D. Inquiries into Truth and Interpretation.
   I. Hacking, 453(NYRB):20Dec84-54
Davidson, E. Henrik Ibsen og Det Kongelige Teater.
   J. Northam, 562(Scan):Nov83-223
Davidson, F.P., with J.S. Cox. Macro.
   H. Goodman, 441:19Feb84-23
Davidson, H. Hot Tongue, Cold Shoulder.
   T.B. Vincent, 198:Jan83-133
Davidson, H.E. - see "Saxo Grammaticus: History of the Danes"
Davidson, H.M. and P.H. Dubé. A Concordance to Pascal's "Les Provinciales."
   J.H. Broome, 208(FS):Apr83-214
Davidson, H.R.E. and W.M.S. Russell, eds. The Folklore of Ghosts.
   C.L. Edwards, 292(JAF):Jul-Sep83-357
Davidson, J. Sideways from the Page.
   M. Duwell, 71(ALS):Oct83-284

Davidson, S. Friends of the Opposite Sex.
   J. Mellors, 362:5Apr84-28
   F. Schumer, 441:22Jan84-22
   442(NY):23Apr84-129
Davie, D. Collected Poems 1970-1983.
   T. Weiss, 441:7Oct84-15
Davie, D. Collected Poems 1971-1983.*
   H. Haughton, 617(TLS):16Mar84-271
   D. O'Driscoll, 493:Sep84-66
Davie, D., ed. The New Oxford Book of Christian Verse.
   J. Blondel, 189(EA):Jan-Mar83-67
Davie, D. These the Companions.*
   P. Robinson, 175:Spring83-88
   A. Shapiro, 569(SR):Fall83-lxviii
Davie, D. Three for Water Music.
   E. Grosholz, 249(HudR):Autumn83-583
Davies, A. An Annotated Critical Bibliography of Modernism.*
   295(JML):Nov83-357
Davies, A. Where did the Forties go?
   D. Smith, 362:21Jun84-24
Davies, B. An Introduction to the Philosophy of Religion.
   P. Helm, 518:Jul83-172
Davies, C. Latin Writers of the Renaissance.*
   L.V.R., 563(SCN):Fall83-63
   J. Rowland, 112:Vol 15-177
Davies, D.H. The Welsh Nationalist Party 1925-1945.
   M. Hurst, 617(TLS):2Mar84-225
Davies, G. Welsh Rugby Scrapbook.
   N. Kinnock, 617(TLS):2Mar84-224
Davies, H. William Wordsworth.
   K. Zaretzke, 396(ModA):Summer/Fall83-370
Davies, J. - see Esenin, S.
Davies, J.G. Temples, Churches and Mosques.
   A. Whittick, 89(BJA):Autumn83-368
Davies, J.I. Growing Up Among Sailors.
   S. Mills, 617(TLS):2Mar84-213
Davies, M. Meaning, Quantification, Necessity.
   J. Campbell, 479(PhQ):Jan83-107
   J. Heal, 393(Mind):Oct83-615
   E.P. Martin, 63:Dec83-459
Davies, N. God's Playground.* (Vol 1)
   M. Hughes, 83:Autumn83-231
Davies, N. Heart of Europe.
   Z. Nagorski, 441:23Dec84-5
Davies, P. E. Tegla Davies.
   K.O. Morgan, 617(TLS):2Mar84-223
Davies, P. Superforce.
   D.N. Schramm, 441:23Dec84-12
Davies, P. and B. Neve, eds. Cinema, Politics and Society in America.
   D. Culbert, 488:Sep83-397
Davies, R. The Rebel Angels.*
   D. Brydon, 102(CanL):Summer83-115
   L.T. Lemon, 502(PrS):Summer83-101
Davies, R.A., ed. On Thomas Chandler Haliburton.
   A. Mitchell, 102(CanL):Autumn83-73
Davies, R.C. and J.H. Denton, eds. The English Parliament in the Middle Ages.
   S.D. White, 589:Jul83-803
Davies, R.R. and others, eds. Welsh Society and Nationhood.
   P.R. Roberts, 617(TLS):10Aug84-899
Davies, S. Emily Brontë.*
   V. Tiger, 441:19Feb84-11

Davies, S. Images of Kingship in "Paradise Lost."
L. Mackinnon, 617(TLS):20Apr84-438
Davies, W.D. and L. Finkelstein, eds. The Cambridge History of Judaism. (Vol 1)
F. Millar, 617(TLS):16Nov84-1299
Davis, B. and D. Arnof. How to Fix What's Wrong with Our Schools.
C.E. Finn, Jr., 441:26Feb84-33
Davis, B.H. and R.K. O'Cain, eds. First Person Singular.*
R. Darnell, 355(LSoc):Sep83-377
Davis, C.T. Dante's Italy.
G. Holmes, 617(TLS):17Aug84-914
Davis, C.T. and M. Fabre. Richard Wright.
R.A. Day, 189(EA):Jul-Sep84-358
Davis, D. Wisdom and Wilderness.*
M. Dodsworth, 175:Summer83-191
Davis, D.B. Slavery and Human Progress.
E.D. Genovese, 61:Dec84-141
442(NY):10Dec84-192
Davis, D.S. Lullaby of Murder.
N. Callendar, 441:13May84-35
Davis, J. Machine Knitting to Suit Your Mood.
V.R. Edwards, 614:Fall84-20
Davis, J. - see Byron, H.J.
Davis, J.B. La Quête de Paul Gadenne.*
J. Roach, 208(FS):Jul83-359
Davis, J.C. Utopia and the Ideal Society.*
J. Stephens, 568(SCN):Spring/Summer83-1
Davis, J.E. The Spanish of Argentina and Uruguay.
G. Dmitrowich, 263(RIB):Vol33No2-255
E.A. Ebbinghaus, 215(GL):Spring83-62
Davis, J.H. The Kennedys.
R. Nalley, 441:15Jul84-19
Davis, J.H. and M.J. Evans. Theatre, Children and Youth.
A. Cornish, 157:Summer83-31
J.R. Wills, 615(TJ):May83-270
Davis, J.H., Jr. Fénelon.
F. Assaf, 475:Vol 10No19-890
Davis, K.C. Two-Bit Culture.
A. Barnet, 441:1Jul84-21
Davis, L. Story and Other Stories.
M. Perloff, 29:May/Jun84-15
Davis, L.J. Factual Fictions.
W.J. Burling, 454:Spring84-282
R. Moss, 617(TLS):13Jan84-44
Davis, L.M. English Dialectology.
R. King, 350:Dec84-990
Davis, L.N. The Corporate Alchemists.
P.V. Danckwerts, 617(TLS):7Sep84-985
Davis, M.E. Voces del Purgatorio.
M. Peña, 292(JAF):Jul-Sep83-342
Davis, N., ed. Non-Cycle Plays and the Winchester Dialogues.*
G.C. Britton, 447(N&Q):Jun82-241
Davis, N.Z. The Return of Martin Guerre.*
E. Benson, 207(FR):Apr84-753
D. Parker, 617(TLS):15Jun84-670
Davis, P. Hometown.*
D.W. Hoover, 42(AR):Spring83-246
Davis, P. Memory and Writing.
L. Mackinnon, 617(TLS):3Aug84-862
Davis, P.J. and R. Hersh. The Mathematical Experience.
D. Pedoe, 529(QQ):Summer83-449
42(AR):Winter83-123
Davis, R. The English Rothschilds.*
S. Schama, 453(NYRB):20Dec84-59

Davis, R.C., ed. The Fictional Father.*
M. Cusin, 189(EA):Apr-Sep83-320
Davis, R.C., ed. Twentieth Century Interpretations of "The Grapes of Wrath."
R. Astro, 649(WAL):Feb84-346
Davis, R.J. Samuel Beckett.
A.R. Jones, 208(FS):Apr83-247
Davis, R.M. A Catalogue of the Evelyn Waugh Collection at the Humanities Research Center, the University of Texas at Austin.*
A. Rosenheim, 447(N&Q):Oct82-470
Davis, R.M. Evelyn Waugh, Writer.*
K. Cushman, 301(JEGP):Apr83-267
B. Stovel, 49:Jul83-60
Davis, T.M. Faulkner's "Negro."*
295(JML):Nov83-470
639(VQR):Summer83-88
Davis, T.M. and V.L., with B.L. Parks - see Taylor, E.
Davis, W.A. The Act of Interpretation.
J. Phelan, 153:Summer83-39
Davis, W.C., ed. The Image of War, 1861-1865.* (Vol 1)
R. Reed, 529(QQ):Summer83-585
Davis, W.C., ed. The Image of War, 1861-1865. (Vol 6)
442(NY):10ct84-136
Davis-Friedmann, D. Long Lives.
D. Davin, 617(TLS):14Sep84-1013
Davison, P. Barn Fever and Other Poems.*
W. Harmon, 569(SR):Summer83-457
Davison, P. Contemporary Drama and the Popular Dramatic Tradition in England.
L. Senelick, 612(ThS):May/Nov83-151
Davison, P. Popular Appeal in English Drama to 1850.
A.B. Cowan, 615(TJ):May83-272
Davydov, S. "Teksty-Matreški" Vladimira Nabokova.
J.H. Katsell, 574(SEEJ):Winter83-494
Dawe, G., ed. The Younger Irish Poets.
T. Eagleton, 565:Vol124No2-66
Dawe, R.D., ed. Sophocles: "Oedipus Rex."
W.M. Calder 3d, 121(CJ):Apr/May84-367
J. O'Brien, 124:Mar-Apr84-253
Dawe, R.D. and J. Diggle - see Page, D.L.
Dawes, F.V. Inheritance.
T. Fitton, 617(TLS):27Jul84-847
Dawidowicz, L.S. On Equal Terms.
B. Levine, 287:Nov83-25
Dawkins, R. The Extended Phenotype.
D. Papineau, 617(TLS):20Jul84-799
Dawson, P.G., C.B. Drover and D.W. Parkes. Early English Clocks.
G. Wills, 39:Oct83-353
Dawson, P.M.S. The Unacknowledged Legislator.*
E.D. Mackerness, 447(N&Q):Apr82-182
C. Woodring, 125:Spring83-296
Day, A.G. Modern Australian Prose, 1901-1975.*
A. Lawson, 402(MLR):Jul83-692
Day, D. The Scarlet Coat Serial.
R. Potter, 137:Sep83-37
P.M. St. Pierre, 102(CanL):Spring83-124
Day, F. Sir William Empson.
J. Culler, 617(TLS):23Nov84-1327
Day, G.M. The Identity of the Saint Francis Indians.
W. Cowan, 269(IJAL):Oct83-444

De George, R.T., ed. Semiotic Themes.
P.W. Jones, 478:Apr83-139
De George, R.T. and J.A. Pichler, eds.
Ethics, Free Enterprise, and Public
Policy.
L.J. Jost, 543:Dec82-445
Degering, K. Defoes Gesellschaftskonzeption.*
D. Mehl, 72:Band219Heft2-477
Degering, T. Das Verhältnis von Individuum und Gesellschaft in Fontanes "Effi
Brest" und Flauberts "Madame Bovary."
F. Wolfzettel, 224(GRM):Band33Heft1-117
Dégh, L., ed. Indiana Folklore.*
J.H. Brunvand, 292(JAF):Jan-Mar83-76
Degrada, F. Il palazzo incantato.
C. Timms, 410(M&L):Jul/Oct83-257
Degrada, F., ed. Vivaldi veneziano
europeo.*
C. Timms, 410(M&L):Jul/Oct83-255
De Grand, A. Italian Fascism.
639(VQR):Spring83-55
De Grazia, E. and R.K. Newman. Banned
Films.
J. Nangle, 200:Mar83-186
Deguise, A. Trois femmes.*
K. Kloocke, 547(RF):Band95Heft4-494
P.H. Meyer, 173(ECS):Winter83/84-193
Deguy, M. La Machine matrimoniale ou
Marivaux.
M. Bishop, 207(FR):May84-877
De Hart, S. The Meininger Theatre 1776-
1926.
E. Braun, 610:Summer83-169
R.K. Sarlós, 615(TJ):Mar83-139
Dehousse, F. and M. Pauchen - see Defrance,
L.
Deichmann, F.W., ed. Corpus der Kapitelle
der Kirche von San Marco zu Venedig.
L.A. Ling, 313:Vol73-225
Deicke, W. and others. Materialien für
die Sekundarstufe. (Vol 2)
A.K.D. Lorenzen, 489(PJGG):Band90Heft2-
431
Deighton, L. Berlin Game.*
M. Laski, 362:12Jan84-26
D. Quammen, 441:8Jan84-24
442(NY):6Feb84-129
Deighton, L. Mexico Set.
T.J. Binyon, 617(TLS):14Dec84-1457
De Jean, J. Libertine Strategies, Freedom
and the Novel in Seventeenth-Century
France.
A. Gabriel, 475:Vol 10No18-313
G. Verdier, 207(FR):Dec83-246
Dekker, G. Coleridge and the Literature
of Sensibility.*
L. Tyler, 591(SIR):Winter83-648
Dekker, G., ed. Donald Davie and the
Responsibilities of Literature.
H. Haughton, 617(TLS):16Mar84-271
De Koven, M. A Different Language.
295(JML):Nov83-572
Delacorta. Nana. Diva.
M. Laski, 362:19Jul84-27
Delacroix, E. La Liberté sur les barricades.
J. Revol, 450(NRF):Apr83-147
Delage, R. Chabrier.
J-M. Nectoux, 537:Vol69No2-238
R. Nichols, 415:Jul83-428

Delahaye, M. On the Third Day. (British
title: The Third Day.)
T.J. Binyon, 617(TLS):26Oct84-1225
D.G. Myers, 441:12Aug84-20
Delalande, M-R. De Profundis Grand Motet
for Soloists, Chorus, Woodwinds, Strings,
and Continuo. (J.R. Anthony, ed)
G. Dixon, 161(DUJ):Dec82-123
Delamaide, D. Debt Shock.
A. Crittenden, 441:8Jul84-6
G. Szamuely, 617(TLS):30Nov84-1371
Delamater, J. Dance in the Hollywood Musical.*
M. Keller, 127:Fall83-284
Delaney, F. and J. Lewinski. James
Joyce's Odyssey.*
295(JML):Nov83-509
De-la-Noy, M. Elgar.*
R. Anderson, 415:Nov83-682
De-la-Noy, M. Denton Welch.
R. Blythe, 362:6Dec84-30
A. Hollinghurst, 617(TLS):21Dec84-1479
De-la-Noy, M. - see Welch, D.
Delany, S. Writing Woman.
B.F. Williamson, 441:17Jun84-21
Delarue, C. Le Dragon dans la glace.
F. de Martinoir, 450(NRF):Dec83-103
Delas, D. Poétique/Pratique.
G. Cesbron, 356(LR):Nov83-343
Delatte, C. Lucy Audubon.
639(VQR):Autumn83-124
Delattre, P. Studies in Comparative
Phonetics. (B. Malmberg, ed)
M.C. Jacobs, 399(MLJ):Spring83-86
Delay, F. Riche et légère.
D. Boreham, 617(TLS):3Feb84-117
A. Clerval, 450(NRF):Oct83-124
Delay, J. Avant-Mémoire.
M. Mohrt, 450(NRF):Jan83-109
E. Roussel, 98:May83-428
Delbanco, N. About My Table.*
W.H. Pritchard, 249(HudR):Winter83/84-
751
Delbanco, N. Group Portrait.
T.C. Moser, 569(SR):Spring83-282
E. Nettels, 284:Fall83-70
R. Stevens, 177(ELT):Vol26No4-319
295(JML):Nov83-363
Delblanc, S. Speranza.*
A. Hollinghurst, 617(TLS):17Feb84-159
Delclos, J-C. Le Témoignage de Georges
Chastellain, historiographe de Philippe
le Bon et de Charles le Téméraire.*
M.J. Freeman, 208(FS):Apr83-202
K. Heitmann, 72:Band219Heft2-461
Delcorno-Branca, D. L'Orlando furioso e
il romanzo cavalleresco medievale.
A.R. Ascoli, 276:Autumn83-278
Delcourt, M. Héphaïstos ou la légende du
magicien.
A. Reix, 542:Oct-Dec83-456
Delcourt, M. - see More, T.
Delcroix, M. and W. Geerts, eds. "Les
Chats" de Baudelaire.
M. Evans, 208(FS):Apr83-232
J.P. Plottel, 546(RR):Jan83-91
De León, A. They Called Them Greasers.
L. Milazzo, 584(SWR):Autumn83-viii
Deleule, D. - see Berkeley, G.
Deleuze, G. and F. Guattari. Anti-Oedipus.
B.A. Farrell, 176:Nov84-58

92

van Delft, L. Le moraliste classique.
E.D. James, 208(FS):Oct83-455
J. von Stackelberg, 475:Vol 10No19-893
Delgatty, E. - see Ringwood, G.
D'Elia, P.B. and others - see under Belli
D'Elia, P. and others
Delière, J. and R. Lafayette. Connaître
la France.
A.G. Suozzo, Jr., 207(FR):Mar84-570
De Lillo, D. The Names.*
42(AR):Winter83-117
Delius, F. Delius: A Life in Letters.
(Vol 1) (L. Carley, ed)
L. Foreman, 617(TLS):16Mar84-281
Dell, H.J., ed. Ancient Macedonian
Studies in Honor of Charles F. Edson.
A.R. Burn, 303(JoHS):Vol 103-208
Dellheim, C. The Face of the Past.*
639(VQR):Autumn83-120
Del Litto, V. - see Stendhal
Dello Buono, C.J., ed. Rare Early Essays
on Walt Whitman.
W. White, 646:Sep83-40
Del Mar, N. Anatomy of the Orchestra.*
A. de Almeida, 537:Vol69No1-99
J.B., 412:Aug-Nov82-267
Del Mar, N. Orchestral Variations.*
J.B., 412:Aug-Nov82-267
Deloche, J., ed. Les Mémoires de Wendel
sur les Jāṭ. les Paṭhān et les Sikh.
C.S.J. White, 318(JAOS):Apr-Jun82-417
Deloffre, F. - see de Voltaire, F.M.A.
De Long, T.A. Pops.
I. Gitler, 441:29Jul84-17
Delord, J. Roland Barthes et la photo-
graphie.
F. de Mèredieu, 450(NRF):Apr83-155
Delpar, H. Red against Blue.
J. Fisher, 86(BHS):Jan83-93
J.L. Helguera, 263(RIB):Vol33No1-36
Delteil, J. La Belle Aude.
J. Laurans, 450(NRF):Apr83-119
De Luca, V.A. Thomas De Quincey.*
T. Rajan, 178:Mar83-105
Delumeau, J. Le Péché et la peur.
J. Bossy, 617(TLS):24Feb84-180
Dem, T. Masseni.
639(VQR):Winter83-18
Demac, D.A. Keeping America Uninformed.
A. Barnet, 441:30Dec84-17
De Mallie, R.J. - see Black Elk
De Mallie, R.J. and E.A. Jahner - see
Walker, J.R.
Demand, N.H. Thebes in the Fifth Century.
K.V. Hartigan, 124:Sep-Oct83-60
Demandt, A. Metaphern für Geschichte.
W. Harms, 52:Band17Heft2-200
Demaray, J.G. Milton's Theatrical Epic.*
G. Campbell, 402(MLR):Jul83-679
De Martino, F. Omero agonista in Delo.
C. Segal, 124:Nov-Dec84-196
Demerson, G. - see Dorat, J.
Demerson, G. and C. Lauvergnat-Gagnière -
see Rabelais, F.
Demesse, L. Changements techno-écono-
miques et sociaux chez les Pygmées
Babinga.
N. Kazadi, 69:Vol53No1-92
Demesse, L. Techniques et économie des
Pygmées Babinga.
N. Kazadi, 69:Vol53No1-92

D'Emilio, J. Sexual Politics, Sexual Com-
munities.*
J. Hughes, 176:Nov84-55
De Mille, N. The Talbot Odyssey.
T. Rutkowski, 441:17Jun84-20
Demos, J.P. Entertaining Satan.*
E. Current-Garcia, 577(SHR):Fall83-369
P.F. Gura, 639(VQR):Autumn83-725
C. Hansen, 656(WMQ):Jul83-466
T. Laidlaw and R. Krut, 99:Oct83-33
Demosthenes. Rede für Ktesiphon über den
Kranz. (W. Zürcher, ed and trans)
G.O. Rowe, 124:Jul-Aug84-377
De Mott, B. Dogon Masks.
P.J. Imperato, 2(AfrA):Feb83-13
De Mouy, J.K. Katherine Anne Porter's
Women.
J. Givner, 27(AL):Dec83-660
D. Kramer, 573(SSF):Fall83-337
W.J. Stuckey, 395(MFS):Winter83-722
J. Wiesenfarth, 659(ConL):Fall84-363
295(JML):Nov83-554
Dempsey, H.A. Red Crow, Warrior Chief.
R. Maud, 106:Spring83-71
Dempster, B. Fables for Isolated Men.*
J. Bell, 526:Autumn83-90
Dempster, W.J. Patrick Matthew and
Natural Selection.
W. George, 617(TLS):9Mar84-254
Demus, O., with R.M. Kloss and K. Weitz-
mann. The Mosaics of San Marco in
Venice.
J.J. Norwich, 441:2Dec84-20
Denbigh, K.G. Three Concepts of Time.
J. Largeault, 542:Jul-Sep83-354
d'Encausse, H.C. - see under Carrère d'En-
causse, H.
Dendle, B.J. Galdós: The Mature Thought.*
G. Gullón, 240(HR):Winter83-108
F.D. López-Herrera, 552(REH):May83-318
E. Rodgers, 86(BHS):Jul83-259
Denecke, L., ed. Brüder Grimm Gedanken.
(Vol 3)
E. Moser-Rath, 196:Band24Heft1/2-137
De Neef, A.L. Spenser and the Motives of
Metaphor.*
H.M., 604:Fall83-58
A.L. Prescott, 539:Nov83-302
639(VQR):Summer83-89
Denhardt, B., ed. The Quarter Horse.
L. Milazzo, 584(SWR):Summer83-vi
Denison, C.B. and H.B. Mules. European
Drawings, 1375-1825, in the Pierpont
Morgan Library.
M. Kemp, 59:Mar83-107
D. Thistlewood, 89(BJA):Spring83-178
Denk, R. "Musica getutscht."
L. Jessel, 301(JEGP):Jul83-412
Denkler, H., ed. Romane und Erzählungen
des bürgerlichen Realismus.*
S. Mews, 400(MLN):Apr83-509
Denkler, H. and others - see Glassbrenner,
A.
Dennerline, J. The Chia-ting Loyalists.
K-C. Liu, 293(JASt):Nov82-130
Dennett, D.C. Brainstorms.*
P. Engel, 98:May83-384
Lord Denning. The Closing Chapter.
D. Pannick, 362:12Jan84-24
Lord Denning. The Due Process of Law.
A. Shenfield, 396(ModA):Spring83-191
Lord Denning. Landmarks in the Law.
D. Pannick, 617(TLS):9Nov84-1279

Dennis, A., P. Foote and R. Perkins - see "Laws of Early Iceland: Grágás I"
Dennis, G.T. - see Maurikios
Dennis, R. English Industrial Cities of the Nineteenth Century.
  P.J. Waller, 617(TLS):9Nov84-1292
Dennison, S. Scandalize My Name.
  M. Fabre, 189(EA):Apr-Jun84-229
  N.E. Tawa, 498:Vol19No2-91
Den Ouden, B., ed. A Symposium on Ethics.
  R.M.M., 185:Apr84-546
Dens, J-P. L'Honnête Homme et la critique du goût.*
  M. Moriarty, 208(FS):Apr83-216
  B. Norman, 210(FrF):May83-184
  C. Rosso, 547(RF):Band95Heft1/2-189
  Z. Youssef, 535(RHL):Sep/Dec83-931
Dent, P. From the Flow.
  T. Dooley, 617(TLS):28Sep84-1105
Dent, R.W. Shakespeare's Proverbial Language.
  H. Heuer, 156(JDSh):Jahrbuch1983-258
  J. Schiffer, 405(MP):Aug83-68
Dentinger, J. First Hit of the Season.
  N. Callendar, 441:22Jul84-32
Denton, J.H. Robert Winchelsey and the Crown, 1294-1313.
  G.L. Harriss, 382(MAE):1983/1-185
  J.R. Wright, 589:Jan83-163
Denton, R.E., Jr. The Symbolic Dimensions of the American Presidency.
  H.L. Ewbank, 583:Spring84-334
Denvir, B. Art Treasures of Italy.
  F. Russell, 39:Feb83-147
Denvir, B., ed. A Documentary History of Taste in Britain: The Eighteenth Century.
  J.P. Hodin, 324:Jun84-479
Denyer, N. Time, Action and Necessity.*
  R.A. Girle, 518:Jan83-47
  L. Humberstone, 393(Mind):Jul83-461
Denz, J. Die Mundart von Windisch-Eschenbach.
  K.L. Rein, 685(ZDL):2/1983-254
Déon, M. Where are you dying tonight?
  D. Coward, 617(TLS):6Jan84-19
  J. Mellors, 364:Oct83-97
Depierris, J-L. Bas-Empire.
  A.O. Sullivan, 207(FR):Dec83-267
Deppermann, M. Andrej Belyjs ästhetische Theorie des schöpferischen Bewusstseins.
  A. Steinberg, 575(SEER):Jul83-429
Dermody, S., J. Docker and D. Modjeska, eds. Nellie Melba, Ginger Meggs and Friends.
  B.C. Ross, 71(ALS):May83-126
Derricotte, T. Natural Birth.
  J.F. Cotter, 249(HudR):Winter83/84-716
Derrida, J. Dissemination.* (B. Johnson, ed and trans) Positions.* (A. Bass, ed and trans)
  W.G. Regier, 502(PrS):Fall83-92
Desai, A. In Custody.
  D. May, 362:18Oct84-31
  J. Motion, 617(TLS):19Oct84-1178
Desai, S.N. Hinduism in Thai Life.
  A.T. Kirsch, 293(JASt):Aug83-1013
De Salvo, L. and M.A. Leaska - see Sackville-West, V.
De Salvo, L.A. Virginia Woolf's First Voyage.*
  R. Miles, 677(YES):Vol 13-346
Desanti, J-T. Un destin philosophique.
  P. Trotignon, 542:Jul-Sep83-375

Desbonnets, T. and others - see Francis of Assisi
Descartes, R. Gespräch mit Burman. (H.W. Arndt, ed and trans)
  J. Ecole, 192(EP):Jul-Sep83-366
Descharnes, R. Dali.
  J. Russell, 441:2Dec84-11
Deschaux, R., ed. Les Oeuvres de Pierre Chastellain et de Vaillant, poètes du XVe siècle.*
  K. Heitmann, 72:Band220Heft1-210
Deschoux, M. Comprendre Platon.*
  M. Narcy, 192(EP):Jul-Sep83-367
  R.W., 555:Vol57fasc2-305
Deschoux, M. Platon ou le jeu philosophique.*
  J. Laborderie, 555:Vol57fasc1-127
Descotes, M. Histoire de la critique dramatique en France.
  F. Bassan, 446(NCFS):Fall-Winter83/84-264
  A. Blanc, 535(RHL):Jan/Feb83-133
"The Desert Fathers." (H. Waddell, trans)
  D. Park, 135:Jul83-103
Deshpande, M.M. Sociolinguistic Attitudes in India.
  F.C. Southworth, 355(LSoc):Jun83-283
"Design in America: The Cranbrook Vision 1925-1950."
  R.L. Shep, 614:Summer84-15
Desika Char, S.V. Readings in the Constitutional History of India 1757-1947.
  H. Tinker, 617(TLS):24Aug84-934
Desmond, A. Archetypes and Ancestors.
  M. Peters, 441:12Aug84-21
Desmond, R. The India Museum 1801-1879.
  G. Eyre, 39:Oct83-353
Desnoes, E., ed. Los dispositivos en la flor, Cuba.*
  E. Alba, 238:Sep83-442
Des Périers, B. Nouvelles Récréations et joyeux Devis: I-XC.* (K. Kasprzyk, ed)
  D.G. Coleman, 208(FS):Jan83-71
Dessain, C.S. John Henry Newman. (3rd ed)
  W. Myers, 569(SR):Spring83-275
Dessaix, R. and M. Ulman - see Svirski, G.
Dessen, A. - see "Renaissance Drama XII"
Dessen, A.C. Elizabethan Stage Conventions and Modern Interpreters.
  S. Wells, 617(TLS):30Nov84-1390
D'Este, C. Decision in Normandy.
  D. Middleton, 441:22Jan84-10
Destler, I.M., L.H. Gelb and A. Lake. Our Own Worst Enemy.
  K.N. Waltz, 441:9Sep84-7
Destler, I.M. and Hideo Sato, eds. Coping with US-Japanese Economic Conflicts.
  Ōkita Saburō, 285(JapQ):Jan-Mar83-79
Desvignes, L. - see Mareschal, A.
De Sylva, G. John Ruskin's "Modern Painters" I and II.
  P. Fontaney, 189(EA):Apr-Jun84-210
Detel, W. Scientia rerum natura occultarum.
  M. Cariou, 542:Oct-Dec83-465
Detering, K., J. Schmidt-Radefeldt and W. Sucharowski, eds. Sprache beschreiben und erklären. Sprache erkennen und verstehen.
  B.J. Koekkoek, 221(GQ):May83-490
  T.F. Shannon, 350:Dec84-983

Dethier, V.G. The Ecology of a Summer
House.
  R.B. Swain, 441:3Jun84-14
Detienne, M. Dionysos mis à mort.*
  L. Scubla, 98:Oct83-796
Detienne, M. L'invention de la myth-
ologie.*
  R.G.A. Buxton, 303(JoHS):Vol 103-193
Detienne, M. and J-P. Vernant. La Cuisine
du sacrifice en pays grec.
  L. Scubla, 98:Oct83-796
Detmold, M.J. The Unity of Law and Moral-
ity.
  T. Baldwin, 176:Nov84-65
Detournay, B. and others. Fouilles exécu-
tées à Mallia. (Vol 2)
  S. Hood, 303(JoHS):Vol 103-216
Detsch, R. Georg Trakl's Poetry.
  M. Hofmann, 617(TLS):27Apr84-449
Detsicas, A. The Cantiaci.
  J. Wacher, 617(TLS):6Jul84-751
Deuchar, M. British Sign Language.
  R. Harris, 617(TLS):20Jul84-807
Deuchar, S. Noble Exercise.
  J.E., 90:Apr83-237
Deudon, E.H. Nietzsche en France.
  C.H. Moore, 107(CRCL):Sep83-447
Deudon, E.H. - see Seignolle, C.
Deussen, P. Sixty Upaniṣads of the Veda.
  J.W. de Jong, 259(IIJ):Mar83-136
Deutsch, E. Personhood, Creativity and
Freedom.
  A.L. Herman, 485(PE&W):Jul83-301
  A. Paskow, 518:Jul83-183
Deutsch, W., ed. The Child's Construction
of Language.
  R.M. Golinkoff and K. Hirsh-Pasek,
355(LSoc):Dec83-548
"Deutsch-polnische Literaturbeziehungen
des XIX. und XX. Jahrhunderts."
  D. Arendt, 52:Band17Heft2-217
Deutscher, M. Subjecting and Objecting.
  R. Lindley, 617(TLS):9Mar84-258
Deutscher, T. - see Carr, E.H.
"Deutsches Literaturarchiv — Schiller-
Nationalmuseum — Die Institute der
Deutschen Schillergesellschaft in
Marbach am Neckar."
  F. Stock, 52:Band18Heft2-222
"Deutsches Literatur-Lexikon." (Vol 8)
(3rd ed) (H. Rupp and C.L. Lang, eds)
  P.M. Mitchell, 301(JEGP):Jul83-405
Devarrieux, C. Les Acteurs au travail.
  J. Van Baelen, 207(FR):May84-901
Devas, N. Two Flamboyant Fathers.
  617(TLS):28Dec84-1511
Devaulx, N. Le Vase de Gurgan.
  F. de Martinoir, 450(NRF):Sep83-133
De Vecchi, P.L. Raffaello, La Pittura.
  M. Bury, 90:Jan83-62
De Vitis, A.A. and A.E. Kalson. J.B.
Priestley.*
  B. Gasser, 447(N&Q):Jun82-269
  L. Löb, 677(YES):Vol 13-349
  T. Paterson, 610:Winter81/82-66
Devitt, M. Designation.
  G. Currie, 63:Jun83-202
  G. McCulloch, 393(Mind):Oct83-622
  D.E. Over, 518:Jan83-51
Devlin, A.J. Eudora Welty's Chronicle.*
  G. Core, 598(SoR):Autumn84-951
  T.D. Young, 392:Fall83-592

Devlin, D.D. Wordsworth and the Poetry of
Epitaphs.*
  J.D. Gutteridge, 447(N&Q):Aug82-361
The Duchess of Devonshire. The House.
  V. Powell, 39:May83-415
Lord Devonshire - see Cavendish, W.
De Voogd, P.J. Henry Fielding and William
Hogarth.*
  S.C. Behrendt, 173(ECS):Spring84-342
  P-G. Boucé, 189(EA):Jan-Mar83-78
  I. Grundy, 447(N&Q):Oct82-449
  R. Paulson, 402(MLR):Jan83-146
De Vos, A. and M. Pompei, Ercolano,
Stabia.
  R. Ling, 313:Vol73-248
Devos, M. and H. Ryckeboer. Woordenboek
van de Vlaamse Dialekten. (Pt 1, fasc 1)
  H. Heestermans, 204(FdL):Sep82-229
De Voto, M. - see Piston, W.
Dew, R.F. The Time of Her Life.
  C. Seebohm, 441:7Oct84-14
  442(NY):5Nov84-170
Dewdney, A.K. The Planiverse.
  G. Strawson, 617(TLS):15Jun84-658
De Windt, A.R. and E.B., eds and trans.
Royal Justice and the Medieval English
Countryside.
  R.C. Palmer, 589:Jul83-745
De Woskin, K.J. A Song for One or Two.
  J. Chaves, 116:Jul82-252
Dexter, C. The Riddle of the Third Mile.
  N. Callendar, 441:20May84-39
Dexter, P. God's Pocket.
  J. Lester, 441:19Feb84-22
Dexter, T. and D. Lemmon. A Walk to the
Wicket.
  A.L. Le Quesne, 617(TLS):21Dec84-1487
Dez, J. Structures de la langue malgache.
  B. Schmidt, 682(ZPSK):Band36Heft2-235
Dezső, L. Studies In Syntactic Typology
and Contrastive Grammar.
  G. Corbett, 353:Vol20No11/12-763
  E.A. Moravcsik, 350:Sep84-653
Dezső, L. Typological Studies in Old
Serbo-Croatian Syntax.
  H. Birnbaum, 350:Mar84-194
Dhanens, E. Hubert and Jan van Eyck.*
  J. Giltay, 600:Vol 13No1-54
D'Hollander, P. Colette, ses apprentis-
sages.
  A.C. Ritchie, 546(RR):Jan83-114
D'Hondt, J. Hegel et l'hégélianisme.
  A. Reix, 542:Jan-Mar83-135
d'Hulst, R-A. Jacob Jordaens.*
  C. Brown, 324:Jul84-550
  U. Hoff, 39:Feb83-144
Diamond, E. and S. Bates. The Spot.
  A. Clymer, 441:26Aug84-17
  P. Whitehead, 617(TLS):9Nov84-1275
Diamond, M. The Ziggy Effect.
  A. Ravel, 102(CanL):Winter82-140
Díaz, H.B. - see under Bejarano Díaz, H.
Díaz Tejera, A. - see Polybius
Di Battista, M. Virginia Woolf's Major
Novels.*
  A. McLaurin, 447(N&Q):Apr82-189
  R. Miles, 677(YES):Vol 13-346
Dibbelt, U. Vom Mysterium der Gnade zur
Korruption durch Macht.
  A. Schlösser, 654(WB):4/1983-749
Dibbets, G.R.W. - see Kók, A.L.

Dick, K. The Shelf.
   A. Duchêne, 617(TLS):24Feb84-184
   442(NY):31Dec84-71
Dick, M. Der junge Heinse in seiner Zeit.
   E. Chevallier, 549(RLC):Apr-Jun83-231
Dick, S. - see Woolf, V.
Dick, S.J. Plurality of Worlds.
   L.W. Beck, 319:Jul84-365
Dickens, C. Un Alberto di Natale.*
   K.J. Fielding, 155:Spring83-45
   S. Monod, 189(EA):Jan-Mar83-91
Dickens, C. David Copperfield.* (N.
   Burgis, ed)
   S. Gill, 541(RES):Aug83-352
   S. Manning, 445(NCF):Jun83-101
   A. Sadrin, 189(EA):Jan-Mar83-98
Dickens, C. Charles Dickens' Book of
   Memoranda.* (F. Kaplan, ed)
   R.L. Caserio, 445(NCF):Dec83-337
   S. Monod, 189(EA):Jan-Mar83-101
Dickens, C. The Letters of Charles Dick-
   ens.* (Vol 5) (G. Storey and K.J. Field-
   ing, eds)
   A. Sadrin, 189(EA):Jan-Mar83-97
   A. Shelston, 366:Spring83-123
Dickens, C. Little Dorrit.* (H.P. Suck-
   smith, ed) The Mystery of Edwin Drood.
   (M. Cardwell, ed)
   M. Reynolds, 155:Summer83-110
Dickens, C. Martin Chuzzlewit. (M. Card-
   well, ed)
   A. Sadrin, 189(EA):Oct-Dec84-469
Dickens, C. Il mistero di Edwin Drood.
   (S. Manferlotti, ed)
   J. McRae, 155:Autumn83-170
Dickens, C. Nicholas Nickleby. [facsim-
   ile]
   T.C. Holyoke, 42(AR):Spring83-247
Dickens, P. SAS: The Jungle Frontier.*
   R. O'Hanlon, 617(TLS):13Jul84-792
"Dickens Studies Annual." (Vol 8) (M.
   Timko, F. Kaplan and E. Guiliano, eds)
   E. Hollahan, 594:Summer83-147
   S. Monod, 189(EA):Jan-Mar83-92
"Dickens Studies Annual."* (Vol 9) (M.
   Timko, F. Kaplan and E. Guiliano, eds)
   E. Hollahan, 594:Summer83-147
   S. Monod, 189(EA):Jan-Mar83-92
   H. Reinhold, 155:Spring83-48
"Dickens Studies Annual."* (Vol 10) (M.
   Timko, F. Kaplan and F. Guiliano, eds)
   S. Monod, 189(EA):Jul-Sep84-340
Dicker, C. Perceptual Knowledge.*
   D. McQueen, 518:Jan83-58
   J.W. Roxbee Cox, 393(Mind):Apr83-279
Dickey, J. The Central Motion.
   L.D. Rubin, Jr., 441:3Jun84-23
Dickey, J. Night Hurdling.*
   L.D. Rubin, Jr., 441:3Jun84-23
Dickey, J. Puella.
   P. Balakian, 363(LitR):Fall83-135
   639(VQR):Winter83-25
Dickey, W. The Sacrifice Consenting.*
   M. Boruch, 271:Vol 13No3/4-251
Dickie, A. Group Farming in North-West
   Nigeria.
   M. Tiffen, 69:Vol53No1-101
Dickinson, A. and M.L. Todd. Austin and
   Mabel. (P. Longsworth, ed)
   P-L. Adams, 61:Apr84-149
   H. Beaver, 617(TLS):26Oct84-1204
   D. Johnson, 441:4Mar84-3

Dickinson, E. The Manuscript Books of
   Emily Dickinson.* (R.W. Franklin, ed)
   S. Juhasz, 191(ELN):Dec83-57
   D. Porter, 517(PBSA):Vol77No1-84
Dickinson, H.T. - see Spence, T.
Dickinson, P. The Last Houseparty.*
   G.W. Oldham, 42(AR):Winter83-115
Dickson, D. The New Politics of Science.
   P.M. Boffey, 441:7Oct84-27
Dickson, K.A. Theology in Africa.
   S. Barrington-Ward, 617(TLS):30Nov84-
   1394
Dickson, M. Octavia's Hill.
   42(AR):Fall83-509
Dickson, M.B. and S.C. Welch - see "The
   Houghton 'Shahnameh'"
"Dictionary of Business Biography." (Vol
   1) (D.J. Jeremy, ed)
   D.G.C.A., 324:Nov84-814
   S. Checkland, 617(TLS):6Apr84-380
"Dictionary of Business Biography."
   (Vol 2) (D.J. Jeremy, ed)
   S. Checkland, 617(TLS):26Oct84-1209
"Dictionary of Canadian Biography/Diction-
   naire Biographique du Canada." (Vol 11)
   (F.G. Halpenny and J. Hamelin, eds)
   529(QQ):Spring83-281
"Dictionary of Literary Biography." (Vol
   12) (D. Pizer and E.N. Harbert, eds)
   P.D. Morrow, 649(WAL):Nov83-273
"Dictionnaire International des Termes
   Littéraires." (fasc 1 and 2) (R.
   Escarpit, ed)
   E. Caramaschi, 549(RLC):Apr-Jun83-216
Diderot, D. Diderot: "Le Neveu de Rameau."
   (J. and A-M. Chouillet, eds)
   D. Fletcher, 83:Autumn83-227
   P. France, 208(FS):Jul83-343
Diderot, D. Oeuvres romanesques. (H.
   Bénac, ed; rev by L. Perol)
   J. Whatley, 207(FR):Mar84-556
"Diderot Studies XX."* (O. Fellows and
   D.G. Carr, eds)
   J.A. Perkins, 173(ECS):Spring84-391
Didi-Huberman, G. Invention de l'hystérie.
   F. de Mèredieu, 450(NRF):Jan83-149
Didier, B. Stendhal autobiographe.
   P-L. Rey, 450(NRF):Oct83-137
Didion, J. Democracy.
   P-L. Adams, 61:May84-122
   T.R. Edwards, 453(NYRB):10May84-23
   J. Epstein, 129:Jun84-62
   C. Hitchens, 617(TLS):14Sep84-1018
   M. McCarthy, 441:22Apr84-1
   K.C. O'Brien, 362:29Nov84-25
Didsbury, P. The Butchers of Hull.*
   T. Eagleton, 565:Vol124No2-66
Diebold, J. Making the Future Work.
   R. Lekachman, 441:21Oct84-39
Dieckmann, F. Theaterbilder.
   H-J. Irmer, 654(WB):8/1982-184
Diederichsen, D. and B. Rudin, eds. Less-
   ing im Spiegel der Theaterkritik, 1945-
   1979.
   F.A. Brown, 301(JEGP):Jan83-109
Diefendorf, J.M. Business and Politics in
   the Rhineland, 1789-1834.
   D.H. Barry, 161(DUJ):Jun83-122
Diego, G. Poemas mayores.
   P.H. Dust, 552(REH):Oct83-437
Diego, G. Poemas menores.
   R. Muñoz, 552(REH):Jan83-159

Diehl, C. Americans and German Scholarship, 1770-1870.
J.W. Halporn, 121(CJ):Dec83/Jan84-171
Diehl, J.F. Dickinson and the Romantic Imagination.*
L.Y. Gossett, 569(SR):Summer83-445
S.K. Harris, 301(JEGP):Jan83-143
M. Homans, 591(SIR):Fall83-445
Diehl, R.A. Tula.
C. Tickell, 617(TLS):27Jul84-852
Diehl, W. Hooligans.
N. Callendar, 441:19Aug84-20
Dienes, L., comp. Bibliographie des oeuvres de Gaïto Gazdanov. (T.A. Ossorguine, ed)
D.M. Fiene, 574(SEEJ):Spring83-119
Dienes, L. Russian Literature in Exile.
W. Kasack, 688(ZSP):Band43Heft2-434
G.S. Smith, 575(SEER):Oct83-609
Dienhart, J.W. A Cognitive Approach to the Ethics of Counseling Psychology.
D.T.O., 185:Jul84-747
Dietrich, M. Marlene Dietrich's ABC. (rev) Marlene D.
P. O'Connor, 617(TLS):28Dec84-1507
Dietrich, W. Bibliografia da Língua Portuguesa do Brasil.
D. Woll, 72:Band220Heft1-201
Dietz, L. Franz Kafka: Die Veröffentlichungen zu seinen Lebzeiten (1908-1924).
G. Guntermann, 52:Band18Heft3-306
Dietze, R. Ralph Ellison.
M. Fabre, 189(EA):Jan-Mar84-113
Dietze, W. Kleine Welt, grosse Welt.
H. Hartmann, 654(WB):10/1982-187
Dietze, W. and P. Goldammer - see "Impulse"
Díez Borque, J.M., ed. Historia de la literatura española. (Vol 3)
P. Deacon, 86(BHS):Jan83-71
Díez Borque, J.M., ed. Historia de las literaturas hispánicas no castellanas.*
A. Porqueras-Mayo, 240(HR):Winter83-120
Di Gaetani, J.L., ed. Penetrating Wagner's Ring.
I.P., 412:Feb82-65
Digard, F. and others. Répertoire analytique des cylindres orientaux publiés dans des sources bibliographiques éparses (sur ordinateur).
E. Porada, 318(JAOS):Jul-Sep82-501
Digby, G.W., with W. Hefford - see under Wingfield Digby, G., with W. Hefford
Diggory, T. Yeats and American Poetry.*
T.F. Merrill, 305(JIL):Sep83-86
Dihle, A. The Theory of Will in Classical Antiquity.
P.F., 185:Jan84-375
J.M. Rist, 487:Autumn83-275
van Dijk, T.A. Studies in the Pragmatics of Discourse.
J. Verschueren, 350:Mar84-172
van Dijk, T.A. Textwissenschaft.
S. Stojanova-Jovčeva, 260(IF):Band88-298
Dik, S.C. Studies in Functional Grammar.
R. Goodwin, 353:Vol20No9/10-662
D.H., 355(LSoc):Mar83-137
R. Hudson, 596(SL):Vol137No1-89
Dike, C. Cane Curiosa.
A. North, 617(TLS):20Jul84-820
Dil, A.S. - see Frake, C.O.
Dil, A.S. - see Grimshaw, A.D.

Dil, A.S. - see McDavid, R.I., Jr.
Dil, A.S. - see McQuown, N.A.
Diletskii, N. Idea Grammatiki Musikiiskoi. (V.V. Protopopov, ed and trans)
C.R. Jensen, 317:Fall83-526
Dilks, D. Neville Chamberlain. (Vol 1)
P. Clarke, 617(TLS):21Dec84-1463
Dillard, A. Encounters With Chinese Writers.
P-L. Adams, 61:Oct84-126
A. Barnet, 441:23Sep84-29
Dillard, A. Living by Fiction.
K. Cushman, 573(SSF):Winter83-65
Dillard, A. Pilgrim at Tinker Creek.
M.L. Reimer, 145(Crit):Vol24No3-182
Dillard, J.L., ed. Perspectives on American English.*
D. Wepman, 660(Word):Apr83-48
Diller, H-J. Metrik und Verslehre.*
W. Bernhart, 224(GRM):Band33Heft1-120
D. Mehl, 72:Band219Heft2-476
Diller, K.C., ed. Individual Differences and Universals in Language Learning Aptitude.*
S.M. Embleton, 320(CJL):Fall83-185
P. Hagiwara, 207(FR):Apr84-725
Dillon, E. Citizen Burke.
S. Altinel, 617(TLS):7Dec84-1420
Dillon, G. Constructing Texts.* Language Processing and the Reading of Literature.
A.C. Purves, 128(CE):Feb83-129
Dillon, J. Shakespeare and the Solitary Man.*
R. Berry, 301(JEGP):Jan83-127
Dilman, I. Freud and the Mind.
B.A. Farrell, 176:Nov84-60
K. Lennon, 617(TLS):21Sep84-1060
Dilman, I. Morality and the Inner Life.*
C.C.W. Taylor, 393(Mind):Jan83-124
Dilnot, A.W., J.A. Kay and C.N. Morris. The Reform of Social Security.
T.C. Cooper, 617(TLS):50Oct84-1123
Dilthey, W. Gesammelte Schriften. (Vol 19) (H. Johach and F. Rodi, eds)
J. Owensby, 319:Jan84-128
Dilworth, C. Scientific Progress.
R. Phillips, 63:Jun83-213
Dima, N. Bessarabia and Bukovina.
D. Deletant, 617(TLS):13Jul84-777
Di Maio, I.S. The Multiple Perspective.
H. Helmers, 133:Band16Heft2/3-258
Di Michele, M. Mimosa and Other Poems.
C. Hlus, 137:Sep83-18
Dimler, G.R. - see Spee, F.
Dimnik, M. Mikhail, Prince of Chernigov and Grand Prince of Kiev, 1223-1246.*
W.K. Hanak, 589:Apr83-450
D. Ostrowski, 575(SEER):Apr83-279
Dimond, P. Music Made Simple.
P. Standford, 415:Jun83-359
Dinh, T.V. Blue Dragon White Tiger.
J. Lester, 441:5Feb84-18
Dini, M. Renzo Piano.
D.J.R. Bruckner, 441:15Jul84-18
Dinkin, R.J. Voting in Revolutionary America.
R.A. Becker, 656(WMQ):Jul83-486
Dinter, A. Der Pygmalion-Stoff in der europäischen Literatur.
F. Wagner, 196:Band24Heft1/2-139

Dinzelbacher, P. Vision und Visionslitera-
tur im Mittelalter.*
  W. Blank, 684(ZDA):Band112Heft1-27
  G.J. Lewis, 564:May83-151
Di Orio, A. Barbara Stanwyck.
  W. Murray, 441:11Mar84-16
de Dìos Vial, J. Tres ideas de la filoso-
fía y una teoría.
  A. Reix, 542:Oct-Dec83-494
Di Piero, W.S. The First Hour.
  E. Grosholz, 249(HudR):Autumn83-591
  W. Prunty, 598(SoR):Autumn84-958
Di Pierro, J.C. Structures in Beckett's
"Watt."*
  K. Schoell, 547(RF):Band95Heft1/2-217
Di Pietro, R.J., ed. Linguistics and the
Professions.*
  S.B. Heath, 355(LSoc):Dec83-517
Di Pinto, M., M. Fabbri and R. Froldi,
  eds. Coloquio Internacional sobre Lean-
dro Fernández de Moratín.
  D.T. Gies, 240(HR):Autumn83-469
Dippie, B.W. The Vanishing American.
  J.W. Bailey, 649(WAL):Aug83-169
Dipple, E. Iris Murdoch.*
  F. Baldanza, 301(JEGP):Apr83-268
  P. Lamarque, 478:Apr83-131
"Directory of British Oral History Collec-
tions."
  D. Gittins, 637(VS):Summer83-431
Dirnecker, R. Sowjetische Weltpolitik
unter Breschnew.
  A. Dallin, 550(RusR):Jan83-119
Di Scala, S. Dilemmas of Italian Social-
ism.
  C.M. Lovett, 276:Winter83-381
Disch, T. Burn This.
  D. Gioia, 461:Fall/Winter83/84-99
Disch, T. Here I am, There you are, Where
were we.
  D. Constantine, 176:Sep/Oct84-42
  B. Morrison, 617(TLS):25May84-573
Disch, T.M. The Businessman.
  M.Z. Bradley, 441:26Aug84-31
  J. Clute, 617(TLS):3Aug84-864
  J. Mellors, 362:23Aug84-27
"Discoveries from Kurdish Looms."
  R.L. Shep, 614:Fall184-15
Diskin, M., ed. Trouble in Our Backyard.
  R. Radosh, 441:19Feb84-5
  R.E. White, 61:Jan84-94
Disraeli, B. Benjamin Disraeli: Letters.*
  (Vols 1 and 2) (J.A.W. Gunn and others,
  eds)
  R. O'Kell, 529(QQ):Autumn83-676
Di Stasi, L. Mal Occhio [The Evil Eye].
  J. Gleason, 472:Fall/Winter83Spring/
  Summer84-265
  C. Speroni, 650(WF):Jan83-73
Di Teodoro, F. and others. Una Ipotesi
sui Rapporti Dimensionali del Ponte a
Santa Trinita.
  S.B.B., 90:Jan83-62
Ditsky, J. The Onstage Christ.*
  G. Bas, 189(EA):Apr-Sep83-334
Dixon, A. The Immaculate Magpies.
  L. Mackinnon, 617(TLS):23Mar84-312
Dixon, J. The Chinese Welfare System,
1949-1979.
  D. Bachman, 293(JASt):Feb83-384

Dixon, L.S. Alchemical Imagery in Bosch's
Garden of Delights.
  W.S. Gibson, 551(RenQ):Spring83-112
  J.F. Moffitt, 111:Spring84-4
Dixon, P.R., Jr. and H.M. Dixon - see
Hübner, K.
Dixon, R.M.W. and B.J. Blake, eds. Hand-
book of Australian Languages, II.
  J. Heath, 350:Jun84-465
Dixon, S. Movies.
  P. Bricklebank, 110:Spring84-85
Dixon, S. Time to Go.
  J. Domini, 441:14Oct84-34
Dixon, V. - see de Vega Carpio, L.
Dizer, J.T., Jr. Tom Swift and Company.
  S. Pickering, Jr., 517(PBSA):Vol177No1-
  67
Djuretić, V. Vlada na Bespuću.
  E. Barker, 617(TLS):10Aug84-897
Djursaa, M. DNSAP.
  J. Logue, 563(SS):Autumn83-392
Djwa, S. and R.S. Macdonald, eds. On F.R.
Scott.
  R. Mathews, 99:Nov83-33
Doane, A.N., ed. Genesis A.* (new ed)
  H. Sauer, 38:Band101Heft3/4-497
Doane, M. The Legends of Jesse Dark.
  R. Banks, 441:4Nov84-37
Dobbs, K. Pride and Fall.*
  P. Barclay, 102(CanL):Winter82-129
  A.T. Seaman, 198:Jun83-95
Dobereiner, P. The Book of Golf Disasters.
  R.R. Harris, 441:21Oct84-31
Döblin, A. Ausgewählte Werke in Einzel-
bänden, 20. (A.W. Riley, ed)
  H. Regensteiner, 221(GQ):Jan83-163
Döblin, A. Bourgeois et soldats (Novembre
1918).
  L. Arénilla, 450(NRF):Jul/Aug83-242
Döblin, A. Tales of a Long Night.
  M. Esslin, 441:30Dec84-10
Dobroszycki, L., ed. The Chronicle of the
Lodz Ghetto, 1941-1944.
  M. Gilbert, 453(NYRB):27Sep84-32
  H. Maccoby, 362:11Oct84-26
  S.S. Prawer, 617(TLS):26Oct84-1208
  E. Wiesel, 441:19Aug84-1
Dobry, C. Make Custom Drapery, Yes You
Can!
  P. Bach, 614:Winter84-19
Dobson, C. and R. Payne. The Dictionary
of Espionage.
  Z. Steiner, 617(TLS):12Oct84-1162
Dobyns, S. The Balthus Poems.
  P. Stitt, 491:Oct83-39
  639(VQR):Winter83-25
Dobyns, S. Black Dog, Red Dog.
  A. Brumer, 441:23Sep84-14
Docherty, T. Reading (Absent) Character.
  B. Bergonzi, 176:Jul/Aug84-50
  T. Tanner, 617(TLS):27Apr84-470
Doctorow, E.L. Lives of the Poets.
  B. De Mott, 441:11Nov84-1
  R. Towers, 453(NYRB):6Dec84-33
"Doctrine de la non-dualité (advaita-vâda)
et christianisme."
  M. Adam, 542:Jan-Mar83-55
Dodd, P., ed. The Art of Travel.
  A. Blayac, 189(EA):Oct-Dec84-451
Dodd, R.M. - see Wells, E.H.
Dodd, S. Old Wives' Tales.
  G. Weaver, 344:Fall84-107

Dodge, E. Dau.
    M. Bell, 441:25Mar84-20
Dodge, J. Fup.
    E.R. Lipson, 441:8Jul84-20
Doe, P. A Warbler's Song in the Dusk.
    T.B. Hare, 407(MN):Spring83-91
    E. Kerkham, 293(JASt):Aug83-953
    M. Morris, 244(HJAS):Dec83-699
Doering, B.E. Jacques Maritain and the
    French Catholic Intellectuals.
    D. O'Connell, 207(FR):May84-900
Doerr, H. Stones for Ibarra.
    L.M. Silko, 441:8Jan84-8
    442(NY):16Jan84-107
d'Offay, D. and G. Lionnet. Diksyonner
    kreol-franse.
    A. Valdman, 207(FR):Feb84-435
Dōgen and K. Uchiyama. Refining Your Life.
    J.C. Maraldo, 407(MN):Winter83-469
Dogliani, P. La Scuola delle reclute.
    M. Clark, 617(TLS):10Feb84-147
Döhl, H. Heinrich Schliemann - Mythos und
    Ärgernis.
    D.F. Easton, 123:Vol33No2-286
Doi Tadao, Morita Takeshi and Chōnan
    Minoru, eds and trans. Vocabvlario da
    Lingoa de Iapam.
    R.A. Miller, 545(RPh):Aug83-74
Doï Takeo. Amae No Kozo.
    F. Davoine and J-M. Gaudillière,
    98:Jan-Feb83-55
Doig, I. The Sea Runners.
    K. Ahearn, 649(WAL):Feb84-347
Dolan, C. Entre tours et clochers.
    B.S. Tinsley, 551(RenQ):Winter83-610
Dolan, T.P. - see Dunning, T.P.
Dolder, U., W. Dolder and D. Rothermund.
    India.
    639(VQR):Autumn83-136
Dolet, É. Correspondance. (C. Longeon,
    ed)
    J. Bailbé, 535(RHL):Sep/Dec83-910
    J.C. Nash, 207(FR):Mar84-551
Dolet, É. Préfaces françaises.* (C.
    Longeon, ed)
    K. Baldinger, 72:Band220Heft1-216
Dolfi, A. - see Jacobbi, R.
Dollimore, J. Radical Tragedy.
    G. Bradshaw, 617(TLS):17Aug84-924
von Döllinger, I. Briefwechsel 1820-1890.
    (Vol 4) (V. Conzemius, ed)
    D. Beales, 617(TLS):23Mar84-297
Dollinger, P. Der bayerische Bauernstand
    vom 9. bis zum 13. Jahrhundert. (F.
    Irsigler, ed)
    H. Schüppert, 684(ZDA):Band112Heft2-63
Dollot, L. La France dans le monde actuel.
    J. Paulhan, 207(FR):Oct83-120
Dolphin, B. Modèles mathématiques pour
    une linguistique quantitative.
    R. Jolivet, 209(FM):Jan83-90
Domanski, D. War in an Empty House.*
    P. Mitcham, 102(CanL):Summer83-144
    A. Munton, 198:Jun83-81
Domenach, J-M. Enquête sur les idées con-
    temporaines.
    L. Duisit, 207(FR):Oct83-118
Domergue, D. Artists Design Furniture.
    A. Shapiro, 441:22Jul84-21
Domínguez, J.I., ed. Mexico's Political
    Economy.
    W.P. Glade, 263(RIB):Vol33No2-256

Dominic, R.B. Unexpected Developments.
    N. Callendar, 441:11Mar84-21
    442(NY):27Feb84-135
Donadio, S. Nietzsche, Henry James, and
    the Artistic Will.*
    R.K. Martin, 106:Winter83-457
Donagan, A. The Theory of Morality.
    R. Wertheimer, 449:May83-303
Donald, A. Hannah At Thirty-Five.
    L. Taylor, 617(TLS):27Apr84-476
Donald, K. Creative Feltmaking.
    G. Brown, 614:Summer84-14
Donaldson, F. The British Council.
    D.J. Enright, 617(TLS):7Dec84-1407
    A. Quinton, 362:20/27Dec84-54
Donaldson, F. P.G. Wodehouse.*
    A. Blayac, 189(EA):Oct-Dec84-479
    295(JML):Nov83-592
Donaldson, G. Books.
    J.B. Nicholson, Jr., 87(BB):Dec83-258
Donaldson, I. The Rapes of Lucretia.*
    K.W. Gransden, 123:Vol33No2-306
    E.H. Hageman, 551(RenQ):Winter83-604
    A. Moss, 83:Autumn83-219
Donaldson, I., ed. Transformations in
    Modern European Drama.
    K. Worth, 617(TLS):15Jun84-663
Donaldson, S. Fool for Love.
    R.A. Martin, 385(MQR):Fall84-612
    B.F. Williamson, 441:15Jan84-19
Donaldson, T. Corporations and Morality.*
    T. Digby, 543:Jun83-921
    V. Di Norcia, 154:Jun83-364
Donaldson, T. Ngiyambaa.
    D.H., 355(LSoc):Mar83-138
Donaldson, W. - see Rorie, D.
Donaldson-Evans, L.K. Love's Fatal
    Glance.*
    A. Saunders, 208(FS):Oct83-449
Donawerth, J. Shakespeare and the Six-
    teenth-Century Study of Language.
    V. Salmon, 617(TLS):24Aug84-940
Donguk, K. - see under Kim Donguk
Doni, A.F. La Zucca del Doni (Venetia
    1551, Francesco Marcolini). (M.
    Chevalier, ed)
    B.M. Damiani, 240(HR):Spring83-229
    M. Davie, 86(BHS):Apr83-145
Donington, R. Music and its Instruments.
    N. O'Loughlin, 415:May83-301
Donington, R. The Rise of Opera.*
    B.R. Hanning, 317:Summer83-316
Donini, A. and J. Novack, eds. Origins
    and Growth of Sociological Theory.
    K.E.S., 185:Oct83-168
Donini, G. - see Thucydides
Donlan, W. The Aristocratic Ideal in
    Ancient Greece.
    A.R. Burn, 123:Vol33No1-147
Donleavy, J.P. De Alfonce Tennis.
    J. Mellors, 362:13Dec84-30
    J. Melmoth, 617(TLS):16Nov84-1302
Donleavy, J.P. Le Destin de Darcy Dancer,
    Gentleman.
    C. Jordis, 450(NRF):Jun83-145
Donleavy, J.P. Leila.*
    K.C. O'Brien, 362:5Jan84-25
Donne, J. Paradoxes and Problems.*
    (H. Peters, ed)
    D.F. Bratchell, 447(N&Q):Feb82-76
    G.R. Evans, 541(RES):Feb83-73

Donnelly, H.M., with R.N. Billings. Sara
and Gerald.*
  M. Secrest, 364:Oct83-70
Donner, F.M. The Early Islamic Conquests.
  I. Shahîd, 589:Apr83-453
Donnet, D. Le "Traité de la construction
de la phrase" de Michel le Syncelle de
Jérusalem.
  É. des Places, 555:Vol57fasc2-323
Donno, D.J. - see Campanella, T.
D'Onofrio, M. and V. Pace. La Campania.
  D.F. Glass, 54:Jun83-340
Donoghue, D. The Arts Without Mystery.
  R. Gilman, 441:20May84-36
Donoghue, D. Ferocious Alphabets.
  H. Bredin, 478:Apr83-124
  L. Gent, 175:Autumn83-280
Donoso, A. Julián Marías.
  A.A. Borrás, 238:Sep83-437
  P. Zancanaro, 258:Dec83-450
Donoso, J. A House in the Country.
  P-L. Adams, 61:Mar84-132
  J. Butt, 617(TLS):6Apr84-369
  R. Towers, 441:26Feb84-7
  442(NY):30Apr84-118
Donovan, D.G., M.G.H. Herman and A.E.
Imbrie. Sir Thomas Browne and Robert
Burton.
  P.J. Klemp, 365:Summer/Fall83-123
Donovan, R.J. Nemesis.
  D. Middleton, 441:4Nov84-30
Donow, H.S. The Sonnet in England and
America.
  D. Redding, 604:Winter83-3
de Donville, L.G. - see under Godard de
Donville, L.
Doppo, K. River Mist and Other Stories.
  A. Cheuse, 441:26Feb84-22
Dor, G. Du Sang bleu dans les veines.*
  J. Ripley, 102(CanL):Winter82-137
Dorais, L-J. The Inuit Language in South-
ern Labrador from 1694-1785.
  Osahito Miyaoka, 269(IJAL):Jul83-344
Dorat, J. Les Odes latines. (G. Demerson,
ed and trans)
  P.J. Ford, 208(FS):Oct83-448
  W. Stroh, 547(RF):Band95Heft1/2-179
Dorfman, A. The Empire's Old Clothes.*
  42(AR):Fall83-504
Dorfman, A. Het kind als onderontwikkeld
gebied.
  R. Bouckaert-Ghesquiere, 204(FdL):
  Mar82-77
Dorian, N.C. Language Death.*
  J.D. McClure, 355(LSoc):Jun83-268
  S. Romaine, 297(JL):Mar83-272
d'Ormesson, J., ed. Grand Hotel.
  P. Goldberger, 441:2Dec84-18
  E.S. Turner, 617(TLS):23Nov84-1334
d'Ormesson, J. Mon dernier rêve sera pour
vous.*
  F. Bassan, 446(NCFS):Fall-Winter83/84-
  254
Dorsett, L.W. Franklin D. Roosevelt and
the City Bosses.
  K. Cassidy, 106:Spring83-97
Dorson, R.M., ed. Handbook of American
Folklore.
  J. Porter, 187:Sep84-558
Dorson, R.M. Land of the Millrats.*
  R.H. Byington and R.S. McCarl,
  292(JAF):Jul-Sep83-353
  D.K. Wilgus, 27(AL):May83-280

Dorson, R.M. Man and Beast in American
Comic Legend.
  R.E. Meyer, 649(WAL):Nov83-270
van Dorsten, J.A. Op het kritieke moment.
  F.J. Warnke, 551(RenQ):Autumn83-467
Doskow, M. William Blake's "Jerusalem."
  P. Hamilton, 617(TLS):15Jun84-674
Dostoevsky, F. The Village of Stepanchi-
kovo. (I. Avsey, ed and trans)
  R. Hingley, 617(TLS):17Aug84-920
Doty, R. Will Barnet.
  J. Russell, 441:2Dec84-11
Dougherty, D.M. and E.B. Barnes, eds. Le
"Galien" de Cheltenham.*
  P.E. Bennett, 402(MLR):Oct83-918
  W.W. Kibler, 589:Oct83-1033
  D.D.R. Owen, 382(MAE):1983/2-323
Douglas, C. Douglas Jardine.
  M. Bose, 362:28Jun84-27
  A.L. Le Quesne, 617(TLS):24Aug84-941
Douglas, D.C. and G.W. Greenaway, eds.
English Historical Documents, 1042-1189.
(Vol 2) (2nd ed)
  B. Lyon, 589:Jan83-165
Douglas, J.S. Gardening Without Soil.
  J.M. Bristow, 529(QQ):Autumn83-712
Douglas, M., ed. Essays in the Sociology
of Perception.
  K.E.S. 185:Oct83-166
Douglas, M. In the Active Voice.
  R.E. Goodin, 185:Jan84-346
Douglass, F. Cavaillé-Coll and the Musi-
cians.
  L. Archbold, 451:Fall83-171
Douglass, J.D., Jr. Soviet Military
Strategy in Europe.
  S.K. Gupta, 550(RusR):Apr83-239
Doumet, C. Les thèmes aériens dans
l'oeuvre de Saint-John Perse.
  C. Marchal, 356(LR):Feb-May83-152
Dourado, A. Pattern for a Tapestry.
  N. Rankin, 617(TLS):6Jul84-761
Dove, G.N. The Police Procedural.
  P. Wolfe, 395(MFS):Autumn83-389
Dove, R. Museum.
  G. Waller, 152(UDQ):Autumn83-123
Dover, K.J., ed. Ancient Greek Literature.
  E. Asmis, 122:Jul83-254
Dover, K.J. - see Plato
Dovlatov, S. The Compromise.*
  J. Bayley, 453(NYRB):22Nov84-28
  P. Lewis, 364:Feb84-101
Dovlatov, S. Zona.
  D.M. Fiene, 574(SEEJ):Summer83-272
Dower, N. World Poverty.
  P.A. McAuliffe, 518:Oct83-229
Dowler, W. Dostoevsky, Grigor'ev, and
Native Soil Conservatism.
  J. Frank, 617(TLS):9Mar84-249
Dowley, T. Schumann.
  R. Anderson, 415:Jan83-35
Dowley, T., ed. Taking Off.
  R. Boston, 617(TLS):21Dec84-1482
Dowling, B.T. and M. McDougal. Business
Concepts for English Practice.
  M.K. Morray, 608:Jun84-329
Dowling, J. - see de la Cruz, R.
Dowling, W.C. Language and Logos in Bos-
well's "Life of Johnson."*
  J.J. Gold, 301(JEGP):Jan83-131
  F.A. Nussbaum, 173(ECS):Spring84-336
  A. Pailler, 189(EA):Apr-Jun84-203
  J. Svilpis, 49:Jul83-91

Dreyfus, J. Aspects of French Eighteenth
Century Typography.
  N. Barker, 617(TLS):10Feb84-151
Drieu la Rochelle, P. Cahiers de l'Herne.
  M.F. Meurice, 450(NRF):Jul/Aug83-207
Drieu la Rochelle, P. Fragment de
mémoires, 1940-1941.*
  P-L. Rey, 450(NRF):Jan83-104
Drinka, G.F. The Birth of Neurosis.
  P-L. Adams, 61:Sep84-128
  R. Dinnage, 441:9Sep84-12
Drinnon, R. Facing West.
  F.E. Hoxie, 658:Spring83-104
Driscoll, J. "The China Cantos" of Ezra
Pound.
  M. Troy, 597(SN):Vol55No2-212
Driscoll, J. The Language of Bone.
  J. Schiff, 584(SWR):Spring83-198
Driver, C. The British at Table 1940-
1980.*
  C. Hawtree, 364:Jul83-100
Dröge, K. Die Fachsprache des Buchdrucks
im 19. Jahrhundert.
  K. Kehr, 685(ZDL):3/1983-403
Droixhe, D. La Linguistique et l'appel de
l'histoire (1600-1800).
  G. Lepschy, 545(RPh):Feb83-461
Dronke, P. Woman Writers of the Middle
Ages.
  P. Neuss, 617(TLS):17Feb84-172
Dronke, U. and others, eds. Specvlvm
Norroenvm.*
  C.D.M. Cossar, 402(MLR):Oct83-994
  A. Liberman, 563(SS):Spring83-189
Drower, G.M.F. Neil Kinnock.
  B. Pimlott, 617(TLS):12Oct84-1165
Droysen, J.G. Historik. (P. Leyh, ed)
  F. Gilbert, 322(JHI):Apr-Jun83-327
Drozdowski, M.M. Z dziejów stosunków
polsko-amerykańskich 1776-1944.
  A.A. Hetnal, 497(PolR):Vol28No2-115
Drucker, P.F. The Temptation to Do Good.
  J. Kaufman, 441:13May84-22
Drudy, P.J., ed. Irish Studies 2.
  C. Ó Gráda, 272(IUR):Spring83-119
Drummond, J.D. Opera in Perspective.*
  C. Crawley, 529(QQ):Spring83-194
Drummond, P. The German Concerto.*
  F.H., 412:May82-142
Drummond de Andrade, C. Nova Reunião.
  J. Gledson, 617(TLS):27Apr84-461
Drury, A. The Roads of Earth.
  R. Elman, 441:30Sep84-28
Druskin, M. Igor Stravinsky.*
  J. Pasler, 415:Oct83-605
Dryden, D.M. Fabric Painting and Dyeing
for the Theatre.
  P. Scheinman, 139:Feb/Mar83-33
Dryden, E.A. Melville's Thematics of Form.
  A. Wrobel, 70:Nov/Dec81-61
Dryden, J. The Beauties of Dryden. (D.
Hopkins and T. Mason, eds)
  M. Dodsworth, 175:Summer83-189
  W.W. Robson, 97(CQ):Vol 12No1-74
Dryden, J. The Works of John Dryden.*
(Vol 19) (A. Roper and V.A. Dearing,
eds)
  G.D. Atkins, 566:Autumn83-51
  D. Hopkins, 447(N&Q):Dec82-551
Dryden, K. The Game.*
  M. Martin, 99:Feb84-36

Dryfhout, J.H. The Work of Augustus Saint-
Gaudens.
  M.H. Bogart, 658:Summer/Autumn83-219
  A.I. Ludwig, 432(NEQ):Dec83-609
  L.M. Roth, 576:Oct83-304
Drysdall, D.L. - see de Rojas, F.
Drzewieniecki, W.M. Samodzielna Brygada
Strzelcow Karpackich i 3 Dywizja Strzel-
cow Karpackich w literaturze i prasie.
  S. Dąbrowski, 497(PolR):Vol28No4-116
D'Sa, F.X. Śabdaprāmāṇyam in Śabara and
Kumārila.
  J. Taber, 485(PE&W):Oct83-407
D'Souza, D. Falwell.
  M. Zupan, 441:30Dec84-18
Dubal, D. Reflections from the Keyboard.
  E. Strickland, 441:30Dec84-13
Du Bartas, G.D. The Divine Weeks and
Works of Guillaume de Saluste, Sieur Du
Bartas, Translated by Joshua Sylvester.
(S. Snyder, ed)
  J. Carscallen, 568(SCN):Fall83-47
Du Bartas, G.D. La Sepmaine (Texte de
1581).* (Y. Bellenger, ed)
  S. Bisarello, 356(LR):Feb-May83-134
Dubé, L. La Mariakèche.
  Y. Bellemare, 102(CanL):Winter82-113
Dube, W-D. Expressionists and Expression-
ism.*
  P-L. Adams, 61:Feb84-104
Dubenetzky, V., ed. The Fiber Book. (2nd
ed)
  E. Thomas, 614:Winter84-17
Dubie, N. Selected and New Poems.
  D. St. John, 29:Sep/Oct84-17
  P. Stitt, 441:15Apr84-31
  D. Young, 199:Spring84-83
Dubinski, R.R. - see Brome, A.
Dubois, C-G. Le maniérisme.
  M. Hugues, 549(RLC):Apr-Jun83-219
Du Bois, E.C. - see Stanton, E.C. and S.B.
Anthony
Dubois, J. L'institution de la littéra-
ture.
  G. Cesbron, 356(LR):Aug83-225
Du Bois, P. History, Rhetorical Descrip-
tion and the Epic.
  H. Kellner, 400(MLN):Dec83-1339
  M. O'Connell, 604:Fall83-65
Dubois, R-D. Adieu, docteur Münch . . .
  E.R. Hopkins, 207(FR):Dec83-268
  J. Moss, 102(CanL):Autumn83-87
Du Bos, C. Robert et Elizabeth Browning
ou la plénitude de l'amour humaine.
  C. Jordis, 450(NRF):Apr83-140
Du Boulay, F.R.H. Germany in the Later
Middle Ages.
  J. Gillingham, 617(TLS):18May84-556
Dubreucq, A. Les concours de chants de
coqs.
  P. Rézeau, 553(RLiR):Jul-Dec83-483
Dubus, A. The Times Are Never So Bad.*
  W.H. Pritchard, 249(HudR):Winter83/84-
752
Dubus, A. Voices From the Moon.
  L. Zeidner, 441:18Nov84-26
Duby, G. The Age of the Cathedrals.* The
Three Orders.
  N.Z. Davis, 453(NYRB):2Feb84-32
Duby, G. The Knight, the Lady and the
Priest.* (French title: Le Chevalier,
la femme et le prêtre.)
  M. Vale, 617(TLS):4May84-491

Ducellier, A. La façade maritime de
l'Albanie au moyen âge.
  B. Krekić, 589:Oct83-1036
Ducháček, O. L'evolution de l'articula-
tion linguistique du domaine esthétique
du latin au français contemporain.*
  V. Vlasák, 554:Vol 103No2/3-402
Duchamp, M. Die Schriften. (Vol 1) (P.
Zimmermann, ed and trans)
  J. Hanimann, 471:Jan/Feb/Mar83-86
Duchêne, R. Ecrire au temps de Mme. de
Sévigné.
  N. Aronson, 475:Vol 10No18-316
  B. Beugnot, 535(RHL):Jan/Feb83-122
Duchêne, R. Ninon de Lenclos.
  A. Levi, 617(TLS):11May84-521
Duchêne, R. Madame de Sévigné ou la
chance d'être femme.
  H.T. Barnwell, 208(FS):Oct83-453
  E. Kuhs, 475:Vol 10No18-319
  M-O. Sweetser, 207(FR):May84-873
  M-O. Sweetser, 535(RHL):Sep/Dec83-926
Duchesneau, F. La Physiologie des Lumi-
ères.
  P.L. Farber, 173(ECS):Spring84-374
Duchet, C. and J. Neefs, eds. Balzac:
l'invention du roman.*
  K. Wingård, 547(RF):Band95Heft1/2-200
Ducornet, R. The Stain.
  D. Durrant, 364:Mar84-111
  J. Grossman, 441:16Dec84-26
  J. Pilling, 617(TLS):2Mar84-227
Dudden, F.E. Serving Women.*
  S. Strasser, 432(NEQ):Dec83-615
Dudek, L. Continuation I.*
  T. Goldie, 168(ECW):Winter83/84-86
  B. Whiteman, 526:Winter83-69
Dudman, J. - see "International Music
Guide 1983"
Duerr, H.P., ed. Der Wissenschaftler und
das Irrationale.
  P.E. Stüben, 679:Band14Heft1-167
Duff, A. - see Galbraith, J.K., R. Jenkins
and R. Wainwright
Duffy, C. Russia's Military Way to the
West.*
  J. Keep, 550(RusR):Jan83-102
Duffy, D. Gardens, Covenants, Exiles.*
  R. Lecker, 627(UTQ):Summer83-475
  S. Solecki, 529(QQ):Winter83-1026
Duffy, E. Challoner and his Church.
  G. Rupp, 83:Autumn83-244
Duffy, E. Rousseau in England.*
  E.B. Murray, 591(SIR):Fall83-474
Duffy, M. Londoners.*
  K.C. O'Brien, 362:5Jan84-25
Dufournet, J. Nouvelles Recherches sur
Villon.
  H. Braet, 356(LR):Aug83-238
  A. Micha, 554:Vol 103No2/3-400
Dufrenne, M. L'inventaire des "a priori."
  A. Reix, 542:Jan-Mar83-59
Dufwa, J. Winds from the East.*
  H. Adams, 54:Sep83-495
  P. Grate, 341:Vol152No3-139
Dugan, A. New and Collected Poems, 1961-
1983.
  J. Hollander, 676(YR):Spring84-xvii
Dugan, M., B. Giles and J.S. Hamilton,
eds. The Hat Trick.
  E. Webby, 381:Mar83-34

Dugast, D. Vocabulaire et stylistique.
(Vol 1)
  A. Raphael, 353:Vol20No7/8-569
Duggan, M. Runcie.
  D. Nineham, 617(TLS):24Feb84-198
Dugger, R. On Reagan.
  D.E. Rosenbaum, 441:8Jan84-16
  D.H. Wrong, 617(TLS):19Oct84-1175
Duhamel, A. Les Prétendants.
  P. Thody, 617(TLS):9Mar84-237
Duhamel, G. Le Livre de l'amertume. (B.
Duhamel, ed)
  D. Johnson, 617(TLS):6Jul84-747
Duijker, H. The Great Wine Château of
Bordeaux. The Good Wines of Bordeaux.
  E. Penning-Rowsell, 617(TLS):17Feb84-
175
Duisit, L. Satire, Parodie, Calembour.*
  J.M. Cocking, 208(FS):Jan83-111
Duke, D.C. Distant Obligations.*
  J.J. Waldmeir, 395(MFS):Winter83-750
Duke, M., J.R. Bryer and M.T. Inge, eds.
American Women Writers.
  L. Simon, 365:Summer/Fall83-128
Dukes, P. The Making of Russian Absolu-
tism, 1613-1801.
  R.P. Bartlett, 575(SEER):Oct83-618
Dukore, B.F. Harold Pinter.*
  L. Back, 397(MD):Sep83-389
  C. Edwards, 157:Autumn83-29
  R. Strang, 610:Autumn83-276
Dukore, B.F. - see Shaw, G.B.
Dukore, M.M. A Novel Called Heritage.
  J. Helbert, 649(WAL):Feb84-348
Dulay, H., M. Burt and S. Krashen. Lan-
guage Two.
  E. Bialystok, 399(MLJ):Autumn83-273
Dulong, G. and G. Bergeron. Le parler
populaire du Québec et de ses régions
voisines.
  M. Juneau, 553(RLiR):Jan-Jun83-235
Dumas, A. Le Comte de Monte-Cristo. (G.
Sigaux, ed)
  C. Schopp, 535(RHL):Jan/Feb83-132
Dumas, A. The Great Lover and Other Plays.
(B. Shaw, ed and trans)
  W.D. Howarth, 208(FS):Oct83-473
Dumas, A. Lettres d'Alexandre Dumas à
Mélanie Waldor. (C. Schopp, ed)
  D.C. Spinelli, 446(NCFS):Fall-
Winter83/84-260
Dumas, M. L'actualisation du Nouveau Test-
ament.
  A. Reix, 542:Jan-Mar83-81
Dumas, M-C. Robert Desnos ou l'explora-
tion des limites.*
  M.A. Caws, 207(FR):Feb84-405
  F.R. Smith, 208(FS):Oct83-485
Dumbleton, W.A. James Cousins.
  A.B., 189(EA):Jul-Sep84-367
Dumézil, G. Camillus. (U. Strutynski, ed)
  A.F. Lacy, 292(JAF):Jan-Mar83-91
Dummett, M. Frege: Philosophy of Lan-
guage.* (2nd ed)
  D. Gorman, 153:Winter83-43
  C.W. Gowans, 258:Mar83-99
  M. Schirn, 53(AGP):Band65Heft2-210
Dummett, M. The Interpretation of Frege's
Philosophy.*
  C.W. Gowans, 258:Mar83-99
  W. Gustason, 543:Mar83-706
  M. Schirn, 167:Sep83-243

[continued]

Dummett, M. The Interpretation of Frege's
Philosophy. [continuing]
J.E. Tiles, 518:Jan83-29
C. Wright, 262:Sep83-363
Dummett, M. Truth and Other Enigmas.
D. Gorman, 153:Winter83-43
Dumont, F. and Y. Martin, eds. Imaginaire
social et représentations collectives,
mélanges offerts à Jean-Charles Falar-
deau.
B-Z. Shek, 627(UTQ):Summer83-505
Dumont, F., J. Hamelin and J-P. Montminy,
eds. Idéologies au Canada français 1940-
1976.
B-Z. Shek, 627(UTQ):Summer83-505
Dumont, L. Essais sur l'individualisme.
A. Wooldridge, 617(TLS):13Jul84-776
Dumont, M. and others. L'Histoire des
femmes au Québec depuis quatre siècles.
G.R. Montbertrand, 207(FR):May84-897
Dumoulin, B. Recherches sur le premier
Aristote.
R. Brague, 192(EP):Oct-Dec83-489
Dunae, P.A. Gentlemen Emigrants.*
E. Hopkins, 298:Fall83-158
C. Kent, 637(VS):Winter83-237
T.J. Regehr, 529(QQ):Autumn83-870
Dunaway, D.K. How Can I Keep from Sing-
ing.*
C. Seemann, 650(WF):Oct83-319
Dunaway, J.M. Jacques Maritain.*
G. Cesbron, 535(RHL):Mar/Apr83-305
J. Collins, 543:Mar83-709
Dunbar, L.W., ed. Minority Report.
W. Kaminer, 441:23Dec84-17
Dunbar, P. William Blake's Illustrations
to the Poetry of Milton.*
D. Hirst, 541(RES):May83-222
Dunbar, W. The Poems of William Dunbar.*
(J. Kinsley, ed)
K. Bitterling, 38:Band101Heft1/2-235
Duncan, D.J. The River Why.*
P. Wild, 649(WAL):Nov83-269
Duncan, F. Dragonhunt.
T. Goldie, 102(CanL):Summer83-104
"Isadora Duncan: Isadora Speaks." (F.
Rosemont, ed)
R. Philp, 151:Oct82-96
Duncan, J.A., ed. L'Époque symboliste et
le monde proustien à travers la Corre-
spondance de Paul Adam, 1884-1920.
J. Kearns, 402(MLR):Jul83-717
Dundee, A. I Only Talk Winning.
V. Scannell, 617(TLS):13Jan84-35
Dundes, A., ed. The Evil Eye.
W.K. McNeil, 292(JAF):Jul-Sep83-359
Dundes, A. Interpreting Folklore.*
B.D.H. Miller, 447(N&Q):Dec82-575
E. Oring, 292(JAF):Jan-Mar83-84
Dundes, A., ed. Mother Wit from the Laugh-
ing Barrel.
M. Fabre, 189(EA):Apr-Jun84-228
Dundes, A. and C.A. Stibbe. The Art of
Mixing Metaphors.
W. Mieder, 196:Band24Heft3/4-293
W. Mieder, 650(WF):Oct83-315
Duneton, C. Le Diable sans porte.
M.G. Hydak, 207(FR):Apr84-735
Dunkel, P. and F. Pialorsi. Advanced
Listening Comprehension.
M. Martin, 399(MLJ):Summer83-183
Dunkley, J. - see de Crébillon, P.J.

Dunlap, H.G. Social Aspects of a Verb
Form.
W. Viereck, 685(ZDL):2/1983-222
Dunlap, S. An Equal Opportunity Death.
N. Callendar, 441:14Oct84-46
Dunlop, D.M., ed. The Muntakhab Ṣiwân
al-Ḥikmah of Abû Sulaimân as-Sijistānī.
D. Gutas, 318(JAOS):Oct-Dec82-645
Dunlop, J.B. The Faces of Contemporary
Russian Nationalism.
G.W. Lapidus, 441:1Apr84-6
H. Seton-Watson, 617(TLS):1Jun84-616
Dunn, D. Europa's Lover.*
M. O'Neill, 493:Mar83-57
Dunn, D., ed. A Rumoured City.*
T. Eagleton, 565:Vol24No2-66
Dunn, D. St. Kilda's Parliament.*
R. Pybus, 565:Vol24No2-73
Dunn, J. Locke.
J. Cottingham, 617(TLS):21Sep84-1061
M. Warnock, 362:5Jul84-26
Dunn, J. The Politics of Socialism.
P. Whitehead, 362:1Nov84-27
Dunn, J.A., Jr. Miles to Go.
C.E. Law, 529(QQ):Summer83-579
Dunn, L.A. Controlling the Bomb.*
T.D., 185:Apr84-568
Dunn, M.M. and R.S. - see Penn, W.
Dunn, R.J. "David Copperfield."
D. Paroissien, 155:Autumn83-165
R.L. Patten, 517(PBSA):Vol77No2-209
Dunn, S. Nerval et le roman historique.*
B.L. Knapp, 593:Winter83/84-324
N. Rinsler, 208(FS):Oct83-474
Dunn, S.P. - see Klibanov, A.I.
Dunn, W.N., ed. Values, Ethics and the
Practice of Policy Analysis.
R.E.G., 185:Apr84-565
Dunne, C. Retrieval.
T.J. Binyon, 617(TLS):18May84-557
Dunnett, D. Dolly and the Bird of Para-
dise.
T.J. Binyon, 617(TLS):17Feb84-159
M. Laski, 362:12Jan84-26
Dünnhaupt, G. Bibliographisches Handbuch
der Barockliteratur.* (Pt 1)
J. Hardin, 301(JEGP):Jan83-106
W. Kaiser, 70:Sep/Oct81-27
P. Skrine, 402(MLR):Oct83-969
Dünnhaupt, G. Bibliographisches Handbuch
der Barockliteratur.* (Pt 2)
J. Hardin, 301(JEGP):Jan83-106
P. Skrine, 402(MLR):Oct83-969
Dünnhaupt, G. Bibliographisches Handbuch
der Barockliteratur.* (Pt 3)
J. Hardin, 301(JEGP):Jan83-106
J.R. Paas, 221(GQ):Nov83-645
P. Skrine, 402(MLR):Oct83-969
Dunning, A. Pietro Antonio Locatelli.
B. Schwarz, 317:Spring83-157
Dunning, S. Walking Home Dead. Do You
Fear No One?
R.F. Willson, 436(NewL):Summer84-109
Dunning, T.P. "Piers Plowman": an Inter-
pretation of the A Text.* (2nd ed) (T.P.
Dolan, ed)
P.M. Kean, 541(RES):May83-202
Dunsdorfs, E. The Livonian Estates of
Axel Oxenstierna.
E. Anderson, 563(SS):Summer83-255
Dunsmore, S. Weaving in Nepal.
A.L. Mayer, 614:Spring84-30

Dutu, A. Romanian Humanists and European Culture.
G. van de Louw, 549(RLC):Apr-Jun83-247
Duval, E.M. Poesis and Poetic Tradition in the Early Works of Saint-Amant.*
J. Bailbé, 535(RHL):Jan/Feb83-120
Du Val, J. - see "Cuckolds, Clerics, and Countrymen"
Duvert, T. Un Anneau d'argent à l'oreille.
S. Smith, 207(FR):Mar84-586
Duwell, M., ed. A Possible Contemporary Poetry.*
J. Tulip, 71(ALS):May83-121
Dworkin, S. Double De Palma.
S. Gold, 441:30Dec84-17
Dwyer, E.J. Pompeian Domestic Sculpture.
R. Brilliant, 124:May-Jun84-320
R. Ling, 313:Vol73-229
Dwyer, W.M. The Day is Ours!
S.W. Sears, 441:8Jan84-10
Dyer, A. A Biography of James Parker, Colonial Printer.
M.A. McCorison, 354:Dec83-434
Dyke, C. Philosophy of Economics.
C.W. Morris, 154:Mar83-180
D-H. Ruben, 483:Oct81-582
Dyson, F. Weapons and Hope.
M. Howard, 441:8Apr84-7
Lord Zuckerman, 453(NYRB):14Jun84-5
Dziemidok, B. Teoria przeżyć i wartości estetycznych w polskiej estetyce dwudziestolecia miedzywojennego.
E.M. Swiderski, 290(JAAC):Winter83-225

Eagleton, T. Criticism and Ideology.*
J.W. Davidson, 477(PLL):Winter83-93
Eagleton, T. The Function of Criticism.
C. Baldick, 617(TLS):23Nov84-1339
Eagleton, T. Literary Theory.*
R. Alter, 129:Mar84-50
P.H. Fry, 676(YR):Summer84-603
L. Hutcheon, 153:Winter83-33
R. King, 344:Fall84-114
Eagleton, T. The Rape of Clarissa.*
J.A. Dussinger, 173(ECS):Spring84-350
A. Gibson, 175:Summer83-166
I. Grundy, 566:Spring84-153
W.B. Warner, 153:Winter83-12
639(VQR):Summer83-90
Eaker, H.L. - see di Conversino, G.
Eames, E.R. and K. Blackwell - see Russell, B.
Earhart, H.B. The New Religions of Japan. (2nd ed)
H. Hardacre, 407(MN):Winter83-473
Earle, P.G., ed. Gabriel García Márquez.
M.A. Aaron, 238:Dec83-647
Early, E. Joy in Exile.
A.J. Vetrano, 238:Sep83-446
Earnshaw, P. Bobbin and Needle Laces.
P. Grappe, 614:Fall84-12
Easlea, B. Witch-Hunting, Magic and the New Philosophy.*
J.C. Eade, 447(N&Q):Apr82-162
Eaton, C.E. The Thing King.
R.W. Hill, 580(SCR):Fall83-123
W. Shear, 389(MQ):Spring84-350
Eatough, G. - see Fracastoro, G.
Eaves, M. William Blake's Theory of Art.*
H. Adams, 88:Winter83/84-107
E. Larrissy, 59:Dec83-478
[continued]

[continuing]
R. Lister, 324:Dec83-86
D. Wagenknecht, 661(WC):Summer83-157
Eban, A. The New Diplomacy.*
S. Jacobson, 362:1Mar84-24
M. Sieff, 129:Aug84-69
A. Watson, 617(TLS):29Jun84-735
Ebbatson, R. The Evolutionary Self.
D.R. Schwarz, 395(MFS):Winter83-782
Ebding, J. Tendenzen der Entwicklung des sowjetischen satirischen Romans (1919-1931).
P. Henry, 575(SEER):Jul83-433
Ebel, E., ed. Die Waräger.
G. Kvaran, 260(IF):Band87-327
Ebel, U. Studien zur skandinavischen Reisebeschreibung von Linné bis Andersen.
M. Lee, 563(SS):Winter83-96
Ebeling, H. and L. Lütkehaus, eds. Schopenhauer und Marx.
R. Zimmer and M. Morgenstern, 53(AGP):Band65Heft3-338
Ebeling, R.A. Over de namen van de Middeleeuwse streekdorpen in Oostfriesland.
J.B. Berns, 685(ZDL):1/1983-125
Eber, I. Voices from Afar.
R.E. Hegel, 116:Jan82-145
Eberline, C.N. Studies in the Manuscript Tradition of the Ranae of Aristophanes.
K.J. Dover, 123:Vol33No1-127
Eberly, P.K. Music in the Air.
S.S. Brylawski, 187:Sep84-567
Ebersole, A.B., ed. Perspectivas de la comedia II.
M. Pérez-Erdélyi, 552(REH):Oct83-452
Ebert, R. A Kiss Is Still a Kiss.
K. Turan, 441:16Dec84-21
Eble, K.E. William Dean Howells. (2nd ed)
L.J. Budd, 651(WHR):Winter83-368
Ebneter, T. Angewandte Linguistik.
G.F. Meier, 682(ZPSK):Band36Heft3-350
Ebneter, T. Wörterbuch des Romanischen von Obervaz Lenzerheide Valbella.
P. Swiggers, 350:Sep84-661
Ebon, M. The Andropov File.*
A. Brown, 617(TLS):6Jul84-750
Ebrey, P.B. The Aristocratic Families of Early Imperial China.
W. Eberhard, 318(JAOS):Jul-Sep82-574
Eça de Queirós. Les Maia. (P. Teyssier, trans)
R. Bréchon, 98:Oct83-829
"Eccentrics in Netsuke."
E.A. Wrangham, 463:Summer83-187
Eccles, A. Obstetrics and Gynaecology in Tudor and Stuart England.
639(VQR):Winter83-8
Eccles, J. and D.N. Robinson. The Wonder of Being Human.
G.A. Miller, 441:26Aug84-22
Eccles, J.C. Le mystère humain.
M. Adam, 542:Jan-Mar83-59
Eccles, M. - see Shakespeare, W.
Eccleshall, R. Order or Reason in Politics.
K. Sharpe, 161(DUJ):Jun83-114
Echard, W.E. Napoleon III and the Concert of Europe.
639(VQR):Autumn83-120
Échenoz, J. Cherokee.*
C. Dis, 450(NRF):Dec83-105

Echlin, E. An Alternative Ending to Richardson's "Clarissa." (D. Daphinoff, ed)
  S. Soupel, 189(EA):Apr-Jun84-205
Eck, D.L. Banaras.*
  C. de Beaurepaire, 364:Jun83-102
Ecke, T.Y-H. Poetry on the Wind.
  M. Hutchinson, 60:Mar-Apr83-134
Ecker, D.W., ed. Qualitative Evaluation in the Arts.
  M. Day, 289:Fall83-123
Eckert, M. Transzendieren und immanente Transzendenz.
  H. Kimmerle, 489(PJGG):Band90Heft2-422
Eckey, L.F., M.A. Schoyer and W.T. Schoyer. 1,001 Broadways.
  G. Maschio, 615(TJ):Dec83-564
Eckhardt, C.M. Fanny Wright.
  D.S. Reynolds, 441:22Apr84-11
Eckley, G. Finley Peter Dunne.
  B. Dolan, 305(JIL):Jan83-111
  B. Gallagher, 26(ALR):Spring83-142
Eckstein, O. and others. The DRI Report on US Manufacturing Industries.
  L.C. Thurow, 453(NYRB):27Sep84-29
Eco, U. The Name of the Rose.* (Italian title: Il nome della rosa; French title: Le Nom de la rose.)
  A. Hartley, 176:Mar84-37
  G. Kearns, 249(HudR):Autumn83-554
  F. de Martinoir, 450(NRF):Mar83-143
  W.E. Stephens, 153:Summer83-51
  P. Vansittart, 364:Oct83-100
Eco, U. Postscript to "The Name of the Rose."
  R. Craft, 453(NYRB):20Dec84-49
Eco, U. Semiotics and the Philosophy of Language.
  R. Posner, 617(TLS):15Jun84-660
  J. Sturrock, 617(TLS):13May84-17
Eco, U. Sette anni di desiderio.
  G. Reid, 617(TLS):5Oct84-1130
"Economic Report of the President Transmitted to the Congress February 1984."
  E. Rothschild, 453(NYRB):15Mar84-14
"Les Ecrivains normands de l'âge classique et le goût de leur temps."
  G. Forestier, 475:Vol 10No18-283
Eddleman, F.E., comp. American Drama Criticism.
  A.P. Hinchliffe, 677(YES):Vol 13-343
Ede, J. A Way of Life: Kettle's Yard.
  F. Spalding, 617(TLS):2Mar84-214
Edel, A. Analyzing Concepts in Social Science.
  W. Gerber, 543:Jun83-924
Edel, A. Aristotle and His Philosophy.
  D.W. Hamlyn, 123:Vol133No2-229
  A. Madigan, 258:Jun83-218
  R.K. Sprague, 319:Apr84-231
Edel, L. Stuff of Sleep and Dreams.*
  M. Gorra, 569(SR):Winter83-vii
  J. Martin, 27(AL):Mar83-96
  S.B. Purdy, 395(MFS):Summer83-371
  G.S. Reed, 473(PR):4/1983-629
  S. Weiland, 128(CE):Nov83-705
  295(JML):Nov83-403
Edel, L. Writing Lives.
  J. Atlas, 441:28Oct84-15
Edel, L. - see James, H.

Edel, L. and D.H. Laurence. A Bibliography of Henry James. (3rd ed rev with J. Rambeau)
  E. James, 354:Dec83-438
  J. Roberts, 617(TLS):4May84-503
  A.J. Shelston, 148:Winter83-92
Edelman, D.I. The Dardic and Nuristani Languages.
  J.A.C. Greppin, 617(TLS):23Mar84-295
Eden, E. Up the Country.*
  J. Mellors, 364:Oct83-102
Eder, K. Kalender-Geschichten.
  W. Theiss, 196:Band24Heft3/4-295
Edgar, D. Maydays.
  J. Spurling, 176:Jan84-55
HRH The Duke of Edinburgh - see under Prince Philip, the Duke of Edinburgh
Edinger, H.G. Index Analyticus Graecitatis Aeschyleae.
  R.D. Dawe, 487:Spring83-83
Edmond, M. End Wall.
  C. Wallace-Crabbe, 617(TLS):20Jul84-819
Edmond, M. Hilliard and Oliver.*
  C. Betsky, 441:8Jul84-20
  S. Foister, 90:Nov83-698
Edmondson, J.A. Einführung in die Transformationssyntax des Deutschen.
  M. Johnson, 350:Sep84-668
Edmonson, W. Spoken Discourse.
  P.L. Carrell, 399(MLJ):Spring83-84
  N. Fairclough, 506(PSt):Sep83-180
  M. Maxwell, 350:Sep84-689
Edmunds, L. The Silver Bullet.*
  P. Buitenhuis, 106:Winter83-475
Edmunds, R.D. Tecumseh and the Quest for Indian Leadership.
  R.F. Berkhofer, Jr., 441:16Sep84-22
Edsall, T.B. The New Politics of Inequality.
  E. Cowan, 441:1Jul84-21
  442(NY):20Aug84-93
Edwards, A. Matriarch.
  N. Annan, 453(NYRB):25Oct84-24
  F. Donaldson, 617(TLS):2Nov84-1254
  J. Kaufman, 441:5Aug84-19
Edwards, A. The Road to Tara.*
  R.F. Durden, 27(AL):Dec83-659
  B.H. Gelfant, 578:Spring84-125
Edwards, A.M. The Design of Suburbia.
  J. Brandon-Jones, 324:Feb84-213
Edwards, A.S.G., ed. Skelton: The Critical Heritage.
  P. Ingham, 541(RES):Aug83-325
Edwards, A.S.G. - see Cavendish, G.
Edwards, A.S.G. and D. Pearsall, eds. Middle English Prose.
  E. Wilson, 447(N&Q):Feb82-65
Edwards, C.S. Hugo Grotius, the Miracle of Holland.
  42(AR):Winter83-125
Edwards, D.L. Christian England. (Vol 2)
  E. Duffy, 617(TLS):24Feb84-197
Edwards, D.L. Christian England. (Vol 3)
  O. Chadwick, 617(TLS):21Sep84-1052
Edwards, G.B. Sarnia.
  F. de Martinoir, 450(NRF):Jun83-142
Edwards, M. Towards a Christian Poetics.
  C.H. Sisson, 617(TLS):21Dec84-1468
Edwards, M. Upholstery and Canework.
  P. Bach, 614:Fall84-26
Edwards, M., ed. Words/Music.
  P.J.P., 412:Feb82-72

Edwards, M.U., Jr. Luther's Last Battles.
  G. Strauss, 551(RenQ):Winter83-612
Edwards, P. Heidegger on Death.*
  A.W.J. Harper, 154:Jun83-371
Edwards, P. and others. The Revels History of Drama in English. (Vol 4)
  C. Hill, 366:Autumn83-250
  R. Jacobs, 175:Spring83-69
Edwards, P., I-S. Ewbank and G.K. Hunter, eds. Shakespeare's Styles.*
  J. Rees, 402(MLR):Jan83-136
  K. Spinner, 179(ES):Aug83-361
Edwards, P.D. Anthony Trollope's Son in Australia.
  A. Wright, 445(NCF):Jun83-104
Edwards, R.B. Kadmos the Phoenician.*
  H. Vos, 394:Vol36fasc1/2-232
Edwards, R.B. A Return to Moral and Religious Philosophy in Early America.
  N. Fiering, 619:Winter83-106
Edwards, R.D. The Saint Valentine's Day Murders.
  R. Hill, 617(TLS):26Oct84-1225
Edwards, T.R.N. Three Russian Writers and the Irrational.*
  J. Grayson, 575(SEER):Jul83-432
  P.R. Hart, 574(SEEJ):Spring83-115
  W.F. Kolonosky, 395(MFS):Summer83-306
  A. McMillin, 402(MLR):Oct83-1000
Eells, E. Rational Decision and Causality.
  S.W., 185:Oct83-167
Eells, G. Robert Mitchum.
  F. Hirsch, 441:1Jul84-13
Eells, G. and S. Musgrove. Mae West.
  C. Brown, 617(TLS):15Jun84-675
van Eemeren, F. and R. Grootendorst. Regels voor redelijke discussies.
  A. Verbiest, 204(FdL):Mar83-74
Efimov, I. Arxivy Strašnogo Suda.
  R. Bowie, 558(RLJ):Fall83-243
Efron, A. and J. Herold, eds. Root Metaphor.
  A.S.C., 543:Sep82-162
Efron, E. The Apocalyptics.
  D.S. Greenberg, 441:5Aug84-8
  S. McCracken, 129:Nov84-60
Egan, D. Seeing Double.
  M. O'Neill, 617(TLS):11May84-516
Egan, L. Crime for Christmas.
  N. Callendar, 441:4Mar84-19
Egan, S. Patterns of Experience in Autobiography.
  J. Sturrock, 617(TLS):16Nov84-1307
Eggebrecht, A., ed. Die zornigen alten Männer.
  J. Kuczynski, 654(WB):2/1982-148
Eggebrecht, H.H., ed. Handwörterbuch der musikalischen Terminologie.* (Pts 7 and 11)
  J. Caldwell, 410(M&L):Jan/Apr83-67
Eggebrecht, H.H. Die Musik Gustav Mahlers.
  S. Gut, 537:Vol69No2-240
  J. Williamson, 410(M&L):Jan/Apr83-81
Eggers-Lan de Teleki, B. Carriego y su poesía de barrio del 900.
  R. Escandón, 552(REH):Jan83-157
Eğit, K. Ferdinand von Saar.
  W. Nehring, 680(ZDP):Band102Heft4-624
Egleton, C. A Conflict of Interests.*
  T.J. Binyon, 617(TLS):30Mar84-354
von Ehingen, G. Reisen nach der Ritterschaft.* (G. Ehrmann, ed)
  S. Schmitz, 680(ZDP):Band102Heft1-149

Ehle, J. Last One Home.
  E. Douglas, 441:23Sep84-49
Ehle, J. The Winter People.
  G. Davenport, 569(SR):Summer83-439
Ehlert, T. Konvention — Variation — Innovation.
  X. von Ertzdorff, 680(ZDP):Band102 Heft1-138
  A. Groos, 589:Jan83-167
Ehrenpreis, I. Swift. (Vols 1 and 2)
  R.M. Adams, 453(NYRB):25Oct84-37
Ehrenpreis, I. Swift. (Vol 3)
  R.M. Adams, 453(NYRB):25Oct84-37
  D. Donoghue, 617(TLS):10Feb84-143
  D.A.N. Jones, 362:31May84-22
Ehrismann, O., ed. Der mittelhochdeutsche Reinhart Fuchs.*
  D. Blamires, 402(MLR):Oct83-961
Ehrlich, E. and others - see "Oxford American Dictionary"
Ehrlich, P.R. and others. The Cold and the Dark.
  W.J. Broad, 441:12Aug84-21
Ehrmann, G. - see von Ehingen, G.
Eibl, K. Kritisch-rationale Literaturwissenschaft.
  L. Martens, 107(CRCL):Sep83-392
Eichhorn, W., E. Hahn and F. Rupprecht, eds. Wertauffassungen im Sozialismus.
  M. Rammler, 654(WB):5/1982-182
Eichner, H. - see Schlegel, F.
Eigeldinger, F. and others, eds. Table de concordances rythmique et syntaxique des "Poésies" d'Arthur Rimbaud. (Vols 1 and 2)
  A. Guyaux, 535(RHL):Sep/Dec83-951
"Eight Dynasties of Chinese Painting."*
  R. Vinograd, 54:Mar83-167
"The Eighteenth Century: A Current Bibliography."* (Vol 4) (R.R. Allen, ed)
  P-G.B., 189(EA):Apr-Jun84-235
"The Eighteenth Century: A Current Bibliography." (Vol 5) (R.R. Allen and P.J. Korshin, eds)
  P-G.B., 189(EA):Oct-Dec84-490
Eikhenbaum, B. Tolstoi in the Seventies.*
  N.O. Warner, 574(SEEJ):Spring83-102
Eikhenbaum, B. Tolstoi in the Sixties.*
  S. Pratt, 574(SEEJ):Spring83-101
Eiko Ishioka. Eiko by Eiko.
  I. Sischy and Eiko Ishioka, 62:Mar84-80
Eimer, H., ed and trans. Bodhipathapradīpa.
  A. Wayman, 318(JAOS):Jan-Mar82-138
"Einführung in die deutsche Literatur des 12. bis 16. Jahrhunderts." (Vol 1)
  R. Hahn, 654(WB):3/1983-569
Eisele, C. Studies in the Scientific and Mathematical Philosophy of Charles S. Peirce.* (R.M. Martin, ed)
  V.G. Potter, 258:Jun83-205
Eisele, U. Der Dichter und sein Detektiv.*
  L.A. Lensing, 221(GQ):May83-517
Eisenach, E.J. Two Worlds of Liberalism.
  R.P. Kraynak, 543:Mar83-710
Eisenberg, D. Romances of Chivalry in the Spanish Golden Age.*
  J.R. Green, Jr., 400(MLN):Mar83-287
  K. Whinnom, 402(MLR):Oct83-941
Eisenberg, D. - see Ortúñez de Calahorra, D.

Elliott, R.C. and A.H. Scouten. The
Poetry of Jonathan Swift.
P-G. Boucé, 189(EA):Apr-Jun84-200
R. Quintana, 402(MLR):Apr83-428
Elliott, R.W.V. Thomas Hardy's English.
C. Peters, 617(TLS):3Aug84-860
Elliott, S.L. Signs of Life.
L. Ricou, 529(QQ):Summer83-532
Ellis, B.D. Rational Belief Systems.*
M.E. Greer, 543:Mar83-711
Ellis, E.F. The British Museum in Fiction.
517(PBSA):Vol77No2-252
Ellis, G. Napoleon's Continental Blockade.
J. Lough, 83:Spring83-116
Ellis, J. Cassino.
M. Carver, 441:12Aug84-16
D. Hunt, 617(TLS):8Jun84-634
R. Trevelyan, 362:17May84-25
442(NY):9Jul84-94
Ellis, J.M. One Fairy Story Too Many.*
P. Jordan-Smith, 469:Vol9No1-124
S.S. Prawer, 617(TLS):30Mar84-343
J. Schmidt, 268(IFR):Summer84-134
Ellis, P.J. The Poetry of Emilio Prados.
D. Harris, 402(MLR):Jan83-211
M.P. Predmore, 240(HR):Summer83-350
Ellis, R. The Book of Sharks.
P.H. Greenwood, 617(TLS):30Mar84-353
Ellis, R.H., comp. Catalogue of Seals in
the Public Record Office: Personal Seals.
(Vol 2)
B.M.B. Rezak, 589:Jul83-793
Ellis, S. Dante and English Poetry.
C.H. Sisson, 617(TLS):13Jul84-789
Ellis-Fermor, U. Shakespeare's Drama.*
(K. Muir, ed)
M. O'Neill, 161(DUJ):Dec82-107
Ellison, D. The Reading of Proust.
E. Hughes, 617(TLS):27Jul84-830
Ellison, E.A. The Innocent Child in
Dickens and Other Writers.
H. Shepherd, 155:Autumn83-164
Ellison, H.J., ed. The Sino-Soviet Con-
flict.
W.D. Mills, 293(JASt):Aug83-913
J. Radvanyi, 550(RusR):Jan83-116
Ellison, R. Invisible Man, Thirtieth
Anniversary Edition.
A. Nadel, 219(GaR):Summer83-438
Elliston, F. and N. Bowie, eds. Ethics,
Public Policy, and Criminal Justice.
R.S.G., 185:Jan84-380
Ellmann, R. James Joyce. (rev)
F.J.M. Blom, 179(ES):Oct83-409
P. Gaskell, 184(EIC):Jul83-252
C.H., 148:Spring83-93
R.M. Kain, 395(MFS):Summer83-278
J-M. Rabaté, 98:Aug-Sep83-691
Ellmann, R. - see Joyce, J.
Ellmann, R. - see Wilde, O.
Ellos, W.J. Thomas Reid's Newtonian Real-
ism.
P.B. Wood, 518:Jul83-147
Ellroy, J. Blood on the Moon.
N. Callendar, 441:22Jul84-32
Ellsworth, J.D. Reading Ancient Greek.
D.H. Kelly, 124:Jul-Aug84-386
Ellsworth, L.E. Charles Lowder and The
Ritualist Movement.*
A.O.J. Cockshut, 637(VS):Summer83-458

Ellsworth, R.H. and H.A. Link. Chinese
Hardwood Furniture in Hawaiian Collec-
tions.
R.R. Jones, 60:May-Jun83-140
Ellul, J. Perspectives on Our Age. (W.H.
Vandenberg, ed)
T.P. Moran, 186(ETC.):Summer83-230
W.T. Stevenson, 396(ModA):Summer/
Fall83-360
Elmer, W. Diachronic Grammar.
G. Bourcier, 189(EA):Jan-Mar84-85
Elon, A. The Israelis.
A. Dowty, 617(TLS):27Jul84-836
"Éloquence et rhétorique chez Cicéron."
H.C. Gotoff, 124:Mar-Apr84-262
Elrod, J.W. Kierkegaard and Christendom.*
J.H. Thomas, 301(JEGP):Apr83-303
J. Walker, 529(QQ):Spring83-255
Elsbree, L. The Ritual of Life.
H.H. Watts, 395(MFS):Summer83-367
Elsen, A., ed. Rodin Rediscovered.
D. Cottington, 59:Sep83-387
Elshtain, J.B. Public Man, Private Woman.*
D. Réaume, 529(QQ):Autumn83-919
Elsom, J., ed. Post-War British Theatre
Criticism.*
G. Bas, 189(EA):Apr-Sep83-340
Elster, J. Explaining Technical Change.*
Sour Grapes.*
S. Walt, 185:Jul84-680
Elster, J. Ulysses and the Sirens.
M.E. Greer, 543:Mar83-713
Elsworth, J.D. Andrey Bely.
G.S. Smith, 617(TLS):5Oct84-1135
Eltis, W. The Classical Theory of
Economic Growth.
T.W. Hutchison, 617(TLS):20Jul84-808
Elton, W.R., with G. Schlesinger. Shake-
speare's World.*
L.S. Champion, 179(ES):Jun83-276
W. Habicht, 402(MLR):Apr83-426
G. Schmitz, 156(JDSh):Jahrbuch1983-255
Elwert, W.T. Die italienische Literatur
des Mittelalters.
L.R. Rossi, 589:Jan83-170
Elwert, W.T. Die romanischen Sprachen und
Literaturen.*
H. Kahane, 545(RPh):Aug82-104
Elytis, O. Maria Nephele.
M.B. Raizis, 678(YCGL):No31-151
Elytis, O. Selected Poems.* (E. Keeley
and P. Sherrard, eds)
R. Pybus, 565:Vol124No2-73
Emanuel, D. and E. Style For All Seasons.
R.L. Shep, 614:Spring84-28
van Emden, W., ed. "Girart de Vienne,"
par Bertrand de Bar-sur-Aube.
A. Iker-Gittleman, 545(RPh):May83-633
Emecheta, B. Destination Biafra.
639(VQR):Winter83-21
Emecheta, B. Double Yoke.
J. Updike, 442(NY):23Apr84-124
Emecheta, B. The Rape of Shavi.
R. Kerridge, 617(TLS):3Feb84-116
K.C. O'Brien, 362:22Mar84-25
Emerson, E.T. The Letters of Ellen Tucker
Emerson. (E.E.W. Gregg, ed)
N. Baym, 432(NEQ):Sep83-465
H.H. Waggoner, 27(AL):Oct83-458
Emerson, R.L., G. Girard and R. Runte, eds.
Man and Nature/L'Homme et la nature.
D. Greene, 627(UTQ):Summer83-416
S. Soupel, 189(EA):Jul-Sep84-327

Emerson, R.W. Emerson in His Journals.*
(J. Porte, ed)
    J. Myerson, 432(NEQ):Jun83-275
    R. Sattelmeyer, 579(SAQ):Autumn83-460
Emerson, R.W. The Journals and Miscel-
laneous Notebooks of Ralph Waldo Emerson.
(Vol 15 ed by L. Allardt and D.W. Hill,
with R.N. Bennett; Vol 16 ed by R.A.
Bosco and G.M. Johnson)
    L.J. Budd, 579(SAQ):Summer83-348
    J. Myerson, 432(NEQ):Jun83-275
Emery, W.B. Life in Archaic Egypt.
    A.A., 617(TLS):20Jul84-822
"Pierre Emmanuel, introduction générale à
l'oeuvre."
    J. Onimus, 535(RHL):May/Jun83-482
Emmen, P.A. - see Olivi, P.I.
Emmens, J.A. Verzameld werk. (M.E.
Vijlbrief and others, eds)
    D. Freedberg, 600:Vol 13No2-142
Emmerich, W. Kleine Literaturgeschichte
der DDR.
    P.U. Hohendahl, 221(GQ):Mar83-347
Emmerich, W. Heinrich Mann: "Der Unter-
tan."
    W. Herden, 654(WB):9/1983-1673
    U. Weisstein, 221(GQ):Jan83-165
Emmers, R. and Ninegishi Yuki, eds. Mus-
ical Voices of Asia.
    Trân Van Khê, 537:Vol69No2-224
Emmerson, J.S., comp. Catalogue of the
Pybus Collection of Medical Books,
Letters and Engravings, 15th-20th
Centuries, Held in the University
Library, Newcastle upon Tyne.
    E. Brodman, 517(PBSA):Vol77No2-245
Emmons, T. and W.S. Vucinich, eds. The
Zemstvo in Russia.
    D.T. Orlovsky, 104(CASS):Summer83-279
Emons, R. Englische Nominale.
    G. Bourcier, 189(EA):Oct-Dec84-455
Empaytaz, D. Antología de Albas, Albor-
adas y poemas afines en la Península
Ibérica hasta 1625.
    G. Beutler, 547(RF):Band95Heft1/2-
227
Empaytaz de Croome, D. Albor.*
    G. Beutler, 547(RF):Band95Heft1/2-227
Empson, W. Seven Types of Ambiguity.
Collected Poems.
    J. Culler, 617(TLS):23Nov84-1327
Empson, W. Using Biography.
    J. Culler, 617(TLS):23Nov84-1327
    E. Griffiths, 362:15Nov84-27
Emrich, E. Macht und Geist im Werk Hein-
rich Manns.
    W. Herden, 654(WB):9/1983-1673
    U. Weisstein, 133:Band16Heft2/3-268
Emrich, W. Freiheit und Nihilismus in der
Literatur des 20. Jahrhunderts.
    R. Nägele, 221(GQ):Mar83-286
von Ems, R. Weltchronik/Der Stricker,
Karl der Grosse.
    E.M. Vetter, 471:Apr/May/Jun83-175
Encarnación, A.M. Cuaderno de Juglaría
Veintiuno.
    I. López Jiménez, 701(SinN):Apr-Jun83-
97
Enchi, F. Masks.
    G. Kearns, 249(HudR):Autumn83-551
    J. Updike, 442(NY):2Jan84-88

Encrevé, A. and M. Richard, eds. Les Pro-
testants dans les débuts de la Troisième
République (1871-1885).
    B. Rigby, 208(FS):Oct83-480
"Encyclopedia of Library and Information
Science." (A. Kent, H. Lancour and J.E.
Daily, eds)
    J.D. Marshall, 70:Jan-Feb83-91
Endo, S. The Samurai.*
    J.B. Gordon, 560:Fall83-99
    42(AR):Winter83-119
    639(VQR):Winter83-20
Endo, S. Stained Glass Elegies.
    L. Allen, 617(TLS):26Oct84-1223
Endres, C. Joannes Secundus.*
    P.J. Ford, 402(MLR):Apr83-407
Engberg, S. Pastorale.*
    J. Tobin, 573(SSF):Fall83-326
Engel, B.A. Mothers and Daughters.*
    639(VQR):Autumn83-122
Engel, E.J. - see Mendelssohn, M.
Engel, H. The Suicide Murders.
    T.J. Binyon, 617(TLS):30Nov84-1391
    N. Callendar, 441:8Apr84-18
    442(NY):18Jun84-116
Engel, M. Fish.*
    M. Dekoven, 473(PR):2/1983-303
Engel, M. and J.A. Kraulis. The Islands
of Canada.*
    D. Brydon, 102(CanL):Winter82-168
Engel, U. - see Tesnière, L.
Engell, J. and W.J. Bate - see Coleridge,
S.T.
Engelmann, B. Im Gleichschritt marsch.
    P. Schoonover, 221(GQ):Nov83-713
Engelmann, R. Leaf House.
    M. Ellmann, 569(SR):Winter83-120
Engels, J. Weather-Fear.
    D. Baker, 434:Winter83-342
    639(VQR):Autumn83-134
Engelstein, L. Moscow, 1905.
    H. Hogan, 550(RusR):Oct83-433
Engen, R. Kate Greenaway.*
    S. Rudikoff, 31(ASch):Summer83-406
Enggass, R. and M. Stokstad, eds. Hortus
Imaginum.
    E. Young, 39:Jan83-73
England, A. Scripted Drama.
    J. Doolittle, 108:Fall83-134
England, A.B. Energy and Order in the
Poetry of Swift.*
    H.A. Marshall, 447(N&Q):Apr82-178
    A. Messenger, 178:Jun83-226
Englebretsen, G. Logical Negation.
    I. Angelelli, 543:Jun83-925
Englebretsen, G. Three Logicians.
    I. Angelelli, 543:Jun83-926
Engler, B. Reading and Listening.
    A.H., 189(EA):Apr-Jun84-231
English, B. and J. Saville. Strict Settle-
ment.
    L. Stone, 453(NYRB):29Mar84-42
Englund, S. Grace of Monaco.
    J. Barthel, 441:27May84-13
    E. Sirkin, 18:Jul-Aug84-43
Englund, S. Man Slaughter.
    D. Johnson, 453(NYRB):16Feb84-38
    C. Verderese, 441:22Jan84-23
Engs, R.F. Freedom's First Generation.
    R. Reid, 106:Spring83-89
Ennabli, L. Les inscriptions funéraires
chrétiennes de Carthage. (Vol 2)
    W.H.C. Frend, 313:Vol73-222

"The Entry of Henri II into Paris, 16 June 1549." (I.D. McFarlane, ed)
  P. Ford, 208(FS):Apr83-209
  B. Mitchell, 551(RenQ):Summer83-276
  L.V.R., 568(SCN):Spring/Summer83-27
Enyeart, J.L. Edward Weston's California Landscapes.
  A. Grundberg, 441:2Dec84-17
Enzensberger, H.M. The Sinking of the Titanic.*
  P. Martin, 381:Jun83-181
"Enzyklopädie Philosophie und Wissenschaftstheorie." (Vol 1) (J. Mittelstrass, ed)
  L.W. Beck, 486:Jun83-349
Ephron, A. Cool Shades.
  M. Bell, 617(TLS):13May84-19
"La época de Fernando VI."
  I.L. McClelland, 86(BHS):Oct83-343
Epp, R. Kinoshita Yūji.
  V.C. Gessel, 293(JASt):Aug83-955
  S. Rabson, 407(MN):Autumn83-326
Eppard, P.B. and G. Monteiro. A Guide to the Atlantic Monthly Contributors' Club.
  27(AL):Dec83-680
Eppelsheimer, R. Goethes Faust.
  J. Gearey, 222(GR):Fall83-162
Epstein, B.L. The Politics of Domesticity.
  A.F. Scott, 579(SAQ):Winter83-103
  P.G. Skidmore, 106:Winter84-437
Epstein, D.M. The Book of Fortune.
  L. Goldstein, 385(MQR):Winter84-145
Epstein, J. The Lion of Freedom.
  J.F.C. Harrison, 637(VS):Winter83-223
Epstein, J. The Middle of My Tether.
  P. Larkin, 617(TLS):13Jan84-29
Epstein, R.A. A Theory of Strict Liability.
  J.L. Coleman, 482(PhR):Oct83-613
Erasmus. Adagia. (S.S. Menchi, ed)
  J.F. D'Amico, 551(RenQ):Summer83-237
Erasmus. Collected Works of Erasmus.* (Vols 1-5 and 23-24) (W.K. Ferguson and others, eds)
  B.E. Mansfield, 70:Nov/Dec82-59
Erasmus. The Correspondence of Erasmus. (Vols 5 and 6) (R.A.B. Mynors and D.F.S. Thomson, eds) Collected Works of Erasmus. (Vol 31) (M.M. Phillips, ed)
  H. Trevor-Roper, 617(TLS):10Feb84-127
Erb, G. Zu Komposition und Aufbau im ersten Buch Martials.
  P. Howell, 123:Vol33No1-34
Erdman, D.V. - see Blake, W.
Erdman, P. Paul Erdman's Money Book.
  K.W. Arenson, 441:26Aug84-19
Erdrich, L. Love Medicine.
  M. Portales, 441:23Dec84-6
Erenberg, L.A. Steppin' Out.
  P. Buitenhuis, 106:Winter83-475
  C. Simpson, 658:Spring83-110
Erfurth, S. Harry Martinsons barndomsvärld.*
  P. Holmes, 562(Scan):Nov82-202
Erhart, A. Indoevropské jazyky.
  W. Cowgill, 350:Sep84-655
Erickson, C. Mistress Anne.
  L. Charlton, 441:8Jul84-21
Erickson, J. The Road to Berlin.
  D. Holloway, 453(NYRB):22Nov84-48
  A. Sella, 617(TLS):28Sep84-1098

Erickson, J. The Road to Stalingrad. (Vol 1)
  D. Holloway, 453(NYRB):22Nov84-48
Erickson, J.D. and I. Pagès, eds. Proust et le texte producteur.*
  J.M. Cocking, 208(FS):Oct83-482
  A. Corbineau-Hoffmann, 547(RF):Band95 Heft3-373
Ericsson, C.H. Roman Architecture Expressed in Sketches by Francesco di Giorgio Martini.
  F.P. Fiore, 576:May83-201
  90:Jun83-374
Eriksson, O. L'attribut de localisation et les nexus locatifs en français moderne.
  K. Hunnius, 547(RF):Band95Heft3-323
Erisman, F. and R.W. Etulain, eds. Fifty Western Writers.
  M. Bucco, 649(WAL):Aug83-155
  27(AL):Mar83-128
Erisman, H.M. and J.D. Martz, eds. Colossus Challenged.
  B. Zagaris, 263(RIB):Vol33No2-257
Eriugena, J.S. Periphyseon (De diuisione naturae), 3. (I.P. Sheldon-Williams, ed and trans)
  T.M. Tomasic, 589:Apr83-489
Erkkila, B. Walt Whitman among the French.*
  J.A. Hiddleston, 208(FS):Oct83-479
  M. Shaw, 546(RR):Nov83-505
Erlebach, P. Die zusammengesetzten englischen Zunamen französischer Herkunft.
  K. Forster, 38:Band101Heft1/2-188
Ermarth, E.D. Realism and Consensus in the English Novel.
  R. Moss, 617(TLS):13Jan84-44
  G.B. Tennyson, 445(NCF):Dec83-360
Ermolaev, H. Mikhail Sholokhov and his Art.*
  M. Dewhirst, 402(MLR):Oct83-1002
  W.F. Kolonosky, 395(MFS):Summer83-306
  A.B. Murphy, 575(SEER):Jul83-439
Ernst, G. and A. Stefenelli, eds. Sprache und Mensch in der Romania.
  G. Price, 208(FS):Jan83-121
Ernst, J. A Not-So-Still Life.
  P. Frank, 441:11Mar84-17
Erny, P. Ethnologie de l'éducation.
  P. Pénigault-Duhet, 189(EA):Apr-Jun84-170
Erouart, G. L'architecture au Pinceau.
  R. Middleton, 90:Dec83-766
Erpenbeck, J. Was kann Kunst?
  W. Höppner, 654(WB):3/1982-185
Erskine-Hill, H. The Augustan Idea in English Literature.*
  F. Kermode, 344:Spring84-132
Erwin, E. Behaviour Therapy.
  M.N. Eagle, 488:Sep83-335
Erznkatsi, Y. Hawak'umn meknut'ean k'erakani. (L.G. Khacherian, ed)
  J.A.C. Greppin, 617(TLS):24Aug84-940
Escarpit, D. La Littérature d'enfance et de jeunesse.*
  P. Pénigault-Duhet, 189(EA):Jan-Mar83-69
Escarpit, R. - see "Dictionnaire International des Termes Littéraires"
Eschbach, A., ed. Zeichen über Zeichen über Zeichen.
  H. Pape, 619:Winter83-100

Eschenburg, T. Geschichte der Bundesrepublik Deutschland. (Vol 1)
    W. Laqueur, 617(TLS):17Aug84-921
Escher, W., E. Liebl and A. Niederer - see Weiss, R. and P. Geiger
Escribano, J.G. and T. Lambert. Por Aquí.
    M.S. Finch, 399(MLJ):Autumn83-307
Esenin, S. A Biography in Memoirs, Letters, and Documents.* (J. Davies, ed and trans)
    D. Whelan, 550(RusR):Oct83-420
Eshleman, C. Hades in Manganese.
    A.J. Arnold, 639(VQR):Winter83-172
Eshleman, C. and A. Smith - see Césaire, A.
Espermann, I. Antenor, Theano, Antenoriden.
    F.M. Combellack, 122:Oct83-349
    J.B. Hainsworth, 123:Vol33No1-124
Espinosa Elerick, M.L. Annotated Bibliography of Technical and Specialized Dictionaries in Spanish-Spanish and Spanish-....
    B.A. Shaw, 238:Dec83-652
de Espronceda, J. El estudiante de Salamanca and Other Poems.* (R.A. Cardwell, ed)
    M. Camarero, 240(HR):Spring83-232
    M.A. Rees, 86(BHS):Jan83-72
Espy, W.R. The Garden of Eloquence.*
    G.A. De Candido, 441:12Feb84-21
Esselborn, H. Georg Trakl.
    M. Anderle, 400(MLN):Apr83-511
van Essen, A.J. E. Kruisinga.
    F. Stuurman, 361:Dec83-369
    R.W. Zandvoort, 179(ES):Dec83-576
Esser, J. Englische Prosodie.
    A. Wollmann, 38:Band101Heft1/2-172
Esser, K. - see Francis of Assisi
Essick, R.N. William Blake, Printmaker.*
    N. Hilton, 173(ECS):Fall83-64
Esslin, M. The Age of Television.
    H.J. Boyle, 529(QQ):Winter83-1015
Estang, L. Corps à coeur.
    Y-A. Favre, 450(NRF):Jun83-120
Esteban, C. Conjoncture du corps et du jardin.
    D. Leuwers, 450(NRF):Jul/Aug83-206
Esteras Martín, C. Orfebrería de Teruel y su provincia.
    D. Angulo Íñiguez, 48:Jul-Sep80-396
Estermann, A. Die deutschen Literatur-Zeitschriften 1815-1850.* (Vol 10)
    S. Seifert, 654(WB):8/1982-167
Estes, J.M. Christian Magistrate and State Church.
    J.W. Baker, 539:May84-136
    M.U. Edwards, Jr., 551(RenQ):Autumn83-436
Estes, J.W. Hall Jackson and the Purple Foxglove.
    M. Kaufman, 106:Fall83-287
Estève, M. Cinéma et condition humaine.
    S.I. Spencer, 207(FR):Oct83-128
Estienne, H. Deux dialogues du nouveau langage françois italianizé. (P.M. Smith, ed)
    G. Roques, 553(RLiR):Jul-Dec83-506
Estleman, L.D. Kill Zone.
    N. Callendar, 441:2Dec84-62
Estrada, F.L. - see under López Estrada, F.
Estroff, S.E. Making It Crazy.
    G.R. Lowe, 529(QQ):Summer83-295

Etcheson, C. The Rise and Demise of Democratic Kampuchea.
    A. Barnett, 617(TLS):14Sep84-1016
Etherton, M. The Development of African Drama.*
    C. Kamlongera, 69:Vol53No3-94
Étiemble. Rimbaud, système solaire ou trou noir?
    C. Scott, 617(TLS):29Jun84-730
Étienne de Fougères. Le Livre des Manières. (R.A. Lodge, ed)
    P.F. Dembowski, 545(RPh):May83-624
Etienne-Nugue, J. Crafts and the Arts of Living in the Cameroon.
    F.T. Smith, 2(AfrA):May83-20
Ettling, J. The Germ of Laziness.
    M. Kaufman, 106:Fall83-287
"Études rabelaisiennes."* (Vol 15)
    D.G. Coleman, 208(FS):Apr83-205
"Etudes sur le XIIIe siècle." (Vol 8) (R. Mortier and H. Hasquin, eds)
    R. Waller, 83:Spring83-73
Etzkorn, G.I. and F.E. Kelly - see Ockham, William of
"Eubulus: The Fragments" - see under Hunter, R.L.
Eulenburg, D.S. The Music of Elliott Carter.
    D. Harvey, 415:Jul83-426
Euripides. Trojan Women. (G. MacEwen, with N. Tsingos, trans)
    T. Marshall, 529(QQ):Winter83-1152
"European Paintings of the 16th, 17th and 18th Centuries." [Cleveland Museum of Art]
    E. Young, 39:Sep83-271
Eustathius. Eustathii archiepiscopi Thessalonicensis Commentarii ad Homeri "Iliadem" pertinentes.* (Vol 3) (M. van der Valk, ed)
    D. Holwerda, 394:Vol36fasc1/2-210
Evan, W.M., ed. The Sociology of Law.
    C.S., 185:Jul84-734
Evans, A.C. - see Bruce-Mitford, R. and others
Evans, B. Freedom to Choose.
    R. Porter, 617(TLS):16Mar84-265
Evans, B.L. and G.L. - see under Lloyd Evans, B. and G.
Evans, C. Landscapes of the Night.* (P. Evans, ed)
    P-L. Adams, 61:Aug84-112
Evans, C. Looking Ahead.
    A. Stevenson, 617(TLS):2Mar84-226
Evans, D. Big Road Blues.
    B. Feintuch, 292(JAF):Oct-Dec83-488
    W.K. McNeil, 650(WF):Oct83-297
    B.L. Pearson, 187:Jan84-143
Evans, D. Mather Brown.*
    I.B. Jaffe, 432(NEQ):Jun83-311
    J.M. Neil, 656(WMQ):Oct83-655
Evans, E. Ring Lardner.
    T.J. Matheson, 106:Fall83-321
Evans, E.J. The Forging of the Modern State.
    R.J. Morris, 617(TLS):16Mar84-283
Evans, E.L. The German Center Party 1870-1933.
    J. Doerr, 150(DR):Summer83-341
Evans, G.B. - see Shakespeare, W.
Evans, G.E. The Strength of the Hills.
    D.A.N. Jones, 617(TLS):2Mar84-225

Evans, G.E. Where Beards Wag All.
   D. Gittins, 637(VS):Summer83-431
Evans, G.R. Anselm and a New Generation.
   J. McCarthy, 543:Dec82-446
Evans, G.R. Augustine on Evil.*
   R.M.M., 185:Jul84-733
Evans, H. Good Times, Bad Times.*
   R.W. Apple, Jr., 441:8Jan84-22
Evans, H. Publica Carmina.
   R.F. Thomas, 124:May-Jun84-331
Evans, J., ed. London Tales.*
   J. Mellors, 362:19Jan84-26
Evans, J.A.S. Herodotus.
   J.M. Bigwood, 487:Spring83-86
   S. West, 123:Vol33No1-132
Evans, J.M. - see Milton, J.
Evans, M., ed. Black Women Writers (1950-
   1980).
   R. Brown, 441:23Sep84-15
Evans, M. Fearless Cooking against the
   Clock.
   W. and C. Cowen, 639(VQR):Spring83-65
Evans, M. Lucien Goldmann.*
   M. Kelly, 402(MLR):Jan83-196
Evans, P. The Englishman's Daughter.*
   639(VQR):Autumn83-128
Evans, P. Sweet Lucy.
   M. Hulse, 617(TLS):12Oct84-1169
Evans, R. The Fabrication of Virtue.
   A. Forty, 59:Dec83-481
Evans, R.J.W. The Making of the Habsburg
   Monarchy 1550-1700.
   J. Black, 161(DUJ):Jun83-112
   J.W., 617(TLS):20Jul84-822
Evans, S. Houses on the Site.
   P. Lewis, 617(TLS):9Nov84-1288
   J. Mellors, 362:11Oct84-30
Evans, W.A. Management Ethics.
   J.H.C., 185:Apr84-574
Evans, W.R. - see "Robert Frost and Sidney
   Cox"
"Walker Evans at Work."
   A. Ross, 364:Jul83-98
Evans-Wentz, W.Y. Cuchama and Sacred
   Mountains. (F. Waters and C.L. Adams,
   eds)
   J.L. Davis, 649(WAL):May83-46
Everhart, R.B. Reading, Writing and Resis-
   tance.
   B. Holmes, 617(TLS):6Jul84-749
Everson, W. Birth of a Poet. (L. Bart-
   lett, ed)
   D.A. Carpenter, 649(WAL):May83-49
"Everyday Matters 2."
   M. Wandor, 362:12Jul84-28
"Everyman."* (G. Cooper and C. Wortham,
   eds)
   J. Conley, 589:Jan83-158
Evett, A. Understanding the Space-Time
   Concepts of Special Relativity.
   B. Mundy, 486:Sep83-518
Ewald, W.B., Jr. Who Killed Joe McCarthy?
   J. Rosenthal, 441:7Oct84-39
Ewans, M. Wagner and Aeschylus.*
   R. Hollinrake, 410(M&L):Jul/Oct83-283
   R.L.J., 412:Aug-Nov82-271
Ewart, G. The Ewart Quarto.
   B. Constantine, 176:Sep/Oct84-43
Ewart-Biggs, J. "Pay, Pack and Follow."
   J. Simpson, 362:25Oct84-27
Ewell, J. Venezuela.
   J. Lynch, 617(TLS):31Aug84-966

Ewers, H-H., ed. Kinder- und Jugendlitera-
   tur der Aufklärung.*
   G. Opie, 402(MLR):Jul83-755
Ewin, R.E. Co-Operation and Human Values.*
   A. Ellis, 518:Jan83-38
   D.H. Monro, 63:Mar83-118
"Exodus." (P.J. Lucas, ed)
   A. Lutz, 72:Band219Heft2-424
von Eyb, A. - see under Albrecht von Eyb
Eyffinger, A. Inventory of the Poetry of
   Hugo Grotius.
   J.A. Parente, Jr., 568(SCN):Winter83-
   86
Eyles, A. James Stewart.
   S. Gold, 441:4Nov84-13
Eyssen, J. Buchkunst in Deutschland vom
   Jugendstil zum Malerbuch.
   L.S. Thompson, 70:Sep/Oct82-31
Ezekiel, T.O. Floaters.
   S. Koch, 441:22Jul84-12
Ezrahi, S.D. By Words Alone.*
   J.E. Young, 390:Apr83-60

Faaland, J., ed. Aid and Influence.
   J. Das Gupta, 293(JASt):Nov82-105
Faas, E. Ted Hughes.
   J.R. Watson, 677(YES):Vol 13-363
Fabbri, M. A Bibliography of Hispanic
   Dictionaries.
   B.A. Shaw, 238:Sep83-449
von Faber, H., ed. Beziehungen zwischen
   Sprachrezeption-Sprachproduktion im
   Fremdsprachenunterricht.
   M.P. Alter, 399(MLJ):Autumn83-272
Fabian, R. and H-C. Adam. Masters of
   Early Travel Photography.*
   M.M. Hambourg, 617(TLS):20Jul84-821
Fabiny, T., ed. Shakespeare and the
   Emblem.
   W. Schleiner, 111:Fall84-7
Fabre, G. Libertus.*
   K.R. Bradley, 487:Summer83-184
Fabre, G. Le Théâtre noir aux États-Unis.
   R.A. Day, 189(EA):Jul-Sep84-359
Fabre, J. Idées sur le roman de Madame de
   Lafayette au Marquis de Sade.
   V. Mylne, 208(FS):Oct83-465
Fabricant, C. Swift's Landscape.
   P. Rogers, 566:Autumn83-49
de Fabry, A.S. Jeux de Miroirs.
   A. Rosenberg, 627(UTQ):Summer83-460
Facco, M.L. Metafisica e diaristica in
   Gabriel Marcel.
   M. Adam, 542:Oct-Dec83-492
Fackler, E. Arson.
   N. Callendar, 441:20May84-39
"The Facsimile Edition of the Nag Hammadi
   Codices: Cartonnage." "The Facsimile
   Edition of the Nag Hammadi Codices:
   Codices IX and X."
   B. Layton, 318(JAOS):Apr-Jun82-397
Fages, J-B. Comprendre René Girard.
   M. Adam, 542:Oct-Dec83-492
Fagg, W. African Majesty from Grassland
   and Forest.
   A. Rubin, 2(AfrA):May83-23
Fagg, W. and J. Pemberton 3d. Yoruba.
   R. Poynor, 2(AfrA):Nov82-8
Faghfoury, M., ed. Analytical Philosophy
   of Religion in Canada.
   J.R. Horne, 154:Dec83-750

Fagunwa, D.O. Forest of a Thousand Dae-
mons.
  B.L. Knapp, 469:Vol9No2-118
  C.R. Larson, 441:15Jan84-11
  J. Updike, 442(NY):23Apr84-119
Fahmy, J.M. Voltaire et Paris.*
  N. Perry, 208(FS):Apr83-218
  J. Renwick, 402(MLR):Jan83-186
Fainlight, R. Climates.
  H. Davies, 617(TLS):13Apr84-413
Fainlight, R. Fifteenth to Infinity.
  H. Davies, 617(TLS):13Apr84-413
  H. Lomas, 364:Feb84-83
Fair, A.A. The Bigger They Come.
  N. Callendar, 441:24Jun84-41
Fairbairns, Z. Here Today.
  S. Altinel, 617(TLS):15Jun84-676
Fairbairns, Z. Stand We at Last.*
  K. Goldsworthy, 381:Sep83-397
Fairbank, J.K., ed. The Cambridge History
  of China. (Vol 10, Pt 1)
  D.H. Bays, 318(JAOS):Apr-Jun82-429
Fairbank, J.K. Chinabound.*
  L.H.D. Gordon, 293(JASt):Aug83-914
Fairbank, J.K. and K-C. Liu, eds. The Cam-
  bridge History of China. (Vol 11)
  Wang Gungwu, 244(HJAS):Jun83-365
Fairbank, W. - see Liang Ssu-ch'eng
Fairbanks, J.L. and E.B. Bates. American
  Furniture.
  G. Wills, 39:Feb83-147
Fairbrother, J. and R. Moore. Testing the
  Wicket.
  A.L. Le Quesne, 617(TLS):21Dec84-1487
"Faire croire."
  E. Peters, 589:Jan83-260
Fairley, A. Flutes, Flautists and Makers
  (active or born before 1900).
  N. O'Loughlin, 415:Jul83-429
Fairley, J. and S. Welfare. Arthur C.
  Clarke's World of Strange Powers.
  N.S. Sutherland, 617(TLS):2Nov84-1259
Fairlie, A. Imagination and Language.*
  (M. Bowie, ed)
  N. King, 402(MLR):Oct83-926
Fairweather, J. Seneca the Elder.*
  E. Noë, 313:Vol73-241
  J.E.G. Zetzel, 24:Summer83-207
Faivre, A. and R.C. Zimmermann, eds.
  Epochen der Naturmystik.
  G. Keil, 680(ZDP):Band102Heft1-154
Falc'hun, F. and M. Oftedal - see Sommer-
  felt, A.
Falcoff, M. and F.B. Pike, eds. The
  Spanish Civil War, 1936-39.*
  P.B. Taylor, Jr., 263(RIB):Vol33No3-
  401
Falcoff, M. and R. Royal, eds. Crisis and
  Opportunity.
  P.S. Falk, 441:9Sep84-31
Falcón, N. and others. Huelga y sociedad.
  C. Gautier Mayoral, 701(SinN):Jul-
  Sep83-73
Falcón Márquez, T. La Catedral de Sevilla
  (Estudio arquitectónico).*
  F. Marías, 48:Oct-Dec80-506
Faler, P.G. Mechanics and Manufacturers
  in the Early Industrial Revolution.
  R.D. Brown, 432(NEQ):Mar83-117
Falk, C. Love, Anarchy, and Emma Goldman.
  C. Gilligan, 441:4Nov84-28
Falk, E.H. The Poetics of Roman Ingarden.*
  G. Prince, 593:Spring83-87

Falk, R., S.S. Kim and S.H. Mendlovitz,
  eds. Studies on a Just World Order.
  (Vol 1)
  J.G., 185:Oct83-186
Falk, T. and M. Archer. Indian Miniatures
  in the India Office Library.*
  J.P. Losty, 463:Spring83-69
Fall, A.S. L'Appel des arènes.
  T.N. Hammond, 207(FR):May84-907
Falla, P.S., ed. The Oxford English-
  Russian Dictionary.
  C.R. Pike, 617(TLS):17Aug84-920
Fallier, J.H. Traditional Rug Hooking
  Manual.
  P. Bach, 614:Summer84-30
Fallon, I. and J. Srodes. Dream Maker.*
  (British title: De Lorean.)
  D. Sharp, 129:Jan84-76
Fallows, D. Dufay.
  H.M. Brown, 415:Oct83-617
  D. Stevens, 414(MusQ):Fall83-601
  R. Strohm, 410(M&L):Jul/Oct83-246
Fantham, E. Seneca's "Troades."*
  W.M. Calder 3d, 24:Winter83-415
  G.A. Kennedy, 124:Sep-Oct83-46
Fantosme, J. Chronicle. (R.C. Johnston,
  ed and trans)
  E.A. Hanawalt, 589:Apr83-456
  M.D. Legge, 382(MAE):1983/1-167
  B. Merrilees, 447(N&Q):Aug82-354
al-Farabi. Al-Farabi's Commentary and
  Short Treatise on Aristotle's "De Inter-
  pretatione."* (F.W. Zimmermann, ed and
  trans)
  T-A.D., 543:Sep82-212
Farah, N. Close Sesame.*
  P. Lewis, 364:Feb84-101
Farber, J. A Field Guide to the Aesthetic
  Experience.
  S.T. Viguers, 290(JAAC):Winter83-241
Farber, S. and M. Green. Hollywood Dynas-
  ties.
  J. Lardner, 441:19Aug84-7
Farber, T. Curves of Pursuit.
  R. Elman, 441:8Jan84-18
Farber, W. Beschwörungsrituale an Ištar
  und Dumuzi.
  D.A. Foxvog, 318(JAOS):Jan-Mar82-160
Farge, A. and M. Foucault. Le Désordre
  des familles.*
  J-P. Guinle, 450(NRF):May83-137
Fargeaud, M. - see de Balzac, H.
Farington, J. The Diary of Joseph Far-
  ington. (Vols 1-6) (K. Garlick and A.
  Macintyre, eds)
  D. Irwin, 161(DUJ):Dec82-89
Farington, J. The Diary of Joseph Faring-
  ton. (Vols 7-10) (K. Cave, ed)
  L. Herrmann, 90:Apr83-235
Faris, W.B. Carlos Fuentes.
  E.J. Mullen, 263(RIB):Vol33No4-586
Farkas, A., ed. Titta Ruffo.
  J. Steane, 617(TLS):12Oct84-1157
Farkas, E. From Here To Here.
  D. Daymond, 102(CanL):Summer83-140
Farley-Hills, D. The Comic in Renaissance
  Comedy.*
  S. Henning, 405(MP):May84-415
  P. Hyland, 568(SCN):Fall83-50
  R.A. Kimbrough, 125:Fall82-108
Farmer, A.D. Jessamyn West.
  R.W. Etulain, 649(WAL):Aug83-176

Farmer, N.K. Poets and the Visual Arts in Renaissance England.
A. Fowler, 617(TLS):19Oct84-1181
Farmer, P. Standing in the Shadow.
L. Taylor, 617(TLS):27Apr84-476
Farnan, D.J. Auden in Love.
R. Craft, 453(NYRB):27Sep84-7
J. Fuller, 441:2Sep84-6
Farnsworth, D.N. and J.W. McKenney. U.S.-Panama Relations, 1903-1978.
L.D. Langley, 263(RIB):Vol133No4-587
Farnsworth, R.M. - see Tolson, M.B.
Farr, W., ed. Hume und Kant.
R. Meerbote, 319:Jul84-375
Farrar, M. and E.T. Maleska, eds. Series 133 Simon and Schuster Crossword Puzzle Book.
S.B. Flexner, 441:8Jul84-17
Farrell, B.A. The Standing of Psychoanalysis.*
H.S. Ruttenberg, 185:Jan84-350
Farrell, J.G. Troubles.
P. Craig, 617(TLS):21Sep84-1066
Farrell, J.P. Revolution as Tragedy.*
J.L. Spear, 125:Spring83-292
Farrell, J.T. On Irish Themes. (D. Flynn, ed)
B. Dolan, 305(JIL):Jan83-111
Farrell, M.J. (M. Keane) The Rising Tide. Devoted Ladies.
P. Craig, 617(TLS):1Jun84-623
Farrell, R.T., ed. Bede and Anglo-Saxon England.
A. Lutz, 38:Band101Heft1/2-204
Farriss, N.M. Maya Society Under Colonial Rule.
D. Brading, 617(TLS):19Oct84-1185
Farson, D. Henry.*
J.W. Blench, 161(DUJ):Dec82-86
Farwell, B. Mr. Kipling's Army. (British title: For Queen and Country.)
L.J. Satre, 637(VS):Autumn82-85
Fassò, A., ed. Cantari d'Aspramonte inediti (Magl. VII 682).
M. Marti, 228(GSLI):Vol 160fasc510-290
Fast, H. The Outsider.
J. Berry, 441:23Sep84-28
Fasulo, L.M. Representing America.
D. Newell, 441:18Nov84-33
Fattori, M. Lessico del "Novum Organum" di Francesco Bacone.
G. Costa, 480(P&R):Vol 16No2-140
Fattori, M. and M. Bianchi, eds. Res: III° Colloquio Internazionale, Roma, 7-9 gennaio 1980.
G. Costa, 480(P&R):Vol 16No2-140
Faulhaber, C. - see Gil de Zamora, J.
Faulhaber, C.B., comp. Medieval Manuscripts in the Library of the Hispanic Society of America.
A. Deyermond, 617(TLS):14Sep84-1022
Faulkes, A., ed. Two Versions of Snorra Edda from the 17th Century.*
J. Lindow, 301(JEGP):Jan83-116
Faulkes, A. - see Snorri Sturluson
Faulkner, A.O. and others. When I Was Comin' Up.
42(AR):Fall83-504
Faulkner, P. Against the Age.*
I. Britain, 637(VS):Autumn82-103
Faulkner, P. Angus Wilson.*
K. Watson, 447(N&Q):Jun82-270

Faulkner, V., with F.C. Luebke, eds. Vision and Refuge.
B.K. Morton, 649(WAL):May83-95
Faulkner, W. Sanctuary.* (N. Polk, ed)
R.A., 189(EA):Apr-Jun84-238
Faulkner, W. Vision in Spring.
H. Kenner, 441:12Aug84-26
Faulks, S. A Trick of the Light.
P. Keegan, 617(TLS):27Jul84-848
J. Mantle, 362:26Jul84-28
Fauré, G. Gabriel Fauré: His Life through His Letters. (J-M. Nectoux, ed)
R. Nichols, 617(TLS):14Sep84-1012
Faust, D.G. James Henry Hammond and the Old South.*
F. Hobson, 392:Fall83-585
Favier, J. François Villon.*
J. Fox, 208(FS):Apr83-204
Fawcett, R.P. Cognitive Linguistics and Social Interaction.
D. Nehls, 257(IRAL):May83-170
Fay, M. A Mortal Condition.
F. Mullan, 441:15Jan84-23
Fay, S. and R. Wood. The Ring.
A. Hollinghurst, 617(TLS):24Aug84-936
Febles, J. Cuentos olvidados de Alfonso Hernández Catá.
O. de la Suarée, 238:Dec83-648
Febvre, L. The Problem of Unbelief in the Sixteenth Century.*
P.R. Berk, 539:May84-123
Febvre, L. and H-J. Martin. The Coming of the Book.
G.N., 617(TLS):17Aug84-927
Fechin, E. Fechin.
D. Phillips, 50(ArQ):Autumn83-287
Federhofer, H. Akkord und Stimmführung in den Musiktheoretischen Systemen von Hugo Riemann, Ernst Kurth und Heinrich Schenker.
D. Neumeyer, 308:Spring83-99
Federman, R. The Twofold Vibration.*
L. Chamberlain, 114(ChiR):Summer83-117
Federspiel, J.F. The Ballad of Typhoid Mary.
J.C. Batchelor, 441:12Feb84-11
E.S. Turner, 617(TLS):12Oct84-1153
442(NY):13Feb84-129
Fedorowicz, J.K., ed and trans. A Republic of Nobles.*
E.B. Fryde, 575(SEER):Oct83-617
639(VQR):Spring84-55
Feenberg, A. Lukács, Marx and the Sources of Critical Theory.*
S.R., 543:Sep82-165
Fegert, H. Die Morphonologie der Präfixe "v(o)z-" und "v(o)s-" in der russischen Schriftsprache der Gegenwart.
N.B. Thelin, 260(IF):Band88-362
Fehér, F. and Á. Heller. Hungary 1956 Revisited.
G. Schöpflin, 617(TLS):27Jan84-80
Fehrenbach, R.J., L.A. Boone and M.A. Di Cesare. A Concordance to the Plays, Poems, and Translations of Christopher Marlowe.
H.S. Donow, 365:Summer/Fall83-130
Fehrenbach, T.R. Lone Star.
L. Milazzo, 584(SWR):Spring83-vi
Fehrman, C. Poetic Creation.
R. Jayne, 52:Band17Heft1-87
Fei-kan, L. - see under Li Fei-kan

Feiffer, J. Jules Feiffer's America.*
(S. Heller, ed)
639(VQR):Spring83-59
Feigin, S.I. Legal and Administrative
Texts of the Reign of Samsu-iluna.
M. Stol, 318(JAOS):Jan-Mar82-161
Feigl, H. Inquiries and Provocations.
R.J. Matthews, 486:Jun83-339
Feijoo, B.J. Obras completas. (Vol 1)
(J.M. Caso González and S. Cerra Suárez,
eds)
P. Ilie, 173(ECS):Spring84-387
Feilden, B.G. Conservation of Historic
Buildings.
J.M. Fitch, 576:May83-197
Fein, R.J. Robert Lowell.
R. Pooley, 402(MLR):Apr83-440
Feinberg, J. Rights, Justice, and the
Bounds of Liberty.*
S.J. Massey, 482(PhR):Jul83-438
Feinberg, R.E. The Intemperate Zone.*
S. McConnell, 129:Feb84-72
Feingold, M. The Mathematicians' Appren-
ticeship.
R. Hall, 617(TLS):20Apr84-442
Feingold, R. Nature and Society.
I. Simon, 179(ES):Feb83-86
Feinstein, E. The Border.
T. Dooley, 617(TLS):8Jun84-632
J. Lasdun, 176:Sep/Oct84-51
J. Mantle, 362:21Jun84-27
Feinstein, H.M. Becoming William James.
R. Dinnage, 453(NYRB):31May84-3
W. Gaylin, 441:14Oct84-45
R.W.B. Lewis, 617(TLS):26Oct84-1203
Feirstein, F. Fathering.
J.F. Cotter, 249(HudR):Winter83/84-716
Feld, A.L., M. O'Hare and J.M.D. Schuster.
Patrons Despite Themselves.
D. Kuspit, 62:Apr84-73
Feld, F. and E. Kobrin. Judaic Symbols
and Mottos for Cross Stitch and Needle-
point.
P. Bach, 614:Summer84-20
Feld, S. Sound and Sentiment.
D.M. Neuman, 187:Sep84-551
Feldman, F.B. The Artist.
G.A. Clark, 289:Fall83-121
Feldman, I. Teach Me, Dear Sister.
S. Burris, 344:Summer84-127
J.F. Cotter, 249(HudR):Winter83/84-711
J. Hollander, 676(YR):Autumn83-xix
639(VQR):Summer83-97
Felix, W. Byzanz und die islamische Welt
im früheren 11. Jahrhundert.
J.H. Forsyth, 589:Apr83-458
Fell, M. The Persistence of Memory.
W. Logan, 441:26Aug84-13
Feller, J.Q. Chinese Export Porcelains in
the 19th Century.
U. Roberts, 60:Jul-Aug83-119
Fellini, F. Moraldo in the City [&] A
Journey with Anita.* (J.C. Stubbs, ed
and trans)
J. Mellors, 362:19Jan84-26
Fellman, A.C. and M. Making Sense of
Self.*
M. Kaufman, 106:Fall83-287
S.E.D. Shortt, 529(QQ):Summer83-557
Fellows, J. Ruskin's Maze.*
E.K. Helsinger, 405(MP):May84-432
H.W., 636(VP):Summer83-197

Fellows, O. and D.G. Carr - see "Diderot
Studies"
Felman, S. La Folie et la chose littér-
aire.
G. Cesbron, 356(LR):Nov83-341
Felman, S., ed. Literature and Psycho-
analysis.
S. Weiland, 128(CE):Nov83-705
Felsenstein, F. - see Smollett, T.
Felten, F.J. Äbte und Laienäbte im Frank-
enreich.
G. Constable, 589:Jan83-172
van der Feltz, A.C.A.W. Charles Howard
Hodges 1764-1837.
R. Walker, 90:Mar83-168
Femenias, B. and J.A. Raducha, with C.C.
Cort. Two Faces of South Asian Art.
R.L. Shep, 614:Spring84-28
Femiano, S. Ricerca su Michelangelo Far-
della, Filosofo e matematico (1650-1718).
R. Sasso, 192(EP):Apr-Jun83-232
"Feminist Readings."
M. Whitford, 208(FS):Jul83-372
Fender, S. Plotting the Golden West.
H.N. Smith, 402(MLR):Oct83-906
Fénelon, F. Oeuvres I. (J. Le Brun, ed)
F.W. Vogler, 207(FR):May84-875
Fenger, H. Kierkegaard.*
W. Greve, 53(AGP):Band65Heft3-331
Fenlon, I., ed. Cambridge Music Manu-
scripts, 900-1700.
D. Fallows, 415:Sep83-550
Fenlon, I., ed. Early Music History.*
(Vol 1)
A.W. Atlas, 551(RenQ):Summer83-259
N.K. Moran, 539:Nov83-282
Fenlon, I. Music and Patronage in Six-
teenth-Century Mantua.* (Vol 1)
L. Lockwood, 551(RenQ):Spring83-100
Fenlon, I. Music and Patronage in Six-
teenth-Century Mantua.* (Vol 2)
J. Chater, 415:Jun83-363
Fenlon, I., ed. Music in Medieval and
Early Modern Europe.*
D. Fallows, 415:Mar83-169
J.A. Owens, 551(RenQ):Spring83-97
Fennell, F.L. Dante Gabriel Rossetti.
I. Small, 89(BJA):Spring83-187
Fennell, T.G. and H. Gelsen. A Grammar
of Modern Latvian.*
B. Comrie, 353:Vol20No7/8-559
Fenoaltea, D. "Si haulte Architecture."
W.J. Beck, 207(FR):May84-871
M. Tetel, 551(RenQ):Winter83-625
Fenton, A. and G. Stell, eds. Loads and
Roads in Scotland and Beyond.
R.H. Campbell, 617(TLS):19Oct84-1194
Fenton, A. and B. Walker. The Rural Archi-
tecture of Scotland.
C. McWilliam, 576:Dec83-394
Fenton, E. Scorched Earth.
C. Hawtree, 617(TLS):13Apr84-396
Fenton, J. Children in Exile.
S. Heaney, 453(NYRB):25Oct84-40
B. Morrison, 617(TLS):27Jan84-76
A. Poulin, Jr., 441:30Sep84-45
Fenton, J. A German Requiem.
J. Saunders, 565:Vol24No1-73
Fenton, J. The Memory of War.*
S. Featherstone, 148:Winter83-85

Fenton, J. You Were Marvellous.*
　J. Lahr, 157:Winter83-36
　C. Ludlow, 364:Jul83-72
　J. Spurling, 176:Jan84-55
Fenton, J. - see Frayn, M.
Ferguson, C.A. and S.B. Heath, eds. Language in the USA.
　P. Beade, 361:Jan83-99
　C.C. Eble, 355(LSoc):Jun83-272
　G-J. Forgue, 189(EA):Jan-Mar83-104
　J. Sledd, 35(AS):Spring83-42
Ferguson, E.J. and others - see Morris, R.
Ferguson, J. Callimachus.*
　E. Jenkinson, 161(DUJ):Dec82-93
Ferguson, J. Jesus in the Tide of Time.
　J.C. Fenton, 161(DUJ):Jul83-146
Ferguson, J. Juvenal, "The Satires."
　R.A. La Fleur, 121(CJ):Feb/Mar84-257
　M.D. Reeve, 123:Vol33No1-27
Ferguson, J.P., ed. Essays on Burma.
　M.E. Spiro, 293(JASt):Nov82-211
Ferguson, M.A.H. Bibliography of English Translations from Medieval Sources, 1943-1967.
　K. Kish, 545(RPh):Aug82-116
Ferguson, N. Right Plant, Right Place.
　L. Yang, 441:3Jun84-9
Ferguson, R.H. Laforgue y Lugones.*
　P.W. Borgeson, Jr., 238:Mar83-139
　J. Wilson, 86(BHS):Jan83-86
Ferguson, W. Freedom and Other Fictions.
　J. Penner, 441:4Mar84-9
Ferguson, W. La versificatión imitativa en Fernando de Herrera.
　A. Carreño, 86(BHS):Jul83-256
　B.W. Ife, 402(MLR):Jul83-734
　M.G. Randel, 238:Mar83-131
Ferguson, W.K. and others - see Erasmus
Ferguson-Lees, J. Shell Guide to the Birds of Britain and Ireland.
　R.O., 617(TLS):17Feb84-174
Fergusson, P. Architecture of Solitude.
　J. Harvey, 617(TLS):16Nov84-1319
Fermor, P.L. Mani.
　G.S., 617(TLS):22Jun84-711
Fern, A. and J. O'Sullivan. The Complete Prints of Leonard Baskin.
　D.J.R. Bruckner, 441:21Oct84-30
Fern, D.E. God Nijinsky.
　R. Philp, 151:Oct82-97
Fernández, A.L. - see under Labandeira Fernández, A.
Fernandez, D. Dans la main de l'Ange.*
　A. Clerval, 450(NRF):Jan83-117
Fernandez, D. Signor Giovanni.
　J. Daviron, 98:Aug-Sep83-745
Fernandez, D.G. The Iloilo Zarzuela 1903-1930.*
　M.D. Zamora, 302:Vol 19No2-225
Fernández, J.B. and N. García. Nuevos horizontes.
　V. Benmaman, 399(MLJ):Summer83-206
　E.C. Torbert, 238:Mar83-151
Fernández, P.H. Ideario etimológico de José Ortega y Gasset.
　A. Donoso, 258:Jun83-224
　L. Lorenzo-Rivero, 238:Mar83-134
Fernández, P.H. Ideario etimológico de Miguel de Unamuno.
　C. Galerstein, 238:May83-296
Fernández, P.H. Ideario etimológico de Ramón Pérez de Ayala.
　C.A. Longhurst, 86(BHS):Oct83-346

Fernández, P.H., ed. Simposio Internacional Ramón Pérez de Ayala (1880-1980).
　J.J. Macklin, 86(BHS):Oct83-345
　R.L. Sheehan, 238:May83-297
Fernández, R.M.A. - see under Aguilar Fernández, R.M.
Fernández de Avellaneda, A. Don Quixote de La Mancha (Part II) Being the Spurious Continuation of Miguel Cervantes' Part I.* (A.W. Server and J.E. Keller, eds and trans)
　G. Martínez Lacalle, 86(BHS):Jan83-66
Fernández González, J.R. El habla de Ancares (León).
　H. Meier, 72:Band220Heft2-434
Fernández Jiménez, J. - see de Medina, P.
Fernández-Morera, D. The Lyre and the Oaten Flute.*
　B.M. Damiani, 240(HR):Autumn83-463
　B.W. Ife, 402(MLR):Oct83-943
Fernández Olmos, M. La cuentística de Juan Bosch.
　F. Jiménez, 238:Dec83-649
Fernández Santos, J. Extramuros.
　D. Lodge, 441:15Jul84-25
Fernández-Sosa, L. Comunicación.
　M. Iglesias, 399(MLJ):Summer83-204
Fernando, C. and R. Flavell. On Idiom.
　R. Gläser, 682(ZPSK):Band36Heft5-602
Fernie, E. The Architecture of the Anglo-Saxons.
　R. Gem, 617(TLS):3Feb84-119
Ferns, C.S. Aldous Huxley: Novelist.*
　T.A. Shippey, 541(RES):Feb83-94
Ferrán, J. Alfonso Costafreda.
　J.M. Naharro, 240(HR):Summer83-355
Ferrard, J. Orgues du Brabant Wallon.*
　L. Jambou, 537:Vol169No2-226
de Ferraresci, A.C. De amor y poesía en la España medieval.
　S. Fleischman, 457(NRFH):Tomo31núm1-123
Ferrars, E.X. Something Wicked.
　N. Callendar, 441:18Mar84-27
　442(NY):30Apr84-123
Ferrell, R.H. Truman.
　D.R. Jones, 441:10Jun84-25
Ferrier, J., ed. Les Fioretti du Quadricentenaire de Fabri de Peiresc.
　M-O. Sweetser, 535(RHL):Jan/Feb83-121
Ferrier-Caverivière, N. L'Image de Louis XIV dans la littérature française de 1660 à 1715.*
　Y. Coirault, 535(RHL):Mar/Apr83-275
　R. Parish, 208(FS):Apr83-217
　M-O. Sweetser, 207(FR):Mar84-552
Ferril, T.H. Anvil of Roses.
　F. Chappell, 651(WHR):Autumn83-251
　J.R. Saucerman, 649(WAL):Feb84-379
Ferris, P. Gentlemen of Fortune.
　J. Hardie, 617(TLS):14Dec84-1438
Ferris, W. and M. Hart, eds. Folk Music and Modern Sound.
　R. Allen, 650(WF):Oct83-296
Ferro, M. The Use and Abuse of History.
　S. Bann, 617(TLS):10Aug84-899
Ferron, M. Histoires édifiantes.
　J.M. Paterson, 102(CanL):Autumn83-67
Ferrucci, F. The Poetics of Disguise.*
　W.J. Kennedy, 400(MLN):Jan83-139

Ferry, D. Strangers.
  A. Brumer, 441:23Sep84-14
  J. Hollander, 676(YR):Spring84-xiv
  M. Kinzie, 29:Mar/Apr84-38
Ferry, L. and A. Renaut - see Fichte, J-G.
Fertey, A. - see Jarvis-Sladky, K.
Fettner, A.G. and W.A. Check. The Truth
  About AIDS.
  K. Ray, 441:17Jun84-21
Fetz, R.L. Whitehead.
  L.S. Ford, 258:Sep83-340
Fetzer, G. Wertungsprobleme in der Trivi-
  alliteraturforschung.
  B. Svane, 462(OL):Vol37No4-372
Fetzer, J.F. Clemens Brentano.
  H.M.K. Riley, 133:Band16Heft1-68
  E. Stopp, 402(MLR):Oct83-981
Fetzer, J.H. Scientific Knowledge.
  D. Shrader, 486:Dec83-660
Feuerbach, L. Thoughts on Death and
  Immortality.
  H. Laycock, 529(QQ):Autumn83-905
Feuerlicht, R.S. The Fate of the Jews.
  A.J. Sherman, 617(TLS):14Sep84-1032
Feuerwerker, Y-T.M. Ding Ling's Fiction.*
  S.W. Chen, 244(HJAS):Dec83-665
"Feydeau, First to Last."
  E. Salmon, 529(QQ):Winter83-1217
Feyder, V. Caldeiras.
  G.R. Besser, 207(FR):Oct83-137
Feyerabend, P.K. Philosophical Papers.
  W. Suchting, 63:Mar83-106
  M. Tiles, 483:Jan83-121
Fichte, J-G. Machiavel et autres écrits
  philosophiques et politiques de 1806-
  1807.* (L. Ferry and A. Renaut, eds and
  trans)
  J-M. Gabaude, 542:Jan-Mar83-131
Fichte, J.O. Alt- und Mittelenglische
  Literatur.
  K. Dietz, 72:Band220Heft2-390
Fichte, J.O. Chaucer's "Art Poetical."*
  P. Hardman, 541(RES):Feb83-55
  T. Turville-Petre, 677(YES):Vol 13-296
Fichter, A. Poets Historical.*
  H.M., 604:Winter83-4
  J.V. Mirollo, 551(RenQ):Winter83-619
Fichtner, P.S. Ferdinand I of Austria.
  J.M. Headley, 551(RenQ):Autumn83-445
Ficino, M. Marsilio Ficino and the Phaed-
  ran Charioteer.* (M.J.B. Allen, ed and
  trans)
  F. Purnell, Jr., 319:Jan84-119
  A. Sheppard, 123:Vol33No1-158
Fickert, K.J. Franz Kafka.
  A. Bloch, 268(IFR):Spring84-118
Ficowski, J. A Reading of Ashes.
  D. McDuff, 565:Vol24No3-67
Fiddian, R. Ignacio Aldecoa.*
  B. Jordan, 86(BHS):Jan83-82
Fiedler, L. What Was Literature?*
  N. Baym, 271:Vol 13No3/4-221
  D.L. Eder, 152(UDQ):Spring83-107
  R.F. Lucid, 385(MQR):Spring84-289
  S. Pinsker, 219(GaR):Spring83-192
  D. Pizer, 27(AL):Oct83-446
  V. Young, 31(ASch):Autumn83-563
  295(JML):Nov83-403
  639(VQR):Spring83-44
Field, G.G. Evangelist of Race.*
  R. Furness, 402(MLR):Oct83-985
  R. Rinard, 221(GQ):Jan83-183

Field, H.H. Science without Numbers.*
  M.D. Resnik, 449:Sep83-514
Field, H.J. Toward a Programme of Imper-
  ial Life.
  W.B. Cohen, 637(VS):Summer83-449
Field, L. - see Wolfe, T.
Fieldhouse, D.K. Colonialism, 1870-1945.
  D. Kennedy, 637(VS):Autumn82-90
Fieldhouse, H. Everyman's Good English
  Guide.
  G. Bourcier, 189(EA):Apr-Jun84-181
  E. Standop, 38:Band101Heft3/4-478
Fielding, H. Jonathan Wild. (D. Nokes,
  ed)
  P-G.B., 189(EA):Jul-Sep84-362
Fields, M.G., with K. Fields. Lemon Swamp
  and Other Places.
  M. Peters, 441:22Jan84-23
  442(NY):16Jan84-110
Fiengo, R. Surface Structure.
  R.R.B., 35(AS):Summer83-189
Fiennes, R. To the Ends of the Earth.
  D. Thomas, 362:12Jan84-22
Fiering, N. Jonathan Edwards's Moral
  Thought and its British Context.*
  A.O. Aldridge, 173(ECS):Fall83-89
  J.L. Blau, 619:Winter83-83
  D. Laurence, 165(EAL):Fall83-187
  W.U. Solberg, 579(SAQ):Spring83-230
  D.O. Thomas, 518:Apr83-79
Fiering, N. Moral Philosophy at Seven-
  teenth-Century Harvard.*
  D. Laurence, 165(EAL):Fall83-187
"Fiestas of San Juan Nuevo."
  R.L. Shep, 614:Fall84-17
Fietz, L. Funktionaler Strukturalismus.
  B. Hüppauf, 67:May83-156
Fife, A. and A. Saints of Sage and Saddle.
  T. Sinclair-Faulkner, 106:Fall83-315
"Fifty Years."
  M.G. Wynne, 517(PBSA):Vol77No2-247
Figes, E. Light.*
  M. Howard, 676(YR):Winter83-ix
  W. Scammell, 364:Aug/Sep83-129
Filbeck, D. T'in.
  L.C. Thompson, 318(JAOS):Jul-Sep82-581
Filby, W., ed. Philadelphia Naturaliza-
  tion Records, 1789-1880.
  K.B. Harder, 424:Sep83-222
Filin, F.P. Istori i sud'by russkogo
  literaturnogo jazyka.
  D.S. Worth, 279:Vol28-186
Fill, A. Wortdurchsichtigkeit im Englis-
  chen.*
  K. Faiss, 257(IRAL):Feb83-71
Finch, A. Stendhal: la Chartreuse de
  Parme.
  V.D.L., 605(SC):15Jul84-375
Finch, C. Norman Rockwell.
  M.S. Young, 39:Feb83-148
Finch, R. Has and Is.
  D. Stephens, 102(CanL):Winter82-150
Fincham, A.A. Basic Marine Biology.
  E.W. Knight-Jones, 617(TLS):29Jun84-
  738
Fincher, J.H. Chinese Democracy.
  P.A. Cohen, 293(JASt):Feb83-386
"The Findern Manuscript (Cambridge Univer-
  sity Library MS Ff.1.6)."*
  T.F. Mustanoja, 439(NM):1983/2-269
Findlater, R., ed. Author! Author!
  N. Berry, 617(TLS):23Nov84-1329

Findlay, J.N. Kant and the Transcendental Object.*
  J.V. Buroker, 479(PhQ):Jan83-95
  G.H.R. Parkinson, 393(Mind):Jul83-438
  E. Potter, 482(PhR):Jul83-422
  A. Stanguennec, 542:Jan-Mar83-124
  G. Stock, 518:Jan83-24
  D. Whewell, 83:Autumn83-197
Findlay, J.N. Plato.
  G. Leroux, 154:Sep83-555
Findley, T. Famous Last Words.*
  G. Davenport, 569(SR):Winter83-xviii
Fine, E.S. Legacy of Night.*
  W. Buchanan, 573(SSF):Fall83-341
Fine, J.V.A. The Ancient Greeks.
  P. Cartledge, 617(TLS):29Jun84-725
  M. Gorra, 441:6May84-45
Finegan, E. Attitudes Toward English Usage.*
  J. Algeo, 300:Mar83-81
  C.C. Doyle, 35(AS):Spring83-46
Fingesten, P. The Eclipse of Symbolism.
  W. Levy, 567:Vol44No1/2-171
Fingleton, D. Kiri Te Kanawa.*
  E. Forbes, 415:Apr83-239
Fingleton, J.H. Cricket Crisis.
  A.L. Le Quesne, 617(TLS):24Aug84-941
Fink, A. I — Mary.
  L. Milazzo, 584(SWR):Summer83-vi
Finkel, D. What Manner of Beast.*
  J. Howard, 436(NewL):Summer84-107
Finlayson, G.B.A.M. The Seventh Earl of Shaftsbury, 1801-1885.
  J.W. Osborne, 637(VS):Spring83-359
Finlayson, I. The Moth and the Candle.
  D. Daiches, 617(TLS):1Jun84-617
Finlayson, M.G. Historians, Puritanism, and the English Revolution.
  N. Malcolm, 617(TLS):1Jun84-605
Finley, G. Landscapes of Memory.*
  D.A. Low, 541(RES):Feb83-86
  J. McCoubrey, 54:Mar84-165
  R. Paulson, 402(MLR):Jan83-157
Finley, G. Turner and George the Fourth in Edinburgh, 1822.*
  J.H. Alexander, 571(ScLJ):Winter83-53
  D. Brown, 59:Dec83-485
  L. Herrmann, 90:Jan83-42
  M. Pointon, 89(BJA):Spring83-184
Finley, M.I. Economy and Society in Ancient Greece.* (B.D. Shaw and R.P. Saller, eds)
  J.A.S. Evans, 639(VQR):Spring83-345
Finley, M.I., ed. The Legacy of Greece.*
  K.A.M., 617(TLS):18May84-562
  P. MacKendrick, 121(CJ):Oct/Nov83-59
  R. Padel, 303(JoHS):Vol 103-233
Finn, C.E., Jr., D. Ravitch and R.T. Fancher. Against Mediocrity.
  T.S. Healy, 441:13May84-14
Finneran, R.J. Editing Yeats's Poems.
  W. Gould, 617(TLS):29Jun84-731
  S. Heaney, 441:18Mar84-1
Finneran, R.J. - see Yeats, W.B.
Finney, B. - see Lawrence, D.H.
Finnis, J. Fundamentals of Ethics.
  J.E.J. Altham, 617(TLS):17Aug84-923
Finnis, J.M. Natural Law and Natural Rights.*
  T. Molnar, 396(ModA):Spring83-211
  W.H. Wilcox, 482(PhR):Oct83-599

Finocchiaro, M. and C. Brumfit. The Functional-Notional Approach.
  M.S. Berns, 608:Jun84-325
Finocchiaro, M.A. Galileo and the Art of Reasoning.*
  P. Strømholm, 262:Mar83-135
Finucane, R.C. Appearances of the Dead.
  B. Aldiss, 617(TLS):3Aug84-863
Finucane, R.C. Soldiers of the Faith.
  J. Sumption, 617(TLS):9Mar84-242
Fiorato, A.C. Bandello entre l'histoire et l'écriture.
  P. Cola, 356(LR):Aug83-239
Fiore, P.A. Milton and Augustine.*
  R.L. Entzminger, 539:Nov83-287
da Fiorenza, M.A. - see under Monte Andrea da Fiorenza
Firestone, B.J. The Quest for Nuclear Stability.
  A.R. De Luca, 550(RusR):Oct83-448
Firmat, G.P. - see under Pérez Firmat, G.
Firpo, M., ed. Il processo inquisitoriale del Cardinal Giovanni Morone. (Vol 1)
  P.F. Grendler, 551(RenQ):Autumn83-408
First, R. One Hundred and Seventeen Days. (2nd ed)
  J. Kimble, 69:Vol53No4-95
Fiscal, M.R. La imagen de la mujer en la narrativa de Rosario Castellanos.
  H. Wozniak-Brayman, 238:Mar83-143
Fisch, H. The Zionist Revolution.
  E. Alexander, 390:Feb83-59
Fisch, M.H. - see Peirce, C.S.
Fischborn, G. Stückeschreiben.
  P. Reichel, 654(WB):1/1983-179
Fischer, B. Verzeichnis der Sigel für Kirchenschriftsteller. (3rd ed)
  M-J. Rondeau, 555:Vol157fasc2-347
Fischer, G.B. Gedroht — Bewahrt. (2nd ed)
  K. Phillips, 221(GQ):Nov83-710
Fischer, J.I. and D.C. Mell, Jr., with D.M. Vieth, eds. Contemporary Studies of Swift's Poetry.
  C. Fabricant, 301(JEGP):Apr83-245
Fischer, J.M., ed. Psychoanalytische Literaturinterpretationen.
  U. Mahlendorf, 221(GQ):May84-468
Fischer, M.S. Nationale Images als Gegenstand Vergleichender Literaturgeschichte.
  K. Heitmann, 72:Band219Heft2-404
Fischer, P.M. Applications of Technical Devices in Archaeology.
  J-C. Margueron, 318(JAOS):Oct-Dec82-666
Fischer, R.E. Bradenburgisches Namenbuch. (Pt 4)
  A. Greule, 685(ZDL):1/1983-121
Fischer, U. Il mondo come letteratura.
  R. Scalmana-Roos, 52:Band17Heft3-324
Fischer-Galati, S., ed. The Communist Parties of Eastern Europe.
  P.J. Best, 497(PolR):Vol28No4-115
Fischer-Lichte, E. Bedeutung.
  L. Hermodsson, 597(SN):Vol55No1-89
Fischhoff, B. and others. Acceptable Risk.
  R.G., 185:Oct83-178
Fischler, B-Z. and R. Nir, eds. Ki-l'shon 'ammo.
  J.A. Reif, 399(MLJ):Spring83-81
Fish, M. Gardening in the Shade.
  A.P., 617(TLS):24Feb84-203

Fish, S. Is There a Text in This Class?*
  J.C. Faris, 355(LSoc):Jun83-252
  J. Phelan, 153:Summer83-39
  E. Proffitt, 289:Summer83-123
  R. Scholes, 454:Winter84-171
  A. Schwarz, 196:Band24Heft1/2-140
  S. Weber, 153:Summer83-14
Fish, S. The Living Temple.*
  I. Leimberg, 38:Band101Heft1/2-263
Fishbein, L. Rebels in Bohemia.
  639(VQR):Spring83-56
Fishburn, E. The Portrayal of Immigration
  in Nineteenth-Century Argentine Fiction
  (1845-1902).*
  J.M. Flint, 402(MLR):Oct83-952
Fishburn, P.C. The Foundations of Ex-
  pected Utility.
  R.H., 185:Oct83-167
Fisher, A. Africa Adorned.
  G. Plimpton, 441:2Dec84-12
Fisher, B.F. 4th, ed. The University of
  Mississippi Studies in English. (new
  Ser, Vol 3)
  J.B. Reece, 495(PoeS):Dec83-41
Fisher, D. and R.B. Stepto, eds. Afro-
  American Literature.
  M. Diedrich, 72:Band220Heft1-188
Fisher, J., ed. Essays on Aesthetics.
  A. Hayward, 290(JAAC):Winter83-217
Fisher, J., ed. Perceiving Artworks.
  J. Cauvel, 289:Summer83-125
Fisher, M.F.K. The Art of Eating.
  K.A.M., 617(TLS):27Jan84-95
Fisher, M.F.K. Not Now But Now.
  L. Duguid, 617(TLS):27Jan84-93
  D. Durrant, 364:Mar84-111
Fisher, M.F.K. Sister Age.*
  D. Durrant, 364:Mar84-111
  639(VQR):Autumn83-129
Fisher, R. and J.M. Bumstead - see Walker,
  A.
Fisher, S. and R.P. Greenberg, eds. The
  Scientific Evaluation of Freud's
  Theories and Therapy.
  M.N. Eagle, 488:Sep83-335
Fishkin, J.S. Justice, Equal Opportunity
  and the Family.
  J. Narveson, 185:Jul84-713
  J. Teichman, 518:Oct83-238
Fishkin, J.S. The Limits of Obligation.
  D. Lyons, 185:Jan84-327
Fishlock, T. India File.
  F. Dinshaw, 617(TLS):13Apr84-400
Fishman, J.A. and G.D. Keller, eds. Bilin-
  gual Education for Hispanic Students in
  the United States.
  M.E. Barker, 238:Sep83-451
Fishman, J.S. Boerenverdriet.
  I.G., 90:Aug83-505
Fishman, R. Urban Utopias in the Twenti-
  eth Century.
  D. Watkin, 39:Feb83-144
Fisiak, J., ed. Historical Morphology.*
  D.C. Walker, 320(CJL):Spring83-101
Fisiak, J., ed. Papers and Studies in Con-
  trastive Linguistics. (Vol 13)
  G. Bourcier, 189(EA):Jan-Mar84-84
Fisiak, J., ed. Papers and Studies in
  Contrastive Linguistics. (Vols 14 and
  15)
  G. Bourcier, 189(EA):Apr-Jun84-177

Fisiak, J., ed. Recent Developments in
  Historical Phonology.*
  A. Tovar, 685(ZDL):3/1983-378
Fisk, M. Ethics and Society.*
  S. Benhabib, 482(PhR):Apr83-246
Fiske, P.L., W.R. Pickering and R.S. Yohe,
  eds. From the Far West/De l'extrême
  Occident.
  Y.K. Stillman, 318(JAOS):Jul-Sep82-570
Fiszman, S. Polish Renaissance in its
  European Context.
  J. Krzyżanowska, 497(PolR):Vol28No1-89
Fitch, B.T. Monde à l'envers/text révers-
  ible.
  L.S. Roudiez, 546(RR):May83-380
Fitch, B.T. The Narcissistic Text.*
  R. Dole, 529(QQ):Spring83-232
  R. le Huenen, 627(UTQ):Summer83-465
  R. Jones, 402(MLR):Jul83-723
  T. Keefe, 208(FS):Oct83-485
  J. Kolbert, 207(FR):May84-885
  B. Stoltzfus, 210(FrF):Jan83-95
  R. Wilcocks, 107(CRCL):Jun83-285
Fitch, J.M. Historic Preservation.
  M.L. Ferro, 576:May83-196
  J.M. Neil, 658:Spring83-91
Fitch, N.R. Sylvia Beach and The Lost
  Generation.*
  S. Benstock, 329(JJQ):Summer84-375
  R. Blythe, 362:5Apr84-25
  H. Kenner, 617(TLS):25May84-590
Fitch, R.E. The Poison Sky.*
  H.P. Bauer, 651(WHR):Winter83-352
  H.W., 636(VP):Summer83-197
Fittschen, K. Die Bildnistypen der Faus-
  tina Minor und die Fecunditas Augustae.
  M.A.R. Colledge, 123:Vol33No2-366
  R.R.R. Smith, 313:Vol73-228
FitzGerald, E. The Letters of Edward
  FitzGerald.* (Vols 1-4) (A.M. and
  A.B. Terhune, eds)
  R.L. Brett, 541(RES):Feb83-89
  A. Easson, 366:Autumn83-246
  R.B. Martin, 31(ASch):Autumn83-540
Fitzgerald, F.S. Correspondence of F.
  Scott Fitzgerald. (M.J. Bruccoli and
  M.M. Duggan, eds)
  L. Willson, 569(SR):Summer83-490
Fitzgerald, J., ed. Un Dozen.
  G.P. Greenwood, 526:Autumn83-92
Fitzgerald, J.T. and L.M. White, eds and
  trans. The Tabula of Cebes.
  S.F. Wiltshire, 124:Mar-Apr84-265
Fitzgerald, M. - see Lady Gregory
Fitzgerald, M., C. Guberman and M. Wolfe,
  eds. Still Ain't Satisfied!
  S. Munro, 99:Apr83-30
Fitzgerald, P. Charlotte Mew and Her
  Friends.
  H. Haughton, 617(TLS):19Oct84-1190
  M. Walters, 362:2Aug84-25
Fitzgibbon, R.H. The Agatha Christie
  Companion.
  P. Wolfe, 395(MFS):Autumn83-389
Fitzherbert, M. The Man Who Was Green-
  mantle.*
  K. Hillier, 364:Dec83/Jan84-132
Fitzmaurice, J. Politics in Denmark.
  J. Logue, 563(SS):Summer83-245
Fitzmaurice, J. The Politics of Belgium.
  D. Leonard, 617(TLS):6Jan84-11

Fitzmyer, J.A. and D.J. Harrington. A Manual of Palestinian Aramaic Texts.
P.E. Dion, 318(JAOS):Jan–Mar82–181
Fitzpatrick, K. Solid Bluestone Foundations.
M. Lake, 381:Sep83–380
Fitzpatrick, P. After "The Doll."*
D. Biggins, 402(MLR):Jan83–174
Fitzpatrick, S. The Russian Revolution.*
R.G. Suny, 550(RusR):Oct83–417
Fitzpatrick, T.J. Rafinesque. (rev by C. Boewe)
L.S. Thompson, 87(BB):Dec83–259
Fitzsimons, M.A. The Past Recaptured.
J.P. Kenyon, 617(TLS):2Mar84–222
Fjeldstad, A. and others. Gruppeteater i Norden.
J. Garton, 610:Spring83–74
Flahaut, F. La parole intermédiaire.
J-C. Margolin, 192(EP):Apr–Jun83–233
Flaherty, D.H., ed. Essays in the History of Canadian Law. (Vol 1)
D. Kettler, 298:Spring83–136
Flaherty, J. Tin Wife.
D. Wakefield, 441:19Feb84–6
Flake, C.J. A Mormon Bibliography, 1830–1930.
R.B. Hancock, 70:Jan–Feb81–97
H.G. Stocks, 517(PBSA):Vol77No1–113
Flanagan, M. Bad Girls.
R. Kaveney, 617(TLS):9Nov84–1289
J. Mellors, 362:8Nov84–28
Flanagan, O.J. The Science of the Mind.
P.N. Johnson-Laird, 617(TLS):14Dec84–1441
Flanary, D.A. Champfleury.
K.G. McWatters, 208(FS):Oct83–476
Flanders, J. The Students of Snow.*
W.H. Pritchard, 491:Jan84–228
V. Young, 249(HudR):Summer83–403
Flandrau, C.M. Viva Mexico!
S.O., 617(TLS):22Jun84–711
Flannery, P. Our Friends in the North.
D. Devlin, 157:Spring83–52
Flathman, R.E. The Practice of Political Authority.*
R.A. Shiner, 482(PhR):Apr83–261
Flaubert, G. Corpus Flaubertianum I: "Un Coeur Simple." (G. Bonaccorso and others, eds)
P.M. Wetherill, 617(TLS):16Mar84–285
Flaubert, G. The Letters of Gustave Flaubert.* (Vol 2: 1857–1880.) (F. Steegmuller, ed and trans)
V. Brombert, 31(ASch):Summer83–418
W. Fowlie, 569(SR):Fall83–lxxii
J.T. Harskamp, 89(BJA):Autumn83–376
M.K. Lazarus, 446(NCFS):Fall-Winter83/84–261
G.S., 617(TLS):12Oct84–1171
639(VQR):Spring83–45
Flaubert, G. and G. Sand. Correspondance. (A. Jacobs, ed)
A. Fairlie, 208(FS):Apr83–234
"Flaubert et Maupassant écrivains normands."
P. Danger, 535(RHL):Jul/Aug83–654
Flaxman, J. Flaxman's Illustrations to Homer.
J. Warner, 88:Summer83–24

Fleeman, J.D. A Preliminary Handlist of Copies of Books Associated with Dr. Samuel Johnson.
P. Rogers, 617(TLS):14Sep84–1039
Fleischman, S. The Future in Thought and Language.
P.M. Lloyd, 350:Mar84–138
C.G. Lyons, 297(JL):Sep83–481
H. Meier, 547(RF):Band95Heft3–307
F. Nuessel, 361:Oct/Nov83–276
Fleishman, A. Figures of Autobiography.*
C.G. Heilbrun, 344:Winter84–136
T.R. Smith, 598(SoR):Spring84–474
G.B. Tennyson, 445(NCF):Dec83–361
Fleishman, L. Boris Pasternak v dvadtsatyye gody.*
J. Grayson, 575(SEER):Apr83–271
le Fleming, C. Journey into Music.
S. Banfield, 415:Mar83–171
Fleming, J.V. Reason and The Lover.
N. Mann, 617(TLS):10Aug84–890
Fleming, R.E. Charles F. Lummis.*
H. Crosby, 26(ALR):Spring83–157
Fleming-Williams, I. and L. Parris. The Discovery of Constable.
D. Thomas, 362:6Dec84–28
Flemming, D.N. and R.G. Mowry. Sobre héroes y rumbos.*
M.A. Salgado, 238:May83–313
Flesch, S. and B. Baselt. Händel-Handbuch. (Vol 1)
W. Dean, 410(M&L):Jul/Oct83–232
Fletcher, C. The Complete Walker III.
P. Hagan, 441:3Jun84–13
Fletcher, I. – see Johnson, L.
Fletcher, J. Novel and Reader.*
J. Preston, 402(MLR):Apr83–389
Fletcher, R.A. Saint James's Catapult.
J. Catto, 617(TLS):26Oct84–1222
Fleuret, M., ed. Regards sur Iannis Xenakis.
B. Schiffer, 607:Mar83–25
Flew, A.G.N. The Politics of Procrustes.*
T.R. Machan, 518:Oct83–245
Flexner, J.T. An American Saga.
R. Varney, 441:4Mar84–18
Flexner, J.T. America's Old Masters.
M.S. Young, 39:Feb83–148
Flexner, S.B. Listening to America.*
42(AR):Spring83–250
Fliegelman, J. Prodigals and Pilgrims.*
J. Auerbach, 141:Spring83–174
E.G. Burrows, 656(WMQ):Jul83–481
L.D. Cress, 432(NEQ):Sep83–455
J. Hurt, 27(AL):Oct83–454
B.S. Schlenther, 83:Autumn83–232
K.E. Smith, 161(DUJ):Jun83–119
Flinn, M.W. and D. Stoker. The History of the British Coal Industry. (Vol 2)
T.C. Barker, 617(TLS):15Jun84–668
Flint, A. Semantic Structure in the Finnish Lexicon.
J.E. Cathey, 563(SS):Spring83–178
J. Verschueren, 350:Mar84–194
Flint, R. Resuming Green.*
P. Stitt, 219(GaR):Winter83–894
Floeck, W. Die Literarästhetik des französischen Barock.*
C.N. Smith, 208(FS):Oct83–452
M. Tietz, 356(LR):Feb–May83–136
Flood, C.B. Lee: The Last Years.*
T.G. Alexander, 529(QQ):Summer83–511

Flook, M. Reckless Wedding.*
  J.D. McClatchy, 491:Dec83-168
Flora, J.M. Hemingway's Nick Adams.*
  M.S. Reynolds, 587(SAF):Spring83-119
  S. Trachtenberg, 27(AL):Mar83-112
  D.E. Wylder, 649(WAL):May83-94
Flores, Á. Narrativa hispanoamericana,
  1816-1981.
  J.B. Fernández, 238:May83-300
Flores, A. Orígenes del cuento hispano-
  americano.
  M. Herrera-Sobek, 552(REH):May83-298
Flores, C. Gaudi, Jujol y el modernismo
  Catalan.
  M.K. Meade, 46:Jul83-60
Flores, E., ed. La critica testuale greco-
  latina, oggi.
  P. Hoffmann, 555:Vol57fasc1-144
Flores, E. Le scoperte di Poggio e il
  testo di Lucrezio.*
  P. Jal, 555:Vol57fasc1-167
de Flores, J. Triunfo de Amor. (A. Gar-
  gano, ed)
  K. Whinnom, 86(BHS):Jan83-61
Flores, R.M. Sancho Panza Through Three
  Hundred Seventy-five Years of Continua-
  tions, Imitations, and Criticism, 1605-
  1980.
  E. Urbina, 304(JHP):Spring83-224
Florit, E. Obras completas. (Vol 3) (L.
  González-del-Valle and R. Esquenazi-Mayo,
  eds)
  O. de la Suarée, 238:Dec83-648
Flory, W.S. Ezra Pound and "The Cantos."*
  A. Woodward, 541(RES):Feb83-102
Flower, J.E. Literature and the Left in
  France.
  P. McCarthy, 617(TLS):16Mar84-285
Flower, M.E. John Dickinson.
  B.H. Newcomb, 656(WMQ):Oct83-644
Floyd, V., ed. Eugene O'Neill.*
  E.G. Griffin, 397(MD):Jun83-236
Floyd, V. - see O'Neill, E.
Fluchère, M-L. L'Oeuvre dramatique de Sir
  John Vanbrugh.
  M. Cordner, 189(EA):Oct-Dec83-471
Fluck, H-R. Fachsprachen. (2nd ed)
  W. Seibicke, 685(ZDL):1/1983-109
Fludd, R. Mosaical Philosophy — Cabala.
  (A. McLean, ed)
  J. Godwin, 111:Fall83-6
Fludd, R. The Origin and Structure of the
  Cosmos. (A. McLean, ed)
  J. Godwin, 111:Spring84-6
Flynn, C.H. Samuel Richardson.*
  T. Castle, 405(MP):Aug83-76
  J.A. Dussinger, 49:Jul83-86
  T.C.D. Eaves and B.D. Kimpel,
  301(JEGP):Jul83-451
  S. Soupel, 189(EA):Apr-Jun84-206
Flynn, C.L., Jr. White Land, Black Labor.
  G.M. Fredrickson, 453(NYRB):8Nov84-39
Flynn, D. - see Farrell, J.T.
Flynt, C. Chasing Dad.
  G.W. Jarecke, 577(SHR):Summer83-285
Flynt, C. Sins of Omission.
  J. Maynard, 441:14Oct84-13
Foa, S.M. Feminismo y forma narrativa.
  D.E. Carpenter, 552(REH):May83-299
Fodor, A. Tolstoy and the Russians.
  J. Bayley, 441:4Nov84-34
  J.B. Dunlop, 617(TLS):5Oct84-1134

Fodor, J.A. The Language of Thought.
  P. Jacob, 98:Oct83-774
Fodor, J.A. The Modularity of Mind.*
  E.H. Matthei, 350:Dec84-976
Fodor, J.A. Representations.*
  P. Jacob, 98:Oct83-774
  K.V. Wilkes, 84:Jun83-175
Foelix, R.F. Biology of Spiders.
  S. Caveney, 529(QQ):Autumn83-913
Foelkel, F. and C.L. Cergoly. Trieste
  provincia imperiale.
  M-A. Lescourret, 98:Aug-Sep83-734
Fogarási, M. Storia di parole.
  L.V. Fainberg, 545(RPh):Nov82-237
Fogarty, R.S. Dictionary of American Com-
  munal and Utopian History.
  L. Perry, 529(QQ):Autumn83-768
Fogel, D.M. Henry James and the Structure
  of the Romantic Imagination.*
  S. Brodwin, 27(AL):Mar83-106
  W.R. Goetz, 594:Fall83-280
  S.K. Harris, 301(JEGP):Jan83-143
  S. Johnson, 591(SIR):Fall83-451
  J.C. Rowe, 405(MP):Nov83-207
  D. Schneider, 284:Winter84-149
Fogel, R.W. and G.R. Elton, eds. Which
  Road to the Past?
  J.P. Kenyon, 617(TLS):2Mar84-222
Fohrmann, J. Abenteuer und Bürgertum.
  W.R. Berger, 52:Band17Heft3-313
  J. Rutledge, 221(GQ):Mar83-313
Fokkelman, J.P. Narrative Art and Poetry
  in the Books of Samuel. (Vol 1)
  F. van Dijk, 204(FdL):Dec82-299
Folejewski, Z. Futurism and Its Place in
  the Development of Modern Poetry.*
  E. Możejko, 107(CRCL):Mar83-118
Folejewski, Z. and others, eds. Canadian
  Contributions to the VIII International
  Congress of Slavists.
  R.S. Struc, 107(CRCL):Sep83-458
Folena, G. L'italiano in Europa.
  P. Grossi, 597(SN):Vol155No2-241
de Foletier, F.D. - see under de Vaux de
  Foletier, F.
Foley, H.P., ed. Reflections of Women in
  Antiquity.
  J.P.H., 185:Jan84-375
Foley, J., ed. Oral Traditional Litera-
  ture.*
  M. Curschmann, 589:Apr83-460
  I.P. Foote, 575(SEER):Apr83-263
Foley, J.M. and others. Approaches to
  Beowulfian Scansion. (A. Renoir and
  A. Hernandez, eds)
  D.C. Baker, 191(ELN):Mar84-60
Foley, M. The Go Situation.*
  T. Eagleton, 565:Vol124No2-66
Folsom, M.B. and S.D. Lubar, eds. The Phi-
  losophy of Manufactures.
  G. Porter, 432(NEQ):Mar83-126
Fónagy, I. Situation et signification.
  C.R. Pons, 207(FR):Feb84-431
  A.R. Tellier, 189(EA):Oct-Dec84-452
  M. Yaeger-Dror, 350:Dec84-996
Fonda Savio, L.S. and B. Maier, eds. Icon-
  ografia sveviana.
  E. Saccone, 400(MLN):Jan83-160
Foner, E. Nothing But Freedom.
  C. Bolt, 617(TLS):25May84-592
  G.M. Fredrickson, 453(NYRB):8Nov84-39
Foner, P.S. - see Martí, J.

Fong, M.L.　The Sociology of Secret
Societies.
　G.W. Skinner, 293(JASt):May83-717
Fong, W. - see under Wen Fong
Fontanella de Weinberg, M.B.　Adquisición
fonológica en español bonaerense.
　C. Pye, 350:Mar84-187
Fontanella de Weinberg, M.B.　Dinámica
social de un cambio lingüístico.*
　P. Quijas Corzo, 457(NRFH):Tomo31núm2-
331
de Fontenay, E.　Diderot.
　J.H. Mason, 617(TLS):6Jan84-6
Fontenrose, J.　The Delphic Oracle.*
　J.N. Bremmer, 394:Vol36fasc3/4-441
　D.E. Bynum, 650(WF):Oct83-308
Fontenrose, J.　Orion.
　R. Parker, 123:Vol33No1-69
Fontes, M.D.　Romanceiro Português do
Canadá.　Romanceiro Português dos
Estados Unidos.　(Vol 1)
　M.L. Daniel, 238:Mar83-136
Fonteyn, M., R. Lazzarini and J. Lazzarini,
eds.　Pavlova.
　J. Dunning, 441:18Nov84-32
Fontius, M. - see de Voltaire, F.M.A.
di Fonzo, L.　St. Peter's Banker.
　R. Cornwell, 617(TLS):30Nov84-1371
Foot, M.　Another Heart and Other Pulses.
　M. Jones, 362:7Jun84-22
　H. Young, 617(TLS):22Jun84-685
Foot, M.R.D.　SOE.
　E. Barker, 617(TLS):23Nov84-1347
Foot, P.　Virtues and Vices and Other
Essays in Moral Philosophy.*
　B. Vermazen, 449:Mar83-117
Forbes, H.A.C.　Yang-ts'ai: The Foreign
Colours.
　M. Medley, 39:Oct83-351
Forbes, P.　Abolishing the Dark.
　B. O'Donoghue, 617(TLS):14Dec84-1456
Forché, G.　The Country Between Us.*
　T. Diggory, 560:Fall83-112
　E. Larrissy, 493:Jun83-64
Ford, B., ed.　The Age of Shakespeare.
　R.D.S., 604:Winter83-8
Ford, B., ed.　The New Pelican Guide to
English Literature.　(Vol 1, Pt 2)
　A. Bruten, 617(TLS):6Jan84-20
Ford, C.　Pierre Fresnay.
　R.M. Webster, 207(FR):Apr84-742
Ford, D.　The Cult of the Atom.
　R. Wilson, 61:Aug84-104
Ford, D., H. Kendall and S. Nadis.　Beyond
the Freeze.
　639(VQR):Spring83-59
Ford, F.M.　The English Novel.*
　A. Phillips, 364:Nov83-116
Ford, J.　Ackermann 1783-1983.
　T. Russell-Cobb, 324:Aug84-640
Ford, M.P.　William James's Philosophy.
　J.T. Temps, 619:Winter83-111
Ford, P.J.　George Buchanan.*
　G.P. Edwards, 571(ScLJ):Autumn83-9
　F.J. Nichols, 551(RenQ):Autumn83-452
　L.V.R., 568(SCN):Winter83-87
　P. Rollinson, 588(SSL):Vol 18-313
Ford, P.R.J.　Oriental Carpet Design.
　M. Beattie, 463:Spring83-70
Ford, R.　Dramatisations of Scott's Novels.
　D. Hewitt, 447(N&Q):Jun82-246

Foreman, L., ed.　The Percy Grainger Com-
panion.*
　P. Driver, 607:Mar83-22
Foreman, P.　Quanah.
　J. Hoggard, 584(SWR):Autumn83-410
Forer, L.G.　Money and Justice.
　N. Dorsen, 441:17Jun84-26
　442(NY):18Jun84-115
Foresti, L.A. - see under Aigner Foresti,
L.
Forestier, G.　Le théâtre dans le théâtre
sur la scène française du XVIIème
siècle.*
　P. Ginestier, 475:Vol 10No18-331
　F. Siguret, 535(RHL):Sep/Dec83-923
Forestier, L. - see de Maupassant, G.
Forestier, L. - see Verlaine, P.
Forge, S.　Victorian Splendour.*
　G. Herbert, 576:Dec83-394
Forgue, G.J. - see Mencken, H.L.
"Formations of Pleasure."
　M. Poole, 362:23Feb84-28
Formisano, R.P.　The Transformation of
Political Culture.
　L. Handlin, 432(NEQ):Sep83-462
Fornara, C.W.　The Nature of History in
Ancient Greece and Rome.
　R. Seager, 617(TLS):24Aug84-951
Forrer, M., ed.　Essays on Japanese Art
Presented to Jack Hillier.
　C. French, 407(MN):Winter83-477
Forrest, A.　The French Revolution and the
Poor.
　J.C. White, 173(ECS):Winter83/84-210
Forrest, L.　Two Wings to Veil My Face.
　B. De Mott, 441:26Feb84-15
Forschner, M.　Die stoische Ethik.
　F. Ricken, 687:Oct-Dec83-640
Forsgren, M.　La Place de l'adjectif
épithète en français contemporain.*
　N.L. Corbett, 545(RPh):Nov82-253
Forss, G.　New York/New York.
　A. Quindlen, 441:4Nov84-24
Forssman, E.　Karl Friedrich Schinkel: Bau-
werke und Baugedanken.*
　R. Carter, 576:Dec83-401
　T. Mellinghof, 90:Dec83-770
Forstenzer, T.R.　French Provincial Police
and the Fall of the Second Republic.
　D.H. Barry, 161(DUJ):Jun83-120
Forster, E.M.　Selected Letters of E.M.
Forster.*　(Vol 1)　(M. Lago and P.N.
Furbank, eds)
　M. Kakutani, 441:8Jan84-3
　V.S. Pritchett, 442(NY):2Apr84-130
　S. Spender, 453(NYRB):10May84-31
　F. Tuohy, 364:Aug/Sep83-117
Forster, H.　Supplements to Dodsley's Col-
lection of Poems.
　J.E. Tierney, 517(PBSA):Vol77No2-219
Förster, J.　Literaturunterricht zwischen
Aufklärung und Gegen-Aufklärung.
　J. Herbst, 406:Winter83-427
Forster, K.　A Pronouncing Dictionary of
English Place-Names.
　S. Soupel, 189(EA):Apr-Jun84-170
Forster, L.　Iter Bohemicum.
　J. Leighton, 402(MLR):Jan83-226
　D.L. Paisey, 447(N&Q):Oct82-474
Forster, M.　Significant Sisters.
　S. Rowbotham, 617(TLS):28Sep84-1080

Fowles, J. Mantissa.*
  R. Campbell, 148:Autumn83-84
  J. Epstein, 249(HudR):Spring83-181
  S. Monod, 189(EA):Apr-Sep83-356
Fowles, J. Television Viewers vs. Media
  Snobs.
  S.C. Schick, 186(ETC.):Winter83-478
Fowlie, W. Aubade.
  J.F. Jones, Jr., 207(FR):May84-899
  E. Morot-Sir, 441:13May84-33
Fowlie, W. Characters from Proust.
  J.F. Cotter, 249(HudR):Winter83/84-718
  E. Morot-Sir, 441:13May84-33
Fowlie, W. Journal of Rehearsals.
  J.F. Jones, Jr., 207(FR):May84-899
Fowlie, W. A Reading of Dante's
  "Inferno."*
  T.G. Bergin, 569(SR):Spring83-261
  M. Davie, 402(MLR):Apr83-466
  C.S. Lonergan, 276:Winter83-369
  S. Noakes, 589:Apr83-540
Fox, A. Thomas More.*
  G. Marc'hadour, 539:May84-138
Fox, D. - see Henryson, R.
Fox, E., ed and trans. In the Beginning.*
  E. Rauch, 469:Vol9No1-98
Fox, J. Comeback.*
  B.A. Young, 157:Autumn83-30
Fox, J.J., ed. The Flow of Life.
  M.Z. Rosaldo, 293(JASt):Nov82-213
Fox, J.J. and others, eds. Indonesia:
  Australian Perspectives.
  R. McVey, 293(JASt):May83-719
Fox, J.P. Germany and the Far Eastern
  Crisis, 1931-1938.
  G. Krebs, 407(MN):Summer83-214
Fox, M., ed. Schopenhauer.
  P. Preuss, 154:Sep83-559
Fox, P. A Servant's Tale.
  P. Giddings, 441:18Nov84-9
  442(NY):12Nov84-192
Fox, S. The Mirror Makers.
  A. Hacker, 441:24Jun84-1
Fox, T. Showtime at the Apollo.
  J. Haskins, 441:8Jan84-19
Fox-Genovese, E. and E.D. Genovese.
  Fruits of Merchant Capital.
  G.M. Fredrickson, 453(NYRB):19Jan84-39
Foxley, A., ed. Reconstrucción económica
  para la democracía.
  D. Gallagher, 617(TLS):20Jan84-66
Foy, G. Asia Rip.
  N. Callendar, 441:9Sep84-40
van Fraassen, B.C. The Scientific Image.*
  A. Rosenberg, 154:Jun83-311
  R. Trigg, 393(Mind):Apr83-291
Fracastoro, G. Fracastoro's "Syphilis."
  (G. Eatough, ed and trans)
  J. Scarborough, 617(TLS):31Aug84-978
Fragonard, M.M. Précis d'histoire de la
  littérature française.
  B.L. Knapp, 207(FR):May84-865
Frake, C.O. Language and Cultural Descrip-
  tion.* (A.S. Dil, ed)
  S.A. Tyler, 355(LSoc):Jun83-242
Frame, D.M. - see "Marthe"
Frame, D.M. and M.B. McKinley, eds. Colum-
  bia Montaigne Conference Papers.*
  F.S. Brown, 210(FrF):Jan83-89
  I.W.F. Maclean, 402(MLR):Jan83-179
  F. Rigolot, 400(MLN):Dec83-1363
  M. Simonin, 535(RHL):Sep/Dec83-915

Frame, J. An Angel at My Table.
  F. Adcock, 617(TLS):9Nov84-1281
  H. Bevington, 441:7Oct84-26
Frame, J. You Are Now Entering the Human
  Heart.
  F. Adcock, 617(TLS):9Nov84-1281
Frame, R. Winter Journey.
  C. Hawtree, 617(TLS):21Sep84-1065
Frampton, K. Modern Architecture 1851-
  1945.*
  P. Goldberger, 441:2Dec84-18
  M. Pawley, 46:Nov83-5
France, P. Diderot.
  C. Blum, 617(TLS):16Mar84-285
  R. Blythe, 362:16Feb84-24
France, P. Poets of Modern Russia.*
  D. McDuff, 472:Fall/Winter83Spring/
  Summer84-51
  639(VQR):Autumn83-135
Franchi de Bellis, A. Le Iovile Capuane.
  D. Briquel, 555:Vol57fasc2-325
di Francia, G.T. - see under Toraldo di
  Francia, G.
de Francia, P. Fernand Léger.
  R.L. Herbert, 617(TLS):23Mar84-317
Francis of Assisi. Écrits. (K. Esser, ed
  of latin text; T. Desbonnets and others,
  eds and trans)
  W.R. Cook, 589:Apr83-551
  J. Perret, 555:Vol57fasc2-368
Francis, A. Picaresca, decadencia, his-
  toria.
  R.R. Langebehn, 457(NRFH):Tomo31núml-
  131
Francis, A.F. Hieronimus Bosch: The Temp-
  tation of Saint Anthony.
  W.S. Gibson, 551(RenQ):Spring83-112
Francis, C. Night Sky.
  J. Bass, 441:20May84-31
Francis, D. The Danger.*
  C. Flake, 441:18Mar84-12
  M. Laski, 362:12Jan84-26
  442(NY):16Apr84-161
Francis, D. Proof.
  M. Laski, 362:25Oct84-29
Francis, H. Miners against Fascism.
  K.O. Morgan, 617(TLS):2Mar84-223
Francis, H.E. Naming Things.
  G. Garrett, 569(SR):Winter83-112
Francis, R.H. The Whispering Gallery.
  N. Callendar, 441:2Dec84-62
  J.K.L. Walker, 617(TLS):27Jul84-848
Franck, F., ed. The Buddha Eye.*
  R. Lee, 293(JASt):Aug83-957
Franco, C. La Beatrice di Dante.
  J.C. Nelson, 276:Winter83-370
Franco Arias, F. El vocabulario político
  de algunos periódicos de México D.F.
  desde 1930 hasta 1940 (Introducción).
  L. Vasvari Fainberg, 545(RPh):Feb83-
  463
François, C. Raison et déraison dans le
  théâtre de Pierre Corneille.
  P.S. Noble, 208(FS):Jul83-334
  J. Thomas, 547(RF):Band95Heft3-348
Franey, P. and R. Flaste. Pierre Franey's
  Low-Calorie Gourmet.
  E. Jones, 441:2Dec84-16
Frangi, A. The PLO and Palestine.
  M. Yapp, 617(TLS):11May84-514

126

Freeman, D. The Last Days of Alfred Hitch-
cock.
P. Lopate, 441:30Dec84-9
Freeman, D. Margaret Mead and Samoa.*
T.G. Buchholz, 129:Jan84-78
Freeman, D.C., ed. Essays in Modern
Stylistics.
R. Fowler, 402(MLR):Jul83-643
J. Pauchard, 189(EA):Jan-Mar84-85
E. Vos, 204(FdL):Sep82-237
Freeman, J.A. Milton and the Martial
Muse.*
A. Burnett, 447(N&Q):Oct82-441
D.D.C. Chambers, 541(RES):Aug83-338
J.H. Sims, 568(SCN):Fall83-33
Freeman, L., ed. The Murder Mystique.
P. Wolfe, 395(MFS):Autumn83-389
Freeman, M.A. The Poetics of "Translatio
Studii" and "Conjointure."*
U. Mölk, 72:Band219Heft2-460
Freeman, M.D.A. The Rights and the Wrongs
of Children.
T.D. Campbell, 617(TLS):6Jan84-22
Freeman, R.B. and J.L. Medoff. What Do
Unions Do?
A.R. Weber, 441:10Jun84-22
Freeman, R.E., ed. Bibliographies of
Studies in Victorian Literature for the
Years 1965-1974.
R.A. Colby, 365:Summer/Fall83-140
Freer, C. The Poetics of Jacobean Drama.*
J.R. Brown, 551(RenQ):Summer83-307
M. Shapiro, 130:Winter83/84-383
Freer, M. and K. Goodwin, eds. A Common
Wealth of Words.
S. Walker, 71(ALS):Oct83-280
Freese, P., H. Groene and L. Hermes, eds.
Die Short Story im Englischunterricht
der Sekundarstufe II.
D. Mehl, 72:Band219Heft2-479
Freestone, B. The Horsemen from Beyond.
G.M. Fyle, 69:Vol53No2-78
Freethy, R. Man and Beast.
E. Neal, 617(TLS):20Jan84-69
Frege, G. Philosophical and Mathematical
Correspondence.* (B. McGuinness, ed)
D. Bell, 556:Winter83/84-159
C. Imbert, 540(RIPh):Vol37fasc1/2-199
J. Weiner, 482(PhR):Oct83-591
Frege, G. Posthumous Writings.* (H.
Hermes, F. Kambartel and F. Kaulbach,
eds)
C. Imbert, 540(RIPh):Vol37fasc1/2-199
Freher, D. The Paradoxical Emblems of
Dionysius Freher. (A. McLean, ed)
J. Godwin, 111:Spring84-6
Frei-Lüthy, C. Der Einfluss der griechi-
schen Personennamen auf die Wortbildung.*
J. Udolph, 260(IF):Band87-298
Freiberg, M., ed. Journals of the House
of Representatives of Massachusetts.*
(Vols 44-50)
J.H. Cary, 656(WMQ):Jan83-164
Freisfeld, A. Das Leiden an der Stadt.
B. Pike, 221(GQ):Jan83-123
Fremlin, C. A Lovely Day to Die.
M. Laski, 362:12Apr84-27
Frémont, C. L'être et la relation, avec
trente-cinq lettres de Leibniz au R.P.
Des Bosses.
M. Phillips, 542:Jan-Mar83-111
Frénaud, A. Haeres.
M. Ghirelli, 450(NRF):Mar83-102

French, A. Czech Writers and Politics,
1945-1969.
R.B. Pynsent, 575(SEER):Oct83-614
P.I. Trensky, 574(SEEJ):Summer83-275
French, M. Shakespeare's Division of
Experience.*
R.K. Bank, 615(TJ):Mar83-129
G. Greene, 570(SQ):Winter83-479
French, P., ed. Three Honest Men.
W. Baker, 477(PLL):Fall83-461
French, P.A. The Scope of Morality.*
R.H. Kane, 543:Dec82-448
French, P.A., T.E. Uehling, Jr. and H.K.
Wettstein, eds. Social and Political
Philosophy.
R.H., 185:Jan84-361
A.R. White, 518:Oct83-251
French, P.J. John Dee.
D.M., 617(TLS):16Nov84-1323
Frère, J. Les Grecs et le désir de l'être
des Préplatoniciens à Aristote.
M.R. Wright, 123:Vol33No2-241
Frere, R. Beyond the Highland Line.
B. Hepburn, 617(TLS):22Jun84-690
Freund, B. Capital and Labour in the
Nigerian Tin Mines.
B. Sharpe, 69:Vol53No4-84
Freundlich, Y., ed. Documents on the
Foreign Policy of Israel. (Vol 14)
H. Druks, 390:Nov83-62
Freustie, J. Prosper Mérimée (1803-1870).
B.T. Cooper, 446(NCFS):Fall-
Winter83/84-255
Frey, C. Shakespeare's Vast Romance.
J. Briggs, 447(N&Q):Apr82-167
G.P. Jones, 627(UTQ):Fall82-106
A.P. Slater, 541(RES):Feb83-66
Frey, G. Theorie des Bewusstseins.*
D. Wandschneider, 687:Jul-Sep83-453
Frey, R.G. Interests and Rights.*
R. Elliot, 63:Jun83-219
L.W. Sumner, 482(PhR):Jul83-447
Frey, R.G. Rights, Killing and Suffering.
K. Lennon, 617(TLS):4May84-484
Frey, S. The British Soldier in America.
P.D.G. Thomas, 83:Spring83-105
Freyer, G. W.B. Yeats and the Anti-
Democratic Tradition.*
G.M. Harper, 405(MP):May84-435
B. Tippett, 366:Spring83-127
von Freyhold, M. Ujamaa Villages in Tan-
zania.
D.R.F. Taylor, 69:Vol53No2-86
Fricke, H. Norm and Abweichung.
B. Bjorklund, 221(GQ):May83-478
M.J. Goth, 221(GQ):May83-479
W. Patt, 52:Band18Heft3-313
J.P. Strelka, 133:Band16Heft1-57
Fricker, R. The Unacknowledged Legisla-
tors. (W. Senn and D. Daphinoff, eds)
D. Mehl, 72:Band219Heft2-476
Fried, C. Contract as Promise.*
P.S. Árdal, 529(QQ):Spring83-260
Fried, M. Absorption and Theatricality.*
N. Llewellyn, 89(BJA):Spring83-180
W. Wrage, 207(FR):Dec83-251
Friedemann, J. Alexandre Weill, écrivain
contestataire et historien engagé (1811-
1899).
F.P. Bowman, 210(FrF):May83-186
Frieden, N.M. Russian Physicians in an
Era of Reform and Revolution: 1856-1905.*
B. Haigh, 575(SEER):Jul83-453

Friedenreich, K., ed. Accompaninge the
Players.
T. Hawkes, 617(TLS):27Jul84-846
Friedenreich, K. Henry Vaughan.
R. Ellrodt, 189(EA):Jan-Mar84-93
Friedman, A. - see Wycherley, W.
Friedman, B.J. Let's Hear It For a Beauti-
ful Guy.
D.G. Myers, 441:18Nov84-32
Friedman, C. A Moment's Notice.
M. Watkins, 441:8Apr84-20
Friedman, E.G. Joyce Carol Oates.*
G.F. Manning, 106:Summer83-225
Friedman, E.H. The Unifying Concept.
S.H. Ackerman, 238:Mar83-132
R.J. Oakley, 86(BHS):Oct83-340
Friedman, G. The Political Philosophy of
the Frankfurt School.*
J. Cappio, 529(QQ):Summer83-540
G.L. Mosse, 125:Winter83-186
Friedman, L.J. Gregarious Saints.*
R.O. Curry and L.B. Goodheart,
106:Winter83-401
L.B. Goodheart, 432(NEQ):Mar83-137
Friedman, L.M. American Law.
F.A. Allen, 441:2Dec84-73
Friedman, M. Martin Buber's Life and
Work: The Early Years 1878-1923.*
42(AR):Winter83-120
Friedman, M. Martin Buber's Life and Work:
The Later Years, 1945-1965.
M.E. Marty, 441:15Apr84-11
Friedman, M., ed. De Stijl, 1917-1931.*
R. Padovan, 46:Feb83-70
Friedman, M., ed. Jewish Life in Philadel-
phia 1830-1940.
J.D. Sarna, 129:Oct84-74
Friedman, M. and R. Tyranny of the Status
Quo.
W. Godley, 617(TLS):14Sep84-1017
S. Lee, 441:26Feb84-18
Friedman, M.A. Jewish Marriage in Pales-
tine.
S. Bowman, 589:Jan83-175
Friedman, M.H. The Making of a Tory Human-
ist.
M. Isnard, 189(EA):Jan-Mar83-83
Friedman, R. Rose of Jericho.
M. Haltrecht, 617(TLS):13Apr84-396
Friedman, S.S. Psyche Reborn.*
S. Paul, 301(JEGP):Jan83-149
Friedman, T. James Gibbs.
J. Summerson, 617(TLS):30Nov84-1363
Friedrich, J. and A. Kammenhuber. Hethi-
tisches Wörterbuch. (2nd ed) (fasc 4)
J. Puhvel, 318(JAOS):Jan-Mar82-177
Friedrichs, E. Die deutschsprachigen
Schriftstellerinnen des 18. und 19.
Jahrhunderts.*
S.L. Cocalis, 406:Fall83-340
Friedrichsmeyer, E. Die satirische Kurz-
prosa Heinrich Bölls.
B. Balzer, 133:Band16Heft1-87
G.P. Knapp, 222(GR):Winter83-42
J. Zipes, 400(MLN):Apr83-513
Friel, B. The Communication Cord.
D. Devlin, 157:Winter83-38
Friel, B. The Diviner.*
P. Craig, 617(TLS):1Jun84-623
Friendly, F.W. Minnesota Rag.
F.R.B., 185:Apr84-566

Friendly, F.W. and M.J.H. Elliott. The
Constitution.
T. Lewin, 441:16Sep84-31
Frier, B.W. Landlords and Tenants in
Imperial Rome.*
J. Crook, 313:Vol73-213
Frier, W., ed. Pragmatik.
T.F. Shannon, 350:Sep84-687
Fries, J.F. Dialogues on Morality and
Religion. (D.Z. Phillips, ed)
L. Geldsetzer, 319:Jul84-382
Fries, N. Ambiguität und Vagheit.
K-D. Gottschalk, 189(EA):Jan-Mar83-69
Friggieri, J. Linguaggio e azione.
A.R. White, 518:Jul83-157
Friman, K. Zum angloamerikanischen Ein-
fluss auf die heutige deutsche Werbe-
sprache.
H-W. Eroms, 685(ZDL):3/1983-398
Frisbie, C.J., ed. Southwestern Indian
Ritual Drama.*
M.K. Brady, 292(JAF):Jan-Mar83-105
Frisch, M. Bluebeard.* (German title:
Blaubart.)
D. Myers, 268(IFR):Winter84-59
Frisch, M. Stücke. (Vols 1 and 2) Er-
zählende Prosa 1939-79.
C. Grimm, 654(WB):7/1982-145
Frisch, W. - see Brahms, J.
Frisé, A. - see Musil, R.
Frith, D. The Slow Men.
A.L. Le Quesne, 617(TLS):16Nov84-1314
Frith, S. Sound Effects.*
B.L. Cooper, 498:Vol9No2-92
Fritsch-Bournazel, R., A. Brigot and J.
Cloos. Les Allemands au coeur de
l'Europe.
R. Morgan, 617(TLS):5Oct84-1114
Fritz, J.M. Goldschmiedekunst der Gotik
in Mitteleuropa.
R.W. Lightbown, 90:Nov83-698
R. Suckale, 471:Apr/May/Jun83-175
Fritzen, B. and H.F. Taylor, eds. Fried-
rich Dürrenmatt.*
I.M. Goessl, 406:Fall83-318
Fritzsch, H. The Creation of Matter.
T. Ferris, 441:2Dec84-76
Frobenius, L. and D.C. Fox. African
Genesis.
G. Kiley, 469:Vol9No1-110
Fröberg, I. Une "histoire secrète" à
matière nordique.*
P. Hourcade, 475:Vol 10No18-334
Fróis, L. Historia de Japam. (J. Wicki,
ed)
M. Cooper, 407(MN):Winter83-446
Froissart, J. "Dits" et "Débats."* (A.
Fourrier, ed)
A. Foulet, 545(RPh):May83-628
Froment-Meurice, M. Les intermittences de
la raison.
J-C. Monnet, 542:Jul-Sep83-376
Fromentin, E. and P. Bataillard. Étude
sur l'"Ahasvérus" d'Edgar Quinet. (B.
Wright and T. Mellors, eds)
C. Crossley, 208(FS):Jul83-351
B.L. Knapp, 446(NCFS):Fall-Winter83/84-
228
Fromkin, V. and R. Rodman. An Introduc-
tion to Language. (3rd ed)
T.C. Frazer, 350:Jun84-448

Fromm, H. and H. Sihwo - see "Jahrbuch
für finnisch-deutsche Literaturbezie-
hungen"
Fröschle, H., ed. Die Deutschen in Latein-
amerika.
F. Niedermayer, 72:Band219Heft1-225
Frossard, A. "Be Not Afraid!"
J. Pelikan, 441:22Apr84-12
Frost, C. The Fearful Child.
639(VQR):Autumn83-134
Frost, F.J. Plutarch, "Themistocles."
A.J. Podlecki, 303(JoHS):Vol 103-180
P.A. Stadter, 121(CJ):Apr/May84-356
Frost, R. Stories for Lesley. (R.D. Sell,
ed)
P-L. Adams, 61:Sep84-129
"Robert Frost and Sidney Cox."* (W.R.
Evans, ed)
G. Core, 579(SAQ):Spring83-228
Froude, J.A. Froude's Life of Carlyle.*
(ed and abridged by J. Clubbe)
J.R. Watson, 161(DUJ):Dec82-92
Froula, C. A Guide to Ezra Pound's
Selected Poems.
M. North, 27(AL):Dec83-666
295(JML):Nov83-556
Frowein-Ziroff, V. Die Kaiser-Wilhelm-
Gedächtniskirche.
E. Mai, 471:Jul/Aug/Sep83-286
Frühwald, W. and W. Schieder, with W.
Hinck, eds. Leben im Exil.*
J.M. Ritchie, 402(MLR):Apr83-505
J.P. Strelka, 221(GQ):Jan83-170
Fry, D.B. Acoustic Phonetics.
G.F. Meier, 682(ZPSK):Band36Heft4-471
Fry, D.K. Norse Sagas Translated into
English.*
L.M. Bell, 191(ELN):Dec83-44
Fry, P.H. The Poet's Calling in the
English Ode.*
A. Elliott, 541(RES):Feb83-120
O.F. Sigworth, 402(MLR):Jul83-676
Fry, P.H. The Reach of Criticism.
I. McGilchrist, 617(TLS):25May84-580
I. Massey, 344:Fall84-102
Fryde, E.B. Humanism and Renaissance His-
toriography.
P. Burke, 617(TLS):6Jul84-746
Frye, M. The Politics of Reality.
T.M.R., 185:Jul84-741
Frye, N. Creation and Recreation.*
P. Drew, 402(MLR):Oct83-880
F. McCombie, 447(N&Q):Jun82-282
Frye, N. The Critical Path.
D.S. Kastan, 617(TLS):17Feb84-163
Frye, N. Divisions on a Ground.* (J.
Polk, ed)
S. Kane, 627(UTQ):Summer83-470
S. Solecki, 529(QQ):Winter83-1026
Frye, N. The Great Code.*
A. Ages, 390:Mar83-58
R. Alter, 88:Summer83-20
M.W. Bloomfield, 473(PR):4/1983-633
P-G. Boucé, 189(EA):Oct-Dec84-449
P.J. Cahill, 150(DR):Autumn83-412
L. Dudek, 627(UTQ):Winter82/83-128
A. Globe, 102(CanL):Summer83-182
J. Gold, 150(DR):Autumn83-408
J. Gold, 178:Dec83-487
D.L. Jeffrey, 627(UTQ):Winter82/83-135
A.D. Nuttall, 402(MLR):Oct83-882
P. Richardson, 150(DR):Autumn83-400
[continued]

[continuing]
E. Stiegman, 627(UTQ):Winter82/83-141
G. Woodcock, 627(UTQ):Winter82/83-149
639(VQR):Summer83-86
Frye, N. The Myth of Deliverance.
D.S. Kastan, 617(TLS):17Feb84-163
L. Speirs, 179(ES):Dec83-518
Frye, R.M., ed. Is God a Creationist?
K.A. Briggs, 441:27May84-17
Frye, R.M. Milton's Imagery and the
Visual Arts.*
R.G. Moyles, 107(CRCL):Sep83-418
Frye, R.M. Shakespeare.* (rev)
L.S. Champion, 179(ES):Jun83-276
Fryer, P. Staying Power.
M. Banton, 617(TLS):20Jul84-813
Frykman, J. Horan i bondesamhället.
P. Vinten-Johansen, 563(SS):Summer83-
252
Frykman, J. and O. Löfgren. Den kulti-
verade människan.
P. Vinten-Johansen, 563(SS):Summer83-
252
Fu, K.S., ed. Syntactic Pattern Recogni-
tion.
G.F. Meier, 682(ZPSK):Band36Heft6-753
Fuchs, C. and A-M. Léonard. Vers une
théorie des aspects.*
C. Vet, 209(FM):Jul83-258
Fuchs, D. Saul Bellow.
D.J. Enright, 617(TLS):22Jun84-688
Fuchs, E. Sexual Desire and Love.
H. Oppenheimer, 617(TLS):31Aug84-973
Fuchs, E., with R. Lauth and W. Schieche,
eds. Fichte im Gespräch. (Vol 3)
J-M. Gabaude, 542:Jan-Mar83-132
Fuchs, R. Origine e sviluppo storico
della lingua tedesca.
E. Seebold, 260(IF):Band87-354
Fuchs, R.W. - see Schreiber, W.L.
Fuegi, J., G. Bahr and J. Willett - see
"The Brecht Yearbook"
Fuentes, C. Les Eaux brûlées.
H. Bianciotti, 450(NRF):Jun83-141
Fuentes, N. Hemingway in Cuba.
442(NY):15Oct84-178
Fuentes, V. La marcha al pueblo en las
letras españolas, 1917-1936.
M. Aznar Soler, 86(BHS):Jan83-78
Fues, W.M. Mystik als Erkenntnis?
J.W. Thomas, 221(GQ):Mar83-302
Fugard, A. "Master Harold" ... and the
Boys.
D. Devlin, 157:Winter83-38
Fugard, A. Notebooks 1960-1977. (M.
Benson, ed)
D. Caute, 441:3Jun84-42
D. Walder, 617(TLS):10Feb84-149
442(NY):30Apr84-120
Fugard, S. A Revolutionary Woman.
R. Jones, 362:6Dec84-34
Fugère, J-P. En Quatre Journées.
C.R. La Bossiere, 102(CanL):Autumn83-
80
Fugger, B. La pénétration du français
commun en Franche-Comté d'après l'"Atlas
linguistique et ethnographique de la
Franche-Comté (ALFC)."
C. Dondaine, 553(RLiR):Jan-Jun83-224
Fuhrmann, M., H.R. Jauss and W. Pannenberg,
eds. Text und Applikation.
J.H. Petersen, 52:Band18Heft3-316

Fujiwara Iwaichi. F. Kikan.
  H. Toye, 617(TLS):20Jan84-59
Fujiwara no Sadaie, comp. The Little Trea-
  sury of One Hundred People, One Poem
  Each. (T. Galt, trans)
  P.T. Harries, 407(MN):Summer83-211
Fukuda, N. Survey of Japanese Collections
  in the United States, 1979-1980.
  M.H. Donovan, 407(MN):Autumn83-356
Fukumoto, N., N. Harano and S. Susuki,
  eds. Le Roman de Renart.
  G. Roques, 553(RLiR):Jul-Dec83-499
Fulbrook, M. Piety and Politics.
  P. Lake, 617(TLS):6Apr84-364
Fülleborn, U. and M. Engel. Materialien
  zu Rainer Maria Rilkes "Duineser
  Elegien."
  B.L. Bradley, 221(GQ):Nov83-681
  P. Bridgwater, 402(MLR):Oct83-991
Fuller, C.J. Servants of the Goddess.
  W.D. O'Flaherty, 617(TLS):23Nov84-1357
Fuller, J. The Beautiful Inventions.*
  B. Jones, 364:Jul83-78
  M. O'Neill, 493:Jun83-58
Fuller, J. Flying to Nowhere.*
  E. Mendelson, 441:4Mar84-9
  W. Scammell, 364:Aug/Sep83-129
Fuller, J. Fragments.
  S. Altinel, 617(TLS):6Apr84-368
  M. Laski, 362:12Apr84-27
  D. Myers, 441:12Feb84-37
Fuller, J.G. The Day We Bombed Utah.
  R. Bailey, 441:13May84-23
Fuller, L.L. The Principles of Social
  Order.* (K.I. Winston, ed)
  C.R. Sunstein, 185:Oct83-126
Fuller, M. The Letters of Margaret Ful-
  ler.* (R.N. Hudspeth, ed)
  G.W. Allen, 432(NEQ):Dec83-585
Fuller, P. Art and Psychoanalysis. See-
  ing Berger.
  S. Mitchell, 59:Dec83-499
Fuller, R. Home and Dry.
  V. Scannell, 617(TLS):30Mar84-331
  I.C. Smith, 362:10May84-30
Fulton, R. Fields of Focus.*
  E. Larrissy, 493:Mar83-61
  R. Lattimore, 249(HudR):Spring83-208
Fulton, R. - see Garioch, R.
Fumaroli, M. L'Age de l'Éloquence.*
  V. Kapp, 224(GRM):Band33Heft3-335
  J. Molino, 535(RHL):Mar/Apr83-224
Fumaroli, M., ed. Le Statut de la littéra-
  ture.*
  M-O. Sweetser, 475:Vol 10No18-305
  R. Trousson, 547(RF):Band95Heft4-488
Fumaroli, M. - see de Goncourt, E. and J.
Funck, E. Berättaren från fattighuset.
  B. Morris, 562(Scan):May82-102
Funke, P. Homónoia und Arché.
  H.D. Westlake, 123:Vol33No2-260
Funston, J. Malay Politics in Malaysia.
  J.A. MacDougall, 293(JASt):Nov82-214
Furbee-Losee, L. The Correct Language.
  J.M. Lawler, 269(IJAL):Oct83-447
Furbee-Losee, L., ed. Mayan Texts I.
  Mayan Texts II. Mayan Texts III.
  P. Brown, 269(IJAL):Jul83-337
von Furer-Haimendorf, C. A Himalayan
  Tribe.
  R.J. Young, 318(JAOS):Oct-Dec82-675

Furet, F. Interpreting the French Revo-
  lution.
  J. Dunne, 366:Spring83-118
  P.M. Jones, 83:Autumn83-242
Furley, D.J. and J.S. Wilkie, eds. Galen:
  On Respiration and the Arteries.
  J. Barnes, 617(TLS):2Nov84-1264
Furman, N. La Revue des Deux Mondes et le
  romantisme (1831-1848).
  S.G. Stary, 546(RR):May83-377
Furnée, E.J. Vorgriechisch-Kartvelisches.
  R. Bielmeier, 260(IF):Band88-371
Furness, R. Wagner and Literature.*
  P. Carnegy, 208(FS):Apr83-241
  J.L. Di Gaetani, 395(MFS):Summer83-372
  F.S. Heck, 207(FR):Feb84-401
Furst, L.R. The Contours of European
  Romanticism.*
  E.F. Gal, 447(N&Q):Jun82-281
Furst, L.R., comp. European Romanticism.*
  D. Fuller, 161(DUJ):Jun83-136
  J. Voisine, 549(RLC):Jan-Mar83-119
Furst, P.T. and others. Sweat of the Sun,
  Tears of the Moon.
  M. Graham, 2(AfrA):Nov82-92
Furuya, K. Chiang Kai-shek.
  E. Rhoads, 293(JASt):Aug83-916
Fusco, M. - see Svevo, I.
Fuss, A., F. Jambrina and A. San Miguel.
  ¡Qué barbaridad! (Vol 1)
  C. Schmitt, 553(RLiR):Jul-Dec83-452
Fussell, P. Abroad.*
  A. Bacon, 506(PSt):May83-87
  A. Blayac, 189(EA):Jan-Mar84-101
  P.M.S.D., 148:Spring83-92
  B. Stovel, 49:Jul83-60
Fussell, P. The Boy Scout Handbook and
  Other Observations.*
  J.D. Barber, 579(SAQ):Summer83-325
Fussell, P. Caste Marks.
  N. Andrew, 362:7Jun84-25
  M.R. Lefkowitz, 617(TLS):6Jul84-749
Fussell, P. Class.*
  442(NY):2Jan84-90
Futrell, A.W. and C.R. Wordell - see
  Maurer, D.W.
Fyfield, J.A. Re-educating Chinese Anti-
  Communists.
  J. Kwong, 293(JASt):Aug83-917
Fyvel, T.R. George Orwell.*
  R.J. Voorhees, 395(MFS):Winter83-786

Gabel, G.U. Immanuel Kant.
  R. Malter, 342:Band74Heft3-370
Gabler, H.W., W. Steppe and C. Melchior -
  see Joyce, J.
Gablik, S. Has Modernism Failed?
  C. Ratcliff, 617(TLS):14Dec84-1452
  E.V. Thaw, 441:30Sep84-11
  442(NY):19Nov84-192
Gabriel, T.H. Third Cinema in the Third
  World.
  M. Keller, 127:Fall83-284
Gabrielsen, V. Remuneration of State
  Officials in Fourth Century B.C. Athens.*
  D.M. MacDowell, 123:Vol33No1-75
Gachoud, F. Maurice Clavel du glaive à la
  foi.
  M. Adam, 542:Oct-Dec83-493
Gadamer, H-G. Dialogue and Dialectic.*
  (P.C. Smith, ed and trans)
  I.M. Crombie, 449:May83-330

Gadamer, H-G. L'art de comprendre.
M. Adam, 542:Jan-Mar83-60
Gadamer, H-G. Reason in the Age of
Science.
J.E. Llewelyn, 518:Apr83-93
W.G. Regier, 400(MLN):Dec83-1312
Gadenne, P. La Plage de Scheveningen.
F. de Martinoir, 450(NRF):May83-125
Gagarin, M. Drakon and Early Athenian Hom-
icide Law.*
D. Lateiner, 24:Winter83-404
Gage, J.T. In the Arresting Eye.*
J. Glenn, 221(GQ):May83-476
Gage, N. Eleni.*
P. Green, 617(TLS):20Jan84-51
I. Scott-Kilvert, 364:Dec83/Jan84-123
639(VQR):Autumn83-124
Gaillard, D. Dorothy L. Sayers.
P. Wolfe, 395(MFS):Autumn83-389
Gaines, E.J. A Gathering of Old Men.*
B. Morton, 617(TLS):6Apr84-368
Gaínza, C.G. and others - see under García
Gaínza, C. and others
Gair, R. The Children of Paul's.*
B.S. Hammond, 610:Autumn83-253
Gairdner, W.D. The Critical Wager.
V. Nemoianu, 400(MLN):Dec83-1335
Gajdusek, R.E., ed. Hemingway's Paris.
B.I. Duffey, 579(SAQ):Autumn83-455
Gajek, B. - see Brentano, C.
Gala, A. Noviembre y un poco de yerba
[and] Petra Regalada. (P. Zatlin-
Boring, ed)
M.P. Holt, 238:Sep83-436
Galbraith, J.K. The Voice of the Poor.*
The Anatomy of Power.*
M. Stewart, 617(TLS):20Apr84-421
Galbraith, J.K., R. Jenkins and R. Wain-
wright. John Maynard Keynes. (A. Duff,
ed)
N. Annan, 453(NYRB):19Jul84-35
Galdós, B.P. - see under Pérez Galdós, B.
Gale, R.L. Will Henry/Clay Fisher.
R.W. Etulain, 649(WAL):Aug83-176
Galeano, L., comp. Mujer y trabajo en el
Paraguay.
D. Menanteau-Horta, 263(RIB):Vol133No1-
37
Galembert, P-J. Les Assassins du Nord.
B.G. Hirsch, 399(MLJ):Summer83-191
Galen. Galeno: "Iniciación a la Dialéc-
tia." (A. Ramírez Trejo, trans)
J. Barnes, 123:Vol133No2-336
Galen. Galen's Commentary on the Hippo-
cratic Treatise Airs, Waters, Places in
the Hebrew Translation of Salomon ha-
Me'ati. (A. Wasserstein, ed and trans)
A. Reix, 542:Oct-Dec83-456
Galenson, D.W. White Servitude in Colo-
nial America.
P.G.E. Clemens, 656(WMQ):Jan83-132
Galenson, W. The United Brotherhood of
Carpenters.
P. Renshaw, 617(TLS):15Jun84-673
Galford, E. Moll Cutpurse.
D. Nokes, 617(TLS):3Aug84-864
Galgan, G. The Logic of Modernity.
W.J. Gavin, 258:Dec83-449
Galich, A. Songs and Poems.
F. Williams, 617(TLS):18May84-559
Galinsky, H. Das amerikanische Englisch.*
D. Nehls, 257(IRAL):Feb83-80
H. Penzl, 685(ZDL):3/1983-396

Galisson, R. Recherches de lexicologie
descriptive.
K.E.M. George, 208(FS):Oct83-502
Gall, D. Die Bilder der horazischen Lyrik.
R.G.M. Nisbet, 313:Vol73-238
Gall, S. Behind Russian Lines.*
D. Thomas, 362:12Jan84-22
J. Van Dyk, 441:20May84-30
Gallacher, T. Journeyman.
D. Dunn, 617(TLS):29Jun84-736
Gallagher, D. - see Waugh, E.
Gallagher, E.J. A Thousand Thoughts on
Technology and Human Values.
D. Levin, 125:Spring83-309
Gallagher, J.S. and A.H. Patera. Wyoming
Post Offices 1850-1980. A Checklist of
Wyoming Post Offices.
M.R. Miller, 424:Sep83-217
Gallagher, M. The Irish Labour Party in
Transition 1957-82.
T. Garvin, 272(IUR):Autumn83-263
Gallagher, T. Willingly.
W. Logan, 441:26Aug84-13
Gallais, P. Dialectique du récit médiéval.
G.R. Mermier, 207(FR):Mar84-548
Gallant, M. Home Truths.
J. Harcourt, 529(QQ):Spring83-244
A. Michaels, 526:Spring83-69
"Gallantry A-la-Mode."
566:Autumn83-66
Gállego, J. El cuadro dentro del cuadro.
F. Marías, 48:Jan-Mar79-92
Gallet, M. and Y. Bottineau, eds. Les
Gabriel.
J. Rykwert, 90:Dec83-765
Gallie, D. Social Inequality and Class
Radicalism in France and Britain.
A. Marwick, 617(TLS):10Aug84-896
Gallie, W.B. Philosophers of Peace and
War.
P. Lantz, 192(EP):Apr-Jun83-235
Gallix, F. - see White, T.H.
Gallois, C. Le Coeur en quatre.
R.R. St.-Onge, 207(FR):Dec83-269
Gallop, J. The Daughter's Seduction.*
M.N. Evans, 207(FR):Apr84-703
Gallop, J. Feminism and Psychoanalysis.*
R. Jackson, 208(FS):Jan83-114
Gallop, J. Intersections.*
J. Humphries, 188(ECr):Winter83-84
Galloway, D. and J. Wasson, eds. Records
of Plays and Players in Norfolk and Suf-
folk, 1330-1642.
A.H. Nelson, 130:Spring83-82
Gallup, D. Ezra Pound. (2nd ed)
H. Kenner, 617(TLS):2Mar84-231
C.F. Terrell, 468:Fall/Winter83-513
Gallup, D. - see O'Neill, E.
Gallwitz, K., ed. Die Nazarener in Rom.
C.J. Bailey, 90:Nov83-702
Galston, W.A. Justice and the Human Good.*
D.A. Lloyd Thomas, 479(PhQ):Jul83-301
Galt, G. Trailing Pythagoras.
R.W. Bevis, 102(CanL):Autumn83-114
Galway, J. Flute.
N. O'Loughlin, 415:May83-302
Gamal, A.S. - see Ibn Ridwān
Gamberini, S. Analisi dei Sepolcri fosco-
liani.
J. Lindon, 278(IS):Vol38-112
Gambini, P-A.Q. - see under Quarantotti
Gambini, P-A.

Gambirasio, G. and B. Minardi. Giovanni Muzio.
R.A. Etlin, 127:Summer83-200
Gamerschlag, K. Sir Walter Scott und die Waverley Novels.
E. Mengel, 72:Band220Heft2-403
Gamkrelidze, T.V. and G.I. Mačavariani. Sonantensystem und Ablaut in den Kartwelsprachen.
B.G. Hewitt, 297(JL):Mar83-286
Gamrath, H. København havns historie. (Vol 2)
R. McKnight, 563(SS):Autumn83-383
Gann, E.K. Gentlemen of Adventure.
D. Myers, 441:22Jan84-22
Gans, E. The Origin of Language.
G. Mounin, 567:Vol42No2/4-289
Gantner, J. - see Wölfflin, H.
Ganz, A. George Bernard Shaw.
A. Carpenter, 617(TLS):15Jun84-663
Ganzel, B. Dust Bowl Descent.
S.M. Halpern, 441:5Aug84-18
Ganzel, D. Fortune and Men's Eyes.*
W.M. Baillie, 539:May84-146
Gaos, V. - see de Cervantes Saavedra, M.
Garapon, R. Le Premier Corneille.
M-O. Sweetser, 475:Vol 10No18-338
M-O. Sweetser, 535(RHL):Sep/Dec83-919
Garapon, R. Ronsard chantre de Marie et d'Hélène.
Y. Bellenger, 535(RHL):Jan/Feb83-118
M. Quainton, 208(FS):Apr83-206
Garavini, F. Madame de La Fayette, La Principessa di Clèves.
G.M. Fondi, 475:Vol 10No19-901
Garbe, B., ed. Die deutsche Rechtschreibung und ihre Reform 1722-1974.
W.H. Veith, 685(ZDL):1/1983-111
Garber, E.K. Metaphysical Tales.
G. Garrett, 569(SR):Winter83-112
Garber, F. The Autonomy of the Self from Richardson to Huysmans.*
J. Black, 149(CLS):Winter83-450
L.R. Furst, 131(CL):Spring83-182
A. Gelley, 678(YCGL):No31-144
M. Kipperman, 661(WC):Summer83-149
J. Sitter, 173(ECS):Winter83/84-189
Garber, L. Sirens and Graces.
M. Malone, 441:1Apr84-22
Garber, M. Coming of Age in Shakespeare.
W. Bies, 125:Winter83-204
C.T. Neely, 551(RenQ):Spring83-140
M. Rose, 570(SQ):Autumn83-382
Garbicz, A. and J. Klinowski. Cinema, the Magic Vehicle.
J. Nangle, 200:Nov83-572
García, L.M. - see under Martínez García, L.
García-Amador, F.V., ed. Sistema Interamericano a Través de Tratados, Convenciones y Otros Documentos. (Vol 1)
C. García-Godoy, 263(RIB):Vol33No4-577
J.M. Ribas, 37:Mar-Apr83-60
García Barragán, M.G. El naturalismo en México.
T. Murad, 238:Mar83-145
Garcia de La Huerta, M. La técnica y el estado moderno.
A. Reix, 542:Oct-Dec83-494
García Gaínza, C. and others. Catálogo monumental de Navarra. (Vol 1)
D. Angulo Íñiguez, 48:Oct-Dec80-504

García Gual, C. El Sistema Diatético en ed Verbo Griego.
E. Neu, 260(IF):Band87-308
García Hernández, B. Semántica estructural y lexemática del verbo.
C. Lleó, 260(IF):Band88-331
R. Wright, 545(RPh):May83-619
García Márquez, G. Chronicle of a Death Foretold.* (Spanish title: Crónica de una Muerte Anunciada.)
G. Kearns, 249(HudR):Autumn83-552
M. Tregebov, 99:Jun83-32
García Márquez, G. El coronel no tiene quien le escriba. (G. Pontiero, ed)
J. Labanyi, 86(BHS):Jul83-266
García Márquez, G. and P. Apuleyo Mendoza. El olor de la guayaba.
A. de Arboleda, 37:Jan-Feb83-61
García Martín, J.L., ed. Las voces y los ecos.
A.P. Debicki, 240(HR):Summer83-353
Garcia Merino, C. Poblacion y poblamiento en Hispania romana.
N. Mackie, 313:Vol73-236
García Moreno, L.A. La epoca helenica y helenistica.
É. Will, 555:Vol57fasc1-115
García Novo, E. La entrada de los personajes y su anuncio en la tragedia griega.
E.M. Craik, 303(JoHS):Vol 103-185
García Salinero, F. Viaje de Turquía.
M-S. Ortolá, 551(RenQ):Autumn83-453
García Servet, J. El humanista Cascales y la inquisición murciana.
F. Márquez Villanueva, 545(RPh):Nov82-345
García Tortosa, F. and R. López Ortega, eds. English Literature and the Working Class.
H.G. Klaus, 72:Band219Heft1-202
García Yebra, V. Teoría y práctica de la traducción.
M. Wandruszka, 547(RF):Band95Heft1/2-135
du Gard, R.M. Le Lieutenant-Colonel de Maumort. (A. Daspre, ed)
P. Fawcett, 617(TLS):25May84-595
Gardam, J. The Pangs of Love and Other Stories.*
D. Taylor, 364:Jul83-94
Garde, P. Grammaire russe.* (Vol 1)
N.J. Brown, 575(SEER):Apr83-259
L. Djurovič, 559:Vol7No1-47
Garden, R. - see Jacob, N.
Gardin, B. and J.B. Marcellesi, eds. Sociolinguistique.
N. Gueunier, 209(FM):Jan83-57
Gardin, J-C. Archaeological Constructs.
E. Porada, 318(JAOS):Jul-Sep82-501
Gardin, J-C. and others. La logique du plausible.
C. Péquegnat, 567:Vol145No1/2-181
P. Somville, 542:Jul-Sep83-329
Gardiner, D. and K.S. Walker - see Chandler, R.
Gardiner, J.R. Going On Like This.*
J.L. Idol, Jr., 573(SSF):Fall83-328
42(AR):Fall83-510
Gardiner, M. Footprints on Malekula.
J. Clifford, 617(TLS):16Nov84-1316
Gardiner, S. Kuwait.
A. Briggs, 362:12Apr84-25
G. Fitzpatrick, 364:Feb84-111

Gardner, H. Frames of Mind.*
   P. Johnson-Laird, 617(TLS):11May84-533
Gardner, H. In Defense of the Imagina-
   tion.*
   J. Blondel, 189(EA):Apr-Jun84-174
   L. Gent, 175:Autumn83-280
   D.K. Hedrick, 221(GQ):May83-456
   P. Henry, 478:Oct83-259
   I. McGilchrist, 402(MLR):Oct83-888
   C. McGlinchee, 290(JAAC):Winter83-239
Gardner, J. The Art of Fiction.
   J. Atlas, 61:Jan84-96
   J. L'Heureux, 441:26Feb84-23
Gardner, J. The Art of Living.*
   G. Garrett, 569(SR):Winter83-112
   J. Mellors, 362:2Feb84-28
Gardner, J., ed. The Best Short Stories
   1982.
   639(VQR):Spring83-56
Gardner, J. Flamingo.
   M. Laski, 362:12Jan84-26
Gardner, J. Mickelsson's Ghosts.
   R. Daly, 219(GaR):Summer83-420
   J.P. Hermann, 577(SHR):Summer83-281
Gardner, J. Role of Honor.
   M. Laski, 362:25Oct84-29
   R. Smith, 441:28Oct84-26
Gardner, J. and J. Maier, with R.A. Hen-
   shaw - see "Gilgamesh"
Gardner, J., with S. Ravenel, eds. The
   Best American Short Stories.
   G.L. Morris, 502(PrS):Summer83-96
Gardner, J.W. Excellence. (rev)
   B. Hall, 441:24Jun84-23
Gardner, L.C. Safe for Democracy.
   J.M. Cooper, Jr., 441:18Nov84-24
Gardner, P. The Lost Elementary Schools
   of Victorian England.
   G. Sutherland, 617(TLS):30Nov84-1370
Gardner, S. When Sunday Comes.
   C. Wallace-Crabbe, 617(TLS):20Jul84-
   819
Gardner, W. Alphabet at Work.*
   639(VQR):Winter83-29
Garelli, J. Artaud et la question du lieu.
   P. Hawkins, 208(FS):Apr83-246
   D. Leuwers, 535(RHL):Sep/Dec83-967
Garey, M.R. and D.S. Johnson. Computers
   and Intractability.
   H.R. Lewis, 316:Jun83-498
Garfield, L. and E. Blishen - see Peake, M.
Gargano, A. - see de Flores, J.
Gargett, G. Voltaire and Protestantism.*
   J. Renwick, 402(MLR):Jul83-711
Garin, E. Astrology in the Renaissance.
   M.J.B. Allen, 551(RenQ):Winter83-577
   T.W., 111:Spring83-2
Garioch, R. Complete Poetical Works.* (R.
   Fulton, ed)
   D. McDuff, 565:Vol24No4-62
Garlan, Y. Les Esclaves en Grèce ancienne.
   T.E.J. Wiedemann, 123:Vol33No2-265
Garland, M.M. Cambridge Before Darwin.*
   R.G. Cox, 447(N&Q):Aug82-359
Garlick, K. and A. Macintyre - see Faring-
   ton, J.
Garliński, J. Enigma.
   R.A. Woytak and C. Kasparek, 497(PolR):
   Vol28No2-98
Garmonsway, G.N., J. Simpson and H.E.
   Davidson. "Beowulf" and its Analogues.
   A.C., 189(EA):Jan-Mar83-108

Garms, J., R. Juffinger and B. Ward-
   Perkins. Die Mittelalterlichen Grab-
   mäler in Rom und Latium vom 13. bis
   15. Jahrhundert. (Vol 1)
   J. Gardner, 90:Oct83-623
Garneau, M. Emilie ne sera plus jamais
   cueillie par l'anémone.
   C.F. Coates, 207(FR):Feb84-411
   R. Usmiani, 102(CanL):Autumn83-85
Garneau, M. Sur le matelas.
   C.F. Coates, 207(FR):Feb84-411
Garner, A. A Book of British Fairy Tales.
   I. Parry, 617(TLS):30Nov84-1381
Garner, P. Emile Gallé.
   C.B. McGee, 441:23Sep84-28
Garner, W. Rats' Alley.
   T.J.B., 617(TLS):12Oct84-1167
   M. Laski, 362:19Jul84-27
Garnett, A. Deceived with Kindness.
   A. Storr, 617(TLS):3Aug84-861
Garofalo, S. L'enciclopedismo italiano.
   F. Betti, 276:Winter83-375
Garoutte, S., ed. Uncoverings 1982.
   P. Bach, 614:Spring84-29
Garoux, A. Spinoza.
   G. Brykman, 542:Oct-Dec83-468
Garrard, J. Mikhail Lermontov.
   H. Goscilo-Kostin, 550(RusR):Oct83-438
   J. Mersereau, Jr., 558(RLJ):Fall83-
   225
   D. White, 574(SEEJ):Winter83-488
Garrard, J., ed. The Russian Novel from
   Pushkin to Pasternak.
   J. Grayson, 617(TLS):17Aug84-920
   V.D. Mihailovich, 268(IFR):Summer84-
   123
Garrett, G. James Jones.
   S. Krim, 441:30Sep84-48
   W. Peden, 578:Fall84-101
Garrett, G. The Succession.*
   W. Peden, 578:Fall84-101
   J.G. Shaw, 389(MQ):Summer84-471
   L.W. Wagner, 385(MQR):Summer84-446
Garrett, P.K. The Victorian Multiplot
   Novel.*
   H. Foltinek, 402(MLR):Jul83-696
Garrick, D. The Plays of David Garrick.*
   (Vols 1 and 2) (H.W. Pedicord and F.L.
   Bergmann, eds)
   I. Donaldson, 541(RES):Feb83-81
   P. Rogers, 83:Spring83-81
Garrick, D. The Plays of David Garrick.*
   (Vols 3 and 4) (H.W. Pedicord and F.L.
   Bergmann, eds)
   M.S. Auburn, 570(SQ):Autumn83-377
   P. Rogers, 83:Spring83-81
Garrigues, E. The Grass Rain.
   A. Johnson, 441:30Sep84-28
Garrison, W. Oglethorpe's Folly.
   H.H. Jackson, 656(WMQ):Oct83-632
Garrisson, J. Henri IV.
   R.J. Knecht, 617(TLS):28Sep84-1092
Gärtner, J. The Vibrato with Particular
   Consideration given to the Situation of
   the Flutist.
   N. O'Loughlin, 415:Jul83-429
Garton Ash, T. The Polish Revolution.
   S. Andreski, 617(TLS):4May84-488
   J. Darnton, 441:29Apr84-9
Garuti, G. - see Claudian
Garvey, C. Children's Talk.
   J. Greene, 617(TLS):13Jul84-779

Gary, R. King Solomon.*
639(VQR):Autumn83-126
Gasché, R. System und Metaphorik in der
Philosophie von Georges Bataille.
D. Chaffin, 400(MLN):May83-822
Gascoyne, D. Journal 1936-1937.
506(PSt):Dec83-311
Gash, J. Firefly Gadroon.
N. Callendar, 441:4Nov84-35
442(NY):22Oct84-164
Gash, J. The Gondola Scam.
T.J. Binyon, 617(TLS):18May84-557
N. Callendar, 441:29Apr84-26
M. Laski, 362:12Apr84-27
442(NY):9Jul84-95
Gash, J. Priestly Murders.
N. Callendar, 441:28Oct84-39
Gash, N. Lord Liverpool.
B. Hilton, 617(TLS):28Sep84-1077
Gaspar, L. Sol absolu et autres textes.
R. Little, 450(NRF):Feb83-122
Gassendi, P. Institutio Logica.* (H.
Jones, ed and trans)
O. Bloch, 542:Jan-Mar83-117
Gassin, J. L'Univers symbolique d'Albert
Camus.
P. McCarthy, 208(FS):Apr83-247
Gateau, J-C. Paul Éluard et la peinture
surréaliste (1910-1939).
J.H. Matthews, 593:Summer83-165
J. Pfeiffer, 450(NRF):May83-149
Gatenby, G., ed. Whales.
S. Mills, 617(TLS):30Mar84-353
Gates, H.L., Jr., ed. Black Literature
and Literary Theory.
T. Eagleton, 441:9Dec84-45
Gatewood, W.B. - see Hodges, W.A.
Gathorne-Hardy, J. Doctors.
D. Gould, 617(TLS):13Jul84-780
D. Widgery, 362:21Jun84-25
Gauchat, L., J. Jeanjaquet and E. Tappolet.
Glossaire des patois de la Suisse
romande.
P. Swiggers, 353:Vol20No9/10-657
Gaudiani, C. Teaching Writing in the
Foreign Language Curriculum.*
J.B. Dalbor, 238:Mar83-147
Gaudon, J. - see Hugo, V.
Gauger, H-M., W. Oesterreicher and R.
Windisch. Einführung in die romanische
Sprachwissenschaft.*
D. Nehls, 257(IRAL):Aug83-244
Gaughan, J.A. A Political Odyssey.
C. Davidson, 617(TLS):16Mar84-282
Gaukroger, S., ed. Descartes: Philosophy,
Mathematics and Physics.*
R. Popkin, 84:Jun83-182
Gaul, M. - see Harris, S.
Gaulmier, J. - see de Gobineau, A-J.
Gaulmier, J. - see Volney, C-F.
Gaume, M. - see d'Urfé, H.
Gauna, M. - see Tahureau, J.
Gaustad, E.S., ed. A Documentary History
of Religion in America to the Civil War.
G.L. Wilson, 579(SAQ):Autumn83-465
Gaute, J.H.H. and R. Odell. Murder
"Whatdunit."
N. Callendar, 441:8Jan84-27
Gauteur, C. - see Renoir, J.
Gauthier, M-M. and G. François. Medieval
Enamels.
D.M. Ebitz, 589:Oct83-1038

Gautier, J-J. Une Amitié tenace.
M.B. Kline, 207(FR):May84-908
Gautier, J-Y. Socioécologie.
J-M. Gabaude, 542:Jul-Sep83-357
Gautier, T. Émaux et Camées. (C. Gothot-
Mersch, ed)
H. Cockerham, 208(FS):Oct83-476
Gautier, T. Mademoiselle de Maupin. (J.
Robichez, ed)
P.J. Whyte, 208(FS):Apr83-231
Gautier-Dalché, J. Économie et société
dans les pays de la Couronne de Castille.
D.W. Lomax, 86(BHS):Jul83-253
Gautier de Dargies. Poesie.* (A.M.
Raugei, ed)
M. Bambeck, 547(RF):Band95Heft3-332
Gauvin, L. and others. Guide Culturel du
Québec.
M. Cagnon, 207(FR):Feb84-428
Gavarini, F. - see Madame de Lafayette
Gavaskar, S. Idols.
A.L. Le Quesne, 617(TLS):21Dec84-1487
Gavazzeni, F. - see Foscolo, U.
Gavron, D. Israel After Begin.
T. Jacoby, 441:15Apr84-23
Gavronsky, S. The German Friend.
R. Elman, 441:18Nov84-32
Gavshon, A. and D. Rice. The Sinking of
the Belgrano.
L. Freedman, 617(TLS):9Mar84-244
442(NY):3Sep84-96
Gay, D. Les élites québécoises et l'Amér-
ique latine.
M. Laroche, 193(ELit):Aug83-298
Gay, J. Selected Poems. (M. Walsh, ed)
566:Autumn83-62
Gay, M. Eclaboussures.
A.L. Amprimoz, 102(CanL):Autumn83-110
Gay, M. Plaque tournante.*
D.F. Rogers, 102(CanL):Summer83-157
Gay, P. The Bourgeois Experience.* (Vol
1)
J.W. Burrow, 617(TLS):17Aug84-907
D. Cannadine, 453(NYRB):2Feb84-19
P. Johnson, 129:Jun84-68
N. McKendrick, 441:8Jan84-1
A. Ryan, 362:5Apr84-23
442(NY):13Feb84-129
Gay-Crosier, R., ed. Albert Camus 1980.*
A. Rizzuto, 546(RR):Jan83-117
Gayle, A. Richard Wright.
L. Sanders, 106:Fall83-343
Gaylin, W. and R. Macklin, eds. Who Speaks
for the Child?
B.B., 185:Oct83-181
Gaynor, E. and K. Haavisto. Finland.
P. Goldberger, 441:2Dec84-20
Geach, P.T. Reference and Generality.
(3rd ed)
C.J.F. Williams, 518:Apr83-98
Gearey, J. Goethe's "Faust": The Making
of Part I.*
B. Bennett, 222(GR):Summer83-121
E.A. Blackall, 301(JEGP):Apr83-288
J.K. Brown, 131(CL):Summer83-299
Geary, J.S. Formulaic Diction in the
"Poema de Fernán González" and the
"Mocedades de Rodrigo."*
K. Adams, 382(MAE):1983/2-331
M-A. Börger-Reese, 240(HR):Winter83-92
R.G. Keightley, 547(RF):Band95Heft1/2-
230
S. Lusignan, 589:Oct83-1116

George, F.H. The Science of Philosophy.
  W.A. Davis, 543:Jun83-929
George, J.C. Journey Inward.
  F. Krall, 649(WAL):May83-44
Georgianna, L. The Solitary Self.
  R.H. Green, 589:Apr83-468
Geraint Gruffydd, R., ed. Bardos.
  P. Ó Fiannachta, 112:Vol 15-184
Geraldus Cambrensis. The History and To-
  pography of Ireland.
  J. Lordson, 174(Éire):Fall83-142
Gérard, A.S. African Languages Litera-
  tures.
  B. Lindfors, 678(YCGL):No31-147
  M. Steins, 52:Band18Heft2-201
Gérard, G. Critique et dialectique.
  H. Faes, 542:Oct-Dec83-479
Gérard, J. L'exclamation en français.*
  K. Hunnius, 547(RF):Band95Heft4-482
Geras, N. Marx and Human Nature.
  S. Lukes, 617(TLS):6Apr84-366
  S.W., 185:Jul84-732
Gerber, A. Le Lapin de lune.
  R. Holzberg-Namad, 207(FR):Mar84-587
Gerber, D.E. Pindar's "Olympian One."
  D.A. Campbell, 627(UTQ):Summer83-398
  R. Hamilton, 121(CJ):Dec83/Jan84-157
  A. Köhnken, 487:Winter83-351
Gerber, J.C., P. Baender and T. Firkins
  - see Twain, M.
Gerber, J.S. Jewish Society in Fez, 1450-
  1700.
  N.A. Stillman, 318(JAOS):Jan-Mar82-221
Gerber, M. and others, eds. Studies in
  GDR Culture and Society.
  S. Lennox, 221(GQ):May83-528
Gere, J.A. and P. Pouncey, with R. Wood.
  Italian Drawings in the Department of
  Prints and Drawings at the British
  Museum: Artists Working in Rome c. 1550
  to c. 1640.
  J.B. Shaw, 90:Sep83-550
Gerhard, D. Old Europe.
  L.B.G., 185:Jan84-368
Gerhard, S.F. "Don Quixote" and the Shel-
  ton Translation.
  R.M. Cox, 240(HR):Summer83-323
Gérin, W. Anne Thackeray Ritchie.*
  V. Colby, 405(MP):Aug83-91
Gerlach, I. Der schwierige Fortschritt.*
  E. Röhner, 654(WB):8/1983-1494
Gerlaud, B. - see Triphiodorus
"The Germ: The Literary Magazine of the
  Pre-Raphaelites."*
  E.D. Mackerness, 447(N&Q):Jun82-256
Germain, C. La sémantique fonctionnelle.
  J-C. Boulanger, 320(CJL):Spring83-77
Germaine, M. Artists and Galleries of
  Australia and New Zealand.
  U. Hoff, 39:Oct83-352
German, A.W. Down on T Wharf.
  W.M. Fowler, Jr., 432(NEQ):Sep83-477
Germino, D. Political Philosophy and the
  Open Society.
  639(VQR):Winter83-22
Gerndt, S. Idealisierte Natur.*
  W.R. Berger, 52:Band17Heft3-313
  J. Hallerbach, 72:Band219Heft1-152
  R. Immerwahr, 301(JEGP):Oct83-599
Gernet, J. Chine et Christianisme.*
  H. Cronel, 450(NRF):Feb83-139
  P.W. Fay, 293(JASt):Aug83-919

Gernet, L. The Anthropology of Ancient
  Greece.
  M.B. Arthur, 400(MLN):Dec83-1374
  J. Redfield, 24:Winter83-398
Gerould, D. Witkacy.*
  F.S. Galassi, 497(PolR):Vol28No4-99
Gershator, D. - see Lorca, F.G.
Gerson, J. The Whitehall Sanction.
  J. Berry, 441:26Feb84-22
Gertler, T. Elbowing the Seducer.
  R. Koenig, 61:Jun84-117
  J. O'Reilly, 441:24Jun84-34
Gerus-Tarnawecka, I.I. East Slavic
  Cyrillica in Canadian Repositories.
  W.T. Zyla, 574(SEEJ):Fall83-399
Gervais, C.H. Up Country Lines.
  R. Hatch, 102(CanL):Winter82-144
Gervais, G. Gravité.
  E. Hamblet, 207(FR):Feb84-412
  H.R. Runte, 102(CanL):Summer83-114
Gervers, V. The History of Ottoman Turk-
  ish Textiles and Costume in Eastern
  Europe with Particular Reference to
  Hungary.
  J. Wearden, 90:Nov83-707
"Gesamtkatalog der Wiegendrucke." (Vol 9,
  fasc 1)
  B.M. Rosenthal, 517(PBSA):Vol77No1-115
Gess, D. Good Deeds.
  D. Cole, 441:12Feb84-20
Gessinger, J. Sprache und Bürgertum.*
  K.H. Jäger, 406:Winter83-443
Geta, H. - see under Hosidius Geta
Gethin, D. Wyatt and the Moresby Legacy.
  N. Callendar, 441:4Nov84-35
Gettings, F. Dictionary of Occult, Her-
  matic and Alchemic Sigils.
  N. Barley, 567:Vol42No2/4-285
  R.P. Multhauf, 589:Jan83-261
Getzler, I. Kronstadt 1917-1921.
  R. Conquest, 617(TLS):13Jan84-32
Gevirtz, D. Business Plan for America.
  K.W. Arenson, 441:26Aug84-18
Gewirth, A. Human Rights.
  B.R. Gross, 185:Jan84-324
  M.C. Overvold, 518:Oct83-241
Gewirth, A. Reason and Morality.
  F. Feldman, 449:Sep83-475
Geyer, D. Kautsky's Russisches Dossier.
  G.L. Freeze, 550(RusR):Jul83-330
Geyer, G.A. Buying the Night Flight.*
  W.P. Carty, 37:Jul-Aug83-61
Geyr, H. Sprichwörter und sprichwortnahe
  Bildungen im dreisprachigen Petersburger
  Lexikon von 1731.
  W. Mieder, 196:Band24Heft1/2-142
Ghalem, N. L'Oiseau de fer.
  M. Benson, 102(CanL):Summer83-102
  E. Sellin, 207(FR):Dec83-270
de Ghelderode, M. Le Mystère de la pas-
  sion.
  J. Decock, 207(FR):Apr84-735
de Ghelderode, M. Le Siège d'Ostende.
  J. Decock, 207(FR):May84-909
de Ghelderode, M. Théâtre VI.
  J. Guérin, 450(NRF):Feb83-155
Ghiglione, L., ed. The Buying and Selling
  of America's Newspapers.
  A.S. Jones, 441:25Nov84-37
Ghigo, F. The Provençal Speech of the Wal-
  densian Colonists of Valdese, North
  Carolina.
  M. Peet, 545(RPh):Nov82-326

Ghose, Z. Don Bueno.
  A. Johnson, 441:12Aug84-20
Giamatti, A.B. The University and the
  Public Interest.*
  C.D. Murphy, 396(ModA):Summer/Fall83-
  332
Giancana, A. and T.C. Renner. Mafia
  Princess.
  L. Taylor, 617(TLS):7Sep84-993
Giannakis, G.N. Orpheōs Lithika.
  É. des Places, 555:Vol57fasc2-319
  J.E. Rexine, 124:Jan-Feb84-192
Giannantoni, G., ed. Lo scetticismo
  antico.
  M.R. Stopper, 520:Vol28No3-265
Giantvalley, S. Walt Whitman, 1838-1939.*
  D.D. Kummings, 125:Fall82-109
Giard, J-B. Le Monnayage de l'atelier de
  Lyon.
  M. Crawford, 617(TLS):24Aug84-950
Giardina, A. Men with Debts.
  J. Haskins, 441:10Jun84-24
Giardina, A. and A. Schiavone, eds. Soci-
  età Romana e Produzione Schiavistica.
  (Vols 1-3)
  W.V. Harris, 24:Winter83-418
  D.W. Rathbone, 313:Vol73-160
Giardina, D. Good King Harry.
  B. Tritel, 441:29Jul84-20
Gibaldi, J., ed. Approaches to Teaching
  Chaucer's "Canterbury Tales."*
  D. Mehl, 72:Band219Heft2-477
Gibaud, H., ed. Un inédit d'Erasme.
  A. Rabil, Jr., 551(RenQ):Autumn83-431
Gibault, H. and P. Morère, eds. Écosse:
  Littérature et civilisation.*
  I. Campbell, 571(ScLJ):Autumn83-40
Gibbon, E. Autobiography.
  A. Storr, 135:Nov83-145
Gibbon, E. Memoirs of My Own Life. (B.
  Radice, ed)
  J.S., 617(TLS):18May84-562
Gibbon, L.G. Lewis Grassic Gibbon, "The
  Speak of the Mearns."* (I. Campbell,
  ed)
  D. Young, 571(ScLJ):Autumn83-30
Gibbons, B. How Flowers Work.
  C. Humphries, 617(TLS):7Sep84-985
Gibbons, B. Jacobean City Comedy.* (2nd
  ed)
  M.T. Jones-Davies, 541(RES):Aug83-332
  P. Seltzer, 610:Winter81/82-63
Gibbons, B. - see Shakespeare, W.
Gibbons, R. The Ruined Motel.*
  R. Pybus, 565:Vol24No2-73
Gibbons, R. and A.L. Geist - see Guillén,
  J.
Gibbs, A. and A. Tilson, eds. Frictions.
  E. Webby, 381:Mar83-34
Gibbs, A.M. The Art and Mind of Shaw.
  E. Jones, 617(TLS):30Mar84-325
Gibbs, D.A. Subject and Author Index to
  "Chinese Literature" Monthly (1951-
  1976).
  T.C. Wong, 318(JAOS):Jan-Mar82-150
Gibson, A.M. The Santa Fe and Taos
  Colonies.
  L. Milazzo, 584(SWR):Spring83-vi
  T.M. Pearce, 649(WAL):Feb84-364
Gibson, A.M. - see Kipling, R.
Gibson, D.B. The Politics of Literary
  Expression.*
  R. Hemenway, 395(MFS):Winter83-746

Gibson, G. Perpetual Motion.*
  L. Franks, 461:Fall/Winter83/84-91
  J.A. Wainwright, 198:Jan84-91
Gibson, G.D., T.J. Larson and C.R. McGurk.
  The Kavango Peoples.
  A. Kuper, 69:Vol53No2-90
Gibson, J.C.L. Textbook of Syrian Semitic
  Inscriptions. (Vol 3)
  P. Swiggers, 350:Jun84-461
Gibson, J.M. and R.L. Green - see Doyle,
  A.C.
Gibson, M., ed. Boethius.
  J. Dillon, 123:Vol33No1-117
  P.J. Ford, 402(MLR):Apr83-401
  A. Hughes, 410(M&L):Jul/Oct83-267
  P. Wormald, 313:Vol73-243
Gibson, M. Long Walks in the Afternoon.*
  P. Mesic, 491:Feb84-301
  D. St. John, 42(AR):Spring83-231
  P. Stitt, 219(GaR):Summer83-428
Gibson, M. The Sandman.
  J. Melmoth, 617(TLS):2Mar84-227
Gibson, M.I. The Roots of Russian Through
  Chekhov.
  C.E. Townsend, 574(SEEJ):Fall83-402
Gibson, R.F., Jr. The Philosophy of W.V.
  Quine.
  F.F.S., 185:Jul84-730
  M. Winston, 486:Dec83-673
Gibson, W. Neuromancer.
  C. Greenland, 617(TLS):7Dec84-1420
Giddings, P. When and Where I Enter.
  G. Naylor, 441:8Jul84-10
Gide, A. Journals 1889-1949.
  G.S., 617(TLS):20Jul84-822
Gide, A. and D. Bussy. Selected Letters
  of André Gide and Dorothy Bussy.* (R.
  Tedeschi, ed and trans)
  A. Fitzlyon, 364:Aug/Sep83-120
Giedymin, J. Science and Convention.
  C.W. Kilmister, 84:Dec83-396
Gier, N.F. Wittgenstein and Phenomenol-
  ogy.*
  D. Ihde, 323:May83-209
  R.E. Innis, 543:Dec82-449
Giertych, J. In Defence of My Country.
  A.J. Matejko, 497(PolR):Vol28No1-117
Gies, D.T. Agustín Durán.
  V. Masson de Gómez, 545(RPh):Feb83-483
Gies, F. The Knight in History.
  W. Smith, 441:9Dec84-27
Giffhorn, J. Phonologische Untersuchungen
  zu den altenglischen Kurzdiphthongen.
  A. Lutz, 72:Band219Heft1-184
Gifford, B. An Unfortunate Woman.
  J. McCulloch, 441:23Dec84-16
Gifford, D. Neil M. Gunn and Lewis Gras-
  sic Gibbon.
  J.B. Caird, 571(ScLJ):Autumn83-32
Gifford, H. Tolstoy.*
  T.G.S. Cain, 529(QQ):Autumn83-897
  W.G. Jones, 402(MLR):Oct83-997
Gifford, J., C. McWilliam and D. Walker.
  The Buildings of Scotland: Edinburgh.
  J. Drummond, 362:13Dec84-26
Gifford, T. and N. Roberts. Ted Hughes.*
  J. Press, 189(EA):Jan-Mar84-108
Gigineišvili, B.K. Sravnitel'naja fone-
  tika dagestanskich jazykov.
  G.F. Meier, 682(ZPSK):Band36Heft2-236
Gignoux, P. Catalogue des Sceaux.
  C.J. Brunner, 318(JAOS):Jan-Mar82-206

[continued]

Gilman, S.L., with I. Reichenbach, eds.
Begegnungen mit Nietzsche. [continuing]
  R. Furness, 402(MLR):Apr83-499
  P. Grundlehner, 400(MLN):Apr83-514
  P. Heller, 680(ZDP):Band102Heft2-303
Gilmont, J-F. Bibliographie des éditions
de Jean Crespin, 1550-1572.
  A. Anninger, 517(PBSA):Vol77No3-404
Gilmont, J-F. Jean Crespin.
  R.M. Kingdon, 551(RenQ):Spring83-89
Gilmour, R. The Idea of the Gentleman in
the Victorian Novel.*
  A. Blake, 366:Spring83-134
  L. Lerner, 184(EIC):Jan83-61
  S. Monod, 189(EA):Oct-Dec83-475
  J. Sutherland, 155:Spring83-46
  A. Welsh, 637(VS):Autumn82-83
Gilroy, J.P., ed. Francophone Literatures
of the New World.
  A.D. Barry, 207(FR):Feb84-384
Gilsenan, M. Recognizing Islam.*
  639(VQR):Autumn83-131
Gilson, D. A Bibliography of Jane Austen.
  G.E. Bentley, Jr., 354:Sep83-305
  P. Goubert, 189(EA):Jul-Sep84-333
  S. Ives, 78(BC):Autumn83-358
  J. Kestner, 661(WC):Summer83-148
  D. McKitterick, 78(BC):Winter83-391
  B. Roth, 594:Winter83-387
  A.J. Shelston, 148:Winter83-92
  G. Watson, 184(EIC):Apr83-153
Gilson, E. L'athéisme difficile.*
  A. Reix, 542:Oct-Dec83-460
Gimson, A.C. An Introduction to the Pro-
nunciation of English.* (3rd ed)
  A. Ward, 447(N&Q):Dec82-567
Gimson, A.C. - see Jones, D.
Gingell, S. - see Pratt, E.J.
Ginns, P.M. Snowbird Gravy and Dishpan
Pie.
  J. Brown, 9(AlaR):Jul83-235
  42(AR):Winter83-119
Ginsberg, A. Collected Poems 1947-1980.
  J. Atlas, 61:Dec84-132
  L. Hyde, 441:30Dec84-5
Ginsburg, M. An Introduction to Fashion
Illustration.
  R.L. Shep, 614:Fall84-18
Ginswick, J., ed. Labour and the Poor in
England and Wales 1849-1851. (Vols 1-3)
  I. Prothero, 617(TLS):6Apr84-385
Ginzburg, C. Erkundigungen über Piero.*
  H-O. Boström, 341:Vol52No3-136
Ginzburg, C. Indagini su Piero.*
  E. Borsook, 90:Mar83-163
Ginzburg, C. The Night Battles.
  N.Z. Davis, 617(TLS):24Feb84-179
Ginzburg, E. Within the Whirlwind.
  L. Williams, 396(ModA):Summer/Fall83-
  348
Ginzburg, N. Le voci della sera. (A.
Bullock, ed)
  T. O'Neill, 278(IS):Vol38-124
Gioia, D. - see Kees, W.
Giono, J. Correspondance Jean Giono —
Lucien Jacques (1922-1929). (P. Citron,
ed)
  R. Ricatte, 535(RHL):May/Jun83-484
Giono, J. Oeuvres cinématographiques.
(Vol 1) (J. Mény, ed)
  J.J. Michalczyk, 207(FR):Apr84-744

Giono, J. Oeuvres romanesques complètes
VI. (R. Ricatte and others, eds)
  W.D. Redfern, 617(TLS):25May84-595
"Giono aujourd'hui."*
  J. Decottignies, 535(RHL):Sep/Dec83-
  965
Giordano, M. and J.L. Pallister. Béroalde
de Verville: "Le Moyen de Parvenir."
  F. Lestringant, 535(RHL):Jul/Aug83-623
Giovanelli, P.D., ed. Pirandello poeta.
  F. Rauhut, 547(RF):Band95Heft1/2-240
Giovanelli, R.G. Secrets of the Sun.
  C.A. Ronan, 617(TLS):2Nov84-1247
Giovanni, J. Un Vengeur est passé.
  C. Michael, 207(FR):May84-910
Giraldi Ginzio, G. - see Speroni, S.
Girard, G. Les vrais principes de la
langue française.
  J. Chaurand, 209(FM):Oct83-384
  M.A. Covington, 350:Mar84-185
Girard, S. Funeral Music and Customs in
Venezuela.
  W.J. Gradante, 187:May84-340
Girardet, F. The Cuisine of Fredy Girar-
det.
  M. Burros, 441:2Dec84-16
Girardi, E.N. Studi su Dante.
  M. Trovato, 276:Autumn83-276
Girardot, N.J. Myth and Meaning in Early
Taoism.
  D. Harper, 469:Vol9No1-94
Giraud, Y., ed. La Vie théâtrale dans les
provinces du Midi.*
  G.A. Runnalls, 208(FS):Jan83-110
Giraudoux, J. Théâtre complet. (J. Body,
ed)
  G. May, 207(FR):Feb84-406
Girbal de Blacha, N.M. Historia de la
agricultura argentina a fines del siglo
XIX (1890-1900).
  P.B. Goodwin, Jr., 263(RIB):Vol33No1-
  39
Girdenis, A. Fonologija.
  W.R. Schmalstieg, 215(GL):Vol23No2-161
Girgus, S.B. The New Covenant.
  J. McCulloch, 441:6May84-27
Girling, J.E. Thailand.
  T. Chaloemtiarana, 293(JASt):Nov82-216
Girling, R. The Forest on the Hill.
  42(AR):Winter83-118
Girouard, M. The Return to Camelot.*
  A. Gowans, 43:Band13Heft1-80
  T.W.I.H., 90:Apr83-236
  J. Halperin, 579(SAQ):Spring83-219
  T.B. James, 366:Spring83-102
  R.C. McCoy, 184(EIC):Oct83-348
  A. Welsh, 637(VS):Autumn82-83
Girouard, M. Robert Smythson and the
Elizabethan Country House.*
  M. Bence-Jones, 324:Jul84-551
Girouard, M. Victorian Pubs.
  M. Carroll, 441:29Jul84-20
Giroud, F. Une Femme honorable.
  M-N. Little, 207(FR):Mar84-580
Giroux, E.X. A Death for Adonis.
  N. Callendar, 441:29Apr84-26
Giroux, R. The Book Known as Q.*
  J.P. Hammersmith, 577(SHR):Summer83-
  302
  J. Pequigney, 570(SQ):Winter83-496
  W.B. Piper, 651(WHR):Summer83-157
  C.G. Thayer, 219(GaR):Spring83-214
Giroux, R. - see Bishop, E.

"Glossaire des patois de la Suisse romande."* (Vol 5, fasc 69, 72 and 74; Vol 6, fasc 70, 71 and 73)
P. Rézeau, 553(RLiR):Jul–Dec83–484
Gloton, J-J. Renaissance et Baroque à Aix-en-Provence.
A. Blunt, 90:Sep83–561
B. Tollon, 576:Dec83–400
Glover, D.H. The Mad River and Other Stories.
M.G. Osachoff, 102(CanL):Winter82–165
Glover, J. What Sort of People Should There Be?
S. Clark, 617(TLS):14Sep84–1030
Gloversmith, F., ed. Class, Culture and Social Change.*
M. Wilding, 677(YES):Vol 13–348
Glowczewski, B. and others. La Cité des Cataphiles.
D. Bodanis, 617(TLS):23Nov84–1334
Głowiński, M. Zaświat przedstawiony.
J.T. Baer, 497(PolR):Vol28No1–93
Glucksman, A. La Force du vertige.
M. Ignatieff, 617(TLS):1Jun84–603
Glymour, C.N. Theory and Evidence.*
R. Rynasiewicz, 606:Jul83–107
Gnilka, C. – see Jachmann, G.
Gnoli, G. and J-P. Vernant, eds. La mort, les morts dans les sociétés anciennes.
S.R.F. Price, 303(JoHS):Vol 103–195
Gnüg, H., ed. Literarische Utopie-Entwürfe.
P. Kuon, 72:Band220Heft2–350
de Gobineau, A-J. Oeuvres. (Vol 1)
T. Cordellier, 450(NRF):Nov83–145
de Gobineau, A-J. Oeuvres. (Vol 2) (J. Gaulmier, ed) Adélaïde, Mademoiselle Irnois. (H. Juin, ed) Les Pléiades. Nouvelles Asiatiques.
P. Fawcett, 617(TLS):30Mar84–323
Göbl, R. Antike Numismatik.
A. Burnett, 313:Vol73–218
Gochet, P. Outline of a Nominalist Theory of Propositions.*
P. Butchvarov, 449:Mar83–122
Gockel, H. Mythos und Poesie.
W. Bies, 196:Band24Heft1/2–143
Godakumbura, C.E. Catalogue of Ceylonese Manuscripts.
E. Bender, 318(JAOS):Oct–Dec82–681
J.W. de Jong, 259(IIJ):Mar83–152
Godard de Donville, L., ed. La Mythologie au XVIIe siècle.
J-P. Dens, 356(LR):Feb–May83–139
D.A. Watts, 475:Vol 10No18–344
Godbold, E.S., Jr. and R.H. Woody. Christopher Gadsden and the American Revolution.
C. Vipperman, 656(WMQ):Oct83–638
Godbolt, J. A History of Jazz in Britain 1919-50.
B. Case, 617(TLS):30Nov84–1389
Godbout, J. Les Têtes à Papineau.
E-M. Kroller, 102(CanL):Spring83–111
Goddard, J.A. – see under Adame Goddard, J.
Goddard, L. and B. Judge. The Metaphysics of Wittgenstein's "Tractatus."
H.L. Finch, 518:Jul83–158
Godden, R. Thursday's Children.
A. Marshall, 441:24Jun84–12
442(NY):27Aug84–92

Godefroy, V. The Dramatic Genius of Verdi. (Vol 2)
D. Rosen, 415:Jun83–353
Gödel, K. Obras completas. (J. Mosterín, ed)
R. Chuaqui, 316:Dec83–1199
Godey, J. Fatal Beauty.
M. Mewshaw, 441:9Dec84–27
Godin, G.D. – see under Guillaume de Pierre Godin
Godley, M.R. The Mandarin-Capitalists from Nanyang.
W.K.K. Chan, 293(JASt):Aug83–920
Godman, P. – see "Alcuin: The Bishops, Kings, and Saints of York"
Godovikova, L.A. – see Possevino, A.
"Gods, Saints and Heroes."
I. Gaskell, 59:Jun83–236
Godwin, G. Mr. Bedford and the Muses.*
J. Motion, 617(TLS):17Feb84–159
Goebl, H. Dialektometrie, Prinzipien und Methoden des Einsatzes der numerischen Taxonomie im Bereich der Dialektgeographie.
S.M. Embleton, 350:Sep84–654
G.F. Meier, 682(ZPSK):Band36Heft5–604
Goeppert, S. and H.C. Psychoanalyse interdisziplinär.
U. Mahlendorf, 221(GQ):May83–468
von Goethe, J.W. Goethe: Poems and Epigrams. (M. Hamburger, trans)
D. Davis, 362:6Dec84–33
T. Eagleton, 617(TLS):27Apr84–454
von Goethe, J.W. Wilhelm Meisters Lehrjahre. (E. Bahr, ed) Wilhelm Meisters Wanderjahre oder Die Entsagenden. Wilhelm Meisters Wanderjahre oder Die Entsagenden. (E. Bahr, ed)
H.R. Vaget, 221(GQ):May83–502
"Goethe-Jahrbuch." (Vol 98) (K-H. Hahn, ed)
E. Middell, 654(WB):10/1983–1832
Goetschel, R. Meir Ibn Gabbay.
L.P. Harvey, 86(BHS):Apr83–140
Goetz-Stankiewicz, M. The Silenced Theater.
F. Gaede, 564:Feb83–70
R. Lindheim, 107(CRCL):Mar83–129
Goetzmann, W.H. and W.J. Orr. Karl Bodmer's America.
P-L. Adams, 61:Dec84–146
J. Russell, 441:2Dec84–11
Goetzmann, W.H. and J.C. Porter. The West as Romantic Horizon.*
G. Barth, 649(WAL):May83–92
Goetzmann, W.H. and B.D. Reese. Texas Images and Visions.
L. Milazzo, 584(SWR):Spring83–vi
Goff, B.L. Symbols of Ancient Egypt in the Late Period.
B.S. Lesko, 318(JAOS):Apr–Jun82–393
Goffman, E. Forms of Talk.*
M. Stubbs, 355(LSoc):Mar83–77
Gogisgi/C. Arnett. Rounds.
C.S.S. Chandra, 436(NewL):Summer84–114
Gogol, N. Arabesques. (A. Tulloch, trans)
G.J. Gutsche, 574(SEEJ):Spring83–99
Gohl, G. Die Koreanische Minderheit in Japan als Fall einer "politisch-ethnischen" Minderheitengruppe.
C. Sorensen, 293(JASt):Aug83–981

Gokhale, N. Paro.
A. Davis, 617(TLS):16Mar84-287
J. Mellors, 364:Feb84-99
Golan, M. Shimon Peres.
G. Nahshon, 390:Oct83-61
Gold, H. Mister White Eyes.
P. Hamill, 441:11Nov84-15
Gold, J.R. and J. Burgess, eds. Valued
Environments.
A. Whittick, 89(BJA):Summer83-270
Gold, M.E. A Dialogue on Comparable Worth.
G.A. De Candido, 441:22Jan84-23
Goldbarth, A. Original Light.*
R. Cording, 110:Winter84-91
Goldberg, A. Ilya Ehrenburg. (E. de
Mauny, ed)
A. Austin, 441:30Dec84-21
Goldberg, J. Endlesse Worke.*
T. Comito, 551(RenQ):Spring83-129
Goldberg, J. James I and the Politics of
Literature.
J. Briggs, 617(TLS):27Apr84-472
Goldberg, M. Namesake.
J. Riemer, 390:Feb83-62
Goldberg, R. Sex and Enlightenment.
T. Eagleton, 617(TLS):12Oct84-1170
Goldberg, S.S. Special Education Law.
D.E.S., 185:Jan84-382
Goldberger, P. The City Observed: New
York.
90:Sep83-566
Goldemberg, I. The Fragmented Life of Don
Jacobo Lerner.* (Spanish title: La vida
a plazos de don Jacobo Lerner.)
R.S. Minc, 238:Sep83-445
Goldemberg, I. Hombre de Paso/Just Pass-
ing Through.*
B. Miller, 238:Dec83-646
Goldfield, D.R. Urban Growth in the Age
of Sectionalism.
J.N. Ingham, 106:Summer83-175
Golding, W. A Moving Target.
S. Monod, 189(EA):Oct-Dec84-479
Golding, W. The Paper Men.
R.M. Adams, 441:1Apr84-3
J. Lasdun, 176:May84-65
D. May, 362:9Feb84-23
J. Mellors, 364:Mar84-105
B. Morrison, 617(TLS):2Mar84-215
J. Raban, 61:Apr84-142
442(NY):21May84-132
Golding, W. Rites of Passage.* (French
title: Rites de passage.)
C. Jordis, 450(NRF):Dec83-115
Goldman, A.H. Elvis.*
B. Allan, 529(QQ):Summer83-516
C. Hamm, 317:Summer83-335
Goldman, M. The Demon in the Aether.
J. Calado, 617(TLS):20Apr84-442
Goldman, N. and L. Szymanski. English
Grammar for Students of Latin.
R.A. La Fleur, 121(CJ):Apr/May84-374
J.C. Traupman, 124:Sep-Oct83-49
Goldman, R.M. Search for Consensus.
H.M. Waller, 106:Spring83-79
Goldman, W. Adventures in the Screen
Trade.*
J.V. Card, 500:Spring/Summer84-63
Goldman, W. The Color of Light.
D. Quammen, 441:15Jan84-18
Goldmann, B. Wolf Heinrich Graf Baudissin.
R. Paulin, 402(MLR):Oct83-978

Goldsberry, S. Maui the Demigod.
J. Berry, 441:29Jul84-20
Goldschläger, A. Simone Weil et Spinoza.*
D. Savan, 627(UTQ):Summer83-565
Goldsmith, J. - see Hinks, R.
Goldsmith, M.E. The Figure of Piers Plow-
man.
C. Clark, 179(ES):Jun83-274
Goldsmith, U.K., with T. Schneider and S.S.
Coleman, eds. Rainer Maria Rilke: A
Verse Concordance to His Complete Lyr-
ical Poetry.*
O. Olzien, 224(GRM):Band33Heft3-351
Goldstein, D.I. Dostoevsky and the Jews.*
G.S. Morson, 574(SEEJ):Fall83-302
Goldstein, K.S. and N.V. Rosenberg, with
others, eds. Folklore Studies in Honour
of Herbert Halpert.
I.S. Posen, 292(JAF):Jan-Mar83-72
Goldstein, S.M. Pre-Roman and Early Roman
Glass in the Corning Museum of Glass.
G. Wills, 39:May83-414
"The Goldstein Gallery Collection:
Curators' Choice." "The Goldstein
Gallery Collection: Collecting Navajo
Weaving."
R.L. Shep, 614:Fall84-17
Goldstrom, J.M. and L.A. Clarkson, eds.
Irish Population, Economy and Society.
R.F. Foster, 637(VS):Summer83-466
Goldthwaite, R.A. The Building of Renais-
sance Florence.*
C. Burroughs, 59:Sep83-359
S. Connell, 90:Sep83-558
B.G. Kohl, 539:Feb84-57
R. Starn, 54:Jun83-329
Goldziher, I. Introduction to Islamic
Theology and Law.
S.A. Akbarabadi, 273(IC):Apr83-163
F. Rosenthal, 589:Jan83-262
Golenbock, P. Bums.
S. Padwe, 441:30Dec84-18
Golitsyn, A. New Lies for Old.
I. Elliot, 617(TLS):26Oct84-1207
Göller, K.H., ed. The Alliterative
"Morte Arthure."*
C. Clark, 179(ES):Jun83-275
P. Gradon, 447(N&Q):Aug82-356
V. Krishna, 589:Jan83-177
D. Mehl, 38:Band101Heft3/4-508
Gollin, A. No Longer an Island.
D. French, 617(TLS):16Nov84-1303
J. Grigg, 362:25Oct84-23
Golyakhovsky, V. Russian Doctor.
L. Graham, 441:26Feb84-10
Gom, L. Land of the Peace.*
S.D. Harasym, 137:Nov82-22
Gombrich, E. Nature and Art as Needs of
the Mind.
J. Sweetman, 89(BJA):Summer83-263
Gombrich, E.H. The Image and the Eye.
C. Altieri, 385(MQR):Fall84-587
D. Blinder, 290(JAAC):Fall83-85
N. Bryson, 90:Jun83-373
J.B. Smith, 39:Oct83-354
Gombrich, E.H. Tributes.
S.S. Prawer, 617(TLS):15Jun84-651
Gomes, P.E.S. P.'s Three Women.
R. Hoffman, 441:29Apr84-32
Gomez, L. and H.W. Woodward, Jr., eds.
Barabaḍur.*
F.E. Reynolds, 293(JASt):Nov82-218

Gomez Arcos, A. Un Oiseau brûlé vif.
R. Buss, 617(TLS):30Nov84-1392
Gómez de Castro, Á. Sonetti.* (I. Pepe
Sarno, ed)
N. Griffin, 402(MLR):Apr83-470
Gómez de la Serna, R. Dali.
D. Ades, 617(TLS):27Jul84-834
Gómez-Martínez, J.L. Teoría del ensayo.
S. Horl, 547(RF):Band95Heft3-397
Gómez Ojea, C. Cantiga de agüero.
R. Johnson, 238:Sep83-437
Gomme, A.H., ed. D.H. Lawrence.*
J. Newman, 161(DUJ):Dec82-83
de Goncourt, E. Les Frères Zemganno. (M.
Petrone, ed)
R. Ricatte, 535(RHL):Mar/Apr83-299
de Goncourt, E. and J. Lettres de jeun-
esse inédites. (A. Nicolas, ed) Madame
Gervaisais. (M. Fumaroli, ed)
R. Ricatte, 535(RHL):Mar/Apr83-299
Gonda, J. Medieval Religious Literature
in Sanskrit.
L. Rocher, 318(JAOS):Apr-Jun82-416
Gondebeaud, L. Le Roman "picaresque"
anglais (1650-1730).
J. Harris, 402(MLR):Jul83-650
Gondosch, D., M. Helmle and G. Paul. Lehr-
buch Philosophie.
A.K.D. Lorenzen, 489(PJGG):Band90Heft2-
431
Gong, G.W. The Standard of "Civilization"
in International Society.
D. Pannick, 617(TLS):7Sep84-992
Gonzáles, A.M.C. - see under Cano Gonzáles,
A.M.
González, A. "Harsh World" and Other
Poems.
A. Josephs, 577(SHR):Winter83-94
Gonzalez, A.B. Language and Nationalism.
J-P. Dumont, 293(JASt):Aug83-1014
González, J.M.C. and S. Cerra Suárez - see
under Caso González, J.M. and S. Cerra
Suárez
González, J.R.F. - see under Fernández
González, J.R.
González-Cruz, L.F. Neruda.
F.L. Yudin, 552(REH):Oct83-445
González-del-Valle, L. and R. Esquenazi-
Mayo - see Florit, E.
González-Montes, Y. Pasión y forma en
"Cal y canto" de Rafael Alberti.
V.R. Foster, 238:Dec83-639
Gonzalez Vasquez, J. La imagen en la
poesia de Virgilio.
J. Perret, 555:Vol57fasc1-164
Gooch, B.N.S. and D.S. Thatcher. Musical
Settings of British Romantic Literature.
S. Banfield, 415:Feb83-106
Gooch, J. The Prospect of War.
L.J. Satre, 637(VS):Autumn82-85
Gooch, S. Creatures from Inner Space.
B. Inglis, 617(TLS):10Aug84-885
Good, M. Every Inch A Lear.
R. Berry, 150(DR):Autumn83-526
Goodacre, S.H. - see Carroll, L.
Goode, J. George Gissing.
P. Coustillas, 189(EA):Oct-Dec83-483
Goodin, R.E. Manipulatory Politics.*
F.M. Barnard, 488:Dec83-515
Goodlad, J.I. A Place Called School.
A. Hacker, 453(NYRB):12Apr84-35
Goodman, I. Heart Failure.
C. Sternhell, 441:8Jan84-18

Goodman, J. Huddling Up.
H. Cantelon, 529(QQ):Summer83-574
Goodman, J. The Stabbing of George Harry
Storrs.
J. Symons, 617(TLS):16Mar84-270
Goodman, J. Who He?
R. Davies, 617(TLS):21Dec84-1481
Goodman, L.E. Monotheism.
N. Gillman, 543:Jun83-930
Goodrich, L. Thomas Eakins.*
E. Johns, 54:Dec83-702
C. Juler, 592:Aug83-48
J.V. Turano, 16:Summer83-91
Goodway, D. London Chartism, 1838-1848.*
J.F.C. Harrison, 637(VS):Winter83-223
Goodwin, C. Conversational Organization.
S. Duncan, Jr., 355(LSoc):Mar83-89
Goodwin, J. - see Hall, P.
Goodwin-Gill, G.S. The Refugee in Inter-
national Law.
R. Errera, 617(TLS):11May84-514
Goold, G.P. - see "Catullus"
Gooneratne, Y. Silence, Exile and Cunning.
F. Blackwell, 49:Oct83-91
Goorney, H. The Theatre Workshop Story.*
C. Tighe, 157:Spring83-52
Goossens, J. and T. Sodmann, eds. Rey-
naert Reynard Reynke.*
P.M. Mitchell, 301(JEGP):Jan83-105
Goossens, J. and T. Sodmann, eds. Third
International Beast Epic, Fable and
Fabliau Colloquium.
E.A. Metzger, 221(GQ):Nov83-630
Gopal, S. Jawaharlal Nehru. (Vol 2)
R.J. Young, 318(JAOS):Oct-Dec82-676
Gopal, S. Jawaharlal Nehru. (Vol 3)
J. Grigg, 362:13Dec84-28
C. Philips, 617(TLS):9Nov84-1276
Gopal, S. - see "Jawaharlal Nehru: An
Anthology"
Göpfert, H.G., ed. Das Bild Lessings in
der Geschichte.
B. Kieffer, 221(GQ):Mar83-315
H.B. Nisbet, 402(MLR):Oct83-972
Gordanier, D.A. Rideau Heritage.
M.S. Angus, 529(QQ):Autumn83-867
Gordimer, N. The Lying Days. Occasion
For Loving.
P. Craig, 617(TLS):9Mar84-259
Gordimer, N. Something Out There.
D.J. Enright, 617(TLS):30Mar84-328
E. Hardwick, 453(NYRB):16Aug84-3
M. Jones, 362:29Mar84-29
S. Rushdie, 441:29Jul84-7
Gordon, A. Death Is For The Living.
A. Calder, 617(TLS):28Dec84-1499
Gordon, C. Beyond the Looking Glass.
442(NY):7May84-160
Gordon, K.E. The Well-Tempered Sentence.
639(VQR):Autumn83-117
Gordon, L. Donald Barthelme.
S.I. Bellman, 573(SSF):Winter83-59
Gordon, L. Cossack Rebellions.
P. Avrich, 104(CASS):Winter83-559
Gordon, L. Robert Coover.*
B. Duyfhuizen, 395(MFS):Winter83-741
Gordon, L. Eliot's Early Years.
R. Hindmarsh, 72:Band220Heft1-173
Gordon, L. Virginia Woolf.
H. Lee, 617(TLS):21Dec84-1480
Gordon, M.M. - see Reid, B.J.
Gordon, R. and A. Forge. Monet.*
R.L. Herbert, 453(NYRB):11Oct84-43

Gordon, R.L., ed. Myth, Religion and Society.
M. Heath, 123:Vol33No1-68
P. Walcot, 303(JoHS):Vol 103-193
Gordon, R.L. and D.M. Stillman. Nuevos Rumbos.
M.A. Marks, 399(MLJ):Spring83-98
Gordon, S. Hitler, Germans, and the "Jewish Question."
I. Deak, 453(NYRB):31May84-37
G. Steiner, 617(TLS):13Jul84-793
Gordon, S. Welfare, Justice, and Freedom.
D. Gauthier, 449:Sep83-494
Gordon, W.T. A History of Semantics.
J-C. Choul, 350:Dec84-995
Goreau, A. Reconstructing Aphra.
P. Danchin, 179(ES):Aug83-375
D.W. Pearson, 568(SCN):Spring/Summer83-13
Göres, J. Goethes Leben in Bilddokumenten.
B. Bennett, 221(GQ):May83-501
Gorey, E. Dancing Cats and Neglected Murderesses. The Gilded Bat.
T. Tobias, 151:Feb81-107
Gorgias. Encomium of Helen. (D.M. MacDowell, ed and trans)
G.O. Rowe, 124:Nov-Dec83-135
Gorilovics, T., ed. Studia Romanica.
É. Martonyi, 535(RHL):Sep/Dec83-943
Görlach, M., ed. An East Midland Revision of the South English Legendary.
K. Reichl, 38:Band101Heft1/2-231
Görlach, M. - see von Nolcken, C.
Görler, W. - see Cicero
Gorman, J.L. The Expression of Historical Knowledge.
H. Palmer, 518:Apr83-111
Gorman, S.M., ed. Post-Revolutionary Peru.
C.A. Astiz, 263(RIB):Vol33No3-403
Gormely, S. Commitments.
E.M. Waring, 529(QQ):Spring83-263
Gornick, V. Women in Science.*
R.C. Lewontin, 453(NYRB):12Apr84-21
de Gorog, R. Dictionnaire inverse de l'ancien français.
D.A. Fein, 207(FR):Feb84-386
N.B. Smith, 589:Jul83-753
Görög, V. Littérature Orale d'Afrique Noire.
E. Dammann, 196:Band24Heft3/4-298
L. Todd, 203:Vol194No1-133
Gorovitz, S. Doctors' Dilemmas.
B.B., 185:Oct83-180
Gorra, M. - see Nievo, I.
Görtz, H-J. Franz von Baaders "Anthropologischer Standpunkt."
K. Kienzler, 489(PJGG):Band90Heft2-427
Gorzka, G. A. Bogdanov und der russische Proletkult.
L. Mally, 550(RusR):Apr83-233
Gose, E.B., Jr. The Transformation Process in Joyce's "Ulysses."*
A. Goldman, 541(RES):Feb83-99
R. Mason, 447(N&Q):Jun82-266
Gosling, J.C.B. and C.C.W. Taylor. The Greeks on Pleasure.*
W.J. Cummins, 319:Jul84-366
A.W. Price, 518:Oct83-217
M.G. Sollenberger, 124:May-Jun84-324
Gosner, P. Caribbean Georgian.
H. Fraser, 37:Sep-Oct83-60

Gosori, K., L.A. Noronha and W. Schicho. Kiswahili cha Kisasa. (Vol 1, Pts 1 and 2)
I. Herms and S. Hepach, 682(ZPSK):Band36Heft1-97
Gosselink, R.N. - see Defoe, D.
Gossen, C.T. - see von Wartburg, W.
Gossip, C.J. An Introduction to French Classical Tragedy.*
M-O. Sweetser, 210(FrF):Jan83-91
B. Woshinsky, 546(RR):May83-376
Gossip, C.J. - see de Cyrano de Bergerac, S.
Gossman, L. The Empire Unpossess'd.*
S. Baker, 301(JEGP):Jan83-129
M. Baridon, 83:Spring83-118
J. Smitten, 125:Winter83-195
W.A. Speck, 366:Spring83-115
Gössmann, E. - see Kilwardby, R.
Gostelow, M. Embroidery.
A.L. Mayer, 614:Fall84-16
Goswāmī, S. Śrīla Prabhupāda-Līlāmṛta. (Vols 1-3)
S. Goswami, 293(JASt):Aug83-986
Coth, M. Rilke und Valéry.
E. Schwarz, 133:Band16Heft1-79
K. Wais, 52:Band18Heft2-216
Gothot-Mersch, C. - see Gautier, T.
Götte, C. Das Menschen- und Herrscherbild des Rex Maior im "Ruodlieb."*
D.H. Green, 402(MLR):Jan83-219
Gottfried, M. Jed Harris.
J. Houseman, 441:5Feb84-13
Gottfried, R.K. The Art of Joyce's Syntax in "Ulysses."*
S. Benstock, 149(CLS):Fall83-355
J. Simmons, 599:Winter83-89
Gottfried, R.S. The Black Death.*
J. Hatcher, 617(TLS):13Jan84-36
Gottfried, R.S. Bury St. Edmunds and the Urban Crisis: 1290-1539.
P. Clark, 551(RenQ):Autumn83-425
C. Platt, 589:Oct83-1039
Gottfried von Strassburg. Tristan.* (R. Krohn, ed and trans)
P.W. Tax, 301(JEGP):Jan83-98
Gottlieb, D. Ontological Economy.*
S. Martens, 482(PhR):Oct83-636
Gottlieb, E. Lost Angels of a Ruined Paradise.*
C. Woodring, 130:Spring83-85
Gottlieb, V. Chekhov and the Vaudeville.
D.G. Eisen, 615(TJ):Oct83-426
D. Rayfield, 402(MLR):Oct83-999
L. Senelick, 574(SEEJ):Summer83-262
639(VQR):Spring83-44
Gottschalk, H.B. Heraclides of Pontus.*
J. Scarborough, 121(CJ):Dec83/Jan84-167
Gottsched, J.C. Ausgewählte Werke. (Vol 7, Pt 4) (P.M. Mitchell and R. Scholl, eds)
H. Eichner, 301(JEGP):Jul83-417
Götze, L. Valenzstrukturen deutscher Verben und Adjektive.
H. Eckert, 257(IRAL):Nov83-340
Gotzkowsky, B. - see Kirchhof, H.W.
Goudet, J. La politique de Dante.
M. Marti, 228(GSLI):Vol 160fasc509-130
Goudriaan, T. and S. Gupta. Hindu Tantric and Śākta Literature.
J.W. de Jong, 259(IIJ):Apr83-212

Gouhier, H. Etudes sur l'histoire des idées en France depuis le XVIIe siècle.
  G. Brykman, 542:Jan-Mar83-113
  J-L. Marion, 192(EP):Apr-Jun83-235
Gould, C. Bernini in France.*
  D.R. Coffin, 551(RenQ):Spring83-117
  J. Whiteley, 208(FS):Oct83-457
  B. Wind, 568(SCN):Winter83-80
Gould, E. Mythical Intentions in Modern Literature.*
  A. Haberer, 189(EA):Apr-Sep83-321
Gould, G. The Glenn Gould Reader. (T. Page, ed)
  E. Strickland, 441:30Dec84-13
Gould, J. No Other Place.
  H. Mitgang, 441:22Jul84-20
Gould, P. Les Cadiens d'Asteur/Today's Cajuns.
  N.R. Spitzer, 292(JAF):Jan-Mar83-109
Gould, S.J. Hen's Teeth and Horse's Toes.*
  M. Ridley, 617(TLS):10Feb84-132
Gould, S.J. The Mismeasure of Man.
  A. Janik, 185:Oct83-153
Goulden, J.C., with A.W. Raffio. The Death Merchant.
  B. Shulgasser, 441:9Sep84-31
Goulding, J. The Last Outpost.
  P. Phillips, 99:Apr83-32
Goulet, A. Giovanni Papini juge d'André Gide.
  J.C. McLaren, 207(FR):May84-884
Goulet, A. Le Parcours moebien de l'écriture: "Le Voyeur."
  J-C. Vareille, 535(RHL):Sep/Dec83-971
Goulet, D. Survival with Integrity.
  J.R. Williams, 293(JASt):May83-699
Gourevitch, A.J. Les Catégories de la culture médiévale.
  J-P. Guinle, 450(NRF):Oct83-139
Gourlay, L., ed. The Beaverbrook I Knew.
  R. Klein, 617(TLS):7Dec84-1406
  D. Trelford, 362:27Sep84-27
Gourse, L. Louis' Children.
  S. Holden, 441:8Apr84-21
Gourvish, T.R. Railways and the British Economy 1830-1914.
  H.W. Parris, 637(VS):Autumn82-96
Govinda, A. The Inner Structure of the "I Ching."
  K. Smith, 293(JASt):Feb83-387
  G. Tropea, 485(PE&W):Jul83-314
Gowans, A. Learning to See.
  J.F. O'Leary, 290(JAAC):Spring84-353
Gower, D. and D. Hodgson. Heroes and Contemporaries.
  A.L. Le Quesne, 617(TLS):4May84-493
Gower, J. Confessio Amantis. (R.A. Peck, ed)
  R.F. Yeager, 402(MLR):Jul83-671
Gowing, L. Lucian Freud.*
  R. Bass, 55:Apr83-21
Gowlett, J. Ascent to Civilization.
  D.J.R. Bruckner, 441:13May84-22
Goyard-Fabre, S. - see Hobbes, T.
Goyard-Fabre, S. - see Abbé de Saint-Pierre
Gozzano, G. The Man I Pretend to Be.
  J. Saunders, 565:Vol24No1-73
Grab, W., ed. Deutsche Aufklärung und Judenemanzipation, Internationales Symposium.
  P.F. Veit, 221(GQ):May83-498

Grabo, N.S. The Coincidental Art of Charles Brockenden Brown.*
  P. McCormack, 594:Summer83-158
  B. Rosenthal, 587(SAF):Spring83-123
Grabowicz, G.G. The Poet as Mythmaker.*
  J.A. Barnstead, 550(RusR):Apr83-230
  V. Bennett, 574(SEEJ):Fall83-396
  J. Fizer, 494:Vol4No4-795
  L. Rudnytzky, 497(PolR):Vol28No3-95
  V. Swoboda, 402(MLR):Oct83-1005
Grace, G.W. An Essay on Language.*
  W.H. Goodenough, 355(LSoc):Jun83-250
Grace, J.P. Burning Money.
  R.J. Margolis, 441:21Oct84-50
Grace, M.D., ed. A Festschrift for Albert Seay.
  D. Leech-Wilkinson, 410(M&L):Jan/Apr83-105
Grace, S.E. The Voyage That Never Ends.
  M.C. Bradbrook, 150(DR):Summer83-358
  C.P. Jones, 627(UTQ):Summer83-488
  295(JML):Nov83-529
Grace, S.E. and L. Weir, eds. Margaret Atwood.
  A.E. Davidson, 395(MFS):Winter83-734
  L. Surette, 105:Fall/Winter83-95
  B. Wineapple, 150(DR):Summer83-360
Gracia, J.J.E. - see Eiximenis, F.
Gracián, B. Art et Figures de l'esprit.
  T. Cordellier, 450(NRF):Dec83-107
Gracq, J. En lisant, en écrivant.*
  G. Cesbron, 535(RHL):Mar/Apr83-309
Grad, B.L. and T.A. Riggs. Visions of City and Country.
  J.P. Gilroy, 207(FR):Mar84-578
Grade, C. Rabbis and Wives.
  J. Epstein, 249(HudR):Spring83-179
Gradidge, R. Edwin Lutyens.
  P.F. Norton, 576:Dec83-390
Gradman, B. Metamorphosis in Keats.*
  W.Z. Hirst, 134(CP):Spring83-100
Grady, J. Runner in the Street.
  M. Berkley, 441:21Oct84-30
Graff, G. Literature Against Itself.*
  J.W. Davidson, 477(PLL):Winter83-93
  P. Hobsbaum, 402(MLR):Apr83-385
Graff, H.J., ed. Literacy and Social Development in the West.
  J.M.B., 179(ES):Apr83-182
Gragg, G.B., with others, eds. Oromo Dictionary.
  A. Manaster-Ramer, 350:Jun84-464
Graham, A.C. "Chuang-tzu": Textual Notes to a Partial Translation.
  R.T. Ames, 293(JASt):May83-615
Graham, A.C. Later Mohist Logic, Ethics and Science.
  D. Bodde, 318(JAOS):Jan-Mar82-143
Graham, A.C. - see "Chuang-tzu"
Graham, D., ed. Critical Essays on Frank Norris.
  S.C. Brennan, 594:Winter83-389
Graham, D. The Truth of War.
  D. Hibberd, 617(TLS):17Aug84-925
Graham, D.O. The Non-Nuclear Defense of Cities.
  T. Garden, 176:Apr84-58
Graham, D.O. and G.A. Fossedal. A Defense that Defends.
  M.A. Uhlig, 441:11Mar84-19
Graham, F., Jr. The Dragon Hunters.
  B. Heinrich, 441:14Oct84-18
  442(NY):26Nov84-151

Graham, J. Erosion.*
  P. Stitt, 219(GaR):Winter83-894
  639(VQR):Autumn83-133
Graham, L. and R. Stites - see Bogdanov, A.
Graham, R. A Broken String of Beads.
  G.H. Boggs, 70:Mar-Apr81-129
Graham, R. Spain.
  D. Smyth, 617(TLS):21Sep84-1049
Graham, R.B.C. - see under Cunninghame
  Graham, R.B.
Graham, V.E. and W.M. Johnson. The Royal
  Tour of France by Charles IX and Cather-
  ine de' Medici.
  M.M. McGowan, 208(FS):Apr83-207
Graham, W.T., Jr. "The Lament for the
  South."*
  D. Holzman, 116:Jul82-255
Grainger, M. - see Clare, J.
Grala, M. and W. Przywarska. W Polsce po
  polsku (In Poland in Polish).
  A. Gorski, 497(PolR):Vol28No1-98
Grammaticus, S. - see under Saxo Grammati-
  cus
Gran, G. Development by People.
  T.C. Holyoke, 42(AR):Fall83-502
Granados, T.M. - see under Melendo Gra-
  nados, T.
Granatstein, J.L. The Ottawa Men.*
  G.W., 102(CanL):Summer83-171
Grandi, D. 25 Iuglio: Quarant'anni dopo.
  (R. De Felice, ed)
  C. Seton-Watson, 617(TLS):30Mar84-348
Grandi, M. and A. Pracchi. Milano.
  R.A. Etlin, 127:Summer83-200
Granger, B. The British Cross.
  D. Myers, 441:15Jan84-18
Granger, B. The Zurich Numbers.
  M. Levin, 441:25Nov84-26
Granger, G-G. Formal Thought and the Sci-
  ences of Man.
  M. Tiles, 617(TLS):20Jan84-68
Granier, J. Nietzsche.
  D. Letocha, 154:Dec83-749
Granier, J. Penser la praxis.
  G. Argence, 542:Apr-Jun83-262
Granoff, W. and J-M. Rey. L'Occulte,
  objet de la pensée freudienne.
  A. Calame, 450(NRF):Sep83-151
Grant, C. The Rock Art of the North Ameri-
  can Indians.
  A. Sieveking, 617(TLS):27Jul84-852
Grant, J. Bernard M. Baruch.
  L. Robinson, 441:1Jan84-21
Grant, K.S. Dr. Burney as Critic and His-
  torian of Music.
  C. Hogwood, 617(TLS):24Aug84-936
Grant, M. From Alexander to Cleopatra.*
  E.N. Borza, 124:Mar-Apr84-261
Grant, M. The History of Ancient Israel.
  P. Alexander, 617(TLS):11May84-530
  K. Bouton, 441:12Aug84-21
Grant, M.K. The Tragic Vision of Joyce
  Carol Oates.
  G.F. Manning, 106:Summer83-225
Grant, P. Literature of Mysticism in West-
  ern Tradition.
  C. Thompson, 617(TLS):13Jan84-42
Grant, S.A. and J.A. Brown. The Russian
  Empire and Soviet Union.
  M.T. Choldin, 550(RusR):Apr83-223
Grant, U.S. Personal Memoirs of U.S.
  Grant. (E.B. Long, ed)
  J.G. Dawson 3d, 9(AlaR):Jul83-231

Grass, G. Aufsätze zur Literatur.
  J. Amsler, 549(RLC):Apr-Jun83-256
Grass, G. Les Enfants par la tête ou les
  Allemands se meurent.
  L. Kovacs, 450(NRF):Jul/Aug83-245
Grass, G. Headbirths, or The Germans are
  Dying Out.*
  M. Hollington, 381:Jun83-175
"Günter Grass: Drawings and Words, 1954-
  1977." (A. Dreher, ed)
  442(NY):6Feb84-128
Grass, R. and W.R. Risley, eds. Waiting
  for Pegasus.*
  C.L. King, 552(REH):Oct83-469
Grasselli, M.M. and P. Rosenberg, with N.
  Parmantier. Watteau: 1684-1721.
  F. Haskell, 453(NYRB):20Dec84-25
Grassin, J-M., ed. Mythe et littérature
  africaine.
  J. Mounier, 549(RLC):Apr-Jun83-249
Grassl, W. - see Waismann, F.
Grasso, S. - see Montale, E.
Grathoff, R. - see Schutz, A. and T.
  Parsons
Grauer, N.A. Wits and Sages.
  E.S. Turner, 617(TLS):17Aug84-908
Graumann, G. "La Guerre de Troie" aura
  lieu.*
  E.E. Tory, 208(FS):Jul83-360
Grave, S.A. Locke and Burnet.
  J.W. Yolton, 518:Jul83-144
Gravel, P. Pour une logique du sujet trag-
  ique: Sophocle.
  G. Leroux, 154:Jun83-347
"Michael Graves: Buildings and Projects,
  1966-1981."
  M. Kimmelman, 55:Summer83-27
Graves, O.F. - see Pape, A.
Graves, R. Between Moon and Moon:
  Selected Letters of Robert Graves, 1946-
  1972. (P. O'Oprey, ed)
  V. Glendinning, 362:29Nov84-24
Graves, R. In Broken Images: Selected Let-
  ters of Robert Graves 1914-1946.* (P.
  O'Prey, ed)
  A. Haberer, 189(EA):Jul-Sep84-348
  J. Wiesenfarth, 659(ConL):Spring84-93
Graves, R.P. The Brothers Powys.*
  R.L. Blackmore, 395(MFS):Winter83-777
  42(AR):Fall83-507
Gray, A. 1982 Janine.
  P-L. Adams, 61:Nov84-148
  J. Baumbach, 441:28Oct84-9
  P. Kemp, 617(TLS):13Apr84-397
  442(NY):10Dec84-190
Gray, A. Unlikely Stories, Mostly.*
  P-L. Adams, 61:Nov84-148
  J. Baumbach, 441:28Oct84-9
Gray, C.S. Strategic Studies.
  J.M., 185:Oct83-185
Gray, D. Robert Henryson.*
  F. Alexander, 571(ScLJ):Winter83-47
  R.L. Kindrick, 588(SSL):Vol 18-269
Gray, D. and E.G. Stanley, eds. Middle
  English Studies.
  P. Neuss, 617(TLS):6Jul84-759
Gray, J. Hayek on Liberty.
  J. Dunn, 617(TLS):26Oct84-1205
  A. Kenny, 362:25Oct84-26
Gray, J. Mill on Liberty: A Defence.*
  H.J. McCloskey, 483:Oct83-550

Gray, J., with E. Peterson. Billy Bishop
Goes to War.
W. Butt, 102(CanL):Autumn83-90
Gray, J.C., ed. Mirror up to Shakespeare.
S. Wells, 617(TLS):30Nov84-1390
Gray, J.M. Thro' the Vision of the Night.*
H. Kozicki, 637(VS):Autumn82-109
S. Shatto, 447(N&Q):Jun82-249
Gray, J.M. - see Tennyson, A.
Gray, N. Life Sentence.
P. Binding, 362:2Aug84-27
Gray, P. T.S. Eliot's Intellectual and
Poetic Development, 1909 to 1922.
J.S. Brooker, 598(SoR):Spring84-483
J. King-Farlow, 478:Oct83-260
Gray, R., ed. American Fiction.
B. Greenfield, 150(DR):Autumn83-547
Gray, R. and G. Lehmann, eds. The Younger
Australian Poets.
J. Tranter, 381:Jun83-244
Grayling, A.C. An Introduction to Philo-
sophical Logic.
I.G. McFetridge, 518:Jul83-164
Grayson, C., ed. The World of Dante.*
J.J. Guzzardo, 589:Jan83-180
Grayson, R. Crime Without Passion.
N. Callendar, 441:26Feb84-27
Graziano, F., ed. Georg Trakl.
M. Hofmann, 617(TLS):27Apr84-449
Graziano, F. - see Trakl, G.
"Great Sweaters to Knit."
C.J. Mouton, 614:Summer84-16
"A Great Trial in Chinese History."
J.D. Seymour, 293(JASt):Feb83-397
Greaves, R.L. Society and Religion in
Elizabethan England.
K. Sharpe, 250(HLQ):Spring83-181
Greaves, R.L. - see Bunyan, J.
"Greek Lyric." (Vol 1) (D.A. Campbell,
trans)
D. Arnould, 555:Vol57fasc1-118
R. Hamilton, 124:Sep-Oct83-49
M.L. West, 123:Vol33No2-309
Greeley, A.M. Love and Play.
H. Oppenheimer, 617(TLS):31Aug84-973
Green, A. Flaubert and the Historical
Novel.*
M.P. Ginsburg, 446(NCFS):Fall-
Winter83/84-232
P.M. Wetherill, 402(MLR):Jan83-191
Green, A.E. and J.D.A. Widdowson, eds.
Language, Culture and Tradition.
N. Philip, 203:Vol194No1-130
Green, A.H. The Tunisian Ulama, 1873-1915.
R.W. Bulliet, 318(JAOS):Jan-Mar82-224
Green, D. Great Cobbett.*
N. Berry, 364:Dec83/Jan84-130
442(NY):1Oct84-133
Green, D.H. Irony in the Medieval
Romance.*
E.D. Blodgett, 107(CRCL):Jun83-260
W.A. Quinn, 599:Winter83-72
Green, G. Karpov's Brain.
M. Laski, 362:12Apr84-27
B. Levin, 390:Dec83-59
Green, G. Not in Vain.
M. Buck, 441:4Nov84-24
Green, H. The Light of the Home.
D. Johnson, 453(NYRB):12Apr84-23
Green, J. The Cynic's Lexicon.
R. Davies, 617(TLS):21Dec84-1481

Green, J., comp. Newspeak: A Dictionary
of Jargon.*
D.A.N. Jones, 362:16Feb84-24
Green, J. The Self-Sufficient Weaver.
P. Bach, 614:Summer84-28
Green, L. The Boundary Hunters.
G.W., 102(CanL):Spring83-156
Green, M. Cataloguing Your Needlework
Library.
P. Bach, 614:Summer84-12
Green, M. The Great American Adventure.
R. Slotkin, 441:14Oct84-32
Green, M. Tolstoy and Gandhi, Men of
Peace.*
G. Woodcock, 99:Oct83-26
Green, M.D. The Politics of Indian
Removal.
M.J. McDaniel, 9(AlaR):Jan83-65
Green, M.J.M. Louis Guilloux.*
J. King, 208(FS):Jan83-107
Green, N. Théodore Rousseau 1812-1867.
W. Vaughan, 59:Jun83-249
Green, O.H., ed. Respect for Persons.
R.M.M., 185:Jan84-359
Green, P. The Pursuit of Inequality.
A.G.N. Flew, 518:Oct83-247
D.A. Lloyd Thomas, 479(PhQ):Jul83-301
Green, R. Ford Madox Ford.*
M. Saunders, 184(EIC):Apr83-163
R.C. Schweik, 177(ELT):Vol26No3-205
Green, R. - see Hutchinson, R.C.
Green, R., M-L. Kiljunen and K. Kiljunen,
eds. Namibia.
C. Juma, 69:Vol53No1-90
Green, R.F. Poets and Princepleasers.*
A.V.S. Schmidt, 541(RES):Feb83-52
Green, R.L. and J.M. Gibson. A. Conan
Doyle.
T.D. Smith, 617(TLS):10Feb84-131
Green, R.P.H., ed. Seven Versions of
Carolingian Pastoral.
H. Cooper, 382(MAE):1983/1-139
Green, S. The Great Clowns of Broadway.
H. Teichmann, 441:11Nov84-28
Green, S. Taking Sides.
A.H. Cordesman, 441:25Mar84-22
W.V. O'Brien, 617(TLS):27Jul84-837
Greenbaum, S., G. Leech and J. Svartvik,
eds. Studies in English Linguistics for
Randolph Quirk.*
J.P. Thorne, 541(RES):May83-199
Greenberg, B. How to Run a Traditional
Jewish Household.
J. Riemer, 390:Dec83-57
Greenberg, B.L. Fire Drills.
D. Grumbach, 219(GaR):Fall83-680
J. Schlueter, 573(SSF):Spring-Summer83-
145
Greenberg, R. The Drawings of Alfred Pel-
lan.*
L. Weir, 102(CanL):Autumn83-61
Greenberg, V.D. Literature and Sensibil-
ities in the Weimar Era.*
G.P. Knapp, 222(GR):Summer83-124
K. Petersen, 133:Band16Heft2/3-272
Greenblatt, S., ed. The Power of Forms in
the English Renaissance.*
A.F. Kinney, 551(RenQ):Winter83-641
Greenblatt, S. Renaissance Self-Fashion-
ing.*
D. Adler, 702:Vol 16-348
J.E. Howard, 570(SQ):Autumn83-378

Greene, A.C. Dallas USA.
  W. King, 441:5Aug84-19
Greene, A.C. The Highland Park Woman.
  E.S. Connell, 441:4Mar84-30
Greene, B. Good Morning, Merry Sunshine.
  J. Carroll, 441:10Jun84-18
Greene, D. - see Johnson, S.
Greene, D.B. Mahler, Consciousness and
  Temporality.
  D. Holbrook, 617(TLS):10Aug84-891
Greene, D.B. Temporal Processes in
  Beethoven's Music.
  W. Mellers, 617(TLS):29Jun84-723
Greene, G. Getting to Know the General.
  J. Didion, 453(NYRB):11Oct84-10
  P. Johnson, 362:27Sep84-25
  A. Riding, 441:4Nov84-12
  442(NY):24Dec84-89
Greene, G. Monsignor Quixote.*
  S. Monod, 189(EA):Apr-Sep83-346
Greene, G., ed. The Old School.
  A.S.B., 617(TLS):16Nov84-1323
Greene, G. Ways of Escape.*
  S. Monod, 189(EA):Apr-Sep83-345
Greene, H. Why We Never Danced the
  Charleston.
  E. Milton, 441:24Jun84-29
Greene, J.C. American Science in the Age
  of Jefferson.
  R. Porter, 617(TLS):23Nov84-1340
Greene, J.P. and J.R. Pole, eds. Colonial
  British America.
  P. Marshall, 617(TLS):29Jun84-734
Greene, M.T. Geology in the Nineteenth
  Century.*
  M. Corlett, 529(QQ):Winter83-1174
Greene, R. Robert Greene's "Planetomachia"
  and the Text of the Third Tragedy. (D.F.
  Bratchell, ed)
  J. Feather, 447(N&Q):Feb82-69
Greene, R.L. and others. A Manual of the
  Writings in Middle English 1050-1500.
  (Vol 6)
  H. Cooper, 541(RES):Feb83-118
  A. Hudson, 677(YES):Vol 13-295
Greene, R.W. Six French Poets of Our
  Time.*
  C.A. Hackett, 208(FS):Jan83-108
Greene, T.M. The Light in Troy.*
  S.D., 148:Summer83-95
  M.A. Di Cesare, 604:Spring-Summer83-31
  V. Kahn, 400(MLN):Dec83-1341
Greenfeld, J. The Return of Mr. Hollywood.
  H. Gold, 441:15Apr84-16
Greenfield, C.C. Humanist and Scholastic
  Poetics, 1250-1500.
  P. Frassica, 551(RenQ):Winter83-618
Greenfield, E., R. Layton and I. March.
  The New Penguin Stereo and Cassette
  Guide.
  M. Walker, 415:May83-303
Greenfield, E., R. Layton and I. March.
  The Penguin Cassette Guide.
  P.J.P., 412:May82-156
Greenfield, S.B. - see "A Readable
  'Beowulf'"
Greenfield, S.B. and F.C. Robinson. A
  Bibliography of Publications on Old
  English Literature to the End of 1972.*
  A. Bliss, 447(N&Q):Aug82-353
  R. Frank, 627(UTQ):Spring83-302
  M.R. Godden, 382(MAE):1983/2-311
                                  [continued]

[continuing]
  B. Mitchell, 541(RES):Aug83-320
  M. Rissanen, 439(NM):1983/2-271
Greenfield, T.N. The Eye of Judgment.
  T. Comito, 301(JEGP):Oct83-544
  R.C. McCoy, 551(RenQ):Winter83-652
  R.L. Montgomery, 401(MLQ):Jun83-198
Greengard, C. The Structure of Pindar's
  Epinician Odes.
  J.M. Bremer, 394:Vol36fasc1/2-167
Greengrass, M. France in the Age of Henri
  IV.
  J.K. Powis, 617(TLS):28Sep84-1092
Greenhalgh, M. Donatello and his Sources.
  R. Cocke, 59:Sep83-389
Greening, J. Westerners.
  M. Hulse, 617(TLS):12Oct84-1169
Greenland, C. The Entropy Exhibition.*
  K.L. Spencer, 561(SFS):Nov83-348
Greenough, P.R. Prosperity and Misery in
  Modern Bengal.
  M. Desai, 293(JASt):Aug83-988
Greenslade, M.W., ed. A History of the
  County of Stafford. (Vol 20)
  R. Mander, 617(TLS):12Oct84-1152
Greenstein, F.I. The Hidden-Hand Presi-
  dency.
  639(VQR):Spring83-58
Greenstein, G. Frozen Star.
  442(NY):17Sep84-143
Greenstone, J.D., ed. Public Values and
  Private Power in American Politics.
  S.E., 185:Oct83-174
Greenwood, J. Mosley by Moonlight.
  R. Hill, 617(TLS):26Oct84-1225
Greenwood, J. Murder, Mr. Mosley.
  N. Callendar, 441:15Jan84-29
Greer, A.L. Cuisine of the American South-
  west.
  M. Burros, 441:3Jun84-15
  L. Milazzo, 584(SWR):Autumn83-viii
Greer, G. Sex and Destiny.
  S.M. Gilbert, 617(TLS):8Jun84-645
  J. Hughes, 176:Nov84-55
  C. Iannone, 129:Aug84-71
  S. Lindebaum, 441:29Apr84-3
  P. Singer, 453(NYRB):31May84-15
  M. Warnock, 362:15Mar84-23
  442(NY):30Apr84-121
Gregersen, E. Sexual Practices.
  M. Levine, 441:8Jan84-19
Gregg, E.E.W. - see Emerson, E.T.
Gregg, L. Too Bright to See.*
  T. Diggory, 560:Fall83-112
  G. Johnson, 461:Spring/Summer83-96
Gregg, P. King Charles I.
  G. Schmidgall, 441:16Sep84-14
Gregor, A. Embodiment and Other Poems.*
  J.F. Cotter, 249(HudR):Winter83/84-721
Gregor, I., ed. Reading the Victorian
  Novel.*
  P. Faulkner, 447(N&Q):Apr82-186
Gregor-Dellin, M. Richard Wagner.*
  E. Robbins, 99:Dec83-36
Gregori, M. Giacomo Ceruti.
  K. Garlick, 39:Jul83-113
  E. Waterhouse, 90:Dec83-753
Lady Gregory. Selected Plays of Lady
  Gregory. (M. Fitzgerald, ed)
  A. Carpenter, 617(TLS):29Jun84-733
Gregory, W. Mr. Gregory's Letter-Box.
  (Lady Gregory, ed)
  639(VQR):Winter83-12

Gregson, J.M. Shakespeare: "Twelfth Night."
  M.G., 189(EA):Jul-Sep84-361
  K. Smidt, 179(ES):Feb83-17
Greig, A. Surviving Passages.
  C. Milton, 571(ScLJ):Winter83-66
  S. Regan, 493:Mar83-64
Greimas, A.J. Apie dievus ir žmones.
  N. Strazhas, 361:Sep83-100
Greimas, A.J. Du Sens II.
  J. Sturrock, 617(TLS):3Feb84-105
Greimas, A.J. and J. Courtés. Semiotics and Language.
  R. Schleifer, 141:Summer83-267
  J. Sturrock, 617(TLS):3Feb84-105
Greiner, D.J. The Other John Updike.*
  W.R. Macnaughton, 587(SAF):Autumn83-268
Greiner, S. Hermann Hesse: Jugend in Calw.
  J. Mileck, 221(GQ):Jan83-171
Greiner, U. Der Tod des Nachsommers.
  K. Weissenberger, 133:Band16Heft2/3-286
Grelle Iusco, A., ed. Arte in Basilicata.
  E. Waterhouse, 90:Mar83-165
Grellet, F. Developing Reading Skills.
  D.W. Birckbichler, 399(MLJ):Summer83-172
Grendler, P.F. Culture and Censorship in Late Renaissance Italy and France.
  C. Cairns, 278(IS):Vol38-108
Grene, N. Shakespeare, Jonson, Molière.*
  D.F. Hills, 447(N&Q):Oct82-436
Grene, N. - see Synge, J.M.
Grenfell, N. Switch On, Switch Off.
  D. Regan, 293(JASt):Nov82-219
Grenier, R. La fiancée de Fragonard.
  C. Outie, 98:Mar83-232
Grenier, R. The Marrakesh One-Two.*
  C. Hope, 617(TLS):9Nov84-1288
Grenville, B.P. Kurt Tucholsky.
  295(JML):Nov83-579
Grenz, D. Mädchenliteratur.
  C. Oberfeld, 196:Band24Heft1/2-145
Grenzmann, L. Traumbuch Artemidori.
  N.F. Palmer, 402(MLR):Jan83-226
Greppin, J.A.C. Classical and Middle Armenian Bird Names.
  E. Schütz, 318(JAOS):Jan-Mar82-243
Gresser, J., K. Fujikura and A. Morishima. Environmental Law in Japan.
  H. Befu, 293(JASt):Nov82-162
Gresset, M. Faulkner ou la fascination.*
  C.L. Anderson, 27(AL):Oct83-472
  R.A. Day, 189(EA):Apr-Jun84-227
  J-J. Mayoux, 98:Jun-Jul83-557
  J. Normand, 450(NRF):Sep83-146
Greule, A., ed. Valenztheorie und historische Sprachwissenschaft.
  T. Shannon, 221(GQ):May83-492
Gribbin, J. Future Weather and the Greenhouse Effect.
  R.E. Munn, 529(QQ):Winter83-1167
Gribble, C.E. Russian Root List With a Sketch of Word Formation. (2nd ed)
  J. Gallant, 399(MLJ):Summer83-201
Gribble, J. The Lady of Shalott in the Victorian Novel.
  K. Flint, 617(TLS):27Apr84-472
Gribble, J. Literary Education.
  I. Salusinszky, 617(TLS):16Mar84-278

Grice, F. Francis Kilvert and His World.
  617(TLS):28Dec84-1511
Gridley, R.E. The Brownings and France.*
  P. Daly, 207(FR):Apr84-719
  W.C. Turner, 85(SBHC):Fall83-77
Grieder, J.B. Intellectuals and the State in Modern China.
  C.W. Hayford, 293(JASt):Feb83-401
Grieder, T. Origins of Pre-Columbian Art.
  M.M. Goldstein, 263(RIB):Vol33No1-40
Grieve, M. and W.R. Aitken - see MacDiarmid, H.
Griffeth, R. and C.G. Thomas, eds. The City-State in Five Cultures.
  A.R. Lewis, 589:Apr83-552
Griffin, A. Sikyon.
  A.W. Johnston, 123:Vol33No2-258
  J. Salmon, 303(JoHS):Vol 303-202
Griffin, D.R. Animal Thinking.
  V. Hearne, 441:27May84-8
Griffin, D.R. The Question of Animal Awareness. (rev)
  L. Darden, 84:Dec83-399
Griffin, J. Homer on Life and Death.*
  F.M. Combellack, 122:Jul83-243
  J. van Eck, 394:Vol36fasc3/4-385
Griffith, E. In Her Own Right.
  M. Rugoff, 441:21Oct84-15
Griffiths, P. Bartók.
  D. Matthews, 617(TLS):10Aug84-891
Griffiths, P. György Ligeti.
  J. Deathridge, 617(TLS):8Jun84-646
Griffiths, P., ed. Igor Stravinsky: "The Rake's Progress."*
  J. Pasler, 415:Oct83-605
  A. Whittall, 410(M&L):Jan/Apr83-101
Griffiths, P. The String Quartet.*
  H. Keller, 607:Dec83-32
Griffiths, R.A., ed. Patronage, the Crown and the Provinces.
  S.D. White, 589:Apr83-470
Griffiths, S. How Plays Are Made.
  P. Mulhern, 610:Autumn83-273
  M. Smith, 610:Autumn83-273
Griffiths, T. Oi for England.
  D. Devlin, 157:Spring83-52
Griffiths, T.R., ed. Stagecraft.
  A. Cornish, 157:Summer83-31
Grigera, L.L. - see under López Grigera, L.
Grignani, M.A. Beppe Fenoglio.
  E. Saccone, 400(MLN):Jan83-163
Grigorenko, P.G. Memoirs.* V podpol'e mozhno vstretit' tol'ko krys.
  A. Ulam, 550(RusR):Apr83-197
Grigson, G. The Cornish Dancer and Other Poems.*
  T. Eagleton, 565:Vol124No3-77
Grigson, G. Montaigne's Tower and Other Poems.
  V. Cunningham, 617(TLS):14Dec84-1439
Grigson, G. Notes from an Odd Country.
  J.K.L.W., 617(TLS):22Jun84-711
Grigson, G. Recollections.
  V. Cunningham, 617(TLS):14Dec84-1439
  D. Wright, 362:6Dec84-31
Grill, J.H. The Nazi Movement in Baden, 1920-1945.
  I. Deak, 453(NYRB):31May84-37
  639(VQR):Summer83-86
Grime, K. Jazz Voices.
  I. Gitler, 441:29Jul84-17

Grimes, M. The Dirty Duck.
  N. Callendar, 441:13May84-35
  442(NY):18Jun84-117
Grimm, F.M. La Correspondance littéraire:
  1er janvier-15 juin 1760. (S. Dafgård,
  ed)
  M. Nøjgaard, 597(SN):Vol55No2-244
Grimm, G. Rezeptionsgeschichte.*
  H.A. Pausch, 107(CRCL):Sep83-398
Grimm, G. - see Kerner, J.
Grimm, J. and W. The German Legends of
  the Brothers Grimm. (D. Ward, ed and
  trans)
  W.W. Anthony, 221(GQ):May83-512
  W.F.H. Nicolaisen, 650(WF):Oct83-312
Grimm, J. and W. Grimms' Other Tales.
  (W. Hansen, ed; R. Michaelis-Jena and
  A. Ratcliff, trans)
  T. Shippey, 617(TLS):30Nov84-1384
Grimm, R. and J. Hermand, eds. Faschismus
  und Avantgarde.
  M.H. Gelber, 221(GQ):Nov83-634
Grimm, R. and J. Hermand. Natur und Natür-
  lichkeit.
  U. Heukenkamp, 654(WB):8/1983-1497
  K. Phillips, 221(GQ):Nov83-632
von Grimmelshausen, H.J.C. The Singular
  Life Story of Heedless Hopalong. (R.L.
  Hiller and J.C. Osborne, eds and trans)
  J.W. Thomas, 221(GQ):Mar83-311
Grimshaw, A.D. Language as Social
  Resource.* (A.S. Dil, ed)
  R. Turner, 355(LSoc):Jun83-247
Grimshaw, J.A., Jr. Robert Penn Warren.*
  J.M. Edelstein, 517(PBSA):Vol77No3-377
Grimshaw, J.A., Jr., ed. Robert Penn War-
  ren's Brother to Dragons.
  M.K. Spears, 569(SR):Fall83-655
Grimshaw, P. and L. Strahan, eds. The
  Half Open Door.
  M. Lake, 381:Sep83-380
Grimstad, K. Masks of the Prophet.
  W. Iggers, 529(QQ):Autumn83-899
  A. Obermayer, 564:Sep83-230
Grin, M., ed. Ustami Buninykh.
  R. Davies, 575(SEER):Jul83-436
Grindal, G. Sketches Against the Dark.
  P. Varner, 649(WAL):May83-87
Grinde, N. Contemporary Norwegian Music
  1920-1980.*
  A.J.B., 412:Aug-Nov82-282
Grindle, J. and S. Gatrell - see Hardy, T.
Grinevald, J. and others. La Quadrature
  du CERN.
  M. Gibson, 617(TLS):7Dec84-1425
Grisanti, C. Folklore di Isnello.
  C. Wiesner-Kopp, 196:Band24Heft3/4-299
Grisewood, H. and R. Hague - see Jones, D.
Grmek, M.D. Les maladies à l'aube de la
  civilisation occidentale.
  J. Scarborough, 617(TLS):16Mar84-284
Grob, E. Die Verwilderte Rede in Bren-
  tanos "Godwi" und L. Sternes "Tristram
  Shandy."
  W. Anthony, 221(GQ):Mar83-318
Gröber, B. and L. Müller - see Müller, L.
Groddeck, G. Le Chercheur d'âme.
  H. Cronel, 450(NRF):Dec83-109
Grodecki, L. and others. Les vitraux de
  Paris, de la région parisienne, de la
  Picardie, et du Nord-Pas-de-Calais.
  Les vitraux du Centre et des Pays de
  [continued]

[continuing]
la Loire.
  M.H. Caviness, 54:Sep83-505
Groden, M., comp. James Joyce's Manu-
  scripts.
  M.J. Sidnell, 178:Sep83-380
Groeben, N. Leserpsychologie.
  E. Ibsch, 204(FdL):Sep83-237
Groft, T.K. Cast with Style.
  D.R. Braden, 658:Summer/Autumn83-218
Grojnowski, D. - see Laforgue, J.
Grønbech, B. Hans Christian Andersen.*
  E. Bredsdorff, 562(Scan):Nov82-192
Grønvik, O. Runene på Tunesteinen.
  E.H. Antonsen, 350:Sep84-668
de Groot, I. Landscape Etchings of Dutch
  Masters of the Seventeenth Century.
  C. White, 39:Feb83-146
de Groot, I. and R. Vorstman. Maritime
  Prints by the Dutch Masters.*
  C. White, 39:Feb83-146
Grootaers, J. and J.A. Selling. The 1980
  Synod of Bishops "On the Role of the
  Family."
  P. Hebblethwaite, 617(TLS):30Mar84-327
Grose, C. Ovid's "Metamorphoses": An
  Index to the 1632 Commentary of George
  Sandys.
  L.V.R., 568(SCN):Fall83-62
Grose, P. Israel in the Mind of America.*
  S.L. Spiegel, 129:Mar84-72
Grosholz, E. The River Painter.
  M. Kinzie, 29:Mar/Apr84-38
Grosjean, F. Life with Two Languages.*
  R.L. Cooper, 350:Sep84-633
  T.S. Wilson, 215(GL):Vol23No3-224
Grosjean, J. Darius.
  E. Marty, 98:Apr83-320
Grosjean, J. Élie.*
  E. Marty, 98:Apr83-320
  N.D. Savage, 207(FR):Mar84-588
Gross, J. The Lives of Rachel.
  R.P. Mills, 441:25Nov84-26
Gross, J., ed. The Oxford Book of Aph-
  orisms.*
  639(VQR):Autumn83-115
Gross, N. From Gesture to Idea.
  J.F. Gaines, 207(FR):Apr84-712
Gross, P. Familiars.
  J. Mole, 176:Dec84-61
  M. O'Neill, 493:Sep83-72
  S. Rae, 617(TLS):17Feb84-168
Gross, P. The Ice Factory.
  N. Corcoran, 617(TLS):7Sep84-1004
  J. Mole, 176:Dec84-61
Gross, S. Ernst Robert Curtius und die
  deutsche Romanistik der zwanziger Jahre.
  R. Dumont, 549(RLC):Apr-Jun83-252
Grossberg, K.A. Japan's Renaissance.*
  S. Gay, 293(JASt):May83-664
Grosse, W. - see Lessing, G.E.
"Der Grosse Brockhaus." (18th ed)
  L.S. Thompson, 70:Jan-Feb82-94
Grosser, A. Les Occidentaux.
  H. Peyre, 207(FR):Apr84-751
Grosshans, H. Hitler and the Artists.
  D. Thomas, 324:Jul84-550
Grosskurth, P. - see Symonds, J.A.
Grossman, A. Against Our Vanishing.*
  (M. Halliday, ed)
  D. Davie, 219(GaR):Spring83-196

Grossman, A. Of the Great House.
  B. Costello, 491:May83-106
  D. St. John, 42(AR):Spring83-231
  639(VQR):Winter83-26
Grossman, R. The Animals.
  V. Crummett, 436(NewL):Summer84-106
"George Grosz: An Autobiography."
  J. Willett, 453(NYRB):1Mar84-33
Grotjahn, R. Hexameter Studies.
  J. Hellegouarc'h, 555:Vol57fasc1-153
Grottanelli, V.L. Una società guineana:
  gli Nzema.
  P.P. Viazzo, 69:Vol53No1-99
Grotzer, P. Albert Béguin ou la passion
  des autres. Existence et destinée
  d'Albert Béguin.
  W. Bush, 107(CRCL):Jun83-238
Grotzer, P. - see Raymond, M. and G.
  Poulet
Groult, P. Literatura espiritual española.
  A. Vermeylen, 356(LR):Feb-May83-123
Groupe μ. A General Rhetoric.*
  M. Grimaud, 567:Vol45No1/2-115
Grout, P.B. and others, eds. The Legend
  of Arthur in the Middle Ages.
  M-M. Dubois, 189(EA):Oct-Dec84-457
Grove, D.C. Chalcatzingo.
  N. Hammond, 617(TLS):30Nov84-1369
Grubb, D. Ancient Lights.
  N. Hilton, 88:Summer83-30
  J. Welch, 639(VQR):Spring83-359
Gruen, E.S. The Hellenistic World and the
  Coming of Rome.
  J. Boardman, 441:23Sep84-16
Gruffydd, R.G. - see under Geraint Gruf-
  fydd, R.
Grumbach, D. The Ladies.
  C.R. Stimpson, 441:30Sep84-12
Grumet, R.S. Native American Place Names
  in New York City.
  H. Kenny, 424:Mar83-62
Grunchec, P. Gericault, Dessins et
  Aquarelles de Chevaux.
  C. Sells, 90:Oct83-629
Grunchec, P. The Grand Prix de Rome. Le
  Grand Prix de Peinture.
  B. Knox, 453(NYRB):27Sep84-21
Grundtvig, N.F.S. A Grundtvig Anthology.
  (N.L. Jensen, ed)
  A.M. Allchin, 617(TLS):3Aug84-874
Grundy, K.W. Soldiers Without Politics.
  R. West, 617(TLS):16Mar84-269
Grünfeld, J. Method and Language.
  P. Engel, 542:Jul-Sep83-357
Grüning, U. Spiegelungen.
  D. von Törne, 654(WB):6/1983-1109
de Grunne, B. The Terracotta Statuary of
  the Inland Delta of the Niger in Mali.
  J. Povey, 2(AfrA):Aug83-83
de Grunne, B. Terres Cuites Anciennes de
  l'Ouest Africain/Ancient Terracottas from
  West Africa.*
  M. Gilbert, 69:Vol53No3-99
Grunwell, P. Clinical Phonology.
  M.L. Edwards, 350:Sep84-639
Gruslin, A. Le Théâtre et l'état au
  Québec.*
  E.J. Talbot, 207(FR):May84-896
Gruys, A. and J.P. Gumbert, eds. Codico-
  logica. (Vols 3 and 5)
  J.F. Preston, 589:Jan83-156

Grzegorczyk, A. An Outline of Mathemati-
  cal Logic.
  E.G.K. López-Escobar, 316:Mar83-220
Grzegorczyk, C. La théorie générale des
  valeurs et le droit.
  J-L. Gardies, 542:Jul-Sep83-337
Grzimek, M. Heartstop.
  F. Conroy, 441:18Nov84-9
Gschnitzer, F. Griechische Socialges-
  chichte.
  É. Will, 555:Vol57fasc2-310
Gschwind-Holtzer, G. Analyse sociolinguis-
  tique de la communication et didactique.*
  F. Helgorsky, 209(FM):Apr83-186
Gsell, O. Gegensatzrelationen im Wort-
  schatz romanischer Sprachen.*
  H. and R. Kahane, 545(RPh):Feb83-422
Gsteiger, M. Wandlungen Werthers und
  andere Essays zur vergleichenden Lit-
  eraturgeschichte.
  M. Moog-Grünewald, 52:Band18Heft2-195
  J. Riesz, 678(YCGL):No31-158
Gual, C.G. - see under García Gual, C.
Gualdani, E.N. - see under Norti Gualdani,
  E.
Gualis, G.M.B. - see under Borrás Gualis,
  G.M.
Guenée, B. Histoire et culture historique
  dans l'occident médiéval.
  P. Bourgain, 554:Vol 103No2/3-412
Guenée, S. Bibliographie de l'histoire
  des universités françaises des origines
  à la revolution. (Vol 1)
  J.W. Baldwin, 589:Jul83-747
Guenthner, F. and S.J. Schmidt, eds.
  Formal Semantics and Pragmatics for
  Natural Languages.
  R. Kempson, 297(JL):Mar83-249
Guérin de Bouscal, D. Dom Quixote de la
  Manche, comédie.* (D. Dalla Valle and
  A. Carriat, eds)
  H.G. Hall, 208(FS):Oct83-454
Guérin du Bouscal, D. Le Gouvernement de
  Sanche Pansa.* (C.E.J. Caldicott, ed)
  A. Viala, 535(RHL):Sep/Dec83-924
Guernsey, B. Gaby.
  P. Bach, 614:Winter84-18
Guernsey, B. January Thaw.
  T. Kooser, 502(PrS):Spring83-107
  V. Young, 249(HudR):Summer83-402
Guerra, R., comp. Bibliographie des
  oeuvres de Boris Zaïtsev. (T.A. Ossor-
  guine, ed)
  D.M. Fiene, 574(SEEJ):Spring83-119
Guerreau-Jalabert, A. - see Abbo of Fleury
Guest, B. Herself Defined.
  A. Kazin, 453(NYRB):29Mar84-15
  G. Pearson, 617(TLS):27Apr84-447
  K. Pollitt, 441:11Mar84-7
Guest, H. Lost and Found. The Emperor of
  Outer Space.
  W. Scammell, 617(TLS):27Jul84-838
Guest, I. Jules Perrot.
  J. Hankey, 617(TLS):21Dec84-1485
Guettat, M. La musique classique du
  Maghreb.
  L.J. Jones, 187:Jan84-150
Guetti, J Word-Music.
  C.K. Smith, 599:Winter83-61
Guibal, F. ... et combien de dieux nou-
  veaux: Lévinas.*
  A. Jacob, 192(EP):Apr-Jun83-237

Guicciardi, J-P. and P. Bonnet - see Duc de Choiseul
Guichard-Meili, J. Matisse Paper Cutouts.
  J. Russell, 441:25Nov84-41
Guichemerre, R. La Tragi-comédie.
  R.W. Tobin, 475:Vol 10No18-349
"Guide to Literary Manuscripts in the Huntington Library."
  517(PBSA):Oct-Dec80-419
Guidi, A. Poesie approvate. (B. Maier, ed)
  E. Bonora, 228(GSLI):Vol 160fasc509-145
Guidoni, E. La Ville européenne.
  H. Ballon, 576:Dec83-397
Guierre, L. Essai sur l'accentuation en anglais contemporain.
  B. Malmberg, 189(EA):Jan-Mar83-73
Guiette, R. Forme et senefiance.
  A. Iker-Gittleman, 545(RPh):Feb83-499
Guilbaut, S. How New York Stole the Idea of Modern Art.
  L. Abel, 129:Jul84-62
  T. Bender, 441:1Jan84-7
  T. Lawson, 62:Summer84-83
  D. Rosand, 617(TLS):12Oct84-1155
Guilbert, P. and A. Dorna. Significations du comportementalisme.
  J-M. Gabaude, 542:Jul-Sep83-333
Guild, J.R. and A. Law, eds. Edinburgh University Library 1580-1980.
  A. Bell, 78(BC):Autumn83-363
Guild, N. The Berlin Warning.
  A. Cheuse, 441:3Jun84-41
Guiliano, E., ed. Lewis Carroll: A Celebration.*
  H-P. Breuer, 395(MFS):Summer83-263
  B.L. Clark, 594:Summer83-161
  S. Monod, 189(EA):Apr-Jun84-216
Guiliano, E. and J.R. Kincaid, eds. Soaring with the Dodo.
  W.H. Bond, 517(PBSA):Vol77No4-518
"Guillaume de Machaut."
  E.R. Sienaert, 356(LR):Aug83-236
Guillaume de Pierre Godin. Tractatus de causa immediata ecclesiastice potestatis. (W.D. McCready, ed)
  H. Kaminsky, 589:Oct83-1040
Guillemin-Flescher, J. Syntaxe comparée du français et de l'anglais.*
  B.K. Barnes, 399(MLJ):Autumn83-285
Guillén, J. Guillén on Guillén. (R. Gibbons and A.L. Geist, eds and trans)
  E.A. Maio, 552(REH):May83-309
Guillen, M. Bridges to Infinity.
  M.S. Kaplan, 441:5Feb84-19
Guillerm, J-P. Tombeau de Léonard de Vinci.
  C. Limousin, 98:May83-452
du Guillet, P. Rymes. (F. Charpentier, ed)
  L. Herlin, 450(NRF):Sep83-125
Guillevic. Requis.
  S. Romer, 617(TLS):1Jun84-610
Guillevic/R. Jean. Choses parlées.
  P.J.T. Gormally, 207(FR):May84-911
Guillory, J. Poetic Authority.
  R. Harvey, 391:Dec83-138
  G. Mathis, 189(EA):Jul-Sep84-321
  S. Mullaney, 141:Fall83-383
Guillot, A. La Vraie Cuisine Légère.
  W. and C. Cowen, 639(VQR):Autumn83-137

Guimera, L.M. Ni Dos ni Ventre.
  W. de Mahieu, 69:Vol153No2-80
Guinet, L. Les emprunts gallo-romans au germanique (du 1er à la fin du 5e siècle).
  G. Roques, 553(RLiR):Jan-Jun83-196
  S.N. Rosenberg, 207(FR):Feb84-434
Guinness, J., with C. The House of Mitford.
  E.S. Turner, 617(TLS):14Dec84-1440
Guiol-Benassaya, E. La Presse face au Surréalisme de 1925 à 1938.
  D. Stephens, 207(FR):Mar84-574
Guiomar, M. Trois paysages du "Rivage des Syrtes."
  G. Cesbron, 535(RHL):Mar/Apr83-307
"Guitares, Chefs-d'oeuvre des collections de France."
  H. Charnassé, 537:Vol69No1-103
Guiter, H. and M.V. Arapov, eds. Studies on Zipf's Law.
  L.D. Stephens, 350:Jun84-445
Guittard, J-M. Catalogue du fonds ancien de la Bibliothèque de l'Institut d'études hispaniques de Paris.
  354:Dec83-441
Gulick, S.L. A Chesterfield Bibliography to 1800.* (2nd ed)
  J.D. Fleeman, 541(RES):Feb83-119
Gullace, G. Taine and Brunetière on Criticism.
  L. Bolle, 356(LR):Aug83-242
Gullace, G. - see Croce, B.
Gullón, A. La novela experimental de Miguel Delibes.
  L. Hickey, 86(BHS):Apr83-162
  G. Roberts, 240(HR):Spring83-236
Gullón, G., ed. Poesía de la vanguardia española.
  S. Daydí-Tolson, 240(HR):Summer83-348
Gullón, R. Espacio y novela.
  G. Navajas, 240(HR):Summer83-338
Gullón, R. Técnicas de Galdós.
  J.W. Kronik, 240(HR):Spring83-234
Gullón, R. - see Benet, J.
Gullvåg, I. and J. Wetlesen, eds. In Sceptical Wonder.
  G.G., 185:Oct83-171
Gumbrecht, H.U., with U. Link-Heer and P.M. Spangenberg, eds. Literatur in der Gesellschaft des Spätmittelalters.
  P.F. Dembowski, 589:Jan83-184
Gumperz, J.J. Discourse Strategies.*
  D. Schiffrin, 350:Dec84-953
Gumperz, J.J., ed. Language and Social Identity.
  D. Schiffrin, 350:Dec84-953
Gunby, D.C. Shakespeare: "Richard III."
  M.G., 189(EA):Jul-Sep84-361
  K. Smidt, 179(ES):Feb83-17
Gundy, E. Love, Infidelity and Drinking to Forget.
  J. Kaufman, 441:12Aug84-20
Gundy, H.P. - see Carman, B.
Gungwu, W. - see under Wang Gungwu
Gunn, E.M. Unwelcome Muse.
  D. Holm, 116:Jul182-287
Gunn, G. The Interpretation of Otherness.
Gunn, J.A.W. and others - see Disraeli, B.
  E.H. Redekop, 106:Winter83-415

Guyotat, P. Le Livre. Vivre.
R. Buss, 617(TLS):6Jul84-761
Gwynne, P.N. Pushkin Shove.
F. Schumer, 441:8Apr84-20
Györgyey, C. Ferenc Molnár.
G.F. Cushing, 402(MLR):Oct83-1006
I. Sanders, 397(MD):Mar83-109
Gysseling, M., with W. Pijnenburg. Corpus
van Middelnederlandse teksten. (Ser 1)
P. Swiggers, 350:Jun84-454

H.D. Collected Poems 1912-1944. (L.L.
Martz, ed)
G. Pearson, 617(TLS):27Apr84-447
K. Pollitt, 441:11Mar84-7
H.D. The Gift.
L.M. Freibert, 50(ArQ):Spring83-89
639(VQR):Autumn83-123
Haac, O.A. Jules Michelet.
E.K. Kaplan, 446(NCFS):Fall-
Winter83/84-262
van den Haag, E. and J.P. Conrad. The
Death Penalty.
J.W. Bishop, Jr., 129:Feb84-70
442(NY):23Apr84-132
Haage, B.D. "Das Heidelberger Schicksal-
buch."
F.B. Brévart, 684(ZDA):Band112Heft1-43
Haakonsen, D. Henrik Ibsen.*
H.S. Naess, 563(SS):Winter83-75
Haakonssen, K. The Science of a Legis-
lator.*
R.H., 185:Apr84-558
B. Keenan, 543:Mar83-715
Haan, N. and others, eds. Social Science
as Moral Inquiry.
K. Sołtan, 185:Apr84-539
Haarscher, G. Égalité et Politique.
P. Van Parijs, 540(RIPh):Vol37fascl/2-
206
Haarscher, G. L'ontologie de Marx.*
G. Argence, 542:Apr-Jun83-257
M. Lagueux, 154:Dec83-710
Haarscher, G. and R. Legros - see Lukács,
G.
Haas, A.M., ed. "Der Franckforter"
Theologia Deutsch.
M. Schmidt, 72:Band220Heft2-371
Haas, A.M. Sermo mysticus.
M. Schmidt, 72:Band220Heft2-371
Haas, A.M. and H. Stirnimann, eds. Das
"einig Ein."*
M. Schmidt, 72:Band220Heft2-371
P.W. Tax, 133:Band16Heft1-61
Haas, K. Inside Music.
W.L. Taitte, 441:22Jul84-33
Haas, R. Die mittelenglische Totenklage.
V.B. Richmond, 589:Jan83-186
Haas, V. and H.J. Thiel. Die Beschwörungs-
rituale der Allaituraḫ(ḫ)i und verwandte
Texte.
C. Carter, 318(JAOS):Apr-Jun82-400
Haas, W., ed. Standard Languages Spoken
and Written.
A.R.T., 189(EA):Oct-Dec84-488
Haas, W., ed. Writing without Letters.
G.F. Meier, 682(ZPSK):Band36Heft6-752
Haase, H. Johannes R. Becher.
S. Rönisch, 654(WB):8/1982-179

Haase, W., ed. Aufstieg und Niedergang
der römischen Welt.
M. Smith, 318(JAOS):Apr-Jun82-405
M. Smith, 318(JAOS):Jul-Sep82-544
Haastrup, U., ed. Kristusfremstillinger.
L. Antonsen and M.H. Caviness,
589:Oct83-1045
Habegger, A. Gender, Fantasy, and Realism
in American Literature.*
R.E. Long, 432(NEQ):Jun83-286
P. Prenshaw, 26(ALR):Autumn83-299
295(JML):Nov83-412
Habereder, J. Kurt Hiller und der litera-
rische Aktivismus.
J.M. Ritchie, 402(MLR):Apr83-504
Haberly, D.T. Three Sad Races.*
F.C.H. Garcia, 263(RIB):Vol33No3-404
Habermas, J. Communication and the Evolu-
tion of Society.
L.C. Hawes, 480(P&R):Vol 16No2-130
Habermas, J., ed. Observations on "The
Spiritual Situation of the Age."
M. Rosen, 617(TLS):5Oct84-1132
Habermas, J. Philosophical-Political Pro-
files.
J. Hodge, 617(TLS):18May84-560
Habgood, J. Church and Nation in a Secu-
lar Age.
J. Lawrence, 617(TLS):25May84-599
Habicht, W. and I. Schabert, eds. Sympa-
thielenkung in den Dramen Shakespeares.
D. Daphinoff, 570(SQ):Spring83-117
K. Otten, 72:Band220Heft2-398
Habra, G. Du discernement spirituel.
(Vol 2)
A. Reix, 542:Oct-Dec83-445
Hackel, S., ed. The Byzantine Saint.
E. Piltz, 341:Vol52No3-130
Hackett, C.A. Rimbaud.*
N. Osmond, 402(MLR):Apr83-456
Hacking, I. Representing and Intervening.
W.H. Newton-Smith, 617(TLS):9Mar84-258
Hadamitzy, W. and M. Spain. Kanji and
Kana.
C.M. De Wolf, 474(PIL):Vol 15No1/4-305
Hadas, R. Slow Transparency.
J. Graham, 441:4Mar84-14
A. Stevenson, 617(TLS):20Jul84-818
R. Tillinghast, 385(MQR):Fall84-596
Hadfield, A.M. Charles Williams.
A. Barnet, 441:19Feb84-23
H. Carpenter, 617(TLS):2Mar84-212
Hadingham, E. Early Man and the Cosmos.
P-L. Adams, 61:Jun84-124
Hadjioannou, K. Hē archaia Kypros eis tas
Hellēnikas pēgas, Tomos D, Meros A + B.
F.G. Maier, 123:Vol33No2-345
Haebler, C. - see Schmitt, A.
Haensch, G. and others. La lexicografía.
M.B. Fontanella de Weinberg, 263(RIB):
Vol33No4-590
Haertig, E. Antique Combs and Purses.
I. Joshi, 614:Winter84-15
Haese, R. Rebels and Precursors.*
E. Cross, 592:Oct83-26
90:Apr83-237
Haffenden, J., ed. W.H. Auden: The Criti-
cal Heritage.
H. Haughton, 617(TLS):27Apr84-457
Haffenden, J. John Berryman.*
G. Clarke, 447(N&Q):Jun82-275

Haffenden, J. The Life of John Berryman.*
  J.D. Bloom, 27(AL):Oct83-478
  P.A. Bové, 659(ConL):Spring84-103
  M. Hofmann, 493:Mar83-67
  S. Pinsker, 363(LitR):Winter84-252
    295(JML):Nov83-439
Hafner, D. "Tom Jones."
  D. Mehl, 72:Band219Heft2-478
Hagarty, B. Sad Paradise.
  S. Ruddell, 102(CanL):Winter82-143
Hageberg, O. Frå Camilla Collett til Dag
  Solstad.
  J. Garton, 562(Scan):Nov82-205
Hagen, A.M. Standaardtaal en dialectspre-
  kende kinderen.
  G. Hubers, 204(FdL):Mar82-67
Hagen, W.W. Germans, Poles, and Jews.*
  A. Katz, 497(PolR):Vol28No4-120
Hager, K. Beiträge zur Kulturpolitik.
  H. Haase, 654(WB):3/1982-174
Hagerty, M.J., ed. Los libros plúmbeos
  del Sacromonte.
  T.E. Case, 552(REH):Jan83-154
Hägg, R. and N. Marinatos, eds. Sanctuar-
  ies and Cults in the Aegean Bronze Age.
  S. Hood, 123:Vol33No2-356
Hägg, T. The Novel in Antiquity.
  B. Vickers, 617(TLS):20Apr84-427
"Hagiographie, cultures et sociétés,
  IVe-XIIe siècles."
  P.J. Geary, 589:Apr83-553
Hagstrum, J.H. Sex and Sensibility.*
  D. Daphinoff, 179(ES):Jun83-279
Hahl-Koch, J. - see "Arnold Schoenberg,
  Wassily Kandinsky"
Hahm, D.E. The Origins of Stoic Cosmology.
  J. Mansfeld, 394:Vol36fasc1/2-193
Hahn, K-H., ed. Brief an Goethe. (Vol 1)
  H.G. Haile, 301(JEGP):Apr83-286
Hahn, K-H. - see "Goethe-Jahrbuch"
Hahn, S. The Roots of Southern Populism.*
  G.M. Fredrickson, 453(NYRB):8Nov84-39
Hahn, T., ed. Upright Lives.
  J.B., 189(EA):Oct-Dec84-491
Hahn, W.G. Postwar Soviet Politics.*
  M. McCauley, 575(SEER):Oct83-631
Haig, A.M., Jr. Caveat.
  M. Carver, 617(TLS):25May84-588
  J. Chace, 441:22Apr84-3
  S. Hoffmann, 453(NYRB):31May84-6
  N. Podhoretz, 129:Jul84-56
Haight, G.S. and R.T. Van Arsdel, eds.
  George Eliot.
  G. Levine, 445(NCF):Jun83-111
Haight, J. The Concept of Reason in
  French Classical Literature 1635-1690.
  N. Cronk, 188(ECr):Winter83-83
  W. Doney, 319:Oct84-478
Haight, M.R. A Study of Self-Deception.*
  S. Ross, 482(PhR):Oct83-630
Hailey, A. Strong Medicine.
  M. Watkins, 441:25Nov84-26
Haiman, G. Nicholas Kis.
  D. McKitterick, 617(TLS):27Jul84-856
Haiman, J. Hua.
  W.A. Foley, 350:Jun84-424
Hain, P. Political Trials in Britain.
  D. Pannick, 617(TLS):10Feb84-145
Haines, J. Living Off the Country.
  E.C. Lynskey, 577(SHR):Summer83-296
Haines, J. News From the Glacier.*
  R. Hedin, 649(WAL):Nov83-250
  R. Lattimore, 249(HudR):Spring83-205

Haines, J. Other Days.
  L. Runciman, 649(WAL):May83-70
Haines, R. The Inner Eye of Alfred Stieg-
  litz.
  M. Orvell, 290(JAAC):Spring84-339
Hair, D.S. Domestic and Heroic in Tenny-
  son's Poetry.*
  P. Allen, 627(UTQ):Fall82-114
Hájek z Libočan, V. Kronika česka.
  J-P. Danes, 549(RLC):Oct-Dec83-503
Haksar, V. Equality, Liberty, and Perfec-
  tionism.*
  N.S. Care, 449:May83-308
Halbfass, W. Indien und Europa.
  H.P. Alper, 485(PE&W):Apr83-189
Haldas, G. - see Saba, U.
Haldeman, J. Worlds Apart.
  G. Jonas, 441:15Jan84-29
Hale, A. Research on Tibeto-Burman Lan-
  guages.
  R.A. Miller, 350:Sep84-676
Hale, J. The Whistle Blower.
  P. Lewis, 617(TLS):12Oct84-1167
Hale, J.R., ed. A Concise Encyclopaedia
  of the Italian Renaissance.*
  C.H. Clough, 324:Apr84-345
Hale, J.R. Renaissance War Studies.
  J. Keegan, 617(TLS):9Mar84-242
Halem, L.C. Divorce Reform.
  J.L.H., 185:Jan84-383
Hales, P.B. Silver Cities.
  T. Bender, 441:21Oct84-13
  J. Hunter, 676(YR):Spring84-433
Halewood, W.H. Six Subjects of Reforma-
  tion Art.*
  R.M. Frye, 627(UTQ):Summer83-411
Haliburton, T.C. The Old Judge, or Life
  in a Colony. (M.G. Parks, ed)
  A. Mitchell, 102(CanL):Autumn83-73
Haliczer, S. The Comuneros of Castile.
  J.S. Amelang, 589:Apr83-474
Halkett, S. and J. Laing. A Dictionary of
  Anonymous and Pseudonymous Publications
  in the English Language, 1475-1640.
  (3rd ed) (J. Horden, ed)
  W.P. Smothers, 70:May-Jun81-161
Hall, A.R. Philosophers at War.
  C.B. Schmitt, 84:Mar83-71
Hall, A.R. Science for Industry.
  J. Taylor, 324:Sep84-698
Hall, A.R. and H.K. Kenward, eds. Environ-
  mental Archaeology in the Urban Context.
  F.L. Cheyette, 589:Oct83-1120
Hall, D. Joyce Cary.
  D. Bradshaw, 617(TLS):2Nov84-1240
Hall, D. The Weather for Poetry.
  D.E. Middleton, 385(MQR):Summer84-434
Hall, H.G. Comedy in Context.
  G. McCarthy, 617(TLS):21Dec84-1485
Hall, H.G., ed. A Critical Bibliography
  of French Literature. (Vol 3A: The
  Seventeenth Century, Supplement.)
  O. Klapp, 475:Vol 10No19-883
  B. Norman, 207(FR):Mar84-553
Hall, J. A History of Ideas and Images
  in Italian Art.
  P. Humfrey, 324:May84-411
Hall, J. Just Relations.
  J. Tulip, 581:Mar83-113
Hall, J. Law, Social Science and Criminal
  Theory.
  R.S.G., 185:Jan84-381

Hampson, N. Will and Circumstance.*
  R. Darnton, 453(NYRB):28Jun84-32
Hampsten, E. Read This Only to Yourself.*
  D.D. Quantic, 649(WAL):Aug83-172
Hampton, C., ed. A Radical Reader.
  J.C., 617(TLS):20Apr84-443
Hanan, P. The Chinese Vernacular Story.*
  K. Carlitz, 116:Jul82-279
Hanbury-Tenison, R. World's Apart.
  H.B. Noble, 441:30Dec84-17
Hancock, G., ed. Magic Realism.
  R. Wilson, 526:Spring83-84
Hand, W.D. Magical Medicine.
  D. Hufford, 650(WF):Jul83-233
"Handbook of Latin American Studies."
  (Vol 42)
  M.E. Venier, 457(NRFH):Tomo31núm2-327
Handelman, S.A. The Slayers of Moses.
  D. Keesey, 478:Oct83-280
Handke, P. Der Chinese des Schmerzes.
  Phantasien der Wiederholung.
  P. Labanyi, 617(TLS):5Oct84-1136
Handke, P. The Weight of the World.
  R. Locke, 441:22Jul84-10
Handlin, L. George Bancroft.
  P-T. Adams, 61:Aug84-112
  M. Peters, 441:23Sep84-29
Hane, M. Peasants, Rebels, and Outcastes.
  R.J. Smith, 293(JASt):Feb83-410
  D.E. Westney, 407(MN):Spring83-95
Hanfling, O., ed. Essential Readings in
  Logical Positivism.*
  R. Haller, 53(AGP):Band65Heft3-345
Hanfling, O. Logical Positivism.*
  R. Haller, 53(AGP):Band65Heft3-345
  A. O'Hear, 84:Sep83-303
Hankin, C.A. Katherine Mansfield and her
  Confessional Stories.
  R. Brown, 617(TLS):13Jul84-772
Hankin, C.A. - see Murry, J.M.
Hankins, J.E. Backgrounds of Shake-
  speare's Thought.*
  E. Auberlen, 38:Band101Heft1/2-252
  J. Wilders, 447(N&Q):Feb82-71
Hankins, T.L. Sir William Rowan Hamilton.
  R.G. Olson, 486:Jun83-348
Hanks, D.A. Innovative Furniture in
  America from 1800 to the Present.
  K.L. Ames, 576:May83-194
Hanks, J.M. Ronsard and Biblical Tradi-
  tion.
  D.G. Coleman, 551(RenQ):Winter83-624
Hanley, A. Hart Crane's Holy Vision.*
  R.P. Sugg, 70:May-Jun83-154
Hanley, D.L., A.P. Kerr and N.H. Waites.
  Contemporary France.
  P.A. Ouston, 208(FS):Oct83-495
Hanley, J. What Farrar Saw and Other
  Stories.
  J.P. Durix, 617(TLS):29Jun84-716
Hanley, K. - see Meredith, G.
Hanley, S. The Lit de Justice of the
  Kings of France.
  R. Bonney, 617(TLS):6Jan84-21
Hanna, P.R. and J.S. Frank Lloyd Wright's
  Hanna House.*
  R.G. Wilson, 505:Jan83-170
Hannaford, R.G. Samuel Richardson.*
  A. Varney, 447(N&Q):Oct82-447
Hannay, A. Kierkegaard.
  M.H.W., 185:Apr84-557

Hannerz, U. Exploring the City.* (French
  title: Explorer la ville.)
  J. Gutwirth, 98:Nov83-872
Hanning, R.W. and D. Rosand, eds. Castig-
  lione, the Ideal and the Real in Renais-
  sance Culture.
  J. Woodhouse, 324:Mar84-279
Hanrahan, B. Kewpie Doll.
  J. Neville, 617(TLS):20Jan84-70
Hanse, J. Nouveau dictionnaire des diffi-
  cultés du français moderne.
  G. Straka, 553(RLiR):Jul-Dec83-469
Hansen, A., ed-in-chief. Holberg-ordbog.
  (Vol 1)
  B. Glienke, 562(Scan):May83-77
  C. Henriksen, 563(SS):Winter83-67
Hansen, B. and others. Barnets kulturhis-
  torie i norden.
  C. Daxelmüller, 196:Band24Heft1/2-146
Hansen, E. Skrift, stavning og retstav-
  ning.
  R. Baudusch, 682(ZPSK):Band36Heft3-354
Hansen, G.E., ed. Agricultural and Rural
  Development in Indonesia.
  F. Hüsken, 293(JASt):Nov82-221
Hansen, J. Nightwork.
  T.J. Binyon, 617(TLS):26Oct84-1225
  N. Callendar, 441:8Apr84-18
Hansen, K. and C. Maggs. Salik.
  P. Pénigault-Duhet, 189(EA):Oct-Dec84-
  483
Hansen, K.J. Mormonism and the American
  Experience.
  T. Sinclair-Faulkner, 106:Fall83-315
Hansen, R. The Assassination of Jesse
  James by the Coward Robert Ford.
  S. Altinel, 617(TLS):3Aug84-875
  D. Freeman, 441:5Feb84-18
  G. Garrett, 385(MQR):Fall84-606
Hansen, T.L. and E.J. Wilkins. Español a
  lo vivo. (5th ed)
  L.E. Haughton, 399(MLJ):Summer83-209
Hansen, W. - see Grimm, J. and W.
Hansen, W.F. Saxo Grammaticus and the
  Life of Hamlet.*
  E.S. de Angeli, 124:Sep-Oct83-50
Hansen-Löve, A.A. Der russische Formal-
  ismus.
  H-J. Lehnert, 654(WB):2/1983-378
Hanson, F.A. and L. Counterpoint in
  Maori Culture.
  P. Gathercole, 617(TLS):2Mar84-230
Hanson, J.K.M. The Civilian Population
  and the Warsaw Uprising of 1944.
  639(VQR):Summer83-82
Hanson, W.S. and G.S. Maxwell. Rome's
  Northwest Frontier.*
  T.H. Watkins, 124:Jul-Aug84-381
Hansson, C. and K. Liden. Moscow Women.*
  L. Chamberlain, 617(TLS):6Jul84-750
Hanzlicek, C.G. Calling the Dead.
  R. Lattimore, 249(HudR):Spring83-207
Hao, Q., Chen Heyi and Ru Suichu - see
  under Qian Hao, Chen Heyi and Ru Suichu
Hapgood, D. and D. Richardson. Monte
  Cassino.
  B. Mauldin, 441:25Mar84-7
Harari, J.V., ed. Textual Strategies.*
  J-P. Sueur, 447(N&Q):Dec82-560
Harari, J.V. and D.F. Bell - see Serres, M.
Haraszti-Takács, M. Spanish Genre Paint-
  ing in the Seventeenth Century.
  R.E. Spear, 617(TLS):23Mar84-318

159

Harbsmeier, C. Wilhelm von Humboldts
Brief an Abel Rémusat und die philos-
ophische Grammatik des Altchinesischen.
  G.F. Meier, 682(ZPSK):Band36Heft5-605
Härd, J.E. Studien zur Struktur mehrglied-
riger deutscher Nebensatzprädikate.*
  H. Graser, 72:Band219Heft2-409
Harden, D.B., with V.A. Tatton-Brown.
Catalogue of Greek and Roman Glass in
the British Museum.* (Vol 1)
  J. Price, 303(JoHS):Vol 103-224
Harden, E.F. The Emergence of Thackeray's
Serial Fiction.*
  T.J. Winnifrith, 402(MLR):Jan83-163
Harden, T. Untersuchungen zur r-Realisa-
tion im Ruhrgebiet.
  D. Karch, 133:Band16Heft2/3-223
Harder, H-B. and H. Rothe, eds. Goethe
und die Welt der Slawen.*
  G. Donchin, 402(MLR):Apr83-509
  P. Thiergen, 52:Band18Heft2-207
Harder, J. Klassenkampf und "linke"
Kunsttheorien.
  E. Kunz, 654(WB):2/1982-183
Hardie, F. and I. Herrman. Britain and
Zion.
  A.P. Thornton, 529(QQ):Summer83-590
Hardiman, D. Peasant Nationalists of
Gujarat.
  E.F. Irschick, 293(JASt):May83-700
Hardin, R. Collective Action.
  R.J. Arneson, 185:Jan84-336
Harding, B. American Literature in Con-
text. (Vol 2)
  L. Buell, 27(AL):May83-252
Harding, S.F. Remaking Ibieca.
  G.W. McDonogh, 441:21Oct84-31
Hardinge, G., ed. Winter's Crimes 15.
  T.J. Binyon, 617(TLS):16Mar84-270
Hardison, O.B., Jr. Entering the Maze.*
  J.S. Allen, 569(SR):Summer83-426
  G.M. Harper, 579(SAQ):Spring83-221
Hardman, J. The French Revolution.
  G. Lewis, 83:Spring83-113
Hardman, M.J., ed. The Aymara Language In
Its Social and Cultural Context.
  J. Verschueren, 350:Mar84-197
Hardt, H., E. Hilscher and W.B. Lerg, eds.
Presse im Exil.
  T.S. Hansen, 406:Winter83-455
Hardwick, C.S., with J. Cook - see Peirce,
C.S.
Hardwick, E. Bartleby in Manhattan and
Other Essays.*
  W. Lesser, 249(HudR):Winter83/84-737
Hardwick, M. The Private Life of Dr.
Watson.
  C. Ricks, 441:1Jan84-24
Hardy, B. Particularities.
  F. Bolton, 189(EA):Jul-Sep84-342
  D.P. Deneau, 268(IFR):Winter84-62
  G. Levine, 445(NCF):Jun83-112
Hardy, D. and C. Ward. Arcadia for All.
  A. Saint, 617(TLS):26Oct84-1218
Hardy, E. The Countryman's Ear and other
Essays on Thomas Hardy.*
  R.C. Schweik, 445(NCF):Jun83-117
Hardy, H. - see Berlin, I.
Hardy, J.C. A Catalogue of English Prose
Fiction Mainly of the Eighteenth Century
from a Private Library.
  T. Hofmann, 78(BC):Autumn83-356

Hardy, T. The Collected Letters of Thomas
Hardy. (Vol 1) (R.L. Purdy and M. Mill-
gate, eds)
  M. Jones, 344:Summer84-103
Hardy, T. The Collected Letters of Thomas
Hardy.* (Vol 2) (R.L. Purdy and M. Mill-
gate, eds)
  M. Jones, 344:Summer84-103
  M. Thorpe, 179(ES):Apr83-181
  M. Williams, 447(N&Q):Apr82-189
Hardy, T. The Collected Letters of Thomas
Hardy. (Vol 3) (R.L. Purdy and M. Mill-
gate, eds)
  P. Coustillas, 189(EA):Jul-Sep84-344
  M. Jones, 344:Summer84-103
  D. Kramer, 177(ELT):Vol26No3-200
  H. Orel, 395(MFS):Winter83-759
Hardy, T. The Collected Letters of Thomas
Hardy. (Vol 4) (R.L. Purdy and M. Mill-
gate, eds)
  J.I.M. Stewart, 617(TLS):23Mar84-294
Hardy, T. The Complete Poetical Works of
Thomas Hardy. (Vol 1) (S. Hynes, ed)
  M. Dodsworth, 175:Summer83-193
  M. Jones, 344:Summer84-103
Hardy, T. The Literary Notebooks of
Thomas Hardy. (L. Björk, ed)
  M. Jones, 344:Summer84-103
Hardy, T. The Oxford Authors: Thomas
Hardy. (S. Hynes, ed)
  W.W. Robson, 617(TLS):26Oct84-1221
Hardy, T. Tess of the d'Urbervilles. (J.
Grindle and S. Gatrell, eds)
  P. Coustillas, 189(EA):Oct-Dec84-472
  M. Dodsworth, 175:Summer83-194
  M. Jones, 344:Summer84-103
Hardy, T. The Woodlanders.* (D. Kramer,
ed)
  P. Coustillas, 189(EA):Oct-Dec84-472
  M. Jones, 344:Summer84-103
  D.J. Nordloh, 301(JEGP):Apr83-260
"Thomas Hardy Annual No. 1." (N. Page, ed)
  K. Brady, 150(DR):Summer83-364
Hare, A. George Frederick Cooke.*
  M. Jones, 447(N&Q):Dec82-558
  A. Toyne, 610:Spring82-143
Hare, A. The Years With Mother.
  T.G.D.F., 617(TLS):17Aug84-927
Hare, J.E. and C.B. Joynt. Ethics and
International Affairs.
  R.L.S., 185:Jul84-738
Hare, P. Aeroplanes in Childhood.
  J. Mole, 176:Dec84-62
  B. O'Donoghue, 617(TLS):14Dec84-1456
Hare, R.M. Moral Thinking.*
  I. Craemer-Ruegenberg, 687:Oct-Dec83-
643
  F. Feldman, 484(PPR):Sep83-131
  A.P. Griffiths, 483:Oct83-497
  J. Howes, 63:Sep83-333
  P. Millican, 479(PhQ):Apr83-207
Hare, R.M. Plato.*
  H. Ruttenberg, 185:Jul84-724
  483:Apr83-277
Hareide, J. Protest, desillusjonering,
resignasjon.
  I.N. Hennel, 172(Edda):1983/3-188
Harford, B. and S. Hopkins, eds. Greenham
Common.
  L. Heron, 362:28Jun84-26
Hargrove, R.J., Jr. General John Burgoyne.
  S.R. Frey, 656(WMQ):Oct83-640

Harington, J.   A Supplie or Addicion to
the Catalogue of Bishops to the Yeare
1608.* (R.H. Miller, ed)
   M-M. Martinet, 189(EA):Jan-Mar84-91
Harkabi, Y.   The Bar Kokhba Syndrome.
   A. Dowty, 617(TLS):27Jul84-836
   E. Lederhendler, 287:Nov83-23
Harlan, L.R. and R.W. Smock - see Washing-
ton, B.T.
Harlfinger, D., ed.   Griechische Kodi-
kologie und Textüberlieferung.*
   P.E. Easterling, 123:Vol33No1-112
Harlow, R.   Paul Nolan.
   R.D. Callahan, 648(WCR):Apr84-50
Harman, B.L.   Costly Monuments.*
   I. Bell, 401(MLQ):Mar83-95
   J.H. Ottenhoff, 568(SCN):Winter83-65
Harman, C. - see Warner, S.T.
Harman, P.M.   Metaphysics and Natural
Philosophy.
   H. Duncan, 486:Dec83-668
Harmetz, A.   The Making of the Wizard of
Oz.
   P. Dowell, 18:Jul-Aug84-56
Harmon, M., ed.   Irish Poetry After Yeats.
   V. Young, 472:Fall/Winter83Spring/
Summer84-323
Harmon, W.   One Long Poem.
   M.M. Clark, 577(SHR):Summer83-294
   W.H. Pritchard, 491:Jan84-228
   P. Stitt, 219(GaR):Summer83-428
Harms, W. and others, eds.   Illustrierte
Flugblätter des Barock.
   70:May-Jun83-165
Harms, W. and H. Reinitzer, eds.   Natura
loquax.*
   J. Knape, 52:Band18Heft1-93
Harms, W., with M. Schilling and A. Wang,
eds.   Deutsche illustrierte Flugblätter
des 16. und 17. Jahrhunderts.* (Vol 2)
   L.S. Thompson, 70:May-Jun83-155
Harner, J.L.   Samuel Daniel and Michael
Drayton.
   J. Robertson, 161(DUJ):Jun83-128
Harnett, B.   Law, Lawyers, and Laymen.
   N. Johnston, 441:2Sep84-15
Harnischfeger, E.   Mystik im Barock.
   P. Deghaye, 684(ZDA):Band112Heft1-58
Harper, F. and D.E. Presley.   Okefinokee
Album.*
   J.A. Burrison, 292(JAF):Oct-Dec83-494
Harper, H.   Between Language and Silence.
   M.M. Rowe, 395(MFS):Summer83-286
   639(VQR):Summer83-88
Harper, J.R.   Krieghoff.
   M.S. Young, 39:May83-414
Harper, M.S. - see Brown, S.A.
Harper, R.H.   Victorian Architectural Com-
petitions.
   A. Whittick, 324:Mar84-277
Harper, W.L., R. Stalnaker and G. Pearce,
eds.   Ifs, Conditionals, Belief, Deci-
sion, Chance and Time.*
   J. Dancy, 479(PhQ):Jan83-96
   D. Nute, 486:Sep83-518
Harrauer, H. and P.J. Sijpesteijn.   Mediz-
inische Rezepte und Verwandtes.
   W. Luppe, 123:Vol33No2-371
Harré, R.   Personal Being.
   A.C. Danto, 441:29Jul84-14
   R. Littlewood, 617(TLS):6Apr84-386

Harrell, J.   Origins and Early Traditions
of Storytelling.
   F. Mench, 124:Jan-Feb84-202
Harrer, H.   Return to Tibet.
   J.H. Crook, 617(TLS):22Jun84-692
Harries, K.   The Bavarian Rococo Church.*
   S. Laeuchli, 290(JAAC):Spring84-455
Harries, M. and S.   The War Artists.
   C. de Beaurepaire, 364:Feb84-110
   A. Brumer, 441:7Oct84-22
Harrigan, S.   Jacob's Well.
   R. Smith, 441:6May84-26
Harrington, M.   The New American Poverty.
   M. Sviridoff, 441:26Aug84-7
   T. Wicker, 61:Oct84-123
   442(NY):22Oct84-160
Harrington, M.   The Politics at God's
Funeral.*
   W.J. Dannhauser, 129:Mar84-77
Harrington, R.   The Inuit.
   D. Brydon, 102(CanL):Winter82-168
Harrington, T.M.   Pascal philosophe.
   L. Greene, 210(FrF):Sep83-274
   A.J. Krailsheimer, 208(FS):Apr83-215
Harris, A.   Night's Black Agents.*
   M.L. Williamson, 702: Vol 16-352
Harris, A.C.   Georgian Syntax.
   B.G. Hewitt, 361:Feb/Mar83-247
   D. Rayfield, 575(SEER):Oct83-597
Harris, D.A.   Inspirations Unbidden.*
   J. Bump, 401(MLQ):Mar83-102
Harris, E.   Velázquez.*
   J. López-Rey, 39:Aug83-192
   P. Troutman, 90:Mar83-166
Harris, F.J.   Encounters with Darkness.*
   C. Hall, 590:Jun84-75
   D. Stephens, 207(FR):May84-895
   639(VQR):Autumn83-115
Harris, H. - see Koestler, A. and C.
Harris, H.S.   Hegel's Development. (Vol 2)
   R. Scruton, 617(TLS):21Sep84-1059
Harris, J., ed.   Roothog.
   L.R. Ricou, 102(CanL):Summer83-118
Harris, J.   William Talman, Maverick Archi-
tect.
   G. Clarke, 324:Mar84-280
   J. Newman, 90:Oct83-627
Harris, J.   Violence and Responsibility.*
   M. Goldinger, 543:Jun83-932
Harris, J. and A. Lévêque.   Basic Conversa-
tional French. (7th ed)
   M. Donaldson-Evans, 399(MLJ):Autumn83-
286
Harris, J.W.   Syllable Structure and
Stress in Spanish.
   D.H., 355(LSoc):Sep83-421
   R. Núñez-Cedeño, 350:Dec84-933
Harris, L., ed.   Philosophy Born of Strug-
gle.
   R. Birt, 142:Fall-Winter82-373
Harris, L.L. - see "Nineteenth-Century
Literature Criticism"
Harris, M.   Lying in Bed.
   J. Charyn, 441:17Jun84-23
Harris, M.   Tenth.
   M. Steinberg, 441:18Mar84-26
Harris, M.R.   Index inverse du Petit
dictionnaire provençal-français.
   M. Pfister, 72:Band220Heft2-433
   N.B. Smith, 589:Jul83-753
Harris, R.   The Language Myth.
   A.V. Cicourel, 355(LSoc):Sep83-356

Harris, R. The Making of Neil Kinnock.
    B. Pimlott, 617(TLS):12Oct84-1165
Harris, R.B., ed. Neoplatonism and Indian
  Thought.
    R.T. Blackwood, 485(PE&W):Apr83-208
Harris, R.W. Clarendon and the English
  Revolution.
    B. Greenslade, 617(TLS):6Jan84-4
    J. Grigg, 362:19Jan84-24
Harris, S. Charles Kingsley. (M. Gaul,
  ed)
    M. Reboul, 189(EA):Jan-Mar83-90
Harris, S.K. Mark Twain's Escape from
  Time.
    B. Michelson, 27(AL):Oct83-466
    D.E.E. Sloane, 26(ALR):Autumn83-312
    J.S. Tuckey, 395(MFS):Summer83-331
Harris, T. From Mammies to Militants.*
    J. Sekora, 27(AL):Dec83-669
    C. Werner, 395(MFS):Winter83-749
Harris, W. Explorations.
    W.J. Howard, 49:Jan83-90
Harris, W.F. The Basic Patterns of Plot.
    H. Charney, 363(LitR):Winter84-279
Harris, W.V. The Omnipresent Debate.*
    E.R. August, 637(VS):Spring83-346
    R.H. Super, 405(MP):Nov83-205
Harris, Z. A Grammar of English on Mathe-
  matical Principles.
    W. Frawley, 350:Mar84-150
Harris-Warrick, R. - see M. de Saint
  Lambert
Harrison, A.T., ed. The Graham Mutiny
  Papers.*
    G.R.G. Hambly, 637(VS):Winter83-228
Harrison, B. Peaceable Kingdom.*
    639(VQR):Autumn83-122
Harrison, B. and B. Hutton. Vernacular
  Houses in North Yorkshire and Cleveland.
    J. Munby, 617(TLS):18May84-544
Harrison, B.G. Foreign Bodies.
    C. Sigal, 441:1Jul84-11
Harrison, F. The Power in the Land.
    S. Alderson, 324:Jan84-135
Harrison, F.F., ed. The Yellow Book.
    M-C. Hamard, 189(EA):Apr-Jun84-218
Harrison, H. How to Play the Flute.
    N. O'Loughlin, 415:Jun83-362
Harrison, H. West of Eden.
    C. Greenland, 617(TLS):7Dec84-1420
Harrison, J. Hume's Theory of Justice.*
    N.S. Arnold, 449:Mar83-139
    B. Harrison, 393(Mind):Oct83-604
    G.B. Herbert, 543:Jun83-932
    J.P. Wright, 518:Oct83-219
Harrison, J. Sundog.
    A.C. Greene, 441:15Jul84-14
Harrison, J. Warlock.
    T.M. Gilligan, 145(Crit):Spring84-147
Harrison, J.F.C. The Common People.
    P. Whitehead, 362:19Apr84-23
Harrison, K. Dead Ends.
    S. Ruddell, 102(CanL):Winter82-143
Harrison, M.J. The Ice Monkey.*
    J. Mellors, 362:2Feb84-28
Harrison, R. Bentham.
    J. Raz, 617(TLS):13Jan84-40
Harrison, R. Death of an Honourable Mem-
  ber.
    R. Hill, 617(TLS):26Oct84-1225
Harrison, R., ed. Rational Action.
    I.G. McFetridge, 393(Mind):Oct83-626

Harrison, R. Why Kill Arthur Potter?
    N. Callendar, 441:19Aug84-20
Harrison, R., M. Harrison and H. Cástulo
  García. Diccionario Zoque de Copainalá.
    R. Rhodes, 350:Jun84-467
Harrison, T. Continuous.* U.S. Martial.*
    R. Pybus, 565:Vol24No2-73
Harrison, W. and S. le Fleming, comps.
  Routledge Russian-English and English-
  Russian Pocket Dictionary.*
    F. Knowles, 402(MLR):Jul83-759
Harriss, W. The Bay Psalm Book Murder.
    M. Laski, 362:25Oct84-29
Harron, F., J. Burnside and T. Beauchamp.
  Biomedical-Ethical Issues. Health and
  Human Values. Human Values in Medicine
  and Health Care.
    S.G.P., 185:Apr84-573
Harrop, J. and S.R. Epstein. Acting with
  Style.
    R. Barton, 615(TJ):Mar83-138
Harsent, D. Mister Punch.
    R. Garfitt, 617(TLS):16Nov84-1318
Hart, B. Poisoned Ivy.
    E.B. Fiske, 441:16Dec84-27
Hart, F.R. and J.B. Pick. Neil M. Gunn.
    N. Mitchison, 588(SSL):Vol 18-257
Hart, H.L.A. Essays in Jurisprudence and
  Philosophy.
    A.J. Ayer, 362:5Jan84-23
    D. Lyons, 617(TLS):18May84-539
Hart, H.L.A. Essays on Bentham.*
    D.R. Knowles, 518:Oct83-220
    C. Silver, 185:Jan84-355
Hart, J. Herodotus and Greek History.
    S. West, 123:Vol33No1-132
Hart, J.D., ed. The Oxford Companion to
  American Literature. (5th ed)
    A. Kazin, 441:29Jan84-3
Hart, T.R. Gil Vicente: "Casandra" and
  "Don Duardos."
    N. Griffin, 402(MLR):Oct83-942
Hart-Davis, R. - see Lyttelton, G. and R.
  Hart-Davis
Hartcup, A. Love and Marriage in the
  Great Country House.
    I. Colegate, 617(TLS):30Nov84-1365
Hartcup, G. and T.E. Allibone. Cockcroft
  and the Atom.
    J. Calado, 617(TLS):3Aug84-867
Harter, H.A. Gertrudis Gómez de Avella-
  neda.*
    M. Hemingway, 86(BHS):Jul83-259
Hartig, M., ed. Angewandte Soziolinguis-
  tik.
    U.M. Quasthoff, 355(LSoc):Dec83-510
Hartig, M. Sozialer Wandel und Sprach-
  wandel.*
    J. Holm, 355(LSoc):Sep83-358
Hartley, R.A., ed. Keats, Shelley,
  Byron, Hunt, and their Circles.
    R.P. Lessenich, 72:Band220Heft1-172
Hartman, C.O. Free Verse.*
    W. Blissett, 529(QQ):Spring83-237
    H. Gross, 599:Winter83-75
    D. Wesling and E. Bollobás, 405(MP):
      Aug83-53
Hartman, G.H. Criticism in the Wilder-
  ness.*
    J.W. Davidson, 477(PLL):Winter83-93
    P.S. Hawkins, 577(SHR):Summer83-265
    J. van Luxemburg, 204(FdL):Dec82-292
    C. Uhlig, 490:Band14Heft1/2-178

Hauerwas, S. and A. MacIntyre, eds. Revisions.
R.M. McCleary, 185:Apr84-515
Haug, W., ed. Formen und Funktionen der Allegorie.*
H.A. Pausch, 107(CRCL):Sep83-456
Haugeland, J., ed. Mind Design.*
D. Barnouw, 561(SFS):Nov83-333
C. Mitchell, 529(QQ):Winter83-1061
Haugen, E. and K. Chapman. Spoken Norwegian. (3rd ed)
D. Buttry, 399(MLJ):Spring83-90
Haugen, E., J.D. McClure and D. Thomson, eds. Minority Languages Today.
W.W. Bostock, 67:May83-161
N.C. Dorian, 350:Mar84-165
J. Göschel, 685(ZDL):1/1983-81
Haugen, J. Diktersfinxen.*
I.M. Gabrieli, 563(SS):Spring83-195
A. Van Marken, 562(Scan):Nov83-220
Hauner, M. India in Axis Strategy.
L.A. Gordon, 293(JASt):Aug83-989
Haupt, G.E. - see More, T.
Haupt, H. - see Kindermann, B.
Hauptmann, G. Notiz-Kalender 1889 bis 1891. (M. Machatzke, ed)
P. Sprengel, 680(ZDP):Band102Heft2-309
Hauschild, B. Gesellingkeitsformen und Erzählstrukur.
P.K. Jansen, 221(GQ):May83-515
Hauser, A. The Sociology of Art.
P. Burke, 90:Nov83-707
P. Conrad, 31(ASch):Winter82/83-128
H. Lenneberg, 414(MusQ):Winter83-125
Häusle, H. Das Denkmal als Garant des Nachruhms.
N.M. Horsfall, 123:Vol33No1-154
J.A. North, 313:Vol73-169
Hausman, D.M. Capital, Profits, and Prices.*
L.A. Boland, 84:Dec83-387
E.J. Green, 311(JP):Dec83-825
I.M. Kirzner, 258:Jun83-220
Hausmann, F.J. Louis Meigret, humaniste et linguiste.*
A. Sancier-Chateau, 209(FM):Jul83-269
P. Wunderli, 553(RLiR):Jan-Jun83-216
de Hauteville, P. La Confession et Testament de l'amant trespassé de deuil. (R.M. Bidler, ed)
G. Roques, 553(RLiR):Jul-Dec83-501
Havard, W.C. and W. Sullivan, eds. A Band of Prophets.*
C. Bohner, 392:Fall83-603
J.M. Cox, 569(SR):Winter83-135
M. O'Brien, 579(SAQ):Summer83-333
M.R. Winchell, 585(SoQ):Spring83-79
Havelock, E.A. The Literate Revolution in Greece and its Cultural Consequences.*
L. Edmunds, 478:Oct83-271
R.L. Enos, 480(P&R):Vol 16No4-265
Havely, N.R. - see Boccaccio, G.
Havens, T.R.H. Artist and Patron in Postwar Japan.*
E.J. Gangloff, 407(MN):Autumn83-351
L.E. Scanlon, 293(JASt):Aug83-958
Tōno Yoshiaki, 285(JapQ):Jul-Sep83-318
Haverkamp, A. Theorie der Metapher.
G. Kleiber, 553(RLiR):Jul-Dec83-427
Haverkamp, W. Aspekte der Modernität.
R. Grimm, 133:Band16Heft2/3-260

Haviaras, S. The Heroic Age.
M. Thiébaux, 441:10Jun84-14
442(NY):13Aug84-92
Haw, J. and others. Stormy Patriot.
J.H. Broussard, 656(WMQ):Jan83-162
Hawes, L. Presences of Nature.*
J.R. Watson, 83:Autumn83-211
Hawkes, J. Humors of Blood and Skin.
A.C. Danto, 441:25Nov84-3
Hawkes, N. Early Scientific Instruments.
G. Wills, 39:Feb83-147
Hawkins, E. Modern Language in the Curriculum.
D.L. Lange, 399(MLJ):Summer83-174
Hawkins, G.S. Mindsteps to the Cosmos.
P. Zaleski, 469:Vol9No1-82
Hawkins, P.S. The Language of Grace.
R. Rhodes, 344:Spring84-129
Hawley, J.S. Krishan, the Butter Thief.
H.D. Smith, 469:Vol9No1-106
Hawley, J.S., with S. Goswani. At Play with Krishna.
A. Entwistle, 293(JASt):Feb83-434
F. Richmond, 130:Spring83-87
Haworth, L. Decadence and Objectivity.
C.G. Normore, 154:Dec83-743
Haworth-Booth, M., ed. The Golden Age of British Photography.
442(NY):26Nov84-152
Hawthorn, J. - see Conrad, J.
Hawthorne, N. Tales and Sketches. (R.H. Pearce, ed)
W.H. Pritchard, 249(HudR):Summer83-352
Hay, E.K. T.S. Eliot's Negative Way.
P. Gray, 617(TLS):27Jan84-90
295(JML):Nov83-466
Hay, J.M. and W.D. Howells. John Hay — Howells Letters. (G. Monteiro and B. Murphy, eds)
L. Willson, 569(SR):Summer83-490
Hay, M. and P. Roberts. Bond.
G. Bas, 189(EA):Apr-Sep83-341
A.P. Hinchliffe, 148:Spring83-82
Hayashima, K. and others, eds. Tibetan Tripiṭaka, Sde dge edition, Bstan ḫgyur.* (Vols 15-17)
J.W. de Jong, 259(IIJ):Mar83-154
Hayden, D. The Grand Domestic Revolution.*
A.C. Fellman, 106:Fall83-297
D. Gorham, 529(QQ):Spring83-273
Hayden, D. Redesigning the American Dream.
A.R. Hochschild, 441:25Mar84-13
Hayden, G.A. Crime and Punishment in Medieval Chinese Drama.
R.J. Lynn, 318(JAOS):Jan-Mar82-139
Hayden, T. The Sunflower Forest.
M. L'Engle, 441:25Nov84-16
Hayek, F.A. Law, Legislation and Liberty.* (French title: Droit, législation et liberté.) (Vol 2)
A. Reix, 542:Jul-Sep83-340
Hayer, G., ed. Die deutschen Handschriften des Mittelalters der Erzabtei St. Peter zu Salzburg.
G.F. Jones, 221(GQ):May83-495
Hayes, A.W. Roberto Arlt.
J.M. Flint, 86(BHS):Oct83-351
Hayes, J. The Landscape Paintings of Thomas Gainsborough.*
M. Butlin, 90:Apr83-232
Hayes, J.H. and J.M. Miller, eds. Israelite and Judaean History.
M.C. Astour, 318(JAOS):Jan-Mar82-192

Hayford, H., H. Parker and G.T. Tanselle -
see Melville, H.
Hayim, G.J. The Existential Sociology of
Jean-Paul Sartre.
W.D., 543:Sep82-167
Hayman, J. - see Ruskin, J.
Hayman, R. Brecht.*
J. Fenton, 453(NYRB):15Mar84-25
M. Hulse, 176:Mar84-36
Hayman, R. K.
C.A.M. Noble, 529(QQ):Summer83-509
Hayman, R. Kafka.*
E. Glass, 590:Jun84-78
R.E. Helbling, 651(WHR):Summer83-169
C. Koelb, 680(ZDP):Band102Heft4-628
P.W. Nutting, 221(GQ):Jan83-168
H. Salinger, 579(SAQ):Spring83-227
L. Williams, 396(ModA):Summer/Fall83-
353
Hayman, R. Nietzsche.*
S. Debevec-Henning, 125:Fall82-103
A.P. Fell, 529(QQ):Spring83-203
M.P., 543:Sep82-163
Haymann, E. Le Camp du Bout du Monde.
M. Gilbert, 617(TLS):7Dec84-1426
Haymon, S.T. Ritual Murder.*
639(VQR):Summer83-93
Haymon, S.T. Stately Homicide.
M. Laski, 362:25Oct84-29
Hayne, P.H. A Man of Letters in the
Nineteenth-Century South. (R.S. Moore,
ed)
N. Polk, 27(AL):Oct83-467
T.D. Young, 392:Winter82/83-77
Haynes, D. Greek Art and the Idea of Free-
dom.*
R. Ling, 303(JoHS):Vol 103-224
Haynes, J. Thanks for Coming!
S. French, 617(TLS):6Apr84-367
C. Sigal, 362:16Feb84-22
Haynes, J.E. Dubious Alliance.
H. Klehr, 129:Dec84-72
R. Radosh, 441:23Sep84-29
Haynes, R.D. H.G. Wells.*
J.R. Reed, 125:Fall82-93
T.A. Shippey, 541(RES):Feb83-94
Hayward, J. and others. Radiance and
Reflection.
J. Oliver, 589:Oct83-1120
Hayward, M. Writers in Russia: 1917-1978.*
(P. Blake, ed)
D.M. Thomas, 176:Mar84-44
Hazard, J.N. Managing Change in the USSR.
A. Brown, 617(TLS):13Jan84-32
Hazlehurst, F.H. Gardens of Illusion.*
C. Thacker, 90:Jul83-430
Hazlitt, W. Liber Amoris.
P.C., 189(EA):Jul-Sep84-364
Headington, C. Britten.
J.B., 412:May82-152
Headington, C. The Listener's Guide to
Chamber Music.
P. Standford, 415:Jun83-359
Headrick, D.R. The Tools of Empire.*
D. Kennedy, 637(VS):Autumn82-90
Heald, T. Class Distinctions.
P. Smelt, 617(TLS):9Nov84-1288
Healey, R., ed. Reduction, Time and
Reality.*
P. Enfield, 486:Mar83-168
Healy, D. Banished Misfortune.*
P. Lewis, 565:Vol24No1-58

Healy, D.D. America's Vice-Presidents.
M.F. Nolan, 441:1Jul84-21
Healy, J.F. Blunt Darts.
N. Callendar, 441:18Nov84-36
Heaney, S. Preoccupations.* Poems: 1965-
1975.*
A. Shapiro, 472:Fall/Winter83Spring/
Summer84-336
Heaney, S. Station Island.
D. May, 362:20/27Dec84-53
B. Morrison, 617(TLS):19Oct84-1191
Heaney, S. Sweeney Astray.
B. Kennelly, 441:27May84-14
D. May, 362:20/27Dec84-53
B. Morrison, 617(TLS):19Oct84-1191
Heaney, S. and T. Hughes, eds. The Rattle
Bag.
N. Rhodes, 493:Mar83-73
Heaps, L. Thirty Years with the KGB.
I. Elliot, 617(TLS):26Oct84-1207
Hearn, M.P. - see Twain, M.
Hearnden, A. Red Robert.
D. Pryce-Jones, 617(TLS):3Feb84-108
Hearon, S. Group Therapy.
V. Miner, 441:18Mar84-18
Heath, C. Behaving Badly.
P. Craig, 617(TLS):20Apr84-422
Heath, J. The Picturesque Prison.*
P. Hinchcliffe, 627(UTQ):Summer83-445
B. Stovel, 49:Jul83-60
B. Stovel, 529(QQ):Winter83-1188
Heath, R.A.K. Kwaku.
C.R. Larson, 441:15Jan84-11
Heath, R.A.K. Orealla.
P. Binding, 362:2Aug84-27
T. Sutcliffe, 617(TLS):27Jul84-847
Heath, S. The Sexual Fix.*
A. Ross, 153:Winter83-2
Heath-Stubbs, J. Naming the Beasts.*
J. Saunders, 565:Vol24No4-71
Hebblethwaite, M. Motherhood and God.
J. Hughes, 176:Nov84-54
H. Oppenheimer, 617(TLS):31Aug84-973
Hebblethwaite, P. John XXIII.
S. Runciman, 617(TLS):?8Dec84-1510
Hebden, M. Pel and the Pirates.
M. Laski, 362:25Oct84-29
Hebden, M. Pel and the Predators.
M. Laski, 362:12Apr84-27
Hebden, M. Pel and the Staghound.
N. Callendar, 441:9Sep84-40
Hebel, J.P. Der Rheinländische Haus-
freund.* (L. Rohner, ed)
E.F. Hoffmann, 221(GQ):Jan83-142
Hébert, A. Les fous de Bassan.*
L. Cossé, 450(NRF):Feb83-130
L. Séjor, 98:Mar83-242
Hébert, A. Héloïse.*
G. Merler, 648(WCR):Jun83-60
Hébert, A. In the Shadow of the Wind.
P. Binding, 362:2Aug84-27
C.D.B. Bryan, 441:22Jul84-7
P. Smart, 99:Mar84-37
Hébert, C. Le Burlesque au Québec.
C.F. Coates, 207(FR):Oct83-99
Hebert, E. Whisper My Name.
T. Le Clair, 441:16Dec84-15
Hébert, M., ed. Ainsi disent-elles.
N. Aronson, 207(FR):Feb84-426
Hecht, A. and J. Hollander, eds. Jiggery-
Pokery.
J. Gross, 441:29Jan84-8

Hecht, H. Cuisine for All Seasons.
  W. and C. Cowen, 639(VQR):Autumn83-138
Hecht, J. Beam Weapons.
  M.R. Gordon, 441:16Sep84-22
Hecker, H. Die deutsche Sprachlandschaft
  in den Kantonen Malmedy und St. Vith.
  P. Wiesinger, 685(ZDL):1/1983-91
Hedges, I. Languages of Revolt.*
  295(JML):Nov83-371
Hedin, M. Fly Away Home.
  G. Garrett, 569(SR):Winter83-112
Hedin, T. The Sculpture of Gaspard and
  Balthazard Marsy.
  F. Haskell, 617(TLS):29Jun84-724
Hedlund, T. Dikten som liv.
  K. Petherick, 563(SS):Spring83-188
Hedrick, H.L. Theo van Doesburg.
  R. Padovan, 46:Feb83-70
Hedrick, J.D. Solitary Comrade.*
  G. Beauchamp, 26(ALR):Spring83-138
  C. Johnston, 649(WAL):May83-77
  R.C. Leitz, 27(AL):Mar83-108
  D. Pizer, 301(JEGP):Apr83-272
Heelan, P.A. Space Perception and the
  Philosophy of Science.
  J.L. Ward, 290(JAAC):Summer84-459
von Hees-Landwehr, C. Griechische Meister-
  werke in römischen Abgüssen.
  R. Ling, 313:Vol73-232
Heffernan, T. The Liam Poems.
  B. Quinn, 577(SHR):Summer83-297
Heffernan, T.F. Stove by a Whale.*
  R. Milder, 183(ESQ):Vol129No2-99
Hefti, P., ed. Codex Dresden M68.*
  A. Robertshaw, 402(MLR):Oct83-965
Hegel, G.W.F. Les écrits de Hamann. (J.
  Colette, ed and trans)
  H. Faes, 542:Jan-Mar83-133
Hegel, G.W.F. Gesammelte Werke. (Vol 4
  ed by H. Buchner and O. Pöggeler; Vol 6
  ed by K. Düsing and H. Kimmerle; Vols 7
  and 8 ed by R-P. Horstmann and J.H.
  Trede)
  G. Krämling, 489(PJGG):Band90Heft2-
  394
Hegel, G.W.F. La philosophie de l'Esprit
  de la Realphilosophie, 1805. (G. Planty-
  Bonjour, trans)
  A. Reix, 542:Jan-Mar83-135
Hegel, R.E. The Novel in Seventeenth-
  Century China.*
  D. Roy, 116:Jan82-120
Heggie, D.C. Megalithic Science.
  J.A.S. Evans, 529(QQ):Spring83-57
Hegyi, O. Cinco leyendas y otros relatos
  moriscos.*
  C. López-Morillas, 240(HR):Autumn83-
  458
  R. Penny, 86(BHS):Apr83-139
Heiberg, J.L. Kjøbenhavns flyvende Post,
  1827-29, 1830.
  P. Vinten-Johansen, 563(SS):Autumn83-
  384
Heid, M., ed. New Yorker Werkstattge-
  spräch 1981.
  R.W. Walker, 399(MLJ):Autumn83-275
Heidegger, M. Gesamtausgabe. (Vols 54
  and 55)
  J-L. Chrétien, 98:Apr83-327
Heidegger, M. Interprétation phénoménol-
  ogique de la "Critique de la raison pure"
  de Kant. (E. Martineau, trans)
  V. Descombes, 98:Mar83-261

Heidegger, M. Nietzsche. (Vol 4) (D.
  Krell, ed)
  M.G., 185:Oct83-172
  R. Nicholls, 529(QQ):Winter83-1204
Heidenreich, R. and H., eds. Daniel
  Defoe.
  P-G.B., 189(EA):Jul-Sep84-362
Heidish, M. Miracles.
  M. Simpson, 441:17Jun84-20
Heidolph, K.E., W. Flämig and W. Motsch,
  eds. Grundzüge einer deutschen Gramma-
  tik.*
  E.H. Antonsen, 301(JEGP):Oct83-586
Heier, E. Ludwig Heinrich von Nicolay
  (1737-1820) as an Exponent of Neo-
  Classicism.
  W. Paulsen, 564:Sep83-218
Heikal, M. Autumn of Fury.*
  B. Lewis, 453(NYRB):31May84-21
Heilbron, J.L. Elements of Early Modern
  Physics.
  E.M. Melhado, 173(ECS):Winter83/84-196
Heilbut, A. Exiled in Paradise.*
  M. Ophuls, 18:Dec83-60
Heilman, W. Ethische Reflexion und
  römische Lebenswirklichkeit in Ciceros
  Schrift De officiis.
  J-P. Richard, 555:Vol57fasc2-335
Heimerdinger, J.W. Sumerian Literary Frag-
  ments from Nippur.
  W. Heimpel, 318(JAOS):Oct-Dec82-660
Hein, R. The Harmony Within.
  R. McGillis, 571(ScLJ):Autumn83-21
Heine, B. The Nubi Language of Kibera.
  J. Heath, 350:Dec84-991
Heine, B. The Waata Dialect of Oromo.
  Boni Dialects.
  D. Biber, 350:Dec84-992
Heine, H. The Complete Poems of Heinrich
  Heine.* (H. Draper, trans)
  G. Annan, 453(NYRB):16Feb84-11
  H. Hatfield, 591(SIR):Winter83-647
  T. Ziolkowski, 249(HudR):Spring83-217
Heine, H. Werke. (S. Atkins, ed)
  R.C. Holub, 221(GQ):Nov83-660
Heinemann, M. Puritanism and Theatre.*
  B.S. Hammond, 610:Autumn83-253
  G.B. Shand, 301(JEGP):Jul83-443
Heinhold-Krahmer, S. and others, eds.
  Probleme der Textdatierung in der Hethi-
  tologie.
  H.C. Melchert, 318(JAOS):Jan-Mar82-176
Heinlein, R.A. Job.
  G. Jonas, 441:11Nov84-22
Heinrich, B. In a Patch of Fireweed.
  P-L. Adams, 61:May84-122
  B. Lopez, 441:22Apr84-16
Heinrichs, J. Reflexionstheoretische
  Semiotik. (Pt 1)
  L.L. Duroche, 221(GQ):Nov83-625
Heinz, R. Psychoanalyse und Kantianismus.
  H. Drüe, 342:Band74Heft1-94
Heinzle, J., ed. Heldenbuch.
  E.R. Haymes, 406:Winter83-439
Heinzmann, G. Schematisierte Strukturen.
  Y. Gauthier, 154:Jun83-368
Heiter, H. Vom friedlichen Weg zum Sozial-
  ismus zur Diktatur des Proletariats.
  M. McCauley, 575(SEER):Oct83-636
Heitmann, A. Noras Schwestern.
  Å.H. Lervik, 172(Edda):1983/4-253

Henderson, A.G. - see Congreve, W.
Henderson, B., with others, eds. The Push-
cart Prize, IX.
    B. Weber, 441:25Nov84-33
Henderson, D.C. and G.R. Perez, comps and
trans. Literature and Politics.
    S. Lipp, 263(RIB):Vol33No3-405
Henderson, G.E. and M.S. Cohen. The Chi-
nese Hospital.
    M. Goldman, 441:7Oct84-20
Henderson, H. The Politics of the Solar
Age.
    M. Bradfield, 529(QQ):Summer83-538
Henderson, J., ed. Aristophanes: Essays
in Interpretation.*
    I.C. Storey, 123:Vol33No2-177
    R.G. Ussher, 303(JoHS):Vol 103-168
Henderson, P.V.N. Félix Díaz, the Porfir-
ians, and the Mexican Revolution.
    J. Fisher, 86(BHS):Jan83-92
Henderson, W.M. Stark Raving Elvis.
    N. Giovanni, 441:9Dec84-26
Hendry, J., ed. Cambridge Physics in the
Thirties.
    J. Calado, 617(TLS):2Nov84-1244
Hendry, J. The Creation of Quantum
Mechanics and the Bohr-Pauli Dialogue.
    J. Calado, 617(TLS):2Nov84-1244
Hendry, J. Marriage in Changing Japan.
    T.S. Lebra, 293(JASt):Feb83-412
Hendry, J.F. The Sacred Threshold.*
    G. Annan, 453(NYRB):27Sep84-17
    E. Heller, 441:7Oct84-24
    M. Hulse, 176:Mar84-36
Henege, T. Skim.
    L.S. Ritter, 441:15Apr84-22
Henig, M., ed. A Handbook of Roman Art.
    R. Higgins, 39:Dec83-527
    D.L. Thompson, 124:Nov-Dec83-137
Henig, R.M. The Myth of Senility.
    E. Beck, 529(QQ):Autumn83-850
Henke, D. Gott and Grammatik.
    R. Margreiter, 489(PJGG):Band90Heft2-
    418
Henke, S. and E. Unkeless, eds. Women in
Joyce.
    J.E. Dunleavy, 301(JEGP):Oct83-573
    R.M. Kain, 395(MFS):Summer83-278
    M. Power, 329(JJQ):Fall83-85
    M.J. Sidnell, 529(QQ):Autumn83-921
    J. Willet-Shoptaw, 594:Summer83-162
    295(JML):Nov83-510
Henkle, R.B. Comedy and Culture: England
1820-1900.*
    J. Bayley, 541(RES):May83-234
    S.M. Smith, 677(YES):Vol 13-332
Henn, F.A. and H.A. Nasrallan, eds. Schiz-
ophrenia as a Brain Disease.
    M.V. Seeman, 529(QQ):Winter83-1211
Henne, H. Sprachpragmatik.
    M. Hartig, 685(ZDL):2/1983-229
Hennebo, D., ed. Geschichte des Stadt-
grüns. (Vols 1-5)
    U. Hassler, 43:Band13Heft2-202
Hennenberg, F. - see Brecht, B.
Hennesey, J. American Catholics.
    J.B. McGloin, 377:Mar83-54
Hennessy, M. The Bright Blue Sky.
    639(VQR):Summer83-92
Hennessy, M. The Crimson Wind.
    S. Altinel, 617(TLS):7Dec84-1420
Hennig, B. "Maere" und "werc."
    D.H. Green, 382(MAE):1983/1-176

Henning, B.D., ed. The House of Commons
1660-1690.
    G. Holmes, 617(TLS):6Jan84-3
Henreid, P., with J. Fast. Ladies Man.
    W. Murray, 441:11Mar84-16
Henri, A. Penny Arcade.
    T. Dooley, 617(TLS):13Apr84-413
Henriksson, A. The Tsar's Loyal Germans.
    J.A. Armstrong, 104(CASS):Winter83-561
    N. Naimark, 550(RusR):Oct83-454
Henriot, J. Champagne Charlie.
    J-M. Guieu, 207(FR):Mar84-589
Henry, A. "Amers" de Saint-John Perse —
une poésie du mouvement.
    A. Berrie, 402(MLR):Jul83-722
Henry, E.P. Chinese Amusement.*
    D.R. Johnson, 293(JASt):Feb83-380
Henry, F. Victims and Neighbors.
    S. Lietzmann, 441:28Oct84-38
Henry, M. Marx.
    U. Santamaria, 488:Dec83-501
Henry, M. - see Vinaver, M.
Henry, M. and R. De Sourdis. The Films
of Alan Ladd.
    J. Beaver, 200:May83-314
Henry, P. A Hamlet of his Time.
    H. Pitcher, 617(TLS):25May84-568
Henry, P. and H-R. Schwyzer - see Plotinus
Henryson, R. The Poems of Robert Henry-
son.* (D. Fox, ed)
    L. Ebin, 588(SSL):Vol 18-301
    D. Mehl, 72:Band220Heft1-154
    D. Murison, 447(N&Q):Apr82-160
Henslee, H. Pretty Redwing.*
    L. Franks, 461:Fall/Winter83/84-91
    42(AR):Spring83-249
Henson, L. In a Dark Mist.
    G.S.S. Chandra, 436(NewL):Summer84-114
Henson, R. Transports and Disgraces.*
    G. Garrett, 569(SR):Winter83-112
Heny, F., ed. Ambiguities in Intensional
Contexts.
    T. Schiebe, 603:Vol7No1-119
Heny, F., ed. Binding and Filtering.*
    R.D. Borsley, 297(JL):Mar83-285
    E. Woolford, 474(PIL):Vol 15No1/4-325
Henze, H.W. Music and Politics.
    S. Hinton, 410(M&L):Jul/Oct83-287
    N. Osborne, 607:Jun83-41
Henze, P.B. The Plot to Kill the Pope.*
    E.J. Epstein, 441:15Jan84-6
    R. Kaplan, 129:Apr84-79
Hepburn, J., ed. Arnold Bennett: The
Critical Heritage.*
    C.P. Havely, 541(RES):Aug83-358
Hepokoski, J.A. Giuseppe Verdi: "Fal-
staff."
    R. Osborne, 617(TLS):10Feb84-133
Hepp, N. and J. Hennequin, eds. Les
Valeurs chez les Mémorialistes français
du XVIIe siècle avant la Fronde.*
    L.K. Horowitz, 546(RR):Jan83-84
Heppenheimer, T.A. The Man-Made Sun.
    R. Bailey, 441:1Apr84-23
Heptner, A.M. and S. Sternburg. Vista His-
panica.
    J.N. Harris, 399(MLJ):Summer83-207
Heptner, A.M. and S.G. Sternburg. Multi-
vista Cultural.
    W. Jassey, 399(MLJ):Spring83-96
Hepworth, M. and B.S. Turner. Confession.
    R.M.M., 185:Jan84-376

Heraclitus. The Art and Thought of Hera-
clitus. (C.H. Kahn, ed and trans)
   C. Emlyn-Jones, 303(JoHS):Vol 103-161
   G.B. Kerferd, 53(AGP):Band65Heft2-187
Herald, J. Renaissance Dress in Italy
1400-1500.*
   J.G. Bernasconi, 278(IS):Vol38-99
   S. Blum, 551(RenQ):Autumn83-418
   J. Harris, 59:Mar83-110
   90:May83-307
"Herbarium Apulei (1481) e Herbolario Vol-
gare (1522)."
   H.W. Peterson, 70:Nov/Dec81-60
Herbermann, C-P. Wort, Basis, Lexem und
die Grenze zwischen Lexikon und Gram-
matik.
   J. Splett, 680(ZDP):Band102Heft3-471
Herbert, F. Heretics of Dune.
   G. Jonas, 441:10Jun84-24
Herbert, G. The Country Parson; The
Temple. (J.N. Wall, Jr., ed)
   W.H. Halewood, 539:Feb84-67
Herbert, I., with C. Baxter and R.E. Fin-
ley - see "Who's Who in the Theatre"
Herbert, J. Approaching Snow.
   A. Stevenson, 617(TLS):2Mar84-226
Herbert, J. L'hindouisme vivant.
   A. Reix, 542:Jul-Sep83-377
Herbert, T.W., Jr. Marquesan Encounters.*
   R. Milder, 183(ESQ):Vol29No2-99
Herbst, J. From Crisis to Crisis.
   J.F. Roche, 656(WMQ):Jul83-492
Herbst, T., D. Heath and H-M. Dedering.
Grimm's Grandchildren.*
   J. Udolph, 260(IF):Band88-342
Herdeg, K. The Decorated Diagram.*
   R. Harbison, 617(TLS):13Apr84-409
Hereth, M. and J. Höffken, eds. Alexis de
Tocqueville — zur Politik in der Demo-
kratie.
   R.L., 185:Oct83-173
Heri Akhmadi. Breaking the Chains of
Oppression of the Indonesian People.
   D.S. Lev, 293(JASt):May83-720
Hering, C. Die Rekonstruktion der Revolu-
tion.
   J. Roberts, 617(TLS):27Jul84-851
Heringer, H.J., B. Strecker and R. Wimmer.
Syntax.*
   F. Hundsnurscher, 685(ZDL):2/1983-230
Héritier, F. L'exercice de la parenté.
   L. Scubla, 98:Oct83-796
Herles, W., ed. "Garel von dem blûnden
tal" von dem Pleier.
   P. Kern, 684(ZDA):Band112Heft3-128
Hermand, J. Orte.
   B. Bennett, 221(GQ):Jan83-106
Hermann, J.P. and J.J. Burke, Jr., eds.
Signs and Symbols in Chaucer's Poetry.
   C. Clark, 179(ES):Dec83-570
   D.C. Fowler, 405(MP):May84-407
   G. Olson, 589:Jan83-263
Hermann, L. L'Utopien et le Lanternois.
   J. Voisine, 549(RLC):Jan-Mar83-113
Hermann, P., ed. Tituli Asiae Minoris.
(Vol 5, fasc 1)
   C. Foss, 24:Summer83-210
Hermansen, G. Ostia.
   G.E. Rickman, 123:Vol33No1-151
Hermes, H., F. Kambartel and F. Kaulbach -
see Frege, G.
"The Hermitage: Western European Drawings."
   K. Andrews, 39:Oct83-355

Hermsdorf, K., H. Fetting and S. Schlen-
stedt. Exil in den Niederlanden und in
Spanien.
   G. Müller-Waldeck, 654(WB):12/1982-183
Hernadi, P., ed. The Horizon of Litera-
ture.*
   W. Bache, 395(MFS):Summer83-356
   M. Steinmann, Jr., 290(JAAC):Spring84-
   347
Hernández, B.G. - see under García Her-
nández, B.
Hernández, J.A. and E. Guillermo - see
Matute, A.M.
Hernández, J.L.A. and others - see under
Alonso Hernández, J.L. and others
Hernández, M. - see Lorca, F.G.
Herndon, M. Native American Music.
   B. Toelken, 292(JAF):Apr-Jun83-242
Herr, L.G. The Scripts of Ancient North-
west Semitic Seals.
   V. Sasson, 318(JAOS):Jan-Mar82-185
Herr, S.S. Rights and Advocacy for Re-
tarded People.
   J.M.G., 185:Jul84-742
Herren, M.W., ed and trans. The Hesperica
Famina. (Vol 1: The A-Text)
   P.A. Breatnach, 112:Vol 15-158
Herren, M.W., ed. Insular Latin Studies.
   J.F. Kelly, 377:Mar83-45
Herrera, H. Frida.*
   M. Kimmelman, 55:May83-27
   42(AR):Summer83-374
Herrera-Sobek, M. The Bracero Experience.
   D. Sheehy, 187:May84-351
Herrera Zapién, T. - see Ovid
Herrick, W. ...Kill Memory...
   A. Cheuse, 441:8Jan84-24
Herrmann-Schneider, H. Status und Funk-
tion des Hofkapellmeisters in Wien
(1848-1918).
   P. Banks, 410(M&L):Jan/Apr83-83
Hersh, S.M. The Price of Power.* (Brit-
ish title: Kissinger: The Price of
Power.)
   P. Roazen, 99:Dec83-30
Herslund, M., O. Mørdrup and F. Sørensen,
eds. Analyses grammaticales du fran-
çais.
   C. Wimmer, 553(RLiR):Jul-Dec83-423
Hertel, H. and S.M. Kristensen, eds. The
Activist Critic.*
   E.M. Christensen, 562(Scan):May83-82
Herting, H. Geschichte für die Gegenwart.
   J. Rosellini, 406:Fall83-320
Hertz, J.S. and R.K. Martin, eds. E.M.
Forster.
   J.W. Weaver, 177(ELT):Vol26No1-62
Hervey, E. The Governess.
   T.J. Binyon, 617(TLS):18May84-557
Hervey, S. Semiotic Perspectives.*
   J-C. Choul, 350:Dec84-1000
   B. Malmberg, 596(SL):Vol137No2-193
Herz, J.S. and R.K. Martin, eds. E.M.
Forster.*
   J.H. Stape, 627(UTQ):Summer83-441
Herzel, R.W. The Original Casting of
Molière's Plays.
   J. Lough, 610:Spring83-65
Herzfeld, M. Ours Once More.
   K. Boklund-Lagopoulou, 567:Vol145No3/4-
   345
   A. Caraveli, 292(JAF):Oct-Dec83-476
                        [continued]

Herzfeld, M. Ours Once More. [continuing]
  J. Du Boulay, 617(TLS):23Mar84-295
  P. Mackridge, 575(SEER):Oct83-622
Herzinger, K.A. D.H. Lawrence in his Time:
  1908-1915.*
  K. Cushman, 651(WHR):Winter83-361
  D.R. Schwarz, 395(MFS):Winter83-782
von Herzmanovsky-Orlando, F. Sämtliche
  Werke in zehn Bänden. (Vols 1 and 2)
  S.S. Prawer, 617(TLS):20Jul84-816
Herzog, C. The Arab-Israeli Wars.
  D. Stone, 287:Nov83-27
Herzog, M. Annapurna.
  D. Roberts, 135:Oct83-143
Heschel, A.J. Maimonides.
  A.J. Bingham, 577(SHR):Spring83-183
Hesiod. The Poems of Hesiod. (R.M.
  Frazer, trans)
  W. Donlan, 124:Jul-Aug84-387
Hess, A.C. The Forgotten Frontier.
  R.W. Bulliet, 318(JAOS):Jan-Mar82-223
Hess, K., ed. Martha Washington's Booke
  of Cookery.*
  P. Buitenhuis, 106:Winter83-475
Hess, S. Ramón Menéndez Pidal.*
  J.E. Keller, 86(BHS):Jul83-255
Hess, W. Das Problem der Farbe in Selbst-
  zeugnissen der Maler.
  H. Matile, 471:Jan/Feb/Mar83-88
Hess-Lüttich, E.W.B., ed. Literatur und
  Konversation.
  S. Jansen, 462(OL):Vol37No3-281
Hesse, M. Revolutions and Reconstructions
  in the Philosophy of Science.*
  R. Bunn, 486:Dec83-657
Hession, C.H. John Maynard Keynes.
  N. Annan, 453(NYRB):19Jul84-35
  T.W. Hutchison, 617(TLS):14Dec84-1438
  P. Stanksy, 441:20May84-7
Hester, M.T. Kinde Pitty and Brave Scorn.*
  D. Novarr, 551(RenQ):Winter83-667
Heth, C., ed. Selected Reports in Ethno-
  musicology. (Vol 3, No 2)
  L.J. Goodman, 292(JAF):Apr-Jun83-214
Hetherington, M.S. The Beginnings of Old
  English Lexicography.*
  F.C. Robinson, 589:Oct83-1121
  E.G. Stanley, 447(N&Q):Jun82-238
Hetman, F., ed and trans. Märchen aus
  Wales.
  K.H. Schmidt, 196:Band24Heft1/2-149
Heubeck, A. Schrift.
  C.J. Ruijgh, 394:Vol36fasc1/2-162
Heubeck, A., S. West and G.A. Privitera -
  see Homer
Heubner, H. P. Cornelius Tacitus, "Die
  Historien." (Kommentar, Vol 5)
  R.H. Martin, 123:Vol133No2-218
Heukenkamp, U. Die Sprache der schönen
  Natur.
  P.D. Sweet, 221(GQ):Nov83-709
de Heusch, L. The Drunken King.
  R. Farron, 69:Vol53No4-102
de Heusch, L. Rois nés d'un coeur de
  vache.*
  H. Cronel, 450(NRF):Jan83-127
de Heusch, L. Why Marry Her?
  R. Fardon, 69:Vol53No1-81
Heussler, R. British Rule in Malaya.
  J.N. Parmer, 293(JASt):May83-721
Hewett, C.A. English Historic Carpentry.
  R. Brunskill, 44:Vol26-105

Hewins, A., ed. The Dillen.
  L.D., 617(TLS):16Nov84-1323
  D. Gittins, 637(VS):Summer83-431
Hewison, R., ed. New Approaches to Rus-
  kin.*
  E.K. Helsinger, 405(MP):May84-432
  P. Morgan, 179(ES):Jun83-284
  H.W., 636(VP):Summer83-198
Hewitt, D. and M. Spiller, eds. Litera-
  ture of the North.
  D. Buchan, 571(ScLJ):Winter83-44
Hewitt, G. Ytek and the Arctic Orchid.
  J.K. Kealy, 102(CanL):Winter82-160
Hewitt, J. The Selected John Hewitt. (A.
  Warner, ed)
  T. Eagleton, 565:Vol124No1-69
Hewitt, K. and L. Roomet. Educational
  Toys in America: 1800 to the Present.
  K. Calvert, 658:Spring83-110
Hewryk, T.D. The Lost Architecture of
  Kiev.
  D. Buxton, 46:Aug83-74
Hewson, J. Beothuk Vocabularies.*
  P. Proulx, 269(IJAL):Apr83-217
Hexelschneider, E. and W.I. Borstschukow.
  Sowjetliteratur in bürgerlicher Sicht.
  R. Göbner, 654(WB):8/1982-175
Heyck, T.W. The Transformation of Intel-
  lectual Life in Victorian England.
  F.M. Turner, 637(VS):Summer83-465
Heyd, D. Supererogation.
  J. Dancy, 479(PhQ):Oct83-405
  N.J.H. Dent, 518:Apr83-65
  N.F., 185:Oct83-158
Heydenreich, L.H., B. Dibner and L. Reti.
  Leonardo the Inventor.
  C. Gould, 39:Feb83-145
Heyen, W. Lord Dragonfly.
  B. Costello, 491:May83-106
Heyer, P. Nature, Human Nature, and
  Society.
  O.J.F., 185:Jan84-370
Heym, S. The Wandering Jew.
  D.J. Enright, 453(NYRB):26Apr84-45
  E. Pawel, 441:26Feb84-14
Heyworth, P. Otto Klemperer. (Vol 1)
  P. Carnegy, 617(TLS):6Apr84-376
  442(NY):22Oct84-162
Heyworth, P.L., ed. Medieval Studies for
  J.A.W. Bennett aetatis suae LXX.*
  E.G. Stanley, 402(MLR):Oct83-894
Hibbard, G.R. The Making of Shakespeare's
  Dramatic Poetry.*
  R. Berry, 529(QQ):Summer83-372
  H.S. Weil, Jr., 178:Dec83-502
Hibbard, H. Caravaggio.*
  L. Gowing, 617(TLS):23Mar84-313
Hibben, C.C. Gouda in Revolt.
  H.H. Rowen, 617(TLS):9Nov84-1293
Hibberd, D., ed. Poetry of the First
  World War.
  G. David, 189(EA):Jan-Mar84-100
  D. Hewitt, 447(N&Q):Aug82-371
Hibbert, C. The Days of the French Revolu-
  tion.
  A.J. Bingham, 399(MLJ):Summer83-193
  J.A. Settanni, 396(ModA):Summer/Fall83-
  373
Hibbert, C. The Personal History of
  Samuel Johnson.
  A.S.B., 617(TLS):17Aug84-927

Hickey, G.C. Sons of the Mountains. Free
in the Forest.
N.D. Volk, 293(JASt):Aug83-1015
Hickl-Szabo, H. Portrait Miniatures in
the Royal Ontario Museum.
B. Scott, 39:Feb83-152
Hickman, H. Robert Musil and the Culture
of Vienna.
E. Timms, 617(TLS):5Oct84-1120
Hicks, B.E. Plots and Characters in
Classic French Fiction.
H. Peyre, 207(FR):Oct83-103
Hieronymus, F. Basler Buchillustration
1500-1545.
617(TLS):8Jun84-647
Higgins, A. Bornholm Night-Ferry.*
C. de Beaurepaire, 364:Aug/Sep83-140
Higgins, D.S. Rider Haggard.
N. Etherington, 637(VS):Summer83-463
Higgins, G.V. A Choice of Enemies.
P-L. Adams, 61:Feb84-104
P. Andrews, 441:12Feb84-18
Higgins, G.V. The Rat on Fire.
W. Domnarski, 639(VQR):Summer83-523
Higgins, G.V. Style Versus Substance.
E. Diamond, 441:11Nov84-33
Higgins, I., ed. Anthology of Second
World War French Poetry.
K. Aspley, 402(MLR):Oct83-934
M. Davies, 208(FS):Oct83-491
Higgins, J., ed. Glyndebourne.
H. Cole, 362:31May84-26
Higgins, J. The Poet in Peru.
P.W. Borgeson, Jr., 238:Sep83-447
R.K. Britton, 402(MLR):Oct83-954
W.W. Rowe, 86(BHS):Apr83-163
Higgins, R. Greek and Roman Jewellery.*
(2nd ed)
G. Wills, 39:Feb83-147
Higgins, S. The Benn Inheritance.
D. Steel, 362:11Oct84-25
Higgins, W.R., ed. The Revolutionary War
in the South.
B. Tucker, 106:Spring83-49
Higgs, R.J. Laurel and Thorn.*
A. Guttmann, 587(SAF):Autumn83-263
G. Haslam, 649(WAL):May83-63
Higgs, T.V., ed. Curriculum, Competence,
and the Foreign Language Teacher.
M.S. Finch, 399(MLJ):Spring83-68
Higham, C. Audrey.
S. Gold, 441:4Nov84-13
Higham, C. Sisters.
F. Hirsch, 441:1Jul84-13
Highet, G. Classical Papers. (R.J. Ball,
ed)
P. Howell, 617(TLS):6Jul84-751
Highfield, A. and A. Valdman, eds. Histor-
icity and Variation in Creole Studies.*
A. Hull, 35(AS):Spring83-49
Highfield, A.R. The French Dialect of St.
Thomas, U.S. Virgin Islands.
R.A. Hall, Jr., 205(ForL):Aug81-88
Highfill, P.H., Jr., ed. Shakespeare's
Craft.
M.C. Bradbrook, 570(SQ):Winter83-491
R.W. Dent, 551(RenQ):Autumn83-469
Highfill, P.H., Jr., K.A. Burnim and E.A.
Langhans. A Biographical Dictionary of
Actors, Actresses, Musicians, Dancers,
Managers, and other Stage Personnel in
London, 1660-1800.* (Vols 7 and 8)
R. Fiske, 410(M&L):Jan/Mar83-104

Highwater, J. Arts of the Indian Americas.
P-L. Adams, 61:Feb84-103
M.J. Lenz, 469:Vol9No2-120
Higonnet, P. Class, Ideology and the
Rights of Nobles during the French
Revolution.
J. Popkin, 173(ECS):Spring84-358
Hikmet, N. Human Landscapes.
639(VQR):Autumn83-133
Hildebidle, J. Thoreau.
R. De Bacco, 590:Dec83-102
W. Howarth, 432(NEQ):Dec83-593
Hildebrand, J. and C. Theuerkauff, eds.
Die Brandenburgishe-Preussische Kunst-
kammer.*
I.K. Rogoff, 59:Jun83-250
Hildebrandt, F., O.A. Beckerlegge and J.
Dale - see Wesley, J.
Hildebrandt, H-H. Becketts Proust-Bilder.
G.R. Kaiser, 52:Band17Heft2-220
Hildesheimer, W. Mozart.*
J.D. Durant, 577(SHR):Summer83-299
J.D. McClatchy, 676(YR):Autumn83-115
S. Sadie, 415:Oct83-616
M. Solomon, 414(MusQ):Spring83-270
Hilen, A. - see Longfellow, H.W.
Hilg, H. Das "Marienleben" des Heinrich
von St. Gallen.
J.W. Marchand, 301(JEGP):Oct83-594
Hilgartner, S., R.C. Bell and R. O'Connor.
Nukespeak.*
E. Battistella, 350:Dec84-1005
Hill, A.G. - see Wordsworth, W. and D.
Hill, B.S. Incunabula, Hebraica and
Judaica.
M. Schmelzer, 517(PBSA):Vol77No3-386
Hill, C. The Experience of Defeat.
H. Horwitz, 441:18Nov84-46
J.G.A. Pocock, 617(TLS):28Dec84-1494
Hill, C., with B. Reay and W. Lamont. The
World of the Muggletonians.*
R.T. Fallon, 391:Oct83-97
Hill, D. A History of Engineering in Clas-
sical and Medieval Times.
L. White, Jr., 617(TLS):2Nov84-1247
Hill, D. - see Spenser, E.
Hill, G. The Lords of Limit.
A. Burgess, 617(TLS):4May84-487
E. Griffiths, 176:Jul/Aug84-59
Hill, G. The Mystery of the Charity of
Charles Péguy.*
D. Dunn, 364:Aug/Sep83-109
D. Gervais, 97(CQ):Vol 12No2/3-201
D. McDuff, 565:Vol124No4-62
S. Medcalf, 617(TLS):27Jan84-76
P. Robinson, 175:Autumn83-262
M. Warner, 493:Sep83-64
Hill, G. - see Ibsen, H.
Hill, I. - see Antoine de la Sale
Hill, J. Rita Hayworth.*
G. Kaufman, 362:19Apr84-26
Hill, J. The Letters and Papers of Sir
John Hill (1714-1775).* (G.S. Rousseau,
ed)
B. Boyce, 579(SAQ):Summer83-343
W.P. Jones, 173(ECS):Winter83/84-195
R.G. Peterson, 405(MP):Nov83-203
P. Rogers, 83:Autumn83-217
S. Soupel, 189(EA):Oct-Dec83-472
Hill, J.E. and J.D. Smith. Bats.
S. Mills, 617(TLS):9Nov84-1296
Hill, J.S., ed. Keats: Narrative Poems.
J. Bayley, 617(TLS):2Mar84-207

Hill, N.K. A Reformer's Art.*
R.L. Caserio, 445(NCF):Dec83-337
D. David, 637(VS):Autumn82-93
Hill, P. Children of Lucifer.
S. Altinel, 617(TLS):7Dec84-1420
Hill, P. Dry Grain Farming Families.
B. Harriss, 69:Vol53No1-84
Hill, R. A Clubbable Woman.
442(NY):24Dec84-90
Hill, R. Deadheads.
P-L. Adams, 61:Jun84-124
T.J. Binyon, 617(TLS):30Mar84-354
N. Callendar, 441:24Jun84-41
Hill, R.A., ed. The Marcus Garvey and
Universal Negro Improvement Association
Papers.
E. Foner, 441:5Feb84-1
Hill, R.M. and E.C. In the Wake of War.
G.B. Pickett, Jr., 9(AlaR):Jan83-61
Hill, S. Saying Hello at the Station.
N. Corcoran, 617(TLS):7Sep84-1004
J. Mole, 176:Dec84-60
Hill, S. The Woman in Black.*
P. Craig, 617(TLS):28Dec84-1506
Hillenaar, H. Roland Barthes.
F. de Haan, 204(FdL):Dec83-313
Hiller, R.L. and J.C. Osborne - see von
Grimmelshausen, H.J.C.
Hilles, R. Look the Lovely Animal
Speaks.*
R. Hatch, 102(CanL):Winter82-144
Hilles, R. The Surprise Element.*
A. Knight, 137:Sep83-7
Hillesum, E. An Interrupted Life. (Brit-
ish title: Etty.)
N. Ascherson, 453(NYRB):19Jul84-9
C. Bermant, 617(TLS):17Feb84-156
T. Des Pres, 441:29Jan84-1
Hillgarth, J.N. The Spanish Kingdoms,
1250-1516. (Vol 2)
G. McKendrick, 161(DUJ):Dec82-94
Hillgruber, A. Germany and the Two World
Wars.
R.F. Hopwood, 529(QQ):Summer83-587
Hilliard, N. Art of Limning. (A.F. Kin-
ney and L.B. Salamon, eds)
P-L. Adams, 61:Jan84-100
442(NY):2Jan84-90
Hilliard, N. The Arte of Limning.*
(R.K.R. Thornton and T.G.S. Cain, eds)
T.W. Craik, 161(DUJ):Dec82-89
Hillman, J. Le polythéisme de l'âme.
M. Adam, 542:Jul-Sep83-378
Hills, D. The Rock of the Wind.
R. Fuller, 364:Mar84-110
D.A.N. Jones, 362:12Jul84-27
Hilman, E., ed. Ernst Krenek Katalog zur
Ausstellung der Wiener Stadt- und Landes-
bibliothek, May/Jun 1982.
M. Carner, 415:Jul83-427
Hiltbrunner, O. Bibliographie zur latein-
ischen Wortforschung. (Vol 1)
P.G.W. Glare, 123:Vol33No2-343
Hilton, J. Georg Büchner.*
D.G. Richards, 397(MD):Sep83-391
L. Sharpe, 610:Autumn83-260
Hilton, J.B. Corridors of Guilt.
T.J. Binyon, 617(TLS):30Mar84-354
N. Callendar, 441:15Apr84-26
Hilton, S.E. Hitler's Secret War in
South America.
U-K. Ketelsen, 221(GQ):Jan83-188
Hilton, S.L. - see Abbad y Lasierra, I.

Hilton, W. Dance of Court and Theater.
W. Burdick, 615(TJ):Oct82-411
Hilvert, J. Blue Pencil Warriors.
M. Davie, 617(TLS):10Aug84-898
Hily-Mane, G. Le Style de Ernest Heming-
way.
K.Z. Derounian, 234:Spring84-53
V. Meyers, 395(MFS):Winter83-731
Himmelfarb, G. The Idea of Poverty.
N. Annan, 453(NYRB):1Mar84-12
M. Cranston, 129:Mar84-70
J. Grigg, 362:5Jul84-26
H. Perkin, 617(TLS):25May84-569
G.J. Stigler, 441:1Jan84-6
442(NY):6Feb84-126
Himmelmann, N. Über Hirten-Genre in der
antiken Kunst.
A. Geyer, 52:Band17Heft3-302
Hinck, W., ed. Rolf Hochhuth — Eingriff
in die Zeitgeschichte.
G.B. Mathieu, 221(GQ):Nov83-704
Hindelang, G. Auffordern.
K. Madsen, 361:Jun/Jul83-215
Hinderer, W., ed. Goethes Dramen.*
C. Brodsky, 221(GQ):Mar83-316
Hinderer, W., ed. Kleists Dramen.*
J.M. Ellis, 301(JEGP):Apr83-289
M. Hoppe, 221(GQ):May83-510
Hinderer, W., ed. Schillers Dramen.
G. Marahrens, 564:Feb83-63
Hinderer, W. Über deutsche Literatur und
Rede.
H.M.K. Riley, 406:Winter83-429
Hinderer, W. - see von Kleist, H.
Hindle, B. Emulation and Invention.
T.M. Doerflinger, 656(WMQ):Apr83-302
R.I. Goler, 658:Spring83-96
Hindley, A. and B.J. Levy. The Old French
Epic.
G. Roques, 553(RLiR):Jul-Dec83-498
Hindman, S., ed. The Early Illustrated
Book.
H-J. Wertheimer, 70:Mar-Apr83-126
Hinds, J. Ellipsis in Japanese.
K. Matsumoto, 350:Sep84-679
Hines, J. Great Singers on Great Singing.*
E. Forbes, 415:Aug83-486
Hines, T.S. Richard Neutra and the Search
for Modern Architecture.
R. Banham, 576:May83-194
D. Gebhard, 617(TLS):4May84-485
R.G. Wilson, 505:Jun83-125
Hingley, R. Nightingale Fever.*
J. Graffy, 402(MLR):Oct83-1003
H. McLean, 550(RusR):Apr83-227
G.S. Smith, 575(SEER):Apr83-274
Hinkemeyer, M.T. A Time to Reap.
N. Callendar, 441:30Sep84-22
Hinkle, R.C. Founding Theory of American
Sociology.
H.N. Tuttle, 543:Jun83-934
Hinks, P. Twentieth Century British Jewel-
lery 1900-1980.
C. Gere, 617(TLS):6Jan84-23
T. Hughes, 324:Nov84-818
Hinks, R. The Gymnasium of the Mind. (J.
Goldsmith, ed)
S. Spender, 617(TLS):29Jun84-715
Hinman, P.G. Recursion-Theoretic Hier-
archies.
W. Richter, 316:Jun83-497
Hinnant, C.H. Thomas Hobbes.
C. Cantalupo, 568(SCN):Winter83-76

172

Hino, S. Sureśvara's "Vartika on Yājña-valkya-Maitreyī Dialogue."
A. Wayman, 485(PE&W):Jan83-95
Hinojosa, R. Mi querido Rafa.
H.L. Johnson, 238:Mar83-147
Hinrichsen, D. The Attraction of Heavenly Bodies.
P. Mesic, 491:Feb84-304
Hinrup, H.J. An Index to "Chinese Literature" 1951-1976.
T.C. Wong, 318(JAOS):Jan-Mar82-150
Hinske, N., ed. Ich handle mit Vernunft...
G. Gawlick, 489(PJGG):Band90Heft1-206
Hinske, N. Kant als Herausforderung an die Gegenwart.
M. Forschner, 687:Jan-Mar83-150
A. von Schoenborn, 543:Dec82-453
Hinsley, F.H., with others. British Intelligence in the Second World War. (Vol 3, Pt 1)
D. Hunt, 362:3May84-24
J. Keegan, 617(TLS):12Oct84-1163
Hinson, D.A. Quilts for Babies and Children.
P. Grappe, 614:Winter84-21
Hinson, D.A. The Sunbonnet Family of Quilt Patterns.
P. Grappe, 614:Winter84-23
von Hinten, W., ed. Der Franckforter (Theologia Deutsch).
H. Bluhm, 589:Oct83-1139
Hinterhäuser, H. Fin de Siècle. (Spanish title: Fin de siglo.)
J-L. Marfany, 86(BHS):Jan83-74
M.M. Sinka, 221(GQ):Mar83-294
Hinterhäuser, H., ed. Jahrhundertende — Jahrhundertwende II.
L. Marx, 563(SS):Spring83-199
Hinton, W. Shenfan.*
D. Pollard, 176:Apr84-53
Hinz, E.J., ed. Beyond Nationalism.
J. Kertzer, 627(UTQ):Summer83-486
Hinze, C. and U. Diederichs, eds. Fränkische Sagen.
L. Petzoldt, 196:Band24Heft1/2-150
Hippocrates. Ippocrate, "Epidemie," libro sesto. (D. Manetti and A. Roselli, eds and trans)
V. Nutton, 123:Vol33No2-187
Hirdina, K. Pathos der Sachlichkeit.
B. Flierl, 654(WB):4/1983-738
Hirsch, E. The Concept of Identity.
R.M. Gale, 311(JP):Apr83-247
R.G. Swinburne, 518:Jan83-54
Hirsch, F. For the Sleepwalkers.*
W. Harmon, 569(SR):Summer83-457
R. Tillinghast, 385(MQR):Fall84-596
Hirsch, E.D., Jr. The Aims of Interpretation.
M.J. Valdés, 107(CRCL):Sep83-389
Hirsch, F. Love, Sex, Death and the Meaning of Life.
S. Feldman, 106:Fall83-353
Hirsch, F. A Method to Their Madness.
M.W. Mason, 441:4Nov84-31
Hirschen, J., ed. Art in the Ancient World.*
H. Plommer, 123:Vol33No1-148
Hirschhorn, J. and others. Rating the Movie Stars.
T. Wiener, 18:Mar84-58

Hirschhorn, L. Beyond Mechanization.
R. Wright, 441:21Oct84-51
Hirschman, A.O. Shifting Involvements.*
D. Usher, 529(QQ):Winter83-1157
Hirschmann, E. "White Mutiny."
A.J. Greenberger, 293(JASt):Nov82-183
Hirsh, A. The French New Left.
C.J. Stivale, 207(FR):Oct83-121
Hirsh, J.E. The Structure of Shakespearean Scenes.*
M. Grivelet, 189(EA):Apr-Jun84-186
H. Levin, 570(SQ):Winter83-486
C.B. Lower, 702:Vol 16-359
M. Rose, 301(JEGP):Apr83-230
Hirsh, S.L. Ferdinand Hodler.*
J.B. Smith, 39:Feb83-144
Hirshaut, J. Jewish Martyrs of Pawiak.
D. Abramowicz, 390:May83-79
Hirshey, G. Nowhere to Run.
R. Williams, 617(TLS):7Dec84-1419
Hirshfield, J. Alaya.
G. Johnson, 461:Spring/Summer83-96
Hirst, D. The Gun and the Olive Branch.
W.V. O'Brien, 617(TLS):27Jul84-837
Hirst, M. Sebastiano del Piombo.*
I. Cheney, 551(RenQ):Summer83-243
Hirst, W.Z. John Keats.
H. de Almeida, 661(WC):Summer83-172
C.W. Miller, 134(CP):Fall83-84
R.A. Sharp, 340(KSJ):Vol32-223
Hirtle, W.H. Number and Inner Space.
G. Bourcier, 189(EA):Apr-Jun84-178
Hiskes, R.P. Community without Coercion.*
T.R. Machan, 518:Jul83-190
Hissette, R. Enquête sur les 219 articles condamnés à Paris le 7 Mars 1277.
A. Zimmermann, 53(AGP):Band65Heft1-91
"Histoire littéraire de la France." (Vol 41)
R.E. Lerner, 589:Apr83-476
"De historia e historiadores."
D. Bushnell, 263(RIB):Vol33No4-596
"Historia von D. Johann Fausten, dem weitbeschreyten Zauberer und Schwartzkünstler."
H. Henning, 196:Band24Heft1-151
"Historizität und gesellschaftliche Bedingtheit der Sprache."
C.V.J. Russ, 685(ZDL):3/1983-375
"The History of Printing from its Beginning to 1930."
M.A. McCorison, 517(PBSA):Vol77No1-93
Hitchcock, H-R. German Renaissance Architecture.*
T.D. Kaufmann, 576:Mar83-76
C.F. Otto, 551(RenQ):Summer83-253
Hitchcock, H.W. Marc-Antoine Charpentier.
A.V. Jones, 410(M&L):Jul/Oct83-241
J.A. Sadie, 415:Sep83-550
Hitchens, C. Cyprus.
S.F. Larrabee, 441:11Nov84-20
C.M. Woodhouse, 617(TLS):13Jul84-777
Hitzler, E. Sel- Untersuchungen zur Geschichte des isländischen Sennwesens seit der Landnahmezeit.*
S. Oakley, 562(Scan):May82-93
Hlynsky, D. Salvage.
L. Daniel, 102(CanL):Spring83-113
Hoagland, E. The Tugman's Passage.*
639(VQR):Winter83-28

173

Hoare, R.C. The Journeys of Sir Richard
Colt Hoare through Wales and England
1793-1810. (M.W. Thompson, ed)
K.O. Morgan, 617(TLS):22Jun84-701
Hobart, M.E. Science and Religion in the
Thought of Nicolas Malebranche.*
J.W. Yolton, 518:Apr83-77
Hobbes, T. Computatio sive Logica: De
Corpore, Part I.* (I.C. Hungerland and
G.R. Vick, eds)
W. von Leyden, 84:Mar83-72
Hobbes, T. De Cive. (H. Warrender, ed)
J. Dunn, 362:30Aug84-24
B. Worden, 617(TLS):6Jul84-746
Hobbes, T. De cive ou les fondements de
la politique. (R. Polin, ed) Le cito-
yen ou les fondements de la politique.
(S. Goyard-Fabre, ed)
J. Bernhardi, 542:Jan-Mar83-115
Hobbs, R., with others. Robert Smithson:
Sculpture.
D. Craven, 59:Dec83-488
Hoberman, G. The Art of Coins and their
Photography.
W. Gardner, 324:Feb84-211
Hobhouse, H. Prince Albert.*
D. Cannadine, 453(NYRB):8Nov84-22
J. Grigg, 176:Jun84-64
T. Russell-Cobb, 324:Feb84-212
Hobhouse, J. Dancing in the Dark.*
L. Chernaik, 364:Jul83-102
Hobsbaum, P. A Reader's Guide to D.H.
Lawrence.
D.R. Schwarz, 395(MFS):Summer83-288
Hobsbawm, E. and T. Ranger, eds. The In-
vention of Tradition.*
P.N. Furbank, 362:1Mar84-23
Hobson, A. John William Waterhouse.
C. Wood, 637(VS):Winter83-243
Hobson, F. Tell About the South.
R.L. Phillips, Jr., 578:Fall84-112
442(NY):26Mar84-135
Hobson, F. - see Johnson, G.W.
Hobson, H. Theatre in Britain.
M. Billington, 362:13Sep84-26
A. Marshall, 617(TLS):7Dec84-1418
Hobson, M. The Object of Art.*
V. Mylne, 402(MLR):Oct83-921
P. Roger, 208(FS):Apr83-223
B. Scott, 39:Jan83-69
C. Sherman, 207(FR):Apr84-715
Hoccleve, T. Selections from Hoccleve.*
(M.C. Seymour, ed)
J. Mitchell, 589:Apr83-477
Hochman, B. The Test of Character.*
J.V. Knapp, 395(MFS):Winter83-772
Hocking, M. Good Daughters.
A. Duchêne, 617(TLS):14Sep84-1020
K.C. O'Brien, 362:16Aug84-26
Hockney, D. and L. Weschler. Cameraworks.
A. Grundberg, 441:2Dec84-17
Hocquard, M. Les verbes d'état en -ē- du
latin.
P. Flobert, 555:Vol57fasc2-326
Hodcroft, F.W. and others, eds. Mediaeval
and Renaissance Studies on Spain and
Portugal in Honour of P.E. Russell.
P.N. Dunn, 86(BHS):Jan83-60
C.F. Fraker, 345(KRQ):Vol30No3-331
F. Pierce, 402(MLR):Jul83-728
Hodder, I., ed. Symbolic and Structural
Archaeology.
J-C. Gardin, 567:Vol145No3/4-339

Hodder, I. Symbols in Action.*
J-C. Gardin, 567:Vol145No3/4-339
Hodge, J.A. The Private World of Georg-
ette Heyer.
G. Avery, 617(TLS):21Sep84-1064
Hodges, A. Alan Turing.*
S. Toulmin, 453(NYRB):19Jan84-3
Hodges, C.W., S. Schoenbaum and L. Leone,
eds. The Third Globe.
R.K. Sarlós, 610:Summer83-160
Hodges, R. and D. Whitehouse. Mohammed,
Charlemagne and the Origins of Europe.
K.J. Leyser, 617(TLS):6Jul84-758
R.J. Rowland, Jr., 124:Jul-Aug84-377
Hodges, T. Western Sahara.
F. Ghiles, 617(TLS):20Jul84-809
A. Horne, 453(NYRB):6Dec84-37
J.S. Whitaker, 441:2Sep84-15
Hodges, W.A. Free Man of Color. (W.B.
Gatewood, ed)
639(VQR):Spring83-51
Hodgins, J. The Barclay Family Theatre.*
J. Harcourt, 529(QQ):Spring83-244
D.L. Jeffrey, 168(ECW):Summer83-80
Hodgkin, T. Vietnam.
A. Woodside, 293(JASt):Nov82-223
Hodgson, G. Lloyd's of London.
R. Cornwell, 362:28Jun84-25
J. Eidus, 441:4Nov84-25
B. Supple, 617(TLS):6Jul84-745
Hodgson, J.A. Wordsworth's Philosophical
Poetry, 1797-1814.*
J. Arac, 591(SIR):Spring83-136
L. Newlyn, 447(N&Q):Aug82-362
R. Sharrock, 191(ELN):Jun84-76
Hodne, B. Eventyret og tradisjonsbaererne.
R. Bjersby, 64(Arv):Vol137-179
Hodne, Ø. Jørgen Moe og folkeeventyrene.
R. Bjersby, 64(Arv):Vol137-179
Hodnett, E. Image and Text.
C. Fox, 59:Sep83-373
Hodson, J.D. The Ethics of Legal Coercion.
G.D., 185:Jul84-728
van Hoecke, W. and A. Welkenhuysen, eds.
Love and Marriage in the Twelfth Cen-
tury.
P. Dinzelbacher, 684(ZDA):Band112Heft3-
111
Høedt, J. and R. Turner, eds. The World
of LSP. New Bearings in LSP.
J. Palmer, 355(LSoc):Mar83-122
Hoek, L.H. La marque du titre.
I. Tamba-Mecz, 567:Vol144No3/4-383
Hoekstra, T., H. van der Hulst and M.
Moortgat, eds. Perspectives on Func-
tional Grammar.
J. Heath, 355(LSoc):Mar83-111
R. Hudson, 596(SL):Vol137No1-89
Hoenigswald, H.M., ed. The European Back-
ground of American Linguistics.*
J. Leopold, 545(RPh):Aug82-58
Hoepfner, I., ed. Märchen aus Persien.
U. Marzolph, 196:Band24Heft1/2-151
Hoey, A. Hymns to a Tree.
E.C. Lynskey, 50(ArQ):Winter83-421
Hoffer, P.C. and N.E.H. Hull. Impeachment
in America, 1635-1805.
G. Marshall, 617(TLS):19Oct84-1176
Hoffman, A. White Horses.
D. Durrant, 364:Aug/Sep83-133
Hoffman, D. Brotherly Love.*
G. Johnson, 461:Spring/Summer83-96
D. Kirby, 502(PrS):Summer83-94

Holden, A.J. - see Hue de Rotelande
Holden, F.M. Lambshead before Interwoven.
  L. Clayton, 649(WAL):May83-75
  L. Milazzo, 584(SWR):Winter83-v
Holden, J. The Rhetoric of the Contemporary Lyric.*
  A. Dunn, 191(ELN):Dec83-66
Holden, U. Eric's Choice.
  L. Taylor, 617(TLS):12Oct84-1168
Holden, U. Wider Pools.*
  D. Durrant, 364:Jul83-91
Hölderlin, F. Hymns and Fragments. (R. Sieburth, trans)
  W.S. Merwin, 441:30Dec84-12
Holderness, G. D.H. Lawrence.*
  J. Gomez, 141:Winter83-79
  D.R. Schwarz, 395(MFS):Summer83-288
  295(JML):Nov83-520
Holdheim, W.W. Die Suche nach dem Epos.*
  V. Nemoianu, 107(CRCL):Mar83-111
Holdsworth, C.A. Modern Minstrelsy.
  K. Eller, 552(REH):May83-289
Holisky, D.A. Aspect and Georgian Medial Verbs.
  B.G. Hewitt, 361:Aug83-363
Holkeboer, K.S. Patterns for Theatrical Costumes.
  R.L. Shep, 614:Fall84-22
Holland, C. The Belt of Gold.
  S. Altinel, 617(TLS):3Aug84-875
  C. Seebohm, 441:8Jul84-20
  442(NY):20Aug84-92
Holland, I. A Death at St. Anselm's.
  N. Callendar, 441:11Mar84-21
Holland, N.N. Laughing.*
  S.I. Bellman, 584(SWR):Summer83-286
Holland, P. Living in France Today.
  P. Lennon, 362:19Jan84-24
Holland, P. - see Wycherley, W.
Holland, R.F. Against Empiricism.*
  K. Strike, 482(PhR):Apr83-307
Holland, W.E. Let a Soldier Die.
  W. Ferguson, 441:28Oct84-26
Hollander, J. The Figure of Echo.*
  E. Cook, 627(UTQ):Spring83-312
  K. Horowitz, 184(EIC):Jul83-246
  J. Humphries, 153:Summer83-29
  D. Krause, 568(SCN):Spring/Summer83-1
  J. Parisi, 405(MP):Aug83-100
Hollander, J. Powers of Thirteen.
  M. Garcia-Simms, 584(SWR):Autumn83-400
  J. Mole, 176:Jun84-55
Hollander, J. Rhyme's Reason.*
  W. Blissett, 529(QQ):Spring83-237
  H. Suhamy, 189(EA):Jan-Mar84-83
Hollander, P. Political Pilgrims.*
  T.J. Jamieson, 396(ModA):Spring83-207
  J. Sleeper, 560:Spring-Summer82-195
  M. Stanton, 575(SEER):Jul83-458
Hollander, R. Studies in Dante.*
  J.J. Guzzardo, 589:Jan83-180
Holledge, J. Innocent Flowers.*
  C. Barker, 611(TN):Vol37No1-44
Hollenbach, D. Nuclear Ethics.
  R.H., 185:Jul84-739
Holley, H.L. A History of Medicine in Alabama.
  J. Duffy, 9(AlaR):Apr83-143
Hollier, D. Politique de la prose.
  T. Cordellier, 450(NRF):Mar83-126
  A. Lavers, 617(TLS):11May84-511
  J-F. Lyotard, 98:Mar83-177

Hollingsworth, J., ed. Hollingsworth.
  J.H. Bonner, 585(SoQ):Winter83-84
Hollington, M., with L. Wilkinson - see Milton, J.
Hollinrake, R. Nietzsche, Wagner, and the Philosophy of Pessimism.*
  412:Aug-Nov82-270
Hollis, C.C. Language and Style in "Leaves of Grass."
  A. Golden, 646:Dec83-56
Hollis, M. and S. Lukes, eds. Rationality and Relativism.*
  J.R. Brown, 154:Jun83-369
  L. Code, 154:Dec83-714
  483:Jan83-133
Holloway, D. The Soviet Union and the Arms Race.*
  639(VQR):Autumn83-129
Holloway, J. Narrative and Structure.*
  J. Preston, 402(MLR):Apr83-389
Holm, B. Fredrika Bremer och den borgerliga romanens födelse.
  R.S. ten Cate, 562(Scan):Nov83-212
  F.H. König, 563(SS):Spring83-183
Holm, J.A., with A.W. Shilling. Dictionary of Bahamian English.
  E.K. Brathwaite, 617(TLS):3Feb84-102
  P. Christie, 35(AS):Fall83-270
  Y. Malkiel, 350:Sep84-683
Holmberg, E.J. Delphi and Olympia.
  A.R. Burn, 123:Vol33No1-149
Holmes, G. Augustan England.*
  L. Stone, 453(NYRB):29Mar84-42
  P.D.G. Thomas, 83:Spring83-98
Holmes, G. Dante.
  T.G. Bergin, 569(SR):Spring83-261
Holmes, J.L. Conductors on Record.
  M. Walker, 415:Aug83-485
Holmes, J.W. Life With Uncle.
  D.G. Haglund, 529(QQ):Spring83-208
Holmes, O. - see Parker, H.T.
Holmes, R. Coleridge.
  P.M.S. Dawson, 148:Spring83-79
Holquist, M. - see Bakhtin, M.M.
Hölscher, F. Corpus Vasorum Antiquorum. (Deutschland, Band 46)
  D.C. Kurtz, 303(JoHS):Vol 103-219
Holst, G. Theodorakis.
  S. Auerbach, 187:May84-349
  N. Osborne, 607:Jun83-41
Holt, H. and H. Pym - see Pym, B.
Holt, J.C. Discipline.
  R.E. Buswell, Jr., 293(JASt):Feb83-436
Holt, J.C. Robin Hood.
  C. Brown, 529(QQ):Winter83-1179
Holt, V. Verna's Stained Glass in Fabric.
  P. Grappe, 614:Fall84-27
Höltgen, K.J. Francis Quarles 1592-1644.
  G. Parfitt, 447(N&Q):Oct82-444
  G.F. Strasser, 568(SCN):Spring/Summer83-7
Holtus, G. Lexikalische Untersuchungen zur Interferenz.*
  E.J. Richards, 545(RPh):May83-610
Holtz, L. Donat et la tradition de l'enseignement grammatical.
  R.A. Kaster, 589:Apr83-478
  J. Perret, 555:Vol57fasc1-168
Holum, K.G. Theodosian Empresses.
  J.W. Barker, 377:Jul83-120
Holzapfel, O. Det balladeske.
  A. Gardner-Medwin, 562(Scan):May82-96
  K. Schier, 196:Band24Heft1/2-153

Holzberg, N. Willibald Pirckheimer.
W.P. Eckert, 52:Band18Heft1-96
Holzberg, R. L'Oeil du serpent.
S. Smith, 207(FR):Oct83-116
Holzer, H., G.S. Boritt and M.E. Neely, Jr.
The Lincoln Image.
442(NY):7May84-160
Hölzle, P. Die Kreuzzüge in der okzitan-
ischen und deutschen Lyrik des 12. Jahr-
hunderts.
D.H. Green, 402(MLR):Apr83-480
A. Wolf, 547(RF):Band95Heft1/2-162
Holzman, D. Poetry and Politics.
K.J.D. Woskin, 318(JAOS):Apr-Jun82-425
Homan, S. Beckett's Theaters.
D. Sexton, 617(TLS):21Dec84-1485
Homan, S., ed. Shakespeare's "More than
Words Can Witness."*
D. Bevington, 677(YES):Vol 13-308
A.P. Slater, 541(RES):Feb83-66
Homan, S. When the Theater Turns to
Itself.
B. Hogden, 481(PQ):Winter83-116
J.D. Huston, 301(JEGP):Oct83-550
W.M. Jones, 130:Spring83-84
Homans, M. Women Writers and Poetic
Identity.*
S. Hudson, 577(SHR):Fall83-382
D. Rosenblum, 637(VS):Summer83-446
J. Wilt, 591(SIR):Fall83-437
Homer. Homer's "Iliad." (D.B. Hull,
trans)
J.A. Dutra, 124:Nov-Dec83-131
Homer. Omero "Odissea." (Vol 1) (A.
Heubeck, S. West and G.A. Privitera, eds)
H. van Thiel, 123:Vol33No2-164
"Hommage des hispanistes français à Noël
Salomon."
H. Klüppelholz, 356(LR):Feb-May83-117
Homolya, I. Valentine Bakfark.
D. Poulton, 617(TLS):10Aug84-891
Honan, P. Matthew Arnold.*
M. Millgate, 301(JEGP):Jan83-138
S. Monod, 189(EA):Oct-Dec83-477
W. Myers, 569(SR):Spring83-275
Hone, J. The Valley of the Fox.
N. Callendar, 441:14Oct84-46
442(NY):30Apr84-123
Honegger, C. and B. Heintz, eds. Listen
der Ohnmacht.
I. Dölling, 654(WB):10/1983-1850
Hong-dao, Y. - see under Yuan Hong-dao
Hongo, G.K. Yellow Light.
D. St. John, 42(AR):Spring83-231
R. Tillinghast, 569(SR):Summer83-473
639(VQR):Winter83-26
Honig, E. Interrupted Praise.
L. Goldstein, 385(MQR):Spring84-305
Honigmann, E.A.J. Shakespeare's Impact on
his Contemporaries.
R. McDonald, 570(SQ):Winter83-488
S. Wells, 617(TLS):30Nov84-1390
Honjō Shigeru. Emperor Hirohito and His
Chief Aide-de-Camp.
D.A. Titus, 407(MN):Winter83-462
Honko, L. and V. Voigt, eds. Adaptation,
Change and Decline in Oral Literature.
A. Bihari-Andersson, 196:Band24Heft3/4-
305
Honko, L. and V. Voigt, eds. Genre, Struc-
ture and Reproduction in Oral Litera-
ture.*
E. Schön, 64(Arv):Vol37-177

Honoré, T. Tribonian.
P. Birks, 123:Vol33No2-246
Honour, H. and J. Fleming. The Visual
Arts.
M. Secrest, 55:Dec83-33
M. Secrest, 364:Oct83-72
Honour, H. and J. Fleming. A World His-
tory of Art.*
P. Burke, 59:Jun83-214
M. Levey, 90:Oct83-619
Hont, I. and M. Ignatieff, eds. Wealth
and Virtue.
D.D. Raphael, 617(TLS):15Jun84-672
Hood, C.C. The Tools of Government.
W. Plowden, 617(TLS):6Jan84-11
Hood, H. Black and White Keys.*
W.J. Keith, 198:Jan83-93
Hood, M. How Far She Went.
G. Weaver, 344:Fall84-107
Hoogeveen, J. and G. Labroisse, eds. DDR
Roman und Literaturgesellschaft.
P.U. Hohendahl, 133:Band16Heft2/3-287
R. Terras, 221(GQ):Nov83-688
Hook, J. Lorenzo de' Medici.
M. Mallett, 617(TLS):17Aug84-914
Hook, J. Siena.
B. Cole, 39:Jun83-514
Hook, S. Marxism and Beyond.*
L.S. Feuer, 31(ASch):Autumn83-558
L.S. Feuer, 390:Vol83-51
Hooker, J. The Bush Soldiers.
C. McGregor, 441:9Dec84-35
Hooker, J. A View from the Source.* The
Poetry of Place.*
J. Saunders, 565:Vol124No4-71
Hooker, J.T. The Ancient Spartans.*
C.M. Stibbe, 394:Vol36fasc3/4-425
Hooker, J.T. The Origin of the Linear B
Script.
A. Heubeck, 260(IF):Band88-322
Hooker, M., ed. Descartes.
D.C. Long, 449:Mar83-99
Hooker, R. Attack and Response. (J.E.
Booty, ed)
F.B. Williams, Jr., 354:Dec83-426
Hooker, R. Of the Laws of Ecclesiastical
Polity.* (Vol 3, Bks 6-8) (P.G. Stan-
wood, ed)
P.E. Forte, 570(SQ):Autumn83-374
Hooper, D. and K. Whyld. The Oxford Com-
panion to Chess.
P. Snowdon, 617(TLS):21Dec84-1487
Hooper, W. - see Lewis, C.S.
Hoopes, R. Cain.*
R.B. Browne, 27(AL):May83-264
Hope, A.D. Antechinus.
R. Pybus, 381:Jun83-253
Hope, C. Kruger's Alp.
D.J. Enright, 617(TLS):28Sep84-1085
R. Jones, 362:20Sep84-27
Hope, C. Titian.*
D. McTavish, 529(QQ):Spring83-198
Höpfl, H. The Christian Polity of John
Calvin.*
F.M. Higman, 208(FS):Oct83-446
Hopkins, A. Sounds of Music.* The Nine
Symphonies of Beethoven.*
J.B., 412:Aug-Nov82-267
Hopkins, D. and T. Mason - see Dryden, J.
Hopkins, D.R. Princes and Peasants.
P. Slack, 617(TLS):15Jun84-670

Hopkins, G.M. Gerard Manley Hopkins:
Selected Prose. (G. Roberts, ed)
  P.M. Ball, 402(MLR):Jan83-170
  J.A. Davies, 506(PSt):May83-85
Hopkins, J. The Flight of the Pelican.*
  J. Mellors, 364:Apr/May83-133
Hopkins, J. Nicholas of Cusa on Learned
Ignorance.* Nicholas of Cusa's Debate
with John Wenck.*
  J. Longeway, 125:Fall82-110
Hopkins, J. Nicholas of Cusa's Metaphysic
of Contraction.
  D.F. Duclow, 589:Oct83-1050
  J. Vuillemin, 540(RIPh):Vol37fasc1/2-
  214
Hopkins, J. and E. Napper - see Dalai Lama
Hopkins, J.K. A Woman to Deliver Her
People.
  W.R. Ward, 83:Spring83-109
Hopkins, K. Death and Renewal.
  M. Crawford, 617(TLS):24Feb84-196
Hopkins, K. Gamel and Rex. Introits and
Indulgences.
  A. Haberer, 189(EA):Jul-Sep84-349
Hopkins, K. - see Woolsey, G.
Hopkinson, C. A Bibliography of the Works
of Giuseppe Verdi 1813-1901. (Vol 2)
  D. Rosen, 415:Jun83-353
Hopkinson, T. Under the Tropic.
  M. Crowder, 617(TLS):2Nov84-1240
  D.A.N. Jones, 362:12Jul84-27
Hoppen, K.T. Elections, Politics and
Society in Ireland 1832-1885.
  D. Cannadine, 617(TLS):7Dec84-1403
Hoppenstand, G., ed. The Dime Novel Detec-
tive.
  P. Wolfe, 395(MFS):Autumn83-389
Hopper, P.J., ed. Tense Aspect.
  N.V. Smith, 297(JL):Sep83-105
  A.R. Tellier, 189(EA):Oct-Dec84-453
Horace. The Complete Works of Horace.
(C.E. Passage, trans) The Essential
Horace. (B. Raffel, trans)
  D.S. Carne-Ross, 453(NYRB):10May84-7
Horace. The Odes.* (K. Quinn, ed)
  J.E.G. Zetzel, 122:Jul83-256
Horak, S.M., ed. Guide to the Study of
the Soviet Nationalities.*
  J.E.O. Screen, 575(SEER):Oct83-637
Horden, L. - see Halkett, S. and J. Laing
Horecký, H. Základy jazykovedy.
  G.F. Meier, 682(ZPSK):Band36Heft3-356
Horgan, P. Mexico Bay.
  M. Westbrook, 649(WAL):May83-80
Horgan, P. Of America East and West.
  D. McCullough, 441:8Apr84-3
Horii, K. Rice Economy and Land Tenure in
West Malaysia.
  R. De Koninck, 293(JASt):Aug83-1018
Horikoshi, J. Eagles of Mitsubishi.
  D.G. Egler, 293(JASt):May83-670
Hörisch-Helligrath, R. Reflexionssnobis-
mus.
  A. Corbineau-Hoffmann, 547(RF):Band95
  Heft3-374
Hörmann, H. To Mean — To Understand.
  M. Bamberg, 603:Vol7No3-431
Horn, H-J. and H. Laufhütte, eds. Ares
und Dionysos.
  W. Ross, 52:Band18Heft1-90
Horn, P. Kleist-Chronik.
  M. Totten, 406:Fall83-346

Horn, P. William Marshall (1745-1818) and
the Georgian Countryside.
  D.G.C.A., 324:Dec83-85
Hornback, B.G. "The Hero of My Life."*
  M. Shelden, 637(VS):Summer83-459
Hornbeck, D., P. Kane and D.L. Fuller.
California Patterns.
  R. Paul, 250(HLQ):Summer83-276
Hornblower, J. Hieronymus of Cardia.
  M.M. Austin, 123:Vol133No1-77
  A.B. Bosworth, 303(JoHS):Vol 103-209
Hornblower, S. The Greek World 479-323 BC.
  P.J. Rhodes, 617(TLS):13Jan84-30
Hornblower, S. Mausolus.
  C.G. Starr, 303(JoHS):Vol 103-206
Hornby, R. Patterns in Ibsen's Middle
Plays.*
  J.S. Chamberlain, 397(MD):Mar83-122
  O.I. Holtan, 563(SS):Summer83-269
Horne, A. The French Army and Politics,
1870-1970.
  J. Grigg, 362:20Sep84-26
Horne, L. The Seventh Day.
  F.W. Kaye, 649(WAL):Nov83-271
Horne, M., with J. Scovell. Marilyn Horne:
My Life.
  A. Quindlen, 441:15Jan84-18
Horner, T. Terriers of the World.
  J. Clutton-Brock, 617(TLS):29Jun84-738
Hornung, E., ed. Das Buch von den Pforten
des Jenseits. (Pt 1)
  V. Condon, 318(JAOS):Oct-Dec82-667
Hornung, E.W. The Complete Short Stories
of Raffles — The Amateur Cracksman.
  T.J. Binyon, 617(TLS):21Dec84-1484
Hornung, M. - see Kranzmayer, E.
Horovitz, F. Snow Light, Water Light.
  H. Davies, 617(TLS):13Apr84-413
Horowitz, D.L. Coup Theories and Officers'
Motives.
  R. Oberst, 293(JASt):Aug83-991
Horowitz, H.L. Alma Mater.
  D. Ravitch, 441:28Oct84-12
Horowitz, J. Conversations with Arrau.*
  A. Coleman, 414(MusQ):Summer83-449
  C. Ehrlich, 415:Nov83-685
Horrall, S.M., ed. The Southern Version
of "Cursor Mundi." (Vol 1)
  E.G. Stanley, 447(N&Q):Apr82-158
Horrent, J. Chanson de Roland et Geste de
Charlemagne.
  H. Klüppelholz, 356(LR):Feb-May83-126
Horrent, J. - see "Cantar de Mío Cid/
Chanson de mon Cid"
Horrocks, J. My Dearest Parents. (A.S.
Lewis, ed)
  P-L. Adams, 61:Jan84-100
Horsley, G.H.R., ed. Hellenika.
  G.W. Bowersock, 124:Mar-Apr84-255
Horsman, R. Race and Manifest Destiny.
  D. Kirby, 639(VQR):Spring83-335
  R. Slotkin, 656(WMQ):Jul83-487
Horst, O.H. and J.P. Stoltman, eds. New
Themes in Instruction for Latin American
Geography.
  R.L. Layton, 263(RIB):Vol33No1-42
ter Horst, R. Calderón: The Secular
Plays.*
  G. Edwards, 610:Autumn83-256
  S. Lipmann, 400(MLN):Mar83-305
  J.H. Parker, 238:Dec83-635
Horstmann, R-P. and J.H. Trede - see
Hegel, G.W.F.

Horton, J. Grieg.
A.F.L.T., 412:Aug-Nov82-272
Horton, R. An Amish Adventure.
B. King, 614:Summer84-9
Horton, S.R. Interpreting Interpreting.*
J.R. Kincaid, 599:Winter83-44
Horton, S.R. The Reader in the Dickens World.*
D. David, 637(VS):Autumn82-93
Horton, S.R. Thinking Through Writing.
W.S. Chisholm, 474(PIL):Vol 15No1/4-321
Horvat, B. The Political Economy of Socialism.
M. Connock, 575(SEER):Jul83-471
K.E. Soltan, 185:Jan84-333
Horwich, P. Probability and Evidence.
A. Morton, 486:Dec83-659
Hörz, H. and U. Röseberg, eds. Materialistische Dialektik in der physikalischen und biologischen Erkenntnis.
A. Bartels, 687:Apr-Jun83-331
Hosidius Geta. Medea. (G. Salanitro, ed and trans)
J. Perret, 555:Vol57fasc2-343
Hoskins, P. Two Men Were Acquitted.
P.D. James, 617(TLS):11May84-515
Hösle, J. Grundzüge der italienischen Literatur des 19. und 20. Jahrhunderts.*
B. König, 72:Band219Heft1-234
Hosler, B.H. Changing Aesthetic Views of Instrumental Music in Eighteenth-Century Germany.
J.M. Tudor, 83:Autumn83-287
Hosmer, S.T., K. Kellen and B.M. Jenkins. The Fall of South Vietnam.
W.J. Duiker, 293(JASt):Feb83-453
Hospers, J. Human Conduct. (2nd ed)
S.G.P., 185:Apr84-545
Hospital, J.T. The Tiger in the Tiger Pit.
M. Simpson, 441:15Apr84-22
Hotchner, A.E. Choice People.
E. Nemy, 441:8Apr84-16
Houart, V. Miniature Silver Toys.
G. Wills, 39:Feb83-147
Houck, C. Nova Scotia Patchwork Patterns.
M. Cowan, 614:Winter84-20
Hougan, C. Shooting in the Dark.
M. Simpson, 441:18Mar84-18
Hougan, J. Secret Agenda.
J.A. Lukas, 441:11Nov84-7
Hough, G. The Mystery Religion of W.B. Yeats.
P. Redgrove, 617(TLS):30Nov84-1366
Hough, R. Bullers' Victory.
S. Altinel, 617(TLS):7Dec84-1420
Hough, R. Edwina, Countess Mountbatten of Burma.*
D.R. Thorpe, 362:26Jan84-20
442(NY):25Jun84-109
Hough, R. The Great War at Sea, 1914-1918.*
D.R. Thorpe, 362:26Jan84-20
"The Houghton 'Shahnameh.'"* (M.B. Dickson and S.C. Welch, eds)
B.W. Robinson, 90:Jun83-372
Houm, P. En mann forut for vår tid.
J. Sjåvik, 563(SS):Spring83-197
Houm, P. Kritikere i en gullalder.
R. Eide, 172(Edda):1983/4-248

Hounshell, D.A. From the American System to Mass Production 1800-1932.
E. Robinson, 617(TLS):7Dec84-1402
W. Skinner, 441:2Sep84-10
Hourani, C. An Unfinished Odyssey.
B. Wasserstein, 617(TLS):7Sep84-1002
Houseley, N. The Italian Crusades.
D.E. Queller, 589:Oct83-1052
"Housman Society Journal." (Vol 7) (J. Pugh, ed)
B. Gasser, 447(N&Q):Jun82-260
Houston, C.J. and W.J. Smyth. The Sash Canada Wore.
P. Brode, 174(Éire):Fall83-152
Houston, G.W. Sources for a History of the bSam yas Debate.
J.W. de Jong, 259(IIJ):Apr83-218
Houston, J. Eagle Song.
K. Echlin, 99:Aug-Sep83-41
Houston, J.D. Californians.
G. Haslam, 649(WAL):Feb84-363
Houston, J.P. French Symbolism and the Modernist Movement.*
P. Collier, 402(MLR):Apr83-415
C. Scott, 208(FS):Apr83-239
Houston, J.P. The Rhetoric of Poetry in the Renaissance and Seventeenth Century.
D.L. Rubin, 207(FR):Apr84-710
Houston, J.P. The Shape and Style of Proust's Novel.
J. Murray, 207(FR):Mar84-562
Houston, J.P. The Traditions of French Prose Style.*
P.J. Bayley, 402(MLR):Jul83-705
H. Godin, 208(FS):Jan83-109
Houston, J.P. and M.T., eds and trans. French Symbolist Poetry.
C. Scott, 208(FS):Apr83-239
Houston, R. The Nation Thief.
R. Elman, 441:22Jan84-22
Houtart, F. and G. Lemercinier. Sociologie d'une Commune vietnamienne.
G.C. Hickey, 293(JASt):Aug83-1020
Hovannisian, R.G., ed. The Armenian Image in History and Literature.
R. Wilkinson, 575(SEER):Apr83-264
Hovannisian, R.G. The Republic of Armenia. (Vol 2)
R.A. Pierce, 104(CASS):Winter83-566
R.G. Suny, 550(RusR):Oct83-450
Hovde, C.F., W.L. Howarth and E.H. Witherell - see Thoreau, H.D.
Hovdhaugen, E. Foundations of Western Linguistics.
M. Covington, 350:Jun84-448
E.A. Ebbinghaus, 215(GL):Vol23No3-232
Hovdhaugen, E., ed. The Nordic Languages and Modern Linguistics.
K. Nilsson, 563(SS):Spring83-180
Howard, C.M. Les Fortunes de Madame de Sévigné au XVIIème et XVIIIème siècles.
N. Bonvalet, 475:Vol 10No18-351
Howard, D. The Architectural History of Venice.*
P.D. du Prey, 529(QQ):Summer83-406
Howard, E.J. Getting It Right.*
P. Craig, 617(TLS):9Mar84-259
D. Flower, 249(HudR):Summer83-373
639(VQR):Spring83-58
Howard, H.A. American Frontier Tales.
K. Ames, 649(WAL):Aug83-174

Howard, J. Margaret Mead.
  M. Sahlins, 441:26Aug84-1
  R. Sandall, 129:Dec84-68
  S. Toulmin, 453(NYRB):6Dec84-3
  M. Warnock, 362:15Nov84-30
  442(NY):15Oct84-179
Howard, J. Wry and Ginger.
  L.K. MacKendrick, 102(CanL):Winter82-
  149
Howard, J.H. Shawnee!
  J.D. Sweet, 187:Jan84-140
Howard, J.T., Jr. A Bibliography of
  Theatre Technology.
  P.S. Grayson, 615(TJ):May83-279
Howard, M. The Causes of Wars and Other
  Essays.*
  L. Robinson, 441:29Jan84-23
Howard, M. Grace Abounding.
  D. Flower, 249(HudR):Summer83-372
Howard, M. Nuclear Weapons and the Preser-
  vation of Peace.
  P. Towle, 617(TLS):9Mar84-241
Howard, P. A Word in Your Ear.*
  C. Trillin, 441:8Jan84-7
Howard, R. Lining Up.
  H. Beaver, 441:18Mar84-30
  J. Hollander, 676(YR):Spring84-xiii
  M. Kinzie, 29:Mar/Apr84-38
Howard, R.J. Three Faces of Hermeneutics.
  R.S., 185:Oct83-168
  S. Wells, 141:Summer83-290
Howard, V.A. Artistry.
  G. Iseminger, 289:Fall83-120
  M.J. Parsons, 290(JAAC):Fall83-89
  F. Sparshott, 529(QQ):Autumn83-883
Howarth, D. Tahiti.
  C. McGregor, 441:22Jan84-27
Howarth, S. Morning Glory.
  I. McGeoch, 617(TLS):9Mar84-244
Howarth, T. Charles Rennie Mackintosh and
  the Modern Movement.
  D. Watkin, 39:Feb83-144
Howarth, W.D. Molière.
  P.V. Conroy, Jr., 130:Fall83-281
  H.G. Hall, 208(FS):Jan83-75
  D.P. Scales, 67:Nov83-319
  R.W. Tobin, 207(FR):Dec83-247
Howarth, W.D., I. McFarlane and M. McGowan,
  eds. Form and Meaning.
  G. Forestier, 475:Vol 10No19-907
Howat, G. Walter Hammond.
  A. Ross, 617(TLS):29Jun84-722
Howatch, S. The Wheel of Fortune.
  B. Helfgott, 441:26Aug84-16
Howe, C. Acquiring Language in a Conversa-
  tional Context.*
  C. Genishi, 355(LSoc):Mar83-129
Howe, C., ed. Shanghai.
  C.K. Leung, 302:Vol 19No2-255
  K. Lieberthal, 293(JASt):Feb83-389
Howe, F. In the Middle of Nowhere.
  S. Laschever, 441:20May84-30
Howe, I., ed. Alternatives.
  R. Margolis, 441:1Jul84-15
Howe, I. A Margin of Hope.*
  J. O'Brian, 99:May83-32
  S. Pinsker, 390:May83-77
  S. Pinsker, 560:Spring-Summer83-186
  F. Tuohy, 364:Jul83-86
  295(JML):Nov83-365
Howe, L.K. Moments on Maple Avenue.
  M. Abrams, 441:18Nov84-42

Howell, A. Notions of a Mirror.
  L. Mackinnon, 617(TLS):27Jul84-838
Howell, B. In a White Shirt.
  A. Munton, 198:Jun83-81
  G. Woodcock, 102(CanL):Summer83-163
Howell, J.M. John Gardner.*
  M.F. Schulz, 677(YES):Vol 13-359
Howell, W.S. The Empathic Communicator.
  D.K. Darnell, 583:Fall83-90
Howells, W.D. A Foregone Conclusion, A
  Modern Instance, Indian Summer, The Rise
  of Silas Lapham.* [shown in prev under
  "Novels, 1875-1886."] (E.H. Cady, ed)
  W.H. Pritchard, 249(HudR):Summer83-352
Howells, W.D. Selected Letters of W.D.
  Howells.* (Vols 1 and 2) (G. Arms and
  others, eds)
  T.H. Towers, 395(MFS):Winter83-707
  E. Wagenknecht, 402(MLR):Jul83-700
Howells, W.D. Selected Letters of W.D.
  Howells.* (Vol 3 ed by R.C. Leitz 3d,
  R.H. Ballinger and C.K. Lohmann; Vol 4
  ed by T. Wortham, with others)
  T. Cooley, 27(AL):Mar83-91
  T.H. Towers, 395(MFS):Winter83-707
  E. Wagenknecht, 402(MLR):Jul83-700
Howes, M. Lying in Bed.*
  A. Mandel, 102(CanL):Winter82-132
Howie, J., ed. Ethical Principles for
  Social Policy.
  R.E.L., 185:Jan84-377
Howland, B. Things To Come and Go.*
  S. Pinsker, 573(SSF):Fall83-329
  E. Turner, 110:Fall83-76
Hoy, C. Introductions, Notes, and Commen-
  taries to Texts in "The Dramatic Works
  of Thomas Dekker."
  A.R. Braunmuller, 301(JEGP):Apr83-235
  G.K. Hunter, 402(MLR):Oct83-899
Hoy, D.C. The Critical Circle.
  L.M. Hinman, 484(PPR):Dec83-282
Hoyle, F. The Intelligent Universe.*
  T. Ferrell, 441:29Apr84-33
Hoyle, P. The Man in the Iron Mask.
  J. Mantle, 362:21Jun84-27
  J. Melmoth, 617(TLS):27Apr84-476
Hoyle, T. Vail.
  N. Shack, 617(TLS):23Nov84-1359
Hoyt, E.P. The Pusan Perimeter.
  R. Trumbull, 441:25Nov84-27
Hoyt, R. Cool Runnings.
  A. Krystal, 441:9Sep84-30
Hrdy, S.B. The Woman that Never Evolved.
  H. Hood, 529(QQ):Autumn83-887
Hroswitha. The Plays of Hroswitha of
  Gandersheim. (L. Bonfante, with A.
  Bonfante-Warren, trans)
  P. Godman, 123:Vol133No2-373
Hsi, W. - see under Wang Hsi
Hsia, A., ed. Hermann Hesse Heute.
  D.G. Daviau, 221(GQ):Jan83-173
Hsia, R.P-C. Society and Religion in
  Münster, 1535-1618.
  H.J. Cohn, 617(TLS):16Nov84-1320
Hsiang-hsiang, W. - see under Wu Hsiang-
  hsiang
Hsiao, K-C. A History of Chinese Politi-
  cal Thought. (Vol 1)
  C-Y. Hsu, 318(JAOS):Apr-Jun82-426
Hsiung, J.C., ed. Contemporary Republic
  of China.
  R.E. Barrett, 293(JASt):May83-617

Hsiung, J.C. and S.S. Kim, eds. China in
the Global Community.
J.F. Copper, 293(JASt):Nov82-133
Hsü Chin-hsiung. Oracle Bones from the
White and Other Collections.
K. Takashima, 318(JAOS):Apr-Jun82-428
Hsü, K.J. The Mediterranean Was a Desert.
C. Vita-Finzi, 617(TLS):27Apr84-479
Hsu, K-Y. and T. Wang, eds. Literature in
the People's Republic of China.*
D.E. Pollard, 116:Jan82-146
Hsu, V.L., ed. Born of the Same Roots.
J.L. Faurot, 293(JASt):Feb83-391
Hu, K-Z. Der Gebrauch des Artikels in der
deutschen Gegenwartssprache.
D. Hartmann, 685(ZDL):3/1983-389
Hu, S-Y., with Y.C. Kong and P.P.H. But.
An Enumeration of Chinese Materia Medica.
P.W. Kroll, 116:Jan82-138
Huang San, A. Pino and L. Epstein - see
"Un Bol de Nids d'Hirondelles ne fait
pas le Printemps de Pékin"
Huang Shu-Min. Agricultural Degradation.
D.C. Schak, 293(JASt):May83-619
Hubbard, B.A.F. and E.S. Karnofsky.
Plato's "Protagoras:" A Socratic Commen-
tary.
K.A.M., 617(TLS):27Jan84-95
D. Sider, 124:Jul-Aug84-384
C.C.W. Taylor, 123:Vol33No2-332
Hubbard, F. Encyclopedia of North Ameri-
can Railroading.
G.F. Ackerman, 649(WAL):May83-81
Huber, T.M. The Revolutionary Origins of
Modern Japan.*
H. Conroy, 407(MN):Winter83-458
S. Vlastos, 293(JASt):Aug83-959
Hubin, A.J. Crime Fiction, 1749-1980.*
(rev)
70:May-Jun83-165
Hübner, I. Kulturzentren.
G. Zahn, 654(WB):10/1983-1847
Hübner, K. Critique of Scientific Reason.
(P.R. Dixon, Jr. and H.M. Dixon, eds)
B. Barnes, 617(TLS):22Jun84-710
Huchel, P. The Garden of Theophrastus.*
D. Davie, 362:6Dec84-33
Huchon, M. Rabelais grammairien.*
K. Varty, 402(MLR):Jul83-708
Hucker, B.U. Hermann Allmers und sein
Marschenhof.
E. Moser-Rath, 196:Band24Heft1/2-154
Huddle, N. Surviving.
D. Emblidge, 441:9Sep84-31
Huddleston, J. Sarah Grand (Mrs. Frances
Elizabeth McFall, née Clarke 1854-1943).
S. Foster, 677(YES):Vol 13-339
Hudson, K. The Language of the Teenage
Revolution.
E. Battistella, 350:Dec84-1006
Hudson, M. Afterlight.
D. Hopes, 236:Spring-Summer83-34
Hudson, R.V. The Writing Game.
G. Weales, 569(SR):Fall83-lxxxii
Hudson, W.D. A Century of Moral Philos-
ophy.
C. Cherry, 393(Mind):Jan83-132
Hudson, W.S. The Cambridge Connection and
the Elizabethan Settlement of 1559.*
R. Tittler, 539:Nov83-285
Hudspeth, R.N. - see Fuller, M.

Hue de Rotelande. Ipomedon.* (A.J.
Holden, ed)
U. Mölk, 72:Band219Heft1-221
Huebner, T. A Longitudinal Analysis of
the Acquisition of English.
T.C. Frazer, 350:Dec84-1001
Huerta, J.A. Chicano Theater.
J.W. Brokaw, 615(TJ):Dec83-561
E. McCracken, 238:Dec83-645
Huet, M-H. Rehearsing the Revolution.*
M.F. O'Meara, 400(MLN):May83-804
Huffaker, R. John Fowles.
J.L. Halio, 677(YES):Vol 13-357
P. Lewis, 161(DUJ):Dec82-116
S. Monod, 189(EA):Apr-Sep83-354
K. Watson, 447(N&Q):Oct82-473
Huffer, V., with E. Roughsey and others.
The Sweetness of the Fig.
P. Stewart, 292(JAF):Apr-Jun83-221
Huffman, C. Montale and the Occasions of
Poetry.
C. Tomlinson, 364:Feb84-73
Hugedé, N. Saint Paul en la Grèce.
É. des Places, 555:Vol57fasc2-323
Hughart, B. Bridge of Birds.
P-L. Adams, 61:Jul84-116
442(NY):4Jun84-132
Hughes, A. Henry Irving, Shakespearean.*
I.G. Dash, 702:Vol 16-366
M. Rubin, 130:Spring83-90
D.J. Watermeier, 615(TJ):May82-282
S. Wells, 447(N&Q):Feb82-73
Hughes, A. Medieval Manuscripts for Mass
and Office.*
R.L. Crocker, 589:Oct83-1054
Hughes, A. Medieval Music. (rev)
D.S., 412:Feb82-63
Hughes, B.B. - see Jordanus de Nemore
Hughes, D. Dryden's Heroic Plays.*
R. Blattès, 189(EA):Oct-Dec83-469
W. Myers, 447(N&Q):Dec82-546
Hughes, D. The Pork Butcher.
T. Fitton, 617(TLS):1Jun84-622
J. Mellors, 362:26Apr84-31
Hughes, D. - see Bulgakov, M.
Hughes, E.J. Marcel Proust.*
M. Bowie, 617(TLS):17Feb84-155
Hughes, G. The Hawthorn Goddess.
V. Cunningham, 617(TLS):4May84-502
J. Mellors, 362:26Apr84-31
Hughes, G. The Poetry of Francisco de la
Torre.
C. Maurer, 304(JHP):Spring83-229
Hughes, G. Where I Used to Play on the
Green.*
P. Craig, 617(TLS):1Jun84-623
Hughes, G.E. and M.J. Cresswell. Einfüh-
rung in die Modallogik.
G.F. Meier, 682(ZPSK):Band36Heft5-
607
Hughes, H.S. Prisoners of Hope.*
A. Lyttelton, 617(TLS):20Apr84-428
Hughes, J.M. Emotion and High Politics.
R.T. Shannon, 617(TLS):6Jan84-9
Hughes, K., ed and trans. Franz Kafka.*
S. Corngold, 221(GQ):May83-521
R. Gray, 400(MLN):Apr83-516
Hughes, M.C. The Calling.*
G. Garrett, 569(SR):Winter83-112
Hughes, P., with J. Hemlow - see Burney, F.
Hughes, R. and M. Rowe. The Colouring,
Bronzing and Patination of Metals.
H. Helwig, 139:Dec83/Jan84-40

Hunt, G.W.   John Updike and the Three
  Great Secret Things.*
    P. Balbert, 594:Fall83-265
    W.R. Macnaughton, 587(SAF):Autumn83-
    268
Hunt, H.   The Abbey.*
    J.W. Flannery, 612(ThS):May/Nov83-145
Hunt, H.A. and T.L.   Human Resource Impli-
  cations of Robotics.
    J. Fallows, 453(NYRB):27Sep84-11
Hunt, J.D. and F.M. Holland, eds.   The
  Ruskin Polygon.*
    P. Conner, 89(BJA):Winter83-88
Hunt, M.   The Universe Within.
    R.L. Sheverbush, 389(MQ):Autumn83-102
Hunt, M.H.   The Making of a Special Rela-
  tionship.*
    J. Spence, 453(NYRB):27Sep84-59
Hunter, A.   The Unhung Man.
    T.J.B., 617(TLS):13Apr84-397
Hunter, A.A.   Class Tells.
    G. Teeple, 529(QQ):Summer83-523
Hunter, B.   Benchmark.
    R. Dubanski, 102(CanL):Spring83-117
    M. Harry, 198:Jan83-115
    W. Latta, 137:Apr83-41
Hunter, C.   The Life and Letters of Alex-
  ander Wilson.
    B. Campbell, 617(TLS):11May84-534
Hunter, E.   Lizzie.
    P-L. Adams, 61:Jul84-116
    J. House, 441:17Jun84-20
Hunter, G.K.   Dramatic Identities and Cul-
  tural Tradition.
    M. Trousdale, 570(SQ):Autumn83-376
    J. Wilders, 447(N&Q):Feb82-71
Hunter, G.K.   "Paradise Lost."
    A. Burnett, 447(N&Q):Feb82-79
    D.D.C. Chambers, 541(RES):Aug83-338
    O.W. Ferguson, 579(SAQ):Winter83-112
    D. Fuller, 161(DUJ):Dec82-108
Hunter, G.K. and C.J. Rawson, with J.
  Mezciems - see "The Yearbook of English
  Studies"
Hunter, J.   Edwardian Fiction.*
    T.E.M. Boll, 177(ELT):Vol26No1-54
    J. McClure, 405(MP):Aug83-97
    T.C. Moser, 569(SR):Spring83-282
Hunter, J.   The Gospel of Gentility.
    R. Harris, 617(TLS):3Aug84-872
    J. Spence, 453(NYRB):27Sep84-59
Hunter, J.A. - see Sevigny, A.M.
Hunter, J.F.M.   Thinking About Sex and
  Love.
    R. Campbell, 150(DR):Spring83-186
    D. Gallop, 154:Mar83-113
Hunter, M.   Science and Society in Restora-
  tion England.*
    J.L. Thorson, 173(ECS):Winter83/84-214
Hunter, R.   And Tomorrow Comes.
    A. Haberer, 189(EA):Jul-Sep84-349
Hunter, R.L., ed.   Eubulus: The Fragments.*
    [shown in prev under title]
    R. Hamilton, 124:May-Jun84-319
Hunter, R.L.   A Study of "Daphnis and
  Chloe."
    B. Vickers, 617(TLS):20Apr84-427
Hunter, V.J.   Past and Process in Herodo-
  tus and Thucydides.
    A.W.H.A., 185:Apr84-560
    J.W. Allison, 24:Fall83-298
                              [continued]

[continuing]
    L. Canfora and A. Corcella,
    487:Summer83-166
    H.D. Westlake, 123:Vol33No1-15
Hunter, W.B., Jr., general ed.   A Milton
  Encyclopedia.
    M.A. Radzinowicz, 551(RenQ):Spring83-
    157
Hunter, W.B., Jr.   Milton's "Comus."
    L. Mackinnon, 617(TLS):20Apr84-438
Huntington, J.   The Logic of Fantasy.
    R.D. Mullen, 177(ELT):Vol26No4-326
Huntley, F.L.   Bishop Joseph Hall and
  Protestant Meditation in Seventeenth-
  Century England.*
    C.L., 189(EA):Oct-Dec84-489
    B.K. Lewalski, 551(RenQ):Spring83-155
    J. Wands, 405(MP):Nov83-199
Huot, H.   Constructions infinitives du
  français.
    F.M. Jenkins, 207(FR):May84-920
Hupka, W.   Das Wortfeld "schlagen" im Alt-
  französischen unter besonderer Berück-
  sichtigung der Entwicklung von "ferir."
    H. Meier, 72:Band219Heft2-447
Hüppauf, B.   "Die Mühen der Ebenen."
    F.D. Hirschbach, 221(GQ):Jan83-180
Huppertsberg, C.   Das Irland-Bild im
  Erzählwerk von Sommerville and Ross.
    R. Noll-Wiemann, 72:Band219Heft1-204
Huppertz, J. and H. Köster.   Kleine China-
  Beiträge.
    W. Franke, 302:Vol 19No2-246
le Huray, P. and J. Day, eds.   Music and
  Aesthetics in the Eighteenth and Early
  Nineteenth Centuries.*
    M. Peckham, 339(KSMB):No34-91
    J.M. Tudor, 83:Autumn83-287
Hurlebusch, K. - see Klopstock, F.G.
Hurlebusch, K. and K.L. Schneider - see
  Stadler, E.
Hurst, C.   Catalogue of the Wren Library
  of Lincoln Cathedral: Books Printed
  Before 1801.*
    J.F. Fuggles, 354:Dec83-432
Hurtado, M.D., C. Ochsenius and H. Vidal,
  eds.   Teatro chileno de la crisis inter-
  nacional: 1973-1980.
    J. Miranda, 352(LATR):Fall83-90
Hurtado, O.   Political Power in Ecuador.*
    D.R. Corkill, 86(BHS):Jan83-84
Hurvitz, L., ed. and trans.   Scripture of
  the Lotus Blossom of the Fine Dharma
  (The Lotus Sūtra).
    D.W. Chappell, 318(JAOS):Jul-Sep82-573
Husain, I.   Bastī.
    M. Salim-ur-Rahman, 314:Summer-Fall83-
    206
Husain, I.   Din aur dāstān.   Ākhrī admī.
  Shahr-e-afsōs.   Kachvē.
    M. Salim-ur-Rahman, 314:Summer-Fall83-
    200
Husain, S. and S.A. Ashraf, eds.   Crisis
  in Muslim Education.
    R. Kemal, 273(IC):Apr83-164
Ḥusain, Ṭ.   The Call of the Curlew.
    F.X. Paz, 318(JAOS):Oct-Dec82-670
Huseboe, A.R., ed.   Siouxland Heritage.
    R.C. Steensma, 649(WAL):Aug83-175

Husserl, E. Aufsätze und Rezensionen (1890-1910).* (B. Rang, ed) Phantasie, Bildewusstsein, Erinnerung.* (E. Marbach, ed)
J.C. Evans, 687:Jul-Sep83-462
Husserl, E. Husserl: Shorter Works. (P. McCormick and F.A. Elliston, eds)
R. Sokolowski, 453:Dec82-459
Husserl, E. Recherches phénoménologiques pour la constitution.
G. Granel, 98:Jun-Jul83-579
Hussey, S.S. The Literary Language of Shakespeare.
J.J.A., 148:Autumn83-93
Huston, J. Répertoire national. (R. Mélançon, ed)
D.M. Hayne, 627(UTQ):Summer83-516
Hutcheon, L. Narcissistic Narrative.*
R. Hunt, 178:Jun83-241
J.H. Petersen, 52:Band18Heft2-209
Hutchings, A. Purcell.
D. Stevens, 415:Apr83-236
Hutchins, J., ed. The Fiberarts Design Book II.
S. Garoutte, 614:Spring84-23
Hutchinson, P. Games Authors Play.
C. Baldick, 617(TLS):25May84-580
B. Bergonzi, 176:Jul/Aug84-50
Hutchinson, R.C. The Quixotes. (R. Green, ed)
D.J. Enright, 617(TLS):27Jul84-847
Hutchinson, S. Henry James.
D. Seed, 189(EA):Jul-Sep84-354
639(VQR):Summer83-88
Hutchinson, T. Niven's Hollywood.
E. Mordden, 441:23Dec84-8
Huters, T. Qian Zhongshu.
M.S. Duke, 293(JASt):Aug83-922
Huth, A. Wanting.
S. Altinel, 617(TLS):15Jun84-676
J. Mellors, 362:24May84-28
Hutson, J.H. John Adams and the Diplomacy of the American Revolution.*
G. Bilson, 106:Spring83-61
Hutt, M. Chouannerie and Counter-Revolution.
A. Forrest, 617(TLS):27Apr84-478
Hutton, J. Accidental Crimes.*
N. Callendar, 441:22Jul84-32
Huxley, A. Brave New World [and] Brave New World Revisited.
D.J. Enright, 617(TLS):17Feb84-160
Huxley, J. Judith Huxley's Table for Eight.
M. Burros, 441:3Jun84-15
Huygens, L. The English Journal, 1651-1652.* (A.G.H. Bachrach and R.G. Collmer, eds and trans)
T.A.B., 179(ES):Jun83-200
L. Miller, 391:Mar83-20
Huysmans, J-K. A Rebours.* (R. Fortassier, ed)
P. Cogny, 535(RHL):Mar/Apr83-303
Huyssen, A. Drama des Sturm und Drang.*
H. Marshall, 400(MLN):Apr83-517
K. Scherpe, 406:Summer83-206
Hwang Chun-ming. The Drowning of an Old Cat and Other Stories.*
J. Wong, 116:Jul82-291
Hyatt, S.L., ed. The Greek Vase.
A. Johnston, 123:Vol33No1-92
Hyde, C. The Tenth Crusade.
M. Laski, 362:12Apr84-27

Hyde, H.M. - see Wilde, O.
Hyde, L. The Gift.*
J. Gleason, 472:Fall/Winter83Spring/Summer84-265
I. McGilchrist, 617(TLS):27Jan84-77
Hyde, M. - see Shaw, G.B. and A. Douglas
Hyde, M.J., ed. Communication Philosophy and the Technological Age.
W.R. Elliott, 583:Fall83-93
Hyde, R. The Regent's Park Colosseum.
H. Hobhouse, 617(TLS):13Apr84-409
Hyland, D.A. The Virtue of Philosophy.
D.C. Lindenmuth, 543:Jun83-935
Hyland, G. Just Off Main.
M.T. Lane, 198:Jun83-75
Hyland, P. The Stubborn Forest.
J. Mole, 176:Dec84-60
S. Rae, 617(TLS):14Dec84-1456
Hymes, D. "In vain I tried to tell you."
W. Bloodworth, 649(WAL):May83-48
R. Maud, 106:Spring83-71
C. Mishler, 292(JAF):Oct-Dec83-481
G.L. Ulmer, 582(SFQ):Vol144-215
Hymes, D. and J. Fought. American Structuralism.
G. Prince, 307:Oct83-89
P. Swiggers, 355(LSoc):Sep83-371
"Hymns and Psalms."
R. Trickett, 617(TLS):21Dec84-1467
Hyneman, C.S. and D.S. Lutz, eds. American Political Writing during the Founding Era, 1760-1805.
K. Silverman, 165(EAL):Spring84-98
Hynes, S. - see Hardy, T.
Hyoe, M. - see under Murakami Hyoe
Hyslop, L.B. Baudelaire.*
J.E. Jackson, 535(RHL):Jul/Aug83-651

Iacocca, L., with W. Novak. Iacocca.
R. Townsend, 441:11Nov84-30
Iatrides, J.O., ed. Greece in the 1940s.
M. Ebon, 396(ModA):Spring83-222
Ibanez, C.V. - see under Velez Ibanez, C.
Ibargüengoitia, J. The Dead Girls.*
J. Mellors, 364:Apr/May83-133
Ibargüengoitia, J. Two Crimes.
S. Altinel, 617(TLS):10Aug84-901
J. Koslow, 441:23Sep84-28
J. Sutherland, 362:9Aug84-26
"Iberiul-k'avk'azuri enatmecniereba XXII."
G.F. Meier, 682(ZPSK):Band36Heft2-237
Ibn 'Arabi, M. Journey to the Lord of Power.
G. Webb, 469:Vol9No2-104
Ibn Ridwān. Medieval Islamic Medicine. (A.S. Gamal, ed)
A.Z. Iskandar, 617(TLS):2Nov84-1264
Ibsen, H. Brand. (2nd ed) (G. Hill, ed and trans)
G.S. Argetsinger, 563(SS):Winter83-81
Ibsen, H. Peer Gynt.* (2nd ed) (R. Fjelde, trans)
A. Simpson, 563(SS):Winter83-78
Ide, R.S. Possessed with Greatness.*
A.W. Bellringer, 447(N&Q):Apr82-164
P. Bement, 541(RES):Nov83-498
"Ideals of the Samurai." (W.S. Wilson, trans)
C. Steenstrup, 407(MN):Autumn83-342
Idiens, D. The Hausa of Northern Nigeria. Pacific Art in the Royal Scottish Museum.
K. Nicklin, 2(AfrA):Feb83-88

Idone, C. Glorious Food.
 W. and C. Cowen, 639(VQR):Spring83-67
Ienaga, S. Japanese Art.
 E.D. Swinton, 318(JAOS):Jul-Sep82-579
Ienaga, S. The Pacific War.
 J.F. Howes, 529(QQ):Summer83-414
Ifri, P.A. Proust et son narrataire.
 J.M. Cocking, 617(TLS):25May84-595
de la Iglesia, M.R. El hambre y las
 revueltas populares en Galicia (1836-
 1856).
 A. Wright, 86(BHS):Jan83-89
Ignatieff, M. The Needs of Strangers.
 J. Waldron, 617(TLS):21Dec84-1471
Ignatow, D. Whisper to the Earth.*
 W. Harmon, 569(SR):Summer83-457
Ignatow, Y. The Flaw.
 G.S.S. Chandra, 436(NewL):Summer84-114
Ihering, H. Bert Brecht hat das dichter-
 ische Antlitz Deutschlands verändert.
 (K. Völker, ed)
 M. Morley, 221(GQ):Jan83-160
Ihnken, T., ed. Die Inschriften von Mag-
 nesia am Sipylos.*
 P. Roesch, 555:Vol57fasc2-309
Ihrie, M. Skepticism in Cervantes.
 B.W. Wardropper, 551(RenQ):Winter83-
 635
Ike, N. A Theory of Japanese Democracy.
 A.D. George, 302:Vol 19No2-232
Ikin, V. Australian Science Fiction.
 R. Blackford, 381:Sep83-403
Ilardi, V., ed. Dispatches with Related
 Documents of Milanese Ambassadors in
 France. (Vol 3)
 F.L. Cheyette, 589:Oct83-1122
 M. Mallett, 551(RenQ):Spring83-79
Ilie, P. Authoritarian Spain, 1939-1975.
 J. Butt, 86(BHS):Oct83-347
Ilie, P. Literature and Inner Exile.*
 L. Hickey, 402(MLR):Jul83-737
 R.S. Thornberry, 107(CRCL):Sep83-452
 H.T. Young, 240(HR):Spring83-238
Iliffe, J. The Emergence of African Capi-
 talism.
 J.F. Munro, 617(TLS):13Apr84-410
Iliffe, S. The NHS.
 E.G. Knox, 617(TLS):17Feb84-169
Illiano, A. Metapsichica e letteratura in
 Pirandello.
 O. Ragusa, 276:Spring83-71
Illich, I. Gender.*
 S. Munro, 99:Jun83-31
"The Illustrated Rock Handbook."
 E.M. Thomson, 362:19Apr84-27
Imaeda, Y. Histoire du cycle de la nais-
 sance et de la mort.
 J.W. de Jong, 259(IIJ):Apr83-222
Imart, G. Le kirghiz (Turk d'Asie Cen-
 trale Soviétique).
 B. Comrie, 353:Vol20No3/4-363
"Immagini del Settecento in Italia."
 A.N. Mancini, 173(ECS):Fall83-85
"Impulse." (Vols 1-5) (W. Dietze and P.
 Goldammer, eds)
 D. Grohnert, 654(WB):12/1983-2185
"In the Chips."
 E. Zureik, 529(QQ):Autumn83-779
Inbar, E.M. Shakespeare in Deutschland:
 Der Fall Lenz.
 W. Bies, 52:Band18Heft3-328
 T.E. Goldsmith-Reber, 564:May83-154
 E. McInnes, 680(ZDP):Band102Heft4-608

Inchbald, P. Short Break in Venice.*
 N. Callendar, 441:1Jan84-26
 442(NY):13Feb84-131
"Incontro di studio in onore di Massimo
 Pallottino (Roma, 11-13 décembre 1979)."
 A. Hus, 555:Vol57fasc2-352
Indelli, G. - see Polystratus
"An Index to Book Reviews in the Humani-
 ties." (Vol 21)
 G. Breuer, 547(RF):Band95Heft4-479
"Index to Reviews of Bibliographical Pub-
 lications." (Vol 2) (L.T. Oggel and R.
 Hewitt, eds)
 517(PBSA):Oct-Dec80-419
Indich, W.M. Consciousness in Advaita
 Vedānta.*
 J.M. Koller, 293(JASt):Nov82-184
"Indochinese Students in U.S. Schools."
 J. Bordie, 399(MLJ):Autumn83-278
Ineichen, G. Allgemeine Sprachtypologie.
 H-J. Sasse, 361:Oct/Nov83-265
 A. Tovar, 682(ZDL):1/1983-61
Ineichen, G. - see Renzi, L.
Inés de la Cruz, J. A Woman of Genius.
 N.M. Scott, 37:Jan-Feb83-60
Infante, G.C. - see under Cabrera Infante,
 G.
"Influences: Traditional and Contemporary
 Quilts."
 S.J. Garoutte, 614:Summer84-17
Ingalls, R. Binstead's Safari.*
 W. Scammell, 364:Aug/Sep83-129
Inge, M.T., ed. Handbook of American Pop-
 ular Culture. (Vols 1 and 2)
 L.J. Budd, 365:Summer/Fall83-126
van Ingen, F. - see von Zesen, P.
Ingersoll, S.M. Intensive and Restrictive
 Modification in Old English.
 E.G. Stanley, 72:Band219Heft2-419
Inglis, B. Science and Parascience.
 J.R. Durant, 617(TLS):2Nov84-1259
Inglis, S. The Football Grounds of
 England and Wales.
 P. Smith, 617(TLS):13Jan84-35
Ingold, F.P. Literatur und Aviatik.
 W.G. Cunliffe, 406:Winter83-434
Ingram, A. Boswell's Creative Gloom.
 F.A. Nussbaum, 173(ECS):Spring84-336
Ingram, R.W., ed. Records of Early
 English Drama: Coventry.
 J.M. Cowen, 611(TN):Vol37No2-87
 C. Gauvin, 189(EA):Oct-Dec84-459
 D. Pearsall, 179(ES):Feb83-81
Ingrams, R. - see Thrale, H.
"'Ingrid' and Other Studies." [National
 Maritime Museum]
 P. Cannon-Brookes, 39:Feb83-146
Inkster, T. Blue Angel.*
 R. Hatch, 102(CanL):Winter82-144
 N. Zacharin, 137:Sep83-23
Innes, C. Edward Gordon Craig.
 P. Holland, 617(TLS):10Feb84-149
Innes, C. Holy Theater.*
 P. Auslander, 107(CRCL):Mar83-126
 R. Cohn, 402(MLR):Apr83-420
 A. Graham-White, 615(TJ):Mar83-140
Innes, D. Anglo American and the Rise of
 Modern South Africa.
 D. Welsh, 617(TLS):28Sep84-1099
Innes, M. Carson's Conspiracy.
 T.J. Binyon, 617(TLS):30Nov84-1391
Innis, R.E. Karl Bühler.*
 R. Cobb-Stevens, 258:Dec83-447

Inoue, Y. Chronicle of my Mother.*
J. Kirkup, 617(TLS):17Feb84-157
M. Ury, 407(MN):Winter83-445
Inoue, Y. Le fusil de chasse.
S. Ludvige, 98:Jan-Feb83-173
Insall, D.W. and others. Conservation in
Action: Chester's Bridgegate.
J.S. Curl, 324:Feb84-213
Insdorf, A. Indelible Shadows.*
M. Dickstein, 18:Oct83-88
A. Goldfarb, 615(TJ):Dec83-567
"International Music Guide 1983." (J. Dud-
man, ed)
N. Goodwin, 415:Apr83-235
"Internationale Germanistische Bibliogra-
phie 1980."* (H-A. and U. Koch, eds)
[shown in prev under eds]
J. Hardin, 222(GR):Winter83-40
W.A. Reichart, 301(JEGP):Apr83-276
S. Seifert, 654(WB):9/1983-1670
H. Weddige, 72:Band220Heft1-142
"Internationale Germanistische Biblio-
graphie 1981." (H-A. and U. Koch, eds)
K. Nyholm, 439(NM):1983/4-541
"Inventaire des collections publiques
françaises." (No 26 and 27)
A. Blunt, 90:Sep83-562
"Inventaris van incunabelen gedrukt te
Antwerpen 1481-1500."
354:Sep83-314
van Inwagen, P. An Essay on Free Will.
N. Denyer, 617(TLS):8Jun84-642
H. Kornblith, 185:Jul84-711
Inwood, M.J. Hegel.
R. Scruton, 617(TLS):21Sep84-1059
Ionesco, E. Voyages chez les morts,
thèmes et variations.
R.C. Lamont, 207(FR):Mar84-590
Ionescu, G. Politics and the Pursuit of
Happiness.
I. Kristol, 617(TLS):23Nov84-1333
Ionescu, O. La notion de droit subjectif
dans le droit privé. (2nd ed)
G. Kalinowski, 192(EP):Apr-Jun83-239
Iooss, W., Jr. and R. Angell. Baseball.
442(NY):5Nov84-172
Irace, F. Ca' Brutta. Precursors of Post-
Modernism.
R.A. Etlin, 127:Summer83-200
Iranzo, C. Antonio García Gutiérrez.*
R.A. Cardwell, 402(MLR):Apr83-474
T. Ruiz-Fábrega, 552(REH):May83-300
'Iraqi, F. Divine Flashes.
J. Baldick, 617(TLS):7Sep84-1001
Irey, E.F. A Concordance to Herman Mel-
ville's "Moby Dick."
H.G. Worthington, 70:Sep/Oct82-30
Irfani, S. Iran's Islamic Revolution.
J.D. Gurney, 617(TLS):7Sep84-998
Irick, R.L. Ch'ing Policy toward the
Coolie Trade, 1847-1878.
J.K. Leonard, 293(JASt):Aug83-923
Irigaray, L. Passions élémentaires.
P. Moran, 208(FS):Jan83-115
"Irish Renaissance Annual III." (D.
Jackson, ed)
K.E. Marre, 395(MFS):Summer83-292
Irizarry, E. Rafael Dieste.*
N.M. Valis, 552(REH):May83-290
Irizarry, E. Enrique A. Laguerre.
F.H. Schiminovich, 238:Sep83-448
Irons, P. Justice at War.
O. Schell, 441:1Jan84-22

Ironside, E. A Very Private Enterprise.
T.J. Binyon, 617(TLS):26Oct84-1225
Irsigler, F. - see Dollinger, P.
Irvin, D. Mytharion.
D. Ben-Amos, 318(JAOS):Jan-Mar82-188
Irvin, E. Australian Melodrama.
V. Kelly, 71(ALS):May83-136
Irvine, L. Castaway.
V. Geng, 441:8Apr84-27
442(NY):14May84-149
Irving, C. Tom Mix and Pancho Villa.*
R.M. Davis, 577(SHR):Summer83-292
Irving, R.G. Indian Summer.*
P.F. Norton, 576:Dec83-390
Irving, T.B., ed and trans. "Kalilah and
Dimnah."*
R.G. Keightley, 547(RF):Band95Heft3-
395
Irwin, J.T. American Hieroglyphics.*
H. Claridge, 447(N&Q):Oct82-467
E.H. Redekop, 106:Winter83-415
N. Schmitz, 529(QQ):Winter83-1191
D. Tallack, 541(RES):May83-247
Irwin, J.V. and S.P. Wong, eds. Phonologi-
cal Development in Children.
L. Menn, 350:Sep84-686
Irwin, T. - see Plato
Isaac, D. - see Proclus
Isaac, R. The Transformation of Virginia,
1740-1790.*
T.H. Breen, 656(WMQ):Apr83-298
Isaac, R.J. and E. The Coercive Utopians.
R. Nisbet, 129:Mar84-79
Isaacs, A. and E. Martin, eds. Dictionary
of Music.
M. Rochester, 415:Apr83-235
Isaacs, A.R. Without Honor.*
R.B. Smith, 617(TLS):25May84-593
Isaacs, N.D. and R.A. Zimbardo, eds.
Tolkien.*
D. Barbour, 529(QQ):Spring83-230
M. Chassagnol, 189(EA):Apr-Sep83-344
Isaacs, S. Almost Paradise.
A. Shapiro, 441:12Feb84-20
Isaacson, W. Pro and Con.
P-L. Adams, 61:Mar84-132
Isaev, M.I. Jazyk Äsperanto.
G.F. Meier, 682(ZPSK):Band36Heft4-478
Isaksson, U. and E.H. Linder. Elin Wägner.
I. Claréus, 563(SS):Winter83-84
Isaku, P.R. Mountain Storm, Pine Breeze.
F. Hoff, 293(JASt):Nov82-165
Isherwood, C. My Guru and His Disciple.
A. Wilde, 506(PSt):May83-89
Isherwood, C. Prater Violet. The World
in the Evening. A Meeting by the River.
Exhumations.
J.C.H. Thompson, 617(TLS):7Dec84-1408
"Ishikawa Tadao Kyōju Kanreki Kinen Rombun-
shū."
H. Fukui, 293(JASt):Aug83-925
Ishioka, E. - see under Eiko Ishioka
Isichei, E. Entirely for God.
A. Redmayne, 69:Vol53No3-90
Isichei, E. A History of Nigeria.
M. Lynn, 617(TLS):11May84-531
Isichei, E., ed. Studies in the History
of Plateau State, Nigeria.
B. Sharpe, 69:Vol53No4-84
Saint Isidore of Seville. Isidorus His-
palensis, "Etymologiae XVII," de l'agri-
culture.* (J. André, ed and trans)
P.K. Marshall, 589:Jan83-264

Iskander, F. The Gospel According to Chegem.
  J. Laber, 441:10Jun84-14
Iskander, F. Sandro of Chegem.*
  D. Taylor, 364:Nov83-109
Israeli, R., ed. The Crescent in the East.
  W.R. Roff, 293(JASt):Aug83-1021
Issacharoff, M. and J-C. Vilquin, eds. Sartre et la mise en signe.
  O. Avni, 400(MLN):May83-829
  K. Kohut, 547(RF):Band95Heft1/2-210
  H. Wardman, 402(MLR):Apr83-463
Issatschenko, A. Geschichte der russischen Sprache. (Vol 1)
  H. Galton, 361:Jun/Jul83-266
Istrati, P. Le Pèlerin du coeur. (A. Talex, ed)
  V. Nemoianu, 617(TLS):5Oct84-1133
Italicus, T.C.S. - see under Silius Italicus, T.C.
Itasaka, G., ed-in-chief. Kondansha Encyclopedia of Japan.
  W.G. Beasley, 617(TLS):18May84-548
Itaya, K. Tengu Child.
  G. Kearns, 249(HudR):Autumn83-549
Ito, M. and A. Inoue. Kimono.
  R.L. Shep, 614:Summer84-21
Itwaru, A. Shattered Songs.
  I. Davies, 99:Apr83-33
Iusco, A.G. - see under Grelle Iusco, A.
Ivancich, A. La Torre Bianca.
  V. Meyers, 234:Fall83-66
Ivanov, V. Sobranie Sočinenij. (D.V. Ivanova and O. Dešart, eds)
  G. Ivask, 558(RLJ):Winter-Spring83-255
Ivanov, V. Sobranie sočinenij. (Vol 3) (D.V. Ivanov and O. Deschartes, eds)
  R.D.B. Thomson, 574(SEEJ):Spring83-112
Ivanova, I.P., V.V. Burlakova and G.G. Počepcov. Teoretičeskaja grammatika sovremennogo anglijskogo jazyka.
  J. Fronek, 361:Oct/Nov83-293
Iversen, G., ed. Corpus troporum IV, Tropes de l'Agnus Dei.*
  É. Weber, 555:Vol57fasc2-367
Ives, E.D. Joe Scott.*
  E. Danielson, 64(Arv):Vol37-191
Iwaichi, F. - see under Fujiwara Iwaichi
Iwaniuk, W. Evenings on Lake Ontario.
  A.C. Lupack, 497(PolR):Vol128No2-111
Izbicki, T.M. Protector of the Faith.
  W.D. McCready, 589:Jul83-759
Izikowitz, K.G. and P. Sørensen, eds. The House in East and Southeast Asia.
  P. Rabinow, 293(JASt):Aug83-895
Izmirlian, H., Jr. The Politics of Passion.
  J. Pettigrew, 293(JASt):Feb83-437
Izzo, H.J., ed. Italic and Romance.*
  M.W. Wheeler, 545(RPh):Nov82-229

Jaanus, M. She.
  E.R. Lipson, 441:29Jan84-22
Jabs, C. The Heirloom Gardener.
  L. Yang, 441:3Jun84-7
Jaccottet, P. Paysage avec figures absentes.
  G. Quinsat, 450(NRF):May83-123
Jaccottet, P. Pensées sous les nuages.
  S. Romer, 617(TLS):1Jun84-610

Jaccottet, P. A travers un verger. La Semaison: 1954-1979.
  R. Buss, 617(TLS):7Dec84-1412
Jaccottet, P. - see Musil, R.
Jachmann, G. Ausgewählte Schriften. (C. Gnilka, ed)
  P. Flobert, 555:Vol57fasc1-161
Jack, D. Rogues, Rebels and Geniuses.*
  W.C. Gibson, 102(CanL):Spring83-111
Jack, I. The Poet and His Audience.
  D. Donoghue, 617(TLS):7Sep84-987
Jack, I. and M. Smith - see Browning, R.
Jack, R.D.S. and R.J. Lyall - see Urquhart, T.
Jack, R.D.S. and A. Noble, eds. The Art of Robert Burns.*
  E. Letley, 617(TLS):6Apr84-383
Jackel, S., ed. A Flannel Shirt and Liberty.*
  T.J. Regehr, 529(QQ):Autumn83-870
  M. Stobie, 102(CanL):Autumn83-98
Jackman, S.W. The People's Princess.
  S. Runciman, 617(TLS):10Aug84-888
Jackowska, N. Earthwalks.* Doctor Marbles and Marianne.
  E. Larrissy, 493:Jun83-64
Jackson, A.M. Illustration and the Novels of Thomas Hardy.*
  J.B. Bullen, 301(JEGP):Apr83-256
  L. Elsbree, 637(VS):Summer83-454
  C. Fox, 59:Sep83-373
Jackson, A.Y. The Arctic 1927.
  529(QQ):Spring83-280
Jackson, B. Fatherhood.
  M. Kettle, 362:26Jul84-25
Jackson, C. The Dreadful Month.
  M.E. Reed, 9(AlaR):Jul83-238
Jackson, C.T. The Oriental Religions and American Thought.
  J. Ryder, 619:Winter83-115
Jackson, D. - see "Irish Renaissance Annual III"
Jackson, E. Middle East Mission.
  J.K. Davison, 441:11Mar84-19
Jackson, G. Leonardo Sciascia: 1956-1976.
  A. Ghezzi, 276:Spring83-80
Jackson, J.A. The Fish People.
  P. Henley, 617(TLS):27Jul84-853
Jackson, J.B. Discovering the Vernacular Landscape.
  J. Raban, 441:12Aug84-29
Jackson, J.H. and J.H. Baumert. Pictorial Guide to the Planets. (3rd ed)
  E. Argyle, 529(QQ):Summer83-312
Jackson, J.R.D. Poetry of the Romantic Period.*
  C. Sherry, 402(MLR):Jan83-153
Jackson, J.R.D. - see Coleridge, S.T.
Jackson, K.D. Traditional Authority, Islam, and Rebellion.
  M.K. Hassan, 318(JAOS):Jul-Sep82-571
Jackson, M. Allegories of the Wilderness.
  E. Tonkin, 69:Vol153No3-93
Jackson, M. Wall.
  T. James, 49:Jan83-86
Jackson, M.L. Style and Rhetoric in Bertrand Russell's Work.
  M. Moran, 556:Winter83/84-185
Jackson, N.S. Vinegar Pie and Chicken Bread. (M.J. Bolsterli, ed)
  639(VQR):Autumn83-124
Jackson, R., ed. Acts of Mind.
  C. Hall, 590:Dec83-104

Jackson, R. Fantasy.*
  C. Fierobe, 189(EA):Apr-Sep83-329
Jackson, R. - see Jones, H.A.
Jackson, R., with M. Lupica. Reggie.
  L.S. Ritter, 441:19Aug84-19
Jackson, R.L. The Art of Dostoevsky.*
  H.M. Curtler, 478:Apr83-138
  R. Freeborn, 402(MLR):Jul83-761
  G. Gibian, 574(SEEJ):Spring83-100
  A. McMillin, 575(SEER):Jul83-427
  N. Perlina, 558(RLJ):Fall83-221
  E. Wasiolek, 131(CL):Spring83-184
Jackson, S. J.P. Morgan.
  A. Sinclair, 617(TLS):25May84-590
Jackson, W. Vision and Re-Vision in
  Alexander Pope.
  G. Rousseau, 617(TLS):13Jul84-789
  J.A. Winn, 566:Spring84-158
Jackson, W. - see Molony, C.J.C., with
  others
Jackson, W.E. Reinmar's Women.
  H. Heinen, 589:Apr83-485
  H. Tervooren, 133:Band16Heft2/3-229
Jackson, W.T.H., ed. European Writers:
  The Middle Ages and the Renaissance.
  70:May-Jun83-165
Jackson, W.T.H. The Hero and the King.*
  R.G. Benson, 569(SR):Winter83-ix
  D.H. Green, 402(MLR):Oct83-879
  G.F. Jones, 222(GR):Summer83-123
  P.H. Stäblein, 589:Oct83-1057
Jacob, A. Cheminements.
  J.B. Ayoub, 154:Sep83-565
Jacob, M. and J., eds. The Origins of
  Anglo-American Radicalism.
  R. Thompson, 617(TLS):24Aug84-939
Jacob, M.C. The Radical Enlightenment.
  N.R. Gelbart, 173(ECS):Winter83/84-184
  R.H. Popkin, 319:Apr84-241
Jacob, P., ed and trans. Poèmes des Tang.
  G. Sartoris, 450(NRF):Nov83-154
Jacob, V. The Lum Hat and Other Stories.
  (R. Garden, ed)
  J.G. Roberts, 571(ScLJ):Winter83-70
Jacobbi, R. L'Avventura del Novecento.
  (A. Dolfi, ed)
  P. Hainsworth, 617(TLS):28Sep84-1097
Jacobi, R.L. Heinrich Heines jüdisches
  Erbe.
  C.A. Lea, 221(GQ):Mar83-324
Jacobowitz, E.S. and S.L. Stepanek. The
  Prints of Lucas van Leyden and His Con-
  temporaries.
  J. Nash, 617(TLS):11May84-528
Jacobs, A. Arthur Sullivan.
  A. Burgess, 441:26Aug84-8
  M. Kennedy, 362:9Aug84-28
  R.T. Shannon, 617(TLS):24Aug84-937
Jacobs, A. - see Flaubert, G. and G. Sand
Jacobs, D.N. Borodin.*
  J.D. Armstrong, 575(SEER):Apr83-300
Jacobs, H., ed. Documenta Malucensia III
  (1606-1682).
  C.R. Boxer, 617(TLS):27Jul84-844
Jacobs, H.C. Stendhal und die Musik.
  K. Ringger, 605(SC):15Jan84-196
Jacobs, J. Cities and the Wealth of
  Nations.
  J.R. Adams, 129:Nov84-71
  R.J. Barnet, 441:27May84-1
  N. Bliven, 442(NY):27Aug84-89

Jacobs, M. and M. Warner. The Phaidon Com-
  panion to Art and Artists in the British
  Isles.
  W. Baron, 39:Jul83-112
Jacobsen, J. The Chinese Insomniacs.*
  W.H. Pritchard, 560:Spring-Summer83-
  176
Jacobson, D. The Story of the Stories.*
  M.W. Bloomfield, 473(PR):4/1983-633
  J. Goldin, 31(ASch):Spring83-261
  H. Maccoby, 176:Feb84-62
  P. Swinden, 148:Winter83-93
Jacobson, H. Coming from Behind.*
  M. Leapman, 441:15Jan84-8
Jacobson, H. The "Exagoge" of Ezekiel.
  É. Des Places, 555:Vol157fasc2-316
Jacobson, H. Peeping Tom.
  A. Franks, 617(TLS):12Oct84-1167
Jacobson, M. Henry James and the Mass
  Market.
  M. Seymour, 617(TLS):25May84-594
Jacobson, N.P. Buddhism and the Contempo-
  rary World.
  N.F., 185:Oct83-165
Jacobson, P. and G.K. Pullum, eds. The
  Nature of Syntactic Representation.
  R.D. Borsley, 297(JL):Sep83-495
  M.S. Dryer, 320(CJL):Fall83-179
  E. Engdahl, 596(SL):Vol137No1-92
Jacobson, S. Preverbal Adverbs and Auxil-
  iaries.
  S.H. Elgin, 350:Jun84-457
Jacobson-Widding, A. Red-White-Black as a
  Mode of Thought.
  J.W. Burton, 69:Vol53No2-82
Jacobus, M., ed. Women Writing and Writ-
  ing about Women.*
  S. Foster, 677(YES):Vol 13-339
Jacoby, R. Social Amnesia.
  J. Shearmur, 488:Mar83-87
Jacoby, S. Wild Justice.*
  D. Johnson, 453(NYRB):16Feb84-38
Jacquart, D. Le milieu médical en France
  du XIIe au XVe siècle.
  L. Demaitre, 589:Apr83-486
Jacques, D. Georgian Gardens.
  D. Stroud, 617(TLS):13Jan84-43
Jacques, F. Différence et subjectivité.
  T. Cordellier, 450(NRF):Feb83-136
  J. Largeault, 542:Jul-Sep83-378
Jacques-Chaquin, N. - see de Lancre, P.
Jaeggli, O. Topics in Romance Syntax.
  H. Contreras, 350:Mar84-143
Jaffa, H.D. Modern Australian Poetry,
  1920-1970.
  A. Lawson, 402(MLR):Jul83-692
Jaffe, S. The Unexamined Wife.
  W.H. Pritchard, 249(HudR):Winter83/84-
  746
Jäger, G. Schule und literarische Kultur.
  (Vol 1)
  J. Herbst, 406:Winter83-427
Jager, G. and J. Schönert, eds. Die Leih-
  bibliothek als Institution des literar-
  ischen Lebens im 18. und 19. Jahrhundert.
  D. Paisey, 78(BC):Winter83-484
Jägerskiöld, S. Viimeiset vuodet: Manner-
  heim 1944-1951.
  M. Rintala, 550(RusR):Oct83-451
Jagger, B. Days of Grace.
  E.R. Lipson, 441:1Jan84-20
Jagger, C. Royal Clocks.
  G. Wills, 39:Oct83-353

188

Jay, E. The Religion of the Heart.*
  W. Franke, 38:Band101Heft1/2-278
Jay, G.S. T.S. Eliot and the Poetics of
  Literary History.
  L. Mackinnon, 617(TLS):30Mar84-350
Jay, J. The Winning of the Peace. (Vol 2)
  (R.B. Morris, with E. Sirvet, eds)
  D. Roper, 656(WMQ):Jan83-160
"Louis-Joseph Jay, sa vie, son oeuvre."
  V.D.L., 605(SC):15Jul84-377
Jay, P. The Crisis for Western Political
  Economy and Other Essays.
  S. Brittan, 617(TLS):28Dec84-1503
Jayakar, P. The Earthen Drum.
  S. Kramrisch, 57:Vol44No1-96
Jayavanta-Sūri. Jayavanta Sūri's Ṛṣidattā
  Rāsa. (N.A. Dalal, ed) Jayavanta
  Sūri's Śṛṅgāramañjarī (Śīlavatīcaritra
  Rāsa). (K.V. Sheth, ed)
  E. Bender, 318(JAOS):Oct-Dec82-679
Jaye, M.C. and A.C. Watts, eds. Litera-
  ture and the Urban Experience.
  W. Sharpe, 435:Spring83-79
Jazayery, M.A., E.C. Polomé and W. Winter,
  eds. Linguistic and Literary Studies in
  Honor of Archibald A. Hill.* (Vols 1-4)
  U. Fries, 38:Band101Heft3/4-456
"Jazykovĕda a příprava ucitelů jazyků,
  teoretické problémy."
  G.F. Meier, 682(ZPSK):Band36Heft5-609
Jeannotte, M. Le Vent n'a pas d'écho.
  E-M. Kroller, 102(CanL):Summer83-131
Jędruch, J. Constitutions, Elections and
  Legislatures of Poland, 1493-1977.
  W.J. Wagner, 497(PolR):Vol28No3-101
Jędrzejewicz, W. Józef Piłsudski, 1867-
  1935.
  D. Dyrcz-Freeman, 574(SEEJ):Winter83-
  499
Jeffares, A.N. Anglo-Irish Literature.
  A. Boué, 189(EA):Apr-Jun84-226
Jeffares, A.N. A New Commentary on the
  Poems of W.B. Yeats.
  W. Gould, 617(TLS):29Jun84-731
Jeffares, A.N., ed. Yeats, Sligo and
  Ireland.
  D.T. O'Hara, 637(VS):Autumn82-99
Jeffers, T.L. Samuel Butler Revalued.*
  R. Gounelas, 637(VS):Winter83-232
Jefferson, A. The Nouveau Roman and the
  Poetics of Fiction.*
  P.H. Solomon, 395(MFS):Summer83-305
Jefferson, A. and D. Robey, eds. Modern
  Literary Theory.
  S. Bassnett-McGuire, 307:Oct83-90
  M. Evans, 208(FS):Jul83-371
  I. Konigsberg, 478:Apr83-117
Jeffrey, D.L., ed. By Things Seen.
  M.G. Randel, 545(RPh):Nov82-263
Jeffrey, F. Jeffrey's Criticism.* (P.F.
  Morgan, ed)
  639(VQR):Autumn83-115
Jeffrey, R., ed. Asia — The Winning of
  Independence.
  A.A. Bliss, Jr., 293(JASt):Feb83-455
Jeffrey, R.C. The Logic of Decision.
  (2nd ed)
  S.W., 185:Apr84-549
Jeffrey, R.C., ed. Studies in Inductive
  Logic and Probability.* (Vol 2)
  I. Levi, 472(PhR):Jan83-116
Jeffreys, J.G. The Pangersbourne Murder.
  N. Callendar, 441:17Jun84-22

Jeffreys-Jones, R. and B. Collins, eds.
  The Growth of Federal Power in American
  History.
  H. Brogan, 617(TLS):29Jun84-734
Jeffri, J. The Emerging Arts.
  M.E. Rutenberg, 397(MD):Jun83-241
  W.M. Weiss, 615(TJ):May82-281
Jeffries, R. Deadly Petard.
  N. Callendar, 441:8Jan84-27
Jeffries, R. Three and One Make Five.
  T.J. Binyon, 617(TLS):13Jul84-790
Jehenson, M.Y. The Golden World of the
  Pastoral.*
  W.R. Davis, 551(RenQ):Summer83-288
  A. Desprechins, 535(RHL):Jul/Aug83-631
Jehmlich, R. Science Fiction.*
  A. Habermann, 561(SFS):Jul83-251
  W. Kluge, 72:Band220Heft2-427
  W.A. O'Brien, 221(GQ):Jan83-112
Jelavich, B. History of the Balkans.
  N. Stone, 617(TLS):16Mar84-277
Jelinek, E.C., ed. Women's Autobiography.
  V. Shaw, 506(PSt):May83-91
Jellicoe, M. The Long Path.
  B. Wisner, 69:Vol153No1-96
Jencks, C., ed. Post-Modern Classicism.
  P. Gough, 46:Mar81-317
Jencks, C. and W. Chaitkin. Current Archi-
  tecture.*
  J. Summerson, 46:May83-75
Jencks, H.W. From Muskets to Missiles.
  B. Esposito, 293(JASt):May83-621
Jenkins, A., ed. The Isle of Ladies or
  The Ile of Pleasaunce.
  J.M. Cowen, 541(RES):Feb83-61
Jenkins, B. Britain and the War for the
  Union.
  D.P. Crook, 637(VS):Winter83-230
Jenkins, D. Life Its Ownself.
  D.G. Myers, 441:21Oct84-30
  442(NY):10Dec84-190
Jenkins, H. - see Shakespeare, W.
Jenkins, I. Social Order and the Limits
  of Law.*
  A. Peczenik, 449:Nov83-711
Jenkins, M. Empire of Smoke.
  A. Stevenson, 617(TLS):2Mar84-226
Jenkins, R., ed. Britain and the EEC.
  E. Roll, 617(TLS):27Jan84-79
Jenkins, R. The Victorians and Ancient
  Greece.
  R.H. Evans, 366:Spring83-121
Jenner, W.J.F. Memories of Loyang.
  D. Grafflin, 293(JASt):Nov82-135
  V.H. Mair, 244(HJAS):Dec83-687
Jenney, C., Jr. and others. First Year
  Latin. Second Year Latin. Third Year
  Latin. Fourth Year Latin.
  F. Burke, 124:Jul-Aug84-382
Jennings, F. The Ambiguous Iroquois
  Empire.
  R. Sanders, 441:11Mar84-6
Jennings, G. The Journeyer.
  P-L. Adams, 61:Feb84-104
  J. Sullivan, 441:15Jan84-18
Jennings, L.B. Justinus Kerners Weg nach
  Weinsberg (1809-1819).
  A.P. Cottrell, 564:Nov83-296
  J. Rissmann, 133:Band16Heft2/3-251
Jennings, P. An End to Terrorism.
  P. Hebblethwaite, 617(TLS):14Dec84-
  1437

191

Johnson, C. Oxherding Tale.*
  S. Altinel, 617(TLS):6Jan84-19
Johnson, D. Angels.*
  J. Clute, 617(TLS):4May84-486
Johnson, D. Dashiell Hammett.*
  M. Colyer, 362:9Feb84-26
  J. Symons, 617(TLS):27Jan84-78
Johnson, D. The Incognito Lounge and
Other Poems.*
  W. Harmon, 569(SR):Summer83-457
  J.D. McClatchy, 491:Dec83-170
  R. Miklitsch, 271:Vol 13No3/4-246
  D. St. John, 42(AR):Spring83-231
Johnson, D. Stratemeyer Pseudonyms and
Series Books.
  S. Pickering, Jr., 517(PBSA):Vol77No1-
  67
Johnson, D.E. and P.M. Postal. Arc Pair
Grammar.
  G. Sampson, 307:Oct82-120
Johnson, D.G. The Medieval Chinese Oligar-
chy.
  T.H.C. Lee, 302:Vol 19No2-249
Johnson, D.R. Yuan Music Dramas.
  J.I. Crump, Jr., 116:Jul82-233
  D. Holm, 293(JASt):Feb83-392
Johnson, E. and D. Moggridge - see Keynes,
J.M.
Johnson, F. - see "Rockwell Kent: An
Anthology of his Works"
Johnson, G.W. South-Watching. (F. Hobson,
ed)
  J.S. Reed, 578:Spring84-110
Johnson, H. Wine Companion.
  R. Ockenden, 617(TLS):17Feb84-175
Johnson, J. Minor Characters.*
  42(AR):Summer83-374
Johnson, J.L. Mark Twain and the Limits
of Power.
  P.D. Beidler, 27(AL):Mar83-105
  J.W. Gargano, 573(SSF):Spring-Summer83-
  148
  D.E.E. Sloane, 26(ALR):Autumn83-312
  J.S. Tuckey, 395(MFS):Summer83-331
  J.S. Tuckey, 445(NCF):Sep83-247
  J.J. Wydeven, 649(WAL):Aug83-178
Johnson, K. Communicative Syllabus Design
and Methodology.
  C.K. Knop, 399(MLJ):Autumn83-275
Johnson, K.A. Women, the Family and
Peasant Revolution in China.
  D. Davin, 617(TLS):14Sep84-1013
Johnson, L. The Collected Poems of Lionel
Johnson. (2nd ed) (I. Fletcher, ed)
  R. Fréchet, 189(EA):Jul-Sep84-350
  W. Harris, 177(ELT):Vol26No4-313
Johnson, L.M. The Metaphor of Painting.
  N. Bryson, 208(FS):Apr83-240
Johnson, L.M. Wordsworth's Metaphysical
Verse.
  C.H. Ketcham, 50(ArQ):Summer83-184
  R. Lessa, 627(UTQ):Summer83-422
  G. Woodcock, 569(SR):Fall83-664
Johnson, M., ed. Philosophical Perspec-
tives on Metaphor.*
  R.D. Cureton, 35(AS):Fall83-267
Johnson, M.K., ed and trans. Recycling
the Prague Linguistic Circle.
  P.L. Garvin, 205(ForL):Aug81-90
  H. Penzl, 685(ZDL):2/1983-215
Johnson, M.P. and J.L. Roark. Black
Masters.
  I. Berlin, 441:16Dec84-12

Johnson, M.P. and J.L. Roark, eds. No
Chariot Let Down.
  I. Berlin, 441:16Dec84-12
Johnson, N. The Letters of Nunnally John-
son. (D. Johnson and E. Leventhal, eds)
  L. Willson, 569(SR):Summer83-490
Johnson, N. The Two of Us.
  C. Seebohm, 441:19Feb84-15
  442(NY):6Feb84-126
Johnson, O.A. Skepticism and Cognitivism.*
  N. Capaldi, 543:Dec82-455
Johnson, P. The Aerofilms Book of London
From the Air.
  G. Plimpton, 441:2Dec84-12
Johnson, P.D. Prayer, Patronage, and
Power.
  D.F. Callahan, 589:Apr83-492
Johnson, R. Carmen Laforet.*
  L. Hickey, 402(MLR):Jan83-213
Johnson, S. The Oxford Authors: Samuel
Johnson. (D. Greene, ed)
  W.W. Robson, 617(TLS):26Oct84-1221
Johnson, S. Johnson's Juvenal. (N. Rudd,
ed)
  W.W. Robson, 97(CQ):Vol 12No1-74
Johnson, T.O. Synge.*
  E. Benson, 150(DR):Summer83-368
  A. Roche, 272(IUR):Autumn83-257
Johnson, W. Poetry and Speculation of the
Ṛg Veda.*
  H.W. Bodewitz, 259(IIJ):Jun83-277
Johnson, W.R. The Idea of Lyric.*
  C.S. Brown, 131(CL):Fall83-374
  C.A. Rubino, 124:May-Jun84-326
Johnson-Davis, D., ed and trans. Arabic
Short Stories.
  R. Irwin, 617(TLS):13Jan84-46
Johnson-Laird, P.N. Mental Models.
  S. Stich, 617(TLS):24Feb84-189
Johnston, A. Of Earth and Darkness.*
  I. Gregor, 447(N&Q):Jun82-271
Johnston, A.F. and M. Rogerson, eds.
Records of Early English Drama: York.*
  R. Axton, 402(MLR):Oct83-892
Johnston, C. The Irish Lights.
  W. Scammell, 364:Dec83/Jan84-118
  G. Szirtes, 617(TLS):22Jun84-705
Johnston, G. Auk Redivivus.
  S. Morrissey, 137:Sep83-26
Johnston, G., comp and trans. Rocky
Shores.
  W.G. Jones, 562(Scan):Nov82-207
  S. Morrissey, 137:Sep83-26
  H. Roe, 102(CanL):Winter82-128
Johnston, J. The Railway Station Man.
  P. Craig, 617(TLS):5Oct84-1140
  R. Jones, 362:6Dec84-34
Johnston, K. The Lions in Winter.
  N. Kinnock, 617(TLS):2Mar84-224
Johnston, K.R. Wordsworth and "The
Recluse."
  K. Hanley, 617(TLS):3Aug84-862
Johnston, M. The Cuisine of the Rose.
  W. and C. Cowen, 639(VQR):Autumn83-137
Johnston, R.C. - see Fantosme, J.
Johnston, T.C. Carry The Wind.
  B.K. Morton, 649(WAL):Nov83-262
Johnston, W.R. The Nineteenth Century
Paintings in the Walters Art Gallery.
  J. Ingamells, 90:Nov83-695
Johnstone, R. The Will to Believe.*
  J. Meckier, 659(ConL):Spring84-110

193

Johnstone, R. and B. Kirk. Images of Belfast.
P. Craig, 617(TLS):31Aug84-979
Joiner, E.G. The Older Foreign Language Learner.
D.T. Stephens, 399(MLJ):Spring83-67
Jolley, E. Miss Peabody's Inheritance. Mr. Scobie's Riddle.
T.M. Disch, 441:18Nov84-14
442(NY):24Dec84-88
Jomaron, J. La Mise en scène contemporaine, II.
D. Bradby, 402(MLR):Oct83-932
R. Laubreaux, 535(RHL):May/Jun83-492
Jonas, G. Final Decree.*
J. Kertzer, 198:Jan83-125
Jonas, G. Vengeance.
K. Follett, 441:3Jun84-24
Jonas, H. Das Prinzip Verantwortung.
D. Birnbacher, 687:Jan-Mar83-144
Jonas, K.W. and others. Die Thomas-Mann-Literatur. (Vol 1)
H. Matter, 654(WB):5/1983-953
Jonas, K.W. and others. Die Thomas-Mann-Literatur.* (Vol 2)
H. Matter, 654(WB):5/1983-953
H.R. Vaget, 406:Summer83-230
Jonas, M. and R.V. Wells, eds. New Opportunities in a New Nation.
R.E. Carp, 656(WMQ):Oct83-658
Jonas, O. Introduction to the Theory of Heinrich Schenker. (J. Rothgeb, ed and trans)
W. Rothstein, 308:Fall83-273
G. Wintle, 617(TLS):1Jul83-697 [inadvertently omitted from prev]
Jones, A.G. Tomorrow is Another Day.*
B. Erkkila, 26(ALR):Spring83-154
M.F., 189(EA):Jul-Sep84-368
C.S. Manning, 585(SoQ):Spring83-80
W.J. Stuckey, 395(MFS):Winter83-722
Jones, B. For the Ancestors. (J. Stewart, ed)
E.S. Meadows, 187:Sep84-565
Jones, B.W. The Emperor Titus.
A. Wallace-Hadrill, 617(TLS):28Sep84-1102
Jones, D. Everyman's English Pronouncing Dictionary. (rev by A.C. Gimson)
A. Ward, 447(N&Q):Dec82-567
Jones, D. The Roman Quarry and Other Sequences.* (H. Grisewood and R. Hague, eds)
A. Cazade, 189(EA):Jan-Mar83-102
Jones, D.B. Movies and Memoranda.
D. Clandfield, 627(UTQ):Summer83-544
Jones, D.G., ed. Business, Religion, and Ethics.
D.S., 185:Jan84-378
Jones, D.R., ed. The Military-Naval Encyclopedia of Russia and the Soviet Union. (Vol 3)
W.F. Ryan, 575(SEER):Apr83-309
Jones, D.V. License for Empire.
Y. Kawashima, 656(WMQ):Jul83-483
Jones, E. and C. Woodward. A Guide to the Architecture of London.
A. Hollinghurst, 617(TLS):6Jan84-8
Jones, G., ed. The Oxford Book of Welsh Verse in English.
D. McDuff, 565:Vol24No4-62

Jones, G. Social Darwinism and English Thought.*
D. Watt, 506(PSt):Dec83-299
Jones, G. and M. Quinn. Fountains of Praise.
K.O. Morgan, 617(TLS):2Mar84-223
Jones, G.S. - see under Stedman Jones, G.
Jones, H. Pierre Gassendi 1591-1655.*
O. Bloch, 542:Jan-Mar83-117
Jones, H. - see Gassendi, P.
Jones, H.A. Plays by Henry Arthur Jones. (R. Jackson, ed)
H.F. Salerno, 177(ELT):Vol26No3-213
Jones, H.G. Hispanic Manuscripts and Printed Books in the Barberini Collection.*
F. Domínguez, 241:Jan83-62
Jones, J. Dostoevsky.
K. Fitzlyon, 364:Aug/Sep83-124
J. Frank, 617(TLS):9Mar84-249
V. Terras, 268(IFR):Summer84-117
Jones, J. Soldiers of Light and Love.
R. Reid, 106:Spring83-89
Jones, J. - see Alas, L.
Jones, J. and E. The Book of Bread.
W. and C. Cowen, 639(VQR):Spring83-70
Jones, J.D. - see Pseudo-Dionysius Areopagite
Jones, J.G., ed. Mississippi Writers Talking.* (Vol 1) [entry in prev was of Vols 1 and 2]
L.E. McDaniel, 585(SoQ):Spring83-78
N. Polk, 392:Spring83-133
W.J. Stuckey, 395(MFS):Summer83-334
Jones, J.H. Bad Blood.*
D.W. Bowen, 9(AlaR):Jul83-224
Jones, J.R., ed. Medieval, Renaissance and Folklore Studies in Honor of John Esten Keller.*
D.L. Heiple, 552(REH):May83-303
K. Kohut, 547(RF):Band95Heft3-392
V. Masson de Gómez, 545(RPh):May83-591
H.C. Woodbridge, 70:Jan-Feb81-95
Jones, L./A. Baraka. The Autobiography of Leroi Jones/Amiri Baraka.
H.L. Gates, Jr., 441:11Mar84-11
D. Pinckney, 453(NYRB):14Jun84-19
Jones, L.P. and I. Sa Kong. Government, Business and Entrepreneurship in Economic Development.
K. Moskowitz, 293(JASt):Nov82-63
D.I. Steinberg, 293(JASt):Nov82-91
Jones, M. Season of the Strangler.
J.N. Gretlund, 219(GaR):Spring83-219
M.R. Winchell, 569(SR):Winter83-xvi
Jones, M.A. The Limits of Liberty.
H. Temperley, 617(TLS):25May84-592
Jones, M.V. and G.M. Terry, eds. New Essays on Dostoyevsky.
J. Frank, 617(TLS):9Mar84-249
Jones, N. Fish Tales.
C. Gaiser, 441:29Apr84-42
D. Pinckney, 453(NYRB):8Nov84-12
Jones, P. Hume's Sentiments.*
P.A., 185:Jan84-374
E. Griffin-Collart, 540(RIPh):Vol137 fasc1/2-216
D. Livingston, 319:Oct84-482
Jones, R. Camus: "L'Étranger" and "La Chute."*
M. Bowie, 402(MLR):Apr83-461
Jones, R. Windows and Walls.
639(VQR):Spring83-61

Jones, R. and K. Daniels, eds. Of Soli-
tude and Silence.*
  J.R. Saucerman, 649(WAL):May83-91
Jones, R. and N. Penny. Raphael.*
  C. Gould, 39:Aug83-193
  C. Gould, 324:Jan84-138
Jones, R.A. The British Diplomatic Serv-
ice 1815-1914.
  J. Ure, 617(TLS):16Mar84-273
Jones, R.A. and H. Kuklick, eds. Research
in Sociology of Knowledge Sciences and
Art. (Vol 2)
  J. Wettersten, 488:Sep83-325
Jones, R.H. Medieval Houses at Flaxengate,
Lincoln.
  R. Brunskill, 44:Vol26-105
Jones, S., ed. Webfoots and Bunch-
grassers.*
  H. Cannon, 292(JAF):Apr-Jun83-220
Jones, S.M., ed. Select Papers from the
Center for Far Eastern Studies. (No 3)
  V.C. Falkenheim, 293(JASt):Aug83-927
Jones, T. Chaucer's Knight.*
  G.C. Britton, 447(N&Q):Oct82-431
  G.A. Lester, 382(MAE):1983/1-122
Jones, W.F. Nature and Natural Science.
  J. Gutmann, 311(JP):Dec83-817
Jones-Davies, M.T. Victimes et rebelles.*
  J. Briggs, 541(RES):Nov83-487
Jong, E. Parachutes and Kisses.
  C.D.B. Bryan, 441:21Oct84-14
  P. Kemp, 617(TLS):16Nov84-1302
  442(NY):19Nov84-190
Jönsjö, J. Studies on Middle English Nick-
names.* (Vol 1)
  P. Erlebach, 72:Band219Heft2-430
Jönsson, C. Superpower.
  G. Szamuely, 617(TLS):2Nov84-1253
Jordan, D.P. Political Leadership in
Jefferson's Virginia.
  E.S. Morgan, 441:15Jan84-16
Jordan, J.M. Paul Klee and Cubism.
  S. Ringbom, 617(TLS):8Jun84-630
Jordan, N. The Dream of a Beast.*
  P. Lewis, 364:Oct83-94
Jordan, N. The Past. Night in Tunisia.
  R. Bonaccorso, 174(Éire):Summer83-147
Jordan, P. The Cheat.
  R.W. Creamer, 441:28Oct84-20
Jordan, T.G. Texas Graveyards.
  G.E. Lich, 585(SoQ):Winter83-85
Jordanus de Nemore. De numeris datis.
  (B.B. Hughes, ed and trans)
  D.C. Lindberg, 589:Oct83-1123
Jorden, W.J. Panama Odyssey.
  J.A. Cabranes, 441:29Jul84-26
Jordens, C. Pierre Emmanuel poète cos-
mique.
  J. Onimus, 535(RHL):May/Jun83-482
Jordens, J.T.F. Dayānanda Sarasvatī.
  R. Rocher, 318(JAOS):Apr-Jun82-420
Jörg, C.J.A. Porcelain and the Dutch
China Trade.*
  G. Wills, 39:Nov83-455
Jorgens, E.B. The Well-Tun'd Word.*
  E. Doughtie, 308:Fall83-294
  D. Ostrom, 134(CP):Spring83-96
  C. Wilson, 410(M&L):Jan/Apr83-113
Jørgensen, J., ed. Taarnet (1893-94).
  G. Albeck, 562(Scan):Nov83-225
Jorion, P. Les Pêcheurs d'Houat.
  M. Chapman, 617(TLS):12Oct84-1154
  J.P., 98:May83-446

Josefson, E-K. La Vision citadine et
sociale dans l'oeuvre d'Émile Verhaeren.
  A. Vandegans, 535(RHL):Jul/Aug83-658
  R.C. Williamson, 207(FR):Apr84-721
Joselit, J.W. Our Gang.
  J.D. Sarna, 129:Aug84-53
Joseph, G. Mission sans retour.
  A. Suied, 450(NRF):Feb83-148
Joseph, J. Beyond Descartes.*
  S. Chambers, 493:Jun83-61
Joseph, L. Shouting At No One.
  J.F. Cotter, 249(HudR):Winter83/84-712
  R. Tillinghast, 385(MQR):Fall84-596
Joseph, T. George Grossmith.
  J.W. Steadman, 611(TN):Vol137No3-143
Josephs, L.S. Palauan Reference Grammar.
  G.F. Meier, 682(ZPSK):Band36Heft4-478
Josephy, A.M., Jr. Now That the Buffalo's
Gone.*
  T. King, 649(WAL):Nov83-258
Joshee, O.K. Mr. Surie.
  N. Callendar, 441:17Jun84-22
  442(NY):18Jun84-113
Joshi, A.K., B.L. Webber and I.A. Sag, eds.
Elements of Discourse Understanding.*
  M. Owen, 297(JL):Mar83-241
Joshi, S.D. - see Kiparsky, P.
Joshi, V. Problems in Sanskrit Grammar.
  R. Rocher, 318(JAOS):Oct-Dec82-672
Josipovici, G. The Air We Breathe.
  C. Baranger, 189(EA):Oct-Dec84-482
Josipovici, G. Conversations in Another
Room.
  A.J. Fitzgerald, 617(TLS):30Nov84-1392
Josipovici, G. The Echo Chamber.
  C. Baranger, 189(EA):Apr-Sep83-349
Josipovici, G. The Mirror of Criticism.
  P. Kemp, 362:26Jan84-20
Josipovici, G. Writing and the Body.*
  P. Kemp, 362:26Jan84-20
  H.E. Lusher, 268(IFR):Winter84-69
Jöst, E. Bauernfeindlichkeit.
  H-D. Mück, 680(ZDP):Band102Heft3-456
Jöst, E., ed. Die Historien des Neithart
Fuchs.*
  I. Bennewitz-Behr, 680(ZDP):Band102
  Heft3-459
Jouas, A.E. Le pédagogie de la révolte
politique dans les publications de Weis-
mann Verlag, de 1970 à 1975.
  G.P. Knapp, 221(GQ):Nov83-678
Joubert, J. The Notebooks of Joseph Jou-
bert.* (P. Auster, ed and trans)
  639(VQR):Autumn83-123
Joubert, L. Treatise on Laughter.* (G.D.
de Rocher, ed and trans)
  W.G.A. Brooks, 208(FS):Oct83-450
Jouhandeau, M. Dans l'épouvante le sou-
rire aux lèvres.
  C. Dis, 450(NRF):May83-115
Joukovsky, F. Le regard intérieur.
  P. Magnard, 192(EP):Jul-Sep83-368
Journet, R. and G. Robert. Contribution
aux études sur Victor Hugo. (Vols 1-4)
  Y. Gohin, 535(RHL):Jul/Aug83-647
Jouve, P.J. La Scène capitale.
  C. Dis, 450(NRF):Mar83-122
Jover Zamora, J.M., ed. España romana
(218 a. de J.C. - 414 de J.C.).
  N. Mackie, 123:Vol33No2-267
Jowell, J.L. and J.P.W.B. McAuslan, eds.
Lord Denning.
  D. Pannick, 617(TLS):9Nov84-1279

Joyce, C. Designing for Printed Textiles.
P. Scheinman, 139:Feb/Mar83-33
Joyce, J. Giacomo Joyce. (R. Ellmann, ed)
The Dead. (illustrated by P. Annigoni)
Finnegans Wake. (Chapter One) (T. Ahern,
ed)
R. Brown, 617(TLS):10Feb84-135
Joyce, J. Oeuvres, I. (J. Aubert, ed)
J-M. Rabaté, 98:Aug-Sep83-691
Joyce, J. Ulysses. (H.W. Gabler, W.
Steppe and C. Melchior, eds)
R. Ellmann, 453(NYRB):25Oct84-30
H. Kenner, 617(TLS):13Jul84-771
Joyce, J. and P. Murtagh. The Boss.
J. Vaizey, 362:9Feb84-24
Joyce, P. Work, Society and Politics.*
M. Mudrick, 249(HudR):Spring83-189
Joyce, W.L. and others, eds. Printing and
Society in Early America.
C.N. Davidson, 165(EAL):Winter83/84-
299
R.E. Stoddard, 617(TLS):10Feb84-151
Jrade, C.L. Rubén Darío and the Romantic
Search for Unity.
H.C. Woodbridge, 263(RIB):Vol33No4-591
Jucquois, G. and B. Devlamminck. Die
Sprache 1 (1949) — 20 (1974): Index des
formes.
R. Schmitt, 260(IF):Band88-287
Jucquois, G. and R. Lebrun, with B. Devlam-
minck, eds. Hethitica 2.
G.C. Moore, 318(JAOS):Jan-Mar82-180
Judd, A. Short of Glory.
T. Fitton, 617(TLS):19Oct84-1180
Judd, C. and A. Ray, eds. Old Trails and
New Directions.
A. Tanner, 529(QQ):Spring83-176
Judge, A. and F.G. Healey. A Reference
Grammar of Modern French.*
S.N. Rosenberg, 207(FR):Apr84-726
Judge, E.A. Rank and Status in the World
of the Caesars and St. Paul.
A.E. Hanson, 124:Jan-Feb84-195
Juergensmeyer, M. and N.G. Barrier, eds.
Sikh Studies.
N. Singh, 293(JASt):Aug83-991
Juhász, J., ed. Kontrastive Studien Ungar-
isch-Deutsch.
R. Radomski, 260(IF):Band88-383
Juhasz, S. The Undiscovered Continent.
M.L. Rosenthal, 617(TLS):15Jun84-669
Juhl, M. and B.H. Jørgensen. Dianas Haevn
— to spor i Karen Blixens forfatterskab.*
(2nd ed)
S.E. Larsen, 562(Scan):May83-85
Juhl, P.D. Interpretation.*
J.A.V. Chapple, 447(N&Q):Oct82-478
R.D. Denham, 405(MP):Nov83-217
G.P. Knapp, 221(GQ):May83-462
J. Margolis, 482(PhR):Apr83-269
B.A. Wilson, 529(QQ):Summer83-552
Juin, H. - see de Gobineau, A-J.
Julia, D. Les Trois Couleurs du tableau
noir: La Révolution.*
C. Garaud, 207(FR):Dec83-284
Juliá, E.R. - see under Rodríguez Juliá, E.
Jully, J.J. Labraunda. (Vol 2, Pt 3)
J. Boardman, 123:Vol33No2-359
Jung, C.G. The Seminars. (Vol 1: Dream
Analysis 1928-1930) The Zofingia Lec-
tures. (W. McGuire, ed of both)
A. Storr, 617(TLS):20Jul84-803

Jung, F. Gott verschläft die Zeit. (K.
Ramm, ed)
H. Bänziger, 221(GQ):Jan83-159
Jungandreas, W. Zur Geschichte des Mosel-
romanischen.*
H.J. Wolf, 72:Band219Heft1-213
Junger, E. L'auteur et l'écriture.
J. Théodoridès, 605(SC):15Jan84-197
Junger, E. Soixante-dix s'efface.
J. Théodoridès, 605(SC):15Jul84-376
Jungraithmayr, H., ed and trans. Märchen
aus dem Tschad.
E. Ettlinger, 203:Vol94No2-262
P. Fuchs, 196:Band24Heft1/2-155
Jungraithmayr, H. and J-P. Caprile, eds.
Cinq textes Tchadiques (Cameroun et
Tchad).
G.F. Meier, 682(ZPSK):Band36Heft2-239
Junk-Ok, T. Jeanne d'Arc dans l'oeuvre
de Péguy de 1910 à 1914.
J. Onimus, 535(RHL):Sep/Dec83-956
Junquera, J.J. La decoración y el mobili-
ario de los palacios de Carlos IV.
V. Tovar Martín, 48:Jul-Sep80-398
Jurgens, M. Documents du Minutier central
des notaires de Paris.
354:Dec83-442
Jurgensen, M., ed. Thomas Bernhard.*
J. Donnenberg, 133:Band16Heft2/3-290
Jurgensen, M. Erzählformen des fiktional-
en Ich.*
F. Voit, 406:Winter83-434
Jurgensen, M. Das fiktionale Ich.*
K. Mommsen, 149(CLS):Fal183-350
G.F. Probst, 133:Band16Heft2/3-283
Jurt, J. La Réception de la littérature
par la critique journalistique.
A. Gier, 72:Band220Heft2-456
Jusefovich, V. David Oistrakh: Conversa-
tions with Igor Oistrakh.
H.B.R., 412:May82-151
Just, W. The American Blues.
J. House, 441:8Jul84-14
Just, W. In the City of Fear.
J. Epstein, 249(HudR):Spring83-180
Justus, J.H. The Achievement of Robert
Penn Warren.*
V.D. Balitas, 579(SAQ):Winter83-105
M.K. Spears, 569(SR):Fal183-655
Juvenal. Sixteen Satires Upon the Ancient
Harlot.* (S. Robinson, trans)
W. Raschke, 124:May-Jun84-329
Juxon, J. Lewis and Lewis.*
M. Peters, 441:18Mar84-19

van Kaam, B. The South Moluccans.
R. Van Niel, 293(JASt):May83-733
Kaan, O. - see Saba, U.
Kabir, M.G. Minority Politics in Bangla-
desh.
H.H. Khondker, 293(JASt):May83-701
Kachru, B.B., ed. The Other Tongue.
M.E. Call, 399(MLJ):Summer83-181
W.C. Ritchie, 350:Dec84-937
Kael, P. 5001 Nights at the Movies.
G. Kaufman, 362:19Apr84-26
A. White, 200:Jan83-61
Kael, P. Taking It All In.
G. Mast, 441:15Apr84-15
Kaelble, B. Untersuchungen zur grossfig-
urigen Plastik des Samsonmeisters.
K. Niehr, 683:Band46Heft1-115

Kamph, J. A Collector's Guide to Book-
binding.
   S. Borghese, 517(PBSA):Vol77No3-390
   F. Broomhead, 503:Spring83-48
Kamuf, P. Fictions of Feminine Desire.*
   S. Rava, 207(FR):Feb84-394
Kandell, J. Passage through El Dorado.
   A. Shoumatoff, 441:18Mar84-8
Kandinsky, W. Complete Writings on Art.*
   (K.C. Lindsay and P. Vergo, eds and
   trans)
   C. Lodder, 90:Nov83-705
   P. Overy, 592:Jan-Feb83-61
Kane, G.S. Anselm's Doctrine of Freedom
   and the Will.
   S.P. Marrone, 589:Oct83-1060
Kanellos, N., ed. A Decade of Hispanic
   Literature.
   A.F. Murphy, 238:Dec83-645
Kanellos, N., ed. Mexican American Thea-
   tre.
   O.U. Somoza, 352(LATR):Spring84-105
Kanner, B., ed. The Women of England from
   Anglo-Saxon Times to the Present.*
   S. Foster, 677(YES):Vol 13-338
Kant, H. Zu den Unterlagen.
   H. Kähler, 654(WB):3/1982-125
Kant, I. Fondements de la métaphysique
   des moeurs. (V. Delbos, trans)
   O. Masson, 192(EP):Oct-Dec83-498
Kant, I. Idée d'une Histoire universelle
   au point de vue cosmopolitique. (J-M.
   Muglioni, ed and trans)
   A. Stanguennec, 542:Jan-Mar83-125
Kant, I. Kants gesammelte Schriften.
   (Vol 27)
   W. Marx, 53(AGP):Band65Heft1-101
Kant, I. Kants gesammelte Schriften.
   (Vol 29)
   W. Steinbeck, 342:Band74Heft4-504
Kant, I. Immanuel Kants Schriften zur
   Religion. (M. Thom, ed)
   R. Malter, 342:Band74Heft4-507
Kant, I. Kritik der reinen Vernunft.
   R. Malter, 342:Band74Heft4-505
Kant, I. Por qué no es inútil una nueva
   Crítica de la Razón Pura (Respuesta a
   Eberhard). (A. Castaño Piñan, trans)
   M.P.M. Caimi, 342:Band74Heft4-508
Kant, I. Traité de pédagogie. (P-J.
   About, ed)
   A. Stanguennec, 542:Jan-Mar83-126
Kantaris, S. The Tenth Muse.
   H. Davies, 617(TLS):13Apr84-413
   H. Lomas, 364:Feb84-83
Kantowsky, D. Sarvodaya.
   J. Das Gupta, 293(JASt):Nov82-105
Kao, G., ed. The Translation of Things
   Past.
   A.T. Grunfeld, 293(JASt):May83-622
Kao Ming. The Lute.* (J. Mulligan, trans)
   C-H. Perng, 116:Jan82-113
Kaplan, E.A. Women and Film.
   B.R. Rich, 18:Dec83-68
Kaplan, E.K. - see Michelet, J.
Kaplan, F. Thomas Carlyle.
   J. Clive, 617(TLS):20Apr84-419
   R.H. Super, 385(MQR):Fall84-609
   D. Thomas, 441:8Jan84-14
   442(NY):16Jan84-111
Kaplan, F. - see Dickens, C.
Kaplan, F.S., ed. Images of Power.
   P. Ben-Amos, 2(AfrA):Feb83-17

Kaplan, H. Power and Order.*
   R.W. Harvey, 106:Winter83-467
Kaplan, J. The Court-Martial of the Kao-
   hsiung Defendants.
   J.D. Seymour, 293(JASt):Feb83-397
Kaplan, J. Mark Twain and His World.
   P. Wolfe, 395(MFS):Summer83-332
Kaplan, J. - see Whitman, W.
Kaplan, S.L. "La Bagarre": Galiani's
   "Lost" Parody.
   W.D. Howarth, 208(FS):Oct83-464
Kapp, V. "Télémaque" de Fénelon.
   D. Fricke, 475:Vol 10No19-913
Kappeler, S. Writing and Reading in Henry
   James.*
   P.B. Armstrong, 445(NCF):Jun83-122
   W.R. Goetz, 594:Fall83-280
   R.K. Martin, 106:Winter83-457
Kappler, C. Monstres, Démons et Mer-
   veilles à la Fin du Moyen Âge.*
   W. Rothwell, 208(FS):Oct83-444
Kapschutschenko, L. El labertino en la
   narrativa hispanoamericana contemporánea.
   G.D. Carrillo, 238:Sep83-439
   U. Schulz-Buschhaus, 547(RF):Band95
   Heft3-401
Kapur, H. The Awakening Giant.
   J. Grasso, 293(JASt):May83-624
Karageorghis, V. and others. Excavations
   at Kition. (Vol 4)
   J. Boardman, 123:Vol33No1-148
Karalaschwili, R. Hermann-Hesse-Studien.
   R. Koester, 221(GQ):Jan83-175
Karch, P.P. Nuits blanches.
   A.L. Amprimoz, 102(CanL):Summer83-126
Kärki, I. Die sumerischen und akkadischen
   Königsinschriften der Altbabylonischen
   Zeit.
   G.F. Meier, 682(ZPSK):Band36Heft4-491
Karl, B.D. The Uneasy State.
   E.R. May, 441:7Oct84-30
Karl, F.R. American Fictions 1940/1980.
   J.W. Aldridge, 441:8Jan84-11
Karl, F.R. and L. Davies - see Conrad, J.
"Karlamagnús saga: Branches I, III, VII et
   IX."* (A. Loth, ed; A. Patron-Godefroit,
   trans)
   A. de Mandach, 301(JEGP):Jan83-122
   I. Short, 208(FS):Apr83-202
Karlin, W. Crossover.
   S.D. Smith, 441:25Mar84-20
   442(NY):23Apr84-134
Karlsen, C.F. and L. Crumpacker - see Burr,
   E.E.
Karlsson, K.E. Syntax and Affixation.*
   H. Van den Bussche, 553(RLiR):
   Jul-Dec83-443
Karnein, A., ed. Salman und Morolf.*
   C. Gellinek, 680(ZDP):Band102Heft3-451
Karnick, M. Rollenspiel und Welttheater.
   H.A. Glaser, 490:Band14Heft3/4-345
   W. Theile, 52:Band17Heft2-204
Karnow, S. Vietnam.*
   N. Podhoretz, 129:Apr84-35
Karpel, B., ed. Arts in America.
   R. Philp, 151:Feb81-107
Karpiński, J. Count-Down.*
   A.M. Cienciala, 497(PolR):Vol28No1-106
   J. Woodall, 575(SEER):Oct83-633
Karpozilos, A. Symbothē stē meletē toy
   ergoy toy Iōannē Mayropodos.
   A. Kazhdan, 589:Jul83-763

Keith, W.J., ed. A Voice in the Land.*
  P. Morley, 178:Jun83-249
Kell, R. The Broken Circle.
  R. Pybus, 565:Vol24No2-73
Kellenberger, I. Der Jugendstil und Rob-
  ert Walser.
  M. Holona, 133:Band16Heft2/3-262
Keller, B. Pauline.
  M. Whitaker, 102(CanL):Spring83-132
Keller, E.F. A Feeling for the Organism.*
  S.J. Gould, 453(NYRB):29Mar84-3
Keller, G. Academic Strategy.
  D.L. Eder, 31(ASch):Autumn83-567
Keller, H. and M. Cosman. Stravinsky:
  Seen and Heard.*
  J.B., 412:Aug-Nov82-267
Keller, O. Döblins Montageroman als Epos
  der Moderne.*
  J. Amsler, 549(RLC):Apr-Jun83-253
  O. Durrani, 402(MLR):Jan83-245
  M.S. Fries, 406:Winter83-451
Keller, R.E. The German Language.
  J. Göschel, 685(ZDL):1/1983-67
Keller, U. Fiktionalität als literaturwis-
  senschaftliche Kategorie.
  J. Anderregg, 490:Band14Heft3/4-317
  M. Knapp, 221(GQ):May83-467
Kelley, M. Private Woman, Public Stage.
  D. Johnson, 453(NYRB):12Apr84-23
  C. Smith-Rosenberg, 441:22Jan84-16
Kellner, M.M. - see Abravanel, I.
Kelly, A. Mikhail Bakunin.*
  S. Monas, 453(NYRB):16Feb84-32
  P. Pomper, 550(RusR):Oct83-430
Kelly, B. and M. London. Amazon.
  P. Henley, 617(TLS):30Nov84-1368
  E. Hoagland, 441:22Jan84-26
  442(NY):23Jan84-105
Kelly, D., comp. Chrétien de Troyes.
  G.M. Armstrong, 545(RPh):Nov82-302
Kelly, G.A. Victims, Authority and
  Terror.
  B.G. Garnham, 83:Autumn83-228
  J. Popkin, 173(ECS):Spring84-358
Kelly, L., ed. Moscow.
  K. FitzLyon, 617(TLS):6Apr84-378
  E. Newman, 441:3Jun84-11
Kelly, L.G. The True Interpreter.*
  D. Bellos, 447(N&Q):Dec82-563
  C. Kasparek, 497(PolR):Vol28No2-83
  K. Reiss, 72:Band219Heft1-157
Kelly, M. Modern French Marxism.
  M.A. Caws, 478:Oct83-268
Kelly, P. Fighting for Hope.
  L. Heron, 362:28Jun84-26
Kelly, W.W. Irrigation Management in
  Japan. Water Control in Tokugawa Japan.
  D.H. Kornhauser, 407(MN):Winter83-465
Kelman, J. The Busconductor Hines.
  E. Morgan, 617(TLS):13Apr84-397
Kelsall, M. Congreve: "The Way of the
  World."
  566:Spring84-164
Kelsall, M. Christopher Marlowe.
  E. Jones, 184(EIC):Oct83-339
Kelsay, I.T. Joseph Brant.
  N.S. Momaday, 441:13May84-7
Kelsey, W.M. Konjaku Monogatari-shū.
  Takeda Katsuhiko, 285(JapQ):Apr-Jun83-
  209
  S.D. Videen, 407(MN):Summer83-207
Kelterborn, R. Zum Beispiel Mozart.
  J. Brand, 308:Fall83-306

Kelvin, N. - see Morris, W.
Kemal, Y. Tu écraseras le serpent.
  L. Kovacs, 450(NRF):Jan83-139
Kemp, I. Tippett.
  A. Whittall, 617(TLS):28Dec84-1493
Kemp, J.A. - see Lepsius, R.
Kemp, M. Leonardo da Vinci.*
  S. Kiernan, 67:May83-152
  M. Podro, 90:Jan83-35
  J. Wasserman, 551(RenQ):Spring83-106
Kemp, P. H.G. Wells and the Culminating
  Ape.*
  R.H. Costa, 395(MFS):Summer83-266
  295(JML):Nov83-585
Kemp, S. No Escape.
  N. Callendar, 441:13May84-35
Kempowski, W. Days of Greatness.*
  P. Lewis, 565:Vol24No3-36
Kendon, A., ed. Nonverbal Communication,
  Interaction and Gesture.
  M. Davis, 567:Vol42No2/4-319
Kendrick, W.M. The Novel-Machine.*
  J. Halperin, 125:Spring83-275
Keneally, T. A Cut-Rate Kingdom.
  J. Mellors, 362:5Jul84-27
  M. Wood, 617(TLS):24Aug84-935
Keneally, T. Outback.*
  J. Neville, 364:Mar84-109
Kenech'du, T. - see Pagels, E.
Kennan, G.F. The Fateful Alliance.
  P-L. Adams, 61:Dec84-145
  J. Joll, 453(NYRB):22Nov84-33
  P. Kennedy, 441:21Oct84-1
Kennan, G.F. The Nuclear Delusion.*
  L. Freedman, 617(TLS):25May84-588
  T. Garden, 176:Apr84-57
  639(VQR):Summer83-96
Kennedy, A. The Domino Vendetta.
  N. Callendar, 441:17Jun84-22
Kennedy, E., ed. "Lancelot do Lac."*
  N. Mann, 447(N&Q):Dec82-533
  L.D. Wolfgang, 589:Oct83-1061
Kennedy, G.A. Greek Rhetoric Under the
  Christian Emperors.*
  H.F. North, 124:Jan-Feb84-191
Kennedy, H.C. Peano.
  P. Odifreddi, 316:Jun83-503
Kennedy, J. Nubian Ceremonial Life.
  J.W. Burton, 69:Vol53No2-82
Kennedy, M. Britten.
  J.B., 412:May82-152
  S. Banfield, 410(M&L):Jan/Apr83-87
Kennedy, M. A Catalogue of the Works of
  Ralph Vaughan Williams. (rev)
  S. Banfield, 415:Apr83-239
  P. Jones, 410(M&L):Jul/Oct83-269
Kennedy, M. The Hallé 1858-1983.
  D. Fanning, 415:Aug83-484
Kennedy, M. Portrait of Elgar. (2nd ed)
  S. Banfield, 410(M&L):Jan/Apr83-107
Kennedy, M.L. The Jacobin Clubs in the
  French Revolution: The First Years.
  F. Busi, 207(FR):Dec83-285
  W. Doyle, 83:Spring83-114
Kennedy, P. Strategy and Diplomacy 1870-
  1945.
  C.S. Maier, 441:18Mar84-16
  Z. Steiner, 617(TLS):16Mar84-273
Kennedy, P. The War Plans of the Great
  Powers, 1880-1914.
  A. Katz, 497(PolR):Vol28No4-118
Kennedy, P.T. Ghanaian Businessmen.
  H.L. van der Laan, 69:Vol53No2-78

Kennedy, R., ed. Australian Welfare History.
  K. Tsokhas, 381:Sep83-390
Kennedy, R.S. - see Wolfe, T.
Kennedy, R.S. - see Wolfe, T. and E. Nowell
Kennedy, W. The Ink Truck.
  J. Conarroe, 441:30Sep84-11
Kennedy, W. Ironweed.*
  D. Flower, 249(HudR):Summer83-375
  P. French, 617(TLS):5Oct84-1116
  J. Mellors, 362:11Oct84-30
Kennedy, W. Legs. Billy Phelan's Greatest Game.
  D. Flower, 249(HudR):Summer83-375
  P. French, 617(TLS):5Oct84-1116
Kennedy, W. O Albany!
  T. Fleming, 441:1Jan84-11
Kennedy, W.J. Rhetorical Norms in Renaissance Literature.
  R. Ahrens, 38:Band101Heft1/2-243
Kennedy, W.J. Jacopo Sannazaro and the Uses of Pastoral.
  H. Cooper, 617(TLS):19Oct84-1181
Kenner, F.M. The Chain of Becoming.*
  D. Pollard, 478:Oct83-258
Kenner, H. A Colder Eye.*
  D. O'Brien, 329(JJQ):Winter84-179
  V. Young, 472:Fall/Winter83Spring/Summer84-323
  42(AR):Fall83-507
Kenner, H. "Ulysses."*
  P.M.S. Dawson, 541(RES):Feb83-96
  O.W. Ferguson, 579(SAQ):Winter83-112
  R.D. Jordan, 161(DUJ):Dec82-113
  E. Lobsien, 38:Band101Heft3/4-536
  R. Mason, 447(N&Q):Jun82-266
Kennett, L. A History of Strategic Bombing.
  639(VQR):Summer83-84
Kenney, E.J. and W.V. Clausen, eds. The Cambridge History of Classical Literature. (Vol 2)
  J.A. Barsby, 67:May83-126
  E. Fantham, 487:Summer83-168
  S.M. Goldberg, 121(CJ):Apr/May84-368
  R.G.M. Nisbet, 313:Vol73-175
  G.B. Townend, 123:Vol33No1-44
Kenney, R. The Evolution of the Flightless Bird.
  J. Hollander, 676(YR):Spring84-ix
  W. Logan, 441:26Aug84-13
Kenney, S. In Another Country.
  M.K. Benet, 617(TLS):2Nov84-1239
  A. Tyler, 441:5Aug84-8
  442(NY):27Aug84-92
Kennington, R., ed. The Philosophy of Baruch Spinoza.
  T.C. Mark, 543:Mar83-717
Kenny, A. The Computation of Style.
  D.C. Spinelli, 399(MLJ):Summer83-176
Kenny, A. Thomas More.
  R. Blythe, 362:16Feb84-24
Kent, A., H. Lancour and J.E. Daily - see "Encyclopedia of Library and Information Science"
Kent, D.V. and F.W. Neighbours and Neighbourhood in Renaissance Florence.
  D. Herlihy, 551(RenQ):Winter83-583
Kent, F.W. and others. Giovanni Rucellai ed il suo Zibaldone. (Vol 2)
  G. Brucker, 551(RenQ):Spring83-86
  R.A. Goldthwaite, 90:Jan83-34

Kent, J.P.C. The Roman Imperial Coinage.* (Vol 8)
  D. Nash, 123:Vol133No1-108
Kent, K.P. Pueblo Indian Textiles.
  R.L. Shep, 614:Summer84-25
"Rockwell Kent: An Anthology of his Works."* (F. Johnson, ed)
  M.S. Young, 39:Sep83-272
Kenyon, J. The History Men.*
  R.C. Richardson, 366:Autumn83-255
  L. Stone, 441:18Mar84-22
Keohane, N.O. Philosophy and the State in France.*
  M. Hulliung, 173(ECS):Fall83-69
Keohane, N.O., M.Z. Rosaldo and B.C. Gelpi, eds. Feminist Theory.
  S.M. Okin, 185:Jul84-723
Kępiński, Z. Veit Stoss.
  J. Kębłowski, 471:Apr/May/Jun83-176
Keppel-Jones, A. Rhodes and Rhodesia.
  R. Gray, 617(TLS):6Jul84-764
Keppie, L. The Making of the Roman Army.
  A. Birley, 617(TLS):23Nov84-1332
Ker, I. and T. Gornall - see Newman, J.H.
Ker, N.R. Medieval Manuscripts in British Libraries. (Vol 3)
  D.G. Vaisey, 617(TLS):16Mar84-286
Kerber, L.K. Women of the Republic.*
  B. Tucker, 106:Spring83-49
Kerbrat-Orecchioni, C. L'énonciation.
  J-C. Gagnon, 193(ELit):Apr83-169
Kerferd, G.B. The Sophistic Movement.*
  M.M. MacKenzie, 123:Vol33No2-220
  T.M. Robinson, 518:Jan83-7
  R.K. Sprague, 303(JoHS):Vol 103-189
Kerferd, G.B., ed. The Sophists and Their Legacy.
  L. Golden, 124:Sep-Oct83-51
  M. Schofield, 123:Vol33No1-141
de Kermadec, J-M.H. The Way to Chinese Astrology.
  D. Walters, 617(TLS):6Apr84-360
Kerman, J. The Masses and Motets of William Byrd.
  P.F., 412:May82-140
Kermode, F. Essays on Fiction 1971-82.*
  B. Bergonzi, 176:Jul/Aug84-47
  A. Phillips, 364:Nov83-116
Kermode, F. The Genesis of Secrecy.* The Art of Telling.
  R. Scholes, 454:Spring84-266
Kern, E. The Absolute Comic.*
  P. Petro, 107(CRCL):Jun83-251
Kern, L.J. An Ordered Love.
  L. Perry, 529(QQ):Autumn83-768
  A.F. Scott, 579(SAQ):Spring83-224
  T. Sinclair-Faulkner, 106:Fall83-315
Kern, M., P.W. Levering and R.B. Levering. The Kennedy Crises.
  P. Braestrup, 441:18Mar84-28
  C. Seymour-Ure, 617(TLS):17Aug84-908
Kern-Simirenko, C.A. - see Simirenko, A.
Kernan, A.B. The Imaginary Library.*
  R.W. Daniel, 569(SR):Spring83-xxxviii
  R. Helgerson, 131(CL):Summer83-289
Kernan, A.B. The Playwright as Magician.*
  I. Schabert, 38:Band101Heft1/2-255
Kerner, J. Ausgewählte Werke.* (G. Grimm, ed)
  M. Gelus, 221(GQ):Jan83-146
  J. Purver, 402(MLR):Apr83-494

Kierkegaard, S. L'Instant.
T. Cordellier, 450(NRF):May83-134
Kiernan, B. Patrick White.*
J. Croft, 71(ALS):May83-141
Kiernan, K.S. "Beowulf" and the "Beowulf"
Manuscript.*
N.F. Blake, 179(ES):Dec83-72
J.D. Niles, 589:Jul83-765
Kiernan, R.F. Gore Vidal.
J.Z. Guzlowski, 395(MFS):Winter83-737
Kiernan, V.G. From Conquest to Collapse.
639(VQR):Winter83-8
Kieser, R. Erzwungene Symbiose.
M. Davies, 617(TLS):7Dec84-1429
Kightly, C. Folk Heroes of Britain.
A.C. Percival, 203:Vol194No2-265
Kilbury, J. The Development of Morpho-
phonemic Theory.
G.F. Meier, 682(ZPSK):Band36Heft5-610
Kilbury-Meissner, U. Die portugiesischen
Anredeformen in soziolinguistischer
Sicht.
H. Meier, 547(RF):Band95Heft1/2-150
Kiley, D. The Wendy Dilemma.
D. Barry, 441:23Sep84-43
Kilian, R., K. Funk and P. Fassl, eds.
Eschatologie.
B. Casper, 489(PJGG):Band90Heft1-220
Kiljunen, K., ed. Kampuchea.
A. Barnett, 617(TLS):14Sep84-1016
Killam, B., with C. Phillips. It's About
Japan.
60:Jul-Aug83-117
Killens, J.O. Youngblood.
M.F., 189(EA):Apr-Jun84-238
Killingley, S-Y. Cantonese Classifiers.
S. Johnson, 350:Sep84-678
Kilmartin, T. A Guide to Proust: Remem-
brance of Things Past.
J.M. Cocking, 617(TLS):25May84-595
R. Fuller, 362:23Feb84-30
Kilpatrick, J.J. The Writer's Art.
A. Brumer, 441:26Aug84-17
Kilwardby, R. Quaestiones in librum ter-
tium Sententiarum. (Vol 1) (E. Gössmann,
ed)
P.O. Lewry, 589:Oct83-1064
Kilworth, G. The Songbirds of Pain.
C. Greenland, 617(TLS):7Dec84-1420
Kilworth, G. A Theatre of Timesmiths.
C. Greenland, 617(TLS):18May84-557
Kim, B-W. and W-J. Rho, eds. Korean
Public Bureaucracy.
M.J. Cha, 293(JASt):Aug83-982
Kim, C.L. and S.T. Pai. The Legislative
Process in Korea.
K.S. Oh, 293(JASt):May83-685
Kim Donguk. History of Korean Literature.
P.H. Lee, 244(HJAS):Jun83-357
Kim, K.S. and M. Roemer. Growth and
Structural Transformation.
K. Moskowitz, 293(JASt):Nov82-63
D.I. Steinberg, 293(JASt):Nov82-91
Kimball, P. The File.*
I. Elliot, 617(TLS):26Oct84-1207
Kimball, R. - see Porter, C.
Kimball, W.F. - see Churchill, W.S. and
F.D. Roosevelt
Kimbell, D.R.B. Verdi in the Age of
Italian Romanticism.*
D. Rosen, 415:Jun83-353

Kimbrough, S.T., Jr. Israelite Religion
in Sociological Perspective.
M.J. Buss, 318(JAOS):Oct-Dec82-658
Kincaid, A.N. - see Buck, G.
Kincaid, J. At the Bottom of the River.
E. Milton, 441:15Jan84-22
Kinch, M.B. Q.D. Leavis 1906-1981.
W. Baker, 477(PLL):Fall83-461
Kinder, K. Techniques in Machine Knitting.
P. Grappe, 614:Fall84-24
Kindermann, B. Der Deutsche Redner. (H.
Haupt, ed)
J.W. Van Cleve, 221(GQ):Nov83-643
Kindleberger, C.P. A Financial History of
Western Europe.
B. Supple, 617(TLS):1Jun84-609
Kindstrand, J.F. Anacharsis.*
L. Pernot, 555:Vol157fasc1-121
Kindstrand, J.F. The Stylistic Evaluation
of Aeschines in Antiquity.
D. Lateiner, 124:Sep-Oct83-59
Kindstrand, J.F. - see Koolmeister, R. and
T. Tallmeister
Kindstrand, J.F. - see Porphyrogenitus, I.
Kindt, O., ed. Heinrich Tessenow.
R. Rosner, 46:Aug83-74
King, A.Y.C. and R.P. Lee, eds. Social
Life and Development in Hong Kong.
M.K. Chan, 293(JASt):May83-589
King, B., ed. West Indian Literature.*
J.A. Ramsaran, 677(YES):Vol 13-361
K. Williamson, 447(N&Q):Feb82-92
King, D.J.C. Castellarium Anglicanum.
B.K. Davison, 617(TLS):14Dec84-1451
King, F. Act of Darkness.*
D. Taylor, 364:Oct83-89
King, F. Voices in an Empty Room.
A. Becker, 441:9Dec84-26
J. Mellors, 362:6Sep84-26
J. Symons, 617(TLS):31Aug84-964
King, F. When Sisterhood Was in Flower.
639(VQR):Autumn83-128
King, F.H.H., ed. Eastern Banking.
S. Checkland, 617(TLS):30Mar84-330
King, J. and C. Ryskamp - see Cowper, W.
King, J.H. - see Camus, A.
King, J.N. English Reformation Litera-
ture.*
J. Dees, 604:Spring-Summer83-37
A. Sinfield, 141:Summer83-280
639(VQR):Spring83-54
King, K. Cricket Sings.
F.W. Kaye, 502(PrS):Winter83-94
King, L.L. The Whorehouse Papers.*
S.M. Archer, 615(TJ):May83-274
King, L.S. Medical Thinking.
G. Bilson, 529(QQ):Winter83-1196
King, M.H. and W.M. Stevens, eds. Saints,
Scholars and Heroes.
M.R. Godden, 541(RES):Aug83-321
King, N. Abel Gance.
J. Ellis, 362:9Aug84-27
King, P.R. Nine Contemporary Poets.*
A. Motion, 541(RES):Feb83-109
King, S. and P. Straub. The Talisman.
A. Shapiro, 441:4Nov84-24
King, S.B., Jr. Darien.
E.S. Nathans, 9(AlaR):Apr83-151
King-Hele, D. - see Darwin, E.
Kingdon, R.M. The Political Thought of
Peter Martyr Vermigli.
W.F. Bense, 551(RenQ):Winter83-614

Kitcher, P. The Nature of Mathematical Knowledge.
  I. Hacking, 453(NYRB):16Feb84-36
Kittel, B. The Hymns of Qumran.
  L.H. Schiefman, 318(JAOS):Oct-Dec82-667
Kittredge, W. We Are Not in This Together. (R. Carver, ed)
  J. Penner, 441:9Sep84-16
Kiyota, M., ed. Mahāyāna Buddhist Meditation.
  G.R. Elder, 318(JAOS):Apr-Jun82-423
Kizer, C. Mermaids in the Basement. Yin.
  P. Hampl, 441:25Nov84-36
Kjaer, I. and E. Petersen, eds. Danmarks gamle Ordsprog I.
  U. Palmenfelt, 64(Arv):Vol137-193
  P. Ries, 562(Scan):May83-75
Kjaer, I. and J.K. Sørensen, eds. Danmarks gamle ordsprog. (Vols 2 and 6)
  U. Palmenfelt, 64(Arv):Vol137-193
Kjersgaard, E. Københavns historie. (Vol 1)
  R. McKnight, 563(SS):Autumn83-383
Klabsbald, V., with R. Attal. Catalogue des manuscrits marocains de la collection Klagsbald.
  N.A. Stillman, 318(JAOS):Jul-Sep82-569
Klami, H.T. The Legalists.
  W.E. Butler, 575(SEER):Jul83-475
Klaniczay, T., ed. A History of Hungarian Literature.
  G. Gömöri, 617(TLS):6Jul84-766
Klappenbach, R. and H. Malige-Klappenbach. Studien zur modernen deutschen Lexikographie.* (W. Abraham, with J.F. Brand, eds)
  D. Herberg, 682(ZPSK):Band36Heft6-737
Klappert, P. The Idiot Princess of the Last Dynasty.
  J.D. McClatchy, 441:2Dec84-54
Klassen, W., ed. Anabaptism in Outline.
  A.M., 125:Fall82-108
Klauber, L.M. Rattlesnakes. (abridged by K.H. McClung)
  N.J. Engberg, 649(WAL):May83-56
Klaus, H.G., ed. The Socialist Novel in Britain.*
  J.R. Reed, 395(MFS):Winter83-774
  Y. Tosser, 189(EA):Apr-Sep83-329
Klavans, J.K. It's a Little Too Late for a Love Song.
  C. Fein, 441:30Sep84-28
Klébaner, D. L'Art du peu.
  F. Wybrands, 450(NRF):Jun83-125
Klehr, H. The Heyday of American Communism.
  E.M. Breindel, 129:Jun84-78
  H. Draper, 453(NYRB):10May84-25
  G. Tyler, 441:29Jan84-9
Kleiber, W., K. Kunze and H. Löffler. Historischer Südwestdeutscher Sprachatlas.*
  A.W. Stanforth, 402(MLR):Jul83-738
Kleiman, C. Sean O'Casey's Bridge of Vision.
  B. Benstock, 397(MD):Sep83-398
  B. Dolan, 305(JIL):May83-114
  C. Murray, 272(IUR):Spring83-128
  M. Sidnell, 627(UTQ):Summer83-437
Klein, A. Figurenkonzeption und Erzählform in den Kurzgeschichten Sherwood Andersons.*
  G.F. Scharnhorst, 72:Band219Heft2-441

Klein, A.M. Beyond Sambation.* (M.W. Steinberg and U. Caplan, eds)
  E.S. Fisher, 627(UTQ):Summer83-492
  A.L. Kagedan, 287:Dec83-26
  F.W. Watt, 105:Spring/Summer83-87
Klein, C. Mothers and Sons.
  B.F. Williamson, 441:13May84-23
Klein, D.M. Magic Time.
  D. Evanier, 441:13May84-22
Klein, F-J. Lexematische Untersuchungen zum französischen Verbalwortschatz im Sinnbezirk von Wahrnehmung und Einschätzung.
  E. Radtke, 547(RF):Band95Heft3-321
Klein, J. Woody Guthrie.
  C. Seemann, 650(WF):Oct83-318
Klein, J. Payback.
  S. Karnow, 441:14Oct84-7
Klein, K. Aspekte des Tragischen im Drama Shakespeares und seiner Zeit.
  D. Mehl, 72:Band220Heft1-163
Klein, M. Foreigners.*
  R. Adolph, 106:Winter83-481
  J.D. Saldívar, 594:Fall83-283
  P. Shaw, 569(SR):Spring83-299
Klein, M., ed. Taal Kundig Beschouwd.
  A. van Santen, 204(FdL):Mar82-70
Klein, N. Lovers.
  A.P. Harris, 441:30Dec84-16
Klein, P.D. Certainty.*
  R. Foley, 484(PPR):Jun84-560
Klein, R., ed. Marc Aurel.*
  P. Hadot, 192(EP):Oct-Dec83-498
Klein, R. The Politics of the National Health Service.
  E.G. Knox, 617(TLS):17Feb84-169
Klein, T.E.D. The Ceremonies.
  A. Krystal, 441:29Jul84-20
Klein-Terrada, R. Der Diebsthal der Lotusfasern.
  A.J. Gail, 259(IIJ):Jun83-285
Kleine, P. Zur Figurencharakteristik in Shakespeares "Henry VI."
  J. Hasler, 156(JDSh):Jahrbuch1983-268
Kleiner, B. Sprache und Entfremdung.
  G. Lehnert-Rodiek, 52:Band17Heft3-332
Kleiner, D. The Monument of Philopappos in Athens.
  S.I. Rotroff, 124:Jul-Aug84-389
Kleiner, J. Korea.
  G. Henderson, 293(JASt):May83-686
Kleinert, A. Die frühen Modejournale in Frankreich.
  H. Kröll, 72:Band220Heft2-451
Kleinfield, S. The Traders.
  J. Brooks, 441:5Feb84-24
Kleinig, J. Philosophical Issues in Education.
  R.T.H., 185:Oct83-182
  J. Harris, 479(PhQ):Apr83-202
Kleinknecht, R. Grundlagen der modernen Definitionstheorie.
  P. Peppinghaus, 167:Sep83-233
Kleinstück, J. Die Erfindung der Realität.
  S. Kohl, 490:Band14Heft3/4-332
von Kleist, H. An Abyss Deep Enough.* (P.B. Miller, ed and trans)
  S. Magee, 114(ChiR):Summer83-127
  M. Mudrick, 249(HudR):Summer83-378
  639(VQR):Winter83-10
von Kleist, H. Anecdotes et petits récits. (J. Ruffet, ed and trans)
  M.D. de Launay, 192(EP):Oct-Dec83-494

von Kleist, H. Heinrich von Kleist: Plays.* (W. Hinderer, ed)
S. Magee, 114(ChiR):Summer83-127
Klemming, G.E. and J.G. Nordin. Svensk boktryckeri-histori, 1483-1883.
70:May-Jun83-166
Klenke, M.A. Chrétien de Troyes and "Le Conte du Graal."*
K. Busby, 547(RF):Band95Heft3-337
P. Nykrog, 589:Apr83-556
Kleppner, P. The Third Electoral System, 1853-1892.
H.M. Waller, 106:Spring83-79
Klessmann, C. and F. Pingel, eds. Gegner des Nationalsozialismus.
U-K. Ketelsen, 221(GQ):Mar83-353
Klibanov, A.I. History of Religious Sectarianism in Russia (1860s to 1917). (S.P. Dunn, ed)
G.L. Freeze, 550(RusR):Jul83-329
Klibansky, R. The Continuity of the Platonic Tradition during the Middle Ages, together with Plato's "Parmenides" in the Middle Ages and the Renaissance. (2nd ed)
A. Sheppard, 123:Vol33No1-157
Klibansky, R. and I.G. Senger - see Nicholas of Cusa
Klieneberger, H.R. The Novel in England and Germany.*
W.P. Hanson, 402(MLR):Oct83-984
E.W. Herd, 564:Nov83-295
I. Schuster, 268(IFR):Summer84-126
Klier, B. Poker Pari.
J.B. Davis, 207(FR):Feb84-437
Kline, M-J. and J.W. Ryan - see Burr, A.
Klingenstein, G. Der Aufsteig des Hauses Kaunitz.
W.R. Ward, 83:Autumn83-234
Klinkenberg, J-M., D. Racelle-Latin and G. Connolly, eds. Langages et Collectivités: le cas du Quebec.*
N. Gueunier, 209(FM):Jan83-54
Kloefkorn, W. Platte Valley Homestead.*
M. Sanders, 649(WAL):May83-96
Klocke, M.U.S.V. Deutsche Phonologie und Morphologie.*
R. Lieber, 603:Vol7No2-320
Kloepfer, R. and G. Janetzke-Dillner, eds. Erzählung und Erzählforschung im 20. Jahrhundert.
J.L. Atkinson, 221(GQ):May83-475
D. Myers, 67:Nov83-328
H.A. Pausch, 107(CRCL):Jun83-278
Klopsch, P. Einführung in die Dichtungslehren der lateinischen Mittelalters.
J. Marenbon, 382(MAE):1983/1-140
J.H. Marshall, 208(FS):Oct83-443
Klopstock, F.G. Epigramme. (K. Hurlebusch, ed)
P.M. Mitchell, 301(JEGP):Jul83-417
"Friedrich Gottlieb Klopstock: Wissenschaftliche Konferenz der Martin-Luther-Universität, Halle-Wittenberg, im Juli 1974."
R.H. Stephenson, 221(GQ):Jan83-134
Klose, K. Russia and the Russians.
M.A. Uhlig, 441:25Mar84-28
Klossowski de Rola, S. Balthus.
A. Ross, 364:Jun83-101
Klotsch, A. Betriebsausflug.
B. Schick, 654(WB):11/1982-137

Klotz, G. Britische Dramatiker der Gegenwart.
J. Krehayn, 654(WB):6/1983-1147
Kluge, P.F. Season for War.
M. Simpson, 441:30Dec84-17
Kluger, S. Changing Pitches.
B. Atkinson, 441:15Jul84-18
Klussmann, P.G. and H. Mohr - see "Jahrbuch zur Literatur in der DDR"
Kluxen, W. Philosophische Ethik bei Thomas von Aquin.* (2nd ed)
L.J. Elders, 543:Dec82-456
Knapp, B.L. Theatre and Alchemy.*
D. Whitton, 610:Spring82-144
Knapp, B.L. Émile Zola.
R. Lethbridge, 208(FS):Apr83-236
Knapp, F.P. Der Selbstmord in der abendländischen Epik des Hochmittelalters.
W. McConnell, 400(MLN):Apr83-519
Knapp, G.P. Die Literatur des deutschen Expressionismus.
H.F. Pfanner, 406:Summer83-227
Knapp, G.P., ed. Studien zum Werk Max Frischs.
K. Schimanski, 654(WB):7/1982-183
Knapp, G.P. and M. Gabriele Wohmann.
L. Hill, 222(GR):Summer83-123
K. Hughes, 133:Band16Heft2/3-292
K. Hughes, 400(MLN):Apr83-521
Knapp-Tepperberg, E-M. Literatur und Unbewusstes.
V. Roloff, 547(RF):Band95Heft3-343
Knecht, R.J. Francis I.
S. Hanley, 551(RenQ):Autumn83-441
Knelman, M. A Stratford Tempest.*
W.T. Liston, 570(SQ):Winter83-499
Knevitt, C. Connections.
H. Winterbotham, 617(TLS):4May84-485
Kneževič, B. History.
G. Oakes, 125:Fall82-91
Knezhević, R. and Z. Sloboda ili Smrt.
E. Barker, 617(TLS):10Aug84-897
Knibbe, D. Forschungen in Ephesos veröffentlicht vom österreichischen archäologischen Institut in Wien. (Vol 9, Pt 1, fasc 1)
A.G. Woodhead, 303(JoHS):Vol 103-228
Knight, D. - see Cobbett, W.
Knight, G. and A. McLean. Commentary on The Chymical Wedding of Christian Rozenkreutz.
J. Godwin, 111:Spring84-6
Knight, G.W. Shakespearean Dimensions.
S. Wells, 617(TLS):30Nov84-1390
Knight, R. Edwin Muir.*
R. Robertson, 541(RES):May83-244
Knight, R.C. Corneille: "Horace."*
L. Picciola, 535(RHL):Sep/Dec83-921
Knight, S. Form and Ideology in Crime Fiction.*
S. Snyder, 106:Summer83-185
P. Wolfe, 395(MFS):Autumn83-389
Knirk, J.E. Oratory in the Kings' Sagas.
M. Ciklamini, 563(SS):Winter83-70
P. Hallberg, 562(Scan):May83-69
Knodel, A.J. - see Perse, S.
Knopp, K. Französischer Schülerargot.*
P. Pupier, 545(RPh):Feb83-474
Knörrich, O., ed. Formen der Literatur in Einzeldarstellungen.
W. Ruttkowski, 133:Band16Heft1-56
W. Theiss, 196:Band24Heft3/4-308

Knott, B. Becos.*
  P. Stitt, 219(GaR):Winter83-894
Knott, J.R., Jr. The Sword of the Spirit.*
  J. Morrill, 541(RES):Aug83-336
  V. Newey, 402(MLR):Apr83-427
  J.C. Ulreich, Jr., 50(ArQ):Spring83-83
Knowland, A.S. W.B. Yeats.
  A. Carpenter, 617(TLS):29Jun84-733
Knowler, D. The Falconer of Central Park.
  A. Heckscher, 441:5Aug84-29
Knowles, A.V. - see Turgenev, I.
Knowles, J. A Stolen Past.*
  B. Morton, 617(TLS):31Aug84-964
Knowlton, C. The Real World.
  C. Fein, 441:1Jul84-20
  R. Koenig, 61:Jun84-117
  442(NY):18Jun84-113
Knox, B. The Hanging Tree.
  M. Callendar, 441:8Jan84-27
Knox, B. Word and Action.*
  W.M. Calder 3d, 122:Jul83-251
Knox, B. - see Sophocles
Knox, M. Mussolini Unleashed, 1939-1941.*
  M. Palla, 278(IS):Vol38-120
Knox, W., ed. Scottish Labour Leaders
  1918-39.
  A. Calder, 617(TLS):6Apr84-380
Knuuttila, S., ed. Reforging the Great
  Chain of Being.
  S. Waterlow, 393(Mind):Jul83-448
Kocan, P. The Cure.
  P. Pierce, 381:Sep83-407
Koch, E.I., with W. Rauch. Mayor.
  N. Podhoretz, 129:May84-60
  A. Schlesinger, Jr., 453(NYRB):12Apr84-
  15
  G. Talese, 441:12Feb84-1
Koch, H-A. and U. - see "Internationale
Germanistische Bibliographie"
Kochan, M. Britain's Internees in the
Second World War.
  B. Wasserstein, 617(TLS):6Jul84-760
Kochman, T. Black and White Styles in Con-
flict.*
  K. Reisman, 355(LSoc):Dec83-521
Koebner, T., ed. Zwischen den Weltkriegen.
  S. Gastineau, 70:May-Jun83-166
Koehl, R.L. The Black Corps.
  I. Deak, 453(NYRB):31May84-37
Koehler, B. Ästhetik der Politik.
  G.F. Peters, 406:Summer83-217
Koenen, L., H. Riad and A.E. Selim - see
Menander
Koenigsberger, D. Renaissance Man.
  E.H. Ramsden, 39:Jan83-69
Koenker, D. Moscow Workers and the 1917
Revolution.*
  N. Stone, 575(SEER):Apr83-315
  J.W. Strong, 529(QQ):Summer83-551
  P. Waldron, 161(DUJ):Jun83-125
Koerner, E.F.K., H-J. Niederehe and R.H.
Robins, eds. Studies in Medieval Lin-
guistic Thought, dedicated to Geoffrey L.
Bursill-Hall.
  J. Stéfanini, 567:Vol43No3/4-371
Koertge, R. Life on the Edge of the
Continent.*
  R.S. Gwynn, 502(PrS):Spring83-102
Koestler, A. Bricks to Babel.
  S.J. Whitfield, 385(MQR):Winter84-110

Koestler, A. and C. Stranger on the
Square. (H. Harris, ed)
  P-L. Adams, 61:Oct84-126
  R. Dinnage, 617(TLS):2Mar84-212
  H. Kramer, 441:7Oct84-11
  W. Scammell, 364:Mar84-103
  S. Spender, 362:23Feb84-26
Koethe, J. The Late Wisconsin Spring.
  J.D. McClatchy, 441:2Dec84-54
Kogan, V. The Flowers of Fiction.
  C. Krance, 210(FrF):May83-187
  F. Rechsteiner, 400(MLN):May83-819
Kogawa, J. Obasan.
  H.L. Thomas, 102(CanL):Spring83-103
Koh, H.C. Korean and Japanese Women.
  L. Kendall, 293(JASt):Aug83-984
Kohl, K-H. Entzauberter Blick.
  M. Steins, 52:Band18Heft1-99
Kohl, N. Oscar Wilde.*
  R.P. Lessenich, 72:Band220Heft2-414
  M. Pfister, 490:Band14Heft3/4-358
Kohl, N. - see Wilde, O.
Kohlberg, L. The Philosophy of Moral
Development. (Vol 1)
  D.W.J. Galon, 529(QQ):Summer83-563
Kohlenbach, M. Günter Eichs späte Prosa.
  J. Ramin, 221(GQ):Nov83-698
Köhler, H-J., ed. Flugschriften als Mass-
enmedium der Reformationszeit.
  G. Brandt, 682(ZPSK):Band36Heft3-352
Köhler, I. Baudelaire et Hoffmann.
  W. Kreutzer, 72:Band219Heft2-468
Köhler, U. Čonbilal Č'ulelal.
  U. Canger, 269(IJAL):Jul83-334
Kohls, J. Aspekte der Naturthematik und
Wirklichkeitserfassung bei Théophile de
Viau, Saint-Amant und Tristan l'Hermite.
  J. Marmier, 475:Vol 10No18-354
Kojève, A. Esquisse d'une phénoménologie
du droit.*
  A. Stanguennec, 542:Apr-Jun83-270
Kojève, A. Introduction to the Reading of
Hegel.
  H.S. Harris, 488:Jun83-247
Kók, A.L. Ont-werp der Neder-duitse let-
terkonst. (G.R.W. Dibbets, ed)
  C.S.M. Rademaker, 204(FdL):Dec82-297
Kolakowski, L. Main Currents of Marxism.*
  A. Giles-Peters, 63:Sep83-310
  A.J. Matejko, 497(PolR):Vol28No1-74
Kolar, W.W. and Á.H. Várdy, eds. The Folk
Arts of Hungary.*
  Y.R. Lockwood, 292(JAF):Apr-Jun83-235
Kolb, E. and others, eds. Atlas of
English Sounds.
  B. Diensberg, 38:Band101Heft3/4-462
Kolb, F. Agora und Theater, Volks- und
Festversammlung.
  R. Seaford, 123:Vol33No2-288
Kolb, H. and H. Lauffer, eds. Sprachliche
Interferenz.*
  D. Nehls, 257(IRAL):Feb83-81
Kolb, J. - see Hallam, A.H.
Kolb, P. - see Proust, M.
Kolbe, H. Wilhelm Raabe.
  H.S. Daemmrich, 400(MLN):Apr83-522
  H.J. Geerdts, 654(WB):9/1983-1667
  M. Swales, 402(MLR):Apr83-497
Kolbenschlag, M. Goodbye Sleeping Beauty.
  J. Hughes, 176:Nov84-54
Kolde, G. Sprachkontakte in gemischt-
sprachigen Städten.
  B.J. Koekkoek, 221(GQ):Mar83-362

Kort, W.A. Moral Fiber.
  J.Z. Guzlowski, 395(MFS):Winter83-737
Kortland, F.H.H. Slavic Accentuation.
  H. Birnbaum, 279:Vol27-175
Kortländer, B. Annette von Droste-Hüls-
  hoff und die deutsche Literatur.
  R.D. Hacken, 406:Summer83-221
Koschorreck, W. and W. Werner, eds. Codex
  Manesse.
  U. Müller, 680(ZDP):Band102Heft1-134
Koshal, S. Conversational Ladakhi.
  S. De Lancey, 350:Sep84-678
Koshal, S. Ladakhi Grammar.* (B.G. Misra,
  ed)
  H. Berger, 260(IF):Band88-318
Koslowski, P. Ethik des Kapitalismus.
  M.G., 185:Oct83-163
Kosmac, C. Une journée de printemps.
  L. Kovacs, 450(NRF):Nov83-159
Kosok, H., ed. Drama und Theater im
  England des 20. Jahrhunderts.
  M. Patterson, 610:Spring82-146
Koss, S. The Rise and Fall of The Politi-
  cal Press in Britain. (Vol 2: The
  Twentieth Century.)
  A. Sampson, 441:20May84-32
  D. Trelford, 362:29Mar84-23
  J.A. Turner, 617(TLS):6Apr84-361
Kosslyn, S.M. Image and Mind.
  D.P. Perkins, 494:Vol4No2-309
Koster, D.N., ed. American Literature and
  Language.*
  R.R.B., 35(AS):Summer83-188
Koster, S. Die Invektive in der griech-
  ischen und römischen Literatur.
  M. Winterbottom, 123:Vol33No1-137
Kostiuk, H. - see Vynnychenko, V.
Koszarski, R. The Man You Loved to Hate.*
  A. Brownjohn, 176:Jan84-65
Kosztolnyik, Z.J. Five Eleventh Century
  Hungarian Kings.*
  M.C. Rady, 575(SEER):Jul83-445
  J.R. Sweeney, 589:Jan83-194
Kotošixin, G. O Rossii v tsarstvovanie
  Alekseja Mixajloviča.* (A.E. Penning-
  ton, ed)
  T.A. Greenan, 402(MLR):Apr83-507
  V. Živov and B. Uspenskij, 279:Vol28-
  149
Kotschi, T., ed. Beiträge zur Linguistik
  des Französischen.
  C. Lange, 682(ZPSK):Band36Heft5-595
Kotsyubinskyj, M. Fata Morgana and Other
  Stories.
  M. Kuchar, 399(MLJ):Spring83-103
Kottak, C.P. The Past in the Present.
  G.M. Berg, 69:Vol53No3-107
Kotvan, I. Slavika XVI storočia Univerzit-
  nej knižnice v Bratislave.
  354:Mar83-85
Kotzor, G., ed. Das altenglische Martyr-
  ologium.
  J. Frankis, 382(MAE):1983/2-313
Kotzwinkle, W. Queen of Swords.
  J. Kaufman, 441:20May84-15
Kouidis, A.P. "Le Neveu de Rameau" and
  "The Praise of Folly."
  H. Cohen, 207(FR):Feb84-397
Kousser, J.M. and J.M. McPherson, eds.
  Region, Race, and Reconstruction.
  P.M. Gaston, 639(VQR):Spring83-327

Kouwenhoven, J.A. Half a Truth is Better
  Than None.*
  D.A. Johnson, 139:Jun/Jul83-30
  R.B. Nye, 27(AL):Oct83-445
Kouwenhoven, J.K. Apparent Narrative as
  Thematic Metaphor.
  A. Hume, 617(TLS):28Sep84-1104
Kovach, F.J. and R.W. Shahan, eds. Albert
  the Great.
  J.V.B., 543:Sep82-169
Kovács, É. and Z. Lovag. The Hungarian
  Crown and Other Regalia.
  E. Piltz, 341:Vol52No3-130
Kovacs, S. From Enchantment to Rage.
  R. Cardinal, 208(FS):Oct83-488
Kowalk, W. Alexander Pope.
  566:Spring84-164
Kowet, D. A Matter of Honor.
  A.R. Miller, 441:3Jun84-38
Koyama, K. Mount Fuji and Mount Siani.
  O. Bowcock, 617(TLS):26Oct84-1227
Kozaczuk, W. Enigma. (C. Kasparek, ed
  and trans)
  M.S. Kaplan, 441:24Jun84-23
Kozicki, H. Tennyson and Clio.*
  E.D. Mackerness, 447(N&Q):Oct82-458
Kozielecki, J. Psychological Decision
  Theory.
  R.H., 185:Oct83-166
Kozma, J.M. Carosello. (2nd ed)
  A.C. Pease, 399(MLJ):Spring83-82
van der Kraan, A. Lombok.
  R.E. Elson, 293(JASt):Nov82-237
Kracauer, S. Le Roman policier.
  E. Blondel, 542:Jul-Sep83-331
  M.D. de Launay, 192(EP):Oct-Dec83-494
Kraft, C.H. Chadic Wordlists. (Vols 1-3)
  S. Brauner, 682(ZPSK):Band36Heft1-98
Kraft, J. - see Bynner, W.
Kraft, W. Stefan George.
  B. Bjorklund, 221(GQ):Jan83-150
  M. Landmann, 224(GRM):Band33Heft3-346
Kragelund, P. Prophecy, Populism and Prop-
  aganda in the "Octavia."
  M. Griffin, 123:Vol133No2-321
  J.P. Sullivan, 124:Sep-Oct83-45
Kraggerud, E. Der Namensatz der tacite-
  ischen Germania.
  M. Winterbottom, 123:Vol133No2-328
Kramer, D. - see Hardy, T.
Kramer, J., ed. Studien zum Ampezzan-
  ischen.*
  G. Schlemmer, 547(RF):Band95Heft1/2-
  147
Kramer, K. A Handbook for Visitors from
  Outer Space.
  C. Sternhell, 441:5Aug84-10
Kramer, L., ed. The Oxford History of
  Australian Literature.*
  J.B. Beston, 49:Apr83-89
  J. Scheckter, 481(PQ):Fall83-542
Krämer, W. Das Leben des schlesischen
  Dichters Johann Christian Günther 1695-
  1723. (2nd ed)
  R.J. Alexander, 406:Summer83-203
  B.L. Spahr, 221(GQ):Nov83-646
Kramrisch, S. Exploring India's Sacred
  Art.* (B.S. Miller, ed)
  V.K. Chari, 290(JAAC):Summer84-463
Kramrisch, S. The Presence of Śiva.
  P. Chandra, 293(JASt):Nov82-187
Kranz, G. Das Bildgedicht.
  H. Zeman, 52:Band18Heft1-88

Kranzmayer, E. Laut- und Flexionslehre der deutschen zimbrischen Mundart.* (M. Hornung, ed)
  A. Rowley, 685(ZDL):2/1983-257
Krapf, L. and C. Wagenknecht - see Weckherlin, G.R.
Krashen, S.D. Principles and Practice in Second Language Acquisition.*
  T.V. Higgs, 399(MLJ):Summer83-168
Krashen, S.D. Second Language Acquisition and Second Language Learning.
  J. Leather, 257(IRAL):May83-165
Krashen, S.D., R.C. Scarcella and M.H. Long. Child-Adult Differences in Second Language Acquisition.
  V.J. Cook, 660(Word):Aug83-122
Krasner, W. Death of a Minor Poet.
  N. Callendar, 441:9Sep84-40
  442(NY):16Jul84-92
Krasnobaev, B.I., ed. Reisen und Reisenbeschreibungen im 18. und 19. Jahrhundert als Quellen der Kulturbeziehungsforschung.
  J.M. Tudor, 83:Spring83-127
Kratz, D.M. Mocking Epic.*
  P. Godman, 123:Vol33No2-374
Kratzmann, G. Anglo-Scottish Literary Relations 1430-1550.*
  P. Bawcutt, 447(N&Q):Apr82-159
Kraus, H.P. Sir Francis Drake.
  L.S. Thompson, 70:Mar-Apr81-128
Kraus, H.P. A Rare Book Saga.
  517(PBSA):Oct-Dec80-419
Kraus, K. In These Great Times. (H. Zohn, ed)
  D.J. Enright, 617(TLS):5Oct84-1121
  S. Taylor, 362:26Jul84-27
Kraus, R.C. Class Conflict in Chinese Socialism.
  R. Baum, 293(JASt):May83-625
Krause, D. The Profane Book of Irish Comedy.
  R. Burnham, 397(MD):Sep83-397
  S. Connelly, 174(Éire):Summer83-141
  W.J. Feeney, 305(JIL):May83-108
  C. Murray, 272(IUR):Spring83-128
Krause, D. and R.G. Lowery, eds. Sean O'Casey: Centenary Essays.*
  A.B., 189(EA):Jul-Sep84-367
  D. Kiberd, 541(RES):Aug83-366
Krause, S.J. and S.W. Reid - see Brown, C.B.
Krausnick, H. and H-H. Wilhelm. Die Truppe des Weltanschauungskrieges.
  F.L. Carsten, 575(SEER):Apr83-298
Krauss, H., ed. Europäisches Hochmittelalter.*
  M. Curschmann, 564:Feb83-59
  M.E. Kalinke, 301(JEGP):Jul83-409
  W. Schröder, 684(ZDA):Band112Heft4-151
Krauss, M.E., ed. In Honor of Eyak.
  W. Bright, 350:Jun84-467
Kraut, R. Socrates and the State.
  G. Vlastos, 617(TLS):24Aug84-931
Krautheimer, R. Rome.
  G.B. Ladner, 54:Jun83-336
  N. Purcell, 313:Vol73-210
Krautheimer, R. Three Christian Capitals.
  M.A. Alexander, 124:Jul-Aug84-387
  R. Cormack, 617(TLS):3Feb84-119
Krebs, H., with R. Schmid. Otto Warburg.
  R. Rinard, 221(GQ):Mar83-355

Krech, S., 3d, ed. Indians, Animals, and the Fur Trade.
  A.J. Ray, 656(WMQ):Jul83-461
Krechel, H-L. Strukturen des Vokabulars in den Maigret-Romanen Georges Simenons.
  G. Matoré, 209(FM):Oct83-374
Kreckel, M. Communicative Acts and Shared Knowledge in Natural Discourse.
  R.E. Longacre, 567:Vol45No3/4-331
Krefetz, G. How to Read and Profit from Financial News.
  L.S. Ritter, 441:21Oct84-46
Kreindler, I., ed. The Changing Status of Russian in the Soviet Union.
  S.M. Embleton, 350:Mar84-159
Kreisel, H. The Almost Meeting and Other Stories.*
  M. Greenstein, 168(ECW):Summer83-64
  A.T. Seaman, 198:Jun83-95
Kreisky, B. Die Zeit in der wir Leben.
  N. Rotenstreich, 390:May83-71
Kreitman, E. Deborah.*
  M. Hulse, 364:Oct83-108
Krell, D. - see Heidegger, M.
Kremer, U.M. Die reformation als Problem der amerikanischen Historiographie.
  L.J. Reith, 125:Spring83-281
Kremer-Marietti, A. La morale.
  M. Adam, 542:Jan-Mar83-61
Kremer-Marietti, A. Le Projet anthropologique d'Auguste Comte.
  D. Giovannangeli, 540(RIPh):Vol137 fasc1/2-219
Kremer-Marietti, A. La Symbolicité.
  M. Adam, 542:Oct-Dec83-446
  D. Giovannangeli and P. Gochet, 540(RIPh):Vol137fasc4-529
Kremnitz, G. Das Okzitanische.*
  J. Albrecht, 547(RF):Band95Heft1/2-144
Kren, T., ed. Renaissance Painting in Manuscripts.
  J.J.G. Alexander, 617(TLS):11May84-528
Kresic, S., ed. Contemporary Literary Hermeneutics and Interpretation of Classical Texts/Herméneutique littéraire contemporaine et interprétation des textes classiques.*
  J-P. Levet, 555:Vol57fasc1-136
  C.A. Rubino, 487:Spring83-87
  F.F. Schwarz, 52:Band18Heft3-300
Kress, G. and R. Hodge. Language as Ideology.*
  R. Helgerson, 131(CL):Fall83-362
  T.J. Taylor, 307:Apr83-92
Kress, H., ed. Drøm om virkelighet.
  E. Johns, 562(Scan):May82-105
Kretzenbacher, L. Legendenbilder aus dem Feuerjenseits.
  M. Lantz, 64(Arv):Vol137-208
Kretzmann, N., A. Kenny and J. Pinborg, eds. The Cambridge History of Later Medieval Philosophy.
  J.J.E. Gracia, 319:Apr84-233
  E.A. Synan, 154:Dec83-741
Kreuzer, H., ed. Jahrhundertende — Jahrhundertwende I.
  L. Marx, 563(SS):Spring83-199
Kreuziger, F.A. Apocalypse and Science Fiction.
  D. Ketterer, 561(SFS):Mar83-110
Kreyling, M. Eudora Welty's Achievement of Order.*
  R. Godden, 447(N&Q):Jun82-277

211

Kribbs, J.K., ed. Critical Essays on
John Greenleaf Whittier.
R. Gray, 677(YES):Vol 13-333
Krich, J. Music in Every Room.
R. Shaplen, 441:6May84-17
Kriedte, P., H. Medick and J. Schlumbohm.
Industrialization before Industrializa-
tion.
L. Stone, 453(NYRB):29Mar84-42
Krieger, E. A Marxist Study of Shake-
speare's Comedies.*
R.D. Sell, 597(SN):Vol55No2-209
Kriegsman, S.A. Modern Dance in America:
The Bennington Years.
S.J. Cohen, 615(TJ):May82-279
Krier, R. Rob Krier on Architecture. Rob
Krier: Urban Projects 1968-1982.
R.J. Findley, 505:Sep83-231
Krige, J. Science, Revolution and Discon-
tinuity.*
J. Blackmore, 488:Dec83-513
N. Koertge, 84:Jun83-185
Krimm, B.G. W.B. Yeats and the Emergence
of the Irish Free State, 1918-1939.
C.W. Barrow, 174(Éire):Fall83-147
G.M. Harper, 405(MP):May84-435
Kripke, S.A. Wittgenstein on Rules and
Private Language.*
B. Abbott, 350:Sep84-646
C.J. Diamond, 518:Apr83-96
P. Engel, 542:Oct-Dec83-496
P. Winch, 479(PhQ):Oct83-398
Kristeller, P.O. Marsilio Ficino letter-
ato e le glosse attribuite a lui nel
codice Caetani di Dante.
E. Bigi, 228(GSLI):Vol 160fasc509-133
Kristeller, P.O. Studien zur Geschichte
der Rhetorik und zum Begriff des Men-
schen in der Renaissance.
R. Düchting, 72:Band219Heft2-479
Kristol, A.M. Color.*
G. Murillo P., 457(NRFH):Tomo31núml-
117
Kristol, I. Reflections of a Neoconserva-
tive.*
A. Sen, 453(NYRB):1Mar84-31
Kritzman, L.D. Destruction/Découverte.*
C. Blum, 535(RHL):Sep/Dec83-916
M.M. McGowan, 402(MLR):Jan83-178
R.J. Morrissey, 405(MP):Nov83-194
Kroeber, K. Traditional Literatures of the
American Indian.
E.C. Fine, 292(JAF):Apr-Jun83-225
D.M. Hines, 650(WF):Jan83-60
A. Krupat, 153:Summer83-2
R. Maud, 106:Spring83-71
van der Kroef, J.M. Communism in South-
East Asia.
P.A. Poole, 293(JASt):Feb83-464
Kroetsch, R. Alibi.
J. Mills, 648(WCR):Apr84-57
Kroetsch, R. Field Notes.*
L.K. MacKendrick, 168(ECW):Summer83-99
Kroetsch, R., ed. Sundogs.
D. Jackel, 102(CanL):Spring83-151
Kröger, W. Das Publikum als Richter.
H.H.F. Henning, 406:Spring83-83
Krohn, R. - see Gottfried von Strassburg
Kröhnke, F. Jungen in schlechter Gesell-
schaft.*
D.C.G. Lorenz, 221(GQ):May83-534

Kröll, F., S. Bartjes and R. Wiengarn.
Vereine.
H. Groschopp, 654(WB):10/1983-1845
Kronen, T. De store årene 1880-1900.
B. Christensen, 172(Edda):1983/6-373
Kronholm, T. Motifs from Genesis I-II in
the Genuine Hymns of Ephrem the Syrian.
J.C. Greenfield, 318(JAOS):Jan-Mar82-
190
Kruck, W.E. Looking for Dr. Condom.
R.R. Butters, 579(SAQ):Summer83-348
O.W. Ferguson, 35(AS):Spring83-54
Krueger, A.O. The Developmental Role of
the Foreign Sector and Aid.
K. Moskowitz, 293(JASt):Nov82-63
D.I. Steinberg, 293(JASt):Nov82-91
Krüger, H. A Crack in the Wall.
A.H. Rosenfeld, 390:Apr83-63
Kruks, S. The Political Philosophy of
Merleau-Ponty.*
B.P. Dauenhauer, 484(PPR):Sep83-137
Krulik, D. and B. Zaffran. Everyday
English.
B. Powell, 399(MLJ):Summer83-182
Krüll, M. Sigmund, fils de Jacob.
J. le Hardi, 450(NRF):Jul/Aug83-235
Krumbholz, M. Ironie im zeitgenössischen
Ich-Roman.
H. Dunkle, 221(GQ):May83-484
Krummacher, H.-H., ed. Beiträge zur bib-
liographischen Lage in der germanistis-
chen Literaturwissenschaft.
P.M. Mitchell, 301(JEGP):Apr83-280
Krupnick, M., ed. Displacement.
S.L. Baughn, 389(MQ):Spring84-345
M. Sprinker, 617(TLS):3Feb84-105
Kruse, H.H. Mark Twain and "Life on the
Mississippi."*
E.J. Burde, 26(ALR):Spring83-134
T. Scanlan, 651(WHR):Winter83-349
Kruskal, W.H., ed. The Social Sciences.
K.S., 185:Oct83-176
Krynski, M.J. and R.A. Maguire - see
Szymborska, W.
Krysinski, W. Carrefours de signes.
G. Brée, 678(YCGL):No31-137
Kubiński, T. An Outline of the Logical
Theory of Questions.
D. Harrah, 316:Sep83-874
Kübler, G. Die soziale Aufsteigerin.
S.L. Cocalis, 221(GQ):Nov83-668
Kucher, G. Thomas Mann und Heimito von
Doderer.
K.L. Komar, 221(GQ):Nov83-691
Kucich, J. Excess and Restraint in the
Novels of Charles Dickens.*
R.L. Caserio, 445(NCF):Dec83-337
P. Schlicke, 155:Summer83-117
M. Shelden, 637(VS):Summer83-459
Kuczynski, J. Geschichte des Alltags des
deutschen Volkes. (Pts 1 and 2)
W. Heise, 654(WB):3/1982-157
Kuehn, T. Emancipation in Late Medieval
Florence.
D.J. Wilcox, 589:Oct83-1126
Kugel, J.J. The Idea of Biblical Poetry.*
R. Polzin, 107(CRCL):Jun83-258
Kügel, W. Besitzdenken in der Frühzeit
der deutschen Aufklärung.
J.W. Van Cleve, 406:Fall83-337

Kuppner, F. A Bad Day for the Sung Dynasty.
  L. Mackinnon, 617(TLS):30Nov84-1393
  J. Mole, 176:Dec84-63
Kurczaba, A. Gombrowicz and Frisch.
  G.F. Probst, 133:Band16Heft2/3-285
Kurismmootil, K.C.J. Heaven and Hell on Earth.
  A.A. De Vitis, 395(MFS):Winter83-788
Kuritz, P. Playing.
  R.A. Adubato, 615(TJ):May83-271
Kuriyama, C.B. Hammer or Anvil.*
  T. McAlindon, 541(RES):May83-210
  J. Weil, 402(MLR):Jul83-675
Kurth, P. Anastasia.
  N. Tolstoy, 617(TLS):24Feb84-186
  C. Verderese, 441:8Jan84-18
Kurtz, D. The Berlin Painter.
  R. Higgins, 39:Dec83-507
Kurtz, M.L. Crime of the Century.
  J.F. Heath, 579(SAQ):Spring83-222
"Kurze deutsche Grammatik."
  K-E. Sommerfeldt, 682(ZPSK):Band36 Heft4-479
Kurzke, H. Auf der Suche nach der verlorenen Irrationalität.*
  U. Karthaus, 52:Band17Heft1-100
Kushner, E. and R. Struc, eds. Actes du VIIe Congrès de l'Association Internationale de Littérature Comparée/Proceedings of the 7th Congress of the International Comparative Literature Association.*
  J. Hervier, 549(RLC):Apr-Jun83-213
Kuśniewicz, A. Le Chemin de Corinthe.
  L. Kovacs, 450(NRF):Feb83-152
Kuspit, D. The Critic is Artist.
  R. Baranik, 62:Summer84-81
Kutler, S.I. The American Inquisition.
  H. Brogan, 617(TLS):25May84-574
Kuttner, R. The Economic Illusion.
  B.P. Bosworth, 441:21Oct84-44
  442(NY):19Nov84-190
Kux, M. Moderne Dichterdramen.*
  T.R. Nadar, 406:Winter83-461
Kuyk, D., Jr. Threads Cable-strong.
  A.F. Kinney, 587(SAF):Autumn83-261
Kuyper, W. Dutch Classicist Architecture.
  K. Downes, 90:Jun83-367
Kuznetsov, A. The Journey.
  442(NY):3Sep84-94
Kvaran, G. Die Zuflüsse zur Nord- und Ostsee von der Ems bis zur Trave.
  W. Laur, 260(IF):Band87-361
Kvart, G. Arbetsglädje och gemenskapstro.
  P. Graves, 562(Scan):May82-101
  R. McKnight, 563(SS):Summer83-278
Kwanten, L. Imperial Nomads.*
  D. Sinor, 318(JAOS):Jan-Mar82-240
Kwitny, J. Endless Enemies.
  M.F. Nolan, 441:29Jul84-8
  442(NY):3Sep84-95
Kydd, A.S. - see under Shand Kydd, A.
Kyle, D. The King's Commissar.
  S. Epstein, 441:20May84-30

Laâbi, A. Le Chemin des Ordalies.
  L. Kovacs, 450(NRF):May83-132
Labandeira Fernández, A. - see Rodríguez de Lena, P.

Labarrière, P-J. Le discours de l'altérité.
  A. Reix, 542:Oct-Dec83-446
Labé, L. Oeuvres complètes.* (E. Giudici, ed)
  P. Sharratt, 402(MLR):Jan83-177
Labé, L. Oeuvres poétiques.
  L. Herlin, 450(NRF):Sep83-125
Laberge, M. Aux Mouvances du temps.
  H.R. Runte, 102(CanL):Summer83-114
Laberge, M. Ils étaient venus pour.
  R. Usmiani, 102(CanL):Autumn83-85
Labica, G. Marxism and the Status of Philosophy.
  W.H. Shaw, 185:Apr84-529
Labica, G., with G. Bensussan, eds. Dictionnaire critique du marxisme.
  J. Bernhardt, 542:Oct-Dec83-485
Labisch, A. Frumentum commeatusque.
  M. Rambaud, 555:Vol57fasc2-356
Labov, W., ed. Locating Language in Time and Space.
  F. Anshen, 35(AS):Fall83-273
  L. Milroy, 355(LSoc):Mar83-82
  S. Romaine, 361:May83-87
Labrador, J.J., C.Á. Zorita and R.A. Di Franco. Cancionero de poesías varias, Biblioteca de Palacio, MS. 617.
  N.F. Marino, 304(JHP):Fall83-73
Labrecque-Pervouchine, N. L'iconostase.
  A.W. Epstein, 589:Jul83-767
Labrie, R. James Merrill.
  C.N. Parker, 50(ArQ):Spring83-91
Labrie, R. Howard Nemerov.
  J.M. Reibetanz, 106:Winter83-497
  R. White, 178:Mar83-115
Laburthe-Tolra, P. Les Seigneurs de la Forêt.
  J.I. Guyer, 69:Vol53No2-81
Lacan, J. Les Complexes familiaux dans la formation de l'individu.
  C. Gordon, 617(TLS):13Jul84-779
La Capra, D. "Madame Bovary" on Trial.*
  K. McSweeney, 529(QQ):Winter83-1184
  B. Nelson, 446(NCFS):Fall-Winter83/84-234
Lacarra, M.J. - see Pedro Alfonso
Lacassagne, J-P. - see Leroux, P.
Lacey, A.R. Modern Philosophy.*
  S. Orde, 84:Dec83-404
Lacey, R. Aristocrats.
  I. Moncreiffe of that Ilk, 617(TLS):6Jan84-7
Lacharité, N. Le modèle E-R. (Chapitre 1)
  Y. Gauthier, 154:Sep83-551
de La Chaussée, F. Initiation à la morphologie historique de l'ancien français.
  J.A. Creore, 545(RPh):Feb83-471
de La Chaussée, P.C.N. L'École des mères, comédie (1744). (I. Bernard, ed)
  R. Waller, 83:Autumn83-259
Lachs, M. The Teacher in International Law.
  D.C.T., 185:Jan84-378
de Laclos, P-A.C. Les Liaisons dangereuses. (R. Pomeau, ed)
  V. Mylne, 535(RHL):Jan/Feb83-128
Lacombe, A. Des Compositeurs pour l'image.*
  J-R. Julien, 537:Vol69No2-251
de La Combe, P.J., ed. Agamemnon 2.
  B. Knox, 124:Nov-Dec83-133

Lacoue-Labarthe, P. and J-L. Nancy, eds.
Rejouer le politique.
N. Lukacher, 400(MLN):May83-750
Lacouture, S. and J. En passant par la
France.
M.A. Garnett, 207(FR):Dec83-281
Lacy, A. Home Ground.
L. Yang, 441:3Jun84-7
Lacy, N.J. The Craft of Chrétien de
Troyes.*
C.J. Chase, 405(MP):Feb84-300
Lacy, N.J. and J.C. Nash, eds. Essays in
Early French Literature Presented to
Barbara M. Craig.
W.W. Kibler, 188(ECr):Spring83-106
Ladbury, A. Dressmaking with Basic Pat-
terns.
G. Brown, 614:Summer84-15
Ladd, D.R., Jr. The Structure of Intona-
tional Meaning.*
S.D. Isard, 353:Vol20No7/8-566
Ladefoged, P. A Course in Phonetics.
(2nd ed)
F. Chevillet, 189(EA):Jul-Sep84-317
Ladin, W. Der elsässische Dialekt —
museumsreif?
K. Hammächer, 685(ZDL):2/1983-250
J. Kramer, 547(RF):Band95Heft1/2-153
Ladis, A. Taddeo Gaddi.
R. Jones, 617(TLS):23Mar84-314
F. Russell, 324:Mar84-278
Ladurie, E.L. - see under Le Roy Ladurie,
E.
Madame de Lafayette. The Princess of
Clèves. (M.S. Greene, trans)
J. Campbell, 208(FS):Jan83-78
Madame de Lafayette. La Princesse de
Clèves. (J. Mesnard, ed)
S. Tiefenbrun, 475:Vol 10No18-372
Madame de Lafayette. La Principessa di
Clèves. (F. Gavarini, ed) (S. Aleramo,
trans)
A. Niderst, 535(RHL):Mar/Apr83-272
La Feber, W. Inevitable Revolutions.*
J. Chace, 453(NYRB):1Mar84-40
Laflamme, J. and R. Tourangeau. L'Eglise
et le Théâtre au Québec.
R. Usmiani, 102(CanL):Spring83-139
Lafleur, J. Décors à l'envers.
A.L. Amprimoz, 102(CanL):Summer83-126
Lafond, J. and A. Redondo, eds. L'image
du monde renversé et ses représentations
littéraires et para-littéraires de la
fin du xvie siècle au milieu du xviie
siècle.*
M. Joly, 457(NRFH):Tomo31núm2-312
Lafond, J. and A. Stegmann, eds.
L'Automne de la Renaissance 1580-1630.
Y. Bellenger, 535(RHL):Mar/Apr83-263
U. Langer, 475:Vol 10No19-917
Laforgue, J. Feuilles volantes. (D.
Grojnowski, ed)
J-L. Debauve, 535(RHL):Sep/Dec83-953
Laforte, C. Survivances médiévales dans
la chanson folklorique.
E.A. Heinemann, 627(UTQ):Summer83-454
S. Laîné, 292(JAF):Oct-Dec83-497
Lafourcade, B. - see Lewis, W.
Lafrance, Y. La théorie platonicienne de
la doxa.*
L. Brisson, 154:Mar83-131
H. Cherniss, 154:Mar83-137
N. Gulley, 303(JoHS):Vol 103-173

Lagarde, P.L., ed. Le Verbe huron.
M. Mithun, 269(IJAL):Jul83-341
Lagerkrantz, O. August Strindberg.
R. Dinnage, 617(TLS):9Nov84-1286
Laget, M. Naissances.
A. Lafortune-Martel, 539:May84-134
Lago, M. - see Burne-Jones, E.C.
Lago, M. and P.N. Furbank - see Forster,
E.M.
Lagorio, V.M. and R. Bradley. The 14th-
Century English Mystics.
M.G. Sargent, 589:Jan83-196
Laguarda Trías, R.A. El hallazgo del Río
de la Plata por Amerigo Vespucci en 1502.
H.J. Tanzi, 263(RIB):Vol33No1-28
La Guardia, D.M. Advance on Chaos.
H. Smith, 250(HLQ):Autumn83-337
Laguerre, M.S., comp. The Complete Hai-
tiana.
F.J. Malval, 263(RIB):Vol33No2-260
Lahana, J. Les mondes parallèles de la
science-fiction soviétique.
D. Gerould, 561(SFS):Nov83-341
de La Harpe, C-F. Correspondance sous la
République Helvétique. (Vol 1) (J.C.
Biaudet and M-C. Jequier, eds)
P. Higonnet, 617(TLS):7Dec84-1424
Lahr, J. Automatic Vaudeville.
S. French, 617(TLS):21Sep84-1050
F. Rich, 441:25Mar84-11
Lahr, J. Coward the Playwright.*
A. Strachan, 157:Spring83-47
de La Huerta, M.G. - see under Garcia de
La Huerta, M.
Lainé, P. Terre des ombres.*
P.A. Mankin, 207(FR):Feb84-414
Láinez, M.M. - see under Mujica Láinez, M.
Laker, R. Jewelled Path.
S. Altinel, 617(TLS):3Aug84-875
Lakoff, G. and M. Johnson. Metaphors We
Live By.*
J. Penelope, 599:Winter83-77
J.O. Thompson, 506(PSt):Sep83-184
J.P. Thorne, 297(JL):Mar83-245
Lal, M. Life of the Amir Dost Muhammed
Khan of Kabul.
S. Rittenberg, 318(JAOS):Apr-Jun82-373
Lalić, I.V. The Works of Love.
R. Pybus, 565:Vol124No2-73
V. Young, 249(HudR):Summer83-399
Lalli, B.T. Repertorio Bibliografico
della Letteratura Americana in Italia.
(Vol 4)
R.A., 189(EA):Apr-Jun84-238
Lalonde, M. and D. Monière. Cause commune,
manifeste pour une internationale des
petites cultures.
B-Z. Shek, 627(UTQ):Summer83-505
Lalonde, R. La Belle épouvante.
Y. Bellemare, 102(CanL):Winter82-113
Lamar, H. and L. Thompson, eds. The Fron-
tier in History.
W.F. Lye, 649(WAL):Aug83-158
R. Rathbone, 69:Vol53No1-89
Lamb, D. The Africans.*
C. Hope, 364:Nov83-78
T.M. Shaw, 150(DR):Summer83-371
Lamb, D. Hegel.*
J.L., 543:Sep82-172
Lamb, M.E. and B. Sutton-Smith, eds. Sib-
ling Relationships.
E. Bermann, 385(MQR):Winter84-119

Lamb, P.F. and K.J. Hohlwein. Touch-
stones.*
  F.W. Kaye, 502(PrS):Winter83-91
Lamb, R. Montgomery in Europe 1943-1945.
  442(NY):31Dec84-71
Lamb, T. The Penguin Guide to Freshwater
Fishing in Britain and Ireland. The
Penguin Guide to Sea Fishing in Britain
and Ireland.
  617(TLS):28Dec84-1511
Lamb, V. and A. Cameroun Weaving.
  D. Idiens, 2(AfrA):Nov82-87
Lambardi, N. Il "Timaeus" ciceroniano.
  J.G.F. Powell, 123:Vol33No2-326
Lambert, A. Unquiet Souls.
  M. Fitz Herbert, 617(TLS):30Nov84-1365
Lambert, D. The Golden Express.
  442(NY):24Dec84-90
Lambert, D. The Judas Code.
  442(NY):27Oct84-93
Lambert, J-C. Cobra, un art libre.
  M. Dachy, 98:Nov83-913
Lambert, M. Dickens and the Suspended
Quotation.*
  R.L. Caserio, 445(NCF):Dec83-337
  D. David, 637(VS):Autumn82-93
  J. Gattégno, 189(EA):Jan-Mar83-95
  S.R. Horton, 131(CL):Winter83-85
  S. Monod, 402(MLR):Jan83-164
  G.J. Worth, 301(JEGP):Jan83-134
Lambert, R.D. and B.F. Freed, eds. The
Loss of Language Skills.
  M. Prokop, 399(MLJ):Summer83-169
Lambert, W.R. Drink and Sobriety in Vic-
torian Wales c. 1820-1895.
  K.O. Morgan, 617(TLS):2Mar84-223
Lambertino, A. Max Scheler.*
  M. Dupuy, 542:Oct-Dec83-499
Lamblin, B. Peinture et Temps.
  B. Lamblin, 192(EP):Jul-Sep83-371
Lambourne, L. Utopian Craftsmen.*
  E. Boris, 658:Spring83-117
Lambrecht, K. Topic, Antitopic and Verb
Agreement in Non-Standard French.
  G. Mallinson, 350:Jun84-453
Lambrechts, R. Les miroirs étrusques et
prénestins des Musées Royaux d'Art et
d'Histoire à Bruxelles.
  G. Lloyd-Morgan, 313:Vol73-233
Lambro, D. Washington — City of Scandals.
  M. Tolchin, 441:9Dec84-27
Lamm, J. De Lorean.
  D. Sharp, 129:Jan84-76
Lamming, R.M. The Notebook of Gismondo
Cavalletti.*
  K.C. O'Brien, 362:22Mar84-25
Lamont, C. Yes to Life.
  M. Ellmann, 569(SR):Winter83-120
Lamont, C. - see Scott, W.
Lamont, W.D. Law and the Moral Order.*
  B.K., 543:Sep82-175
Lamott, A. Rosie.*
  D. Cole, 441:29Jan84-22
L'Amour, L. The Walking Drum.
  R. Nalley, 441:1Jul84-20
Lamport, F.J. Lessing and the Drama.
  G. Hillen, 301(JEGP):Oct83-598
  C.P. Magill, 402(MLR):Apr83-491
Lancaster, C.S. The Goba of the Zambezi.
  G. Prins, 69:Vol53No2-89
Lancaster, O. The Littlehampton Saga.
  T.G.D.F., 617(TLS):12Oct84-1171

Lancel, S., ed. Mission archéologique
française à Carthage: Byrsa II.
  D. Ridgway, 123:Vol33No2-363
"Lancelot, roman en prose du XIIIe siècle."
(Vol 7) (A. Micha, ed)
  F. Lecoy, 554:Vol 103No2/3-376
"Lancelot, roman en prose du XIIIe siècle."
(Vol 8) (A. Micha, ed)
  F. Bogdanow, 208(FS):Oct83-441
  F. Lecoy, 554:Vol 103No2/3-376
Lanchester, E. Elsa Lanchester Herself.*
  J. Nangle, 200:Dec83-625
de Lancre, P. Tableau de l'inconstance
des mauvais anges et démons. (N.
Jacques-Chaquin, ed)
  C. Dis, 450(NRF):Feb83-143
Landa, L.A. Essays in Eighteenth-Century
English Literature.*
  P. Rogers, 541(RES):Aug83-340
Landeck, U. Der fünfte Akt von Goethes
Faust II.
  O. Durrani, 402(MLR):Oct83-976
Landeira, R., ed. Critical Essays on
Gabriel Miró.*
  A. Román, 552(REH):May83-291
Landes, D.S. Revolution in Time.*
  R. Coles, 442(NY):24Sep84-123
  J. North, 617(TLS):6Apr84-359
Landes-Fuss, M.G. A Red Brick Building,
Ugly as Hell, in Venice, California.
  S. Laschever, 441:8Apr84-21
Landgrebe, L. Faktizität und Individua-
tion.
  Kah Kyung Cho, 484(PPR):Jun84-552
Landgrebe, L. The Phenomenology of Edmund
Husserl.
  L. O'Dwyer, 63:Sep83-313
Landgren, B. - see Strindberg, A.
"Landhaus und Villa in Niederösterreich
1840-1914."
  D. Klein, 471:Jul/Aug/Sep83-288
Landon, H.C.R. Mozart and the Masons.
  S. Sadie, 415:Oct83-616
Landow, G.P., ed. Approaches to Victorian
Autobiography.*
  R.J. Dingley, 447(N&Q):Oct82-468
Landow, G.P. Images of Crisis.
  D.J. De Laura, 637(VS):Spring83-339
  S. Prickett, 89(BJA):Summer83-279
Landow, G.P. Victorian Types, Victorian
Shadows.*
  R.L. Brett, 506(PSt):May83-83
  C.L. Brooks, 541(RES):Aug83-351
  D.J. De Laura, 637(VS):Spring83-339
Landreau, A.N. and R.S. Yohe, with others.
Flowers of the Yayla.
  A.L. Mayer, 614:Spring84-23
Landy, F. - see "The Tale of Aqhat"
Lane, C.W. Evelyn Waugh.
  I. Murray, 161(DUJ):Jun83-145
  B. Stovel, 49:Jul83-60
Lane, H., ed. The Deaf Experience.
  S. Chess, 441:21Oct84-3
Lane, H. When the Mind Hears.
  S. Chess, 441:21Oct84-3
Lane, J. Return Fare.
  P. Holland, 102(CanL):Spring83-115
Lane, M. Architecture of the Old South:
South Carolina.
  P. Goldberger, 441:2Dec84-20
Lane, P. The Measure.*
  F. Cogswell, 198:Jan83-129
  C. Levenson, 526:Spring83-76

Lane, P. Old Mother.*
  C. Levenson, 526:Spring83-76
Lang, B., ed. Philosophical Style.
  J. Hospers, 290(JAAC):Fall83-104
Lang, C.Y. and E.F. Shannon, Jr. - see
  Tennyson, A.
Lang, E., G. Sauer and R. Steinitz - see
  Steinitz, E.
Lång, H. Kvinnor, vagabonder och vision-
  ärer.
  K. Petherick, 563(SS):Spring83-184
von Lang, J., ed. Eichmann Interrogated.
  A.J. Sherman, 617(TLS):13Apr84-407
de Langbehn, R.R. - see under Rohland de
  Langbehn, R.
"Dorothea Lange: Photographs of a Life-
  time."
  R. Adams, 617(TLS):6Apr84-371
Lange, M. Las casetas de baño.
  M.A. Robatto, 701(SinN):Apr-Jun83-98
Lange, M. Zur epischen Kinder- und Jugend-
  literatur in der BRD.
  C. Emmrich, 654(WB):9/1983-1664
Lange, W-D., ed. Französische Literatur
  des 19. Jahrhunderts.* (Vols 1 and 2)
  M. Kesting, 547(RF):Band95Heft3-360
Lange, W-D., ed. Französische Literatur
  des 19. Jahrhunderts.* (Vol 3)
  A. Gier, 72:Band220Heft2-453
  M. Kesting, 547(RF):Band95Heft3-360
Langendoen, D.T. and P.M. Postal. The
  Vastness of Natural Languages.
  Y. Wilks, 617(TLS):15Jun84-660
"Langenscheidts Enzyklopädisches Wörter-
  buch Deutsch-Englisch A-Z." (Pt 2) (O.
  Springer, ed)
  D. and K. Duckworth, 72:Band219Heft1-
  175
Langer, E. Josephine Herbst.
  R.G. Davis, 441:5Aug84-3
  442(NY):17Sep84-142
Langer, S.K. Mind. (Vol 3)
  G.P., 185:Jan84-364
  639(VQR):Summer83-100
Langevin, G. Le Fou solidaire.
  D.F. Rogers, 102(CanL):Summer83-157
Langevin, G. Issue de secours.*
  D.F. Rogers, 102(CanL):Summer83-157
  J. Viswanathan, 102(CanL):Autumn83-108
Langford, P. - see Burke, E.
Langham, R. A Letter. (R.J.P. Kuin, ed)
  C.E. McGee, 539:Aug84-228
Langhans, E.A. Restoration Promptbooks.*
  J. Milhous, 173(ECS):Winter83/84-238
  H.W. Pedicord, 611(TN):Vol137No1-43
Langkabel, H. Die Staatsbriefe Coluccio
  Salutatis.
  R.G. Witt, 589:Apr83-498
Langlois, J.D., Jr., ed. China under
  Mongol Rule.
  L.H. Kwanten, 293(JASt):Nov82-138
Langner, H. Untersuchungen zur Mundart
  und zur Umgangssprache im Raum von Wit-
  tenberg.*
  G. Lerchner, 682(ZPSK):Band36Heft4-483
Langton, J. Emily Dickinson is Dead.
  N. Callendar, 441:15Jul84-27
  442(NY):13Aug84-94
Langworthy, H.W. - see Wiese, C.
Lanham, L.W. and C.A. Macdonald. The
  Standard in South African English and
  its Social History.
  F.W. Gester, 72:Band219Heft1-178

Lankheit, K. Die Modellsammlung der Por-
  zellanmanufaktur Doccia.
  J. Montagu, 90:Dec83-757
"L'année 1778 à travers la presse traitée
  par ordinateur."
  P. Rétat, 535(RHL):Jul/Aug83-644
Lannoy, R. - see Thompson, L.
Lansbury, C. The Reasonable Man.*
  R. ap Roberts, 385(MQR):Winter84-138
Lanser, S.S. The Narrative Act.
  D.J. Depew, 478:Apr83-134
  B. Duyfhuizen, 477(PLL):Spring83-218
  P. Lawley, 402(MLR):Jul83-642
  J. Phelan, 141:Winter83-69
  S. Praet, 204(FdL):Jun83-149
Lantz, M., ed. Emigrantvisor.
  R. Wright, 563(SS):Winter83-82
Lanza, D. Lingua e discorso nell'Atene
  delle professioni.
  F.D. Harvey, 303(JoHS):Vol 103-191
Lao She. Ma and Son. (J.M. James, trans)
  R.E. Hegel, 116:Jul82-299
Lapalme, M. Éperdument.
  M.E. Kidd, 102(CanL):Spring83-141
de La Peña, J. De bello contra insulanos.
  A. Reix, 542:Jan-Mar83-96
Lapeyre, P. Le Vertige de Rimbaud.
  M.E. Birkett, 446(NCFS):Fall-
  Winter83/84-237
  C.A. Hackett, 208(FS):Jul83-354
Lapidge, M. and P.H. Blair - see Blair,
  P.H.
Lapidus, G.W., ed. Women, Work, and Fam-
  ily in the Soviet Union.
  M.E. Fischer, 550(RusR):Oct83-434
Lapière, M-R. La lettre ornée dans les
  manuscrits mosans d'origine bénédictine
  (XIe-XIIe siècles).
  L. Nees, 589:Jul83-768
Lapierre, A. L'Ontario français du sud-
  ouest.
  C.A. Demharter, 207(FR):Apr84-727
  A. Thomas, 320(CJL):Fall83-202
La Pierre, A. Toponymie française en
  Ontario.
  R. Coulet du Gard, 424:Sep83-215
Lapierre, R. Hubert Aquin.
  P. Merivale, 188(ECr):Fall83-105
Lapierre, R. L'Imaginaire captif.*
  F.M. Iqbal, 102(CanL):Summer83-170
Lapointe, G. Arbre-Radar.
  D.F. Rogers, 102(CanL):Summer83-162
Lappin, S. Sorts, Ontology and Metaphor.
  F.G. Droste, 353:Vol20No1/2-133
  A. Günther, 603:Vol7No2-313
  P. Hanna, 543:Mar83-719
Laprevotte, G. Science et poésie de
  Dryden à Pope.
  I. Simon, 189(EA):Apr-Jun84-193
Larbaud, V. and M. Ray. Correspondance
  1899-1937. (F. Lioure, ed)
  A. Connell, 107(CRCL):Mar83-137
Lardy, N.R. Agriculture in China's Mod-
  ern Economic Development.
  N. Eberstadt, 129:Mar84-47
Lardy, N.R. Economic Growth and Distribu-
  tion in China.
  Chun Hwa Chai, 302:Vol 19No2-243
Large, P. The Micro Revolution Revisited.
  L. Burnard, 617(TLS):14Dec84-1444
Large, S.S. Organized Workers and Social-
  ist Politics in Interwar Japan.*
  S.M. Garon, 293(JASt):Nov82-167

217

Lariviere, R.W. The Divyatattva of Raghunandana Bhaṭṭācārya.
J.D.M. Derrett, 259(IIJ):Jun83-287
Larkin, E. The Roman Catholic Church and the Plan of Campaign, 1886-1888.
M.E. Daly, 272(IUR):Autumn83-268
Larkin, P. Required Writing.*
J. Barnes, 617(TLS):6Jan84-5
R. Craft, 453(NYRB):28Jun84-30
B. Morrison, 176:Feb84-43
R. Pinsky, 441:12Aug84-9
R. Richman, 129:Oct84-78
W. Scammell, 364:Feb84-107
442(NY):13Aug84-93
Larminie, V.M. The Godly Magistrate.
D. McKitterick, 354:Dec83-426
Larner, C. Enemies of God.*
L.F. Barmann, 377:Mar83-51
R.B. Manning, 551(RenQ):Spring83-96
La Rocque, G. Les Masques.*
P. Merivale, 102(CanL):Spring83-147
Larrue, J-M. Le Théâtre à Montréal à la fin de la XIXe siècle.
L.E. Doucette, 627(UTQ):Summer83-527
L. Shouldice, 102(CanL):Autumn83-84
Larsen, J.P. Haydn.*
L. Salter, 415:May83-298
Larson, G.O. The Reluctant Patron.*
T. Russell-Cobb, 324:Apr84-343
Larsson, L.O. Albert Speer: Le Plan de Berlin 1937-1943.
M. Pawley, 46:Jun83-57
Laruelle, F. Au-delà du principe de pouvoir.
C. Chalier, 192(EP):Apr-Jun83-241
Lasch, C. The Minimal Self.
M.C. Miller, 61:Nov84-141
D.H. Wrong, 441:28Oct84-7
Lasdun, S. Victorians at Home.*
S. Monod, 189(EA):Oct-Dec83-475
Lasierra, I.A. - see under Abbad y Lasierra, I.
Lasker-Schüler, E. Hebrew Ballads and Other Poems. (A. Durchslag and J. Litman-Demeestère, eds and trans)
S. Bauschinger, 221(GQ):Mar83-336
Laslett, P. The World We Have Lost: Further Explored.
G. Himmelfarb, 441:24Jun84-20
de Lasry, A.B. El judío como héroe de novela.
F.G. Ilárraz, 552(REH):Oct83-465
de Lasry, A.B. Two Romances.
D.S. Severin, 86(BHS):Oct83-339
Lass, R. On Explaining Language Change.*
U. Fries, 38:Band101Heft1/2-164
S. Romaine, 355(LSoc):Jun83-223
C.V.J. Russ, 402(MLR):Apr83-388
Lassalle, G. Chasing the Chattel.
J.K.L. Walker, 617(TLS):19Oct84-1180
Lassalle, J-P. and T. Lassalle-Maraval. Un Manuscrit des "Lettres d'une religieuse portugaise."
M. Alcover, 207(FR):Feb84-390
Lasserre, F. - see Strabo
Lassner, J. The Shaping of 'Abbāsid Rule.
E. Kohlberg, 318(JAOS):Apr-Jun82-371
Latacz, J., ed. Homer: Tradition und Neuerung.
E. Heitsch, 260(IF):Band87-301
"Lateinisches Hexameter-Lexikon." (Pts 4 and 5) (O. Schumann, comp)
J. Soubiran, 555:Vol57fasc2-327

"L'atelier de Jackson Pollock."
C. Finkelsztajn, 98:May83-440
"L'atelier de Mondrian."
J-C. Lebensztejn, 98:Nov83-893
Lathem, E.C. - see Caldwell, E.
Lathrop, T.A. The Evolution of Spanish.*
N.J. Dyer, 240(HR):Autumn83-455
"Il latino nell'italiano."
F. Murru, 260(IF):Band87-311
La Tourette, A. Nuns and Mothers.
E. Fisher, 617(TLS):26Oct84-1224
Lattimore, R. Continuing Conclusions.
N. Tredell, 617(TLS):27Apr84-454
Lau, J.S.M., C.T. Hsia and L.O-F. Lee, eds. Modern Chinese Stories and Novellas 1919-1949.*
P.G. Pickowicz, 293(JASt):May83-652
Lauber, V. The Political Economy of France from Pompidou to Mitterrand.
P. McCarthy, 617(TLS):8Jun84-643
Laubich, A. and R. Spencer. Art Tatum.
F. Hoffmann, 498:Vol9No2-88
Lauer, Q. Hegel's Concept of God.
H.S. Harris, 518:Jul83-153
J.L. Marsh, 258:Mar83-91
A. Reix, 542:Jan-Mar83-136
W.E. Steinkraus, 319:Apr84-247
Lauer, R., ed. Europäischer Realismus.*
P. Brang, 688(ZSP):Band43Heft2-436
Lauer, R., with others, eds. Neues Handbuch der Literaturwissenschaft. (Vol 17)
Z. Konstantinović, 52:Band17Heft3-328
Laufs, M. Walter Jens.*
A. Otten, 406:Spring83-86
Laughlan, W.F. - see Hogg, J.
Laugier, J. Le Verbe et la semence.
D. Festa-McCormick, 207(FR):Dec83-270
Laugwitz, D. Infinitesimalkalkül.
H.J.M. Bos, 316:Mar83-217
Lauha, A. Kohelet.
A. Lacocque, 318(JAOS):Oct-Dec82-661
Laundy, P. The Office of Speaker in the Parliaments of the Commonwealth.
B. Cocks, 617(TLS):2Nov84-1236
Launitz-Schürer, L.S., Jr. Loyal Whigs and Revolutionaries.*
B. Tucker, 106:Spring83-49
Laupin, P. Le Jour l'aurore.
F. Coulange, 450(NRF):Jan83-103
Laur, W. Die Ortsnamen im Kreis Pinneberg.
E. Felder, 685(ZDL):1/1983-122
Laurence, D.H. Bernard Shaw: A Bibliography.
S. Weintraub, 617(TLS):18May84-563
Laurence, F.M. Hemingway and the Movies.
M. Deutelbaum, 395(MFS):Winter83-733
Laurent, V. Le corpus des sceaux de l'empire byzantin. (Vol 2)
J.W. Nesbitt, 589:Jul83-771
Laurenti, J.L. Ensayo de una bibliografía de la novela picaresca española: años 1554-1964.
Y.M., 545(RPh):Nov82-322
Laurenti, J.L. and A. Porqueras-Mayo. The Spanish Golden Age (1472-1700).*
C. Griffin, 86(BHS):Apr83-144
Lauritzen, M. Jane Austen's "Emma" on Television.
P.G., 189(EA):Apr-Jun84-236
Lausberg, M. Das Einzeldistichon.
J. Soubiran, 555:Vol57fasc2-337
Lauverjat, R-M. - see Verlaine, P.

Lavabre, S. La Mélancolie et la poésie victorienne.
P. Marshall, 189(EA):Oct-Dec83-478
Lavagetto, M., ed. Per conoscere Saba.
E. Favretti, 228(GSLI):Vol 160fasc509-122
Laver, J. The Phonetic Description of Voice Quality.*
D.H., 355(LSoc):Mar83-134
Lavers, A. Roland Barthes.
R.A. Carter, 89(BJA):Autumn83-372
A. Jefferson, 494:Vol4No2-373
B.R. McGraw, 141:Spring83-177
C. Prendergast, 208(FS):Jul83-365
C. Reichler, 546(RR):Nov83-502
M.B. Wiseman, 478:Apr83-106
295(JML):Nov83-433
Lavin, M.A. Piero della Francesca's Baptism of Christ.*
G.L. Geiger, 90:May83-301
Lavis, G. and M. Stasse. Les chansons de Thibaut de Champagne: Concordances et index.
K.J. Brahney, 589:Jul83-846
G. Roques, 553(RLiR):Jul-Dec83-482
"Lavori ispanistici." (Ser 4)
C.B. Faulhaber, 545(RPh):May83-639
Lavroukine, N. and L. Tchertkov, with C. Robert. D.S. Mirsky.*
L. Dienes, 558(RLJ):Winter-Spring83-290
R. Sheldon, 550(RusR):Jan83-125
Law-Yone, W. The Coffin Tree.*
L. Marcus, 617(TLS):9Mar94-252
Lawford, V. Horst.
A. Grundberg, 441:2Dec84-17
Lawler, J.R. René Char, The Myth and The Poem.
S. Metzidakis, 546(RR):Nov83-500
Lawler, T. The One and the Many in the "Canterbury Tales."*
C. Clark, 179(ES):Feb83-92
S.S. Hussey, 677(YES):Vol 13-297
P. Neuss, 541(RES):Nov83-483
D. Staines, 597(SN):Vol55No2-206
Lawler, T.M.C., G. Marc'hadour and R.C. Marius - see More, T.
Lawless, R. and A. Findlay, eds. North Africa.
F. Ghiles, 617(TLS):20Jul84-809
Lawlor, R. Sacred Geometry.*
D. Pedoe, 529(QQ):Winter83-1176
Lawlor, S. Britain and Ireland 1914-23.
R. Foster, 617(TLS):24Feb84-194
Lawrence, A.W. Greek Aims in Fortification.
J.J. Coulton, 123:Vol33No2-257
J. Ober, 122:Jan83-56
Lawrence, D.H. Apocalypse and the Writings on Revelation.* (M. Kalnins, ed)
A. Fothergill, 506(PSt):Sep83-195
K.M. Hewitt, 541(RES):Aug83-360
Lawrence, D.H. The Letters of D.H. Lawrence.* (Vol 1) (J.T. Boulton, ed)
P. Preston, 447(N&Q):Jun82-261
Lawrence, D.H. The Letters of D.H. Lawrence.* (Vol 2) (G.J. Zytaruk and J.T. Boulton, eds)
É. Delavenay, 189(EA):Jul-Sep84-346
D. Mehl, 72:Band220Heft2-420
M.L. Ross, 556:Summer83-54

Lawrence, D.H. The Lost Girl. (J. Worthen, ed)
J.F. Stewart, 577(SHR):Fall83-361
Lawrence, D.H. Mr. Noon. (L. Vasey, ed)
G. Hough, 617(TLS):14Sep84-1028
M. Poole, 362:13Sep84-24
V.S. Pritchett, 453(NYRB):25Oct84-18
D. Trilling, 441:16Dec84-3
Lawrence, D.H. The Portable D.H. Lawrence. (D. Trilling, ed)
J. Newman, 161(DUJ):Dec82-83
Lawrence, D.H. The Prussian Officer and Other Stories. (J. Worthen, ed)
M. Dodsworth, 175:Autumn83-300
Lawrence, D.H. Ten Paintings.
J. Meyers, 290(JAAC):Summer84-465
M. Shaw, 148:Autumn83-23
Lawrence, D.H. The Trespasser. (E. Mansfield, ed) St. Mawr and Other Stories. (B. Finney, ed)
D. Mehl, 72:Band220Heft2-420
Lawrence, E.A. Rodeo.
B.J. Stoeltje, 567:Vol44No1/2-137
Lawrence, F.L., ed. Visages de Molière.
G. Defaux, 400(MLN):May83-834
Lawrence, K.R. The Odyssey of Style in "Ulysses."*
S. Benstock, 329(JJQ):Spring84-290
R. Boyle, 305(JIL):May83-110
Lawrence, R.G. and S.L. Macey, eds. Studies in Robertson Davies' Deptford Trilogy.
E. Cameron, 178:Mar83-119
Lawrence, R.Z. Can America Compete?
L.C. Thurow, 453(NYRB):27Sep84-29
"Laws of Early Iceland: Grágás I." (A. Dennis, P. Foote and R. Perkins, trans)
F. Scott, 382(MAE):1983/2-343
Lawson, C. The Chalumeau in Eighteenth-Century Music.*
A. Baines, 410(M&L):Jul/Oct83-259
Lawson, J. Robert Bloomfield.
P. Marshall, 677(YES):Vol 13-325
Lawson, P. George Grenville.
L. Colley, 617(TLS):14Sep84-1033
Lawson, S. and B. Soasey. Apron Makin'.
G. Brown, 614:Spring84-19
Lawson, S.K. Amish Inspirations.
P. Bach, 614:Winter84-15
Lawson, W. The Western Scar.*
A. Dzidzienyo, 395(MFS):Winter83-825
Lax, E. Life and Death on 10 West.
A. Barnet, 441:25Mar84-12
Lax, E. On Being Funny.
S. Feldman, 106:Fall83-353
Laye, C. The Guardian of the Word.
M. Tucker, 441:24Jun84-24
Layman, R. Shadow Man.
P. Wolfe, 395(MFS):Autumn83-389
Layton, I. Taking Sides. (H. Aster, ed)
A.J. Harding, 102(CanL):Autumn83-102
Layton, P. Designer Jeans. (Bks 1 and 2) Slip-Fit Method of Pattern Making. Pocket Shapes and Designs.
M. Cowan, 614:Spring84-22
Lazarnick, G. Netsuke and Inro Artists, and How to Read their Signatures.
E.A. Wrangham, 60:Mar-Apr83-136
Lazaroff, A. The Theology of Abraham Bibago.
B. Septimus, 589:Apr83-556

Lea, J. and J. Young. What is to be done about Law and Order?
  L. Taylor, 617(TLS):21Sep84-1046
Lea, K.M. and T.M. Gang - see Tasso, T.
Lea, S. The Floating Candles.
  S.C. Behrendt, 502(PrS):Spring83-105
  E. Grosholz, 249(HudR):Autumn83-585
  W. Prunty, 598(SoR):Autumn84-958
Leach, D., ed. Generative Literature and Generative Art.*
  S.G. Kellman, 395(MFS):Winter83-812
Leach, E. and D.A. Aycock. Structuralist Interpretations of Biblical Myth.
  M. Douglas, 453(NYRB):20Dec84-43
Leade, J. The Revelation of Revelations.
  J. Godwin, 111:Spring84-6
Leader, Z. Reading Blake's Songs.*
  H. Adams, 591(SIR):Fall83-458
  S. Gill, 184(EIC):Jan83-49
  N. Hilton, 173(ECS):Fall83-64
  J.C. Robinson, 661(WC):Summer83-160
Leake, R.E., D.B. and A.E. Concordance des "Essais" de Montaigne.*
  R.D. Cottrell, 207(FR):Feb84-387
  F.J. Hausmann, 547(RF):Band95Heft1/2-143
  M.B. McKinley, 551(RenQ):Autumn83-465
Leakey, M. Africa's Vanishing Art.
  A. Sieveking, 617(TLS):27Jul84-852
Leakey, M. Disclosing the Past.
  K. Bouton, 441:4Nov84-26
  442(NY):12Nov84-194
Leakey, R.E. One Life.
  K. Bouton, 441:4Nov84-26
  R. Martin, 617(TLS):28Dec84-1497
Leal, L. and others, eds. A Decade of Chicano Literature (1970-1979).
  D. Gerdes, 238:Sep83-441
Leale, B.C. Leviathan.
  L. Mackinnon, 617(TLS):30Nov84-1393
  J. Mole, 176:Dec84-63
Leamer, L. Ascent.
  M. Cohen, 649(WAL):May83-47
Leandicho Lopez, M. A Study of Philippine Games.
  W.W. Anderson, 650(WF):Apr83-153
  H.Q. Meñez, 292(JAF):Jan-Mar83-103
Leapman, M. Treachery?
  D.A.N. Jones, 617(TLS):7Sep84-993
Lear, J. Aristotle and Logical Theory.*
  A.W. Price, 393(Mind):Jan83-126
Leary, D., ed. Shaw's Plays in Performance.
  A. Carpenter, 617(TLS):15Jun84-663
Leary, L. The Book-Peddling Parson.
  R. Nalley, 441:10Jun84-25
Lease, B. Anglo-American Encounters.
  H.W. Emerson, Jr., 366:Spring83-130
  W.L. Hedges, 27(AL):Mar83-102
  A.E. Stone, 131(CL):Spring83-191
Lease, B. and H-J. Lang - see Neal, J.
Least Heat Moon, W. Blue Highways.*
  R. McDowell, 249(HudR):Summer83-420
Leatherbarrow, W.J. Fedor Dostoevsky.*
  R. Freeborn, 575(SEER):Jul83-425
  S. Hackel, 402(MLR):Jan83-249
Leaton, A. Good Friends, Just.*
  A. Ross, 364:Oct83-105
Leaton, A. Mayakovsky, My Love.
  J. Clute, 617(TLS):25May84-598
Leavis, F.R. The Critic as Anti-Philosopher.* (G. Singh, ed)
  W. Baker, 477(PLL):Fall83-461

Leavis, Q.D. Collected Essays. (Vol 1) (G. Singh, ed)
  E. Griffiths, 362:12Jan84-21
Leavitt, D. Family Dancing.
  W. Lesser, 441:2Sep84-7
Leavitt, D.L. Feminist Theatre Groups.
  G. Crane, 615(TJ):May82-273
Lebano, E.A. and P.R. Baldini. Buon Giorno a Tutti!
  L.F. Farina, 399(MLJ):Autumn83-297
Le Blanc, B.B. Faut Divorcer!*
  J. Ripley, 102(CanL):Winter82-137
Leblanc, B.B. Horace du l'art de porter la redingote.
  K. Mezei, 102(CanL):Summer83-128
Le Blanc, C. and D. Borei - see Bodde, D.
Leblanc, H. Existence, Truth, and Provability.
  E.J. Ashworth, 154:Sep83-570
Le Blanc, S.A. The Mimbres People.
  W. Bray, 617(TLS):27Jul84-852
  L. Milazzo, 584(SWR):Autumn83-viii
Le Bonniec, H. - see Arnobius
Le Bossu, R. Traité du poème épique.*
  R. Zuber, 535(RHL):Jan/Feb83-125
Lebra, T.S. Japanese Women.
  J. McCulloch, 441:19Aug84-19
Lebrecht, N. Discord.
  L. Salter, 415:Jun83-359
Le Bris, M. Romantics and Romanticism.
  D.M. Read, 88:Winter83/84-114
Le Brun, A. Les Châteaux de la subversion.
  R.J. Golsan, 207(FR):Apr84-717
  J.H. Matthews, 593:Fall83-245
Le Brun, J. - see Fénelon, F.
Lebsock, S. The Free Women of Petersburg.
  W. Kaminer, 441:26Feb84-23
Lecker, R. On the Line.
  B. Cameron, 627(UTQ):Summer83-500
  A.E. Davidson, 395(MFS):Winter83-734
Lecker, R. and J. David, eds. The Annotated Bibliography of Canada's Major Authors. (Vol 3)
  T. Goldie, 102(CanL):Spring83-153
Lecker, R., J. David and E. Quigley, eds. Canadian Writers and Their Works.
  R. Mathews, 99:Dec83-33
Leckie, R.W., Jr. The Passage of Dominion.
  R.W. Hanning, 589:Jan83-198
Le Clair, T. and L. McCaffery, eds. Anything Can Happen.*
  B. Duyfhuizen, 395(MFS):Winter83-741
  P.B. McElwain, 590:Dec83-105
Leclanche, J-L., ed. Le Conte de Floire et Blancheflor.
  A.J. Holden, 208(FS):Jul83-326
Leclant, J., ed. Ägypten. (Vols 1-3)
  D. Wildung, 471:Jul/Aug/Sep83-287
"Le Corbusier Sketchbooks."
  W.H. Jordy, 576:Mar83-83
Le Corsu, F. Plutarque et les femmes dans les Vies parallèles.
  O.D. Watkins, 303(JoHS):Vol 103-181
Lecourt, D. La philosophie sans feinte.
  M. Barthélémy-Madaule, 542:Jul-Sep83-380
Lecouteux, C. Les Monstres dans la littérature allemande du moyen âge.
  A. Closs, 402(MLR):Oct83-963
Ledbetter, K. Too Many Blackbirds.
  R. Hoffman, 441:27May84-16
Lederer, D.P. Drapery Top Treatments.
  G. Brown, 614:Spring84-22

Lederer, W.J. I, Giorghos.
R.P. Mills, 441:8Apr84-20
Lederman, W.R. Continuing Canadian Consti-
tutional Dilemmas.
R.E. Bilson, 529(QQ):Summer83-520
de Ledezma, M. and L. Álvarez. Dos en-
sayos de lingüística.
F. Nuessel, 350:Mar84-186
Leduc-Park, R. Réjean Ducharme —
Nietzsche et Dionysos.
P. Hébert, 627(UTQ):Summer83-523
Ledwidge, B. De Gaulle.*
639(VQR):Summer83-79
Lee, A. Sarah Phillips.
S.R. Shreve, 441:18Nov84-13
Lee, A.R., ed. Black Fiction.*
M. Fabre, 189(EA):Jan-Mar83-106
Lee, A.R., ed. Ernest Hemingway.
V. Meyers, 395(MFS):Winter83-731
Lee, A.R., ed. Herman Melville.
L. Mackinnon, 617(TLS):31Aug84-965
Lee, B., with D. Lally. The Wrong Stuff.
L.S. Ritter, 441:3Jun84-11
Lee, C. and G. De Vos, with others.
Koreans in Japan.*
G. Scoggins, 293(JASt):Feb83-422
Lee, D. Drinking and Driving.
L.L. Lee, 649(WAL):Nov83-255
Lee, E. Folksong and Music Hall.
A. Lamb, 415:Oct83-619
Lee, G. - see Tibullus
Lee, H. Elizabeth Bowen.*
D. Gauthier, 189(EA):Jan-Mar84-104
Lee, J.Y. Korean Shamanistic Rituals.
L. Kendall, 293(JASt):May83-687
Lee, L. Mourning into Dancing.
B. Rollin, 441:2Sep84-22
Lee, L. and B. Gifford. Saroyan.
M. Norman, 441:25Nov84-14
Lee, P.H., ed. The Silence of Love.*
A.S-H. Lee, 293(JASt):Feb83-424
Lee, S.E., ed. The Sketchbooks of Hiro-
shige.
P-L. Adams, 61:Dec84-148
Lee, S.Y. and Y.C. Jao. Financial Struc-
tures and Monetary Policies in Southeast
Asia.
D. Feeny, 293(JASt):Aug83-1022
Leech, G. Semantics.
R. Martin, 553(RLiR):Jul-Dec83-433
Leech, G.N. and M.H. Short. Style in Fic-
tion.*
R. Fowler, 38:Band101Heft1/2-198
R.S. Sharma, 257(IRAL):Nov83-333
Leed, R.L., A.D. Nakhimovsky and A.S.
Nakhimovsky. Beginning Russian. (Vol 2)
M.I. Levin, 558(RLJ):Fall83-208
Leeker, J. Existentialistische Motive im
Werk Alberto Moravias.
J. Hösle, 52:Band17Heft1-105
Leeman, A.D. and H. Pinkster. M. Tullius
Cicero, "De Oratore" Libri III. (Vol 1)
M. Winterbottom, 123:Vol33No1-36
Lees-Milne, J. Another Self. Ancestral
Voices. Prophesying Peace.
T.G.D.F., 617(TLS):12Oct84-1171
Lees-Milne, J. Caves of Ice.*
T.G.D.F., 617(TLS):12Oct84-1171
R. Kingzett, 39:Aug83-196
N. Woodin, 364:Jul83-99
Lees-Milne, J. The Last Stuarts.*
G. Schmidgall, 441:16Sep84-14

Lees-Milne, J. Harold Nicolson.
E. Perényi, 453(NYRB):29Mar84-33
G.S. Rousseau, 579(SAQ):Autumn83-445
Le Fanu, J.S. The Cock and Anchor, being
A Chronicle of Old Dublin City. The
House by the Church-Yard. The Purcell
Papers.
R. Tracy, 445(NCF):Dec83-354
Lefay-Toury, M-N. La Tentation du suicide
dans le roman français du XIIe siècle.
A.H. Diverres, 208(FS):Apr83-200
Lefebvre, C. La Syntaxe comparée du fran-
çais standard et du français populaire.
F. des Roches, 627(UTQ):Summer83-538
Lefebvre, C., H. Magloire-Holly and N.
Piou. Syntaxe de l'haïtien.*
Y. Dejean, 207(FR):Oct83-147
Lefebvre, V.A. Algebra of Conscience.
H.R. Alker, Jr., 185:Apr84-520
Lefkowitz, M.K. and M.B. Fant, eds. Wom-
en's Life in Greece and Rome.
639(VQR):Spring83-56
Lefkowitz, M.R. The Lives of the Greek
Poets.*
J.M. Bell, 487:Summer83-159
D.L. Clayman, 24:Spring83-96
Lefrançois, T. Nicolas Bertin, 1668-
1736.*
D. Posner, 54:Dec83-701
Leftwich, A. Redefining Politics.
G. Sampson, 617(TLS):24Aug84-946
Légaré, H. Brun marine.
E. Hamblet, 207(FR):Mar84-591
Le Garrec, E. Séverine, une rebelle (1855-
1929).
S. Tarrow, 446(NCFS):Fall-Winter83/84-
256
Le Gassick, T., ed. Major Themes in Mod-
ern Arabic Thought.
M.N. Mikhail, 318(JAOS):Oct-Dec82-671
Legendre, P. Paroles poétiques échappées
du texte.*
G.L., 185:Oct83-162
Léger, F. La Jeunesse d'Hippolyte Taine.
C. Evans, 208(FS):Jan83-95
Leggatt, A. Ben Jonson.*
J.B. Bamborough, 541(RES):Aug83-334
R. Finkelstein, 405(MP):Nov83-197
C. Hill, 366:Autumn83-250
W.D. Kay, 401(MLQ):Dec82-395
B. King, 569(SR):Winter83-149
Leggett, T. - see Sankaracarya
Legner, A. Deutsche Kunst der Romanik.
70:May-Jun83-167
Le Goff, J. and J-C. Schmitt, eds. Le
Charivari.
B. Bushaway, 203:Vol94No1-133
Legon, R.P. Megara.*
J. Salmon, 303(JoHS):Vol 103-202
Leheny, J. - see Addison, J.
Lehfeldt, W. Formenbildung des russischen
Verbs.
G.F. Meier, 682(ZPSK):Band36Heft3-359
Lehman, D. and C. Berger, eds. James
Merrill.*
V. Shetley, 491:Nov83-101
Lehmann, A.G. The European Heritage.
D. Thomas, 362:19Apr84-24
Lehmann, G. Kants Tugenden.*
V. Gerhardt, 53(AGP):Band65Heft1-97
Lehmann, G.A. Reformvorschläge in der
Krise der späten römischen Republik.
L. de Blois, 394:Vol36fasc3/4-421

Lehmann, H.G. Chronik der Bundesrepublik
Deutschland 1945/49 bis 1981.
B.H. Decker, 221(GQ):Jan83-184
Lehmann, J. Strandgesellschaft.
F. Albrecht, 654(WB):1/1982-140
Lehmann, J. Three Literary Friendships.
P. Sourian, 441:15Jul84-19
Lehmann, R.P.M., ed and trans. Early
Irish Verse.
J. Dunn, 174(Éire):Fall83-136
A. Harrison, 272(IUR):Spring83-123
Lehnert, H. Geschichte der deutschen Lit-
eratur vom Jugendstil zum Expressionis-
mus.
W. Wucherpfennig, 406:Summer83-224
Lehrer, A. Wine and Conversation.
B.J. Koch, 350:Dec84-997
Lehrman, J. Earthly Paradise.
R. Fonseca, 576:May83-201
Le Huenen, R. and P. Perron. Balzac —
Sémiotique du personnage romanesque.*
P. Imbert, 107(CRCL):Jun83-269
Leif, J. Pièges et mystifications de la
parole.
H. Bonnard, 209(FM):Oct83-379
Leigh, D. High Time.
A.W.B. Simpson, 617(TLS):12Oct84-1153
Leigh, J. There Really Was a Hollywood.
S. Gold, 441:4Nov84-13
Leigh, R.A., ed. Rousseau after Two Hun-
dred Years.
M. Carroll, 402(MLR):Apr83-449
M. Delon, 535(RHL):Jul/Aug83-641
P. Robinson, 83:Spring83-124
Leigh, R.A. - see Rousseau, J-J.
Leighton, A. Shelley and the Sublime.
I. Armstrong, 617(TLS):1Jun84-606
Leighton, L.G. - see Chukovsky, K.I.
Leiken, R.S., ed. Central America.
J. Chace, 453(NYRB):1Mar84-40
R. Radosh, 441:19Feb84-5
Leiner, J. Imaginaire — Langage —
Identité culturelle — Négritude.*
J.S.T. Garfitt, 208(FS):Oct83-498
Leinfellner, W., E. Kraemer and J. Schank,
eds. Language and Ontology.
483:Jul83-420
Leinonen, M. Russian Aspect, "Temporal-
'naja Lokalizacija" and Definiteness/
Indefiniteness.
K.T. Holden, 558(RLJ):Fall83-212
Leinsdorf, E. The Composer's Advocate.
N. Goodwin, 415:Aug83-485
Leisi, E. Paar und Sprache.
P. Seidensticker, 685(ZDL):3/1983-367
Leitch, D. Family Secrets.
D.A.N. Jones, 617(TLS):9Nov84-1281
Leitch, V.B. Deconstructive Criticism.*
J.T. Matthews, 141:Fall83-381
Leiter, S. Akhmatova's Petersburg.
C. Barnes, 617(TLS):8Jun84-635
J. Bayley, 453(NYRB):19Jan84-21
D. McDuff, 472:Fall/Winter83Spring/
Summer84-51
Leiter, S.L., ed and trans. The Art of
Kabuki.
H. Burger, 302:Vol 19No2-236
Leith-Ross, P. The John Tradescants.
J. Buxton, 617(TLS):22Jun84-709
Leithauser, B. Equal Distance.
A. Broyard, 441:30Dec84-4
Leithauser, B. Hundreds of Fireflies.*
R. Tillinghast, 569(SR):Summer83-473

Leitner, G. Denominale Verbalisierung im
Englischen.
K. Reichl, 38:Band101Heft1/2-185
Leitz, R.C. 3d, R.H. Ballinger and C.K.
Lohmann - see Howells, W.D.
Lele, J. Elite Pluralism and Class Rule.
G. Omvedt, 293(JASt):Feb83-438
Lellis, G. Bertolt Brecht.
M. Keller, 127:Fall83-284
Lem, S. Imaginary Magnitude.
P.J. Farmer, 441:2Sep84-4
Leman, B., ed. Patchwork Sampler Legacy
Quilt.
B. King, 614:Summer84-25
Lemann, N. Out of the Forties.*
J. Hunter, 676(YR):Spring84-433
Lemay, J.A.L. and P.M. Zall - see Franklin,
B.
Lemberg, H. and F. Seibt, eds. Deutsch-
tschechische Beziehungen in der Schul-
literatur und im populären Geschichts-
bild.*
J.J. Tomiak, 575(SEER):Oct83-625
Lemerle, P. The Agrarian History of
Byzantium.
J.W. Barker, 589:Jan83-202
Lemert, C.C. and G. Gillan. Michel
Foucault.*
G.P. Bennington, 208(FS):Jul83-366
A. Thiher, 207(FR):Feb84-430
Lemieux, D. and L. Mercier. La Recherche
sur les femmes au Québec.
C. Verduyn, 298:Fall83-162
Lemieux, G. La vie paysanne 1860-1900.
A.B. Chartier, 207(FR):May84-895
Lemire, M., ed. Dictionnaire des oeuvres
littéraires du Québec. (Vol 3)
A.B. Chartier, 207(FR):Dec83-238
B-Z. Shek, 627(UTQ):Summer83-520
Lemire, M. Introduction à la littérature
québécoise (1900-1939).
L. Shouldice, 102(CanL):Autumn83-84
Lemke, G.H. Sonne Mond und Sterne in der
deutschen Literatur seit dem Mittelal-
ter.*
K.H. Spinner, 564:Feb83-73
Lemm, R. Dancing in Asylum.
B.K. Filson, 526:Winter83-80
A. Munton, 198:Jun83-81
Lémonon, J-P. Pilate et le gouvernement
de la Judée.
T. Rajak, 313:Vol73-207
de Lena, P.R. - see under Rodríguez de
Lena, P.
Lenard, Y. Parole et pensée.* (4th ed)
M.A. Barnett, 399(MLJ):Spring83-75
Lenburg, J., J.H. Maurer and G. Lenburg.
The Three Stooges Scrapbook.
P.H. Broeske, 200:May83-317
Lenders, W. and K-P. Wegera, eds. Maschi-
nelle Auswertung sprachhistorischer
Quellen.
S.M. Embleton, 350:Sep84-667
H. Fix, 680(ZDP):Band102Heft3-473
L'Enfant, J. The Dancers of Sycamore
Street.
J.H. Wildman, 598(SoR):Spring84-488
Leniaud, J-M. Jean-Baptiste Lassus (1807-
1857), ou le temps retrouvé des cathé-
drales.*
C. Mead, 54:Sep83-523

Lenkersdorf, C. B'omak'umal Tojol Ab'al-Kastiya 1. B'omak'umal Kastiya-Tojol Ab'al 2.
  L. Furbee, 269(IJAL):Apr83-214
Lennon, T.M., J.M. Nicholas and J.W. Davis, eds. Problems of Cartesianism.*
  E.J. Ashworth, 154:Jun83-363
Lenoir, T. The Strategy of Life.
  F. Duchesneau, 154:Dec83-738
Le Normand, A. La Tradition classique et l'esprit romantique.*
  A. Potts, 90:Mar83-173
Lensing, L.A. and H-W. Peter, eds. Wilhelm Raabe.
  E. Meyer-Krentler, 680(ZDP):Band102 Heft2-296
  H. Steinecke, 221(GQ):Nov83-667
Lentricchia, F. After the New Criticism.*
  J.W. Davidson, 477(PLL):Winter83-93
  P. Hobsbaum, 402(MLR):Apr83-385
  S.R. Horton, 599:Winter83-37
Lentricchia, F. Criticism and Social Change.
  C. Baldick, 617(TLS):22Jun84-707
Lenz, A. Das Proöm des frühen griechischen Epos.
  F.M. Combellack, 122:Jul83-245
  P.V. Jones, 123:Vol133No1-125
Lenz, C.R.S., G. Greene and C.T. Neely, eds. The Woman's Part.*
  R.K. Bank, 615(TJ):Mar83-129
Lenz, S. The Heritage.*
  P. Lewis, 565:Vol124No3-36
Leon, J.M. - see under Messer Leon, J.
de León, L. - see under Luis de León
Leonard, E. Stick.*
  T.J. Binyon, 617(TLS):24Aug84-953
Leonard, F.M. Laughter in the Courts of Love.
  G.D. Economou, 589:Jul83-772
  D.A. Northrop, 405(MP):Feb84-306
Leonard, G. The Ice Cathedral.
  B. Atkinson, 441:28Oct84-26
Leonard, R. South Africa at War.
  J. de St. Jorre, 441:30Sep84-24
Leonhardt, F. Brücken/Bridges.
  P. Rice, 46:Jul83-60
Leoni, F.A. - see Albano Leoni, F.
Leopardi, G. Les Chants.
  L. Herlin, 450(NRF):Mar83-137
Leopardi, G. A Leopardi Reader. (O.M. Casale, ed and trans)
  D. Rolfs, 276:Autumn83-283
Leopardi, G. Moral Tales.*
  J. Davies, 617(TLS):10Feb84-146
Leopardi, G. Pensieri.*
  O.M. Casale, 276:Winter83-377
Lepage, Y.G. - see Richard de Fournival
Lepelley, R., ed. Dialectologie et littérature du domaine d'oïl occidentale.
  J. Joseph, 350:Dec84-987
Lepère, P. Les Antipodes.
  J. Réda, 450(NRF):Jun83-118
Leppmann, W. Rilke.*
  G. Annan, 453(NYRB):27Sep84-17
  P.P. Brodsky, 221(GQ):Jan83-157
  E. Heller, 441:7Oct84-24
  G. Steiner, 442(NY):8Oct84-133
Lepschy, G.C. Mutamenti di prospettiva nella linguistica.
  F. Murru, 260(IF):Band88-269

Lepschy, G.C. Saggi di linguistica italiana.*
  A. Stussi, 545(RPh):Feb83-467
Lepsius, R. Standard Alphabet for Reducing Unwritten Languages and Foreign Graphic Systems to a Uniform Orthography in European Letters.* (2nd ed) (J.A. Kemp, ed)
  P. Swiggers, 353:Vol20No9/10-658
Le Quesne, L. The Bodyline Controversy.*
  J.L. Carr, 364:Nov83-119
Lerat, P. Le ridicule et son expression dans les comédies françaises de Scarron à Molière.*
  J. Chaurand, 209(FM):Jul83-273
Le Rider, J. Le cas Otto Weininger.
  A. Reix, 542:Oct-Dec83-488
Lerman, R. The Book of the Night.
  V. Miner, 441:28Oct84-27
Lermontov, M. Mikhail Lermontov: Major Poetical Works. (A. Liberman, ed and trans)
  D. Bethea, 441:21Oct84-61
  H. Gifford, 453(NYRB):31May84-28
Lerner, L. Bible Poems.
  J. Mole, 176:Jun84-60
Lerner, L. Chapter and Verse.
  S. Rae, 617(TLS):7Sep84-1004
Lerner, L. The Literary Imagination.
  G.D. Martin, 89(BJA):Autumn83-375
  N. Pervukhina, 395(MFS):Winter83-819
  D. Schenker, 569(SR):Fall83-xc
Lerner, L., ed. Reconstructing Literature.*
  P. Kemp, 362:26Jan84-20
Lerner, L. Selected Poems.
  J. Mole, 176:Jun84-59
  S. Rae, 617(TLS):7Sep84-1004
Lernoux, P. In Banks We Trust.
  J. Gerth, 441:1Apr84-23
Lerond, A. Dictionnaire de la prononciation française.*
  A. Valdman, 545(RPh):Feb83-470
Leroux, J-P. Dans l'intervalle.
  D.F. Rogers, 102(CanL):Summer83-159
Leroux, P. La Grève de Samarez. (J-P. Lacassagne, ed)
  B. Rigby, 208(FS):Jan83-90
  J-J. Wunenburger, 192(EP):Jan-Mar83-101
Leroy, G. Péguy entre l'ordre et la révolution.
  K. Bieber, 207(FR):Feb84-425
  S. Fraisse, 535(RHL):Sep/Dec83-954
Le Roy Ladurie, E. Love, Death and Money in the Pays d'Oc.* (French title: L'argent, l'amour et la mort en pays d'oc.)
  L.M. Paterson, 208(FS):Oct83-462
Le Roy Ladurie, E. The Mind and Method of the Historian.*
  G. McLennan, 366:Spring83-107
Le Roy Ladurie, E. Paris-Montpellier, P.C.-P.S.U. 1945-1963.*
  H. Cronel, 450(NRF):May83-140
Le Roy Ladurie, E. La Sorcière de Jasmin.
  N.Z. Davis, 617(TLS):24Feb84-179
Leach, J.E. Science and Medicine in France.
  R. Fox, 617(TLS):2Nov84-1264
Lescure, P. Liwanaï au seuil de l'âge d'or.
  M. Naudin, 207(FR):Apr84-736

Leslau, W. Etymological Dictionary of
Gurage (Ethiopic).*
  R. Hetzron, 361:Apr83-378
  G. Hudson, 318(JAOS):Apr-Jun82-377
Lesley, C. Winterkill.
  R. Nalley, 441:29Jul84-20
Leslie, J. Value and Existence.*
  D. Ratzsch, 449:Mar83-113
Leslie, M. Spenser's "Fierce Warres and
Faithfull Loves."
  A. Hume, 617(TLS):28Sep84-1104
Lessa, W.A. More Tales From Ulithi Atoll.
  R.E. Mitchell, 292(JAF):Jan-Mar83-69
Lessard, P. Les petites images dévotes.
  P. Greenhill, 292(JAF):Jul-Sep83-352
Lesser, R. Etruscan Things.*
  E. Grosholz, 249(HudR):Autumn83-587
  J. Hollander, 676(YR):Autumn83-xvi
  P. Mesic, 491:Feb84-300
Lessing, D. The Diaries of Jane Somers.
  C. Greenland, 617(TLS):23Nov84-1358
  R. Jones, 362:6Dec84-34
Lessing, D. The Making of the Representa-
tive for Planet 8.
  L.T. Lemon, 502(PrS):Summer83-102
Lessing, G.E. Die Erziehung des Mensch-
engeschlechts.* (L.F. Helbig, ed)
  H.B. Nisbet, 402(MLR):Jan83-232
Lessing, G.E. Hamburgische Dramaturgie.
(K.L. Berghahn, ed) Die Juden. (W.
Grosse, ed)
  J.M. Tudor, 83:Autumn83-279
Lester, G.A. Sir John Paston's "Grete
Boke."
  N. Orme, 617(TLS):6Jul84-767
Le Tourneux, J-H. Pylônes.
  D.F. Rogers, 102(CanL):Summer83-160
Le Touzé, P. Le Mystère du réel dans les
romans de Bernanos.
  E.M. O'Sharkey, 208(FS):Jan83-104
Lettau, E.U. Faulkners "Intruder in the
Dust."
  W. Schlepper, 72:Band220Heft1-186
Lettenbauer, W. Der Baumkult bei den
Slaven.
  A. Měšťan, 688(ZSP):Band43Heft2-420
Léturmy, M. Abraham a vu mon jour.
  S.H. Léger, 207(FR):Feb84-414
Letwin, S.R. The Gentleman in Trollope.*
  S. Botros, 479(PhQ):Oct83-408
  E. Hollahan, 594:Summer83-147
  R. Kiely, 473(PR):4/1983-625
  R. ap Roberts, 385(MQR):Winter84-138
  A. Wright, 445(NCF):Jun83-104
Leube, E. and A. Noyer-Weidner, eds. Apol-
linaire.*
  V. Kapp, 547(RF):Band95Heft3-377
Leuchtenberg, W.E. In the Shadow of
F.D.R.*
  J.C. Chalberg, 129:May84-74
  E. Wright, 617(TLS):15Jun84-673
Leung Chi-keung, J.W. Cushman and Wang
Gungwu, eds. Hong Kong.
  M.K. Chan, 293(JASt):May83-589
Leung, S.M.R. Discover China.
  U. Roberts, 60:Nov-Dec83-150
Leupen, P. Philip of Leyden.
  J. Muldoon, 589:Jul83-775
Leuthner, S. The Railroaders.
  R. Starr, 129:Feb84-77
Leveille, L. Le Livre des marges.
  M.E. Kidd, 102(CanL):Spring83-141

Levenson, C., ed and trans. Seeking
Heart's Solace.
  C. Shields, 137:Sep83-25
Levenson, J.C. and others - see Adams, H.
Levenstein, A. Escape to Freedom.
  S. Miller, 129:Jan84-74
Lever, M. Le Roman français au XVIIème
siècle.*
  F. Assaf, 475:Vol 10No18-359
  J. Prévot, 535(RHL):Jan/Feb83-125
Levere, T.H. Poetry Realized in Nature.*
  C.W. Miller, 661(WC):Summer83-136
  B. Ross, 529(QQ):Summer83-554
Levernier, J.A. and D.R. Wilmes, eds.
American Writers before 1800.
  J.A.L. Lemay, 165(EAL):Fall84-215
Levertov, D. Candles in Babylon.
  P. Stitt, 491:Oct83-39
Lévesque, C. and C.V. McDonald, eds.
L'Oreille de l'autre.
  N. Lukacher, 400(MLN):May83-750
Levesque, L. Quand j'y ai dit ça, à parti
de rire ...
  A.D. Barry, 207(FR):Mar84-592
Levett, J. Changing Sides.
  M. O'Neill, 493:Sep83-72
  S. Rae, 617(TLS):17Feb84-168
Levey, M. An Affair on the Appian Way.
  C. Hawtree, 617(TLS):31Aug84-977
  J. Mellors, 362:13Dec84-30
Levi, I. The Enterprise of Knowledge.*
  W.L. Harper, 311(JP):Jun83-367
  M. Kaplan, 482(PhR):Apr83-310
Levi, J.N. Linguistics, Language, and Law.
  E. Finegan, 350:Mar84-199
Levi, P. The Echoing Green.
  L. Mackinnon, 617(TLS):27Jul84-838
Levi, P. The Flutes of Autumn.
  P. Dickinson, 364:Nov83-118
  W. Harrod, 617(TLS):4May84-504
Levi, P. The Periodic Table.
  A.H. Rosenfeld, 441:23Dec84-9
  442(NY):24Dec84-88
Lévi-Strauss, C. Myth and Meaning.
  J.F. Nagy, 650(WF):Oct83-306
Lévi-Strauss, C. The Naked Man.
  B. Toelken, 649(WAL):May83-39
Lévi-Strauss, C. Le Regard éloigné.
  J-P. Naugrette, 98:Dec83-948
  R. Needham, 617(TLS):13Apr84-393
Lévi-Strauss, C. The Way of the Masks.*
  J. Cove, 529(QQ):Winter83-1145
  W. Muensterberger, 90:Dec83-773
  W.N., 102(CanL):Spring83-188
Levin, B. Enthusiasms.*
  442(NY):4Jun84-134
Levin, B. The Way We Live Now.
  N. Berry, 617(TLS):28Dec84-1505
Levin, H. Grand Delusions.*
  D. Sharp, 129:Jan84-76
Levin, I., with U. Masing, eds. Armen-
ische Märchen.
  L. Röhrich, 196:Band24Heft3/4-312
Levin, I., D. Rabiev and M. Yavič, eds.
Svod tadžikskogo fol'klora. (Vol 1)
  H. Jason, 196:Band24Heft1/2-157
  M. Zand, 196:Band24Heft1/2-160
Levin, J. Snow.
  C. Verderese, 441:11Mar84-18
Levin, M.E. Metaphysics and the Mind-Body
Problem.*
  R.F.H., 543:Sep82-176

Lichem, K. and H.J. Simon, eds. Hugo
Schuchardt *Gotha 1842-†Graz 1927.
G. Ineichen, 260(IF):Band87-321
Licht, F. and D. Finn. Canova.
D. Irwin, 617(TLS):29Jun84-724
Lichtenstein, N. Labor's War at Home.
A. Wald, 385(MQR):Winter84-147
Lichtheim, M. Ancient Egyptian Literature.
(Vol 3)
H. Goedicke, 318(JAOS):Jan-Mar82-173
Lichtman, A.J. Prejudice and the Old
Politics.
H.M. Waller, 106:Spring83-79
Lickteig, F-B. The German Carmelites at
the Medieval Universities.
B. Smalley, 382(MAE):1983/2-356
Lida, R. Letras hispánicas.
H.B. Wescott, 238:May83-293
Liddell, V.G. With a Southern Accent.
G.H. Gates, 9(AlaR):Jul83-219
Lieb, H-H., ed. Oberflächensyntax und
Semantik.
G. Koller, 685(ZDL):3/1983-388
Lieb, M. Poetics of the Holy.*
B.K. Lewalski, 301(JEGP):Oct83-560
J.H. Sims, 568(SCN):Fall83-33
R.B. Waddington, 551(RenQ):Autumn83-
485
S. Wintle, 175:Summer83-160
Lieb, S. Mother of the Blues.
B. Harrah-Conforth, 187:Sep84-566
W.K. McNeil, 650(WF):Oct83-321
Lieberman, H. Nightbloom.
M. Buck, 441:24Jun84-22
Lieberman, L. Eros at the World Kite
Pageant.
J.F. Cotter, 249(HudR):Winter83/84-720
R.W. Hill, 580(SCR):Fall83-123
M. McFee, 472:Fall/Winter83Spring/
Summer84-367
Lieberman, L. God's Measurements.* Un-
assigned Frequencies.
M. McFee, 472:Fall/Winter83Spring/
Summer84-367
Lieberman, R. Renaissance Architecture in
Venice.
B. Boucher, 39:Sep83-270
D. Howard, 90:Sep83-559
Lieberman, S. The Contemporary Spanish
Economy.
J. Harrison, 86(BHS):Apr83-161
Lieberman, S.J., ed. Sumerological Stud-
ies in Honor of Thorkild Jacobsen on his
Seventieth Birthday June 7, 1974.
W. Heimpel, 318(JAOS):Jan-Mar82-152
Liebert, R.S. Michelangelo.*
L. Steinberg, 453(NYRB):28Jun84-41
Liebertz-Grün, U. Seifried Helbling.*
R.F.M. Byrn, 402(MLR):Apr83-487
J. Goheen, 589:Jul83-778
Liebich, A. Between Ideology and Utopia.
P. Smale, 154:Dec83-717
Lieblich, A. Kibbutz Makom.
A.J. Rawick, 287:Nov83-24
Liebman, C.S. and E. Don-Yehia. Civil
Religion in Israel.
D. Vital, 129:May84-70
Liebow, E.M. Dr. Joe Bell.
P. Wolfe, 395(MFS):Autumn83-389
Liehm, A. and P. Kussi, eds. The Writing
on the Wall.
G. Theiner, 617(TLS):28Sep84-1098

Liehm, M. Passion and Defiance.
W. Murray, 441:16Sep84-35
Lienhard, S. Die Legende vom Prinzen Viś-
vantara.
R. Morris, 318(JAOS):Apr-Jun82-415
Liersch, W. Hans Fallada.
T. Rietzschel, 654(WB):5/1983-951
Lietz, R. At Park and East Division.*
S.C. Behrendt, 502(PrS):Spring83-105
Lieven, D.C.B. Russia and the Origins of
The First World War.
J. Joll, 453(NYRB):29Mar84-21
J. Keep, 617(TLS):9Mar84-243
Lifshin, L. Blue Dust, New Mexico.
G. Burns, 584(SWR):Winter83-101
Lifton, R.J. and R. Falk. Indefensible
Weapons.*
D.L., 185:Oct83-184
"Ligeti in Conversation."
J. Deathridge, 617(TLS):8Jun84-646
Lightfoot, D. The Language Lottery.
L. Jenkins, 350:Dec84-979
W. O'Grady, 320(CJL):Fall83-161
Lightfoot, D.W. Principles of Diachronic
Syntax.*
S. Romaine, 355(LSoc):Jun83-223
A.R. Warner, 297(JL):Mar83-187
Lightfoot, S.L. The Good High School.
J.K. Davison, 441:25Mar84-21
Lightman, A.P. Time Travel and Papa Joe's
Pipe.
S. Boxer, 441:13May84-16
Lihani, J. Bartolomé de Torres Naharro.*
C. Stern, 545(RPh):May83-640
Lijphart, A. Democracies.
V. Bogdanor, 617(TLS):8Jun84-631
Likhachov, D. The Great Heritage.
O. Frink, 399(MLJ):Autumn83-304
Lilja Norrlind, E. Studier i svensk fri
versen.
I. Scobbie, 562(Scan):May83-87
A. Swanson, 563(SS):Winter83-69
Lill, R. Geschichte Italiens vom 16.
Jahrhundert bis zu den Anfängen des
Faschismus.
C. Dipper, 72:Band220Heft1-227
Lilliu, G. La civiltà nuragica.
D. Ridgway, 617(TLS):5Oct84-1131
Lillo, G. Der Kaufmann von Londen oder
Begebenheiten Georg Barnwells; Ein
bürgerliches Trauerspiel. (K-D. Mül-
ler, ed)
H.I. Dunkle, 221(GQ):Jan83-136
Lilly, M. The National Council for Civil
Liberties.
D. Pannick, 362:30Aug84-27
Lim Mah Hui. Ownership and Control of
the One Hundred Largest Corporations in
Malaysia.
L.Y.C. Lim, 293(JASt):May83-722
Lima, J.M. La sílaba en la piel.
L. Ramos Collado, 701(SinN):Jul-Sep83-
88
Limb, S. Up The Garden Path.
C. Hawtree, 617(TLS):13Apr84-396
J. Mellors, 362:26Apr84-31
Limentani, A. L'Eccezione narrativa.*
S. Kay, 382(MAE):1983/2-329
Limonov, E. It's Me, Eddie.* (Russian
title: Èto ja — Èdička.)
J. Bayley, 453(NYRB):22Nov84-28
Z. Zinik, 617(TLS):16Mar84-267

227

Lin, H.T. Essential Grammar for Modern Chinese.
 P.F-M. Yang, 293(JASt):May83-629
Lin Manshu, Hai Feng and Cheng Hai. Zhongguo dangdai wenxue shi gao.
 B. Lum, 116:Jan82-134
Lin, T-B., R.P. Lee and U-E. Simonis, eds. Hong Kong.
 M.K. Chan, 293(JASt):May83-589
Lincoln, B. Priests, Warriors, and Cattle.
 U. Strutynski, 292(JAF):Jul-Sep83-347
Lindberg, G. The Confidence Man in American Literature.*
 D. Jarrett, 366:Spring83-133
 J.H. Justus, 401(MLQ):Mar83-105
 W.R. Macnaughton, 27(AL):May83-266
 J.R. Russo, 594:Fall83-285
Lindberg-Seyersted, G. - see Pound, E. and F.M. Ford
Lindeman, F.O. The Triple Representation of Schwa in Greek and Some Related Problems of Indo-European Phonology.
 L.A. Connolly, 660(Word):Aug83-115
 B.D. Joseph, 350:Sep84-656
Lindenberger, H. Opera.
 J.S. Hans, 344:Summer84-123
Linder, J. Pasolini als Dramatiker.
 E. Brissa, 72:Band220Heft2-475
Linder, O. and H. Hand Spinning Cotton.
 W.P. Mickle, 614:Summer84-17
Lindheim, N. The Structures of Sidney's "Arcadia."
 T. Comito, 301(JEGP):Oct83-544
 T. Greenfield, 604:Fall83-64
 R. Kimbrough, 551(RenQ):Winter83-650
 H. MacLachlan, 627(UTQ):Summer83-407
 R.L. Montgomery, 401(MLQ):Jun83-198
Lindken, H-U. - see Schnitzler, A.
Lindner, G. Grundlagen der pädagogischen Audiologie. (2nd ed)
 G.F. Meier, 682(ZPSK):Band36Heft4-484
Lindop, G. The Opium-Eater.*
 P. Morgan, 179(ES):Dec83-573
Lindow, J. Swedish Legends and Folktales.
 U. Palmenfelt, 64(Arv):Vol37-184
Lindqvist, C. L'emploi temporel dans la complétive au subjonctif introduite par un temps du passé en français contemporain.
 M. Offord, 208(FS):Oct83-501
Lindsay, K.C. and P. Vergo - see Kandinsky, W.
Lindsay, L. Cocktails and Laughter.
 A. Forbes, 617(TLS):6Jan84-7
Lindstrom, N. Macedonio Fernández.
 S. Boldy, 86(BHS):Jan83-86
 M. Goldman, 238:May83-303
Lindström, O. Aspects of English Intonation.*
 F.W. Gester, 72:Band219Heft2-416
Linehan, P. Spanish Church and Society 1150-1300.
 R. Fletcher, 617(TLS):3Feb84-115
Ling, T. Buddhist Revival in India.
 M. Moffatt, 293(JASt):Nov82-189
Ling, T. Karl Marx and Religion.
 G. Russell, 485(PE&W):Jul83-311
Lingard, J. Sisters By Rite.
 P. Craig, 617(TLS):29Jun84-736
Lings, M. Muhammad.*
 S.H. Nasr, 469:Vol9No1-92
Lings, M. The Secret of Shakespeare.
 P. Jordan-Smith, 469:Vol9No3-111

"Linguistique et mathématiques."
 R. Martin, 553(RLiR):Jul-Dec83-416
Link, E.P., Jr. Mandarin Ducks and Butterflies.
 J.B. Grieder, 293(JASt):Feb83-394
Link, F.H. Zwei amerikanische Dichterinnen.
 H. Friedl, 72:Band220Heft1-181
Linker, R.W. A Bibliography of Old French Lyrics.*
 K. Varty, 208(FS):Jul83-330
Links, J.G. Canaletto.
 R. Bromberg, 90:Jul83-433
 42(AR):Winter83-121
Links, R. Alfred Döblin.
 O.F. Best, 301(JEGP):Oct83-607
Linley, J. The Georgia Catalog.
 C.M. Howett, 576:Oct83-308
 H.B. Owens, 219(GaR):Spring83-211
von Linné, K. Voyage en Laponie.
 J-L. Trassard, 450(NRF):Sep83-159
Linnér, S. Dostojevskij.
 V. Terras, 574(SEEJ):Winter83-489
Linscott, G. A Healthy Body.
 T.J. Binyon, 617(TLS):20Jul84-801
Linsen, E. Subjekt-Objekt-Beziehungen bei Balzac, Flaubert und Nathalie Sarraute unter besonderer Berücksichtigung der Sprachproblematik.
 G.W. Frey, 72:Band220Heft1-223
Linsley, L. America's Favorite Quilts.
 B. Self, 614:Summer84-11
Lintott, A. Violence, Civil Strife and Revolution in the Classical City 750-330 B.C.*
 N.R.E. Fisher, 123:Vol33No2-255
Lintvelt, J. Essai de Typologie Narrative.
 S. Praet, 204(FdL):Sep83-239
"L'Inventaire Suisse d'Architecture, 1850-1920." (Vols 3 and 4)
 R.J. Lawrence, 576:Dec83-403
Lion, F. Geist und Politik in Europa. (F. Martini and P. de Mendelssohn, eds)
 S. Hoefert, 406:Summer83-234
 K. Sontheimer, 52:Band17Heft1-98
"Lion de Bourges." (W.W. Kibler, J-L.G. Picherit and T.S. Fenster, eds)
 C. Roussel, 356(LR):Feb-May83-131
Lioure, F. - see Larbaud, V. and M. Ray
Lipka, L. and H. Günther, eds. Wortbildung.
 L. Seppänen, 439(NM):1983/4-535
Lipking, L., ed. High Romantic Argument.*
 J.H. Averill, 591(SIR):Winter83-632
 C. Clausen, 569(SR):Fall83-672
Lipking, L. The Life of the Poet.*
 M.G. Hamilton, 107(CRCL):Sep83-407
 H.J. Levine, 219(GaR):Summer83-446
Lipman, M. La découverte d'Harry Stottlemeier.
 J. Lefranc, 192(EP):Jan-Mar83-102
Lipman, S. The House of Music.
 W.L. Taitte, 441:16Dec84-20
Lipow, A. Authoritarian Socialism in America.
 S.J. Whitfield, 432(NEQ):Mar83-145
Lipp, S. Leopoldo Zea.*
 F. Avendaño, 552(REH):Oct83-471
Lippard, L.R. Get the Message?
 R. Baranik, 62:Summer84-81
Lippard, L.R. Overlay.*
 C. Rickey, 62:Sep83-65

Lipphardt, W., ed. Lateinische Oster-
feiern und Osterspiele. (Pts 1-6)
  H. Linke, 684(ZDA):Band112Heft1-33
Lippincott, L. Selling Art in Georgian
London.*
  D.G.C.A., 324:Aug84-640
Lippit, N.M. Reality and Fiction in
Modern Japanese Literature.*
  B. Thornbury, 149(CLS):Winter83-456
Lippit, N.M. and K.I. Selden, eds and
trans. Stories by Contemporary Japanese
Women Writers.
  Y. McClain, 407(NM):Winter83-442
  H. Matsui, 648(WCR):Oct83-57
Lippy, C.H. Seasonable Revolutionary.
  C.E. Wright, 656(WMQ):Jan83-147
Lipson, A., with S.J. Molinsky. A Russian
Course.* (Pts 1 and 2)
  D.M. Fiene, 399(MLJ):Autumn83-304
  M.I. Levin, 558(RLJ):Winter-Spring83-
  223
Lipson, A. and S.J. Molinsky. A Russian
Course. (Pt 3)
  D.M. Fiene, 399(MLJ):Autumn83-304
Lipton, D.R. Ernst Cassirer.*
  S. Mayer and W.F. Eggers, Jr.,
  125:Fall82-83
Lish, G. What I Know So Far.
  A. Friedman, 441:22Apr84-13
Liska, G. Russia and the Road to Appease-
ment.*
  R.C. North, 550(RusR):Oct83-457
de l'Isle-Adam, P.A.M.D. - see under de
Villiers de l'Isle-Adam, P.A.M.
Liss, P.K. Atlantic Empires.*
  J. Lynch, 263(RIB):Vol33No3-407
Lissak, M., ed. Israeli Society and Its
Defence Establishment.
  A. Shlaim, 617(TLS):14Sep84-1032
Lissorgues, Y. - see Alas, L.
List, R.N. Dedalus in Harlem.
  S. Benstock, 395(MFS):Summer83-284
  A. Nadel, 219(GaR):Summer83-438
  S.R. Parr, 329(JJQ):Summer84-388
  295(JML):Nov83-390
Lister, E. Portal Painters.
  M. Amaya, 592:Apr/May83-49
Lister, R. George Richmond.*
  S.M. Bennett, 88:Summer83-22
  D. Brown, 59:Dec83-485
Listfield, E. It Was Gonna Be Like Paris.
  C. Gaiser, 441:26Aug84-10
  R. Koenig, 61:Jun84-117
"Literary Communication and Reception."
  F. Meregalli, 107(CRCL):Mar83-86
"Literatur für Kinder und Jugendliche in
der DDR."
  K. Kögel, 654(WB):9/1982-171
"Literature and the Other Arts."
  F. Meregalli, 107(CRCL):Mar83-91
Litman, T.A. Les Comédies de Corneille.*
  M-O. Sweetser, 475:Vol 10No18-361
Little, I.M.D. Economic Development.
  S.A. Marglin, 453(NYRB):19Jul84-41
Little, J. Comedy and the Woman Writer.
  J. Batchelor, 617(TLS):10Aug84-900
  L.A. De Salvo, 659(ConL):Winter84-494
Little, J.P. Beckett: "En attendant Godot"
and "Fin de partie."
  L. Hill, 402(MLR):Oct83-936
  H. Peyre, 207(FR):Oct83-114

Little, K. The Sociology of Urban Women's
Image in African Literature.
  G. Moore, 447(N&Q):Aug82-382
Littlejohn, D. Architect.
  J. Giovannini, 441:28Oct84-27
Littleton, C.S. The New Comparative Myth-
ology. (3rd ed)
  J.F. Nagy, 650(WF):Oct83-306
Littlewood, I. The Writings of Evelyn
Waugh.
  A. Blayac, 189(EA):Jul-Sep84-347
  A.A. De Vitis, 395(MFS):Winter83-788
Littlewood, J. Milady Vine.
  D. Pryce-Jones, 617(TLS):29Jun84-719
Litvinoff, E. Falls the Shadow.*
  J. Sullivan, 441:1Jan84-20
Litweiler, J. The Freedom Principle.
  I. Gitler, 441:29Jul84-16
Liu, M-T. Chinesisch-deutsches Stilwörter-
buch für Konversation.
  G. Richter, 682(ZPSK):Band36Heft1-100
Liu Qing. J'accuse devant le Tribunal de
la Société.
  J.P. Harrison, 293(JASt):Aug83-869
Lively, P. According to Mark.
  D. May, 362:18Oct84-31
  G. Strawson, 617(TLS):19Oct84-1179
Lively, P. Corruption.
  C. Hawtree, 617(TLS):9Mar84-251
Lively, P. Next to Nature.* (British
title: Next to Nature, Art.)
  P. Craig, 617(TLS):1Jun84-623
  C. Sigal, 441:1Jan84-20
Lively, P. Perfect Happiness.*
  A. Becker, 441:21Oct84-34
  D. Taylor, 364:Dec83/Jan84-143
Liver, R. Manuel pratique de romanche
(sursilvan-vallader).
  M. Ulleland, 597(SN):Vol55No2-243
Liver, R. Die Nachwirkung der antiken
Sakralsprache im christlichen Gebet des
lateinischen und italienischen Mittel-
alters.
  E.J. Richards, 545(RPh):May83-610
Livermore, H., ed. University of British
Columbia Hispanic Studies.
  C.B. Faulhaber, 545(RPh):Feb83-489
Livesay, D. The Phases of Love.*
  K. Mezei, 648(WCR):Oct83-51
  J. Peirce, 99:Oct83-28
"Living with Nuclear Weapons."
  R.H., 185:Jul84-740
Livingston, J. Die Again, Macready.
  N. Callendar, 441:18Mar84-27
  442(NY):7May84-161
Livingston, J. and J. Beardsley. Black
Folk Art in America, 1930-1980.
  J.W. Ward, Jr., 585(SoQ):Winter83-82
Livingston, P. Ingmar Bergman and the
Rituals of Art.*
  L. Giannetti, 651(WHR):Summer83-158
  J. Nelson, 529(QQ):Autumn83-892
  P. Walsh, 108:Fall83-132
Livrea, H. - see Triphiodorus
Livrea, H., with P. Eleuteri - see Musaeus
Livy. Tite-Live, "Histoire romaine," Tome
28, Livre 38. (R. Adam, ed and trans)
  J.W. Rich, 313:Vol73-239
Livy. T. Livius, "Ab urbe condita," Libri
xxvi-xxvii. (P.G. Walsh, ed)
  S. Oakley, 123:Vol33No2-215

Lizé, É. Voltaire, Grimm et la Correspondance littéraire.
D. Fletcher, 208(FS):Jan83-82
J. Sareil, 546(RR):Jan83-107
Ljung, M. Reflections on the English Progressive.*
R.A. Close, 596(SL):Vol37No2-209
E. König, 38:Band101Heft1/2-178
A. Schopf, 603:Vol7No2-283
Ljung, P.E. Vilhelm Ekelund och den problematiska författarrollen.
S. Linnér, 562(Scan):Nov82-204
Lleó Cañal, V. Nueva Roma.
D. Angulo Iñiguez, 48:Jul-Sep80-399
Llorach, E.A. - see under Alarcos Llorach, E.
Lloréns, V. El romanticismo español.*
L. Fernández Cifuentes, 701(SinN): Jan-Mar83-77
I.M. Zavala, 240(HR):Winter83-105
Llosa, M.V. - see under Vargas Llosa, M.
Lloyd, C., ed. Social Theory and Political Practices.*
R.H., 185:Apr84-547
Lloyd, C. The Well-Chosen Garden.
L. Yang, 441:3Jun84-7
Lloyd, D.W. The Making of English Towns.
A. Clifton-Taylor, 617(TLS):18May84-544
Lloyd, G.E.R. Magic, Reason and Experience.*
D. Pingree, 122:Jan83-70
Lloyd, R. Baudelaire's Literary Criticism.*
J.E. Jackson, 535(RHL):Jul/Aug83-652
E.K. Kaplan, 207(FR):Feb84-399
G. Rees, 208(FS):Apr83-233
Lloyd, S. The Archaeology of Mesopotamia from the Old Stone Age to the Persian Conquest.
M-H. Gates, 318(JAOS):Jan-Mar82-170
Lloyd, S. H. Balfour Gardiner.
L. Foreman, 617(TLS):16Nov84-1309
Lloyd, S. An Indian Attachment.
S.S. Klass, 441:9Dec84-18
D. Murphy, 617(TLS):13Jul84-786
Lloyd, T.O. The British Empire 1558-1983.
D.K. Fieldhouse, 617(TLS):16Nov84-1321
Lloyd Evans, B. and G. Everyman's Companion to the Brontës.
S. Davies, 148:Summer83-88
Lloyd-Jones, H. Blood for the Ghosts.*
W.M. Calder 3d, 124:Sep-Oct83-55
Lloyd-Jones, H. - see von Wilamowitz-Moellendorff, U.
Lo, S.D. - see under de Mundo Lo, S.
Loar, B. Mind and Meaning.*
J. Bigelow, 63:Sep83-316
Lobanova, N.A. and I.P. Slesareva. Učebnik Russkogo Jazyka Dlja Inostrannyx Studentov-Filologov.
N.M. Baranova, 558(RLJ):Winter-Spring83-235
Lobb, E. T.S. Eliot and the Romantic Critical Tradition.*
E. Larrissy, 506(PSt):Dec83-303
F. McCombie, 447(N&Q):Aug82-372
Lobo, A. and H. Kapadia. Three Monographs on Music.
F. Berberich, 187:Jan84-153
Lobo, J. The Itinerário of Jerónimo Lobo.
J.J. Gold, 617(TLS):22Jun84-695

Lobo, S. A House of My Own.*
S.B. Brush, 37:Jan-Feb83-63
Locey, L., and M., eds. Le Mistere d'une jeune fille laquelle se voulut habandonner a peché.
A. Knapton, 545(RPh):Nov82-334
Lochhead, I.J. The Spectator and the Landscape in the Art Criticism of Diderot and His Contemporaries.
P.C., 90:Dec83-774
M.A. Cheetham, 127:Winter83-419
Lock, F.P. Swift's Tory Politics.
D.A.N. Jones, 362:31May84-22
P. Langford, 617(TLS):10Feb84-144
Lock, G. The State and I.
W.H., 185:Jan84-372
Locke, D. A Fantasy of Reason.*
N.L. Rosenblum, 543:Jun83-938
Locke, J. The Correspondence of John Locke. (Vol 6) (E.S. de Beer, ed)
M. Phillips, 192(EP):Apr-Jun83-242
Locke, R. Seldom Sung Songs.
N. Ramsey, 441:16Sep84-30
Lockspeiser, E. Claude Debussy.
S. Gut, 537:Vol69No2-241
Lodder, C. Russian Constructivism.
J.E. Bowlt, 453(NYRB):16Feb84-27
P. Vergo, 617(TLS):13Jan84-41
Lodgaard, S. and M. Thee, eds. Nuclear Disengagement in Europe.
M. Ignatieff, 617(TLS):1Jun84-603
Lodge, D. Ginger, You're Barmy.
P. Craig, 617(TLS):1Jun84-623
Lodge, D. Small World.
P. Larkin, 362:29Mar84-24
B. Morrison, 617(TLS):23Mar84-293
Lodge, D. Working with Structuralism.*
N. Armstrong, 567:Vol42No2/4-247
J. Lothe, 172(Edda):1983/1-58
S. Monod, 189(EA):Apr-Sep83-318
W.G. Weststeijn, 204(FdL):Sep82-235
Lodge, G.C. The American Disease.
R.D. Hormats, 441:11Mar84-20
Lodge, R.A. - see Étienne de Fougères
Loeb, L.E. From Descartes to Hume.*
M.B. Bolton, 482(PhR):Jan83-89
Loeser, K. A Thousand Pardons.
D. Grumbach, 219(GaR):Fall83-680
R. Orodenker, 573(SSF):Winter83-62
639(VQR):Spring83-58
Loewe, M. Ways to Paradise.*
A.C. Soper, 57:Vol44No4-326
Loewenstein, J.I. Marx Against Marxism.
L.D. Walker, 125:Fall82-104
Loewinsohn, R. Magnetic Field(s).*
W.H. Pritchard, 249(HudR):Winter83/84-753
Löffler, A., ed. "... an seinem Platz geprüft."
E. Mehnert, 654(WB):1/1982-184
Löffler, A., ed. Märchen aus Australien.
E. Schlesier, 196:Band24Heft1/2-161
Löffler, A. "The Rebel Muse."
P. Wagner, 189(EA):Apr-Jun84-201
Logan, C. Selected Poems of Christine Logan.*
A. Brooks, 102(CanL):Autumn83-62
Logan, F.D. The Vikings in History.
H. Davidson, 617(TLS):6Jul84-758
Logan, G.M. The Meaning of More's "Utopia."
G.M. Logan, 617(TLS):10Feb84-129

Lugnani, L. and G-L. Goggi. "La Parure" di Maupassant.
G. Hainsworth, 208(FS):Jul83-353
Luhr, W. Raymond Chandler on Film.
P. Wolfe, 395(MFS):Autumn83-389
Luhrmann, T. The Objects in the Garden.
E. Grosholz, 249(HudR):Autumn83-592
Lui, A.Y-C. The Hanlin Academy.*
E-T.Z. Sun, 244(HJAS):Jun83-359
Luis de León. The Unknown Light. (W. Barnstone, trans)
A. Lumsden-Kouvel, 552(REH):Jan83-148
Luizzi, V. A Naturalistic Theory of Justice.
R.A.P., 185:Jan84-371
Lukach, J.M. Hilla Rebay.
C. Betsky, 441:15Apr84-23
Lukács, G. Le jeune Hegel.* (G. Haarscher and R. Legros, eds and trans)
A. Reix, 542:Apr-Jun83-269
Lukacs, J. Outgrowing Democracy.
N. Bliven, 442(NY):16Jul84-88
J.C. Furnas, 441:30Sep84-34
Lukas, R.C. Bitter Legacy.
M.B. Biskupski, 550(RusR):Oct83-456
639(VQR):Winter83-23
Luke, H.M. Woman: Earth and Spirit.
S.F. Wiltshire, 577(SHR):Spring83-179
Luker, K. Abortion and the Politics of Motherhood.
P. Robinson, 441:6May84-3
Luker, N., ed and trans. An Anthology of Russian Neo-Realism.
J.W. Connolly, 399(MLJ):Spring83-92
B.Y. Forman, 574(SEEJ):Spring83-113
Lukes, S. - see Durkheim, É.
Lukić, G. Basic Serbo-Croatian Language. (2nd ed)
R. Bogert, 574(SEEJ):Spring83-131
Lumsden, C.J. and E.O. Wilson. Genes, Mind, and Culture.
D. Rancour-Laferriere, 307:Oct82-113
A. Rosenberg, 311(JP):Apr83-304
Luna, F. Buenos Aires y el país.
O.C. Stoetzer, 263(RIB):Vol33No1-43
Lunardi, E. and R. Nugent - see Pascoli, G.
Lunde, L. - see Kielland, A.L.
Lundestad, G. America, Scandinavia, and the Cold War, 1945-1949.
E.S. Einhorn, 563(SS):Winter83-103
Lundgren, M-B. and L. Wendt. Acquarossa. (Vol 3)
D. Ridgway, 123:Vol33No2-365
Lundquist, L. La cohérence textuelle.
M. Silenstam, 597(SN):Vol55No2-218
Lundqvist, Å. Från sextital till åttital.
G. Orton, 562(Scan):Nov83-232
Lundström, S. Ein textkritisches Problem in den Tusculanen.
M. Winterbottom, 123:Vol33No1-134
Lundström-Burghoorn, W. Minahasa Civilization.
J.M. Atkinson, 293(JASt):Nov82-224
Lundwell, H.J. - see Ailman, H.B.
Luneau, M. Folle alliée.
C. Mackey, 207(FR):Mar84-592
Lunn, E. Marxism and Modernism.
639(VQR):Autumn83-129
Lunt, J. Glubb Pasha.
M. Carver, 617(TLS):20Apr84-429
P. Johnson, 362:8Mar84-22

Lunzer, H. Hofmannsthals politische Tätigkeit in den Jahren 1914-1917.
W. Nehring, 221(GQ):Mar83-334
Luoma, J.R. Troubled Skies, Troubled Waters.
L. Robinson, 441:22Apr84-15
Luperini, R. Il Novecento.
R.S. Dombroski, 400(MLN):Jan83-151
Luplow, C. Isaac Babel's "Red Cavalry."
M. Ehre, 574(SEEJ):Fall83-389
Luria, A.R. Language and Cognition. (J.V. Wertch, ed)
J.J. Pilotta and T. Widman, 583: Summer84-438
Luria, S.E. A Slot Machine, A Broken Test Tube.
A.M. Cunningham, 441:8Apr84-23
Lurie, A. Foreign Affairs.
G. Annan, 453(NYRB):11Oct84-37
A. Bernays, 441:16Sep84-9
442(NY):5Nov84-170
Lurie, A. The Language of Clothes.
J.M. Fayer, 583:Winter84-217
Lurie, A.T. and others. European Paintings of the 16th, 17th and 18th Centuries.
J. Hayes, 324:May84-409
Lustig, I.S. and F.A. Pottle - see Boswell, J.
Lustig, R.J. Corporate Liberalism.
C.W. Anderson, 185:Jan84-353
Lüthi, H.J. Max Frisch.*
G.B. Pickar, 133:Band16Heft1-89
Lüthi, M. The European Folktale.
R. Bendix, 650(WF):Oct83-311
Luttwak, E. and D. Horowitz. The Israeli Army, 1948-73.
T.R. Fyvel, 176:Apr84-62
Luttwak, E.N. The Grand Strategy of the Soviet Union.*
R.H. Ullman, 441:5Feb84-29
Lutyens, M. and M. Warner. Rainy Days at Brig o' Turk.
R. Mander, 39:Nov83-454
von Lutz, B. Dramatische Hamlet-Bearbeitungen des 20. Jahrhunderts in England und den USA.
W. Erzgräber, 156(JDSh):Jahrbuch 1983-248
Lutz, D.S. Weltkrieg wieder willen?
M. Ignatieff, 617(TLS):1Jun84-603
Lutz, G. Die Stellung Marieluise Fleissers in der bayerischen Literatur des 20. Jahrhunderts.
M. Meyer, 406:Spring83-87
Lutz, L. Zum Thema "Thema."
R. Pasch, 682(ZPSK):Band36Heft6-738
Lützeler, P.M., ed. Herman Broch: Briefe — Dokumente und Kommentare zu Leben und Werk.
G. Roethke, 221(GQ):May83-519
Lützeler, P.M., ed. Romane und Erzählungen der deutschen Romantik.
R. Immerwahr, 564:Nov83-293
S. Mews, 221(GQ):Jan83-113
Lutzhöft, H-J. Deutsche Militärpolitik und schwedische Neutralität 1939-1942.
M. Geyer, 563(SS):Autumn83-399
Luukkainen, M. Untersuchungen zur morphematischen Transferenz im Frühdeutschen dargestellt an den Tegernseer Vergilglossen.
E. Erämetsä, 439(NM):1983/1-155

Lux, F. Text, Situation, Textsorte.
    Z. Szabó, 353:Vol20No11/12-768
Lydon, J., ed. England and Ireland in the
    Later Middle Ages.
    S.D. White, 589:Apr83-501
Lynch, D. Yeats.*
    J.P. Frayne, 301(JEGP):Jul83-457
Lynch, J., ed. Andrés Bello: The London
    Years.
    H.E. Davis, 263(RIB):Vol33No1-44
Lynch, J. Spain under the Habsburgs.
    R.A. Stradling, 86(BHS):Jan83-62
Lynch, K. A Theory of Good City Form.*
    M.S. Foster, 658:Spring83-98
Lynch, M. The Interrogation of Ambrose
    Fogarty.
    272(IUR):Autumn83-273
Lyne, R.O.A.M. The Latin Love Poets from
    Catullus to Horace.*
    J.F. Miller, 121(CJ):Oct/Nov83-73
Lynn, J. and A. Jay, eds. The Complete
    "Yes, Minister."
    P. Worthstone, 362:25Oct84-28
Lynn, K.S. The Air-Line to Seattle.
    P.J. Parish, 617(TLS):10Feb84-130
    P. Shaw, 31(ASch):Autumn83-546
Lyon, J. The Theatre of Valle-Inclán.
    C. Wheatley, 617(TLS):24Feb84-201
Lyon, J.K. Bertolt Brecht in America.*
    D. Constantine, 161(DUJ):Dec82-118
    P. Gontrum, 131(CL):Fall83-393
    M. Morley, 221(GQ):Jan83-161
    G. Tracy, 106:Winter83-469
Lyon, R. Zolas "Foi nouvelle."
    H-J. Müller, 547(RF):Band95Heft3-370
Lyons, D. Ethics and the Rule of Law.
    J. Waldron, 617(TLS):7Sep84-992
Lyons, D., ed. Rights.
    D.Z. Phillips, 453:Dec82-457
Lyons, F.S.L. and R.A.J. Hawkins, eds.
    Ireland Under the Union, Varieties of
    Tension.*
    D. Bowen, 637(VS):Autumn82-97
Lyons, J. Language, Meaning and Context.*
    P.L. Carrell, 399(MLJ):Spring83-88
    R. Singh, 320(CJL):Spring83-99
Lyons, J. Semantik. (Vol 1)
    L. Hermodsson, 597(SN):Vol55No1-89
    G. Stötzel, 685(ZDL):3/1983-379
Lyons, J.B. Oliver St. John Gogarty.
    E. Kennedy, 174(Éire):Summer83-139
Lyons, W.E. Emotion.*
    A. Skillen, 393(Mind):Apr83-310
Lyons, W.E. Gilbert Ryle.*
    L.W. Forguson, 393(Mind):Apr83-277
Lytle, G.F., ed. Reform and Authority in
    the Medieval and Reformation Church.*
    S.H. Hendrix, 551(RenQ):Spring83-73
Lytle, G.F. and S. Orgel, eds. Patronage
    in the Renaissance.
    R.L. Montgomery, 702:Vol 16-374
Lyttelton, G. and R. Hart-Davis. The
    Lyttelton/Hart-Davis Letters. (Vol 1)
    (R. Hart-Davis, ed)
    G. Lewis, 441:30Dec84-17
Lyttelton, G. and R. Hart-Davis. The
    Lyttelton Hart-Davis Letters. (Vol 6)
    (R. Hart-Davis, ed)
    A. Bell, 617(TLS):25May84-579

Ma, L.J.C. and E.W. Hanten, eds. Urban
    Development in Modern China.
    R. Murphey, 293(JASt):Nov82-139
Ma, L.J.C. and A.G. Noble, eds. The Envi-
    ronment.
    R. Murphey, 293(JASt):Nov82-139
Maalouf, A. The Crusades Through Arab
    Eyes.
    R. Irwin, 617(TLS):16Nov84-1300
Maas, J. The Victorian Art World in Photo-
    graphs.
    442(NY):27Aug84-92
Maas, U. Grundkurs Sprachwissenschaft.
    (Pt 1) (3rd ed)
    K-E. Sommerfeldt, 682(ZPSK):Band36
    Heft5-611
Maass, J. Kleist.*
    M. Hulse, 176:Mar84-36
    S.S. Prawer, 617(TLS):27Jan84-91
Mabey, R. In a Green Shade.
    S. Mills, 617(TLS):26Oct84-1218
Mabry, D.J. The Mexican University and
    the State.
    M.E. Burke, 263(RIB):Vol33No3-408
MacAfee, N., with L. Martinengo - see
    Pasolini, P.P.
McAleer, J. Ralph Waldo Emerson.
    H. Bloom, 453(NYRB):22Nov84-19
    B.L. Packer, 441:30Sep84-41
McAlester, V. and L. A Field Guide to
    American Houses.
    D. Guimaraes, 441:9Sep84-30
McAlexander, H.H. The Prodigal Daughter.*
    M. Jacobson, 577(SHR):Fall83-386
McAllester, D.P., ed and trans. Hogans,
    Navajo Houses and House Songs.*
    D.M. Hines, 650(WF):Jan83-58
    J. Vander, 187:Jan84-142
McAllister, J.O. The Right Hand of Power.
    R. Manning, 441:23Sep84-30
McAllister, P.A. Umsindleko.
    D.H., 355(LSoc):Mar83-142
McAloon, K., ed. Modèles de l'arithmé-
    tique, Séminaire Paris VII.
    J.B. Paris, 316:Jun83-483
MacAndrew, E. The Gothic Tradition in Fic-
    tion.*
    S. Prickett, 402(MLR):Jul83-683
McAndrew, J. Venetian Architecture of the
    Early Renaissance.*
    A. Blunt, 46:May81-318
    C. Kolb, 576:Mar83-75
    D. Pincus, 54:Jun83-342
    P.D. du Prey, 529(QQ):Summer83-406
MacAndrew, M-C. and J.H. Moore - see
    Zaleski, E.
Macaulay, A. Dr. Russell of Maynooth.
    S. Gilley, 617(TLS):3Aug84-874
Macaulay, T.B. The Letters of Thomas Bab-
    ington Macaulay. (Vols 5 and 6) (T.
    Pinney, ed)
    J. Clive, 31(ASch):Winter82/83-119
McAuley, J. Recital.
    M. Harmon, 272(IUR):Spring83-114
McAuley, J. What Henry Hudson Found.*
    R. Hatch, 102(CanL):Winter82-144
McBain, E. Jack and the Beanstalk.
    T.J. Binyon, 617(TLS):26Oct84-1225
MacBeth, G. Anna's Book.
    P-L. Adams, 61:May84-123
    P. Lewis, 364:Oct83-94
    442(NY):14May84-148

MacBeth, G. The Lion of Pescara.
  R. Jones, 362:6Dec84-34
  J. Rosselli, 617(TLS):12Oct84-1166
MacBeth, G. The Long Darkness.
  G. Lindop, 617(TLS):27Apr84-459
  J. Mole, 176:Jun84-59
MacBeth, G. Poems from Oby.*
  D. McDuff, 565:Vol24No3-67
McBride, M. The Going Under of the Even-
  ing Land.
  639(VQR):Autumn83-134
McBride, M.F. Folklore of Dryden's
  England.
  P.E. Parnell, 568(SCN):Winter83-75
McBride, W.L. Social Theory at a Cross-
  roads.*
  D. Lamb, 323:May83-206
MacCabe, C., ed. James Joyce.
  S. Benstock, 329(JJQ):Winter84-184
  J.L., 617(TLS):23Mar84-319
  W. Potts, 305(JIL):Sep83-83
MacCabe, C. James Joyce and the Revolu-
  tion of the Word.*
  J. Willet-Shoptaw, 594:Summer83-162
MacCabe, C., ed. The Talking Cure.*
  A. Davison, 350:Dec84-1004
  H. Rapaport, 355(LSoc):Jun83-256
MacCabe, C., with M. Eaton and L. Mulvey.
  Godard.*
  M. Kernan, 500:Fall83-61
McCabe, R.A. Joseph Hall.
  C.L., 189(EA):Oct-Dec84-490
McCaffery, L. The Metafictional Muse.*
  S. Fogel, 395(MFS):Summer83-340
  M. Davidson, 27(AL):Oct83-484
McCaffrey, A. Moreta.
  R. Hoffman, 441:8Jan84-18
MacCaffrey, W.T. Queen Elizabeth and the
  Making of Policy, 1572-1588.*
  D.M. Loades, 551(RenQ):Spring83-93
McCaig, D. Nop's Trials.
  P-L. Adams, 61:May84-122
  J. Sullivan, 441:15Apr84-22
MacCaig, N. A World of Difference.*
  D. Davis, 362:19Jul84-25
  H. Lomas, 364:Oct83-73
  J. Mole, 176:Mar84-51
  D. O'Driscoll, 493:Sep83-66
McCaldin, D. Mahler.
  412:Feb82-67
McCallum, A. Fun with Stagecraft.
  J. Doolittle, 108:Fall83-134
MacCameron, R. Bananas, Labor, and Pol-
  itics in Honduras.
  J.F. McCamant, 263(RIB):Vol33No3-409
McCarney, J. The Real World of Ideology.
  R. Hudelson, 482(PhR):Oct83-625
McCarter, P.K., Jr., ed and trans. I Sam-
  uel.
  A. Caquot, 318(JAOS):Jul-Sep82-535
McCarthy, B.E. William Wycherley.*
  H. Love, 677(YES):Vol 13-319
MacCarthy, F. - see Pritchard, J.
McCarthy, M.S. Balzac and his Reader.*
  G. Falconer, 446(NCFS):Fall-
  Winter83/84-220
  A. Fischler, 268(IFR):Winter84-66
  A.R. Pugh, 651(WHR):Winter83-346
McCarthy, P. Camus.
  B. Stoltzfus, 395(MFS):Winter83-795
  295(JML):Nov83-447
  639(VQR):Summer83-79

McCarthy, P.A. The Riddles of "Finnegans
  Wake."*
  Z. Bowen, 305(JIL):May83-112
McCarthy, P.A. Olaf Stapledon.
  S.A. Cowan, 150(DR):Spring83-173
McCarthy, R.J. Freedom and Fulfillment.
  F. Shehadi, 318(JAOS):Apr-Jun82-374
McCarthy, T. The Sorrow Garden.
  T. Eagleton, 565:Vol24No2-66
MacCary, W.T. Childlike Achilles.
  D.M. Halperin, 121(CJ):Apr/May84-363
McCash, W.B. Thomas R.R. Cobb.
  639(VQR):Autumn83-125
McCaslin, D.E. Stone Anchors in Antiquity.
  A.B. Knapp, 318(JAOS):Jul-Sep82-543
McCaughey, P. Australian Painters of the
  Heidelberg School.*
  U. Hoff, 39:Oct83-352
McCaughey, P. Fred Williams.*
  E. Cross, 592:Oct83-28
McCaughey, R.A. International Studies
  and Academic Enterprise.
  T. Bender, 441:18Nov84-33
McCauley, M. The German Democratic
  Republic Since 1945.
  T.G. Ash, 617(TLS):8Jun84-644
McCauley, M., ed. The Soviet Union after
  Brezhnev.
  R.G. Suny, 385(MQR):Fall84-576
McCauley, M. The Soviet Union Since 1917.
  P. Kenez, 550(RusR):Jan83-112
McCawley, J.D. Everything that Linguists
  Have Always Wanted to Know about Logic,
  (but were ashamed to ask).*
  D.H., 355(LSoc):Mar83-142
McCawley, J.D. Thirty Million Theories of
  Grammar.
  W. O'Grady, 320(CJL):Fall83-190
Macchia, G. Saggi italiani.
  F. Donini, 617(TLS):10Feb84-146
McClain, J.L. Kanazawa.
  R.P. Toby, 407(MN):Autumn83-338
McClanahan, E. The Natural Man.*
  J. Saari, 42(AR):Fall83-502
McClatchy, J.D. Scenes from Another Life.*
  W. Harmon, 569(SR):Summer83-457
  E. Larrissy, 493:Jun83-64
McCleave, H. The Life and Death of Liam
  Faulds.
  R. Hoffman, 441:19Aug84-18
McClelland, C.E. State, Society, and
  University in Germany 1700-1914.
  A. Thimme, 529(QQ):Spring83-217
McClelland, D. Hollywood on Ronald Reagan.
  A.H. Marrill, 200:Nov83-572
McClelland, E.M. The Cult of Ifá among
  the Yoruba.* (Vol 1)
  J.M. Borgatti, 2(AfrA):Nov82-88
McClintock, C. and A.F. Lowenthal, eds.
  The Peruvian Experiment Reconsidered.
  E.H. Stephens, 263(RIB):Vol33No4-592
McCloskey, D.N. Enterprise and Trade in
  Victorian Britain.
  W. Ashworth, 637(VS):Autumn82-87
McCloskey, H.J. Ecological Ethics and
  Politics.
  R.E. Goodin, 185:Jan84-344
McCloskey, J. Transformational Syntax and
  Model Theoretic Semantics.*
  D.P. Ó Baoill, 112:Vol 15-165
McClosky, H. and A. Brill. Dimensions of
  Tolerance.
  P. Brest, 441:1Jan84-12

McClung, K.H. - see Klauber, L.M.

McClung, W.A. The Architecture of Paradise.
  J. Rykwert, 617(TLS):14Sep84-1029

McClure, J. Cop World.
  M. Cain, 617(TLS):14Dec84-1455

McClure, J.A. Kipling and Conrad.*
  T.K. Bender, 577(SHR):Winter83-87
  J.R. Cox, 177(ELT):Vol26No1-58
  J. Meyers, 136:Vol 15No2-156
  S. Monod, 189(EA):Apr-Jun84-220
  Z.T. Sullivan, 301(JEGP):Apr83-264
  L. Thornton, 131(CL):Summer83-302

McClure, M. Scratching the Beat Surface.
  L. Bartlett, 649(WAL):May83-57

McClure, R.K. Coram's Children.
  A.D. Barker, 447(N&Q):Dec82-553

McCluskey, J., Jr. Mr. America's Last Season Blues.
  J. Haskins, 441:1Apr84-22

McColgan, J. British Policy and the Irish Administration 1920-22.
  R. Foster, 617(TLS):24Feb84-194

McColley, D.K. Milton's Eve.
  L. Mackinnon, 617(TLS):20Apr84-438

McConkey, J. Court of Memory.*
  M. Kreyling, 573(SSF):Spring-Summer83-141

McConkey, J. To a Distant Island.
  V.L. Smith, 441:22Jul84-25

McConnell, F. Murder Among Friends.
  N. Callendar, 441:8Jan84-27

McConnell, F. The Science Fiction of H.G. Wells.*
  M. Duperray, 189(EA):Apr-Jun84-219

McConville, S. A History of English Prison Administration. (Vol 1)
  J.E. Thomas, 637(VS):Autumn82-109

McCord, N. Strikes.*
  M.J. Daunton, 161(DUJ):Jun83-127

McCorkle, J. The Cheer Leader. July 7th.
  A. Gottlieb, 441:7Oct84-9

McCormack, M.H. What They Don't Teach You at Harvard Business School.
  S. Salmans, 441:21Oct84-49

MacCormack, S.G. Art and Ceremony in Late Antiquity.
  E.D. Hunt, 123:Vol33No1-83

McCormack, W.J. and A. Stead, eds. James Joyce and Modern Literature.
  B. Benstock, 395(MFS):Summer83-281
  S. Benstock, 329(JJQ):Winter84-181
  M.P. Gillespie, 594:Winter83-364

McCormick, C. The Club Paradis Murders.
  N. Callendar, 441:29Jan84-17

MacCormick, N. Legal Right and Social Democracy.*
  B. Barry, 185:Apr84-525
  R.H.S. Tur, 518:Oct83-193

McCormick, P. and F.A. Elliston - see Husserl, E.

McCormmach, R. Night Thoughts of a Classical Physicist.
  B. Castel, 529(QQ):Spring83-264

McCorquodale, C. Bronzino.*
  E.H. Ramsden, 39:Feb83-150

McCorquodale, C. The History of Interior Decoration.
  B. Scott, 324:Aug84-642

McCourt, J. Kaye Wayfaring in "Avenged."
  M. Harris, 441:8Jul84-12

McCoy, A.W., ed. Southeast Asia Under Japanese Occupation.
  B.R.O. Anderson, 293(JASt):Feb83-456

McCoy, S. Album.
  D. Gunn, 617(TLS):12Oct84-1168

McCracken, C. Malebranche and British Philosophy.
  G. Brykman, 542:Oct-Dec83-467

McCracken, D. Wordsworth and the Lake District.
  J. Keates, 617(TLS):22Jun84-690

McCracken, S. The War Against the Atom.
  R. Wilson, 61:Aug84-104

McCrary, W.C. and J.A. Madrigal. Studies in Honor of Everett W. Hesse.
  J. Fernández Jiménez, 238:Mar83-129

McCraw, T.K. Prophets of Regulation.
  M. Wexler, 441:21Oct84-51

McCrea, B. Henry Fielding and the Politics of Mid-Eighteenth-Century England.
  J. Cannon, 366:Spring83-116
  M. Golden, 173(ECS):Fall83-92
  C.J. Rawson, 447(N&Q):Dec82-555

McCreadie, A., ed. Karl Amadeus Hartmann.
  M. Anderson, 607:Dec83-35

McCreadie, M. Women on Film.
  R. Simon, 200:Apr83-253

McCreadie, S., ed. Classical Guitar Companion.
  M. Criswick, 415:Jun83-363

McCready, W.D. - see Guillaume de Pierre Godin

McCreight, T. The Complete Metalsmith.
  H. Helwig, 139:Dec83/Jan84-40

McCreless, P. Wagner's "Siegfried."*
  D. Puffett, 617(TLS):8Jun84-646

McCrum, R. The Fabulous Englishman.
  B. Morrison, 617(TLS):7Sep84-988

McCully, M. Els Quatre Gats.
  E. Casado, 48:Jan-Mar79-96

McCunn, R.L. Thousand Pieces of Gold.
  B. Wahlstrom, 649(WAL):May83-78

MacCurdy, G.G. Jorge Guillén.
  A. Byrum, 238:Sep83-435
  D. Harris, 402(MLR):Oct83-949

McDaniel, G.W. Hearth and Home.
  T.J. Davis, 658:Spring83-119

McDavid, R.I., Jr. Varieties of American English. (A.S. Dil, ed)
  H.H. Perritt, 583:Winter84-218

McDermott, R.A. - see Steiner, R.

MacDiarmid, H. The Letters of Hugh MacDiarmid. (A. Bold, ed)
  J. Campbell, 617(TLS):5Oct84-1125
  D. Craig, 362:23Aug84-23

MacDiarmid, H. Hugh MacDiarmid Complete Poems 1920-1976. (M. Grieve and W.R. Aitken, eds)
  R. McQuillan, 588(SSL):Vol 18-177

MacDiarmid, H. The Thistle Rises. (A. Bold, ed)
  J. Campbell, 617(TLS):5Oct84-1125

McDiarmid, M.P. Robert Henryson.
  F. Alexander, 571(ScLJ):Winter83-47

MacDonagh, O. States of Mind.
  J.C. Beckett, 617(TLS):16Mar84-282

Macdonald, A. A Different Lens.*
  R. Hatch, 102(CanL):Winter82-144

MacDonald, C. Emma Albani.
  R. Christiansen, 617(TLS):21Dec84-1469

MacDonald, C.B. The Battle of the Bulge.
  M. Carver, 617(TLS):28Dec84-1496

McGann, J.J. The Romantic Ideology.
P.H. Fry, 676(YR):Summer84-603
McGann, J.J. - see Lord Byron
McGerr, C. René Clair.
J-P. Boon, 207(FR):Dec83-277
McGhee, G. Envoy to the Middle World.
J.K. Davison, 441:12Feb84-21
MacGibbon, J. I Meant to Marry Him.
R. Fuller, 362:24May84-25
P. Willmott, 617(TLS):18May84-547
McGilchrist, I. Against Criticism.
P. Barry, 175:Spring83-104
C. Norris, 402(MLR):Oct83-889
McGill, P. Children of the Dead End. The
Rat Pit.
P. Craig, 617(TLS):21Dec84-1066
McGinley, P. Foggage.*
P-L. Adams, 61:Jan84-100
P. Craig, 617(TLS):7Sep84-988
R. Koenig, 231:Jan84-76
McGinn, C. The Character of Mind.*
B. Harrison, 483:Oct83-549
R. Kirk, 518:Jul83-177
McGinn, D.J. Thomas Nashe.
J.J.M. Tobin, 447(N&Q):Dec82-543
McGinn, N.E. and others. Education and
Development in Korea.
K. Moskowitz, 293(JASt):Nov82-63
D.I. Steinberg, 293(JASt):Nov82-91
McGinnis, B. Sweet Cane.
L. Rodenberger, 649(WAL):Aug83-181
McGinniss, J. Fatal Vision.*
C. Sigal, 617(TLS):17Aug84-915
McGivern, W.P. A Matter of Honor.
442(NY):4Jun84-137
McGlathery, J.M. Mysticism and Sexuality.
(Pt 1)
K.G. Negus, 564:Nov83-297
McGrady, D. - see de Vega Carpio, L.
McGrath, J. A Good Night Out.*
M. Page, 397(MD):Mar83-111
McGrath, R.D. Gunfighters, Highwaymen and
Vigilantes.
W. Broyles, Jr., 441:9Sep84-36
McGraw, C. Piano Duet Repertoire.
A.F.L.T., 412:May82-154
MacGregor, A. Anglo-Scandinavian Finds
from Lloyds Bank, Pavement, and Other
Sites.
R.T. Farrell, 589:Oct83-1128
MacGregor, A., ed. Tradescant's Rarities.*
E. Waterhouse, 90:Nov83-695
McGregor, R.S. Outline of Hindi Grammar.
(2nd ed)
M.K. Verma, 293(JASt):Nov82-190
McGregor, S. Traditional Knitting.
V.R. Edwards, 614:Fall84-26
McGuane, T. Something to be Desired.
R. Roper, 441:16Dec84-11
442(NY):24Dec84-88
McGuckian, M. The Flower Master.*
T. Eagleton, 565:Vol24No3-77
McGuckian, M. Venus and the Rain.
J. Mole, 176:Dec84-58
M. O'Neill, 617(TLS):30Nov84-1393
McGuinness, B., ed. Wittgenstein and His
Times.*
B. Frohmann, 556:Summer83-71
McGuinness, B. - see Frege, G.
McGuire, M.C. Milton's Puritan Masque.
L. Mackinnon, 617(TLS):20Apr84-438
McGuire, W. Bollingen.
R.E. Spiller, 27(AL):May83-281

McGuire, W. - see Jung, C.G.
McGurk, P. and others, eds. Early English
Manuscripts in Facsimile. (Vol 21)
C.R. Dodwell, 617(TLS):30Mar84-355
Mach, R., with R.D. McChesney. Catalogue
of Arabic Manuscripts (Yahuda Section)
in the Garrett Collection.
S.A. Spectorsky, 318(JAOS):Oct-Dec82-
670
Machado, A. Selected Poems.*
P.L. Ullman, 399(MLJ):Summer83-202
Machado de Assis, J.M. Dom Casmurro.
J-L. Gautier, 450(NRF):Jun83-139
Machatschek, A. and M. Schwarz. Baufor-
schungen in Selge.
J.S. Crawford, 589:Jul83-779
Machatzke, M. - see Hauptmann, G.
Maché, U. and V. Meid, eds. Gedichte des
Barock.
J. Hardin, 406:Spring83-74
Macherey, M.P. Hegel ou Spinoza.*
D. Souche-Dagues, 192(EP):Jan-Mar83-87
Machiavelli, N. Discorso intorno alla
nostra lingua. (P. Trovato, ed)
B.T. Sozzi, 228(GSLI):Vol 160fasc512-
599
Machin, A. Cohérence et continuité dans
le théâtre de Sophocle.*
A.L. Brown, 303(JoHS):Vol 103-166
J.C. Kamerbeek, 394:Vol136fasc3/4-404
McHugh, R. Annotations to "Finnegans
Wake."*
P.M.S. Dawson, 541(RES):Feb83-96
McHugh, R. The Sigla of "Finnegans Wake."
M. Hodgart, 447(N&Q):Dec82-559
McHugh, R. and M. Harmon. Short History
of Anglo-Irish Literature.*
R.G. Yeed, 305(JIL):May83-110
McIlwaine, I., J. McIlwaine and P.G. New,
eds. Bibliography and Reading.
A.R. Rogers, 87(BB):Dec83-258
McInerney, J. Bright Lights, Big City.
P-L. Adams, 61:Dec84-145
W. Kotzwinkle, 441:25Nov84-9
D. Pinckney, 453(NYRB):8Nov84-12
McInerny, R. St. Thomas Aquinas.
P. King, 258:Jun83-227
McInerny, R. Ethica Thomistica.
R. Hittinger, 543:Jun83-939
MacInnes, H. Ride a Pale Horse.
J. Kaufman, 441:11Nov84-32
MacIntyre, A. After Virtue.*
R.L. Arrington, 569(SR):Spring83-309
J. Casey, 479(PhQ):Jul83-296
S.R.L. Clark, 262:Dec83-425
R. Gaita, 262:Dec83-407
G. McKenzie, 63:Dec83-450
O. O'Neill, 262:Dec83-387
D.M. Rasmussen, 142:Fall-Winter82-383
S. Scheffler, 482(PhR):Jul83-443
McIntyre, H.G. The Theatre of Jean
Anouilh.*
R. Champigny, 397(MD):Sep83-396
Mack, C.W. Polynesian Art at Auction.
T. Barrow, 2(AfrA):Aug83-83
Mack, D.S. - see Hogg, J.
Mack, M. Collected in Himself.
C. Rawson, 617(TLS):13Apr84-412
J. Sitter, 566:Autumn83-55
Mack, M., ed. The Last and Greatest Art.
H. Erskine-Hill, 617(TLS):2Nov84-1241

Mack, M. and G.D. Lord, eds. Poetic Traditions of the English Renaissance.*
  S. Stewart, 551(RenQ):Winter83-645
Mack, M. and J.A. Winn, eds. Pope: Recent Essays by Several Hands.
  W.B. Carnochan, 402(MLR):Jan83-145
MacKay, A. and D.S. Severin, eds. Cosas sacadas de la historia del Rey Don Juan el Segundo.
  R.B. Tate, 86(BHS):Apr83-141
MacKay, A.F. Arrow's Theorem.
  W.D. Hart, 393(Mind):Jul83-471
  L. Sowden, 479(PhQ):Jan83-104
McKay, J.H. Narration and Discourse in American Realistic Fiction.*
  E. Ammons, 26(ALR):Autumn83-301
  R.A. Cassell, 395(MFS):Summer83-328
  295(JML):Nov83-414
McKay, P. Electric Empire.
  H.V. Nelles, 298:Summer83-152
Mackay, R. and J.D. Palmer, eds. Languages for Specific Purposes.*
  T. Pica, 355(LSoc):Mar83-127
MacKay, S. An Advent Calendar.
  P. Craig, 617(TLS):9Mar84-259
Mackay, S. Babies in Rhinestones.*
  J. Mellors, 362:2Feb84-28
Mackay, S. A Bowl of Cherries.
  B. Hardy, 617(TLS):19Oct84-1180
  K.C. O'Brien, 362:29Nov84-25
Mackay, T., ed. A Plea for Liberty.
  A.T. Bouscaren, 396(ModA):Spring83-199
Mackay Brown, G. - see under Brown, G.M.
McKean, C. and D. Walker, comps. The Edinburgh Architectural Guide.
  P.D., 46:Feb83-71
  592:Jan-Feb83-64
McKean, M.A. Environmental Protest and Citizen Politics in Japan.*
  T. MacDougall, 293(JASt):May83-665
McKeehnie, S. British Silhouette Artists and Their Work.
  G. Wills, 39:Nov83-455
McKendrick, N., J. Brewer and J.H. Plumb. The Birth of a Consumer Society.
  S. Mackiewicz, 658:Winter83-303
  P. Rogers, 617(TLS):15Jun84-668
  L. Stone, 453(NYRB):29Mar84-42
MacKendrick, P. The Mute Stones Speak.
  M.T., 617(TLS):17Aug84-927
McKenna, F. The Railway Workers 1840-1970.
  H.W. Parris, 637(VS):Autumn82-96
McKenna, R. Portrait of Dylan.
  295(JML):Nov83-578
Mackenzie, C.C. Sarah Barnwell Elliott.*
  R.A., 189(EA):Jan-Mar83-109
MacKenzie, D. Raven's Longest Night.
  N. Callendar, 441:8Jan84-27
MacKenzie, D. Raven's Shadow.
  M. Laski, 362:25Oct84-29
Mackenzie, D. - see Rodríguez de Almela, D.
MacKenzie, D.A. Statistics in Britain, 1865-1930.
  S. Kingsland, 637(VS):Spring83-357
MacKenzie, J.M. Propaganda and Empire.
  A. Barnett, 362:23Aug84-24
  V. Bogdanor, 617(TLS):21Dec84-1464
Mackenzie, M.M. Plato on Punishment.*
  M.F. Rousseau, 543:Jun83-941
  T.J. Saunders, 303(JoHS):Vol 103-173
MacKenzie, N. Le Prix du Silence.
  K. Mezei, 102(CanL):Summer83-128
MacKenzie, N. and J. - see Webb, B.

Mackenzie, N.H. A Reader's Guide to Gerard Manley Hopkins.*
  R. Beum, 569(SR):Winter83-xiii
  W.D. Shaw, 178:Sep83-375
McKeon, Z.K. Novels and Arguments.*
  V. Aarons, 395(MFS):Summer83-360
  295(JML):Nov83-414
Mackerras, C. The Performing Arts in Contemporary China.
  S.M. Goldstein, 293(JASt):May83-630
  Rulan Chao Pian, 187:Sep84-574
McKerrow, M. The Faeds.*
  M. Pointon, 90:Apr83-236
Mackesy, P. War without Victory.
  J.S. Bromley, 617(TLS):14Sep84-1033
Mackey, W.F. and J. Ornstein, eds. Sociolinguistic Studies in Language Contact.
  A. Tovar, 685(ZDL):2/1983-216
Mackie, J.L. Ethics.*
  T. Airaksinen, 262:Dec83-467
Mackie, J.L. Hume's Moral Theory.*
  B. Harrison, 393(Mind):Jan83-129
  D.O. Thomas, 83:Autumn83-280
Mackie, J.L. The Miracle of Theism.*
  H. Meynell, 483:Jul83-414
  S.L. Ross, 185:Jul84-718
McKillop, A.B. - see Morton, W.L.
McKinley, M.B. Words in a Corner.*
  D.M. Frame, 551(RenQ):Spring83-123
  I.W.F. Maclean, 402(MLR):Jan83-179
  T.A. Perry, 210(FrF):Jan83-90
  F. Rigolot, 400(MLN):Dec83-1363
McKinley, R.A. The Surnames of Lancashire.
  E.C. Smith, 424:Jun83-124
Mackinnon, L. Eliot, Auden, Lowell.
  A. Thwaite, 617(TLS):27Apr84-458
McKitterick, D. - see Morison, S.
Macklin, J.J. Pérez de Ayala: "Tigre Juan" and "El curandero de su honra."*
  C.A. Longhurst, 86(BHS):Jul83-260
McLachlan, I. Helen in Exile.*
  J. Kertzer, 198:Jan83-125
MacLaine, S. Out on a Limb.*
  G. Kaufman, 362:19Apr84-26
McLaren, C.A. The Warriors Under the Stone.
  C. Hope, 617(TLS):3Feb84-116
McLaren, I.F. Marcus Clarke.
  M. Wilding, 581:Sep83-358
Maclaren-Ross, J. Memoirs of the Forties.
  T.G.D.F., 617(TLS):16Nov84-1323
McLaughlin, R., ed. What? Where? When? Why?
  C.A. Hooker, 63:Dec83-448
MacLaverty, B. Cal.*
  P. Craig, 617(TLS):21Sep84-1066
  M. Howard, 676(YR):Winter84-xiii
  J. Moynahan, 453(NYRB):16Feb84-40
  W.H. Pritchard, 249(HudR):Winter83/84-750
MacLaverty, B. Secrets.
  W. Boyd, 441:11Nov84-12
McLaverty, M. The Three Brothers. The Road to the Shore and Other Stories.
  S. Hillan, 272(IUR):Autumn83-266
McLean, A. A Commentary on the Mutus Liber. A Commentary on Goethe's Fairy Tale.
  J. Godwin, 111:Spring84-6
MacLean, A. Floodgate.
  R. Smith, 441:18Mar84-18

McLean, A., ed. The Magical Calendar.
(2nd ed) The Crowning of Nature. The
Rosicrucian Emblems of Daniel Cramer.
The Rosary of the Philosophers. The
Amphitheatre Engravings of Heinrich
Khunrath.
J. Godwin, 111:Fall83-6
MacLean, A. Night Falls on Ardnamurchan.
D. Craig, 362:11Oct84-28
G. Mangan, 617(TLS):28Dec84-1499
McLean, A. - see Fludd, R.
McLean, A. - see Freher, D.
McLean, A. - see Dr. Rudd
McLean, A. - see Stolcius, D.
McLean, A. - see Trismosin, S.
McLean, A. - see Trithemius, J.
McLean, A.M. Shakespeare.
D.E. Litt, 539:Nov83-295
MacLean, D. and P.G. Brown, eds. Energy
and the Future.
R.E. Goodin, 185:Apr84-542
McLean, R. Victorian Publishers' Book-
Bindings in Paper.*
F. Broomhead, 503:Autumn83-140
MacLean, S-B. Chester Art.
P.W. Travis, 627(UTQ):Summer83-406
McLean, T. The English at Play In the
Middle Ages.
B. Bolton, 617(TLS):9Mar84-256
Maclean, V. A Short-Title Catalogue of
Household and Cookery Books Published
in the English Tongue, 1701-1800.*
J. Archibald, 354:Mar83-75
P. Grinke, 78(BC):Spring83-108
S. Soupel, 189(EA):Apr-Jun84-194
B.K. Wheaton, 517(PBSA):Vol77No2-242
Maclear, M. The Ten Thousand Day War.
G.S. Smith, 529(QQ):Winter83-972
McLeave, H. The Life and Death of Liam
Faulds.
442(NY):30Jul84-88
MacLeish, A. Letters of Archibald Mac-
Leish, 1907-1982.* (R.H. Winnick, ed)
B. Duffey, 27(AL):Oct83-475
R.E. Spiller, 651(WHR):Autumn83-268
McLeish, K. and V. The Oxford First Com-
panion to Music.
P. Standford, 415:Apr83-236
McLellan, D. Karl Marx: His Life and
Thought.
W.L. McBride, 390:Jan83-53
McLendon, W.L. Une ténébreuse affaire
sous l'Empire et la Restauration.
F.P. Bowman, 210(FrF):Sep83-280
Macleod, C. Collected Essays. (O. Taplin,
ed)
N.M. Horsfall, 617(TLS):3Feb84-103
MacLeod, C. Something the Cat Dragged In.
T.J. Binyon, 617(TLS):24Aug84-953
MacLeod, C.W. Homer: "Iliad" Book XXIV.
J. Griffin, 123:Vol33No1-1
T. Van Nortwick, 24:Summer83-199
Macleod, D.I. Building Character in the
American Boy.
W. Kaminer, 441:15Jan84-19
McLeod, G.D. Essentially Canadian.
C. Thomas, 102(CanL):Autumn83-60
Macleod, J. The Actor's Right to Act.*
G. Rowell, 610:Spring83-72
M. Vicinus, 637(VS):Winter83-225
McLeod, K. The Last Summer.*
442(NY):20Aug84-93
Macleod, M.D. - see Lucian

MacLeod, R. - see Owen, D.
Macleod, S. Axioms.
K.C. O'Brien, 362:7Jun84-25
McLeod, W.H. Early Sikh Tradition.
C.S.J. White, 318(JAOS):Apr-Jun82-418
McLeod, W.R. and V.B. A Graphical Direc-
tory of English Newspapers and Period-
icals, 1702-1714.*
P.J. Guskin, 173(ECS):Winter83/84-201
McLeod, W.T., ed. The New Collins Thesau-
rus.
J. Crowther, 617(TLS):28Dec84-1492
McLoughlin, W.G. - see Backus, I.
MacLulich, T.D. Voyages.
M. Harry, 198:Jan83-115
M.T. Lane, 102(CanL):Winter82-154
Maclure, S. Educational Development and
School Building.
G. Oddie, 617(TLS):30Nov84-1370
McMackin, L. Thoughts on Freedom.
R.M.M., 185:Jan84-362
McMahan, J. British Nuclear Weapons.
D.L., 185:Oct83-185
McMahon, D. Republicans and Imperialists.
C. Townshend, 617(TLS):24Aug84-939
McManners, J. Death and the Enlightenment.
B. Redford, 173(ECS):Spring84-369
D. Schier, 569(SR):Summer83-lx
D. Williams, 83:Spring83-71
639(VQR):Winter83-7
McManus, E.G., L.S. Josephs and M.
Emesiochel. Palauan-English Dictionary.
G.F. Meier, 682(ZPSK):Band36Heft4-487
McManus, J. Out of the Blue.
C. Seebohm, 441:26Feb84-22
McMaster, G. Scott and Society.*
N.S. Bushnell, 588(SSL):Vol 18-278
F. Jordan, 661(WC):Summer83-145
W. Ruddick, 366:Spring83-120
McMaster, J. and R. The Novel from Sterne
to James.*
G. Levine, 637(VS):Spring83-354
S. Monod, 189(EA):Apr-Sep83-330
McMillan, C. Women, Reason and Nature.
S.M.O., 185:Jan84-359
A.E. Seller, 518:Oct83-236
Macmillan, H. War Diaries.
A.J. Ayer, 362:28Jun84-24
G. Smith, 441:16Sep84-7
C.M. Woodhouse, 617(TLS):17Aug84-912
McMillan, I. How the Hornpipe Failed.
M. O'Neill, 493:Sep83-72
McMillan, I. Now It Can Be Told.
C. Boyle, 364:Dec83/Jan84-120
T. Dooley, 617(TLS):13Apr84-413
J. Mole, 176:Mar84-52
McMullen, L. An Odd Attempt in a Woman.
R. Fothergill, 617(TLS):21Dec84-1485
McMullen, L. Sinclair Ross.*
M. Peterman, 102(CanL):Spring83-136
McMullen, L., ed. The Ethel Wilson Sympo-
sium.
H. Dahlie, 627(UTQ):Summer83-496
MacMullen, R. Christianizing the Roman
Empire.
R.M. Grant, 441:28Oct84-36
MacMullen, R. Paganism in the Roman
Empire.*
D. Fishwick, 24:Fall83-306
McMurrin, S.M. Religion, Reason, and
Truth.
D.S., 185:Oct83-173

McMurrin, S.M., ed. The Tanner Lectures
on Human Values.* (Vols 1 and 2)
483:Oct81-593
McMurrin, S.M., ed. The Tanner Lectures
on Human Values. (Vol 3)
T.M. Reed, 185:Jan84-325
McMurry, L.O. George Washington Carver.
A. Hornsby, Jr., 9(AlaR):Apr83-147
McMurry, R.M. John Bell Hood and the War
for Southern Independence.*
F.L. Byrne, 9(AlaR):Jul83-227
McNally, R.T. Dracula was a Woman.
D.P. Varma, 150(DR):Spring83-175
MacNamara, E. Forcing the Field.*
P. Mitcham, 102(CanL):Summer83-144
Macnamara, J. Names for Things.*
J.M. Carroll, 350:Sep84-636
McNamee, K. Abbreviations in Greek Liter-
ary Papyri and Ostraca.
H.M. Cockle, 303(JoHS):Vol 103-229
McNaughton, H. - see Baxter, J.K.
McNee, D. McNee's Law.
M. Cain, 617(TLS):27Jan84-89
MacNeice, L. The Strings Are False.
A. Haberer, 189(EA):Apr-Jun84-223
McNeil, F. The Overlanders.
F.W. Kaye, 649(WAL):Nov83-271
R. Miles, 102(CanL):Autumn83-95
McNeil, G.R. Groundwork.
D.L. Watson, 441:29Jun84-23
MacNeilage, P.F., ed. The Production of
Speech.
M. MacDonald and D.G. MacKay, 350:
Sep84-684
McNerney, K. The Influence of Ausiàs
March on Early Golden Age Castilian
Poetry.
E.L. Rivers, 304(JHP):Spring83-216
MacNicholas, J. James Joyce's "Exiles."*
J. Lewis, 397(MD):Jun83-249
MacNiven, I.S. and H.T. Moore - see Alding-
ton, R. and L. Durrell
McPartland, P. Take it Easy. (3rd ed)
C. Greenberg, 351(LL):Dec83-551
McPeck, J.E. Critical Thinking and Educa-
tion.
T. Govier, 154:Mar83-170
McPhee, J. In Suspect Terrain.*
A. Hallam, 617(TLS):6Jan84-18
42(AR):Spring83-249
McPhee, J. La Place de la Concorde Suisse.
(British title: The Swiss Army.)
C.H. Church, 617(TLS):7Dec84-1413
J. Steinberg, 441:6May84-41
Macpherson, I., ed. Juan Manuel Studies.
G. Perissinotto, 457(NRFH):Tomo31núm1-
121
Macpherson, I. - see Manuel, J.
Macpherson, J. Dzheyms Makferson, "Poemy
Ossiana." (Y.D. Levin, ed and trans)
A. McMillin, 617(TLS):6Apr84-362
Macpherson, J. The Spirit of Solitude.*
W.B. Carnochan, 301(JEGP):Oct83-541
A. McWhir, 627(UTQ):Summer83-420
McPherson, J.M. Ordeal by Fire.
J.G. Taylor, 9(AlaR):Jul83-229
MacPherson, M. Long Time Passing.
D. Knox, 441:24Jun84-9
MacPherson, M.C. The Blood of His
Servants.
R. Samuel, 441:29Apr84-7

McPherson, S. Patron Happiness.*
J. Graham, 441:4Mar84-14
P. Mesic, 491:Feb84-298
McPherson, W. Testing the Current.
R. Banks, 441:18Mar84-3
MacPike, L. Dostoevsky's Dickens.*
M. Futrell, 402(MLR):Jan83-252
N.M. Lary, 637(VS):Winter83-242
A. McMillin, 575(SEER):Jul83-427
L. Ormond, 155:Summer83-115
McQuade, W. Architecture in the Real
World.
P. Goldberger, 441:2Dec84-20
MacQueen, B.D. Plato's "Republic" in the
Monographs of Sallust.
E. Rawson, 123:Vol33No2-327
MacQueen, J. Progress and Poetry.
D.S. Thomson, 571(ScLJ):Autumn83-11
McQuown, N.A. Language, Culture, and
Education. (A.S. Dil, ed)
J.P. Lantolf, 215(GL):Vol123No3-226
MacRéamoinn, S., ed. The Pleasures of
Gaelic Poetry.*
J. Cronin, 174(Éire):Fall83-139
Macrí, O. Il Foscolo negli scrittori
italiani del Novecento.
T. O'Neill, 276:Autumn83-281
Macrí, O. La obra poética de Jorge Guil-
lén.
B. Gicovate, 457(NRFH):Tomo31núm1-
135
Macrorie, K. Twenty Teachers.
G.I. Maeroff, 441:18Nov84-33
MacShane, F. - see Chandler, R.
McSweeney, K. Four Contemporary Novelists.
M. Casserley, 617(TLS):5Oct84-1112
McSweeney, K. Tennyson and Swinburne as
Romantic Naturalists.*
P. Allen, 627(UTQ):Fall82-114
D. Hair, 178:Jun83-237
McSweeney, K. - see Wilson, A.
McTaggart, L. Kathleen Kennedy.*
H. Fraser, 362:1Mar84-27
McTague, M. The Businessman in Literature.
C. Leach, 447(N&Q):Feb82-85
Mactoux, M-M. Douleia.
T.E.J. Wiedemann, 303(JoHS):Vol 103-
200
MacVicar, A. Golf in My Gallowses.
B. Hepburn, 617(TLS):4May84-493
McWatters, K.G. - see Stendhal
McWhirter, G. God's Eye.*
P. Morley, 102(CanL):Summer83-101
McWilliams, D. The Narratives of Michel
Butor.
P.A. Robberecht, 107(CRCL):Jun83-288
McWilliams, J.R. Brother Artist.
295(JML):Nov83-533
Madden, D. The New Orleans of Possibil-
ities.
M. Kreyling, 573(SSF):Winter83-61
Madden, D. and R. Powers. Writers' Revi-
sions.
P. Gaskell, 677(YES):Vol 13-362
Madden, E.H. and J.E. Hamilton. Freedom
and Grace.
D.F. Kinlaw, 619:Winter83-94
Maddock, M. - see "Three Russian Women
Poets"
Maddox, L. Nabokov's Novels in English.*
C.S. Ross, 395(MFS):Winter83-736

Madell, G.C. The Identity of the Self.*
  B. Aune, 543:Mar83-724
  J.M. Howarth, 393(Mind):Oct83-629
  A. Lyon, 483:Jan83-130
  S. Priest, 323:May83-211
Maehler, H. - see Bacchylides
van Maerlant, J. Historie van den Grale
  und Boek van Merline. (T. Sodmann, ed)
  H. Kolb, 72:Band219Heft1-171
Magarotto, L., M. Marzaduri and G. Pagani
  Cesa, eds. L'Avanguardia a Tiflis.
  E.K. Beaujour, 550(RusR):Oct83-421
  D. Rayfield, 575(SEER):Oct83-605
Magee, B. The Philosophy of Schopenhauer.*
  A. Landor, 364:Feb84-93
Maginnis, H.B.J. - see Offner, R.
Magnard, P. - see de Bovelles, C.
Magnússon, S.A. - see "The Postwar Poetry
  of Iceland"
Magraw, R. France 1814-1915.
  E. Weber, 617(TLS):2Mar84-229
Maguire, H. Art and Eloquence in Byzan-
  tium.
  A.W. Epstein, 589:Apr83-503
  C. Mango, 90:Feb83-97
Maher, J.P., A.R. Bomhard and E.F.K.
  Koerner, eds. Papers from the Third
  International Conference on Historical
  Linguistics.
  S.G. Thomason, 350:Sep84-611
Mahfouz, N. Children of Gebelawi (Awlād
  Ḥāritnā).
  P. Cachia, 194:Vol 14-101
Mahindra, I. The Club.
  J. Motion, 617(TLS):27Jul84-849
Mahler, G. and R. Strauss. Gustav Mahler —
  Richard Strauss: Correspondence 1888-
  1911. (H. Blaukopf, ed)
  N. Del Mar, 617(TLS):7Dec84-1401
"Gustav Mahler and Guido Adler: Records of
  a Friendship."* (E.R. Reilly, ed and
  trans)
  F.W. Sternfeld, 410(M&L):Jan/Apr83-95
Mahon, D. The Chimeras.
  M. Harmon, 272(IUR):Spring83-114
Mahon, D. The Hunt by Night.*
  C. Boyle, 364:Nov83-84
  A. Frazier, 174(Éire):Winter83-136
  M. Harmon, 272(IUR):Spring83-114
  M. O'Neill, 493:Mar83-57
  V. Young, 249(HudR):Summer83-407
Mahoney, R.D. JFK: Ordeal in Africa.
  H. Goodman, 441:29Jan84-23
  R. Jeffreys-Jones, 617(TLS):25May84-
  593
Maida, P.B. and N.B. Spornick. Murder She
  Wrote.
  P. Wolfe, 395(MFS):Autumn83-389
Maiden, J. The Terms.
  J. Tulip, 581:Mar83-113
Maier, A. On the Threshold of Exact
  Science. (S.D. Sargent, ed and trans)
  D.C. Lindberg, 589:Oct83-1129
  E. McMullin, 319:Jul84-368
Maier, B. - see Guidi, A.
Mailer, N. Ancient Evenings.*
  G. Kearns, 249(HudR):Autumn83-560
  L.W. Wagner, 385(MQR):Summer84-446
Mailer, N. Tough Guys Don't Dance.
  P-L. Adams, 61:Sep84-128
  J. Campbell, 617(TLS):19Oct84-1178
  D. Donoghue, 441:29Jul84-1
  P. Kemp, 362:22Nov84-28

Maillet, A. Cent Ans dans les bois.
  E-M. Kroller, 102(CanL):Winter82-172
Maillet, A. La Contrebandière.
  J. Ripley, 102(CanL):Winter82-137
Mailloux, S. Interpretive Conventions.*
  D.H. Hirsch, 569(SR):Summer83-417
  P.C. Hogan, 651(WHR):Summer83-172
  M. Rapisarda, 395(MFS):Summer83-362
  L. Stern, 290(JAAC):Fall83-96
Maimonides, M. Maimonides' Commentary on
  the Mishnah "Tractate Sanhedrin." (F.
  Rosner, ed and trans)
  M. Kellner, 589:Oct83-1129
Main, G.L. Tobacco Colony.*
  639(VQR):Spring83-55
Maisel, L.S. From Obscurity to Oblivion.
  639(VQR):Autumn83-131
Maital, S. and S.L. Economic Games People
  Play.
  R.D. Luce, 441:26Aug84-10
Maitland, S. Virgin Territory.
  J. Rogers, 617(TLS):9Nov84-1289
Majidi, M-R. Strukturelle Beschreibung
  des iranischen Dialekts der Stadt Semnan.
  D.N. MacKenzie, 260(IF):Band88-320
  G.F. Meier, 682(ZPSK):Band36Heft1-100
Major, G. Le Cinéma québécois à la
  recherche d'un public.
  B-Z. Shek, 627(UTQ):Summer83-505
Major, J-L. Anne Hébert et le miracle de
  la parole.
  A.D. Barry, 188(ECr):Fall83-106
Major, J.R. Representative Government in
  Early Modern France.*
  H.G. Koenigsberger, 161(DUJ):Dec82-98
Majum'dār, B. and N. Jānā. Baiṣṇab
  padābalīr anukramaṇikā.
  R.P. Das, 259(IIJ):Apr83-216
Makin, J.H. The Global Debt Crisis.
  H. Goodman, 441:21Oct84-50
Makin, P. Provence and Pound.
  D. Seed, 447(N&Q):Aug82-375
Makkreel, R. Dilthey.
  O. Pöggeler, 125:Summer83-397
  H.N. Tuttle, 125:Summer83-396
Makoto, Ō. - see under Ōoka Makoto
Makouta M'Boukou, J-P. Introduction à
  l'étude du roman négro-africain de lan-
  gue française.
  C.L. Dehon, 207(FR):Oct83-101
Makowsky, V.A. - see Blackmur, R.P.
Makuck, P. Breaking and Entering.*
  G.W. Jarecke, 577(SHR):Summer83-285
Makuck, P. Where We Live.
  V. Young, 249(HudR):Summer83-402
Malamud, B. God's Grace.*
  S. Pinsker, 577(SHR):Summer83-275
Malamud, B. The Stories of Bernard Mala-
  mud.*
  G. Josipovici, 617(TLS):24Feb84-184
  J. Leonard, 453(NYRB):19Jan84-14
Malandain, P. La Fable et l'intertexte.
  M. Vincent, 207(FR):Oct83-106
Malbin, M.J., ed. Money and Politics in
  the United States.
  H.G. Nicholas, 617(TLS):19Oct84-1177
Malcolm, J. A Back Room in Somers Town.
  T.J. Binyon, 617(TLS):22Jun84-706
  M. Laski, 362:19Jul84-27
Malcolm, J. In the Freud Archives.
  H. Bloom, 441:27May84-3
Malcolm, J.L. Caesar's Due.
  R. Lockyer, 617(TLS):21Sep84-1062

Malcomson, R.M. Daisy Ashford.
  I. Hayes, 362:8Nov84-30
Male, R.R., ed. Money Talks.*
  K. Kinnamon, 651(WHR):Winter83-359
Malebranche, N. The Search after Truth
  [and] Elucidations of the Search after
  Truth.* Dialogue between a Christian
  Philosopher and a Chinese Philosopher on
  the Existence and Nature of God.*
  Entretiens sur la Métaphysique.
  H.A.S. Schankula, 518:Jan83-17
Malekin, P. Liberty and Love.*
  C. Cantalupo, 568(SCN):Winter83-77
  C. Hill, 366:Autumn83-266
Malenfant, P.C. Le Mot à mot.
  E. Hamblet, 207(FR):Apr84-737
de Malesherbes, C-G.D. Mémoires sur la
  librairie et sur la liberté de la
  presse.* (G.E. Rodmell, ed)
  J.H. Brumfitt, 208(FS):Oct83-463
Maleska, E.T. Across and Down.
  S.B. Flexner, 441:8Jul84-17
Malet, M. Nestor Makhno in the Russian
  Civil War.*
  P. Avrich, 550(RusR):Jan83-113
  J.F.N. Bradley, 575(SEER):Apr83-292
  P. Kenez, 104(CASS):Winter83-565
Maley, A. and S. Moulding. Learning to
  Listen.
  R.J. Melpignano, 399(MLJ):Spring83-67
Malfèr, S., ed. Die Protokolle des öster-
  reichischen Ministerrates, 1848-1867.
  (Pt 5, Vol 2)
  T.V. Thomas, 575(SEER):Apr83-283
Malherbe, J.F. Epistémologies anglo-
  saxonnes.
  A. Boyer, 542:Jul-Sep83-359
Malherbe, M. Kant ou Hume, ou la raison
  et le sensible.
  L. Marcil-Lacoste, 154:Mar83-167
Malicet, M. Lecture psychanalytique de
  l'oeuvre de Claudel.*
  B. Howells, 208(FS):Apr83-243
Malin, D. and P. Murdin. Colours of the
  Stars.
  C.A. Ronan, 617(TLS):2Nov84-1247
Malina, J. The Diaries of Judith Malina:
  1947-1957.
  J. Novick, 441:24Jun84-23
Malino, F. and P.C. Albert, eds. Essays
  in Modern Jewish History.*
  M.I. Urofsky, 390:Dec83-58
Malinowski, B. and J. De la Fuente. Malin-
  owski in Mexico.
  C. Silver, 185:Jul84-721
Malkiel, Y. - see Richter, E.
Malkowski, R. Zu Gast.
  J. Adler, 617(TLS):9Mar84-239
de Mallac, G. Boris Pasternak.*
  E.C. Brody, 363(LitR):Spring84-372
  J. Grayson, 575(SEER):Apr83-272
  W.F. Kolonosky, 395(MFS):Summer83-306
  D. Milivojević, 558(RLJ):Winter-
  Spring83-260
  G.S. Smith, 402(MLR):Jan83-255
Mallarmé, S. Correspondance.* (Vol 5)
  (H. Mondor and L.J. Austin, eds)
  C. Chadwick, 402(MLR):Jan83-192
Mallarmé, S. Correspondance.* (Vol 6)
  (H. Mondor and L.J. Austin, eds)
  C. Chadwick, 402(MLR):Jan83-192
  U. Franklin, 207(FR):May84-882

Mallarmé, S. Correspondance.* (Vol 7)
  (H. Mondor and L.J. Austin, eds)
  U. Franklin, 207(FR):May84-882
Mallarmé, S. Correspondance.* (Vol 8)
  (H. Mondor and L.J. Austin, eds)
  U. Franklin, 207(FR):May84-882
  E. Souffrin-Le Breton, 208(FS):Jul83-
  354
Mallarmé, S. Correspondance. (Vol 10)
  (H. Mondor and L.J. Austin, eds)
  J.M. Cocking, 617(TLS):3Aug84-866
Mallarmé, S. A Tomb for Anatole. (P.
  Auster, trans)
  L. Bersani, 441:15Jan84-10
  R. Craft, 453(NYRB):15Mar84-38
  M. Perloff, 29:Jan/Feb84-40
Mallet-Joris, F. Le Clin d'oeil de l'ange.
  J. Aeply, 450(NRF):Jun83-128
Mallett, M.E. and J.R. Hale. The Military
  Organization of a Renaissance State.
  P. Laven, 617(TLS):9Nov84-1293
Mallette, R. Spenser, Milton and Renais-
  sance Pastoral.*
  H. Cooper, 447(N&Q):Oct82-448
Mallin, S. Merleau-Ponty's Philosophy.*
  A. Montefiore, 447(N&Q):Feb82-93
Mallinson, G.J. The Comedies of Corneille.
  G. Hall, 617(TLS):10Aug84-890
Mallon, F.E. The Defense of Community in
  Peru's Central Highlands.
  G. Philip, 617(TLS):10Feb84-142
Mallon, T. Edmund Blunden.
  R. Queen, 134(CP):Fall83-82
Malmanger, M. Form og forestilling.
  G. Danbolt, 341:Vol52No2-92
Malmberg, B. - see Delattre, P.
Malmstad, J.E. - see Bugayeva, K.N.
Malone, D. Jefferson and His Time.*
  (Vols 1-6)
  B. Raffel, 385(MQR):Winter84-130
Maloney, G. and R. Savoie. Cinq cents ans
  de bibliographie hippocratique 1473-1982.
  V. Nutton, 123:Vol133No2-339
  J. Scarborough, 487:Summer83-180
Maloney, J.J. I Speak for the Dead.
  D. Weiser, 436(NewL):Summer84-109
Malory, T. Caxton's Malory. (J.W. Spisak
  and W. Matthews, eds)
  C. La Farge, 617(TLS):28Sep84-1104
Malouf, D. Fly Away Peter.
  J. Tulip, 581:Mar83-113
Malouf, D. Harland's Half Acre.
  P-L. Adams, 61:Oct84-126
  M. Gorra, 441:14Oct84-9
  J. Crace, 617(TLS):15Jun84-658
  J. Mellors, 362:5Jul84-27
Malpede, K., ed. Women in Theatre.
  N.B. Lenz, 615(TJ):Dec83-563
Maltby, W.S. Alba.
  D.J.R. Bruckner, 441:5Feb84-31
  H.G. Koenigsberger, 617(TLS):27Jul84-
  844
  H.R. Trevor-Roper, 453(NYRB):27Sep84-3
Maltman, K. Branch Lines.
  R. Dubanski, 102(CanL):Spring83-117
Mamdani, M. Imperialism and Fascism in
  Uganda.
  K. Ingham, 617(TLS):20Jan84-65
Mamonova, T., with S. Matilsky, eds.
  Women and Russia.
  J. Daynard, 441:27May84-17
de Man, P. Allegories of Reading.*
  R. Poole, 447(N&Q):Jun82-283

Mancing, H. The Chivalric World of "Don Quijote."*
  H. Ettinghausen, 400(MLN):Mar83-297
  J.A. Parr, 238:Sep83-433
  R.L. Predmore, 551(RenQ):Summer83-286
  B.W. Wardropper, 131(CL):Winter83-79
Mancini, A.N. Romanzi e romanzieri del Seicento.
  G. Costa, 593:Winter83/84-319
  N.J. Perella, 400(MLN):Jan83-144
  R.J. Rodini, 405(MP):May84-422
Mancini, G. Teresa de Avila.
  C.P. Thompson, 86(BHS):Apr83-147
de Mandach, A., ed and trans. Le Jeu des Trois Rois de Neuchâtel.
  C. Foxton, 402(MLR):Jul83-707
  G.A. Runnalls, 382(MAE):1983/2-327
de Mandach, A. Naissance et développement de la chanson de geste en Europe. (Vols 3 and 4)
  L.S. Crist, 589:Jan83-204
Mandel, E. Life Sentence.* Dreaming Backwards.
  D. Barbour, 102(CanL):Winter82-125
Mandel, O. Annotations to "Vanity Fair."
  P. Coustillas, 189(EA):Oct-Dec84-470
Mandel, O. Philoctetes and the Fall of Troy.
  P.G. Mason, 123:Vol33No2-314
Mandelbaum, A., ed and trans. Chelmaxioms.
  M.D. Lammon, 436(NewL):Fall83-111
Mandelbaum, A. - see Dante Alighieri
Mandelbaum, M. The Nuclear Future.
  R.H., 185:Jul84-740
  S.M. Halpern, 441:8Jan84-19
  P. Towle, 617(TLS):9Mar84-241
Mandelkow, K.R., ed. Europäische Romantik I.
  G. Hoffmeister, 107(CRCL):Sep83-429
Mandelkow, K.R. Goethe in Deutschland.* (Vol 1)
  H. Reiss, 133:Band16Heft2/3-238
Mandell, J. and S. Rubin. Trump Tower.
  P. Goldberger, 441:2Dec84-18
Mandell, R.D. Sport.
  L.S. Ritter, 441:3Jun84-11
  P. Smith, 617(TLS):16Nov84-1314
Mandeville, B. Free Thoughts on Religion, the Church, and National Happiness.
  566:Spring84-176
de Mandiargues, A.P. Le Deuil des roses.
  R. Buss, 617(TLS):11May84-529
Mandilaras, B.G. Papyroi kai papyrologia.
  J.D. Thomas, 123:Vol33No2-372
Manekeller, W. Briefe schreibt man heute so. (9th ed)
  J. Göschel, 685(ZDL):3/1983-407
Maneli, M. Juridical Positivism and Human Rights.
  A.W. Rudzinski, 185:Jul84-719
Manetti, D. and A. Roselli - see Hippocrates
Manferlotti, S. - see Dickens, C.
Manfredi, J. The Social Limits of Art.
  C. Dyke, 290(JAAC):Spring84-350
Mangan, J.A. Athleticism in the Victorian and Edwardian Public School.
  P. Scott, 637(VS):Spring83-342
Manganiello, D. Joyce's Politics.*
  P.M.S. Dawson, 541(RES):Feb83-96
  B. Forkner, 125:Fall82-95
Mango, C. Byzantium and its Image.
  R. Browning, 617(TLS):13Apr84-395

Manguel, A., ed. Black Water.
  J. Sullivan, 441:26Aug84-16
Manguel, A. and G. Guadalupi. The Dictionary of Imaginary Places.
  K.B. Harder, 424:Sep83-220
Manheim, M. Eugene O'Neill's New Language of Kinship.
  J.R. Bryer, 27(AL):May83-257
Manion, M.M. and V.F. Vines. Medieval and Renaissance Illuminated Manuscripts in Australian Collections.
  C. de Hamel, 617(TLS):14Sep84-1037
Maniruzzaman, T. The Bangladesh Revolution and its Aftermath.
  B.S. Gupta, 293(JASt):May83-702
Manitt, O. Adam 2000.
  D. Daymond, 102(CanL):Summer83-140
Mankowitz, W. The Devil in Texas.
  D. Montrose, 617(TLS):19Oct84-1178
Manley, L. Convention: 1500-1750.*
  F.J. Warnke, 401(MLQ):Dec82-405
Manlove, C.N. The Gap in Shakespeare.
  H. Keyishian, 551(RenQ):Spring83-137
  E. Pechter, 447(N&Q):Dec82-541
Manlove, C.N. The Impulse of Fantasy Literature.*
  C.C. Smith, 395(MFS):Summer83-350
Manlove, C.N. Literature and Reality, 1600-1800.*
  L.G. Black, 447(N&Q):Oct82-446
Mann, C. New Shades.
  J. Povey, 2(AfrA):Aug83-85
Mann, J. No Man's Island.*
  N. Callendar, 441:15Jan84-29
Mann, K. Mephisto.*
  D. Johnson, 617(TLS):28Sep84-1095
Mann, N. Petrarch.
  D. Robey, 617(TLS):16Nov84-1317
Mann, T. Thomas Mann Diaries 1918-1939.* (H. Kesten, ed)
  295(JML):Nov83-533
Mann, T. Reflections of a Nonpolitical Man.*
  295(JML):Nov83-534
Mann, W. James Galway's Music in Time.
  L. Salter, 415:Aug83-486
Manna, Z. Lectures on the Logic of Computer Programming.
  E.L. Bull, Jr., 316:Mar83-213
Mannheim, K. Structures of Thinking.
  I.S., 185:Jan84-365
Manning, K.R. Black Apollo of Science.*
  D.L. Hall, 441:1Jan84-9
  P. Weindling, 617(TLS):20Jul84-800
Manning, O. The Doves of Venus. The Play Room.
  P. Craig, 617(TLS):21Sep84-1066
Manning, R. Open the Door.*
  W. Scammell, 364:Aug/Sep83-129
Mannoni, O. Un commencement qui n'en finit pas. Ça n'empêche pas d'exister.
  F. Roustang, 98:Mar83-201
Manoliu-Manea, M., ed. The Tragic Plight of a Border Area.
  D. Deletant, 617(TLS):13Jul84-777
Manser, A. and G. Stock, eds. The Philosophy of F.H. Bradley.
  T. Baldwin, 176:Nov84-63
  H.M. Robinson, 617(TLS):9Nov84-1277
Mansfield, B.E. Phoenix of His Age.*
  P.G. Bietenholz, 539:Nov83-294
Mansfield, E. - see Lawrence, D.H.

Mansfield, K. The Collected Letters of
  Katherine Mansfield. (Vol 1) (V.
  O'Sullivan and M. Scott, eds)
    R. Dinnage, 617(TLS):14Sep84-1028
    V. Glendinning, 362:13Sep84-23
Mansfield, K. Journal. Short Stories.
  (J.M. Murry, ed of both) Short Stories.
  (C. Tomalin, ed)
    J. Uglow, 617(TLS):13Jan84-47
Mansfield, K. The Letters and Journals of
  Katherine Mansfield. (C.K. Stead, ed)
    P.A. Packer, 161(DUJ):Dec82-115
Manshu, L., Hai Feng and Cheng Hai - see
  under Lin Manshu, Hai Feng and Cheng Hai
Manteuffel, T. The Formation of the
  Polish State.
    E.B. Fryde, 575(SEER):Jul83-444
    W.K. Hanak, 589:Oct83-1069
Mantou, R. Le vocabulaire des actes origi-
  naux rédigés en français dans la partie
  flamingante du Comté de Flandre (1250-
  1350). (Pt 6)
    G. Roques, 553(RLiR):Jul-Dec83-482
Mantovanelli, P. Profundus.
    C. Moussy, 555:Vol57fasc1-150
Manuel, J. Juan Manuel: A Selection.* (I.
  Macpherson, ed)
    R.G. Keightley, 547(RF):Band95Heft3-
    395
Manuwald, B. Der Aufbau der lukrezischen
  Kulturentstehungslehre ("Da rerum
  natura" 5. 925-1457).*
    J-C. Richard, 555:Vol57fasc1-168
Manvell, R. Ingmar Bergman.
    M.J. Blackwell, 563(SS):Winter83-93
Manzoni, A. On the Historical Novel.
    B.F. Williamson, 441:8Jul84-21
"Mao Zedong's 'Talks at the Yan'an Confer-
  ence on Literature and Art.'"* (B.S.
  McDougall, ed and trans)
    L.S. Chang, 485(PE&W):Jan83-87
Mapanje, J. Of Chameleons and Gods.*
    I. Banda, 565:Vol124No2-14
Mapplethorpe, R. Lady: Lisa Lyon.
    E. Simson, 55:Nov83-53
Maracotta, L. Everything We Wanted.
    R. Koenig, 61:Jun84-117
Maraini, D. Woman at War.
    M. Wandor, 362:12Jul84-28
Maravall, J.A. Utopía y reformismo en la
  España de los Austrias.
    R.L. Kagan, 551(RenQ):Winter83-631
Marazza, C. - see Ysambert de Saint-Léger
Marbach, E. - see Husserl, E.
Marbeck, G. Hautefaye.
    G.J. Barberet, 207(FR):Mar84-593
Marc, D. Demographic Vistas.
    B. Brown, 18:Jul-Aug84-53
    T. Gitlin, 441:22Apr84-15
Marc, D. and W., eds. Linguistique romane
  et linguistique française: Hommages à
  Jacques Pohl.
    G. Ineichen, 260(IF):Band88-328
Marchand, L.A., ed. Byron's Letters and
  Journals.* (Vol 12: Index)
    J. Clubbe, 579(SAQ):Summer83-314
    C.W. Hagelman, Jr., 340(KSJ):Vol132-212
Marchand, L.A. - see Lord Byron
Marchessault, J. Lettre de Californie.
    C-L. Rogers, 102(CanL):Autumn83-69

Marcil-Lacoste, L. Claude Buffier and
  Thomas Reid, Two Common-Sense Philos-
  ophers.
    F. Duchesneau, 154:Sep83-513
    P.B. Wood, 518:Jul83-147
Marciszewski, W., ed. Dictionary of Logic
  as Applied in the Study of Language.
    J.D. McCawley, 567:Vol42No2/4-279
Marcolungo, F.L. Wolff e il possibile.
    J. Ecole, 192(EP):Oct-Dec83-495
Marcos, J.C. - see under Cascon Marcos, J.
Marcos Marín, F. Estudios sobre el pro-
  nombre.
    M. Torreblanca, 545(RPh):Aug82-44
Marcus, G.J. The Conquest of the North
  Atlantic.
    J.A.B. Townsend, 447(N&Q):Dec82-572
Marcus, I.G. Piety and Society.
    Y. Shamir, 589:Apr83-505
Marcus, J., ed. Virginia Woolf.
    J. Batchelor, 617(TLS):10Aug84-900
Marcus, M.J. An Allegory of Form.
    E.B. Weaver, 276:Summer83-169
Marcus, P.L., W. Gould and M.J. Sidnell -
  see Yeats, W.B.
Marcus, S. Freud and the Culture of Psy-
  choanalysis.
    B.A. Farrell, 176:Nov84-59
Marcus, S.E. David Smith.
    L. Ellmann, 617(TLS):29Jun84-724
Marcuse, H. The Aesthetic Dimension.
    R. Castiglione, 453:Dec82-460
de Maré, E. The Victorian Woodblock Illus-
  trators.
    V. Dailey, 517(PBSA):Vol77No4-504
van Maren, J.W. - see Marquard von Lindau
Marenbon, J. From the Circle of Alcuin
  to the School of Auxerre.*
    S. Gersh, 589:Jan83-207
Mareschal, A. La Cour Bergère ou l'Arca-
  die de Messire Philippes Sidney.* (L.
  Desvignes, ed)
    H.B. McDermott, 207(FR):Feb84-389
    G. Verdier, 475:Vol 10No18-367
Margalit, A., ed. Meaning and Use.*
    K. Bach and R.M. Harnish, 606:Mar83-
    469
Margarotto, L., M. Marzaduri and G.P. Cesa,
  eds. L'avanguardia a Tiflis.
    J.R. Stapanian, 574(SEEJ):Fall83-394
Margenau, H. Physics and Philosophy.*
    J. Bub, 486:Sep83-515
de Margerie, B. Les perfections du Dieu
  de Jésus-Christ.
    A. Reix, 192(EP):Apr-Jun83-245
Margitić, M.R., ed. Corneille comique.
    L. Picciola, 535(RHL):Sep/Dec83-920
Margitić, M.R. - see Corneille, P.
Margolies, E. Which Way Did He Go?*
    S. Dutruch, 189(EA):Oct-Dec84-484
    L.O. Sauerberg, 462(OL):Vol38No2-185
    P. Wolfe, 395(MFS):Autumn83-389
    295(JML):Nov83-391
Margolin, J-C. L'humanisme en Europe au
  temps de la Renaissance.
    A. Reix, 542:Jan-Mar83-95
    A. Tissoni Benvenuti, 547(RF):Band95
    Heft1/2-174
Margolin, J-C. and R. Sauzet, eds. Pra-
  tiques et discours alimentaires à la
  Renaissance.
    Y. Bellenger, 535(RHL):May/Jun83-464

Margolis, G. The Day We Still Stand Here.
R.W. Hill, 580(SCR):Fall83-123
Margolis, H. Selfishness, Altruism, and
Rationality.
M. Taylor, 185:Oct83-150
Margolis, J. Art and Philosophy.*
P. Jones, 483:Jan83-128
P. Lamarque, 482(PhR):Apr83-266
E. Schaper, 89(BJA):Autumn83-360
Margolis, J. Persons and Minds.
F. Jackson, 449:Mar83-94
Margolis, M.L. Mothers and Such.
R.W. Schram, 441:16Sep84-43
Margreiter, R. Ontologie und Gottesbe-
griffe bei Nietzsche.
K. Leidlmair, 489(PJGG):Band90Heft2-
420
Marguerite de Navarre. The Heptameron.
(P.A. Chilton, trans)
T. Cave, 617(TLS):27Jul84-830
Marguerite de Navarre. Oraison a nostre
Seigneur Jésus Christ.* (R. Salminen,
ed)
L. Löfstedt, 439(NM):1983/2-276
Marho. Visions of History.
L. Robinson, 441:18Mar84-19
Mariani, P. Crossing Cocytus.*
F. Chappell, 651(WHR):Autumn83-251
R. Lattimore, 249(HudR):Spring83-209
Mariani, P. William Carlos Williams.*
R. Nelson, 639(VQR):Spring83-354
S. Pinsker, 363(LitR):Fall83-128
M.L. Rosenthal, 27(AL):Mar83-89
Marías, F. and A. Bustamante García. Las
ideas artísticas de El Greco.
J. Bury, 90:Jun83-366
Marie de France. Die Lais.* (D. Rieger,
with R. Kroll, eds and trans)
F. Olef-Krafft, 72:Band220Heft2-448
Marienstras, R. Le Proche et le lointain.
L. Salingar, 189(EA):Apr-Jun84-187
Maril, R.L. Texas Shrimpers.
L. Milazzo, 584(SWR):Autumn83-viii
Marín, F.M. - see under Marcos Marín, F.
Marín, J.L.M. - see under Morales y Marín,
J.L.
Marin, L. Le portrait du roi.*
O. Ranum, 400(MLN):May83-745
Marin, L. Utopics.
J.N. Gray, 617(TLS):13Jul84-776
Marin, L. La Voix excommuniée.
C. Lang, 400(MLN):May83-791
Marini, S.A. Radical Sects of Revolution-
ary New England.
M.L. Bradbury, 432(NEQ):Sep83-457
E.S. Gaustad, 656(WMQ):Apr83-330
Marino, A. Étiemble ou le comparatisme
militant.*
H. Peyre, 678(YCGL):No31-150
Marino, A. L'Hermeneutique de Mircea
Eliade.
R.J. Schoeck, 125:Spring83-301
Marino, L. The "Decameron" 'Cornice.'
G. Costa, 545(RPh):Nov82-343
M. Marcus, 276:Autumn83-277
Marion, J-L. Dieu sans l'être.
D. Janicaud, 192(EP):Oct-Dec83-496
Marion, J-L. Théologiques.
A. Reix, 542:Oct-Dec83-460
Maritain, J. Distinguer pour unir ou les
degrés du savoir.
T. Cordellier, 450(NRF):Apr83-134

de Marivaux, P.C.D. Up from the Country,
Infidelities, The Game of Love and
Chance.
S. Harvey, 208(FS):Jul83-341
Marker, F.J. and L-L. Edward Gordon Craig
and "The Pretenders."*
A. Rood, 397(MD):Mar83-121
J.M. Walton, 610:Summer83-177
J. Wiingaard, 612(ThS):May/Nov83-150
Marker, L-L. and F.J. Ingmar Bergman.*
M.J. Blackwell, 563(SS):Winter83-91
H. Lane, 627(UTQ):Summer83-561
P. Walsh, 108:Fall83-132
Markey, T.L. Frisian.*
R.H. Bremmer, Jr., 133:Band16Heft1-93
S. Johnson, 353:Vol20No3/4-345
A. Petersen, 204(FdL):Mar82-75
P.M. Tiersma, 361:Apr83-375
Markham, E.A. Human Rites.
T. Eagleton, 617(TLS):9Nov84-1290
Markham, E.A. Love, Politics and Food.
S. Brown, 493:Jun83-67
Markham, E.J. Saibara.
R. Widdess, 617(TLS):9Mar84-240
Markham, S. John Loveday of Caversham
1711-1789.
J. Carswell, 617(TLS):19Oct84-1196
Markis, D. Quine und das Problem der
Übersetzung.*
J. Simon, 489(PJGG):Band90Heft1-208
Markov, G. The Truth That Killed.*
W.F. Buckley, Jr., 441:8Jul84-7
E. de Mauny, 617(TLS):27Jan84-80
442(NY):9Jul84-94
Markov, V. Russian Imagism, 1919-1924.*
G. Ivask, 558(RLJ):Winter-Spring83-263
Markovits, A.S. and F.E. Sysyn, eds.
Nationbuilding and the Politics of
Nationalism.
T.W. Simons, Jr., 550(RusR):Jul83-327
Marks, B. and R. Puppet Plays and Puppet
Making.
R. Hoffman, 614:Summer84-26
Marks, C.E. Commissurotomy, Consciousness
and Unity of Mind.
R. Double, 543:Mar83-726
Marks, E. and I. de Courtivron, eds. New
French Feminisms.
J.L. Beizer, 188(ECr):Summer83-119
M. Whitford, 208(FS):Jul83-372
Marks, E.R. Coleridge on the Language of
Verse.*
R. Modiano, 191(ELN):Sep83-63
F.W. Shilstone, 134(CP):Spring83-93
Marks, G.A. and C.B. Johnson. Harrap's
Slang Dictionary: English-French/French-
English. (rev) (J. Pratt, ed)
D. Coward, 617(TLS):6Apr84-377
Marks, H.S. and M.K. Alabama Past Leaders.
L.R. Atkins, 9(AlaR):Jan83-57
Marks, R. Burrell.*
S. Gardiner, 362:26Jan84-19
Marks, R. and others. The Burrell Collec-
tion.*
S. Gardiner, 362:26Jan84-19
Marks, R. and N. Morgan. The Golden Age
of English Manuscript Painting, 1200-
1500.
J. Backhouse, 90:Jun83-363
Marks, S. Innocent Abroad.
A. Orde, 161(DUJ):Dec82-103

Marks, S. and A. Atmore, eds. Economy and Society in Pre-Industrial South Africa.
  D. Hedges, 69:Vol53No1-87
Marks, V. Somerset County Cricket Scrapbook.
  A.L. Le Quesne, 617(TLS):4May84-493
Markus, T.A., ed. Order in Space and Society.*
  H. Colvin, 46:Jun83-57
  A. Forty, 59:Dec83-481
Marlatt, D. Our Lives.
  D. O'Rourke, 102(CanL):Winter82-130
Marling, K.A. Wall-to-Wall America.
  J.C. Carlisle, 658:Winter83-312
Marling, W. William Carlos Williams and the Painters, 1909-1923.
  K. Eble, 651(WHR):Autumn83-272
Marlowe, C. The Complete Works of Christopher Marlowe. (2nd ed) (F. Bowers, ed)
  P.J. Croft, 541(RES):Nov83-492
Marlowe, C. Tamburlaine the Great. (J.S. Cunningham, ed)
  J.L. Selzer, 568(SCN):Winter83-74
de Marly, D. Costume on the Stage 1600-1940.
  M. Carlson, 612(ThS):May/Nov83-168
Marowitz, C. Sex Wars.
  D. Devlin, 157:Autumn83-31
Marquard von Lindau. Die zehn Gebot (Strassburg 1516 und 1520). (J.W. van Maren, ed)
  N.F. Palmer, 447(N&Q):Dec82-574
Marquardt, A. and H. Rathsack, eds. Preussen. (Vol 5)
  I.K. Rogoff, 59:Jun83-250
Marquet, J-F. - see Schelling, F.W.J.
Márquez, A. Literatura e Inquisición en España (1478-1834).*
  F. Fernández-Turienzo, 240(HR): Spring83-227
Márquez, G.G. - see under García Márquez, G.
Márquez, G.G. and P. Apuleyo Mendoza - see under García Márquez, G. and P. Apuleyo Mendoza
Márquez, T.F. - see under Falcón Márquez, T.
Marr, D. Vision.
  I. Rosenfield, 453(NYRB):11Oct84-53
Marranca, B., ed. American Dreams.*
  P. Grego, 615(TJ):May82-278
Marranca, B. Theatrewritings.
  M. Gussow, 441:15Jul84-19
Marranca, B. and C. Dasgupta. American Playwrights.*
  P. Auslander, 615(TJ):May83-277
Marroni, G. Nuovo repertorio bibliografico della prima lirica galego-portoghese (1814-1977).
  Y.M., 545(RPh):Nov82-321
Marrow, J.H. and A. Shestack, eds. Hans Baldung Grien: Prints and Drawings.*
  M. Wolff, 551(RenQ):Summer83-251
Marrus, M.R. and R.O. Paxton. Vichy France and the Jews.
  E. Weber, 31(ASch):Winter82/83-107
Mars, G. and M. Nicod. The World of Waiters.
  C. Driver, 617(TLS):15Jun84-659

Marsack, R. The Cave of Making.*
  A. Haberer, 189(EA):Apr-Jun84-224
  J. Mole, 493:Mar83-70
  272(IUR):Autumn83-273
Marschall, H-G. Die Kathedrale von Verdun.
  W. Haas, 43:Band13Heft1-78
Marschall, R. - see Perelman, S.J.
Marsh, D. Before I Get Old.
  T.D.S., 617(TLS):13Jan84-33
Marsh, D. The Quattrocento Dialogue.*
  A.F. Nagel, 481(PQ):Winter83-109
Marshall, A. Life's Rich Pageant.
  N. Annan, 362:20Sep84-24
Marshall, C. Julie.
  J. Eidus, 441:28Oct84-26
Marshall, D.J., Jr. Prinzipien der Descartes-Exegese.
  H. Caton, 319:Oct84-480
Marshall, G. Constitutional Conventions.
  H.W.R. Wade, 617(TLS):20Apr84-439
Marshall, G. In Search of the Spirit of Capitalism.
  J.K., 185:Apr84-556
Marshall, H. Masters of the Soviet Cinema.
  G. Kaufman, 362:19Apr84-26
Marshall, H.W. Folk Architecture in Little Dixie.
  Y.J. Milspaw, 650(WF):Oct83-309
  G.L. Pocius, 292(JAF):Jul-Sep83-350
Marshall, H.W. and R. Ahlborn. Buckaroos in Paradise.*
  H. Cannon, 292(JAF):Apr-Jun83-220
Marshall, J. The Papers of John Marshall. (Vol 3) (W.C. Stinchcombe, C.T. Cullen and L. Tobias, eds)
  H.L. Coles, 161(DUJ):Jun83-117
Marshall, L. Cooking with Lydie Marshall.
  W. and C. Cowen, 639(VQR):Autumn83-137
Marshall, M.F. and J. Todd. English Congregational Hymns in the Eighteenth Century.
  D.R. Anderson, 566:Spring84-174
  F. Baker, 579(SAQ):Autumn85-462
Marshall, P. Praisesong for the Widow.*
  C.G. Holloway, 95(CLAJ):Jun84-460
Marshall, P. Reena and Other Stories.
  C. Sternhell, 441:19Feb84-22
Marshall, P. and G. Williams, eds. The British Atlantic Empire before the American Revolution.*
  R.R. Johnson, 173(ECS):Winter83/84-221
Marshall, P.H. William Godwin.
  D. Bromwich, 441:21Oct84-24
  D. Locke, 617(TLS):21Sep84-1061
  J. Lucas, 362:12Jul84-24
Marshall, P.J. - see Burke, E.
Marshall, P.J. and G. Williams. The Great Map of Mankind.*
  R. Janes, 173(ECS):Spring84-354
  P. Rogers, 83:Spring83-75
Marshall, R. The Haunted Major.
  442(NY):19Mar84-146
Marshall, R.K. Virgins and Viragos.*
  42(AR):Fall83-505
Marshall, S. Everyman's Book of English Folk Tales.
  C.W. Joyner, 292(JAF):Apr-Jun83-230
Marshall, W. The Far Away Man.
  T.J. Binyon, 617(TLS):24Aug84-953
Marsot, A.L.A. Egypt in the Reign of Muhammad Ali.
  P.J. Vatikiotis, 617(TLS):18May84-549

Martens, E. Dialogisch-pragmatische
Philosophiedidaktik.
  A.K.D. Lorenzen, 489(PJGG):Band90Heft2-
431
"Marthe."* (D.M. Frame, trans)
  P. Gay, 441:23Dec84-13
Martí, J. Major Poems. (P.S. Foner, ed)
  J.M. Kirk, 150(DR):Summer83-366
Martí, J. José Martí: Thoughts/Pensamien-
tos. (C. Ripoll, ed and trans)
  S.H. Gale and C. Carney, 552(REH):
    Oct83-438
Martin, A. Anthologie du conte en France,
1750-1799.
  J. Barchilon, 535(RHL):Sep/Dec83-937
  K. Sasse, 547(RF):Band95Heft3-350
Martin, C. Passages from Friday.
  D. Gioia, 461:Fall/Winter83/84-99
  E. Grosholz, 249(HudR):Autumn83-584
Martín, C.E. - see Esteras Martín, C.
Martin, D. Final Harbor.
  N. Ramsey, 441:7Oct84-22
Martin, D. The Road to Ballyshannon.
  P. Craig, 617(TLS):9Mar84-259
Martin, D. and P. Johnson. The Struggle
for Zimbabwe.
  T.M. Shaw, 529(QQ):Autumn83-880
Martin, D. and P. Mullen, eds. Unholy War-
fare.
  T. Garden, 176:Apr84-60
  P. Towle, 617(TLS):9Mar84-241
Martin, D.M., ed. Handbook of Latin Amer-
ican Studies. (No 43)
  N.J. Pearson, 263(RIB):Vol33No3-410
Martin, E.A., ed. A Concise Dictionary of
Law.
  A. Whitaker, 617(TLS):6Apr84-382
Martin, F.D. Sculpture and Enlivened
Space.*
  L.R. Rogers, 89(BJA):Spring83-164
Martin, F.X. - see Tierney, M.
Martin, G. The Damrosch Dynasty.
  J. Novick, 441:22Jan84-23
Martin, G. The Opera Companion.
  A.J.G.H., 617(TLS):17Aug84-927
Martin, G.D. The Architecture of Experi-
ence.*
  R.W. Beardsmore, 483:Apr83-271
  J. King-Farlow, 478:Apr83-136
Martin, H. and G. Pflug, eds. Deutsche
Fernostbibliographie 1979/German Far
East Bibliography 1979.
  W.H.N., 116:Jan82-148
Martin, H-J., R. Chartier and J-P. Vivet,
eds. Histoire de l'édition française.
(Vol 1)
  R. Briggs, 617(TLS):20Apr84-435
Martin, J. William Barclay.
  J. Whale, 617(TLS):28Dec84-1510
Martin, J. Gilbert.*
  J.K.L. Walker, 617(TLS):27Jan84-93
Martin, J. Miss Manners' Guide to Excruci-
atingly Correct Behavior.*
  639(VQR):Spring83-63
Martin, J. Miss Manners' Guide to Rearing
Perfect Children.
  E. Abeel, 441:21Oct84-16
  P-L. Adams, 61:Dec84-146
Martin, J. Patchworkbook.
  B. Self, 614:Spring84-25
Martín, J.L. Bomba de tiempo.
  M. Gardón, 701(SinN):Oct-Dec82-86

Martín, J.L.G. - see under García Martín,
J.L.
Martin, L. Buildings and Ideas 1933-83
from the Studio of Leslie Martin and His
Associates.
  S. Cantacuzino, 617(TLS):13Jan84-41
Martin, P. "Piers Plowman."
  T.D. Hill, 447(N&Q):Jun82-240
Martin, P., A. Gregg and G. Perlin. Con-
tenders.
  J. Hutcheson, 99:Dec83-29
Martin, P.P. Images and Conversations.
  L. Milazzo, 584(SWR):Autumn83-x
Martin, P.W. Byron.*
  C.T. Goode, 661(WC):Summer83-164
  W. Ruddick, 366:Autumn83-271
  M. Storey, 175:Spring83-75
  G. Woodcock, 569(SR):Fall83-664
Martin, R. Pour une logique du sens.
  G. Kleiber, 553(RLiR):Jul-Dec83-428
Martin, R. Tacitus.*
  E. Keitel, 24:Spring83-102
Martin, R.B. Tennyson.*
  P. Allen, 627(UTQ):Fall82-114
  J. Kolb, 405(MP):Nov83-173
  S. Shatto, 447(N&Q):Jun82-247
Martin, R.E. American Literature and the
Universe of Force.*
  Y. Hakutani, 26(ALR):Spring83-145
  R.W. Harvey, 106:Winter83-467
  J.C. Levenson, 27(AL):Mar83-94
  A.M. Woodlief, 577(SHR):Fall83-374
Martin, R.H. Evangelicals United.
  S. Gilley, 617(TLS):30Mar84-327
Martin, R.K. The Homosexual Tradition in
American Poetry.
  R. Kroetsch, 106:Summer83-219
Martin, R.M. Events, Reference, and Log-
ical Form.
  C.F.K., 543:Sep82-178
Martin, R.M. Logico-Linguistic Papers.*
  H. Hiż, 355(LSoc):Jun83-286
Martin, R.M. Primordiality, Science and
Value.
  S.B. Rosenthal, 543:Dec82-461
Martin, R.M. - see Eisele, C.
Martin, S. California Writers.
  A. Sinclair, 617(TLS):13Apr84-392
Martin, S. Wagner to "The Waste Land."
  P. Carnegy, 208(FS):Apr83-241
  M. Magalaner, 395(MFS):Summer83-261
Martin, V.J. and W.R. Mitchell, Jr. Land-
mark Homes of Georgia, 1733-1983.
  C.M. Howett, 576:Oct83-308
  H.B. Owens, 219(GaR):Spring83-211
Martin, W. An American Triptych.
  S. Gubar, 441:19Feb84-26
  M.L. Rosenthal, 617(TLS):15Jun84-669
Martin, W. Nerve Endings.
  J. Bass, 441:19Feb84-22
Martin-Fugier, A. La Bourgeoise, femme au
temps de Paul Bourget.
  A-C. Faitrop, 207(FR):Dec83-287
Martin-Jenkins, C. Twenty Years On.
  A.L. Le Quesne, 617(TLS):21Dec84-1487
Martín Zorraquino, M.A. Las construc-
ciones pronominales en español.
  M. Torreblanca, 545(RPh):Aug82-44
Martindale, J.R. The Prosopography of the
Later Roman Empire. (Vol 2)
  T.D. Barnes, 487:Autumn83-248
  F.M. Clover, 122:Apr83-162

Mason, M. and T.F. Rigelhof. A Beast With Two Backs.*
  L. Daniel, 102(CanL):Spring83-113
Mason, P. The English Gentleman.*
  42(AR):Winter83-121
Maspero, H. China in Antiquity.
  D. Holzman, 318(JAOS):Apr-Jun82-430
Maspero, H. Taoism and Chinese Religion.
  J.R. Kirkland, 293(JASt):Feb83-395
Massa, I. A Short History of the Beginnings and Origins of These Present Wars in Moscow under the Reign of Various Sovereigns down to the Year 1610. (G.E. Orchard, ed and trans)
  D. Rowland, 550(RusR):Jan83-101
  J. Spicer, 627(UTQ):Summer83-560
Massie, A. One Night in Winter.
  T. Fitton, 617(TLS):8Jun84-632
Massie, S. Land of the Firebird.
  A.K. Donchenko, 558(RLJ):Winter-Spring83-269
Masson, A. The Pictorial Catalogue: Mural Decoration in Libraries.*
  A. Hobson, 354:Mar83-82
Masson, J.M. The Assault on Truth.
  F. Cioffi, 617(TLS):6Jul84-743
  B.A. Farrell, 176:Nov84-57
  C. Rycroft, 453(NYRB):12Apr84-3
  A. Storr, 441:12Feb84-3
Masson, J.M. The Oceanic Feeling.*
  F.B.J. Kuiper, 259(IIJ):Jan83-53
Mastai, M-L.D. Illusion in Art.
  C.H. Clough, 39:Jan83-67
Mastandrea, P. Un Neoplatonico Latino: Cornelio Labeone.
  J. Mansfield, 394:Vol36fasc3/4-437
Masters, H. Last Stands.
  M.D. Riley, 219(GaR):Winter83-914
  639(VQR):Summer83-80
Masters, O. The Home Girls.
  E. Webby, 381:Mar83-34
Mastny, V. Russia's Road to the Cold War.*
  J. Radvanyi, 396(ModA):Spring83-205
Mastronarde, D.J. Contact and Discontinuity.*
  E.M. Craik, 303(JoHS):Vol 103-185
Mastronarde, D.J. and J.M. Bremer. The Textual Tradition of Euripides' Phoinissai.
  C.E. Cowherd, 124:Mar-Apr84-264
Masur, H.Q. Bury Me Deep.
  N. Callendar, 441:24Jun84-41
Mat-Hasquin, M. Voltaire et l'antiquité grecque.
  R.C. Knight, 402(MLR):Apr83-449
  C. Poulouin, 535(RHL):Jul/Aug83-638
Matas, J. La cuestión del género literario.
  V. Cano, 238:May83-298
  A.K. Kaminsky, 552(REH):Oct83-461
Matejič, M. and others. A Biobibliographical Handbook of Bulgarian Authors.* (K. Black, ed)
  C.A. Moser, 574(SEEJ):Spring83-120
Mateo, M.S. Razon y sensibilidad en la ética de Kant.
  N. Demé, 542:Jan-Mar83-129
"Matériaux pour l'histoire du vocabulaire français." (Vol 19)
  P. Larthomas, 535(RHL):Sep/Dec83-977

Mates, B. Skeptical Essays.*
  J. Benardete, 543:Dec82-463
  R. Feldman, 449:Sep83-508
  F.F. Schmitt, 482(PhR):Jul83-466
  483:Oct81-593
Matheopoulos, H. Maestro.*
  N. Goodwin, 415:Aug83-485
Mathes, J., ed. Prosa des Jugendstils.
  H. Lehnert, 133:Band16Heft2/3-264
Mathes, J. - see Brentano, C.
Matheson, S. Time Off to Dig.
  D. Thomas, 362:12Jan84-22
Mathews, J. and L. One Billion.
  J.K. Davison, 441:26Feb84-23
  J.K. Fairbank, 453(NYRB):19Jan84-17
Mathias, R. Burning Brambles.
  A. Stevenson, 617(TLS):2Mar84-226
Mathieu, R., ed and trans. Le Mu tianzi zhuan.
  W.H. Nienhauser, Jr., 116:Jul82-247
Mathieu-Castellani, G., ed. La Métamorphose dans la poésie baroque française et anglaise.*
  B. Guthmüller, 72:Band220Heft1-131
Mathieu-Castellani, G. Mythes de l'éros baroque.*
  J.D. Lyons, 207(FR):Oct83-105
Mathis, R. In the Land of the Living.
  K.R. Johnson, 9(AlaR):Jan83-58
Matisse, H. Jazz.*
  J.D. Flam, 62:Feb84-72
"Henri Matisse, Das Goldene Zeitalter." "Henri Matisse 1869-1954, Gravures et lithographies." "Henri Matisse."
  N. Watkins, 90:Dec83-771
Matos Paoli, F. Jardín vedado.
  I. López Jiménez, 701(SinN):Jul-Sep83-86
Matossian, N. Iannis Xenakis.
  B. Schiffer, 607:Mar83-25
Matsumura, T. The Labour Aristocracy.
  T.C. Barker, 617(TLS):6Apr84-385
Matte, E.J. Histoire des Modes phonetiques du français.
  J. Klausenburger, 350:Jun84-452
  J. Kramer, 547(RF):Band95Heft4-479
  B. Rochet, 320(CJL):Fall83-197
Matthee, D. Circles in a Forest.
  C.R. Larson, 441:28Oct84-31
  442(NY):26Nov84-148
Mattheier, K.J. Pragmatik und Soziologie der Dialekte.
  H.L. Kufner, 221(GQ):Mar83-360
  D. Stellmacher, 680(ZDP):Band102Heft3-469
Matthew, H.C.G. - see Gladstone, W.E.
Matthews, D. Michael Tippitt.
  412:Feb82-67
Matthews, D. Arturo Toscanini.
  N. Goodwin, 415:May83-300
Matthews, J. Sassafras.
  C.R. Larson, 441:19Feb84-22
  442(NY):26Mar84-134
Matthews, J. Voices.*
  42(AR):Fall83-507
  295(JML):Nov83-546
  639(VQR):Autumn83-125
Matthews, J.H. Eight Painters.
  D. Festa-McCormick, 593:Fall83-242
  A. Otten, 42(AR):Summer83-369

Matthews, J.H. Surrealism, Insanity, and
Poetry.
M. Bishop, 150(DR):Spring83-177
B.L. Knapp, 593:Spring83-84
A. Otten, 42(AR):Summer83-369
Matthews, J.J. Talking to the Moon.
R. and G. Laubin, 649(WAL):Aug83-179
Matthews, J.T. The Play of Faulkner's
Language.*
P.G. Hogan, Jr., 573(SSF):Winter83-55
D. Krause, 594:Fall83-287
J.M. Mellard, 301(JEGP):Oct83-581
D. Minter, 27(AL):Mar83-110
K.F. Zender, 141:Winter83-80
Matthews, M. Education in the Soviet
Union.
J. Dunstan, 575(SEER):Jul83-470
I. Kreindler, 550(RusR):Oct83-443
Matthews, P.H. Generative Grammar and Lin-
guistic Competence.*
D.H., 355(LSoc):Mar83-141
Matthews, P.H. Syntax.*
R.I. Binnick, 320(CJL):Fall83-171
L. Haegeman, 179(ES):Feb83-79
D. Kilby, 361:Jan83-95
J. Miller, 297(JL):Mar83-233
Matthews, S.R. Interwoven.
L. Clayton, 649(WAL):May83-75
L. Milazzo, 584(SWR):Winter83-v
Matthews, W. Flood.*
B. Costello, 491:May83-106
Matthews, W. A Happy Childhood.
D. Kalstone, 441:1Jul84-14
Matthiessen, P. Indian Country.
P-L. Adams, 61:Jun84-124
P. Nabokov, 453(NYRB):27Sep84-44
D. Wagoner, 441:29Jul84-9
442(NY):4Jun84-134
Matthieu, P. Tablettes de la vie et de la
mort.* (C.N. Smith, ed)
J. Trethewey, 208(FS):Jan83-75
Mattusch, C.C. Bronzeworkers in the
Athenian Agora.
E. Davis, 124:May-Jun84-311
Matusow, A.J. The Unraveling of America.
W.E. Leuchtenburg, 61:Apr84-138
L. Walsh, 441:26Feb84-14
Matute, A.M. Selecciones de Ana María
Matute. (J.A. Hernández and E. Guillermo, eds)
C.M. Cherry, 238:Dec83-641
Matz, F. and H-G. Buchholz, eds. Archae-
ologia Homerica. (Vol 3, Pt 10)
J.T. Hooker, 260(IF):Band87-304
Maung Maung, U. From Sangha to Laity.
J.P. Ferguson, 293(JASt):Nov82-226
de Mauny, E. - see Goldberg, A.
de Maupassant, G. Contes et nouvelles.
(Vol 2) (L. Forestier, ed)
G. Hainsworth, 208(FS):Oct83-477
Maupin, A. Babycakes.
J. Austin, 441:18Nov84-32
Maurel, S. - see Tirso de Molina
Maurer, D.W. Language of the Underworld.*
(A.W. Futrell and C.R. Wordell, eds)
J.H. Hall, 579(SAQ):Summer83-341
L. Pederson, 405(MP):Aug83-105
L.E. Seits, 424:Sep83-211
Maurer, F. and H. Rupp, eds. Deutsche
Wortgeschichte. (3rd ed)
P. Wiesinger, 685(ZDL):2/1983-235
Maurer, H. Das Bistum Konstanz. (Vol 1)
J.B. Freed, 589:Jul83-780

Maurer, J. Italienische Lyrik aus sieben
Jahrhunderten von Dante bis Quasimodo.
H. Köhler, 224(GRM):Band33Heft1-116
Maurer, P. Wunsch und Maske.
P.K. Jansen, 301(JEGP):Apr83-292
Mauriac, C. Zabé.
R. Buss, 617(TLS):6Jul84-761
Mauriac, F. Lettres d'une vie (1904-1969).
(C. Mauriac, ed)
A. Séailles, 535(RHL):May/Jun83-487
Maurikios. Das Strategikon des Maurikios.
(G.T. Dennis, ed)
J.W. Barker, 589:Jul83-782
Maurin, M.S. - see under Simpson Maurin, M.
Mavor, E., ed. Life with the Ladies of
Llangollen.
P. Beer, 617(TLS):30Nov84-1365
Mavrogordatos, G.T. Stillborn Republic.
R. Clogg, 617(TLS):15Jun84-679
Maximov, V. La Ballade de Savva et autres
nouvelles.
J. Blot, 450(NRF):May83-147
Maxton, H. Jubilee for Renegades.
M. Harmon, 272(IUR):Spring83-114
Maxwell, R.S. and R.D. Baker. Sawdust
Empire.
L. Milazzo, 584(SWR):Summer84-vii
Maxwell, W. - see Warner, S.T.
May, C. Breaking the Silence.
J. Decreus, 208(FS):Oct83-497
May, D. Proust.*
R. Fuller, 364:Jun83-99
May, D. The Times Nature Diary.
M.F., 617(TLS):12Oct84-1171
May, E., ed. Music of Many Cultures.
J. Montagu, 410(M&L):Jan/Apr83-94
T. Vennum, Jr., 292(JAF):Apr-Jun83-216
May, J. Curious Facts 2.
R. Davies, 617(TLS):21Dec84-1481
May, J.R. and M. Bird, eds. Religion in
Film.
P. Valenti, 500:Fall83-59
May, R. and J. Koster, eds. Levels of
Syntactic Representation.
R.D. Borsley, 297(JL):Mar83-285
D.J. Napoli, 350:Sep84-605
A. Verhagen, 204(FdL):Mar83-64
Mayeda, S. - see Śaṅkara
Mayer, A. One Who Came Back.
S. Neuman, 102(CanL):Winter82-118
Mayer, A. La Persistance de l'Ancien
Régime.
H. Cronel, 450(NRF):Oct83-145
Mayer, A.L. Clothing from the Hands That
Weave.
P. Bach, 614:Summer84-13
Mayer, D., ed. Henry Irving and "The
Bells."*
M. Vicinus, 637(VS):Winter83-225
Mayer, F. and P. Nečaev. Die Orthodoxe
Kirche in Russland.
G.L. Freeze, 550(RusR):Oct83-428
Mayer, G. and W. Schmitz - see Brentano, C.
Mayer, M. The Diplomats.
W.E. Schaufele, Jr., 441:19Feb84-16
Mayer, M. The Money Bazaars.
L. Caplan, 441:16Sep84-28
Mayer, R. The Grace of Shortstops.
M. Bell, 441:7Oct84-22
Mayer, R. Ontologische Aspekte der Nomin-
alsemantik.
F. Hundsnurscher, 685(ZDL):3/1983-381
Mayer, R. - see Lucan

Mayer, T.M. - see "Georg Büchner Jahrbuch 1, 1981"
Mayer, W. Nuzi-Studien, I.
  M.P. Maidman, 318(JAOS):Jan-Mar82-168
Mayer-Prokop, I. Die gravierten etruskischen Griffspiegel archaischen Stils.
  G. Lloyd-Morgan, 313:Vol73-234
Mayer-Tasch, P.C., ed. Im Gewitter der Geraden.
  I.M. Goessl, 221(GQ):May83-531
Mayerthaler, E. Unbetonter Vokalismus und Silbenstruktur im Romanischen.
  G.S. Nathan, 350:Jun84-451
Mayerthaler, W. Morphologische Natürlichkeit.*
  B. Comrie, 353:Vol20No9/10-666
Mayhew, E.D. and M. Myers, Jr. A Documentary History of American Interiors from the Colonial Era to 1915.
  W. Seale, 658:Spring83-95
Maynard, K. Lieutenant Lamb.
  S. Altinel, 617(TLS):7Dec84-1420
Mayne, S. The Impossible Promised Land.*
  M. Thorpe, 102(CanL):Winter82-170
  B. Whiteman, 198:Jan83-122
Mayo, A.P. - see under Porqueras Mayo, A.
Mayo, C. and N.M. Henley, eds. Gender and Nonverbal Behavior.
  A.G. Halberstadt, 567:Vol145No3/4-351
Mayr, E. The Growth of Biological Thought.*
  J. Bernstein, 442(NY):23Jan84-98
Mayrhofer, M. Zur Gestaltung des etymologischen Wörterbuches einer "Grosscorpus-Sprache."
  Y.M., 545(RPh):Nov82-324
de la Maza, F. Sor Juana Inés de la Cruz ante la historia.
  M.C. González, 457(NRFH):Tomo31núm2-332
Mazer, C.M. Shakespeare Refashioned.
  R. Berry, 150(DR):Autumn83-526
  R.A. Cave, 611(TN):Vol37No3-140
Mazumdar, D. The Urban Labor Market and Income Distribution.
  D.R. Snodgrass, 293(JASt):Nov82-227
Mazzaoui, M.F. The Italian Cotton Industry in the Later Middle Ages (1100-1600).
  S. Cohn, Jr., 589:Apr83-506
  M. Mallett, 551(RenQ):Autumn83-406
Mazzarella, M. Myt och verklighet.
  G. Orton, 562(Scan):Nov82-199
  M. Setterwall, 563(SS):Summer83-276
Mazzarella, M. and others, eds. Författare om författare.
  W.G. Jones, 562(Scan):May83-92
Mazzaro, J. The Figure of Dante.*
  T. Barolini, 551(RenQ):Spring83-75
  T.G. Bergin, 569(SR):Spring83-261
  R. Jacoff, 405(MP):Feb84-303
  J.A. Scott, 402(MLR):Jul83-724
Mazzaro, J. Postmodern American Poetry.*
  R. Kroetsch, 106:Summer83-219
M'Boukou, J-P.M. - see under Makouta M'Boukou, J-P.
Mead, W.R. An Historical Geography of Scandinavia.
  S.P. Oakley, 562(Scan):Nov82-191
Meades, J. Filthy English.
  J. Melmoth, 617(TLS):27Jul84-849
Meaney, A.L. Anglo-Saxon Amulets and Curing Stones.
  H.R.E. Davidson, 203:Vol194No1-131

Mearsheimer, J.J. Conventional Deterrence.
  M. Ignatieff, 617(TLS):1Jun84-603
Meckel, C. The Figure on the Boundary Line.
  D. Shapiro, 441:25Nov84-22
Medawar, P.B. and J.S. Aristotle to Zoos.*
  R. Dawkins, 617(TLS):9Mar84-254
  J. Weightman, 176:Dec84-53
Medcalf, S., ed. The Later Middle Ages.
  L. Ebin, 589:Apr83-509
de Medeiros, M-T. Jacques et Chroniqueurs.
  J. Dufournet, 554:Vol 103No2/3-406
Medhurst, K.N. The Church and Labour in Colombia.
  A. Angell, 617(TLS):12Oct84-1151
Medina, A.L. - see under Lorente Medina, A.
Medina, J.A.O. - see under Ortega y Medina, J.A.
Medina, J.T. Spanish Realism.*
  J.H. Hoddie, 552(REH):May83-317
de Medina, P. Svma de cosmographía. (J. Fernández Jiménez, ed)
  D. Finello, 552(REH):May83-307
  N.G. Round, 86(BHS):Jan83-63
Medish, V. The Soviet Union.*
  J. Cracraft, 550(RusR):Jul83-332
Medley, R. Drawn from the Life.*
  J. Darracott, 364:Nov83-104
  F. Spalding, 362:12Jan84-23
Medlicott, P. - see Palmer, T.
Medvedev, F.A. Rannyaya istoriya askiomi vibora.
  I. Grattan-Guinness, 556:Winter83/84-180
Medvedev, P.N. and M.M. Bakhtin. The Formal Method in Literary Scholarship.
  D. Carroll, 153:Summer83-65
Medvedev, R. All Stalin's Men.
  A. Brown, 617(TLS):23Mar84-296
  442(NY):16Apr84-160
Medvedev, Z.A. Andropov.*
  R.G. Suny, 385(MQR):Fall84-576
Medwall, H. The Plays of Henry Medwall.* (A.H. Nelson, ed)
  C. Belsey, 402(MLR):Jul83-672
  S. Carpenter, 541(RES):May83-208
Mee, C.L., Jr. The Marshall Plan.
  A.W. De Porte, 441:9Sep84-44
Meehan, R.L. The Atom and the Fault.
  M.L. Wald, 441:23Dec84-17
Meehan-Waters, B. Autocracy and Aristocracy.
  R.H. Warner, 550(RusR):Jan83-104
Meek, M. and J. Miller, eds. Changing English.
  R. Harris, 617(TLS):14Sep84-1031
Meek, M.R.D. The Sitting Ducks.
  T.J. Binyon, 617(TLS):20Jul84-801
Meeks, W.A. The First Urban Christians.*
  R.J. Rowland, Jr., 124:Jan-Feb84-189
van der Meer, L.B. Corpus Speculorum Etruscorum; The Netherlands.
  G. Lloyd-Morgan, 313:Vol73-233
Mehlman, J. Cataract.*
  P. Jimack, 208(FS):Oct83-461
Mehra, P. The North-Eastern Frontier. (Vol 2)
  R.J. Young, 318(JAOS):Oct-Dec82-677
Mehringer, A. Bedeutende Skulturen.
  N. Powell, 39:Jan83-66
Mehta, S.S. Productivity, Production Function and Technical Change.
  J. Das Gupta, 293(JASt):Nov82-105

Mehta, V. The Ledge Between the Streams.
    A. Embree, 441:6May84-14
    R.K. Narayan, 617(TLS):6Jul84-748
    E.S. Turner, 362:23Aug84-26
Mehta, V.R. Beyond Marxism.
    K.L. Deutsch, 321:Vol 17No2-165
Meid, W. Gallisch oder Lateinisch?
    K.H. Schmidt, 260(IF):Band88-335
Meier, A. Georg Büchner: "Woyzeck."
    W.B. Armstrong, 406:Spring83-84
Meier, C. Die Entstehung des Politischen
  bei den Griechen.*
    E. Vollrath, 687:Jan-Mar83-147
Meier, E., ed. Deutsche Kinder-Reime und
  Kinder-Spiele aus Schwaben.
    E. Moser-Rath, 196:Band24Heft1/2-161
Meier, F. Abū Saʻīd-i Abū l-Hayr (357-
  440/967-1049).
    H. Moayyad, 318(JAOS):Apr-Jun82-381
Meier, H. Lateinisch-romanische Etymol-
  ogien.
    H. Bursch, 72:Band220Heft1-194
Meiggs, R. Trees and Timber in the
  Ancient Mediterranean World.*
    L. Casson, 124:May-Jun84-321
Meigret, L. Traité touchant le commun
  usage de l'escriture françoise. (K.
  Cameron, ed)
    P. Rickard, 208(FS):Jan83-73
van der Meijden, A.G.H.A. - see under
  Anbeek van der Meijden, A.G.H.
Meiland, J.W. and M. Krausz, eds. Relativ-
  ism.
    483:Jan83-133
Meili, D. Schweizer Bauernhaus.
    I.B. Whyte, 617(TLS):7Dec84-1413
Meillassoux, C. Maidens, Meal and Money.
    C. Silver, 185:Jul84-721
Meillier, C. Callimaque et son temps.*
    F. Williams, 303(JoHS):Vol 103-178
Meinck, W. Warten auf den lautlosen Augen-
  blick.
    K. Richter, 654(WB):3/1982-131
Meinel, A. and M. Sunsets, Twilights and
  Evening Skies.
    O.M. Ashford, 617(TLS):17Feb84-174
Meininger, A-M. - see Stendhal
Meirion-Jones, G.I. The Vernacular Archi-
  tecture of Brittany.
    A. Clifton-Taylor, 46:May83-75
Meisel, M. Realizations.
    S. Wall, 617(TLS):10Aug84-883
Meisel, P. The Absent Father.*
    A. McLaurin, 447(N&Q):Apr82-189
Meissner, F-J. Wortgeschichtliche Unter-
  suchung im Umkreis von französisch
  "Enthousiasme" und "Genie."*
    H-L. Scheel, 72:Band219Heft2-450
Meister, B. Nineteenth-Century French
  Song.*
    412:May82-150
Mélançon, R. - see Huston, J.
Mélandri, P. La Politique extérieure des
  États-Unis de 1945 à nos jours.
    R.A. Day, 189(EA):Oct-Dec84-485
"Mélanges à la mémoire de Franco Simone."
    B. Beugnot, 475:Vol 10No18-397
"Mélanges de littérature du moyen âge au
  XXe siècle offerts à Mademoiselle Jeanne
  Lods, Professeur honoraire de littéra-
  ture médiévale à l'École Normale Supér-
  ieure de Jeunes Filles, par ses col-
                          [continued]

[continuing]
  lègues, ses élèves et ses amis." (Vol 1)
    B. Cazelles, 545(RPh):Nov82-294
Melanson, L. Zélika à Cochon Vert.
    M. Greenstein, 102(CanL):Autumn83-92
    R.R. St.-Onge, 207(FR):May84-912
Melchinger, S. Die Welt als Tragödie.*
  (Vols 1 and 2)
    D.J. Mastronarde, 122:Jan83-61
Meléndez Valdés, J. Obras en verso. (Vol
  1) (J.H.R. Polt and J. Demerson, eds)
    P. Ilie, 173(ECS):Spring84-387
Melendo Granados, T. Ontología de los
  opuestos.
    A. Reix, 542:Oct-Dec83-449
Melfi, M. A Queen is Holding a Mummified
  Cat.
    D. Daymond, 102(CanL):Summer83-140
Melikian-Chirvani, A.S. Islamic Metalwork
  from the Iranian World, 8th-18th Cen-
  turies.
    J.M. Rogers, 90:Nov83-706
Melillo, M. Le conguinzioni dei dialetti
  di Puglia nelle versioni della parabola
  del figliuol prodigo.
    M. Contini, 553(RLiR):Jan-Jun83-186
Melillo, M. L'articolo, l'aggettivo, il
  nome dei dialetti di Puglia nelle ver-
  sioni della Parabola del figliuol prod-
  igo.
    H. Lausberg, 547(RF):Band95Heft1/2-147
Melinkoff, E. What We Wore.
    I. Joshi, 614:Summer84-30
Mell, D.C., Jr. English Poetry, 1660-1800.
    566:Autumn83-63
Mellard, J.M. The Exploded Form.*
    D. Seed, 677(YES):Vol 13-345
    G.F. Waller, 106:Summer83-207
Meller, H. London Cemeteries.*
    L. Walker, 576:Dec83-393
Mellers, W. A Darker Shade of Pale.
    T. Russell, 617(TLS):7Dec84-1419
Mellinkoff, R. The Mark of Cain.*
    S.S. Jones, 292(JAF):Apr-Jun83-234
Mellor, A.K. English Romantic Irony.*
    J. Haney-Peritz, 591(SIR):Spring83-111
Mellor, B. The University of Hong Kong.
    E.F. Candlin, 324:Dec83-85
Mellor, D.H. The Possibility of Predic-
  tion.
    G. Lloyd, 518:Jan83-44
Mellor, D.H. Real Time.*
    M. Chandler, 486:Dec83-663
    W. Godfrey-Smith, 63:Mar83-109
    C.W. Kilmister, 84:Jun83-197
    G. Lloyd, 518:Jan83-44
    M. Macbeath, 479(PhQ):Jan83-92
Mellor, J.E. and T. Pearce. The Austin
  Friars, Leicester.
    K. Biddick, 589:Oct83-1073
Mellow, J.R. Nathaniel Hawthorne in His
  Times.*
    R.B. Hovey, 396(ModA):Spring83-215
Mellow, J.R. Invented Lives.
    M. Dickstein, 441:4Nov84-7
    442(NY):26Nov84-151
Melly, G. Scouse Mouse, or I Never Got
  Over It.
    F. Spiegl, 362:29Mar84-25
Melman, S. Profits Without Production.
    H. Goodman, 441:15Jan84-19
Melot, M. and others. Prints.
    D. Kunzle, 59:Mar83-125

Meltzer, M. and P.G. Holland - see Child,
L.M.
Melvern, L., N. Anning and D. Hebditch.
Techno-Bandits.
D. Burnham, 441:28Oct84-27
Melville, H. Moby-Dick; or, The Whale.*
(H. Hayford, H. Parker and G.T. Tanselle,
eds)
J. Espey, 445(NCF):Sep83-238
Melville, H. Typee, Omoo, Mardi. (G.T.
Tanselle, ed)
R. Milder, 183(ESQ):Vol29No2-99
W.H. Pritchard, 249(HudR):Summer83-352
Melville, J. Death of a Daimyo.
T.J. Binyon, 617(TLS):22Jun84-706
M. Laski, 362:19Jul84-27
Melville, J. The Ninth Netsuke.*
639(VQR):Summer83-93
"Memoria: Segundo Congreso Iberoamericano
de Periodismo Científico."
K.H. Cárdenas, 552(REH):Oct83-433
Mena, L.I. La función de la historia en
"Cien años de soledad."
D. Wise, 238:Mar83-141
Ménager, L-R. Recueil des actes des ducs
normands d'Italie (1046-1127). (Vol 1)
E.Z. Tabuteau, 589:Apr89-512
"Le Menagier de Paris."* (G.E. Brereton
and J.M. Ferrier, eds)
N. Mann, 447(N&Q):Dec82-535
Menander. The Cairo Codex of Menander (P.
Cair.J. 43227). (L. Koenen, H. Riad and
A.E. Selim, eds)
P.G.M. Brown, 123:Vol33No2-180
"Menander."* (Loeb, Vol 1) (W.G. Arnott,
ed and trans)
P.G.M. Brown, 123:Vol33No2-180
Menant, S. La Chute d'Icare.*
A. Goodden, 402(MLR):Jan83-185
J.P. Houston, 207(FR):Feb84-395
Ménard, P. Les fabliaux, contes à rire du
moyen âge.
G. Roques, 553(RLiR):Jan-Jun83-249
Menchi, S.S. - see Erasmus
Menchú, R. I...Rigoberta Menchú. (E.
Burgos-Debray, ed)
C. Henfrey, 617(TLS):31Aug84-966
Mencken, H.L. Letters from Baltimore.
(P.E. Cleator, ed)
G. Monteiro, 27(AL):May83-267
Mencken, H.L. Letters of H.L. Mencken.
(G.J. Forgue, ed)
L. Willson, 569(SR):Summer83-490
Mendelsohn, E. The Jews of East Central
Europe Between the World Wars.
M. Friedberg, 129:Jun84-74
Mendelsohn, E. and Y. Elkana, eds. Sci-
ences and Cultures.
M. Heidelberger, 84:Dec83-406
Mendelsohn, L. Paragoni.
E. Cropper, 551(RenQ):Winter83-598
Mendelson, D. Metaphor in Babel's Short
Stories.
A.R. Durkin, 395(MFS):Summer83-311
M. Ehre, 574(SEEJ):Fall83-389
Mendelson, E. Early Auden.*
S. Corey, 219(GaR):Summer83-442
Mendelson, L. Robert Breer.
M. Keller, 127:Fall83-284
Mendelssohn, M. Gesammelte Schriften.
(Vol 6, Pt 1 ed by A. Altmann; Vol 6,
Pt 2 ed by E.J. Engel)
S.S. Schwarzschild, 319:Jan84-124

Mendonsa, E.L. The Politics of Divination.
D. Parkin, 617(TLS):2Mar84-230
Menefee, S.P. Wives For Sale.
M.J. Lovelace, 292(JAF):Jul-Sep83-361
R. Palmer, 203:Vol194No1-126
Meneghini, G.B., with R. Allegri. My Wife
Maria Callas.*
E. Forbes, 415:Aug83-486
Menegoni, F. Moralità e morale in Hegel.
H. Faes, 542:Oct-Dec83-479
Menéndez Pidal, R. Reliquias de la poesía
épica española.* (Vol 1) (2nd ed) (D.
Catalán, ed)
H.R. Stone, 589:Jul83-847
Ménétra, J-L. Journal de ma vie. (D.
Roche, ed)
R. Darnton, 453(NYRB):28Jun84-32
Menges, M. Abstrakte Welt und Eigen-
schaftslosigkeit.
M. Knapp, 221(GQ):Nov83-689
Menke, H., ed. Von Reinicken Fuchs, Frank-
furt 1544. Reineke Fuchs am Ende des
philosophischen Jahrhunderts.
T.W. Best, 221(GQ):Mar83-303
D. Blamires, 402(MLR):Oct83-961
Menke, K-H. Vernunft und Offenbarung nach
Antonio Rosmini.
K. Kienzler, 687:Apr-Jun83-335
Mennemeier, F.N. Bertolt Brechts Lyrik.
R. Pohl, 680(ZDP):Band102Heft4-631
Mennemeier, F.N. and F. Trapp. Deutsche
Exildramatik 1933-1950.
T.S. Hansen, 221(GQ):Mar83-343
Mensch, J.R. The Question of Being in
Husserl's Logical Investigations.*
L. O'Dwyer, 63:Sep83-313
Mentrup, W., ed. Konzepte zur Lexiko-
graphie.*
D. Herberg, 685(ZDL):2/1983-239
Mény, J. Jean Giono et la cinéma.
J.J. Michalczyk, 207(FR):Apr84-744
Mény, J. - see Giono, J.
Menzel, P. Medical Costs, Moral Choices.
J.C., 185:Jul84-743
Menzies, H. Computers on the Job.
E. Zureik, 529(QQ):Autumn83-779
Menzies, H. Women and the Chip.
L. Marcil-Lacoste, 529(QQ):Spring83-
275
Mercanton, J. Le siècle des grandes
ombres.
Y. Coirault, 535(RHL):Sep/Dec83-928
P. Ronzeaud, 475:Vol 10No18-370
Merchant, W.M. R.S. Thomas.
A. Motion, 541(RES):Feb83-109
Mercier, A. L'Habitation Saint-Ybars ou
maîtres et esclaves en Louisiane (Récit
social). (R. Hamel, ed)
A. Nabarra, 207(FR):Mar84-595
Mercier, L-S. Parallèle de Paris et de
Londres. (C. Bruneteau and B. Cotteret,
eds)
J. Pappas, 207(FR):Mar84-555
Mercier-Josa, S. Pour lire Hegel et Marx.
M. Vadée, 192(EP):Jan-Mar83-105
Meredith, G. Selected Poems. (K. Hanley,
ed)
S. Rae, 617(TLS):6Apr84-383
Meriç, R. Metropolis in Ionien.
S. Mitchell, 123:Vol33No2-360

Merin, J., with E.B. Burdick. International Directory of Theatre, Dance and Folklore Festivals.*
J. Fowler, 611(TN):Vol37No1-40
Merino, C.G. - see under Garcia Merino, C.
Meriwether, J.B. and M. Millgate, eds. Lion in the Garden.*
D. Hewitt, 447(N&Q):Apr82-191
Merker, N. Die Aufklärung in Deutschland.
W. Albrecht, 654(WB):11/1983-2018
Merklinger, E.S. Indian Islamic Architecture: The Deccan 1347-1686.
C.B. Asher, 293(JASt):Feb83-439
Merl, S. Der Agrarmarkt und die Neue Ökonomische Politik.
M. McCauley, 575(SEER):Oct83-628
Merle, G. Lytton Strachey (1880-1932).
L. Edel, 189(EA):Oct-Dec83-487
Merrell, F. Semiotic Foundations.
D.E. Wellbery, 494:Vol4No2-369
Merrett, R.J. Daniel Defoe's Moral and Rhetorical Ideas.*
H. Rinehart, 178:Jun83-229
P. Rogers, 677(YES):Vol 13-321
Merrifield, R. London: City of the Romans.
B.W. Cunliffe, 617(TLS):13Jan84-31
Merrill, J. The Changing Light at Sandover.*
D. Flower, 249(HudR):Winter83/84-724
D. St. John, 42(AR):Spring83-231
V. Shetley, 491:Nov83-101
Merrill, J. From the First Nine.*
D. Flower, 249(HudR):Winter83/84-731
D. St. John, 42(AR):Spring83-231
V. Shetley, 491:Nov83-101
H. Vendler, 442(NY):21May84-124
639(VQR):Autumn83-135
Merrill, T.F. The Poetry of Charles Olson.
D. Pope, 27(AL):Oct83-479
"The Merry-Thought: or, The Class-Window and Bog-House Miscellany (1731)."
P-G.B., 189(EA):Jul-Sep84-362
566:Autumn83-67
Mersereau, J. Russian Romantic Fiction.
R. Freeborn, 617(TLS):8Jun84-635
Merwin, W.S. Finding the Islands.
639(VQR):Spring83-62
Merwin, W.S. Opening the Hand.*
M. Garcia-Simms, 584(SWR):Autumn83-400
Merwin, W.S. Unframed Originals.*
S.P. Edelman, 584(SWR):Winter83-92
W. Mitgutsch, 651(WHR):Spring83-91
Merwin, W.S. and J.M. Masson - see "Sanskrit Love Poetry"
Meryman, R. Broken Promises, Mended Dreams.
C. Kitman, 441:9Sep84-14
Meserve, W.J. American Drama to 1900.
P. Drew, 610:Spring83-71
Meskill, J. Academies in Ming China.
E.L. Farmer, 293(JASt):May83-631
Meskill, J.M. A Chinese Pioneer Family.
R.P. Weller, 318(JAOS):Jul-Sep82-576
Mesnard, J. - see Madame de Lafayette
Messenger, C. "Bomber" Harris and the Strategic Bombing Offensive, 1939-1945.
B. Bond, 617(TLS):12Oct84-1164
Messenger, C.F. Sport and the Spirit of Play in American Fiction.*
A. Guttmann, 587(SAF):Autumn83-263
M. Oriard, 587(SAF):Spring83-127

Messent, P. and T. Paulin - see James, H.
Messer Leon, J. The Book of the Honeycomb's Flow. (I. Rabinowitz, ed and trans)
G.A. Kennedy, 539:May84-154
Messerli, D., ed. Contemporary American Fiction.
B. Morton, 617(TLS):30Nov84-1391
Messerli, D. River to Rivet.
M. Perloff, 29:May/Jun84-15
Metcalf, B.D. Islamic Revival in British India.
W.R. Roff, 293(JASt):May83-703
Metcalf, J. Kicking against the Pricks.
B. Cameron, 627(UTQ):Summer83-482
Metcalf, J., ed. Second Impressions.*
P. Klovan, 102(CanL):Winter82-136
D.O. Spettigue, 529(QQ):Autumn83-878
Metcalf, J., ed. Third Impressions.
M.S. Dyment, 526:Spring83-72
D. Watmough, 102(CanL):Summer83-96
Metcalf, J. and L. Rooke, eds. 81: Best Canadian Stories.*
P. Klovan, 102(CanL):Winter82-136
D.O. Spettigue, 529(QQ):Autumn83-878
Metcalf, T.R. Land, Landlords, and the British Raj.*
R. Rocher, 318(JAOS):Jan-Mar82-239
Metcalf, W.E. The Cistophori of Hadrian.
I. Carradice, 313:Vol73-218
Métellus, J. Une Eau-forte.
R. Buss, 617(TLS):3Feb84-117
Methuen-Campbell, J. Chopin Playing from the Composer to the Present Day.
R.L.J., 412:Feb82-63
Metuh, E.I. God and Man in African Religion.
J.W. Burton, 69:Vol53No2-83
Metz, C. Psychoanalysis and Cinema.
J.P., 617(TLS):23Mar84-319
E. and E. Wright, 494:Vol4No2-360
Metzger, B.A. - see "The Reader's Digest Bible"
Metzger, B.M. Manuscripts of the Greek Bible.
J.N. Birdsall, 123:Vol133No2-302
Metzger, T. and M. Jewish Life in the Middle Ages.
D. Goldstein, 617(TLS):13Apr84-415
L. Wieseltier, 441:15Jan84-9
Metzing, D., ed. Frame Conceptions and Text Understanding.
U.L. Figge, 307:Oct82-116
Meunier, C. and L. Saia. Appelez-moi Stéphane.
M. Allain, 207(FR):Dec83-271
R. Usmiani, 102(CanL):Autumn83-82
Meunier, C. and L. Saia. Les Voisins.
T.H. Brown, 207(FR):May84-913
R. Usmiani, 102(CanL):Autumn83-82
Mewe, W. Pseudomagia. (J.C. Coldewey and B.P. Copenhaver, eds and trans)
J. Feather, 447(N&Q):Feb82-69
Mews, S. Carl Zuckmayer.
J. Hein, 133:Band16Heft1-85
Mewshaw, M. Year of the Gun.
C. Verderese, 441:20May84-23
442(NY):30Jul84-87
Meyer, B. The Tongues Between Us.
R. Dubanski, 102(CanL):Spring83-117
Meyer, D. Victoria Ocampo.*
P.G. Earle, 240(HR):Summer83-359

Meyer, E.H. Early English Chamber Music
from the Middle Ages to Purcell. (2nd
ed rev by E.H. Meyer and D. Poulton)
  A. Ashbee, 410(M&L):Jan/Apr83-99
Meyer, H., ed. Bibliographie der Buch-
und Bibliotheksgeschichte. (Vol 1)
  J.L. Flood, 354:Dec83-435
Meyer, H. Medeia und die Peliaden.
  S. Woodford, 303(JoHS):Vol 103-225
Meyer, P.H.G. Die Strophenfolge und ihre
Gesetzmässigkeiten im Minnelied Walthers
von der Vogelweide.
  G. Lohse, 684(ZDA):Band112Heft1-22
Meyer, M. Logique, langage et argumenta-
tion.
  L. Apostel, 540(RIPh):Vol37fasc1/2-221
Meyer, P. The Child and the State.
  A. Brown, 617(TLS):1Jun84-621
Meyer, P. Kunst und Religion der Lobi.
  C.D. Roy, 2(AfrA):Feb83-23
Meyers, J. The Enemy.*
  R. Currie, 541(RES):Feb83-100
  M. Goldstein, 569(SR):Winter83-iv
  295(JML):Nov83-526
Meyers, J. D.H. Lawrence and the Experi-
ence of Italy.
  D.R. Schwarz, 395(MFS):Winter83-782
  J. Voelker, 573(SSF):Spring-Summer83-
  147
  295(JML):Nov83-521
Meyers, J. - see Lewis, W.
Meyers, W. The Image-Makers.
  S. Fox, 441:23Dec84-11
Meynell, H. Freud, Marx and Morals.*
  M. Hughes, 483:Apr83-273
  J.N. Loughran, 258:Mar83-101
Meynell, H.A. The Intelligible Universe.*
  P. Sherry, 483:Jan83-129
Mezei, A. Magyar Kocka.
  G. Mikes, 617(TLS):12Oct84-1154
Mezger, W. Hofnarren im Mittelalter.
  E. Moser-Rath, 196:Band24Heft1/2-162
de Mézières, P. - see under Philippe de
Mézières
Mezzatesta, M.P. Henri Matisse, Sculptor/
Painter.
  T. Hilton, 617(TLS):23Nov84-1344
Micewski, A. Cardinal Wyszynski.
  Z. Nagorski, 441:23Dec84-5
Micha, A. - see "Lancelot, roman en prose
du XIIIe siècle"
Micha, A. - see Robert de Boron
Michael, C.A. Ho kōmikos logos toy Aris-
tophanoys.
  R.G. Ussher, 303(JoHS):Vol 103-168
Michael, F. Rule by Incarnation.
  G.W. Houston, 293(JASt):Aug83-932
Michael, P. The Academy Awards.
  M. Buckley, 200:Jun/Jul83-380
Michaelis-Jena, R. Heritage of the
Kaiser's Children.
  N. Roberts, 617(TLS):6Jan84-9
Michaud, Y. Hume et la fin de la philos-
ophie.
  P. Engel, 98:Dec83-960
Michaux, H. Chemins cherchés, chemins
perdus, transgressions.
  M. Bishop, 207(FR):Dec83-272
  J-M. Maulpoix, 98:May83-448
Michaux, H. Les Commencements.
  J. Laurans, 450(NRF):Oct83-114
Michaux, J.P., ed. George Gissing.*
  C. Cook, 447(N&Q):Oct82-464

Michel, A. La parole et la beauté (rhé-
torique et esthétique dans la tradition
occidentale).
  P. Somville, 542:Jan-Mar83-90
Michel, M., ed. Pouvoir et vérité.*
  A. Reix, 192(EP):Jan-Mar83-108
Michel, O. and others. Sebastiano Conca
(1680-1764).
  E.P. Bowron, 90:Apr83-231
Michel, P. Les Barbares, 1789-1848.
  B.T. Cooper, 207(FR):Dec83-287
Michel, P. Un mythe romantique.
  J. Gaulmier, 535(RHL):May/Jun83-475
Michelangelo. Il carteggio di Michel-
angelo. (Vol 4) (G. Poggi, with P.
Barocchi and R. Ristori, eds)
  F. Hartt, 551(RenQ):Summer83-248
Michelet, J. Mother Death. (E.K. Kaplan,
ed)
  E. Weber, 617(TLS):28Sep84-1072
Michell, G. Brick Temples of Bengal.
  A. Topsfield, 617(TLS):14Sep84-1029
Michelmore, D.J.H., ed. The Fountains
Abbey Lease Book.
  C.H. Berman, 589:Oct83-1074
Michels, V. Mittelhochdeutsch Grammatik.*
  (5th ed) (H. Stopp, ed)
  J. Udolph, 260(IF):Band88-354
Michelsen, P. Der Bruch mit der Vater-
Welt.
  H. Moenkemeyer, 406:Summer83-209
  N. Oellers, 52:Band17Heft2-215
Michelson, K., ed. Three Stories in
Oneida.
  M. Mithun, 269(IJAL):Jan83-109
Michie, J. New and Selected Poems.*
  C. Boyle, 364:Dec83/Jan84-120
  J. Mole, 176:Mar84-51
Mickel, E.J. Eugène Fromentin.
  B. Wright, 535(RHL):Mar/Apr83-298
"Microelectronics."
  E. Zureik, 529(QQ):Autumn83-779
Middlekauff, R. The Glorious Cause.
  C. Bridenbaugh, 432(NEQ):Mar83-132
  D. Higginbotham, 656(WMQ):Jul83-455
  P.D.G. Thomas, 83:Autumn83-236
Middleton, C. The Pursuit of the King-
fisher.
  M. Hulse, 176:Mar84-35
  G. Steiner, 617(TLS):9Mar84-239
Middleton, C. III Poems.
  D. Dunn, 364:Aug/Sep83-109
  G. Steiner, 617(TLS):9Mar84-239
Middleton, R., ed. The Beaux-Arts and
Nineteenth-Century French Architecture.*
  B. Scott, 39:Dec83-530
  D.T. Stephens, 207(FR):Dec83-285
Middleton, R. and D. Horn - see "Popular
Music"
Middleton, S. The Daysman.
  J. Mellors, 362:1Mar84-28
  J.K.L. Walker, 617(TLS):2Mar84-216
Midgley, D.R. Arnold Zweig.
  P.F. Veit, 406:Winter83-454
Midgley, M. Animals and Why They Matter.
  M. Furness, 617(TLS):1Jun84-618
Midgley, M. Beast and Man.
  J. Agassi, 488:Jun83-235
Midgley, M. Heart and Mind.*
  D. Collinson, 479(PhQ):Oct83-410
Midgley, M. Wickedness.
  A.J. Ayer, 362:13Sep84-25
  A.C. Danto, 617(TLS):21Dec84-1472

Midgley, M. and J. Hughes. Women's Choices.
S.M. Gilbert, 617(TLS):8Jun84-645
"Midwest Studies in Philosophy V."
J. Bacon, 449:Nov83-663
M. Devitt, 449:Nov83-669
Mieder, W. Grimms Märchen — modern.*
Deutsche Sprichwörter und Redensarten.*
Deutsche Volkslieder.
H.F. Taylor, 399(MLJ):Spring83-77
Mieder, W. International Proverb Scholarship.
F.J. Oinas, 574(SEEJ):Winter83-504
Mieder, W. and A. Dundes, eds. The Wisdom of Many.
S.L. Arora, 650(WF):Jul83-231
W.K. McNeil, 292(JAF):Jul-Sep83-359
Mies, M. Indian Women and Patriarchy.
A. Bandarage, 293(JASt):May83-694
Mies, M. The Lace Makers of Narsapur.
R. Hamilton, 614:Summer84-22
Miethe, T.L., comp. Augustinian Bibliography, 1970-1980.
R.J. O'Connell, 258:Dec83-451
Miething, C. Marivaux.
W.D. Howarth, 208(FS):Jul83-339
Migliorini, B. and T.G. Griffith. The Italian Language.
G. Lepschy, 617(TLS):11May84-527
Mignone, M.B. Anormalità e angoscia nella narrativa di Dino Buzzati.
G.O. de Stefanis, 276:Spring83-84
Mignot, C. Architecture of the Nineteenth Century in Europe.
P. Goldberger, 441:2Dec84-18
Mikalson, J.D. Athenian Popular Religion.
R. Buxton, 617(TLS):2Mar84-209
Mikes, G. Arthur Koestler.
R. Dinnage, 617(TLS):2Mar84-212
H. Kramer, 441:7Oct84-11
G. Steiner, 442(NY):11Jun84-121
Mikhail, E.H., ed. Brendan Behan: Interviews and Recollections.*
R. Imhof, 272(IUR):Autumn83-261
Mikhanovsky, V. The Doubles.
J.W. Connolly, 399(MLJ):Autumn83-305
Mikoś, M.J. Early Maps of Poland (1508-1772) in the American Geographical Society Collection.
J. Krzyżanowska, 497(PolR):Vol28No1-90
Milam, L.W. The Cripple Liberation Front Marching Band Blues.
W. Kendrick, 441:6May84-21
Milanini, C. - see Saba, U.
Milbury-Steen, S.L. European and African Stereotypes in Twentieth-Century Fiction.*
G. Moore, 447(N&Q):Aug82-382
Milde, W., ed. Gesamtverzeichnis der Lessing-Handschriften. (Vol 1)
H.B. Nisbet, 83:Autumn83-278
Mileck, J. Hermann Hesse.
H. Stegemann, 529(QQ):Spring83-227
Mileham, J.W. The Conspiracy Novel.
J.S. Allen, 446(NCFS):Fall-Winter83/84-223
Miles, A. and G. Finn, eds. Feminism in Canada.
B. Godard, 99:Jul83-30
Miles, G.B. Virgil's "Georgics."
L.M. Styler, 447(N&Q):Dec82-568
Miles, M.A. Beyond Monetarism.
P. Passell, 441:16Sep84-19

Miles, P. and H. Pitcher - see Chekhov, A.
Mileur, J-P. Vision and Revision.
F. McConnell, 661(WC):Summer83-133
P. Magnuson, 401(MLQ):Mar83-99
A.K. Mellor, 301(JEGP):Jul83-453
Milhous, J. and R.D. Hume - see Coke, T.
Miliband, R. Capitalist Democracy in Britain.*
J.K., 185:Apr84-564
Mill, J.S. The Collected Works of John Stuart Mill.* (Vol 1: Autobiography and Literary Essays) (J.M. Robson and J. Stillinger, eds)
K. Britton, 483:Apr83-263
L. Hartveit, 179(ES):Jun83-286
S. Neuman, 178:Dec83-507
Mill, J.S. The Collected Works of John Stuart Mill. (Vol 6: Essays on England, Ireland, and the Empire) (J.M. Robson, ed)
K. Britton, 483:Apr83-263
Millar, F. and E. Segal, eds. Caesar Augustus.
T.P. Wiseman, 617(TLS):24Aug84-950
Millard, P. - see North, R.
Miller, A. The American Clock.
D. Devlin, 157:Winter83-38
Miller, A. and I. Morath. "Salesman" in Beijing.
P-L. Adams, 61:Jun84-124
J. Hiley, 362:19Jul84-26
N. Houghton, 441:24Jun84-37
Miller, A.I. Albert Einstein's Special Theory of Relativity.
G.J. Whitrow, 84:Mar83-78
Miller, B.S. - see Kramrisch, S.
Miller, C. Who's Really Who.
A. Forbes, 617(TLS):6Jan84-7
Miller, C.H. Auden.*
42(AR):Summer83-374
Miller, D. Philosophy and Ideology in Hume's Political Thought.*
A. Baier, 482(PhR):Apr83-241
R. Hardin, 185:Apr84-534
F.J. McLynn, 83:Spring83-87
Miller, D. and L. Siedentop, eds. The Nature of Political Theory.*
J.G. Cottingham, 518:Oct83-252
Miller, D.A. Narrative and Its Discontents.*
F. Bolton, 189(EA):Apr-Sep83-324
E.B. Holtsmark, 149(CLS):Winter83-466
L. Lerner, 131(CL):Winter83-82
G. Levine, 637(VS):Spring83-354
J. van Luxemburg, 204(FdL):Mar83-76
P. Swinden, 148:Spring83-78
Miller, D.G. Homer and the Ionian Epic Tradition.
B.D. Joseph, 350:Sep84-657
Miller, D.G. Improvisation, Typology, Culture, and "The New Orthodoxy."
J.P. Holoka, 124:Sep-Oct83-56
Miller, D.M. Frank Herbert.
W.E. Meyers, 561(SFS):Mar83-106
Miller, E. Drudgerie Divine.
J.M. Patrick, 568(SCN):Spring/Summer83-5
H. Wilcox, 447(N&Q):Apr82-171
Miller, E. Textiles.
G. Brown, 614:Fall84-25
Miller, H. From Your Capricorn Friend.
E. Jong, 441:1Apr84-23

Miller, H. Opus Pistorum.
R. Hewison, 617(TLS):4May84-494
Miller, H. The Time of the Assassins.
P. Redgrove, 617(TLS):50ct84-1124
Miller, H.B. and W.H. Williams, eds.
Ethics and Animals.
T.D., 185:Jul84-745
Miller, I. Seesaw.
639(VQR):Summer83-92
Miller, J. Rousseau.
K.M. Baker, 441:16Sep84-9
Miller, J. These Are The Women.
C. Hlus, 137:Sep83-18
Miller, J. and D. Pelham. The Facts of
Life.
E. Le Shan, 441:18Nov84-28
Miller, J.C., ed. Poe's Helen Remembers.*
A.M. Emery, 506(PSt):Dec83-296
Miller, J.H. Fiction and Repetition.*
H. Charney, 363(LitR):Winter84-279
M. Magalaner, 395(MFS):Summer83-261
R. Scholes, 445(NCF):Jun83-97
J.V. Smyth, 494:Vol4No4-783
Miller, J.P. The Skook.
W. Ferguson, 441:30Sep84-28
Miller, J.W. The Paradox of Cause and
Other Essays. The Definition of the
Thing. The Philosophy of History. The
Midworld of Symbols and Functioning
Objects. In Defense of the Psycholog-
ical.
T. Friend, 676(YR):Spring84-446
Miller, K., ed. New Stories 8.
J. Mellors, 362:19Jan84-26
Miller, K.E. Principles of Singing.
J. Bridges, 498:Vol9No2-90
Miller, M. Gardening in Small Places.
L. Yang, 441:3Jun84-9
Miller, M. Jazz in Canada.
J. Doyle, 102(CanL):Autumn83-106
P. Stevens, 99:May83-34
Miller, M. The Saints of Gwynedd.
J. Rowland, 112:Vol 15-176
Miller, N.K. The Heroine's Text.*
566:Spring84-168
Miller, P.B. - see von Kleist, H.
Miller, P.J. Amy, Wendy and Beth.
J.W. Lindfors, 355(LSoc):Dec83-551
C.E. Snow, 355(LSoc):Sep83-381
Miller, P.M. Parlons de tout.
R. Danner, 207(FR):Dec83-262
L. Vines, 399(MLJ):Autumn83-288
Miller, R. Snail.
A. Codrescu, 441:25Nov84-26
Miller, R.A. Japan's Modern Myth.*
L. Allen, 407(MN):Autumn83-333
Miller, R.A. Origins of the Japanese Lan-
guage.*
J. Street, 318(JAOS):Apr-Jun82-431
Miller, R.B., ed. Black American Litera-
ture and Humanism.*
M.F., 189(EA):Apr-Jun84-237
H. Spillers, 301(JEGP):Oct83-583
Miller, R.B. City and Hinterland.
J.N. Ingham, 106:Summer83-175
Miller, R.F. Dostoevsky and "The Idiot."*
R. Freeborn, 575(SEER):Apr83-266
W.J. Leatherbarrow, 402(MLR):Jan83-250
Miller, R.H. - see Harington, J.
Miller, R.K. Mark Twain.
H. Beaver, 617(TLS):15Jun84-657
L. Leary, 578:Spring84-107

Miller, R.K. Oscar Wilde.
G.A. Cevasco, 397(MD):Mar83-115
R.J. Voorhees, 395(MFS):Summer83-271
Miller, S. Excellence and Equity.
C.E. Finn, Jr., 129:Sep84-77
Miller, S. and J. Cull. Quilted Collage
Jackets and Vests.
M. Cowan, 614:Winter84-21
Miller, S.M. and D. Tomaskovic-Devey. Re-
capitalizing America.
R.J. Margolis, 441:12Feb84-21
Miller, T. Standing By.
N. Callendar, 441:9Sep84-40
Miller, T.L. Bohemians and Critics.
P.A. Davis, 615(TJ):May83-275
R. Jackson, 610:Spring83-68
Miller, W.M., Jr. A Canticle for Leibo-
witz.
N. Perrin, 135:Mar83-116
Millett, B., ed. Hali Meidhad.
F. Chevillet, 189(EA):Jul-Sep84-318
Millett, R. The Vultures and the Phoenix.
J. Meyers, 290(JAAC):Summer84-465
Millgate, M. Thomas Hardy.*
J.B. Bullen, 177(ELT):Vol26No2-133
K. Flint, 175:Spring83-81
E. Guiliano, 219(GaR):Summer83-456
J. Halperin, 395(MFS):Summer83-274
M. Jones, 344:Summer84-103
R.S. Kennedy, 295(JML):Nov83-490
G.G. Wickens, 627(UTQ):Summer83-429
K. Wilson, 529(QQ):Winter83-1148
G. Wing, 49:Jan83-92
Milligan, D. Reasoning and the Explana-
tion of Actions.*
J. Bishop, 63:Mar83-114
C. Macdonald, 393(Mind):Oct83-624
Millones, L. and Hiroyasu Tomoeda, eds.
El Hombre y Su Ambiente en los Andes
Centrales.
F.L. Phelps, 37:Mar-Apr83-61
Mills, A.D. The Place-Names of Dorset.*
(Pt 2)
B. Cottle, 541(RES):Aug83-316
Mills, E.S. and B-N. Song. Urbanization
and Urban Problems.
K. Moskowitz, 293(JASt):Nov82-63
D.I. Steinberg, 293(JASt):Nov82-91
Mills, H. Mailer.*
T. Ludington, 27(AL):Dec83-662
295(JML):Nov83-532
639(VQR):Spring83-48
Mills, J. Lizard in the Grass.*
K. Fraser, 168(ECW):Summer83-138
Milne, C. The Enchanted Places.
L.D., 617(TLS):24Feb84-203
Milne, J. London Fields.*
R. Hogan, 441:5Aug84-18
Milne, R.S. and D. Mauzy. Politics and
Government in Malaysia.
J. Funston, 293(JASt):Feb83-459
Milner, A. John Milton and the English
Revolution.*
A. Burnett, 447(N&Q):Oct82-441
H. Richmond, 125:Winter83-198
Milner, C.A., 2d. With Good Intentions.
W. Bloodworth, 649(WAL):Feb84-361
Milner, J. Vladimir Tatlin and the Rus-
sian Avant-Garde.
J.E. Bowlt, 453(NYRB):16Feb84-27
P. Vergo, 617(TLS):13Jan84-41

Milner, J.C. De la Syntaxe à l'interprétation.*
    N.L. Corbett, 545(RPh):Feb83-443
Milner, M. - see Bertrand, A.
Milo, R.D. Immorality.
    A.C. Danto, 617(TLS):21Dec84-1472
Miloslavskij, I.G. Morfologičeskie kategorii sovremennogo russkogo jazyka.
    W. Lehfeldt, 559:Vol7No3-277
Milosz, C. The Land of Ulro.
    N. Davies, 441:2Sep84-1
    442(NY):17Sep84-142
Miłosz, C., ed. Pieśń niepodległa/The Invincible Song.
    R. Grol-Prokopczyk, 497(PolR):Vol28No1-86
Milosz, C., ed. Postwar Polish Poetry. (new ed)
    H.J.F. de Aguilar, 472:Fall/Winter83 Spring/Summer84-127
Milosz, C. The Separate Notebooks.
    H.J.F. de Aguilar, 472:Fall/Winter83 Spring/Summer84-127
    D.J. Enright, 617(TLS):13Jul84-778
    H. Vendler, 442(NY):19Mar84-138
Milosz, C. Visions from San Francisco Bay. The Seizure of Power.
    H.J.F. de Aguilar, 472:Fall/Winter83 Spring/Summer84-127
    J-A. Mort, 287:Apr83-25
Milosz, C. The Witness of Poetry.*
    H.J.F. de Aguilar, 472:Fall/Winter83 Spring/Summer84-127
    J. Cary, 469:Vol9No4-104
    G. Waller, 152(UDQ):Autumn83-123
Milroy, J. Regional Accents of English: Belfast.
    D. Britton and H.J. Giegerich, 361:Feb/Mar83-292
Milsark, G.L. Existential Sentences in English.
    L.E. Breivik, 361:Dec83-353
Milton, J. The Complete Poems.* (B.A. Wright, ed)
    T.N. Corns, 677(YES):Vol 13-316
Milton, J. Complete Prose Works of John Milton.* (rev) (Vol 7) (R.W. Ayers, ed)
    A. Burnett, 447(N&Q):Apr82-175
    G. Campbell, 506(PSt):May83-75
    M. Fixler, 541(RES):Aug83-364
Milton, J. John Milton: "Paradise Lost." (Bks 1 and 2 ed by J. Broadbent, Bks 3 and 4 ed by L. Potter and J. Broadbent, Bks 9 and 10 ed by J.M. Evans, Bks 11 and 12 ed by M. Hollington, with L. Wilkinson)
    C. Schaar, 179(ES):Feb83-83
Milton, N.D. The China Option.*
    639(VQR):Spring83-57
"Milton Studies."* (Vol 12) "Milton Studies." (Vol 13) (J.D. Simmonds, ed of both) "Milton Studies Index, I-XII." (B.E. Luey, ed)
    W.A. McQueen, 577(SHR):Winter83-78
"Milton Studies." (Vol 15) (J.D. Simmonds, ed)
    D.S. Berkeley, 568(SCN):Fall83-36
"Milton Studies." (Vol 16) (J.D. Simmonds, ed)
    L.S. Young, 568(SCN):Fall83-40
    639(VQR):Autumn83-116

Milward, A.S. The Reconstruction of Western Europe 1945-51.
    S. Strange, 617(TLS):23Nov84-1347
Milward, P. Religious Controversies of the Elizabethan Age. Religious Controversies of the Jacobean Age.
    T.A.B., 179(ES):Dec83-502
    N. Tyacke, 447(N&Q):Dec82-544
Minahan, J. The Great Diamond Robbery.
    N. Callendar, 441:26Feb84-27
Minasian, S.M., K.C. Balcomb 3d and L. Foster. The World's Whales.
    G. Plimpton, 441:2Dec84-14
Minc, A. L'après-crise est commencé.
    A.D. Ketchum, 207(FR):May84-894
    M.F. Meurice, 450(NRF):Mar83-134
"The Mind and Art of C.P. Cavafy."
    R. Beaton, 617(TLS):24Aug84-938
Minden, M.R. Arno Schmidt.*
    G.P. Knapp, 222(GR):Fall83-161
    S. Mandel, 395(MFS):Summer83-299
Minear, P.S. Matthew.
    G.N. Stanton, 617(TLS):19Oct84-1199
Miner, E., ed. Literary Uses of Typology from the Late Middle Ages to the Present.
    M. Stocker, 677(YES):Vol 13-366
Miner, E. and H. Odagiri, eds and trans. The Monkey's Straw Raincoat and Other Poetry of the Bashō School.*
    L.M. Zolbrod, 293(JASt):Aug83-961
Miner, V. Blood Sisters.
    M.R. Farwell, 448:Vol21No1-167
Miner, V. Winter's Edge.
    M.K. Benet, 617(TLS):27Jul84-848
    M. Wandor, 362:12Jul84-28
Minetti, F.F. - see Monte Andrea da Fiorenza
Ming, K. - see under Kao Ming
Mingay, G.F., ed. The Victorian Countryside.
    J.F.C. Harrison, 637(VS):Summer83-444
Minh-ha, T.T. Un Art sans oeuvre ou l'anonymat dans les arts contemporains.
    M.W. Blades, 207(FR):Feb84-409
    F.L. Coppay, 210(FrF):May83-189
Minhinnick, R. Life Sentences.
    A. Stevenson, 617(TLS):2Mar84-226
"Des Minnesangs Frühling."* (Pt 3) (H. Moser and H. Tervooren, eds)
    O. Sayce, 402(MLR):Jul83-740
Minnis, A.J. Chaucer and Pagan Antiquity.
    B. O'Donoghue, 617(TLS):18May84-555
Minnis, A.J. Medieval Theory of Authorship.
    H. Cooper, 617(TLS):6Jul84-759
Minogue, V. Nathalie Sarraute and the War of the Words.*
    B.L. Knapp, 405(MP):Feb84-326
Minta, S. Petrarch and Petrarchism.*
    G. Capone, 541(RES):Feb83-54
Miola, R.S. Shakespeare's Rome.
    S. Wells, 617(TLS):30Nov84-1390
Mirashi, V.V. Inscriptions of the Śilāhāras.
    R. Salomon, 318(JAOS):Apr-Jun82-410
"The Mirroure of the Worlde: MS Bodley 283."*
    J. Griffiths, 78(BC):Summer83-235
Mirza, T. and others, eds. Folclor Muzical din Zona Huedin.
    L. Kürti, 187:May84-346

Misan, J. L'Italie des Doctrinaires (1817–1830).
P. Cola, 356(LR):Feb–May83–142
A. Pallotta, 276:Autumn83–284
Mischel, T., ed. The Self.
J.W. Yolton, 488:Dec83–519
Mishima, Y. La Mort en été.
C. Jordis, 450(NRF):Sep83–168
Mishima, Y. Une soif d'amour.*
M-A. Lescourret, 98:Jan–Feb83–170
Miskimin, H.A. Money and Power in Fifteenth-Century France.
M. Vale, 617(TLS):5Oct84–1122
Misra, B.G. - see Koshal, S.
Misra, S.S. The Avestan.
N. Sen, 261:Mar–Dec81–136
Misrahi, R. Traité du bonheur, II.
T. Cordellier, 450(NRF):Oct83–131
Mistry, F. Nietzsche and Buddhism.*
R. Furness, 402(MLR):Apr83–500
S.L. Gilman, 107(CRCL):Sep83–445
Mitcham, A. The Literary Achievement of Gabrielle Roy.
T. Quigley, 268(IFR):Summer84–120
Mitcham, S.W., Jr. Triumphant Fox.
D. Middleton, 441:4Mar84–23
Mitchell, A. On the Beach at Cambridge.
D. Constantine, 176:Sep/Oct84–43
Mitchell, B. Morality: Religious and Secular.
P. Masterson, 393(Mind):Apr83–313
Mitchell, B. - see Morand, P.
Mitchell, B.L. Edmund Ruffin.*
J.W. Cooke, 396(ModA):Winter83–98
A.V. Huff, Jr., 579(SAQ):Summer83–345
Mitchell, D. Britten and Auden in the Thirties: The Year 1936.*
J.B., 412:May82–152
J. Michon, 189(EA):Oct–Dec84–475
Mitchell, E. Furnished Rooms.
J. Mole, 176:Mar84–51
Mitchell, E.A. Fort Timiskaming and the Fur Trade.
A. Tanner, 529(QQ):Spring83–176
Mitchell, G. Cold, Lone and Still.
N. Callendar, 441:13May84–35
Mitchell, G. The Crozier Pharaohs.
T.J. Binyon, 617(TLS):26Oct84–1125
Mitchell, G. The Saltmarsh Murders.
R. Hill, 617(TLS):26Oct84–1225
Mitchell, G. No Winding-Sheet.
T.J. Binyon, 617(TLS):16Mar84–270
Mitchell, J. The Walter Scott Operas.
J. Kolb, 107(CRCL):Sep83–440
Mitchell, J. Women: The Longest Revolution.
J. Hughes, 176:Nov84–51
M. Midgley, 617(TLS):28Sep84–1080
Mitchell, J. and J. Rose, eds. Feminine Sexuality.
A. Ross, 153:Winter83–2
Mitchell, J.H. Ceremonial Time.
J.A. West, 441:12Aug84–27
Mitchell, J.T. A Thematic Analysis of Mme. d'Aulnoy's "Contes de fées."*
M.M. Welch, 546(RR):Mar83–247
Mitchell, K. Sinclair Ross.*
D. O'Rourke, 102(CanL):Summer83–136
Mitchell, L. Holland House.
M. Butler, 339(KSMB):No34–80
Mitchell, L.C. Witnesses to a Vanishing America.*
C.L. Miller, 529(QQ):Summer83–544

Mitchell, M. Tally Ho!
L.K. MacKendrick, 102(CanL):Winter82–149
Mitchell, P.M. and R. Scholl - see Gottsched, J.C.
Mitchell, R. The Leaning Tower of Babel.
P-L. Adams, 61:Nov84–149
Mitchell, R.J. Ideology of a Superpower.
T. Remington, 550(RusR):Jan83–120
Mitchell, R.L. Corbière, Mallarmé, Valéry.*
P. Broome, 208(FS):Jan83–98
Mitchell, S. The Token.
J. Rogers, 617(TLS):13Jul84–790
Mitchell, S. The Water Inside the Water.
A. Corn, 441:11Mar84–26
Mitchell, S. - see Rilke, R.M.
Mitchell, S., with D. French and J. Greenhalgh. Regional Epigraphic Catalogues of Asia Minor. (Vol 2)
J. Reynolds, 123:Vol33No2–298
Mitchell, W.J.T., ed. The Language of Images.*
C. Dussère, 221(GQ):May83–477
Mitchell, W.J.T., ed. On Narrative.*
H. Charney, 363(LitR):Winter84–279
O. Miller, 599:Spring83–294
Mitchiner, J.E. Studies in the Indus Valley Inscriptions.
W. Bright, 318(JAOS):Jan–Mar82–233
Mitford, J. Faces of Philip.
A.J. Ayer, 362:12Jul84–25
D.A.N. Jones, 617(TLS):27Jul84–850
442(NY):10Dec84–192
Mitford, M.R. Our Village.
P-G.B., 189(EA):Jul–Sep84–364
Mitroff, I.I. and R.H. Kilmann. Methodological Approaches to Social Science.
J.J. Hartman, 488:Mar83–115
Mittal, A.C. The Inscriptions of Imperial Paramāras (800 A.D. to 1320 A.D.) (Paramār Abhilekh).
R. Salomon, 318(JAOS):Jul–Sep82–556
Mittelstrass, J. - see "Enzyklopädie Philosophie und Wissenschaftstheorie"
Mitterand, H. Le discours du roman.*
M-T. Ligot, 209(FM):Oct83–377
P. Nykrog, 546(RR):Nov83–501
Mitterand, H. - see Zola, É.
Mitterauer, M. Grundtypen alteuropäischer Sozialformen.
A. Neef, 654(WB):6/1982–185
Mitterauer, M. and R. Sieder. The European Family.
V.L. Bullough, 551(RenQ):Winter83–582
Mitterrand, F. The Wheat and the Chaff.
H. Thorburn, 529(QQ):Winter83–1150
Miura, D. The Forgotten Child.
O. Bowcock, 617(TLS):9Nov84–1273
Miyasaka Kazuo. Bokugei no Shiori.
J. Clark, 463:Summer83–181
Miyauchi, B. Immortal Longings.
W. Rosen, 570(SQ):Autumn83–366
Miyazaki Tōten. My Thirty-Three Years' Dream.* (Etō Shinkichi and M.B. Jansen, trans)
P. Duus, 407(MN):Spring83–97
Ihara Kichinosuke, 285(JapQ):Jul–Sep83–316
Miyoshi, M. As We Saw Them.
M.D. Ericson, 293(JASt):Aug83–963
Mizón, L. Poème du sud et autres poèmes.
J. Ancet, 450(NRF):Sep83–173

"Mladopis'mennye jazyki Afriki."
    I. Herms, 682(ZPSK):Band36Heft2-244
Mo, T. Sour Sweet.
    R. Boscombe, 364:Apr/May83-141
Mo-jo, K. - see under Kuo Mo-jo
Moch, C. and V. Virga. Deals.
    J. McCulloch, 441:21Oct84-50
"Francesco Mochi 1580-1654."
    J. Montagu, 90:Jul83-432
Mochulsky, K. Aleksandr Blok.
    G. Donchin, 617(TLS):5Oct84-1135
Mockler, A. Haile Selassie's War.
    R. Pankhurst, 617(TLS):21Dec84-1464
"Modèles et moyens de la réflexion poli-
    tique au XVIIIe siècle."* (Vols 1-3)
    D-H. Pageaux, 549(RLC):Apr-Jun83-229
Modell, J.S. Ruth Benedict.*
    M. Strathern, 617(TLS):29Jun84-721
Modersohn-Becker, P. Paula Modersohn-
    Becker: The Letters and Journals. (G.
    Busch and L. von Reinken, eds; newly
    ed and trans by A.S. Wensinger and C.C.
    Hoey)
    H. Yglesias, 441:26Feb84-1
    442(NY):9Apr84-146
Modiano, P. De si braves garçons.*
    A. Thiher, 207(FR):Apr84-737
Modick, K. Lion Feuchtwanger im Kontext
    der zwanziger Jahre.
    H. Dahlke, 654(WB):11/1982-179
Modleski, T. Loving With a Vengeance.
    M. De Koven, 395(MFS):Summer83-344
Modlin, C.E. - see Anderson, S.
Moeller, J., H. Liedloff and C.J. Kent.
    German Today 1. German Today 2. (both
    3rd ed)
    S.L. Hahn, 399(MLJ):Spring83-79
Moes, R. Les hellénismes de l'époque
    théodosienne.
    J. André, 555:Vol57fasc1-151
Moeschler, J. Dire et contredire.
    R. Martin, 553(RLiR):Jan-Jun83-178
Moeseneder, K. Philipp Otto Runge und
    Jakob Boehme — Über Runges "Quelle und
    Dichter" und den "Kleinen Morgen."
    U. Finke, 90:Oct83-630
Moffat, G. Last Chance Country.
    T.J. Binyon, 617(TLS):30Mar84-354
    N. Callendar, 441:1Jan84-26
Moffett, J. James Merrill.
    D.W. Hartnett, 617(TLS):9Nov84-1290
Moffett, J. Whinny Moor Crossing.
    M. Kinzie, 29:Sep/Oct84-38
Mogen, D. Wilderness Visions.
    P. Fitting, 561(SFS):Nov83-353
    J.K. Folsom, 649(WAL):Feb84-360
Moggach, D. Porky.*
    D. Durrant, 364:Jul83-91
Mohapatra, R.P. Udayagiri and Khandagiri
    Caves.
    R.L. Brown, 293(JASt):Nov82-193
Mohlenbrock, R.H. The Field Guide to U.S.
    National Forests.
    P. Hagan, 441:3Jun84-13
Mohr, W. Wolfram von Eschenbach.*
    H.A. Hilgers, 684(ZDA):Band112Heft2-66
von Mohrenschildt, D. Towards a United
    States of Russia.*
    A. Wood, 575(SEER):Jul83-451
Moir, A. Caravaggio.*
    C. Gilbert, 55:Dec83-35
    L. Gowing, 617(TLS):23Mar84-313

Moisés, M. and J.P. Paes. Pequeno
    Dicionário de Literatura Brasileira.
    (2nd ed)
    A. Aiex, 238:Sep83-448
Mojtabai, A.G. Autumn.
    V. Middleton, 577(SHR):Summer83-288
    42(AR):Winter83-118
    639(VQR):Spring83-58
Mokrzycki, E. Philosophy of Science and
    Sociology.
    F.W., 185:Jul84-735
Molander, B. The Order There Is and the
    Order We Make.
    A.G.N. Flew, 518:Jan83-63
Moldenhauer, J.J. - see Thoreau, H.D.
Mole, J. In and Out of the Apple.
    D. Constantine, 176:Sep/Oct84-43
    B. O'Donoghue, 617(TLS):14Dec84-1456
Molesworth, C. Donald Barthelme's Fic-
    tion.*
    S.I. Bellman, 573(SSF):Spring-Summer83-
    150
    R.M. Davis, 651(WHR):Summer83-177
    A. Wilde, 560:Spring-Summer83-165
Molesworth, C. The Fierce Embrace.
    P. Kroetsch, 106:Summer83-219
Molière. Molière: Five Plays. (R.
    Wilbur, trans)
    D. Devlin, 157:Spring83-52
de Molina, T. - see under Tirso de Molina
Moline, J. Plato's Theory of Understand-
    ing.*
    R.F. Stalley, 123:Vol33No2-222
    S.J. Waterlow, 518:Jul83-139
Molinié, G. Du roman grec au roman
    baroque.
    J. Serroy, 475:Vol 10No18-379
    G. Verdier, 207(FR):May84-872
Molino, J. and J. Tamine. Introduction à
    l'analyse linguistique de la poésie.*
    R. Adamson, 402(MLR):Jul83-704
Moll, K. Der junge Leibniz. (Vol 2)
    G. Hunter, 319:Jul84-371
Molland, E. Norges kirkehistorie i det 19.
    Århundre.
    T.R. Skarsten, 563(SS):Autumn83-386
Mollinger, R. Psychoanalysis and Litera-
    ture.
    S.A. Black, 149(CLS):Winter83-456
    S. Weiland, 128(CE):Nov83-705
Mollison, J. and N. Bonham. Albert Tucker.
    G. Catalano, 381:Dec83-449
Mollison, J. and L. Murray, eds. Austra-
    lian National Gallery.
    U. Hoff, 39:Mar83-263
Molnar, T. Tiers-Monde, Idéologie et
    Réalité.
    P. Gottfried, 396(ModA):Summer/Fall83-
    326
Molony, C.J.C., with others. The Mediter-
    ranean and Middle East. (Vol 6, Pt 1)
    (rev by W. Jackson)
    D. Hunt, 617(TLS):9Nov84-1278
Molyneaux, G. Charlie Chaplin's "City
    Lights."
    C. Maland, 500:Spring/Summer84-55
Mombello, G. La Raccolte francesi di
    favole esopiane dal 1480 alla fine del
    secolo XVI.
    P. Malandain, 535(RHL):Mar/Apr83-258
Momigliano, A. Problèmes d'historiogra-
    phie ancienne et moderne.
    M. Jarrety, 450(NRF):Nov83-148

Mommsen, K. Goethe und 1001 Nacht.*
    M-V. Leistner, 654(WB):11/1983-2022
Monaco, J. American Film Now.
    S. Feldman, 106:Fall83-353
Monaco, P. Modern European Culture and
Consciousness.
    R. Hauptman, 395(MFS):Winter83-817
Monaghan, D. Jane Austen.*
    V. Jones, 447(N&Q):Aug82-360
    F.M. Keener, 402(MLR):Apr83-433
Monaghan, D., ed. Jane Austen in a Social
Context.*
    M.A. Doody, 445(NCF):Sep83-220
"Monastica." (Vol 1)
    C.V. Franklin, 589:Oct83-1075
Mondor, H. and L.J. Austin - see Mallarmé,
S.
Moneta, G.C. On Identity.
    C.G. Swain, 543:Dec82-464
Monge, P.R. and J.N. Capella, eds. Multi-
varate Techniques in Human Communication.
    H. Petrie, 353:Vol20No3/4-351
Monière, D. Ideologies in Quebec.
    J.T. Stevenson, 154:Mar83-163
Moñino, A.R.R. - see under Rodríguez
Moñino, A.R.
Monk, P. The Smaller Infinity.*
    J.S. Grant, 627(UTQ):Summer83-498
Monkman, L. A Native Heritage.*
    T. Goldie, 178:Dec83-514
    T.D. MacLulich, 168(ECW):Summer83-130
Monnier, A. Un Publiciste frondeur sous
Catherine II.
    W.G. Jones, 575(SEER):Jul83-421
    T. Page, 574(SEEJ):Summer83-257
    N.V. Riasanovsky, 550(RusR):Jan83-105
Monnier, G. Pastels.
    P-L. Adams, 61:Aug84-112
Monod-Fontaine, I. The Sculpture of Henri
Matisse.
    T. Hilton, 617(TLS):23Nov84-1344
Monshi, E.B. History of Shāh 'Abbās the
Great (Tārīk-e 'Ālamārā-ye 'Abbāsī) by
Eskandar Beg Monshi. (R.M. Savory,
trans)
    M.M. Mazzaoui, 318(JAOS):Apr-Jun82-382
Monsman, G. Walter Pater's Art of Auto-
biography.*
    E. Block, 481(PQ):Fall83-537
    P. Clements, 402(MLR):Oct83-911
Monson, C. Voices and Viols in England,
1600-1650.
    A. Ashbee, 410(M&L):Jul/Oct83-252
Monson, K. Alma Mahler.*
    R. Dyer, 441:11Mar84-14
    H. Lee, 617(TLS):11May84-520
    H. Wackett, 362:1Mar84-22
Monson, N. and D. Scott. The Nouveaux
Pauvres.
    H. Wackett, 362:8Nov84-25
Montague, J., ed. The Book of Irish Verse.
    V. Young, 472:Fall/Winter83Spring/
    Summer84-323
Montague, J. The Dead Kingdom.
    D. Constantine, 176:Sep/Oct84-42
    D. Davis, 362:19Jul84-25
    D. Dunn, 617(TLS):5Oct84-1124
Montague, J. Selected Poems.*
    T. Eagleton, 565:Vol124No3-77
    R. Skelton, 134(CP):Spring83-87
    V. Young, 249(HudR):Summer83-405
Montalban, M.V. - see under Vazquez Montal-
ban, M.

Montalbano, W.D. and C. Hiaasen. A Death
in China.
    H. Mitgang, 441:24Jun84-22
Montale, E. Lettere a Salvatore Quasimodo.
(S. Grasso, ed)
    E. Bonora, 228(GSLI):Vol 160fasc509-
    148
Montale, E. Otherwise.
    W. Kaiser, 441:18Nov84-21
de Montalvo, J. Siete tratados. (J.L.
Abellán, ed)
    E.H. Friedman, 552(REH):May83-310
Montalvo, S.R.M. - see under Rodríguez M.
Montalvo, S.
Montanari, F. Studi di Filologia Omerica
Antica I.
    D.M. Schenkeveld, 394:Vol36fasc3/4-389
Montanaro, J.S. Chinese/English Phrase
Book for Travellers.
    T. Light, 399(MLJ):Spring83-69
Monte Andrea da Fiorenza. Le rime. (F.F.
Minetti, ed)
    W. Storey, 276:Summer83-162
Montefiore, A., ed. Philosophy in France
Today.
    P. Horden, 617(TLS):27Jan84-83
Montefusco, L.C. - see under Calboli
Montefusco, L.
Monteiro, G. - see de Sena, J.
Monteiro, G. and B. Murphy - see Hay, J.M.
and W.D. Howells
Montero, G. Billy Higgins Rides the
Freights.
    P. Nodelman, 102(CanL):Spring83-149
Montes Huidobro, M. Poesía compartida.
    J. Febles, 238:Sep83-443
Montes Huidobro, M. Segar a los muertos.
    C. Gariano, 238:Mar83-142
Montesinos, J. La pasión amorosa de Que-
vedo.
    A. Carreño, 238:Mar83-133
Montgomery, B. Monty's Grandfather.
    H. Tinker, 617(TLS):16Nov84-1322
Montgomery, M. Why Flannery O'Connor
Stayed Home.*
    L.A. Lawson, 396(ModA):Summer/Fall83-
    319
Montgomery, M. Why Poe Drank Liquor.
    R. Rash, 580(SCR):Spring84-140
Montgomery, M.R. In Search of L.L. Bean.
    D. Traxel, 441:30Dec84-17
Montias, J.M. Artists and Artisans in
Delft.
    C. Brown, 90:Feb83-101
    A.K. Wheelock, Jr., 551(RenQ):Spring83-
    119
    C. White, 39:Jan83-64
Montoya Martínez, J. Las colecciones de
milagros de la Virgen en la Edad Media.
    M.S. Delpy, 547(RF):Band95Heft1/2-167
Montross, C.M. Virtue or Vice?
    C.P. Thompson, 86(BHS):Oct83-349
"Monumenta Musicae in Polonia." (Ser D,
fasc I-X) (J. Morawsky, ed)
    C. Meyer, 537:Vol69No1-107
Moody, S. Penny Black.
    T.J. Binyon, 617(TLS):30Nov84-1391
Moon, M. A Supplement to "John Harris's
Books for Youth 1801-1843."
    P. Stockham, 503:Autumn83-142
Moon, W.G., ed. Ancient Greek Art and
Iconography.
    B.F. Cook, 617(TLS):24Aug84-949

263

Moon, W.L.H. - see under Least Heat Moon,
W.
Moorcock, M. The Laughter of Carthage.
   V. Cunningham, 617(TLS):7Sep84-1005
Moorcock, M. The Opium General and Other
Stories.
   D. Montrose, 617(TLS):23Nov84-1358
Moore, B. Cold Heaven.*
   M. Howard, 676(YR):Winter84-xiii
   K. McSweeney, 99:Nov83-32
   J. Mellors, 364:Oct83-97
   K.C. O'Brien, 362:5Jan84-25
Moore, C. Louisbourg Portraits.
   G.W., 102(CanL):Spring83-189
Moore, D. Twinkle, Twinkle, Little Star.
   A. Harmetz, 441:23Sep84-20
Moore, D.R. The Torres Strait Collections
of A.C. Haddon.
   R.L. Shep, 614:Fall84-25
Moore, F.S. Vassilieff and his Art.
   G. Catalano, 381:Dec83-449
Moore, G. Furthermoore.
   E. Forbes, 415:Aug83-485
Moore, G. Poet's Love. Singer and
Accompanist.
   E. Forbes, 415:Apr83-237
Moore, G.H. Zermelo's Axiom of Choice.
   I. Grattan-Guinness, 556:Winter83/84-
   180
Moore, H.T. The Priest of Love.
   J. Newman, 161(DUJ):Dec82-83
"Henry Moore: Animals."
   C. Simmons, 441:19Feb84-22
Moore, J.N. Edward Elgar.
   H. Cole, 362:28Jun84-28
   D. Mitchell, 617(TLS):14Sep84-1011
Moore, J.N. Spirit of England.
   D. Mitchell, 617(TLS):14Sep84-1011
Moore, M. The Short Season Between Two
Silences.
   J. Batchelor, 617(TLS):10Aug84-900
Moore, P. and others. The Atlas of the
Solar System.
   C. Ronan, 617(TLS):17Feb84-174
Moore, R.A., ed. Culture and Religion in
Japanese-American Relations.
   W.M. Fridell, 407(MN):Spring83-107
Moore, R.S. That Cunning Alphabet.
   T.W. Herbert, 70:May-Jun83-152
Moore, R.S. - see Hayne, P.H.
Moore, S. My Old Sweetheart.
   J. Mellors, 364:Apr/May83-133
Moore, S. A Reader's Guide to William
Gaddis's "The Recognitions."
   J.Z. Guzlowski, 395(MFS):Winter83-737
   J. Kuehl, 141:Winter83-83
Moore, S.R. The Drama of Discrimination
in Henry James.
   J.K. Hale, 67:Nov83-317
Moore, T. and C. Carling. Language Under-
standing.* (British title: Understand-
ing Language.)
   S.D. Guttenplan, 483:Oct83-557
   D.H., 355(LSoc):Sep83-422
   F.J. Newmeyer, 350:Mar84-123
Moore, T.W. Philosophy of Education.
   W.H., 185:Jan84-379
Moorehead, C. Sidney Bernstein.
   J. Isaacs, 362:2Feb84-24
   P. Smith, 617(TLS):3Feb84-109
Moorhouse, A.C. The Syntax of Sophocles.
   H. Lloyd-Jones, 123:Vol33No2-171
   P. Monteil, 555:Vol157fasc2-301

Moorhouse, F. Selected Stories.
   D. Taylor, 364:Jul83-94
Moorhouse, G. Lord's.
   M. Meyer, 364:Oct83-103
Moortgat, M., H. van der Hulst and T.
Hoekstra, eds. The Scope of Lexical
Rules.*
   R. Hudson, 603:Vol7No3-439
Mora, C.J. Mexican Cinema.
   W.P. Carty, 37:Jan-Feb83-62
   D. Meson-Sosnowski, 263(RIB):Vol33No2-
   261
Mora, G. and B. Plossu. New Mexico Re-
visited.
   L. Milazzo, 584(SWR):Autumn83-viii
Mora, P. and L., with P. Philippot. Con-
servation of Wall Paintings.
   D. Winfield, 617(TLS):19Oct84-1182
Morabito, P. Bibliografia Montaignana.
   H. Sonneville, 356(LR):Nov83-356
Morace, R.A. and K. Van Spanckeren, eds.
John Gardner.
   J.P. Hermann, 577(SHR):Summer83-281
Morales y Marín, J.L. La pintura aragon-
esa en el siglo XVII.
   I. Mateo, 48:Oct-Dec80-507
Moran, E.F., ed. The Dilemma of Amazonian
Development.
   P. Henley, 617(TLS):27Jul84-853
Moran, R. Knowing Right from Wrong.
   R. Harris, 637(VS):Spring83-343
Morand, P. Fancy Goods [and] Open All
Night. (B. Mitchell, ed)
   R. Sieburth, 441:17Jun84-10
   J. Updike, 442(NY):10Sep84-136
Moravcsik, E.A. and J.R. Wirth, eds. Cur-
rent Approaches to Syntax.
   R. Hudson, 361:Jun/Jul83-249
Morawsky, J. - see "Monumenta Musicae in
Polonia"
Mörchen, H. Adorno und Heidegger.
   R. Wiggershaus, 687:Oct-Dec83-653
Mordden, E. The American Theatre.*
   E. Salmon, 529(QQ):Summer83-576
   R.K. Sarlós, 610:Summer83-181
   R. Toscan, 615(TJ):May82-272
Mordden, E. Broadway Babies.
   R. Cushman, 617(TLS):5Oct84-1137
   J. Novick, 441:26Feb84-23
More, T. The Complete Works of St. Thomas
More.* (Vol 6: A Dialogue Concerning
Heresies.) (T.M.C. Lawler, G. Marc'-
hadour and R.C. Marius, eds)
   W. Allen, 569(SR):Winter83-143
   J.S. McGee, 377:Mar83-49
More, T. The Complete Works of St. Thomas
More.* (Vol 9: The Apology.) (J.B.
Trapp, ed)
   E. McCutcheon, 506(PSt):Sep83-187
More, T. L'Utopie, ou Le traité de la
meilleure forme de gouvernement. (M.
Delcourt, ed and trans)
   G. Marc'hadour, 539:Nov83-292
More, T. St. Thomas More: The Tower Works,
Devotional Writings.* (G.E. Haupt, ed)
   E. McCutcheon, 506(PSt):Sep83-187
   J. Mezciems, 447(N&Q):Oct82-432
Moreau, F. L'Image littéraire.
   B.L. Knapp, 207(FR):May84-865
Moreau, P-F. Le Récit utopique, droit
naturel et roman de l'état.
   M. Angenot, 561(SFS):Nov83-344
                                [continued]

Moreau, P-F. Le Récit utopique, droit naturel et roman de l'état. [continuing]
P. Macherey, 540(RIPh):Vol37fascl/2-228

Morejón, N. Nación y mestizaje en Nicolás Guillén.
V.M. Kutzinski, 400(MLN):Mar83-275

Morel, J-P. Céramique campanienne.
F.R.S. Ridgway, 123:Vol33No1-105

Morell, D. and Chai-Anan Samudavinija. Political Conflict in Thailand.
A. Ramsay, 293(JASt):Aug83-1024

Moreno, L.A.G. - see under García Moreno, L.A.

Morère, P. - see Beattie, J.

Moretti, I. and R. Stopani. La Toscana.
D.F. Glass, 54:Jun83-340

Morewedge, P., ed. Philosophies of Existence.
S. Gaukroger, 63:Dec83-461

Lady Morgan - see Owenson, S.

Morgan, C. Future Man.
R. Dwyer, 561(SFS):Jul83-254

Morgan, E. Grafts/Takes.
D. Dunn, 617(TLS):20Jan84-54
D. O'Driscoll, 493:Sep83-66

Morgan, E. Poems of Thirty Years.
D. McDuff, 565:Vol24No3-67
S. Regan, 493:Mar83-64
J. Wain, 364:Jul83-74

Morgan, F. Northbook.*
W. Harmon, 569(SR):Summer83-457
G. Johnson, 461:Spring/Summer83-96
P. Stitt, 491:Oct83-39
639(VQR):Winter83-24

Morgan, G. - see Chaucer, G.

Morgan, J. Agatha Christie.
R. Barnard, 617(TLS):21Sep84-1063
M. Drabble, 362:27Sep84-26

Morgan, K.L. Children of Strangers.*
M.M. White, 292(JAF):Jan-Mar83-99

Morgan, K.O. Consensus and Disunity.
P. Williamson, 161(DUJ):Dec82-101

Morgan, K.O. Labour in Power 1945-1951.
P. Clarke, 617(TLS):16Mar84-263
A. Howard, 362:15Mar84-26

Morgan, K.O., ed. The Oxford Illustrated History of Britain.
J. Ridley, 617(TLS):21Sep84-1062

Morgan, M.R., ed. La Continuation de Guillaume de Tyr (1184-1197).
A.H. Diverres, 402(MLR):Jul83-706
J. Tattersall, 208(FS):Apr83-199

Morgan, P. The Eighteenth Century Renaissance.
G.H. Jenkins, 83:Autumn83-230

Morgan, P. A Winter Visitor.
T. Dooley, 617(TLS):13Apr84-413
H. Lomas, 364:Feb84-83

Morgan, P.F. - see Jeffrey, F.

Morgan, S. In the Meantime.*
F.M. Keener, 402(MLR):Apr83-433

Morganti, A. Poul Anderson, tecnocrate e bardo.
P.G. Mastrodonato, 561(SFS):Jul83-252

Morgenstein, G. The Man Who Wanted to Play Centerfield for the New York Yankees.
639(VQR):Autumn83-127

Morgenthaler, W. Bedrängte Positivität.
H-G. Richert, 133:Band16Heft1-71

Moriconi, V. The Princes of Q.
J. Motion, 617(TLS):25May84-598
K.C. O'Brien, 362:7Jun84-25

Morin, M. L'Amérique de nord et la culture.
P. Coleman, 207(FR):May84-898

Morishima, M. Why Has Japan "Succeeded"?
L. Lynn, 293(JASt):Aug83-966

Morison, S. Selected Essays on the History of Letter-Forms in Manuscript and Print. (D. McKitterick, ed)
N. Barker, 354:Jun83-197
W.H. Bond, 589:Jul83-787

Morison, W.L. John Austin.
R.H., 185:Jan84-373

Moritz, A.F. Black Orchid.*
J. Garratt, 137:Nov82-10
P.K. Smith, 102(CanL):Summer83-138

Moritz, A.F. Signs and Certainties.*
D. Daymond, 102(CanL):Summer83-140

Moritz, C.P. Journeys of a German in England.
K.A.M., 617(TLS):24Feb84-203

Moritz, M. The Little Kingdom.
W. Stockton, 441:21Oct84-50

Morley, D. and K. Worpole, eds. The Republic of Letters.
B. Roberts, 381:Sep83-283

Morley, P. Margaret Laurence.*
J. Ferns, 178:Dec83-516

Morley, S. Tales from the Hollywood Raj.*
442(NY):20Aug84-93

Morony, M.G. Iraq after the Muslim Conquest.
H. Kennedy, 617(TLS):7Sep84-999

Morpurgo-Tagliabue, G. Demetrio: dello stile.
J-P. Levet, 555:Vol57fascl-135

Morreall, J. Taking Laughter Seriously.
R.M.M., 185:Apr84-550

Morrell, D. The Brotherhood of the Rose.
M. Buck, 441:13May84-22
442(NY):16Jul84-93

Morrell, O. and D. Cresswell. Dear Lady Ginger. (H. Shaw, ed)
K. Walker, 617(TLS):4May84-504

Morresi, R. Introduzione a Hamelin.
M. Adam, 542:Oct-Dec83-501

Morrill, J., ed. Reactions to the English Civil War 1642-1649.*
J. Blondel, 189(EA):Oct-Dec84-464

Morris, A.J.A. The Scaremongers.
H. Goodman, 441:9Dec84-27

Morris, B. - see Shakespeare, W.

Morris, C.B. García Lorca "Bodas de sangre."
C. Pulpeiro, 547(RF):Band95Heft1/2-232

Morris, C.R. A Time of Passion.
M. Kinsley, 441:25Mar84-12
W.E. Leuchtenburg, 61:Apr84-138

Morris, E. Salerno.
A.O.J. Cockshut, 617(TLS):8Jun84-634

Morris, H. Peru.*
J. Hollander, 676(YR):Autumn83-xiv
W.H. Pritchard, 491:Jan84-228
639(VQR):Autumn83-135

Morris, J. Journeys.
E. Newman, 441:3Jun84-11

Morris, J. Stones of Empire.
G. Fitzpatrick, 364:Feb84-111
442(NY):9Apr84-147

Morris, J. The Venetian Empire.
P.D. du Prey, 529(QQ):Summer83-406

265

Morris, K.L.   The Image of the Middle Ages
in Romantic and Victorian Literature.
  E. Archibald, 617(TLS):14Dec84-1450
Morris, M.   Saying and Meaning in Puerto
Rico.
  A. Pousada, 355(LSoc):Jun83-262
  M. Solá, 701(SinN):Oct-Dec82-83
Morris, R.   The Devil's Butcher Shop.
  D.C. Anderson, 441:26Feb84-28
Morris, R.   The Papers of Robert Morris,
1781-1784.   (Vols 2-5) (E.J. Ferguson
and others, eds)
  J.A. Ernst, 656(WMQ):Jan83-156
Morris, R.B., with E. Sirvet – see Jay, J.
Morris, S.P.   The Black and White Style.
  J. Boardman, 617(TLS):24Aug84-948
Morris, W.   The Collected Letters of Wil-
liam Morris.   (Vol 1) (N. Kelvin, ed)
  J. Harris, 617(TLS):31Aug84-963
  W.S. Peterson, 441:29Apr84-15
Morris, W.   The Courting of Marcus Dupree.*
  S. Lardner, 5Mar84-136
Morris, W.   Political Writings of William
Morris.   (A.L. Morton, ed)
  J. Harris, 617(TLS):31Aug84-963
Morris, W.   Solo.*
  42(AR):Summer83-375
Morris, W.   Will's Boy.*
  M. Ellmann, 569(SR):Winter83-120
  D.E. Wylder, 395(MFS):Winter83-719
Morrison, B.   Dark Glasses.
  N. Corcoran, 617(TLS):16Nov84-1318
Morrison, B.   Seamus Heaney.*
  R.F., 189(EA):Jul-Sep84-367
Morrison, B.   The Movement.
  D. Howard, 366:Spring83-128
Morrison, B. and A. Motion, eds.   The
Penguin Book of Contemporary British
Poetry.*
  M. Blackburn, 565:Vol24No4-8
  M. Hulse, 148:Autumn83-61
  R. Kerridge, 97(CQ):Vol 12No1-66
  H. Lomas, 364:Apr/May83-123
  N. Rhodes, 493:Mar83-73
Morrison, T.   Sula.
  M.R. Farwell, 448:Vol21No1-167
Morrison, W.H.   Fortress Without a Roof.
  639(VQR):Spring83-54
Morrison-Reed, M.D.   Black Pioneers in a
White Denomination.
  B. Atkinson, 441:5Aug84-19
Morrissette, G.   Finding Mom at Eaton's.
  D. Daymond, 102(CanL):Summer83-140
Morrissey, L.J.   Henry Fielding.*
  H. Amory, 447(N&Q):Feb82-82
  P-G. Boucé, 189(EA):Jan-Mar83-78
  M. Irwin, 541(RES):May83-221
Morscher, E. and R. Stranzinger, eds.
Ethics.
  R.H., 185:Jan84-358
Morse, D.   Perspectives on Romanticism.*
  C. Clausen, 569(SR):Fall83-672
  D. Simpson, 591(SIR):Fall83-462
Morse, E.S.   Catalogue of the Morse Col-
lection of Japanese Pottery.   (new ed)
  M. Medley, 39:Feb83-150
Morse, R.A., ed.   The Politics of Japan's
Energy Strategy.*
  M.A. McKean, 293(JASt):May83-668
Morselli, M.   Amedeo Avogadro.
  D. Knight, 617(TLS):31Aug84-978

Morsley, C.   News from the English Country-
side 1851-1950.
  J. Cherrington, 617(TLS):13Jan84-39
Morson, G.S.   The Boundaries of Genre.*
  S.L. Baehr, 550(RusR):Jan83-123
  R. Freeborn, 575(SEER):Apr83-266
  R. Teeuwen, 204(FdL):Jun83-156
Morsy, M.   North Africa 1800-1900.
  F. Ghiles, 617(TLS):20Jul84-809
Mortier, R.   Diderot and the "Grand Goût."
  D. Fletcher, 83:Spring83-123
Mortier, R. and H. Hasquin – see "Etudes
sur le XIIIe siècle"
Mortimer, E.   Faith and Power.*
  G. Thaiss, 99:Nov83-35
Mortimer, E.   The Rise of the French Com-
munist Party 1920-1947.
  H. Brogan, 362:29Mar84-26
  D. Johnson, 617(TLS):9Mar84-237
Mortimer, J.   Clinging to the Wreckage.
  42(AR):Spring83-250
  639(VQR):Spring83-51
Mortimer, J.   Rumpole's Return.
  W. Domnarski, 639(VQR):Summer83-523
Morton, A.   Frames of Mind.*
  K.V. Wilkes, 393(Mind):Jan83-147
Morton, A.L. – see Morris, W.
Morton, D.   Canada and War.
  W.A.B. Douglas, 529(QQ):Spring83-206
Morton, F.   The Forever Street.
  R. Plant, 441:10Jun84-9
  442(NY):16Jul84-91
Morton, H.   The Whale's Wake.
  B.M. Gough, 150(DR):Winter83/84-688
  S. Mills, 617(TLS):30Mar84-353
Morton, H.V.   In Search of England.   In
Search of Ireland.
  J.C., 617(TLS):22Jun84-711
Morton, W.L.   Contexts of Canada's Past.
  (A.B. McKillop, ed)
  G.W., 102(CanL):Winter82-174
Mosca, L.   Il Madagascar nella vita di
Raombana primo storico malgascio (1809-
1855).
  M. Bloch, 69:Vol53No3-106
Moscadi, L.B. and others – see under
Baldini Moscadi, L. and others
Moscato, M. and L. Le Blanc, eds.   The
United States of America v. One Book
Entitled "Ulysses" by James Joyce.
  A. Boyer, 329(JJQ):Summer84-373
Moscovitch, H.   New Poems.
  G. Woodcock, 102(CanL):Summer83-163
Moser, C.A.   Dmitrov of Bulgaria.
  H. Seton-Watson, 575(SEER):Apr83-299
Moser, H. and H. Tervooren – see "Des
Minnesangs Frühling"
Moser, T.C.   The Life in the Fiction of
Ford Madox Ford.*
  R. Brebach, 301(JEGP):Jul83-462
  K. Cushman, 405(MP):Nov83-212
  E. Hollahan, 594:Winter83-391
  D. Lemarchal, 189(EA):Oct-Dec83-484
  M. Saunders, 184(EIC):Apr83-163
Moses, E.   Astonishment of Heart.
  R. Hoffman, 441:8Apr84-25
Moses, J.   The Novelist as Comedian.
  M. Gorra, 31(ASch):Summer83-413
  H. Orel, 395(MFS):Winter83-759
Moshansky, M.   Mendelssohn.
  R. Anderson, 415:Jan83-35
Mosher, S.W.   Broken Earth.*
  N. Eberstadt, 129:Mar84-44

Moskalew, W. Formular Language and Poetic Design in the Aeneid.
N.M. Horsfall, 123:Vol33No2-320
Moskal'skaja, O.I. Grammatika teksta.
W. Mühlner, 682(ZPSK):Band36Heft5-613
Mosley, L. Zanuck.
C. Chase, 441:6May84-28
P. Dunne, 18:Jul-Aug84-45
442(NY):30Ju184-88
Mosley, P. Ingmar Bergman.
M.J. Blackwell, 563(SS):Summer83-282
Moss, A. Ovid in Renaissance France.
P. Ford, 208(FS):Apr83-211
M. Moog-Grünewald, 547(RF):Band95Heft3-341
L.V.R., 568(SCN):Spring/Summer83-30
D. Shaw, 354:Mar83-71
Moss, H. Rules of Sleep.
H. Beaver, 441:11Nov84-18
Moss, J. A Reader's Guide to the Canadian Novel.
W.J. Keith, 627(UTQ):Summer83-481
Moss, J.D. "Godded with God."
J. van Dorsten, 551(RenQ):Summer83-269
T.W. Hayes, 568(SCN):Spring/Summer83-15
Moss, L. Arthur Miller.
M.C., 189(EA):Jan-Mar83-109
M. Rudman, 610:Winter81/82-67
Moss, R. Rudyard Kipling and the Fiction of Adolescence.
H-P. Breuer, 395(MFS):Summer83-263
H. Orel, 177(ELT):Vol26No1-52
Moss, S. Skull of Adam.
P. Balakian, 363(LitR):Fall83-135
Mossberg, B.A.C. Emily Dickinson.
J. Loving, 27(AL):Dec83-649
295(JML):Nov83-459
639(VQR):Autumn83-116
Mossberg, C.L. Scandinavian Immigrant Literature.*
H. Crosby, 26(ALR):Spring83-157
Mosshammer, A.A. The "Chronicle" of Eusebius and Greek Chronographic Tradition.*
J. Mansfeld, 394:Vol36fasc1/2-202
Mossiker, F. Madame de Sévigné.*
N. Bliven, 442(NY):16Jan84-102
F. du Plessix Gray, 441:8Jan84-25
Mossman, E. - see Pasternak, B.
Mossman, J., ed. Pseudonyms and Nicknames Dictionary.*
K.B. Harder, 424:Jun83-127
P. Larkin, 402(MLR):Oct83-884
Mossner, E.C. The Life of David Hume.* (2nd ed)
D.T. Siebert, 588(SSL):Vol 18-288
Mosterín, J. La ortografía fonémica del español.
J.M. Sharp, 238:May83-310
Mosterín, J. - see Gödel, K.
Motion, A. The Poetry of Edward Thomas.
A. Nicholson, 677(YES):Vol 13-343
Motion, A. Secret Narratives.*
M. Hulse, 364:Nov83-88
C. Rawson, 493:Sep83-58
Mott, M. The Seven Mountains of Thomas Merton.
R. Coles, 441:23Dec84-1
Mottahedeh, R.P. Loyalty and Leadership in an Early Islamic Society.
I.M. Lapidus, 318(JAOS):Jan-Mar82-210
Mottram, E. A Book of Herne.
J. Saunders, 565:Vol24No4-71

Mottram, E. Elegies.
J. Saunders, 565:Vol24No1-73
Motzan, P., ed. Ein halbes Semester Sommer.
H. Nalewski, 654(WB):10/1983-1803
Motzan, P. Die rumäniendeutsche Lyrik nach 1944.
K. Schuhmann, 654(WB):9/1982-188
Mouligneau, G. Madame de la Fayette, romancière?
D. Beyerle, 547(RF):Band95Heft1/2-191
J. De Jean, 188(ECr):Spring83-118
Moulton, C. Aristophanic Poetry.*
T. Long, 121(CJ):Oct/Nov83-71
R.G. Ussher, 303(JoHS):Vol 103-168
Moulton, J. and G.M. Robinson. The Organisation of Language.
E. Briscoe, 297(JL):Sep83-475
J.P. Stemberger, 361:Jun/Jul83-244
Mouré, E. Wanted Alive.
T. Marshall, 99:Aug-Sep83-43
Mouré, E. The Whisky Vigil.
P.K. Smith, 102(CanL):Summer83-138
Moure Casas, A.M. - see Palladius
Moureau, F. and R. Bernoulli. Autour du Journal de voyage de Montaigne 1580-1980.
A. Reix, 542:Oct-Dec83-463
Mouret, F.J.L. Les Traducteurs anglais de Pétrarque: 1754-1798.
J.A. Scott, 545(RPh):Feb83-482
de Mourgues, O. Quelques paradoxes sur le classicisme.*
J. Morel, 535(RHL):Mar/Apr83-271
Moynihan, D.P. Loyalties.
W.V. Shannon, 441:8Apr84-17
Mozet, N. La Ville de province dans l'oeuvre de Balzac — l'espace romanesque.
P.P. Clark, 207(FR):May84-880
Mück, H-D. and U. Müller - see "Jahrbuch der Oswald-von-Wolkenstein-Gesellschaft"
Muecke, S. - see Roe, P.
Mueller, I. Philosophy of Mathematics and Deductive Structure in Euclid's "Elements."
M. Boylan, 486:Dec83-665
D.H. Fowler, 84:Mar83-57
S. Rosen, 543:Dec82-465
Mueller, M. Children of Oedipus and other Essays on the Imitation of Greek Tragedy 1550-1800.
R. Jenkyns, 541(RES):Feb83-62
Mueller, M. "The Iliad."
B. Hainsworth, 617(TLS):28Dec84-1498
Mugdan, J. Flexionsmorphologie und Psycholinguistik.
G. Koller, 685(ZDL):1/1983-118
Muglioni, J-M. - see Kant, I.
Muhadjir. Morphology of Jakarta Dialect.
D.C. Walker, 350:Sep84-681
Muhammad, I.H. The Prince of Mount Tahan.
M.H. Salleh, 293(JASt):Aug83-1008
Mühlpfordt, H.M. Königsberger Leben im Rokoko.
R. Malter, 342:Band74Heft4-513
Muhlstein, A. Baron James.*
R. Kaplan, 129:Jan84-72
Muhr, R. Sprachwandel als soziales Phänomen.
H.L. Kufner, 221(GQ):Jan83-125
Muir, E. Uncollected Scottish Criticism.* (A. Noble, ed)
A-M. Le Bon-Dodat, 189(EA):Apr-Jun84-222

Muñoz Cadina, O. Teatro Boliviano Contemp-
  oraneo.
    J. Otero, 37:Sep-Oct83-60
    J. Otero, 263(RIB):Vol33No1-46
Munro, A. Dance of the Happy Shades.
    P. Craig, 617(TLS):9Mar84-259
Munro, A. Lives of Girls and Women.
    P. Craig, 617(TLS):21Sep84-1066
Munro, A. The Moons of Jupiter.*
    E.D. Blodgett, 102(CanL):Summer83-98
    D. Flower, 249(HudR):Summer83-366
    L. Franks, 461:Fall/Winter83/84-91
    L. McMullen, 198:Jan84-77
    D. Taylor, 364:Jul83-94
    639(VQR):Autumn83-128
Munro, C., ed. The First UQP Story Book.
    E. Webby, 381:Mar83-34
Munro, J. Daughters.
    I. Sowton, 102(CanL):Summer83-124
Munson, H., Jr., ed and trans. The House
  of Si Abd Allah.
    M. Gilsenan, 617(TLS):7Sep84-1002
    A. Rassam, 441:15Apr84-23
Munton, A. and A. Young. Seven Writers of
  the English Left.
    A. Haberer, 189(EA):Jan-Mar84-106
Munz, P. The Shapes of Time.
    J. Lyon, 396(ModA):Summer/Fall83-343
Murail, L. La Grande Roue.
    A.D. Cordero, 207(FR):May84-914
Murakami Hyoe. Japan.
    D.G. Egler, 293(JASt):May83-670
"Murasaki Shikibu: Her Diary and Poetic
  Memoirs."* (R. Bowring, trans)
    M. Ury, 407(MN):Summer83-175
Murat, I. Napoleon and the American Dream.
    H. Peyre, 207(FR):Oct83-123
Muratore, M.J. The Evolution of the
  Cornelian Heroine.
    J. Cairncross, 475:Vol 10No19-929
Murck, C.F., ed. Artists and Traditions.
    J.W. Best, 318(JAOS):Jan-Mar82-151
Murdoch, I. The Philosopher's Pupil.*
    C. Hawtree, 364:Apr/May83-130
    J. Lasdun, 176:Jan84-71
    W.H. Pritchard, 249(HudR):Winter83/84-
      748
    J. Sturrock, 648(WCR):Apr84-60
    42(AR):Fall83-509
Murdoch, I. and R. Stone. A Year of Birds.
    G. Reynolds, 39:Feb83-145
Murdoch, J. and others. The English Mini-
  ature.*
    O. Millar, 90:Jul83-426
    R.R. Wark, 551(RenQ):Spring83-104
Murdoch, P.C. Der Sakramentalphiloso-
  phische Aspekt im Denken Nikolaj Aleksan-
  drovitsch Berdjaevs.
    E. Lampert, 575(SEER):Jul83-456
Mure, D. The Last Temptation.
    P. Craig, 617(TLS):22Jun84-706
Murgatroyd, P. A Commentary of the First
  Book of the "Elegies" of Albius Tibullus.
    J. Soubiran, 555:Vol57fasc1-158
Murison, D. Scots Saws.
    A.A. MacDonald, 179(ES):Feb83-94
Murnane, W.J. The Penguin Guide to
  Ancient Egypt.
    K. Kitchen, 617(TLS):27Jan84-88
Murphey, R. The Fading of the Maoist
  Vision.
    R. Vohra, 293(JASt):Aug83-933

Murphy, C.J. Alienation and Absence in
  the Novels of Marguerite Duras.
    A.E. Babcock, 210(FrF):Sep83-286
    L. Bishop, 207(FR):May84-890
Murphy, D. Eight Feet in the Andes.*
    D. Thomas, 362:12Jan84-22
Murphy, G.R. Brecht and the Bible.
    H. Knust, 301(JEGP):Jul83-423
    A. Tatlow, 133:Band16Heft2/3-274
Murphy, J.G. Evolution, Morality and the
  Meaning of Life.
    P.S. Wenz, 185:Oct83-140
Murphy, J.J., ed. Medieval Eloquence.
    E.W. Poe, 545(RPh):Aug82-117
Murphy, J.J., with K.P. Roddy, eds. Ren-
  aissance Rhetoric.*
    R.J. Schoeck, 191(ELN):Mar84-66
Murphy, L.R. Lucien Bonaparte Maxwell.
    L. Milazzo, 584(SWR):Summer83-vi
Murphy, O.T. Charles Gravier, Comte de
  Vergennes.
    F. Busi, 207(FR):Feb84-427
Murphy, S. The Complete Knowledge of
  Sally Fry.*
    J. Daynard, 441:1Jul84-20
Murray, A.D. - see Ludlow, J.
Murray, C. Losing Ground.
    L.M. Mead, 441:16Dec84-7
Murray, D. Odious Commerce.
    J. Fisher, 86(BHS):Jan83-92
Murray, J. The Proustian Comedy.*
    A. Corbineau-Hoffmann, 547(RF):Band95
      Heft3-374
Murray, L.A. The Vernacular Republic.*
    C. Benfey, 472:Fall/Winter83Spring/
      Summer84/236
    J.D. McClatchy, 491:Dec83-172
Murray, O. Early Greece.*
    R. Sealey, 122:Apr83-167
Murray, P. - see Burckhardt, J.
Murray, R. Journey.*
    F. Cogswell, 198:Jan83-129
    L. Hutchman, 137:Sep83-15
    L.R. Ricou, 102(CanL):Summer83-118
Murray, S. La Mère morte.
    A.D. Barry, 207(FR):Apr84-738
    E-M. Kroller, 102(CanL):Winter82-172
Murray, W. Tip on a Dead Crab.
    J. Richardson, 441:22Apr84-16
    442(NY):23Apr84-130
Murrin, M. The Allegorical Epic.*
    C. Jordan, 276:Winter83-373
    K.M. Lea, 541(RES):Feb83-59
    H.K. Moss, 131(CL):Fall83-384
Murry, J.M. The Letters of John Middleton
  Murry to Katherine Mansfield.* (C.A.
  Hankin, ed)
    R. Brown, 617(TLS):13Jul84-772
Murry, J.M. - see Mansfield, K.
Mursell, N. Green and Pleasant Land.
    S. Mills, 617(TLS):26Oct84-1218
Mursia, U. Scritti Conradiani. (M.
  Curreli, ed)
    S. Monod, 189(EA):Jul-Sep84-345
Mursia, U. - see Conrad, J.
de Murville, M.N.L.C. and P. Jenkins - see
  under Couve de Murville, M.N.L. and P.
  Jenkins
Musa, M. - see Dante Alighieri
Musaeus. Hero et Leander. (H. Livrea,
  with P. Eleuteri, eds)
    M.L. West, 123:Vol33No2-184

Musallam, B.F. Sex and Society in Islam.
  R. Irwin, 617(TLS):17Feb84-161
Musarra-Schrøder, U. Le Roman-mémoires
  moderne.
  H-P. Bayerdörfer, 52:Band18Heft2-212
Musat, M. and I. Ardeleanu. Political
  Life in Romania, 1918-1921.
  D. Deletant, 617(TLS):13Jul84-777
Muscarella, O.W. The Catalogue of Ivories
  from Hasanlu, Iran.
  G. Herrmann, 318(JAOS):Jul-Sep82-542
Musgrave, S. Tarts and Muggers.*
  A. Brooks, 102(CanL):Autumn83-62
  P. Stuewe, 529(QQ):Winter83-1034
Mushabac, J. Melville's Humor.*
  W.B. Dillingham, 569(SR):Fall83-lxxxvi
  42(AR):Winter83-120
Musil, R. Beitrag zur Beurteilung der
  Lehren Machs und Studien zur Technik
  und Psychotechnik. (A. Frisé, ed)
  H. Reiss, 402(MLR):Apr83-502
Musil, R. Briefe 1901-1942. (A. Frisé,
  ed)
  H. Reiss, 402(MLR):Apr83-502
  J. Strelka, 133:Band16Heft1-80
  J.J. White, 220(GL&L):Apr84-232
Musil, R. Journaux. (P. Jaccottet, ed
  and trans)
  W. Moser, 98:Jun-Jul83-459
Musil, R. L'homme sans qualités.
  H. Weinmann, 98:Jun-Jul83-477
Mussell, K. Women's Gothic and Romantic
  Fiction.
  G.R. Thompson, 395(MFS):Summer83-349
Muthesius, S. The English Terraced House.*
  S. Pepper, 90:Jul83-429
Muthman, F. Der Granatapfel.
  C.R. Phillips 3d, 124:Jan-Feb84-200
Mutsu Munemitsu. Kenkenroku.* (G.M.
  Berger, ed)
  Fujimura Michio, 285(JapQ):Jan-Mar83-
    81
Muyskens, J.L. Moral Problems in Nursing.
  R.S. Downie, 479(PhQ):Jul83-312
  D.O., 185:Oct83-180
Muyskens, J.L. The Sufficiency of Hope.
  W.P.A., 543:Sep82-182
Muzio, G. Tre case a Milano, 1922, 1930,
  1936.
  R.A. Etlin, 127:Summer83-200
"My Secret Life."
  M. Lerner, 135:Oct82-138
Myant, M.R. Socialism and Democracy in
  Czechoslovakia, 1945-1948.
  M. Hauner, 575(SEER):Apr83-302
Myers, G.M., ed. Les chétifs.
  R.F. Cook, 589:Apr83-514
Myers, J.B. Tracking the Marvelous.
  J. Frumkin, 129:Apr84-74
  442(NY):19Mar84-148
Myers, J.J. Texas Electric Railway.
  L. Milazzo, 584(SWR):Winter83-v
Myers, J.P., ed. Elizabethan Ireland.
  N. Canny, 617(TLS):10Feb84-144
Myers, N. The Primary Source.
  J.E. Maslow, 441:2Sep84-8
Myers, R. and M. Harris, eds. Development
  of the English Book Trade, 1700-1899.
  E. James, 354:Mar83-75
  P.J. Korshin, 566:Spring84-173
  E.A. Swaim, 517(PBSA):Vol77No1-111
Myers, R.L. Racine's "La Thébaïde."
  A. Viala, 535(RHL):Sep/Dec83-928

Myers, R.M., ed. The Children of Pride.
  (abridged)
  H. Mitgang, 441:15Apr84-23
Myers, W. The Teaching of George Eliot.
  P. Boumelha, 617(TLS):20Jul84-818
Myerson, J. Ralph Waldo Emerson.
  J.C. Broderick, 365:Summer/Fall83-119
  G. Goodspeed, 78(BC):Winter83-488
  M.M. Sealts, Jr., 517(PBSA):Vol77No1-
    87
Myerson, J. The New England Transcenden-
  talists and the "Dial."
  A.M. Woodlief, 577(SHR):Fall83-376
Myerson, J. Theodore Parker.
  517(PBSA):Vol77No4-518
Myerson, J., ed. Studies in the American
  Renaissance 1979.
  D.M. Van Leer, 677(YES):Vol 13-329
Mylne, V. Diderot: La Religieuse.
  R. Niklaus, 83:Autumn83-269
  A. Strugnell, 208(FS):Apr83-219
Mylne, V.G. The Eighteenth-Century French
  Novel.*
  E. Showalter, Jr., 207(FR):Dec83-249
  P. Testud, 535(RHL):Jan/Feb83-129
Mynors, R.A.B. and D.F.S. Thomson - see
  Erasmus
Myres, S.L. Westering Women and the Fron-
  tier Experience, 1800-1915.
  C.A. O'Connor, 649(WAL):Nov83-260
"Le Mystère de sainte Venice."* (G.A.
  Runnalls, ed)
  A. Foulet, 545(RPh):May83-627
"Mystique and Identity."
  R.L. Shep, 614:Fall84-21
"Le Mythe d'Étiemble."*
  D.W. Fokkema, 107(CRCL):Jun83-241

Nabb, M. Death in Springtime.*
  M. Laski, 362:9Feb84-26
Nabokov, V. Lectures on Don Quixote.*
  (F. Bowers, ed)
  A. Close, 304(JHP):Spring83-227
  C.S. Ross, 395(MFS):Winter83-736
Nabokov, V. Mademoiselle O.
  J. Aeply, 450(NRF):May83-145
Naccarato, F. - see Eiximenis, F.
Nadeau, R. Readings from the New Book of
  Nature.*
  J.M. Mellard, 587(SAF):Autumn83-264
Nadelhaft, J.J. The Disorders of War.
  J.J. Crow, 656(WMQ):Oct83-635
Nadolny, S. Die Entdeckung der Langsam-
  keit.
  J.J. White, 617(TLS):20Jul84-816
Nagel, B. Kleine Schriften zur deutschen
  Literatur.
  F. Shaw, 402(MLR):Oct83-957
Nagel, G. The Structure of Experience.
  R.C.S. Walker, 617(TLS):27Jul84-851
Nagel, J. Stephen Crane and Literary Im-
  pressionism.*
  J. Cazemajou, 189(EA):Jan-Mar83-105
  T.J. Matheson, 106:Fall83-321
Nagel, J., ed. Ernest Hemingway.
  J. Campbell, 617(TLS):20Jul84-806
Nagel, P.C. Descent from Glory.*
  V.H. Winner, 27(AL):Oct83-457
  639(VQR):Spring83-48
Nagy, G. The Best of the Achaeans.*
  C. Leach, 447(N&Q):Feb82-89

Nagy, P. Vous et nous.
G.M. Vajda, 52:Band18Heft3-323
J. Voisine, 549(RLC):Apr-Jun83-247
El-Nahal, G.H. The Judicial Administra-
tion of Ottoman Egypt in the Seventeenth
Century.
F.J. Ziadeh, 318(JAOS):Jul-Sep82-563
Nahmias, D. The Cuisine of Olympe.
M. Burros, 441:3Jun84-15
Nahum, P. Monograms of Victorian and
Edwardian Artists.
T. Crombie, 39:Sep83-273
Naidoo, I. Island in Chains.
J. Kimble, 69:Vol53No4-95
Naik, M.K., ed. Perspectives on Indian
Prose in English.
A.P. Cappon, 436(NewL):Fall83-107
Naimark, N.M. Terrorists and Social Demo-
crats.
P. Pomper, 104(CASS):Summer83-283
Naipaul, S. Beyond the Dragon's Mouth.
I. Hislop, 362:11Oct84-29
Naipaul, S. A Hot Country.*
P. Craig, 617(TLS):28Dec84-1506
C. Hope, 364:Dec83/Jan84-139
Naipaul, S. Love and Death in a Hot Coun-
try.
P-L. Adams, 61:Jun84-124
J. Yglesias, 441:12Aug84-26
Naipaul, V.S. Among the Believers.*
M. Bayat, 31(ASch):Winter82/83-124
G.M. Wickens, 529(QQ):Summer83-570
Naipaul, V.S. Finding the Centre.
A. Burgess, 617(TLS):22Jun84-691
J. Didion, 453(NYRB):11Oct84-10
D.J. Enright, 362:3May84-22
E. Hoagland, 441:16Sep84-1
J. Lasdun, 176:Sep/Oct84-48
Naipaul, V.S. A House for Mr. Biswas.
(new ed)
D.J. Enright, 362:3May84-22
Najder, Z. Joseph Conrad.*
F. Crews, 453(NYRB):1Mar84-3
P. Kemp, 362:15Mar84-24
R. O'Hanlon, 617(TLS):24Feb84-185
Najder, Z. Conrad under Familial Eyes.
P. Kemp, 362:15Mar84-24
R. O'Hanlon, 617(TLS):24Feb84-185
Najemy, J.M. Corporatism and Consensus in
Florentine Electoral Politics, 1280-1400.
W.M. Bowsky, 377:Nov83-186
Najita, T. and J.V. Koschmann, eds. Con-
flict in Modern Japanese History.
M. Fletcher, 407(MN):Autumn83-346
Nakadate, N., ed. Robert Penn Warren.*
M.E. Cook, 392:Winter82/83-85
A. Gelpi, 405(MP):May84-447
M.K. Spears, 569(SR):Fall83-655
Nakahara Chūya. Depilautumn. (K.L.
Richard and J.L. Riley, trans)
J.R. Morita, 293(JASt):Aug83-968
Nakam, G. Montaigne et son temps.
J. Brody, 551(RenQ):Winter83-627
A. Reix, 542:Oct-Dec83-463
Nakamura, H. Indian Buddhism.
P.S. Jaini, 293(JASt):Aug83-994
J.P. McDermott, 318(JAOS):Jul-Sep82-
547
Nakamura, H. Shoki no Vedānta tetsugaku.
J.W. de Jong, 259(IIJ):Mar83-137
Nakamura Tetsurō. Seiyōjin no Kabuki Hak-
ken.
L.C. Pronko, 407(MN):Spring83-109

Nakano, E., with B.B. Stephan. Japanese
Stencil Dyeing — Paste-Resist Tech-
niques.*
P. Bach, 614:Summer84-19
Nakhimovsky, A. and S. Paperno. An
English-Russian Dictionary of Nabokov's
"Lolita."
C. Brown, 550(RusR):Oct83-418
S.J. Parker, 574(SEEJ):Winter83-496
Nakhimovsky, A.S. Laughter in the Void.
E. Chances, 574(SEEJ):Fall83-391
Nalimov, V.V. Faces of Science.* (R.G.
Colodny, ed)
A.B. Stewart, 42(AR):Spring83-247
Nalimov, V.V. In the Laybrinths of Lan-
guage.*
G. Pirog, 558(RLJ):Winter-Spring83-247
Naman, A.A. The Jew in the Victorian
Novel.*
J. Bayley, 541(RES):May83-234
"Namibia: The Facts."
B. Wisner, 69:Vol53No1-106
Namjoshi, S. The Authentic Lie.
I. Sowton, 102(CanL):Summer83-124
Namuth, H. Pollock Painting. (B. Rose,
ed) L'Atelier de Jackson Pollock.
F. Orton and G. Pollock, 59:Mar83-114
Nance, J.J. Splash of Colors.
A. Salpukas, 441:21Oct84-51
Nancy, J-L. L'Impératif catégorique.
F. Trémolières, 450(NRF):Jul/Aug83-234
Nanda, B.R., ed. Essays in Modern Indian
History.
D. Haynes, 293(JASt):Feb83-441
Naqvi, S. Quṭb Shāhī 'Āshūr Khānās of
Hyderabad City.
S. Kazim, 273(IC):Jul83-248
Narahara, Y., T. Okamoto and H. Shimoda.
Beiträge zur Phonetik des Deutschen.
G.F. Meier, 682(ZPSK):Band36Heft3-362
Narasimhacharya, M.S., ed. Mahābhāsya
Pradīpa Vyākhyānāni. (Vols 6 and 7)
R. Rocher, 318(JAOS):Oct-Dec82-672
Narasimhaiah, C.D., ed. An Introduction
to Australian Literature.
S. Walker, 71(ALS):Oct83-280
Narasimhan, R. Modelling Language Behav-
iour.
D.D. Mahulkar, 261:Mar-Dec81-141
Narayan, J. Towards Total Revolution.
(Brahmanand, ed)
R.J. Young, 318(JAOS):Oct-Dec82-677
Nardo, A.K. Milton's Sonnets and the
Ideal Community.*
A. Burnett, 447(N&Q):Feb82-79
von Naredi-Rainer, P. Architektur und
Harmonie.
F. Bucher, 54:Dec83-704
Narkiewicz, O.A. Marxism and Reality of
Power, 1919-1980.
M. Waller, 575(SEER):Apr83-293
Narkiss, B. Hebrew Illuminated Manu-
scripts in the British Isles. (Pt 1)
G.N., 617(TLS):13Apr84-415
Narvarte, C. Problemas de método y teoría.
A. Reix, 542:Oct-Dec83-494
Nash, E. Always First Class.
E. Forbes, 415:May83-300
Nash, M.I. Canadian Occupational Health
and Safety Law Handbook.
D. Leitch, 99:Oct83-34

Nash, O. I Wouldn't Have Missed It. (L.
  Smith and I. Eberstadt, eds)
    T. Disch, 617(TLS):3Feb84-118
Nash, S. Paul Valéry's "Album de vers
  anciens."
    A.J. Arnold, 210(FrF):Sep83-285
    295(JML):Nov83-580
Nash, W. Designs in Prose.
    R. Carter, 447(N&Q):Jun82-282
    M. Rose, 506(PSt):Sep83-176
Nasr, S.H., ed. Ismā'īlī Contributions
  to Islamic Culture.
    H. Landolt, 318(JAOS):Jan-Mar82-213
Nassar, E.P. Essays Critical and Meta-
  critical.
    W.B. Bache, 395(MFS):Winter83-815
Nathan, J. An American Folklife Cookbook.
    M. Burros, 441:2Dec84-16
Nathan, L. Holding Patterns.*
    C. Dennis, 219(GaR):Fall83-688
    T. Diggory, 560:Fall83-112
Nathan, P. The Nervous System.
    R.O., 617(TLS):20Jul84-822
"A Nation at Risk."
    A. Hacker, 453(NYRB):12Apr84-35
    T.S. Healy, 441:13May84-14
"National Parks of the Desert Southwest."
    P. Hagan, 441:3Jun84-14
Natsuki, S. Murder at Mt. Fuji.
    N. Callendar, 441:17Jun84-22
Naudeau, O. - see Aumeric
Naughtie, J., ed. Playing the Palace.
    J. Critchley, 362:20/27Dec84-56
Nauhaus, G. - see Schumann, R.
Naumann, O. Frans van Mieris (1635-1681)
  The Elder.
    I. Gaskell, 59:Jun83-236
    P. Hecht, 90:Aug83-501
    D.R. Smith, 54:Dec83-694
    C. White, 39:Jan83-64
Naumann, U. Adalbert Stifter.
    C.O. Sjögren, 406:Summer83-219
Naumann, U. - see "Sammlung"
Naumann, W. Die Dramen Shakespeares.
    H-J. Weckermann, 72:Band220Heft1-156
de Navacelle, T. Sublime Marlene.
    P. O'Connor, 617(TLS):28Dec84-1507
de Navarre, M. - see under Marguerite de
  Navarre
Navasky, V.S. Naming Names.*
    G.D. Black, 488:Mar83-123
Naville, P. Sociologie et logique.
    A. Reix, 542:Jul-Sep83-340
Naylor, J.F. A Man and an Institution.
    J.A. Turner, 617(TLS):28Sep84-1073
Neal, J. The Genius of John Neal. (B.
  Lease and H-J. Lang, eds)
    J.E. Reilly, 495(PoeS):Dec83-44
Neal, J. The Kentucky Shakers.
    P. Bach, 614:Winter84-19
Neal, S. Dark Horse.
    R. Bendiner, 441:15Jan84-27
Neale, R.S. Bath 1680-1850.
    L. Stone, 453(NYRB):29Mar84-42
Neale, S. Genre.
    B.K. Grant, 106:Spring83-107
Neaman, J. and C.G. Silver. A Dictionary
  of Euphemisms.
    R. Davies, 617(TLS):21Dec84-1481
Neave, E.H. Canada's Financial System.
    T. Powrie, 529(QQ):Summer83-525
Nebel, H.M., Jr. - see Sumarokov, A.P. and
  N.M. Karamzin

Nebreda, J.J. La fenomenologia del
  lenguaje de M. Merleau-Ponty.
    G. Hottois, 540(RIPh):Vol137fasc1/2-
    239
Nectoux, J-M. - see Fauré, G.
Needham, J. "The Completest Mode."*
    639(VQR):Winter83-14
Needham, J. Science in Traditional China.
    J.T. Wilson, 529(QQ):Winter83-1213
Needham, J., with others. Science and
  Civilization in China. (Vol 5, Pt 4)
    D.S. Payne, 302:Vol 19No2-257
Needham, J. and F. Bray. Science and
  Civilisation in China. (Vol 6, Pt 2)
    D. Rimmington, 617(TLS):2Nov84-1245
Needham, R. Essential Perplexities.
    J. Agassi, 488:Mar83-116
Neesen, L. Untersuchungen zu den direkten
  Staatsabgaben der römischen Kaiserzeit
  27 v. Chr. bis 284 n. Chr.
    R.P. Duncan-Jones, 123:Vol33No2-353
Neff, D. Warriors for Jerusalem.
    M. Viorst, 441:6May84-46
Nehls, D., ed. Studies in Contrastive Lin-
  guistics and Error Analysis. (Vol 2)
    S. Eliasson, 257(IRAL):Feb83-76
"Jawaharlal Nehru: An Anthology."* (S.
  Gopal, ed)
    R.J. Young, 318(JAOS):Oct-Dec82-675
Neider, C. - see Twain, M.
Neiers, M.D. The Peoples of the Jos
  Plateau, Nigeria.
    B. Sharpe, 69:Vol53No4-84
Neill, S. A History of Christianity in
  India.
    P.J. Marshall, 617(TLS):4May84-501
Nelde, P.H., ed. Deutsch als Mutter-
  sprache in Belgien.
    J. Eichhoff, 685(ZDL):2/1983-246
Nelsen, H.W. The Chinese Military System.
  (2nd ed)
    R. Weidenbaum, 293(JASt):Nov82-141
Nelson, A.H. The Medieval English Stage.
    H-J. Diller, 38:Band101Heft3/4-511
Nelson, A.H. - see Medwall, H.
Nelson, C. Our Last First Poets.*
    E. Folsom, 301(JEGP):Apr83-273
    W. Harmon, 651(WHR):Spring83-79
    J.M. Reibetanz, 106:Winter83-497
    K. Shevelow, 405(MP):Feb84-337
Nelson, D.A. - see de Berceo, G.
Nelson, H. Robert Bly.
    D.W. Hartnett, 617(TLS):9Nov84-1290
Nelson, H.L.W. Überlieferung, Aufbau und
  Stil von Gai Institutiones.
    J. Crook, 313:Vol73-212
Nelson, H.S. Charles Dickens.*
    R. Barnard, 179(ES):Aug83-377
    A. Sadrin, 189(EA):Apr-Jun84-213
Nelson, J. Mabel Dodge Luhan.
    R.W. Etulain, 649(WAL):Aug83-176
Nelson, J.I. Economic Inequality.
    T.D., 185:Apr84-560
Nelson, R.J. Pascal.*
    J. Alter, 400(MLN):May83-809
    J-J. Demorest, 210(FrF):Jan83-94
    B. Norman, 475:Vol 10No18-381
    H.L. Shapiro, 529(QQ):Spring83-204
Nelson, T.A. Kubrick.*
    M. Kernan, 18:Oct83-90
Nelson, W.A. The Dutch Forts of Sri Lanka.
    J.M. Richards, 617(TLS):23Nov84-1341

Nelson, W.N. On Justifying Democracy.*
  T.D. Campbell, 393(Mind):Apr83-301
  C. Pateman, 482(PhR):Apr83-255
de Nemore, J. - see under Jordanus de
  Nemore
Nencioni, G. Lessicografia e letteratura
  italiana.
  M. Contini, 553(RLiR):Jan-Jun83-180
Neruda, P. Passions and Impressions. (M.
  Neruda and M. Otero Silva, eds)
  J. Chaves, 37:Sep-Oct83-61
de Nerval, G. Léo Burckart. (J. Richer,
  ed)
  F. Bassan, 597(SN):Vol55No2-244
Nessen, R. The Hour.
  W. Ferguson, 441:22Jul84-20
Nessi, A. Terra Matta.
  J. Steinberg, 617(TLS):7Dec84-1410
Nesteby, J.R. Black Images in American
  Films, 1896-1954.
  S. Bryant-Johnson, 18:Jan-Feb84-74
Neto, P.D. - see under de Carvalho Neto, P.
Nettles, G. and P. Golenbock. Balls.
  L.S. Ritter, 441:3Jun84-9
Nettum, R.N., ed. I diktningens brenn-
  punkt.
  J. Sjåvik, 563(SS):Summer83-280
Neubauer, F. Die Struktur der Explika-
  tionen in deutschen einsprachigen Wörter-
  büchern.
  D. Herberg, 682(ZPSK):Band36Heft6-739
Neubauer, J. Novalis.*
  P.M. Lützeler, 406:Summer83-219
Neubecker, A.J. Altgriechische Musik.
  W.A., 412:Feb82-57
  J. Solomon, 122:Jul83-236
Neubuhr, E., ed. Geschichtsdrama.*
  E. Lehmann, 490:Band14Heft3/4-340
  H.S. Lindenberger, 133:Band16Heft1-60
  K. Tetzeli von Rosador, 72:Band220
    Heft2-418
Neufeldt, L. The House of Emerson.
  J. Myerson, 432(NEQ):Jun83-275
  M.M. Sealts, Jr., 301(JEGP):Oct83-579
  D. Yannella, 27(AL):Dec83-646
Neugeboren, J. The Stolen Jew.
  S. Goldleaf, 473(PR):3/1983-454
  S.G. Kellman, 390:Feb83-61
Neuhaus, H. The Art of Piano Playing.
  J. Methuen-Campbell, 415:Nov83-683
Neuhaus, R.J. The Naked Public Square.
  J.M. Cameron, 453(NYRB):11Oct84-39
  H. Cox, 441:26Aug84-11
Neuhaus, V. Die zeitgeschichtliche Sen-
  sationsroman in Deutschland 1855 bis
  1878.
  L.A. Lensing, 221(GQ):Mar83-326
  H. Schmiedt, 52:Band17Heft1-93
Neuland, L. Motif-Index of Latvian Folk-
  tales and Legends.
  H-J. Uther, 196:Band24Heft1/2-164
Neuman, D.M. The Life of Music in North
  India.
  N.A. Jairazbhoy, 293(JASt):Nov82-194
Neuman, S. Some One Myth.
  S. Connelly, 174(Éire):Winter83-152
Neumann, F. Manoeuvres.
  T.J. Binyon, 617(TLS):30Mar84-354
Neumann, F. Ornamentation in Baroque and
  Post-Baroque Music.*
  D. Collins, 537:Vol69No1-109
Neumann, G. Herman the German.
  R. Bailey, 441:5Aug84-19

Neuse, E.K. Die deutsche Kurzgeschichte.*
  W.D. Elfe, 221(GQ):May83-489
Neuser, K. Anemoi.
  M.B. Trapp, 313:Vol73-235
Neville, G.H. A Memoir of D.H. Lawrence.*
  (C. Baron, ed)
  R.H. Costa, 177(ELT):Vol26No1-66
Neville, R.C. Reconstruction of Thinking.*
  P. Dubois, 542:Jan-Mar83-63
Neville, R.C. Soldier, Sage, Saint.
  D.L. Hall, 485(PE&W):Apr83-206
Neville, R.C. The Tao and the Daimon.
  E.M. Kraus, 258:Dec83-441
Neville, S. The Invention of Flight.
  G. Weaver, 344:Fall84-107
Nevin, D. Dream West.
  M. Cunliffe, 441:29Jan84-10
New, M. and J. - see Sterne, L.
"A New Look for Needlework."
  J. Zarbaugh, 614:Fall84-21
"A New Wave in Fashion."
  R.L. Shep, 614:Summer84-24
Newall, V.J., ed. Folklore Studies in the
  Twentieth Century.
  R. Wehse, 196:Band24Heft3/4-316
Newberg, P.R., ed. The Politics of Human
  Rights.
  J.H.C., 185:Apr84-567
Newbury, M. Reminiscences of a Bradford
  Mill Girl.
  D. Gittins, 637(VS):Summer83-431
Newby, E. On the Shores of the Mediter-
  ranean.
  R. Fox, 362:8Nov84-26
Newby, P.H. Saladin in His Time.*
  L. Robinson, 441:26Aug84-17
  J. Sumption, 617(TLS):9Mar84-242
Newcomb, H. and R.S. Alley. The Pro-
  ducer's Medium.*
  B. Brown, 18:Jul-Aug84-53
Newcombe, W.W., with M.S. Carnahan. Ger-
  man Artist of the Western Frontier:
  Friedrich Richard Petri.
  M.S. Young, 39:Feb83-148
Newell, N.D. Creation and Evolution.
  K.S., 185:Apr84-554
  639(VQR):Winter83-28
Newey, V. Cowper's Poetry.*
  W. Hutchings, 148:Summer83-84
  S. Soupel, 189(EA):Jul-Sep84-331
  J.R. Watson, 83:Autumn83-213
Newey, V., ed. "The Pilgrim's Progress":
  Critical and Historical Views.
  J.B.H. Alblas, 179(ES):Apr83-191
  J. Blondel, 189(EA):Oct-Dec83-465
  G.R. Evans, 541(RES):May83-217
  C. Hill, 447(N&Q):Apr82-176
  O.C. Watkins, 161(DUJ):Jun83-129
Newfarmer, R., ed. From Gunboats to
  Diplomacy.
  J. Le Moyne, 441:15Apr84-24
Newlin, D. Schoenberg Remembered.*
  E.S., 412:Aug-Nov82-273
Newman, C. White Jazz.
  R. Loewinsohn, 441:15Jan84-14
Newman, J. Saul Bellow and History.
  D.J. Enright, 617(TLS):22Jun84-688
Newman, J.H. An Essay in Aid of a Grammar
  of Assent.
  W. Myers, 569(SR):Spring83-275

Newman, J.H. The Letters and Diaries of
John Henry Newman.* (Vols 2-4) (I. Ker
and T. Gornall, eds)
H.R. Woudhuysen, 447(N&Q):Jun82-254
Newman, J.H. The Letters and Diaries of
John Henry Newman. (Vol 6) (G. Tracey,
ed)
A.O.J. Cockshut, 617(TLS):19Oct84-1186
Newman, M. Socialism and European Unity.
P. McCarthy, 617(TLS):8Jun84-643
Newman, S.J. Dickens at Play.*
D. David, 637(VS):Autumn82-93
Newmark, L., P. Hubbard and P. Prifti.
Standard Albanian.*
V.A. Friedman, 399(MLJ):Summer83-178
Newmark, P. Approaches to Translation.
R.L. Tinsley, Jr., 399(MLJ):Summer83-
210
Newmeyer, F.J. Linguistic Theory in Amer-
ica.*
R.A. Hall, Jr., 205(ForL):Dec81-177
Newth, R. Finding the Lamb.
E. Grosholz, 249(HudR):Autumn83-588
Newton, I. The Optical Papers of Isaac
Newton. (Vol 1) (A. Shapiro, ed)
I.B. Cohen, 617(TLS):2Nov84-1242
Newton, J.L. Women, Power, and Subversion.
D. Rosenblum, 637(VS):Summer83-446
Newton, K.M. George Eliot, Romantic Human-
ist.
C. Gallagher, 637(VS):Autumn82-89
M.C. Henberg, 478:Apr83-120
Newton, S.M. Fashion in the Age of the
Black Prince.
J. Harris, 59:Mar83-110
Newton-Smith, W.H. The Rationality of
Science.*
J.E. Adler, 479(PhQ):Jan83-90
J.R. Brown, 154:Jun83-299
M. Detlefsen, 540(RIPh):Vol137fasc3-364
J.A. Kourany, 311(JP):Aug83-474
C.B. Wright, 518:Apr83-118
Newton-Smith, W.H. The Structure of Time.*
J. Butterfield, 482(PhR):Jul83-468
G.N. Schlesinger, 393(Mind):Apr83-293
Neyt, F. L'Art Holo du Haut-Kwango.
A.P. Bourgeois, 2(AfrA):Aug83-26
Ničev, A. La catharsis tragique
d'Aristote.
R.V. Schoder, 124:May-Jun84-330
Nichol, B.P. As Elected. (B.P. Nichol
and J. David, eds)
G. Boire, 102(CanL):Summer83-166
Nichol, B.P. Extreme Positions.
A. Mandel, 102(CanL):Winter82-132
Nichol, B.P. - see Davey, F.
Nicholas of Cusa. Nicolai de Cusa: Opera
omnia. (Vol 12: De venatione sapientiae,
De apice theoriae.) (R. Klibansky and
I.G. Senger, eds)
G. von Bredow, 687:Jul-Sep83-456
Nicholas I, Patriarch of Constantinople.
Miscellaneous Writings. (L.G. Westerink,
ed and trans)
J. Meyendorff, 589:Apr83-517
Nicholl, C. The Chemical Theatre.
R.M. Schuler, 541(RES):Aug83-328
Nicholl, C. A Cup of News.
E. Jones, 617(TLS):18May84-540
Nichols, B. Ideology and the Image.*
R.A. Berman, 221(GQ):Jan83-182
S. Feldman, 529(QQ):Autumn83-890

Nichols, C.H. - see Bontemps, A. and L.
Hughes
Nichols, F.D. and R.E. Griswold. Thomas
Jefferson.
639(VQR):Spring83-64
Nichols, F.J., ed and trans. An Anthology
of Neo-Latin Poetry.*
W. Adam, 72:Band220Heft1-115
Nichols, J. The Last Beautiful Days of
Autumn.
D. Rawlings, 649(WAL):May83-54
Nichols, J. Predicate Nominals.
C.V. Chvany, 350:Sep84-591
Nichols, P. Feeling You're Behind.
J. Hiley, 362:31May84-24
H. Hobson, 617(TLS):13Jul84-781
Nichols, S.G., Jr. Romanesque Signs.
N.J. Lacy, 207(FR):May84-867
Nicholson, J. The Heartache of Motherhood.
M. Lake, 381:Sep83-380
Nickel, G., ed. "Beowulf" und die klein-
eren Denkmäler der altenglischen Helden-
sage Waldere und Finnsburg.
K.R. Grinda, 260(IF):Band87-328
Nickel, G. Einführung in die Linguistik.
L. Lipka, 38:Band101Heft1/2-158
Nickell, J. Inquest on the Shroud of
Turin.
D. Dutton, 385(MQR):Summer84-422
Nickles, T., ed. Scientific Discovery,
Logic and Rationality.* Scientific
Discovery: Case Studies.*
P.L. Mott, 84:Sep83-306
Nicolaisen, P. Ernest Hemingway.*
G. Ahrends, 72:Band220Heft1-184
Nicolas, A. - see de Goncourt, E. and J.
Nicolet, C., ed. Insula sacra.
J-C. Richard, 555:Vol57fasc1-179
Nicolet, C. L'Idée républicaine en
France.*
H. Cronel, 450(NRF):Sep83-157
Nicolet, C. The World of the Citizen in
Republican Rome.
G.W. Bowersock, 453(NYRB):14Jun84-45
Nicoll, A. The Garrick Stage.* (S.
Rosenfeld, ed)
C. Price, 402(MLR):Oct83-904
Nicolodi, F., ed. Musica italiana del
primo Novecento.
J. Budden, 410(M&L):Jan/Apr83-119
Nicolson, H. Diaries and Letters 1930-
1964. (S. Olson, ed)
L.D., 617(TLS):18May84-562
Niederauer, D.J. Pierre Louÿs.*
E. Lehouck, 627(UTQ):Summer83-464
Niederehe, H-J. - see Stengel, E.
Nieh, H., ed. Literature of the Hundred
Flowers Period.
H-Y.L. Mowry, 293(JASt):Nov82-142
Nielsen, E. Glo Ikke Så Romantisk.
G. Pattison, 89(BJA):Autumn83-378
Nielsen, K. Ethics Without God.
R.Z. Friedman, 258:Sep83-321
Nielsen, K. An Introduction to the Philos-
ophy of Religion.
P. Helm, 518:Jul83-172
Nielsen, K. and S.C. Patten, eds. Marx
and Morality.*
J. Narveson, 154:Sep83-523
Nielsen, S. Stability in Musical Improvi-
sation.
P. Gronow, 187:May84-342

Nobori Shomu and Akamatsu Katsumaro. The
Russian Impact on Japan. (P. Berton,
P.F. Langer and G.O. Totten, eds and
trans)
Tsuguo Togawa, 550(RusR):Apr83-237
Noccioli, G. Duse on Tour. (G. Pontiero,
ed and trans)
L. Richards, 610:Summer83-174
Noddings, N. Caring.
L. Kuhmerker, 441:19Aug84-19
"Charles Nodier."
B. Juden, 402(MLR):Jul83-714
Noel, G. Ena.
S. Runciman, 617(TLS):10Aug84-888
Noel, T.J. The City and the Saloon.
L. Milazzo, 584(SWR):Winter84-v
Noethlicus, K.L. Beamtentum und Dienst-
vergehen.
A. Chastagnol, 555:Vol57fasc2-361
Noiray, J. Le Romancier et la machine.
(Vol 2)
A. Martin, 208(FS):Oct83-480
Nokes, D. - see Fielding, H.
Nolan, B. The Gothic Visionary Perspec-
tive.
S.P. Coy, 545(RPh):Feb83-452
Nolan, D., ed. Dante Commentaries.
A.A-M. Paasonen, 545(RPh):Aug82-122
Nolan, W.F. Dashiell Hammett.*
M. Colyer, 362:9Feb84-26
Nolan, W.F. McQueen.
P. Craig, 18:Jul-Aug84-56
W. Murray, 441:11Mar84-16
von Nolcken, C. The Middle English Trans-
lation of the Rosarium Theologie. (M.
Görlach, ed)
A. Zettersten, 72:Band219Heft1-187
Nølke, H. Les adverbes paradigmatisants.
R. Martin, 553(RLiR):Jul-Dec83-479
Nolte, E. Marxismus und industrielle
Revolution.
S. Pollard, 617(TLS):20Jul84-802
Nomez, N., ed. Chilean Literature in
Canada/Literatura Chilena en Canada.
B. Mogridge, 99:Jul83-37
A. Percival, 627(UTQ):Summer83-541
Noonan, H.W. Objects and Identity.*
C.D.C. Reeve, 482(PhR):Oct83-633
Noone, J.B., Jr. Rousseau's Social Con-
tract.*
A. Levine, 482(PhR):Oct83-620
Noordman, L.G.M. Inferring from Language.
J.F. Kess, 257(IRAL):Feb83-70
Noort, E. Untersuchungen zum Gottesbes-
cheid in Mari.
I. Nakata, 318(JAOS):Jan-Mar82-166
Nooteboom, C. Rituals. A Song of Truth
and Semblance.
T. Fitton, 617(TLS):28Dec84-1506
Nooy-Palm, B. The Sa'dan-Toraja. (Vol 1)
T. Bigalke, 293(JASt):Aug83-1025
Norcliffe, G. and T. Pinfold, eds. Plan-
ning African Development.
D.R.F. Taylor, 69:Vol53No2-84
Nordan, L. Welcome to the Arrow-Catcher
Fair.
E. Milton, 441:15Jan84-22
von Nordheim, E. Die Lehre der Alten.
(Vol 1)
A.B. Kolenkow, 318(JAOS):Oct-Dec82-663
Nordholt, J.W.S. The Dutch Republic and
American Independence.
J. Popkin, 656(WMQ):Jul83-479

Nordon, H. The Education of a Polish Jew.
A. Shulman, 390:May83-76
Noret, J., ed. Vitae duae antiquae sancti
Athanasii Athonitae.
M. Whitby, 303(JoHS):Vol 103-231
Norman, B. Here's Looking at You.
A. Smith, 362:5Jul84-24
Norman, D.A., ed. Perspectives on Cogni-
tive Science.
E.M. Segal, 474(PIL):Vol 15No1/4-291
Norman, E. The English Catholic Church in
the Nineteenth Century.
J. Bossy, 617(TLS):11May84-513
G. Priestland, 362:8Mar84-25
Norman, P. The Stones.
N. Fountain, 362:31May84-23
Norman, P. Symphony for the Devil.
R. Palmer, 441:11Nov84-34
J. Wolcott, 453(NYRB):22Nov84-15
442(NY):12Nov84-194
Norn, O. At se det usynlige — Mysterie-
kult og ridderidealer.
S. Kaspersen, 341:Vol52No3-134
Norrick, N.R. Semiotic Principles in
Semantic Theory.*
M.K.L. Ching, 215(GL):Spring83-71
Norris, C. Deconstruction.
G.D. Atkins, 400(MLN):Dec83-1308
M. Bell, 402(MLR):Jul83-637
W.E. Cain, 131(CL):Summer83-283
D. Donoghue, 478:Oct83-248
T. Eagleton, 366:Autumn83-260
M.A.R. Habib, 89(BJA):Summer83-277
J. van Luxemburg, 204(FdL):Dec82-292
T. Rajan, 529(QQ):Winter83-1193
Norris, C. The Deconstructive Turn.
P. Hamilton, 617(TLS):17Aug84-923
Norris, K. To Sleep, To Love.
P. Mitcham, 102(CanL):Summer83-144
Norris, M. The Decentrated Universe of
"Finnegans Wake."
M. Hodgart, 447(N&Q):Dec82-559
Norris, W. Willful Misconduct.
R. Witkin, 441:1Jul84-21
Norrlind, E.L. - see under Lilja Norrlind,
E.
Norrman, M. I livets hand.
K.W. Berg, 562(Scan):Nov82-193
Norrman, R. The Insecure World of Henry
James's Fiction.*
P. Horne, 184(EIC):Oct83-353
E. Nettels, 445(NCF):Jun83-124
Norrman, R. and J. Haarberg. Nature and
Language.
C. Norris, 402(MLR):Apr83-395
B. Sunesen, 179(ES):Feb83-67
Norstedt, J. Thomas MacDonagh.*
M. Harmon, 447(N&Q):Feb82-94
North, H.F. From Myth to Icon.*
J.E. Herrin, 447(N&Q):Jun82-287
J.E. Rexine, 121(CJ):Oct/Nov83-78
North, R. The Animals Report.
M. Furness, 617(TLS):1Jun84-618
North, R. General Preface and Life of Dr.
John North. (P. Millard, ed)
P. Rogers, 617(TLS):19Oct84-1196
Northedge, F.S. and A. Wells. Britain and
Soviet Communism.
R.H. McNeal, 550(RusR):Oct83-458
Norti Gualdani, E. - see de Padilla, J.
Norton, C.A. Writing "Tom Sawyer."
27(AL):Oct83-489

Norton, D.F. David Hume.
  A. Baier, 484(PPR):Sep83-127
  R. Hardin, 185:Apr84-534
  P.H. Jones, 518:Apr83-82
  R.D. Stock, 405(MP):Aug83-80
Norton, D.F., N. Capaldi and W.L. Robison,
  eds. McGill Hume Studies.
  J.P. Wright, 518:Jan83-22
Norton-Smith, J. - see "James I of Scot-
  land: 'The Kingis Quair'"
Norwood, C. At Highest Risk.
  J.H. Roberts, 529(QQ):Winter83-1165
Nössig, M., J. Rosenberg and B. Schrader.
  Literaturdebatten in der Weimarer
  Republik.
  K. Kändler, 654(WB):6/1982-163
Nöth, W. Dynamik semiotischer Systeme.
  W. Kühlwein, 307:Oct80-116
  M. Thornton, 107(CRCL):Jun83-226
Nothofer, B. Dialektgeographische Unter-
  suchungen in West-Java und im westlichen
  Zentral-Java.
  J.U. Wolff, 318(JAOS):Jul-Sep82-558
Notker der Deutsche. Die Werke Notkers
  des Deutschen. (Vols 8 and 9) (P.W. Tax,
  ed)
  H.D. Schlosser, 133:Band16Heft2/3-226
Nott, D. - see Sartre, J-P.
Nova, C. The Good Son.*
  D. Smith, 344:Winter84-121
Novak, B. Nature and Culture.*
  A. Wallach, 59:Sep83-380
Novak, M. Freedom with Justice.
  A. Wildavsky, 441:9Dec84-14
Novak, M. The Spirit of Democratic Capi-
  talism.*
  W. McGurn, 396(ModA):Winter83-91
Novak, M.E. Realism, Myth, and History in
  Defoe's Fiction.
  R. Moss, 617(TLS):13Jan84-44
Novales, R.G. - see under Gil Novales, R.
Novarr, D. The Disinterred Muse.*
  J. Baumgaertner, 541(RES):Nov83-503
  P.R. Sellin, 301(JEGP):Apr83-240
Novo, E.G. - see under García Novo, E.
Novotny, J.L. English-German Dictionary
  of American Verbal Idioms.
  P.J.E. Hyams, 179(ES):Aug83-370
Nowak, J. Courier from Warsaw.*
  639(VQR):Spring83-50
Nowak, M. and S. Durrant. The Tale of the
  Nišan Shamaness.
  Chieh-Hsien Ch'en, 302:Vol 19No2-239
Nowakowski, M. The Canary.*
  J. Mellors, 362:2Feb84-28
  T. Swick, 441:9Sep84-30
Nowlan, A. Early Poems.
  E. Trethewey, 150(DR):Autumn83-540
Nowlan, A. I might not tell everybody
  this.*
  A. Munton, 198:Jun83-81
Nozick, R. Philosophical Explanations.*
  R.L. Arrington, 569(SR):Spring83-309
  R.J. Fogelin, 311(JP):Dec83-819
  A.I. Goldman, 482(PhR):Jan83-81
  R. Hardin, 185:Jan84-326
  R.F. Holland, 483:Jan83-118
  G.J. Nathan, 529(QQ):Summer83-560
  R.C. Neville, 396(ModA):Summer/Fall83-
    322
  H.M. Solomon, 577(SHR):Spring83-188
  R. Swinburne, 63:Sep83-303

Nuchelmans, G. Late Scholastic and Human-
  ist Theories of the Proposition.*
  J. Longeway, 482(PhR):Apr83-302
Nuessel, F.H., Jr., ed. Contemporary
  Studies in Romance Languages.
  M.E. Winters, 350:Jun84-450
Nugel, B. The Just Design.
  G. Stratmann, 490:Band14Heft3/4-348
Nunes, M.L. The Craft of an Absolute
  Winner.
  E.E. Fitz, 263(RIB):Vol33No3-412
Nunn, K. Tapping the Source.
  W. Lesser, 441:4Mar84-22
Nusbaum, M.A. and L. Verdier. Parlez sans
  peur!
  E. Doss-Quinby, 207(FR):Feb84-438
  R.J. Melpignano, 399(MLJ):Autumn83-289
Nussbaum, F.A. The Brink of All We Hate.
  D. Brooks-Davies, 617(TLS):15Jun84-678
Nussbaum, M.C. - see Aristotle
Nuttall, A.D. A New Mimesis.
  T. Hawkes, 617(TLS):11May84-518
  R. Hayman, 176:Jan84-62
Nuttall, A.D. Overheard by God.*
  H. Wilcox, 447(N&Q):Apr82-169
Nuttall, A.D. Pope's Essay on Man.
  D. Nokes, 617(TLS):17Aug84-925
Nuttall, Z. - see "The Codex Magliabech-
  iano"
Nutton, V., ed. Galen: Problems and Pros-
  pects.
  J. Longrigg, 123:Vol33No2-244
Nwankwo, N. My Mercedes is Bigger Than
  Yours.
  E. Okeke-Ezigbo, 145(Crit):Summer84-
    199
Nyangoni, W.W. The OECD and Western Min-
  ing Multinational Corporations in the
  Republic of South Africa.
  W.M. Freund, 69:Vol53No4-94
Nye, J.S., Jr., ed. The Making of Amer-
  ica's Soviet Policy.
  A. Tonelson, 441:16Sep84-34
Nye, R. The Facts of Life.*
  J. Mellors, 362:2Feb84-28
Nylander, J.C. Fabrics for Historic Build-
  ings.
  P. Bach, 614:Fall84-16
Nylander, R.C. Wallpapers for Historic
  Buildings.
  P. Bach, 614:Fall84-27
Nyman, M. Experimental Music.
  A. Gillmor, 529(QQ):Winter83-990
Nyssen, H. Des arbres dans la tête.
  R. Robe, 207(FR):May84-915
Nystedt, J. - see Savonarola, M.
Nystrand, M., ed. What Writers Know.
  L. Brodkey, 355(LSoc):Sep83-391
Nystrom, P. Mary Wollstonecraft's Scandi-
  navian Journey.
  P. Honan, 447(N&Q):Apr82-182

Oakes, G. - see Simmel, G.
Oakes, J. The Ruling Race.*
  R.F. Durden, 579(SAQ):Autumn83-458
Oakes, P. At the Jazz Band Ball.*
  J. Mellors, 364:Feb84-109
Oakes, P. Dwellers All in Time and Space.
  S. Newell, 441:22Jul84-21

Oakley, A. Taking it Like a Woman.
  A. Huth, 362:8Mar84-23
  J.H. Murray, 441:3Jun84-26
  P. Willmott, 617(TLS):17Feb84-157
Oates, J. Babylon.
  M-H. Gates, 318(JAOS):Jan-Mar82-170
Oates, J.C. A Bloodsmoor Romance.*
  639(VQR):Spring83-58
Oates, J.C., comp. First Person Singular.
  J. Atlas, 61:Jan84-96
Oates, J.C. Last Days.
  E. Jong, 441:5Aug84-7
Oates, J.C. Mysteries of Winterthurn.
  P. Craig, 441:12Feb84-7
  L. Sage, 617(TLS):20Jul84-801
  L.W. Wagner, 385(MQR):Summer84-446
  M. Wandor, 362:12Jul84-28
  442(NY):27Feb84-133
Oates, J.C. Wild Saturday.
  P. Craig, 617(TLS):24Aug84-935
Oates, S.B. Let The Trumpet Sound.*
  D.J. Garrow, 579(SAQ):Summer83-328
Oates, S.B. Abraham Lincoln.
  P-L. Adams, 61:Jun84-124
Ober, W.U., ed. The Story of the Three
  Bears.
  P. Pénigault-Duhet, 189(EA):Oct-Dec84-
  448
Oberhelman, H.D. The Presence of Faulkner
  in the Writings of García Márquez.
  J. Higgins, 86(BHS):Jan83-93
Oberman, H.A. Masters of the Reformation.
  G. Strauss, 589:Jan83-210
Oberman, H.A. Wurzeln des Antisemitismus.
  J.J. Petuchowski, 221(GQ):Mar83-357
Obermeier, O.P. Poppers "Kritischer Ra-
  tionalismus."
  J. Wettersten, 489(PJGG):Band90Heft1-
  198
Obeyesekere, G. Medusa's Hair.
  M.T. Egnor, 293(JASt):Feb83-442
Obler, L.K. and L. Menn, eds. Exceptional
  Language and Linguistics.
  F.J. Newmeyer, 350:Dec84-969
Obolensky, D. The Byzantine Inheritance
  of Eastern Europe.
  W.T. Treadgold, 550(RusR):Jan83-100
O'Brian, J. David Milne and the Modern
  Tradition of Painting.
  E. Milroy, 99:Jan84-31
O'Brien, D. Theories of Weight in the
  Ancient World.* (Vol 1)
  P. Pellegrin, 542:Jan-Mar83-81
O'Brien, E. A Fanatic Heart.
  M. Gordon, 441:18Nov84-1
O'Brien, K. Mary Lavelle.
  P. Craig, 617(TLS):1Jun84-623
O'Brien, M., ed. All Clever Men, Who Make
  Their Way.
  J.S. Reed, 578:Spring84-110
  639(VQR):Summer83-82
O'Brien, S. The Indoor Park.*
  B. Jones, 364:Jul83-78
  E. Larrissy, 493:Jun83-64
O'Callaghan, J. Edible Anecdotes and
  Other Poems.
  C. Boyle, 364:Mar84-95
  M. O'Neill, 617(TLS):11May84-516
O'Carroll, J.P. and J.A. Murphy, eds. De
  Valera and His Times.
  R. Foster, 617(TLS):24Feb84-194
"O'Casey Annual No. 1."* (R.G. Lowery, ed)
  B. Dolan, 305(JIL):May83-114

Ochsner, J.K. H.H. Richardson: Complete
  Architectural Works.*
  P.R. Baker, 658:Summer/Autumn83-222
  P.C. Harrell, 432(NEQ):Dec83-613
  A. Saint, 59:Sep83-376
Ochwadt, C. and E. Tecklenborg, eds. Das
  Mass des Verborgenen.
  B. Casper, 489(PJGG):Band90Heft1-219
de Ockham, N. Quaestiones disputatae de
  dilectione Dei. (C. Saco Alarcón, ed)
  G.J. Etzkorn, 589:Jul83-789
Ockham, William of. Guillelmi de Ockham:
  Scriptum in Librum Primum Sententiarum:
  Ordinatio, Distinctiones XIX-XLVIII.
  (G.I. Etzkorn and F.E. Kelly, eds)
  M.M. Adams, 482(PhR):Apr83-93
Ockham, William of. Ockham's Theory of
  Propositions. (A.J. Freddoso and H.
  Schuurman, trans)
  J. Longeway, 482(PhR):Apr83-302
Ockham, William of. Venerabilis Inceptor-
  is Guillelmi de Ockham: Quodlibeta
  Septem. (J.C. Wey, ed)
  M.M. Adams, 482(PhR):Jan83-98
O'Connell, D., ed. The Instructions of
  Saint Louis.*
  W. Rothwell, 208(FS):Oct83-441
O'Connor, A. The African City.
  R. Oliver, 617(TLS):13Apr84-410
O'Connor, A. Unfinished Work.
  G. Catalano, 381:Dec83-449
O'Connor, F. Frank O'Connor: Collected
  Stories.*
  42(AR):Fall83-507
O'Connor, G. Darlings of the Gods.
  J. Neville, 617(TLS):11May84-520
O'Connor, G. Ralph Richardson.
  J. Lahr, 157:Spring83-49
O'Connor, J. Come Day — Go Day.
  P. Craig, 617(TLS):10Aug84-901
O'Connor, J. and D. Bensky, eds and trans.
  Acupuncture.
  R.D. Sawyer, 293(JASt):Aug83-942
O'Connor, M. Hebrew Verse Structure.
  A. Berlin, 318(JAOS):Apr-Jun82-392
  T. Collins, 307:Oct83-91
O'Connor, P.W. - see "Plays of Protest
  from the Franco Era"
O'Conor, C. The Letters of Charles
  O'Conor of Belanagare. (C.C. and R.E.
  Ward, eds)
  W.D. Griffin, 173(ECS):Fall83-75
Oda, T. - see under Takuji Oda
Odegard, D. Knowledge and Scepticism.
  M. Smithurst, 518:Jul83-170
Odmark, J., ed. Language, Literature and
  Meaning I.*
  C.E. Reeves, 599:Winter83-59
Odmark, J. An Understanding of Jane
  Austen's Novels.
  M.A. Doody, 445(NCF):Sep83-220
  P.G., 189(EA):Apr-Jun84-235
"Odna ili dve russkix literatury?"
  S. Kryzytski, 574(SEEJ):Spring83-117
O'Donnell, C. Cooking with Cornelius.
  W. and C. Cowen, 639(VQR):Spring83-65
O'Donnell, V. and J. Kable. Persuasion.
  J.L. Lucaites, 583:Spring84-331
O'Donnell, W.J. and D.A. Jones. The Law
  of Marriage and Marital Alternatives.
  E.M., 185:Oct83-182

278

O'Donoghue, B., ed. The Courtly Love Tradition.
  A. Bruten, 617(TLS):6Jan84-20
O'Donoghue, B. Razorblades and Pencils.
  T. Dooley, 617(TLS):28Sep84-1105
O'Driscoll, D. Kist.
  M. Harmon, 272(IUR):Spring83-114
O'Driscoll, R., ed. The Celtic Consciousness.*
  S.F. Gallagher, 627(UTQ):Summer83-431
Ó Dufaigh, S. and B.E. Rainey, eds. Comhairle Mhic Clamha ó Achadh na Muilleann.
  B. Ó Cuív, 112:Vol 15-180
Oe, K., ed. Atomic Aftermath.
  J. Kirkup, 617(TLS):26Oct84-1227
Oehlenschläger, E. Närrische Phantasie.*
  D.F. Mahoney, 406:Fall83-343
Oehler, L. Staatliche Kunstsammlungen Kassel, niederländische Zeichnungen des 16. bis 18. Jahrhunderts.
  E. Llewellyn, 39:Nov83-456
Oelmüller, W. and others. Philosophische Arbeitsbücher.
  A.K.D. Lorenzen, 489(PJGG):Band90Heft2-431
Oesch, M. Das Handlungsproblem.
  J-M. Gabaude, 542:Jan-Mar83-138
Oesterby, M. - see Ornatskij, A.A.
Oetinger, F.C. Die Lehrtafel der Prinzessin Antonia. (R. Breymayer and F. Häussermann, eds)
  P. Deghaye, 684(ZDA):Band112Heft1-52
Oetinger, F.C. Theologia ex idea vitae deducta. (K. Ohly, ed)
  P. Deghaye, 684(ZDA):Band112Heft1-54
O'Fahey, R.S. State and Society in Dar Fur.
  L. Sanneh, 69:Vol53No1-105
O'Faolain, J. The Irish Signorina.
  K.C. O'Brien, 362:4Oct84-28
  L. Taylor, 617(TLS):26Oct84-1224
Offer, A. Property and Politics 1870-1914.
  D.H. Aldcroft, 637(VS):Spring83-362
Offner, R. A Critical and Historical Corpus of Florentine Painting: A Legacy of Attributions, The Fourteenth Century, Supplement. (H.B.J. Maginnis, ed)
  J.H. Stubblebine, 54:Sep83-506
O'Flaherty, W.D. Dreams, Illusions and Other Realities.
  M.C. Taylor, 441:18Nov84-11
O'Flaherty, W.D., ed. Karma and Rebirth in Classical Indian Traditions.*
  J.W. de Jong, 259(IIJ):Mar83-135
  R. Salomon, 318(JAOS):Apr-Jun82-407
O'Flaherty, W.D. Women, Androgynes, and Other Mythical Beasts.*
  H.B. Reynolds, 259(IIJ):Jun83-281
O'Flaherty, W.D., G. Michell and C. Berkson. Elephanta.
  J.C. Harle, 617(TLS):13Apr84-400
O'Flynn, J.M. Generalissimos of the Western Roman Empire.
  R.K. Sherk, 124:Jul-Aug84-380
Ogburn, C. The Mysterious William Shakespeare.
  R. Giroux, 441:9Dec84-13
Oggel, L.T. and R. Hewitt - see "Index to Reviews of Bibliographical Publications"
O'Gorman, F. The Emergence of the British Two-Party System 1760-1832.
  W.A. Speck, 83:Spring83-95

Oh, S. and D. Falkner. Sadaharu Oh.
  L.S. Ritter, 441:3Jun84-9
O'Hanlon, R. Joseph Conrad and Charles Darwin.
  J. Lucas, 617(TLS):6Jul84-763
O'Hanlon, R. Into the Heart of Borneo.
  P. Metcalf, 617(TLS):30Nov84-1368
O'Hara, D.T. Tragic Knowledge.
  E. Block, Jr., 651(WHR):Spring83-86
  G.M. Harper, 405(MP):May84-435
  R.C. Petersen, 177(ELT):Vol26No2-143
O'Hare, D., ed. Psychology and the Arts.
  G.M. Mayes, 89(BJA):Spring83-176
O'Hear, A. Education, Society and Human Nature.
  J. Harris, 479(PhQ):Apr83-202
  R.F. Holland, 479(PhQ):Apr83-197
  G. Langford, 84:Jun83-188
O'Hear, A. Karl Popper.*
  T. Horgan, 482(PhR):Jan83-126
O'Hehir, D. I Wish This War Were Over.
  B.F. Williamson, 441:6May84-24
  442(NY):16Apr84-158
Ohly, K. - see Oetinger, F.C.
Ohnuki-Tierney, E. Illness and Healing among the Sakhalin Ainu.
  W.P. Lebra, 293(JASt):Aug83-974
Ohrn, K.B. Dorothea Lange and the Documentary Tradition.
  J.C. Curtis, 658:Spring83-116
Oinas, F.J., ed. Heroic Epic and Saga.*
  B.R. Jonsson, 64(Arv):Vol37-175
  P.N. Richardson, 149(CLS):Winter83-446
Oja, C.J., ed. Stravinsky in "Modern Music" (1924-1946).*
  J. Pasler, 415:Oct83-605
Ojea, C.G. - see under Gómez Ojea, C.
Oka, Y. Konoe Fumimaro.
  B-A. Shillony, 407(MN):Winter83-460
Okada, B.T. and V. Reynolds. Japan.
  R.L. Shep, 614:Summer84-18
Okali, C. Cocoa and Kinship in Ghana.
  M. Johnson, 617(TLS):11May84-531
Okeke, U. Art in Development.
  F.T. Smith, 2(AfrA):Feb83-84
Okken, L. and H-D. Mück. Die satirischen Lieder Oswalds von Wolkenstein wider die Bauern.
  E. Jöst, 680(ZDP):Band102Heft1-140
Okpewho, I. Myth in Africa.
  R. Brain, 617(TLS):11May84-531
Okun, A.M. Economics for Policymaking. (J.A. Pechman, ed)
  A. Cairncross, 617(TLS):29Jun84-718
Ola, C.S. Town and Country Planning Law in Nigeria.
  R. Home, 69:Vol53No2-76
Ólason, V., ed. Sagnadansar.
  B.R. Jonsson, 64(Arv):Vol37-189
Oldenbourg, Z. Que nous est Hécube?
  P. Thody, 617(TLS):10Aug84-890
Olderogge, D.A. and S. Brauner, eds. Sozialer Wandel in Afrika und die Entwicklung von Formen und Funktionen afrikanischer Sprachen.
  M. Gross, 682(ZPSK):Band36Heft1-102
Oldfield, S. Spinsters of This Parish.
  V. Glendinning, 617(TLS):9Mar84-238
  D. Taylor, 364:Feb84-96
Oldham, R. and J. George Temple-Poole.
  G. Herbert, 576:Dec83-394

Olds, M.C. Desire Seeking Expression.
   R. Stanley, 446(NCFS):Fall-Winter83/84-
   239
Olds, S. The Dead and the Living.
   H. Beaver, 441:18Mar84-30
   M. Kinzie, 29:Sep/Oct84-38
Olds, S. Satan Says.*
   S.P. Estess, 577(SHR):Winter83-92
Olechowska, E.M. - see Claudian
Oles, C. Quarry.
   T. Kooser, 502(PrS):Fall83-86
Olesch, R. and P. Šimunović, eds. Čaka-
   visch-deutsches Lexikon. (Pt 2)
   P. Herrity, 575(SEER):Apr83-262
Oleson, J. The Sources of Innovation in
   Later Etruscan Tomb Design (ca. 350-100
   B.C.).
   J.P. Small, 124:May-Jun84-313
Olinder, B. and I. Pohl, with C. Sorren-
   tino. San Giovenale. (Vol 2, fasc 4)
   D. Ridgway, 123:Vol33No2-364
Oliner, S.P. Restless Memories.
   M.Z. Rosensaft, 390:Mar83-62
Mrs. Oliphant. Hester.
   P. Craig, 617(TLS):21Sep84-1066
Oliphant, D. and L. Ramos-Garcia, eds.
   Washing the Cow's Skull.
   A. Struthers, 436(NewL):Fall83-117
Olivares, J. The Love Poetry of Francisco
   de Quevedo.
   A. Paterson, 617(TLS):13Apr84-399
Oliver, A. Michel, Job, Pierre, Paul.
   D.H. Walker, 208(FS):Jul83-360
Oliver, A. and J.B. Peabody, eds. The
   Records of Trinity Church, Boston, 1728-
   1830. (Vol 2)
   J.M. O'Toole, 432(NEQ):Jun83-293
Oliver, H.J. - see Shakespeare, W.
Oliver, P., I. Davis and I. Bentley. Dun-
   roamin.
   S. Izenour, 576:Mar83-81
Oliver, R.W. Dreams of Passion.*
   J. Davies, 402(MLR):Jan83-200
   O. Ragusa, 276:Spring83-71
Olivero, A. - see Audebert, N.
Olivi, P.I. Quaestiones de incarnatione
   et redemptione. (P.A. Emmen, ed) Quaes-
   tiones de virtutibus. (E. Stadter, ed)
   S.P. Marrone, 589:Apr83-518
Olivier, L. Confessions of an Actor.*
   J.W. Lambert, 157:Spring83-48
   639(VQR):Summer83-79
Ollard, R. Pepys.
   G.N., 617(TLS):16Nov84-1323
Oller, J.W., Jr. Language Tests at
   School.
   M. Olsson, 597(SN):Vol55No1-105
Oller, J.W., Jr. and K. Perkins. Research
   in Language Testing.*
   J.B. Carroll, 257(IRAL):Aug83-235
Olleson, E., ed. Modern Musical Scholar-
   ship.*
   P.J.P., 412:Aug-Nov82-284
Ollivier, J., M. Morran and C.M. Howard.
   Appel.
   M-N. Little, 207(FR):May84-926
Olmos, M.F. - see under Fernández Olmos, M.
Olmstead, F.L. The Papers of Frederick
   Law Olmstead.* (Vol 2) (C.E. Beveridge
   and C.C. McLaughlin, with D. Schuyler,
   eds)
   R.F. Durden, 579(SAQ):Summer83-336

Olofsson, A. Relative Junctions in
   Written American English.
   A.R. Tellier, 189(EA):Oct-Dec84-453
Olofsson, T. Frigörelse eller sammanbrott.
   J. Lutz, 563(SS):Spring83-186
O'Loughlin, M. Atlantic Blues.
   M. Harmon, 272(IUR):Spring83-114
Olsen, A.H. Guthlac of Croyland.
   G. Russom, 589:Apr83-519
Olsen, J. "Son."
   W. Kaminer, 441:5Feb84-19
   C. Sigal, 617(TLS):17Aug84-915
Olsen, M.E. Participatory Pluralism.
   R.F. Tomasson, 563(SS):Summer83-250
Olsen, S. Problems of "seem/scheinen" Con-
   structions and their Implications for
   the Theory of Predicate Sentential Com-
   plementation.
   A. Davison, 350:Dec84-988
   R. Schreyer, 38:Band101Heft1/2-182
   M. Viel, 189(EA):Jan-Mar83-73
Olshen, B.N. and T.A. John Fowles.
   J.L. Halio, 677(YES):Vol 13-357
   P. Lewis, 161(DUJ):Dec82-116
   S. Monod, 189(EA):Apr-Sep83-354
   J.G. Watson, 447(N&Q):Oct82-474
Olson, C., ed. The Book of the Goddess,
   Past and Present.
   R. Kraemer, 124:Jul-Aug84-373
Olson, M. The Rise and Decline of
   Nations.*
   M. Wallerstein, 185:Jan84-348
Olson, S. - see Nicolson, H.
Olson, T. Millennialism, Utopianism, and
   Progress.
   M.G. Kalin, 529(QQ):Winter83-1202
Olsson, T. Idealism och klassicism.
   L. Koch, 562(Scan):May83-79
Olszewski, E.J., with J. Glaubinger. The
   Draftsman's Eye.*
   M. Kemp, 59:Mar83-107
O'Malley, P. The Uncivil Wars.
   S. O'Rourke, 441:5Feb84-16
   442(NY):13Feb84-130
Oman, C.C. and J. Hamilton. Wallpapers.*
   A. Budge, 90:May83-304
Omar Khayyám. Edward Fitzgerald: La
   "Robajoj" de Omar Kajam. (W. Auld,
   trans)
   M. Boulton, 447(N&Q):Oct82-457
O'Meally, R.G. The Craft of Ralph Elli-
   son.*
   A. Nadel, 219(GaR):Summer83-438
   L. Sanders, 106:Fall83-343
O'Meara, D.J., ed. Neoplatonism and Chris-
   tian Thought.*
   G.A. Kennedy, 480(P&R):Vol 16No3-208
O'Meara, D.J., ed. Studies in Aristotle.
   J.D.G. Evans, 123:Vol33No2-236
O'Meara, P. K.F. Ryleev.
   T. Briggs, 617(TLS):7Dec84-1421
Omohundro, J.T. Chinese Merchant Families
   in Iloilo.
   C. Szanton, 293(JASt):Nov82-229
Ondaatje, M. Running in the Family.*
   M. Mudrick, 249(HudR):Autumn83-569
O'Neal, H. Berenice Abbott.*
   A. Berman, 55:May83-29
O'Neil, D., ed. Life: The Second Decade,
   1946-1955.
   A. Grundberg, 441:2Dec84-16
O'Neil, L.T. Towards the Life Divine.
   J. O'Connor, 293(JASt):Feb83-444

O'Neill, E. The Calms of Capricorn. Work Diary 1924-1943. (D. Gallup, ed of both)
M. Hinden, 130:Summer83-195
O'Neill, E. Eugene O'Neill at Work.* (V. Floyd, ed)
D.P. Deneau, 577(SHR):Fall83-387
M. Hinden, 130:Summer83-195
O'Neill, E. "The Theatre We Worked For."* (J.R. Bryer, ed)
V. Floyd, 397(MD):Sep83-385
M. Manheim, 130:Fall83-289
O'Neill, G.K. The Technology Edge.
H. Weil, 441:29Apr84-33
O'Neill, G.K. 2081.
C.A.L. Prager, 529(QQ):Winter83-1167
O'Neill, J. Essaying Montaigne.*
P. Henry, 207(FR):Dec83-243
O'Neill, J. For Marx against Althusser and Other Essays.
J.J., 185:Apr84-552
O'Neill, P. German Literature in English Translation.*
P.S. Seadle, 221(GQ):Mar83-288
O'Neill, T. Of Virgin Muses and of Love.
J. Lindon, 278(IS):Vol38-115
C.A. McCormick, 67:May83-153
O'Neill, W.L. A Better World.*
639(VQR):Spring83-54
Ong, W.J. Orality and Literacy.*
J.M.B., 179(ES):Apr83-182
W.A. Bacon, 480(P&R):Vol 16No4-270
R.A. Hall, Jr., 350:Sep84-625
M.C. Tuman, 128(CE):Dec83-769
Onwuejeogwu, M.A. An Igbo Civilization.
E.N. Quarcoopome, 2(AfrA):Nov82-90
Ōoka Makoto. A String Around Autumn.
J.R. Morita, 293(JASt):Aug83-968
Oommen, T.K. Doctors and Nurses.
P.K-M. New, 293(JASt):Nov82-186
Oosting, J.T. Andrea Palladio's "Teatro Olimpico."
S. Orgel, 612(ThS):May/Nov83-160
van Oostrom, F.P. Reinaert Primair.
H. Pleij, 204(FdL):Sep83-233
Opel, A., ed. Anthology of Modern Austrian Literature.
J. Glenn, 221(GQ):Mar83-290
Openshaw, S., P. Steadman and O. Greene. Doomsday.
T. Garden, 176:Apr84-59
Opie, I. and P., eds. The Oxford Book of Narrative Verse.*
442(NY):9Jan84-109
Opland, J. Anglo-Saxon Oral Poetry.*
R. Frank, 447(N&Q):Apr82-153
R.F. Leslie, 405(MP):Feb84-298
B. Mitchell, 541(RES):May83-200
P.B. Taylor, 179(ES):Dec83-567
Oppenheim, F.E. Political Concepts.*
D.T. Meyers, 482(PhR):Apr83-249
Opperby, P. Leopold Stokowski.
N. Goodwin, 415:May83-300
O'Prey, P. - see Graves, R.
Orchard, G.E. - see Massa, I.
"Ordbok över Finlands svenska folkmål av Olav Ahlbäck." (Vol 1, Pt 2)
H.H. Ronge, 260(IF):Band87-355
O'Regan, M. The Mannerist Aesthetic.*
A.T. Gable, 208(FS):Jul83-336
R.N. Nicolich, 475:Vol 10No18-384
O'Reilly, T. Frank Herbert.
W.E. Meyers, 561(SFS):Mar83-106

Orel, H., ed. Kipling: Interviews and Recollections.
N. Andrew, 362:22Mar84-23
T.J. Binyon, 617(TLS):25May84-579
Orel, H. Victorian Literary Critics.
C. Baldick, 617(TLS):26Oct84-1211
von Orelli, M. Der altfranzösische Bibelwortschatz des Neuen Testaments im Berner Cod. 28 (13. Jh.).
R. Blumenfeld-Kosinski, 545(RPh):Feb83-515
Orgel, S. The Jonsonian Masque.
B. King, 569(SR):Winter83-149
Oriard, M.V. Dreaming of Heroes.*
A. Guttmann, 587(SAF):Autumn83-263
D. Peters, 27(AL):Mar83-119
Origen. Homilies on Genesis and Exodus. (R. Heine, trans)
A. Tripolitis, 124:May-Jun84-328
Origo, I. A Need to Testify.
P.N. Furbank, 617(TLS):20Apr84-428
H.S. Hughes, 441:1Jul84-10
Origo, I. War in Val d'Orcia.
H.S. Hughes, 441:1Jul84-10
M. Panter-Downes, 442(NY):17Dec84-148
Oring, E. Israeli Humor.
G.A. Fine, 292(JAF):Apr-Jun83-229
J.P. Leary, 650(WF):Jan83-65
Orizet, J. Le Voyageur absent.
A.M. Russo, 207(FR):Oct83-139
Orleans, L., ed. Science in Contemporary China.
D.F. Simon, 293(JASt):Nov82-143
Orledge, R. Debussy and the Theater.*
M. Chimènes, 537:Vol69No2-245
R. Holloway, 607:Jun83-45
Orlova, R. Memoirs.
A. Austin, 441:12Feb84-16
Orme, N. Early British Swimming, 55 BC - AD 1719.
J. Catto, 617(TLS):21Sep84-1062
Ormrod, R. Una Troubridge.
V. Glendinning, 617(TLS):20Jul84-804
"Ornamental Conifers."
L. Yang, 441:3Jun84-7
Ornatskij, A.A. Istorija rossijskoj ierarchii. (M. Oesterby, ed)
E. Bryner, 688(ZSP):Band43Heft2-426
O'Rourke, B. The Conscience of the Race.
R. Hauptman, 395(MFS):Winter83-817
O'Rourke, M. L'Article de Charles Du Bos sur Proust.
M. Mein, 208(FS):Jan83-102
Orr, J. Tragic Drama and Modern Society.
N. Berlin, 397(MD):Jun83-234
V.L. Cahn, 363(LitR):Spring84-384
Orrell, J. Fallen Empires.*
D. Gardner, 627(UTQ):Summer83-478
Orringer, N.R. Ortega y sus fuentes germánicas.*
L.C. Belby, 552(REH):May83-315
Orser, W.E. Searching for a Viable Alternative.
C.P. Le Warne, 579(SAQ):Spring83-225
Ortega y Medina, J.A. El conflicto anglo-español por el dominio oceánico (siglos XVI y XVII).
D. Ramos, 263(RIB):Vol33No2-263
Orth, W. Königlicher Machtanspruch und städtische Freiheit.
S.M. Sherwin-White, 303(JoHS):Vol 103-214

Ortiz, S.J. Fightin'.
D. Cole, 441:29Apr84-32
Ortiz Armengol, P. - see Pérez Galdós, B.
Ortolano, S. Rafaello.
C. Gould, 39:Aug83-193
Ortoleva, M.Y. Joris-Karl Huysmans
romancier du salut.
J. Lethève, 535(RHL):Jan/Feb83-133
Orton, H., S. Sanderson and J. Widdowson,
eds. The Linguistic Atlas of England.
B. Diensberg, 38:Band101Heft3/4-462
Orton, L.D. Polish Detroit and the Koła-
sinski Affair.
D.S. Buczek, 497(PolR):Vol28No3-105
Ortony, A., ed. Metaphor and Thought.*
J. Penelope, 599:Winter83-77
D.E.B. Pollard, 307:Oct80-113
Ortúñez de Calahorra, D. Espejo de prín-
cipes y cavalleros. (D. Eisenberg, ed)
S.G. Dahlgren, 545(RPh):May83-577
Orwen, G.P. Jean-François Regnard.
W.D. Howarth, 610:Summer83-163
F. Moureau, 535(RHL):Sep/Dec83-933
Ory, P. L'Entre-deux-mai.
H.B. Sutton, 207(FR):Mar84-573
Osberg, L. Economic Inequality in Canada.
G. Teeple, 529(QQ):Summer83-523
Osborn, J.J., Jr. The Man Who Owned New
York.
W. Domnarski, 639(VQR):Summer83-523
Osborn, M. and S. Longland. Rune Games.
J. Simpson, 203:Vol194No2-260
Osborn, R. - see Wordsworth, W.
Osborne, H. Abstraction and Artifice in
Twentieth-Century Art.
P. McCormick, 290(JAAC):Summer84-467
Osborne, J., ed. Die Meininger.
E. McInnes, 402(MLR):Jan83-240
S. Williams, 221(GQ):Jan83-120
Osborne, J. Meyer or Fontane?
M. Swales, 617(TLS):31Aug84-965
Osborne, M.J. Naturalization in Athens.
(Vol 1)
M.B. Walbank, 303(JoHS):Vol 103-204
Osburn, C.B. Research and Reference
Guide to French Studies.* (2nd ed)
C. Blanche-Benveniste, 353:Vol20No7/8-
563
A.D. Hytier, 399(MLJ):Spring83-70
R. Rancoeur, 535(RHL):Jan/Feb83-138
Osgood, C.E. Lectures on Language Perfor-
mance.*
P.H. Salus, 567:Vol42No2/4-311
O'Shaughnessy, B. The Will.*
A. Donagan, 311(JP):May83-298
G. Marshall, 63:Mar83-88
O'Shaughnessy, H. Grenada.
R. Fox, 362:2Aug84-26
L. Whitehead, 617(TLS):27Jul84-827
Ó Siadhail, M. Learning Irish.
M. Murphy, 174(Éire):Spring83-149
Ó Siadhail, M. Springnight.
M. O'Neill, 617(TLS):11May84-516
Osman, N. Kleines Lexikon deutscher
Wörter arabischer Herkunft.
P. Kunitzsch, 684(ZDA):Band112Heft3-
105
Ospovat, D. The Development of Darwin's
Theory.
N.C. Gillespie, 637(VS):Winter83-229
Ossorguine, T.A. - see Dienes, L.
Ossorguine, T.A. - see Frank, V.

Ossorguine, T.A. - see Gladkova, T. and L.
Mnukhin
Ossorguine, T.A. - see Guerra, R.
Ostendorf, B. Black Literature in White
America.
C. Werner, 395(MFS):Summer83-319
Ostenfeld, E. Forms, Matter and Mind.
H.E. Samuel, 124:Nov-Dec83-136
Oster, D. Monsieur Valéry.*
R. Galand, 207(FR):Dec83-254
Osterwalder, P. Das althochdeutsche Gal-
luslied Ratperts und seine lateinischen
Übersetzungen durch Ekkehart IV.
D.H. Green, 402(MLR):Oct83-958
Östman, J-O. "You Know."
L. Schourup, 350:Sep84-665
Ostrom, E., ed. Strategies of Political
Inquiry.
K.S., 185:Oct83-176
O'Sullivan, V. The Butcher Papers.
T. Irwin, 381:Jun83-262
O'Sullivan, V. and M. Scott - see Mans-
field, K.
Osuna, R. Los sonetos de Calderón en sus
obras dramáticas.
S. Herpoel, 356(LR):Feb-May83-135
Oswald, A., with R.C.J. Hildyard and R.G.
Hughes. English Brown Stoneware 1670-
1900.
J.V.G. Mallet, 324:Aug84-639
N. Stretton, 90:May83-305
G. Wills, 39:Sep83-273
Otaka, T. Lovable Mini-Dolls.
M.Z. Cowan, 614:Summer84-22
Otaka, Y. and H. Fukui, eds. Apocalypse
(Bibliothèque nationale, fonds français,
403).
G.J. Brault, 589:Jul83-849
Otaka, Y. and H. Fukui, eds. Apocalypse
anglo-normande (Cambridge Trinity
College Ms. R.16.2).
B. Cazelles, 545(RPh):Nov82-331
Otero, C.P. - see Chomsky, N.
Otis, B. Cosmos and Tragedy.* (E.C.
Kopff, ed)
P. Demont, 555:Vol57fascl-122
A.F. Garvie, 303(JoHS):Vol 103-162
A.G. McKay, 121(CJ):Dec83/Jan84-155
O'Toole, G.J.A. The Spanish War.
S.C. Miller, 441:2Sep84-9
O'Toole, L.M. Structure, Style and Inter-
pretation in the Russian Short Story.
J. Andrew, 575(SEER):Oct83-599
P. Debreczeny, 268(IFR):Summer84-115
A.R. Durkin, 395(MFS):Summer83-311
D.B. Johnson, 574(SEEJ):Fall83-385
V.D. Mihailovich, 573(SSF):Spring-
Summer83-155
C. Popkin, 550(RusR):Apr83-224
O'Toole, P. Corporate Messiah.
K.W. Arenson, 441:26Aug84-18
Ott, K.A. Der Rosenroman.*
B. Schmolke-Hasselmann, 72:Band220
Heft1-208
Ott, W. Metrische Analysen zu Vergil
"Aeneis" Buch IV. Metrische Analysen
zu Vergil "Aeneis" Buch X.
J. Soubiran, 555:Vol57fasc2-328
Ott-Meimberg, M. Kreuzzugsepos oder
Staatsroman?*
U. Peters, 684(ZDA):Band112Heft1-14
F. Shaw, 402(MLR):Jan83-224

Ottaway, M. Soviet and American Influence in the Horn of Africa.
F. Halliday, 69:Vol53No1-104
Otten, T. After Innocence.*
H.H. Watts, 395(MFS):Summer83-367
Ottenberg, S., ed. African Religious Groups and Beliefs.
J. Povey, 2(AfrA):May83-11
den Otter, A.A. Civilizing the West.
E. Waterston, 102(CanL):Spring83-105
Otto, C.F. Space into Light.*
A. Laing, 90:Jan83-41
Otto, R. Aufsätze zur Ethik. (J.S. Boozer, ed)
H.O.T., 185:Apr84-545
Ottonello, F. Cultura filosofica nella stampa periodica dell'Italia meridionale della prima metà dell'ottocento.
C. Cesa, 53(AGP):Band65Heft3-322
Ó Tuama, S., ed. An Duanaire.*
V. Young, 472:Fall/Winter83Spring/Summer84-323
Oudot, S. and others. French Today 2.
P. Silberman, 399(MLJ):Autumn83-290
Oudot, S. and R. Hunt. French Today 1.*
P. Silberman, 399(MLJ):Autumn83-290
Ouellette, H.T. - see William of Malmesbury
Ouimette, V. José Ortega y Gasset.
A. Donoso, 258:Jun83-222
H.B. Wescott, 238:Sep83-435
Outhwaite, W. Concept Formation in Social Science.*
F.C., 185:Jan84-367
Outram, D. Georges Cuvier.
M. Rudwick, 617(TLS):2Nov84-1263
Øverland, J. Cora Sandel om seg selv.
S. Gimnes, 172(Edda):1983/4-251
Oversteegen, J.J. Berperkingen, Methodologische recepten en andere vooronderstellingen en vooroordelen in de moderne literatuurwetenschap.
R. van der Paardt, 204(FdL):Dec83-318
Overton, B. The Unofficial Trollope.
R. ap Roberts, 385(MQR):Winter84-138
A. Wright, 445(NCF):Jun83-104
Ovid. Publio Ovidio Nasón: "Heroidas." (T. Herrera Zapién, ed and trans)
P. Cherchi, 122:Jul83-261
Ovid. P. Ovidi Nasonis "Remedia Amoris."* (A.A.R. Henderson, ed)
J. den Boeft, 394:Vol36fasc1/2-217
Owen, A. The Whalers of Anglesey.
S. Mills, 617(TLS):2Mar84-213
Owen, D. A Future That Will Work.
J. Campbell, 617(TLS):2Nov84-1236
Owen, D. The Government of Victorian London 1855-1889. (R. MacLeod, ed)
A. Briggs, 617(TLS):9Mar84-255
Owen, G.R. Rites and Religions of the Anglo-Saxons.
H. Chickering, 589:Jan83-267
Owen, S. The Great Age of Chinese Poetry: The High T'ang.
J.J.Y. Liu, 116:Jan82-94
A.C. Yu, 293(JASt):May83-599
Owen, U., ed. Fathers.
J. Hughes, 176:Nov84-52
Owen, W. The Complete Poems of Wilfred Owen. (J. Stallworthy, ed)
N. Corcoran, 617(TLS):10Feb84-131
Owens, A. Gentlemen of the West.
G. Mangan, 617(TLS):15Jun84-676

Owens, I. Hope Diamond Refuses.
R. Hogan, 441:3Jun84-45
442(NY):13Aug84-91
Owens, J. St. Thomas Aquinas on the Existence of God.* (J.R. Catan, ed)
K. Konyndyk, Jr., 482(PhR):Apr83-297
A. Zimmermann, 53(AGP):Band65Heft3-315
Owens, J. Aristotle.* (J.R. Catan, ed)
J.L. Ackrill, 123:Vol33No1-64
W.M.A. Grimaldi, 480(P&R):Vol 16No4-275
Owens, M. and D. Cry of the Kalahari.
J. Hillaby, 441:9Dec84-15
Owens, W.A. Tell Me a Story, Sing Me a Song.
J.O. West, 187:Sep84-563
Owenson, S. [Lady Morgan]. The Wild Irish Girl. O'Donnel. Florence Macarthy. The O'Briens and the O'Flahertys. Dramatic Scenes from Real Life.
R. Tracy, 445(NCF):Sep83-235
Owram, D.R., ed. The Formation of Alberta.
D. Swainson, 529(QQ):Winter83-1229
Oxenhorn, H. Elemental Things.
D. Craig, 617(TLS):6Jul84-753
"Oxford American Dictionary."* (E. Ehrlich and others, eds)
M. Montgomery, 35(AS):Spring83-55
"The Oxford Dictionary for Writers and Editors."
P-G. Boucé, 189(EA):Jan-Mar83-67
"The Oxford Dictionary of Quotations." (3rd ed)
A.W. Shipps, 447(N&Q):Feb82-86
"The Oxford-Duden Pictorial German-English Dictionary." (J. Pheby and W. Scholze, eds-in-chief)
A.W. Stanforth, 402(MLR):Oct83-955
"Oxford Latin Dictionary."* [complete] (P.G.W. Glare, ed)
P. Flobert, 555:Vol157fasc2-293
L.S. Thompson, 70:Jan-Feb83-93
J.C. Traupman, 124:Jan-Feb84-190
"Oxford Latin Dictionary." (fasc 8) (P.G.W. Glare, ed)
J. André, 555:Vol157fasc1-154
Oyola, E. Los pecados capitales en la literatura medieval española.
C. Stern, 545(RPh):Aug82-98
Oz, A. In the Land of Israel.*
A. Dowty, 617(TLS):27Jul84-836
T.R. Fyvel, 176:Apr84-64
I. Kalka, 362:23Feb84-28
R.R. Wisse, 129:Apr84-68
Oz, A. Where the Jackals Howl and Other Stories.*
N. Aschkenasy, 390:Jan83-58
Ozick, C. Art and Ardor.*
J. Parini, 434:Summer84-630
S. Pinsker, 219(GaR):Fall83-676
639(VQR):Autumn83-115
Ozick, C. The Cannibal Galaxy.*
J. Epstein, 129:Mar84-64
J. Lasdun, 176:May84-64
D. Montrose, 617(TLS):20Jan84-71
Ozigi, A. and L. Ocho. Education in Northern Nigeria.
R.F. Stock, 69:Vol53No3-105
Ozment, S. When Fathers Ruled.
G.R. Elton, 453(NYRB):14Jun84-39

van der Paardt, R.T. and others. 2000
    Jaar Vergilius.
    J. van Luxemburg, 204(FdL):Jun83-158
Paarlberg, D. Farmers of Five Continents.
    D. Unger, 441:17Jun84-14
Paasivirta, J. Finland and Europe.
    R.G. Selleck, 563(SS):Spring83-175
Pacey, A. The Culture of Technology.
    L. Tiger, 441:26Feb84-13
Pacey, P. David Jones and the Other
    Wonder Voyagers.*
    T. Stoneburner, 344:Fall84-119
Pache, W. Einführung in die Kanadistik.
    H-M. Militz, 682(ZPSK):Band36Heft6-741
    W. Riedel, 107(CRCL):Jun83-290
Pacheco, J.E. Signal From the Flames.
    B.T. Osiek, 238:May83-305
Pachet, P. Le Premier Venu.
    A.J. McKenna, 435:Winter83-99
Pachet, P. Le Voyageur d'Occident.
    M. Deguy, 450(NRF):Mar83-129
Pachmuss, T. A Russian Cultural Revival.
    O. Matich, 550(RusR):Jul83-346
Pachmuss, T. Women Writers in Russian
    Modernism.
    M. Bayuk, 558(RLJ):Fall83-232
Pacho, J. Ontologie und Erkenntnistheorie.
    M. Schneider, 543:Jun83-943
Pächt, O., U. Jenni and D. Thoss. Fläm-
    ische Schule.
    70:May-Jun83-169
Pächt, O., U. Jenni and D. Thoss. Fläm-
    ische Schule I.
    J.J.G. Alexander, 617(TLS):11May84-528
Pachter, H. Socialism in History. (S.E.
    Bronner, ed)
    P.H. Stone, 441:14Oct84-27
Pachter, H. Weimar Etudes.*
    G.L. Mosse, 560:Spring-Summer83-170
Packer, B.L. Emerson's Fall.
    G.W. Allen, 27(AL):Oct83-460
    K.C. Larson, 400(MLN):Dec83-1352
    S. Paul, 301(JEGP):Jul83-466
Packman, D. Vladimir Nabokov.*
    J.P. Levine, 268(IFR):Summer84-129
    S.J. Parker, 550(RusR):Jul83-348
    C.S. Ross, 395(MFS):Winter83-736
    B. Stonehill, 659(ConL):Summer84-235
Pādalipta. Saṃkhitta-Taraṃgavaī-Kahā.
    (H.C. Bhayani, trans)
    E. Bender, 318(JAOS):Oct-Dec82-679
Paddock, H. A Dialect Survey of Carbonear,
    Newfoundland.
    A.M. Kinloch, 35(AS):Summer83-186
Padel, J. New Poems by Shakespeare.
    J. Pequigney, 570(SQ):Winter83-496
Padfield, P. Dönitz.
    A.O.J. Cockshut, 617(TLS):20Apr84-429
    N. Polmar, 441:23Sep84-48
Padgett, R. Triangles in the Afternoon.
    M. Boruch, 271:Vol 13No3/4-251
Padilla, H. Legacies: Selected Poems.*
    D. McDuff, 565:Vol24No3-67
de Padilla, J. Los doce triunfos de los
    doce apóstoles. (Vol 2, Pt 1) (E.
    Norti Gualdani, ed)
    C. Stern, 545(RPh):Nov82-289
Paduano, G. Tragedie e Frammenti di
    Sofocle.
    H. Lloyd-Jones, 123:Vol33No2-311
Page, B.I. Who Gets What from Govern-
    ment.*
    C.N.S., 185:Apr84-561

Page, D.L., ed. Further Greek Epigrams.*
    (rev by R.D. Dawe and J. Diggle)
    J. Clack, 124:May-Jun84-323
    M.L. West, 303(JoHS):Vol 103-186
Page, E. Cold Light of Day.
    T.J. Binyon, 617(TLS):16Mar84-270
Page, M. The Man Who Stole the Mona Lisa.
    S. Epstein, 441:11Nov84-32
    442(NY):15Oct84-180
Page, N. A Dickens Companion.
    A. Sanders, 617(TLS):6Apr84-379
Page, N., ed. Thomas Hardy.*
    P.C., 189(EA):Jul-Sep84-365
    S. Hunter, 677(YES):Vol 13-336
    F.B. Pinion, 541(RES):Feb83-92
Page, N. A.E. Housman.
    B. Knox, 453(NYRB):15Mar84-11
    A. Motion, 617(TLS):10Feb84-131
Page, N., ed. Nabokov: The Critical Heri-
    tage.
    B. Stonehill, 659(ConL):Summer84-235
Page, N. - see "Thomas Hardy Annual No. 1"
Page, P.K. Evening Dance of the Grey
    Flies.*
    B. Whitman, 529(QQ):Autumn83-876
Page, T. - see Gould, G.
Pagels, E. Les Évangiles secrets. (T.
    Kenech'du, ed and trans)
    M.F. Meurice, 450(NRF):Feb83-146
Pagels, E. The Gnostic Gospels.
    A.F. Segal, 318(JAOS):Jan-Mar82-202
Pagnamenta, P. and R. Overy. All Our Work-
    ing Lives.
    A. Marwick, 617(TLS):7Sep84-991
Pagnol, M. Confidences.
    B. Cap, 207(FR):Feb84-431
Paillet, J-P. and A. Dugas. Approaches to
    Syntax.
    M.E. Winters, 350:Sep84-652
Paillochet, C. Unmentionables.
    R.L. Shep, 614:Summer84-30
Pain, B. The Eliza Stories.
    E.S. Turner, 617(TLS):21Dec84-1482
Paine, J.H.E. Theory and Criticism of the
    Novella.
    H.H.H. Remak, 149(CLS):Fall83-346
Paine, R., ed. Politically Speaking.
    C.W., 185:Oct83-175
Paine, S. Beckett, Nabokov, Nin.
    F.N. Smith, 395(MFS):Spring83-127
Pak, P-H. and others. Modernization and
    its Impact upon Korean Law.
    S.B. Young, 293(JASt):May83-682
Pal, P. and L. Fournier. A Buddhist Para-
    dise.
    A. Chase, 60:Jul-Aug83-116
    B. Gray, 39:May83-412
Palacin, R. Les "Comprehensive Schools"
    britanniques à travers l'expérience du
    bourg-comté de Bristol.
    J. Honey, 189(EA):Jul-Sep84-303
de Palacio, J. William Godwin et son
    monde intérieur.*
    D. McCracken, 173(ECS):Spring84-380
de Palacio, J., ed. Max Jacob 3.
    G. Cesbron, 535(RHL):May/Jun83-480
Palais, J.B. Politics and Policy in Tradi-
    tional Korea.
    G.C. Hurst 3d, 318(JAOS):Jan-Mar82-148
Paley, M. The Continuing City.
    P. Hamilton, 617(TLS):15Jun84-674
Palla, R. - see Prudentius

284

Palladius. Palladius, Liber Primus. (A.M. Moure Casas, ed)
P.K. Marshall, 123:Vol33No2-329
Pallister, J.L. - see Paré, A.
Pallot, J. and D.J.B. Shaw. Planning in the Soviet Union.*
R.E.H. Mellor, 575(SEER):Jul83-469
Pallottino, M. La langue étrusque.
R. Pfister, 260(IF):Band87-376
Pallottino, M., H. Blanck and S. Steingräber, eds. Miscellanea Archaeologica Tobias Dohrn Dedicata.
J.G. Pedley, 124:Jul-Aug84-374
Pallucchini, R. and others. Gli affreschi nelle ville venete dal seicento all'ottocento.
B. Hannegan, 54:Jun83-347
Pallucchini, R. and P. Rossi. Tintoretto.
C. Gould, 39:Jan83-72
Palma-Cayet, P-V. L'Histoire prodigieuse du docteur Fauste. (Y. Cazaux, ed)
R.C. Cholakian, 207(FR):Apr84-708
Palmer, A. The Chancelleries of Europe.
D. Hunt, 362:2Feb84-26
Palmer, A. Movable Feasts.
617(TLS):28Dec84-1511
Palmer, A. and V. Who's Who in Shakespeare's England.
G. Schmitz, 156(JDSh):Jahrbuch1983-255
Palmer, A.S., P.J.M. Groot and G.A. Trosper, eds. The Construct Validation of Tests of Communicative Competence.*
S.B. Ross, 608:Sep84-515
Palmer, C., ed. The Britten Companion.
A. Whittall, 617(TLS):13Jul84-773
Palmer, C.A. Human Cargoes.
J. Fisher, 86(BHS):Jan83-92
M. Monteón, 83:Spring83-108
Palmer, F. Encyclopaedia of Oil Painting.
S. Gardiner, 362:15Mar84-25
Palmer, F.R. Semantics.* (2nd ed)
P.L. Carrell, 399(MLJ):Spring83-88
Palmer, G., ed. A Bibliography of Loyalist Source Material in the United States, Canada, and Great Britain.
P. Marshall, 617(TLS):13Jul84-795
Palmer, J.J.N., ed. Froissart, Historian.*
T.B. James, 366:Spring83-102
N. Mann, 447(N&Q):Dec82-534
M.R. Powicke, 589:Jan83-267
Palmer, K. - see Shakespeare, W.
Palmer, L.R. The Greek Language.*
J-C. Billigmeier, 24:Fall83-303
G. Nagy, 121(CJ):Oct/Nov83-64
Palmer, R., ed. Everyman's Book of British Ballads.*
C.W. Joyner, 292(JAF):Apr-Jun83-230
Palmer, S., with S. Palmer. The Hurdy-Gurdy.
J.S. Griffith, 292(JAF):Apr-Jun83-240
Palmer, T. All You Need Is Love. (P. Medlicott, ed)
D. Duncalfe, 529(QQ):Winter83-1200
Palmquist, P.E. Carleton E. Watkins.
L. Milazzo, 584(SWR):Autumn83-viii
Paludan-Müller, F. Adam Homo.
N.L. Jensen, 562(Scan):Nov83-214
K.H. Ober, 563(SS):Winter83-73
Panati, C. The Browser's Book of Beginnings.
T. Ferrell, 441:22Jul84-20
442(NY):3Sep84-96

Pancake, B.D'J. The Stories of Breece D'J Pancake.*
L. Franks, 461:Fall/Winter83/84-91
G. Morris, 502(PrS):Fall83-89
Pandey, B.N. South and South-east Asia, 1945-1979.
T.L. Wilborn, 293(JASt):Nov82-231
Panek, L. The Special Branch.
P. Wolfe, 395(MFS):Autumn83-389
de Pange, V. - see Madame de Staël and E. Hervey
Panichas, G.A. - see Babbitt, I.
Paniker, K.A. and Z.P. Thundy, eds. Malayalam Anthology.
R.E. Asher, 293(JASt):Nov82-196
Panofsky, E. Meaning in the Visual Arts.
M. Larsen, 324:Jun84-477
Pantigoso, E.J. La rebelión contra el indigenismo y la afirmación del pueblo en el mundo de José María Arguedas.
A.J. Vetrano, 238:Dec83-651
Paoli, F.M. - see under Matos Paoli, F.
Pap, L. The Portuguese-Americans.*
J.A. Kerr, Jr., 238:Mar83-137
Papadiamantis, A. The Murderess.*
D. Taylor, 364:Nov83-109
Papageorgiou-Venetas, A. Délos, Recherches urbaine sur une ville antique.*
J.E. Jones, 303(JoHS):Vol 103-217
Papanek, G.F., ed. The Indonesian Economy.
D.S. Paauw, 293(JASt):Nov82-233
Papazoglou, O. Sweet, Savage Death.
N. Callendar, 441:25Mar84-24
Pape, A. Bettel und Garteteuffel. (O.F. Graves, ed)
F.H. Bäuml, 221(GQ):Mar83-308
H. Bluhm, 406:Fall83-332
A. Elschenbroich, 133:Band16Heft1-63
Pape, W. Das literarische Kinderbuch.
R. Bouckaert-Ghesquire, 204(FdL):Mar83-72
H. ten Doornkaat, 196:Band24Heft3/4-320
G. Opie, 402(MLR):Jul83-755
"Papers on Monetary Economics."
D. Feeny, 293(JASt):Aug83-1022
"Papers Presented at the Longfellow Commemorative Conference, April 1-3, 1982."
H.H. Waggoner, 432(NEQ):Jun83-295
Papineau, D. Theory and Meaning.*
C. Wright, 393(Mind):Oct83-618
Papmehl, K.A. Metropolitan Platon of Moscow (Petr Levshin 1737-1812).
G.L. Freeze, 550(RusR):Oct83-427
Papp, E., ed. Codex Vindobonensis 2721.*
B. Murdoch, 402(MLR):Jan83-218
Paquet, L. Les Cyniques grecs.
G. Leroux, 154:Jun83-361
Paquet, M. Magritte ou l'éclipse de l'être.
M. Adam, 542:Jul-Sep83-332
Paradis, J. and T. Postlewait, eds. Victorian Science and Victorian Values.*
R.A. Soloway, 637(VS):Winter83-244
Paradis, S. Emmanuelle en noir.
C.R. La Bossiere, 102(CanL):Autumn83-80
Paradis, S. Les Hauts cris.
Y. Bellemare, 102(CanL):Winter82-113
de Paradis, V. Tunis et Alger au XVIIIe siècle.
F. Ghiles, 617(TLS):20Jul84-809

Parain, B. Joseph.
  F. de Martinoir, 450(NRF):Oct83-121
Parain-Vial, J. Tendances nouvelles de
la philosophie.
  T. Lacour, 192(EP):Apr-Jun83-246
Paramasivam, K. Effectivity and Causativ-
ity in Tamil.
  S.B. Steever, 350:Mar84-195
Parássoglou, G.M. The Archive of Aurelius
Sakaon.
  G. Mussies, 394:Vol36fasc3/4-454
"Parcours symboliques chez Julien Gracq."
  M. Murat, 535(RHL):Sep/Dec83-969
Paré, A. On Monsters and Marvels. (J.L.
Pallister, ed and trans)
  M.J. Giordano, 188(ECr):Spring83-111
Pare, R. Photography and Architecture,
1839-1939.
  J. Herschman, 576:Dec83-405
Pareles, J. and P. Romanowski, eds. The
Rolling Stone Encyclopedia of Rock 'n'
Roll.
  E.M. Thomson, 362:19Apr84-27
Parent, G. A Little Bit Married.
  A. Shapiro, 441:1Jul84-20
Parent-Lardeur, F. Les Cabinets de lec-
ture.
  D. Bellos, 402(MLR):Apr83-453
Parent-Lardeur, F. Lire à Paris au temps
de Balzac.
  D. Bellos, 402(MLR):Apr83-453
  D. Bellos, 535(RHL):Mar/Apr83-286
Paretsky, S. Deadlock.
  T.J. Binyon, 617(TLS):30Nov84-1391
  N. Callendar, 441:18Mar84-27
  M. Laski, 362:25Oct84-29
Parfit, D. Reasons and Persons.
  T. Baldwin, 176:Nov84-61
  S. Scheffler, 617(TLS):4May84-483
  P.F. Strawson, 453(NYRB):14Jun84-42
  M. Warnock, 362:26Apr84-26
Parimoo, B.N. The Ascent of Self.
  B.B. Kachru, 293(JASt):May83-705
Parini, G. La Gazzetta di Milano [1769].
(A. Bruni, ed)
  E. Bonora, 228(GSLI):Vol 160fasc510-
  307
Parini, J. Anthracite Country.
  W.H. Pritchard, 560:Spring-Summer83-
  176
  R. Tillinghast, 569(SR):Summer83-473
  639(VQR):Summer83-96
Parini, J. Theodore Roethke.*
  N. McCleery, 649(WAL):Nov83-252
  R. Pooley, 402(MLR):Apr83-439
  G. Reeves, 161(DUJ):Dec82-112
Paris, B.J. Character and Conflict in
Jane Austen's Novels.*
  F.M. Keener, 402(MLR):Apr83-434
  G.S. Rousseau, 72:Band219Heft1-192
Paris, R-M. Camille Claudel 1864-1943.
  R. Dinnage, 617(TLS):21Dec84-1473
"Paris au temps de Stendhal."
  V.D.L., 605(SC):15Jul84-377
"Paris 1935 — Erster Internationaler
Schriftstellerkongress zur Verteidigung
der Kultur."
  K. Kändler, 654(WB):5/1983-940
"Paris-Rome-Athens: Travels in Greece by
French Architects in the Nineteenth and
Twentieth Centuries."
  B. Knox, 453(NYRB):27Sep84-21

Parish, H.R. Las Casas as a Bishop/Las
Casas, Obispo.
  R.B. Klein, 238:Sep83-440
Parisien, J-E. Nadeige.
  M. Benson, 102(CanL):Summer83-102
Park, C.C. The Siege.
  B. Caplan, 219(GaR):Spring83-221
Parker, A. and A. Neal. Los Ambulantes.
  K. Shaw, 37:Mar-Apr83-60
Parker, A.A. Luis de Góngora, "Poly-
phemus and Galatea."
  A. Terry, 86(BHS):Apr83-151
Parker, H.T. Motion Arrested.* (O.
Holmes, ed)
  I.M. Fanger, 151:May83-152
Parker, P.A. Inescapable Romance.*
  K.M. Lea, 541(RES):Feb83-59
Parker, R. Miasma.
  G.S. Kirk, 617(TLS):2Mar84-209
Parker, R. - see Baldini, G.
Parker, R. and G. Pollock. Old Mistres-
ses.*
  B. Scott, 39:Jul83-113
  F. Spalding, 90:Jan83-43
Parker, R.B. Valediction.
  N. Callendar, 441:20May84-39
Parkinson, N. Lifework.
  M. Jordan, 617(TLS):20Jul84-821
Parkinson, T. Hart Crane and Yvor Winters.
  R. Whittemore, 31(ASch):Spring83-258
Parks, M.G. - see Haliburton, T.C.
Parks, S. and P.J. Croft. Literary Auto-
graphs.
  K. Duncan-Jones, 617(TLS):2Mar84-231
Parmalee, P.L. Brecht's America.*
  G. Tracy, 106:Winter83-489
Parmée, D. - see Zola, É.
Parmée, M.A. Ivan Goll.
  R. Cardinal, 402(MLR):Apr83-466
  E.E. Reed, 221(GQ):May83-520
Parnell, M. Eric Linklater.
  D.A.N. Jones, 362:29Nov84-25
Parr, J., ed. Manitoba Stories.
  D. Jackel, 102(CanL):Spring83-151
Parr, N. James Hogg at Home.*
  I. Campbell, 447(N&Q):Aug82-364
Parret, H. and J. Bouveresse, eds. Mean-
ing and Understanding.*
  F. Recanati, 192(EP):Jan-Mar83-106
Parrinder, P. Science Fiction.*
  C. Greenland, 541(RES):Aug83-362
Parrish, F. Face at the Window.
  T.J.B., 617(TLS):5Oct84-1140
Parrish, J.R. Between Loaded Guns.
  R. Tuerk, 649(WAL):Aug83-191
Parrish, P.A. Richard Crashaw.
  P. Palmer, 677(YES):Vol 13-318
Parrott, C. Jaroslav Hašek.
  A. French, 67:Nov83-332
  M. Heim, 574(SEEJ):Fall83-398
  639(VQR):Winter83-18
Parrott, D.M., ed. Nag Hammadi Codices
V.2-5 and VI with Papyrus Berolinensis
8502. 1 and 4.
  M.W. Meyer, 318(JAOS):Jan-Mar82-205
Parry, A.J.A., ed. La Passion des Jong-
leurs.
  L.R. Muir, 382(MAE):1983/2-324
Parry, B. Conrad and Imperialism.
  E.W. Said, 617(TLS):12Oct84-1149
Parry, G. The Golden Age Restor'd.
  C. Hill, 366:Spring83-112
  D. Howarth, 39:Feb83-153

Parry, L. William Morris Textiles.
  R. Mander, 39:Sep83-271
Parry-Crooke, C., ed. Mr. Gamage's Great
  Toy Bazaar.
  V. Powell, 39:Mar83-261
Parshall, L.B. The Art of Narration in
  Wolfram's "Parzival" and Albrecht's
  "Jüngerer Titurel."*
  D.H. Green, 402(MLR):Jul83-743
  W.T.H. Jackson, 222(GR):Winter83-43
  S.M. Johnson, 221(GQ):Mar83-302
  R.W. Leckie, Jr., 589:Jul83-791
  J.W. Marchand, 301(JEGP):Jul83-411
Parsons, A. The Pride and the Fall.
  J. Grigg, 362:24May84-24
  J.D. Gurney, 617(TLS):7Sep84-998
Parsons, D.S.J. Roy Campbell.
  P. Le Bon, 189(EA):Apr-Jun84-222
  N.H. MacKenzie, 627(UTQ):Summer83-444
Parsons, T. Nonexistent Objects.*
  N. Griffin, 154:Mar83-178
  R. Howell, 311(JP):Mar83-163
Parssinen, T.M. Secret Passions, Secret
  Remedies.
  A. Hayter, 617(TLS):17Feb84-161
Partee, B.H. Fundamentals of Mathematics
  for Linguists.*
  A. Zwicky, 297(JL):Mar83-211
Partee, M.H. Plato's Poetics.
  J.L. Jarrett, 651(WHR):Spring83-71
Parth, W.W. Goethes Christiane.
  O. Durrani, 402(MLR):Jan83-235
Partridge, C. - see Gissing, G.
Partridge, E. A Dictionary of Slang and
  Unconventional English. (8th ed) (P.
  Beale, ed)
  J. Barnes, 617(TLS):3Aug84-860
Partridge, J.G. Semantic, Pragmatic and
  Syntactic Correlates.
  M. Celce-Murcia, 350:Dec84-989
Pascal, N. Ensayo crítico.
  S.N. Harper, 552(REH):Oct83-449
Pascal, R. Kafka's Narrators.*
  C. Koelb, 395(MFS):Summer83-297
Pascall, R., ed. Brahms.*
  R. Anderson, 415:May83-297
Pascasio, E.M. The Filipino Bilingual.
  J. Gibbons, 302:Vol 19No2-226
Pascoli, G. Convivial Poems. (Pt 1) (E.
  Lunardi and R. Nugent, eds and trans)
  P. Baker, 276:Autumn83-288
Pashuto, V.T., ed. Rossiia na putiakh
  tsentralizatsii.
  R. Croskey, 550(RusR):Jul83-325
Paskoff, P.F. and D.J. Wilson, eds. The
  Cause of the South.
  639(VQR):Spring83-55
Pasley, M. - see Kafka, F.
Pasolini, P.P. Lutheran Letters.
  N.S. Thompson, 617(TLS):25May84-596
Pasolini, P.P. Poems. (N. MacAfee, with
  L. Martinengo, eds and trans)
  J. Ahern, 472:Fall/Winter83Spring/
    Summer84-103
Pasolini, P.P. Selected Poems.
  R. Wells, 617(TLS):5Oct84-1130
Pasquier, E. Le Catéchisme des Jésuites.
  (C. Sutto, ed)
  F. Gray, 207(FR):Mar84-550
Pasquini, K. Mandala for Contemporary
  Quilt Designs and Other Mediums.
  B. Self, 614:Fall84-20

Passage, C.E. Character Names in
  Dostoevsky's Fiction.*
  L.R.N. Ashley, 424:Sep83-217
Passfield, R.W. Building the Rideau Canal.
  M.S. Angus, 529(QQ):Autumn83-867
  G.W., 102(CanL):Winter82-175
Passmore, J. The Philosophy of Teaching.
  K. Strike, 482(PhR):Apr83-307
Pastan, L. PM/AM.*
  W.H. Pritchard, 491:Jan84-228
  P. Stitt, 219(GaR):Spring83-201
  639(VQR):Spring83-62
Pasternak, A. A Vanished Present. (A.P.
  Slater, ed and trans)
  G. Annan, 362:4Oct84-26
  H. Pitcher, 617(TLS):21Dec84-1478
Pasternak, B. Guests in the Dragon.
  D. Davin, 617(TLS):14Sep84-1013
Pasternak, B. Ma soeur la vie, et autres
  poèmes.
  J. Blot, 450(NRF):Jan83-137
Pasternak, B. My Sister — Life and a Sub-
  lime Malady.*
  639(VQR):Summer83-98
Pasternak, B. Perepiska s Ol'goy Freyden-
  berg.* (E. Mossman, ed)
  C. Barnes, 575(SEER):Jul83-435
Pasternak, B. Poems.
  H. Gifford, 617(TLS):8Jun84-635
Pastor, B. Roberto Arlt y la rebelión
  alienada.
  J.M. Flint, 86(BHS):Oct83-351
Pastor Poppe, R. Los mejores cuentos boli-
  vianos del siglo XX.
  R.L. Acevedo, 238:Mar83-139
Pastore, J. Inequality and Social Mobil-
  ity in Brazil.
  C.S. Knowlton, 263(RIB):Vol33No3-413
Pastori, J-P. Patrick Dupond.
  A. Barzel, 151:Apr83-46
Pastoureau, M. Les sceaux.
  B.M.B. Rezak, 589:Jul83-793
Pater, W. Selected Writings of Walter
  Pater. (H. Bloom, ed)
  506(PSt):Dec83-310
Paterculus, V. - see under Velleius
  Paterculus
Patočka, J. Essais hérétiques sur la
  philosophie de l'histoire.
  E. Kohák, 543:Dec82-468
  A. Reix, 542:Oct-Dec83-502
Patočka, J. Platon et l'Europe.
  F. Wybrands, 450(NRF):Sep83-149
Patrick, J. Architecture in Tennessee:
  1768-1897.*
  M.J. Bolsterli, 585(SoQ):Spring83-77
Patrides, C.A., ed. Approaches to Sir
  Thomas Browne.
  A. Favre, 189(EA):Jul-Sep84-326
  A.E. Imbrie, 551(RenQ):Summer83-309
Patrides, C.A. Promises and Motifs in
  Renaissance Thought and Literature.*
  G.B. Christopher, 551(RenQ):Autumn83-
    450
Patrides, C.A. and R.B. Waddington, eds.
  The Age of Milton.*
  J. Blondel, 189(EA):Oct-Dec83-464
  D.D.C. Chambers, 541(RES):Aug83-338
Patrie, J. The Genetic Relationship of
  the Ainu Language.*
  H.A. Dettmer, 407(MN):Autumn83-331
  G.F. Meier, 682(ZPSK):Band36Heft1-103
  J.M. Unger, 474(PIL):Vol 15No1/4-317

"Le Patromoine Monumental de la Belgique: Wallomie."
    M.K. Meade, 46:Aug83-74
Patten, B. Love Poems.
    B. Constantine, 176:Sep/Oct84-43
Patten, R.L. Charles Dickens and his Publishers.*
    H. Reinhold, 38:Band101Heft1/2-280
Patterson, E.C. Mary Somerville and the Cultivation of Science, 1815-1840.
    M. Neve, 617(TLS):28Dec84-1497
Patterson, F. Photography of Natural Things.
    W.N., 102(CanL):Spring83-155
Patterson, M. The Revolution in German Theatre, 1900-1933.*
    P. Meech, 610:Autumn82-245
    J. Rouse, 615(TJ):May83-268
Patterson, M. Peter Stein.*
    M. Andre, 108:Spring83-131
    J. Zipes, 397(MD):Dec83-580
Patterson, M.L.P. South Asian Civilizations.
    L. Rocher, 293(JASt):Aug83-995
Patterson, O. Slavery and Social Death.*
    R. Hellie, 550(RusR):Oct83-424
    639(VQR):Summer83-84
Patterson, W.T. The Genealogical Structure of Spanish.
    J. Klausenburger, 350:Jun84-453
    H. Meier, 547(RF):Band95Heft4-486
    C. Schmitt, 553(RLiR):Jul-Dec83-453
Patti, A.L.A. Why Viet Nam?
    P. Stuchen, 529(QQ):Autumn83-882
Pattison, R. On Literacy.
    H.J. Graff, 355(LSoc):Dec83-559
Patton, P. Razzle-Dazzle.
    D. Anderson, 441:19Aug84-19
Patton, P.C. and R.A. Holoien, eds. Computing in the Humanities.
    S.M. Embleton, 320(CJL):Spring83-79
Paucker, A. - see "Leo Baeck Institute: Year Book XXVI"
Paul, B. A Cadenza for Caruso.
    442(NY):3Sep84-98
Paul, B. The Renewable Virgin.
    T.J. Binyon, 617(TLS):22Jun84-706
    M. Laski, 362:12Apr84-27
Paul, C.B. Science and Immortality.*
    P. Saint-Amand, 400(MLN):May83-839
Paul, F., ed. Grundzüge der neueren skandinavischen Literaturen.
    F-M. Kirsch, 654(WB):12/1982-180
    S.H. Rossel, 221(GQ):Nov83-629
Paul, F. August Strindberg.
    F. Sammern-Frankenegg, 563(SS):Summer83-271
Paul, H. - see Marzell, H.
Paul, R. "Fire in Our Hearts."
    J.R. Reed, 395(MFS):Winter83-774
    P. Yvard, 189(EA):Oct-Dec84-477
Paul, R. The Tragedy at Tiverton.
    J. Lester, 441:1Apr84-15
Paul, R.A. The Tibetan Symbolic World.
    G. Samuel, 293(JASt):May83-633
Paul, W. Ernst Lubitsch's American Comedy.
    R. Koenig, 453(NYRB):16Feb84-34
    J.E. Siegel, 18:Jan-Feb84-54
Paul of Venice. Logica Magna. (Pt 1, fasc 7) (P. Clarke, trans)
    G. Nuchelmans, 518:Jan83-15
Paulhan, J. Traité du Ravissement.
    G. Quinsat, 450(NRF):Jul/Aug83-210

Paulin, T. The Book of Juniper.*
    T. Eagleton, 565:Vol24No2-66
Paulin, T. Liberty Tree.*
    D. Davis, 362:19Jul84-25
    H. Lomas, 364:Oct83-73
    J. Mole, 176:Mar84-49
    C. Rawson, 493:Sep83-58
Paulsen, W. and H.G. Hermann, eds. Sinn aus Unsinn.
    E.E. Reed, 221(GQ):Nov83-675
Paulson, M.G. and T. Alvarez-Detrell - see de Vega Carpio, L.
Paulson, R. Book and Painting.
    D. Bindman, 617(TLS):6Jan84-10
    E. Schoenberg, 391:May83-51
Paulson, R. Literary Landscape: Turner and Constable.*
    D. Brooks-Davies, 148:Winter83-89
    C. Fabricant, 661(WC):Summer83-130
    K. Kroeber, 141:Spring83-165
    G. Reynolds, 39:Jul83-111
    639(VQR):Winter83-14
Paulson, R. Popular and Polite Art in the Age of Hogarth and Fielding.*
    M. Coleman, 179(ES):Jun83-285
Paulson, R. Representations of Revolution (1789-1820).*
    D. Carrier, 290(JAAC):Winter83-223
    L. Goldstein, 385(MQR):Summer84-455
Paulus, R. Lyrik und Poetik Karl Krolows 1940-1970.
    K. Schuhmann, 654(WB):6/1983-1143
Paulus, R., ed. Maler-Müller Almanach 1980.
    F.A. Brown, 406:Spring83-90
Pauly, M. Doctors and Their Workshops.
    J.A.M., 185:Oct83-179
Pavis, P. Dictionnaire du Théâtre.
    M. de Rougemont, 610:Spring82-150
Pavis, P. Languages of the Stage.
    R.F. Gross, 615(TJ):Oct83-422
    A. Zanger, 400(MLN):Dec83-1359
Pavlovsky, E. La mueca; El señor Galíndez; Telarañas.* (G.O. Schanzer, ed)
    R. McCormick, 552(REH):Oct83-435
Pawel, E. The Nightmare of Reason.
    P-L. Adams, 61:Aug84-112
    L. Michaels, 441:10Jun84-1
    M. Swales, 617(TLS):5Oct84-1120
    J. Updike, 442(NY):18Jun84-108
    A. Vivis, 362:9Aug84-27
    R.R. Wisse, 129:Nov84-62
Pawełczyńska, A. Values and Violence in Auschwitz.
    B.T. Lupack, 497(PolR):Vol28No2-88
Pawley, M. Building for Tomorrow.*
    J.M. Fitch, 505:Apr83-159
Paxton, J., ed. Everyman's Dictionary of Abbreviations.
    L. Burnett, 447(N&Q):Dec82-565
Payen, J-C. Le Prince d'Aquitaine.*
    F.M. Chambers, 545(RPh):Aug82-120
    E.R. Sienaert, 356(LR):Feb-May83-130
Payet-Burin, R. Émerveillement et lucidité poétique.
    G. Cesbron, 356(LR):Nov83-346
Payn, G. and S. Morley - see Coward, N.
Payne, A., P. Sutton and T. Thorndike. Grenada.
    L. Whitehead, 617(TLS):27Jul84-827
Payne, D. Confessions of a Taoist on Wall Street.
    M. Wexler, 441:21Oct84-30

288

Payne, F.A. Chaucer and Menippean Satire.*
C. Clark, 179(ES):Apr83-189
H. Cooper, 382(MAE):1983/1-134
W. Frost, 131(CL):Fall83-382
W. von Koppenfels, 38:Band101Heft1/2-239
D. Staines, 597(SN):Vol55No2-206
Payne, H.C. - see "Studies in Eighteenth-Century Culture"
Payne, L. Black Novelists and the Southern Literary Tradition.*
R. Yarborough, 219(GaR):Summer83-449
Payne, R. By Me, William Shakespeare.
L. Daugherty, 570(SQ):Autumn83-372
Paynter, J. Music in the Secondary School Curriculum.
P. Standford, 415:Jul83-427
"Le paysage normand dans la littérature et dans l'art."
J. Voisine, 549(RLC):Apr-Jun83-251
Paz, O. Selected Poems. (E. Weinberger, ed)
C. Bedient, 441:19Aug84-13
Peace, R. Chekhov.
K. FitzLyon, 617(TLS):27Apr84-471
Peace, R. The Enigma of Gogol.*
B. Heldt, 402(MLR):Apr83-509
A. McMillin, 575(SEER):Jul83-424
Peach, B., ed. Richard Price and the Ethical Foundations of the American Revolution.
M. Jack, 319:Oct84-486
Peach, L. British Influence on the Birth of American Literature.
L. Buell, 27(AL):May83-252
Peacock, D.P.S. Pottery in the Roman World.
R. Reece, 123:Vol33No2-296
Peacock, M. Raw Heaven.
J.D. McClatchy, 441:2Dec84-54
Peacocke, C. Sense and Content.
A. Margalit, 617(TLS):18May84-560
Peake, M. Sketches from "Bleak House."
(L. Garfield and E. Blishen, eds)
B. Sibley, 362:16Aug84-24
Pearce, A., ed. Critical Essays on Thomas Pynchon.*
P. Balbert, 594:Fall83-265
D. Seed, 184(EIC):Jan83-75
Pearce, R. The Novel in Motion.
K. Tölölyan, 454:Spring84-279
A. Wilde, 659(ConL):Winter84-478
Pearce, R.H. - see Hawthorne, N.
Pearcy, R.J., ed. Studies in the Age of Chaucer. (Vol 2)
J.A. Burrow, 541(RES):May83-203
Pears, D. Motivated Irrationality.
J. Elster, 617(TLS):30Nov84-1388
Pearsall, D., ed. Manuscripts and Readers in Fifteenth-Century England.
B. Cottle, 617(TLS):13Jul84-795
B. Windeatt, 176:Jul/Aug84-55
Pearsall, D. and N. Zeeman - see Salter, E.
Pearsall, R. Tell Me, Pretty Maiden.
L. Nead, 59:Jun83-227
Pearson, B.A., ed. Nag Hammadi Codices: IX and X.
B. Layton, 318(JAOS):Apr-Jun82-397
Pearson, D. The Summer of the Barshinskeys.
M. Wexler, 441:4Nov84-25
Pearson, J. Stags and Serpents.
F.M.L. Thompson, 617(TLS):16Mar84-283

Pearson, J. Tragedy and Tragicomedy in the Plays of John Webster.*
E.M. Yearling, 541(RES):May83-214
Pearson, M.N. Coastal Western India.
G.D. Winius, 293(JASt):May83-706
R. Young, 318(JAOS):Oct-Dec82-676
Pearson, W. "Chessplayer."
M. Kaylan, 441:22Jul84-20
Peary, D., ed. Omni's Screen Flights/Screen Fantasies.
F. Hirsch, 441:7Oct84-16
Peattie, L. and M. Rein. Women's Claims.
W. Kaminer, 441:29Apr84-33
Pêcheux, M. Language, Semantics and Ideology.* (French title: Les Vérités de la Palice.)
D.H., 355(LSoc):Jun83-288
P. Lamarque, 307:Oct83-83
T. Pateman, 297(JL):Sep83-500
G. Seidel, 208(FS):Oct83-498
Pechman, J.A. - see Okun, A.M.
Peck, G.T. The Fool of God.*
P. Hainsworth, 447(N&Q):Dec82-569
S.E. Moran, 276:Summer83-164
Peck, M.S. People of the Lie.
J. Loudon, 469:Vol9No3-104
J. Rascoe, 441:1Jan84-10
Peck, M.S. The Road Less Traveled.
J. Loudon, 469:Vol9No3-104
Peck, R.A. Chaucer's Lyrics and Anelida and Arcite.
A. Bruten, 617(TLS):6Jan84-20
Peck, R.A. - see Gower, J.
Pecknold, A. Mime.
R. East, 108:Fall83-133
"Pecos to Rio Grande."
L. Milazzo, 584(SWR):Autumn83-viii
Peddy, G.W. and K.F. Saddle Bag and Spinning Wheel. (G.P. Cuttino, ed)
G. Rable, 9(AlaR):Jul83-234
Pedicord, H.W. and F.L. Bergmann - see Garrick, D.
Pedretti, C. The Literary Works of Leonardo da Vinci.
C. Gould, 39:Feb83-145
Pedro Alfonso. Disciplina clericalis. (M.J. Lacarra, ed)
R. Ayerbe-Chaux, 238:Mar83-131
Peek, W. Attische Versinschriften.*
P.A. Hansen, 123:Vol33No2-370
Peel, C. Firestorm.
N. Callendar, 441:4Nov84-35
Peel, J.D.Y. Ijeshas and Nigerians.
M. Lynn, 617(TLS):12Oct84-1150
Peele, G. The Old Wives Tale. (P. Binnie, ed)
P. Cheney, 568(SCN):Fall83-52
M. Hattaway, 541(RES):Feb83-64
Peele, G. Revival and Reaction.
D.H. Wrong, 617(TLS):19Oct84-1175
Peinovich, M.P. Old English Noun Morphology.*
T.F. Hoad, 447(N&Q):Feb82-64
Peirce, C.S. Semiotic and Significs. (C.S. Hardwick, with J. Cook, eds)
H. Buczynska-Garewicz, 567:Vol45No3/4-315
Peirce, C.S. Writings of Charles S. Peirce. (Vol 1) (M.H. Fisch, general ed)
R. Almeder, 319:Oct84-494
C. Hartshorne, 619:Winter83-64
P. Weiss, 619:Winter83-71
483:Apr83-276

Peirce, N.R. and J. Hagstrom. The Book of America.
E. Fawcett, 617(TLS):25May84-591
J. Herbers, 441:8Jan84-37
Peiter, H. - see Schleiermacher, F.D.E.
Pekarik, A., ed. Ukifune.*
R. Bowring, 407(MN):Summer83-209
Pelagia, O. Euphranor.
R. Higgins, 39:Jan83-71
Pelikan, J. The Christian Tradition. (Vol 4)
J.M. Todd, 441:30Sep84-36
Pelinka, P. Erbe und Neubeginn.
F.L. Carsten, 575(SEER):Apr83-316
Pelinski, R. La musique des Inuit du Caribou.
T.F. Johnston, 187:May84-336
Pellaprat, H.P. The Great Book of French Cuisine.
W. and C. Cowen, 639(VQR):Spring83-68
Pellegrin, P. La Classification des animaux chez Aristote.
J. Barnes, 123:Vol33No2-334
Pellegrini, A. Il profondo ieri.
U. Schulz-Buschhaus, 52:Band18Heft2-193
Pellegrino, E.D. and D.C. Thomasma. A Philosophical Basis of Medical Practice.*
J. Fletcher, 529(QQ):Spring83-251
Pelletier, F.J. and C.G. Normore, eds. New Essays in Philosophy of Language.
M. Stack, 154:Dec83-725
Pellew, J. The Home Office 1848-1914.
H. Parris, 637(VS):Summer83-456
Pelling, H. The Labour Governments, 1945-51.
P. Addison, 617(TLS):31Aug84-960
D. Smith, 362:21Jun84-24
Pelous, J-M. Amour précieux, amour galant (1654-1675).*
N. Aronson, 475:Vol 10No18-387
Peltenburg, E.J. Recent Developments in the Later Prehistory of Cyprus.
S. Hood, 123:Vol33No2-357
Pemberton, J.M. - see Ruffner, H.
de la Peña, J.A. Aguayo Expedition into Texas, 1721. (R.G. Santos, ed)
L. Milazzo, 584(SWR):Spring83-vi
Penkower, M.N. The Jews Were Expendable.
A.J. Sherman, 617(TLS):14Sep84-1032
Penn, J. Stag Dinner Death.
N. Callendar, 441:8Jan84-27
Penn, W. The Papers of William Penn.* (Vol 1) (M.M. and R.S. Dunn, eds)
S.V. James, 656(WMQ):Apr83-314
Penna, S. This Strange Joy.
D. Gioia, 461:Fall/Winter83/84-99
Penner, J. Private Parties.
E. Milton, 441:15Jan84-22
Penninger, F.E. William Caxton.*
K. Ward-Perkins, 447(N&Q):Jun82-243
Pennington, A. and P. Levi. Marko the Prince.
E.D. Goy, 617(TLS):24Aug84-938
Pennington, A.E. - see Kotošixin, G.
Pennington, M.B. and N. Sapieha. Monastery.
V. Rossi, 469:Vol9No2-108
"Pensée hispanique et Philosophie française des Lumières."*
D-H. Pageaux, 549(RLC):Apr-Jun83-230
"La pensée juridique de Paul Foriers."
J-L. Gardies, 542:Jul-Sep83-339

Pensom, R. Literary Technique in the "Chanson de Roland."
I. Short, 382(MAE):1983/2-321
Pentecost, H. Murder Out of Wedlock.
N. Callendar, 441:29Jan84-17
Pepe Sarno, I. - see Gómez de Castro, Á.
Pépin, J. Everyday Cooking with Jacques Pépin.
W. and C. Cowen, 639(VQR):Spring83-68
Pepper, C.B. We the Victors.
S. Offit, 441:1Apr84-17
Peppin, B. and L. Micklethwait. Dictionary of British Book Illustrators: The Twentieth Century.
D.J.C., 503:Autumn83-98
W. Feaver, 617(TLS):20Jan84-71
T. Russell-Cobb, 324:Nov84-815
B. Sibley, 362:2Feb84-25
Pepys, S. Tagebuch aus dem London des 17. Jahrhunderts.* (H. Winter, ed and trans)
G. Pascoe, 38:Band101Heft3/4-523
Pera, M. Apologia del Metodo.
W.R. Shea, 486:Dec83-662
Pera, M. Hume, Kant e l'induzione.
M.A. Finocchiaro, 319:Oct84-484
Percival, J. Theatre in My Blood.
S. Gold, 441:19Feb84-23
Perdome, M.T. El lector activo y la comunicación en "Rayuela."
W. Imo, 72:Band220Heft2-462
de Pereda, J.M. La puchera.* (L. Bonet, ed)
E. Rodgers, 86(BHS):Jan83-73
Pereira, N.G.O. Tsar-Liberator Alexander II of Russia, 1818-1881.
A.J. Rieber, 104(CASS):Summer83-277
Pereire, A. and G. van Zuylen. Private Gardens of France.
H. Winterbotham, 617(TLS):13Jan84-43
Perelli, L. Il movimento popolare nell'ultimo secolo della repubblica.
P.A. Brunt, 313:Vol73-206
A. Lintott, 123:Vol33No2-349
D.R. Shackleton Bailey, 124:Mar-Apr84-255
Perelman, C. Justice, Law, and Argument.*
J. Beatty, 321:Vol 17No4-325
A. Reix, 192(EP):Jan-Mar83-108
Perelman, C. The New Rhetoric and the Humanities.*
J. Beatty, 321:Vol 17No4-325
Perelman, C. The Realm of Rhetoric.* (German title: Das Reich der Rhetorik.)
C.H.W., 185:Apr84-548
Perelman, S.J. That Old Gang o' Mine. (R. Marschall, ed)
P. Crowther, 453(NYRB):8Nov84-37
P. De Vries, 442(NY):13Aug84-88
S.D. Smith, 441:8Jul84-16
Perera, H. Plantado.*
R. Romeu, 238:Sep83-442
Perera, V. and R.D. Bruce. The Last Lords of Palenque.
D. Johnson, 649(WAL):Nov83-263
Pérez, L.A., Jr. Historiography of the Revolution.
M.H. Sable, 263:Vol33No1-47
Pérez Firmat, G. Idle Fictions.
R.A. Gonzales Torres, 395(MFS):Winter83-809

Pérez Galdós, B. Fortunata y Jacinta (Dos historias de casadas). (P. Ortiz Armengol, ed)
 T.A. Sackett, 238:Sep83-434
Pérez-Gómez, A. Architecture and the Crisis of Modern Science.
 R. Evans, 617(TLS):3Aug84-876
Pérez-Rioja, J.A., M. Fernández-Galiano and A. Amorós. Humanismo español en el siglo XIX.
 S. Herpoel, 356(LR):Feb-May83-141
Pérez Rivera, F. and M. Hurtado. Introducción a la literatura española. (rev)
 D.R. McKay, 399(MLJ):Autumn83-309
Pérez Sánchez, A.E. El dibujo español de los siglos de Oro.
 D. Angulo Íñiguez, 48:Jul-Sep80-401
Perham, M. West African Passage. (A.H.M. Kirk-Greene, ed)
 R. Oliver, 617(TLS):20Jan84-65
Peri, J. Euridice. (H.M. Brown, ed)
 H.W. Hitchcock, 317:Spring83-150
Peri, Y. Between Battles and Ballots.
 C.C. O'Brien, 362:26Apr84-29
Perillo, G. and S. Delauro. Perillo.
 M.S. Young, 39:Feb83-148
"Perissotera Ellēnika."
 J.E. Rexine, 399(MLJ):Autumn83-294
Perkey, E.A. Perkey's Nebraska Place Names.
 P.J. Cosgrave, 424:Sep83-214
Perkin, M.R., ed. The Book Trade in Liverpool to 1805.
 A. Mason, 517(PBSA):Vol77No2-250
 A.D. Sterenberg, 354:Jun83-190
Perkins, D.N. The Mind's Best Work.*
 H. Osborne, 89(BJA):Winter83-91
Perkins, E.J. The Economy of Colonial America.
 C.D. Clowse, 656(WMQ):Oct83-630
Perl, R. The Falkland Islands Dispute in International Law and Politics.
 R. Etchepareborda, 263(RIB):Vol33No2-265
Perl, W.R. Operation Action.
 A.J. Sherman, 617(TLS):27Jan84-92
Perle, G. The Operas of Alban Berg. (Vol 2)
 R. Craft, 453(NYRB):20Dec84-52
Perlman, A.S. Sorting It Out.
 R. Lattimore, 249(HudR):Spring83-206
Perlmutter, D.M., ed. Studies in Relational Grammar 1.
 S. Johnson, 350:Sep84-652
Perlmutter, D.M. and S. Soames. Syntactic Argumentation and the Structure of English.*
 P.H. Matthews, 205(ForL):Dec81-171
Perloff, M. The Poetics of Indeterminacy.*
 P. Breslin, 405(MP):Feb84-333
 G.F. Butterick, 301(JEGP):Apr83-215
 M. Calinescu, 678(YCGL):No31-141
 P. Makin, 402(MLR):Jul83-657
Perman, M. The Road to Redemption.
 C.N. Degler, 441:29Jul84-11
Perng, C-H. Double Jeopardy.
 H. Shadick, 116:Jan82-109
Pernoud, R. Christine de Pisan.
 M.J. Ward, 207(FR):Mar84-549
Pérol, J. Histoire contemporaine.*
 M. Guiney, 207(FR):Feb84-416
Perol, L. - see Diderot, D.

Perosa, S. Henry James and the Experimental Novel.*
 M. Seymour, 617(TLS):25May84-594
Perrault, C. Contes, suivis du Miroir ou la Métamorphose d'Orante, de la Peinture, poème et du Labyrinthe de Versailles.* (J-P. Collinet, ed)
 D.L. Rubin, 208(FS):Jan83-77
Perrault, P. La Bête lumineuse.
 D. Clandfield, 627(UTQ):Summer83-546
Perrie, W. Out of Conflict.
 C. Milton, 571(ScLJ):Winter83-65
Perrin, N. Third Person Rural.
 P. Hagan, 441:8Jan84-21
Perrin, N.A. Reification and the Development of Realism in Late Minnesang.
 S.L. Wailes, 221(GQ):Mar83-300
du Perron, E. Le pays d'origine.
 Y. Guérin, 549(RLC):Apr-Jun83-255
Perros, G. Lettres à Michel Butor.
 J. Pfeiffer, 450(NRF):Feb83-126
Perros, J.P-G. Correspondance 1953-1967.
 J. Aeply, 450(NRF):Mar83-116
Perrow, C. Normal Accidents.
 J. Pfeiffer, 441:8Apr84-19
Perry, A., ed. La Passion des Jongleurs.
 C. Foxton, 402(MLR):Apr83-445
Perry, C. The Haight-Ashbury.
 H. Gold, 441:12Aug84-10
 442(NY):3Sep84-96
Perry, J.C. and B.L. Smith, eds. Essays on T'ang Society.
 C.A. Peterson, 318(JAOS):Jan-Mar82-142
Perry, L. Childhood, Marriage, and Reform.*
 R.O. Curry and L.B. Goodheart, 106:Winter83-401
Perry, M. The Harlem Renaissance.
 H.C. Woodbridge, 70:May-Jun82-159
Perry, M.J. The Constitution, the Courts, and Human Rights.
 A.A. Morris, 185:Apr84-501
Perry, R. MacAllister.
 N. Callendar, 441:15Apr84-26
Perry, R. Montgomery's Children.
 W. Balliett, 442(NY):6Feb84-124
 M. Watkins, 441:5Aug84-18
Perry, R. The Programming of the President.
 N. Fountain, 362:5Jul84-25
 H.G. Nicholas, 617(TLS):19Oct84-1177
Perry, R. Women, Letters, and the Novel.*
 P. Boumelha, 541(RES):Aug83-342
Perry, T. Metzger's Dog.*
 T.J. Binyon, 617(TLS):26Oct84-1225
 M. Laski, 362:19Jul84-27
Perse, S. St.-John Perse: Letters. (A.J. Knodel, ed and trans)
 J. Cruickshank, 396(ModA):Summer/Fall83-345
Pertschuk, M. Revolt against Regulation.
 639(VQR):Spring83-60
Peschel, E.R., ed. Medicine and Literature.
 R.A., 189(EA):Apr-Jun84-234
Peschken, G. Karl Friedrich Schinkel — Das Architektonische Lehrbuch.
 T. Mellinghoff, 90:Nov83-701
Pesetsky, B. Digs.
 P-L. Adams, 61:Dec84-148
 L.A. Schreiber, 441:4Nov84-9
 442(NY):17Dec84-156

291

Pesot, J. Silence, on parle.*
  B.H. Davis, 350:Mar84-203
Pessen, E. The Log Cabin Myth.
  P-L. Adams, 61:Jun84-124
Pestelli, G. The Age of Mozart and Beethoven.
  H.C.R. Landon, 617(TLS):27Apr84-474
Peter, H-W. - see Raabe, W.
Peter, K., ed. Romantikforschung seit 1945.
  D.P. Haase, 406:Summer83-216
Peters, E. Dead Man's Ransom.
  T.J. Binyon, 617(TLS):13Jul84-790
Peters, E. The Devil's Novice.*
  442(NY):5Nov84-172
Peters, E. Die for Love.
  J. Kaufman, 441:24Jun84-22
Peters, E., ed. Heresy and Authority in Medieval Europe.*
  A. Murray, 382(MAE):1983/2-358
Peters, H. - see Donne, J.
Peters, J., ed. Collectible Books.
  P.B. Eppard, 517(PBSA):Oct-Dec80-415
Peters, J. Farbe und Licht.
  A. Pyman, 575(SEER):Apr83-269
Peters, J. From Time Immemorial.
  J.C. Campbell, 441:13May84-9
  D. Pipes, 129:Jul84-60
  W. Reich, 61:Jul84-110
Peters, M. Mrs. Pat.
  P-L. Adams, 61:Apr84-148
  R. Findlater, 617(TLS):31Aug84-961
  W. Weaver, 441:4Mar84-13
Peters, M. Pitt and Popularity.
  J. Black, 161(DUJ):Jun83-115
  C.L.H. Knight, 656(WMQ):Apr83-319
Peters, M. Untersuchungen zur Vertretung der indogermanische Laryngale im Griechischen.*
  P. Flobert, 555:Vol57fasc1-109
  G.R. Hart, 123:Vol33No2-342
  C.J. Ruijgh, 394:Vol36fasc3/4-373
  W.F. Wyatt, Jr., 122:Oct83-363
Peters, R. The Great American Poetry Bake-Off. (2nd Ser)
  G. Burns, 584(SWR):Winter83-101
Peters, R., ed and trans. Jihad in Medieval and Modern Islam.
  U. Abd-Allāh, 318(JAOS):Jul-Sep82-567
Peters, R. Mammalian Communication.
  M. Bekoff, 567:Vol44No1/2-195
Petersen, A. Die Rezeption von Bölls "Katharina Blum" in den Massenmedien der Bundesrepublik Deutschland.
  K.E. Kuhn-Osius, 406:Fall83-322
Petersen, G. Stitches and Decorative Seams.
  P. Bach, 614:Fall84-23
Petersen, H., ed. Erkundungen.
  R. Ulbrich, 654(WB):4/1982-132
Petersen, K. Die "Gruppe 1925."
  A. Arnold, 564:Sep83-225
Petersen, S.H., ed. Voces nuevas del romancero castellano-leonés.
  E. Rogers, 238:Dec83-642
Peterson, L.S. The Canyons of Grace.
  P. La Salle, 573(SSF):Fall83-325
  J. Sanders, 649(WAL):Nov83-242
Peterson, M.D. Olive Branch and Sword.
  J.H. Pease, 579(SAQ):Summer83-340
Peterson, R.E. Andrei Bely's Short Prose.
  J.D. Elsworth, 575(SEER):Apr83-268

Peterson, R.F., A.M. Cohn and E.L. Epstein, eds. Work in Progress: Joyce Centenary Essays.
  M. Libertin, 329(JJQ):Summer84-381
Peterson, R.S. Imitation and Praise in the Poems of Ben Jonson.*
  I. Donaldson, 184(EIC):Apr83-148
  A. Guibbory, 301(JEGP):Oct83-554
  W.D. Kay, 401(MLQ):Dec82-395
  B. King, 569(SR):Winter83-149
Peterson, W.S. - see "Browning Institute Studies"
Petesch, N.L.M. Duncan's Colony. Soul Clap Its Hands and Sing.
  M.D. Lammon, 436(NewL):Fall83-109
Petherick, K. Per Gunnar Evander.
  B. Nolin, 562(Scan):Nov83-231
Petievich, G. To Live and Die in L.A.
  M. Buck, 441:29Apr84-32
  442(NY):4Jun84-136
Petiot, G. Le Robert des Sports.*
  R. Holt, 208(FS):Oct83-503
Petit, J. Claudel et la Bible.
  M. Wood, 208(FS):Jan83-101
"Petit Larousse Illustré 1983."
  S.F. Noreiko, 208(FS):Oct83-504
Petitfils, P., ed. Album Verlaine.
  J-H. Bornecque, 535(RHL):May/Jun83-478
Petitfils, P. Verlaine.
  J. Aeply, 450(NRF):Jun83-129
Petitmengin, P. and others. Pélagie la Pénitente. (Vol 1)
  P. Pattenden, 123:Vol33No1-114
Petits, J-P. La Terrasse du roi lépreux.
  A.L. Amprimoz, 102(CanL):Autumn83-110
Petonnet, C. Espaces habités.
  J. Gutwirth, 98:Nov83-872
Petrey, S. History in the Text.*
  D.M. Bickerton, 208(FS):Apr83-230
Petrie, D.W. Ultimately Fiction.*
  T.D. Adams, 77:Spring83-176
  D. Novarr, 506(PSt):Sep83-203
Petrone, M. - see de Goncourt, E.
Petroski, C. Gravity and Other Stories.
  E. Klein, 502(PrS):Winter83-89
Pettersson, T. Consciousness and Time.
  R.O. Evans, 569(SR):Spring83-291
  D.L. Higdon, 395(MFS):Winter83-766
  J. Lothe, 172(Edda):1983/3-185
  S. Monod, 189(EA):Apr-Jun84-219
  S.L. Ross, 478:Oct83-267
  G. Stewart, 651(WHR):Winter83-364
Pettigrew, J. and T.J. Collins - see Browning, R.
Pettigrew, T. British Film Character Actors.
  200:Oct83-493
Petty, A.C. One Ring to Bind Them All.
  H. Ilsemann, 38:Band101Heft3/4-538
Petty, E.P. Journey to Pleasant Hill. (N.D. Brown, ed)
  L. Milazzo, 584(SWR):Summer83-vi
Petzl, G. Die Inschriften von Smyrna. (Vol 1)
  J. Pouilloux, 555:Vol57fasc2-307
Peucker, B. Arcadia to Elysium.
  P. Salm, 221(GQ):Mar83-297
  H.J. Schneider, 52:Band17Heft1-89
Pevsner, N. Studies in Art, Architecture and Design.
  N. Burton, 59:Mar83-127

Pfaffel, W. Quartus gradus etymologiae.
  P. Flobert, 555:Vol57fasc2-335
  E. Laughton, 123:Vol33No2-325
Pfeiffer, B.B. - see Wright, F.L.
Pfister, M. Einführung in die romanische
Etymologie.*
  D. Evans, 447(N&Q):Jun82-288
  H. Petermann, 682(ZPSK):Band36Heft5-
  615
Pfister-Roesgen, G. Die etruskischen
Spiegel des 5 Jahrhunderts v. Chr.
  G. Lloyd-Morgan, 313:Vol73-234
Pfitzner, J. Der Anglizismus im Deutschen.
  A.W. Stanforth, 72:Band219Heft1-163
Pfoser, A. Literatur und Austromarxis-
mus.*
  F. Achberger, 406:Fall83-419
Pheby, J. and W. Scholze - see "The Oxford-
Duden Pictorial German-English Diction-
ary"
Phelan, J. Worlds From Words.*
  M.D. Springer, 284:Fall83-73
Phelan, N. The Swift Foot of Time.
  J. Neville, 617(TLS):24Aug84-937
Phelps, R. - see Colette
Pheto, M. And Night Fell.
  M. Hope, 441:14Oct84-27
Philbrick, S. No Goodbye.
  M. Williams, 651(WHR):Spring83-53
Philbrick, W.R. Slow Dancer.
  N. Callendar, 441:28Oct84-39
Prince Philip, the Duke of Edinburgh. Men,
Machines and Sacred Cows.
  J. Grigg, 362:8Mar84-24
Philip, I. The Bodleian Library in the
Seventeenth and Eighteenth Centuries.
  P. Quarrie, 617(TLS):3Aug84-879
Philip, N. A Fine Anger.
  H.R.E. Davidson, 203:Vol194No1-129
Philipe, A. Les Résonances de l'amour.
  G.P. Ashley, 207(FR):Mar84-596
Philipp, H. Bronzeschmuck aus Olympia.
  C.A. Picón, 123:Vol33No1-100
Philipp, T. Ğurğī Zaidān.
  M.M. Badawi, 294:Vol 14-98
Philippe, B. Être juif dans la société
française.
  J. Paulhan, 207(FR):May84-892
Philippe, R. Political Graphics.*
  P. Overy, 592:Aug83-49
Philippe de Mézières. Philippe de
Mézières' Campaign for the Feast of
Mary's Presentation. (W.E. Coleman,
ed)
  R.W. Pfaff, 589:Apr83-521
Philippi, D.L. Songs of Gods, Songs of
Humans.*
  W. Eberhard, 318(JAOS):Jul-Sep82-580
Philippi, K-P. Volk des Zorns.
  H. Müssener, 406:Summer83-228
Phillips, B. Conran and the Habitat Story.
  R. Coward, 362:31May84-25
  J. Rutherford, 617(TLS):20Jul84-820
Phillips, D.D. Spook or Spoof?
  D. Milivojević, 558(RLJ):Winter-
  Spring83-288
  M.J. Smith, 50(ArQ):Summer83-173
  A.J. Wehrle, 574(SEEJ):Summer83-260
Phillips, D.Z. Through a Darkening Glass.*
  J.J. Stuhr, 478:Apr83-116
Phillips, D.Z. - see Anderson, J.
Phillips, D.Z. - see Fries, J.F.

Phillips, E., ed. The Left and the
Erotic.*
  M. Poole, 362:23Feb84-28
Phillips, G.D. George Cukor.*
  J.A. Gallagher, 200:Jan83-61
Phillips, G.D. Hemingway and Film.
  M. Deutelbaum, 395(MFS):Winter83-733
Phillips, H. The Theatre and its Critics
in Seventeenth-Century France.
  H.C. Knutson, 615(TJ):Oct82-410
Phillips, J.A. Electoral Behavior in
Unreformed England.*
  L. Stone, 453(NYRB):29Mar84-42
Phillips, J.A. Eve.
  J. Boswell, 441:15Jul84-7
Phillips, J.A. Machine Dreams.
  M.K. Benet, 617(TLS):23Nov84-1359
  J. Mellors, 362:13Dec84-30
  A. Tyler, 441:1Jul84-3
  442(NY):30Jul84-87
Phillips, K.P. Post-Conservative America.
  S.T. Francis, 396(ModA):Spring83-201
  639(VQR):Winter83-22
Phillips, K.P. Staying On Top.
  L. Silk, 441:21Oct84-37
Phillips, M.M. - see Erasmus
Phillips, N. Sijobang.
  J. Siegel, 293(JASt):Aug83-1027
  R.A. Sutton, 187:May84-355
Phillips, P. and E. Women and Work.
  R.R. Pierson, 99:Oct83-29
Phillips, R. Running on Empty.*
  W.H. Pritchard, 491:Jan84-228
Phillips, R. - see Schwartz, D.
Phillips, W. A Partisan View.
  D.M. Oshinsky, 441:8Jan84-28
Phillips, W.J. Phillips in Print. (M.
Tippett and D. Cole, eds)
  E. Milroy, 99:Feb84-34
Physick, J. The Victoria and Albert
Museum.*
  C. Gere, 39:Aug83-195
Pi, W. - see under Wang Pi
Piaget, J. Les formes élémentaires de la
dialectique.
  R.L. Fetz, 687:Oct-Dec83-650
Piaget, J. and R. Garcia. Psychogénèse et
histoire des sciences.
  J.C. Piguet, 540(RIPh):Vol37fasc3-371
Pianu, G. Ceramiche etrusche sovradipinte.
  D. Von Bothmer, 124:Jan-Feb84-199
Piatigorsky, A. The Buddhist Philosophy
of Thought.
  B.K. Matilal, 617(TLS):4May84-501
Piattelli-Palmarini, M., ed. Language and
Learning.* (French title: Théories du
langage, Théories de l'apprentissage.)
  S. Haroutunian, 393(Mind):Jan83-138
  A. Marras, 486:Mar83-173
Picabia, L. and A. Zribi-Hertz. Découvrir
la grammaire française.
  J-P. Beaujot, 209(FM):Jan83-60
Picano, F. House of Cards.
  M.S. Kaplan, 441:15Jul84-18
Picat-Guinoiseau, G. Une oeuvre méconnue
de Charles Nodier: "Faust" imité de
Goethe.*
  P.J. Whyte, 208(FS):Jul83-349
Picchio, L.S. - see under Stegagno Picchio,
L.
Piccone, P. Italian Marxism.
  J.V. Femia, 617(TLS):8Jun84-643
Picherot, A. - see de Vigny, A.

Pine, L.G. A Dictionary of Nicknames.
R. Davies, 617(TLS):21Dec84-1481
Pineau, J. Le Mouvement rythmique en
français.
G. Cesbron, 356(LR):Nov83-349
Pinedo, F.Á. and J.M. Ramírez Martínez -
see under Álvarez Pinedo, F. and J.M.
Ramírez Martínez
Pinion, F.B., ed. A George Eliot Miscel-
lany.
G. Levine, 445(NCF):Jun83-112
Pinkney, A. The Myth of Black Progress.
B. Rustin, 61:Oct84-121
Pinkney, T. Women in the Poetry of T.S.
Eliot.
D. Davie, 617(TLS):21Sep84-1043
Pinkster, H., ed. Latin Linguistics and
Linguistic Theory.
M.E. Winters, 350:Dec84-986
Pinkus, B. The Soviet Government and the
Jews 1948-1967.
M. Gilbert, 617(TLS):21Dec84-1478
Pinney, S. - see Warner, S.T.
Pinney, T. - see Macaulay, T.B.
del Pino, S.R. - see under Rodríguez del
Pino, S.
Pins, J. The Japanese Pillar Print,
Hashira-e.
S. Addiss, 60:Mar-Apr83-132
Pinsker, S. Between Two Worlds.
G.F. Waller, 106:Summer83-207
Pinsky, R. History of My Heart.
R.W. Flint, 441:8Apr84-14
M. Kinzie, 29:Sep/Oct84-38
Pintacuda, M. Interpretazioni musicali
sul teatro di Aristofane.
E.K. Borthwick, 123:Vol33No1-128
J. Yudkin, 24:Fall83-302
Piotrovsky, B. The Hermitage.
M. Chamot, 39:Mar83-261
Piper, D., general ed. The Mitchell Beaz-
ley Library of Art.
G. Waterfield, 39:Apr83-335
Piper, J. and R. Ingrams. Piper's Places.
C. de Beaurepaire, 364:Feb84-110
Pipes, D. In the Path of God.
E. Kedourie, 129:Aug84-65
Pipes, R. Survival is Not Enough.
H. Sonnenfeldt, 441:18Nov84-12
Pippin, R.B. Kant's Theory of Form.
P. Guyer, 319:Jul84-377
R. Meerbote, 482(PhR):Jul83-419
W.H. Walsh, 518:Apr83-91
"Pirandello/Martoglio." (S. Zappulla, ed)
O. Ragusa, 276:Spring83-71
Pirazzoli-t'Serstevens, M. The Han Civili-
sation of China.
"Skipjack," 463:Winter83/84-392
Pirie, D.B. William Wordsworth.*
P.J. Manning, 661(WC):Summer83-120
S.M. Sperry, 301(JEGP):Oct83-564
Pirler, P. Friedrich von Gentzens Ausein-
andersetzung mit Immanuel Kant.
P. Burg, 342:Band74Heft3-368
Piron, M., ed. Anthologie de la littéra-
ture dialectale de Wallonie.
A. Goosse, 356(LR):Aug83-233
A. Sakari, 553(RLiR):Jan-Jun83-233
Pirrotta, N. and E. Povoledo. Music and
Theatre from Poliziano to Monteverdi.*
G.J. Buelow, 414(MusQ):Fall83-607
T. Carter, 278(IS):Vol38-104
[continued]

[continuing]
J.W. Hill, 317:Fall83-519
F.W. Sternfeld, 410(M&L):Jul/Oct83-250
de Pisan, C. - see under Christine de
Pisan
Pisi, G. - see Blass, F. and A. Debrunner
Pissarro, C. Correspondance de Camille
Pissarro. (Vol 1) (J. Bailly-Herzberg,
ed)
R. Pickvance, 90:Oct83-630
Piston, W. Harmony.* (4th ed rev by M.
De Voto)
A.W., 412:Feb82-68
Pistorius, G. Marcel Proust und Deutsch-
land.*
R. Birn, 678(YCGL):No31-136
A. Corbineau-Hoffmann, 547(RF):Band95
Heft3-373
G.R. Kaiser, 52:Band18Heft1-111
W.A. Strauss, 221(GQ):Nov83-697
Pitavy, F.L. William Faulkner's "Light in
August."
R.A. Day, 189(EA):Jul-Sep84-358
Pitcher, J. Samuel Daniel: The Brotherton
Manuscript.*
P. Cronewett, 517(PBSA):Vol77No3-409
B. Juel-Jensen, 354:Dec83-428
D.B.J. Randall, 551(RenQ):Spring83-145
Pitt, A. Shakespeare's Women.*
R.K. Bank, 615(TJ):Mar83-129
I. Leimberg, 156(JDSh):Jahrbuch
1983-242
Pitt, J.C., ed. The Philosophy of Wilfrid
Sellars.
F. Wilson, 543:Dec82-469
Pitt, J.C. Pictures, Images and Concep-
tual Change.
W.S. Robinson, 486:Dec83-671
Piva, P. Da Cluny a Polirone.
C.B. McClendon, 589:Jan83-212
Piven, F.F. and R. Cloward. The New
Class War.
639(VQR):Winter83-24
Pizer, D. Twentieth-Century American Lit-
erary Naturalism.*
S.C. Brennan, 594:Summer83-166
T. Ludington, 577(SHR):Fall83-384
R. Martin, 179(ES):Aug83-380
Pizer, D. - see London, J.
Pizer, D. and E.N. Harbert - see "Diction-
ary of Literary Biography"
Pla, J. Guía fundamentada y popular del
Monasterio de Poblet.
R. Cómez, 576:Mar83-74
Placella Somella, P. Marcel Proust e i
Movimenti Pittorici d'Avanguardia.
B. Brun, 535(RHL):Sep/Dec83-962
Plaidy, J. Myself My Enemy.
J. Bass, 441:15Jan84-18
Plain, B. Crescent City.
E.N. Evans, 441:7Oct84-18
Plank, F., ed. Ergativity.
G.F. Meier, 682(ZPSK):Band36Heft5-597
Plank, F. Morphologische (Ir-) Regularitä-
ten.
P.H. Matthews, 297(JL):Mar83-281
"Planning Now for an Information Society."
E. Zureik, 529(QQ):Autumn83-779
Plante, D. The Foreigner.
A. Friedman, 441:7Oct84-12
A. Mars-Jones, 617(TLS):16Nov84-1301
Plantinga, A. Does God Have a Nature?*
W.L. Rowe, 482(PhR):Apr83-305

Plantinga, T. Historical Understanding in the Thought of Wilhelm Dilthey.*
  H. Ineichen, 687:Jan-Mar83-153
Plantos, T. Passchendaele.
  P.K. Smith, 99:Mar84-38
Planty-Bonjour, G., ed. Hegel et la religion.
  D. Janicaud, 192(EP):Jul-Sep83-372
  A. Reix, 542:Jan-Mar83-134
Plaskin, G. Horowitz.*
  J. Methuen-Campbell, 415:Nov83-685
von Platen, M. Innanläsning.
  L. Thompson, 562(Scan):May83-98
Plater, W.M. The Grim Phoenix.
  P. Balbert, 594:Fall83-265
Plath, S. The Collected Poems.* (T. Hughes, ed)
  D. Seed, 189(EA):Jan-Mar84-108
  A. Williamson, 491:Jun83-170
Platis, E.N. Oi katēgoroi tou Sōkratē.
  G. Vlastos, 24:Summer83-201
Plato. Gorgias.* (T. Irwin, ed and trans)
  A. Nehamas, 449:Sep83-497
  J. Sisson, 479(PhQ):Oct83-406
  W.J. Verdenius, 394:Vol136fasc3/4-413
Plato. Hippias Major.* (P. Woodruff, ed and trans)
  L. Ballew, 319:Apr84-229
  M.J. O'Brien, 529(QQ):Winter83-1221
Plato. Symposium.* (K.J. Dover, ed)
  S.R. Slings, 394:Vol136fasc3/4-414
Platt, C. The Abbeys and Priories of Medieval England.
  J.H. Harvey, 617(TLS):18May84-544
Platt, J. Reformed Thought and Scholasticum.
  R.A. Muller, 551(RenQ):Autumn83-438
Plattner, S.W. Roy Stryker: U.S.A., 1943-1950.
  J. Hunter, 676(YR):Spring84-433
Platts, M., ed. Reference, Truth and Reality.
  J. Dancy, 393(Mind):Apr83-288
  A. Morton, 316:Mar83-208
  R. Wachbroit, 482(PhR):Jul83-474
Plautus. The Darker Comedies. (J. Tatum, trans)
  M. Hammond, 124:Jul-Aug84-378
Plautus. Rudens, Curculio, Casina. (C. Stace, trans)
  H.J.K. Usher, 123:Vol33No1-158
Playfair, G. The Flash of Lightning.
  R. Findlater, 617(TLS):27Jan84-87
"Plays of Protest from the Franco Era." (P.W. O'Connor, trans)
  M-E. Bravo, 552(REH):Oct83-463
Pleeth, W. Cello. (N. Pyron, ed)
  R. Anderson, 415:Jan83-36
Pleij, H. De wereld volgens Thomas van der Noot.
  S. Levie, 204(FdL):Dec83-309
Pleket, H.W. and R.S. Stroud. Supplementum Epigraphicum Graecum. (Vol 28)
  P.M. Fraser, 123:Vol33No1-153
Plessen, M. and D. Spoerri. Le Musée Sentimental de Preusse.
  I.K. Rogoff, 59:Jun83-250
Plessner, H. Gesammelte Schriften II.
  W. Steinbeck, 342:Band74Heft1-88
Plett, H.F., ed. Englisches Drama von Beckett bis Bond.
  E. Auberlen, 189(EA):Apr-Sep83-314

Plimpton, G. Fireworks.
  F. Ferretti, 441:23Sep84-13
Plimpton, G. and C. Hemphill - see Vreeland, D.
Pliny the Elder. Plinivs Secvndvs d. A.C., "Naturkunde." (Bks 14 and 15) (R. König, with G. Winkler, eds and trans)
  J. André, 555:Vol57fasc2-332
Plomley, R., with D. Drescher. Desert Island Lists.
  R. Twisk, 362:1Nov84-31
Plotinus. Enneas. (Vol 6) (P. Henry and H-R. Schwyzer, eds)
  É. des Places, 555:Vol57fasc2-318
Plott, J.C., with J.M. Dolin. Global History of Philosophy. (Vol 3)
  W. Gray, with S. Nonken, 485(PE&W):Jan83-100
"Ploutizō ta Ellēnika mou (Advanced Level)."
  J.E. Rexine, 399(MLJ):Autumn83-294
Plowden, G.F.C. Pope on Classic Ground.
  N. Berry, 364:Nov83-113
  G. Rousseau, 617(TLS):13Jul84-789
Plumly, S. Summer Celestial.*
  D. Wojahn, 434:Spring84-489
  D. Young, 199:Spring84-83
Plummer, J. and G. Clark. The Last Flowering.
  J.J.G. Alexander, 617(TLS):11May84-528
Plummer, J.F., ed. Vox Feminae.
  W.T.H. Jackson, 589:Jan83-216
Plunket, R. My Search for Warren Harding.*
  M.K. Benet, 617(TLS):27Jul84-848
  J. Mellors, 362:5Apr84-28
  639(VQR):Autumn83-127
Plutarch. Plutarque, "Oeuvres Morales." (Vol 12, Pt 1) (M. Cuvigny and G. Lachenand, eds)
  D.A. Russell, 123:Vol33No2-316
Po Chü-i. Translations from Po Chü-i's Collected Works. (Vol 4) (H.S. Levy and H.W. Wells, trans)
  J.M. Boltz, 116:Jul82-269
Pochmann, H.A. Bibliography of German Culture in America to 1940.
  L.S. Thompson, 70:Mar-Apr83-127
"Pocket Dictionary of Music."
  M. Rochester, 415:Apr83-235
Pocock, D.C., ed. Humanistic Geography and Literature.*
  W.N., 102(CanL):Spring83-155
Podeschi, J.B. Dickens and Dickensiana.
  R.L. Patten, 517(PBSA):Vol77No2-209
Podgorecki, A. and C.J. Whelan, eds. Sociological Approaches to Law.
  C.S., 185:Apr84-562
Podhoretz, N. Why We Were in Vietnam.*
  G.S. Smith, 529(QQ):Winter83-972
Podro, M. The Critical Historians of Art.*
  D. Carrier, 290(JAAC):Fall83-94
  M.A. Cheetham, 127:Winter83-419
  P. Crowther, 89(BJA):Autumn83-363
Poe, E.A. Collected Writings of Edgar Allan Poe.* (Vol 1) (B.R. Pollin, ed)
  R. Asselineau, 189(EA):Jan-Mar84-112
  W. Goldhurst, 579(SAQ):Summer83-346
  P.F. Quinn, 495(PoeS):Jun83-14
Poe, E.A. Edgar Allan Poe: Essays and Reviews. (G.R. Thompson, ed)
  H. Bloom, 453(NYRB):11Oct84-23
  R. Wilbur, 441:9Sep84-3

Ponge, F. The Making of the Pré.
R. de Gorog, 545(RPh):May83-621
M. Perloff, 29:Jan/Feb84-40
Ponge, F. Nioque de l'Avant-Printemps.*
G. Sartoris, 450(NRF):May83-118
Pons, A. - see Vico, G.
Pons, C.R. - see under Reyes Pons, C.
Pontiero, G. - see García Márquez, G.
Pontiero, G. - see Noccioli, G.
"Ponto Baltica." (Vol 1)
R. Eckert, 682(ZPSK):Band36Heft6-742
Pontus de Tyard - see under de Tyard, P.
Poole, F. and M. Vanzi. Revolution in the
Philippines.
J. Bresnan, 441:15Jul84-19
442(NY):13Aug84-93
Poole, M. and J. Wyver. Powerplays.
D. Edgar, 362:5Apr84-27
Poole, R.W., Jr., ed. Instead of Regula-
tion.
W.H. Peterson, 396(ModA):Winter83-101
Poortinga, Y. De prins op frijersfuotten.
H.L. Cox, 196:Band24Heft1/2-167
Poovey, M. The Proper Lady and the Woman
Writer.
D. Kaplan, 454:Fall83-81
Popa, M. Geschichte der rumänischen
Literatur.
I. Gregori, 72:Band220Heft1-233
Pope, N. Dickens and Charity.
R. Bennett, 541(RES):May83-236
Pope-Hennessy, J. Verandah.
A.J.G.H., 617(TLS):20Jul84-822
Popelar, I. - see Baldinger, K.
Popkin, R.H. The High Road to Pyrrhonism.*
(R.A. Watson and J.E. Force, eds)
G. Gawlick, 53(AGP):Band65Heft2-190
Poppe, R.P. - see under Pastor Poppe, R.
Popper, K.R. Die beiden Grundprobleme der
Erkenntnistheorie.
E.G. Zahar, 84:Jun83-149
Popper, K.R. The Open Universe. (W.W.
Bartley 3d, ed)
O.F., 185:Oct83-165
N.D. Mermin, 486:Dec83-651
Popper, K.R. Quantum Theory and the
Schism in Physics.
N.D. Mermin, 486:Dec83-651
Popper, K.R. Realism and the Aim of Sci-
ence. (W.W. Bartley 3d, ed)
R.A. Healey, 486:Dec83-669
Poppitz, K., ed. Von Odysseus bis Felix
Krull.
70:May-Jun83-170
"Popular Music 2." (R. Middleton and D.
Horn, eds)
J. Porter, 187:Jan84-137
"Popular Music 3." (R. Middleton and D.
Horn, eds)
E.M. Thomson, 362:19Apr84-27
Porch, D. The Conquest of Morocco.*
639(VQR):Summer83-84
Porges, H. Wagner Rehearsing the "Ring."*
R. Anderson, 415:Oct83-618
Pörn, I. Action Theory and Social Science.
R. Martin, 488:Mar83-94
Porphyrios, D., ed. Classicism Is Not a
Style.
639(VQR):Winter83-29
Porphyrios, D. Sources of Modern Eclecti-
cism.
639(VQR):Winter83-27

Porphyrogenitus, I. Praefatio in Homerum.*
(J.F. Kindstrand, ed)
D.M. Schenkeveld, 394:Vol36fasc3/4-389
Porqueras Mayo, A. - see Calderón de la
Barca, P.
Porte, J., ed. Emerson.
L.A. Lange, 529(QQ):Autumn83-901
J. Myerson, 432(NEQ):Jun83-275
D. Yannella, 27(AL):Dec83-646
Porte, J. - see Emerson, R.W.
Porter, C. The Complete Lyrics of Cole
Porter.* (R. Kimball, ed)
R. Davies, 617(TLS):13Jan84-33
Porter, C. Seeing and Being.*
J.A. Ward, 284:Fall83-68
Porter, D. Dickinson.*
L.Y. Gossett, 569(SR):Summer83-445
Porter, D. Frommer's Dollarwise Guide to
the Caribbean (including Bermuda and the
Bahamas).
B.F. Carruthers, 37:Nov-Dec83-62
Porter, D. The Pursuit of Crime.*
S.D., 189(EA):Apr-Jun84-234
G. Falconer, 529(QQ):Spring83-223
D.I. Grossvogel, 131(CL):Fall83-380
P. Wolfe, 395(MFS):Autumn83-389
Porter, D.H. The Emergence of the Past.
R.S. Dupree, 543:Jun83-945
J.L. Gorman, 518:Apr83-113
W.H. Walsh, 125:Spring83-278
Porter, H. Lies, Damned Lies and Some
Exclusives.
D. Trelford, 362:22Nov84-26
Porter, J. and E. All Under Heaven.
D. Davin, 617(TLS):26Oct84-1206
Porter, J., M. Porter and B. Blishen.
Stations and Callings.
J.F. Ellis, 529(QQ):Winter83-1163
Porter, J.A. The Drama of Speech Acts.*
I. Schabert, 38:Band101Heft1/2-255
J. Wilders, 447(N&Q):Feb82-71
Porter, J.A. The Kentucky Stories.
J. Mellors, 362:2Feb84-28
G. Monteiro, 573(SSF):Fall83-323
Porter, M.G. The Art of Grit.
R. Curran, 649(WAL):Nov83-244
T. Martin, 27(AL):Mar83-115
Porter, P. Collected Poems.*
D. Dunn, 364:Jun83-74
G. Szirtes, 493:Mar83-34
Porter, R. English Society in the Eigh-
teenth Century.
D. Jarrett, 83:Spring83-100
L. Stone, 453(NYRB):29Mar84-42
Porter, R. Milan Kundera.
J. Rupnik, 575(SEER):Jul83-441
Porter, R. and M. Teich, eds. The Enlight-
enment in National Context.*
W. Stafford, 366:Spring83-117
Porterfield, N. Jimmie Rodgers.
C. Seemann, 650(WF):Oct83-318
D.K. Wilgus, 187:Jan84-146
M.R. Winchell, 585(SoQ):Winter83-77
Portillo Trambley, E. Sor Juana and Other
Plays.
D. Devlin, 157:Winter83-38
E.C. Ramírez, 352(LATR):Spring84-103
Portoghesi, P. L'angelo della storia,
Teoria e linguaggi dell'architettura.
P.G. Raman, 576:May83-203

298

Porzio, D., with R. and M. Tabanelli, eds.
Lithography.
  J. Kainen, 441:8Jan84-9
  442(NY):9Jan84-110
Posner, D. Antoine Watteau.
  A. Brookner, 617(TLS):23Mar84-299
  F. Haskell, 453(NYRB):20Dec84-25
  J. Russell, 441:2Dec84-11
Posner, R. and J.N. Green, eds. Trends in
Romance Linguistics and Philology.*
(Vols 1 and 2)
  M. Iliescu, 553(RLiR):Jan-Jun83-166
  C. Price, 208(FS):Jan83-117
Posner, R. and J.N. Green, eds. Trends in
Romance Linguistics and Philology.
(Vols 3 and 4)
  J. Klausenburger, 399(MLJ):Autumn83-
    300
  G. Price, 208(FS):Jan83-117
Possevino, A. Istoricheskie sochineniia o
Rossii XVI v. (L.A. Godovikova, ed and
trans)
  H.F. Graham, 550(RusR):Oct83-431
Post, J.F.S. Henry Vaughan.*
  B. Berry, 141:Spring83-171
  R. Ellrodt, 189(EA):Jan-Mar84-94
    639(VQR):Summer83-89
"The Postwar Poetry of Iceland." (S.A.
Magnússon, trans)
  J. Gudmundsson, 529(QQ):Winter83-1227
Potash, R.A. Mexican Government and Indus-
trial Development in the Early Republic.
  I.E. Cadenhead, Jr., 263(RIB):Vol133No3-
    414
Pothast, U. Die eigentlich metaphysische
Tätigkeit.
  M. Hielscher, 489(PJGG):Band90Heft2-
    430
Pothast, U. Die Unzulänglichkeit der Frei-
heitsbeweise.
  R. Hesse, 687:Apr-Jun83-320
Pothet, L. Mythe et tradition populaire
dans l'imaginaire dickensien.
  G.H. Ford, 189(EA):Jan-Mar83-93
Potok, C. The Book of Lights.*
  B. Elson, 529(QQ):Spring83-219
  S.G. Kellman, 390:Aug/Sep83-58
    42(AR):Winter83-120
Pott, H-G. Die schöne Freiheit.
  A.J. Camigliano, 406:Fall83-342
  W. Wittkowski, 221(GQ):Jan83-141
Potter, J. The Liberty We Seek.
  J.W. Tyler, 432(NEQ):Dec83-622
Potter, J.H. Five Frames for the "Decam-
eron."
  S. Deligiorgis, 402(MLQ):Dec82-404
  K.J. Harty, 573(SSF):Spring-Summer83-
    154
  D.R. Howard, 551(RenQ):Autumn83-410
  A. di Tommaso, 141:Winter83-71
Potter, K.H., ed. Encyclopedia of Indian
Philosophies: Advaita Vedānta Up to
Śaṃkara and His Pupils.
  P. Granoff, 293(JASt):Nov82-198
  A.L. Herman, 485(PE&W):Apr83-197
Potter, L. and J. Broadbent - see Milton,
J.
Potthoff, K. Einführung in die Modell-
theorie und ihre Anwendungen.
  G. Fuhrken, 316:Mar83-219
Pottle, F.A. Pride and Negligence.*
  C.J. Rawson, 569(SR):Spring83-269

Potts, T.C. Conscience in Medieval Philos-
ophy.*
  P.A. Clarke, 393(Mind):Jan83-128
Potts, W., ed. Portraits of the Artist in
Exile.
  J-M. Rabaté, 98:Aug-Sep83-691
Potulicki, E.B. La modernité de la pensée
de Diderot dans les oeuvres philoso-
phiques.*
  A. Vartanian, 173(ECS):Winter83/84-244
Pou, P.J. - see under Jauralde Pou, P.
Poulat, É. Une Église Ébranlée.
  W.R. Ward, 161(DUJ):Dec82-125
Poulenc, F. Emmanuel Chabrier.*
  R. Nichols, 415:Jul83-428
Poulenc, F. My Friends and Myself. (S.
Audel, ed)
  A.W., 412:Feb82-68
Poulle, E. Les sources astronomiques.
  B.R. Goldstein, 589:Apr83-522
Poulsen, R.C. The Pure Experience of
Order.
  S.J. Bronner, 649(WAL):Aug83-189
Poulton, D. John Dowland. (2nd ed)
  J. Steele, 415:Mar83-171
  C. Wilson, 410(M&L):Jan/Apr83-96
Pouncey, P.R. The Necessities of War.*
  V. Hunter, 487:Spring83-66
Pound, E. Collected Shorter Poems.
  A.J., 617(TLS):20Jul84-822
Pound, E. and F.M. Ford. Pound/Ford.*
(B. Lindberg-Seyersted, ed)
  F. Tuohy, 364:Jul83-86
    42(AR):Summer83-374
    295(JML):Nov83-390
"Ezra Pound and Dorothy Shakespear: Their
Letters, 1909-1914." (O. Pound and A.W.
Litz, eds)
  H. Carpenter, 441:16Sep84-3
Poupart, J-M. Angoisse Play.
  K. Mezei, 102(CanL):Summer83-128
Pourrat, H. and G. Roud. Sur la route des
hauts jardins.
  H. Godin, 208(FS):Jul83-362
Pouthier, P. Ops et la conception divine
de l'abondance dans la religion romaine
jusqu'à la mort d'Auguste.*
  M. Beard, 313:Vol73-215
Povejšil, J. Das Prager Deutsch des 17.
und 18. Jahrhunderts.*
  P. Trost, 685(ZDL):2/1983-264
Povey, J.F. Literature for Discussion.
  I. Leki, 608:Dec84-729
Powe, B.A. The Aberhart Summer.
  M. Thorpe, 99:Oct83-25
Powell, A. Faces in My Time.*
  G. Merle, 189(EA):Apr-Sep83-347
Powell, A. O, How the Wheel Becomes It!*
  P. Craig, 617(TLS):28Dec84-1506
  C. Michener, 441:22Jan84-25
    442(NY):9Jan84-109
Powell, A. Venusburg.
  P. Craig, 617(TLS):21Sep84-1066
Powell, B. Epic and Chronicle.
  G. West, 304(JHP):Fall83-68
Powell, J. The Other Side of the Story.
  L. Bernstein, 441:1Apr84-7
  J. Muravchik, 129:Aug84-63
    442(NY):23Apr84-131
Powell, P. Edisto.
  R. Loewinsohn, 441:15Apr84-14
  G. Strawson, 617(TLS):31Aug84-964
  R. Towers, 453(NYRB):31May84-35

Powell, P.J. People of the Sacred Moun-
tain.
  G. Brotherston, 617(TLS):23Nov84-1336
  L. Evers, 649(WAL):Aug83-151
Powell, S., ed. The Advent and Nativity
Sermons from a Fifteenth-Century Revi-
sion of John Mirk's Festial.
  C. von Nolcken, 589:Oct83-1078
  M.F. Wakelin, 38:Band101Heft1/2-233
Powell, V. The Constant Novelist.*
  R. Usborne, 364:Oct83-110
Powell, V. Flora Annie Steel, Novelist
of India.
  F.M. Mannsaker, 637(VS):Autumn82-105
Power, M.S. Hunt for the Autumn Clowns.*
  D. Durrant, 364:Aug/Sep83-133
Powers, T. Thinking about the Next War.*
  639(VQR):Summer83-93
Powers, W.K. Yuwipi.
  C.R. Farrer, 187:May84-338
  J.W. Schneider, 649(WAL):May83-71
Powledge, F. Fat of the Land.
  B. Miller, 441:24Jun84-25
Pozuelo Yvancos, J.M. El lenguaje poético
de la lírica amorosa de Quevedo.
  P.J. Smith, 402(MLR):Jan83-210
Pozzi, G. La parola dipinta.
  K. Ley, 547(RF):Band95Heft3-404
  F. Meregalli, 52:Band18Heft1-88
Pradines, M. Le beau voyage.
  M. Adam, 542:Oct-Dec83-450
  A. Reix, 542:Jan-Mar83-65
Pradines, M. La fonction perceptive. (R.
Guyot, ed)
  A. Reix, 542:Jul-Sep83-334
Praestgaard Andersen, L. Skjoldmøer.
  J.M. Jochens, 563(SS):Summer83-262
Prall, D.W. Aesthetic Judgment.
  G. Dickie, 290(JAAC):Fall83-83
Pramoedya Ananta Toer. Child of All
Nations.
  J. Crace, 617(TLS):28Dec84-1506
Prandi, A. and others. L'Umbria.
  D.F. Glass, 54:Jun83-340
Prange, G.W., with D.M. Goldstein and K.V.
Dillon. At Dawn We Slept.
  E.S. Shapiro, 396(ModA):Summer/Fall83-
  334
Prange, G.W., with D.M. Goldstein and K.V.
Dillon. Target Tokyo.
  D. Ghitelman, 441:18Nov84-33
Prantera, A. Strange Loop.
  M. Furness, 617(TLS):29Jun84-717
  J. Mellors, 362:5Jul84-27
Prāsādika, B. and L.M. Joshi, eds and
trans. Vimalakírtinirdeśasútra.
  J.W. de Jong, 259(IIJ):Mar83-160
Praschek, H., ed. Gerhart Hauptmanns
"Weber."*
  J. Osborne, 402(MLR):Oct83-986
Pratt, A. Archetypal Patterns in Women's
Fiction.*
  E.B. Jordan, 395(MFS):Summer83-347
  A-M. Roman, 189(EA):Apr-Sep83-325
Pratt, C. El anglicismo en el español pen-
insular contemporáneo.*
  R. Wright, 545(RPh):Feb83-465
Pratt, E.J. E.J. Pratt on His Life and
Poetry. (S. Gingell, ed)
  E.J. Devereux, 105:Fall/Winter83-92
Pratt, J. - see Marks, G.A. and C.B.
Johnson

Pratt, J.C., ed. Vietnam Voices.
  C. Trueheart, 441:7Oct84-23
Pratt, J.C. and V.A. Neufeldt - see Eliot,
G.
Praveček, J. Instrumentationslehre für
Blasorchester.
  N. O'Loughlin, 415:Mar83-172
Prawer, S.S. Caligari's Children.
  P.V. Brady, 402(MLR):Jul83-758
Prawer, S.S. Heine's Jewish Comedy.*
  G. Annan, 453(NYRB):16Feb84-11
"The Prayer Book of Michelino da Besozzo."
  J. Oliver, 589:Jul83-797
Préaux, C. Le monde hellénistique.
  S.M. Sherwin-White, 303(JoHS):Vol 103-
  212
Prebble, J. John Prebble's Scotland.
  A. Smith, 617(TLS):19Oct84-1194
Pred, A. Urban Growth and City Systems in
the United States, 1840-1860.*
  J.N. Ingham, 106:Summer83-175
Prédal, R. Le Cinéma.
  M. Cottenet-Hage, 207(FR):May84-903
Predmore, M.P. Una España joven en la
poesía de Antonio Machado.
  D.P. Hill, 238:Dec83-637
  G. Ribbans, 240(HR):Summer83-344
Predmore, R.L. Lorca's New York Poetry.*
  A. Josephs, 345(KRQ):Vol30No2-218
  E.L. King, 149(CLS):Fall83-353
Prelog, J. Die Chronik Alfons' III.
  B. Löfstedt, 260(IF):Band88-329
Premack, D. and A.J. The Mind of an Ape.
  T.A. Sebeok, 617(TLS):29Jun84-738
Preminger, E.L. Gypsy and Me.
  S. Bolotin, 441:18Nov84-13
Prescott, F.C. - see Poe, E.A.
Pressly, W.L. The Life and Art of James
Barry.*
  S.M. Bennett, 88:Summer83-22
  D. Brown, 59:Dec83-485
Prévot, J. La Première institutrice de
France.
  C. Garaud, 207(FR):Dec83-284
du Prey, P.D. John Soane.
  M. Girouard, 453(NYRB):19Jan84-19
  E. McParland, 90:Apr83-235
Price, A. Gunner Kelly.
  T.J. Binyon, 617(TLS):18May84-557
  N. Callendar, 441:17Jun84-22
  M. Laski, 362:12Jan84-26
Price, C.A. Music in the Restoration
Theatre.*
  E.A. Matter, 566:Spring84-174
Price, C.A. Henry Purcell and the London
Stage.
  W. Dean, 617(TLS):12Oct84-1157
Price, D.C. Patrons and Musicians of the
English Renaissance.*
  C. Wilson, 551(RenQ):Summer83-262
Price, G. The Languages of Britain.
  B. Cottle, 617(TLS):11May84-527
Price, G. and D.A. Wells - see "The Year's
Work in Modern Language Studies"
Price, K., ed. On Criticizing Music.*
  E.A. Lippman, 414(MusQ):Winter83-144
  F. Sparshott, 415:Feb83-103
Price, M. Forms of Life.*
  W.B. Bache, 395(MFS):Winter83-815
  L.D. Bloom, 454:Winter84-181
  A. Welsh, 445(NCF):Sep83-326
Price, P. Bells and Man.
  W. Mellers, 617(TLS):3Feb84-101

Price, R. An Annotated Catalogue of
Medical Americana in the Library of the
Wellcome Institute for the History of
Medicine.
R.A. McNeil, 617(TLS):6Jul84-767
Price, R. The Breaks.*
42(AR):Spring83-249
Price, R. The Correspondence of Richard
Price. (Vol 1) (D.O. Thomas and B.
Peach, eds)
M. Jack, 319:Oct84-486
Price, R. Vital Provisions.
W.H. Pritchard, 491:Jan84-228
Price, S. Co-Wives and Calabashes.
A. Schlegel, 441:17Jun84-21
Price, S.R.F. Rituals and Power.
A.N. Sherwin-White, 617(TLS):23Nov84-
1332
Price-Mars, J. So Spoke the Uncle.
R.A. Rosenstone, 441:29Apr84-33
Prichard, K.S. Straight Left. (R.
Throssell, ed)
S. Walker, 71(ALS):Oct83-280
Pride, J.B., ed. New Englishes.
M.E. Call, 399(MLJ):Summer83-181
A. Dada, 355(LSoc):Sep83-410
J.T. Platt, 361:Aug83-351
Priessnitz, H., ed. Anglo-amerikanische
Shakespeare-Bearbeitungen des 20. Jahr-
hunderts.
W. Erzgräber, 156(JDSh):Jahrbuch
1983-248
M. Pfister, 72:Band220Heft1-168
Priest, C. The Glamour.
P. Kemp, 617(TLS):12Oct84-1167
Priest, R. Sadness of Spacemen.*
N. Zacharin, 137:Sep83-23
Priestley, J.B. English Journey.
J. Raban, 453(NYRB):25Oct84-46
Priestley, J.B. Three Men in New Suits.
The Image Men.
J.C.H. Thompson, 617(TLS):26Oct84-1211
Prigogine, I. and I. Stengers. Order
Out of Chaos.
C. Gardner, 362:2Aug84-24
Prijma, K. S vekom naravne.
H. Ermolaev, 574(SEEJ):Summer83-266
Primeau, R. Beyond "Spoon River."*
K. Carabine, 191(ELN):Sep83-68
Prince, F.T. Later On.
J. Mole, 176:Jun84-56
A. Poulin, Jr., 441:30Sep84-45
W. Scammell, 617(TLS):27Jul84-838
Prince, G. Narratology.
H.F. Mosher, Jr., 599:Spring83-290
S. Praet, 204(FdL):Jun83-150
Pringle, P. and W. Arkin. S.I.O.P., The
Secret U.S. Plan for Nuclear War.
S.M. Halpern, 441:15Jan84-19
Prins, G., ed. The Nuclear Crisis Reader.
C.R. Herron, 441:11Nov84-33
"Printed by Taunus Textildruck."
R.L. Shep, 614:Spring84-26
Printz-Påhlson, G. CCRI.
J. Saunders, 565:Vol124No1-73
Prioleau, E.S. The Circle of Eros.
E. Ammons, 27(AL):May83-262
J.W. Crowley, 26(ALR):Autumn83-317
J.K. Folsom, 191(ELN):Jun84-82
T.A. Gullason, 395(MFS):Winter83-716
Prior, A., ed. Catholics in Apartheid
Society.
C. Hope, 617(TLS):16Mar84-269

Pritchard, J. View from a Long Chair.
(F. MacCarthy, ed)
F. Spalding, 617(TLS):9Nov84-1280
Pritchard, W.H. Frost.
H. Vendler, 441:14Oct84-1
Pritchard, W.H. Lives of the Modern Poets.
M. Woodfield, 72:Band219Heft1-195
Pritchett, V.S. Collected Stories.*
D.A. Hughes, 573(SSF):Spring-Summer83-
139
S.S. Prawer, 617(TLS):17Aug84-926
Pritchett, V.S. More Collected Stories.*
J. Mellors, 362:2Feb84-228
Pritchett, V.S. The Other Side of The
Frontier.
S.S. Prawer, 617(TLS):17Aug84-926
Pritchett, V.S. The Spanish Temper.
J.F.T.R., 617(TLS):22Jun84-711
Pritchett, W.K. Studies in Ancient Greek
Topography. (Vol 3)
J.F. Lazenby, 303(JoHS):Vol 103-201
Pritsak, O. The Origin of Rus'. (Vol 1)
C.E. Fell, 575(SEER):Oct83-615
A. Liberman, 589:Oct83-1079
Privat, B. L'Itinéraire.
F. de Martinoir, 450(NRF):Jan83-114
J. Moss, 207(FR):Mar84-597
"Private Press Books 1977."
W.G. Hammond, 517(PBSA):Vol177No1-112
Privitera, G.A. - see Pindar
Probst, G.F. and J.F. Bodine, eds. Per-
spectives on Max Frisch.
E.N. Elstun, 395(MFS):Winter83-805
"Proceedings of the National Conference on
Professional Priorities."
J.F. Lalande 2d, 399(MLJ):Autumn83-276
Prochaska, F.K. Women and Philanthropy in
Nineteenth-Century England.*
E. Jay, 447(N&Q):Oct82-466
Proclus. Commentaire sur le Parménide de
Platon. (Vol 1) (G. de Moerbeke, trans;
C. Steel, ed)
É. des Places, 555:Vol157fasc2-320
Proclus. Théologie platonicienne. (Bk 4)
(H.D. Saffrey and L.G. Westerink, eds)
A. Meredith, 123:Vol133No2-318
Proclus. Trois études sur la Providence.
(Vol 3) (D. Isaac, ed and trans)
É. des Places, 555:Vol157fasc2-321
Prodi, P. Il sovrano pontifice, un corpo
e due anime.
D. Hay, 551(RenQ):Autumn83-402
Proffer, E. Bulgakov.
R. Hingley, 441:9Dec84-30
Proffer, E., ed. A Pictorial Biography of
Mikhail Bulgakov.
R. Hingley, 441:9Dec84-30
Proffer, E. - see Bulgakov, M.A.
Proffitt, N. Gardens of Stone.*
W. Balliett, 442(NY):6Feb84-125
Prohl, J. Elemente und Formen der Person-
albibliographien zur deutschen Litera-
turgeschichte.
M.L. Caputo-Mayr, 406:Spring83-71
Prokosch, F. Voices.*
C. Osborne, 364:Dec83/Jan84-135
D.P. Slattery, 584(SWR):Autumn83-411
639(VQR):Autumn83-125
Prokudin-Gorskii, S.M. Photographs for
the Tsar.* (R.H. Allshouse, ed)
M. Winokur, 558(RLJ):Winter-Spring83-
270

Pronko, L.C. Eugène Labiche and Georges
Feydeau.*
    O.G. Brockett, 130:Winter83/84-394
    W.D. Howarth, 610:Summer83-172
    E. Kern, 397(MD):Sep83-392
    J. Kestner, 446(NCFS):Fall-Winter83/84-
    265
Pronzini, B. Gun in Cheek.
    P. Wolfe, 395(MFS):Autumn83-389
Prophète, J. Les Para-personnages dans
les tragédies de Racine.*
    M-O. Sweetser, 475:Vol 10No18-393
von Proschwitz, G. Alexis Piron épisto-
lier.*
    J-P. Seguin, 209(FM):Jul83-282
Prosser, E. Shakespeare's Anonymous
Editors.*
    J. Gerritsen, 179(ES):Apr83-185
    E.A.J. Honigmann, 447(N&Q):Dec82-539
    P. Werstine, 405(MP):May84-419
Protopopov, V.V. - see Diletskii, N.
Proust, J. L'Objet et le texte.*
    J.H. Brumfitt, 208(FS):Oct83-466
Proust, J. - see de Bougainville, L.A.
Proust, M. Correspondance. (Vol 5) (P.
Kolb, ed)
    A. Corbineau-Hoffmann, 547(RF):Band95
    Heft3-373
Proust, M. Correspondance. (Vol 10) (P.
Kolb, ed)
    J.M. Cocking, 617(TLS):25May84-595
Proust, M. Matinée chez la Princesse de
Guermantes.* (H. Bonnet, with B. Brun,
eds)
    P-L. Rey, 450(NRF):Apr83-114
Proust, M. A Search for Lost Time:
Swann's Way.* (J. Grieve, trans)
    M. Bowie, 617(TLS):17Feb84-155
Proust, M. Selected Letters, 1880-1903.
(P. Kolb, ed)
    M. Bowie, 617(TLS):17Feb84-155
    J. Mellors, 364:Nov83-99
Provencher, J. C'était l'été.
    A.B. Chartier, 207(FR):May84-895
Provencher, J. and J. Blanchet. C'était
le printemps.
    A.B. Chartier, 207(FR):May84-895
Pruche, B. Existant et acte d'être. (Vol
2)
    M.D. Jordan, 543:Dec82-470
    A. Reix, 192(EP):Jan-Mar83-109
Prudentius. Prudenzio, "Hamartigenia."*
(R. Palla, ed and trans)
    J-L. Charlet, 555:Vol157fasc1-175
Prudhomme, P. Chef Paul Prudhomme's
Louisiana Kitchen.
    M. Burros, 441:3Jun84-15
von Prüm, W. - see under Wandalbert von
Prüm
de Prunes, M.I.S.C. - see under Santa Cruz
de Prunes, M.I.
Prunty, W. The Times Between.*
    R. Tillinghast, 569(SR):Summer83-473
Prutz, R.E. Zu Theorie und Geschichte der
Literatur.
    W. Heise, 654(WB):3/1983-551
Pryce-Jones, D. Cyril Connolly.
    G. Ewart, 364:Jul83-88
    V.S. Pritchett, 453(NYRB):15Mar84-6
Pryce-Jones, D. Paris in the Third Reich.*
    D.T. Stephens, 207(FR):Feb84-422
Pryce-Jones, D. - see Connolly, C.

Przybylski, R. To jest Klasycyzm.
    J.T. Baer, 497(PolR):Vol28No1-95
Pseudo-Dionysius Areopagite. The Divine
Names and Mystical Theology. (J.D.
Jones, ed and trans)
    W.J. Carroll, 543:Jun83-936
    D.F. Duclow, 258:Jun83-225
Psychopedis, K. Untersuchungen zur
politischen Theorie von Immanuel Kant.
    P. Burg, 342:Band74Heft4-512
Ptolemy. Ptolemey's "Almagest." (G.J.
Toomer, ed)
    G.E.R. Lloyd, 617(TLS):28Sep84-1101
Pucci, M. La rivolta ebraica al tempo di
Traiano.
    M.D. Goodman, 313:Vol73-209
Puffett, D. The Song Cycles of Othmar
Schoeck.
    M. Anderson, 607:Dec83-35
    P. Evans, 410(M&L):Jan/Apr83-109
    P. Franklin, 415:Jan83-36
    C. Wintle, 617(TLS):20Apr84-436
Pugh, J. - see "Housman Society Journal"
Pugh, S. Earth Studies and Other Voyages.
    A. Stevenson, 617(TLS):2Mar84-226
Puhvel, M. "Beowulf" and Celtic Tradi-
tion.*
    A.A. Lee, 178:Sep83-363
    B. Lindström, 597(SN):Vol155No2-204
    R.W. McTurk, 677(YES):Vol 13-294
Puig, M. Betrayed by Rita Hayworth. Kiss
of the Spider Woman.
    M. Gee, 617(TLS):21Sep84-1066
Puig, M. Blood of Requited Love.
    J. Franco, 441:23Sep84-11
Puig, M. Eternal Curse on the Reader of
These Pages.* (Spanish title: Maldición
Eterna a Quien Lea Esta Páginas.)
    R. Christ, 473(PR):3/1983-463
Pulatow, T. Der Stammgast.
    S. Kleinmichel, 654(WB):11/1982-146
Pullan, B. The Jews of Europe and the
Inquisition of Venice, 1550-1670.
    F. Gilbert, 617(TLS):20Jan84-57
Pulman, S.G. Word Meaning and Belief.
    A. Lehrer, 350:Dec84-998
Pulos, A.J. American Design Ethic.
    J.F. Pile, 139:Jun/Jul83-30
Punshon, J. Portrait in Grey.
    B. Godlee, 617(TLS):23Nov84-1356
Punter, D. Blake, Hegel and Dialectic.
    P. Dubois, 542:Jan-Mar83-139
    M. Fischer, 478:Oct83-265
    N. Hilton, 88:Spring84-164
    F. Piquet, 189(EA):Apr-Jun84-208
Punter, D. The Literature of Terror.*
    K. Hume, 402(MLR):Jan83-152
    M. Lévy, 189(EA):Apr-Sep83-326
    P. Thomson, 541(RES):May83-224
Pupino, A.R. "Il vero solo è bello."
    C. Godt, 400(MLN):Jan83-118
Pupo-Walker, E. La vocación literaria del
pensamiento histórico en América.
    R. Adorno, 238:Sep83-439
    I.M. Zuleta, 263(RIB):Vol33No1-48
Puppo, M. Poesia e verità.
    C. Godt, 400(MLN):Jan83-118
Purdy, A. Bursting into Song.
    A.L. Amprimoz, 526:Winter83-73
    G. Woodcock, 102(CanL):Summer83-163
Purdy, J. Mourners Below.*
    T.O. Treadwell, 617(TLS):31Aug84-977

Purdy, J. On Glory's Course.
R.J. Seidman, 441:26Feb84-25
Purdy, R.L. and M. Millgate - see Hardy, T.
"Pure and Applied Science Books, 1876-
1982."
D. Utley, 70:Sep/Oct82-30
Purkis, J. The World of the English Roman-
tic Poets.*
J. Raimond, 189(EA):Jul-Sep84-336
Purtle, C.J. The Marian Paintings of Jan
van Eyck.
D. Goodgal, 551(RenQ):Winter83-590
L. Silver, 471:Oct/Nov/Dec83-397
90:Aug83-505
Pusch, E.B. Das Senet-Brettspiel im Alten
Ägypten. (Pt 1)
V.L. Davis, 318(JAOS):Jan-Mar82-174
Püschel, U. Mit allen Sinnen.
O. Winkler, 654(WB):9/1982-177
Pusey, J.R. China and Charles Darwin.
J.B. Grieder, 617(TLS):2Nov84-1246
Pushkin, A.S. Boris Godounov. (A. Hayes,
trans)
J. Drummond, 592:Jul83-56
Pushkin, A.S. Collected Narrative and
Lyrical Poetry. (W. Arndt, trans)
J. Bayley, 441:25Mar84-15
Pushkin, A.S. Complete Prose Fiction. (P.
Debreczeny and W. Arndt, trans)
J. Bayley, 441:25Mar84-15
V.S. Pritchett, 442(NY):14May84-145
639(VQR):Autumn83-116
Pushkin, A.S. The History of Pugachev.
(E. Sampson, trans)
J. Bayley, 441:25Mar84-15
Pushkin, A.S. Mozart and Salieri, and the
Little Tragedies.* (A. Wood, trans)
D. Devlin, 157:Autumn83-31
Pushkin, A.S. and M. Lermontov. Narrative
Poems by Alexander Pushkin and by Mik-
hail Lermontov. (C. Johnston, trans)
H. Gifford, 453(NYRB):31May84-28
"Puteoli: Studi di storia antica I, III."
R. Ling, 313:Vol73-232
Putmans, J.L.C. Verskonkordanz zum Herzog
Ernst (B, A und Kl).
A. Schnyder, 680(ZDP):Band102Heft1-152
Putnam, H. Meaning and the Moral Sciences.
M. Devitt, 449:May83-291
Putnam, H. Reason, Truth and History.
G.A. Malinas, 63:Sep83-300
H.E. Matthews, 518:Apr83-114
S. Nathanson, 258:Jun83-211
A. Polakow, 479(PhQ):Jan83-108
R. Rorty, 98:Dec83-923
M. Thompson, 185:Oct83-143
Putnam, M.C.J. Essays on Latin Lyric
Elegy and Epic.
J. Chomarat, 555:Vol57fasc1-161
Putnam, M.C.J. Virgil's Poem of the
Earth.*
W.W. Briggs, Jr., 121(CJ):Apr/May84-
371
Putnam, R.D. and N. Bayne. Hanging
Together.
P. Lewis, 441:8Jul84-13
Putt, S.G. The Golden Age of English
Drama.*
R. Jacobs, 175:Spring83-69
Pütz, P., ed. Erforschung der deutschen
Aufklärung.*
C. Siegrist, 406:Summer83-205

Puyraimond, J-M. Catalogue du fonds mand-
chou.
J.L. Mish, 318(JAOS):Jan-Mar82-241
Puyuelo, R. L'anxiété de l'enfant ou le
bonheur difficile.
J-M. Gabaude, 542:Jul-Sep83-334
Puzo, M. The Sicilian.
G. Talese, 441:9Dec84-1
442(NY):31Dec84-71
Puzo, V., ed. Fodor's Caribbean and the
Bahamas 1983. Fodor's Budget Caribbean
'83.
B.F. Carruthers, 37:Nov-Dec83-60
Pye-Smith, C. and C. Rose. Crisis and
Conservation.
A. Manning, 362:13Sep84-27
Pyles, T. Thomas Pyles: Selected Essays
on English Usage.* (J. Algeo, ed)
G. Kristensson, 179(ES):Jun83-287
Pym, B. No Fond Return of Love.*
J. Epstein, 249(HudR):Spring83-185
Pym, B. An Unsuitable Attachment.*
639(VQR):Winter83-18
Pym, B. A Very Private Eye. (H. Holt and
H. Pym, eds)
P. Ackroyd, 617(TLS):3Aug84-861
R. Dinnage, 453(NYRB):16Aug84-15
V. Glendinning, 441:8Jul84-3
P. Howe, 362:5Jul84-14
P. Kemp, 362:2Aug84-23
442(NY):16Jul84-91
Pym, F. The Politics of Consent.
V. Bogdanor, 617(TLS):17Aug84-912
J. Cole, 362:5Jul84-24
Pynchon, J. The Pynchon Papers. (Vol 1)
(C. Bridenbaugh, ed)
S. Innes, 656(WMQ):Oct83-628
R.J. Taylor, 432(NEQ):Jun83-290
Pynchon, T. Slow Learner.
M. Wood, 441:15Apr84-1
442(NY):23Apr84-130
Pyne, S.J. Fire in America.
639(VQR):Winter83-8
Pyritz, H. and I. Bibliographie zur deut-
schen Literaturgeschichte des Barockzeit-
alters.* (Pt 2, fasc 1 and 2)
R.J. Alexander, 406:Fall83-333
Pyritz, H. and I. Bibliographie zur deut-
schen Literaturgeschichte des Barockzeit-
alters. (Pt 2, fasc 3 and 4)
R.E. Schade, 133:Band16Heft1-65
Pyron, N. - see Pleeth, W.

al-Qalyoûbî, A. Le Fantastique et le
Quotidien.
D.S. Richards, 294:Vol 14-96
Qian Hao, Chen Heyi and Ru Suichu. Out of
China's Earth.
J. Rawson, 59:Jun83-217
Qing, L. - see under Liu Qing
Quadrio-Curzio, A., ed. The Gold Problem.
A.J. Sherman, 617(TLS):1Jun84-609
Quaini, M. Geography and Marxism.
D.H., 185:Oct83-161
Quainton, M. Ronsard's Ordered Chaos.*
L. Terreaux, 535(RHL):Jul/Aug83-624
Quak, A. Die altmittel- und altnieder-
fränkischen Psalmen und Glossen.
E.H. Bartelmez, 221(GQ):Mar83-299
R.L. Kyes, 133:Band16Heft2/3-224
H. Mayer, 564:Sep83-215
W. Sanders, 684(ZDA):Band112Heft1-10

Qualls, B.V. The Secular Pilgrims of Victorian Fiction.*
  B. Hardy, 155:Summer83-113
  A. Jumeau, 189(EA):Apr-Jun84-212
  S. Pickering, Jr., 445(NCF):Dec83-324
  639(VQR):Spring83-45
Quantrill, M. Alvar Aalto.*
  M. Pawley, 46:Oct83-84
Quarantotti Gambini, P-A. Les régates de San Francisco. La rose rouge. Nos semblables. Le cheval Tripoli. La vie ardente. Printemps à Trieste.
  P. Barucco, 98:Aug-Sep83-678
Quasimodo, S. Complete Poems.
  D. Davis, 362:6Dec84-33
  L. Pertile, 617(TLS):27Apr84-450
Quayle, E. Early Children's Books.
  L.G.E. Bell, 503:Summer83-93
Quednau, R. Die Sala di Costantino im Vatikanischen Palast.*
  L. Partridge, 54:Sep83-515
Queffelec, A. and F. Jouannet. Inventaire des particularités lexicales du français du Mali.
  R. Chaudenson, 553(RLiR):Jan-Jun83-240
de Queirós, E. - see under Eça de Queirós
Quemada, B., ed. Matériaux pour l'histoire du vocabulaire français. (2nd Ser, fasc 21)
  R. Arveiller, 553(RLiR):Jan-Jun83-198
Quemada, B., ed. Matériaux pour l'histoire du vocabulaire français. (2nd Ser, fasc 22)
  R. Arveiller, 553(RLiR):Jul-Dec83-459
Queneau, R. Exercises in Style.
  M.H. Begnal, 480(P&R):Vol 16No1-60
Quennell, P. - see Connolly, C.
Questal, V.D. Hard Stares.
  S. Brown, 493:Jun83-67
Quested, R.K.I. "Matey" Imperialists.
  S.I. Levine, 104(CASS):Winter83-562
Quet, M-H. La Mosaïque cosmologique de Mérida.
  K.M.D. Dunbabin, 487:Spring83-78
  R.J. Ling, 123:Vol33No2-368
"La Quête du Saint Graal." (E. Baumgartner, trans)
  D.D.R. Owen, 208(FS):Jul83-329
  D. Robertson, 545(RPh):May83-637
de Quevedo, F. El Buscón. (D. Ynduráin, ed)
  G. Díaz-Migoyo, 240(HR):Winter83-103
de Quevedo, F. L'heure de tous et la fortune raisonable/La hora de todos y la fortuna con seso.* (J. Bourg, P. Dupont and P. Geneste, eds) La hora de todos y la fortuna con seso. (L. López Grigera, ed)
  P. Jauralde Pou, 457(NRFH):Tomo31núm2-319
de Quevedo, F. Poesía varia. (J.O. Crosby, ed)
  G. Díaz-Migoyo, 240(HR):Summer83-332
  P.J. Smith, 402(MLR):Jan83-209
  B.W. Wardropper, 400(MLN):Mar83-294
de Quevedo, F. Songs of Love and Death. (D.M. Gitlitz, ed and trans)
  R.W. Listerman, 238:Mar83-133
de Quevedo, F. Songs of Love and Death and In Between.
  R.M. Price, 86(BHS):Jan83-68

Quick, M., M. Sadik and W. Gerdts. American Portraiture in the Grand Manner.
  R. Ormond, 90:Mar83-168
Quicoli, A.C. The Structure of Complementation.
  A.R.T., 189(EA):Oct-Dec84-488
Quignard, P. Les Tablettes de buis d'Apronenia Avitia.
  R. Buss, 617(TLS):6Jul84-761
Quijano, J.A.C. and others - see under Calderón Quijano, J.A. and others
Quill, M. And Then There Was Nun.
  N. Callendar, 441:1Apr84-27
Quillen, E. L'Angleterre et l'Amérique dans la vie et la poésie d'André Chénier.
  J. Gury, 549(RLC):Jan-Mar83-117
Quillet, P. - see Cassirer, E.
Quilligan, M. The Language of Allegory.*
  G. Clifford, 599:Winter83-68
  R.M. Cummings, 402(MLR):Oct83-878
  M-M. Martinet, 189(EA):Jan-Mar84-82
"The Quilt."
  S.J. Garoutte, 614:Summer84-26
"The Quilt Digest." (1984) (R. Kiracofe and M. Kile, eds)
  P. Bach, 614:Spring84-26
Quine, W.V. Theories and Things.*
  J.B., 543:Sep82-184
  C. McGinn, 311(JP):Apr83-239
  G. Nerlich, 63:Jun83-216
Quinn, D.B., ed. Early Maryland in a Wider World.
  D.W. Jordan, 656(WMQ):Jul83-463
Quinn, E.C., ed. The Penitence of Adam.*
  S. Kay, 545(RPh):Feb83-512
  M. Rigby, 541(RES):Feb83-49
Quinn, J. American Tongue and Cheek.*
  R.R.B., 35(AS):Winter83-371
Quinn, K. - see Horace
Quinn, P.F. - see Poe, E.A.
Quinn, P.L. Divine Commands and Moral Requirements.
  T.O. Buford, 543:Jun83-946
Quinn, T.J. Athens and Samos, Lesbos and Chios: 478-404 B.C.
  D.M. Lewis, 123:Vol33No1-146
Quinn, W.A. and A.S. Hall. Jongleur.
  A.H. Olsen, 589:Jul83-799
Quinney, R. Social Existence.
  D.G.C., 185:Jan84-373
Quinsac, A-P. Segantini.
  S.H. Berresford, 90:Nov83-704
Quint, D. Origins and Originality in Renaissance Literature.
  A. Bruten, 617(TLS):6Jan84-20
  D. Stone, Jr., 207(FR):May84-870
Quintana, A., ed and trans. Poesía alemanna del barroco.
  C. Rodiek, 52:Band18Heft2-206
Quintanilla, M.A. Idealismo y filosofía de la ciencia.
  Z. Kouřím, 542:Jul-Sep83-362
Quintas, E.R. - see under Rivas Quintas, E.
Quirk, R. Style and Communication in the English Language.*
  A. Easthope, 349:Fall83-504
Quirk, T. Melville's Confidence Man.*
  G. Van Cromphout, 27(AL):Oct83-463

Raab, R., A. Klingborg and A. Fant. Eloquent Concrete.
P.B. Jones, 46:May81-318

Raabe, P., ed. Bücher und Bibliotheken im 17. Jahrhundert in Deutschland.
G. Dünnhaupt, 221(GQ):Mar83-312
D. Paisey, 78(BC):Winter83-484

Raabe, P., ed. Buchgestaltung in Deutschland 1740 bis 1890.
D. Paisey, 78(BC):Winter83-484

Raabe, W. Werke in Auswahl. (H-W. Peter, ed)
W.P. Hanson, 402(MLR):Oct83-985
E. Meyer-Krentler, 680(ZDP):Band102 Heft2-296

Raat, W.D. The Mexican Revolution.
D.A. Brading, 263(RIB):Vol33No4-593

Rabassa, C.C. Demetrio Aguilera-Malta and Social Justice.*
J. Walker, 107(CRCL):Mar83-133

Rabassa, C.C. En torno a Aguilera Malta.
M.K. Cobb, 238:Sep83-443

"Rabbits, Crabs, Etc." (P. Birnbaum, trans)
C. Mulhern, 407(MN):Autumn83-329

Rabelais, F. Le Disciple de Pantagruel (Les Navigations de Panurge). (G. Demerson and C. Lauvergnat-Gagnière, eds)
P.R. Berk, 539:May84-123
R. Cholakian, 207(FR):Feb84-386

Rabil, A., Jr. Laura Cereta.
B.G. Kohl, 551(RenQ):Summer83-231

Rabinovich, I. The War for Lebanon, 1970-1983.
L. Robinson, 441:17Jun84-21

Rabinowitz, H.N., ed. Southern Black Leaders of the Reconstruction Era.
J.H. Shofner, 9(AlaR):Jul83-232
639(VQR):Winter83-9

Rabinowitz, I. - see Messer Leon, J.

Rabkin, N. Shakespeare and the Problem of Meaning.*
G. Aggeler, 651(WHR):Winter83-356
R. Berry, 529(QQ):Summer83-372
B. Cullen, 175:Spring83-61
G.P. Jones, 627(UTQ):Fall82-106

Raby, P. "Fair Ophelia."
D.K. Holoman, 415:Dec83-749
M.J. Nurnberg, 208(FS):Apr83-231
S. Wells, 157:Summer83-32
639(VQR):Summer83-81

Race, W.H. The Classical Priamel From Homer to Boethius.*
T.F. Curley 3d, 24:Summer83-211
N. Horsfall, 123:Vol33No1-136

Racelle-Latin, D., ed. Inventaire des particularités lexicales du français en Afrique noire. (fasc 3)
N. Gueunier, 209(FM):Jan83-74

Rachow, L.A., ed. Theatre and Performing Arts Collections.
L. Mackenney, 610:Spring83-75

Racine, D.L., ed. Leon-Gontran Damas, 1912-78.
T.N. Hammond, 207(FR):Dec83-239

Racine, J. Andromache. (R. Wilbur, trans)
R. Lattimore, 249(HudR):Spring83-215
A. Shaw, 385(MQR):Summer84-458

Racine, J. Four Greek Plays. (R.C. Knight, trans)
D. Devlin, 157:Spring83-52
J. Moravcevich, 207(FR):Apr84-713

Raczymow, H. "On ne part pas."
C. Dis, 450(NRF):Oct83-126

Radden, G. Ein Profil soziolinguistischer Variation in einer amerikanischen Kleinstadt.
D. Karch, 685(ZDL):2/1983-223

Raddysh, G. White Noise.
B. Pell, 102(CanL):Summer83-112

Rader, M. Marx's Interpretation of History.*
D. Merllié, 542:Apr-Jun83-259

Radford, A. Transformational Syntax.
R.I. Binnick, 320(CJL):Fall83-171
R.P. Ebert, 399(MLJ):Spring83-87
R. Salkie, 353:Vol20No3/4-347

Radford, C.J. and S. Minogue. The Nature of Criticism.*
F. Cioffi, 518:Apr83-108
M. Wreen, 478:Apr83-142

Radic, T. G.W.L. Marshall-Hall.
J.M. Thomson, 415:Nov83-683

Radice, B. - see Gibbon, E.

Radice, L. Beatrice and Sidney Webb.
B. Pimlott, 617(TLS):23Nov84-1331
F. Wheen, 362:2Aug84-25

Radin, G. Virginia Woolf's "The Years."*
E.F. Cornwell, 268(IFR):Summer84-116

Radji, P.C. In the Service of the Peacock Throne.*
S. Jenkins, 441:29Jul84-31

Radley, S. The Quiet Road to Death.
N. Callendar, 441:20May84-39
442(NY):27Aug84-93

Radnitzky, G. and G. Andersson, eds. Voraussetzungen und Grenzen der Wissenschaft.
A. Sandor, 221(GQ):May83-466

Radway, J.A. Reading the Romance.
S.M. Gilbert, 441:30Dec84-11

Raeburn, J. Fame Became of Him.
J. Campbell, 617(TLS):20Jul84-806

Raether, M. Der "Acte gratuit," Revolte und Literatur.*
J.H. Petersen, 52:Band17Heft1-95

Rafael, G. Destination Peace.
M.I. Urofsky, 390:Jun/Jul83-63

Raffel, S. Matters of Fact.
A. Walker, 488:Mar83-73

Rafroidi, P. Irish Literature in English: The Romantic Period, 1789-1850.*
M.H. Thuente, 125:Fall82-107

Ragland, M.E. Rabelais and Panurge.
P. Henry, 546(RR):May83-374

Ragon, M. The Space of Death.*
E. Weber, 617(TLS):20Jul84-802

Ragotzky, H. Gattungserneuerung und Laienunterweisung in Texten Des Strickers.
D.H. Green, 402(MLR):Apr83-484
L.S., 382(MAE):1983/2-341
E. Stutz, 684(ZDA):Band112Heft3-116

Raguin, V.C. Stained Glass in Thirteenth-Century Burgundy.
N. Kline, 576:Oct83-301

Ragusa, O. Pirandello.*
J. Davies, 402(MLR):Jan83-200
L. Richards, 610:Winter81/82-64

Rahner, K. The Love of Jesus and the Love of Neighbour. Theological Investigations. (Vols 18 and 19)
P. Hebblethwaite, 617(TLS):24Feb84-200

Rahner, K. and H. Vorgrimler. Concise
  Theological Dictionary. (2nd ed)
  P. Hebblethwaite, 617(TLS):24Feb84-200
Raikes, P.L. Livestock Development and
  Policy in East Africa.
  R. Baker, 69:Vol53No2-87
Raina, P. Independent Social Movements in
  Poland.
  A.M. Cienciala, 497(PolR):Vol28No1-106
  J. Woodall, 575(SEER):Oct83-632
Rainbow, B. and others. English Psalmody
  Prefaces.
  N. Temperley, 415:Sep83-575
Raine, C. A Free Translation.
  J. Saunders, 565:Vol24No1-73
Raine, C. Rich.
  D. Bromwich, 617(TLS):19Oct84-1193
Raine, K. The Human Face of God.*
  D. Fuller, 83:Spring83-76
Raine, K. The Inner Journey of the Poet
  and Other Papers. (B. Keeble, ed)
  P.M.S.D., 148:Spring83-93
Raison, L., comp. Tuscany.
  E. Newman, 441:3Jun84-12
Raitt, A.W. The Life of Villiers de
  l'Isle Adam.*
  J.B. Anzalone, 207(FR):Apr84-720
  R. Griffiths, 402(MLR):Jul83-716
Raizis, M.B. From Caucasus to Pittsburgh.
  S.F. Wiltshire, 124:Sep-Oct83-57
Rajak, T. Josephus.
  P. Alexander, 617(TLS):11May84-530
Rajec, E.M. The Study of Names in Litera-
  ture. (Supp)
  W.F.H. Nicolaisen, 424:Jun83-126
Rakosi, C. Spiritus, I.
  M. Hulse, 617(TLS):12Oct84-1169
Ralegh, W. Selected Writings. (G. Ham-
  mond, ed)
  K. Duncan-Jones, 617(TLS):26Oct84-1220
Rallis, G. Ores Efthynis. Khoris prokat-
  alipsi gia to paron kai to mellon.
  R. Clogg, 617(TLS):13Apr84-401
Ralph, D. Work and Madness.
  R. Labonté, 99:Oct83-36
Ram, A., ed. Perspectives on R.K. Narayan.
  U. Parameswaran, 268(IFR):Summer84-123
Ramallo Asensio, G. El Fontán.
  A. Bustamante García, 48:Oct-Dec80-506
Ramanathan, A.A. The Saṃnyāsa Upaniṣads.
  J.P. Olivelle, 318(JAOS):Jan-Mar82-228
Ramat, P. Einführung in das Germanische.*
  M. Durrell, 402(MLR):Apr83-477
  H. Penzl, 685(ZDL):1/1983-63
Ramazani, R.K. The United States and Iran.
  S. Simpson, 639(VQR):Summer83-540
Rambeau, J. - see Edel, L. and D.H.
  Laurence
Ramchand, K., ed. Best West Indian
  Stories.
  H. Barratt, 49:Jul83-89
Ramm, K. - see Jung, F.
Ramraj, V.J. Mordecai Richler.
  A. Mitcham, 268(IFR):Summer84-133
Ramsden, J. - see Sanders, R.
Ramsey, L.C. Chivalric Romances.
  B. O'Donoghue, 617(TLS):3Feb84-122
Ramstedt, G.J. Paralipomena of Korean
  Etymologies. (S. Kho, ed)
  R.A. Miller, 350:Dec84-993

Rancour-Laferriere, D. Out from under
  Gogol's Overcoat.
  S. Cassedy, 550(RusR):Oct83-442
  J.M. Mills, 574(SEEJ):Fall83-380
Randall, G. The English Parish Church.
  D. Guinness, 576:Dec83-390
Randers-Pehrson, J.D. Barbarians and
  Romans.
  M. Hammond, 124:Nov-Dec83-136
Randisi, J.L. A Tissue of Lies.
  W.J. Stuckey, 395(MFS):Summer83-334
Rando, E.N. and D.J. Napoli, eds. Meli-
  glossa.
  L. Menn, 350:Sep84-690
Randolph, L.I. and others. The Regional
  Imperative.
  R.G.C. Thomas, 293(JASt):Nov82-203
Randolph, V., ed. Ozark Folksongs. (rev)
  T.C. Humphrey, 650(WF):Oct83-304
Randolph, V. and G.P. Wilson. Down in the
  Holler.
  T.C. Humphrey, 650(WF):Oct83-304
Rang, B. - see Husserl, E.
Range, J.D., ed and trans. Litauische
  Volksmärchen.
  B. Kerbelytė, 196:Band24Heft1/2-168
Rangeon, F. Hobbes.
  L. Roux, 189(EA):Apr-Jun84-190
Ranke, K. and others, eds. Enzyklopädie
  des Märchens.* (Vol 1, Pts 4 and 5;
  Vol 2)
  R.L. Welsch, 301(JEGP):Oct83-612
Ranke, K. and others, eds. Enzyklopädie
  des Märchens.* (Vol 3)
  R.L. Welsch, 301(JEGP):Oct83-612
  M. Zender, 196:Band24Heft3/4-296
Rankka, E. Li ver del Juïse.
  F. Lecoy, 554:Vol 103No4-561
  L. Löfstedt, 439(NM):1983/2-277
Ranney, A. Channels of Power.*
  A.L. Chickering, 129:Feb84-79
Ransom, J.C. Selected Essays on John
  Crowe Ransom. (T.D. Young and J. Hindle,
  eds)
  D. Davie, 441:20May84-11
Ransome, A. Bohemia in London. Old
  Peter's Russian Tales.
  N. Stone, 617(TLS):3Feb84-107
Ranwez, A.D. Jean-Paul Sartre's "Les
  Temps Modernes."*
  S. Ungar, 546(RR):May83-381
Rao, K.B. Paul Scott.
  M.M. Mahood, 677(YES):Vol 13-355
Rao, M.S.N. Kirātārjunīyam in Indian
  Art (With Special Reference to Karna-
  taka).
  M.W. Meister, 318(JAOS):Jan-Mar82-236
Rao, M.S.N., ed. Madhu.
  H.O. Thompson, 57:Vol44No1-94
Rapaport, H. Milton and the Postmodern.
  L. Mackinnon, 617(TLS):20Apr84-438
Raper, J.R. From the Sunken Garden.*
  P. Leary, 447(N&Q):Oct82-471
Raphael, C. The Springs of Jewish Life.*
  R. Patai, 390:Dec83-48
Raphael, D.D. Justice and Liberty.*
  A. Collier, 393(Mind):Apr83-303
  W.N. Nelson, 482(PhR):Apr83-252
Raphael, F. Oxbridge Blues.
  J. Epstein, 249(HudR):Spring83-176
Raphael, M. Proudhon, Marx, Picasso.
  S. Mitchell, 59:Dec83-499

Raphaelson, S. Three Screen Comedies.
 R. Koenig, 453(NYRB):16Feb84-34
 J.E. Siegel, 18:Jan-Feb84-54
Rapin, N. Oeuvres. (Vol 1) (J. Brunel,
 ed)
 R. Zuber, 535(RHL):Jul/Aug83-626
Rapin, N. Oeuvres V. (J. Brunel, ed)
 F. Rigolot, 207(FR):Mar84-552
Rapp, F. Analytical Philosophy of Technol-
 ogy.
 A. Franklin, 84:Jun83-190
Rasponi, L. The Last Prima Donnas.
 A. FitzLyon, 617(TLS):20Apr84-436
Ratcliff, C. John Singer Sargent.*
 M. Amaya, 592:Vol 196No1003-56
 J.V. Turano, 16:Spring83-78
Ratcliffe, F.W., with D. Patterson. Pres-
 ervation Policies and Conversation in
 British Libraries.
 H. Forde, 617(TLS):5Oct84-1143
Ratcliffe, S. Campion: On Song.*
 C. Wilson, 410(M&L):Jul/Oct83-264
Rathbone, J. Nasty, Very.
 J.K.L. Walker, 617(TLS):7Sep84-1005
Rathbone, J. Watching the Detectives.
 N. Callendar, 441:26Feb84-27
 M. Laski, 362:12Jan84-26
Rathbone, J. Wellington's War.
 E. Davies, 617(TLS):13Jul84-792
"Walther Rathenau — Maximilian Harden:
 Briefwechsel 1897-1920." (H.D. Hellige,
 ed)
 J. Joll, 617(TLS):17Feb84-162
Rather, L.J. The Dream of Self-Destruc-
 tion.
 U. Weissstein, 107(CRCL):Mar83-113
Rathmann, B. Der Einfluss Boileaus auf
 die Rezeption der Lyrik des frühen 17.
 Jahrhunderts in Frankreich.
 C.N. Smith, 208(FS):Jan83-78
Rathmann, J. Zur Geschichtsphilosophie
 J.G. Herders.
 J-M. Gabaude, 542:Jan-Mar83-129
Ratliff, W.F. and others. Cara a cara.
 (2nd ed)
 M.E. Beeson, 238:May83-311
 M.A. Marks, 399(MLJ):Autumn83-310
Ratnakīrti. Der allwissende Buddha. (G.
 Bühnemann, ed and trans)
 J.P. McDermott, 318(JAOS):Jul-Sep82-
 549
Ratner, L.G. Classic Music.*
 J.W. Hill, 173(ECS):Fall83-78
 J. Stevens, 308:Spring83-121
Rau, F. Zur Verbreitung und Nachahmung
 des "Tatler" und "Spectator."
 D.F. Bond, 405(MP):May84-427
 W. Martens, 52:Band18Heft1-102
Rau, W. - see "Bhartṛharis Vākyapadīya"
Rauch, I. and G.F. Carr, eds. Linguistic
 Method.*
 T.F. Shannon, 350:Mar84-128
Rauch, I. and G.F. Carr, eds. The Signify-
 ing Animal.
 J. Fought, 355(LSoc):Mar83-92
Raugei, A.M. Rifrazioni e Metamorfosi.
 K. Busby, 547(RF):Band95Heft1/2-170
Raugei, A.M. - see Gautier de Dargies
Raupach, M. and M. Französierte Trobador-
 lyrik.
 J.H. Marshall, 545(RPh):Aug82-83

Rauschenberger, M. Shakespeares "Imagery."
 T. Finkenstaedt, 156(JDSh):Jahrbuch
 1983-262
Raval, S. Metacriticism.*
 H. Adams, 301(JEGP):Jul83-427
 W.E. Cain, 131(CL):Spring83-167
 D. Novitz, 478:Apr83-121
 R. Shusterman, 89(BJA):Winter83-89
 P. Stewart, 579(SAQ):Spring83-229
 M.S. Strine, 583:Summer84-436
Raven, S. Morning Star.
 T. Fitton, 617(TLS):13Jul84-791
 K.C. O'Brien, 362:16Aug84-26
Ravitch, D. The Troubled Crusade.*
 B. Holmes, 617(TLS):6Jul84-749
Rawlings, H.R. 3d. The Structure of Thu-
 cydides' History.*
 J.R. Ellis, 303(JoHS):Vol 103-167
 V. Hunter, 487:Spring83-66
 D.P. Tompkins, 24:Spring83-93
Rawlins, C.L. William Barclay.
 J. Whale, 617(TLS):28Dec84-1510
Raworth, T. Writing.*
 M. Perloff, 29:May/Jun84-15
Rawson, C., ed. English Satire and the
 Satiric Tradition.
 D. Nokes, 617(TLS):23Nov84-1355
Rawson, H. A Dictionary of Euphemisms and
 Other Doubletalk.
 R.R.B., 35(AS):Spring83-60
Ray, A.J. and D. Freeman. "Give Us Good
 Measure."
 A. Tanner, 529(QQ):Spring83-176
Ray, G.N. The Art of the French Illus-
 trated Book, 1700 to 1914.
 G. Barber, 90:Oct83-628
 D.P. Becker, 517(PBSA):Vol77No2-226
"Man Ray, Photographs."*
 M. Amaya, 592:Jul83-58
Raychaudhuri, T. and I. Habib, eds. The
 Cambridge Economic History of India.
 (Vol 1)
 P.J. Marshall, 293(JASt):Aug83-997
Raymond, M. and G. Poulet. Marcel Raymond —
 Georges Poulet, Correspondance: 1950-
 1977.* (P. Grotzer, ed)
 S.P. Posch, 547(RF):Band95Heft3-380
Raymond, P. La résistible fatalité de
 l'histoire.
 M. Adam, 542:Oct-Dec83-451
Raynor, D.R., ed. Sister Peg.
 C.B., 189(EA):Jul-Sep84-363
 R. McRae, 627(UTQ):Summer83-419
 R.B. Sher, 518:Apr83-85
 K.E. Smith, 83:Autumn83-282
Rea, A.M. Once a River.
 L. Milazzo, 584(SWR):Summer83-vi
Read, A. and D. Fisher. Colonel Z.
 J. Keegan, 617(TLS):28Dec84-1496
Read, B. Victorian Sculpture.*
 C. Ashwin, 592:Apr/May83-50
Read, F. '76: One World and "The Cantos"
 of Ezra Pound.*
 S.M. Gall, 301(JEGP):Jan83-147
 B.D. Kimpel, 579(SAQ):Winter83-107
Read, G. Modern Rythmic Notation.
 D.C., 412:Feb82-73
"Jenny Read: In Pursuit of Art and Life."
 (K. Doyle, ed)
 N. Miller, 42(AR):Spring83-245
Read, M.K. Juan Huarte de San Juan.
 N. Griffin, 86(BHS):Apr83-146

307

"A Readable 'Beowulf.'" (S.B. Greenfield, trans)
D.C. Baker, 191(ELN):Mar84-58
H. Chickering, 589:Oct83-1118
A.H. Olsen, 152(UDQ):Spring83-119
"The Reader's Digest Bible." (B.A. Metzger, general ed)
A.J. Bingham, 577(SHR):Spring83-181
Reading, P. Diplopic.*
M. O'Neill, 493:Sep83-72
Reading, P. Tom o'Bedlam's Beauties.
J. Saunders, 565:Vol24No1-73
Reagan, R. Abortion and the Conscience of the Nation.
R.G. Kaiser, 453(NYRB):28Jun84-38
Real, J. - see Swift, J.
Reale, G. Storia della filosofia antica.*
J-L. Poirier, 542:Jan-Mar83-74
Reardon, J.J. Peyton Randolph, 1721-1775.
G.S. Cowden, 656(WMQ):Oct83-642
Reardon, K.K. Persuasion.
J.L. Lucaites, 583:Spring84-331
Reavell, C. and T. E.F. Benson.
617(TLS):28Dec84-1511
Reaver, J.R. Moments of Transition.
J.L. Di Gaetani, 395(MFS):Summer83-372
Rebholz, R.A. - see Wyatt, T.
Rebuffat-Emmanuel, D. Le miroir étrusque d'après la collection du cabinet des médailles.
G. Lloyd-Morgan, 313:Vol73-233
Rector, M., ed. Cowboy Life on the Texas Plains.*
L. Clayton, 649(WAL):Nov83-261
Réda, J. Hors les murs.
L. Ray, 450(NRF):Feb83-119
Réda, J. L'Herbe des talus.
I. Bell, 617(TLS):5Oct84-1117
Redeker, H. Abbildung und Wertung.
D. Posdzech, 654(WB):4/1982-176
Redenbarger, W.J. Articulator Features and Portuguese Vowel Height.
J.B. Jensen, 238:Mar83-148
Redfern, R. The Making of a Continent.*
A. Hallam, 617(TLS):6Jan84-18
Redfern, W.D. Queneau: "Zazie dans le métro."
M. Bowie, 402(MLR):Apr83-461
Redgrave, M. In My Mind's I.* (British title: In My Mind's Eye.)
G. Kaufman, 362:19Apr84-26
J. Novick, 441:11Mar84-19
Redmond, D.A. Sherlock Holmes.
E.S. Lauterbach, 177(ELT):Vol126No4-334
295(JML):Nov83-462
Redmond, J., ed. Drama and Symbolism.
J. Coakley, 130:Winter83/84-396
Redmond, J. - see "Themes in Drama 4"
Redner, H. In the Beginning Was the Deed.
295(JML):Nov83-373
Redondo, A., ed. XIXe Colloque International d'Études Humanistes, Tours 5-17 juillet 1976: L'Humanisme dans les lettres espagnoles.*
F. Domínguez, 241:Jan83-63
N. Griffin, 402(MLR):Jan83-203
M. Joly, 457(NRFH):Tomo3lnúm2-312
Redwood, C., ed. An Elgar Companion.*
R. Anderson, 415:Jul83-428
Redwood, J. Going For Broke ...
J. Hardie, 617(TLS):4May84-500
Reed, A. Romantic Weather.
L. Mackinnon, 617(TLS):15Jun84-678

Reed, J. By the Fisheries.
D. Profumo, 617(TLS):27Apr84-459
Reed, J. The Lipstick Boys.
S. Pickles, 617(TLS):9Nov84-1289
Reed, J. The Missionary Mind and American East Asia Policy, 1911-1915.*
J. Spence, 453(NYRB):27Sep84-59
Reed, J. Sir Walter Scott.*
D.A. Low, 541(RES):Feb83-86
R. Paulson, 402(MLR):Jan83-157
Reed, J.R. The Natural History of H.G. Wells.*
R.H. Costa, 395(MFS):Summer83-266
R.D. Mullen, 177(ELT):Vol126No4-326
D.C. Smith, 366:Spring83-132
295(JML):Nov83-585
Reed, J.S. and D.J. Singal - see Vance, R.
Reed, M. The Georgian Triumph, 1700-1830.*
L. Stone, 453(NYRB):29Mar84-42
Reed, W.L. An Exemplary History of the Novel.*
A. Morvan, 189(EA):Apr-Sep83-322
P. Sabor, 529(QQ):Spring83-157
566:Spring84-167
Rees, A. Striking a Balance.
P.T. Kilborn, 441:15Apr84-25
Rees, J. The Poetry of Dante Gabriel Rossetti.
A.H. Harrison, 481(PQ):Winter83-122
A.J. Sambrook, 402(MLR):Apr83-436
Reeves, A.C. Lancastrian Englishmen.
J.R. Lander, 589:Apr83-524
Reeves, H. Atoms of Silence.
T. Ferris, 441:23Sep84-12
Reeves, J. Murder before Matins.
N. Callendar, 441:2Sep84-12
Reeves, R. Passage to Peshawar.
G. Utley, 441:9Dec84-39
Reeves, T.D. An Index to the Sermons of John Donne.
J.M. Shami, 539:Feb84-59
Regaldo, N.F. Poetic Patterns in Rutebeuf.
E.R. Sienaert, 356(LR):Feb-May83-130
Regan, D.H. Utilitarianism and Co-operation.*
E. Conee, 311(JP):Jul83-415
D. Copp, 482(PhR):Oct83-617
R.G. Frey, 393(Mind):Apr83-296
G.W. Harrison, 479(PhQ):Oct83-412
R.L. Holmes, 543:Mar83-729
Regan, M.S. Love Words.
S. Minta, 208(FS):Apr83-210
Regan, T. All That Dwell Therein.
T.M.R., 185:Oct83-160
Regan, T. and D. Van De Veer, eds. And Justice for All.
J.D., 185:Oct83-178
A. Flew, 479(PhQ):Jul83-313
Regensteiner, E. Weaving Sourcebook Ideas and Techniques. (2nd ed)
P. Bach, 614:Winter84-24
Regényi, I. and A. Scherer. Donauschwäbisches Ortsnamenbuch für die ehemals und teilweise noch deutsch besiedelten Orte in Ungarn, Jugoslawien (ohne Slowenien) sowie West-Rumänien (Banat und Sathmar).
A. Gommermann, 685(ZDL):1/1983-123
Reggiani, A.M. Rieti.
F.R.S. Ridgway, 123:Vol33No2-364
Reginin, A.I. Indiyskiy Natsional'nyy Kongress.
T.P. Thornton, 293(JASt):May83-707

Regnard, J-F. Comédies du Théâtre italien.
(A. Calame, ed)
W. Henning, 72:Band220Heft1-220
H.B. McDermott, 207(FR):Oct83-109
F. Moureau, 535(RHL):Sep/Dec83-932
Régnier, C. Les parlers du Morvan.
J.M., 554:Vol 103No1-135
Regosin, R.L. The Matter of My Book.
B. Croquette, 535(RHL):Mar/Apr83-259
Reh, A.M. Die Rettung der Menschlichkeit.*
F.J. Lamport, 402(MLR):Oct83-971
P. von Matt, 133:Band16Heft2/3-236
H.B. Nisbet, 301(JEGP):Jul83-418
Rehbock, P.F. The Philosophical Natural-
ists.
M. Ridley, 617(TLS):9Mar84-254
Rehder, R. Wordsworth and the Beginnings
of Modern Poetry.*
P. Swaab, 184(EIC):Jan83-55
Rehfus, W.D. Didaktik der Philosophie.
A.K.D. Lorenzen, 489(PJGG):Band90Heft2-
431
Rehkopf, F. - see Blass, F. and A. Debrun-
ner
Reich, W. A Stranger in My House.
D.K. Shipler, 441:28Oct84-18
Reichenbach, H. Selected Writings 1909-
1953. (M. Reichenbach and R.S. Cohen,
eds) Gesammelte Werke. (Vol 3) (A.
Kamlah and M. Reichenbach, eds)
W. Balzer, 53(AGP):Band65Heft3-343
Reichl, K. Categorial Grammar and Word-
Formation.
J. Lavédrine, 189(EA):Jul-Sep84-315
M. Stong-Jensen, 350:Mar84-187
Reichl, K. Religiöse Dichtung im eng-
lischen Hochmittelalter.
D. Gray, 382(MAE):1983/1-151
Reid, A. - see Wang Gungwu
Reid, B.J. Overland to California with
the Pioneer Line. (M.M. Gordon, ed)
P.A.M. Taylor, 617(TLS):23Mar84-310
Reid, C. The Music Monster.
A. Jacobs, 617(TLS):28Sep84-1074
R. Morrison, 362:30Aug84-26
Reid, C. Pea Soup.*
J. Saunders, 565:Vol24No4-71
Reid, D. Our Own Country Canada.
G.W., 102(CanL):Winter82-175
M.S. Young, 39:Feb83-148
Reid, J.M. The Process of Composition.
J.J. Kohn, 399(MLJ):Spring83-101
Reid, J.P. In Defiance of the Law.*
H.F. Bell, 656(WMQ):Jan83-151
P. Lawson, 106:Summer83-165
Reid, M. The Life of Ryley.*
R. Hatch, 102(CanL):Winter82-144
Reidel, H. Emanuel Joseph von Herigoyen.
A. von Buttlar, 471:Oct/Nov/Dec83-397
Reif, S.C. Shabbethat Sofer and his
Prayer-book.
W. Weinberg, 318(JAOS):Apr-Jun82-402
Reiffenstein, I. and P. Gereke - see Kon-
rad von Würzburg
Reiger, G. Wanderer on My Native Shore.*
639(VQR):Autumn83-136
Reilly, B.F. The Kingdom of León-Castilla
under Queen Urraca, 1190-1126.
J.F. Powers, 377:Mar83-48
Reilly, E.R. - see "Gustav Mahler and
Guido Adler: Records of a Friendship"
Reilly, P. A Private Practice.
D.X. Freedman, 441:29Apr84-22

Reilly, P. Jonathan Swift.
P. Danchin, 189(EA):Apr-Jun84-199
R.J. Dingley, 67:Nov83-313
P. Hammond, 83:Autumn83-221
L.D. Peterson, 173(ECS):Winter83/84-
233
F.N. Smith, 566:Autumn83-53
Reindl, N. Die poetische Funktion des
Mittelalters in der Dichtung Clemens
Brentanos.
H.M.K. Riley, 133:Band16Heft2/3-250
Reiner, E. Die etymologischen Dubletten
des Französischen.*
O. Soutet, 209(FM):Jan83-77
Reinharz, J. and D. Swetschinski, eds.
Mystics, Philosophers, and Politicians.
D.R. Blumenthal, 319:Jul84-385
Reinitz, R. Irony and Historical Con-
sciousness.
D. Levin, 125:Fall82-97
Reisch, E.M., ed. Agricultura Sinica.
B. Ward, 293(JASt):Aug83-935
Reiser, S.A. Russkaia paleografiia novogo
vremeni.
E. Kasinec, 550(RusR):Jul83-328
Reiss, E. Boethius.
J.C. Ziolkowski, 124:Sep-Oct83-54
Reiss, T.J. The Discourse of Modernism.
L. Hutcheon, 153:Winter83-33
L. Hutcheon, 627(UTQ):Summer83-553
D.R. Kelley, 551(RenQ):Summer83-278
R. Lockwood, 400(MLN):May83-799
W. Sypher, 569(SR):Summer83-lviii
Reiss, T.J. Tragedy and Truth.*
M. Mueller, 402(MLR):Apr83-408
Remak, H.H.H. Der Weg zur Weltliteratur.*
G.W. Field, 406:Summer83-223
P-P. Sagave, 549(RLC):Apr-Jun83-239
H.S. Schultz, 564:Nov83-304
Remeikis, T. Opposition to Soviet Rule in
Lithuania, 1945-1980.
T. Venclova, 104(CASS):Winter83-568
Remini, R.V. Andrew Jackson and the
Course of American Democracy, 1833-1845.
N. Bliven, 442(NY):6Aug84-92
J.A. Garraty, 441:28Oct84-33
Remini, R.V. Andrew Jackson and the
Course of American Freedom, 1822-1832.*
H.C. Owsley, 396(ModA):Spring83-213
"Renaissance Drama X." (L. Barkan, ed)
B. Gibbons, 541(RES):Nov83-490
"Renaissance Drama XII." (A. Dessen, ed)
M. Axton, 130:Summer83-192
Renardy, C. Les maîtres universitaires
dans le diocèse de Liège.
J.J. Contreni, 589:Jan83-268
Renault, M. The Friendly Young Ladies.
P. Craig, 617(TLS):21Sep84-1066
Rendell, R. The Fever Tree.
639(VQR):Summer83-92
Rendell, R. The Killing Doll.
P. Craig, 617(TLS):16Mar84-287
Rendell, R. Master of the Moor.
639(VQR):Winter83-20
Rendell, R. Speaker of Mandarin.*
N. Callendar, 441:29Jan84-17
M. Laski, 362:9Feb84-26
de Renéville, J.R. - see under Rolland de
Renéville, J.
Rennie, N. The Cargo.
T. Dooley, 617(TLS):28Sep84-1105
Rennison, J.R. Bidialektale Phonologie.*
G. Lerchner, 682(ZPSK):Band36Heft6-747

Renoir, A. and A. Hernandez - see Foley, J.M. and others
Renoir, J. Julienne et son amour suivi d'En avant Rosalie! Oeuvres de cinéma inédites. (C. Gauteur, ed of both)
J. Paulhan, 207(FR):Dec83-278
Renouard, P., ed. Imprimeurs et libraires parisiens du XVIe siècle. (fasc Breyer)
P.O. Kristeller, 551(RenQ):Winter83-587
D. Shaw, 354:Dec83-419
Rentschler, M. Liudprand von Cremona.
M. Arbagi, 589:Jul83-850
Renwick, R.D. English Folk Poetry.*
D. Buchan, 292(JAF):Jan-Mar83-95
Renzi, L. Einführung in die romanische Sprachwissenschaft.* (G. Ineichen, ed)
H. and R. Kahane, 545(RPh):Feb83-418
Repetto, R. and others. Economic Development, Population Policy, and Demographic Transition in the Republic of Korea.
K. Moskowitz, 293(JASt):Nov82-63
D.I. Steinberg, 293(JASt):Nov82-91
"Report of the Federal Cultural Policy Review Committee."
T. Hathaway, 529(QQ):Summer83-466
"The Report of the President's National Bipartisan Commission on Central America."
J. Chace, 453(NYRB):1Mar84-40
R. Radosh, 441:19Feb84-5
Reps, J.W. Cities of the American West.
P.C. Papademetriou, 46:May81-319
Reps, J.W. The Forgotten Frontier.
P.L. Goss, 651(WHR):Summer83-179
Reps, J.W. Views and Viewmakers of Urban America.
W. Morgan, 441:15Apr84-13
Requardt, W. and M. Machatzke. Gerhart Hauptmann und Erkner.*
W.A. Reichart, 406:Spring83-79
Resch, G. Die Weinbauterminologie des Burgenlandes.
L. Zehetner, 685(ZDL):2/1983-255
Rescher, N. Leibniz's Metaphysics of Nature.*
G. Lloyd, 63:Mar83-102
J.R. Milton, 84:Jun83-193
R.J. Mulvaney, 319:Jan84-121
Rescher, N. Scepticism.*
R. Trigg, 483:Oct81-591
Rescher, N. Unpopular Essays on Technological Progress.*
M. Sagoff, 482(PhR):Jul83-450
Resh, H.M. Hydroponic Food Production.
J.M. Bristow, 529(QQ):Autumn83-712
Resnick, M.C. Introducción a la historia de la lengua española.*
H. Meier, 547(RF):Band95Heft3-324
F. Nuessel, 361:Jun/Jul83-262
J.L. Palmer, 238:May83-309
Resnick, S. and W. Giuliano. En Breve.
T.R. Arrington, 399(MLJ):Summer83-205
H.J. Dennis, 238:May83-312
Resnik, M.D. Frege and the Philosophy of Mathematics.*
L. Wetzel, 482(PhR):Jan83-114
Ressel, G. Syntaktische Struktur und semantische Eigenschaften russischer Sätze.
H. Fegert, 260(IF):Band88-359
Restak, R.M. The Brain.
E.G. Joiner, 399(MLJ):Summer83-171
H.M. Schmeck, Jr., 441:25Nov84-27

Restak, R.M. The Self Seekers.
G.R. Lowe, 529(QQ):Spring83-261
Restrepo, F. El castellano naciente y otros estudios filológicos. (H. Bejarano Díaz, ed)
O.T. Myers, 545(RPh):Aug82-107
Rétat, P., ed. Le Journalisme d'Ancien Régime.
J.R. Censer, 173(ECS):Spring84-383
Revard, S.P. The War in Heaven.*
G. Campbell, 402(MLR):Jan83-140
D.D.C. Chambers, 541(RES):Aug83-338
Revel, J-F., with B. Lazitch. How Democracies Perish.
D. Owen, 441:9Dec84-12
Reveley, E. In Good Faith.*
D. Durrant, 364:Aug/Sep83-133
Revell, D. From the Abandoned Cities.*
639(VQR):Autumn83-134
Revell, P. Quest in Modern American Poetry.*
L. Keller, 405(MP):May84-441
J. Ollier, 189(EA):Apr-Jun84-228
Rey-Debove, J. and others. Le Robert méthodique.
J-P. Colin, 209(FM):Apr83-179
Reyes, C. The Shingle Weaver's Journal.
C.L. Rawlins, 649(WAL):May83-53
Reyes Pons, C. Petrograd.
J. Hancock, 238:Mar83-146
Reynaert, J. De Beeldspraak van Hadewijch.*
P. Dinzelbacher, 684(ZDA):Band112Heft2-87
Reynes, R. The Commonplace Book of Robert Reynes of Acle. (C. Louis, ed)
P. Gradon, 541(RES):May83-206
O.S. Pickering, 72:Band219Heft2-432
Reynolds, B. - see "Seven"
Reynolds, C.H.B. - see Wijayaratne, D.J., with A.S. Kulasuriya
Reynolds, D.M. The Architecture of New York City.
S. Ferrell, 441:1Jul84-20
Reynolds, D.S. Faith in Fiction.*
N. Baym, 301(JEGP):Apr83-270
J.M. Cameron, 627(UTQ):Winter82/83-217
G.O. Carey, 579(SAQ):Summer83-347
T. Werge, 432(NEQ):Mar83-142
Reynolds, D.S. George Lippard.
R. Asselineau, 189(EA):Oct-Dec84-484
C.J. Forbes, 495(PoeS):Jun83-16
Reynolds, F.E., with J. Holt and J. Strong, eds. Guide to Buddhist Religion.
K.P. Pedersen, 485(PE&W):Apr83-201
Reynolds, G. The Later Paintings and Drawings of John Constable.
D. Thomas, 362:6Dec84-28
Reynolds, J. Aphrodisias and Rome.
A.N. Sherwin-White, 313:Vol73-220
Reynolds, J. William Callow, R.W.S.
D. Farr, 39:Apr83-337
Reynolds, J. Discourses on Art. (R.R. Wark, ed)
D. Mannings, 83:Spring83-129
Reynolds, J. The Great Paternalist.
A. Briggs, 617(TLS):9Mar84-255
Reynolds, J.H. and others. Letters from Lambeth. (J. Richardson, ed)
L.M. Jones, 340(KSJ):Vol132-226
D.H. Reiman, 591(SIR):Fall83-470

Reynolds, L.D., ed. Texts and Transmission.
E.J. Kenney, 617(TLS):16Mar84-272
Reynolds, L.D. - see Seneca
Reynolds, M.S., ed. Critical Essays on Ernest Hemingway's "In Our Time."
M. Westbrook, 234:Spring84-52
Reynolds, M.T. Joyce and Dante.*
T.G. Bergin, 569(SR):Spring83-261
W. Fowlie, 569(SR):Spring83-xxx
L.V. Harrod, 174(Éire):Summer83-144
Reynolds, S. Kingdoms and Communities in Western Europe, 900-1300.
M.T. Clanchy, 617(TLS):14Dec84-1451
Reynolds, V. and R. Tanner. The Biology of Religion.
I.M. Lewis, 617(TLS):31Aug84-973
Reynolds, W.J. The Nebraska Quotient.
N. Callendar, 441:18Nov84-36
Reznikova, N.V. Ognennaja pamjat'.*
G.N. Slobin, 574(SEEJ):Fall83-384
von Rezzori, G. Memoirs of an Anti-Semite.*
J. Mellors, 362:1Mar84-28
S.S. Prawer, 617(TLS):17Feb84-160
Rheault, R. - see Sand, G.
Rhees, R., ed. Recollections of Wittgenstein. (new ed)
G.S., 617(TLS):24Feb84-203
Rheinfelder, H., P. Christophorov and E. Müller-Bochat, eds. Literatur und Spiritualität.
M. Tietz, 356(LR):Aug83-227
Rhoads, M.E.G. The Fan Directory.
R.L. Shep, 614:Summer84-16
Rhode, J. and others. Ask a Policeman.
T.J. Binyon, 617(TLS):18May84-557
Rhodes, D.E. A Catalogue of Incunabula in all the Libraries of Oxford University Outside the Bodleian.*
R.C. Alston, 354:Mar83-65
N. Barker, 78(BC):Autumn83-360
Rhodes, D.E. Incunabula in Greece.
R.C. Alston, 354:Sep83-280
Rhodes, N. Elizabethan Grotesque.*
P. Drew, 541(RES):Nov83-488
Rhodes, P.J. A Commentary on the Aristotelian "Athenaion Politeia."*
B.M. Caven, 303(JoHS):Vol 103-177
A. Lintott, 123:Vol33No2-262
P. MacKendrick, 121(CJ):Feb/Mar84-262
R.W., 555:Vol57fasc1-129
Rhys, J. The Letters of Jean Rhys. (F. Wyndham and D. Melly, eds)
W. Balliett, 442(NY):10Dec84-184
V. Gornick, 441:30Sep84-3
P. Rose, 61:Aug84-109
Riasanovsky, N.V. and E. Kasinec, comps. Old Cyrillic and Russian Books.
W.F. Ryan, 575(SEER):Oct83-594
Ribbans, G. Pérez Galdós: "Fortunata y Jacinta."
R. Gutiérrez Girardot, 72:Band219Heft2-473
Ribbat, E., ed. Romantik.
H. Scholz, 654(WB):3/1983-559
Ribeiro, A. A Visual History of Costume: The Eighteenth Century.
R.L. Shep, 614:Spring84-29
Ribeiro, D. Maíra.
P-L. Adams, 61:Apr84-148
J.F. Riegelhaupt, 441:3Jun84-20
Riberette, P. - see de Chateaubriand, F.R.

Ricapito, J.V. Bibliografía razonada y anotada de los obras maestras de la picaresca española.
D. McGrady, 400(MLN):Mar83-301
Ricardou, J. Nouveaux problèmes du roman.
G. Cesbron, 356(LR):Aug83-231
Ricatte, R. and others - see Giono, J.
Ricciuti, E.R. The New York City Wildlife Guide.
T. Ferrell, 441:8Apr84-21
Madame Riccoboni. Lettres de Mistriss Fanni Butlerd. (J.H. Stewart, ed)
V. Mylne, 208(FS):Jan83-84
Rice, E.E. The Grand Procession of Ptolemy Philadelphus.
J. Ray, 617(TLS):11May84-530
Rice, F.A. and M.F. Sa'id. Eastern Arabic.
F. Cadora, 399(MLJ):Summer83-179
Rice, M. Cognition to Language.
R. Schreck, 351(LL):Jun83-247
Rich, A. Sources.
A. Stevenson, 617(TLS):20Jul84-818
Rich, P.B. White Power and the Liberal Conscience.
G. Sampson, 617(TLS):6Jul84-764
Richard, D. Les Chagrins d'aimer.
D. Aury, 450(NRF):Sep83-137
Richard, J. Les récits de voyages et de pèlerinages.
D.R. Howard, 589:Apr83-558
Richard, J-P. Pages paysages: Microlectures II.
C. Prendergast, 617(TLS):28Sep84-1096
Richard de Fournival. L'Oeuvre lyrique de Richard de Fournival.* (Y.G. Lepage, ed)
J.H. Marshall, 382(MAE):1983/1-164
D. Nelson, 589:Apr83-526
Richards, B., ed. English Verse 1830-1890.
J.R. Watson, 402(MLR):Apr83-430
Richards, B. - see James, H.
Richards, D.A. Lives of Short Duration.*
L. Ricou, 529(QQ):Summer83-532
M. Taylor, 198:Jan83-107
Richards, D.A.J. Sex, Drugs, Death and the Law.
G. Dworkin, 185:Oct83-155
R.G. Frey, 518:Oct83-234
Richards, E.J. Dante and the "Roman de la Rose."
R.H. Lansing, 589:Jul83-801
J. Took, 402(MLR):Jan83-199
Richards, F. Old Soldiers Never Die. Old Soldier Sahib.
J.K.L.W., 617(TLS):18May84-562
Richards, H.J. and T. Cajiao Salas. Asedios a la poesía de Nicomedes Santa Cruz.
M.D. Compton, 263(RIB):Vol33No3-415
Richards, J. The Age of the Dream Palace.
A. Smith, 362:5Jul84-24
P. Smith, 617(TLS):17Aug84-909
Richards, J.M. The National Trust Book of Bridges.
H. Macdonald, 617(TLS):3Aug84-876
Richards, J.R. The Sceptical Feminist.*
C.A., 543:Sep82-184
L.M. Broughton, 483:Apr83-259
R. Lindley, 393(Mind):Jan83-149
M. Weinzweig, 518:Jul83-129
Richards, S. Philosophy and Sociology of Science.
B. Barnes, 617(TLS):22Jun84-710

Ridgway, B.S. Fifth Century Styles in Greek Sculpture.*
C.A. Picón, 123:Vol33No1-94
A. Stewart, 54:Mar83-172
G.B. Waywell, 90:Jun83-363
Ridler, A. - see Austin, W.
Ridley, H. Images of Imperial Rule.
J.R. Reed, 395(MFS):Winter83-774
Ridley, M. The Explanation of Organic Diversity.
J. Alcock, 617(TLS):27Apr84-479
Rieber, A.J. Merchants and Entrepreneurs in Imperial Russia.*
P. Gatrell, 575(SEER):Jul83-449
J.L. West, 550(RusR):Jan83-107
Riede, D.G. Dante Gabriel Rossetti and the Limits of Victorian Vision.
639(VQR):Autumn83-117
Riedel, N. Uwe Johnson: Bibliographie 1959-1980.* (Vol 1) (2nd ed)
U.K. Faulhaber, 222(GR):Summer83-125
W. Schwarz, 133:Band16Heft1-91
Rieger, D., with R. Kroll - see Marie de France
Rieger, H.C. and B. Bhadra. Comparative Evaluation of Road Construction Techniques in Nepal.
J. Das Gupta, 293(JASt):Nov82-105
Riehle, W. The Middle English Mystics.*
N.F. Blake, 72:Band219Heft2-434
J.P.H. Clark, 481(PQ):Fall83-539
R. Ellis, 382(MAE):1983/1-154
Riemer, A.P. Antic Fables.
M. Coyle, 447(N&Q):Apr82-163
Rietra, M., ed. Jung Österreich.
F. Achberger, 406:Summer83-222
E. Wangermann, 447(N&Q):Jun82-279
Riewald, J.G. and J. Bakker. The Critical Reception of American Literature in the Netherlands 1824-1900.
R.A., 189(EA):Oct-Dec84-492
T.A.B., 179(ES):Apr83-187
Rifaat, A. Distant View of Minarate and Other Stories.
R. Irwin, 617(TLS):13Jan84-46
Riffaterre, M. Semiotics of Poetry.*
(French title: Sémiotique de la poésie.)
L. Edson, 494:Vol4No2-355
Riffaterre, M. Text Production. (French title: La Production du texte.)
D.F. Bell, 599:Spring83-297
T. Cave, 617(TLS):16Mar84-278
Rifkin, J. Algeny.
P. Zaleski, 469:Vol9No1-82
Rifkin, N. Antonioni's Visual Language.
M. Keller, 127:Fall83-284
Rigby, T.H. and F. Fehér. Political Legitimation in Communist States.
M. McCauley, 575(SEER):Jul83-462
Rigg, D., comp. No Turn Unstoned.
G. Playfair, 157:Summer83-28
Riggan, R. Free Fire Zone.
C.R. Larson, 441:11Mar84-18
Riggio, T.P., J.L.W. West 3d and N.M. Westlake - see Dreiser, T.
Riggs, J. The Last Laugh.
N. Callendar, 441:17Jun84-22
Righter, R.W. Crucible for Conservation.
P.M. Hocker, 649(WAL):Aug83-162
Rigney, B.H. Lilith's Daughters.
M. De Koven, 395(MFS):Summer83-344
Rihoit, C. La Favorite.
C. Michael, 207(FR):Oct83-140

Rihoit, C. La Nuit de Varennes.
I. Kohn, 207(FR):Dec83-273
de Rijk, L.M., ed. Anonymi auctoris Franciscani logica "Ad rudium."
E.J. Ashworth, 589:Apr83-549
Riley, A.W. - see Döblin, A.
Riley, P. Kant's Political Philosophy.*
J.S., 185:Jan84-373
Riley, P. Will and Political Legitimacy.*
J.M.G., 185:Apr84-558
Rilke, R.M. Duino Elegies. (G. Miranda, trans)
S. Hamill, 448:Vol21No2/3-169
Rilke, R.M. Letters to a Young Poet. (S. Mitchell, trans)
G. Annan, 453(NYRB):27Sep84-17
Rilke, R.M. The Selected Poetry of Rainer Maria Rilke.* (S. Mitchell, ed and trans)
P. Wild, 50(ArQ):Summer83-172
Rilke, R.M. Le Testament. (P. Jaccottet, trans)
J. Aeply, 450(NRF):Sep83-166
Rimbaud, A. Oeuvres.* (S. Bernard and A. Guyaux, eds)
W.C. Carter, 207(FR):Dec83-253
Rimer, J.T. and Yamazaki Masakazu, eds and trans. On the Art of the Nō Drama.
P.S. Plowright, 617(TLS):5Oct84-1138
Rinaldi, N. We Have Lost Our Fathers and Other Poems.*
W. Zander, 363(LitR):Winter84-272
Ringe, D.A. American Gothic.*
N.S. Grabo, 445(NCF):Sep83-224
T. Martin, 27(AL):Dec83-644
Ringger, K. L'Ame et la page.*
E. Mullady, 546(RR):Nov83-499
Ringle, M.D., ed. Philosophical Perspectives in Artificial Intelligence.
S.P. Stich, 482(PhR):Apr83-280
Ringler, S. Viten- und Offenbarungsliteratur in Frauenklöstern des Mittelalters.
T.R. Jackson, 402(MLR):Jan83-224
P.W. Tax, 589:Jan83-220
Ringrose, D.R. Madrid and the Spanish Economy, 1560-1850.
J. Israel, 617(TLS):26Oct84-1222
Ringwood, G. The Collected Plays of Gwen Ringwood. (E. Delgatty, ed)
J. Hoffman, 108:Spring83-134
Rinner, F. and K. Zerinschek, eds. Komparatistik.
P. Thiergen, 52:Band18Heft3-320
Ríos, A.A. - see under Alvaro Ríos, A.
Ripley, J. "Julius Caesar" on Stage in England and America, 1599-1973.*
T.R. Griffiths, 677(YES):Vol 13-311
A. Humphreys, 541(RES):Aug83-331
Ripoll, A.M. - see under Martínez Ripoll, A.
Ripoll, C. - see Martí, J.
Riquelme, J.P. Teller and Tale in Joyce's Fiction.
M. Magalaner, 395(MFS):Winter83-780
295(JML):Nov83-511
Risch, E. Supplying Washington's Army.
E.W. Carp, 656(WMQ):Apr83-327
Risebero, B. Modern Architecture and Design.
D. Shapiro and L. Stamm, 55:Dec83-35
Rissik, A. The James Bond Man.
G. Kaufman, 362:19Apr84-26

Rist, J.M.   Human Value.
   R.J. Sullivan, 487:Winter83-367
Ritchie, C.   Diplomatic Passport.
   S. Neuman, 102(CanL):Winter82-118
Ritchie, D.   The Binary Brain.
   S.M. Halpern, 441:19Feb84-23
Ritsos, Y.   The Lady of the Vineyards.
   M.B. Raizis, 678(YCGL):No31-151
Ritter, A., ed.   Deutschlands litera-
   risches Amerikabild.
   M. Schulze, 72:Band220Heft2-382
Ritter, A. - see Sealsfield, C.
Ritter, H.   Tūrōyo.   (Pt B)
   J.C. Greenfield, 318(JAOS):Apr-Jun82-
   406
Ritter, J.   Hegel and the French Revolu-
   tion.
   H.S. Harris, 518:Oct83-224
   K.L. Schmitz, 319:Oct84-493
Ritter, J. and K. Gründer, eds.   Histor-
   isches Wörterbuch der Philosophie.
   (Vol 5)
   K. Hartmann, 489(PJGG):Band90Heft1-221
Ritter-Schaumburg, H.   Die Nibelungen
   zogen nordwärts.
   H. Kratz, 221(GQ):Nov83-636
"Das Ritterbuch als Volkslesestoff im
   spanischen und rumänischen Raum."
   F. Meregalli, 52:Band17Heft3-312
Ritz, H.   Die Geschichte vom Rotkäppchen.
   O.F. Gmelin, 196:Band24Heft1/2-170
Ritz, R.   Le Théâtre de Richard Cumberland.
   A. Hare, 189(EA):Jan-Mar83-80
Rivarola, J.L.   Las conjunciones concesi-
   vas en español medieval y clásico.
   O.T. Myers, 545(RPh):May83-604
Rivas, R.A.   Fuentes documentales para el
   estudio de Rufino Blanco Fombona.
   B.T. Osiek, 552(REH):May83-301
Rivas Quintas, E.   Toponimia de Marín.
   H. Kröll, 547(RF):Band95Heft4-487
Rivera, F.P. and M. Hurtado - see under
   Pérez Rivera, F. and M. Hurtado
Rivers, C.   Virgins.
   J. Kaufman, 441:16Dec84-26
Rivers, E.L.   Garcilaso de la Vega: Poems.
   B.W. Ife, 402(MLR):Oct83-943
Rivers, I., ed.   Books and Their Readers
   in Eighteenth-Century England.*
   J.M.B., 179(ES):Apr83-182
   V.E. Neuburg, 366:Autumn83-269
Rivers, J.   The Life and Hard Times of
   Heidi Abromowitz.
   M. Dowd, 441:9Dec84-26
Rivers, J.E.   Proust and the Art of Love.*
   P. Brady, 268(IFR):Summer84-119
   A.J.L. Busst, 535(RHL):Sep/Dec83-957
   M. Muller, 546(RR):Jan83-109
Rivers, J.E. and C. Nicol, eds.   Nabokov's
   Fifth Arc.
   J. Grayson, 575(SEER):Oct83-607
   J.P. Levine, 268(IFR):Summer84-129
   D.W. Madden, 594:Winter83-396
   E. Pifer, 550(RusR):Jul83-347
   C.S. Ross, 395(MFS):Winter83-736
   B. Stonehill, 659(ConL):Summer84-235
Rivers, J.W.   Proud and on My Feet.
   R.W. Hill, 580(SCR):Fall83-123
Rivière, J-C.   Les Poésies du Trouvère
   Jacques de Cambrai.
   A. Iker-Gittleman, 545(RPh):Feb83-507
Rivkin, E.   A Hidden Revolution.
   D.M. Smith, 318(JAOS):Jan-Mar82-204

Rivlin, A.M., ed.   Economic Choices 1984.
   W. Diebold, 441:21Oct84-51
Rix, H.   Historische Grammatik des Griech-
   ischen.
   P. Swiggers, 353:Vol20No1/2-159
Rix, W.T., ed.   Hermann Sudermann.*
   D. Assmann, 439(NM):1983/2-282
   J. Osborne, 402(MLR):Apr83-501
Rizvi, J.   Ladakh.
   C. von Fürer-Haimendorf, 617(TLS):
   24Aug84-934
Rizvi, S.A.A.   Shāh Walī-Allāh and His
   Times.
   W. Fusfeld, 293(JASt):Nov82-201
   A. Schimmel, 318(JAOS):Apr-Jun82-367
Rizzi, L.   Issues in Italian Syntax.*
   C. Dobrovie-Sorin, 361:Sep83-91
   J. Siracusa, 399(MLJ):Summer83-198
Rizzo, V.   Niccolò Tagliacozzi Canale o il
   trionfo dell'ornato nel Settecento
   napoletano.
   A. Blunt, 90:Feb83-102
Rizzuto, A.   Camus' Imperial Vision.*
   E.H. Zepp, 546(RR):Mar83-251
van Rjndt, P.   Last Message to Berlin.
   A. Krystal, 441:18Nov84-32
Roa Bastos, A.   Ich der Allmächtige.
   C. Schnelle, 654(WB):1/1983-161
Roach, E. - see Coudrette
Roaf, C. - see Speroni, S.
Robb, J.D.   Hispanic Folk Music of New
   Mexico and the Southwest.*
   J.O. West, 292(JAF):Apr-Jun83-239
Robb, J.W.   Por los caminos de Alfonso
   Reyes.
   M.V. Ekstrom, 238:May83-305
Robbins, C.A.   The Cuban Threat.
   639(VQR):Autumn83-129
Robbins, D., ed.   Rethinking Social In-
   equality.
   J.L.H., 185:Jan84-363
Robbins, D.   The Vermont State House.
   R. Janson, 576:Oct83-307
Robbins, H.   Descent from Xanadu.
   D. Fitzpatrick, 441:29Apr84-32
Robbins, P.   The British Hegelians, 1875-
   1925.
   M.A.G., 185:Jan84-372
Robbins, R. - see Browne, T.
Robbins, T.   Jitterbug Perfume.
   J. House, 441:9Dec84-11
Robe, S.L., ed.   Hispanic Legends from
   New Mexico.*
   M. Weigle, 292(JAF):Apr-Jun83-238
Robert, L.   À travers l'Asie Mineure.
   S. Mitchell, 303(JoHS):Vol 103-211
Robert, M.   As Lonely as Franz Kafka.
   295(JML):Nov83-515
Robert, M.   Origins of the Novel.*
   J. Preston, 402(MLR):Apr83-390
Robert de Boron.   Merlin, roman du XIIIe
   siècle.   (A. Micha, ed)
   C-A. van Coolput, 356(LR):Nov83-355
   L. Cooper, 545(RPh):Nov82-308
   P.S. Noble, 382(MAE):1983/1-161
Robert de Boron.   Le Roman du Saint Graal.
   (M. Schöler-Beinhauer, ed and trans)
   K. Busby, 547(RF):Band95Heft1/2-171
Roberts, B.   Randolph.
   A. Watkins, 362:12Apr84-23
   C.M. Woodhouse, 617(TLS):13Apr84-394

Roberts, C.H. Manuscript, Society and Belief in Early Christian Egypt.
   M. Smith, 318(JAOS):Jan-Mar82-201
Roberts, C.H. and T.C. Skeat. The Birth of the Codex.
   N.G. Wilson, 617(TLS):30Mar84-355
Roberts, C.W. A Legacy from Victorian Enterprise.
   K.E. Jermy, 324:Oct84-746
Roberts, D. The Indirection of Desire.
   U.H. Gerlach, 301(JEGP):Jan83-113
Roberts, G. - see Hopkins, G.M.
Roberts, G. - see Pole, D.
Roberts, H.S. - see under Salskov Roberts, H.
Roberts, J. Walter Benjamin.*
   J.C.E., 185:Apr84-555
Roberts, J.R. John Donne.*
   G.H. Carrithers, Jr., 539:May84-149
Roberts, J.R., ed. Essential Articles for the Study of George Herbert's Poetry.
   P. Palmer, 402(MLR):Jan83-141
Roberts, J.T. Accountability in Athenian Government.
   M.H. Jameson, 124:May-Jun84-314
Roberts, J.W. Richard Boleslavsky.
   L. Senelick, 610:Summer83-178
Roberts, J.W. City of Sokrates.
   P.J. Rhodes, 617(TLS):27Jul84-831
Roberts, K. Pavane.
   C. Greenland, 617(TLS):18May84-557
Roberts, K. Stonefish and Other Poems.
   L. Lemire-Tostevin, 102(CanL):Summer83-168
Roberts, M. British Diplomacy and Swedish Politics, 1758-1773.
   S.P. Oakley, 562(Scan):May82-97
Roberts, M. The Wild Girl.
   E. Fisher, 617(TLS):26Oct84-1224
Roberts, P. Tender Prey.*
   M. Laski, 362:9Feb84-26
Roberts, P.C. The Supply-Side Revolution.
   J. Fallows, 453(NYRB):12Apr84-8
   M. Kandel, 441:18Mar84-10
   M.J. Ulmer, 129:Jun84-60
Roberts, R. No Bells on Sunday. (A. Walker, ed)
   M. Seldes, 441:14Oct84-14
Roberts, W. A Bibliography of D.H. Lawrence. (2nd ed)
   K. Cushman, 517(PBSA):Vol77No3-382
   E.D., 189(EA):Jul-Sep84-366
   J. Roberts, 617(TLS):4May84-503
Robertson, A.S. Roman Imperial Coins in the Hunter Coin Cabinet, University of Glasgow.* (Vol 5)
   D. Nash, 123:Vol33No1-110
Robertson, C.M. A Shorter History of Greek Art.
   R. Ling, 303(JoHS):Vol 103-224
Robertson, D.W., Jr. Essays in Medieval Culture.
   R.T. Davies, 447(N&Q):Apr82-157
   P. Gradon, 541(RES):Feb83-51
   T.D. Hill, 191(ELN):Mar84-63
   T.A. Shippey, 402(MLR):Jul83-669
Robertson, G. and A.G.L. Nicol. Media Law.
   D. Pannick, 362:25Oct84-25
Robertson, I. Blue Guide France.
   J. Ardagh, 617(TLS):22Jun84-702
Robertson, L., with C. Flinders and B. Godfrey. The Laurel's Kitchen Bread Book.
   M. Burros, 441:2Dec84-16

Robertson, M. A Shorter History of Greek Art.
   D. Williams, 123:Vol33No2-290
Robertson, M.G. The Sculpture of Palenque. (Vol 1)
   W.M. Bray, 617(TLS):17Feb84-170
Robertson, P. An Experience of Women.*
   A.F. Scott, 579(SAQ):Autumn83-448
Robertson, P.J.M. The Leavises on Fiction.*
   W. Baker, 477(PLL):Fall83-461
Robertson, S.M. Rosegarden and Labyrinth.
   L. Selfe, 89(BJA):Summer83-268
Robertson, T. Plays by Tom Robertson. (W. Tydeman, ed)
   D. Devlin, 157:Spring83-52
Robertson-Mellor, G., ed. The Franco-Italian Roland (V4).*
   A.J. Holden, 402(MLR):Oct83-914
Robichez, J. Verlaine entre Rimbaud et Dieu.*
   C. Chadwick, 402(MLR):Apr83-459
Robichez, J. - see Gautier, T.
Robida, A. Le Vingtième siècle.
   M. Angenot, 561(SFS):Jul83-237
Robilliard, S.A. Religion and the Law.
   A. Phillips, 617(TLS):13Jul84-787
Robinet, A. La pensée à l'âge classique.
   J-M. Beyssade, 542:Jan-Mar83-119
Robins, M.H. Promising, Intending, and Moral Autonomy.
   G. Warnock, 617(TLS):7Dec84-1404
Robinson, B.W. Kuniyoshi, The Warrior Prints.
   M. Takeuchi, 293(JASt):Aug83-976
Robinson, C., ed. The Artist and the Quilt.
   I. Joshi, 614:Winter84-16
Robinson, C.E., ed. Lord Byron and His Contemporaries.
   F.L. Beaty, 340(KSJ):Vol32-215
Robinson, D. Apostle of Culture.
   G.W. Allen, 651(WHR):Autumn83-270
   J. Campbell, 619:Winter83-108
   R.D. Habich, 432(NEQ):Sep83-469
   R.E. Spiller, 27(AL):Mar83-103
Robinson, D. Chaplin.*
   C. Maland, 500:Spring/Summer84-55
Robinson, D. William Morris, Edward Burne-Jones and the Kelmscott Chaucer.*
   R. Mander, 39:Jun83-512
Robinson, D. Piece of Cake.
   F. Levy, 441:27May84-18
Robinson, E. and R. Fitter - see Clare, J.
Robinson, E. and D. Powell - see Clare, J.
Robinson, F.J.G. and others. Eighteenth-Century British Books: An Author Union Catalogue.* (Vols 1-5)
   H. Amory, 517(PBSA):Vol77No1-80
Robinson, F.J.G., J.M. Robinson and C. Wadham. Eighteenth-Century British Books: An Index to the Foreign and Provincial Imprints in the Author Union Catalogue.
   H. Amory, 517(PBSA):Vol77No1-80
Robinson, G. Raven the Trickster.
   J. Giltrow, 102(CanL):Spring83-126
Robinson, H. Matter and Sense.*
   G.C. Madell, 518:Jul83-175
Robinson, J. Dr. Rocksinger and The Age of Longing.
   J. Epstein, 249(HudR):Spring83-182

Robinson, J.A. Eugene O'Neill and Oriental Thought.
  C.P. Wilson, 27(AL):May83-269
Robinson, J.C. - see Van Ghent, D.
Robinson, J.M. The Dukes of Norfolk.*
  M. Bence-Jones, 324:Jan84-136
  V. Powell, 39:Apr83-338
Robinson, J.M. Georgian Model Farms.
  D. Walker, 617(TLS):13Apr84-409
  J.N. White, 324:Nov84-817
Robinson, J.M. The Latest Country Houses.
  H.G. Slade, 617(TLS):30Nov84-1364
Robinson, J.M. Royal Residences.
  J. Lees-Milne, 39:Mar83-262
Robinson, J.S. H.D.*
  V.M. Kouidis, 577(SHR):Fall83-378
  G. Pearson, 617(TLS):27Apr84-447
Robinson, L. An American in Leningrad.
  639(VQR):Winter83-28
Robinson, M. Housekeeping.
  K.M. Hammond, 152(UDQ):Spring83-123
Robinson, P.C. Willa.*
  S.J. Rosowski, 502(PrS):Winter83-96
Robinson, R., ed. The Everyman Book of Light Verse.
  N. Lewis, 362:20/27Dec84-55
Robinson, T. The Long Case Clock.*
  G. Wills, 39:Jan83-68
Robinson, W. The English Flower Garden.
  H. Mitchell, 135:Jun83-121
Robinson, W.S. The Southern Colonial Frontier, 1607-1763.
  F.L. Owsley, Jr., 9(AlaR):Apr83-150
Robreau, Y. L'honneur et la honte.*
  W.D. Paden, Jr., 589:Jul83-809
Robson, J.M. - see Mill, J.S.
Robson, J.M. and J. Stillinger - see Mill, J.S.
Robson, W.W. The Definition of Literature and Other Essays.*
  A. Bony, 189(EA):Apr-Jun84-171
  M. Dodsworth, 97(CQ):Vol 12No2/3-215
  E. Robertson, 175:Autumn83-270
Roca-Pons, J. Introduction to Catalan Literature.
  M. Agosín, 241:May83-91
Rocard, M. Les fils du soleil.
  J. Tyler, 238:Mar83-144
Roche, D. La Disparition des lucioles.
  F. de Mèredieu, 450(NRF):Apr83-155
Roche, D. - see Ménétra, J-L.
Roche, J. Lassus.
  J. Blezzard, 415:Mar83-169
  A. Carver, 410(M&L):Jan/Apr83-96
  H.T.E.M., 412:Aug-Nov82-265
Roche, T.P., Jr. and C.P. O'Donnell, Jr. - see Spenser, E.
la Rochelle, P.D. - see under Drieu la Rochelle, P.
de Rocher, G.D. - see Joubert, L.
Rocher, R. Orientalism, Poetry, and the Millennium.
  D.H. Killingley, 617(TLS):19Oct84-1196
Lord Rochester. The Letters of John Wilmot, Earl of Rochester.* (J. Treglown, ed)
  P.E. Hewison, 447(N&Q):Apr82-177
  D.F. Hills, 541(RES):May83-218
  R. Selden, 161(DUJ):Dec82-110
  J.L. Thorson, 568(SCN):Winter83-72
  R. Wilcoxon, 566:Spring84-175

Lord Rochester. John Wilmot, Earl of Rochester: Selected Poems. (P. Hammond, ed)
  M. Dodsworth, 175:Summer83-189
  W.W. Robson, 97(CQ):Vol 12No1-74
Rochester, M.B. René Crevel.*
  R. Cardinal, 208(FS):Jan83-105
Rockefeller, G.C. Books, Pamphlets, and Broadsides Printed or Published in New Jersey, 1801-1819, not Recorded in Shaw and Shoemaker's American Bibliography.
  S. Ferguson, 517(PBSA):Vol77No4-517
Rockmore, T. Fichte, Marx, and the German Philosophical Tradition.*
  S. Crowell, 258:Sep83-338
Rockmore, T. and others. Marxism and Alternatives.
  J.P. Conway, 258:Mar83-96
Rockwell, J. All American Music.*
  R.M. Radano, 187:Jan84-148
Rockwell, J. Evald Tang Kristensen.
  A. Talbot, 203:Vol94No2-263
Rockwell, J. Sinatra.
  M. Lydon, 441:11Nov84-16
Röd, W. Descartes. (new ed)
  H. Caton, 319:Oct84-480
Roda, S. Commento Storico al Libro IX dell'Epistolario di Q. Aurelio Simmaco.
  J-P. Callu, 555:Vol57fasc2-341
Roddick, N. A New Deal in Entertainment.
  T. Balio, 18:Jul-Aug84-51
Roddy, E.G. Mills, Mansions and Mergers.
  L.M. Roth, 576:Dec83-404
Rodee, M.E. Old Navajo Rugs.
  G.N. Johnson, 292(JAF):Jul-Sep83-361
Roderick, C. Miles Franklin.
  V. Kent, 71(ALS):May83-132
Roderick, C. The Real Henry Lawson.
  D. Robinson, 71(ALS):Oct83-277
Rodgers, A.T. The Universal Drum.*
  M. Perloff, 447(N&Q):Jun82-273
  G. Reeves, 161(DUJ):Dec82-112
Rodier, J. L'ordre du coeur.*
  C. Chalier, 192(EP):Jan-Mar83-109
Rodin, A. Art: Conversations with Paul Gsell.
  R. Snell, 617(TLS):21Dec84-1473
Rodman, S. Artists in Tune with Their World.
  F.L. Phelps, 37:May-Jun83-61
Rodmell, G.E. Marivaux: "Le Jeu de l'amour et du hasard" and "Les Fausses Confidences."
  H. Mason, 208(FS):Jul83-340
  R. Niklaus, 83:Autumn83-267
Rodmell, G.E. - see de Malesherbes, C-G.F.
Rodney, R.M., comp. Mark Twain International.*
  L.J. Budd, 579(SAQ):Summer83-349
Rodoreda, M. My Christina.
  G. Rabassa, 441:2Dec84-68
Rodrigues, E.L. Quest for the Human.
  J.Z. Guzlowski, 395(MFS):Winter83-737
Rodríguez, A.T. - see under Trujillo Rodríguez, A.
Rodríguez, I. Poemas de Israel.
  L.T. Perry, 552(REH):Oct83-430
Rodriguez, J. Witch Heart.
  J. Maiden, 381:Jun83-256
Rodríguez, J.L. El Cancionero de Joan Airas de Santiago.*
  G. Tavani, 72:Band220Heft2-467

Rodriguez, R. Hunger of Memory.*
   G.M. Blanco, 399(MLJ):Autumn83-282
   R.B. Kaplan, 351(LL):Mar83-123
   H.A. Porter, 31(ASch):Spring83-278
Rodríguez, R.V. - see under Vélez Rodrí-
   guez, R.
Rodríguez de Almela, D. Cartas. (D.
   Mackenzie, ed)
   D.E. Carpenter, 545(RPh):Aug82-126
   N.G. Round, 402(MLR):Jul83-732
Rodríguez de Lena, P. El Passo honroso
   de Suero de Quiñones.* (A. Labandeira
   Fernández, ed)
   C. González, 457(NRFH):Tomo31núm1-126
Rodríguez del Pino, S. La novela chicana
   escrita en español.
   R.B. Klein, 399(MLJ):Autumn83-310
Rodríguez Juliá, E. El entierro de Cor-
   tijo.
   A. González, 701(SinN):Jul-Sep83-82
Rodríguez-Luis, J. Hermenéutica y praxis
   del indigenismo.
   B.B. Aponte, 240(HR):Summer83-357
Rodríguez M. Montalvo, S. - see Alfonso X
Rodríguez Moñino, A.R. Los poetas ex-
   tremeños del Siglo XVI.* (P. Cañada
   Castillo and others, eds)
   G. Hughes, 552(REH):Oct83-456
Rodway, A. The Craft of Criticism.
   A.H., 189(EA):Apr-Jun84-231
   O.M. Meidner, 89(BJA):Autumn83-373
Roe, J. Frank Matsura, Frontier Photog-
   rapher.
   M. Lewis, 649(WAL):Feb84-362
Roe, P. Gularabulu. (S. Muecke, ed)
   A. Schmidt, 381:Sep83-401
   C. Wallace-Crabbe, 617(TLS):20Jul84-
   819
Roe, S. Estella.
   S. Monod, 189(EA):Apr-Sep83-357
Roe, S.A. Matter, Life, and Generation.
   J. Larson, 173(ECS):Winter83/84-225
Roeber, A.G. Faithful Magistrates and
   Republican Lawyers.
   G. Morgan, 656(WMQ):Apr83-317
Roebuck, G. Clarendon and Cultural Conti-
   nuity.
   J. Egan, 568(SCN):Fall83-55
Roebuck, P. It Never Rains ...
   A.L. Le Quesne, 617(TLS):21Dec84-1487
Roebuck, P., ed. Macartney of Lisanoure
   1737-1806.
   N. Canny, 617(TLS):20Apr84-440
Roehricht, K.H. Waldsommerjahre.
   R. Bernhardt, 654(WB):7/1983-1271
Roesdahl, E. Danmarks Vikingetid.
   J.J. Kudlik, 563(SS):Summer83-264
Roesdahl, E. Viking Age Denmark.
   S.A. Mitchell, 589:Jul83-851
Roethel, H.K. and J.K. Benjamin. Kandin-
   sky: Catalogue Raisonné of the Oil Paint-
   ings.* (Vol 1)
   J.E. Bowlt, 453(NYRB):16Feb84-27
   D.E. Gordon, 90:Nov83-705
   F. Thürlemann, 683:Band46Heft2-223
Roethel, H.K. and J.K. Benjamin. Kandin-
   sky: Catalogue Raisonné of the Oil Paint-
   ings. (Vol 2)
   J. Gage, 617(TLS):27Jul84-834
Roffman, P. and J. Purdy. The Hollywood
   Social Problem Film.
   R. MacMillan, 488:Mar83-119

Rogers, B. The Domestication of Women.
   M. Stivens, 69:Vol53No1-103
Rogers, D. and N.H. Chung. 110 Livingston
   Street Revisited.
   C.E. Finn, Jr., 441:26Feb84-33
   B. Holmes, 617(TLS):6Jul84-749
Rogers, E.M. and J.K. Larsen. Silicon
   Valley Fever.
   W. Stockton, 441:24Jun84-16
Rogers, E.R. The Perilous Hunt.*
   S. Bohnet, 107(CRCL):Jun83-267
   M.S. Finch, 552(REH):Oct83-446
   E.R. Long, 292(JAF):Jan-Mar83-98
Rogers, G.A. An Illustrated History of
   Needlework Tools.
   R.L. Shep, 614:Fall84-18
Rogers, J. Her Living Image.
   L. Marcus, 617(TLS):19Oct84-1180
   K.C. O'Brien, 362:29Nov84-25
Rogers, J. Separate Tracks.*
   D. Durrant, 364:Jul83-91
Rogers, J.M. Islamic Art and Design: 1500-
   1700.
   R.L. Shep, 614:Fall84-19
Rogers, K.M. Feminism in Eighteenth-
   Century England.*
   M.J. Benkovitz, 301(JEGP):Jul83-449
   M.W. Brownley, 566:Spring84-162
   J. Todd, 83:Spring83-86
   42(AR):Winter83-123
Rogers, L. Queens of the Next Hot Star.
   L.R. Ricou, 102(CanL):Summer83-118
Rogers, M. Blue Guide: Museums and Gal-
   leries of London.
   D. Goddard, 324:Apr84-345
Rogers, N. and M. Stanley, eds. In Cele-
   bration of the Curious Mind.
   P. Bach, 614:Fall84-18
Rogers, P., ed. The Eighteenth Century.
   C. Price, 541(RES):May83-220
Rogers, P. The Expectations of Light.*
   J.D. McClatchy, 491:Dec83-174
Rogers, P. Hacks and Dunces.*
   C.T. Wells, Jr., 447(N&Q):Oct82-446
Rogers, P. "Robinson Crusoe."*
   O.W. Ferguson, 579(SAQ):Winter83-112
Rogers, P. - see Swift, J.
Rogger, H. Russia in the Age of Modernisa-
   tion and Revolution 1881-1917.
   D. Lieven, 617(TLS):20Jul84-814
Rogin, M.P. Subversive Genealogy.*
   R.H. Brodhead, 445(NCF):Sep83-214
   W-C. Dimock, 219(GaR):Winter83-912
   B. Thomas, 454:Fall83-85
Rogoziński, J. Power, Caste, and Law.
   A.R. Lewis, 589:Apr83-527
Rohan, K. Pagoda, Skull and Samurai.
   G. Evans, 407(MN):Winter83-436
Rohatyn, F.G. The Twenty-Year Century.
   R.M. Solow, 441:5Feb84-11
   442(NY):19Mar84-149
Rohder, R. Padre to the Papagos.
   K. McCarty, 50(ArQ):Autumn83-286
Rohdich, H. Antigone.
   P.G. Mason, 123:Vol133No2-313
Rohland de Langbehn, R. - see Scrivá, L.
Rohlfs, G. Romanische Lehnübersetzungen
   aus germanischer Grundlage.
   G. Straka, 553(RLiR):Jul-Dec83-440
Rohlich, T.H., ed and trans. A Tale of
   Eleventh-Century Japan.
   C. Hochstedler, 407(MN):Winter83-429

Rohner, L. Kommentarband zum Faksimile-
druck der Jahrgänge 1808-1815 und 1819
des "Rheinländischen Hausfreunds" von
Johann Peter Hebel.
E.F. Hoffmann, 221(GQ):Jan83-142
Rohner, L. - see Hebel, J.P.
Rohr, R. Einführung in das Studium der
Romanistik. (3rd ed)
H. Kröll, 72:Band220Heft2-431
Rohrkemper, J., ed. John Dos Passos.
R. Willett, 677(YES):Vol 13-350
Roider, K.A., Jr. Austria's Eastern Ques-
tion 1700-1789.
J. Black, 83:Autumn83-238
Roider, U., ed. and trans. De Chophur in
Da Muccida.
B. Ó Cuív, 112:Vol 15-175
K.H. Schmidt, 260(IF):Band88-337
Roig, A.A. Esquemas para una historia de
la filosofía ecuatoriana. (2nd ed)
J.C. Torchia Estrada, 263(RIB):Vol133
No3-416
Roitinger, A. Oscar Wilde's Life as
Reflected in his Correspondence and his
Autobiography.
J. Stokes, 677(YES):Vol 13-338
de Rojas, F. "La Celestine" in the French
Translation of 1578 by Jacques de Lavar-
din. (D.L. Drysdall, ed)
D.S. Severin, 545(RPh):Feb83-490
de Rola, S.K. - see under Klossowski de
Rola, S.
Rolf, R. Masamune Hakuchō.
M.G. Ryan, 293(JASt):Nov82-169
Rolfe, L. Literary L.A.
J. Helbert, 649(WAL):May83-65
Rolfs, D. The Last Cross.
F.A. Bassanese, 276:Autumn83-290
M. Caesar, 402(MLR):Apr83-468
Röll, W. Oswald von Wolkenstein.
H. Famira, 564:May83-150
G.F. Jones, 221(GQ):Jan83-133
A. Robertshaw, 402(MLR):Jul83-749
S.L. Wailes, 221(GQ):Mar83-301
Rolland de Renéville, J. Itinéraire du
sens.
M. Adam, 542:Jan-Mar83-65
J. Catesson, 98:May83-409
R. Misrah, 192(EP):Jul-Sep83-373
Rölleke, H. Der Wahre Butt.
E. Ettlinger, 203:Vol194No2-261
Rölleke, H. - see Brentano, C.
Rollin, B.E. Animal Rights and Human
Morality.
R. Elliot, 63:Dec83-454
M.A.F., 185:Jan84-360
R.J. Hall, 484(PPR):Sep83-135
Rollins, R.M. The Long Journey of Noah
Webster.*
G. Bilson, 106:Spring83-61
Rollinson, P., with P. Matsen. Classical
Theories of Allegory and Christian
Culture.*
S.A. Barney, 589:Jul83-852
A. Sheppard, 123:Vol33No1-139
G. Teskey, 627(UTQ):Winter82/83-209
Roloff, H-G. - see "Sophie Elisabeth,
Gräfin zu Braunschweig und Lüneburg:
Dichtungen"
Romaine, S. Socio-historical Linguistics.
P. Bennett, 297(JL):Sep83-484
F. Chevillet, 189(EA):Jul-Sep84-316

Roman, Z. Anton von Webern.
P. Griffiths, 415:Dec83-750
Romanos, G.D. Quine and Analytic Philos-
ophy.
T. Baldwin, 617(TLS):13Jan84-40
Romanyshyn, R.D. Psychological Life.*
G.P., 185:Oct83-170
Römer, J. Naturästhetik in der frühen
römischen Kaiserzeit.
J.C. Bramble, 123:Vol33No1-50
Römer, W.H.P. Das Sumerische Kurzepos
"Bilgameš und Akka."
S.N. Kramer, 318(JAOS):Oct-Dec82-655
Romera Castillo, J. Notas a tres obras de
Lope, Tirso y Calderón.
P.W. Evans, 86(BHS):Oct83-340
Romeralo, A.S. - see under Sánchez Romer-
alo, A.
Romeralo, A.S. and A. Valenciano - see
under Sánchez Romeralo, A. and A.
Valenciano
Romero, L. Agua Negra.*
J. Addiego, 448:Vol21No1-147
de Romilly, J. Précis de littérature
grecque.*
G.J. de Vries, 394:Vol36fasc3/4-371
Romm, S. The Unwelcome Intruder.
L. Goldberger, 441:10Jun84-25
Rommetveit, R. and R.M. Blakar, eds.
Studies of Language, Thought and Verbal
Communication.
R. Veltman, 307:Oct82-134
Ronald, A. The New West of Edward Abbey.
J.R. Hepworth, 649(WAL):Feb84-343
J.H. Maguire, 27(AL):May83-270
D.E. Wylder, 395(MFS):Winter83-719
Ronan, R. Narratives from America.
M. Boruch, 271:Vol 13No3/4-251
Ronen, A. The Peter and Paul Altarpiece
and Friedrich Pacher.
E. Young, 39:Jan83-73
Ronen, D. The Quest for Self-Determina-
tion.
J. Agassi, 488:Mar83-126
Ronfard, J-P. La Mandragore.
S.R. Schulman, 207(FR):Apr84-739
Ronfard, J-P. Vie et mort du roi boîteux.
E. Hamblet, 207(FR):Oct83-141
R. Usmiani, 102(CanL):Winter82-157
Ronzeaud, P. L'Utopie hermaphrodite.
R. Démoris, 475:Vol 10No19-932
Rooke, L. The Birth Control King of the
Upper Volta.*
J. Kertzer, 198:Jan84-85
M. Taylor, 99:Apr83-29
Rooke, L. Death Suite.* Last One Home
Sleeps in the Yellow Bed.
J. Lennox, 102(CanL):Winter82-123
Rooke, L. The Magician in Love.
J. Wasserman, 102(CanL):Winter82-122
Rooke, L. Shakespeare's Dog.*
W.J. Keith, 198:Jan84-88
42(AR):Fall83-509
639(VQR):Autumn83-126
Rooke, L. Sing Me No Love Songs, I'll Say
You No Prayers.
A. Manguel, 441:1Apr84-20
Rooks, G., D. Scholberg and K. Scholberg.
Conversar sin parar.
N. Levy-Konesky, 238:Sep83-452
J. Shreve, 399(MLJ):Summer83-206
Rooney, A.A. Pieces of My Mind.
S.M. Halpern, 441:7Oct84-23

318

Rosenberg, A. Sociobiology and the Pre-
emption of Social Science.*
L.E. Johnson, 63:Mar83-112
V. Pratt, 518:Apr83-121
Rosenberg, B. and E. Goldstein, eds. Cre-
ators and Disturbers.
S. Pinsker, 390:May83-77
Rosenberg, B.A. The Code of the West.
R.M. Davis, 577(SHR):Summer83-292
R.C. Poulsen, 649(WAL):Feb84-359
639(VQR):Winter83-29
Rosenberg, D.M. Oaten Reeds and Trumpets.*
P.J. Klemp, 604:Winter83-9
von Rosenberg, I. Der Weg nach oben.
H.G. Klaus, 72:Band219Heft1-202
Rosenberg, J. Women's Reflections.
M. Keller, 127:Fall83-284
Rosenberg, J.D. - see Ruskin, J.
Rosenberg, J.F. One World and Our Knowl-
edge of It.*
P. Humphreys, 84:Dec83-410
Rosenberg, J.F. Thinking Clearly about
Death.
R.M.M., 185:Jan84-360
Rosenberg, M. The Masks of "Macbeth."*
S. Viswanathan, 38:Band101Heft1/2-260
Rosenberg, N. Inside the Black Box.
S.W., 185:Apr84-562
Rosenberg, P. and U. van de Sandt. Pierre
Peyron, 1744-1814.
P. Conisbee, 90:Dec83-764
Rosenberg, S.N., ed. Chanter M'Estuet.*
(Music ed by H. Tischler)
P.W. Cummins, 589:Jan83-222
A.T. Harrison, 207(FR):Oct83-104
J.H. Marshall, 402(MLR):Jan83-176
Rosenberg, S.N. and others. Harper's
Grammar of French.
J.T. Chamberlain, 207(FR):May84-923
Rosenblum, H.F. Descending Order.
J. McCulloch, 441:16Sep84-30
Rosenblum, N. A World History of Photo-
graphy.
A. Grundberg, 441:2Dec84-17
Rosenblum, R. and H.W. Janson. 19th-Cen-
tury Art. (British title: Art of the
Nineteenth Century.)
F. Haskell, 441:22Apr84-9
W. Vaughan, 617(TLS):23Mar84-316
Rosenfeld, S. Georgian Scene Painters and
Scene Painting.*
G. Barlow, 610:Summer83-165
E. Craig, 611(TN):Vol37No1-41
J. Gage, 59:Jun83-248
A.W. McDonald, 615(TJ):Mar83-135
P. van der Merwe, 90:Oct83-628
Rosenfeld, S. - see Nicoll, A.
Rosenfield, I., E. Ziff and B. Van Loon.
DNA for Beginners.
H.M. Schmeck, Jr., 441:11Mar84-18
Rosenhaft, E. Beating the Fascists?
F.L. Carsten, 617(TLS):10Feb84-147
I. Deak, 453(NYRB):31May84-37
Rosenmeyer, T.G. The Art of Aeschylus.*
D.M. MacDowell, 610:Autumn83-252
639(VQR):Winter83-18
Rosenqvist, J.O. Studien zur Syntax und
Bemerkungen zum Text der "Vita Theodori
Syceotae."
P. Pattenden, 123:Vol33No1-119
É. des Places, 555:Vol57fasc1-140
Rosenstein, J.G. Linear Orderings.
D. Myers, 316:Dec83-1207

Rosenstiel, L. Nadia Boulanger.*
R. Orr, 415:Mar83-171
Rosenstone, S.J., R.L. Behr and E.H. Laza-
rus. Third Parties in America.
H.G. Nicholas, 617(TLS):25May84-589
Rosenthal, L. Heinrich Heines Erbschafts-
streit.
R.W. Hannah, 221(GQ):Nov83-659
Rosenthal, L. The Ticket Out.
D. Stern, 441:1Jan84-20
Rosenthal, M. British Landscape Painting.
C. Ashwin, 592:Apr/May83-26
P. Conisbee, 90:Nov83-701
G. Reynolds, 39:Jan83-65
Rosenthal, M. Constable.*
M. Pointon, 324:Sep84-699
Rosenthal, M. Juan Gris.
P. de Francia, 617(TLS):27Apr84-475
Rosenthal, M.L. and S.M. Gall. The Modern
Poetic Sequence.*
T. Martin, 659(ConL):Winter84-483
42(AR):Summer83-371
Rosenthal, S.B. and P.L. Bourgeois. Prag-
matism and Phenomenology.
G.E. Myers, 484(PPR):Mar84-424
P.H. Spader, 543:Mar83-730
Rosenwein, B.H. Rhinoceros Bound.
J.H. Lynch, 589:Jul83-813
Rosenzweig, R. Eight Hours For What We
Will.
P. Renshaw, 617(TLS):15Jun84-673
Rosie, G. Hugh Miller.
J.A. Secord, 637(VS):Summer83-450
Roskell, J.S. The Impeachment of Michael
de la Pole, Earl of Suffolk, in 1386.
M. Prestwich, 617(TLS):13Apr84-408
Roskies, D.G. Against the Apocalypse.
A.A. Cohen, 441:17Jun84-28
Rösler, W. Dichter und Gruppe.
A.M. Bowie, 303(JoHS):Vol 103-183
A.M. van Erp Taalman Kip, 394:Vol136
fasc3/4-397
T. Gelzer, 490:Band14Heft3/4-321
W.J. Slater, 487:Spring83-69
Rosman, D.M. Evangelicals and Culture.
S. Gilley, 617(TLS):30Mar84-327
Rosner, F. - see Maimonides, M.
Rosow, E. Born to Lose.
B.K. Grant, 106:Spring83-107
Ross, A. - see Addison, J. and R. Steele
Ross, A. and D. Woolley - see Swift, J.
Ross, C. Richard III.
639(VQR):Summer83-81
Ross, C.L. The Composition of "The Rain-
bow" and "Women in Love."*
E. Delavenay, 189(EA):Jan-Mar84-101
J. Worthen, 447(N&Q):Jun82-263
Ross, G.M. Leibniz.
J. Cottingham, 617(TLS):21Sep84-1061
Ross, H.C. The Art of Bedouin Jewellery.
R.L. Shep, 614:Spring84-19
Ross, H.L., ed. Law and Deviance.
D.O., 185:Oct83-183
Ross, I.C. - see Sterne, L.
Ross, I.S. William Dunbar.*
P. Bawcutt, 571(ScLJ):Autumn83-4
A. Hudson, 541(RES):Nov83-485
A.A. MacDonald, 179(ES):Apr83-179
W. Scheps, 588(SSL):Vol 18-297
Ross, J. Dead Eye.
N. Callendar, 441:2Dec84-62
Ross, J., ed. The Vogue Bedside Book.
N. Berry, 617(TLS):28Dec84-1505

Ross, M., ed. The Aesthetic Imperative.
G. McFee, 89(BJA):Winter83-86
Ross, S.D. Perspective in Whitehead's Metaphysics.
D. Gustafson, 619:Fall83-416
Ross, S.D. Philosophical Mysteries.*
M.S.G., 543:Sep82-188
Ross, S.D. A Theory of Art.*
T.R. Martland, 289:Spring83-118
F. Sparshott, 290(JAAC):Spring84-328
Ross, S.R. and T.F. McGann, eds. Buenos Aires.
C.E. Solberg, 263(RIB):Vol33No2-267
Ross, W. Der ängstliche Adler.
H. Reiss, 402(MLR):Jan83-240
Rossbach, J. Ambivalent Conspirators.
639(VQR):Autumn83-121
Rossel, S.H. A History of Scandinavian Literature 1870-1980.
P.M. Mitchell, 562(Scan):May83-96
Rosselli, F., ed. Saggi e Ricerche Ispano-americani.
J. Siracusa, 399(MLJ):Summer83-176
Rosselli, J. The Opera Industry in Italy from Cimarosa to Verdi.
R. Osborne, 617(TLS):11May84-517
Rosser, H.L. Conflict and Transition in Rural Mexico.
M.S. Arrington, Jr., 345(KRQ):Vol30No1-108
C. Tatum, 238:Sep83-444
Rosshandler, F. Passing Through Havana.
M. Simpson, 441:26Feb84-22
442(NY):27Feb84-132
Rossi, A. Serafino Aquilano e la poesia cortigiana.*
R. Russell, 276:Winter83-372
Rossi, A. The Architecture of the City.*
A Scientific Autobiography.
A.M. Vogt, 576:Mar83-86
Rossi, A. Astonish Us in the Morning.
R.L. Coe, 570(SQ):Spring83-115
Rossini. Quelques Riens pour album.
(M. Tartak, ed)
C. Cranna, 451:Fall83-169
Rössler, H. Karl Kraus und Nestroy.
F.H. Mautner, 221(GQ):Nov83-673
Rossner, J. August.*
W.H. Pritchard, 249(HudR):Winter83/84-742
D. Taylor, 364:Dec83/Jan84-143
Rosso, C. Pagine al vento.
U. Schulz-Buschhaus, 547(RF):Band95 Heft3-339
Rosso, J.G. - see under Geffriaud Rosso, J.
van Rossum-Guyon, F. and M. van Brederode, eds. Balzac et "Les Parents pauvres."*
M. Ménard, 535(RHL):Mar/Apr83-289
Rosten, L. Hooray for Yiddish!
J.D. Shulman, 390:Jun/Jul83-61
42(AR):Winter83-122
Rostow, W.W. The Barbaric Counter-Revolution.*
J. Fallows, 453(NYRB):12Apr84-8
R.J. Margolis, 441:25Mar84-21
E.J. Mishan, 617(TLS):25May84-591
de Rotelande, H. - see under Hue de Rotelande
Rotenstreich, N. Man and His Dignity.
R.M.M., 185:Jul84-727
Rotermund, E. Zwischen Exildichtung und Innerer Emigration.
G. Bauer, 406:Winter83-456

Roth, A. Parliamentary Profiles, A-D.
J. Critchley, 362:10May84-29
Roth, B.G. and C. Schulz. The New Handbook of Timesaving Tables for Weavers, Spinners and Dyers.
P. Bach, 614:Winter84-20
Roth, G. Winterreise.
P. Lewis, 565:Vol124No3-36
Roth, H. Call it Sleep.
P. Craig, 617(TLS):9Mar84-259
Roth, J. The Emperor's Tomb.
A. Fothergill, 617(TLS):20Jul84-817
Roth, J. Job.*
D. Durrant, 364:Aug/Sep83-133
Roth, J. La Marche de Radetzky.
B. Bayen, 450(NRF):Jan83-133
Roth, J. Le Poids de la grâce.
J-L. Gautier, 450(NRF):Apr83-142
Roth, L.M. McKim, Mead and White.
H.H. Reed, 441:17Jun84-9
A. Saint, 617(TLS):23Nov84-1341
Roth, M. and V. Cowie, eds. Psychiatry, Genetics and Pathography.
R. Mayou, 447(N&Q):Dec82-564
Roth, M.C. Der "Philotheus" des Laurentius von Schnüffis (1633-1702).
J. Hardin, 406:Spring83-73
Roth, M-L. Biographie et écriture.
H. Weinmann, 98:Jun-Jul83-477
Roth, P. The Anatomy Lesson.*
J. Epstein, 129:Jan84-62
M. Jones, 362:23Feb84-27
J. Mellors, 364:Mar84-105
S. Pinsker, 219(GaR):Winter83-880
S. Pinsker, 390:Dec83-54
C. Sinclair, 617(TLS):24Feb84-183
Roth, P.A. Bram Stoker.
A. Johnson, 177(ELT):Vol26No2-135
Rothenberg, G.E., B.K. Király and P.F. Sugar, eds. East Central European Society and War in the Pre-Revolutionary Eighteenth Century.*
P. Dukes, 83:Autumn83-254
Rothenberg, J. Pre-Faces and Other Writings.*
J. Gleason, 472:Fall/Winter83Spring/Summer84-265
Rothenberg, J. and D. Symposium of the Whole.
J. Gleason, 472:Fall/Winter83Spring/Summer84-265
Rothenberg, R. The Neoliberals.
R. Reeves, 441:29Jul84-12
Rothgeb, J. - see Jonas, O.
Rothman, D.J. and S.M. The Willowbrook Wars.
J.H. Jones, 441:25Nov84-32
Rothman, E.K. Hands and Hearts.
A. Jones, 441:13May84-26
Rothman, S. and S.R. Lichter. Roots of Radicalism.
P. Hollander, 176:Apr84-66
Rothman, W. Hitchcock.*
M.A. Anderegg, 385(MQR):Spring84-281
A. Brownjohn, 176:Jan84-67
Lord Rothschild. Random Variables.
N. Annan, 617(TLS):15Jun84-656
de Rothschild, G. Contre bonne fortune ... *
R. Kaplan, 129:Jan84-72
Rothschild, M. Dear Lord Rothschild.
S. Schama, 453(NYRB):20Dec84-59

321

Rothstein, E. Restoration and Eighteenth-Century Poetry, 1660-1780.*
P-G. Boucé, 189(EA):Apr-Jun84-191
R. Eversole, 173(ECS):Winter83/84-228
Rotili, M. Arte bizantina in Calabria e in Basilicata.
A.W. Epstein, 54:Sep83-503
Rotroff, S.I. Hellenistic Pottery, Athenian and Imported Moldmade Bowls.
R.L. Pounder, 124:Mar-Apr84-254
Rotrou, J. Les Sosies.* (D. Charron, ed)
H.T. Barnwell, 208(FS):Jul83-335
Rott, J. - see Bucer, M.
Rötzer, H.G. and H. Walz, eds. Europäische Lehrdichtung.
I. Marquardt, 196:Band24Heft3/4-323
W. Ross, 52:Band18Heft3-321
Roubaud, J. Dors.*
M. Guiney, 207(FR):Dec83-274
Rouberol, J. L'Esprit du Sud dans l'oeuvre de Faulkner.
J. Templeton, 189(EA):Jul-Sep84-356
Roudinesco, É. La Bataille de Cent Ans. (Vol 1)
J. Forrester, 208(FS):Oct83-494
J. le Hardi, 450(NRF):Jun83-134
G.L., 185:Oct83-170
Roueché, B. Special Places.*
J. Kaufmann, 31(ASch):Spring83-274
Rough, J.Z. Australian Locker Hooking.
P. Bach, 614:Summer84-11
Rouland, N. Rome démocratie impossible?
J-C. Richard, 555:Vol57fasc1-179
Rountree, B. Bonaventure d'Argonne.*
P.J. Bayley, 208(FS):Oct83-455
P. Wolfe, 475:Vol 10No19-935
Rousseau, A.M. L'Angleterre et Voltaire.
E.J.H. Greene, 107(CRCL):Mar83-99
Rousseau, F. La croissance solidaire des droits de l'homme.
M. Adam, 542:Jul-Sep83-341
Rousseau, G. L'Image des Etats-Unis dans la littérature québécoise (1775-1930).*
C.F. Coates, 207(FR):Oct83-98
Rousseau, G.S. Tobias Smollett.*
P-G. Boucé, 189(EA):Jul-Sep84-330
Rousseau, G.S. - see Hill, J.
Rousseau, G.S. and R. Porter, eds. The Ferment of Knowledge.*
P-G. Boucé, 189(EA):Jan-Mar83-77
P. Buck, 84:Mar83-88
Rousseau, J-J. Correspondance complète de Jean-Jacques Rousseau.* (Vols 33-38) (R.A. Leigh, ed)
P. Lefebvre, 535(RHL):Jul/Aug83-639
Rousseau, J-J. Correspondance complète de Jean-Jacques Rousseau.* (Vol 39) (R.A. Leigh, ed)
L. Gasbarrone, 207(FR):May84-878
Rousseau, J-J. Correspondance complète de Jean-Jacques Rousseau.* (Vol 40) (R.A. Leigh, ed)
P. France, 402(MLR):Oct83-923
Rousseau, J-J. The Indispensable Rousseau.* (J.H. Mason, ed)
F. Baker, 402(MLR):Oct83-924
Rousseau-Dujardin, J. Couché par écrit.
G-F. Duportail, 450(NRF):Jul/Aug83-238
Roussel, H. and F. Suard, eds. Alain de Lille, Gautier de Châtillon, Jakemart Gielée et leur temps.*
B.N. Sargent-Baur, 545(RPh):Feb83-508

Rousset, J. Leurs yeux se rencontrèrent.*
K. Hoffman, 400(MLN):May83-787
V. Mylne, 535(RHL):Mar/Apr83-314
Roustang, F. Psychoanalysis Never Lets Go.
P. Roazen, 99:May83-32
Roustang, G. Le travail autrement.
P. Livet, 98:Apr83-341
Routley, R. Exploring Meinong's Jungle and Beyond.*
T. Parsons, 311(JP):Mar83-173
W.J. Rapaport, 484(PPR):Jun84-539
Roux, L. - see de Sorbière, S.
Rovere, R. Final Reports.
D.P. Moynihan, 442(NY):17Sep84-134
R.L. Strout, 441:19Feb84-20
Rovner, A. and others, eds. Gnosis Anthology of Contemporary American and Russian Literature and Art. (Vol 2)
G. Janeček, 574(SEEJ):Summer83-273
Rowan, A.N. Of Mice, Models and Men.
S. Clark, 617(TLS):1Jun84-618
Rowan, S., ed and trans. Germans for a Free Missouri.
J.M. Elukin, 441:15Apr84-23
Rowbotham, S. Im Dunkel der Geschichte.
I. Dölling, 654(WB):8/1983-1501
Rowe, A. A Century of Change in Guatemalen Textiles.
42(AR):Winter83-124
Rowe, A.P. Costumes and Featherwork of the Lords of Chimor.
B. Femenias, 614:Summer84-14
Rowe, C. The Baudelairean Cinema.
M. Keller, 127:Fall83-284
Rowe, J.C. Through the Custom-House.
K. Dauber, 445(NCF):Sep83-243
C. Dolan, 478:Oct83-273
E. Heyne, 432(NEQ):Sep83-474
G.L. Stonum, 284:Winter83-1349
M. Warner, 400(MLN):Dec83-1349
Rowell, G. Theatre in the Age of Irving.
R.A. Cave, 611(TN):Vol37No3-137
C.M. Mazer, 615(TJ):Mar83-136
Rowell, G. The Vision Glorious.
B. Martin, 617(TLS):24Feb84-181
Rowell, G. - see Gilbert, W.S.
Rowell, G. and A. Jackson. The Repertory Movement.
I. Wardle, 617(TLS):7Dec84-1418
Rowell, L. Thinking About Music.
P. Alperson, 290(JAAC):Summer84-452
Rowell, M. and A.Z. Rudenstine. Art of the Avant-Garde in Russia.
G. Janeček, 574(SEEJ):Spring83-124
Rowlands, J. Hercules Segers.
C. White, 39:Feb83-146
Rowley, G. Israel into Palestine.
T.R. Fyvel, 176:Apr84-63
Roy, C. Littérature orale en Gaspésie.
E.J. Talbot, 207(FR):Feb84-429
G. Thomas, 102(CanL):Winter82-161
Roy, G.R. - see "Studies in Scottish Literature"
Roy, J-L. Terre féconde.
D.F. Rogers, 102(CanL):Summer83-159
Roy, L., L. Saia and M. Rivard. Bachelor.*
R. Usmiani, 102(CanL):Winter82-157
Roy, M. Traces.
A.L. Amprimoz, 102(CanL):Autumn83-110
M. Le Clézio, 207(FR):Oct83-142
Roy, S.C. The Birhors.
L.P. Elwell-Sutton, 203:Vol94No1-129

"Royal Commission on Historical Monuments:
An Inventory of Historical Monuments in
the County of Dorset." (Vol 5)
   J. Lees-Milne, 39:Feb83-144
Royce, K. The Crypto Man.
   M. Laski, 362:25Oct84-29
Royce, K. The Stalin Account.
   M. Laski, 362:9Feb84-26
Royle, T. James and Jim.
   A. Ross, 364:Feb84-106
Royle, T. The Macmillan Companion to
Scottish Literature.*
   J.E. Sait, 571(ScLJ):Winter83-76
Royle, T. Precipitous City.
   M. Ash, 571(ScLJ):Autumn83-38
Royot, D. L'humour américain.*
   D.E.E. Sloane, 27(AL):May83-259
Royster, C. Light-Horse Harry Lee and the
Legacy of the American Revolution.
   R. Dawidoff, 656(WMQ):Jan83-154
Roždestvenskij, J.V. Einführung in die
allgemeine Philologie.
   C. Pankow, 682(ZPSK):Band36Heft5-617
Rozenberg, P. Le romantisme anglais.
   H. Viebrock, 72:Band219Heft1-188
Rozewicz, T. Conversations with the
Prince.
   D. Gioia, 461:Fall/Winter83/84-99
   J.R. Krzyżanowski, 574(SEEJ):Winter83-
   498
Rozewicz, T. Mariage Blanc [and] The
Hunger Artist Departs.
   D. Devlin, 157:Winter83-38
Rozman, G., ed. The Modernization of
China.
   S. Mann, 293(JASt):Nov82-146
Rozman, G. Population and Marketing Set-
tlements in Ch'ing China.
   R.K. Schoppa, 293(JASt):Aug83-938
Rózsa, M. Double Life.*
   L. Salter, 415:Jun83-362
Ruark, G. Keeping Company.
   M. Kinzie, 29:Mar/Apr84-38
Rubens, B. Brothers.*
   R. Greenfield, 441:25Mar84-25
Rubenstein, R.L. The Age of Triage.*
   R. Farley, 385(MQR):Summer84-452
Rubin, D.L. The Knot of Artifice.*
   F. Hallyn, 535(RHL):Sep/Dec83-917
   S. Tiefenbrun, 210(FrF):May83-182
   639(VQR):Spring83-43
Rubin, J. and I. Thompson. How to Be a
More Successful Language Learner.
   M-A. Reiss, 399(MLJ):Autumn83-278
   S. Wood, 351(LL):Dec83-555
Rubin, J.H. Realism and Social Vision in
Courbet and Proudhon.*
   A. Rifkin, 59:Sep83-368
Rubin, L.D., Jr. A Gallery of Southern-
ers.*
   J.E. Bassett, 392:Fall83-596
   W.J. Stuckey, 395(MFS):Summer83-334
   639(VQR):Summer83-89
Rubin, L.D., Jr. Surfaces of a Diamond.*
   G.W. Jarecke, 577(SHR):Summer83-285
Rubinger, R. Private Academies of
Tokugawa Japan.
   Kaji Nobuyuki, 285(JapQ):Oct-Dec83-441
   R.M. Spaulding, 407(MN):Winter83-454
Rubino, C.A. and C.W. Shelmerdine, eds.
Approaches to Homer.
   F.R. Bliss, 124:Mar-Apr84-263

Rubinstein, A. The Zionist Dream Revis-
ited.
   A. Dowty, 617(TLS):27Jul84-836
   G. Gottlieb, 441:15Jul84-23
Rubinstein, W.D. Men of Property.
   D.H. Aldcroft, 637(VS):Spring83-362
Rubio, F. and J.L. Falcó, eds. Poesía
española contemporánea (1939-1980).
   D. Barnette, 238:Dec83-638
Ruble, B.A. Soviet Trade Unions.*
   M. Matthews, 575(SEER):Apr83-305
Ruby, J., ed. A Crack in the Mirror.
   C.R. Farrer, 650(WF):Jul83-228
Ruch, E.A. and K.C. Anyanwu, eds. African
Philosophy.*
   I. Onyewuenyi, 258:Jun83-209
Rucker, R. The Fourth Dimension.
   T. Ferris, 441:2Dec84-76
Rückert, R. Die Glassammlung des Bayer-
ischen Nationalmuseums München.
   T.H. Clarke, 39:Mar83-263
Dr. Rudd. A Treatise on Angel Magic. (A.
McLean, ed)
   J. Godwin, 111:Spring84-6
Rudd, N. - see Johnson, S.
Rude, F. Stendhal et la pensée sociale de
son temps. (new ed) La révolte des
canuts 1831-1834.
   V.D.L., 605(SC):15Jul84-386
von Rüden, M. "Wlanc" und Derivate im
Alt- und Mittelenglischen.
   K. Bitterling, 72:Band220Heft1-148
Rudenstine, A.Z., ed. The George Costakis
Collection.
   G. Janeček, 574(SEEJ):Spring83-124
Rudman, M. Robert Lowell.
   D.W. Hartnett, 617(TLS):9Nov84-1290
Rudolf, G. The Theatrical Notation of
Roman and Pre-Shakespearean Comedy.
   L.S. Champion, 179(ES):Jun83-276
Rudolf, M. The Grammar of Conducting.
(2nd ed)
   N. Goodwin, 415:Aug83-485
Rudolph, E.P. William Law.
   A.J. Sambrook, 677(YES):Vol 13-324
Rudolph, K. Gnosis.
   P. Perkins, 469:Vol9No3-118
Rudrum, A. - see Vaughan, H.
Rudrum, A. - see Vaughan, T.
Rudy, S. - see Jakobson, R.
Rudzka, B. and Z. Goczołowa. Wśród
Polaków (Among Poles).
   A. Gorski, 497(PolR):Vol28No1-98
Ruef, H. Augustin über Semiotik und
Sprache.*
   J. Pépin, 555:Vol157fasc2-349
Ruel, F. Les Trois Grâces.
   E.R. Hopkins, 207(FR):Feb84-416
   J. Moss, 102(CanL):Autumn83-87
   R. Usmiani, 102(CanL):Autumn83-85
Ruer, J. and others. Le Roman en Grande-
Bretagne depuis 1945.
   J. Fletcher, 189(EA):Apr-Sep83-331
Ruff, H. Making Money.
   K.W. Arenson, 441:26Aug84-18
Ruff, L.K. Edward Sheldon.
   M.K. Fielder, 615(TJ):May83-276
   J.S. O'Connor, 397(MD):Jun83-238
Ruffet, J. - see von Kleist, H.
Ruffinelli, J. Literatura e ideología.
   T. Murad, 263(RIB):Vol33No4-593

Ruffner, H. Judith Bensaddi and Seclusa-
val. (J.M. Pemberton, ed)
A. Cheuse, 441:20May84-30
Ruggiero, G. Violence in Early Renais-
sance Venice.*
D.O. Hughes, 589:Jan83-223
Ruggiers, P.G., ed. Versions of Medieval
Comedy.
J.L. Grigsby, 545(RPh):May83-584
Ruggiers, P.G. - see Chaucer, G.
Rugoff, M. The Beechers.*
D.S. Miller, 569(SR):Spring83-xxxii
Ruh, K. Höfische Epik des deutschen Mit-
telalters.* (Pt 2)
R.M. Kully, 564:Feb83-62
P.W. Tax, 589:Jan83-226
Ruh, K. and others, eds. Die deutsche Lit-
eratur des Mittelalters: Verfasserlexi-
kon. (Vol 2) (2nd ed)
M. Huby, 680(ZDP):Band102Heft1-121
Ruh, K. and others, eds. Die deutsche
Literatur des Mittelalters: Verfasser-
lexikon. (Vol 3) (2nd ed)
E.A. Philippson, 301(JEGP):Apr83-282
Ruhlen, M. A Guide to the Languages of
the World.
L. Bauer, 603:Vol7No2-328
Rühm, G. - see Behrens, F.R.
Ruiz, J. Juan Ruiz, the Archpriest of
Hita, "The Book of True Love." (A.N.
Zahareas, ed; S.R. Daly, trans)
S. Fleischman, 545(RPh):Nov82-280
Ruiz Barrionuevo, C. El "Paradiso" de
Lezama Lima.
B. Torres Caballero, 240(HR):Autumn83-
482
Rukeyser, L. What's Ahead for the Economy.
R.J. Margolis, 441:4Mar84-23
Ruland, M. A Lexicon of Alchemy.
111:Fall84-8
Rule, J. The Experience of Labour in
Eighteenth-Century English Industry.
L. Stone, 453(NYRB):29Mar84-42
Rullière, R. Abrégé d'histoire de la
médecine.
P-G. Boucé, 189(EA):Jan-Mar84-80
Rumens, C. Scenes from the Gingerbread
House.*
M. O'Neill, 493:Mar83-57
Rumens, C. Star Whisper.*
M. O'Neill, 493:Sep83-72
Rumeu de Armas, A. Origen y fundación del
Museo del Prado.
D. Angulo Íñiguez, 48:Oct-Dec80-507
Rumilly, R. L'Acadie française (1497-
1713).
G.R. Montbertrand, 207(FR):Oct83-126
Runcie, R. Windows onto God.
D. Nineham, 617(TLS):24Feb84-198
Runciman, W.G. A Treatise on Social
Theory.* (Vol 1)
J. Lieberson, 453(NYRB):8Nov84-45
Rundle, B. Grammar in Philosophy.*
T. Burge, 482(PhR):Oct83-639
D. Holdcroft, 483:Oct83-554
Runnalls, G.A., ed. La Passion d'Auvergne.
A. Hindley, 402(MLR):Jul83-707
R.A. Lodge, 553(RLiR):Jul-Dec83-503
L.R. Muir, 382(MAE):1983/2-325
Runnalls, G.A. - see "Le Mystère de sainte
Venice"

Running, T. Borges's Ultraist Movement
and its Poets.
D.T. Jaén, 238:May83-302
Runte, R. - see "Studies in Eighteenth-
Century Culture"
Runyon, R. Fowles/Irving/Barthes.*
295(JML):Nov83-374
Ruoff, A. Häufigkeitswörterbuch gesproche-
ner Sprache, gesondert nach Wortarten,
alphabetisch, rückläufig alphabetisch
und nach Häufigkeit geordnet.
M. Faust, 685(ZDL):2/1983-242
R. Hildebrandt, 260(IF):Band88-357
Rupke, N.A. The Great Chain of History.
J.B. Morrell, 617(TLS):3Feb84-106
Rupp, H. and C.L. Lang - see "Deutsches
Literatur-Lexikon"
Ruppersburg, H.M. Voice and Eye in Faulk-
ner's Fiction.*
J.M. Grimwood, 27(AL):Dec83-661
M. Oriard, 594:Winter83-394
Ruse, M. Is Science Sexist? And Other
Problems in the Biological Sciences.
A. Minas, 154:Mar83-183
Ruse, M.E. Sociobiology.*
T.A. Goudge, 488:Mar83-90
Rush, C. Peace Comes Dropping Slow.
J.A.S. Miller, 571(ScLJ):Winter83-69
"William Rush, American Sculptor."
J.M. Neil, 656(WMQ):Oct83-655
Rushdie, S. Midnight's Children.*
J.T. Hospital, 529(QQ):Spring83-239
Rushdie, S. Shame.*
T. Hyman, 364:Oct83-93
J. Lasdun, 176:Jan84-72
442(NY):9Jan84-109
Rusher, W.A. The Rise of the Right.
L.H. Lapham, 441:15Jul84-9
Rushton, J. W.A. Mozart: "Don Giovanni."
S. Sadie, 415:Oct83-616
Rushton, J. The Musical Language of
Berlioz.
H. Macdonald, 617(TLS):24Feb84-187
C. Rosen, 453(NYRB):26Apr84-40
Rushton, W. W.G. Grace's Last Case or The
War of the Worlds — Part Two.
S. Rae, 617(TLS):24Aug84-941
Rusich, L.G. Un carbonaro molisano nei
due mondi.
P.F. Angiolillo, 276:Winter83-378
Ruskin, J. The Genius of John Ruskin.
(J.D. Rosenberg, ed)
D. Birch, 447(N&Q):Jun82-255
Ruskin, J. Letters from the Continent
1858.* (J. Hayman, ed)
W. Whitla, 627(UTQ):Summer83-427
Russ, C.V.J. Studies in Historical German
Phonology.
H. Penzl, 350:Sep84-618
Russell, B. Building Systems, Industrial-
ization and Architecture.
A.H. Balfour, 46:Oct83-84
Russell, B. The Collected Papers of Ber-
trand Russell. (Vol 1) (K. Blackwell
and others, eds)
S. Hook, 441:29Jan84-7
P.F. Strawson, 617(TLS):3Feb84-104
J. Watling, 362:26Jan84-22
Russell, B. Theory of Knowledge. (E.R.
Eames and K. Blackwell, eds)
A.J. Ayers, 617(TLS):7Dec84-1404

324

Russell, C., ed. The Avant-Garde Today.*
  M. Perloff, 402(MLR):Jul83-663
  N. Zurbrugg, 678(YCGL):No31-162
Russell, C. Parliaments and English Politics 1621-1629.
  S.P. Salt, 161(DUJ):Jun83-113
Russell, D.A. Criticism in Antiquity.*
  M. McCall, 487:Winter83-364
Russell, D.A. Greek Declamation.
  E. Rawson, 617(TLS):25May84-597
Russell, D.W. Anne Hébert.
  P.G. Lewis, 207(FR):Apr84-704
Russell, F., ed. A Century of Chair Design.
  K.L. Ames, 576:May83-194
Russell, J. Communicative Competence in a Minority Group.
  B. Wald, 355(LSoc):Sep83-398
Russell, J. Paris.
  P. Lennon, 362:19Jan84-24
Russell, M. Visions of the Sea.
  J. Nash, 617(TLS):19Oct84-1182
Russell, R. Valentin Kataev.*
  G.A. Hosking, 575(SEER):Jul83-438
Russell, S.A. Semiotics and Lighting.
  M. Keller, 127:Fal183-284
Russett, B. The Prisoners of Insecurity.
  D.P.L., 185:Jul84-740
Russo, L.P., ed. Estetica e Psicologia.
  R. Arnheim, 290(JAAC):Spring84-341
Rusten, J.S. Dionysius Scytobrachion.
  M. Campbell, 123:Vol33No2-314
Rustin, J. Le Vice à la Mode.*
  J.A. Fleming, 627(UTQ):Spring83-303
  V. Mylne, 208(FS):Jul83-343
Ruthrof, H. The Reader's Construction of Narrative.*
  G. Bourcier, 189(EA):Jan-Mar84-84
  A. Freadman, 67:Nov83-295
Ruthven, K.K. Critical Assumptions.
  J. Rutherford, 447(N&Q):Feb82-95
Ruthven, M. Islam in the World.
  M. Hinds, 617(TLS):7Sep84-983
Rutsala, V. Walking Home from the Icehouse.*
  B. Tremblay, 649(WAL):May83-89
Rutter, N.K. Campanian Coinages 475-380 B.C.
  M.H. Crawford, 123:Vol33No1-107
Ruttkowski, W.V., ed. Nomenclator litterarius.*
  F. Nies, 72:Band219Heft1-154
  J. Voisine, 549(RLC):Apr-Jun83-217
Ruud, C.A. Fighting Words.*
  A. Gleason, 550(RusR):Apr83-229
  D. Senese, 104(CASS):Summer83-280
Ryan, A. Property and Political Theory.
  W. Rodgers, 362:27Sep84-29
Ryan, A.A., Jr. Quiet Neighbors.
  R. Blumenthal, 441:11Nov84-31
Ryan, E.B. and H. Giles, eds. Attitudes Towards Language Variation.
  S. Gal, 350:Sep84-630
Ryan, M. In Winter.*
  W. Zander, 363(LitR):Winter84-272
Ryan, M. Marxism and Deconstruction.*
  W.S., 185:Oct83-161
Ryan, M.A. Conjugação e Uso Dos Verbos em Português.
  R. Moody, 238:May83-314
Ryan, N. A Hitch or Two in Afghanistan.*
  D. Thomas, 362:12Jan84-22

Ryan, T.G. Stage Left.*
  S. Grace, 102(CanL):Autumn83-100
Rybakow, A. Heavy Sand.* (German title: Schwerer Sand.)
  P. Kirchner, 654(WB):8/1983-1468
Rydén, B. and V. Bergström, eds. Sweden.
  R.F. Tomasson, 563(SS):Winter83-98
Rydén, M. Shakespearean Plant Names.
  M. Seidel, 72:Band220Heft1-162
  H-J. Weckermann, 570(SQ):Winter83-509
Ryder, M.L. Sheep and Man.
  J. Clutton-Brock, 617(TLS):20Jan84-69
  A. Manning, 362:1Mar84-27
du Ryer, P. Les Vendanges de Suresne.*
  (L. Zilli, ed)
  M.R. Margitić, 475:Vol 10No18-424
Rykwert, J. The First Moderns.*
  D. Wiebenson, 173(ECS):Fal183-61
Ryōkan. The Zen Poems of Ryōkan.* (N. Yuasa, trans)
  S. Arntzen, 293(JASt):Nov82-175
Rywkin, M. Moscow's Muslim Challenge.
  A.S. Donnelly, 104(CASS):Winter83-569
Rzhevski, N. Russian Literature and Ideology.
  P.R. Hart, 395(MFS):Winter83-801

Saagpakk, P.F., comp. Eesti-inglise sõnaraamat.
  I. Lehiste, 350:Jun84-459
Saalman, H. Filippo Brunelleschi: The Cupola of Santa Maria del Fiore.*
  N. Adams, 54:Sep83-513
  M. Trachtenberg, 576:Oct83-292
Saarinen, E., ed. Conceptual Issues in Ecology.
  O.J.F., 185:Jan84-368
Saavedra, M.D. - see under de Cervantes Saavedra, M.
Saba, U. Il Canzoniere. Trieste et autres poèmes. (G. Haldas, ed and trans) Trieste et un poète. (O. Kaan, ed and trans) Comme un vieillard qui rêve. (G. Macé, ed and trans) Prose.
  Y. Hersant, 98:Aug-Sep83-645
Saba, U. Coi miei occhi. (C. Milanini, ed) Il Canzoniere 1921. (G. Castellani, ed)
  E. Favretti, 228(GSLI):Vol 160fasc509-122
Sabais, H.W. The People and the Stones.
  J. Adler, 617(TLS):28Sep84-1094
Sabar, Y., ed and trans. The Folk Literature of the Kurdistani Jews.
  H. Jason, 196:Band24Heft3/4-324
Sabari, S. Mouvements populaires à Bagdad à l'époque "Abbasside," IXe-XIe siècles.
  R.W. Bulliet, 589:Jul83-815
Sabarsky, S. Egon Schiele.
  R. Craft, 453(NYRB):20Dec84-50
Sábato, J.A. and M. Mackenzie. La producción de tecnología autónoma y transnacional.
  C. Fighetti, 263(RIB):Vol33No4-594
Sabato, L. The Democratic Party Primary in Virginia.
  H.M. Waller, 106:Spring83-79
Sabban, A. Gälisch-Englischer Sprachkontakt.
  G. Bourcier, 189(EA):Oct-Dec84-455
Sabbatini Tumolesi, P. Gladiatorum paria.
  R. Ling, 313:Vol73-208

Sabia, D.R., Jr. and J.T. Wallulis, eds.
Changing Social Science.
J.S., 185:Jul84-736
Sabol, A.J., ed. Four Hundred Songs and
Dances from the Stuart Masque.
J. Stevens, 131(CL):Winter83-76
Sabom, M.B. Recollections of Death.
D.N. Walton, 529(QQ):Spring83-248
Sabourin, M. Chansons.
D.F. Rogers, 102(CanL):Summer83-159
Sabourin, P. Quand il pleut sur ma ville.
A.L. Amprimoz, 102(CanL):Summer83-126
Sabra, A.I. Theories of Light from
Descartes to Newton.
M. Bradie, 568(SCN):Spring/Summer83-17
Sachs, B. and B. Ife, eds and trans.
Anthology of Early Keyboard Methods.
H. Schott, 415:May83-301
Sachs, B.T. The Rainbow Box.
J. Domini, 441:15Apr84-22
Sachs, H. Virtuoso.*
C. Ehrlich, 415:Jun83-359
T. Hathaway, 529(QQ):Spring83-172
Sachs, K-J. Mensura fistularum.* (Vols
1 and 2)
W.T. Atcherson, 589:Jan83-231
Sachs, V. The Game of Creation.
R.A. Day, 189(EA):Jul-Sep84-353
T. Philbrick, 27(AL):Mar83-98
Sackett, T.A. Galdós y las máscaras.
L.H. Klibbe, 238:Dec83-636
Sacks, E. Shakespeare's Images of Preg-
nancy.*
M. Crampton-Smith, 447(N&Q):Apr82-167
J. La Belle, 570(SQ):Summer83-254
Sacks, K. Polybius on the Writing of
History.
J.M. Moore, 123:Vol33No2-190
Sacks, O. A Leg to Stand On.
J. Bruner, 453(NYRB):27Sep84-39
D.X. Freeman, 441:11Nov84-11
G. Strawson, 617(TLS):22Jun84-686
Sacks, S., ed. On Metaphor.*
J. Penelope, 599:Winter83-77
Sackville-West, V. The Letters of Vita
Sackville-West to Virginia Woolf. (L.
De Salvo and M.A. Leaska, eds)
H. Lee, 617(TLS):21Dec84-1480
T. Mallon, 441:16Dec84-34
Saco Alarcón, C. - see de Ockham, N.
no Sadaie, F. - see under Fujiwara no
Sadaie
el-Sadat, A. Those I Have Known.
W.E. Farrell, 441:30Sep84-29
Saddlemyer, A., ed. Theatre Business.
C. Markgraf, 177(ELT):Vol26No4-324
Saddlemyer, A. - see Synge, J.M.
Saddlemyer, A. - see Yeats, W.B., Lady
Gregory and J.M. Synge
Saddler, B. and A. Carlson, eds. Environ-
mental Aesthetics.
D.W. Crawford, 290(JAAC):Spring84-335
"Sade, Écrire la crise."
G.P. Bennington, 208(FS):Oct83-466
Sadie, J.A. The Bass Viol in French
Baroque Chamber Music.
L. Sawkins, 415:Sep83-550
Sadie, S. Mozart.*
L. Salter, 415:May83-298

Sadie, S., ed. The New Grove Dictionary
of Music and Musicians.* (Vols 1-20)
L. Botstein, 513:Fall-Winter81/Spring-
Summer82-568
J. Dyer, 589:Apr83-528
Sadji, U., ed. Cadomostos Beschreibung
von Westafrika.
E.J. Morrall, 402(MLR):Apr83-488
Sadler, L.V. John Bunyan.*
M. Heinemann, 402(MLR):Jul83-680
Sadoff, D.F. Monsters of Affection.*
P. Bellis, 400(MLN):Dec83-1332
J. Kucich, 445(NCF):Dec83-347
Sadoff, I. A Northern Calendar.
M. McGovern, 114(ChiR):Summer83-130
Sadoff, I. Uncoupling.
639(VQR):Spring83-56
Saeed, J.I. Central Somali.
D. Biber, 350:Dec84-993
Safdie, M. Form and Purpose.
B. Perkins, 45:Jan83-77
Saffrey, H.D. and L.G. Westerink - see
Proclus
Safir, M. A Woman of Letters.
M. Buck, 441:9Sep84-30
Safire, W. On Language. What's the Good
Word?
J. Algeo, 35(AS):Summer83-182
Sagan, F. Avec mon meilleur souvenir.
J. Weightman, 617(TLS):18May84-547
Sagan, F. Incidental Music.
F. Weldon, 441:11Mar84-12
442(NY):9Apr84-143
Sagan, F. Salad Days.
K. Olson, 441:9Sep84-30
Sagan, F. The Still Storm.
D. Coward, 617(TLS):6Jul84-761
Sagar, K. D.H. Lawrence: A Calendar of
his Works.*
J. Newman, 161(DUJ):Dec82-83
Sagar, K., ed. A D.H. Lawrence Handbook.*
E.D., 189(EA):Jul-Sep84-366
D.G., 148:Autumn83-94
D.R. Schwarz, 395(MFS):Summer83-288
295(JML):Nov83-521
Sagar, K. The Reef.
J. Saunders, 565:Vol124No4-71
Sagarin, E. Raskolnikov and Others.
P. Wolfe, 395(MFS):Autumn83-389
Sage, L. Doris Lessing.
C. Sprague, 659(ConL):Winter84-488
Y. Tosser, 189(EA):Oct-Dec84-483
Sage, V. Dividing Lines.
P. Binding, 362:2Aug84-27
P. Kemp, 617(TLS):20Jul84-817
Sagovsky, N. Between Two Worlds.
S. Prickett, 617(TLS):24Feb84-181
Saham, J. British Investment in Malaysia,
1963-1971.
T.R. Leinbach, 293(JASt):May83-726
Sahi, J. The Child and the Serpent.*
E.A. Singer, 292(JAF):Jan-Mar83-78
Sahni, C.L. Forster's "A Passage to
India."
R.J. Voorhees, 395(MFS):Summer83-271
Saich, T. China.
B-J. Ahn, 293(JASt):May83-636
Said, E.W. Covering Islam.*
R. Berg, 615(TJ):Oct82-417
Said, E.W. The Question of Palestine.*
B. Robbins, 153:Fall83-69

Said, E.W. The World, the Text, and the Critic.*
  B. Bergonzi, 176:Jul/Aug84-49
  I. Ehrenpreis, 453(NYRB):19Jan84-37
  L. Hutcheon, 153:Winter83-33
  D. Lodge, 617(TLS):4May84-487
  B. Robbins, 153:Fall83-69
Said, H.M., ed. New Researches in Biology and Genetics.
  K. Vaidyanath and Y.R. Ahuja, 273(IC):Jul83-249
Sailey, J. The Master Who Embraces Simplicity.
  P.W. Kroll, 116:Jan82-139
Sainsbury, R.M. Russell.*
  W.M.B., 543:Sep82-190
Saint, A. The Image of the Architect.*
  H. Lipstadt, 505:Oct83-122
Saint, A. and others. A History of the Royal Opera House Covent Garden (1732-1982).
  R.D. Hume, 415:May83-303
de Saint-Aubin, C.G. The Art of the Embroiderer.*
  S.M. Newton, 617(TLS):6Jan84-23
St. Clair, L.L. and A.B. Govenar. Stoney Knows How.
  S.K.D. Stahl, 292(JAF):Oct-Dec83-496
Saint-Denis, M. Training for the Theatre.
  J. Spurling, 176:Jan84-52
de Saint-Exupéry, A. Écrits de guerre (1939-1944), [avec la] Lettre à un otage.*
  G. Sartoris, 450(NRF):Mar83-113
St. John-Stevas, N. The Two Cities.
  H. Young, 617(TLS):13Apr84-394
M. de Saint Lambert. Principles of the Harpsichord. (R. Harris-Warrick, ed)
  R. Craft, 453(NYRB):20Dec84-49
  R. Donington, 617(TLS):13Jul84-773
de Saint-Léger, Y. - see under Ysambert de Saint-Léger
St.-Onge, S.S., D.W. King and R.R. St.-Onge. Interaction.
  W. Wrage, 207(FR):May84-928
Abbé de Saint-Pierre. Projet pour rendre la paix perpétuelle en Europe.* (S. Goyard-Fabre, ed)
  E.M. Horsman, 535(RHL):Jul/Aug83-635
  A. Reix, 542:Jan-Mar83-130
St. Pierre, P. Smith and Other Events.
  P-L. Adams, 61:May84-122
  R. Smith, 441:22Jul84-20
Sainte-Beauve, C.A. Livre d'amour. (A.M. Scaiola, ed)
  A. Bonnerot, 535(RHL):Jul/Aug83-647
de Ste. Croix, G.E.M. The Class Struggle in the Ancient Greek World.*
  J.A. Crook, 123:Vol33No1-71
  F.W. Walbank, 303(JoHS):Vol 103-199
  É. Will, 555:Vol157fasc1-111
Sakala, C. Women of South Asia.
  S. Vatuk, 293(JASt):Aug83-999
Sakurai, A. Salmon.
  P-L. Adams, 61:Jun84-125
Sala, M. and others. El léxico indígena del español americano.*
  G. Carrillo-Herrera, 72:Band219Heft2-457
Salaff, J.W. Working Daughters of Hong Kong.
  M.K. Chan, 293(JASt):May83-589
Salanitro, G. - see Hosidius Geta

Salaquarda, J., ed. Nietzsche.*
  S. Antosik, 222(GR):Fall83-159
de la Sale, A. - see under Antoine de la Sale
Saleeby, A. L'Heure bleue.
  E. Sellin, 207(FR):Feb84-417
Salem, L. Die Frau in den Liedern des "Hohen Minnesangs."
  O. Ehrismann, 680(ZDP):Band102Heft1-135
Salgādo, G. English Drama.*
  G. Bas, 189(EA):Apr-Sep83-312
  A.R. Botica, 447(N&Q):Oct82-433
Salinas, L.O. Darkness Under the Trees.
  J. Addiego, 448:Vol21No1-147
Salinero, F.G. - see under García Salinero, F.
Salinger, P. and L. Gross. The Dossier.
  D. Evanier, 441:19Aug84-18
Salisbury, H.E., ed. Vietnam Reconsidered.
  R.H. Ullman, 441:1Jul84-22
Salisbury, N. Manitou and Providence.
  G.W. La Fantasie, 656(WMQ):Apr83-309
  A.T. Vaughan, 432(NEQ):Mar83-129
Salisbury, R. When the Boys Came Out to Play.
  L. Taylor, 617(TLS):29Jun84-736
Sallée, P. Deux études sur la musique du Gabon.
  R.M. Stone, 187:May84-341
Saller, R.P. Personal Patronage Under the Early Empire.
  E. Champlin, 487:Autumn83-280
  A.N. Sherwin-White, 123:Vol33No2-271
Sallis, J. The Gathering of Reason.*
  S. Watson, 323:May83-207
Sallis, J., ed. Jazz Guitars.
  I. Gitler, 441:29Jul84-16
Salminen, R. - see Marguerite de Navarre
Salmon, E., ed. Bernhardt and the Theatre of her Time.
  J.S. Bratton, 617(TLS):9Nov84-1286
Salmon, E. Granville Barker.*
  S. Morley, 157:Autumn83-29
Salmon, E.T. The Making of Roman Italy.
  J. Briscoe, 123:Vol33No2-350
  T.J. Luce, 487:Winter83-356
Salmon, J.B. Wealthy Corinth.
  M.M. Austin, 617(TLS):27Jul84-831
Salmon, J.H.M. Society in Crisis.
  M.M. McGowan, 208(FS):Jul83-333
Salmon, N.U. Reference and Essence.
  M.S. Gram, 543:Dec82-472
  G. Stahl, 542:Jul-Sep83-363
Salmon, V. The Study of Language in 17th-Century England.*
  A. Palacas, 568(SCN):Fall83-55
Saloheimo, V. Pohjois-Karjalan Historia III.
  S.P. Oakley, 562(Scan):Nov82-191
Salom, P. The Projectionist.
  C. Wallace-Crabbe, 617(TLS):20Jul84-819
Salomon, B. Critical Analyses in English Renaissance Drama.*
  G. Schmitz, 156(JDSh):Jahrbuch1983-255
Salomon, C. Charlotte: Life or Theater?
  M. Tane, 639(VQR):Winter83-162
Salomon, M. Future Life.
  442(NY):27Feb84-134
Salomon-Bayet, C. L'institution de la science et l'expérience du vivant.
  R. Prévost, 192(EP):Apr-Jun83-246

Salskov Roberts, H. Corpus Speculorum
Etruscorum; Denmark. (Vol 1, fasc 1)
G. Lloyd-Morgan, 313:Vol73-233
F.R.S. Ridgway, 123:Vol133No2-291
Salt, H.S. Animals' Rights Considered in
Relation to Social Progress.
S. Clark, 479(PhQ):Jan83-98
Salter, C.H. Good Little Thomas Hardy.*
L. Elsbree, 637(VS):Summer83-454
295(JML):Nov83-492
Salter, E. Fourteenth-Century English
Poetry. (D. Pearsall and N. Zeeman,
eds)
D. Fox, 617(TLS):17Feb84-172
Saltzman, E.L. Overshot Weaving.
P. Bach, 614:Winter84-21
Salu, M. and R.T. Farrell, eds. J.R.R.
Tolkien.
H. Ilsemann, 38:Band101Heft3/4-538
Salvatore, N. Eugene V. Debs.*
639(VQR):Summer83-79
Salverson, L.G. Confessions of an Immi-
grant's Daughter.* (K.P. Stich, ed)
L. Good, 529(QQ):Spring83-277
Salway, P. Roman Britain.*
S.L. Dyson, 589:Jul83-816
Samaran, C. and R. Marichal. Catalogue
des manuscrits en écriture latine por-
tant des indications de date, de lieu ou
de copiste. (Vol 4, Pt 1)
J. Krochalis, 589:Jan83-233
Sambrook, J. - see Thomson, J.
"Sammlung." (Vols 1-4) (U. Naumann, ed)
F. Wagner, 654(WB):5/1983-946
Sammons, J.L. Heinrich Heine.*
H. Spencer, 221(GQ):Mar83-323
Samples, G. Lust for Fame.
D.B. Wilmeth, 612(ThS):May/Nov83-157
Sampson, A. Empires of the Sky.
G. Bull, 362:15Nov84-28
M. Goldring, 617(TLS):16Nov84-1303
Sampson, G. An End to Allegiance.
J. Campbell, 617(TLS):2Nov84-1236
Sampson, G. Schools of Linguistics.*
G. Lepschy, 297(JL):Mar83-218
N. Love, 541(RES):May83-197
P.H. Salus, 567:Vol142No2/4-311
W.C. Stokoe, 307:Apr83-98
Sampson, R., ed. Early Romance Texts.*
F.W. Hodcroft, 382(MAE):1983/1-166
C.J. Pountain, 402(MLR):Apr83-405
"Saṃsad bāṅālī caritābhidhān (prāẏ sāṛe
tin sahasra jībanī-sambalita ākar'-
grantha)."
R.P. Das, 259(IIJ):Apr83-216
Samsaris, D.K. Ho exellēnismos tēs
Thrakēs kata tēn Hellēnike kai Hrōmaikē
archaiotēta.
N.G.L. Hammond, 303(JoHS):Vol 103-215
Samson, J. Music in Transition.
D.C., 412:Aug-Nov82-276
Samudavanija, C-A. - see under Chai-Anan
Samudavanija
Samuel, R., ed. East End Underworld.
D. Gittins, 637(VS):Summer83-431
Samuel, R. and G.S. Jones. Culture, Ideol-
ogy and Politics.
D.J.G., 185:Jul84-734
Samuel, R.H. and H.M. Brown. Kleist's
Lost Year and the Quest for Robert
Guiskard.
J.M. Ellis, 564:Feb83-67
W. Wittkowski, 133:Band16Heft2/3-245

Samuels, P. and H. Frederic Remington.*
B.M. Vorpahl, 649(WAL):Aug83-166
Samuelson, A. With Hemingway.
H. Ford, 441:16Dec84-27
San, H., A. Pino and L. Epstein - see
under Huang San, A. Pino and L. Epstein
Sánchez, A.E.P. - see under Pérez Sánchez,
A.E.
Sánchez, M.B. - see under Brioso Sánchez,
M.
Sánchez, R., ed. Homenaje a Enrique Labra-
dor Ruiz.
J.E. Hernández-Miyares, 238:Dec83-649
Sánchez Romeralo, A. - see Jiménez, J.R.
Sánchez Romeralo, A. and A. Valenciano.
Romancero rústico.
A. González, 457(NRFH):Tomo31núm2-308
Sánchez Vidal, A. Las novelas de Joaquín
Costa. (Vol 1)
D.L. Shaw, 86(BHS):Apr83-159
Sand, G. Correspondance. (Vol 16) (G.
Lubin, ed)
L.J. Austin, 208(FS):Jan83-93
J. Gaulmier, 535(RHL):Jul/Aug83-650
Sand, G. Mademoiselle Merquem. (R.
Rheault, ed)
G. Lubin, 535(RHL):Mar/Apr83-296
N. Mozet, 535(RHL):Mar/Apr83-295
Sandahl, B. Middle English Sea Terms.
(Vol 3)
C.G., 189(EA):Oct-Dec84-489
Sandberg, H. - see Dagerman, S.
Sandburg, C. Ever the Winds of Chance.
B.F. Williamson, 441:1Jan84-21
Sandel, M.J. Liberalism and the Limits of
Justice.*
B. Barry, 185:Apr84-523
D.A.L. Thomas, 518:Oct83-249
Sanders, A. Charles Dickens: Resurrection-
ist.*
J.H. Buckley, 445(NCF):Dec83-334
S. Monod, 189(EA):Jul-Sep84-341
D. Walder, 155:Spring83-43
Sanders, A. The Victorian Historical
Novel 1840-1880.
T.J. Winnifrith, 402(MLR):Jan83-163
Sanders, C.R. and K.J. Fielding - see
Carlyle, T. and J.W.
Sanders, I.F. Roman Crete.
S. Hood, 123:Vol133No1-104
A.J.S. Spawforth, 313:Vol73-237
Sanders, J. Other Lips and Other Hearts.
R.E. Morsberger, 649(WAL):Nov83-245
Sanders, L. The Passion of Molly T.
M. Kaylan, 441:30Sep84-28
Sanders, N. - see Shakespeare, W.
Sanders, N. and others. The Revels His-
tory of Drama in English.* (Vol 2)
L. Lieblein, 615(TJ):Mar83-132
Sanders, R. The High Walls of Jerusalem.
P. Johnson, 441:22Jan84-3
C.C. O'Brien, 453(NYRB):15Mar84-34
Sanders, R. Real Old Tory Politics. (J.
Ramsden, ed)
K. Robbins, 617(TLS):17Aug84-912
Sanders, S.R. Fetching the Dead.
J. Cantor, 441:14Oct84-26
G. Weaver, 344:Fall84-108
Sanderson, L.M.P. and N. Education, Reli-
gion and Politics in Southern Sudan 1899-
1964.
J.W. Burton, 69:Vol153No3-88

328

Saroyan, A. William Saroyan.
 H. Keyishian, 363(LitR):Fall83-153
Saroyan, W. Births.*
 H. Keyishian, 363(LitR):Fall83-153
Sarraute, N. Childhood.* (French title:
 Enfance.)
 P-L. Adams, 61:Apr84-148
 F. Kermode, 453(NYRB):25Oct84-49
 F. de Martinoir, 450(NRF):Jul/Aug83-
 212
 R. Shattuck, 441:1Apr84-1
Sarraute, N. L'Usage de la parole.
 C. Dis, 450(NRF):Jun83-122
Sarrazac, J-P. L'Avenir du drame.
 D. Bradby, 402(MLR):Oct83-937
Sarton, M. At Seventy.
 J. McCulloch, 441:20May84-31
Sartre, J-P. Cahiers pour une morale.
 J-L. Chrétien, 98:Nov83-856
 T. Cordellier, 450(NRF):Jul/Aug83-222
 A. Lavers, 617(TLS):11May84-511
Sartre, J-P. Les Carnets de la drôle de
 guerre.
 C. Dis, 450(NRF):Sep83-129
 A. Lavers, 617(TLS):11May84-511
Sartre, J-P. The Family Idiot. (Vol 1)
 W. Fowlie, 569(SR):Winter83-x
 E.F. Gray, 395(MFS):Summer83-300
Sartre, J-P. Lettres au Castor et à
 quelques autres. (S. de Beauvoir, ed)
 A. Lavers, 617(TLS):11May84-511
Sartre, J-P. Les Mots. (D. Nott, ed)
 I.H. Walker, 402(MLR):Apr83-464
Sartre, J-P. Oeuvres romanesques.* (M.
 Contat and M. Rybalka, with others, eds)
 C. Howells, 402(MLR):Apr83-461
 A. Lavers, 617(TLS):11May84-511
Sartre, J-P. Le Scénario Freud.
 A.C. Danto, 617(TLS):6Jul84-744
Saso, M.R. The Teaching of Taoist Master
 Chuang.
 A.P. Cohen, 318(JAOS):Jan-Mar82-138
Sassatelli, G., ed. Corpus Speculorum
 Etruscorum; Italia. (Vol 1, fasc 1
 and 2)
 G. Lloyd-Morgan, 313:Vol73-233
 F.R.S. Ridgway, 123:Vol33No2-291
Satijn, N. Le Labyrinthe de la cité
 radieuse.
 R.C. Lamont, 207(FR):Oct83-116
Sato, H. One Hundred Frogs.
 E.F. Yasuhara, 407(MN):Winter83-440
Sato, H. and B. Watson, eds and trans.
 From the Country of Eight Islands.*
 K. Brazell, 293(JASt):Feb83-417
 W.R. La Fleur, 407(MN):Summer83-191
Sato, N. Retorikku kankaku. Retorikku
 minshiki.
 T. Aino, 209(FM):Oct83-369
Sauder, G. Empfindsamkeit.* (Vol 3)
 L.E. Kurth-Voigt, 400(MLN):Apr83-528
Sauer, M. Parzival auf der Suche nach der
 verlorenen Zeit.
 D.H. Green, 402(MLR):Jul83-743
Sauer, W., ed. The Metrical Life of
 Christ.
 K. Reichl, 38:Band101Heft1/2-231
Sauer, W. - see Hoffmann, H.
Saul, N. Knights and Esquires.
 J.M.W. Bean, 589:Apr83-535
 C. Dyer, 382(MAE):1983/1-121
Saulnier, V.L. Rabelais. (Vol 2)
 F. Rigolot, 535(RHL):May/Jun83-462

Saumur, L. The Humanist Evangel.
 J.R. Horne, 154:Mar83-185
Saunders, A. The Sixteenth-Century
 "Blason poétique."
 L.K. Donaldson-Evans, 551(RenQ):
 Autumn83-463
Saunders, F., with J. Southwood. Torn
 Lace Curtain.
 639(VQR):Spring83-50
Saunders, J.W. A Biographical Dictionary
 of Renaissance Poets and Dramatists,
 1520-1650.
 R.V. Holdsworth, 617(TLS):11May84-518
Saunders, T.J. - see Aristotle
Sauren, H. Les tablettes cunéiformes de
 l'epoque d'Ur des collections de la New
 York Public Library.
 P. Steinkeller, 318(JAOS):Oct-Dec82-
 639
Sauter, W. Theater als Widerstand.
 P. Meech, 610:Autumn82-246
Sautermeister, G. Thomas Mann — "Mario
 und der Zauberer."
 E.E. Reed, 221(GQ):May83-524
de Sauvigny, G.D. - see under de Bertier
 de Sauvigny, G.
Savage, C.W., ed. Perception and Cogni-
 tion.*
 R.C. Richardson, 449:Sep83-482
Savage, J. The Kinks.
 M. Bell, 617(TLS):7Dec84-1419
Savage, T. The Power of the Dog.
 M. Laski, 362:25Oct84-29
Savage, W.W., Jr. Singing Cowboys and All
 That Jazz.
 L. Milazzo, 584(SWR):Spring83-vi
Savard, J.G. and L. Laforge, eds. Proceed-
 ings of the 5th Congress of l'Associa-
 tion Internationale de Linguistique
 Appliquée/Actes du 5e congrès de l'Assoc-
 iation internationale de linguistique
 appliquée.*
 R. Martin, 553(RLiR):Jul-Dec83-417
Savatier, P. Le Photographe.
 F. de Martinoir, 450(NRF):Apr83-127
 S.R. Schulman, 207(FR):Feb84-418
Savić, S. How Twins Learn to Talk.
 R. Goodwin, 353:Vol20No9/10-660
 L.H. Waterhouse, 355(LSoc):Sep83-382
Savile, A. The Test of Time.*
 W. Charlton, 483:Jul83-411
 P. Jones, 89(BJA):Summer83-259
 C. Lord, 289:Fall83-112
 J. Stolnitz, 290(JAAC):Fall83-91
 M.M. Warner, 518:Jan83-40
Saville-Troike, M. The Ethnography of
 Communication.
 J. Jonz, 608:Dec84-725
Savio, L.S.F. and B. Maier - see under
 Fonda Savio, L.S. and B. Maier
Savitski, D. Bons baisers de nulle part.
 J. Blot, 450(NRF):Oct83-147
Savoie, P. Acrobats.
 B.K. Filson, 526:Winter83-80
Savonarola, M. Libreto de tute le cosse
 che se manzano. (Vol 1) (J. Nystedt, ed)
 I. Arthur, 597(SN):Vol55No1-121
 J. Nicolas, 553(RLiR):Jul-Dec83-451
 A. Tissoni Benvenuti, 547(RF):Band95
 Heft3-408
Savoret, A. and others. Alchimie.
 I.M. Kohn, 111:Spring83-2

Savuškinoj, N.I., ed. Obrjadovaja poèzija Pinež'ja.
  J.L. Conrad, 292(JAF):Apr-Jun83-241
Saward, D. Bernard Lovell.
  C.A. Ronan, 617(TLS):28Dec84-1497
Sawatsky, J. For Services Rendered.
  G.W., 102(CanL):Spring83-156
Sawyer, P.H., ed. Charters of Burton Abbey.
  H. Gneuss, 38:Band10lHeftl/2-219
Sawyer, R. Casement.
  D. Fitzpatrick, 617(TLS):1Jun84-611
Sax, R. Cooking Great Meals Every Day.
  W. and C. Cowen, 639(VQR):Spring83-65
Saxena, S.K. Aesthetical Essays.
  V.K. Chari, 290(JAAC):Fall83-105
  N. McAdoo, 89(BJA):Spring83-169
Saxo Grammaticus. Danorum regum heroumque historia. (Bks 10-16) (E. Christiansen, ed and trans)
  J. Martinez-Pizarro, 589:Jan83-234
  H. O'Donoghue, 382(MAE):1983/2-346
"Saxo Grammaticus: History of the Danes."* (H.E. Davidson, ed; P. Fisher, trans)
  K. Johannesson, 64(Arv):Vol37-177
  K. Muir, 570(SQ):Spring83-116
  H. O'Donoghue, 382(MAE):1983/1-184
  R. Perkins, 562(Scan):Nov83-211
Saxon, A.H. - see Barnum, P.T.
Sayce, O. The Medieval German Lyric 1150-1300.
  L.S., 382(MAE):1983/2-339
Sayce, R.A. and D. Maskell. A Descriptive Bibliography of Montaigne's "Essais," 1580-1700.
  J.W. Jolliffe, 617(TLS):6Jul84-767
Sayers, D.L., ed. Great Tales of Detection.
  P. Craig, 617(TLS):28Dec84-1506
Sayle, A. Train to Hell.
  J. Melmoth, 617(TLS):16Mar84-267
Sayre, K.M. Plato's Late Ontology.
  M.F. Burnyeat, 617(TLS):13Jul84-788
Sayre, N. Running Time.*
  P. Shaw, 31(ASch):Spring83-270
Scaffidi Abbate, A. Introduzione allo studio comparativo delle lingue germaniche antiche.
  E. Seebold, 260(IF):Band87-352
Scaglione, A., ed. Francis Petrarch, Six Centuries Later.
  C. Kleinhenz, 545(RPh):Nov82-273
Scaglione, A. The Theory of German Word Order from the Renaissance to the Present.*
  S.M. Embleton, 320(CJL):Spring83-83
Scaiola, A.M. - see Sainte-Beuve, C.A.
Scalamandrè, R. F. Vielé-Griffin e il platonismo.*
  C. Dédéyan, 535(RHL):May/Jun83-479
Scales, J.R. and D. Goble. Oklahoma Politics.
  L. Milazzo, 584(SWR):Winter83-vii
Scammell, G.V. The World Encompassed.
  J. Elliott, 551(RenQ):Spring83-71
Scammell, M. Solzhenitsyn.
  A. Kelly, 453(NYRB):11Oct84-13
  B. Levin, 61:Sep84-124
  N. Stone, 441:28Oct84-1
Scammell, W. A Second Life.*
  B. Jones, 364:Jul83-78

Scarcella, R.C. and S.D. Krashen, eds. Research in Second Language Acquisition.*
  S.M. Embleton, 320(CJL):Fall83-185
Scarisbrick, J.J. The Reformation and the English People.
  P. Collinson, 617(TLS):1Jun84-605
Scarr, D. Ratu Sukuna.
  M. Richards, 617(TLS):27Apr84-477
Scarr, D. - see Sukuna, L.
Scarre, C., ed. Ancient France.
  A.G. Sherratt, 617(TLS):20Apr84-437
Scattergood, J. - see Skelton, J.
Scavnicky, G.E., ed. Dialectología hispanoamericana.*
  R. de Gorog, 545(RPh):Nov82-242
  P. Quijas Corzo, 457(NRFH):Tomo31núm2-302
Schaar, C. "The Full Voic'd Quire Below."
  G. Mathis, 189(EA):Jul-Sep84-322
  M.A. Radzinowicz, 551(RenQ):Winter83-674
  B. Sherry, 67:Nov83-311
  B. Sherry, 391:Oct83-95
Schabert, I. Der historische Roman in England und Amerika.
  E. Mengel, 72:Band220Heft2-403
  T.H. Pickett, 107(CRCL):Sep83-438
Schabert, T. Gewalt und Humanität.*
  J-C. Margolin, 192(EP):Apr-Jun83-247
Schach, P., ed. Languages in Conflict.*
  S. Clausing, 301(JEGP):Apr83-311
Schachermeyer, F. Kreta zur Zeit der Wanderungen.
  S. Hood, 123:Vol33No2-355
Schacht, R. Nietzsche.*
  483:Oct83-559
Schack, C. Die Glaskunst.
  G. Wills, 39:Mar83-263
Schadeberg, T.C. and M.L. Bender, eds. Nilo-Saharan.
  P. Unseth, 350:Jun84-464
Schädler, K-F. Ekoi.
  J. Povey, 2(AfrA):Aug83-83
Schaeffer, G. Espace et temps chez George Sand.
  M. Bossis, 535(RHL):Mar/Apr83-297
Schaeffer, S.F. The Madness of a Seduced Woman.*
  M.K. Benet, 617(TLS):23Mar84-311
Schafer, E.H. Pacing the Void.
  A.P. Cohen, 318(JAOS):Jan-Mar82-137
Schäfer, J. Documentation in the O.E.D.*
  R.W. McConchie, 67:May83-165
  V. Salmon, 402(MLR):Jan83-130
  R.J. Schoeck, 570(SQ):Autumn83-371
Schäfer, J., ed. Phaselis.
  J.M. Cook, 303(JoHS):Vol 103-218
Schäfer, P. Der Bar Kokhba-Aufstand.
  M.D. Goodman, 123:Vol33No2-273
Schaffer, D. Garden Cities for America.
  D. Schuyler, 576:May83-192
Schakhovskoy, D., comp. Bibliographie des oeuvres de Ivan Chmelev.
  L. Dienes, 558(RLJ):Winter-Spring83-289
  D.M. Fiene, 574(SEEJ):Spring83-119
Schalk, D.L. The Spectrum of Political Engagement.
  G. Allardyce, 161(DUJ):Dec82-99
Schall, J.V. Christianity and Politics.
  J.W. Cooper, 396(ModA):Winter83-88

Schaller, H.W. Die Geschichte der Slavis-
tik in Bayern.
  H. Rösel, 688(ZSP):Band43Heft2-419
Schanzer, G.O. - see Pavlovsky, E.
Schaper, E. Studies in Kant's Aesthetics.*
  H. Graubner, 342:Band74Heft2-235
  M. Kuehn, 518:Jul83-150
Schapiro, L. 1917.
  R. Pipes, 617(TLS):20Jul84-814
Schapiro, L. The Russian Revolutions of
1917.
  R.C. Tucker, 441:23Sep84-22
Schaps, D.M. Economic Rights of Women in
Ancient Greece.*
  T.M. de Wit-Tak, 394:Vol36fasc1/2-228
Schareika, H. Der Realismus der aristo-
phanischen Komödie.
  J.T.M.F. Pieters, 394:Vol36fasc3/4-410
Schärer, K. Pour une poétique des
"Chimères" de Nerval.*
  N. Rinsler, 208(FS):Oct83-474
Scharff, S. The Elements of Cinema.
  R. Durgnat, 18:Apr84-57
Scharfstein, B-A. The Philosophers.*
  M. Kroy, 63:Sep83-307
Scharfswerdt, J. Literatur und Literatur-
wissenschaft in der DDR.
  K. Kändler, 654(WB):8/1983-1490
Scharzwald, O., ed. Hebrew Computational
Linguistics.
  A.S. Kaye, 318(JAOS):Jan-Mar82-195
Schatt, R. James Dean.
  A. White, 200:Mar83-187
Schatz, T. Hollywood Genres.*
  J. Fleckenstein, 615(TJ):May82-280
  B.K. Grant, 106:Spring83-107
Schatz, T. Old Hollywood/New Hollywood.
  M. Keller, 127:Fall83-284
Schaub, T.H. Pynchon: The Voice of Ambigu-
ity.*
  P. Balbert, 594:Fall83-265
  W. Harmon, 577(SHR):Fall83-379
  D. Seed, 402(MLR):Jul83-702
  G.F. Waller, 106:Summer83-207
Schauer, F.F. Free Speech.*
  F.R.B., 185:Jan84-380
  H.J. McCloskey, 518:Oct83-231
Scheck, U. Parodie und Eigenständigkeit
in Nestroys "Judith und Holofernes."
  W.E. Yates, 402(MLR):Oct83-983
Scheer, R., with N. Zacchino and C. Mat-
thiessen. With Enough Shovels.*
  E. Hooven, 99:May83-34
  639(VQR):Summer83-93
Scheerer, T.M. Ferdinand de Saussure.*
  U. Bichel, 685(ZDL):2/1983-212
  P. Swiggers, 567:Vol42No2/4-297
Scheffer, C. Acquarossa. (Vol 2, Pt 1)
  D. Ridgway, 123:Vol33No2-365
Scheffer, V.B. Spires of Form.
  N. Wade, 441:11Mar84-19
Scheffler, I. Beyond the Letter.*
  A. Margalit, 311(JP):Feb83-129
Scheffler, L. - see Müller, L.
Scheffler, S. The Rejection of Consequen-
tialism.
  E. Telfer, 518:Jul83-188
Scheffler, W. Goldschmiede des Ostallgäus
(zwischen Iller und Lech).
  G. Schiedlausky, 471:Jan/Feb/Mar83-89
Schefold, K. Die Göttersage in der klass-
ischen und hellenistischen Kunst.
  S. Woodford, 303(JoHS):Vol 103-225

Scheible, H., ed. Arthur Schnitzler in
neuer Sicht.
  J.M. Herz, 221(GQ):Nov83-672
Scheidegger, J. Arbitraire et motivation
en français et en allemand.*
  D. Justice, 545(RPh):Nov82-259
Scheier, L. The Larger Life.
  P.K. Smith, 99:Mar84-38
Schein, S.L. The Mortal Hero.
  B. Hainsworth, 617(TLS):28Dec84-1498
Schele, L. Mayan Glyphs.
  L. Campbell, 350:Sep84-621
Schell, J. The Abolition.
  P.C. Warnke, 441:8Jul84-8
  Lord Zuckerman, 453(NYRB):14Jun84-5
Schell, O. Modern Meat.
  C. Murphy, 441:10Jun84-7
Schelle, H., ed. Christoph Martin Wie-
land.*
  A. Menhennet, 402(MLR):Apr83-490
  H. Rowland, 173(ECS):Winter83/84-218
  P. Schäublin, 680(ZDP):Band102Heft2-
  279
  A.R. Schmitt, 221(GQ):Mar83-314
Schelling, F.W.J. Contribution à l'his-
toire de la philosophie moderne, Leçons
de Munich. (J-F. Marquet, ed and trans)
  J-M. Gabaude, 542:Oct-Dec83-478
Schelling, F.W.J. Historisch-kritische
Ausgabe. (1st Ser, Vol 2) (H. Buchner
and J. Jantzen, eds)
  J-F. Courtine, 192(EP):Jan-Mar83-111
  J-M. Gabaude, 542:Jan-Mar83-140
Schelling, F.W.J. Historish-kritische
Ausgabe. (1st Ser, Vol 3) (H. Buchner,
W.G. Jacobs and A. Pieper, eds)
  J-F. Courtine, 192(EP):Jan-Mar83-111
  J-M. Gabaude, 542:Jan-Mar83-141
Schelling, T.C. Choice and Consequence.
  M. Olson, 441:1Jul84-10
van Schendel, W. Peasant Mobility.
  R. uddin Ahmed, 293(JASt):May83-711
Schenk, G. The Complete Shade Gardener.
  L. Yang, 441:3Jun84-7
Schenkel, S.M. The Tools of Jazz.
  J. Bridges, 498:Vol9No2-90
Scherer, D. and T. Attig, eds. Ethics and
the Environment.
  R.E.G., 185:Apr84-574
Scherer, J., M. Borie and M. de Rougemont,
comps. Esthétique théâtrale.
  H. Allentuch, 207(FR):May84-864
Scherer, K.R. and H. Giles, eds. Social
Markers in Speech.
  P. Mühlhäusler, 307:Oct82-125
  J.R. Rennison, 685(ZDL):2/1983-220
Scherf, W. Lexikon der Zaubermärchen.
  F. Karlinger, 547(RF):Band95Heft3-325
Scherpe, K.R. Poesie der Demokratie.
  J.A. McCarthy, 406:Winter83-431
Scheuer, H. Biographie.
  K.E. Kuhn-Osius, 406:Summer83-204
  M. McKenzie, 221(GQ):May83-470
Scheurer, P. Révolutions de la science et
permanence du réel.
  J. Largeault, 542:Jul-Sep83-364
Scheven, A. Swahili Proverbs.
  L. Todd, 203:Vol94No1-132
Schezen, R. Adolf Loos.
  A. Betsky, 505:Jul83-117

Schiavo, L. Historia y novela en Valle-Inclán.*
B. Entenza de Solare, 547(RF):Band95 Heft3-399
G. Minter, 86(BHS):Jan83-77
Schiavone de Cruz-Sáenz, M., ed. The Life of Saint Mary of Egypt.
P.F. Dembowski, 545(RPh):Feb83-478
R.W. Ramírez de Arellano, 240(HR): Spring83-223
Schickel, R. D.W. Griffith.
P. Bogdanovich, 441:8Apr84-1
T. Gunning, 18:Jun84-57
M. Wood, 453(NYRB):6Dec84-10
442(NY):30Apr84-121
Schickel, R. D.W. Griffith and the Birth of Film.
D.J. Wenden, 617(TLS):15Jun84-675
Schiebe, M.W. - see under Wifstrand Schiebe, M.
Schieder, T. Friedrich der Grosse.
E. Sagarra, 617(TLS):14Sep84-1014
Schiefer, E.F., ed. Explanationes et Tractationes Fenno-Ugricae in Honorem Hans Fromm.
K. Ruppel, 260(IF):Band87-383
Schier, K., ed and trans. Die Saga von Egil.
E.G. Fichtner, 563(SS):Spring83-192
Schierling, M. "Das Kloster der Minne."
I. Glier, 680(ZDP):Band102Heft3-461
Schiff, D. The Music of Elliott Carter.*
B. Northcott, 453(NYRB):31May84-18
C. Wuorinen, 414(MusQ):Fall83-606
Schiff, G. Picasso: The Last Years, 1963-1973.
J. Richardson, 453(NYRB):19Jul84-21
Schiff, Z. and E. Ya'ari. Israel's Lebanon War.
P. Grose, 441:14Oct84-12
von Schilcher, F. and N. Tennant. Philosophy, Evolution and Human Nature.
A. Woodfield, 617(TLS):19Oct84-1197
Schildt, J., ed. Auswirkungen der industriellen Revolution auf die deutsche Sprachentwicklung im 19. Jahrhundert.
G. Schmidt, 682(ZPSK):Band36Heft4-467
Schiller, D. and others. Exil in Frankreich.
W. Klein, 654(WB):5/1982-177
Schiller, F. Kunst, Humanität und Politik in der späten Aufklärung. (W. Wittkowski, ed)
O.W. Johnston, 680(ZDP):Band102Heft4-610
Schilling, R. La religion romaine de Vénus depuis les origines jusqu'au temps d'Auguste. (2nd ed)
P. Flobert, 555:Vol57fasc2-356
Schilpp, P.A., ed. The Philosophy of Brand Blanshard.
H.D. Lewis, 483:Jan83-110
Schilpp, P.A., ed. The Philosophy of Jean-Paul Sartre.
R.P.H., 543:Sep82-192
Schimmel, A. Islam in the Indian Subcontinent. Islam in India and Pakistan.
B. Metcalf, 293(JASt):Feb83-444
Schindler, M. Die Kuenringer in Sage und Legende.
S. Krause, 196:Band24Heft3/4-325
Schine, C. Alice in Bed.*
42(AR):Fall83-509

Schings, H-J. Der mitleidigste Mensch ist der beste Mensch.*
D. Borchmeyer, 490:Band14Heft1/2-171
Schirmacher, W., ed. Zeit der Ernte.
M. Hielscher, 489(PJGG):Band90Heft2-430
Schirmer, G.A. The Poetry of Austin Clarke.
H. Kenner, 617(TLS):20Jan84-54
Schirokauer, A. and P.W. Tax. Hartmann von Aue, Das Bühlein.
H. Zutt, 680(ZDP):Band102Heft3-452
Schiroli, M.G.C. - see under Cavalca Schiroli, M.G.
Schlachter, W. and G. Ganschow, eds. Bibliographie der uralischen Sprachwissenschaft 1830-1970. (Vol 2, Pt 1)
J. Helder-Jastrzębska, 260(IF):Band87-380
Schlaffer, H. Faust Zweiter Teil.*
R. Dau, 654(WB):10/1983-1827
O. Durrani, 402(MLR):Jan83-233
J. Hörisch, 490:Band14Heft3/4-353
Schlaffer, H. Wilhelm Meister.*
J.K. Brown, 301(JEGP):Jan83-110
S.L. Cocalis, 406:Fall83-341
J. Hörisch, 490:Band14Heft3/4-353
H.R. Vaget, 221(GQ):May83-502
Schlanger, J. L'activité théorique.
Y. Gauthier, 154:Dec83-724
A. Reix, 542:Oct-Dec83-452
Schlanke, M., ed. Preussen. (Vol 2)
I.K. Rogoff, 59:Jun83-250
Schlee, A. The Proprietor.*
M.L. Jefferson, 441:22Jan84-22
J. Mellors, 364:Oct83-97
442(NY):16Jan84-109
Schlee, E. German Folk Art.
H. Koppinger, 70:Nov/Dec81-60
Schlegel, F. Kritische Friedrich-Schlegel-Ausgabe. (Vol 1) (E. Behler, ed)
W. Henckmann, 489(PJGG):Band99Heft2-401
M.R. Higonnet, 301(JEGP):Oct83-601
Schlegel, F. Kritische Friedrich-Schlegel-Ausgabe. (Vols 2-6 ed by H. Eichner; Vols 7 and 10 ed by E. Behler; Vol 8 ed by E. Behler and U. Struc-Oppenberg; Vol 9 ed by J-J. Anstett)
W. Henckmann, 489(PJGG):Band99Heft2-401
Schlegel, F. Kritische Friedrich-Schlegel-Ausgabe. (Vols 16, 29 and 30) (E. Behler and others, eds)
M.R. Higonnet, 301(JEGP):Oct83-601
Schleiermacher, F.D.E. Der christliche Glaube nach den Grundsätzen der evangelischen Kirche im Zusammenhange dargestellt (1821/22). (H. Peiter, ed)
G. Hummel, 53(AGP):Band65Heft3-320
Schleifer, J.T. The Making of Tocqueville's "Democracy in America."
D. Kummings, 125:Spring83-309
Schlenstedt, D., ed. Literarische Widerspiegelung.
R.C. Holub, 221(GQ):May83-480
Schlereth, T.J. Artifacts and the American Past.*
W.E. Roberts, 650(WF):Jan83-56
Schlesinger, I.M. Steps to Language.
A. van Kleeck, 350:Jun84-470
Schleyer, W. Die Stücke von Peter Hacks.
E. Glew, 221(GQ):Jan83-176

333

Schneider, S.H. and R. Londer. The Coevolution of Climate and Life.
J.E. Lovelock, 441:19Aug84-11
Schneiders, H-W. Der französische Wortschatz zur Bezeichnung von "Schall."*
D. Justice, 545(RPh):Aug82-71
Schnitzler, A. Flucht in die Finsternis. (H-U. Lindken, ed)
J.B. Berlin, 406:Spring83-82
Schnitzler, A. Tagebuch 1909-1912.* (W. Welzig and others, eds)
W.E. Yates, 402(MLR):Oct83-989
Schnitzler, A. Tagebuch 1913-1916. (W. Welzig and others, eds)
E. Timms, 617(TLS):20Apr84-434
Schnyder, A., ed. Biterolf und Dietleib.*
J. Heinzle, 680(ZDP):Band102Heft1-143
Schober, W. The Lives of Bats.
S. Mills, 617(TLS):9Nov84-1296
Schoen, E. Widower.
L. Bennetts, 441:28Oct84-46
Schoenbaum, S. William Shakespeare: Records and Images.*
P. Davison, 366:Spring83-111
W. Schrickx, 179(ES):Dec83-572
K. Tetzeli von Rosador, 156(JDSh): Jahrbuch1983-260
Schoenbaum, S. Shakespeare: The Globe and the World.*
R. Berry, 529(QQ):Summer83-372
K. Spinner, 179(ES):Aug83-361
Schoenberg, A. Correspondance (1930-1951).
A. Suied, 450(NRF):Sep83-163
"Arnold Schoenberg, Wassily Kandinsky: Letters, Pictures and Documents." (J. Hahl-Koch, ed)
H. Cole, 362:1Nov84-30
J. Willett, 617(TLS):8Jun84-630
Schoenbrun, D. America Inside Out.
H. Giniger, 441:14Oct84-33
Schofield, M., M. Burnyeat and J. Barnes, eds. Doubt and Dogmatism.*
T.H. Irwin, 449:Mar83-126
P. Sanford, 303(JoHS):Vol 103-191
C. Stough, 482(PhR):Oct83-593
Schofield, M. and M.C. Nussbaum, eds. Language and Logos.
R.W. Sharples, 303(JoHS):Vol 103-190
C.J.F. Williams, 123:Vol33No2-331
Scholefield, A. The Sea Cave.
H. Benedict, 441:14Oct84-27
M. Laski, 362:12Jan84-26
442(NY):1Oct84-133
Scholem, G. Walter Benjamin.*
S. Cain, 390:Aug/Sep83-53
R.S. Wistrich, 473(PR):1/1983-154
Schöler-Beinhauer, M. - see Robert de Boron
Scholes, R. Semiotics and Interpretation.*
W. Bache, 395(MFS):Summer83-356
M.C., 189(EA):Apr-Jun84-234
D.H. Hirsch, 569(SR):Summer83-417
A.N. Jeffares, 651(WHR):Summer83-163
C. Norris, 478:Oct83-278
Scholten, T., A. Evers and M. Klein. Inleiding in de transformationeel-generatieve taaltheorie.
J.W. de Vries, 204(FdL):Dec83-311
Scholz, J.J. Blake and Novalis.
D.W. Dörrbecker, 88:Winter83/84-111
Scholz, W. Abbildung und Veränderung durch das Theater im 18. Jahrhundert.
H. Slessarev, 221(GQ):Nov83-648

Schön, I. Neutrum und Kollektivum.
E. Neu, 260(IF):Band87-314
Schönrich, G. Kategorien und transzendentale Argumentation.
W. Hogrebe, 342:Band74Heft2-239
Schönzeler, H-H. Dvorak.
J. Rockwell, 441:23Dec84-17
"Schooling and Language Minority Students."
G. Thurgood, 351(LL):Dec83-541
Schopenhauer, A. De la cuádruple raíz del principio de razón suficiente.
A. Reix, 542:Jan-Mar83-142
Schöpf, A. Sigmund Freud.
A.J., 185:Apr84-555
Schopf, J.W., ed. Earth's Earliest Biosphere.
L. Margulis, 617(TLS):10Aug84-903
Schopp, C. - see Dumas, A.
Schoppa, R.K. Chinese Elites and Political Change.
E.S. Rawski, 293(JASt):Aug83-940
Schottelius, J.G. Ethica.* (J.J. Berns, ed)
J. Leighton, 402(MLR):Jan83-228
H. Rowland, 406:Fall83-335
Schouls, P.A. The Impossible Method.*
H.A.S. Schankula, 393(Mind):Oct83-601
Schouvaloff, A. and V. Borovsky. Stravinsky on Stage.
P. Griffiths, 415:Mar83-168
Schöwerling, R. Chapbooks.*
K. Gamerschlag, 72:Band220Heft2-401
Schrader, B. Introduction to Electro-Acoustic Music.
P. Griffiths, 415:May83-302
Schramm, S.S. Plow Women rather than Reapers.
S. Foster, 677(YES):Vol 13-338
Schreck, J. - see Jandl, E.
Schreiber, B. L'Organeau.
H. Thomas, 450(NRF):Apr83-125
Schreiber, F. The Estiennes.
E. Armstrong, 517(PBSA):Vol77No3-402
G. Guilleminot, 354:Dec83-417
S. Sider, 551(RenQ):Winter83-588
Schreiber, M.H. Last of a Breed.
L. Clayton, 649(WAL):Nov83-261
Schreiber, W.L. Die Kräuterbücher des XV. und XVI. Jahrhunderts. (R.W. Fuchs, ed)
J.L. Flood, 354:Sep83-316
Schreier-Hornung, A. Spielleute, Fahrende, Aussenseiter.
D.H. Green, 402(MLR):Apr83-480
W. Salmen, 680(ZDP):Band102Heft3-455
Schreuders, P. Paperbacks, U.S.A.
517(PBSA):Vol77No2-253
Schrey, H. Das verlorene Paradies.
G. Kalb, 72:Band220Heft2-399
Schricker, G.C. A New Species of Man.
S. Connelly, 174(Éire):Winter83-152
Schrijvers, P.H. Horatius: "Ars Poetica."
J.J.L. Smolenaars, 204(FdL):Jun82-158
Schröder, S. Deutsche Komparatistik im Wilhelminischen Zeitalter 1871-1918.
P. Mellen, 221(GQ):Jan83-118
Schröder, W. Reflektierter Roman.
F.N. Smith, 395(MFS):Spring83-127
Schröder, W. Text und Interpretation.
R. Deist, 406:Winter83-438
Schröder, W. Texte und Untersuchungen zur "Willehalm"-Rezeption.
N.F. Palmer, 402(MLR):Jul83-748

335

Schröder, W. Wolfram-Nachfolge im "Jun-
geren Titurel."
　　A. Ebenbauer, 684(ZDA):Band112Heft4-
　　160
Schroeder, C.L. A Bibliography of Danish
Literature in English Translation 1950-
1980.
　　A. Jørgensen, 172(Edda):1983/4-245
Schroeder, J. Pierre Reverdy.*
　　A.D. Ketchum, 207(FR):Mar84-564
Schröpfer, J. Semantische Hefte IV.
Wörterbuch der vergleichenden Bezeich-
nungslehre.
　　J.T. Baer, 574(SEEJ):Summer83-276
Schubert, D. Die Kunst Lehmbrucks.
　　J. Heusinger von Waldegg, 471:
　　Jul/Aug/Sep83-289
"Schuchardt-Symposium 1977 in Graz."
　　H. Penzl, 685(ZDL):1/1983-62
Schudson, M. Advertising, the Uneasy Per-
suasion.
　　S. Fox, 441:23Dec84-11
Schuh, D. Erlasse und Sendschreiben
mongolischer Herrscher für tibetische
Geistliche.
　　J.W. de Jong, 259(IIJ):Apr83-218
Schuh, D. Grundlagen tibetischer Siegel-
kunde.
　　J.W. de Jong, 259(IIJ):Apr83-218
Schuh, D. Tibetische Handschriften und
Blockdrucke. (Pt 8)
　　J.W. de Jong, 259(IIJ):Mar83-158
Schuh, D., ed. Urkunden und Sendschreiben
aus Zentraltibet, Ladakh und Zanskar.
(Pt 1)
　　J.W. de Jong, 259(IIJ):Apr83-218
Schuh, D. and L.S. Dagyab. Urkunden,
Erlasse und Sendschreiben aus dem Besitz
sikkimesischer Adelshäuser und des
Klosters Phodang.
　　J.W. de Jong, 259(IIJ):Apr83-218
Schuh, D. and J.K. Phukhang. Urkunden und
Sendschreiben aus Zentraltibet, Ladakh
und Zanskar. (Pt 2)
　　J.W. de Jong, 259(IIJ):Apr83-218
Schuh, R.G. A Dictionary of Ngizim.
　　J. Verschueren, 350:Mar84-195
Schuh, W. Richard Strauss: a Chronicle
of the Early Years, 1864-1898.*
　　R. Anderson, 415:Feb83-106
　　B. Gilliam, 451:Fall83-174
Schuhmacher, K. "Weil es geschehen ist."
　　R. Kieser, 406:Fall83-317
Schulberg, B. Moving Pictures.*
　　A. Marlow, 364:Jul83-104
Schulte, B. Ödön von Horváth.
　　B. Zimmermann, 133:Band16Heft2/3-276
Schulte, G. 200 Jahre Vernunftkritik.
　　A. Kudascheff, 342:Band74Heft1-86
Schultheis, R. The Hidden West.
　　J.C. and S. Work, 649(WAL):Nov83-264
　　639(VQR):Winter83-28
Schultz, J.W. Many Strange Characters.
　　(E.L. Silliman, ed)
　　W. Blevins, 649(WAL):Nov83-266
　　R.L. Buckland, 573(SSF):Winter83-64
Schultz, W. Herman Saftleven 1609-1685.
　　C.J.W., 90:Nov83-708
Schultze, S. The Structure of "Anna
Karenina."*
　　P. Mitchell, 574(SEEJ):Spring83-106

Schulz, G. Die Deutsche Literatur zwis-
chen Französischer Revolution und Res-
tauration. (Vol 7, Pt 1)
　　T.J. Reed, 617(TLS):23Mar84-309
Schulz, G., ed. Seltene Texte aus der
deutschen Romantik. (Vols 2-4)
　　A. Stephens, 67:May83-144
Schulz, G-M. Die Überwindung der Bar-
barei.*
　　S.D. Martinson, 406:Fall83-336
Schulz, R.A. and others. Lesen, Lachen,
Lernen.
　　I. Henderson, 399(MLJ):Spring83-78
Schumann, O. - see "Lateinisches Hexameter-
Lexikon"
Schumann, R. Tagebücher. (Vol 3) (G.
Nauhaus, ed)
　　J. Chernaik, 617(TLS):18May84-542
Schurhammer, G. Francis Xavier. (Vol 4)
　　M. Cooper, 407(MN):Winter83-446
　　W.J. Miller, 377:Jul83-122
Schuring, G.K. A Multilingual Society.
　　A. Berteloot, 685(ZDL):3/1983-399
Schürmann, R. Le Principe d'anarchie.
　　T. Cordellier, 450(NRF):Jan83-120
Schusky, R., ed. Das deutsche Singspiel
im 18. Jahrhundert.
　　G. Flaherty, 301(JEGP):Jul83-422
Schüssler, I. Philosophie und Wissen-
schaftspositivismus.
　　P. Rohs, 342:Band74Heft3-359
Schuster, I., ed. Interpretationen zu
Alfred Döblin.
　　M.S. Fries, 221(GQ):Mar83-341
Schuster, I. - see Rose, E.
Schutte, J., ed. Lyrik des Naturalismus.
　　R.C. Cowen, 133:Band16Heft2/3-261
Schutte, W.M. List of Recurrent Elements
in James Joyce's "Ulysses."*
　　R. Boyle, 305(JIL):May83-110
Schütz, A. Life Forms and Meaning Struc-
ture.
　　R.J. Anderson and W.W. Sharrock,
　　323:Jan83-91
　　J.J., 185:Jul84-729
Schutz, A. and T. Parsons. The Theory of
Social Action. (R. Grathoff, ed)
　　P. Lantz, 192(EP):Apr-Jun83-238
Schütz, B. Die Katharinenkirche in Oppen-
heim.
　　N. Borger-Keweloh, 683:Band46Heft4-444
Schütz, E. and others. Einführung in die
deutsche Literatur des 20. Jahrhunderts.
(Vol 3)
　　G. Tracy, 406:Winter83-447
Schütz, H. Martin Luther.
　　S. Streller, 654(WB):11/1983-1983
Schutz, H. The Prehistory of Germanic
Europe.
　　A.G. Sherratt, 617(TLS):20Apr84-437
Schütze, P. Peter Hacks.
　　E. Glew, 221(GQ):Jan83-176
Schützeichel, R. Textgebundenheit.
　　J.A. Davidson, 221(GQ):Jan83-130
Schüwer, H. Wortgeographische und etymol-
ogische Untersuchungen zur Terminologie
des Ackerwagens.
　　J.B. Berns, 685(ZDL):1/1983-90
Schvey, H.I. Oskar Kokoschka.
　　J.M. Ritchie, 397(MD):Dec83-578
　　295(JML):Nov83-517
Schwab, R. The Oriental Renaissance.
　　B. Lewis, 441:23Dec84-15

Schwake, H.P. Der Wortschatz des "Cligés" von Chrétien de Troyes.
M. Offord, 208(FS):Apr83-201
H.J. Wolf, 72:Band219Heft1-222
Schwamm, E. How He Saved Her.*
M.K. Benet, 617(TLS):27Apr84-476
W.H. Pritchard, 249(HudR):Winter83/84-744
Schwarberg, G. The Murders at Bullenhuser Damm.
N. Ascherson, 453(NYRB):19Jul84-9
Schwarcz, V. Long Road Home.
R. Bernstein, 441:29Jul84-21
D. Davin, 617(TLS):26Oct84-1206
Schwartz, D. Letters of Delmore Schwartz. (R. Phillips, ed)
E. Hardwick, 441:30Dec84-1
Schwartz, L. Diderot and the Jews.*
L. Jacobs, 208(FS):Oct83-460
Schwartz, L. These People.*
R. Tillinghast, 569(SR):Summer83-473
Schwartz, L. and S.P. Estess, eds. Elizabeth Bishop and Her Art.*
L. Keller, 659(ConL):Summer84-242
Schwartz, L.H. Marxism and Culture.
C. Kleinhans, 125:Winter83-208
Schwartz, L.S. Acquainted With the Night.
A. Hulbert, 441:26Aug84-9
Schwartz, M.M. and C. Kahn, eds. Representing Shakespeare.*
S. Weiland, 128(CE):Nov83-705
Schwartz, N. Hamlet i klasskampen.
G. Orton, 562(Scan):Nov82-199
Schwartz, S. The Art Presence.*
J. Gilder, 55:Apr83-21
Schwartzman, H.B. Transformations.
F. Elkin, 488:Mar83-99
Schwarz, C. Der nicht-nominale MENT-Ausdruck im Französischen.*
K. Karlsson, 545(RPh):Aug82-111
Schwarz, D.R. Conrad: "Almayer's Folly" to "Under Western Eyes."*
E. Bevan, Jr., 136:Vol 15No2-158
R.O. Evans, 569(SR):Spring83-291
J. Halperin, 637(VS):Winter83-227
A. Hunter, 447(N&Q):Jun82-258
Schwarz, D.R. Conrad: The Later Fiction.
R.O. Evans, 569(SR):Spring83-291
D.L. Higdon, 395(MFS):Winter83-766
D. Kramer, 573(SSF):Spring-Summer83-146
Schwarz, D.R. Disraeli's Fiction.*
P. Coustillas, 189(EA):Apr-Jun84-214
R. O'Kell, 637(VS):Spring83-347
Schwarz, E. Music.
P. Standford, 415:Jun83-359
Schwarz, H-P. Geschichte der Bundesrepublik Deutschland. (Vols 2 and 3)
W. Laqueur, 617(TLS):17Aug84-921
Schwarz, J.A. The Speculator.
E.A. Rosen, 579(SAQ):Summer83-331
Schwarz, J.E. America's Hidden Success.
W.E. Leuchtenburg, 61:Apr84-138
N.W. Polsby, 129:Apr84-77
A.M. Rivlin, 441:1Jan84-16
Schwarz, P.P. Lyrik und Zeitgeschichte.
R. Nägele, 406:Summer83-233
Schwarz, W., comp. Rückläufiges Wörterbuch des Altindischen/Reverse Index of Old Indian. (Pts 1-4)
J.W. de Jong, 259(IIJ):Mar83-140

Schwarzbaum, H. Biblical and Extra-Biblical Legends in Islamic Folk-Literature.
M. Piamenta, 196:Band24Heft3/4-327
Schwarze, C., ed. Analyse des prépositions.*
J. Herschensohn, 660(Word):Apr83-45
Schwarzer, A. Simone de Beauvoir Today.
A. Ryan, 362:24May84-26
Schwarzkopf, E. On and Off the Record.
D.R.P., 412:Aug-Nov82-278
Schweickart, D. Capitalism or Worker Control?*
J. Sensat, 482(PhR):Oct83-622
Schweikle, G. Die mittelhochdeutsche Minnelyrik 1.
N.F. Palmer, 447(N&Q):Feb82-88
Schweitzer, D. Science Fiction Voices 5.
P. Fitting, 561(SFS):Nov83-352
Schweizer, N.R. Hawai'i und die deutschsprachigen Völker.
P.D. Sweet, 221(GQ):Mar83-350
Schwengel, G. Propago sacri ordinis Cartusiensis per Germaniam. (Vol 1)
R.B. Marks, 589:Oct83-1134
Schwenger, P. Phallic Critiques.
C. Gardner, 362:30Aug84-28
Schwertheim, E. Die Inschriften von Kyzikos und Umgebung.* (Pt 1)
H.W. Pleket, 394:Vol36fasc3/4-450
Schwob, A. Historische Realität und literarische Umsetzung.
A. Robertshaw, 402(MLR):Jul83-752
Sciascia, L. Cruciverba.
U. Varnai, 617(TLS):30Mar84-348
Sciascia, L. The Day of the Owl [and] Equal Danger.
M. Laski, 362:25Oct84-29
P. McCarthy, 617(TLS):26Oct84-1223
Scobie, S. A Grand Memory for Forgetting.*
A. Mandel, 102(CanL):Winter82-132
B. Whiteman, 198:Jan83-122
Scoff, A. Le Pantalon.
C. Coll, 207(FR):Apr84-739
Scofield, M. The Ghosts of "Hamlet."*
W. Erzgräber, 156(JDSh):Jahrbuch 1983-248
G.P. Jones, 627(UTQ):Fall82-106
A.D. Moody, 402(MLR):Jul83-673
Scollon, R. and S.B.K. Narrative, Literacy, and Face in Interethnic Communication.
S.E. Jacobs, 608:Sep84-519
M. Solá, 355(LSoc):Dec83-533
Scotellaro, R. The Dawn is Always New.
W.S. Di Piero, 472:Fall/Winter83Spring/Summer84-169
A-M. O'Healy, 276:Spring83-82
Scott, A. The Dynamics of Interdependence.
639(VQR):Autumn83-130
Scott, A., comp. Scotch Passion.*
C. Milton, 571(ScLJ):Winter83-66
Scott, A. and J. Aitchison, eds. New Writing Scotland 1983.
A. Stevenson, 617(TLS):13Apr84-398
Scott, C. Antichthon.
J. Mills, 99:Apr83-29
S. Whaley, 102(CanL):Spring83-122
Scott, C. French Verse-Art.*
A. Fairlie, 208(FS):Jul83-369
Scott, C. A Historian and His World.
G. Bull, 362:3May84-26
B. Fothergill, 617(TLS):10Aug84-899

Scott, D., ed. Bread and Roses.*
    N. Rhodes, 493:Mar83-73
Scott, D. Dreadsong.
    S. Brown, 493:Jun83-67
Scott, F.R. The Collected Poems of F.R.
    Scott.*
    T. Whalen, 198:Jan83-96
Scott, G.D., with B. Trent. Inmate.
    A. Propper, 529(QQ):Winter83-1209
Scott, H.F. and W.F., eds. The Soviet Art
    of War.
    J.R. Adelman, 550(RusR):Jan83-114
Scott, J. All The Pretty People.
    T.J. Binyon, 617(TLS):27Jan84-93
Scott, J. - see William of Malmesbury
Scott, J.S. Corporal Smithers, Deceased.*
    N. Callendar, 441:1Jan84-26
Scott, M. Late Gothic Europe, 1400-1500.*
    J. Harris, 59:Mar83-110
Scott, M. Mauriac.*
    K. Goesch, 535(RHL):Sep/Dec83-966
    B. Lustig, 546(RR):Jan83-111
Scott, P. The Crisis of the University.
    E. Parkes, 617(TLS):31Aug84-959
Scott, P.H. and A.C. Davis, eds. The Age
    of MacDiarmid.
    M. McCulloch, 588(SSL):Vol 18-259
Scott, P.J.M. Jane Austen: A Reassessment.*
    P. Goubert, 189(EA):Jul-Sep84-334
Scott, P.J.M. E.M. Forster.
    L. Mackinnon, 617(TLS):6Jul84-763
Scott, P.J.M. Reality and Comic Confi-
    dence in Charles Dickens.
    R. Bennett, 541(RES):May83-236
Scott, W. The Heart of Midlothian. (C.
    Lamont, ed)
    M. Dodsworth, 175:Summer83-195
Scott, W. Waverley; or, 'Tis Sixty Years
    Since.* (C. Lamont, ed)
    T. Dale, 588(SSL):Vol 18-272
    F. Jordan, 661(WC):Summer83-145
Scott, W.O. The God of Arts.
    A.D. Nuttall, 570(SQ):Spring83-126
Scotto, R. and O. Roca. Scotto.
    B. Holland, 441:11Nov83-33
Scotus, J.D. God and Creatures. (F.
    Alluntis and A.B. Wolter, eds and trans)
    J. Longeway, 482(PhR):Jul83-431
Scragg, D.G., ed. The Battle of Maldon.
    G. Clark, 589:Oct83-1082
    R. Huisman, 67:May83-128
Screech, M.A. Montaigne and Melancholy.
    M. Fumaroli, 617(TLS):6Jan84-6
Screen, J.E.O. Finland.
    D. Barrett, 562(Scan):May83-100
Scribner, R.W. For the Sake of Simple
    Folk.*
    C. Garside, Jr., 551(RenQ):Autumn83-
    439
    M. Hunter, 78(BC):Summer83-229
Scribner, S. and M. Cole. The Psychology
    of Literacy.*
    R.M. Brend, 660(Word):Aug83-135
    D.A. Wagner and K.M. Seeley, 355(LSoc):
    Sep83-394
Scrivá, L. Veneris tribunal. (R. Rohland
    de Langbehn, ed)
    P.E. Grieve, 304(JHP):Spring83-214
Scriven, M. Sartre's Existential Biogra-
    phies.
    A. Lavers, 617(TLS):11May84-511

Scrivener, M.H. Radical Shelley.*
    R.A. Duerksen, 661(WC):Summer83-166
    F. Piquet, 189(EA):Jul-Sep84-338
    G. Woodcock, 569(SR):Fall83-664
    639(VQR):Spring83-45
Scroffa, C. I Cantici di Fidenzio. (P.
    Trifone, ed)
    M. Marti, 228(GSLI):Vol 160fasc509-139
Scroggins, D.C. Las aguafuertes porteñas
    de Roberto Arlt.
    C.S. Mathieu, 238:Dec83-646
Scruggs, C. The Sage of Harlem.
    J. Lester, 441:13May84-23
Scruton, R. The Aesthetics of Architec-
    ture.*
    F. Schier, 479(PhQ):Jan83-100
Scruton, R. From Descartes to Wittgen-
    stein.*
    B. Baxter, 479(PhQ):Oct83-411
    A. Manser, 393(Mind):Jul83-436
    R.N.D. Martin, 84:Jun83-195
    H.M. Solomon, 577(SHR):Spring83-188
Scruton, R. Kant.*
    A. Broadie, 342:Band74Heft4-508
    N. Demê, 542:Jan-Mar83-127
    J.S., 185:Apr84-557
    D. Whewell, 83:Autumn83-197
Scuffil, M. Experiments in Comparative
    Intonation.
    A. Cutler, 353:Vol20No9/10-655
Scull, A., ed. Madhouses, Mad-Doctors,
    and Madmen.
    V. Skultans, 637(VS):Autumn82-106
Scullard, H.H. Festivals and Ceremonies
    of the Roman Republic.*
    E.T. Salmon, 487:Spring83-89
Scupham, P. Winter Quarters.
    H. Lomas, 364:Feb84-83
    J. Mole, 176:Mar84-48
    S. Rae, 617(TLS):17Feb84-168
Seale, D. Vision and Stagecraft in
    Sophocles.
    J. Diggle, 123:Vol33No2-312
Seale, W. The Tasteful Interlude. (2nd
    ed)
    M.Y. Frye, 658:Summer/Autumn83-224
Sealock, R., M.M. Sealock and M.S. Powell.
    Bibliography of Place-Name Literature:
    United States and Canada. (3rd ed)
    K.B. Harder, 424:Sep83-213
Sealsfield, C. Das Kajütenbuch oder Na-
    tionale Charakteristiken. (A. Ritter,
    ed)
    W. Koepke, 133:Band16Heft2/3-257
    H. Steinecke, 221(GQ):Nov83-663
Sealts, M.M., Jr. Pursuing Melville, 1940-
    1980.
    G.W. Allen, 219(GaR):Spring83-216
    R.H. Brodhead, 445(NCF):Sep83-214
    A. Hayman, 395(MFS):Winter83-754
    517(PBSA):Vol77No2-253
Sealy, R.J. The Palace Academy of Henry
    III.
    G. Demerson, 547(RF):Band95Heft3-342
    I.D. McFarlane, 551(RenQ):Autumn83-443
Seaman, D.W. Concrete Poetry in France.
    P.G. Lewis, 207(FR):Dec83-258
"Seamless Knitting from the Top Down."
    M. Fenner, 614:Spring84-28
Sear, F. Roman Architecture.*
    S. Bertman, 124:Sep-Oct83-52
    D. Small, 313:Vol73-223

Searing, H., ed. In Search of Modern
Architecture.
M. Pawley, 46:Aug83-74
D. Watkin, 576:Oct83-304
Searing, H. New American Art Museums.*
M. Jacqz, 55:Dec83-33
Searle, C. Grenada.
R. Fox, 362:2Aug84-26
Searle, C., ed. The Sunflower of Hope.
T. Eagleton, 565:Vol24No3-77
Searle, J. Minds, Brains and Science.
D. Papineau, 617(TLS):14Dec84-1442
Searle, J.R. Expression and Meaning.*
G. Öhlschläger, 72:Band219Heft1-160
Searle, J.R. Intentionality.
J. Hornsby, 617(TLS):2Mar84-217
Searls, H. Blood Song.
M. Buck, 441:22Jul84-20
Sears, D.A. John Neal.
J.E. Reilly, 495(PoeS):Dec83-44
Sears, D.O. and J. Citrin. Tax Revolt.
C.S., 185:Oct83-188
Sears, J.N. The First One Hundred Years
of Town Planning in Georgia.
C.M. Howett, 576:Oct83-308
Sebald, W.G. Der Mythus der Zerstörung
im Werk Döblins.
M.S. Fries, 221(GQ):Mar83-341
Sebbar, L. Schérazade.
M. Sergent, 207(FR):May84-917
Sebeok, T.A. The Sign and its Masters.
B. Lindemann, 307:Oct80-118
Sebeok, T.A. and J. Umiker-Sebeok, eds.
Speaking of Apes.
M.S. Seidenberg, 567:Vol44No1/2-177
Sebeok, T.A. and J. Umiter-Sebeok. "You
Know My Method."*
B. Altshuler, 482(PhR):Jan83-110
V.G. Potter, 258:Jun83-205
Secor, R. John Ruskin and Alfred Hunt.
P. Fontaney, 189(EA):Apr-Jun84-211
Secrest, M. Kenneth Clark.
M. Levey, 362:4Oct84-25
Sedgwick, P. Psychopolitics.
R. Gray, 560:Fall83-125
Sedlar, J.W. India in the Mind of Germany.
P. Gaeffke, 318(JAOS):Jul-Sep82-549
Sedwick, F. Conversation in Spanish.
(3rd ed)
J.R. Green, Jr., 399(MLJ):Spring83-98
von See, K. Skaldendichtung.*
H. Beck, 52:Band17Heft1-83
Seeck, G.A., ed. Das griechische Drama.
D. Babut, 555:Vol57fasc1-122
Seeger, B. Der Harmonikaspieler.
H.J. Geerdts, 654(WB):8/1982-119
Seeley, M. and C. Doll Costuming.
R.L. Shep, 614:Fall84-15
Seelig, S.C. The Shadow of Eternity.*
A.L. Deneef, 579(SAQ):Spring83-233
U.M. Kaufmann, 301(JEGP):Jul83-446
L.L. Martz, 401(MLQ):Dec82-407
J.H. Summers, 551(RenQ):Spring83-151
Seelow, H., ed. Hálfs saga ok Hálfsrekka.
A. Heinrichs, 684(ZDA):Band112Heft4-
149
Seers, D. The Political Economy of Nation-
alism.
C. Ehrlich, 617(TLS):9Nov84-1274
Seferis, G. Collected Poems.
J. Saunders, 565:Vol24No4-71

Segal, C. Dionysiac Poetics and Euripides'
"Bacchae."*
A.N. Michelini, 124:May-Jun84-317
Segal, C. Poetry and Myth in Ancient Pas-
toral.
S. Franchet d'Espèrey, 555:Vol57fasc1-
164
E.M. Jenkinson, 161(DUJ):Jun83-111
Segal, C. Tragedy and Civilization.
P.G. Mason, 123:Vol33No1-5
Segal, G., ed. The China Factor.
W.T. Tow, 293(JASt):Feb83-398
Segalen, M. Love and Power in the Peasant
Family.
G. Wright, 617(TLS):6Jan84-21
Segalen, V. Les Immémoriaux. Peintures.
J. Clifford, 617(TLS):22Jun84-683
Segre, C. Semiotica filologica.
G. Lepschy, 545(RPh):Aug82-80
Segre, C. Structures and Time.*
H.F. Mosher, Jr., 599:Winter83-52
Seibicke, W. Vornamen.
G. Koss, 685(ZDL):1/1983-120
Seide, R. Die mathematischen Stellen bei
Plutarch.
I. Bulmer-Thomas, 123:Vol33No1-143
Seidel, L. Songs of Glory.*
D.M. Ebitz, 576:Oct83-300
Seidenspinner-Núñez, D. The Allegory of
Good Love.
T.R. Hart, 400(MLN):Mar83-285
Seidler, H. Österreichischer Vormärz und
Goethezeit.*
A. Obermayer, 564:Sep83-221
Seifert, A. Untersuchungen zu Hölderlins
Pindar-Rezeption.
H.S. Schultz, 680(ZDP):Band102Heft2-
282
Seifert, J. The Casting of Bells.
R. Scruton, 617(TLS):24Feb84-195
Seifert, J. An Umbrella from Piccadilly.
D. Davis, 362:6Dec84-33
I. Hájek, 364:Nov83-81
R. Scruton, 617(TLS):24Feb84-195
Seignolle, C. The Nightcharmer. (E.H.
Deudon, ed and trans)
J. Sullivan, 441:26Feb84-22
Seiler, R.M., ed. Walter Pater: The Criti-
cal Heritage.
P. Clements, 402(MLR):Oct83-910
Seiler-Franklin, C. Boulder-Pushers.
M.M. Rowe, 395(MFS):Winter83-791
Seitz, W.C. Abstract Expressionist Paint-
ing in America.
D. Rosand, 617(TLS):12Oct84-1155
Sekora, J. Luxury.
W. Franke, 38:Band101Heft1/2-276
Selbourne, D. The Making of "A Midsummer
Night's Dream."*
R. Berry, 150(DR):Autumn83-526
Selby, B. Riding the Mountains Down.
D. Murphy, 617(TLS):22Jun84-692
Seldon, A. and J. Pappworth. By Word of
Mouth.
A. Howkins, 617(TLS):8Jun84-629
Selén, K. C.G.E. Mannerheim ja hänen
puolustusneuvostonsa 1931-1939.
R.G. Selleck, 563(SS):Winter83-101
Sell, R.D. Robert Frost.
A. Massa, 447(N&Q):Aug82-379
M.S., 189(EA):Jan-Mar83-109
Sell, R.D. - see Frost, R.

Sellery, J.M. and W.O. Harris. Elizabeth
Bowen.
  J. Crane, 87(BB):Sep83-193
Sellin, B. The Life and Works of David
Lindsay.
  J.D. McClure, 571(ScLJ):Autumn83-27
  G.D. Martin, 189(EA):Jul-Sep84-350
Sells, A.L.L., with I.L. Sells. Thomas
Gray.
  D. Fairer, 541(RES):Feb83-78
Seltén, B. The Anglo-Saxon Heritage in
Middle English Personal Names: East
Anglia 1100-1399.
  P. Erlebach, 72:Band219Heft2-427
Selwyn, V. and others. From Oasis into
Italy.
  K. Bosley, 617(TLS):6Jul84-760
Selznick, I.M. A Private View.*
  G. Kaufman, 362:19Apr84-26
  S. Laschever, 453(NYRB):19Jan84-34
Semanov, V.I. Lu Hsün and His Predeces-
sors. (C.J. Alber, ed and trans)
  M. Doleželová-Velingerová, 116:Jan82-
  143
Semlak, W.D. Conflict Resolving Communica-
tion.
  T.J. Housel, 583:Summer84-445
Sen, A. Choice, Welfare and Measurement.
  R.H., 185:Oct83-159
Sen, A. Poverty and Famines.
  H. Shue, 185:Jan84-342
Sen, A. and B. Williams, eds. Utilitarian-
ism and Beyond.
  J.J.C. Smart, 483:Jul83-413
Sen, S. Bāṃlā sthān'nām.
  R.P. Das, 259(IIJ):Apr83-215
de Sena, J. Sobre Esta Praia (Over This
Shore). (J. Griffin, trans) The Poetry
of Jorge de Sena. (F.G. Williams, ed)
In Crete, With the Minotaur, and Other
Poems. (G. Monteiro, ed and trans)
  K. Oderman, 50(ArQ):Spring83-77
Senderens, A. The Three-Star Recipes of
Alain Senderens.
  W. and C. Cowen, 639(VQR):Spring83-68
Seneca. Lvcio Anneo Seneca, "De tranquil-
litate animi." (M.G. Cavalca Schiroli,
ed)
  J-C. Fredouille, 555:Vol57fasc2-331
Seneca. L. Annaei Senecae Dialogorum
Libri XII. (L.D. Reynolds, ed)
  B.L. Hijmans, Jr., 394:Vol36fasc3/4-
  429
Sénécal, A. and N. Crane. Québec Studies.
  M. Cagnon, 207(FR):Feb84-428
Senelick, L. Gordon Craig's Moscow
"Hamlet."
  A. Rood, 610:Autumn83-262
Senelick, L., ed and trans. Russian Dra-
matic Theory from Pushkin to the Symbol-
ists.*
  D. Gerould, 397(MD):Dec83-573
  S. Golub, 615(TJ):Oct83-423
Senelick, L., D.F. Cheshire and U. Schnei-
der. British Music Hall 1840-1923.*
  C. Barker, 610:Spring83-70
  M. Vicinus, 637(VS):Winter83-225
Senelier, J. Bibliographie nervalienne
(1968-1980) et compléments antérieurs.
  N. Rinsler, 208(FS):Oct83-474
Senger, M.W. Leonhard Culmann.
  T.I. Bacon, 400(MLN):Apr83-530
  P. Schaeffer, 551(RenQ):Summer83-281

Sengle, F. Biedermeierzeit.* (Vol 3)
  H. Denkler, 680(ZDP):Band102Heft2-266
  N. Oellers, 52:Band17Heft3-324
Senn, H.A. Were-Wolf and Vampire in
Romania.
  J.L. Perkowski, 574(SEEJ):Spring83-126
Senn, W. and D. Daphinoff - see Fricker, R.
Sennett, R. An Evening of Brahms.
  J. Chernaik, 617(TLS):2Nov84-1239
  E. Rothstein, 441:27May84-9
  442(NY):25Jun84-108
Sensibar, J.L. The Origins of Faulkner's
Art.
  H. Kenner, 441:12Aug84-26
Sepamia, S. A Ride on the Whirlwind.
  M. Pollack, 441:2Sep84-14
Šepić, D. Vlada Ivana Šubašića.
  E. Barker, 617(TLS):10Aug84-897
"Les Sept Sages de Rome."
  F. Lecoy, 554:Vol 103No1-143
Serafini, L. Codex Seraphinianus.
  P-L. Adams, 61:Feb84-105
  D.J.R. Bruckner, 441:12Feb84-20
Serafini-Sauli, J.P. Giovanni Boccaccio.
  D.R. Howard, 551(RenQ):Autumn83-410
Serbat, G. Cas et fonctions.*
  R. Martin, 553(RLiR):Jul-Dec83-438
  M. Plénat, 209(FM):Oct83-381
Sereni, V. The Disease of the Elm.
  T. Dooley, 617(TLS):28Sep84-1105
Sergeant, H. Between the Lines.
  G. Wheatcroft, 617(TLS):28Sep84-1099
Sergi, G. Potere e territorio lungo la
strada di Francia.
  E.L. Cox, 589:Oct83-1086
Serjeant, R.B. and R. Lewcock, eds.
San'ā.*
  B. Gray, 39:Jul83-110
de la Serna, R.G. - see under Gómez de la
Serna, R.
Sernin, A. Un philosophe méconnu Georges
Bénézé, 1888-1978.
  M. Adam, 542:Oct-Dec83-503
Serres, M. Hermes. (J.V. Harari and D.F.
Bell, eds)
  J.E. Hogle, 50(ArQ):Summer83-174
Serres, M. The Parasite.*
  J.D. Lyons, 478:Oct83-264
Server, A.W. and J.E. Keller - see Fernán-
dez de Avellaneda, A.
Servet, J.G. - see under García Servet, J.
Service, A. The Architects of London and
their Buildings from 1066 to the Present
Day.
  M.I. Wilson, 39:Jan83-69
Service, A. Edwardian Interiors.*
  P. Davey, 46:Sep83-68
  J. Lees-Milne, 90:Jul83-429
  V. Powell, 39:Mar83-261
Sesonske, A. Jean Renoir, the French
Films, 1924-1939.
  A. Thiher, 207(FR):Oct83-129
Sessions, G.A. Mormon Thunder.
  E.E. Campbell, 651(WHR):Winter83-354
Sessions, R. Roger Sessions on Music.
(E.T. Cone, ed)
  M. Brody, 308:Spring83-111
  A.W., 412:Feb82-68
de Seta, C. Napoli. Architettura, ambi-
ente e società a Napoli nel '700.
  A. Blunt, 90:Feb83-102

Shakespeare, W. The Taming of the Shrew.
(B. Morris, ed) Much Ado About Nothing.
(A.R. Humphreys, ed)
  E.A.J. Honigmann, 161(DUJ):Jun83-95
  W.P. Williams, 570(SQ):Winter83-501
Shakespeare, W. The Taming of the Shrew.*
(H.J. Oliver, ed)
  J. Eberstadt, 129:Dec84-40
  M. Grivelet, 189(EA):Jul-Sep84-319
  A. Gurr, 354:Dec83-430
Shakespeare, W. Titus Andronicus. (E.
Waith, ed) Julius Caesar. (A. Hum-
phreys, ed)
  F. Eberstadt, 129:Dec84-40
Shakespeare, W. Troilus and Cressida.*
(K. Muir, ed)
  J. Eberstadt, 129:Dec84-40
  M. Grivelet, 189(EA):Jul-Sep84-319
  A. Gurr, 354:Dec83-430
  N. Powell, 148:Autumn83-77
Shakespeare, W. Troilus and Cressida.*
(K. Palmer, ed)
  E.A.J. Honigmann, 161(DUJ):Jun83-95
  N. Powell, 148:Autumn83-77
"Shakespeare Survey." (Vol 33) (K. Muir,
ed)
  M. Grivelet, 189(EA):Oct-Dec83-461
  G.P. Jones, 627(UTQ):Fall82-106
  I. Robson, 447(N&Q):Oct82-435
"Shakespeare Survey." (Vol 34) (S. Wells,
ed)
  M. Grivelet, 189(EA):Oct-Dec83-461
  M. Manheim, 130:Summer83-188
  L. Nathanson, 702:Vol 16-377
"Shakespeare Survey."* (Vol 35) (S. Wells,
ed)
  D. Barrett, 610:Autumn83-255
"Shakespeare Survey." (Vol 36) (S. Wells,
ed)
  J. Hankey, 617(TLS):9Mar84-257
Shale, R. Donald Duck Joins Up.
  M. Keller, 127:Fall83-284
Shalhope, R.E. John Taylor of Caroline.
  G. Bilson, 106:Spring83-61
  J.W. Cooke, 396(ModA):Winter83-98
Shallis, M. The Silicon Idol.
  L. Burnard, 617(TLS):14Dec84-1444
Shalom, S. A Marriage Sabbatical.
  B.F. Williamson, 441:28Oct84-27
Shalom, S.R. The United States and the
Philippines.
  R.L. Youngblood, 293(JASt):Nov82-234
El-Shamy, H.M., ed and trans. Folktales
of Egypt.
  F.X. Paz, 318(JAOS):Jan-Mar82-219
  S.J. Webber, 292(JAF):Jan-Mar83-70
Shand Kydd, A. Happy Trails.
  A. Franks, 617(TLS):31Aug84-977
Shank, T. American Alternative Theatre.
  P. Auslander, 615(TJ):May83-277
  J.N. Harris, 610:Autumn83-270
Shankman, S. Pope's "Iliad."
  N. Berry, 364:Nov83-113
  P.J. Connelly, 566:Spring84-160
  J.P. Holoka, 124:May-Jun84-315
  G. Rousseau, 617(TLS):13Jul84-789
  639(VQR):Autumn83-116
Shannon, D. Destiny of Death.
  N. Callendar, 441:13May84-35
Shannon, D. Exploit of Death.
  T.J. Binyon, 617(TLS):30Mar84-354
Shannon, R. Gladstone. (Vol 1)
  S. Rothblatt, 441:5Aug84-20

Shapcott, T. The Birthday Gift.
  J. Tulip, 581:Mar83-113
Shapiro, A. - see Newton, I.
Shapiro, A.M., J.R. Bryer and K. Field.
Carson McCullers.*
  J.S. Crane, 517(PBSA):Vol77No1-102
Shapiro, D. Jasper Johns: Drawings 1954-
1984.
  J. Russell, 441:2Dec84-11
Shapiro, D. To an Idea.
  J. Graham, 441:4Mar84-14
Shapiro, H. The Light Holds.
  D. Ray, 441:1Apr84-26
Shapiro, H.A. Art, Myth and Culture.
  D.C. Kurtz, 303(JoHS):Vol 103-220
Shapiro, M. Hieroglyph of Time.*
  D. Wesling and E. Bollobás, 405(MP):
  Aug83-53
Shapiro, M.H., ed. Biological and Behav-
ioral Technologies and the Law.
  B.F., 185:Oct83-182
Shapiro, M.J. Language and Political
Understanding.*
  S. James, 483:Oct83-552
Sharma, M.M. Inscriptions of Ancient
Assam.
  J.W. de Jong, 259(IIJ):Apr83-211
Sharma, M.N. Wodehouse the Fictionist.
  R.J. Voorhees, 395(MFS):Summer83-271
Sharma, R.S. Śūdras in Ancient India.
(2nd ed)
  S.J.M. Sutherland, 293(JASt):Aug83-
  1004
Sharp, F.M. The Poet's Madness.*
  U. Rainer, 406:Winter83-450
Sharpe, L. Schiller and the Historical
Character.
  C.P. Magill, 610:Summer83-168
  J.W. Smeed, 83:Autumn83-276
  W. Witte, 402(MLR):Oct83-974
Sharpe, T. Vintage Stuff.*
  J.R.B., 148:Autumn83-92
Sharpe, T. Wilt on High.
  J. Mellors, 362:11Oct84-30
  T.O. Treadwell, 617(TLS):12Oct84-1166
Sharples, R.W. Alexander of Aphrodisias
on Fate.
  S. Waterlow, 617(TLS):17Feb84-173
Sharratt, B. Reading Relations.
  C. Norris, 402(MLR):Jul83-640
  R.J. Schoeck, 125:Spring83-301
  S. Smith, 366:Autumn83-257
Sharrer, H.L., ed. The Legendary History
of Britain in Lope García de Salazar's
"Libro de las bienandanzas e fortunas."*
  C. Stern, 545(RPh):May83-645
Shattock, J. and M. Wolff, eds. The Vic-
torian Periodical Press.
  H.W., 636(VP):Summer83-198
  M. Woodfield, 184(EIC):Jan83-68
Shaw, A. Dictionary of American Pop/Rock.
  C.A. and R.R.B., 35(AS):Winter83-372
Shaw, B. Orbitsville Departure.
  M. Rosen, 617(TLS):13Jan84-46
Shaw, B. - see Dumas, A.
Shaw, B.D. and R.P. Saller - see Finley,
M.I.
Shaw, C.M. "Some Vanity of Mine Art."
  W.D. Lehrman, 568(SCN):Fall83-49
Shaw, D. Press Watch.
  P.H. Stone, 441:27May84-17

Sheppard, A.D.R. Studies on the 5th and
6th Essays of Proclus' "Commentary on
the Republic."*
  G.J.P. O'Daly, 123:Vol33No2-242
Sheppard, D.C., general ed. Favorite
Meals From Williamsburg.
  W. and C. Cowen, 639(VQR):Spring83-66
Sheppard, F.H.W., ed. Survey of London.
(Vol 40, Pt 2)
  J. Harris, 90:Apr83-234
Sheppard, F.H.W., ed. Survey of London.*
(Vol 41)
  J. Hayes, 324:Sep84-697
Sheppard, R., ed. Die Schriften des Neuen
Clubs, 1908-1914. (Vol 1)
  M. Pazi, 221(GQ):Nov83-676
Sheraton, M. New York Times Guide to New
York Restaurants.
  639(VQR):Summer83-100
Sheratt, A., ed. The Cambridge Encyclo-
pedia of Archaeology.
  G.H. Hampton, 70:Sep/Oct81-28
Sheridan, E.R. Lewis Morris, 1671-1746.*
  J. Judd, 656(WMQ):Jan83-135
Sheridan, J.J. - see Alan of Lille
Sheridan, P. Penny Theatres of Victorian
London.
  M. Vicinus, 637(VS):Winter83-225
Sherman, C.R., with A.M. Holcomb, eds.
Women as Interpreters of the Visual Arts,
1820-1979.*
  S. ffolliott, 551(RenQ):Autumn83-422
  M. Tippett, 529(QQ):Spring83-276
"Cindy Sherman."
  A. Grundberg, 441:22Jul84-11
Sherman, J. Lords of Shouting.
  B.K. Filson, 526:Winter83-80
  P. Monk, 150(DR):Spring83-179
  A. Munton, 198:Jun83-81
Sherman, K. The Cost of Living.
  D. Daymond, 102(CanL):Summer83-140
Sherman, K. Words for Elephant Man.
  P.K. Smith, 99:Mar84-48
Sherry, C. Wordsworth's Poetry of the
Imagination.*
  J. Arac, 591(SIR):Spring83-136
  J.D. Gutteridge, 447(N&Q):Aug82-361
  M. Isnard, 189(EA):Jan-Mar83-85
  W.J.B. Owen, 541(RES):Aug83-346
Sherwin-White, A.N. Roman Foreign Policy
in the East 168 BC to AD 1.
  E. Badian, 617(TLS):24Aug84-952
Sherwood, J. Green Trigger Fingers.
  T.J.B., 617(TLS):8Jun84-632
Sherwood, S. Venice Simplon Orient-
Express.
  442(NY):26Mar84-134
Sheth, K.V. - see Jayavanta-Sūri
Sheth, N.R. The Social Framework of an
Indian Factory.
  A.M. Weiss, 293(JASt):May83-709
Shevelov, G.Y. A Historical Phonology of
the Ukrainian Language.*
  J. Udolph, 260(IF):Band88-365
Shick, T.W. Behold the Promised Land.
  C. Fyfe, 69:Vol53No1-100
Shields, H. Shamrock, Rose and Thistle.
  P. Cooke, 187:May84-343
Shifflett, C.A. Patronage and Poverty in
the Tobacco South.
  639(VQR):Summer83-82
Shigeo, K. - see under Kishibe Shigeo
Shigeru, H. - see under Honjō Shigeru

Shikatani, G. and D. Aylward, eds. Paper
Doors.
  T. Cullis, 102(CanL):Summer83-150
"Murasaki Shikibu: Her Diary and Poetic
Memoirs" - see under Murasaki
Shillony, B-A. Politics and Culture in
Wartime Japan.*
  A. Gordon, 293(JASt):May83-676
Shils, E. Tradition.
  A. Warren, 396(ModA):Winter83-80
Shimizu, M. Das "Selbst" in Mahāyāna-
Buddhismus in Japanischer Sicht und die
"Person" im Christentum im Licht des
Neuen Testaments.
  J. Van Bragt, 407(MN):Winter83-467
Shimomiya, T. Zur Typologie des Georg-
ischen (verglichen mit dem Indogerman-
ischen).*
  R. Bielmeier, 260(IF):Band87-388
Shimony, A. and H. Feshbach, eds. Physics
as Natural Philosophy.
  A.B. Stewart, 42(AR):Summer83-369
Shine, W. and J. A Bibliography of the
Published Works of John D. MacDonald,
with Selected Biographical Materials
and Critical Essays.
  E. Mason, 517(PBSA):Vol77No1-105
Shinn, R.L. Forced Options.
  R.M., 185:Oct83-175
Shinran. Notes on the Inscriptions on
Sacred Scrolls.
  L.O. Gómez, 407(MN):Spring83-73
Shipley, J.T. The Origins of English
Words.
  P-L. Adams, 61:Aug84-113
  C.R. Sleeth, 617(TLS):14Sep84-1031
Shipley, V. Jack Tales.
  G.S.S. Chandra, 436(NewL):Summer84-114
Shipp, G.P. Modern Greek Evidence for the
Ancient Greek Vocabulary.*
  C.J. Ruijgh, 394:Vol36fasc3/4-380
Shiratori, R., ed. Japan in the 1980s.
  G.D. Hook, 285(JapQ):Oct-Dec83-433
Shirer, W.L. The Nightmare Years: 1930-
1940.
  N. Bliven, 442(NY):2Jul84-99
  J. Chancellor, 441:27May84-10
Shirk, S.L. Competitive Comrades.
  J. Kwong, 293(JASt):May83-646
  W.M., 185:Oct83-177
Shirley, F.A. Swearing and Perjury in
Shakespeare's Plays.
  H-J. Weckermann, 570(SQ):Winter83-510
Shirley, J.W. Thomas Harriot.
  J. Roche, 617(TLS):13Jan84-34
Shivers, L. Here to Get My Baby Out of
Jail.*
  P. Craig, 617(TLS):28Dec84-1506
  639(VQR):Summer83-91
Shklar, J.N. Ordinary Vices.
  A.C. Danto, 617(TLS):21Dec84-1472
Shloss, C. Flannery O'Connor's Dark
Comedies.*
  D. Seed, 447(N&Q):Jun82-276
Shoben, E.J., Jr. Lionel Trilling.
  R. Langbaum, 31(ASch):Winter82/83-132
  J. Martin, 579(SAQ):Spring83-216
Shoemaker, S. and R. Swinburne. Personal
Identity.
  T. Baldwin, 176:Nov84-62
Shoemaker, W.H. The Novelistic Art of
Galdós.*
  R. Landeira, 552(REH):Jan83-151

"Shogun: The Shogun Age Exhibition."
R.L. Shep, 614:Summer84-28
Shomu, N. and A. Katsumaro - see under
Nobori Shomu and Akamatsu Katsumaro
Shonfield, A. In Defence of the Mixed
Economy.
S. Blank, 441:12Oct84-51
Shope, R.K. The Analysis of Knowing.*
F.F.S., 185:Jul84-729
Shore, L. Pure Running.
D. Gittins, 637(VS):Summer83-431
Shorris, E. Jews Without Mercy.
J.V. Mallow, 287:May83-24
Shorris, E., with E. Etheridge and S.
Sasson, eds. While Someone Else is
Eating.
S.V. Roberts, 441:8Jul84-21
Short, A. The First Fair Wind.
S. Altinel, 617(TLS):7Dec84-1420
Shorter, E. A History of Women's Bodies.*
G. Finn, 99:Jul83-33
P.E. Malcolmson, 529(QQ):Autumn83-917
Shotaro, Y. - see under Yasuoka Shotaro
Shotter, J. Social Accountability and
Selfhood.
D. Ingleby, 617(TLS):9Nov84-1287
Showalter, J.C. and J. Driesbach, eds.
Wooton Patent Desks.
P. Bach, 614:Summer84-31
Shōyō, T. The Essence of the Novel.
R. Rolf, 407(MN):Winter83-434
Shreve, S.R. Dreaming of Heroes.
T. Edwards, 441:1Apr84-8
Shtromas, A. Political Change and Social
Development.*
M. McCauley, 575(SEER):Jul83-476
Shu-Min, H. - see under Huang Shu-Min
Shubik, M. Game Theory in the Social
Sciences.
R.H., 185:Jan84-366
Shue, H. Basic Rights.
M.D. Bayles, 543:Jun83-947
P. Dubois, 542:Jul-Sep83-342
A. Kuflik, 185:Jan84-319
Shukla, Y.K. Wall Paintings of Rajasthan.
E. Bender, 318(JAOS):Oct-Dec82-682
Shuldham-Shaw, P. and E.B. Lyle, eds. The
Greig-Duncan Folksong Collection. (Vol
1)
P. Cooke, 187:May84-343
W. Donaldson, 571(ScLJ):Autumn83-1
Shulman, D.D. Tamil Temple Myths.*
P.M. Gardner, 292(JAF):Jan-Mar83-81
Shulman, F.J., ed. Doctoral Dissertations
on Japan and Korea, 1969-1979.
M. Cooper, 407(MN):Summer83-220
Shultz, R.H. and R. Godson. Dezinformat-
sia.
H. Bering-Jensen, 129:Dec84-76
I. Elliot, 617(TLS):26Oct84-1207
Shumaker, W. Renaissance Curiosa.
L.V.R., 568(SCN):Spring/Summer83-27
T.W., 111:Spring83-1
Shurkin, J. Engines of the Mind.
W. Stockton, 441:24Jun84-17
Shurr, W.H. The Marriage of Emily Dickin-
son.
M.L. Rosenthal, 617(TLS):15Jun84-669
Shurr, W.H. Rappaccini's Children.*
A.M. Woodlief, 577(SHR):Fall83-373
Shuter-Dyson, R. and C. Gabriel. The Psy-
chology of Musical Ability.*
F. Berenson, 89(BJA):Winter83-93

Shuttleworth, S. George Eliot and
Nineteenth-Century Science.
M. Mason, 617(TLS):1Jun84-606
Shuy, R.W. and A. Shnukal, eds. Language
Use and the Uses of Language.*
L. D'Amico-Reisner, 355(LSoc):Mar83-96
Shyirambere, S. Contribution à l'étude de
la sociolinguistique du bilinguisme.
K. Legère, 682(ZPSK):Band36Heft1-106
"Sibley's Heir."
W. Bentinck-Smith, 432(NEQ):Jun83-284
Sicard, A. El pensamiento poético de
Pablo Neruda.
J.H. Ward, 238:Mar83-140
Sicherl, M. Johannes Cuno.
G. Billanovich, 52:Band17Heft2-203
Sicherman, B. Alice Hamilton: A Life in
Letters.
P-L. Adams, 61:Oct84-126
Siciliano, E. Pasolini.* (Italian title:
Vita di Pasolini.)
J. Ahern, 472:Fall/Winter83Spring/
Summer84-103
295(JML):Nov83-550
Sidane, V. Le Printemps de Pékin, Opposi-
tions Démocratiques en Chine, Novembre
1978-Mars 1980.
R. Weidenbaum, 293(JASt):May83-639
Sidane, V. and W. Zafanolli. Procès Polit-
iques à Pékin, Wei Jingsheng, Fu Yuehua.
R. Weidenbaum, 293(JASt):May83-639
Sidel, V.W. and R., eds. Reforming
Medicine.
P. Starr, 441:4Mar84-25
Sider, D. - see Anaxagoras
Sidhu, J.S. Administration in the Feder-
ated Malay States: 1896-1920.
C.A. Trocki, 293(JASt):May83-727
Sidney, R. The Poems of Robert Sidney.
(P.J. Croft, ed)
H.R. Woudhuysen, 617(TLS):26Oct84-1219
"Siebenbürgisch-Sächsisches Wörterbuch."
(Vols 4 and 5)
K. Rein, 685(ZDL):1/1983-102
Siebenheller, N. P.D. James.
P. Wolfe, 395(MFS):Autumn83-389
Sieber, R. African Furniture and House-
hold Objects.*
M. Gilbert, 69:Vol153No3-99
Siebers, T. The Romantic Fantastic.
R. Ashton, 617(TLS):12Oct84-1170
Siegel, F.F. Troubled Journey.
J.C. Furnas, 441:30Sep84-34
Siegel, P.J. Alfred de Musset.*
A.V. Bruegge, 615(TJ):Dec83-562
D.G. Charlton, 208(FS):Jul83-350
S. Walton, 402(MLR):Jul83-715
Sieghart, P. The International Law of
Human Rights.*
J.M.G., 185:Apr84-567
Siekmann, A. Drama und sentimentalisches
Bewusstsein.
F. Piedmont, 406:Summer83-210
Siemek, A. La Recherche morale et esthé-
tique dans le roman de Crébillon fils.
J.F. Jones, Jr., 207(FR):Dec83-250
R. Veasey, 402(MLR):Apr83-451
Sienkewicz, T. Classical Gods and Heroes
in the National Gallery of Art.
E. Dwyer, 124:Jan-Feb84-194

Siep, L. Recognition as the Principle of
Practical Philosophy. (German title:
Anerkennung als Prinzip der praktischen
Philosophie.)
    W. Bonsiepen, 125:Summer83-367
    R.R. Williams, 142:Spring82-101
Siepmann, H. Die portugiesische Lyrik des
Segundo Modernismo.
    G.R. Lind, 72:Band219Heft2-474
Siewert, P. Die Trittyen Attikas und die
Heeresreform des Kleisthenes.
    A. Andrewes, 123:Vol33No2-346
    P.J. Rhodes, 303(JoHS):Vol 103-203
Sigaux, G. - see Dumas, A.
Sigouin, G. Théâtre en lutte.
    L.E. Doucette, 627(UTQ):Summer83-527
Silbergeld, J. Chinese Painting Style.
    M. Tregear, 324:May84-413
Silberman, M., ed. Zum Roman in der DDR.
    F.D. Hirschbach, 221(GQ):Jan83-179
    A. Stephan, 406:Winter83-460
Silburn, L. Śivasūtra et Vimarśinī de
Kṣemarāja.
    A. Bharati, 293(JASt):May83-710
Silius Italicus, T.C. La Guerre Punique.
(Bks 5-8) (J. Volpilhac, P. Miniconi and
G. Devallet, eds and trans)
    F. Delarue, 555:Vol57fasc2-322
    D.C. Feeney, 123:Vol33No2-322
Silk, G. and others. Automobile and Cul-
ture.
    P. Goldberger, 441:2Dec84-18
Silk, L. Economics in the Real World.
    R.M. Solow, 441:30Dec84-7
Silk, M.S. and J.P. Stern. Nietzsche on
Tragedy.*
    R. Furness, 402(MLR):Apr83-498
    A. Stephens, 67:May83-146
Silkin, J. Autobiographical Stanzas.
    T. Dooley, 617(TLS):28Sep84-1105
Silko, L.M. Storyteller.
    T. King, 649(WAL):May83-86
"Silks From the Palaces of Napoleon."
    R.L. Shep, 614:Winter84-22
Silliman, E.L. - see Schultz, J.W.
Silliman, R. ABC. Tjanting.
    M. Perloff, 29:May/Jun84-15
Sillitoe, A. Down from the Hill.
    B. Hardy, 617(TLS):16Nov84-1301
Sillitoe, A. The Lost Flying Boat.*
    M. Mewshaw, 441:14Oct84-26
Sillitoe, A. The Second Chance and Other
Stories.
    S. Monod, 189(EA):Apr-Sep83-353
Silver, A. Bernard Shaw.*
    B.M. Fisher, 177(ELT):Vol26No4-315
    A. Turco, Jr., 572:Vol4-185
    J.P. Wearing, 637(VS):Spring83-364
Silver, A.I. The French-Canadian Idea of
Confederation, 1864-1900.
    R. Hudon, 529(QQ):Autumn83-872
Silver, B.R. Virginia Woolf's Reading
Notebooks.
    J. Batchelor, 617(TLS):10Aug84-900
    L.A. De Salvo, 659(ConL):Winter84-494
    C. Hawtree, 364:Nov83-115
Silver, E. Begin.
    S. Jacobson, 362:1Mar84-24
    C.C. O'Brien, 441:25Nov84-7
Silver, I. Ronsard and the Hellenic
Renaissance in France.* (Vol 2, Pt 1)
    D. Stone, Jr., 131(CL):Winter83-78

Silverberg, R. Gilgamesh the King.
    W.L. Moran, 441:11Nov84-13
Silverberg, R. Valentine Pontifex.
    C. Greenland, 617(TLS):3Aug84-875
Silverman, D. and B. Torode. The Mate-
rial Word.*
    A. O'Connor, 488:Dec83-511
Silverman, J. For the World to See.
    J. Hunter, 676(YR):Spring84-433
    J. Sturman, 55:Nov83-53
Silverman, K. The Life and Times of Cot-
ton Mather.
    P-L. Adams, 61:Apr84-148
    U. Brumm, 165(EAL):Fall84-209
    F. Eberstadt, 129:Aug84-67
    E.S. Morgan, 453(NYRB):31May84-33
    L. Ziff, 441:25Mar84-3
    442(NY):23Apr84-131
Silverman, K. The Subject of Semiotics.
    C. Crosby, 454:Fall83-77
    T. Hawkes, 617(TLS):16Mar84-278
Silverman, R., ed. The Dog Observed.
    S.M. Halpern, 441:30Sep84-28
Silvis, R. The Luckiest Man in the World.
    M.B. Tack, 441:21Oct84-30
    G. Weaver, 344:Fall84-108
Sim, K. David Robert R.A. 1796-1864.
    D. Walker, 617(TLS):22Jun84-701
Simenon, G. Intimate Memoirs.
    M. Gallant, 441:1Jul84-1
    J. Symons, 453(NYRB):19Jul84-12
    442(NY):6Aug84-94
Simenon, G. The Lodger.*
    442(NY):26Mar84-133
Simenon, G. The Long Exile.*
    42(AR):Spring83-250
Simenon, G. Maigret in Court.
    442(NY):27Feb84-135
Simenon, G. Maigret's Revolver.
    442(NY):17Dec84-158
Simic, C. Austerities.*
    E. Larrissy, 493:Jun83-64
    P. Stitt, 491:Oct83-39
    639(VQR):Winter83-26
Simirenko, A. The Professionalization of
Soviet Society. (C.A. Kern-Simirenko,
ed)
    M.G. Field, 550(RusR):Oct83-446
Simkin, T. and R.S. Fiske, eds. Krakatau
1883.
    M. Sweeting, 617(TLS):10Aug84-903
Simmel, G. Georg Simmel: Essays on Inter-
pretation in Social Science. (G. Oakes,
ed and trans)
    R.H. Weingartner, 125:Fall82-89
Simmel, G. Georg Simmel: On Women, Sexual-
ity, and Love.
    D. Frisby, 441:9Sep84-13
Simmerman, J. Home.
    T. Stumpf, 110:Fall83-70
Simmonds, J.D. Masques of God.
    R. Ellrodt, 189(EA):Jan-Mar84-93
Simmonds, J.D. - see "Milton Studies"
Simmonds, R.S. The Two Worlds of William
March.
    H. Mitgang, 441:23Dec84-17
Simmonds, S. and S. Digby, eds. The Royal
Asiatic Society.
    E. Whelan, 318(JAOS):Jan-Mar82-224
Simmons, D.L. Margaret Rutherford.
    S. Gold, 441:18Mar84-18
Simmons, G. Peckinpah.*
    G.W. Jones, 584(SWR):Summer83-289

Sinfield, A. Literature in Protestant
England 1560-1660.*
R.D.S., 604:Fall83-67
Sinfield, A., ed. Society and Literature
1945-1970.
D. Trotter, 617(TLS):22Jun84-707
Singal, D.J. The War Within.*
B. Brandon, 9(AlaR):Apr83-148
R.F. Durden, 27(AL):Mar83-116
F. Hobson, 392:Fall83-600
W.J. Stuckey, 395(MFS):Summer83-334
Singer, B. Village Notables in Nineteenth-
Century France.
R.T. Denommé, 207(FR):Dec83-289
Singer, D. The Road to Gdańsk.*
A.J. Matejko, 497(PolR):Vol28No1-109
Singer, I.B. The Collected Stories of
Isaac Bashevis Singer.*
42(AR):Winter83-119
Singer, I.B. Love and Exile.
D. Evanier, 441:7Oct84-23
Singer, I.B. The Penitent.*
J. Mellors, 364:Mar84-105
T. Sutcliffe, 617(TLS):23Mar84-311
Singer, J.F. The Movie Set.
E.R. Lipson, 441:12Aug84-20
Singer, P. The Expanding Circle.*
F.J. Clendinnen, 63:Sep83-326
A. Denman, 42(AR):Winter83-114
N. Hoerster, 167:Nov83-377
A. Manser, 479(PhQ):Jul83-305
Singer, P. Hegel.*
483:Oct83-561
Singer, P. Practical Ethics.*
J.M. Fischer, 482(PhR):Apr83-264
Singh, A., R. Verma and I.M. Joshi, eds.
Indian Literature in English, 1827-1979.
P.L. Gupta, 49:Oct83-87
Singh, G. - see Leavis, F.R.
Singh, G. - see Leavis, Q.D.
Singh, K. Heir Apparent.
T. Raychaudhuri, 617(TLS):13Apr84-400
Singh, R.A. Syntax of Apabhraṃśa.
M.C. Shapiro, 318(JAOS):Jul-Sep82-550
Singh, R.R., ed. Social Work Perspectives
on Poverty.
J. Das Gupta, 293(JASt):Nov82-105
Singhal, D.P. A History of the Indian
People.
H. Tinker, 617(TLS):24Aug84-934
Singko, L., ed. Reunion and Other Stories.
M.H. Salleh, 293(JASt):Aug83-1008
Singleton, C.S. - see Boccaccio, G.
Sinha, A.K. Vedanta and Modern Science.
Science and Tantra Yoga.
A. Malhotra, 485(PE&W):Apr83-203
Sinopoulos, T. Selected Poems.
M.B. Raizis, 678(YCGL):No31-151
Sipala, P.M., ed. Mazzini biografo e auto-
biografo.
A. Pipa, 276:Winter83-380
Sipriot, P. Montherlant sans masque.*
(Vol 1)
R.J. Golsan, 400(MLN):May83-817
Sisson, C.H. Collected Poems 1943-1983.
D. Constantine, 176:Sep/Oct84-40
C. Craig, 617(TLS):26Oct84-1210
D. Davis, 362:14Jun84-26
Sisson, C.H. English Poetry 1900-1950.
T. Mallon, 134(CP):Spring83-89
L. Simpson, 441:15Jul84-13
Sisson, C.H. - see "The Song of Roland"

Sissons, R. and B. Stoddart. Cricket
and Empire.
M. Bose, 362:28Jun84-27
Sitkoff, H. The Struggle for Black Equal-
ity, 1954-1980.
E.F. Haas, 9(AlaR):Jan83-70
Sitter, J. Literary Loneliness in Mid-
Eighteenth-Century England.
D.L. Patey, 566:Spring84-165
E. Rothstein, 401(MLQ):Jun83-212
P.M. Spacks, 579(SAQ):Autumn83-452
639(VQR):Summer83-88
"Situación Revolucionaria y Escalada Inter-
vencionista en la Guerra Salvadoreña."
C. Dickey, 453(NYRB):14Jun84-25
Sitwell, E. Collected Poems.
D. McDuff, 565:Vol124No3-67
Sitwell, S. An Indian Summer.
D. McDuff, 565:Vol124No3-67
Siu, H.F. and Z. Stern, eds. Mao's Har-
vest.
D. Pollard, 176:Apr84-52
Sivaramamurti, C. Sources of History
Illuminated by Literature.
D. Srinivasan, 318(JAOS):Apr-Jun82-
414
de Sivers, F., ed. Structuration de
l'espace dans les langues de la Baltique
orientale.
W.R. Schmalstieg, 215(GL):Spring83-67
Sizer, T.R. Horace's Compromise.
C.E. Finn, Jr., 129:May84-64
A. Hacker, 453(NYRB):Apr84-35
T.S. Healy, 441:13May84-14
Sjoestedt, M-L. Gods and Heroes of the
Celts.
G. Kiley, 469:Vol9No1-110
Sjollema, B. Isolating Apartheid.
W.M. Freund, 69:Vol53No4-94
Skagestad, P. The Road of Inquiry.*
C.J.D., 543:Sep82-196
M. Thompson, 449:Nov83-715
Skard, S. Classical Tradition in Norway.*
H. Beck, 52:Band18Heft2-200
Skármeta, A. La insurreción.
K. Schwartz, 238:Dec83-651
Skei, A.B. Heinrich Schütz.
R. Roberts, 415:May83-299
Skei, H.H. William Faulkner: The Short
Story Career.*
M.V. Peterson, 573(SSF):Fall83-338
S.M. Ross, 395(MFS):Winter83-728
Skelton, G. Richard and Cosima Wagner.*
R.L.J., 412:May82-147
Skelton, J. The Complete English Poems of
Skelton.* (J. Scattergood, ed)
M. Dodsworth, 175:Summer83-190
Skelton, R. Landmarks.*
J. Giltrow, 102(CanL):Spring83-126
Skelton, R. Limits.
F. Cogswell, 198:Jan83-129
L.R. Ricou, 102(CanL):Summer83-118
Skelton, R., ed. Six Poets of British
Columbia.
S. Morrissey, 137:Nov82-51
L.R. Ricou, 102(CanL):Summer83-118
Skelton, R.A. - see Keynes, G.
Skenazy, P. The New Wild West.
R.W. Etulain, 649(WAL):Aug83-176
Skidelsky, R. John Maynard Keynes.*
(Vol 1)
N. Annan, 453(NYRB):19Jul84-35
D. Marquand, 176:Apr84-46

Skidmore, T.E. and P.H. Smith. Modern
Latin America.
  S.K. Purcell, 441:12Feb84-21
Skinner, B.F. and M.E. Vaughan. Enjoy Old
Age.
  J. Rascoe, 441:1Jan84-10
Skirius, J. El ensayo hispanoamericano
del siglo XX.
  S. Lipp, 238:Mar83-138
Skjoldager, E. Den egentlige Kierkegaard.
  M. Plekon, 563(SS):Summer83-266
Skjöldebrand, I. Treasure Chest of
Swedish Weaving.
  P. Bach, 614:Fall84-26
Sklar, K.K. - see Stowe, H.B.
Skloot, R., ed. The Theatre of the Holo-
caust.
  A. Goldfarb, 615(TJ):Dec83-567
Skrine, P.N. The Baroque.*
  G. Hainsworth, 208(FS):Jan83-80
Skully, M.T., ed. Financial Institutions
and Markets in the Far East.
  C. MacDougall, 293(JASt):May83-611
Skulsky, H. Metamorphosis.*
  E. Crasnow, 301(JEGP):Jul83-430
  E. Stein, 478:Apr83-119
Skura, M.A. The Literary Use of the Psy-
choanalytic Process.*
  S.A. Black, 529(QQ):Spring83-234
  S. Weiland, 128(CE):Nov83-705
Skurnowicz, J.S. Romantic Nationalism and
Liberalism.*
  M.B. Biskupski, 497(PolR):Vol28No1-104
Skvorecky, J. The Engineer of Human Souls.
  W. Balliett, 442(NY):15Oct84-175
  D.J. Enright, 453(NYRB):27Sep84-49
  R. Towers, 441:19Aug84-9
Skvorecky, J. The Swell Season.*
  D. Durrant, 364:Aug/Sep83-133
Skyrms, B. Causal Necessity.*
  D.H. Mellor, 84:Mar83-97
  R. Otte, 519(PhS):Nov83-425
Slade, C.A., ed. Approaches to Teaching
Dante's "Divine Comedy."*
  T.G. Bergin, 569(SR):Spring83-261
  B. Weiss, 399(MLJ):Summer83-197
Slataper, S. Il mio carso.
  P. Lombardo, 98:Aug-Sep83-653
Slater, A.P. Shakespeare the Director.*
  D. Bevington, 401(MLQ):Mar83-92
  D. Daniell, 617(TLS):30Nov84-1390
Slater, A.P. - see Pasternak, A.
Slater, C. Defeatists and their Enemies.*
  B. Vardar, 209(FM):Jul83-278
Slater, C. Stories on a String.*
  M.J. Curran, 238:May83-308
Slater, M. Dickens and Women.*
  N. Berry, 364:Jun83-81
  P. Boumelha, 175:Autumn83-257
  J.H. Buckley, 445(NCF):Dec83-334
  J. Korg, 219(GaR):Fall83-685
  S. Monod, 155:Summer83-108
  639(VQR):Autumn83-117
Slater, M. Family Life in the Seventeenth
Century.
  L. Colley, 617(TLS):8Jun84-629
Slater, P. Origins and Significance of
the Frankfurt School.
  B. Agger, 488:Sep83-347
Slatkes, L.J. Rembrandt and Persia.
  J. Nash, 617(TLS):26Oct84-1212

Slatkes, L.J. Vermeer and his Contempor-
aries.
  C. White, 39:Jan83-64
Slatta, R.W. Gauchos and the Vanishing
Frontier.
  W.R. Wright, 263(RIB):Vol133No4-597
Slaughter, C. The Banquet.*
  J. Grossman, 441:15Jul84-18
Slaughter, C. A Perfect Woman.
  J. Motion, 617(TLS):13Jul84-790
Slavick, W.H. Du Bose Heyward.
  V.A. Kramer, 585(SoQ):Spring83-82
Slavin, M. The French Revolution in Minia-
ture.
  W. Scott, 617(TLS):3Aug84-873
Slavitt, D.R. Alice at 80.
  M. Jefferson, 441:19Aug84-12
Slavitt, D.R. Dozens.
  F. Chappell, 651(WHR):Autumn83-251
Slawson, W.D. The New Inflation.
  A.N. McLeod, 529(QQ):Winter83-1160
Sleeman, J.H. and G. Pollet. Lexicon
Plotinianum.
  L.S., 543:Sep82-198
Sleeth, C.R. Studies in "Christ and
Satan."
  J. Chance, 301(JEGP):Apr83-218
Sleigh, T. After One.
  R. Pack, 441:20May84-37
Slerca, A. - see de la Vigne, A.
Slesin, S., S. Cliff and K. Kirkwood.
English Style.
  G. Allen, 441:2Dec84-20
Slights, C.W. The Casuistical Tradition
in Shakespeare, Donne, Herbert, and
Milton.*
  J. Balakier, 391:May83-53
  C. Freer, 551(RenQ):Autumn83-476
  R.D. Lord, 478:Oct83-277
  G.A. Starr, 405(MP):Aug83-70
Slinn, E.W. Browning and the Fictions of
Identity.
  B. Gardiner, 67:Nov83-315
Sloane, D.E.E., ed. The Literary Humor of
the Urban Northeast, 1830-1890.
  A. Gribben, 26(ALR):Autumn83-307
Sloate, D. A Taste of Earth, A Taste of
Flame.*
  A. Mitcham, 102(CanL):Autumn83-112
Slobin, M. Tenement Songs.*
  J. Santino, 292(JAF):Oct-Dec83-472
Slobin, M. - see Beregovski, M.
Slosman, A. La vie extraordinaire de
Pythagore.
  R. Prévost, 192(EP):Jan-Mar83-113
Slosser, B. Reagan Inside Out.
  R.G. Kaiser, 453(NYRB):28Jun84-38
Slote, M. Goods and Virtues.
  J.E.J. Altham, 617(TLS):17Aug84-923
"Slovník slovanské lingvistické termino-
logie."
  I. Ohnheiser, 682(ZPSK):Band36Heft3-
  365
Sluga, H.D. Gottlob Frege.*
  I. Angelelli, 311(JP):Apr83-232
  D.R. Bell, 393(Mind):Jan83-135
  W. Carl, 687:Jul-Sep83-465
  T.C. Potts, 483:Oct81-585
  M.D. Resnik, 482(PhR):Jan83-122
  C. Wright, 262:Sep83-363
Slusser, G.E., E.S. Rabkin and R. Scholes,
eds. Bridges to Fantasy.
  C.C. Smith, 395(MFS):Summer83-350

349

Smith, R.D. - see Wickham, A.
Smith, R.H. Patches of Godlight.*
  S. Monod, 189(EA):Jan-Mar84-107
Smith, R.J. Japanese Society.
  B. Moeran, 617(TLS):18May84-548
Smith, R.N. An Uncommon Man.
  R.S. McElvaine, 441:2Sep84-4
  442(NY):23Jul84-107
Smith, S. Inviolable Voice.*
  P. Didsbury, 493:Sep83-76
  D. Lloyd, 272(IUR):Spring83-131
Smith, S.B. The Great Mental Calculators.
  M. Gardner, 453(NYRB):15Mar84-23
Smith, S.M. The Other Nation.*
  J. Bayley, 541(RES):May83-234
  A. Easson, 402(MLR):Jul83-694
Smith, W.C. Belief and History.
  E.T. Long, 543:Mar83-734
Smith, W.E. Charles Dickens in the
  Original Cloth. (Pt 1)
  R.L. Patten, 517(PBSA):Vol77No2-209
  J. Stephens, 155:Summer83-118
Smith, W.F. and F.W. Medley. Noticiario:
  Segundo Nivel.
  J. Shreve, 399(MLJ):Summer83-202
Smith, W.F. and L.L. Nieman. Noticiario:
  Tercer Nivel.*
  J.F. Ford, 399(MLJ):Autumn83-311
  R. Hoff, 238:Dec83-653
Smith, W.J., comp. A Green Place.
  639(VQR):Spring83-62
Smith, W.L. The One-eyed Goddess.
  E.C. Dimock, Jr., 318(JAOS):Apr-Jun82-
  416
Smith, W.S. Bishop of Everywhere.
  C.A. Berst, 572:Vol4-173
  D. Leary, 177(ELT):Vol26No2-141
  295(JML):Nov83-567
Smitheram, V., D. Milne and S. Dasgupta,
  eds. The Garden Transformed.
  P. Phillips, 99:Apr83-32
Smitherman, G., ed. Black English and the
  Education of Black Children and Youth.*
  G.W. Beattie, 353:Vol20No3/4-354
  R.B. Shuman, 35(AS):Spring83-52
Smithwick, N. The Evolution of a State,
  or Recollections of Old Texas Days.
  L. Milazzo, 584(SWR):Autumn83-x
Smits, K., W. Besch and V. Lange, eds.
  Interpretation und Edition deutscher
  Texte des Mittelalters.
  I.R. Campbell, 67:Nov83-323
  H. Heinen, 589:Jul83-854
  W.C. McDonald, 400(MLN):Apr83-531
Smitten, J.R. and A. Daghistany, eds.
  Spatial Form in Narrative.*
  H. Charney, 363(LitR):Winter84-279
  J. McCormick, 107(CRCL):Jun83-223
Smoldon, W.L. The Music of the Medieval
  Church Dramas.* (C. Bourgeault, ed)
  J. Caldwell, 410(M&L):Jan/Apr83-91
  A.E. Planchart, 414(MusQ):Winter83-120
Smollett, T. Travels through France and
  Italy.* (F. Felsenstein, ed)
  P-G.B., 189(EA):Jul-Sep84-363
Smoot, J.J. A Comparison of Plays by
  John Millington Synge and Federico
  García Lorca.
  R.R. Wilson, 107(CRCL):Sep83-450
Smullyan, R. Alice in Puzzle-Land.*
  S.G. Burstein, 283:Winter82/83-21
  T.C. Holyoke, 42(AR):Winter83-115

Smyers, V.L. and M. Winship - see Blanck,
  J.
Smyth, A.P. Warlords and Holy Men.
  A.A.M. Duncan, 617(TLS):19Oct84-1194
Smyth, G. Loss and Gain.
  M. Harmon, 272(IUR):Spring83-114
Sneddon, J.N. Proto-Minahasan.
  J.U. Wolff, 318(JAOS):Jan-Mar82-147
Snell, G., comp. The Book of Theatre
  Quotes.
  G. Playfair, 157:Summer83-28
Snell, R. Théophile Gautier, a Romantic
  Critic of the Visual Arts.
  F.W.J. Hemmings, 402(MLR):Jul83-715
  P. Joannides, 59:Jun83-252
  B. Kennedy, 89(BJA):Summer83-265
  M. Levey, 90:Jul83-434
Snelling, J. The Sacred Mountain.
  E. Rice, 469:Vol9No3-114
Snitow, A., C. Stansell and S. Thompson,
  eds. Desire.
  J. Hughes, 176:Nov84-55
Snodgrass, D.R. Inequality and Economic
  Development in Malaysia.
  L.Y.C. Lim, 293(JASt):May83-722
Snorri Sturluson. Edda. (A. Faulkes, ed)
  M. Ciklamini, 563(SS):Summer83-261
Snow, E.A. A Study of Vermeer.*
  90:Nov83-708
Snow, H.F. My China Years.
  H.R. Lieberman, 441:27May84-18
Snow, J.T. - see de Valdivielso, J.
Snow, R. and K. Kanai. Coney Island.
  R.F. Shepard, 441:25Nov84-26
Snowden, F.M., Jr. Before Color Preju-
  dice.*
  S.B. Pomeroy, 124:Jul-Aug84-388
Snyder, G. Axe Handles.*
  J. Sheehy, 469:Vol9No1-123
Snyder, S. The Comic Matrix of Shake-
  speare's Tragedies.*
  I. Schabert, 38:Band101Heft1/2-255
Snyder, S. - see Du Bartas, G.D.
Soar, P. and M. Tyler. Encyclopedia of
  British Football.
  P. Smith, 617(TLS):13Jan84-35
Sobejano, G. - see Alas, L.
Sobel, R. Car Wars.
  H. Weil, 441:21Oct84-51
Sobel, R. Gogol's Forgotten Book.*
  L. Amberg, 688(ZSP):Band43Heft2-422
  A. Hippisley, 402(MLR):Jul83-760
  A. McMillin, 575(SEER):Jul83-424
Sobel, R. IBM.
  I. Fallon, 617(TLS):14Dec84-1444
Sobel, R. The Rise and Fall of the Con-
  glomerate Kings.
  J. Koslow, 441:8Jul84-21
Sober, E., ed. Conceptual Issues in Evolu-
  tionary Biology.
  D. Macdonald, 617(TLS):28Sep84-1100
Sobin, A. The Sunday Naturalist.*
  F. Chappell, 651(WHR):Autumn83-251
"Social Classes Action and Historical
  Materialism."
  J-M. Gabaude, 542:Jul-Sep83-343
"Società, politica e cultura a Capri ai
  tempi di Alberto III Pio."
  C.H. Clough, 551(RenQ):Summer83-227
Socken, P.G. Concordance de Bonheur
  d'occasion.
  B-Z. Shek, 627(UTQ):Summer83-520

Söderberg, B. Flykten mot stjärnorna.
  G. Orton, 562(Scan):Nov82-199
  M. Setterwall, 563(SS):Winter83-85
Södergård, Ö., ed. "La Chirurgie de
  l'abbé Poutrel."*
  P. Ménard, 545(RPh):May83-635
Södergård, Ö., ed. Une lettre d'Hippo-
  crate.
  G. Roques, 553(RLiR):Jul-Dec83-499
Södergran, E. The Collected Poems.
  G. Hird, 562(Scan):May82-107
Sodmann, T., ed. Dat narren schyp.
  J.L. Flood, 684(ZDA):Band112Heft2-94
Sodmann, T. - see van Maerlant, J.
Soellner, R. "Timon of Athens."
  I. Schabert, 38:Band101Heft1/2-255
Sogliuzzo, A.R. Luigi Pirandello, Direc-
  tor.
  O. Ragusa, 276:Spring83-71
Sohlman, R. The Legacy of Alfred Nobel.
  E. Abraham, 617(TLS):27Jan84-82
Söhne, R. Pierre de Villier's Werk unter
  besonderer Berücksichtigung seiner
  Beiträge zur französischen Moralistik.
  C. Strosetzki, 475:Vol 10No18-405
Söhnen, R. Untersuchungen zur Komposition
  von Reden und Gesprächen im Rāmāyaṇa.
  J.W. de Jong, 259(IIJ):Mar83-141
Sojcher, J., ed. La Belgique malgré tout.
  J. Van Baelen, 207(FR):Oct83-100
Sola, M.M. Poesía y política en Pablo
  Neruda.*
  M. López-Baralt, 701(SinN):Apr-Jun83-
  94
Sola-Solé, J.M., S.G. Armistead and J.H.
  Silverman, eds. Hispania Judaica.
  (Vol 1)
  W. Mettmann, 547(RF):Band95Heft1/2-225
Sola-Solé, J.M., S.G. Armistead and J.H.
  Silverman, eds. Hispania Judaica.
  (Vol 2)
  L.P. Harvey, 86(BHS):Jul83-254
Solar, G. Jan Hackaert.
  W. Schulz, 683:Band46Heft4-450
Solberg, C. Hubert Humphrey.
  J.P. Lash, 441:12Aug84-13
Soldevila Durante, I. La novela desde
  1936.*
  B. Jordan, 86(BHS):Jan83-80
Solé, C.A. and Y.R. Español.
  L. Martin, 238:Sep83-451
Solé-Leris, A. The Spanish Pastoral
  Novel.*
  M.S. Carrasco Urgoiti, 240(HR):
  Winter83-94
Solin, H. Zu lukanischen Inschriften.
  M.H. Crawford, 313:Vol73-247
Sollers, P. Femmes.*
  A. Clerval, 450(NRF):May83-129
Sollors, W. Amiri Baraka/LeRoi Jones.
  K. Kinnamon, 301(JEGP):Jan83-153
Solmsen, F. Isis among the Greeks and
  Romans.*
  M.N. Nagler, 122:Jan83-81
Solodow, J.B. The Latin Particle Quidem.
  S.M. Goldberg, 121(CJ):Oct/Nov83-67
Solomon, F. and B. Litvinoff. A Woman's
  Way.
  J. Burnley, 441:16Sep84-11
Solomon, L. Breaking Up Ontario Hydro's
  Monopoly.
  C.K. Rush, 529(QQ):Autumn83-865

Solomon, P. Rimbaud — un voyage au centre
  de la parole.
  A. Hagiu, 535(RHL):Jul/Aug83-657
Solomon, R.C. In the Spirit of Hegel.
  R. Scruton, 617(TLS):21Sep84-1059
Solomon, R.H., ed. The China Factor.
  W.T. Tow, 293(JASt):Feb83-398
Solomon, S.G., ed. Pluralism in the
  Soviet Union.
  M. Waller, 617(TLS):1Jun84-616
Solovyov, V. and E. Klepikova. Yuri And-
  ropov.*
  A. Brown, 617(TLS):6Jul84-750
  R.G. Suny, 385(MQR):Fall84-576
Solta, G.R. Einführung in die Balkan-
  linguistik mit besonderer Berücksichti-
  gung des Substrats und des Balkanlatein-
  ischen.*
  P. Flobert, 555:Vol57fasc1-155
  K-H. Schroeder, 72:Band220Heft2-440
Solway, D. The Mulberry Men.
  D. Hine, 102(CanL):Summer83-109
  D.E. Tacium, 137:Nov82-14
Solway, D. Selected Poems.*
  D. Hine, 102(CanL):Summer83-109
  D.E. Tacium, 137:Nov82-14
  R. Whiteman, 526:Winter83-69
Solzhenitsyn, A. Krasnoe koleso. (fasc 1)
  G.A. Hosking, 617(TLS):3Feb84-99
Somcynsky, J-F. Peut-être à Tokyo.
  M. Benson, 102(CanL):Summer83-102
Somella, P.P. - see under Placella Somella,
  P.
Somers, J. If the Old Could ...
  C. Seebohm, 441:24Jun84-14
Somerset, A. Ladies-in-Waiting.
  B. Harvey, 441:12Aug84-21
  S. Runciman, 617(TLS):8Jun84-633
Somerville, R. Scotia pontificia.
  J.W. Alexander, 589:Oct83-1135
Sommella, P. Forma e urbanistica di
  Pozzuoli romana.
  R. Ling, 313:Vol73-232
Sommerfelt, A. Le Breton Parlé à Saint-
  Pol-de-Léon. (rev by F. Falc'hun and
  M. Oftedal)
  M. McKenna, 112:Vol 15-164
Sommers, F. The Logic of Natural Lan-
  guage.*
  J. van Bentham, 518:Apr83-99
  G. Stahl, 542:Jul-Sep83-367
Sommerstein, A.H. - see Aristophanes
Sonderegger, E. Simplikios: "Über die
  Zeit."
  H.J. Blumenthal, 123:Vol33No2-337
Sonderegger, S. Grundzüge deutscher
  Sprachgeschichte. (Vol 1)
  J. Udolph, 260(IF):Band88-345
"The Song of Roland." (C.H. Sisson, trans)
  D.D.R. Owen, 617(TLS):17Feb84-172
Sonnenfeld, A. Crossroads.
  G. Montbertrand, 207(FR):May84-888
Sonnichsen, C.L. Tucson.
  L. Milazzo, 584(SWR):Winter84-v
Sonntag, G. Eva Perón.
  M. Navarro, 263(RIB):Vol33No3-417
Sontag, F. A Kierkegaard Handbook.
  G.J. Stack, 543:Mar83-736
Sontag, S. A Susan Sontag Reader.*
  J. Parini, 249(HudR):Summer83-415
Sontag, S. - see Barthes, R.

Soo, F.Y.K. Mao Tse-tung's Theory of
Dialectic.
  R. Baum, 293(JASt):Nov82-153
Soons, A. Juan de Mariana.
  H. Nader, 551(RenQ):Summer83-285
Soothill, R. My Friend Freud.
  J. Brett, 381:Sep83-404
"Sophie Elisabeth, Gräfin zu Braunschweig
und Lüneburg: Dichtungen." (Vol 1)
(H-G. Roloff, ed)
  J. Leighton, 402(MLR):Jan83-230
Sophocles. The Three Theban Plays. (R.
Fagles, trans; B. Knox, ed)
  J.F. Cotter, 249(HudR):Winter83/84-719
  P.E. Easterling, 617(TLS):13Jan84-30
Sorabji, R. Necessity, Cause, and Blame.*
  J.M. Day, 518:Jan83-8
  J.D.G. Evans, 483:Oct81-584
  G.B. Matthews, 449:Mar83-135
  L.P. Schrenk, 124:May-Jun84-311
  R.W. Sharples, 303(JoHS):Vol 103-176
Sorabji, R. Time, Creation and the Con-
tinuum.
  J. Barnes, 617(TLS):25May84-587
de Sorbière, S. Relation d'un voyage en
Angleterre.* (L. Roux, ed)
  N. Bonvalet, 107(CRCL):Mar83-96
Sorel, N.C. Ever Since Eve.
  A. McCarthy, 441:22Jul84-21
Sørensen, P.M. Norrønt nid.*
  P. Hallberg, 562(Scan):May83-93
  K. Schier, 196:Band24Heft1/2-170
Sorensen, T.C. A Different Kind of Presi-
dency.
  K. Phillips, 441:29Jan84-21
  442(NY):26Mar84-135
Sorescu, M. Selected Poems.
  D. Deletant, 617(TLS):18May84-559
  D. Dunn, 364:Aug/Sep83-109
Sorg, N. Restauration und Rebellion.
  R.J. Alexander, 406:Winter83-441
Soria, R. Dictionary of Nineteenth-Cen-
tury American Artists in Italy, 1760-
1914.
  I. Ragusa, 276:Autumn83-272
Sorley Walker, K. De Basil's Ballets
Russes.
  T. Finch, 151:Jan83-76
Sornicola, R. Sul parlato.
  D.J. Napoli, 545(RPh):Feb83-449
Sornig, K. Lexical Innovation.
  D.H., 355(LSoc):Sep83-423
Sornig, K. Soziosemantik auf der Worte-
bene.
  G. Lerchner, 682(ZPSK):Band36Heft3-368
Sorokin, V.F. A Basic Study of Yüan Drama.
  B.L. Riftin, 116:Jan81-104
Sorrentino, F. Seven Conversations with
Jorge Luis Borges. (C.W. Zlotchew, ed
and trans)
  G. Guinness, 395(MFS):Summer83-315
  M.S. Stabb, 238:May83-302
Sorrentino, G. Blue Pastoral.*
  J. Mellors, 362:13Dec84-30
Sosa, E., ed. The Philosophy of Nicholas
Rescher.*
  T. Airaksinen, 486:Mar83-169
Sötér, I. and I. Neupokoyeva, eds. Euro-
pean Romanticism.*
  V. Nemoianu, 678(YCGL):No31-148
  A. Schnack, 462(OL):Vol137No4-368
Soto, G. Where Sparrows Work Hard.*
  J. Addiego, 448:Vol21No1-147

Soubiran, J. - see Avienus
Souchal, F., with F. de la Moureyre. Les
Frères Coustou et l'évolution de la
sculpture française du Dôme des
Invalides aux Chevaux de Marly.*
  T. Hodgkinson, 90:Jun83-368
Soucy, J-Y. Les Chevaliers de la nuit.
  K. Mezei, 102(CanL):Summer83-128
Soueif, A. Aisha.*
  D. Taylor, 364:Jul83-94
Soupel, S., ed. La Lettre écarlate.
  R.A. Day, 189(EA):Apr-Jun84-226
Soupel, S. - see Sterne, L.
Soupel, S. and R.A. Hambridge. Literature
and Science and Medicine.
  P-G. Boucé, 189(EA):Jul-Sep84-328
"Les Sources en Musicologie."*
  M-N. Colette, 537:Vol69No2-223
Souriau, E. L'avenir de la philosophie.
  M. Adam, 542:Oct-Dec83-452
Souriau, P. The Aesthetics of Movement.
(M. Souriau, ed and trans)
  S.M. Halpern, 441:25Mar84-21
"Sous la Règle de Saint Benoît."
  C. Morris, 382(MAE):1983/2-356
Soustal, P., with J. Koder. Nikopolis und
Kephallēnia.
  C. Foss, 589:Jul83-821
Souster, R. Collected Poems of Raymond
Souster.* (Vols 2 and 4)
  J.A. Wainwright, 102(CanL):Summer83-
148
Souster, R. Collected Poems of Raymond
Souster. (Vol 3)
  M. Darling, 198:Oct83-79
  J.A. Wainwright, 102(CanL):Summer83-
148
South, M. - see Topsell, E.
Southam, B. - see Austen, J.
Southard, D. Bobbin Lacemaking.
  P. Grappe, 614:Spring84-20
Southwell, S.B. Quest for Eros.
  R. Mason, 447(N&Q):Jun82-251
de Souza, A., ed. Children in India.
  J. Das Gupta, 293(JASt):Nov82-105
Souza, R.D. Lino Novás Calvo.*
  A.M. Kapcia, 86(BHS):Jan83-87
de Souza, T.R. Medieval Goa.
  N.J. Lamb, 86(BHS):Jan83-88
Sowell, T. Civil Rights.
  W.J. Wilson, 441:24Jun84-28
Sowerwine, C. Sisters or Citizens?
  N. Aronson, 207(FR):Feb84-426
Soyinka, W. Aké: The Years of Childhood.
  M. Mudrick, 249(HudR):Autumn83-569
Sozzi, L. and V.L. Saulnier, eds. La
nouvelle française à la Renaissance.*
  F. Rigolot, 551(RenQ):Autumn83-461
Spacks, B. Spacks Street.*
  R. Lattimore, 249(HudR):Spring83-211
Spada, J. Hepburn.
  S. Gold, 441:4Nov83-13
Spahr, B.L. Problems and Perspectives.
  D.L. Paisey, 221(GQ):Mar83-309
Spalding, F. Vanessa Bell.*
  P. Lively, 176:Feb84-40
  R. Pickvance, 90:Dec83-772
  A. Ross, 364:Dec83/Jan84-146
Spalding, K. Huarochirí.
  D. Brading, 617(TLS):19Oct84-1185
Spangenberg, E. Karriere eines Romans.
  D. Johnson, 617(TLS):28Sep84-1095

Spangenberg, W. Sämtliche Werke. (Vol 4,
Pt 1 and Vol 7) (A. Vizkelety, ed)
K. Phillips, 301(JEGP):Apr83-283
Spanier, D. Total Chess.
P. Snowdon, 617(TLS):21Dec84-1487
Spanos, W.V., P.A. Bové and D. O'Hara.
The Question of Textuality.
R.C. Holub, 221(GQ):May83-463
Spariosu, M. Literature, Mimesis and Play.
J.D. Black, 494:Vol14No4-773
V. Nemoianu, 400(MLN):Dec83-1338
Spark, M. Loitering with Intent.*
S. Monod, 189(EA):Apr-Sep83-352
Spark, M. The Only Problem.
P-L. Adams, 61:Aug84-113
G. Annan, 362:6Sep84-23
A. Brookner, 441:15Jul84-1
G. Josipovici, 617(TLS):7Sep84-989
J. Updike, 442(NY):23Jul84-104
Sparshott, F.E. The Theory of the Arts.
P.B. Lewis, 518:Jul83-185
Spater, G. William Cobbett.*
L. McCauley, 661(WC):Summer83-168
Spatharakis, I. Corpus of Dated Illumi-
nated Greek Manuscripts to the year 1453.
A. Cutler, 589:Jul83-823
E. Piltz, 341:Vol52No1-44
Spatz, L. Aeschylus.
S.G. Daitz, 124:Sep-Oct83-48
Speaight, G. A History of the Circus.*
A.H. Saxon, 612(ThS):May/Nov83-153
Speakes, R. Hannah's Travels.*
M. Boruch, 271:Vol 13No3/4-251
Spear, F.A. Bibliographie de Diderot.*
P. France, 208(FS):Jan83-84
Spear, J. and M. June, eds. New England
Begins.
H.A. Weinberg, 165(EAL):Spring84-93
Spear, J.C. Presidents and the Press.
J. Deakin, 617(TLS):17Aug84-908
Spear, R.E. Domenichino.*
D. De Grazia, 551(RenQ):Winter83-601
N. Turner, 39:May83-413
Spears, J., ed. Teaching Basic Quiltmak-
ing. (rev)
B. Self, 614:Fall84-24
Specht, H. Chaucer's Franklin in "The
Canterbury Tales."
D.C. Fowler, 405(MP):May84-407
G.D. Gopen, 301(JEGP):Jul83-436
G. Morgan, 382(MAE):1983/1-125
M. Powell, 462(OL):Vol38No3-280
M.T. Tavormina, 589:Jul83-825
Speck, S. Die morphologische Adaptation
der Lehnwörter im Russischen des 18.
Jahrhunderts.
D. Ward, 559:Vol7No2-197
Spector, R.D. Tobias Smollett.*
M. Irwin, 541(RES):May83-221
J.V. Price, 447(N&Q):Oct82-450
Spector, R.H. Eagle Against the Sun.
D.M. Goldstein, 441:16Dec84-8
Spee, F. Trutznachtigall. (G.R. Dimler,
ed)
J. Hardin, 221(GQ):Nov83-644
Speier, H. From the Ashes of Disgrace.*
R.F. Bell, 221(GQ):Jan83-185
S.G. Payne, 406:Fall83-323
Speir, J. Raymond Chandler.
P. Wolfe, 395(MFS):Autumn83-389
Spence, A. Its Colours They Are Fine.
J.A.S. Miller, 571(ScLJ):Winter83-69

Spence, G. Of Murder and Madness.
A.M. Dershowitz, 441:18Mar84-19
Spence, J. The Death of Woman Wang.
K.J. De Woskin, 318(JAOS):Jan-Mar82-
146
Spence, J.D. The Gate of Heavenly Peace.*
C.W. Hayford, 293(JASt):Feb83-401
Spence, J.D. The Memory Palace of Matteo
Ricci.
P. Robinson, 441:25Nov84-11
Spence, T. The Political Works of Thomas
Spence. (H.T. Dickinson, ed)
G.E. Bentley, Jr., 88:Spring84-172
P.J. Corfield, 83:Autumn83-245
Spencer, A.M. In Praise of Heroes.*
K.P. Kent, 2(AfrA):Feb83-85
Spencer, B.T. Patterns of Nationality.*
E. Folsom, 481(PQ):Spring83-274
Spencer, E. The Salt Line.
P-L. Adams, 61:Feb84-104
F. Taliaferro, 441:29Jan84-11
Spencer, J.H. Ethiopia at Bay.
E. Ullendorff, 617(TLS):28Sep84-1079
Spencer, M.A. and M.R. Hall. Group Quilt
Handbook.
P. Bach, 614:Summer84-16
Spencer, M.C. Charles Fourier.*
P. Hambly, 67:May83-132
M. Nathan, 535(RHL):Sep/Dec83-940
Spencer-Noël, G. Zénon ou le thème de
l'alchimie dans "L'Oeuvre au Noir" de
Marguerite Yourcenar.
J. Onimus, 535(RHL):Sep/Dec83-973
Spender, D. Man Made Language.*
P. Randall, 583:Summer84-442
Spender, D. Women of Ideas.
T.C. Holyoke, 42(AR):Summer83-370
Spender, H. Worktown People.
J. Hunter, 676(YR):Spring84-433
Spender, L. Intruders on the Rights of
Men.
J. Hughes, 176:Nov84-50
Spengemann, W.G. The Forms of Autobiog-
raphy.*
P. Hollindale, 541(RES):Feb83-116
A.F.T. Lurcock, 447(N&Q):Oct82-479
L. Simon, 77:Summer83-273
G. Woodcock, 569(SR):Winter83-129
Spenser, E. The Faerie Queene. (T.P.
Roche, Jr. and C.P. O'Donnell, Jr.,
eds)
B. Tannier, 189(EA):Jan-Mar84-90
Spenser, E. The Illustrated "Faerie
Queen." (D. Hill, ed)
M.A. Mikolajczak, 568(SCN):Fall83-57
"Spenser Studies."* (Vol 1) (P. Cullen
and T.P. Roche, Jr., eds)
H. Cooper, 541(RES):Aug83-326
"Spenser Studies." (Vol 2) (P. Cullen and
T.P. Roche, Jr., eds)
L.E. Orange, 568(SCN):Spring/Summer83-
3
B. Tannier, 189(EA):Jan-Mar84-89
"Spenser Studies."* (Vol 3) (P. Cullen
and T.P. Roche, Jr., eds)
639(VQR):Spring83-43
Speroni, S. Canace e Scritti in sua
difesa [together with] Giraldi Cinzio, G.
Scritti contro la Canace. (C. Roaf, ed)
M. Marti, 228(GSLI):Vol 160fasc512-606
Sperry, R. Science and Moral Priority.*
K.S., 185:Jul84-738

Speta, F. and H.L. Werneck. Das Kräuter-
buch des Johannes Hartlieb.
  N.F. Palmer, 382(MAE):1983/1-182
Spevack, M. and J.W. Binns, general eds.
Renaissance Latin Drama in England.
(Vols 1-4)
  L.V.R., 568(SCN):Fall83-62
Spiegelberg, H. The Context of the Phenom-
enological Movement.*
  P.M. Simons, 484(PPR):Mar84-426
Spierenburg, P. The Spectacle of Suffer-
ing.
  E. Weber, 617(TLS):28Dec84-1495
Spiering, F. Lizzie.
  P-L. Adams, 61:Jul84-116
  H. Gardner, 441:1Jul84-21
Spiers, E.M. Radical General.
  H. Strachan, 617(TLS):20Jan84-67
Spies, W. Max Ernst: Loplop.
  T. Hilton, 617(TLS):23Mar84-303
Spiller, R.E. Late Harvest.*
  S.S. Conroy, 125:Spring83-289
Spillman, J.S. American and European
Pressed Glass in the Corning Museum of
Glass.
  G. Wills, 39:May83-414
Spinelli, D.C., ed. A Concordance to
Marivaux's Comedies in Prose.*
  H. Mason, 208(FS):Jul83-340
Spinosa, N., ed. Napoli e la Campania.
  E. Waterhouse, 90:Feb83-103
Spinoza, B. The Ethics and Selected
Letters. (S. Shirley, trans)
  V. Maxwell, 529(QQ):Winter83-1222
Spires, E. Globe.*
  R. Tillinghast, 569(SR):Summer83-473
"Spirit Child." (J. Bierhorst, trans)
  J. Cech, 469:Vol9No4-118
Spirn, A.W. The Granite Garden.
  R. Bender, 441:22Jan84-13
Spisak, J.W. and W. Matthews - see Malory,
T.
Spitaels, P., ed. Studies in South Attica
I.
  J.E. Jones, 303(JoHS):Vol 103-218
Spitz, D. The Real World of Liberalism.
  J.H.C., 185:Apr84-546
Spivack, C. The Comedy of Evil on Shake-
speare's Stage.
  P.A. Cantor, 570(SQ):Summer83-250
Spivey, T.R. The Journey Beyond Tragedy.*
  M.G. Hamilton, 107(CRCL):Jun83-282
"Splicing Life."
  S.G.P., 185:Apr84-572
Splitter, R. Proust's Recherche.
  B. Straus, 149(CLS):Winter83-453
Spore, P. and others, eds. Actes du 8e
congrès des romanistes scandinaves.
  G. Kleiber, 553(RLiR):Jul-Dec83-418
Spoto, D. The Dark Side of Genius.*
  M. Wood, 453(NYRB):26Apr84-22
Spray, C. The Mare's Egg.
  P. Nodelman, 102(CanL):Spring83-149
Sprengel, P., ed. Jean Paul im Urteil
seiner Kritiker.*
  D.F. Mahoney, 406:Fall83-343
Sprengel, P. Die Wirklichkeit der Mythen.*
  R. Bernhardt, 654(WB):11/1983-2027
  C. Eykman, 222(GR):Summer83-121
Sprigg, J., ed. Domestick Beings.
  P-L. Adams, 61:Jul84-117
  F. Randall, 441:29Jul84-21

Sprigge, T.L.S. The Vindication of Abso-
lute Idealism.
  H. Robinson, 617(TLS):9Mar84-258
Springer, M.D. A Rhetoric of Literary
Character.
  R.K. Martin, 106:Winter83-457
Springer, O. - see "Langenscheidts Enzyklo-
pädisches Wörterbuch Deutsch-Englisch
A-Z"
Springorum, T.P.A.F. Dialoogstructuur.
  A. van Berkel, 204(FdL):Dec82-305
Sprinker, M. "A Counterpoint of Disson-
ance."*
  R.K.R. Thornton, 541(RES):Aug83-356
Spritzer, L.N. The Belle of Ashby Street.
  639(VQR):Spring83-48
Sprunger, K.L. Dutch Puritanism.
  M. Lee, Jr., 551(RenQ):Winter83-616
Spruytte, J. Early Harness Systems.
  J. Clutton-Brock, 617(TLS):17Feb84-170
Spufford, M. Small Books and Pleasant His-
tories.*
  J.M.B., 179(ES):Apr83-182
  V. Neuburg, 203:Vol194No1-131
  J.G. Schiller, 517(PBSA):Vol77No2-221
Spurling, H. Ivy.* [US one-vol ed]
  G. Annan, 453(NYRB):20Dec84-19
  J.C. Oates, 441:9Dec84-7
Spurling, H. Secrets of a Woman's Heart.
  P. Kemp, 362:7Jun84-23
  A.N. Wilson, 617(TLS):8Jun84-627
Spurling, J. The British Empire Part One.
  D. Devlin, 157:Spring83-52
Spurlock, J.H. He Sings for Us.
  A. Puckett, 292(JAF):Apr-Jun83-236
Squarotti, G.B. - see under Bàrberi Squar-
otti, G.
Srinivasan, S.A. On the Composition of
the Nāṭyaśāstra.
  T. Venkatacharya, 259(IIJ):Jun83-283
Ssu-ch'eng, L. - see under Liang Ssu-
ch'eng
Stableford, B.M. Masters of Science Fic-
tion.
  P. Fitting, 561(SFS):Nov83-352
Stacey, C.P. Canada and the Age of Con-
flict. (Vols 1 and 2)
  D.M. Schurman, 529(QQ):Spring83-211
Stacey, C.P. A Date with History.
  R. Hall, 99:Dec83-30
Stacey, J. Patriarchy and Socialist Revo-
lution in China.
  D. Davin, 617(TLS):14Sep84-1013
von Stackelberg, J., ed. Europäische Auf-
klärung. (Vol 3)
  M. Moog-Grünewald, 52:Band17Heft2-207
von Stackelberg, J. Klassische Autoren
des schwarzen Erdteils.
  J. Riesz, 52:Band18Heft2-219
  J. Riesz, 547(RF):Band95Heft1/2-219
Stackelberg, R. Idealism Debased.
  S.G. Payne, 406:Fall83-323
Stadler, E. Dichtungen, Schriften,
Briefe.* (K. Hurlebusch and K.L.
Schneider, eds)
  H. Steinecke, 680(ZDP):Band102Heft4-
  626
Stadler, P. Der Kulturkampf in der
Schweiz.
  O. Chadwick, 617(TLS):7Dec84-1422
Stadter, E. - see Olivi, P.I.

Madame de Staël. Correspondance générale.
(Vol 5, Pt 1) (B.W. Jasinski, ed)
  J. Gaulmier, 535(RHL):Sep/Dec83-938
  J. Kitchin, 208(FS):Oct83-468
Madame de Staël and E. Hervey. Le plus
beau de toutes les fêtes. (V. de Pange,
ed)
  M. Gutwirth, 446(NCFS):Fall-
    Winter83/84-259
  J.F. Hamilton, 207(FR):Oct83-111
Staff, L. An Empty Room.*
  J.T. Baer, 497(PolR):Vol28No3-92
  D. Dunn, 364:Aug/Sep83-109
Stafford, B.M. Voyage Into Substance.
  N. Bliven, 442(NY):22Oct84-158
  K. Thomas, 441:14Oct84-22
Stafford, E.P. Little Ship, Big War.
  W.H. Honan, 441:8Jul84-21
Stafford, P. Queens, Concubines and Dow-
agers.
  B. Ward, 617(TLS):3Aug84-865
Stafford, W. A Glass Face in the Rain.*
  B. Howard, 502(PrS):Winter83-81
  R. Lattimore, 249(HudR):Spring83-208
  J. Mazzaro, 385(MQR):Spring84-294
  J.R. Roberts, Sr., 649(WAL):Nov83-253
    639(VQR):Spring83-61
Stafford, W. and M. Bell. Segues.
  R.W. Flint, 441:8Apr84-14
Stagg, J.C.A. Mr. Madison's War.
  P.J. Parish, 617(TLS):25May84-575
Staicar, T., ed. The Feminine Eye.
  L. Leith, 561(SFS):Jul83-247
Staines, D., ed. The Callaghan Symposium.*
  J. Kendle, 168(ECW):Winter83/84-77
  D. O'Rourke, 102(CanL):Summer83-136
Staines, D., ed. Reappraisals.
  J. Ferns, 178:Dec83-516
Štajner, K. 7000 jours en Sibérie.
  L. Kovacs, 450(NRF):Sep83-154
Staley, T.F., ed. Twentieth-Century Women
Novelists.*
  M.M. Rowe, 395(MFS):Winter83-791
Stallman, R.W., ed. The Art of Joseph
Conrad.
  R.O. Evans, 569(SR):Winter83-ii
Stallworth, A.N. Go, Go, Said the Bird.
  R. Hoffman, 441:4Nov84-16
Stallworthy, J., ed. The Oxford Book of
War Poetry.
  R. Fuller, 617(TLS):14Sep84-1015
Stallworthy, J. - see Owen, W.
Stam, T.D. Gavarni and the Critics.
  B.L. Knapp, 207(FR):Feb84-398
Stamm, L.E. Die Rüdiger Schopf-Handschrif-
ten.
  M. Curschmann, 589:Jul83-827
Stammers, N. Civil Liberties in Britain
in the Second World War.
  B. Wasserstein, 617(TLS):6Jul84-760
Stamp, G. The Changing Metropolis.
  S. Gardiner, 362:15Nov84-29
Stamp, G. The Great Perspectivists.*
  J. Zukowsky, 576:May83-198
Stancliffe, C. St. Martin and his Hagio-
grapher.
  R.A. Markus, 617(TLS):13Jan84-42
Standing, J. Exordium.
  D. Chambers, 503:Summer83-89
Stanfill, F. Shadows and Light.
  E.R. Lipson, 441:23Dec84-16
Stanford, D. - see Masefield, J.

Stanford, D.E. Revolution and Convention
in Modern Poetry.
  D.E. Middleton, 385(MQR):Summer84-434
  J.E. Miller, Jr., 659(ConL):Fall84-354
Stanford, D.E. - see Bridges, R.
Stanford, R.A., ed. Rural Development in
Pakistan.
  J. Das Gupta, 293(JASt):Nov82-105
Stanford, W.B. Enemies of Poetry.*
  N. Havely, 447(N&Q):Feb82-95
Stanford, W.B. Greek Tragedy and the Emo-
tions.
  B. Knox, 617(TLS):24Aug84-932
Stang, S.J., ed. The Presence of Ford
Madox Ford.*
  J. Newman, 161(DUJ):Jun83-138
Stanislawski, M. Tsar Nicholas I and the
Jews.
  N.V. Riasanovsky, 104(CASS):Winter83-
    560
Staniszkis, J. Pologne.
  A.J. Matejko, 497(PolR):Vol28No3-85
Stankiewicz, W.J. Approaches to Democ-
racy.*
  P. Dubois, 542:Jul-Sep83-343
Stanley, R.M. Prelude to Pearl Harbor.
    639(VQR):Summer83-82
Stanley, T.A. Ōsugi Sakae, Anarchist in
Taishō Japan.*
  Asukai Masamichi, 285(JapQ):Jan-Mar83-
    83
  F.G. Notehelfer, 293(JASt):May83-678
Stannard, M., ed. Evelyn Waugh: The Crit-
ical Heritage.
  J. Bayley, 617(TLS):5Oct84-1111
Stansky, P. William Morris.
  R. Blythe, 362:16Feb84-24
Stanton, E.C. and S.B. Anthony. Elizabeth
Cady Stanton and Susan B. Anthony: Cor-
respondence, Writings, Speeches. (E.C.
Du Bois, ed)
  S. Levine, 579(SAQ):Spring83-226
Stanton, J. La Nomade.
  H.R. Runte, 102(CanL):Summer83-114
Stanwood, P.G. - see Hooker, R.
Stanzel, F.K. A Theory of Narrative.*
(German title: Theorie des Erzählens.)
  A. Jefferson, 617(TLS):28Dec84-1508
  D. Mehl, 72:Band219Heft2-476
  A. Schwarz and L. Tatlock, 196:Band24
    Heft3/4-329
Stapleton, M. The Cambridge Guide to
English Literature.*
  C.B. Cox, 148:Summer83-2
  M. Dodsworth, 175:Summer83-188
Starbuck, G. The Argot Merchant Disaster.*
  W. Harmon, 491:Sep83-350
  J. Hollander, 676(YR):Autumn83-xix
  R. Lattimore, 249(HudR):Spring83-214
Starck, T. and J.C. Wells, eds. Althoch-
deutsches Glossenwörterbuch.
  H. von Gadow, 72:Band219Heft2-406
  H. von Gadow, 72:Band220Heft1-137
  D.H. Green, 402(MLR):Jan83-219
  D.H. Green, 402(MLR):Oct83-958
Stargell, W. and T. Bird. Willie Stargell.
  L.S. Ritter, 441:3Jun84-11
Stark, D. The Old English Weak Verbs.
  G. Bourcier, 189(EA):Apr-Jun84-183
Stark, F. Alexander's Path.
  G.N., 617(TLS):12Oct84-1171
Stark, G.D. Entrepreneurs of Ideology.
  W.R. Ward, 161(DUJ):Dec82-120

Stark, G.D. and B.K. Lackner, eds. Essays on Culture and Society in Modern Germany.
639(VQR):Summer83-86
Stark, J.O. Pynchon's Fictions.*
E.B. Safer, 677(YES):Vol 13-356
S. Strehle, 599:Winter83-84
G.F. Waller, 106:Summer83-207
Stark, R. The Rare Coin Score. Slayground.
M. Laski, 362:12Apr84-27
Starobinski, J. Montaigne en mouvement.*
P. Burke, 208(FS):Apr83-206
A. Compagnon, 98:Jun-Jul83-522
H. Cronel, 450(NRF):Jul/Aug83-230
L. and C. Welch, 150(DR):Autumn83-533
Starr, C.G. The Beginnings of Imperial Rome.
H.W. Pleket, 394:Vol36fasc3/4-442
Starr, J.B., ed. The Future of U.S.-China Relations.
E.K. Lawson and D. Denny, 293(JASt): Feb83-402
Starr, P. The Social Transformation of American Medicine.*
A.S. Relman, 453(NYRB):29Mar84-29
639(VQR):Summer83-94
Starr, S.F. Red and Hot.*
H.F. Graham, 550(RusR):Oct83-403
M. Slobin, 187:Jan84-149
Stary, P.F. Zur eisenzeitlichen Bewaffnung und Kampfesweise in Mittelitalien.
D. Ridgway, 123:Vol33No2-362
Stati, S., ed. Le teorie sintattiche del Novecento.
F. Murru, 685(ZDL):2/1983-234
Statler, O. Japanese Pilgrimage.
J. Kirkup, 617(TLS):30Nov84-1368
E. Munro, 469:Vol9No1-102
Stäuble, M. and A. - see Bertòla, A.D.
Stauffer, H.W. Mari Sandoz.
M. Graulich, 649(WAL):Nov83-239
J.H. Maguire, 27(AL):May83-270
D.E. Wylder, 395(MFS):Winter83-719
Stauffer, H.W. and S.J. Rosowski, eds. Women and Western American Literature.
D.C. Grover, 649(WAL):Aug83-182
R. Hoople, 651(WHR):Winter83-362
Staves, S. Players' Sceptres.*
E. Späth, 38:Band101Heft1/2-269
Stead, C. The Puzzleheaded Girl.
P. Craig, 617(TLS):28Dec84-1506
Stead, C.K. All Visitors Ashore.
C. Hawtree, 617(TLS):13Jul84-791
Stead, C.K. - see Mansfield, K.
Steadman, R. I, Leonardo.
M. Kemp, 617(TLS):20Jan84-55
Stecher, A. Inschriftliche Grabgedichte auf Krieger und Athleten.
P.A. Hansen, 123:Vol33No2-369
Stedman Jones, G. Languages of Class.
P. Joyce, 617(TLS):11May84-532
Steegmuller, F. - see Flaubert, G.
Steel, C. - see Proclus
Steel, D. Full Circle.
N. Ramsey, 441:19Aug84-18
Steele, H. The Wishdoctor's Song.
J.K.L. Walker, 617(TLS):9Nov84-1288
Steele, H.T. The Hawaiian Shirt.
W. Kaminer, 441:16Sep84-30
Steele, J. World Power.
G. Szamuely, 617(TLS):31Aug84-976

Steele, J. and E. Abraham. Andropov in Power.
R.G. Suny, 385(MQR):Fall84-576
Steele, R. and A.D. Bourlon. Elle.
W. Wrage, 207(FR):Oct83-153
Steele, S. and others. An Encyclopedia of AUX.
E.M. Kaisse, 350:Dec84-924
Steensland, L. A Method for Measuring Perceptual Differences between Different Vowel Qualities — Some Identification Tests Using Russian /e/ Variants and Swedish Subjects.
D. Ward, 559:Vol7No1-73
Steer, G. Hugo Ripelin von Strassburg.
N.F. Palmer, 402(MLR):Apr83-486
Steer, J. Alvise Vivarini.*
J. Anderson, 278(IS):Vol38-102
J. Fletcher, 90:Feb83-99
C. Gould, 39:Apr83-337
Stéfan, J. Lettres tombales.
J. Laurans, 450(NRF):Jul/Aug83-217
Stefanis, J.E. Ho doylos stis kōmōdies toy Aristophanē.
R.G. Ussher, 303(JoHS):Vol 103-168
Stefenelli, A. Geschichte des französischen Kernwortschatzes.*
H. Geckeler, 547(RF):Band95Heft3-314
D.A. Kibbee, 207(FR):May84-922
Stegagno Picchio, L. La Littérature brésilienne.
T.R.H., 131(CL):Spring83-172
Stegner, W. One Way To Spell Man.*
K. Ahearn, 649(WAL):May83-52
Stehle, H. Eastern Politics of the Vatican, 1917-1979.
R.F. Byrnes, 550(RusR):Apr83-234
H. Hanak, 575(SEER):Apr83-294
Steig, W. Ruminations.
442(NY):17Dec84-157
Stein, B. Peasant State and Society in Medieval South India.
J.F. Richards, 293(JASt):Aug83-1005
Stein, B.J. The Manhattan Gambit.*
S. Altinel, 617(TLS):6Apr84-368
Stein, C.W., ed. American Vaudeville.
H. Teichmann, 441:11Nov84-28
Stein, H. Hoopla.
I. Berkow, 441:15Jan84-18
Stein, H. Presidential Economics.
J. Fallows, 453(NYRB):12Apr84-8
R.J. Samuelson, 61:Feb84-98
L. Silk, 441:12Feb84-9
M.J. Ulmer, 129:Jun84-60
Stein, K.W. The Land Question in Palestine, 1917-1939.
J.C. Hurewitz, 441:4Nov84-18
Stein, P. Connaissance et emploi des langues à l'Île Maurice.
C. Corne, 350:Dec84-950
Stein, P.K. and others, eds. Sprache — Text — Geschichte.*
D.H. Green, 402(MLR):Apr83-480
Stein, R.L. The French Slave Trade in the Eighteenth Century.*
J. Lough, 208(FS):Jan83-87
Steinauer, P-H. La logique au service du droit.
J. Woleński, 316:Dec83-1206
Steinberg, A. Word and Music in the Novels of Andrei Bely.
J.D. Elsworth, 575(SEER):Oct83-600

[continued]

Steinberg, A. Word and Music in the Novels of Andrei Bely. [continuing]
  P.R. Hart, 395(MFS):Winter83-801
  G.S. Smith, 617(TLS):5Oct84-1135
  639(VQR):Autumn83-118
Steinberg, D.D. Psycholinguistics.*
  M.S. Seidenberg, 399(MLJ):Autumn83-301
Steinberg, D.I. Burma's Road Toward Development.
  A.D. Moscotti, 293(JASt):May83-729
Steinberg, L. The Sexuality of Christ in Renaissance Art and in Modern Oblivion.
  A. Chastel, 453(NYRB):22Nov84-25
  D. Summers, 617(TLS):23Nov84-1346
  R. Wollheim, 441:29Apr84-13
Steinbrich, S. Gazelle und Büffelkuh.
  E. Dammann, 196:Band24Heft3/4-330
Steinbruckner, B.F. Dialektgeographie des oberen Mühlviertels.
  L. Zehetner, 685(ZDL):1/1983-97
Steinecke, H. Literaturkritik des Jungen Deutschland.
  J.P. Strelka, 221(GQ):Mar83-295
Steinem, G. Outrageous Acts and Everyday Rebellions.*
  S.M. Gilbert, 617(TLS):8Jun84-645
Steiner, G. Antigones.
  D. Grene, 441:16Dec84-13
  O. Murray, 617(TLS):24Aug84-947
  R. Padel, 176:Nov84-44
  F. Raphael, 362:19Jul84-24
  O. Taplin, 453(NYRB):6Dec84-13
  442(NY):26Nov84-150
Steiner, G. Martin Heidegger.
  M.L. Cushman, 480(P&R):Vol 16No3-211
  P. Trotignon, 542:Oct-Dec83-505
Steiner, G. Nach Babel.
  H. Nette, 52:Band18Heft1-85
Steiner, G. The Portage to San Cristóbal of A.H.*
  L. Kahn, 390:Oct83-55
  M. Plotinsky, 287:Apr83-18
Steiner, J. - see Storm, T. and T. Fontane
Steiner, P., ed. The Prague School.
  M. Bílý, 596(SL):Vol137No2-199
  B.H. Davis, 350:Mar84-181
Steiner, R. The Essential Steiner. (R.A. McDermott, ed)
  O. Barfield, 469:Vol9No4-94
Steiner, W. The Colors of Rhetoric.
  C. Altieri, 385(MQR):Fall84-587
  M.A. Caws, 290(JAAC):Fall83-90
  L. Edson, 188(ECr):Winter83-85
  S. Ferguson, 141:Summer83-282
  A. Janowitz, 395(MFS):Summer83-377
  295(JML):Nov83-408
Steiner, W., ed. The Sign in Music and Literature.*
  C. Ayrey, 410(M&L):Jul/Oct83-274
  R. Solie, 317:Summer83-328
  J.A. Winn, 402(MLR):Jul83-644
Steinfeldt, C. Texas Folk Art.
  G.E. Lich, 585(SoQ):Winter83-85
Steinhauer, K., comp. Hegel-Bibliography-Bibliographie.*
  J. D'Hondt, 192(EP):Jan-Mar83-114
Steinhauser, K. Altering Today's Blouse Patterns. Altering Today's Slacks Patterns.
  G. Brown, 614:Fall84-12
Steinhaussen, K., ed. Kein Duft von wilder Minze.
  I. Pawlowitz, 654(WB):9/1982-137

Steininger, R., ed. Deutsche Geschichte 1945-1961.
  W. Laqueur, 617(TLS):17Aug84-921
Steinitz, W. Dialektologisches und etymologisches Wörterbuch der ostjakischen Sprache. (Pt 9)
  E. Schiefer, 260(IF):Band88-379
Steinitz, W. Ostjakologische Arbeiten.* (Vol 4) (E. Lang, G. Sauer and R. Steinitz, eds)
  G.F. Cushing, 575(SEER):Oct83-595
  M.S. Kispál, 682(ZPSK):Band36Heft1-108
Steinmeyer, G. Historische Aspekte des "français avancé."*
  H. Meier, 72:Band219Heft2-453
Steins, M. Blaise Cendrars, bilans nègres.
  M. Watthee-Delmotte, 356(LR):Nov83-359
Steinvorth, U. Stationen der politischen Theorie.
  P. Burg, 342:Band74Heft3-368
Steele, T. The Prudent Heart.
  D. Gioia, 461:Fall/Winter83/84-99
Stellmacher, D. Studien zur gesprochenen Sprache in Niedersachsen.
  K.H. Schmidt, 685(ZDL):1/1983-88
Steltzer, U. Inuit.*
  G.W., 102(CanL):Spring83-188
Stempel, J.D. Inside the Iranian Revolution.
  S. Simpson, 639(VQR):Summer83-540
Stendhal. Chroniques pour l'Angleterre. (Vol 1) (K.G. McWatters, ed)
  F. Claudon, 535(RHL):Mar/Apr83-294
  C. Robinson, 447(N&Q):Oct82-454
Stendhal. Chroniques pour l'Angleterre. (Vols 2 and 3) (K.G. McWatters, ed)
  P. Berthier, 605(SC):15Jan84-197
Stendhal. De l'amour.* (V. Del Litto, ed)
  F.W. Saunders, 208(FS):Oct83-471
Stendhal. Lucien Leuwen. (A-M. Meininger, ed)
  G. Dethan, 605(SC):15Apr84-285
Stendhal. Mémoires d'un touriste en Bretagne.
  V.D.L., 605(SC):15Jul84-385
Stendhal. Oeuvres intimes.* (Vol 2) (V. Del Litto, ed)
  E.J. Talbot, 446(NCFS):Fall-Winter83/84-217
Stendhal. Le Rose et le Vert, Mina de Vanghel et autres nouvelles.* (V. Del Litto, ed)
  I. Simon, 446(NCFS):Fall-Winter83/84-218
"Stendhal et l'Europe."
  V.D.L., 605(SC):15Jul84-377
Stengel, E. Chronologisches Verzeichnis französischer Grammatiken. (rev by H-J. Niederehe)
  Y.M., 545(RPh):Nov82-318
Stephan, A. Die deutsche Exilliteratur 1933-1945.*
  H. Müssener, 133:Band16Heft1-83
Stephan, A. Christa Wolf.
  M. Hannaford, 133:Band16Heft1-92
  R. Hargreaves, 447(N&Q):Feb82-90
Stephan, H. "Lef" and the Left Front of the Arts.*
  J. Graffy, 575(SEER):Apr83-277
Stephan, J.J. Hawaii Under the Rising Sun.
  H. Goodman, 441:8Apr84-21

Stéphane, H. Introduction à l'ésotérisme
chrétien. (Vol 2)
   A. Reix, 542:Oct-Dec83-453
Stéphane, M. Feux de joie.
   M.G. Rose, 207(FR):Dec83-275
Stephanopoulos, T.K. Umgestaltung des
Mythos durch Euripides.*
   W. Pötscher, 394:Vol36fasc3/4-408
Stephany, E. and others. Licht Glas Farbe.
   R. Kehlmann, 139:Dec83/Jan84-39
Stephen, I. Malin, Hebrides, Minches.
   D. McDuff, 565:Vol24No4-62
Stephens, J. Uncollected Prose of James
Stephens. (P.A. McFate, ed)
   P. Craig, 617(TLS):27Jan84-81
Stephens, J.C., ed. The Guardian.*
   E.A. Bloom, 566:Autumn83-57
   A. Bony, 189(EA):Apr-Jun84-197
Stephens, J.R. The Censorship of English
Drama 1824-1901.*
   K. Tetzeli von Rosador, 72:Band220
   Heft2-416
   C. Woodring, 130:Spring83-85
Stephenson, N. The Big U.
   A. Cheuse, 441:30Sep84-18
Steppat, M. The Critical Reception of
Shakespeare's "Antony and Cleopatra"
from 1607 to 1905.
   A.W. Bellringer, 447(N&Q):Apr82-165
   M.G., 189(EA):Jul-Sep84-361
   D. Mehl, 72:Band220Heft1-163
Sterba, J.P. The Demands of Justice.*
   D.A. Lloyd Thomas, 479(PhQ):Jul83-301
   J.T. Rabinowitz, 482(PhR):Oct83-607
Sterchi, B. Blösch.
   M. Hofmann, 617(TLS):5Oct84-1136
Sterling, C. Enguerrand Quarton.
   C. Reynolds, 90:Dec83-755
Sterling, C. The Time of the Assassins.
   E.J. Epstein, 441:15Jan84-6
   R. Kaplan, 129:Apr84-79
Sterling, D., ed. We Are Your Sisters.
   S.M. Halpern, 441:29Apr84-33
   442(NY):16Apr84-159
Stern, D.C. Hilde Domin.
   A.W. Riley, 221(GQ):Jan83-175
Stern, E. Excavations at Tel Mevorakh
(1973-1976). (Pt 1)
   W.G. Dever, 318(JAOS):Apr-Jun82-399
Stern, F.C. F.O. Matthiessen.*
   J.D. Bloom, 579(SAQ):Winter83-102
   M.H. Buxbaum, 191(ELN):Dec83-63
Stern, G. Paradise Poems.
   H. Beaver, 441:11Nov84-18
Stern, H.J. Judgment in Berlin.
   E.R. Fidell, 441:25Mar84-17
Stern, I. and M. Square Meals.
   M. Burros, 441:2Dec84-16
Stern, J.L., ed. Lewis Carroll's Library.*
   M.N. Cohen, 517(PBSA):Vol77No1-89
Stern, J.P., ed. The World of Franz Kafka.
   R.S. Livingstone, 402(MLR):Jan83-241
Stern, M., ed. Expressionismus in der
Schweiz.*
   C. Eykman, 221(GQ):Jan83-116
   C. Eykman, 222(GR):Summer83-125
   C. Eykman, 400(MLN):Apr83-535
   G.P. Knapp, 405(MP):May84-444
   J.M. Ritchie, 402(MLR):Jan83-243
   H.G. Rotzer, 52:Band17Heft3-331
   P. Spycher, 301(JEGP):Apr83-298

Stern, M.B., ed. Publishers for Mass
Entertainment in Nineteenth Century
America.
   M. Winship, 517(PBSA):Vol77No2-229
Stern, M.R., ed. Critical Essays on Her-
man Melville's "Typee."
   R. Milder, 183(ESQ):Vol29No2-99
Stern, R.A.M., G. Gilmartin and J.M. Mas-
sengale. New York 1900.
   P. Goldberger, 441:18Mar84-11
Stern, R.G. The Invention of the Real.
   639(VQR):Winter83-16
Stern, V.F. Gabriel Harvey.
   W.G. Colman, 179(ES):Apr83-169
Sternbach, L. A Descriptive Catalogue of
Poets Quoted in Sanskrit Anthologies and
Inscriptions.* (Vols 1 and 2)
   J.W. de Jong, 259(IIJ):Mar83-138
Sternbach, L. Poësie sanskrite conservée
dans les anthologies et les inscrip-
tions.* (Vol 1)
   J.W. de Jong, 259(IIJ):Mar83-138
Sterne, L. The Life and Opinions of Tris-
tram Shandy, Gentleman. (M. and J. New,
eds) The Life and Opinions of Tristram
Shandy, Gentleman. (I.C. Ross, ed)
   S. Soupel, 189(EA):Jan-Mar84-96
Sterne, L. Vie et opinions de Tristram
Shandy, gentilhomme. (S. Soupel, ed)
   R.A. Day, 189(EA):Jan-Mar84-98
Sterne, L. Le Voyage sentimental. (S.
Soupel, ed)
   R.A. Day, 189(EA):Apr-Jun84-207
Sternlieb, G. and J.W. Hughes. The Atlan-
tic City Gamble.
   R. Roberts, 441:18Mar84-19
Stétié, S. L'Être Poupée [suivi de]
Colombe aquiline.
   M. Baronheid, 450(NRF):Jul/Aug83-204
Steven, S. The Poles.
   G.T. Kapolka, 497(PolR):Vol28No3-88
Stevens, D. Musicology.
   J.B., 412:Aug-Nov82-267
Stevens, M. Summer in the City.
   R. Koenig, 61:Jun84-117
   F. Taliaferro, 441:22Apr84-11
Stevens, P. Coming Back.*
   P. Mitcham, 102(CanL):Summer83-144
Stevens, P. Revenge of the Mistresses.
   P. Stuewe, 529(QQ):Winter83-1034
Stevenson, A. Minute by Glass Minute.*
   M. Kinzie, 29:Mar/Apr84-38
   E. Larrissy, 493:Mar83-61
   J. Saunders, 565:Vol24No4-71
Stevenson, J. British Society 1914-45.
   J. Burnett, 617(TLS):5Oct84-1123
Stevenson, K.E. and G.R. Habermas. Ver-
dict on the Shroud.
   B. Elson, 529(QQ):Summer83-569
Stevenson, R. On the Other Hand, Death.
   N. Callendar, 441:14Oct84-46
Stevenson, R.L. The Amateur Emigrant.
   J.T., 617(TLS):20Apr84-441
Stevenson, W. Intrepid's Last Case.
   J. Bamford, 441:22Jan84-20
Stevenson, W. The Myth of the Golden Age
in English Romantic Poetry.
   V.A. De Luca, 88:Summer83-32
Stevick, P. Alternative Pleasures.*
   D.W. Madden, 594:Winter83-396
Stewart, H. By the Old Walls of Kyoto.
   R. Dunlop, 581:Jun83-167

Stewart, J. So the Night World Spins.
  R. Hatch, 102(CanL):Winter82-144
Stewart, J. - see Jones, B.
Stewart, J.B. The Partners.*
  639(VQR):Summer83-94
Stewart, J.D. Sir Godfrey Kneller and the
  English Baroque Portrait.
  M. Rogers, 617(TLS):23Mar84-300
Stewart, J.H. - see Madame Riccoboni
Stewart, J.I.M. Appleby and Honeybath.
  N. Callendar, 441:1Jan84-26
Stewart, J.I.M. An Open Prison.
  A. Shapiro, 441:29Jul84-20
Stewart, M. Far Cry.
  N. Shack, 617(TLS):13Jul84-791
Stewart, M. The Wicked Day.
  D. Hoffman, 441:1Jan84-20
Stewart, R. Rescue Mission.
  G.S.S. Chandra, 436(NewL):Summer84-114
Stewart, R.F. ...and Always a Detective.
  U. Böker, 72:Band219Heft1-166
Stewart, S. Nonsense.*
  C. Lindahl, 650(WF):Jan83-71
  R.R. Wilson, 107(CRCL):Jun83-254
Steyn, P. Birds of Prey of Southern
  Africa.
  R.O., 617(TLS):22Jun84-711
Stich, K.P. - see Salverson, L.G.
Stich, S.P. From Folk Psychology to Cogni-
  tive Science.
  S. Blackburn, 617(TLS):14Sep84-1030
Stichel, R.H.W. Die römische Kaiserstatue
  am Ausgang der Antike.
  B. Burrell, 124:Mar-Apr84-257
Stichweh, K. and M.B. de Launay - see
  Löwith, K.
Stiene, H.E. - see Wandalbert von Prüm
Stierlin, H. Art of the Incas.
  P-L. Adams, 61:Jul84-117
  T.C. Patterson, 441:14Oct84-30
Stiewe, K. and N. Holzberg, eds. Polybios.
  E.S. Gruen, 124:May-Jun84-312
Stil, A. L'Homme de coeur.
  P.H. Solomon, 207(FR):Feb84-419
Stilgoe, J.R. Common Landscape of America,
  1580-1845.*
  D. Schuyler, 658:Summer/Autumn83-213
Stilgoe, J.R. Metropolitan Corridor.*
  L. Marx, 453(NYRB):15Mar84-28
Stillers, R. Maurice Blanchot: "Thomas
  l'Obscur."
  F. Wolfzettel, 535(RHL):Jul/Aug83-661
Stillman, N.A. The Jews of Arab Lands.
  N. Cigar, 318(JAOS):Jan-Mar82-222
Stimm, H., ed. Zur Geschichte des gespro-
  chenen Französisch und zur Sprachlenkung
  im Gegenwartsfranzösischen.*
  A. Greive, 72:Band219Heft1-218
  O. Välikangas, 439(NM):1983/4-531
Stinchcombe, W.C., C.T. Cullen and L.
  Tobias - see Marshall, J.
Stinchecum, A.M. Kosode.
  R.L. Shep, 614:Summer84-21
Stinson, R. and P. The Long Dying of Baby
  Andrew.
  P. Singer and H. Kuhse, 453(NYRB):
  1Mar84-17
Stipe, R.E., ed. New Directions in Rural
  Preservation.
  S.L. Farley, 650(WF):Jan83-55
Stivers, W. Supremacy and Oil.
  639(VQR):Summer83-95

Stock, I. Fiction as Wisdom.*
  J. McCormick, 107(CRCL):Mar83-106
Stock, R.D. The Holy and the Daemonic
  from Sir Thomas Browne to William Blake.*
  J.M. Aden, 569(SR):Summer83-liv
  J. Blondel, 189(EA):Jul-Sep84-327
  L.J. Swingle, 401(MLQ):Mar83-80
  A. Taylor, 141:Winter83-75
Stockinger, L. Ficta Respublica.
  W. Braungart, 196:Band24Heft3/4-332
  M. Winter, 680(ZDP):Band102Heft2-260
Stoddard, E.R., R.L. Nostrand and J.P.
  West, eds. Borderlands Soucrebook.
  D.E. Chipman, 263(RIB):Vol33No2-269
  L. Milazzo, 584(SWR):Spring83-vi
Stoddard, K.M. Saints and Shrews.
  J. Beerman, 42(AR):Fall83-503
Stoddard, R.E. Poet and Printer in Colo-
  nial and Federal America.
  J.A.L. Lemay, 365:Summer/Fall83-127
Stodelle, E. Deep Song.
  A. Kisselgoff, 441:28Oct84-13
Stöhr, W. Die Altindonesischen Religionen.
  J.A. Boon and J.R. Eidson, 293(JASt):
  May83-730
Stokes, A. With All the Views.
  R. Pybus, 565:Vol24No2-93
Stokes, D.W. A Guide to Observing Insect
  Lives.
  P. Hagan, 441:3Jun84-13
Stokes, G. Pinstripe Pandemonium.
  L.S. Ritter, 441:3Jun84-9
Stokes, R. Esdaile's Manual of Bibliogra-
  phy. (5th ed)
  P.S. Koda, 517(PBSA):Vol77No2-236
Stokker, K. and O. Haddal. Norsk, Nord-
  menn og Norge.
  D. Buttry, 399(MLJ):Spring83-89
  S.R. Smith, 563(SS):Winter83-94
Stokstad, M. Santiago de Compostela in
  the Age of the Pilgrimages.
  I. Mateo Gómez, 48:Jan-Mar79-102
Stokvis, W. Cobra.
  M. Dachy, 98:Nov83-913
Stol, M., with K. van Lerberghe. On Trees,
  Mountains, and Millstones in the Ancient
  Near East.
  R.D. Biggs, 318(JAOS):Oct-Dec82-659
Stolcius, D. The Hermetic Garden of
  Daniel Stolcius. (A. McLean, ed)
  J. Godwin, 111:Fall83-6
Stoler, J.A. and R.D. Fulton. Henry Field-
  ing.*
  P-G. Boucé, 189(EA):Jan-Mar83-78
  C. Price, 610:Spring82-149
Stoller, M.L. and T.J. Steele, eds. Diary
  of the Jesuit Residence of Our Lady of
  Guadalupe Parish, Conejos, Colorado,
  December 1871-December 1875.
  L. Milazzo, 584(SWR):Summer83-vi
Stolzenberg, M. Clowns for Circus and
  Stage.
  A. Cornish, 157:Summer83-31
Stone, A. Antique Furniture.
  G. Wills, 39:Sep83-273
Stone, A.A. Law, Psychiatry, and Morality.
  G.P. Fletcher, 441:9Sep84-42
Stone, A.E., ed. The American Autobiog-
  raphy.
  G. Woodcock, 569(SR):Winter83-129
  506(PSt):Dec83-311

Stone, A.E. Autobiographical Occasions
and Original Acts.
  W.L. Andrews, 26(ALR):Autumn83-303
  R. Gray, 77:Fall83-358
  L.A. Renza, 27(AL):Oct83-450
Stone, B. The Parlement of Paris, 1774-
1789.
  J. Merrick, 173(ECS):Spring84-333
Stone, D.D. The Romantic Impulse in Vic-
torian Fiction.*
  E.M. Eigner, 591(SIR):Fall83-455
Stone, G. An Introduction to Polish.
  A. Gorski, 497(PolR):Vol28No1-98
Stone, G.W., Jr., ed. The Stage and the
Page.*
  P. Dixon, 611(TN):Vol37No2-86
  J.J. Stathis, 570(SQ):Winter83-508
Stone, G.W., Jr. and G.M. Kahrl. David
Garrick.*
  O.M. Brack, Jr., 610:Spring83-66
  J. Donohue, 402(MLR):Jan83-148
  C. Price, 541(RES):Feb83-80
Stone, L. The Past and the Present.
  P. Christianson, 529(QQ):Summer83-546
  G. McLennan, 366:Spring83-107
Stone, L. and J.C.F. An Open Elite?
  H. Brogan, 362:6Sep84-22
  D. Cannadine, 453(NYRB):20Dec84-64
  F.M.L. Thompson, 617(TLS):7Sep84-990
Stone, M.E. Scriptures, Sects, and
Visions.*
  J. Neuser, 318(JAOS):Oct-Dec82-655
Stone, P.W.K. The Textual History of
"King Lear."*
  M.P. Jackson, 570(SQ):Spring83-121
  G. Taylor, 541(RES):Feb83-68
Stoneman, R., ed. Daphne into Laurel.*
  W.H., 148:Autumn83-90
Stonum, G.L. Faulkner's Career.
  E. Gallafent, 677(YES):Vol 13-351
Stonyk, M. Nineteenth-Century English
Literature.
  J. Adlard, 617(TLS):20Apr84-420
Stopp, H., ed. Das Kochbuch der Sabina
Welserin.
  H. Parigger, 684(ZDA):Band112Heft4-185
Stopp, H. Schreibsprachwandel.*
  C.V.J. Russ, 685(ZDL):3/1983-405
Stopp, H. - see Michels, V.
Stoppelli, P. - see Castelletti, C.
Storey, D. Present Times.
  V. Cunningham, 617(TLS):18May84-546
  J. Mellors, 362:24May84-28
Storey, D. A Prodigal Child.*
  M. Théry, 189(EA):Jul-Sep84-349
Storey, E. A Right to Song.
  P.M.S.D., 148:Autumn83-93
Storey, G. and K.J. Fielding - see Dickens,
C.
Storkey, A. A Christian Social Perspec-
tive.
  G.W. Trompf, 488:Dec83-517
Storm, T. and T. Fontane. Theodor Storm —
Theodor Fontane: Briefwechsel.* (J.
Steiner, ed)
  A.T. Alt, 400(MLN):Apr83-533
  H-G. Richert, 133:Band16Heft1-73
  H. Steinecke, 221(GQ):Mar83-329
Story, G. The Book of Thirteen.
  D. O'Rourke, 102(CanL):Winter82-130

Story, G.M., W.J. Kirwin and J.D.A. Widdow-
son, eds. Dictionary of Newfoundland
English.
  A. Cameron, 627(UTQ):Summer83-503
  T.K. Pratt, 320(CJL):Fall83-194
Stössel, A. Keramik aus Westafrika.
  J. Povey, 2(AfrA):Aug83-83
Stout, J. A Family Likeness.
  F.K. Foster, 649(WAL):Nov83-266
Stout, R. The Hand in the Glove.
  R. Hill, 617(TLS):26Oct84-1225
Stove, D. Popper and After.*
  J. Largeault, 542:Jul-Sep83-369
  A. Lugg, 486:Jun83-350
Stow, R. The Suburbs of Hell.
  P-L. Adams, 61:Sep84-128
Stow, R. Tourmaline.
  P. Craig, 617(TLS):24Aug84-935
Stowe, H.B. Uncle Tom's Cabin, The Minis-
ter's Wooing, Oldtown Folks. (K.K.
Sklar, ed)
  W.H. Pritchard, 249(HudR):Summer83-352
Stowe, W.W. Balzac, James, and the Real-
istic Novel.*
  S.B. Daugherty, 27(AL):Dec83-655
Stowell, H.P. Literary Impressionism,
James and Chekhov.*
  R.K. Martin, 106:Winter83-457
van Straaten, Z., ed. Philosophical Sub-
jects.*
  R. Clark, 449:Nov83-694
  J. Heal, 479(PhQ):Jan83-77
Strabo. Strabon, "Géographie." (Vol 9)
(F. Lasserre, ed)
  P. Levi, 123:Vol33No1-17
Strachan, H. Wellington's Legacy.
  P. Towle, 617(TLS):31Aug84-974
Strachan, W.J. Henry Moore: Animals.
  C. Juler, 592:Vol 196No1003-58
Strachan, W.J. Open Air Sculpture in
Britain.
  S. Gardiner, 362:15Nov84-29
Strachey, B. and J. Samuels - see Berenson,
M.
Strachey, J. and F. Partridge. Julia.*
  B.S. Halpern, 556:Winter83/84-177
Strachey, R. A Strachey Boy.
  C. Hawtree, 364:Aug/Sep83-137
Stradling, R.A. Europe and the Decline of
Spain.
  P. Williams, 86(BHS):Apr83-148
Straight, M. After Long Silence.*
  A.P. Cappon, 436(NewL):Summer84-101
Straka, G. Les Sons et les Mots.*
  P. Pupier, 320(CJL):Spring83-90
Strand, M. Selected Poems.*
  P. Stitt, 219(GaR):Spring83-201
Strandberg, V. A Faulkner Overview.*
  T.L. McHaney, 392:Summer83-519
Strange, J. Caphtor/Keftiu.
  M.C. Astour, 318(JAOS):Apr-Jun82-395
  J.T. Hooker, 303(JoHS):Vol 103-216
Strange, K.H. The Climbing Boys.*
  D.G.C.A., 324:Dec83-85
  A.S. Watts, 155:Spring83-49
Strange, R. Newman and the Gospel of
Christ.
  W. Myers, 569(SR):Spring83-275
Strasburger, H. Studien zur Alten Ge-
schichte. (W. Schmitthenner and R.
Zoepffel, eds)
  J. Briscoe, 123:Vol33No2-377

Strasser, P. Wirklichkeitskonstruktion
und Rationalität.
P.E. Stüben, 489(PJGG):Band90Heft2-424
Strassner, E. Graphemsystem und Wortkon-
stituenz.
W.J. Jones, 685(ZDL):1/1983-100
Stratford, J. Catalogue of the Jackson
Collection of Manuscript Fragments in
the Royal Library, Windsor Castle, with
a Memoir of Canon J.E. Jackson and a
List of his Works.
B. Barker-Benfield, 354:Jun83-177
R.A. Linenthal, 517(PBSA):Vol77No2-243
J.F. Preston, 377:Mar83-46
A. Stones, 589:Oct83-1088
Strauch, J. Chinese Village Politics in
the Malaysian State.
R. Trottier, 293(JASt):Nov82-235
Straughan, R. "I Ought To, But . . ."*
J.E.M. Darling, 518:Jan83-35
Straus, B. The Maladies of Marcel Proust.*
R. Splitter, 149(CLS):Winter83-454
Straus, D. Under the Canopy.
S.G. Kellman, 390:Mar83-60
S.S. Pinsker, 395(MFS):Summer83-373
Strauss, B. Tumult.
J. Lasdun, 176:May84-64
Strauss, D. Die erotische Dichtung von
Robert Burns.*
M.P. McDiarmid, 588(SSL):Vol 18-253
Strauss, J., ed. "Beowulf" und die klein-
eren Denkmäler der altenglischen Helden-
sage Waldere und Finnsburg. (Vol 3)
R.P.M. Lehmann, 589:Oct83-1136
Strauss, J. Yehudah Leib Gordon Poète
hébreu (1830-1892).
V. Nikiprowetzky, 549(RLC):Apr-Jun83-
240
Strauss, L. Pensées sur Machiavel.
H. Védrine, 542:Jan-Mar83-97
"Richard Strauss: 'Der Rosenkavalier.'"
(text retold by A. Burgess)
M. Kennedy, 415:Sep83-551
Stravinsky, I. Stravinsky: Selected
Correspondence. (Vol 1) (R. Craft,
ed)
A. Whittall, 410(M&L):Jan/Apr83-102
Stravinsky, I. Stravinsky: Selected Corre-
spondence. (Vol 2) (R. Craft, ed)
J. Drummond, 362:18Oct84-29
D. Hamilton, 441:5Aug84-11
442(NY):30Jul84-87
Stravinsky, I. and R. Craft. Dialogues.
J. Pasler, 415:Oct83-605
Stravinsky, V. and R. McCaffrey, with R.
Craft, eds. Igor and Vera Stravinsky.
J. Pasler, 415:Oct83-605
Strawson, P.F. Etudes de logique et de
linguistique.
D. Zaslawsky, 209(FM):Jan83-71
Strayer, J.R., ed. Dictionary of the Mid-
dle Ages. (Vols 1 and 2)
J.C. Hansford, 70:May-Jun83-164
Strecke, R. Zur geschichtlichen Bedeutung
des altfranzösischen Alexiusliedes.
W. Rothwell, 208(FS):Apr83-198
Streeten, P. Development Perspectives.
M. Lipton, 617(TLS):31Aug84-972
Streeten, P. and others. First Things
First.
M. Lipton, 617(TLS):31Aug84-972
Strelka, J. Esoterik bei Goethe.*
K.G. Negus, 564:May83-155

Strelka, J. Stefan Zweig.*
M. Pazi, 222(GR):Fal183-164
K. Weissenberger, 221(GQ):Nov83-697
Strelka, J.P. Literary Criticism and
Philosophy.
J. Hospers, 290(JAAC):Summer84-461
"Strengthening Conventional Deterrence in
Europe."
T. Garden, 176:Apr84-58
G. Kennedy, 617(TLS):1Jun84-604
Strieber, W. and J.W. Kunetka. Warday.
D.G. Myers, 441:22Apr84-14
Strieder, P. Dürer.
J. Rowlands, 39:Jul83-112
Striker, C.L. The Myrelaion (Bodrum Camii)
in Istanbul.
R. Cormack, 90:Feb83-97
J. Morganstern, 589:Oct83-1090
Strindberg, A. By the Open Sea. (M.
Sandbach, trans) Five Plays. (H.G.
Carlson, trans)
R. Dinnage, 617(TLS):9Nov84-1286
Strindberg, A. Strindberg Plays: Two.
(M. Meyer, trans)
D. Devlin, 157:Spring83-52
Strindberg, A. I vårbrytningen. Röda
rummet. (C.R. Smedmark, ed of both)
Svenska öden och äventyr. (B. Land-
gren, ed)
W. Johnson, 562(Scan):May83-84
Strobel, R. Mittelalterliche Bauplastik
am Bürgerhaus in Regensburg.
F. Bucher, 589:Jan83-269
Stroiński, L. Window.
A.C. Lupack, 497(PolR):Vol28No2-113
Stroker, E. and R. Hahn, eds. Wissen-
schaftstheorie der Naturwissenschaften.
K.O., 543:Sep82-199
Stromberg, R.N. Redemption by War.
L. Lampert, 529(QQ):Summer83-581
Strong, R. The English Renaissance Mini-
ature.*
D. Foskett, 324:Apr84-344
Strong, R. The Renaissance Garden in
England.*
A.P., 617(TLS):20Apr84-443
Strong, T.B. and H. Keyssar. Right In Her
Soul.
J.C. Thomson, Jr., 441:11Mar84-25
Stroud, D. Sir John Soane Architect.
K. Downes, 617(TLS):15Jun84-653
Stroud, J. and G. Thomas, eds. Images of
the Untouched.
T.W., 111:Spring83-2
Stroud, M.D. - see Calderón de la Barca, P.
Stroup, T., ed. Edward Westermarck.
T.M.R., 185:Jul84-731
Strout, C. The Veracious Imagination.*
H. Tulloch, 366:Spring83-126
Struminger, L.S. What Were Little Girls
and Boys Made of?
S.S. Bryson, 207(FR):Mar84-576
Struminskyj, B., comp. Old Ruthenian
Printed Books and Manuscripts in the
Episcopal and Heritage Institute
Libraries of the Byzantine Catholic
Diocese of Passaic.
W.F. Ryan, 575(SEER):Oct83-594
Struminskyj, B., with E. Kasinec, comps.
Kievan, Galician, Volhynian and Trans-
carpathian Old Cyrillic Printed Books
from the Collections of Paul M. Fekula.
W.F. Ryan, 575(SEER):Oct83-594

Strutynski, U. - see Dumézil, G.
Struve, N. Osip Mandelstam.
  J.G. Harris, 574(SEEJ):Winter83-492
Stuart, D. Common Ground.
  639(VQR):Winter83-24
Stuart, F. Black List, Section H.
  F.C. Molloy, 145(Crit):Winter84-115
Stuart, F. States of Mind.
  T.D. White, 617(TLS):29Jun84-733
Stuart, F. We Have Kept the Faith.
  M. Harmon, 272(IUR):Spring83-114
Stuart, I. The Garb of Truth.
  N. Callendar, 441:24Jun84-41
Stuart, R.C. War and American Thought
  from the Revolution to the Monroe Doc-
  trine.
  C. Symonds, 656(WMQ):Oct83-648
Stubbs, J. The Northern Correspondent.
  S. Altinel, 617(TLS):7Dec84-1420
Stubbs, J.C. - see Fellini, F.
Stubbs, P. Women and Fiction.*
  E. Aird, 161(DUJ):Jun83-139
  P. Coustillas, 189(EA):Oct-Dec84-473
  S. Foster, 677(YES):Vol 13-339
Stuckey, W.J. The Pulitzer Prize Novels.*
  (2nd ed)
  F. Milley, 395(MFS):Summer83-324
Stückrath, J. Historische Rezeptionsfor-
  schung.
  J.M. Peck, 107(CRCL):Jun83-235
Stucky, S. Lutosławski and his Music.*
  A.W., 412:Aug-Nov82-280
"Studies in Eighteenth-Century Culture."
  (Vol 6 ed by R. Rosbottom; Vol 8 ed by
  R. Runte)
  J. Mezciems, 402(MLR):Apr83-410
"Studies in Eighteenth-Century Culture."
  (Vol 10) (H.C. Payne, ed)
  E.J.H. Greene, 107(CRCL):Sep83-427
  B.B. Redford, 402(MLR):Jul83-653
  P. Rétat, 535(RHL):Sep/Dec83-935
  P. Rogers, 506(PSt):Sep83-193
"Studies in Scottish Literature." (Vol 15)
  (G.R. Roy, ed)
  A.H. MacLaine, 541(RES):Feb83-112
"Studies in Slavic and General Linguis-
  tics."* (Vol 1) (A.A. Barentsen, B.M.
  Groen and R. Sprenger, eds)
  F.E. Knowles, 575(SEER):Apr83-310
de Stúñiga, L. Poesías. (J. Battesti-
  Pelegrin, ed)
  A. de Colombí-Monguió, 304(JHP):Fall83-
  71
Stunkel, K.R. Relations of Indian, Greek,
  and Christian Thought in Antiquity.
  H.P. Alper, 318(JAOS):Apr-Jun82-421
Sturges, R. and others. Jules Breton and
  the French Rural Tradition.
  R. Jay, 446(NCFS):Fall-Winter83/84-249
  K. McConkey, 90:Nov83-703
Sturluson, S. - see under Snorri Sturluson
Sturrock, J. The Pangersbourne Murders.
  M. Laski, 362:12Apr84-27
Sturrock, J., ed. Structuralism and
  Since.*
  H.F. Mosher, Jr., 599:Winter83-49
Sturz, E.L. Widening Circles.
  J. Howard, 441:29Jan84-15
Stutman, S. - see Wolfe, T. and A. Bern-
  stein
Stutzer, B. Albert Müller und die Basler
  Künstlergruppe Rot-Blau.
  G. Krüger, 471:Jan/Feb/Mar83-90

Styan, J.L. Modern Drama in Theory and
  Practice.* (Vols 1 and 2)
  G. Bas, 189(EA):Apr-Sep83-309
  M. Breslow, 529(QQ):Summer83-364
  P.W. Ferran, 130:Spring83-79
  C. Innes, 397(MD):Mar83-103
Styan, J.L. Modern Drama in Theory and
  Practice.* (Vol 3)
  G. Bas, 189(EA):Apr-Sep83-309
  M. Breslow, 529(QQ):Summer83-364
  P.W. Ferran, 130:Spring83-79
  C. Innes, 397(MD):Mar83-103
  J. O'Connor, 615(TJ):May83-267
Styan, J.L. Max Reinhardt.
  M. Andre, 108:Spring83-131
  H.A. Arnold, 397(MD):Dec83-582
  C.M. Mazer, 130:Winter83/84-386
Stykowa, M.B. Teatralna recepcja Maeter-
  lincka w okresie Młodej Polski.
  F. Mikolajczak-Thyrion, 356(LR):Feb-
  May83-150
Styron, W. This Quiet Dust and Other Writ-
  ings.*
  B. Duyfhuizen, 395(MFS):Winter83-741
Su, J. and Luo Lun - see under Jing Su and
  Luo Lun
Su Yun-feng. Chung-kuo hsien-tai-hua ti
  Ch'ü-ü yen-chiu.
  W.T. Rowe, 293(JASt):May83-641
Suarez, F. De Anima. (Vol 2) (S. Castel-
  lote, ed)
  J-F. Courtine, 542:Jan-Mar83-99
Suarez, F. Suarez on Individuation, Meta-
  physical Disputation V. (J.J.E. Gracia,
  trans)
  A.J. Freddoso, 484(PPR):Mar84-419
  J.F. Ross, 319:Oct84-476
Suárez, J.A. The Mesoamerican Indian Lan-
  guages.
  P. Levy, 350:Sep84-682
Suárez-Murias, M.C. Essays on Hispanic
  Literature/Ensayos de literatura His-
  pana.
  E.A. Azzario, 238:Dec83-643
Subtelny, O. The Mazepists.*
  P. Longworth, 575(SEER):Apr83-280
Suckiel, E.K. The Pragmatic Philosophy of
  William James.
  J.B., 185:Oct83-172
  E.T. Long, 619:Fall83-413
Sucksmith, H.P. - see Dickens, C.
Suerbaum, U., U. Broich and R. Borgmeier.
  Science Fiction.
  M. Nagl, 196:Band24Heft1/2-172
  M. Schwonke, 52:Band17Heft3-334
  O.R. Spittel, 654(WB):12/1982-188
Suetonius. Divus Augustus. (J.M. Carter,
  ed)
  D.L. Stockton, 123:Vol33No2-328
Sugerman, D. The Doors.
  T.D.S., 617(TLS):13Jan84-33
Sugimoto, Y. Popular Disturbances in Post-
  war Japan.
  P.G. Steinhoff, 293(JASt):Aug83-977
Suh, D-S. Korean Communism 1945-1980.
  B.C. Koh, 293(JASt):May83-690
Suits, B. The Grasshopper.
  J.K., 543:Sep82-201
Sukuna, L. Fiji. (D. Scarr, ed)
  M. Richards, 617(TLS):27Apr84-477
al-Sulami, I.H. The Book of Sufi Chivalry.
  G. Webb, 469:Vol9No2-104

Suleiman, S.R. Authoritarian Fictions.
  P. McCarthy, 617(TLS):20Jan84-64
Suleiman, S.R. and I. Crosman, eds. The
  Reader in the Text.*
  D.H. Hirsch, 569(SR):Summer83-417
  S. Mailloux, 131(CL):Spring83-169
  P. Wenzel, 490:Band14Heft1/2-186
Sulitzer, P-L. The Green King.
  P. Andrews, 441:22Jul84-17
Sullivan, A.T. Thomas-Robert Bugeaud,
  France and Algeria, 1784-1849.*
  B.T. Cooper, 207(FR):Apr84-752
Sullivan, D. Navvyman.
  T. Coleman, 617(TLS):23Mar84-310
Sullivan, E. and N.A. Malloy, with J.H.
  Elliott. Painting in Spain 1650-1700
  from North American Collections.
  R.M. Quinn, 50(ArQ):Spring83-80
Sullivan, E.B. American Political Badges
  and Medalets, 1789-1892.
  R.A. Fischer, 658:Spring83-99
Sullivan, H.W. Calderón in the German
  Lands and the Low Countries.
  A.L. Mackenzie, 617(TLS):13Apr84-399
Sullivan, J. Elegant Nightmares.
  J. Briggs, 447(N&Q):Aug82-384
Sullivan, J., ed. Lost Souls.
  R. Atwan, 441:1Apr84-22
Sullivan, M. Symbols of Eternity.*
  D. Sensabaugh, 318(JAOS):Jul-Sep82-578
Sullivan, R., ed. Fine Lines.*
  M.R. Farwell, 448:Vol21No1-167
Sullivan, W. Reconstructing Public Phil-
  osophy.
  M.K., 185:Oct83-174
Sullivan, W.H. Mission to Iran.
  S. Simpson, 639(VQR):Summer83-540
Sullivan, W.H. Obbligato.
  S.J. Ungar, 441:26Aug84-25
Sulloway, F.J. Freud.
  P. Meisel, 473(PR):3/1983-456
Sumarokov, A.P. and N.M. Karamzin.
  Selected Aesthetic Works of Sumarokov
  and Karamzin.* (H.M. Nebel, Jr., ed and
  trans)
  R. Burger, 574(SEEJ):Spring83-98
Sumida, J.T. - see Pollen, A.J.H.
Summerfield, M. The Classical Guitar.
  M. Criswick, 415:Jun83-363
Summerfield, P. Women Workers in the
  Second World War.
  P. Willmott, 617(TLS):28Dec84-1496
Summers, D. Michelangelo and the Language
  of Art.*
  E. Cropper, 54:Mar83-157
  C. Dempsey, 90:Oct83-624
Summers, H. The Burning Book and Other
  Poems.
  L. Mackinnon, 617(TLS):23Mar84-312
Summers, M. Calling Home.
  M.G. Osachoff, 526:Autumn83-86
  D. Watmough, 102(CanL):Summer83-96
Summers, R.S. Instrumentalism and Amer-
  ican Legal Theory.
  R.N. Bronaugh, 518:Oct83-227
  B.R.G., 185:Jan84-370
Summerson, J. The Life and Work of John
  Nash.
  H. Hobhouse, 46:May81-317
Summerson, J., D. Watkin and G-T. Melling-
  hoff. Architectural Monographs: John
  Soane.
  M. Girouard, 453(NYRB):19Jan84-19

Sumner, L.W. Abortion and Moral Theory.*
  S.S. Kleinberg, 479(PhQ):Jul83-310
  L. Thomas, 449:May83-323
Sumner, L.W., J.G. Slater and F. Wilson,
  eds. Pragmatism and Purpose.
  J.L. Esposito, 567:Vol143No3/4-367
  D.R. Koehn, 619:Summer83-291
Sumner, R. Thomas Hardy.*
  M. Williams, 447(N&Q):Aug82-369
Sunahara, A.G. The Politics of Racism.
  H.L. Thomas, 102(CanL):Spring83-103
Sund, R. Ish River.
  J.F. Cotter, 249(HudR):Winter83/84-714
Sundberg, B. Sanningen, myterna och
  intressenas spel.*
  J. Lutz, 563(SS):Summer83-274
Sundberg, H. The Novgorod Kabala Books of
  1614-1616.
  S.S. Lunden, 559:Vol7No2-193
  M. Ziolkowski, 574(SEEJ):Summer83-256
Sundquist, E.J., ed. American Realism.*
  R.A. Cassell, 395(MFS):Summer83-328
  D. Pizer, 651(WHR):Summer83-185
Sundquist, E.J. Faulkner.
  H. Beaver, 617(TLS):30Mar84-350
  E.J. Higgins, 95(CLAJ):Sep83-97
  J.B. Wittenberg, 454:Fall83-88
  295(JML):Nov83-471
Sundquist, E.J. Home as Found.*
  K. Carabine, 402(MLR):Jul83-689
Sung Tz'u. The Washing Away of Wrongs.
  (B.E. McKnight, trans)
  P.K. Bol, 293(JASt):May83-643
Suntharalingam, R. Indian Nationalism.
  H. Tinker, 617(TLS):24Aug84-934
Suomela-Härmä, E. Les Structures narra-
  tives dans le Roman de Renart.
  K. Varty, 402(MLR):Oct83-919
Suozzo, A.G., Jr. The Comic Novels of
  Charles Sorel.
  R. Godenne, 475:Vol 10No19-938
Super, R.H. Trollope in the Post Office.*
  P. Coustillas, 189(EA):Oct-Dec84-470
  R. ap Roberts, 385(MQR):Winter84-138
  A. Wright, 445(NCF):Jun83-104
Super, R.H. - see Trollope, A.
Suppes, P. Probabilistic Metaphysics.
  R.S. Woolhouse, 617(TLS):28Dec84-1509
"A Supplement to the Oxford English Dic-
  tionary."* (Vol 3) (R.W. Burchfield, ed)
  H. Amory, 517(PBSA):Vol77No4-514
  D.C. Baker, 191(ELN):Dec83-65
  G. Stein, 38:Band101Heft3/4-468
Surette, L. A Light from Eleusis.
  R. Morton, 178:Mar83-112
  D. Seed, 447(N&Q):Aug82-375
Surma, S.J. - see Wajsberg, M.
"Le Surnaturalisme français."*
  G. Chesters, 208(FS):Jul83-348
Surtees, V. The Ludovisi Goddess.
  G. Avery, 617(TLS):10Aug84-888
Surtees, V. - see Brown, F.M.
Surtz, R.E. El libro del Conorte.
  N. Griffin, 86(BHS):Apr83-143
Suryadinata, L. Peranakan Chinese Poli-
  tics in Java. (rev)
  M.F.S. Heidhues, 293(JASt):Feb83-460
Suryadinata, L. and S. Siddique, eds.
  Trends in Indonesia II.
  R.W. Liddle, 293(JASt):Aug83-1030
Susnik, B. Los Aborígenes del Paraguay.
  (Vol 2)
  H.E.M. Klein, 269(IJAL):Jul83-345

Swiatecka, M.J. The Ideal of the Symbol.*
  P. Magnuson, 402(MLR):Apr83-432
Swiezawski, S. Dzieje Filozofii Europej-
  skiej w XV wieku. (Vol 3)
  A.N.W., 543:Sep82-202
Swiezawski, S. Dzieje Filozofii Europej-
  skiej w XV wieku. (Vol 4)
  A.N.W., 543:Sep82-204
Swift, G. Waterland.*
  W.H. Pritchard, 441:25Mar84-9
  D. Taylor, 364:Oct83-89
  M. Wood, 453(NYRB):16Aug84-47
Swift, J. The Battle of the Books. (J.
  Real, ed)
  G. Ahrends, 38:Band101Heft1/2-273
Swift, J. The Complete Poems.* (P.
  Rogers, ed)
  M. Dodsworth, 175:Summer83-190
  M. Shinagel, 566:Spring84-170
  639(VQR):Summer83-89
Swift, J. The Oxford Authors: Jonathan
  Swift. (A. Ross and D. Woolley, eds)
  W.W. Robson, 617(TLS):26Oct84-1221
Swinburne, R. Space and Time.* (2nd ed)
  G.N. Schlesinger, 393(Mind):Jul83-464
Swindell, L. The Reluctant Lover.* (Brit-
  ish title: Charles Boyer.)
  J. Nangle, 200:May83-314
Swinden, P. Paul Scott: Images of India.*
  M.M. Mahood, 677(YES):Vol 13-355
Swinfen, A. In Defence of Fantasy.
  R. Jackson, 617(TLS):31Aug84-965
Sydow, B.É., with S. and D. Chainaye –
  see Chopin, F.
Sykes, A. Tariff Reform in British Poli-
  tics 1903-1913.
  M. Bentley, 161(DUJ):Jun83-126
Sykes, S. The Identity of Christianity.
  D. Nineham, 617(TLS):28Dec84-1510
Syllaba, T. and M. Křepinská. Radegast
  Parolek.
  D. Short, 575(SEER):Jul83-475
Sylvander, C.W. James Baldwin.
  L. Sanders, 106:Fall83-343
Sylvère, A. Le Légionnaire Flutsch.
  G.J. Barberet, 207(FR):Mar84-574
Symcox, G. Victor Amadeus II.
  S. Woolf, 617(TLS):18May84-556
Syme, R. Historia Augusta Papers. (A.R.
  Birley, ed) Roman Papers III.
  A. Momigliano, 617(TLS):12Oct84-1147
Symonds, J.A. Memoirs. (P. Grosskurth,
  ed)
  J.R. Vincent, 617(TLS):20Jul84-804
Symons, J., ed. Classic Crime Omnibus.
  P. Craig, 617(TLS):21Dec84-1484
Symons, J. Critical Observations.*
  P. Wolfe, 395(MFS):Autumn83-389
Symons, J. The Name of Annabel Lee.*
  M. Tax, 441:29Jan84-22
  442(NY):27Feb84-136
Symons, J. The Tigers of Subtopia.*
  639(VQR):Autumn83-127
Synge, J.M. The Collected Letters of John
  Millington Synge.* (Vol 1) (A. Saddle-
  myer, ed)
  R. Ellmann, 441:15Jan84-25
Synge, J.M. The Collected Letters of John
  Millington Synge. (Vol 2) (A. Saddle-
  myer, ed)
  P. Craig, 617(TLS):27Jul84-829

Synge, J.M. The Well of the Saints. (N.
  Grene, ed)
  A. Roche, 272(IUR):Autumn83-257
Synge, L. Antique Needlework.
  G. Wills, 39:Sep83-273
Syz, H., J.J. Miller 2d and R. Rückert.
  Catalogue of the Hans Syz Collection.
  (Vol 1)
  J.V.G. Mallet, 39:Jan83-70
Szabo, A. The Beginnings of Greek Mathe-
  matics.
  M. Boylan, 486:Dec83-665
Szabolcsi, M. Attila József.*
  A. Pezold, 654(WB):7/1983-1322
Szacki, J. Spotkania z Utopią.
  A. Blaim, 561(SFS):Jul83-241
Szaivert, W. Die Münzprägung der Kaiser
  Tiberius und Caius.
  M. Crawford, 617(TLS):24Aug84-950
Szajkowski, B. Next to God ... Poland.
  Z. Pelczynski, 617(TLS):2Mar84-211
Szanto, G. The Next Move.
  A. Ravel, 102(CanL):Winter82-140
Szarkowski, J. and M.M. Hambourg. The
  Work of Atget.* (Vol 3)
  T. Papageorge, 617(TLS):6Apr84-371
Szarmach, P.E., ed. Vercelli Homilies
  IX-XXIII.
  R. Boenig, 301(JEGP):Apr83-221
  M. Halsall, 589:Oct83-1136
Szarota, E.M., ed. Das Jesuitendrama im
  deutschen Sprachgebiet.* (Vols 1 and 2)
  J.A. Parente, Jr., 406:Winter83-440
Szasz, T. The Therapeutic State.
  B.A. Farrell, 176:Nov84-56
Szatmary, D.P. Shay's Rebellion.
  P. Lawson, 106:Summer83-165
Szczypiorski, A. The Polish Ordeal.
  J. Woodall, 575(SEER):Oct83-1510
Szemerényi, O. Richtungen der modernen
  Sprachwissenschaft II.
  W.R. Schmalstieg, 215(GL):Vol23No4-283
Szidat, J. Historischer Kommentar zu
  Ammianus Marcellinus Buch XX-XXI. (Pt 2)
  R. Browning, 123:Vol33No1-135
  M. Reydellet, 555:Vol57fasc2-340
Szirtes, G. November and May.
  R. Pybus, 565:Vol24No2-73
Szirtes, G. Short Wave.
  C. Boyle, 364:Mar84-95
  J. Mole, 176:Jun84-57
  S. Rae, 617(TLS):1Jun84-610
Sztompka, P. Sociological Dilemmas.
  M.A. Finocchiaro, 488:Sep83-394
Sztulman, H. and J. Fénelon, eds. La
  curiosité en psychanalyse.
  J-M. Gabaude, 542:Jul-Sep83-335
Szymborska, W. Sounds, Feelings,
  Thoughts.* (M.J. Krynski and R.A.
  Maguire, eds and trans) Selected Poems.
  J. Aaron, 472:Fall/Winter83Spring/
  Summer84-254

Tabachnick, S.E. Charles Doughty.*
  W.N. Rogers 2d, 637(VS):Spring83-358
Tacitus. Empire and Emperors. (G. Tingay,
  trans)
  H.W. Benario, 124:Jan-Feb84-193
Tadao, D., Morita Takeshi and Chōnan
  Minoru – see under Doi Tadao, Morita
  Takeshi and Chōnan Minoru

Tadié, J-Y. Proust.
J.M. Cocking, 617(TLS):25May84-595
Tadié, J-Y. Le roman d'aventures.*
J-P. Naugrette, 98:May83-365
Tähtinen, U. Non-violent Theories of
Punishment.
F.R.B., 185:Apr84-547
Tahureau, J. Les Dialogues Non moins prof-
itables que facetieux.* (M. Gauna, ed)
G. Demerson, 547(RF):Band95Heft4-490
L. Terreaux, 535(RHL):Sep/Dec83-913
Taïeb, E., ed. Hubertine Auclert.
A.D. Ketchum, 207(FR):Mar84-580
Taisbak, S.M. Coloured Quadrangles.
I. Bulmer-Thomas, 123:Vol33No1-143
Tait, A.A. The Landscape Garden in Scot-
land, 1735-1835.*
J.D. Hunt, 90:Mar83-175
Takaki, R.T. Iron Cages.
D.L. Jones, 658:Spring83-102
Takamiya, T. and D. Brewer, eds. Aspects
of Malory.*
J.M. Cowen, 447(N&Q):Aug82-358
M. Lambert, 589:Jan83-235
Takeo, D. - see under Doï Takeo
Takezawa, S-I. and A.M. Whitehill. Work
Ways, Japan and America.*
H. Matsusaki, 293(JASt):Feb83-419
Takuji Oda. A Concordance to the Riddles
of the Exeter Book.
A. Crépin, 189(EA):Apr-Jun84-183
Talbot, É., ed. La critique stendhalienne
de Balzac à Zola.*
F.W. Saunders, 208(FS):Jul83-352
Talbott, S. Deadly Gambits.
G.W. Ball, 453(NYRB):8Nov84-5
M. Bundy, 441:7Oct84-1
T. Draper, 441:9Dec84-3
J. Fallows, 61:Dec84-136
442(NY):5Nov84-171
Talbott, S. The Russians and Reagan.
R.G. Kaiser, 453(NYRB):28Jun84-38
W. Taubman, 441:20May84-17
"The Tale of Aqhat." (F. Landy, trans)
J. Saunders, 565:Vol24No1-73
Talex, A. - see Istrati, P.
Tall, D. Ninth Life.
M. Boruch, 271:Vol 13No3/4-251
Tallent, E. In Constant Flight.*
J. Mellors, 362:19Jan84-26
Tallent, E. Married Men and Magic Tricks.
E. Prioleau, 27(AL):Mar83-114
W.T.S., 395(MFS):Winter83-745
295(JML):Nov83-580
Talmage, F., ed. Studies in Jewish Folk-
lore.
D. Dahbany-Miraglia, 292(JAF):Apr-
Jun83-228
A.A. Schwadron, 187:Sep84-557
Talmon, J.L. The Myth of the Nation and
the Vision of Revolution.
J.H., 185:Oct83-164
Talmor, E. Descartes and Hume.*
J.P. Wright, 518:Apr83-81
Tamaki, N. The Life Cycle of the Union
Bank of Scotland 1830-1954.
B. Lenman, 617(TLS):30Mar84-330
Tamba, A. The Musical Structure of Nô.
M.J. Nearman, 407(MN):Summer83-216
Tamba-Mecz, I. Le Sens figuré.
R. Martin, 209(FM):Oct83-377
Taminiaux, J. Recoupements.
A. Reix, 542:Oct-Dec83-454

Tanahashi, K. Enkū.*
D.F. McCallum, 407(MN):Autumn83-354
Tanaka, I. and K. Koike, eds. Japan Color.
R.L. Shep, 614:Summer84-18
Tanaka, Y. and E. Hanson, eds and trans.
This Kind of Woman.
J.W. Carpenter, 285(JapQ):Jul-Sep83-
320
E.C. Knowlton, 573(SSF):Fall83-331
Y. McClain, 407(MN):Winter83-442
M.J. Salter, 441:16Dec84-26
Tang Xianzu. The Peony Pavillion (Mudan
Ting).* (C. Birch, trans)
R. Strassberg, 116:Jul82-276
S.H. West, 293(JASt):Aug83-944
Tangheroni, M. Aspetti del commercio dei
cereali nei paesi della Corona d'Aragona.
(Vol 1)
J.E. Dotson, 589:Oct83-1137
Tanis, J. and J. Dooley. Bookbinding in
America 1680-1910.
M.A. McCorison, 617(TLS):14Sep84-1034
Tanizaki, J. L'éloge de l'ombre.
P. Lombardo, 98:Jan-Feb83-16
Tanizaki, J. The Secret History of the
Lord of Musashi [and] Arrowroot.*
P. McCarthy, 407(MN):Autumn83-321
Tannen, D., ed. Spoken and Written Lan-
guage.
G.L. Dillon, 350:Jun84-441
D. Kurzon, 215(GL):Spring83-64
Tanner, T. Adultery in the Novel.*
D. Latimer, 577(SHR):Winter83-97
A.K. Thorlby, 402(MLR):Apr83-412
Tanner, T.A. Frank Waters.
C.L. Adams, 649(WAL):Feb84-344
Tanselle, G.T. - see Melville, H.
Taplin, O. - see Macleod, C.
Tapply, W.G. Death at Charity Point.
N. Callendar, 441:8Apr84-18
Tarán, L. Speusippus of Athens.
J. Dillon, 123:Vol33No2-225
Tarbert, G.C. - see "Book Review Index: A
Master Cumulation, 1969-1979"
Tarr, R. and R. Sokan. A Bibliography of
the D.H. Lawrence Collection at Illinois
State University.
K. Cushman, 517(PBSA):Vol77No3-382
de Tarragon, J-M. Le Culte à Ugarit,
d'aprés les textes de la pratique en
cunéiformes alphabétiques.
C.E. L'Heureux, 318(JAOS):Oct-Dec82-
661
Tartak, M. - see Rossini
Taruskin, R. Opera and Drama in Russia as
Preached and Practiced in the 1860s.
G. Abraham, 410(M&L):Jan/Apr83-80
S. Beckwith, 550(RusR):Jul83-321
A. Fitz Lyon, 575(SEER):Jul83-452
H. Robinson, 574(SEEJ):Spring83-122
Tarvainen, K. Dependenzielle Satzglied-
syntax des Deutschen.
G. Koller, 685(ZDL):1/1983-116
Tasolambros, F.L. In Defence of Thucydi-
des.*
G.J.D. Aalders H. Wzn., 394:Vol136
fasc3/4-411
Tasso, T. Creation of the World.* (J.
Tusiani, trans; G. Cipolla, ed)
A. Bullock, 539:May84-128
Tasso, T. Godfrey of Bulloigne. (K.M.
Lea and T.M. Gang, eds)
P. Thomson, 541(RES):Nov83-500

Tatar, M.M. Spellbound.*
  M.V. Dimić, 107(CRCL):Sep83-436
Tate, A. The Poetry Reviews of Allen Tate, 1924-1944.* (A. Brown and F.N. Cheney, eds)
  T.D. Young, 651(WHR):Summer83-189
Tatian. Oratio ad Graecos and Fragments. (M. Whittaker, ed and trans)
  A. Tripolitis, 124:Nov-Dec83-133
Tatu, M. La Bataille des euromissiles.
  M. Ignatieff, 617(TLS):1Jun84-603
Tatum, J. Apuleius and The Golden Ass.*
  R.T. van der Paardt, 394:Vol36fasc1/2-220
Tatum, S. Inventing Billy the Kid.*
  R.M. Davis, 577(SHR):Summer83-292
  R. Hansen, 385(MQR):Winter84-144
  P.A. Hutton, 651(WHR):Winter83-348
  M.T. Marsden, 649(WAL):Feb84-357
Taube, M. Beiträge zur Geschichte der medizinischen Literatur Tibets.
  J.W. de Jong, 259(IIJ):Apr83-218
Taubken, H. Niederdeutsch, Niederländisch, Hochdeutsch.
  H.J. Gernentz, 682(ZPSK):Band36Heft5-619
  W. Sanders, 684(ZDA):Band112Heft1-6
Tauriac, M. La Catastrophe.
  H. Le Mansec, 207(FR):Apr84-740
Tauscher, H., ed and trans. Candrakīrti.
  J.W. de Jong, 259(IIJ):Apr83-214
Tausky, V. and M. - see Janáček, L.
Taussig, M.A. The Devil and Commodity Fetishism in South America.
  J.E. Limón, 292(JAF):Jul-Sep83-340
Taveneaux, R. Le Catholicisme dans la France classique 1610-1715.
  A.H.T. Levi, 208(FS):Jan83-80
Taverdet, G., ed. L'Onomastique, témoins des langues disparues.
  J-P. Chambon, 553(RLiR):Jul-Dec83-418
Tax, P.W. - see Notker der Deutsche
Taylor, A. The Politics of the Yorkshire Miners.
  D. MacIntyre, 617(TLS):12Oct84-1165
Taylor, A. Selected Poems: 1960-1980.
  C. Benfey, 472:Fall/Winter83Spring/Summer84-236
Taylor, A.J.P. An Old Man's Diary.
  R. Foster, 617(TLS):15Jun84-656
  J. Vaizey, 362:26Apr84-25
Taylor, A.J.P. A Personal History.
  R. Baxter, 364:Aug/Sep83-143
Taylor, B. The Green Avenue.*
  H. Pyle, 541(RES):Aug83-365
Taylor, C. Radical Tories.
  D. Duffy, 627(UTQ):Summer83-477
  D. Smiley, 99:Jun83-33
Taylor, C.P. Good.
  D. Devlin, 157:Spring83-52
Taylor, D. Gemini.
  N. Shack, 617(TLS):31Aug84-977
Taylor, D. Hardy's Poetry, 1860-1928.*
  D. Bromwich, 405(MP):Feb84-324
  F.R. Giordano, Jr., 579(SAQ):Winter83-109
  S. Trombley, 447(N&Q):Oct82-462
Taylor, E. Angel.
  P. Craig, 617(TLS):1Jun84-623
Taylor, E. The Sleeping Beauty. Mrs. Palfrey at the Claremont. In the Summer
  [continued]

[continuing]
Season. The Soul of Kindness.
  W.H. Pritchard, 249(HudR):Winter83/84-747
Taylor, E. Edward Taylor's Harmony of the Gospels. (T.M. and V.L. Davis, with B.L. Parks, eds)
  E. Emerson, 165(EAL):Fall84-213
Taylor, E.R. New and Selected Poems.
  R. Tillinghast, 385(MQR):Fall84-596
Taylor, G. - see Shakespeare, W.
Taylor, G. - see under Wells, S.
Taylor, G. and M. Warren, eds. The Division of the Kingdoms.
  P. Edwards, 617(TLS):9Mar84-257
  E.A.J. Honigmann, 453(NYRB):2Feb84-16
Taylor, H.H. The Divorce Sonnets.
  C. Verderese, 441:8Jul84-20
Taylor, I.P. Invisible Man.
  T. Dooley, 617(TLS):28Sep84-1105
Taylor, J., ed. Notebooks/Memoirs/Archives.
  J. Dollimore, 148:Winter83-82
  C. Sprague, 659(ConL):Winter84-488
Taylor, J. A Routine Rape.
  E. Webby, 381:Mar83-34
Taylor, J.H.M., ed. Le Roman de Perceforest. (Pt 1)
  A.H. Diverres, 208(FS):Jul83-327
Taylor, J.R. Ingrid Bergman.
  A. Brownjohn, 176:Jan84-67
Taylor, J.R. Alec Guinness.
  C. Brown, 617(TLS):7Dec84-1418
Taylor, L. In the Underworld.
  J. Fairleigh, 617(TLS):17Aug84-915
  P.P. Read, 362:12Jul84-25
Taylor, L. Mourning Dress.
  R.L. Shep, 614:Spring84-25
Taylor, L.A. One for the Books.
  T.J. Binyon, 617(TLS):30Mar84-354
Taylor, L.A. One Half a Hoax.*
  T.J. Binyon, 617(TLS):13Jul84-790
Taylor, L.J. Henry James, 1866-1916.
  R.L. Gale, 26(ALR):Spring83-151
Taylor, M.C. Journeys to Selfhood.*
  J. Walker, 529(QQ):Spring83-255
Taylor, P. The Smoke Ring.
  J. Eidus, 441:9Dec84-27
  P. Smith, 617(TLS):18May84-541
Taylor, P.E. - see Babb, J., with P.E. Taylor
Taylor, R. Arquitectura Andaluza.
  A. Rodríguez G. de Ceballos, 48:Jan-Mar79-91
Taylor, R. Literature and Society in Germany 1918-1945.*
  A.K. Kuhn, 221(GQ):Jan83-186
  E.F. Timms, 402(MLR):Oct83-991
Taylor, R. A Reader's Guide to the Plays of W.B. Yeats.
  A. Carpenter, 617(TLS):29Jun84-733
Taylor, R. Robert Schumann.*
  G. Abraham, 410(M&L):Jul/Oct83-266
  R. Anderson, 415:Apr83-237
Taylor, R.H. The Neglected Hardy.*
  W.E. Davis, 177(ELT):Vol26No2-145
  J. Halperin, 395(MFS):Summer83-274
  R.C. Schweik, 445(NCF):Jun83-117
  295(JML):Nov83-492
Taylor, R.P. Rural Energy Development in China.
  B.J. Esposito, 293(JASt):Aug83-945

Taylor, S., ed. The Anglo-Saxon Chronicle. (Vol 4)
  B. Windeatt, 176:Jul/Aug84-55
Taylor, S. The Rise of Hitler.
  I. Deak, 453(NYRB):31May84-37
Taylor, S.S.B., ed. The Theater of the French and German Enlightenment.
  E. Martin, 406:Spring84-77
Taylor, T.J. Linguistic Theory and Structural Stylistics.
  C.E. Reeves, 355(LSoc):Mar83-116
  J. Renkema, 361:May83-96
Taylor, W. Faulkner's Search for a South.*
  295(JML):Nov83-471
Taylor-Martin, P. John Betjeman.*
  J. Glancey, 46:Jun83-58
Taylour, W. The Mycenaeans. (rev)
  R. Higgins, 39:Dec83-527
Tazawa, Y., ed. Biographical Dictionary of Japanese Art.
  O.R. Impey, 90:Mar83-176
Tedeschi, R. - see Gide, A. and D. Bussy
Tedlock, B. Time and the Highland Maya.
  T. Grieder, 263(RIB):Vol33No2-270
Teed, C.A., H.C. Raley and J.B. Barber. Conversational Spanish for the Medical and Health Professions.
  J. Shreve, 399(MLJ):Autumn83-312
Tegethoff, W. Mies van der Rohe: Die Villen und Landhausprojekte.*
  F. Schulze, 127:Summer83-206
  A. Windsor, 90:Jul83-430
Teichman, J. Illegitimacy.
  J-L. Gardies, 542:Jul-Sep83-337
  I. Kesarcodi-Watson, 63:Dec83-457
Teigen, P.M., ed. Books, Manuscripts, and the History of Medicine.
  G.D. Hargreaves, 354:Dec83-405
"Teilhard de Chardin, son apport, son actualité."
  M. Adam, 542:Oct-Dec83-506
Teixidor, J. The Pantheon of Palmyra.
  H.J.W. Drijvers, 318(JAOS):Jul-Sep82-538
Tejera, A.D. - see under Díaz Tejera, A.
Tekin, Ş. Buddhistische Uigurica aus der Yüan-Zeit.
  J.W. de Jong, 259(IIJ):Apr83-225
Tekinay, A. Materialien zum vergleichenden Studium von Erzählmotiven in der deutschen Dichtung des Mittelalters und den Literaturen des Orients.*
  P. Gaeffke, 52:Band17Heft2-202
de Teleki, B.E-L. - see under Eggers-Lan de Teleki, B.
Teleky, R., ed. The Oxford Book of French-Canadian Short Stories.
  C. Blaise, 441:9Sep84-26
Telfer, E. Happiness.*
  E.J. Bond, 529(QQ):Summer83-565
  R. Kraut, 482(PhR):Jan83-131
Telle, J. Sol und Luna.
  W. Newman, 589:Jan83-238
Tellegen, J.W. The Roman Law of Succession in the Letters of Pliny the Younger, 1.
  B.W. Frier, 123:Vol33No2-340
Tellenbach, H. Goût et Atmosphère.
  F. Wybrands, 450(NRF):Oct83-134
Tellini, G. Manzoni.
  C. Godt, 400(MLN):Jan83-118
Tellini, G. - see Verga, G.

Teloh, H. The Development of Plato's Metaphysics.*
  D.C. Lindenmuth, 543:Dec82-475
  C.J. McKnight, 518:Jul83-141
Temko, F. New Knitting.
  C. Mouton, 614:Spring84-25
Temperley, N., ed. The Athlone History of Music in Britain.* (Vol 5)
  A. Hutchings, 410(M&L):Jul/Oct83-237
  A. Walker, 414(MusQ):Summer83-446
Temporini, H., ed. Aufstieg und Niedergang der romischen Welt.
  W.E. Metcalf, 24:Spring83-103
Ten, C.L. Mill on Liberty.*
  C.B. Jones, 506(PSt):Dec83-292
  D. Little, 482(PhR):Jul83-434
  D.A. Lloyd Thomas, 393(Mind):Jan83-152
  D. Wells, 63:Sep83-330
Ten Cate, A.G., ed. The Rideau.
  M.S. Angus, 529(QQ):Autumn83-867
"The Ten Thousand Leaves."* (Vol 1) (I.H. Levy, trans)
  E. Rutledge, 244(HJAS):Jun83-263
Tendrjakow, W. Sechzig Kerzen.
  K. Kasper, 654(WB):11/1983-1989
Teng, S-Y. Protest and Crime in China.
  D.E. Kelley, 293(JASt):Feb83-404
Tennant, E. Woman Beware Woman.*
  J. Mellors, 362:1Mar84-28
Tennant, N. Natural Logic.
  W. Sieg, 316:Mar83-215
Tennant, R. Joseph Conrad.*
  B.E. Teets, 177(ELT):Vol26No1-60
Tennant, R. - see Conrad, J.
"Lady Tennyson's Journal."* (J.O. Hoge, ed)
  P.L. Elliott, 637(VS):Winter83-248
Tennyson, A. Idylls of the King. (J.M. Gray, ed)
  M. Dodsworth, 175:Summer83-191
Tennyson, A. The Letters of Alfred Lord Tennyson.* (Vol 1) (C.Y. Lang and E.F. Shannon, Jr., eds)
  C.T. Christ, 405(MP):Feb84-321
  A. Day, 184(EIC):Apr83-158
  P.L. Elliott, 637(VS):Winter83-248
  J. Hepburn, 569(SR):Summer83-503
  W.D. Shaw, 301(JEGP):Jul83-454
Tennyson, G.B. Victorian Devotional Poetry.*
  S. Monod, 189(EA):Oct-Dec83-479
  C. Williams, 591(SIR):Spring83-119
Tennyson, G.B. - see Carlyle, T.
Tennyson, H. The Haunted Mind.
  R. Blythe, 362:14Jun84-25
  A. Motion, 617(TLS):15Jun84-656
Tennyson, H., ed. Studies in Tennyson.
  P.L. Elliott, 637(VS):Winter83-248
Teodorsson, S-T. Anaxagoras' Theory of Matter.
  B. Inwood, 487:Winter83-354
Te Paske, J.J., ed. Research Guide to Andean History: Bolivia, Chile, Ecuador, and Peru.
  R. Miller, 86(BHS):Jan83-83
de Terán, L.S. Keepers of the House.*
  P. Craig, 617(TLS):9Mar84-259
de Terán, L.S. The Slow Train to Milan.*
  M. Bell, 441:22Apr84-14
  P. Craig, 617(TLS):28Dec84-1506
  D. Durrant, 364:Jul83-91
  442(NY):7May84-159

de Terán, L.S. The Tiger.
  T. Fitton, 617(TLS):21Sep84-1065
  K.C. O'Brien, 362:4Oct84-28
Terborgh, J. Five New World Primates.
  D. Macdonald, 617(TLS):9Nov84-1295
Terenzio, S., ed. The Prints of Robert
  Motherwell and a Catalogue Raisonné
  1943-1984.
  D.J.R. Bruckner, 441:9Dec84-26
Terhune, A.M. and A.B. - see FitzGerald, E.
Terkel, S. "The Good War."
  L. Wainwright, 441:7Oct84-7
Ternes, E. Probleme der kontrastiven
  Phonetik.
  G.F. Meier, 682(ZPSK):Band36Heft3-370
Terraine, J. The First World War 1914-
  1918.
  H. Strachan, 617(TLS):9Mar84-243
Terras, V. A Karamazov Companion.*
  A. Slater, 402(MLR):Jul83-763
  J. Tucker, 599:Winter83-91
Terrell, C.F. A Companion to the "Cantos"
  of Ezra Pound.* (Vol 1)
  S.M. Gall, 301(JEGP):Jan83-147
Terrill, R. The White-Boned Demon.
  F. Butterfield, 441:4Mar84-11
  E. Croll, 617(TLS):3Aug84-872
  J. Shapiro and L. Heng, 453(NYRB):
  15Mar84-8
Terry, B. The Watermelon Kid.
  J. House, 441:4Nov84-24
Terry, G.M. East European Languages and
  Literatures, II.
  D. Short, 575(SEER):Oct83-635
Terry, W. Bloods.
  W. Balliett, 442(NY):12Nov84-189
  S. Karnow, 441:14Oct84-7
Teskey, A. Platonov and Fyodorov.
  L. Koehler, 574(SEEJ):Summer83-264
  I. Masing-Delic, 550(RusR):Oct83-449
Tesnière, L. Grundzüge der strukturalen
  Syntax. (U. Engel, ed and trans)
  F. Hundsnurscher, 685(ZDL):1/1983-109
"Tessuti Italiani del Rinascimento: Collezi-
  oni Franchetti Carrand, Museo Nazionale
  del Bargello."
  B. Scott, 39:Feb83-152
Testard, M. Chrétiens latins des premiers
  siècles.*
  T.D. Barnes, 123:Vol33No1-136
Tetreau, F. L'Architecture pressentie.
  D.F. Rogers, 102(CanL):Summer83-158
Tetsurō, N. - see under Nakamura Tetsurō
Tetzner, G. Maxi.
  K. Richter, 654(WB):1/1982-132
Teuchert, H-J. August Graf von Platen in
  Deutschland.
  R. Dove, 402(MLR):Jan83-238
  H. Szépe, 400(MLN):Apr83-537
Tevis, W. The Steps of the Sun.
  C. Greenland, 617(TLS):18May84-557
Teysseire, D. Pédiatrie des Lumières.
  J. Lough, 83:Autumn83-261
Thackara, J. America's Children.
  G. Strawson, 617(TLS):18May84-546
Thaden, E.C., ed. Russification in the
  Baltic Provinces and Finland, 1855-
  1914.*
  A. Orde, 161(DUJ):Jun83-123
Thale, M., ed. Selections from the Papers
  of the London Corresponding Society 1792-
  1799.
  J. Dinwiddy, 617(TLS):6Jan84-4

"Thanatos classique."
  N. Hepp, 475:Vol 10No18-408
Thapliyal, U.P. Foreign Elements in
  Ancient Indian Society.
  R. Salomon, 318(JAOS):Oct-Dec82-673
Tharamangalam, J. Agrarian Class Conflict.
  J. Das Gupta, 293(JASt):Nov82-105
Thavenius, C. Referential Pronouns in
  English Conversation.
  B.A. Fox, 350:Sep84-664
Theelke, A. Faces of Mystery.
  G. Wills, 39:Oct83-353
Theeravit, K. and M. Brown, eds. Indo-
  china and Problems of Security and
  Stability in Southeast Asia.
  G. Porter, 293(JASt):Feb83-462
Theil, A. Les Nouvelles de V.S. Pritchett.
  J. Fletcher, 189(EA):Apr-Sep83-332
Theile, W. Immanente Poetik des Romans.*
  V. Kapp, 72:Band220Heft1-129
"Themes in Drama 4." (J. Redmond, ed)
  G. Bas, 189(EA):Apr-Sep83-315
Theocritus. Idylls and Epigrams. (D.
  Hine, trans)
  J. Hollander, 676(YR):Autumn83-x
  639(VQR):Summer83-98
Theophanes. The Chronicle of Theophanes.
  (H. Turtledove, trans)
  G.T. Dennis, 589:Oct83-1092
Théoret, M. Les Discours de Cicéron.*
  H.C. Gotoff, 487:Summer83-183
Thériault, Y. Oeuvre de chair.
  H. Bouraoui, 207(FR):Dec83-275
Theroux, A. Darconville's Cat.
  T. Treadwell, 617(TLS):3Feb84-116
Theroux, P. Doctor Slaughter.
  P. Kemp, 617(TLS):8Jun84-632
  K.C. O'Brien, 362:7Jun84-25
Theroux, P. Half Moon Street.
  P-L. Adams, 61:Nov84-149
  A. McDermott, 441:28Oct84-35
Theroux, P. The Kingdom by the Sea.*
  C. de Beaurepaire, 364:Dec83/Jan84-
  150
Theroux, P. The London Embassy.*
  D. Flower, 249(HudR):Summer83-368
Theroux, P. The Mosquito Coast.*
  J.L. Davis, 649(WAL):Feb84-354
Theroux, P. Sailing through China.
  W.S. Morton, 441:22Apr84-15
  442(NY):16Apr84-159
Thesing, W.B. The London Muse.*
  I. Campbell, 571(ScLJ):Autumn83-24
  J.J.S., 636(VP):Summer83-196
  G.B. Tennyson, 401(MLQ):Jun83-215
Thesleff, H. Studies in Platonic Chron-
  ology.
  I.M. Crombie, 123:Vol33No1-53
  R.A.H. Waterfield, 303(JoHS):Vol 103-
  174
Thevenon, P. Le Vice roi.
  J. Kolbert, 207(FR):Feb84-420
Thevet, A. Les Singularités de la France
  antarctique.
  F. Lestringant, 535(RHL):Jul/Aug83-621
Thévoz, M. The Painted Body.
  S. Laschever, 441:23Sep84-29
Thiebaux, M. Ellen Glasgow.
  J.L. Idol, Jr., 573(SSF):Spring-Summer
  83-148
van Thiel, H. Iliaden und Ilias.
  J.B. Hainsworth, 123:Vol33No2-163
Thierry, A. - see d'Aubigné, A.

Thierry, Y. Sens et langage.
  A. Reix, 542:Oct-Dec83-454
Thiher, A. The Cinematic Muse.
  R. Lloyd, 208(FS):Oct83-489
Thill, A. "Alter ab illo."*
  R.E.H. Westendorp Boerma, 394:Vol36
  fasc1/2-215
Thinès, G. Phénoménologie et science du
comportement.
  J-M. Gabaude, 542:Jul-Sep83-335
wa Thiong'o, N. Land der flammenden
Blüten.
  R. Arnold, 654(WB):10/1983-1796
Thireau, J-L. Charles Du Moulin (1500-
1566).*
  P. Sharratt, 208(FS):Jan83-70
Thiry, C., ed. Le "Jeu de l'Étoile" du
manuscrit de Cornillon (Liège).
  S. Kay, 545(RPh):Feb83-518
Thivel, A. Cnide et Cos?
  V. Nutton, 123:Vol33No2-338
  P. Pellegrin, 542:Jan-Mar83-85
Thodberg, C. and A.P. Thyssen, eds. N.F.S.
Grundtvig, Tradition and Renewal.
  A.M. Allchin, 617(TLS):3Aug84-874
Thoiron, P. Dynamisme du texte stylosta-
tistique.
  A. Raphael, 353:Vol20No7/8-571
Thom, J.A. From Sea to Shining Sea.
  D.G. Myers, 441:7Oct84-22
Thom, M. - see Kant, I.
Thom, P. The Syllogism.*
  S.L. Read, 518:Jan83-14
  M. von Thun, 63:Dec83-463
Thomas, A. The Phototropic Woman.
  V. Aarons, 363(LitR):Fall83-147
Thomas, A. Real Mothers.*
  B. Godard, 198:Jan83-110
Thomas, B. Astaire.
  E. Mordden, 441:23Dec84-8
Thomas, B. Golden Boy.*
  J. Nangle, 200:Dec83-626
Thomas, B. James Joyce's "Ulysses."
  M. Magalaner, 395(MFS):Winter83-780
  J.P. Riquelme, 329(JJQ):Fall83-88
  295(JML):Nov83-512
Thomas, C. and J. Lennox. William Arthur
Deacon.*
  W.J. Keith, 627(UTQ):Summer83-485
  R.G. Moyles, 168(ECW):Winter83/84-70
Thomas, D. Belladonna.
  J. Symons, 617(TLS):30Mar84-354
Thomas, D. Robert Browning.*
  E. Guiliano, 219(GaR):Fall83-694
  J. Hunter, 249(HudR):Autumn83-577
Thomas, D. The Collected Stories.
  F. Morris, 617(TLS):2Mar84-227
  B. O'Donoghue, 493:Sep83-74
Thomas, D. Mad Hatter Summer.
  C. Ricks, 441:1Jan84-24
Thomas, D. Naturalism and Social Science.*
  D. Little, 482(PhR):Jan83-107
Thomas, D.A. Dickens and the Short Story.
  J.H. Buckley, 445(NCF):Dec83-334
  D.P. Deneau, 573(SSF):Fall83-332
  E. Hollahan, 594:Winter83-391
  P.J. McCarthy, 651(WHR):Summer83-165
  J.R. Reed, 141:Spring83-173
  M. Shelden, 637(VS):Summer83-459
Thomas, D.M. Ararat.*
  A. Clerval, 450(NRF):Sep83-170
  G. Kearns, 249(HudR):Autumn83-556
    [continued]

[continuing]
  P. Lewis, 364:Jun83-95
  J. Mills, 648(WCR):Jun83-58
  S. Solecki, 99:Jun83-30
  42(AR):Fall83-510
  639(VQR):Summer83-91
Thomas, D.M. Selected Poems.*
  G. Ewart, 493:Sep83-62
  E. Grosholz, 249(HudR):Autumn83-586
  D. McDuff, 565:Vol24No4-62
Thomas, D.M. Swallow.
  D.J. Enright, 453(NYRB):22Nov84-45
  J. Leggett, 441:4Nov84-14
  J. Mantle, 362:26Jul84-28
  G. Strawson, 617(TLS):29Jun84-717
Thomas, D.O. and B. Peach - see Price, R.
Thomas, E. Wales.
  J.H., 189(EA):Jul-Sep84-365
Thomas, F.R. Literary Admirers of Alfred
Stieglitz.
  M. Orvell, 290(JAAC):Spring84-339
Thomas, G. The One Place.
  A. Stevenson, 617(TLS):2Mar84-226
Thomas, G. and M. Morgan-Witts. The Year
of Armageddon.
  P. Hebblethwaite, 617(TLS):2Nov84-1252
Thomas, G.S. The Art of Planting.
  C. Lloyd, 617(TLS):22Jun84-709
Thomas, H. Havannah.
  T. Fitton, 617(TLS):2Mar84-216
  J.P. Kenyon, 362:29Mar84-31
Thomas, H. La Migrateur.
  R. Buss, 617(TLS):29Jun84-730
Thomas, J.L. Alternative America.*
  M. Cantor, 432(NEQ):Dec83-618
Thomas, K. Man and the Natural World.*
  H. Ritvo, 676(YR):Spring84-439
  639(VQR):Autumn83-122
Thomas, L. Late Night Thoughts on Listen-
ing to Mahler's Ninth Symphony.*
  R. Bailey, 129:Sep84-72
Thomas, L. The Youngest Science.*
  J.F. Watkins, 617(TLS):18May84-541
Thomas, M.E. Agweddau ar Weithgarwch
Llenyddol Gwent yn y Ganrif Ddiwethaf.
  J. Rowland, 112:Vol 15-177
Thomas, P. Robert Kroetsch.*
  E. Cameron, 178:Mar83-119
  L.K. MacKendrick, 168(ECW):Summer83-99
  M. Peterman, 102(CanL):Spring83-136
Thomas, R. Briarpatch.
  442(NY):10Dec84-194
Thomas, R. Missionary Stew.
  M. Laski, 362:12Apr84-27
Thomas, R.H. Nietzsche in German Politics
and Society, 1890-1918.
  D.E. Cooper, 617(TLS):17Feb84-162
Thomas, R.S. Later Poems, 1972-1982.*
  S. Chambers, 493:Jun83-61
  D. McDuff, 565:Vol24No4-62
Thomas, R.S. Selected Prose. (S. Anstey,
ed)
  P.J. Kavanagh, 617(TLS):2Mar84-226
Thomas, T. That's Dancing!
  E. Mordden, 441:23Dec84-8
Thomas, W.K. The Fizz Inside.*
  R. Smith, 178:Mar83-123
Thomas of Kent. The Anglo-Norman "Alexan-
der (Le roman de toute chevalerie)" by
Thomas of Kent. (B. Foster, with I.
Short, eds)
  A. Iker-Gittleman, 545(RPh):May83-630

Thomason, B.C. Making Sense of Reification.
R.J. Anderson and W.W. Sharrock, 323:Jan83-104
Thomasset, C. Commentaire du dialogue de Placides et Timéo.
D. Evans, 208(FS):Oct83-442
Thomasset, C.A., ed. Placides et Timéo, ou Li secrés as philosophes.
S.M. Taylor, 207(FR):Dec83-241
Thompson, A. - see Shakespeare, W.
Thompson, B. Franz Grillparzer.
J.L. Hodge, 221(GQ):Mar83-319
W.E. Yates, 133:Band16Heft2/3-255
Thompson, C. First Born.
W.H. Pritchard, 249(HudR):Winter83/84-749
Thompson, D., ed. Change and Tradition in Rural England.*
S. Hunter, 677(YES):Vol 13-328
Thompson, D. The Chartists.
P. Joyce, 617(TLS):11May84-532
M.J. Wiener, 441:1Jul84-12
Thompson, D., ed. The Leavises.
G. Hough, 617(TLS):23Nov84-1329
Thompson, D. Cesare Pavese.
T. O'Neill, 278(IS):Vol38-122
Thompson, D. Raphael.*
C. Gould, 39:Aug83-193
Thompson, E.A. Romans and Barbarians.
W.E. Kaegi, Jr., 589:Jul83-831
Thompson, E.P. Beyond the Cold War.*
J. Martin, 584(SWR):Summer83-294
Thompson, G., J. Coldrey and G. Bernard. The Pond.
T. Halliday, 617(TLS):11May84-534
Thompson, G.R. - see Poe, E.A.
Thompson, G.R. and V.L. Lokke, eds. Ruined Eden of the Present.*
B. Hayne, 106:Fall83-309
Thompson, H.S. and R. Steadman. The Curse of Lono.
C. Haas, 441:15Jan84-19
Thompson, J. Conscience Place.
N. Shack, 617(TLS):23Nov84-1359
Thompson, J. The Crackwalker.
A. Ravel, 102(CanL):Winter82-140
Thompson, J.B. Critical Hermeneutics.
M.J. Hyde, 480(P&R):Vol 16No4-272
C.B. McCullagh, 63:Jun83-211
Thompson, J.B. - see Ricoeur, P.
Thompson, J.H. Spiritual Considerations in the Prevention, Treatment and Cure of Disease.
J. Mathers, 617(TLS):23Nov84-1356
Thompson, K. Eisenstein's "Ivan the Terrible."
H. Eagle, 574(SEEJ):Summer83-278
Thompson, L. Mirror to the Light. (R. Lannoy, ed)
C.P. Thompson, 617(TLS):30Nov84-1394
Thompson, L. and A. Prior. Politics in the Republic of South Africa.
K.A. Heard, 150(DR):Spring83-184
Thompson, M.W. - see Hoare, R.C.
Thompson, P. The Edwardians.
D. Gittins, 637(VS):Summer83-431
Thompson, P. Hairpin Crochet.
P. Grappe, 614:Summer84-17
Thompson, P., with T. Wailey and T. Lummis. Living the Fishing.
A. Calder, 617(TLS):2Mar84-213

Thompson, R. Hush, Child! Can't You Hear the Music? (C. Beaumont, ed)
C.L. Perdue, Jr., 292(JAF):Oct-Dec83-474
J.W. Ward, Jr., 585(SoQ):Winter83-82
Thompson, R.F. Flash of the Spirit.
B. Brown, 95(CLAJ):Dec83-230
C.H. Long, 469:Vol9No1-115
J. Olney, 441:12Feb84-13
Thompson, R.F. and J. Cornet. The Four Movements of the Sun.
J. Vansina, 2(AfrA):Nov82-23
Thompson, S. Close-Ups.
A. Shapiro, 441:15Jan84-18
Thompson, T. Edwardian Childhoods.
D. Gittins, 637(VS):Summer83-431
Thompson, W.D.J.C. The Political Thought of Martin Luther. (P. Broadhead, ed)
E. Cameron, 617(TLS):14Sep84-1014
Thomsen, C.W. Das englische Theater der Gegenwart.
M. Patterson, 610:Spring82-146
G. Stratmann, 490:Band14Heft3/4-368
Thomsen, C.W. and J.M. Fischer, eds. Phantastik in der Literatur und Kunst.
I. Gregori, 72:Band220Heft1-123
Thomson, A. Materialism and Society in the Mid-Eighteenth Century.
L.G. Crocker, 173(ECS):Fall83-111
A. Vartanian, 546(RR):Nov83-497
Thomson, D. A Biographical Dictionary of Film. (rev) Overexposures.
R. Carney, 114(ChiR):Summer83-111
Thomson, D. In Camden Town.*
P. Vansittart, 364:Dec83/Jan84-147
Thomson, D.S., ed. The Companion to Gaelic Scotland.
C. McAll, 617(TLS):20Apr84-440
Thomson, F.C. - see Eliot, G.
Thomson, J. The Seasons.* (J. Sambrook, ed)
M. Dodsworth, 175:Summer83-194
R. Inglesfield, 354:Sep83-300
M.J. Scott, 588(SSL):Vol 18-307
J.R. Watson, 161(DUJ):Jun83-134
566:Autumn83-64
Thomson, J. Sound Evidence.
T.J. Binyon, 617(TLS):13Jul84-790
Thomson, J.K.J. Clermont-de-Lodève, 1633-1789.*
T. Kemp, 83:Autumn83-251
Thomson, J.M. A Distant Music.
R. Hollinrake, 410(M&L):Jan/Apr83-69
D. Tunley, 415:Jan83-35
Thomson, P. Shakespeare's Theatre.*
R. Berry, 150(DR):Autumn83-526
R. Hayman, 176:Jan84-59
Thomson, R.M. Manuscripts from St. Albans Abbey 1066-1235.*
N. Barker, 78(BC):Autumn83-352
Thorberg, K., ed. Hørup i Breve og Digte.
E. Bredsdorff, 562(Scan):Nov82-198
Thorburn, D. and H. Eiland, eds. John Updike.*
P. Balbert, 594:Fall83-265
Thoreau, H.D. Journal.* (Vol 1) (J.C. Broderick and others, eds)
W.G. Heath, 106:Winter83-447
Thoreau, H.D. The Maine Woods. (J.J. Moldenhauer, ed)
A.P., 617(TLS):24Feb84-203
Thoreau, H.D. Thoreau in the Mountains.
A. Krupat, 27(AL):May83-255

Tillinghast, R. Our Flag Was Still There.
 P. Breslin, 441:22Jul84-15
 W. Prunty, 598(SoR):Autumn84-958
Tillman, H.C. Utilitarian Confucianism.
 W.W. Lo, 293(JASt):Aug83-947
 C. Schirokauer, 485(PE&W):Oct83-410
Tillmann, H.G. and P. Mansell. Phonetik.
 P. Rösel, 257(IRAL):Nov83-338
Tillot, R. Le Rythme dans la poésie de
 Léopold Sédar Senghor.
 M. Parent, 535(RHL):Mar/Apr83-306
Timberg, T.A. The Marwaris.
 K. Leonard, 293(JASt):Feb83-447
Timerman, J. The Longest War.*
 M. Benazon, 99:Apr83-28
 M. Rosenblum, 287:Aug/Sep83-27
 R. Wistrich, 473(PR):3/1983-475
Timko, M., F. Kaplan and E. Guiliano - see
 "Dickens Studies Annual"
Timpanaro, S. Aspetti e figure della cul-
 tura ottocentesca.*
 P. Treves, 228(GSLI):Vol 160fasc510-
 280
Tinelli, H. Creole Phonology.*
 J. Amastae, 361:Aug83-359
Tinker, H., ed. Burma: The Struggle for
 Independence 1944-1948. (Vol 1)
 D.J. Duncanson, 617(TLS):27Apr84-477
Tinker, H. The Ordeal of Love.
 M. Juergensmeyer, 293(JASt):Feb83-448
Tinkle, L. An American Original.
 J.M. Flora, 578:Fall84-114
Tippett, M. and D. Cole - see Phillips,
 W.J.
Tiresias. Notes from Overground.
 H. Carpenter, 617(TLS):29Jun84-722
Tirso de Molina. Los balcones de Madrid.
 (G. Cazottes, ed)
 G.E. Wade, 238:Dec83-634
Tirso de Molina. La celosa de sí misma,
 La jalouse d'elle-même. (S. Maurel, ed
 and trans)
 M. Wilson, 86(BHS):Oct83-341
Tischler, A., with C. Tomasic. Fifteen
 Black American Composers.
 A.F.L.T., 412:May82-154
Tischler, H. The Earliest Motets (to
 circa 1270).*
 M-D. Popin, 537:Vol69No2-252
Tischler, H. - see Rosenberg, S.N.
Tischler, J. Hethitisches etymologisches
 Glossar. (Pt 3)
 E. Neu, 260(IF):Band88-302
Tismar, J., ed. Das deutsche Kunstmärchen
 des 20. Jahrhunderts.*
 H. ten Doornkaat, 196:Band24Heft1/2-
 173
 E.A. Metzger, 221(GQ):May83-487
 T. Rietzschel, 654(WB):11/1983-2024
 J. Zipes, 406:Fall83-327
Tison-Braun, M. L'Introuvable origine.*
 B.L. Knapp, 400(MLN):May83-826
 A.A. McLees, 207(FR):Oct83-113
 E.R. Peschel, 210(FrF):Sep83-282
 R. Theis, 547(RF):Band95Heft3-367
Titley, N.M. Miniatures from Turkish Manu-
 scripts.
 B.W. Robinson, 90:Sep83-564
Titley, N.M. Persian Miniature Painting.
 B.W. Robinson, 617(TLS):20Apr84-425
Titon, J.T., ed. Downhome Blues Lyrics.*
 W.K. McNeil, 650(WF):Oct83-297

Titone, R. Glottodidattica.
 P.E. Balboni, 351(LL):Sep83-413
Tiwari, K.N. Dimensions of Renunciation
 in Advaita Vedānta.
 P. Olivelle, 318(JAOS):Jan-Mar82-227
Tobias, A. Money Angles.
 K.W. Arenson, 441:16Dec84-27
Tobias, M. Old Dartmouth on Trial.
 J. Herbst, 432(NEQ):Jun83-307
de Tocqueville, A. De la démocratie en
 Amerique.
 S. Wolin, 98:Oct83-749
de Tocqueville, A. Voyages en Angleterre
 et en Irlande.
 A. Clerval, 450(NRF):Mar83-110
Toczek, N. Rock 'n' Roll Terrorism.
 J. Saunders, 565:Vol24No1-73
Todd, A. A Time to Remember.
 J. Calado, 617(TLS):3Aug84-867
Todd, C. Voltaire: "Dictionnaire philo-
 sophique."*
 R. Niklaus, 83:Autumn83-268
Todd, I.A. The Prehistory of Central
 Anatolia I.*
 J. Yakar, 318(JAOS):Jul-Sep82-540
Todd, J., ed. Men by Women.
 M. De Koven, 395(MFS):Summer83-344
Todd, J.M. Women's Friendship in Litera-
 ture.*
 F.M. Oben, 149(CLS):Winter83-458
 C. Parke, 107(CRCL):Mar83-102
Todd, M., Jr. and S.M. A Valuable Prop-
 erty.
 J. Nangle, 200:Nov83-573
Todd, O. Une légère gueule de bois.
 P. Thody, 617(TLS):6Jan84-11
Todd, W.B. The Gutenberg Bible.
 P. Needham, 517(PBSA):Vol77No3-341
Todoran, E. M. Eminescu.
 V. Nemoianu, 617(TLS):18May84-559
Todorov, N. The Balkan City 1400-1900.
 F.W. Carter, 617(TLS):16Mar84-277
Todorov, T. Mikail Bakhtine.
 M. Bal, 204(FdL):Jun83-154
 D. Carroll, 153:Summer83-65
Todorov, T. The Conquest of America.
 (French title: La Conquête de l'Amé-
 rique.)
 J. Culler, 441:5Aug84-22
 J.H. Elliott, 453(NYRB):19Jul84-29
 J. King, 677(YES):Vol 13-299
 I.S. Majer, 400(MLN):May83-771
Todorov, T. Introduction to Poetics.*
 C. Norris, 402(MLR):Jul83-636
Todorov, T. Symbolism and Interpretation.*
 (French title: Symbolisme et Interpréta-
 tion.)
 D. Hult, 400(MLN):May83-765
 639(VQR):Spring83-43
Todorov, T. Theories of the Symbol.*
 (French title: Théories du symbole.)
 G.L. Bruns, 131(CL):Summer83-286
 R.A. Champagne, 399(MLJ):Summer83-177
Toer, P.A. - see under Pramoedya Ananta
 Toer
Toews, J.E. Hegelianism.*
 L.S. Stepelevich, 543:Mar83-737
Toffler, A. The Adaptive Corporation.
 M. Kandel, 441:21Oct84-47
Toffler, A. Previews and Premises.*
 639(VQR):Autumn83-131
Togeby, K. Grammaire française. (Vol 1)
 H. Bonnard, 209(FM):Jul83-266

Tokson, E.H. The Popular Image of the
Black Man in English Drama, 1550–1688.
  E.W. Taylor, 570(SQ):Winter83-506
Toland, J. Infamy.*
  E.S. Shapiro, 396(ModA):Summer/Fall83-
  334
Tolbert, F.X. A Bowl of Red.
  L. Milazzo, 584(SWR):Spring83-vi
"Tolerance et intolérances dans le monde
anglo-américan aux XVIIe et XVIIIe
siècles."
  W.J. Wolfe, 568(SCN):Spring/Summer83-
  17
Toliver, H. The Past that Poets Make.*
  C. Ricks, 184(EIC):Jul83-255
Tolkien, J.R.R. The Book of Lost Tales.
(Pt 1) (C. Tolkien, ed)
  B. Tritel, 441:27May84-7
Tolkien, J.R.R. The Monsters and the
Critics.* (C. Tolkien, ed)
  M. Thiébaux, 441:17Jun84-21
Tolkien, J.R.R. The Old English "Exodus."*
(J. Turville-Petre, ed)
  D.C. Baker, 191(ELN):Mar84-58
  E.B. Irving, Jr., 589:Apr83-538
Tölle-Kasterbein, R. Frühklassische
Peplasfiguren.
  C.E. Vafopoulou-Richardson, 123:
  Vol33No1-89
Tolley, K. Caviar and Commissars.
  H. Goodman, 441:6May84-27
de Tolnay, C. Corpus dei Disegni di
Michelangelo.
  M. Hirst, 90:Sep83-552
Toloudis, C. Jacques Audiberti.* [shown
in prev under both Toloudis and Toulou-
dis]
  H.G. Hall, 208(FS):Jul83-362
Tolson, M.B. Caviar and Cabbage. (R.M.
Farnsworth, ed)
  C. Colter, 436(NewL):Summer84-112
Tolson, M.B. A Gallery of Harlem Por-
traits. (R.M. Farnsworth, ed)
  A. Rampersad, 677(YES):Vol 13-354
Tolstoy, L.N. Tolstoy on Education. (A.
Pinch and M. Armstrong, eds)
  D. Matual, 558(RLJ):Fall83-220
Tomalin, C. - see Mansfield, K.
Tomalin, M. The Fortunes of the Warrior
Heroine in Italian Literature.
  A. Reynolds, 67:Nov83-329
  E.B. Weaver, 551(RenQ):Autumn83-456
Tomkies, M. A Last Wild Place.
  J. Hunter, 617(TLS):9Nov84-1295
Tomlinson, A. and G. Whannel, eds. Five
Ring Circus.
  B. Glanville, 362:14Jun84-22
Tomlinson, C. Notes from New York and
Other Poems.
  D. Constantine, 176:Sep/Oct84-42
  D. Davis, 362:19Jul84-25
  R. Swigg, 617(TLS):27Apr84-452
Tomlinson, C. Poetry and Metamorphosis.*
  P. Dickinson, 364:Aug/Sep83-136
  M. Dodsworth, 175:Summer83-298
  P. Kemp, 362:26Jan84-20
  D. McDuff, 565:Vol124No4-62
Tomlinson, C. Translations.
  D. Davis, 362:6Dec84-33
  R. Swigg, 617(TLS):27Apr84-452
Tomlinson, C. - see Williams, W.C.

Tomlinson, H., ed. Before the English
Civil War.
  R. Lockyer, 617(TLS):21Sep84-1062
Tomlinson, H.M. - see Brodeau, V.
Tomlinson, R. La Fête galante — Watteau
et Marivaux.*
  A. Cismaru, 207(FR):Apr84-716
  P.V. Conroy, Jr., 173(ECS):Fall83-107
  M. Gilot, 535(RHL):Mar/Apr83-278
  H. Wagner, 547(RF):Band95Heft3-354
Tomlinson, R.A. Epidaurus.
  R. Higgins, 39:Dec83-527
Tompert, H., ed. Ethik und Kommunikation.
  C.G.C., 185:Jul84-745
Tondl, L. Problems of Semantics.
  H. Hiz, 355(LSoc):Dec83-565
Toomer, G.J. - see Ptolemy
Toomer, J. The Wayward and the Seeking.
(D. Turner, ed)
  M. Fabre, 189(EA):Jan-Mar83-107
van den Toorn, P.C. The Music of Igor
Stravinsky.*
  J. Pasler, 415:Oct83-605
Toppani, B.D. and others - see under di
Colloredo Toppani, B. and others
Topsell, E. Topsell's Histories of Beasts.
(M. South, ed)
  B.P. O'Donnell, 568(SCN):Spring/
  Summer83-19
Topsfield, L.T. Chrétien de Troyes.*
  D. Evans, 447(N&Q):Dec82-570
  J.H.M. McCash, 131(CL):Summer83-291
  D. Maddox, 589:Jan83-242
  J. Schulze, 72:Band220Heft2-444
Toraldo di Francis, G. The Investigation
of the Physical World.
  R. Arthur, 486:Sep83-516
  N. Cartwright, 84:Sep83-310
Torelli, M. Typology and Structure of
Roman Historical Reliefs.
  R.R.R. Smith, 313:Vol73-225
Torgovnick, M. Closure in the Novel.*
  J. van Luxemburg, 204(FdL):Mar83-76
  P. Swinden, 148:Spring83-78
Törnqvist, E. Strindbergian Drama.
  B. Steene, 563(SS):Summer83-273
Torracinta-Pache, C. Le Pouvoir est pour
demain.
  D. Steiner, 617(TLS):7Dec84-1425
Torrance, T.F. Divine and Contingent
Order.
  C. Ebenreck, 543:Jun83-950
Torres, A. El realismo de "Tirant lo
Blanch" y su influencia en el "Quijote."
  C. Stern, 545(RPh):May83-647
Torretti, R. Philosophy of Geometry from
Riemann to Poincaré.*
  J.A. Coffa, 449:Nov83-683
Torrey, E.F. The Roots of Treason.*
  M. Bradbury, 176:Dec84-47
  H. Carpenter, 617(TLS):27Apr84-448
  E. Griffiths, 362:22Mar84-25
  K.S. Lynn, 129:Jan84-68
Torri, J. Diálogo de los libros. (S.I.
Zaïtzeff, ed)
  A. Blasi, 240(HR):Winter83-119
Tortosa, F.G. and R. López Ortega - see
under García Tortosa, F. and R. López
Ortega
Torvill, J. and C. Dean, with J. Hennessy.
Torvill and Dean.
  S.M. Halpern, 441:20May84-31

Tosaki, H. Bukkyō Ninshikiron no Kenkyū.
    M. Hattori, 259(IIJ):Jan83–58
Toscani, B., ed. Le laude dei Bianchi
    contenute nel codice Vaticano Chigiano
    L.VII.226.
    R. Mignani, 276:Summer83–173
Toscano, F. and J. Hiester, eds. Anti-
    Yankee Feelings in Latin America.
    M.S. Finch, 238:May83–299
Tosches, N. Hellfire.
    M.R. Winchell, 585(SoQ):Winter83–77
Tōten, M. – see Miyazaki Tōten
Toth, S.A. Ivy Days.
    B. Creaturo, 441:17Jun84–31
Totman, C. Japan before Perry.*
    A.H. Ion, 529(QQ):Winter83–1181
    R.P. Toby, 293(JASt):Nov82–171
Totok, W. Handbuch der Geschichte der
    Philosophie. (Vol 3)
    H. Sonneville, 356(LR):Nov83–351
Tougas, G. Destin littéraire du Québec.
    A.B. Chartier, 207(FR):Mar84–546
    D.M. Hayne, 627(UTQ):Summer83–516
Toulet, S. Le Tourment de Dieu dans
    l'oeuvre autobiographique de Julien
    Green.
    J. Onimus, 535(RHL):Sep/Dec83–968
    C.D.E. Tolton, 627(UTQ):Summer83–467
Toulmin, S. The Return to Cosmology.
    D. Duncalfe, 529(QQ):Winter83–1215
Touloudis, C. – see under Toloudis, C.
Touraine, A. The Voice and the Eye.
    W.L.M., 185:Apr84–564
Touré, A. La Civilisation quotidienne en
    Côte-d'Ivoire.
    H. Cronel, 450(NRF):Mar83–132
Tourney, L.D. Joseph Hall.*
    J.E. Platt, 447(N&Q):Apr82–168
Tournier, M. The Fetishist and Other
    Stories.
    V. Brombert, 441:9Sep84–7
    J. Mellors, 362:19Jan84–26
    D. Taylor, 364:Nov83–109
    J. Weightman, 453(NYRB):8Nov84–25
Tournier, M. Gilles et Jeanne.*
    P. Bourgeade, 450(NRF):Sep83–136
Tournier, M. and J-M. Toubeau. Le Vaga-
    bond immobile.
    P. Thody, 617(TLS):24Aug84–946
Tournoy-Thoem, G., ed. Publi Fausti Andre-
    lini Amores sive Livia.
    L.V.R., 568(SCN):Spring/Summer83–28
Toury, G. In Search of a Theory of Trans-
    lation.*
    S.G. Kellman, 462(OL):Vol37No2–199
Tovar, A. Relatos y diálogos de los Mata-
    cos.
    M. Faust, 260(IF):Band87–390
Tovell, R.L. Reflections in a Quiet Pool.
    L. Weir, 102(CanL):Autumn83–61
Tovey, D.F. Essays in Musical Analysis.*
    Concertos and Choral Works.
    M. Tilmouth, 415:Jan83–35
Tovstykh, I.A. – see Mukandarām
Towers, R. The Summoning.*
    J. Moynahan, 453(NYRB):16Feb84–40
    D. Smith, 344:Winter84–121
Towle, P., ed. Estimating Foreign Mili-
    tary Power.
    R.J. Overy, 575(SEER):Jul83–465
Towle, P. Protest and Perish.
    T. Garden, 176:Apr84–58

Townsend, C.E. Czech through Russian.*
    M. Fryščak, 558(RLJ):Winter-Spring83–
    243
Townsend, R. Further Up the Organization.
    S. Salmans, 441:25Mar84–21
Townshend, C. Political Violence in
    Ireland.
    D. Fitzpatrick, 617(TLS):20Jul84–815
Toye, J. Public Expenditure in Indian
    Development Policy 1960–1970.
    J. Das Gupta, 293(JASt):Nov82–105
Toynbee, A. The Greeks and Their Heri-
    tages.
    R.H. Brophy 3d, 396(ModA):Spring83–194
    R. Padel, 303(JoHS):Vol 103–233
    K. Snipes, 123:Vol33No1–156
Tracey, G. – see Newman, J.H.
Tracey, M. A Variety of Lives.*
    P. Dickinson, 364:Dec83/Jan84–137
    D.A.N. Jones, 617(TLS):3Feb84–108
Trachtenberg, A. The Incorporation of
    America.*
    T. Bender, 473(PR):3/1983–459
    P. Shaw, 569(SR):Spring83–299
Tracy, H. The Heart of England.
    D. May, 362:19Jan84–23
Tracy, R., with S. Delano. Balanchine's
    Ballerinas.
    D. Harris, 441:1Jan84–21
Tracy, S.V. Inscriptiones Graecae. (Vol
    2) (2nd ed)
    D.J. Geagan, 303(JoHS):Vol 103–205
Trafford, A. Crazy Time.
    639(VQR):Spring83–60
Träger, F. Herbarts realistisches Denken.
    J-M. Gabaude and E. Harmat, 542:
    Jan-Mar83–143
Traglia, A. and G. Aricò, eds. "Opere" di
    P. Papinio Stazio.
    F. Delarue, 555:Vol57fasc1–159
Trahan, E., ed. Gogol's "Overcoat."
    R. Gregg, 550(RusR):Oct83–441
    J.M. Mills, 574(SEEJ):Fall83–380
Traill, E.L. Sintaxis de los verboides en
    el habla culta de la ciudad de México.
    G. Murillo P., 457(NRFH):Tomo31núm2–
    304
Trakl, G. A Profile. (F. Graziano, ed)
    S. Friebert, 199:Spring84–64
Trambley, E.P. – see under Portillo Tramb-
    ley, E.
Tranel, B. Concreteness in Generative
    Phonology.*
    J. Durand, 297(JL):Sep83–487
    M. Picard, 320(CJL):Spring83–87
    E.R. Van Vliet, 660(Word):Apr83–52
Tranquillo, M.D. Styles of Fashion.
    R.L. Shep, 614:Fall84–23
"Transactions of the Fifth International
    Congress on the Enlightenment."* (Vol
    1)
    J.H. Brumfitt, 208(FS):Jan83–86
"Transactions of the Fifth International
    Congress on the Enlightenment." (Vol 2)
    J.H. Brumfitt, 208(FS):Jan83–86
    H. Duranton, 535(RHL):Jul/Aug83–637
"Transactions of the Fifth International
    Congress on the Enlightenment."* (Vols
    3 and 4)
    J.H. Brumfitt, 208(FS):Jan83–86
Tranströmer, T. Selected Poems.*
    S. Birkerts, 472:Fall/Winter83Spring/
    Summer84/192

Tranter, J.   Selected Poems.
   J. Forbes, 381:Jun83-249
Trapido, B.   Brother of the More Famous
   Jack.*
   42(AR):Winter83-118
Trapido, B.   Noah's Ark.
   C. Hawtree, 617(TLS):12Oct84-1168
   J. Mellors, 362:8Nov84-28
Trapnell, W.H.   Christ and His "Associates"
   in Voltairian Polemic.
   T.E.D. Braun, 207(FR):Apr84-714
Trapnell, W.H.   Voltaire and the Euchar-
   ist.*
   J. Pappas, 207(FR):Feb84-396
Trapp, J.   The Preface to the "Aeneis" of
   Virgil (1718).
   P-G.B., 189(EA):Oct-Dec84-491
Trapp, J.B. - see More, T.
Traubel, H.   With Walt Whitman in Camden.*
   (Vol 6) (G. Traubel and W. White, eds)
   R. Asselineau, 189(EA):Jul-Sep84-353
Traubner, R.   Operetta.
   J. Novick, 441:1Apr84-23
   P. O'Connor, 617(TLS):20Apr84-436
Trautmann, T.R.   Dravidian Kinship.
   M.B. Emeneau, 350:Sep84-675
Travaglini, A.   Inventario dei rinveni-
   menti monetali del Salento.
   F. Van Keuren, 124:Mar-Apr84-266
"The Travels of Sir John Mandeville."
   L. Antonsen, 469:Vol9No1-104
Traven, B.   The Rebellion of the Hanged.
   J. Melmoth, 617(TLS):14Dec84-1457
Traver, R.   People Versus Kirk.
   W. Dommarski, 639(VQR):Summer83-523
Traversi, D.   "The Canterbury Tales:" A
   Reading.
   A. Bruten, 617(TLS):6Jan84-20
   B. Windeatt, 176:Jul/Aug84-55
Traversi, D.   The Literary Imagination.
   A. Bruten, 617(TLS):6Jan84-20
Travis, P.W.   Dramatic Design in the
   Chester Cycle.*
   K. Ashley, 301(JEGP):Jul83-440
   L.M. Clopper, 589:Oct83-1095
   T. Coletti, 130:Winter83/84-390
   M. Twycross, 175:Autumn83-251
Travitsky, B., ed.   The Paradise of Women.*
   E.C. Wright, 539:Feb84-52
Traxel, D.   An American Saga.
   M.S. Young, 39:Jan83-72
Treadway, T.   Wyoming.
   D. Wellenbrock, 649(WAL):May83-82
Trebach, A.S.   The Heroin Solution.
   J.P.C., 185:Jan84-383
Tredell, N.   The Novels of Colin Wilson.
   S. Dutruch, 189(EA):Oct-Dec84-481
   J.V. Knapp, 395(MFS):Winter83-772
Treece, P.   A Man for Others.*
   B.T. Lupack, 497(PoIR):Vol28No2-88
Trefil, J.S.   The Unexpected Vista.*
   42(AR):Fall83-506
Tregear, M.   Song Ceramics.*
   "Skipjack," 463:Spring83-69
   W. Watson, 90:May83-306
Tregear, T.R.   China.
   R.D. Hill, 302:Vol 19No2-241
Tregebov, R.   Remembering History.
   C. Hlus, 137:Sep83-18
   H. Kirkwood, 526:Summer83-76

Treglown, J., ed.   Spirit of Wit.*
   D. Griffin, 566:Spring84-155
   J.V. Guerinot, 568(SCN):Winter83-70
   P. Hammond, 97(CQ):Vol 12No1-56
   A.E. Watson, 148:Spring83-87
Treglown, J. - see Lord Rochester
Treherne, J.   The Galapagos Affair.*
   P-L. Adam, 61:Jan84-101
   A. Ross, 364:Apr/May83-137
   L. Sante, 453(NYRB):2Feb84-22
Treherne, J.   The Strange History of
   Bonnie and Clyde.
   E. Korn, 617(TLS):17Aug84-915
Treib, M. and R. Herman.   A Guide to the
   Gardens of Kyoto.
   592:Jan-Feb83-29
"Treize miracles de Notre-Dame tirés du Ms.
   B. N. fr. 2094."*   (P. Kunstmann, ed)
   M. Boulton, 545(RPh):Feb83-516
   E. Rankka, 597(SN):Vol55No1-118
Trelease, J.   The Read-Aloud Handbook.
   C. Fox, 617(TLS):30Nov84-1374
   T.C. Holyoke, 42(AR):Spring83-246
"Trema No. 5: Anthony Burgess."
   R.A. Day, 189(EA):Apr-Sep83-348
Tremain, R.   The Colonel's Daughter.
   C. James, 441:27May84-12
   J. Motion, 617(TLS):17Feb84-159
   K.C. O'Brien, 362:22Mar84-25
de Tremaudan, A-H.   Hold High Your Heads.
   F.W. Kaye, 649(WAL):Nov83-271
Tremblay, M.   La Duchesse et le roturier.
   E.R. Babby, 207(FR):Oct83-143
Tremblay, M.   The Fat Woman Next Door is
   Pregnant.   The Impromptu of Outremont.*
   Damnée Manon Sacrée Sandra.*   Sainte-
   Carmen of the Main.*   Les Anciennes
   Odeurs.*
   J.J. O'Connor, 102(CanL):Autumn83-76
Trench, C.C.   The Great Dan.
   R. Foster, 617(TLS):19Oct84-1184
Trenckner, V.   A Critical Pāli Dictionary.
   (Vol 2, fasc 10 and 11)   (L. Alsdorf, ed-
   in-chief)
   C. Caillat, 260(IF):Band88-312
Trenton, P. and P.H. Hassrick.   The Rocky
   Mountains.
   R.P. McDonald, 70:May-Jun83-169
   L. Milazzo, 584(SWR):Autumn83-viii
"Trésors des Musées du Nord de la France,
   IV."
   A. Blunt, 90:Sep83-562
Trethowan, I.   Split Screen.
   W. Deedes, 362:17May84-23
Treves, P. - see Cattaneo, C.
Trevor, W.   Fools of Fortune.*
   P. Craig, 617(TLS):28Dec84-1506
   M. Howard, 676(YR):Winter84-xiv
   J. Mellors, 364:Jun83-92
Trevor, W.   A Writer's Ireland.
   P-L. Adams, 61:May84-122
   P. Craig, 617(TLS):31Aug84-979
   V. Young, 472:Fall/Winter83Spring/
      Summer84-323
   442(NY):2Apr84-133
Trewavas, E.   Tilapiine Fishes of the
   genera Sarotherodon, Oreochromis and
   Danakilia.
   P.H. Greenwood, 617(TLS):27Apr84-479
Trexler, R.C.   Public Life in Renaissance
   Florence.*
   D. Bornstein, 539:Nov83-289
      [continued]

Trousson, R. Thèmes et mythes.*
  W. Bies, 196:Band24Heft3/4-335
  D. Madelenat, 535(RHL):Jan/Feb83-137
  C. Rodiek, 52:Band17Heft2-197
  M. Schmeling, 549(RLC):Apr-Jun83-209
Trovato, P. - see Machiavelli, N.
Trow, G.W.S. The City in the Mist.
  R. Koenig, 61:Jun84-117
  J. Leggett, 441:5Feb84-12
Troyat, H. Alexander of Russia.*
  D.C.B. Lieven, 617(TLS):2Mar84-210
Troyat, H. The Web.
  D. Coward, 617(TLS):6Jul84-761
de Troyes, C. - see under Chrétien de
  Troyes
Trubeckoj, G.N. Gody Smuty i Nadežd 1917-
  1919.
  V. Grebenschikov, 558(RLJ):Winter-
  Spring83-283
Trudeau, D. Léandre et son péché.
  T.R. Wooldridge, 627(UTQ):Summer83-535
Trudgill, P. and J. Hannah. International
  English.
  F. Chevillet, 189(EA):Oct-Dec84-454
  E. Finegan, 350:Mar84-188
Trueblood, P.G., ed. Byron's Political
  and Cultural Influence in Nineteenth-
  Century Europe.*
  G. Hoffmeister, 107(CRCL):Mar83-108
  A. Rodway, 447(N&Q):Aug82-366
Truffaut, F., with H.G. Scott. Hitchcock.
  (rev)
  P. Lopate, 441:30Dec84-9
Trujillo Rodríguez, A. El Retablo Barroco
  en Canarias.
  A. Rodríguez G. de Ceballos, 48:Jan-
  Mar79-98
Truman, M. Murder on Embassy Row.
  N. Callendar, 441:5Aug84-21
Truninger, A. Paddy and the Paycock.
  K. Tetzeli von Rosador, 72:Band220
  Heft1-177
Trusted, J. Free Will and Responsibility.
  T. Baldwin, 176:Nov84-64
Trustram, M. Women of the Regiment.
  H. Strachan, 617(TLS):26Oct84-1213
Trypanis, C.A. Greek Poetry.*
  R. Padel, 303(JoHS):Vol 103-233
  N.J. Richardson, 123:Vol33No1-41
  A.G. Robson, 399(MLJ):Summer83-181
Trypučko, J. O pewnym wypadku litewsko-
  polskiej interferencji językowej w
  zakresie onomastyki (lit. przyrostek
  "-utis," pol. "-uć").
  J.I. Press, 575(SEER):Jul83-417
Tsai, M. and I-M. Contemporary Chinese
  Novels and Short Stories, 1949-1974.
  W.A. Lyell, 318(JAOS):Oct-Dec82-669
Ts'ao Yü. The Wilderness. (C.C. Rand and
  J.S.M. Lau, trans)
  C. Tung, 116:Jan82-124
Tsatsos, I. My Brother George Seferis.
  P. Kouidis, 577(SHR):Winter83-93
Tschäni, H. Wer regiert die Schweiz?
  C.J. Hughes, 617(TLS):7Dec84-1425
Tschiedel, H.J. Caesars "Anticato."
  P. Jal, 555:Vol57fasc2-336
Tschimmel, I. Kriminalroman und Gesell-
  schaftsdarstellung.
  V. Neuhaus, 52:Band18Heft2-217

von Tschirnhaus, E.W. Médecine de l'es-
  prit ou Préceptes généraux de l'art de
  découvrir. (J-P. Wurtz, ed and trans)
  A. Reix, 542:Oct-Dec83-471
Tschumi, B. The Manhattan Transcripts.
  L.S. Shapiro, 505:Aug83-126
Tsereteli, K. Grammatik der modernen
  assyrischen Sprache (Neuostaramäish).
  J.C. Greenfield, 318(JAOS):Jan-Mar82-
  209
Tsipis, K. Arsenal.
  S.M. Halpern, 441:5Feb84-19
  T. Powers, 61:Feb84-93
Tsirkas, S. Printemps perdu.
  L. Kovacs, 450(NRF):Mar83-149
Tsitsikli, D., ed. Historia Apollonii
  Regis Tyri.
  J.M. Hunt, 122:Oct83-331
Tsong-yi, J. and P. Ryckmans - see under
  Jao Tsong-yi and P. Ryckmans
Tsou, T., ed. Select Papers from the
  Center for Far Eastern Studies. (No 4)
  V.C. Falkenheim, 293(JASt):Aug83-927
Tsoukalis, L. and M. White, eds. Japan
  and Western Europe.
  Yoshitomi Masaru, 285(JapQ):Apr-Jun83-
  207
Tsuang, M.T. Schizophrenia.
  M.V. Seeman, 529(QQ):Winter83-1211
Ts'ung-wen, S. - see under Shen Ts'ung-wen
Tsurutani, T. Japanese Policy and East
  Asian Security.
  H. Fukui, 293(JASt):May83-680
Tsuzuki, C. Edward Carpenter, 1844-1929.*
  I. Britain, 637(VS):Autumn82-103
  P. Faulkner, 506(PSt):May83-93
Tu, K-C. Li Ho.
  S.S. Wong, 293(JASt):Nov82-154
Tuaillon, G. Les régionalismes du fran-
  çais parlé à Vourey, village dauphinois.
  P. Rézeau, 553(RLiR):Jul-Dec83-486
Tucci, P. La Poesia di Jean Regnier.
  (Vol 1)
  N. Mann, 208(FS):Jul83-332
Tuchman, B.W. The March of Folly.
  P-L. Adams, 61:Apr84-148
  L. Freedman, 617(TLS):22Jun84-687
  D. Gress, 129:Jun84-71
  J. Keegan, 441:11Mar84-1
  G.S. Wood, 453(NYRB):29Mar84-8
Tucker, C.G. Kate Freeman Clark.
  H.H. McAlexander, 392:Winter82/83-81
Tucker, D.F.B. Marxism and Individualism.*
  F. Tricaud, 542:Apr-Jun83-259
Tucker, G.H. A Goodly Heritage.
  A. Shaprio, 441:20May84-31
Tucker, P.H. Monet at Argenteuil.*
  R. Pickvance, 90:Sep83-563
Tucker, P.L. Time and History in Valle-
  Inclán's Historical Novels and "Tirano
  Banderas."*
  N.G. Kobzina, 552(REH):Oct83-453
Tucker, R.W. and D.C. Hendrickson. The
  Fall of the First British Empire.
  B.D. Bargar, 656(WMQ):Jul83-477
Tucker, W. Progress and Privilege.
  D.R., 185:Oct83-187
Tuckwell, B. Horn.
  N. O'Loughlin, 415:Dec83-750
Tudjman, F. Nationalism in Contemporary
  Europe.*
  G. Schöpflin, 575(SEER):Apr83-306

Tudor, A. Beyond Empiricism.
  D.J.G., 185:Jan84-367
Tugendhat, E. Traditional and Analytical
  Philosophy.
  E. Craig, 483:Oct83-555
Tulard, J. Napoleon.
  N. Hampson, 617(TLS):5Oct84-1122
Tulloch, G. The Language of Sir Walter
  Scott.*
  D. Murison, 447(N&Q):Jun82-245
Tullock, G. Economics and Redistribution.
  T.D., 185:Apr84-561
Tuma, G.W. The Fourteenth Century English
  Mystics.
  M. Wakelin, 382(MAE):1983/1-155
Tumarkin, N. Lenin Lives!*
  639(VQR):Autumn83-118
Tumolesi, P.S. - see Sabbatini Tumolesi, P.
Tung Yüeh. The Tower of Myriad Mirrors.
  (S-F. Lin and L.J. Schulz, trans)
  R.E. Hegel, 116:Jan82-140
Tunley, D. Couperin.
  J.A. Sadie, 415:Mar83-170
Tunnicliffe, C.L. Tunnicliffe's Birds.
  G. Plimpton, 441:2Dec84-14
Tuohy, F. The Collected Stories.
  D.J. Enright, 617(TLS):21Dec84-1465
Tuppen, J. The Economic Geography of
  France.
  D. Bell, 617(TLS):10Feb84-148
Tupper, A. and G.B. Doern, eds. Public
  Corporations and Public Policy in Canada.
  G. Cassidy, 529(QQ):Summer83-529
Turani, G. and L. Zanda, eds. L'Annuario
  Italiano.
  G.R., 617(TLS):5Oct84-1144
Turbayne, C.M., ed. Berkeley.
  D.M. Armstrong, 63:Dec83-439
  K.P. Winkler, 319:Jul84-372
Turdeanu, É. Apocryphes slaves et
  roumains de l'Ancien Testament.
  D. Deletant, 575(SEER):Jul83-416
Turgenev, I. Turgenev's Letters.* (A.V.
  Knowles, ed and trans)
  L. Schapiro, 176:Feb84-47
Turing, P. Hans Hotter.
  M. Tanner, 617(TLS):26Oct84-1226
Türk, D.G. School of Clavier Playing.
  P. Whitmore, 410(M&L):Jul/Oct83-284
Turkle, S. The Second Self.
  H. Gardner, 441:22Jul84-3
  S. Sutherland, 617(TLS):14Dec84-1443
Turnbull, C.M. The Human Cycle.*
  I.M. Lewis, 617(TLS):30Mar84-326
Turnbull, G. A Gathering of Poems: 1950-
  1980.
  T. Dooley, 617(TLS):23Mar84-312
Turnbull, P. Big Money.
  T.J. Binyon, 617(TLS):18May84-557
  M. Laski, 362:12Apr84-27
Turner, A. Nathaniel Hawthorne.*
  B. Hayne, 106:Fall83-309
Turner, B. Hot Air, Cool Music.
  B. Case, 617(TLS):30Nov84-1389
  J. Wain, 362:13Dec84-27
Turner, B., with G. Nordquist. The Other
  European Community.
  J. Logue, 563(SS):Summer83-245
Turner, B.S. Religion and Social Theory.
  R. Towler, 617(TLS):1Jun84-619
Turner, D. Marxism and Christianity.*
  M. Adam, 542:Oct-Dec83-483
Turner, D. - see Toomer, J.

Turner, E.S. ABC of Nostalgia.
  D.A.N. Jones, 362:6Sep84-25
Turner, F.C. and J.E. Miguens, eds. Juan
  Perón and the Reshaping of Argentina.*
  A. Ciria, 263(RIB):Vol33No4-598
Turner, F.M. The Greek Heritage in Victor-
  ian Britain.*
  J. Clubbe, 301(JEGP):Apr83-253
  A.O.J. Cockshut, 447(N&Q):Oct82-465
  R.H. Evans, 366:Spring83-121
  M.K. Flavell, 402(MLR):Apr83-413
  R. Tobias, 636(VP):Spring83-98
Turner, G.L. Collecting Microscopes.
  G. Wills, 39:Feb83-147
Turner, G.L. Nineteenth-Century Scien-
  tific Instruments.
  J.S. Curl, 324:Sep84-699
Turner, H.A., with others. The Last
  Colony.
  M.K. Chan, 293(JASt):May83-589
Turner, J., ed. Businessmen and Politics.
  R. Overy, 617(TLS):26Oct84-1209
Turner, J.H. The Myth of Icarus in Span-
  ish Renaissance Poetry.
  M.G. Randel, 545(RPh):Feb83-491
Turner, M.R. and A. Miall, eds. The
  Edwardian Song Book.*
  A. Lamb, 415:Oct83-619
Turner, R. - see Dee, J.
Turner, T. The Diary of Thomas Turner
  1754-1765. (D. Vaisey, ed)
  J.P. Kenyon, 362:22Nov84-28
Turner, V. Focusing.
  L. Marcus, 617(TLS):24Aug84-953
Turner, V. From Ritual to Theatre.
  V. Crapanzano, 617(TLS):27Apr84-473
Túrolo, C.M., ed. Así lucharon.
  M. Deas, 617(TLS):10Feb84-142
Turone, S. Corrotti e corruttori.
  G. Reid, 617(TLS):28Sep84-1097
Turpin, J. John Hogan.
  N. Penny, 90:Jul83-433
Türr, K. Zur Antikenrezeption in der
  französischen Skulptur des 19. und
  frühen 20. Jahrhunderts.
  P. Gerlach, 471:Apr/May/Jun83-177
Turtledove, H. The Chronicle of Theo-
  phanes.
  M. Whitby, 123:Vol33No2-372
Turville-Petre, J. - see Tolkien, J.R.R.
Turyn, A. Dated Greek Manuscripts of the
  Thirteenth and Fourteenth Centuries in
  the Libraries of Great Britain.
  I.C. Cunningham, 303(JoHS):Vol 103-230
Tusa, A. and J. The Nuremberg Trial.*
  W. Mommsen, 617(TLS):3Feb84-120
  W.L. Shirer, 441:30Sep84-7
Tuska, J. and V. Piekarski, eds-in-chief.
  Encyclopedia of Frontier and Western
  Fiction.
  27(AL):Dec83-680
Tussing, M. and J.E. Zimmerman. Deutsch
  im Kontext.
  W.D. Keel, 399(MLJ):Summer83-194
Tute, W., J. Costello and T. Hughes, eds.
  D-Day.
  M. Carver, 617(TLS):8Jun84-634
Tuţescu, M. Les grammaires génératives-
  transformationnelles.
  F. Helgorsky, 209(FM):Oct83-384
Tuţescu, M. La présupposition en français
  contemporain.
  M. Dominicy, 209(FM):Jan83-67

Tuṭescu, M. Le Texte, de la linguistique
à la littérature.
F. Helgorsky, 209(FM):Jan83-67
Tutuola, A. The Witch-Herbalist of the
Remote Town.
J. Updike, 442(NY):23Apr84-121
Tuulio, T. Fredrikan Suomi.
M.N. Deschner, 563(SS):Spring83-177
Tuve, R. Allegorical Imagery.
J.L. Grigsby, 545(RPh):Aug82-113
Tuveson, E.L. The Avatars of Thrice Great
Hermes.
B.L. St. Armand, 111:Fall83-4
L.J. Swingle, 401(MLQ):Mar83-80
Twain, M. Adventures of Huckleberry Finn
...A Facsimile of the Manuscript.
T. Wortham, 445(NCF):Dec83-358
Twain, M. The Adventures of Tom Sawyer: A
Facsimile of the Author's Holograph Manu-
script.* (P. Baender, ed)
T. Wortham, 445(NCF):Dec83-358
27(AL):Oct83-488
Twain, M. The Adventures of Tom Sawyer,
Life on the Mississippi, Adventures of
Huckleberry Finn, Pudd'nhead Wilson.*
[shown in prev under "Mississippi Writ-
ings"] (G. Cardwell, ed)
W.H. Pritchard, 249(HudR):Summer83-352
Twain, M. The Adventures of Tom Sawyer;
Tom Sawyer Abroad; Tom Sawyer, Detec-
tive.* (J.C. Gerber, P. Baender and T.
Firkins, eds)
P. Messent, 541(RES):Aug83-354
Twain, M. The Annotated "Huckleberry
Finn." (M.P. Hearn, ed)
T. Wortham, 445(NCF):Dec83-359
Twain, M. Early Tales and Sketches.*
(Vol 1) (E.M. Branch and R.H. Hirst,
with H.E. Smith, eds)
E. Wagenknecht, 402(MLR):Oct83-908
Twain, M. Early Tales and Sketches.*
(Vol 2) (E.M. Branch and R.H. Hirst,
with H.E. Smith, eds)
S.K. Harris, 26(ALR):Spring83-136
E. Wagenknecht, 402(MLR):Oct83-908
Twain, M. The Selected Letters of Mark
Twain.* (C. Neider, ed)
J.S. Tuckey, 395(MFS):Summer83-331
L. Willson, 569(SR):Summer83-490
Twitchell, J.B. The Living Dead.*
S. Prickett, 402(MLR):Jul83-683
Twitchett, D. Printing and Publishing in
Medieval China.
D. Helliwell, 617(TLS):10Feb84-151
"Two Death Tales from the Ulster Cycle."
(M. Tymoczko, trans)
J. Dunn, 174(Éire):Fall83-136
Twomey, A.C. Needle to the North. (W.C.
James, ed)
G.W., 102(CanL):Spring83-188
de Tyard, P. Solitaire Second.* (C.M.
Yandell, ed) [shown in prev under Pontus
de Tyard]
K.M. Hall, 208(FS):Oct83-448
Tydeman, W. The Theatre in the Middle
Ages.
W.A. Armstrong, 611(TN):Vol137No2-91
Tydeman, W. - see Robertson, T.
Tyler, A. and S. Ravenel, eds. The Year's
Best American Short Stories.
B. Morton, 617(TLS):30Nov84-1391
Tyler, R., ed. Alfred Jacob Miller.
T.D. Hanson, 70:Mar-Apr82-127

Tyler, R. Visions of America.
M. Abley, 617(TLS):23Mar84-302
Tyler, W.T. Rogue's March.
639(VQR):Spring83-57
Tyler, W.T. The Shadow Cabinet.
M. Malone, 441:11Mar84-18
Tymieniecka, A-T., ed. The Philosophical
Reflection of Man in Literature.
P. Crowther, 89(BJA):Autumn83-370
M. Rapisarda, 395(MFS):Summer83-362
Tymoczko, M. - see "Two Death Tales from
the Ulster Cycle"
Tyng, A. Beginnings.
T.S. Hines, 617(TLS):9Nov84-1280
Tyrer, A.K. A Programmed German Grammar
with Exercises.
H.F. Taylor, 399(MLJ):Autumn83-293
Tyrrell, J. and others. Leoš Janáček:
Kát'a Kabanová.
J. Warrack, 415:Jan83-33
Tyrrell, W.B. Amazons.
H. King, 617(TLS):10Aug84-886
Tysdahl, B.J. William Godwin as Novelist.
W.S. Braden, 478:Apr83-130
D. McCracken, 173(ECS):Spring84-380
Tyson, A., ed. Beethoven Studies 3.
B. Cooper, 410(M&L):Jan/Apr83-116
W. Drabkin, 451:Fall83-163
Tyson, B. The Story of Shaw's "Saint
Joan."
B.M. Fisher, 177(ELT):Vol26No4-315
R.B. Parker, 627(UTQ):Summer83-435
J.L. Wisenthal, 397(MD):Sep83-400
S.A. Yorks, 572:Vol4-196
295(JML):Nov83-568
Tyson, N.J. Eugene Aram.
G.B. Tennyson, 445(NCF):Dec83-362
Tytell, P. La plume sur le divan.
A. Jackson, 208(FS):Oct83-493
Tytler, G. Physiognomy in the European
Novel.*
E.Z. Lambert, 591(SIR):Winter83-636
S. Soupel, 189(EA):Apr-Jun84-173
C. Watts, 402(MLR):Jul83-655
Tzara, T. Cinéma calendrier du coeur
abstrait: Maisons.
J.D. Flam, 62:Feb84-72
Tzara, T. Oeuvres complètes. (Vol 5)
D. Leuwers, 450(NRF):Feb83-118
Tz'u, S. - see under Sung Tz'u

de Ubeda, F.L. - see under López de Ubeda,
F.
Ubersfeld, A. Lire le théâtre. L'École
du spectateur.
M. Corvin, 535(RHL):Mar/Apr83-310
Učida, N. Studien zur Hindi-Vokalphonol-
ogie.
M. Gatzlaff, 682(ZPSK):Band36Heft1-110
M.C. Shapiro, 318(JAOS):Jul-Sep82-552
Udelson, J.H. The Great Television Race.
E.C. Clark, 9(AlaR):Jan83-67
Udolph, J. Studien zu slavischen Gewässer-
namen und Gewässerbezeichnungen.*
E. Dickenmann, 260(IF):Band87-369
Uecker, H., ed. Der Wiener Psalter.*
P. Schach, 589:Apr83-560
G.S. Tate, 301(JEGP):Oct83-592
Ueding, G., ed. Friedrich Maximilian
Klinger: Ein verbannter Göttersohn.
T. Salumets, 221(GQ):May83-509

Uffelman, L.K. Charles Kingsley.
  K. Watson, 447(N&Q):Jun82-250
Ugarte, M. Trilogy of Treason.
  F. Wyers, 395(MFS):Winter83-806
  P. Zatlin-Boring, 238:May83-298
Uguay, M. Autoportraits.
  E.G. Lombeida, 207(FR):Oct83-144
Uhlman, F. Beneath the Lightning and the
  Moon.
  T. Fitton, 617(TLS):14Dec84-1457
Ujházy, M. Herman Melville's World of
  Whaling.
  H.C. Horsford, 27(AL):Oct83-464
Ulf, C. - see Weiler, I.
Ullmann, E., ed. Geschichte der deutschen
  Kunst 1350-1470.
  R. Zeitler, 341:Vol52No2-88
Ulloa, J. and L.A. de Ulloa. Graded
  Spanish Reader. (2nd ed)
  M.E. Giles, 238:Dec83-653
Ulmschneider, H. - see von Berlichingen, G.
Ulph, O. The Fiddleback.
  C.L. Rawlins, 649(WAL):Aug83-161
Ulrich, L.T. Good Wives.
  L. Koehler, 656(WMQ):Jul83-471
Umphlett, W.L. The Movies Go to College.
  A. Quinton, 617(TLS):17Aug84-910
"Un Bol de Nids d'Hirondelles ne fait pas
  le Printemps de Pékin." (Huang San, A.
  Pino and L. Epstein, trans)
  J.P. Harrison, 293(JASt):Aug83-869
Underwood, M. Death in Camera.
  N. Callendar, 441:18Nov84-37
Underwood, M. A Party to Murder.
  N. Callendar, 441:29Apr84-26
Underwood, T.L. - see Bunyan, J.
Ungar, S. Roland Barthes.
  C. Norris, 617(TLS):21Sep84-1058
Ungeheuer, G. Sprache und Signal.
  G.F. Meier, 682(ZPSK):Band36Heft6-754
Unger, D. Leaving the Land.
  P-L. Adams, 61:Mar84-133
  S. Altinel, 617(TLS):21Dec84-1484
  J. Moynahan, 441:5Feb84-7
  R. Towers, 453(NYRB):31May84-35
  442(NY):2Apr84-133
Unger, J. Education Under Mao.
  J. Kwong, 293(JASt):May83-646
Unger, L. Eliot's Compound Ghost.*
  B. Rajan, 27(AL):May83-275
Unger, R. Poesía en Voz Alta in the The-
  ater of Mexico.
  J.W. Brokaw, 397(MD):Jun83-245
  A.M. Stanton, 86(BHS):Jan83-94
Unger, R.M. Passion.
  J. Neu, 441:8Jul84-24
Ungerer, M. Country Food.
  M. Burros, 441:3Jun84-15
Ungerer, T. Far Out Isn't Far Enough.
  N. Perrin, 441:2Sep84-5
Unseld, J. Franz Kafka: Ein Schriftstel-
  lerleben.
  G. Guntermann, 52:Band18Heft3-306
Untracht, O. Jewelry Concepts and Technol-
  ogy.
  H. Helwig, 139:Dec83/Jan84-40
Upadhyay, G.P. Brāhmaṇas in Ancient India.
  R. Salomon, 318(JAOS):Jul-Sep82-555
Upadhye, A.N. and others, eds. Mahāvīra
  and His Teachings.
  R.J. Cohen, 318(JAOS):Jan-Mar82-231
Updike, J. Bech is Back.*
  42(AR):Winter83-119

Updike, J., ed. The Best American Short
  Stories 1984.
  J. L'Heureux, 441:7Oct84-41
Updike, J. Hugging the Shore.*
  D. Lodge, 176:Jul/Aug84-63
  L. Sage, 617(TLS):20Jan84-53
Updike, J. The Witches of Eastwick.
  P-L. Adams, 61:Aug84-112
  M. Atwood, 441:13May84-1
  D.J. Enright, 362:27Sep84-29
  D. Johnson, 453(NYRB):14Jun84-3
  C. Raine, 617(TLS):28Sep84-1084
  442(NY):25Jun84-107
Uphaus, R.W. Beyond Tragedy.
  L.S. Champion, 579(SAQ):Spring83-232
  C. Frey, 551(RenQ):Autumn83-474
Uphaus, S.H. John Updike.*
  M.F. Schulz, 677(YES):Vol 13-359
"Upright Lives."
  D.C. Reep, 568(SCN):Spring/Summer83-16
Upton, A.F. The Finnish Revolution.
  P.K. Hämäläinen, 563(SS):Summer83-256
Upton, R. Fade Out.
  N. Callendar, 441:18Nov84-36
Ur, P. Discussions That Work.
  E.K. Horwitz, 399(MLJ):Summer83-173
Urbach, E.E. The Sages.
  H.N. Strickman, 390:Nov83-60
Urban, G.R., ed. Stalinism.*
  J.A. Getty, 550(RusR):Oct83-429
Urban, W. The Prussian Crusade.
  S. Jenks, 589:Jan83-245
Urbanyi, P. The Nowhere Idea.
  A. Percival, 627(UTQ):Summer83-541
Urbas, K. Erhebungen und Analysen zur
  Verbreitung der "liaison facultative" im
  heutigen Französisch.
  J. Klausenburger, 207(FR):May84-923
Urdang, D. Only the World.
  J.F. Cotter, 249(HudR):Winter83/84-714
Urdang, L., ed. Idioms and Phrases Index.
  70:May-Jun83-170
Urdang, L., ed-in-chief. -Ologies and
  -isms. (2nd ed)
  D.H., 355(LSoc):Mar83-145
Urdang, L., A. Humez and H.G. Zettler, eds.
  Suffixes and Other Word-Final Elements
  of English.*
  H. Käsmann, 38:Band101Heft3/4-475
Urdang, L. and F.G. Ruffner, Jr. Allu-
  sions — Cultural, Literary, Biblical and
  Historical.
  K.B. Harder, 424:Jun83-127
Ure, J. The Quest for Captain Morgan.*
  D. Thomas, 362:12Jan84-22
Ureland, P.S., ed. Kulturelle und sprach-
  liche Minderheiten in Europa.
  I. Lehiste, 350:Mar84-169
Ureland, P.S., ed. Die Leistung der Strat-
  aforschung und der Kreolistik.
  Y. Malkiel, 350:Sep84-683
Ureland, P.S., ed. Sprachkontakte im
  Nordseegebiet.*
  G. Kvaran, 260(IF):Band87-327
Ureland, P.S., ed. Sprachvariation und
  Sprachwandel.
  M. Hartig, 257(IRAL):Nov83-335
Ureland, P.S., ed. Standardsprache und
  Dialekte in mehrsprachigen Gebieten
  Europas.
  M. Hartig, 257(IRAL):May83-168

Valis, N.M. The Decadent Vision in Leopoldo Alas.*
   J.E. Dial, 552(REH):Oct83-468
   M.Z. Hafter, 345(KRQ):Vol30No1-109
Valk, G.M., with W. Huder - see Kaiser, G.
de Valk, P. The State and Income Distribution.
   J. Das Gupta, 293(JASt):Nov82-105
van der Valk, M. - see Eustathius
Valkenier, E.K. The Soviet Union and the Third World.
   D.S. Zagoria, 441:15Apr84-23
Valla, L. Laurentii Valle: "Repastinatio Dialectice et Philosophie." (G. Zippel, ed)
   P. Mack, 319:Apr84-236
Vallbona, R. La obra en prosa de Eunice Odio.
   A. Tcachuk, 238:May83-304
Valleau, M.A. The Spanish Civil War in American and European Films.
   M. Keller, 127:Fall83-284
Vallier, D. L'intérieur de l'art.
   C. Limousin, 98:Oct83-831
Vanasco, R.R. La poesia di Giacomo da Lentini.
   R. Russell, 276:Summer83-161
Vanasse, A. La Saga des Lagacé.
   E-M. Kroller, 102(CanL):Summer83-131
Van Buuren-Veenenbos, C.C., ed. The Buke of the Sevyne Sagis.
   P. Bawcutt, 571(ScLJ):Autumn83-6
   A.A. MacDonald, 179(ES):Apr83-176
Vance, C. Hard Choices.*
   E. Kedourie, 176:Nov84-15
Vance, K.A. The Theme of Alienation in the Prose of Peter Weiss.
   T.F. Barry, 221(GQ):Nov83-703
Vance, R. Regionalism and the South. (J.S. Reed and D.J. Singal, eds)
   B. Noggle, 9(AlaR):Jan83-68
Van Cleve, J.W. Harlequin Besieged.
   B. Duncan, 221(GQ):May83-500
   J.G. Stackhouse, 406:Winter83-442
Vandenberg, W.H. - see Ellul, J.
Vanden Berghe, L., with B. de Wulf and E. Haerinck. Bibliographie analytique de l'archéologie de l'Irān ancien.
   E. Porada, 57:Vol44No4-332
Van der Cruysse, D. - see under van der Cruysse, D.
Van Der Dussen, W.J. - see under van der Dussen, W.J.
Vanderhaeghe, G. Man Descending.*
   A. van Herk, 649(WAL):Summer83-267
   R.P. Knowles, 198:Oct83-94
   J.A. Wainwright, 150(DR):Autumn83-544
Vandermeersch, L. Wangdao ou La Voi Royale. (Vol 1)
   C. Schirokauer, 318(JAOS):Apr-Jun82-431
Van Der Rhoer, E. The Shadow Network.
   H.H. Ransom, 441:4Mar84-26
Vander Stelt, J.C., ed. The Challenge of Marxist and Neo-Marxist Ideologies for Christian Scholarship.
   R.B., 185:Apr84-557
Vanderwood, P.J. Disorder and Progress.
   P.T. Bradley, 86(BHS):Jan83-91
Vandromme, P. La Belgique francophone.
   K. Heitmann, 72:Band219Heft2-480

Van Duyn, M. Letters from a Father and Other Poems.*
   R. Lattimore, 249(HudR):Spring83-210
   P. Stitt, 491:Oct83-39
   639(VQR):Winter83-27
Van Engen, J.H. Rupert of Deutz.
   G. Leff, 617(TLS):3Feb84-122
Van Ghent, D. Keats. (J.C. Robinson, ed)
   J. Bayley, 617(TLS):2Mar84-207
   W.H. Evert, 661(WC):Summer83-173
   G. Woodcock, 569(SR):Fall83-664
   639(VQR):Autumn83-115
Van Herk, A. The Tent Peg.
   L. Van Luven, 649(WAL):May83-59
Vanheste, B. Literatuursociologie.
   A. Mertens, 204(FdL):Sep82-230
Van Kley, D.K. The Damiens Affair and the Unraveling of the Ancien Régime 1750-1770.
   C. Jones, 617(TLS):28Dec84-1495
Van Lustbader, E. The Miko.
   M. Levin, 441:23Sep84-28
Vannatta, D. H.E. Bates.
   B. Hooper, 573(SSF):Fall83-335
Van Ness, E. and S. Prawirohardjo. Javanese Wayang Kulit.
   F. Richmond, 130:Spring83-87
Vanneste, H.M.C. Northern Review 1945-1956.
   D. Precosky, 105:Fall/Winter83-98
Vannoy, R. Sex Without Love.*
   R. Campbell, 150(DR):Spring83-186
Vanovitch, K. Female Roles in East German Drama 1949-1977.
   A.D. Langdon, 221(GQ):Nov83-707
Van Parijs, P. Evolutionary Explanation in the Social Sciences.
   H.M. Hoenigswald, 355(LSoc):Sep83-424
   R.B. Le Page, 307:Oct83-87
Vansittart, P., ed. Voices from the Great War.*
   442(NY):4Jun84-135
Vansittart, P. - see Masefield, J.
Van Steenberghen, F. Maître Siger de Brabant.
   R. Hissette, 53(AGP):Band65Heft1-93
Van Steenberghen, F. Le problème de l'existence de Dieu dans les écrits de saint Thomas d'Aquin.
   A. Reix, 542:Oct-Dec83-460
Van Steenberghen, F. Le Thomisme.
   J. Jolivet, 542:Oct-Dec83-458
Van Thienen, G. Incunabula in Dutch Libraries.
   D. McKitterick, 617(TLS):8Jun84-647
Van Toorn, P., ed. Lakeshore Poets.
   K. Norris, 137:Sep83-39
Van Waesberghe, J.S. Codex Oxoniensis Bibl. Bodl. Rawl. C270. (Pt B)
   C. Meyer, 537:Vol69No2-229
Van Walleghen, M. More Trouble With the Obvious.
   G. Allen, 577(SHR):Spring83-171
   T. Swiss, 639(VQR):Spring83-349
Van Wert, W. Tales for Expectant Fathers.
   S. Pinsker, 577(SHR):Summer82-278
Van Wert, W.F. The Film Career of Alain Robbe-Grillet.
   C.J. Murphy, 207(FR):Mar84-568
Van Zandt, H.F. Pioneer American Merchants in Japan.
   J.N. Huddleston, Jr., 293(JASt):Nov82-173

Varadarajan, L. Ajrakh and Related Techniques.
    I. Joshi, 614:Fall84-11
Varanda, F. Art of Building in Yemen.
    P.B., 46:Feb83-71
Vareille, J-C. Alain Robbe-Grillet
l'étrange.*
    E. Smyth, 535(RHL):Sep/Dec83-971
Varey, S. - see "Lord Bolingbroke: Contributions to the 'Craftsman'"
Varg, P.A. New England and Foreign Relations, 1789-1850.
    G. Smith, 432(NEQ):Dec83-583
Varga, A.K. - see under Kibédi Varga, A.
Vargas Llosa, M. Aunt Julia and the
Scriptwriter.* (Spanish title: La tia
Julia y el escribidor.)
    R. Christ, 473(PR):3/1983-463
    J. Epstein, 249(HudR):Spring83-184
    C.B. Fleming, 37:May-Jun83-61
    J. O'Faolain, 364:Aug/Sep83-127
Vargas Llosa, M. The War of the End of
the World.* (Spanish title: La Guerra
del Fin del Mundo.)
    R. Kaplan, 129:Dec84-63
    R. Stone, 441:12Aug84-1
Vasconcelos, J. The Cosmic Race/La raza
cósmica.
    M.S. MacKenzie, 238:May83-304
Vasey, L. - see Lawrence, D.H.
Vásquez, A.B. and others - see under Barrera Vásquez, A. and others
Vasquez, J.G. - see under Gonzalez Vasquez,
J.
Vass, W.K. The Bantu Speaking Heritage of
The United States.
    B. Wald, 355(LSoc):Mar83-106
Vassallo, P., ed. The Magic of Words.
    D.E. Wylder, 395(MFS):Winter83-719
Vassberg, D.E. Land and Society in Golden
Age Castile.
    H. Kamen, 617(TLS):27Jul84-844
Vatsyayan, K. Traditional Indian Theatre.
    S. Kramrisch, 57:Vol44No2/3-235
Vatz, R.E. and L.S. Weinberg, eds. Thomas
Szasz.
    T.M.R., 185:Apr84-550
Vauchez, A. La sainteté en Occident aux
derniers siècles du moyen âge d'après
les procès de canonisation et les documents hagiographiques. Religion et
société dans l'Occident médiéval.
    L.K. Little, 589:Oct83-1097
Vaudrin, B. Tanaina Tales from Alaska.
    F. Buske, 649(WAL):Aug83-183
Vaughan, F. The Tradition of Political
Hedonism from Hobbes to J.S. Mill.
    T. Fuller, 319:Oct84-499
Vaughan, H. The Complete Poems. (A. Rudrum, ed)
    R. Ellrodt, 189(EA):Jan-Mar84-93
Vaughan, P.H. John Updike's Images of
America.
    W.T.S., 395(MFS):Winter83-745
Vaughan, T. The Works of Thomas Vaughan.
(A. Rudrum, ed)
    C.H. Sisson, 617(TLS):24Aug84-933
de Vaux de Foletier, F. Les Bohémiens en
France au XIXe siècle.
    J. Morel, 535(RHL):May/Jun83-477
Vax, L. Les chefs-d'oeuvre de la littérature fantastique.
    J-C. Margolin, 192(EP):Apr-Jun83-248

Vázquez, J.Z. and L. Meyer. México frente
a Estados Unidos.
    E. Ferris, 263(RIB):Vol33No4-599
Vazquez Montalban, M. Murder in the
Central Committee.
    T.J. Binyon, 617(TLS):20Jul84-801
Veatch, R.M. A Theory of Medical Ethics.
    R. O'Neil, 529(QQ):Spring83-249
de Vega Carpio, L. El caballero de Olmedo.
(F. Rico, ed)
    W.F. King, 240(HR):Summer83-325
de Vega Carpio, L. "La Corona Trágica" de
Lope de Vega. (M.G. Paulson and T.
Alvarez-Detrell, eds)
    J.S. Chittenden, 238:Sep83-433
    A.A. Heathcote, 86(BHS):Jul83-257
de Vega Carpio, L. La francesilla.* (D.
McGrady, ed)
    A.A. Heathcote, 86(BHS):Apr83-149
    E.S. Morby, 240(HR):Winter83-101
de Vega Carpio, L. Lírica. (J.M. Blecua,
ed)
    A. Carreño, 86(BHS):Apr83-150
    J.F.G. Gornall, 402(MLR):Jan83-208
    A.S. Trueblood, 240(HR):Spring83-230
de Vega Carpio, L. El perro del hortelano.* (V. Dixon, ed)
    G. Schüler, 547(RF):Band95Heft4-501
    A.S. Trueblood, 240(HR):Summer83-327
Veith, W.H. Der Kleine Deutsche Sprachatlas als Arbeitsmittel.
    G. Van der Elst, 685(ZDL):1/1983-87
Velebit, V. Sečanja.
    E. Barker, 617(TLS):10Aug84-897
Veldman, H. La Tentation de l'inaccessible.*
    D. Bellos, 402(MLR):Jan83-197
Velez Ibanez, C. Bonds of Mutual Trust.
    J.L. Aguilar, 50(ArQ):Summer83-188
Vélez Rodríguez, R. Castilhismo.
    Z. Kouřim, 542:Jan-Mar83-143
Velie, A.R. Four American Indian Literary
Masters.*
    R. Evans, 649(WAL):May83-83
    J.J. Wydeven, 395(MFS):Summer83-322
Vélissaropoulos, J. Les nauclères grecs.
    T. Drew-Bear, 122:Oct83-345
Véliz, C. The Centralist Tradition in
Latin America.*
    P. Cammack, 161(DUJ):Jun83-118
Velleius Paterculus. Histoire romaine.
(Vols 1 and 2) (J. Hellegouarc'h, ed and
trans)
    R. Weil, 555:Vol57fasc2-330
Veltsos, G. and others. Dēmotikē Glōssa.
    J.E. Rexine, 399(MLJ):Autumn83-295
Venantius Fortunatus. A Basket of Chestnuts. (G. Cook, trans)
    G.D. Economou, 589:Apr83-561
    C.F. Natunewicz, 124:May-Jun84-328
Vendler, H. The Odes of John Keats.*
    J. Bayley, 617(TLS):2Mar84-207
    I. Ehrenpreis, 453(NYRB):12Apr84-33
    P.H. Fry, 676(YR):Summer84-603
van Venlo, S. Boexken van der officien
ofte dienst der missen. (L. Simons, ed)
    J.L. Flood, 354:Sep83-314
Ventzel, T.V. The Gypsy Language.
    J.A.C. Greppin, 617(TLS):3Feb84-102
Venuti, L. - see Buzzati, D.
Vera, C. and G.R. McMurray, eds. In Honor
of Boyd G. Carter.
    L.F. Lyday, 238:Dec83-642

Verani, H. Onetti.
　M.R. Frankenthaler, 238:Mar83-146
Verbruggen, H. Le Zeus crétois.
　R. Parker, 123:Vol33No1-144
　R.F. Willetts, 303(JoHS):Vol 103-195
Vercier, B. and J. Lecarme. La Littéra-
　ture en France depuis 1968.
　C.J. Stivale, 207(FR):Feb84-439
Verdaasdonk, H. Literatuur en kapitaal.
　R. van der Paardt, 204(FdL):Dec83-318
Verdaasdonk, H. Literatuurbeschouwing en
　argumentatie.
　E. van Alphen, 204(FdL):Dec82-308
Verdelhan-Bourgade, M., M. Verdelhan and P.
　Dominique. Sans frontières 1.
　E. Doss-Quinby, 207(FR):May84-925
Verdier, R. La Vengeance.
　J. Vanderlinden, 69:Vol53No4-101
Verene, D.P., ed. Symbol, Myth and Cul-
　ture.
　S. Mayer and W.F. Eggers, Jr.,
　125:Fall82-83
Verene, D.P. Vico's Science of Imagina-
　tion.*
　D. Lovekin, 480(P&R):Vol 16No1-55
Veres, G. Opere lui Charles Dickens în
　România.
　R. Bales, 155:Summer83-119
Verey, C.D., T.J. Brown and E. Coatsworth,
　eds. Early English Manuscripts in Fac-
　simile. (Vol 20: The Durham Gospels.)
　W. Provost, 70:Jan-Feb82-91
Verey, D. Cotswold Churches.
　D. Guinness, 576:Dec83-390
Verga, G. The House by the Medlar Tree.
　Mastro-Don Gesualdo. The She-Wolf and
　Other Stories.
　R.M. Adams, 453(NYRB):20Dec84-46
Verga, G. Le novelle. (G. Tellini, ed)
　B.T. Sozzi, 228(GSLI):Vol 160fasc512-
　613
Vergara, G. Guida allo studio della
　poesia barbara italiana.
　V. Kapp, 547(RF):Band95Heft3-411
Vergara, L. Rubens and the Poetics of
　Landscape.*
　G. Martin, 39:Sep83-270
　B. Wind, 568(SCN):Winter83-78
Vergil. The Aeneid.* (R. Fitzgerald,
　trans)
　C.R. Beye, 472:Fall/Winter83Spring/
　Summer84-213
　P. Breslin, 491:Mar84-347
　J. Griffin, 617(TLS):24Feb84-196
　G. Steiner, 176:May84-51
Vergil. The "Aeneid" of Virgil. (A.
　Mandelbaum, trans)
　R. Pybus, 565:Vol24No2-73
Vergil. Virgil: The "Eclogues" and "Geor-
　gics."* (R.D. Williams, ed)
　B. Frischer, 122:Jan83-77
Vergil. Virgil: "The Georgics."* (R.
　Wells, trans)
　R. Lattimore, 249(HudR):Spring83-215
Vergine, L. L'Autre Moitié de l'avant-
　garde (1910-1940).
　F. de Mèredieu, 450(NRF):Mar83-153
Vergo, P. Vienna 1900.
　N. Powell, 39:Dec83-528
　E. Silber, 324:Jun84-478
Verheijen, C.R. Reflexives and Intensi-
　fiers in Modern British English.
　H. Bennis, 204(FdL):Dec83-315

Verheijen, L. - see Saint Augustine
Verhoeff, H. Les Grandes tragédies de
　Corneille.
　H. Allentuch, 615(TJ):Mar83-142
　H.R. Allentuch, 475:Vol 10No18-415
　M-O. Sweetser, 535(RHL):Sep/Dec83-922
Verhoeff, H. De Januskop van Oedipus.
　H. Hillenaar, 204(FdL):Mar83-68
"Vérité et Ethos."
　M. Adam, 542:Jan-Mar83-64
Verlaine, P. La Bonne Chanson, Jadis et
　naguère, Parallèlement. (L. Forestier,
　ed)
　C. Chadwick, 208(FS):Jan83-97
Verlaine, P. Poésies. (R-M. Lauverjat,
　ed)
　M. Schaettel, 356(LR):Nov83-359
Verlet, P. Les meubles français du XVIIIe
　siècle.*
　G. de Bellaigue, 90:May83-302
Verlet, P. The Savonnerie.
　P. Thornton, 90:Nov83-700
Verma, M.K. and T.N. Sharma. Intermediate
　Nepali Structure.
　B. Michailovsky, 293(JASt):Nov82-205
　W.L. Smith, 318(JAOS):Apr-Jun82-422
Vermazen, S. War Torn.
　C. Capa, 441:18Nov84-22
Vermeersch, P.M. L'Elkabien.
　M.A. Hoffman, 318(JAOS):Apr-Jun82-390
Vermes, G. Jesus and the World of Judaism.
　A.E. Harvey, 617(TLS):24Feb84-199
Vermeule, E. Aspects of Death in Early
　Greek Art and Poetry.*
　J. Bremmer, 394:Vol36fasc1/2-235
　S.R.F. Price, 303(JoHS):Vol 103-195
Vermeule, E. and V. Karageorghis. Myce-
　naean Pictorial Vase Painting.
　J.G. Younger, 303(JoHS):Vol 103-220
Vermilye, J. The Films of the Thirties.
　J. Nangle, 200:Jun/Jul83-379
Vernant, J-P. Myth and Society in Ancient
　Greece.
　P. Walcot, 303(JoHS):Vol 103-193
Vernant, J-P. The Origins of Greek
　Thought.
　D.J.F., 185:Jan84-374
Vernay, P., ed. Maugis d'Aigremont,
　chanson de geste.*
　P. Rickard, 382(MAE):1983/1-162
Verne, J. Mathias Sandorf.
　J. Vanves, 98:Aug-Sep83-743
Vernes, J-R. Critique de la raison aléa-
　toire, ou Descartes contre Kant.
　J. Largeault, 542:Jul-Sep83-372
Vernon, F. Gentlemen and Players.
　L. Duguid, 617(TLS):29Jun84-736
da Verona, R. Aquilon de Bavière. (P.
　Wunderli, ed)
　G. Roques, 553(RLiR):Jul-Dec83-500
Verrier, A. Through the Looking Glass.*
　H. Goodman, 441:27May84-17
Versényi, L. Holiness and Justice.
　J. Annas, 123:Vol33No1-56
Versnel, H.S., ed. Faith, Hope and Wor-
　ship.
　N.J. Richardson, 303(JoHS):Vol 103-194
Verstraëte, D. La Chasse spirituelle
　d'Arthur Rimbaud.
　A. Guyaux, 535(RHL):Sep/Dec83-953
Verweyen, T. and G. Witting. Die Parodie
　in der neueren deutschen Dichtung.
　G.B. Pickar, 406:Spring83-72

Vesey, G., ed. Idealism Past and Present.
  G. Brykman, 542:Jan-Mar83-66
  W.V. Doniela, 63:Dec83-442
  M.G., 185:Jul84-732
  J. Lampert, 543:Jun83-951
Vestal, S. Happy Hunting Grounds.
  R. and G. Laubin, 649(WAL):Aug83-186
Vet, C. Temps, aspects et adverbes de
  temps en français contemporain.*
  C. Verbert, 209(FM):Jul83-251
Vetö, M. Eléments d'une doctrine chré-
  tienne du mal.*
  J-F. de Raymond, 192(EP):Jul-Sep83-375
Vetö, M. Le fondement selon Schelling.
  A. Dibi, 542:Apr-Jun83-264
Vetter, H. Stadien der Existenz.
  H-H. Schrey, 53(AGP):Band65Heft3-337
Veyne, P. L'Élégie érotique romaine.
  M. Jarrety, 450(NRF):Dec83-111
Veyne, P. Writing History.
  E. Weber, 441:22Jul84-13
Vial, A. La Dialectique de Chateaubriand.
  J-C. Berchet, 535(RHL):Mar/Apr83-284
Vial, J.D. - see under de Dìos Vial, J.
Viallaneix, P. and J. Ehrard, eds. Aimer
  en France.
  A.B. Hagger, 208(FS):Apr83-229
Viallet, N. Principes d'Analyse Scientif-
  ique Tapisserie Méthode et Vocabulaire.
  90:May83-307
Vian, F. - see Apollonius of Rhodes
Vickers, B., ed. Occult and Scientific
  Mentalities in the Renaissance.
  C.B. Schmitt, 617(TLS):2Nov84-1243
Vickery, M. Cambodia: 1975-1982.
  A. Barnett, 617(TLS):14Sep84-1016
Vico, G. Vico: Selected Writings. (L.
  Pompa, ed and trans)
  G.L.C. Bedani, 89(BJA):Spring83-169
  V. Jones, 278(IS):Vol38-110
Vico, G. Vie de Giambattista Vico écrite
  par lui-même, Lettres, La méthode des
  études de notre temps.* (A. Pons, ed
  and trans)
  G. Costa, 480(P&R):Vol 16No2-143
  H. Védrine, 542:Jan-Mar83-121
Vidal, A.S. - see under Sánchez Vidal, A.
Vidal, G. Duluth.*
  639(VQR):Autumn83-128
Vidal, G. Lincoln.
  H. Bloom, 453(NYRB):19Jul84-5
  A. Burgess, 617(TLS):28Sep84-1082
  J.C. Oates, 441:3Jun84-1
  P. Whitehead, 362:27Sep84-30
Vidal, H. Dar la vida por la vida.
  J.E-G., 185:Oct83-186
Vidal-Naquet, P. Il buon uso del tradi-
  mento.*
  L. Darmezin, 555:Vol57fasc2-317
Vidali, V. Diary of the Twentieth Con-
  gress.
  J. Daynard, 441:29Jul84-21
Vidman, L., ed. Inscriptiones urbis
  Romae Latinae. (Pt 6, fasc 2)
  A.E. Gordon, 122:Jul83-267
Vieillard-Baron, J-L. Platon et l'Ideal-
  isme Allemand.
  D.R. Lachterman, 125:Summer83-389
Vieira, A. António Vieiras Rochuspredigt
  aus dem Restaurationskriegsjahr 1642.
  (R. Hoffmann, ed)
  N. Griffith, 86(BHS):Jul83-262

Viereck, W., ed. Studien zum Einfluss der
  englischen Sprache auf das Deutsche.
  J. Eichhoff, 406:Summer83-197
Vierhaus, R., ed. Bürger und Bürgerlich-
  keit im Zeitalter der Aufklärung.
  W. Albrecht, 654(WB):10/1983-1835
Viertel, P. American Skin.
  C. Seebohm, 441:18Mar84-10
Vieth, D.M. Swift's Poetry, 1900-1980.
  D.C. Mell, Jr., 566:Autumn83-62
de la Vigne, A. Le Voyage de Naples. (A.
  Slerca, ed)
  C. Marchello-Nizia, 554:Vol 103No4-564
  G. Roques, 553(RLiR):Jan-Jun83-260
de Vigny, A. Cinq-Mars. (A. Picherot, ed)
  D.G. Charlton, 208(FS):Jan83-91
Vigueur, J-C.M. Les pâturages de l'église
  et la douane du bétail dans la province
  du Patrimonio (XIVe-XVe siècles).
  W.M. Bowsky, 589:Jul83-833
Vijlbrief, M.E. and others - see Emmens,
  J.A.
Vilares Cepeda, I., ed. Vidas e Paixões
  dos Apóstolos. (Vol 1)
  A. Gier, 553(RLiR):Jan-Jun83-186
Villacañas Berlanga, J.L. La Formación de
  la Crítica de la Razón Pura.
  M. Caimi, 342:Band74Heft2-242
Villar, F. Ergatividad, Acusatividad y
  Género en la Familia Lingüística Indo-
  europea.
  W.R. Schmalstieg, 215(GL):Vol23No4-290
Ville, G. La gladiature en Occident des
  origines à la mort de Domitien.
  J-C. Richard, 555:Vol57fasc2-353
Villegas, F.D. - see under de Quevedo
  Villegas, F.
Villemaire, Y. Adrénaline.
  E.G. Lombeida, 207(FR):Mar84-598
Villemaire, Y. Du côté hiéroglyphe de ce
  qu'on appelle le réel. Ange amazone.
  P.G. Lewis, 207(FR):Feb84-421
Villey, M. Le Droit et les droits de
  l'homme.
  F. Trémolières, 450(NRF):Oct83-143
Villey, M. Philosophie du droit. (Vol 1)
  J-L. Gardies, 542:Jul-Sep83-337
Villien, B. Hitchcock.
  M. Wood, 453(NYRB):26Apr84-22
de Villiers de l'Isle-Adam, P.A.M. L'Eve
  future. (M.G. Rose, trans)
  L.B. Konrad, 446(NCFS):Fall-
    Winter83/84-243
Vinaver, M. Écrits sur le théâtre. (M.
  Henry, ed)
  D. Bradby, 402(MLR):Oct83-937
Vincent, N. and M. Harris, eds. Studies
  in the Romance Verb.
  S. Fleischman, 350:Jun84-419
  L. Pérez, 320(CJL):Fall83-192
  C. Thogmartin, 207(FR):Mar84-582
Vine, P.A.L. Pleasure Boating in the Vic-
  torian Era.
  H. Carpenter, 617(TLS):29Jun84-722
Vinogradov, J. Olbia.
  P.M. Fraser, 123:Vol33No1-150
Vinovskis, M.A. Fertility in Massachu-
  setts from the Revolution to the Civil
  War.
  D.R. Leet, 656(WMQ):Jul83-475
Vinson, J., ed. Contemporary Novelists.
  R.S., 148:Spring83-94

Vinson, J., ed. Twentieth-Century Western Writers.
  J.R. Milton, 649(WAL):Feb84-367
Vinson, J., with D.L. Kirkpatrick, eds. Great Writers of the English Language: Dramatists.
  G. Bas, 189(EA):Apr-Sep83-311
Violato, G. La Principessa Gianseniste, saggi su Madame de La Fayette.
  A. Niderst, 535(RHL):Mar/Apr83-272
Virgil - see under Vergil
Virgouley, R. Blondel et le modernisme.*
  A. Reix, 192(EP):Jul-Sep83-376
Virmaux, O. Les Héroïnes romanesques de Madame de Lafayette.
  J.A. Kreiter, 535(RHL):Mar/Apr83-273
  D. Kuizenga, 207(FR):Feb84-393
Virmond, W. Eulenspiegel und seine Interpreten.
  W. Wunderlich, 196:Band24Heft3/4-336
Vischer, M. Sekunde durch Hirn, Der Teemeister, Der Hase und andere Prosa. (H. Geerken, ed)
  H. Bänziger, 221(GQ):Jan83-159
Vishnevskaya, G. Galina.
  M. Bernheimer, 441:23Sep84-7
  S. Lipman, 129:Dec84-54
Viswanathan, S. The Shakespeare Play as Poem.*
  K. Duncan-Jones, 447(N&Q):Oct82-434
  G.P. Jones, 627(UTQ):Fall82-106
  K. Muir, 402(MLR):Jan83-139
Vita-Finzi, C. Archaeological Sites in Their Setting.
  K.M. Petruso, 576:Dec83-388
Vitale, A.J. Swahili Syntax.
  T.A. Hoekstra and G.J. Dimmendaal, 361:May83-53
Vitale, A.T. Spoken Swahili.
  K. Legère, 682(ZPSK):Band36Heft2-243
Viteritti, J.P. Across the River.
  A.L. Goren, 441:25Nov84-27
Vitse, M. Segismundo et Serafina.
  P.L. Smith, 86(BHS):Jul83-258
Vittucci, P.B. La collezione archeologica nel Casale di Roma Vecchia.
  F.R.S. Ridgway, 123:Vol33No2-364
Vivas, E. Two Roads to Ignorance.
  P. Grim, 543:Jun83-953
Vivekananda, F.C.S. Unemployment in Karnataka, South India.
  J. Das Gupta, 293(JASt):Nov82-105
Vizkelety, A. - see Spangenberg, W.
Vlach, J.M. Charleston Blacksmith.
  A. Govenar, 292(JAF):Oct-Dec83-495
Vogel, E. and others. Bibliografia della musica italiana vocale profana pubblicata dal 1500 al 1700.
  H.M. Brown, 317:Spring83-142
Vogel, H. Bilderbogen, Papiersoldat, Würfelspiel und Lebensrad.
  M. Dauskardt, 196:Band24Heft1/2-175
Vogel, P. and I. Stiegler. Bibliographisches Handbuch zum Philosophieunterricht.
  T. Macho, 687:Jul-Sep83-467
Vogelsang, A. A Planet.
  639(VQR):Summer83-98
Voghera, G. Gli anni della psicanalisi.
  E. Favretti, 228(GSLI):Vol 160fasc509-122
  J. Nobécourt, 98:Aug-Sep83-623

Vogt, E., ed. Neues Handbuch der Literaturwissenschaft. (Vol 2)
  H. Erbse, 52:Band18Heft2-196
Voicu, S.J. and S. D'Alisera. I.M.A.G.E.S.
  P. Pattenden, 123:Vol33No1-156
Voiers, L. Looking at Twills.
  P. Bach, 614:Fall84-20
Voigt, E.B. The Forces of Plenty.*
  P. Mesic, 491:Feb84-295
Voigtländer, H-D. Der Philosoph und die Vielen.
  C.J. Rowe, 123:Vol33No1-140
Voisin, M. Le Soleil et la Nuit.
  D.G. Burnett, 446(NCFS):Fall-Winter83/84-229
Voit, P. Franz Anton Pilgram (1699-1761).
  A. Laing, 90:Jun83-369
Volgyes, I. The Political Reliability of the Warsaw Pact Armies.
  A.R. De Luca, 550(RusR):Oct83-447
Volk, W., ed. Karl Friedrich Schinkel.
  R. Elvin, 46:May81-317
Völker, K. - see Ihering, H.
Volkoff, V. Vladimir, the Russian Viking.
  F. Wigzell, 617(TLS):7Dec84-1421
Vollmer, J., E.J. Keall and E. Nagai-Berthron. Silk Roads, China Ships.
  R.L. Shep, 614:Winter84-21
Volney, C-F. La loi naturelle, Leçons d'histoire. (J. Gaulmier, ed)
  C.J. Betts, 208(FS):Apr83-221
Voloshinov, V.N. Marxism and the Philosophy of Language.
  D. Carroll, 153:Summer83-65
Vološin, M. Stixotvorenija.
  J. Ivask, 558(RLJ):Fall83-236
della Volpe, G. Kritik des Geschmacks.
  S. Kleinschmidt, 654(WB):11/1982-173
Volpilhac, J., P. Miniconi and G. Devallet - see Silius Italicus, T.C.
de Voltaire, F.M.A. Correspondance. (Vols 6 and 7) (T. Besterman, ed; adapted by F. Deloffre)
  J.H. Brumfitt, 208(FS):Apr83-217
de Voltaire, F.M.A. Erzählungen, Dialoge, Streitschriften.* (M. Fontius, ed)
  U. van Runset, 535(RHL):Jan/Feb83-126
"Voltaire and the English."*
  E.J.H. Greene, 107(CRCL):Mar83-99
  J.S. Spink, 549(RLC):Jan-Mar83-115
Voorwinden, N. and M. de Haan, eds. Oral Poetry.*
  W.G. van Emden, 208(FS):Jul83-330
Vorlat, E., ed. Analytical Bibliography of Writings on Modern English Morphology and Syntax. (Vol 5)
  B. Sundby, 597(SN):Vol55No2-199
Vormweg, H. Peter Weiss.
  J. Ricker-Abderhalden, 221(GQ):Mar83-349
Voronova, T., ed. Corpus des notes marginales de Voltaire. (Vol 1)
  W.H. Barber, 208(FS):Jan83-81
Vorster, G. The Textures of Silence.
  S. Laschever, 441:8Jul84-20
Voslensky, M. Nomenklatura.
  C. Gati, 441:9Sep84-31
Voss, P. and others. Die Freizeit der Jugend.
  L. Bisky, 654(WB):1/1983-185
Vosters, S.A. Los Países Bajos en la literatura española.* (Pt 1)
  C. Stern, 545(RPh):Feb83-487

Vouga, D. Nerval et ses Chimères.
  N. Rinsler, 208(FS):Oct83-474
Vovelle, M. The Fall of the French Mon-
  archy.
  W. Scott, 617(TLS):3Aug84-873
Vovelle, M. La Mort et l'Occident de 1300
  à nos jours.
  E. Weber, 617(TLS):20Jul84-802
Voyles, J.B. Gothic, Germanic, and North-
  west Germanic.*
  J.W. Marchand, 133:Band16Heft2/3-219
  N. Wagner, 684(ZDA):Band112Heft1-1
Vranich, S.B. Ensayos sevillanos del
  Siglo de Oro.
  W.C. Bryant, 240(HR):Summer83-321
Vreeland, D. D.V. (G. Plimpton and C.
  Hemphill, eds)
  P-L. Adams, 61:Jul84-116
  C. Curtis, 441:17Jun84-13
  C. Hitchens, 617(TLS):21Dec84-1482
  J. Lieberson, 453(NYRB):28Jun84-15
  442(NY):23Jul84-108
Vroom, N.R.A. A Modest Message as Intim-
  ated by the Painters of the "Monochrome
  Banketje."
  E. Young, 39:Mar83-261
Vucinich, A. Empire of Knowledge.
  L. Graham, 617(TLS):2Nov84-1246
Vucinich, W.S., ed. At the Brink of War
  and Peace.
  639(VQR):Autumn83-120
Vucinich, W.S., ed. The First Serbian
  Uprising, 1804-1813.
  639(VQR):Summer83-82
Vynnychenko, V. Shchodennyk: 1911-20.
  (Vol 1) (H. Kostiuk, ed)
  G.S.N. Luckyj, 104(CASS):Winter83-564

"The WPA Guide to Florida." "The WPA
  Guide to California."
  E. Newman, 441:3Jun84-12
Wachhorst, W. Thomas Alva Edison.
  D.E.E. Sloane, 579(SAQ):Winter83-100
Wachtel, C. Joe the Engineer.*
  42(AR):Spring83-249
Wachtel, P.L. The Poverty of Affluence.
  H. Goodman, 441:22Jan84-23
  442(NY):27Feb84-134
Wackernagel, M. The World of the Floren-
  tine Renaissance Artist.
  F. Ames-Lewis, 161(DUJ):Jun83-109
  C. Lloyd, 278(IS):Vol138-96
  D. Norman, 59:Jun83-223
  J.T. Paoletti, 589:Jul83-835
  R. Starn, 54:Jun83-329
Wacziarg, F. and A. Nath. Rajasthan: The
  Painted Walls of Shekhavati.*
  A. Topsfield, 90:Oct83-630
Wada, Y., M.K. Rice and J. Barton.
  Shibori.
  R. Granich, 139:Oct/Nov83-21
Waddell, H. - see "The Desert Fathers"
Waddington, M. Summer at Lonely Beach and
  Other Stories.
  A. Brooks, 102(CanL):Autumn83-62
  D. Martens, 526:Winter83-67
Waddington, M. The Visitants.
  C. Rooke, 102(CanL):Winter82-116
Waddington, P. Turgenev and England.*
  A.D.P. Briggs, 637(VS):Autumn82-101
  A.V. Knowles, 447(N&Q):Oct82-460

Waddington, P. Turgenev and George Sand.*
  A.V. Knowles, 447(N&Q):Oct82-460
Waddy, C. The Muslim Mind. (2nd ed)
  S. Kazim, 273(IC):Oct83-309
Wade, E. and others. As in a Vision.
  R.L. Shep, 614:Winter84-16
Wade, G. Segovia.
  M. Criswick, 415:Aug83-486
Wädekin, K-E., ed. Current Trends in the
  Soviet and East European Food Economy.
  R.E.F. Smith, 575(SEER):Jul83-473
de Waelens, A. and others. Etudes
  d'anthropologie philosophique.
  J. Lefranc, 192(EP):Jan-Mar83-115
de Waelhens, A. Le Duc de Saint-Simon,
  immuable comme Dieu et d'une suite en-
  ragée.*
  J. Dubu, 535(RHL):Jul/Aug83-634
Waelti-Walters, J. Icare ou l'évasion
  impossible.
  M. Eigeldinger, 535(RHL):Sep/Dec83-972
  S. Smith, 207(FR):Oct83-116
van der Waerden, B.L. Die gemeinsame
  Quelle der erkenntnistheoretischen
  Abhandlungen von Iamblichos und Proklos.
  A. Sheppard, 123:Vol33No1-142
Wagar, W.W. Terminal Visions.*
  G. Beauchamp, 385(MQR):Spring84-299
  H.H. Watts, 395(MFS):Summer83-367
Wagenknecht, C. Deutsche Metrik.*
  L.L. Albertsen, 301(JEGP):Jan83-96
  S.S. Prawer, 402(MLR):Apr83-479
Wagenknecht, E. Eve and Henry James.
  R.K. Martin, 106:Winter83-457
Wagenknecht, E. Henry David Thoreau.*
  R. Wilson, 77:Spring83-181
  T. Woodson, 651(WHR):Spring83-69
Wagenvoort, H. Pietas.
  M. Beard, 313:Vol73-215
Wagg, S. Percy Erskine Nobbs Architecte,
  Artiste, Artisan/Architect, Artist,
  Craftsman.
  A.M. de Fort-Menares, 627(UTQ):
    Summer83-552
Wagle, N.K., ed. Images of Maharashtra.
  F.F. Conlon, 293(JASt):Nov82-207
Wagner, C. and S. Marquez. Cooking Texas
  Style.
  L. Milazzo, 584(SWR):Spring83-vi
Wagner, F. Rudolf Borchardt and the
  Middle Ages.
  J-U. Fechner, 52:Band18Heft3-334
Wagner, H-P. Puritan Attitudes Towards
  Physical Recreation in Early Seventeenth-
  Century New England.
  K.Z. Derounian, 568(SCN):Fall83-44
Wagner, H.R. Alfred Schutz.
  Z. Bauman, 617(TLS):1Jun84-621
Wagner, H.R. and C.L. Camp. The Plains
  and the Rockies. (4th ed) (R.H. Becker,
  ed)
  M.D. Heaston, 517(PBSA):Vol77No2-234
  L.S. Thompson, 70:Mar-Apr82-125
Wagner, K. Herr und Knecht.*
  G.C. Avery, 406:Winter83-448
  D. Borchmeyer, 224(GRM):Band33Heft3-
    356
  R.E. Lorbe, 221(GQ):Nov83-693
Wagner, L.W. Ellen Glasgow.*
  M.T. Inge, 27(AL):Dec83-658
  W.J. Stuckey, 395(MFS):Summer83-334
  295(JML):Nov83-485

Wagner, R. My Life.* (M. Whittall, ed)
P. Gay, 617(TLS):27Jan84-91
Wagner, R. Three Wagner Essays.* (R.L.
Jacobs, trans)
R.D.A., 412:Aug-Nov82-272
Wagner, R-L. Essais de linguistique fran-
çaise.*
K. Hunnius, 547(RF):Band95Heft1/2-142
Wagner-Rieger, R. and M. Reissberger.
Theophil von Hansen.
S. Muthesius, 576:Mar83-80
Wagoner, D. First Light.
J.D. McClatchy, 441:22Jan84-12
Wah, F. Loki is Buried at Smoky Creek.
(G. Bowering, ed)
G. Boire, 102(CanL):Summer83-166
Wahba, M., ed. Centenary Essays on George
Eliot.
F. Bolton, 189(EA):Jul-Sep84-342
Wahsner, R. Das Aktive und das Passive.
K. Gloy, 342:Band74Heft3-361
Waidson, H.M., ed. Anthology of Modern
Swiss Literature.
M. Gsteiger, 617(TLS):7Dec84-1431
Wailes, S.L. Studien zur Kleindichtung
des Stricker.
E. Stutz, 684(ZDA):Band112Heft3-116
Wain, B. - see Allen, T.W.
Wain, J. Young Shoulders.
P. Craig, 617(TLS):9Mar84-259
Waine, A. Martin Walser.
J. Boening, 406:Spring83-88
Wainwright, A. After the War.
M. Thorpe, 102(CanL):Winter82-170
L. Welch, 198:Oct83-98
Wainwright, J. Cul-de-Sac.
N. Callendar, 441:15Jul84-27
Waismann, F. Lectures on the Philosophy
of Mathematics. (W. Grassl, ed)
M.E. Tiles, 518:Jul83-160
Waite, D. Art of the Solomon Islands.
J. Teilhet-Fisk, 2(AfrA):Aug83-82
Waith, E. - see Shakespeare, W.
Wajsberg, M. Logical Works. (S.J. Surma,
ed)
S. McCall, 316:Sep83-873
Wakefield, H. Nineteenth Century British
Glass.
G. Wills, 39:May83-414
Wakefield, T. Mates.
J. Melmoth, 617(TLS):6Jan84-19
Walaskay, P.W. "And So We Came to Rome."
J.L. Houlden, 617(TLS):20Apr84-441
Walbank, F.W. The Hellenistic World.
D.S. Potter, 123:Vol33No2-347
Walbank, F.W. A Historical Commentary on
Polybius. (Vol 3)
G. Schepens, 394:Vol36fasc1/2-198
Walcott, D. The Fortunate Traveller.*
T. Eagleton, 565:Vol24No1-68
B. Howard, 502(PrS):Spring83-93
Walcott, D. Midsummer.
T. Eagleton, 617(TLS):9Nov84-1290
R.W. Flint, 441:8Apr84-14
Wald, A.M. The Revolutionary Imagination.*
L. Lane, Jr., 150(DR):Winter83/84-691
Waldenfels, H. Absolute Nothingness.
D.W. Mitchell, 485(PE&W):Jul83-305
Walder, D. Dickens and Religion.*
J. Halperin, 125:Winter83-190
L. Lerner, 184(EIC):Jan83-61
S. Monod, 189(EA):Jan-Mar83-90
G.J. Worth, 301(JEGP):Oct83-570

Waldman, A. Makeup on Empty Space.
P. Hampl, 441:25Nov84-36
Waley, D. George Eliot's Blotter.*
F.B., 189(EA):Apr-Jun84-236
Waley, P. - see "Curial and Guelfa"
Walker, A. An Account of a Voyage to the
North West Coast of America in 1785 and
1786 by Alexander Walker. (R. Fisher
and J.M. Bumstead, eds)
D. Gutteridge, 99:Apr83-31
Walker, A. The Color Purple.
M.R. Farwell, 448:Vol21No1-167
A. Gussow, 114(ChiR):Summer83-124
E.B. Kelley, 95(CLAJ):Sep83-91
M.K. Mootry-Ikerionwu, 95(CLAJ):Mar84-
345
Walker, A. Dietrich.
P. O'Connor, 617(TLS):28Dec84-1507
Walker, A. In Search of Our Mother's
Gardens.*
M.K. Benet, 617(TLS):20Jul84-818
B. Brown, 95(CLAJ):Mar84-348
J. Parini, 434:Summer84-630
Walker, A. Franz Liszt.* (Vol 1)
C. Rosen, 453(NYRB):12Apr84-17
Walker, A. - see Roberts, R.
Walker, A.G.H. Die nordfriesische Mundart
der Bökingharde.*
H.J. Gernentz, 682(ZPSK):Band36Heft4-
492
Walker, B.G. The Woman's Encyclopedia of
Myths and Secrets.
P-L. Adams, 61:Feb84-105
J.I. Smith, 469:Vol9No4-108
Walker, D.C. Dictionnaire inverse de
l'ancien français.*
F.J. Hausmann, 547(RF):Band95Heft3-312
L. Löfstedt, 439(NM):1983/4-534
N.B. Smith, 589:Jul83-753
T.R. Wooldridge, 627(UTQ):Summer83-456
Walker, D.C. An Introduction to Old
French Morphophonology.*
T.R. Wooldridge, 627(UTQ):Summer83-456
Walker, D.D. Clio's Cowboys.*
E.R. Bingham, 649(WAL):May83-64
Walker, D.H. - see Genet, J.
Walker, E., ed. Explorations in the Biol-
ogy of Language.
H.W. Buckingham, Jr., 474(PIL):Vol 15
No1/4-275
Walker, G., ed. Resources for Soviet,
East European and Slavonic Studies in
British Libraries.
W.F. Ryan, 575(SEER):Apr83-317
Walker, J. - see Cunninghame Graham, R.B.
Walker, J.R. Lakota Belief and Ritual.
(R.J. De Mallie and E.A. Jahner, eds)
M.E. Melody, 292(JAF):Jan-Mar83-107
Walker, J.R. Lakota Myths. (E.A. Jahner,
ed)
J.E. Brown, 469:Vol9No2-99
Walker, J.W.S. A History of Blacks in
Canada.
W.N., 102(CanL):Winter82-175
Walker, K.S. - see under Sorley Walker, K.
Walker, M. Johann Jakob Moser and the
Holy Roman Empire of the German Nation.
W.R. Ward, 161(DUJ):Jun83-147
R. Wines, 377:Mar83-52
Walker, P.F. Moral Choices.
R.O. Curry and L.B. Goodheart,
106:Winter83-401

Walker, P.K. Engineers of Independence.
E.W. Carp, 656(WMQ):Apr83-327
Walker, R.C.S. Kant.
P. Milne, 84:Sep83-312
Walker, R.C.S., ed. Kant on Pure Reason.
N. Demé, 542:Jan-Mar83-127
D. Whewell, 83:Autumn83-197
Walker, R.M., ed. El Cavallero Plaçidas (MS. Esc. h-I-13).
C. González, 304(JHP):Fall83-70
Walker, S. and A. Burnett. The Image of Augustus.*
M.A.R. Colledge, 123:Vol33No2-366
Wall, C.C. George Washington.*
G. Bilson, 106:Spring83-61
Wall, J.N., Jr. - see Herbert, G.
Wallace, A.F.C. The Social Context of Innovation.
S. Bernstein, 42(AR):Spring83-246
Wallace, E. - see Williams, C.W.
Wallace, I. The Miracle.
S. Isaacs, 441:16Sep84-15
Wallace, M. and G.P. Gates. Close Encounters.
J. Kornbluth, 441:30Sep84-15
Wallace, R. and C. Zimmerman, eds. The Work.*
C. Innes, 108:Spring83-133
Wallace, R.K. Jane Austen and Mozart.
B. Brophy, 617(TLS):24Feb84-187
Wallace, W.A. Prelude to Galileo.
S.J. Livesey, 319:Oct84-474
E. McMullin, 486:Mar83-171
E. McMullin, 543:Mar83-738
Wallace-Hadrill, A. Suetonius.
D.J.R. Bruckner, 441:1Apr84-23
T.P. Wiseman, 617(TLS):27Jan84-88
Wallace-Hadrill, J.M. The Frankish Church.
K.F. Morrison, 617(TLS):25May84-572
Wallack, F.B. The Epochal Nature of Process in Whitehead's Metaphysics.
D.W.S., 543:Sep82-207
E. Wolf-Gazo, 53(AGP):Band65Heft2-218
Wallechinsky, D. The Complete Book of the Olympics.
E. Segal, 441:3Jun84-31
Waller, B. L'Ascenseur.
F.J. Greene, 207(FR):May84-918
Waller, G.F. Dreaming America.
G.F. Manning, 106:Summer83-225
Waller, M.R. Petrarch's Poetics and Literary History.*
T.O. Calhoun, 191(ELN):Dec83-49
Waller, R.J. The Dukeries Transformed.
S. Pollard, 617(TLS):13Apr84-411
Wallerstein, N. Language and Culture in Conflict.*
J. Valdes, 351(LL):Jun83-259
Wallis, R. The Elementary Forms of the New Religious Life.
B. Godlee, 617(TLS):1Jun84-619
Wallner, B., ed. The Middle English Translation of Guy de Chauliac's Treatise on Wounds.* (Pts 1 and 2)
K. Bitterling, 72:Band220Heft1-149
Wallop, D. The Other Side of the River.
M. Bell, 441:20May84-26
Wallot, H. Intermèdes, poésie et prose.
J. Viswanathan, 102(CanL):Autumn83-108
Wallrafen, C. Maksimilian Vološin als Künstler und Kritiker.
C. Marsh, 575(SEER):Oct83-603

Walpole, H. The Yale Edition of Horace Walpole's Correspondence.* (Vols 1-48) (W.S. Lewis, ed)
I. Ehrenpreis, 453(NYRB):26Apr84-19
Walpole, R.N. An Anonymous Old French Translation of the Pseudo-Turpin Chronicle.
P. Bourgain, 554:Vol 103No1-138
P.F. Dembowski, 545(RPh):Nov82-327
Walsdorf, J.J. William Morris in Private Press and Limited Edition.
D. McKitterick, 617(TLS):6Apr84-387
H.M. Pisanello, 70:May-Jun83-171
Walser, M. Runaway Horse.
P. Lewis, 565:Vol24No3-36
Walser, R. Maler, Poet und Dame. (D. Keel, ed) Romane und Erzählungen.
S.S. Prawer, 617(TLS):7Dec84-1429
Walser, R. Selected Stories.*
M. Hulse, 364:Apr/May83-143
Walsh, D. Seasonal Bravery.
R. Hatch, 102(CanL):Winter82-144
Walsh, D. and A. Poole, eds. A Dictionary of Criminology.
S. McConville, 617(TLS):27Jan84-89
Walsh, G.B. The Varieties of Enchantment.
R. Padel, 617(TLS):10Aug84-886
Walsh, J. American War Literature, 1914 to Vietnam.*
E. Solomon, 27(AL):Mar83-120
Walsh, K. A Fourteenth-Century Scholar and Primate.
P.R. Szittya, 589:Jan83-249
Walsh, M. - see Gay, J.
Walsh, M. and K. Williamson - see Smart, C.
Walsh, P.G. - see Livy
Walsh, R. The Mycroft Memoranda.
T.J. Binyon, 617(TLS):16Mar84-270
Walsh, W. Introduction to Keats.
G. Woodcock, 569(SR):Fall83-664
Walsh, W. F.R. Leavis.*
G. Singh, 396(ModA):Winter83-105
Walsh, W. R.K. Narayan.*
C. vanden Driesen, 268(IFR):Winter84-60
S.F.D. Hughes, 395(MFS):Winter83-821
Walter, H. La dynamique des phonèmes dans le lexique français contemporain.*
N.L. Corbett, 545(RPh):Aug82-66
Walter, H. Enquête phonologique et variétés régionales du français.
W.J. Ashby, 350:Mar84-185
J. Kramer, 547(RF):Band95Heft3-318
Walter, J.A. The Human Home.
T.J. Diffey, 89(BJA):Summer83-272
Walters, J. Crochet Workshop.
A.L. Mayer, 614:Fall84-14
Walters, T.N. Randolph Silliman Bourne.
J.L. Jarrett, 651(WHR):Winter83-370
Walters, W. and P. Singer. Test-Tube Babies.
J.L. Thompson, 63:Jun83-223
P.S.W., 185:Apr84-571
Walther, E. Modernes Wallfahrtswesen in Westirland am Beispiel von sechs Dörfern der Grafschaften Galway und Mayo.
E. Ettlinger, 203:Vol94No1-127
Walther, F.R. Communication and Expression in Hoofed Mammals.
I. Gordon, 617(TLS):29Jun84-738
Walton, I. Compleat Angler.* (J. Bevan, ed)
M. Dodsworth, 175:Summer83-194

Watt, G. The Fallen Woman in the 19th-
Century English Novel.
　K. Flint, 617(TLS):27Apr84-472
Watt, J., E.J. Freeman and W.F. Bynum, eds.
Starving Sailors.
　P-G. Boucé, 189(EA):Jan-Mar84-81
Watt, W.S. - see Cicero
Wattenberg, B.J. The Good News Is the Bad
News Is Wrong.
　A. Hacker, 441:28Oct84-14
Wattenberg, M.P. The Decline of American
Political Parties 1952-1980.
　H.G. Nicholas, 617(TLS):19Oct84-1177
　W. Schneider, 441:13May84-24
Watters, D.H. "With Bodilie Eyes."*
　J.F. Maclear, 656(WMQ):Jul83-469
Watters, J. and Horst. Return Engagement.
　J. Maslin, 441:16Dec84-26
Watts, C. The Deceptive Text.
　E.W. Said, 617(TLS):12Oct84-1149
Watts, C. A Preface to Conrad.
　J. Lothe, 136:Vol 15No3-237
Watts, C. and L. Davies. Cunninghame
Graham.
　C.J. Rawson, 402(MLR):Oct83-913
Watts, D.A. Cardinal de Retz.*
　P.J. Klemp, 568(SCN):Fall83-53
Watts, E.S. The Businessman in American
Literature.*
　J.W. Halpern, 395(MFS):Winter83-752
　S. Pinsker, 219(GaR):Fall83-697
Watts, G.S. The Revolution of Ideas.
　P. Helm, 518:Oct83-255
　483:Oct83-560
Waugh, C.G. and M.H. Greenberg - see Wool-
rich, C.
Waugh, E. Essays, Articles and Reviews.
(D. Gallagher, ed)
　J. Barnes, 617(TLS):3Feb84-113
　A. Bell, 441:14Oct84-11
　D.J. Enright, 362:2Feb84-23
Waugh, E. The Letters of Evelyn Waugh.*
(M. Amory, ed)
　M. Rosenthal, 473(PR):2/1983-297
　J. Russell, 396(ModA):Spring83-203
　B. Stovel, 49:Jul83-60
Waugh, E. Waugh in Abyssinia.
　J. Bayley, 617(TLS):5Oct84-1111
Waugh, H. Kate's House.*
　M. Wexler, 441:9Sep84-30
　442(NY):10Dec84-190
Waugh, L.R. A Semantic Analysis of Word
Order.
　M. Forsgren, 597(SN):Vol55No2-222
Waugh, L.R. and C.H. van Schooneveld, eds.
The Melody of Language.
　S.D. Isard, 353:Vol20No7/8-565
Waugh, T. Painting Water.
　J. Grant, 617(TLS):27Jan84-93
　K.C. O'Brien, 362:22Mar84-25
Wawrytko, S. The Undercurrent of Feminine
Philosophy in Eastern and Western
Thought.
　S-C. Huang, 485(PE&W):Apr83-199
Way, B. F. Scott Fitzgerald and the Art
of Social Fiction.*
　P. Messent, 541(RES):Feb83-104
Wayman, T. Inside Job.
　S. Delany, 99:Nov83-37
Wayman, T. The Nobel Prize Acceptance
Speech.
　P.K. Smith, 102(CanL):Summer83-138
　B. Whiteman, 198:Jan83-122

"We Believe."
　R. Incledon, 617(TLS):21Sep84-1052
Weale, A. Political Theory and Social
Policy.
　P. Willmott, 617(TLS):6Jan84-22
Wearing, J.P. American and British Theat-
rical Biography.*
　S. Billington, 610:Spring82-152
Wearing, J.P. The London Stage 1900-1909.*
　T.R. Griffiths, 611(TN):Vol137No3-141
　C.M. Mazer, 615(TJ):Mar83-136
Wearing, J.P. The London Stage, 1910-
1919.*
　K. Beckson, 365:Summer/Fall83-122
Weatherford, R. Philosophical Foundations
of Probability Theory.
　J.H. Fetzer, 518:Jul83-165
　S.W., 185:Jan84-366
Weatherhead, A.K. The British Dissonance.
　L. McDiarmid, 134(CP):Fall83-76
Weaver, L., ed. Small Country Houses of
Today.
　P. Davey, 46:Sep83-68
Weaver, R., ed. Small Wonders.
　P. Nightingale, 102(CanL):Summer83-146
　E. Tretheway, 526:Winter83-63
Weaver, W. Duse.
　R. Lewis, 441:30Sep84-13
　J. Russell, 453(NYRB):11Oct84-41
Weaver, W. and M. Chusid, eds. The Verdi
Companion.
　D. Rosen, 415:Jun83-353
Webb, B. All the good things of life.
　I. Thomson, 364:Nov83-106
Webb, B. The Diary of Beatrice Webb.
(Vol 1) (N. and J. MacKenzie, eds)
　639(VQR):Winter83-10
Webb, B. The Diary of Beatrice Webb.*
(Vol 2) (N. and J. MacKenzie, eds)
　R. Clark, 441:29Jan84-14
　J. Harris, 617(TLS):9Mar84-238
　442(NY):23Apr84-133
Webb, B. The Diary of Beatrice Webb.
(Vol 3) (N. and J. MacKenzie, eds)
　M. Warnock, 362:18Oct84-27
Webb, E. Eric Voegelin.
　G. Niemeyer, 396(ModA):Winter83-83
　D.H. Porter, 125:Spring83-285
Webb, I. From Custom to Capital.*
　P. Keating, 637(VS):Summer83-468
Webb, J.C. Mechanism, Mentalism, and Meta-
mathematics.*
　C.S. Hill, 482(PhR):Apr83-276
Webb, M.G. Darling Corey's Dead.
　N. Callendar, 441:22Jul84-32
Webb, P. Wilson's Bowl.*
　A. Mandel, 168(ECW):Summer83-85
Webb, R.C. and S.A. Jean Genet and His
Critics.
　J.L. Savona, 610:Autumn83-268
　H.E. Stewart, 207(FR):May84-887
Webb, S.S. The Governors-General.*
　L.R. Fischer, 106:Fall83-279
　P. Haffenden, 161(DUJ):Dec82-95
Webb, S.S. 1676.
　W.S. McFeely, 441:24Jun84-13
Webb, T., ed. English Romantic Hellenism,
1700-1824.*
　J. Raimond, 189(EA):Jul-Sep84-335
　P. Wheatley, 175:Summer83-176
Webb, W.L., ed. The Bedside "Guardian" 33.
　N. Berry, 617(TLS):28Dec84-1505

Weber, B.N. and H. Heinen, eds. Bertolt Brecht.*
  S.L. Cocalis, 221(GQ):Mar83-340
  J.K. Lyon, 130:Fall83-284
Weber, D.J. The Mexican Frontier, 1821-1846.
  F. Downs, 584(SWR):Winter83-94
Weber, D.J., ed. Troubles in Texas, 1832.
  L. Milazzo, 584(SWR):Summer83-vi
Weber, E. and C. Mithal. Deutsche Originalromane zwischen 1680 und 1780.
  G. Dünnhaupt, 680(ZDP):Band102Heft4-605
Weber, H. Einzug ins Paradies.
  M. Hähnel, 654(WB):4/1982-125
Weber, H. Kleine generative Syntax des Deutschen. (Vol 1)
  G. Van der Elst, 685(ZDL):1/1983-114
Weber, P. and others. Kunstperiode.
  W. Beyer, 654(WB):3/1983-545
Weber, S. The Legend of Freud.
  R. Blood, 400(MLN):Dec83-1327
  J.M. Todd, 478:Oct83-274
Weber, V. Form and Funktion von Sprachspielen.
  W. Helmich, 547(RF):Band95Heft3-383
Webster, B.S. Blake's Prophetic Psychology.
  P. Hamilton, 617(TLS):15Jun84-674
Webster, C., ed. Biology, Medicine and Society: 1840-1940.
  J. Woodward, 637(VS):Summer83-462
Webster, C., ed. Utopian Planning and the Puritan Revolution.
  J. Morrill, 541(RES):Aug83-336
Webster, G. The Republic of Letters.*
  506(PSt):Dec83-311
Webster, J. El Diablo Blanco.
  J. Fernández Jiménez, 552(REH):Oct83-450
Webster, P. and N. Powell. Saint-Germain-des-Prés.
  P. McCarthy, 617(TLS):23Nov84-1334
Wechsler, J. A Human Comedy.
  A.A. McLees, 207(FR):Dec83-286
Wechsler, L. Solidarity.
  A.R. Dadlez, 497(PolR):Vol28No1-108
Weckherlin, G.R. Stuttgarter Hoffeste.*
  Essais van Hulsen/Matthäus Merian.* (L. Krapf and C. Wagenknecht, eds of both)
  M.R. Sperberg-McQueen, 400(MLN):Apr83-524
Wedberg, A. A History of Philosophy. (Vol 3)
  A. Quinton, 617(TLS):8Jun84-641
Wedde, I. Castaly.
  J. Saunders, 565:Vol24No1-73
von Wedel-Wolff, A. Geschichte der Sammlung und Erforschung des deutschsprachigen Volkskinderliedes und Volkskinderreimes im 19. Jahrhundert.
  R. Wehse, 196:Band24Heft3/4-338
"Weegee's New York."
  A. Quindlen, 441:4Nov84-24
  442(NY):3Sep84-97
Weeks, A. The Paradox of the Employee.
  C. Bedwell, 395(MFS):Summer83-376
Weeks, J. Sex, Politics and Society.
  A. McLaren, 637(VS):Winter83-234
  L. Nead, 59:Jun83-227
Wegmann, B. Ocho Mundos. (2nd ed)
  H.G. Tuttle, 399(MLJ):Autumn83-313

Wegner, B. Hitlers Politische Soldaten.
  C.W. Sydnor, 617(TLS):3Feb84-120
Wehle, P. Le Théâtre populaire selon Jean Vilar.
  B.L. Knapp, 615(TJ):Oct82-412
Wehle, W., ed. Nouveau roman.*
  B. Burmeister, 654(WB):5/1982-187
  W. Hollerbach, 72:Band220Heft2-460
  M. Kesting, 547(RF):Band95Heft1/2-213
Wehle, W. Novellenerzählen.*
  O. Millet, 535(RHL):Jan/Feb83-117
Wehlte, K. The Materials and Techniques of Painting.
  J. Burr, 39:Feb83-147
Wehner, W. Weberelend und Weberaufstände in der deutschen Lyrik des 19. Jahrhunderts.
  R.C. Cowen, 406:Winter83-434
Wehnert, W. Heinrich Heine: "Die schlesischen Weber" und andere Texte zum Weberelend.
  A. Sandor, 221(GQ):Mar83-324
Wehrli, M. Geschichte der deutschen Literatur von den Anfängen bis zur Gegenwart.* (Vol 1: Geschichte der deutschen Literatur vom frühen Mittelalter bis zum Ende des 16. Jahrhunderts.)
  K.A. Zaenker, 564:Feb83-57
Wehse, R. Schwanklied und Flugblatt in Grossbritannien.*
  R. Grambo, 64(Arv):Vol137-192
Wei, W. - see under Wang Wei
Weidenfeld, W. Die Identität der Deutschen.
  R. Morgan, 617(TLS):5Oct84-1114
Weidert, A. Tonologie.
  D.L. Goyvaerts, 361:Sep83-47
Weiers, M. Linguistische Feldforschung.
  E. Ternes, 685(ZDL):1/1983-84
Weigand, E. Die Zuordnung von Ausdruck und Inhalt bei den grammatischen Kategorien des Deutschen.
  U. Schwartz, 260(IF):Band87-356
Weigel, S. Flugschriftenliteratur 1848 in Berlin.*
  S.R. Merrill, 221(GQ):May83-513
  A. Wetterer, 406:Summer83-222
Weigelt, K., ed. Heimat und Identität der Deutschen.
  R. Morgan, 617(TLS):5Oct84-1114
Weiger, J. - see de Castro, G.
Weiger, J.G. The Individuated Self.*
  P.E. Russell, 447(N&Q):Dec82-545
Weigl, E. Aufklärung und Skeptizismus.
  W. Koepke, 221(GQ):Nov83-657
Weigle, M. and K. Fiore. Santa Fe and Taos.*
  R. Gish, 649(WAL):Aug83-185
Weigle, M., with C. and S. Larcombe, eds. Hispanic Arts and Ethnohistory in the Southwest.
  L. Milazzo, 584(SWR):Summer83-vi
Weigley, R.F., ed. Philadelphia.
  S.B. Warner, 617(TLS):29Jun84-734
van der Weijden, G. Indonesische Reisrituale.
  J.A. Boon and J.R. Eidson, 293(JASt):May83-730
Weijnen, A. Outlines for an Interlingual European Dialectology.
  A. Tovar, 685(ZDL):1/1983-80
Weil, A. Health and Healing.
  G. Weissmann, 441:29Jan84-23

Weil, R. - see Polybius
Weil-Garris, K. and J.F. D'Amico. The
Renaissance Cardinal's Ideal Palace.
P. Waddy, 576:Dec83-399
Weiler, I. Der Sport bei den Völkern der
alten Welt [together with] Ulf, C.
Sport bei den Naturvölkern.
R.L. Howland, 303(JoHS):Vol 103-198
Weimar, K. Enzyklopädie der Literaturwis-
senschaft.*
G. Mason, 406:Fall83-331
Weinberg, H.G. A Manhattan Odyssey.
J.A. Gallagher, 200:Mar83-188
de Weinberg, M.B.F. - see under Fontanella
de Weinberg, M.B.
Weinberger, C.W. Department of Defense
Annual Report to the Congress, Fiscal
Year 1985.
E. Rothschild, 453(NYRB):15Mar84-14
Weinberger, E. - see Paz, O.
Weinbrot, H.D. Alexander Pope and the
Traditions of Formal Verse Satire.*
P. Dixon, 83:Autumn83-225
D. Griffin, 401(MLQ):Jun83-210
W. Jackson, 141:Winter83-73
G. Laprevotte, 189(EA):Oct-Dec84-466
639(VQR):Spring83-43
Weiner, E.S.C., comp. The Oxford Guide to
English Usage.
D.A.N. Jones, 362:16Feb84-24
Weinreb, B. and C. Hibbert, eds. The
London Encyclopaedia.
V. Pearl, 617(TLS):6Apr84-378
Weinrich, H., ed. Positionen der Negativi-
tät.
H.A. Pausch, 107(CRCL):Sep83-401
Weinstein, A. Fictions of the Self: 1550-
1800.*
J. Harris, 402(MLR):Jul83-650
C. Koelb, 221(GQ):May83-488
P. Sabor, 529(QQ):Spring83-157
J. Sitter, 173(ECS):Winter83/84-189
Weinstein, D. and R.M. Bell. Saints and
Society.
C. Stancliffe, 617(TLS):24Aug84-955
Weinstein, E.A. Woodrow Wilson.*
J. Gilbert, 639(VQR):Winter83-167
Weinstein, F.B. and F. Kamiya, eds. The
Security of Korea.
B. Cumings, 293(JASt):Feb83-428
Weinstein, M.A. The Wilderness and the
City.
B. Kuklick, 619:Spring83-223
Weinstein, M.E., ed. Northeast Asian
Security After Vietnam.
S.C. Yang, 293(JASt):Aug83-896
Weintraub, P., ed. The Omni Interviews.
S. Boxer, 441:19Aug84-19
Weintraub, S., ed. Modern British Drama-
tists, 1900-1945.*
R.A. Cave, 610:Autumn83-267
Weintraub, S. The Unexpected Shaw.*
D. Leary, 572:Vol4-179
R. Nickson, 397(MD):Sep83-402
Weintraub, S. - see Shaw, G.B. and F.
Harris
Weinzierl, U. Er war Zeuge.
F. Achberger, 406:Winter83-419
Weinzierl, U. - see Polgar, A.
Weir, J.E. - see Baxter, J.K.
Weir, R.F. Selective Nontreatment of
Handicapped Newborns.
P. Singer, 441:30Sep84-14

Weisberg, D.B. Texts from the Time of
Nebuchadnezzar.
R.H. Sack, 318(JAOS):Oct-Dec82-664
Weisberg, G.P., ed. The European Realist
Tradition.
R. Ormond, 324:Sep84-700
Weisbrod, P. Literarischer Wandel in der
DDR.
M. Gerber, 221(GQ):May83-529
Weisgerber, J. L'espace romanesque.
H. Jechova, 549(RLC):Apr-Jun83-222
Weisman, R. Witchcraft, Magic, and Reli-
gion in 17th-Century Massachusetts.
M. Peters, 441:13May84-23
Weiss, E. and S. Freud. Lettres sur la
pratique psychanalytique.
J. Nobécourt, 98:Aug-Sep83-623
Weiss, N.J. Farewell to the Party of
Lincoln.*
C. Bolt, 617(TLS):25May84-592
Weiss, P. Privacy.
T.M.R., 185:Jul84-728
Weiss, R. and P. Geiger, eds. Atlas der
schweizerischen Volkskunde. (Pt 2,
section 8) (continued by W. Escher, E.
Liebl and A. Niederer)
R. Bauer, 72:Band219Heft2-413
Weiss, T. The Man from Porlock.*
R. Gibbons, 461:Spring/Summer83-107
Weiss, T. Recoveries.*
R. Gibbons, 461:Spring/Summer83-107
W. Harmon, 569(SR):Summer83-457
Weiss, W. Das Studium der englischen Lit-
eratur.
M. Brunkhorst, 38:Band101Heft3/4-548
Weissel, B., ed. Kultur und Ethnos.
U. Mohrmann, 654(WB):7/1982-187
Weissman, J. - see Carruth, H.
Weissman, N.B. Reform in Tsarist Russia.*
D.C.B. Lieven, 575(SEER):Apr83-288
Weissman, R.F.E. Ritual Brotherhood in
Renaissance Florence.
D. Bornstein, 539:May84-151
F. Gilbert, 589:Jul83-836
D. Weinstein, 551(RenQ):Spring83-81
Weitzmann, K., ed. Age of Spirituality.
D. Buckton, 39:Feb83-153
Weitzmann, K. Art in the Medieval West
and its Contacts with Byzantium.
A. Cutler, 589:Oct83-1141
Weitzmann, K. The Miniatures of the Sacra
Parallela: Parisinus Graecus 923.
A.W. Carr, 54:Mar83-147
Weitzmann, K. Studies in the Arts at
Sinai.
R. Cormack, 90:Nov83-696
Weixlmann, J. American Short-Fiction
Criticism and Scholarship, 1959-1977.
295(JML):Nov83-360
von Weizsäcker, R. Die Deutsche Geschich-
te geht Weiter.
R. Morgan, 617(TLS):5Oct84-1114
Welch, A.T. and P. Cachia, eds. Islam.
J.D. Latham, 294:Vol 14-85
Welch, C. The Art of Art Works.
L. Code, 154:Dec83-756
J. Zemans, 627(UTQ):Summer83-558
Welch, C.B. Liberty and Utility.
W. Scott, 617(TLS):3Aug84-873
Welch, D. The Journals. (M. De-la-Noy,
ed) I Left My Grandfather's House.
R. Blythe, 362:6Dec84-30
A. Hollinghurst, 617(TLS):21Dec84-1479

Welch, H. and A.K. Seidel, eds. Facets of Taoism.
V.B. Cass, 116:Jan82-91
Welch, L. Brush and Trunks.
M.T. Lane, 102(CanL):Winter82-154
Welch, R., ed. The Way Back.
T. Elderman, 305(JIL):May83-110
Welch, T.L., comp. Catálogo de la colección de la literatura chilena en la Biblioteca Colón.
A.E. Gropp, 263(RIB):Vol33No4-600
Weldon, F. Letters to Alice.
J. Motion, 617(TLS):6Jul84-763
Weldon, F. The Life and Loves of a She-Devil.
P. Craig, 617(TLS):20Jan84-70
R. Drexler, 441:30Sep84-1
J. Lasdun, 176:May84-63
Wellbank, J.H., D. Snook and D.T. Mason, eds. John Rawls and His Critics.
B. Barry, 185:Jan84-351
Wellek, R. The Attack on Literature and Other Essays.
T.R.H., 131(CL):Summer83-277
L.W. Hyman, 191(ELN):Jun84-72
A.R. Louch, 478:Apr83-99
639(VQR):Winter83-16
Wellek, R. Four Critics.*
W.W. Holdheim, 52:Band18Heft2-191
W. Martin, 131(CL):Summer83-276
C. Norris, 402(MLR):Jul83-634
Weller, J. History of the Farmstead.
D. Pearce, 324:Jan84-135
Welliver, W. Dante in Hell.
S. Noakes, 589:Apr83-540
Wellman, C. Welfare Rights.
L.M., 185:Jan84-377
A.R. White, 518:Oct83-243
Wells, B.W.P. Body and Personality.
B.A. Farrell, 176:Nov84-60
Wells, D.A. The Literary Index to American Magazines, 1815-1865.
517(PBSA):Oct-Dec80-420
Wells, E.H. Magnificence and Misery. (R.M. Dodd, ed)
P-L. Adams, 61:Aug84-112
Wells, H.G. Experiment in Autobiography.
J. Atlas, 61:Nov84-138
442(NY):17Dec84-157
Wells, H.G. H.G. Wells in Love. (G.P. Wells, ed)
J. Atlas, 61:Nov84-138
P. Kemp, 362:4Oct84-27
P. Larkin, 617(TLS):28Sep84-1075
442(NY):17Dec84-157
Wells, J. Fifty Glorious Years.
R. Boston, 617(TLS):21Dec84-1482
Wells, J.C. Accents of English.
G. Knowles, 297(JL):Sep83-502
R.I. McDavid, Jr., 300:Mar83-88
H. Rogers, 320(CJL):Fall83-199
Wells, R.V. Revolutions in Americans' Lives.
E. Shorter, 656(WMQ):Oct83-626
Wells, S. Modernizing Shakespeare's Spelling [together with] Taylor, G. Three Studies in the Text of "Henry V."*
P. Werstine, 702:Vol 16-382
G.W. Williams, 677(YES):Vol 13-307
Wells, S. - see "Shakespeare Survey"
Welsby, P.A. A History of the Church of England 1945-1980.
D. Martin, 617(TLS):1Jun84-619

Welsch, R.L., ed. Mister, You Got Yourself a Horse.*
G.E. Evans, 203:Vo194No2-266
K.I. Periman, 650(WF):Apr83-154
Welsh, A., ed. Narrative Endings.
J. Preston, 402(MLR):Apr83-389
Welsh, A. Reflections on the Hero as Quixote.*
J.J. Allen, 400(MLN):Mar83-299
J. Harris, 402(MLR):Jul83-650
A. Morvan, 189(EA):Apr-Sep83-322
Welty, E. The Collected Stories of Eudora Welty.*
R. Drake, 396(ModA):Winter83-96
Welty, E. One Writer's Beginnings.
P-L. Adams, 61:Mar84-132
G. Core, 598(SoR):Autumn84-951
E. Homberger, 617(TLS):20Jul84-806
W. Maxwell, 442(NY):20Feb84-133
C.V. Woodward, 441:19Feb84-7
Welzig, W. and others - see Schnitzler, A.
Wen Fong, ed. The Great Bronze Age of China.
J. Rawson, 59:Jun83-217
Wendell, C. Alfred Bester.
P.A. McCarthy, 561(SFS):Mar83-112
Wendell, C. - see al-Bannā, Ḥ.
Wendorf, P. Leo Days.
L. Taylor, 617(TLS):27Jan84-93
Wendorf, R., ed. Articulate Images.
G. Reynolds, 617(TLS):25May84-578
Weng, W-G. and Y. Boda, eds. The Palace Museum, Peking.*
B. Gray, 39:Apr83-334
Wensinger, A.S. and C.C. Hoey - see Modersohn-Becker, P.
Wentzel, T.W. Die Zigeunersprache.
K. Kostov, 682(ZPSK):Band36Heft1-110
Wenzel, H., ed. Adelsherrschaft und Literatur.
D.H. Green, 402(MLR):Jan83-219
Wenzel, H. Höfische Geschichte.
D.H. Green, 402(MLR):Jan83-219
Wenzel, P. Der Lear-Kritik im 20. Jahrhundert.
D. Mehl, 72:Band220Heft1-163
Werenskiold, M. The Concept of Expressionism.
F. Spalding, 617(TLS):8Jun84-630
Wermser, R. Statistische Studien zur Entwicklung des englischen Wortschatzes.
C.V.J. Russ, 685(ZDL):3/1983-401
Werner, C.H. Paradoxical Resolutions.*
J.S. Bakerman, 27(AL):May83-277
S. Fogel, 395(MFS):Summer83-340
J.G. Watson, 329(JJQ):Winter84-189
Werner, D. Amazon Journey.
R. Murphy, 441:12Aug84-34
Werner, D. Bu Mu'yuk Jloktor.
N.A. McQuown, 269(IJAL):Jan83-108
Werner, G. Ripa's Iconologia.
E. McGrath, 59:Sep83-363
Werner, K.F., ed. L'histoire médévale et les ordinateurs.
S. Lusignan, 589:Oct83-1142
Werner, T. Formale Besonderheiten in metrischen Texten des Tocharischen.
R. Dietz, 260(IF):Band87-277
Werner-Jensen, K. Studien zur "Don-Giovanni"-Rezeption im 19. Jahrhundert (1800-1850).
J. Rushton, 410(M&L):Jul/Oct83-260

Wernham, R.B. After the Armada.
  G. Parker, 617(TLS):20Apr84-424
Wernli, A. Studien zum literarischen und
  musikalischen Werk Adriano Banchieris
  (1568-1634).
  C. Marvin, 308:Fall83-282
Wershoven, C. The Female Intruder in the
  Novels of Edith Wharton.
  W.J. Stuckey, 395(MFS):Winter83-722
Wertch, J.V. - see Luria, A.R.
Werth, P., ed. Conversation and Discourse.
  M. Toolan, 307:Oct83-73
Weschler, L. The Passion of Poland.
  J. Darnton, 441:29Apr84-9
Wescott, L. and P. Degen, eds. Wind and
  Sand.
  R. Witkin, 441:29Apr84-32
Wesley, J. The Works. (Vol 7) (F. Hilde-
  brandt, O.A. Beckerlegge and J. Dale,
  eds)
  R. Trickett, 617(TLS):21Dec84-1467
Wesley, M. The Camomile Lawn.
  M. Cantwell, 441:8Jul84-7
  J. Motion, 617(TLS):13Apr84-396
  K.C. O'Brien, 362:7Jun84-25
  442(NY):25Jun84-108
Wessell, L.P., Jr. Karl Marx, Romantic
  Irony, and the Proletariat.*
  M.T. Jones, 222(GR):Fall83-167
Wessell, L.P., Jr. The Philosophical Back-
  ground to Friedrich Schiller's Aesthet-
  ics of Living Form.
  H. Osborne, 89(BJA):Autumn83-362
Wessels, H-F. Lessings "Nathan der Weise."
  W. Albrecht, 654(WB):3/1983-563
Wesson, R., ed. U.S. Influence in Latin
  America in the 1980's.
  J. Child, 263(RIB):Vol33No1-50
West, A. Heritage.
  R. Dinnage, 617(TLS):20Apr84-422
  J. Gross, 441:6May84-7
  M. Wandor, 362:14Jun84-20
West, A. H.G. Wells.
  P-L. Adams, 61:Jun84-125
  B. Brophy, 453(NYRB):6Dec84-31
  J. Gross, 441:6May84-7
  P. Larkin, 617(TLS):28Sep84-1075
  V.S. Pritchett, 442(NY):30Jul84-84
  M. Wandor, 362:14Jun84-20
West, D. and T. Woodman, eds. Creative
  Imitation and Latin Literature.*
  A. Crabbe, 123:Vol33No1-48
West, F. Gilbert Murray.
  H. Corke, 362:3May84-23
  J.E. Powell, 617(TLS):27Apr84-468
West, G.D., comp. An Index of Proper
  Names in French Arthurian Prose Romances.
  E. Kennedy, 545(RPh):Nov82-329
West, J.L.W. 3d and others - see Dreiser,
  T.
West, M. The World Is Made of Glass.*
  D.T. Turner, 405(MP):Feb83-336
  639(VQR):Autumn83-126
West, M.L. Greek Meter.
  P. Monteil, 555:Vol57fasc2-299
  639(VQR):Autumn83-118
West, M.L. The Orphic Poems.
  D.J.R. Bruckner, 441:16Sep84-31
  G.L. Huxley, 617(TLS):25May84-597
West, N. Unreliable Witness.
  A.J. Ayer, 362:11Oct84-27
West, R. This Real Night.
  P. Craig, 617(TLS):23Nov84-1330

West, R.J. Eugenio Montale.
  L.T. Perry, 580(SCR):Spring84-146
Westbrook, W.W. Wall Street in the Ameri-
  can Novel.*
  H. Tulloch, 366:Spring83-126
Westen, K., B. Meissner and F-C. Schro-
  der, eds. Der Schutz individueller
  Rechte und Interessen im Recht sozialis-
  tischer Staaten.
  W.E. Butler, 575(SEER):Apr83-317
Westendorf, W., ed. Aspekte der spätägyp-
  tischen Religion.
  K.A. Kitchen, 318(JAOS):Apr-Jun82-389
Westerink, L.G. - see Nicholas I, Patri-
  arch of Constantinople
Western, J. Outcast Cape Town.
  M. Pigott, 69:Vol53No4-97
von Westernhagen, C. Wagner.
  R.L.J., 412:May82-147
Westin, A. Newswatch.*
  639(VQR):Summer83-94
Westlake, D.E. A Likely Story.
  M. Stasio, 441:2Dec84-69
Westman, R. - see Cicero
Weston, P. The Clarinettist's Companion.
  N. O'Loughlin, 415:Jun83-363
Westwater, M. The Wilson Sisters.
  G. Avery, 617(TLS):10Aug84-888
  J. Grigg, 362:23Aug84-26
Westwood, J.N. Endurance and Endeavour.
  (2nd ed)
  N.V. Riasanovsky, 550(RusR):Jan83-106
Wetherill, P.M., ed. Flaubert: la dimen-
  sion du texte.
  A. Fairlie, 208(FS):Jan83-93
  T.A. Unwin, 402(MLR):Jan83-190
Wetsel, D. L'Ecriture et le reste.*
  B. Norman, 475:Vol 10No18-421
Wettengel, M. Der Streit um die Vogtei
  Kelkheim 1275-1276.
  K. Pennington, 589:Jul83-856
Wetterau, B. Concise Dictionary of World
  History.
  R. Foster, 617(TLS):6Apr84-382
Wetterer, A. Publikumsbezug und Wahrheits-
  anspruch.
  R.R. Heitner, 133:Band16Heft2/3-234
Wetzel, C-D. Die Worttrennung am Zeilen-
  ende in altenglischen Handschriften.
  A. Bammesberger, 38:Band101Heft3/4-500
  C. Sisam, 382(MAE):1983/2-313
Wexler, A. Emma Goldman.
  C. Gilligan, 441:4Nov84-28
Wexler, J.P. Laura Riding's Pursuit of
  Truth.*
  E. Longley, 447(N&Q):Jun82-268
  R.D. Sell, 541(RES):Feb83-105
Wexler, K. and P.W. Culicover. Formal
  Principles of Language Acquisition.
  M. Atkinson, 307:Oct83-76
Wey, J.C. - see Ockham, William of
de Weydenthal, J.B., B.D. Porter and K.
  Devlin. The Polish Drama: 1980-1982.
  A. Brumberg, 617(TLS):21Sep84-1047
Weydt, H., ed. Die Partikeln der deut-
  schen Sprache.*
  L.M. Eichinger, 406:Summer83-198
Weydt, H., ed. Partikeln und Deutschunter-
  richt.
  R.C. Helt, 399(MLJ):Spring83-77
Weyl, H. Symmetry.
  P. Tabor, 46:Jun83-58

White, J.B. When Words Lose Their Meaning.
  L. Bersani, 441:16Sep84-32
White, L. For Capital Stedman.
  M. Hulse, 617(TLS):12Oct84-1169
White, L. Grammatical Theory and Language
  Acquisition.
  J.D. McCawley, 350:Jun84-431
White, M. What Is and What Ought to Be
  Done.*
  L.C. Becker, 543:Jun83-954
  D.M. Hausman, 311(JP):May83-312
  D-H. Ruben, 393(Mind):Oct83-631
White, P. Beyond Domination.
  G. Sampson, 617(TLS):11May84-533
White, P. Benjamin Tompson, Colonial
  Bard.
  R.A. Bosco, 165(EAL):Spring84-92
White, R.A. The Morass.
  C. Dickey, 453(NYRB):14Jun84-25
White, R.S. Shakespeare and the Romance
  Ending.
  K. Smidt, 179(ES):Apr83-190
White, S. De Gaulle.
  S. Jacobson, 362:22Nov84-29
White, S. Sam White's Paris.
  C. Hargrove, 617(TLS):10Feb84-148
White, T. Bleeding Hearts.
  N. Callendar, 441:2Sep84-12
White, T.H. A Joy Proposed.
  639(VQR):Summer83-97
White, T.H. T.H. White, Letters to a
  Friend. (F. Gallix, ed)
  T. Shippey, 617(TLS):19Oct84-1186
  T.O. Treadwell, 189(EA):Oct-Dec84-477
White, W. - see Carter, J. and J. Sparrow
"White Crochet Lace."
  P. Bach, 614:Winter84-24
Whitelaw, W. and others. Home Office 1782-
  1982.
  H. Parris, 637(VS):Summer83-456
Whitelock, D., M. Brett and C.N.L. Brooke,
  eds. Councils and Synods. (Vol 1)
  B.F. Harvey, 382(MAE):1983/2-351
Whitelock, D., R. McKitterick and D. Dum-
  ville, eds. Ireland in Early Medieval
  Europe.
  L. Nees, 589:Oct83-1102
Whiteman, B. The Thera Poems.
  A. Haberer, 189(EA):Jul-Sep84-349
Whitford, F. Japanese Prints and Western
  Painters.
  H. Adams, 54:Sep83-495
Whitford, M. Merleau-Ponty's Critique of
  Sartre's Philosophy.
  C. Howells, 323:May83-205
Whiting, A.S. Siberian Development and
  East Asia.*
  S-E. Koo, 293(JASt):Nov82-156
Whiting, C. Ardennes.
  M. Carver, 617(TLS):28Dec84-1496
Whiting, R.C. The View From Cowley.
  R.J. Overy, 617(TLS):23Mar84-310
Whitington, R.S. Keith Miller.
  A.L. Le Quesne, 617(TLS):13Jan84-35
Whitley, J.S. Detectives and Friends.
  S. Snyder, 106:Summer83-185
  P. Wolfe, 395(MFS):Autumn83-389
Whitlock, R. The English Farm.
  S. Mills, 617(TLS):13Jul84-780
Whitman, F.H. Old English Riddles.
  R. Frank, 627(UTQ):Summer83-404
Whitman, R. Tamsen Donner.
  M. Boruch, 271:Vol 13No3/4-251

Whitman, T.J. Dear Brother Walt. (D.
  Berthold and K.M. Price, eds)
  S.M. Halpern, 441:17Jun84-21
Whitman, W. Complete Poetry and Collected
  Prose. (J. Kaplan, ed)
  E. Folsom, 646:Sep83-37
  W.H. Pritchard, 249(HudR):Summer83-352
Whitmarsh, A. Simone de Beauvoir and the
  Limits of Commitment.*
  295(JML):Nov83-434
Whitney, P.A. Rainsong.
  C. Verderese, 441:5Feb84-18
Whitrow, G.J. The Natural Philosophy of
  Time. (2nd ed)
  C.W. Kilmister, 84:Jun83-200
Whittaker, J.H. Matters of Faith and
  Matters of Principle.
  R.B. Edwards, 543:Jun83-956
Whittaker, M. - see Tatian
Whittaker, R. The Faith and Fiction of
  Muriel Spark.*
  M.M. Rowe, 395(MFS):Winter83-791
Whittall, A. The Music of Britten and
  Tippett.*
  P. Evans, 410(M&L):Jan/Apr83-84
  B. Northcott, 415:Mar83-168
Whittall, M. - see Wagner, R.
Whitton, K.S. The Theatre of Friedrich
  Dürrenmatt.*
  I.M. Goessl, 406:Fall83-319
  W.E. Yates, 402(MLR):Jan83-247
Whitwell, W.L. and L.W. Winborne. The
  Architectural Heritage of the Roanoke
  Valley.
  D. Upton, 576:Oct83-309
Whitworth, J. Poor Butterflies.*
  E. Larrissy, 493:Mar83-61
"Who's Who in the Theatre."* (17th ed)
  (I. Herbert, with C. Baxter and R.E.
  Finley, eds)
  J.P. Wearing, 615(TJ):May83-280
Whyte, I.B. - see under Boyd Whyte, I.
Whyte, J. Gallimaufry.*
  A. Mandel, 102(CanL):Winter82-132
Whyte, J. Homage, Henry Kelsey.
  C. MacCulloch, 526:Winter83-74
  P.M. St. Pierre, 102(CanL):Spring83-
  124
Whyte, R.O. The Industrial Potential of
  Rural Asia.
  J.E. Nickum, 293(JASt):Aug83-893
Wiarda, H.J., ed. Rift and Revolution.
  C. Dickey, 453(NYRB):14Jun84-25
  S.K. Purcell, 441:28Oct84-28
Wichmann, S. Japonisme.*
  H. Adams, 54:Sep83-495
  P. Mauries, 98:Jan-Feb83-157
  T. Watanabe, 59:Sep83-384
Wicht, W. Virginia Woolf, James Joyce,
  T.S. Eliot.*
  U. Riese, 654(WB):4/1983-759
Wickens, G.M. Arabic Grammar: A First
  Workbook.
  W.M. Thackston, 318(JAOS):Jul-Sep82-
  566
Wickens, H. Natural Dyes for Spinners and
  Weavers.
  S. Bill, 614:Spring84-24
Wicker, T. Unto This Hour.
  P-L. Adams, 61:Mar84-132
  S. Altinel, 617(TLS):7Dec84-1420
  J. Beatty, 441:12Feb84-24
  442(NY):19Mar84-146

Wilbur, E. Wind and Birds and Human
Voices.
 W. Kendrick, 441:14Oct84-43
Wilcox, J. Modern Baptists.*
 J. Crace, 617(TLS):20Jan84-70
Wild, P. Heretics. Bitteroots.
 D.A. Carpenter, 649(WAL):Feb84-377
Wild, P. Clarence King.*
 H. Crosby, 26(ALR):Spring83-157
Wild, P. and F. Graziano, eds. New Poetry
of the American West.
 S.E. Marovitz, 649(WAL):Nov83-256
Wilde, O. The Annotated Oscar Wilde.
(H.M. Hyde, ed)
 G.A. Cevasco, 177(ELT):Vol26No3-211
Wilde, O. The Artist as Critic. (R. Ell-
mann, ed)
 D.T. O'Hara, 659(ConL):Summer84-250
Wilde, O. Lady Windermere's Fan. (I.
Small, ed)
 M.R. Booth, 541(RES):May83-242
 N. Grene, 447(N&Q):Oct82-463
Wilde, O. Sämtliche Werke in zehn Bänden.
(N. Kohl, ed)
 M. Pfister, 490:Band14Heft3/4-358
Wilden, A. System and Structure.
 C. Norris, 349:Winter83-107
Wildung, D. Imhotep und Amenhotep.
 D.B. Redford, 318(JAOS):Jan-Mar82-172
Wilen, J. and L. Name Me, I'm Yours!
 R.M. Rennick, 424:Jun83-123
Wiles, D. The Early Plays of Robin Hood.
 A.B. Friedman, 589:Jul83-857
 C. Gauvin, 189(EA):Jan-Mar84-88
Wiles, T.J. The Theater Event.*
 A. Graham-White, 615(TJ):Mar83-140
Wiley, P. and R. Gottlieb. Empires in the
Sun.
 J. Nice, 649(WAL):May83-69
Wilford, J.N. The Mapmakers.
 H.W. Castner, 529(QQ):Autumn83-893
Wilhelm, G. Das Archiv des Šilwa-teššup.
(Pt 2)
 M.P. Maidman, 318(JAOS):Apr-Jun82-391
Wilhelm, J.J. Il Miglior Fabbro.
 J.C. Hirsh, 468:Fall/Winter83-515
Wilhelm, J.J. - see Arnaut Daniel
Wilhelm, K. Welcome, Chaos.
 G. Jonas, 441:3Jun84-50
Wilhelm, P. The Nobel Prize.
 E. Abraham, 617(TLS):27Jan84-82
Wilken, R.L. The Christians as the Romans
Saw Them.
 P-L. Adams, 61:Mar84-133
 R.M. Brown, 441:26Feb84-30
Wilkes, P., ed. Merton.
 R. Coles, 441:23Dec84-1
Wilkes, R. Wallace.
 P.D. James, 617(TLS):27Jul84-832
Wilkes, W. Die Entwicklung der eisernen
Buchdruckerpresse.
 R. Sweet, 70:May-Jun83-172
Wilkie, B. and M.L. Johnson. Blake's
"Four Zoas."
 J. Blondel, 189(EA):Jan-Mar83-82
Wilkinson, A. Midnights.
 639(VQR):Spring83-61
Wilkinson, J.D. The Intellectual Resis-
tance in Europe.*
 R.A., 189(EA):Apr-Jun84-235
 R.F. Bell, 221(GQ):May83-533
 F.J. Breit, 478:Oct83-269

[continued]

[continuing]
 D.M. Ennis, 529(QQ):Summer83-583
 S.G. Payne, 406:Fall83-323
Wilkinson, S. Death on Call.
 N. Callendar, 441:15Jul84-27
Will, É. Histoire politique du monde hel-
lénistique. (Vol 2)
 R.W., 555:Vol157fasc2-310
Will, P-É. Bureaucratie et famine en
Chine au 18e siècle.
 R.B. Wong and P.C. Perdue, 244(HJAS):
Jun83-291
Willan, A. The La Varenne Cooking Course.
 W. and C. Cowen, 639(VQR):Spring83-70
Willard, N. Household Tales of Moon and
Water.*
 J. Mazzaro, 385(MQR):Spring84-294
 639(VQR):Spring83-62
Willcox, A.R. The Rock Art of Africa.
 A. Sieveking, 617(TLS):27Jul84-852
Wille, G. Einführung in das römische
Musikleben.
 W.A., 412:May82-137
Willeford, C. Miami Blues.
 N. Callendar, 441:2Sep84-12
 442(NY):23Apr84-134
Willems, D. Syntaxe, lexique et séman-
tique.*
 H. Huot, 209(FM):Jul83-262
Willems, G. Grossstadt- und Bewusstseins-
poesie.
 R. Alter, 67:Nov83-326
 R.E. Lorbe, 301(JEGP):Jul83-424
 K. Weissenberger, 133:Band16Heft2/3-
278
Willems, G. Das Konzept der literarischen
Gattung.
 M.C. Crichton, 221(GQ):Mar83-293
 H.S. Daemmrich, 301(JEGP):Apr83-281
Willems, M. and others. Aspects du thé-
âtre anglo-saxon.
 L. Salingar, 189(EA):Apr-Jun84-175
Willems, N. English Intonation From a
Dutch Point of View.
 C.W. Kreidler, 350:Sep84-666
Willens, H. The Trimtab Factor.
 A. Frye, 441:18Mar84-25
Willett, J. Brecht in Context.
 P. Brady, 617(TLS):23Mar84-309
 R. Davies, 362:22Mar84-22
 J. Fenton, 453(NYRB):15Mar84-25
Willett, J. The Theatre of Bertolt Brecht.
 D. Constantine, 161(DUJ):Dec82-118
Willett, J. The Weimar Years.
 R. Davies, 362:22Mar84-22
 S. Heller, 441:22Apr84-14
Willett, J. and R. Manheim - see Brecht, B.
Willetts, W. Chinese Calligraphy.*
 M. Tregear, 324:May84-413
William of Conches. Guillaume de Conches:
"Glosae in Iuvenalem."* (B. Wilson, ed)
 P. Dronke, 382(MAE):1983/1-146
William of Malmesbury. The Early History
of Glastonbury. (J. Scott, ed and trans)
 F.C., 189(EA):Apr-Jun84-233
 J.P. Carley, 589:Jul83-819
William of Malmesbury. Polyhistor. (H.T.
Ouellette, ed)
 R.E. Pepin, 589:Oct83-1143
Williams, B. John Henry.
 G. Bluestein, 187:Sep84-562

Williams, B. Moral Luck.
E.J. Bond, 483:Oct83-544
R. Gaita, 479(PhQ):Jul83-288
A. MacIntyre, 185:Oct83-113
Williams, B.B. A Literary History of Ala-
bama: The Nineteenth Century.
C.S. Watson, 392:Winter82/83-83
Williams, C.G.S. Madame de Sévigné.*
R.T. Corum, Jr., 210(FrF):May83-185
M. Gérard, 535(RHL):Sep/Dec83-925
A. Panaghis, 568(SCN):Winter83-77
Williams, C.J.F. What is Existence?
K. Lambert, 518:Apr83-103
Williams, C.J.F. - see Aristotle
Williams, C.K. Tar.*
P. Stitt, 219(GaR):Winter83-894
D. Wojahn, 434:Spring84-489
D. Young, 199:Spring84-83
Williams, C.W. Texas' Last Frontier. (E.
Wallace, ed)
L. Milazzo, 584(SWR):Spring83-vi
Williams, D. Advertise for Treasure.
T.J. Binyon, 617(TLS):20Jul84-801
N. Callendar, 441:28Oct84-39
Williams, D. Cain and Beowulf.
D.G. Calder, 589:Jul83-838
S.B. Greenfield, 405(MP):Nov83-191
Williams, D. Mr. George Eliot.*
B.F. Williamson, 441:12Feb84-21
Williams, D. The River Horsemen.*
L.K. MacKendrick, 198:Jan83-119
Williams, F.G. - see de Sena, J.
Williams, G., ed. Apprenticeship in Craft.
P. Bach, 614:Winter84-15
Williams, G. Figures of Thought in Roman
Poetry.*
J.G. Fitch, 122:Apr83-175
Williams, G. Not for Export.
J. Hutcheson, 99:Aug-Sep83-40
Williams, G. Technique and Ideas in the
"Aeneid."*
J.H. Dee, 124:Sep-Oct83-58
Williams, G.A. Goya and the Impossible
Revolution.
A.P., 617(TLS):20Jul84-822
Williams, G.H., ed and trans. The Polish
Brethren.
W.F. Bense, 551(RenQ):Autumn83-433
L. Krzyżanowski, 497(PolR):Vol28No1-66
Williams, H. Rousseau and Romantic Auto-
biography.
J. Starobinski, 617(TLS):7Dec84-1423
Williams, J. Byng of Vimy.
H. Strachan, 617(TLS):9Mar84-243
Williams, J. Costume and Setting for
Shakespeare's Plays.
A. Cornish, 157:Summer83-31
Williams, J. Get Hot or Get Out.
A. Struthers, 436(NewL):Fall83-115
Williams, J. Taking Care.
P. La Salle, 573(SSF):Winter83-60
639(VQR):Winter83-21
Williams, J., E. Dunning and P. Murphy.
Hooligans Abroad.
B. Glanville, 617(TLS):13Jul84-780
S. Hey, 362:21Jun84-26
Williams, J.F. What is Existence?
M.S. Gram, 543:Jun83-958
Williams, J.G. The Art of Gupta India.
T.S. Maxwell, 90:Sep83-563
G.M. Tartakov, 576:Dec83-388

Williams, J.R. Martin Heidegger's Phi-
losophy of Religion.
A.W.J. Harper, 154:Sep83-567
Williams, K. The New Kit Williams.
A. Fowler, 617(TLS):8Jun84-640
Williams, L.V. Self and Society in the
Poetry of Nicolás Guillén.
H.L. Johnson, 238:Dec83-639
V.M. Kutzinski, 400(MLN):Mar83-275
Williams, M. Groundless Belief.*
J. Hall, 543:Mar83-739
Williams, M. The Jazz Tradition. (rev)
C. Fox, 617(TLS):4May84-490
Williams, M., ed. The Way to Lord's.
A.L. Le Quesne, 617(TLS):4May84-493
Williams, M. Women in the English Novel
1800-1900.
P. Boumelha, 617(TLS):20Jul84-818
Williams, P. Kedymdeithyas Amlyn ac Amic.
P. Ó Fiannachta, 112:Vol 15-187
Williams, P. The Organ Music of J.S.
Bach.* (Vols 1 and 2)
R. Stinson, 414(MusQ):Winter83-134
Williams, P. The Organ Music of J.S.
Bach. (Vol 3)
M. Boyd, 617(TLS):28Sep84-1074
Williams, P.L. The Heart of a Distant
Forest.
C. Fein, 441:5Aug84-18
Williams, R. The Lords of the Isles.
C. Bingham, 617(TLS):14Dec84-1451
Williams, R. Skilful Rugby.
N. Kinnock, 617(TLS):2Mar84-224
Williams, R. Writing in Society.
J. Lucas, 617(TLS):13Jan84-29
Williams, R. The Year 2000.
R. Bendiner, 441:6May84-27
Williams, R.D. - see Vergil
Williams, R.D. and T.S. Pattie. Virgil.
B.C. Barker-Benfield, 123:Vol33No2-321
A.G. McKay, 487:Spring83-91
Williams, R.L. Una década de la novela
colombiana.
L.I. Mena, 238:Mar83-141
Williams, R.M. Sing a Sad Song. (2nd ed)
C. Seemann, 650(WF):Oct83-318
M.R. Winchell, 585(SoQ):Winter83-77
Williams, S.A. Some One Sweet Angel
Chile.*
C.S. Giscombe, 181:Spring-Summer84-208
Williams, T.H. The Selected Essays of T.
Harry Williams.
639(VQR):Autumn83-118
Williams, W. The Tragic Art of Ernest
Hemingway.*
M. Westbrook, 587(SAF):Spring83-116
Williams, W.C. The Doctor Stories. (R.
Coles, comp)
G. Sorrentino, 441:21Oct84-9
Williams, W.C. Selected Poems. (C. Tom-
linson, ed) Paterson.
H. Kenner, 617(TLS):27Apr84-451
Williamson, V.G. The Minor Dramatists of
Seventeenth-Century Spain.*
K.C. Gregg, 238:Dec83-634
Williamson, A. Introspection and Contempo-
rary Poetry.
M.L. Rosenthal, 441:23Sep84-34
Williamson, A. Presence.*
W. Harmon, 110:Spring84-81
J.D. McClatchy, 491:Dec83-178
R. Tillinghast, 385(MQR):Fall84-596
639(VQR):Summer86-96

Williamson, C. A Feast of Creatures.
   N. Barley, 567:Vol44No3/4-395
Williamson, E.C. American Political Writ-
ers: 1801-1973.
   C.L. Grant, 577(SHR):Fall83-377
Williamson, J. The Crucible of Race.
   G.M. Fredrickson, 453(NYRB):6Dec84-28
   L.F. Litwack, 441:16Sep84-12
Williamson, K. - see Smart, C.
Williamson, T. and L. Bellamy. Ley Lines
in Question.
   S. Piggott, 617(TLS):13Jan84-31
Willis, B. The Captain's Diary [1983-84].
   A.L. Le Quesne, 617(TLS):16Nov84-1314
Willis, J. Screen World 1983.
   G. Kaufman, 362:19Apr84-26
Willner, A.R. The Spellbinders.
   B. Mazlish, 441:4Mar84-24
Wills, G. Cincinnatus.
   P. Anderson, 441:5Aug84-9
   M. Cunliffe, 453(NYRB):11Oct84-47
   442(NY):4Jun84-135
Wills, G. The Kennedy Imprisonment.*
   D.J. Garrow, 577(SHR):Spring83-201
   R. Weisbrot, 639(VQR):Autumn83-731
Wills, G.F. Statecraft as Soulcraft.
   G. Marshall, 617(TLS):25May84-589
Wills, J.R. Directing in the Theatre.
   J. Fernald, 610:Spring82-153
Willson, M.F. and N. Burley. Mate Choice
in Plants.
   T. Halliday, 617(TLS):13Jan84-43
Wilmet, M., ed. Sémantique lexicale et
sémantique grammaticale en moyen fran-
çais.
   S.N. Rosenberg, 207(FR):Feb84-436
Wilshire, B. Role Playing and Identity.
   J.R. Hamilton, 290(JAAC):Spring84-337
Wilson, A. Diversity and Depth in Fic-
tion.* (K. McSweeney, ed)
   M. Amis, 61:May84-112
   J. Atlas, 441:19Aug84-22
   B. Bergonzi, 176:Jul/Aug84-46
Wilson, A. Les Quarante Ans de Mrs. Eliot.
   C. Jordis, 450(NRF):Nov83-157
Wilson, A.N. Hilaire Belloc.
   P-L. Adams, 61:Sep84-129
   N. Annan, 617(TLS):27Apr84-467
   R. Blythe, 362:26Apr84-22
   E. Pearce, 129:Nov84-69
   W. Sheed, 441:2Sep84-3
Wilson, A.N. The Life of John Milton.*
   R. Flannagan, 391:May83-49
   G. Hammond, 148:Autumn83-79
Wilson, A.N. Scandal.*
   D. Taylor, 364:Dec83/Jan84-143
Wilson, A.N. Wise Virgin.*
   J.R.B., 148:Summer83-95
   P. Craig, 617(TLS):1Jun84-623
   442(NY):26Mar84-134
Wilson, B. Religion in Sociological Per-
spective.
   42(AR):Winter83-120
Wilson, B. - see William of Conches
Wilson, B.K. Jane Austen in Australia.
   L. Duguid, 617(TLS):26Oct84-1224
Wilson, C. A Criminal History of Mankind.
   W. Kaminer, 441:29Jul84-21
Wilson, C.N., ed. Why the South Will
Survive.*
   D.W. Grantham, 579(SAQ):Winter83-93
Wilson, D. Chou.
   S. Leys, 617(TLS):26Oct84-1206

Wilson, D. Rutherford.
   J. Calado, 617(TLS):18May84-545
Wilson, D.M. Anglo-Saxon Art.
   G. Zarnecki, 617(TLS):14Dec84-1448
Wilson, E. The Portable Edmund Wilson.*
   (L.M. Dabney, ed)
   N. Berry, 364:Aug/Sep83-122
Wilson, E. Erica Wilson's Children's
World.
   P. Grappe, 614:Summer84-15
Wilson, E.A.M. The Modern Russian Dic-
tionary For English Speakers: English-
Russian.
   C.R. Pike, 617(TLS):17Aug84-920
Wilson, E.M. and D.W. Cruickshank. Samuel
Pepys's Spanish Plays.*
   J. Agustín Castañeda, 238:May83-294
   C. Stern, 240(HR):Winter83-99
   517(PBSA):Vol77No4-517
Wilson, E.O. Biophilia.
   S. Boxer, 441:7Oct84-23
Wilson, E.O. On Human Nature.
   D.M.O., 543:Sep82-208
   P.J. Provost, 125:Spring83-311
Wilson, G. and P. Sands. Building a City.
   G. Herbert, 576:Dec83-394
Wilson, I. Mind Out of Time?
   C.G. Hospital, 529(QQ):Autumn83-910
Wilson, J., ed. Disability Prevention.
   A. Darnbrough, 324:Feb84-209
Wilson, J., ed. Entertainments for
Elizabeth I.*
   D.M. Bergeron, 677(YES):Vol 13-304
   D. Norbrook, 541(RES):Feb83-74
Wilson, J. Joinings, Edges and Trims.
   A.L. Mayer, 614:Summer84-20
Wilson, J. Jean Wilson's Soumak Workbook.
   V.R. Edwards, 614:Summer84-30
Wilson, J.B., comp. Children's Writings.
   A.M. Hildebrand, 87(BB):Dec83-256
Wilson, J.D. The Romantic Heroic Ideal.
   R.F. Gleckner, 27(AL):Oct83-448
   639(VQR):Summer83-88
Wilson, L.A. From the Bottom Up.
   D. Grumbach, 219(GaR):Winter83-889
   639(VQR):Summer83-90
Wilson, M.I. William Kent.
   H. Colvin, 617(TLS):31Aug84-967
Wilson, P.L. and G.R. Aavani, eds and
trans. Nasir-i Khusraw.
   H. Landolt, 318(JAOS):Jan-Mar82-214
Wilson, R.B.J. Henry James's Ultimate Nar-
rative: "The Golden Bowl."*
   S. Brodwin, 27(AL):Mar83-106
   T.H. Getz, 284:Winter84-146
Wilson, R.G. McKim, Mead and White.
   H.H. Reed, 441:17Jun84-9
Wilson, R.J.A. Piazza Armerina.
   R. Higgins, 39:Dec83-527
Wilson, R.L. and G. Loyola, eds. Rescue
Archeology.
   A.R. Williams, 37:Jul-Aug83-60
Wilson, R.M., ed. The Future of Coptic
Studies.
   O. Wintermute, 318(JAOS):Jan-Mar82-183
Wilson, R.N. The Writer as Social Seer.
   J. Preston, 402(MLR):Apr83-389
Wilson, R.T. The Camel.
   R. Irwin, 617(TLS):7Sep84-984
Wilson, S. The Man in the Gray Flannel
Suit II.
   J. Chamberlain, 441:25Mar84-20

Wilson, S., ed. Saints and their Cults.
C. Stancliffe, 617(TLS):24Aug84-955
Wilson, S. Spaceache.
J. Melmoth, 617(TLS):16Mar84-267
Wilson, S.G. Luke and the Law.
J.L. Houlden, 617(TLS):20Apr84-441
Wilson, T.J. Sein als Text.
Q. Lauer, 258:Sep83-344
Wilson, W.D. The Narrative Strategy of
Wieland's "Don Sylvio von Rosalva."*
A. Menhennet, 402(MLR):Jan83-231
T.C. Starnes, 221(GQ):Jan83-137
Wilson, W.S. - see "Ideals of the Samurai"
Wilt, J. Ghosts of the Gothic.*
S. Prickett, 402(MLR):Jul83-683
P. Thomson, 541(RES):May83-224
Wilton, A. Turner Abroad.
G. Reynolds, 39:Dec83-529
Wilton, A. Turner and the Sublime.
J. McCoubrey, 54:Mar83-165
Wimsatt, J.I. Chaucer and the Poems of
"Ch" in University of Pennsylvania MS
French 15.
B. O'Donoghue, 617(TLS):18May84-555
Winchell, M.R. Joan Didion.*
C.M. Fulmer, 577(SHR):Winter83-90
G.F. Waller, 106:Summer83-207
Winchell, M.R. Horace McCoy.
R.W. Etulain, 649(WAL):Aug83-176
Winchester, S. Prison Diary, Argentina.
M. Deas, 617(TLS):10Feb84-142
Winckler, P.A., ed. History of Books and
Printing.
R.G. Silver, 517(PBSA):Oct-Dec80-413
Windeatt, B.A., ed and trans. Chaucer's
Dream Poetry.
D. Staines, 589:Oct83-1143
Windsor, A. Peter Behrens.*
J.B. Smith, 39:Jan83-68
Wingate, J. William the Conqueror.
S. Altinel, 617(TLS):3Aug84-875
Wingfield, S. Collected Poems 1938-1983.
W. Scammell, 617(TLS):27Jul84-838
Wingfield Digby, G., with W. Hefford. Vic-
toria and Albert Museum: The Tapestry
Collection, Medieval and Renaissance.
A.S. Cavallo, 90:May83-303
Winiarczyk, M., ed. "Diagorae Melii" et
"Theodori Cyrenaei" reliquiae.
É. des Places, 555:Vol57fasc1-126
Winiger, J. Feuerbachs Weg zum Humanis-
mus.*
C. Salvi, 53(AGP):Band65Heft2-206
Winitz, H., ed. The Comprehensive
Approach to Foreign Language Instruc-
tion.
L.A. Briscoe, 399(MLJ):Spring83-66
Winitz, H., ed. Native Language and
Foreign Language Acquisition.
E. Bialystok, 399(MLJ):Summer83-170
Winkler, B. Wirkstrategische Verwendung
populärliterarischer Elemente in Sean
O'Caseys dramatischem Werk unter beson-
derer Berücksichtigung des Melodramas.
K. Tetzeli von Rosador, 72:Band220
Heft1-177
Winkler, E.H. The Clown in Modern Anglo-
Irish Drama.
H. Kosok, 72:Band219Heft1-206
Winkler, J.J. and G. Williams, eds. Later
Greek Literature.
R.C. McCail, 123:Vol33No2-192

Winks, R.W. Modus Operandi.
R. Hill, 617(TLS):16Mar84-270
Winn, J.A. Unsuspected Eloquence.*
N.A. Brittin, 577(SHR):Spring83-197
A. Howell, 107(CRCL):Sep83-410
J. Mazzaro, 308:Fall83-290
J. Stevens, 402(MLR):Apr83-397
Winner, E. Invented Worlds.
C.L. Doyle, 289:Fall83-110
F. Williams, 290(JAAC):Fall83-99
Winnick, R.H. - see MacLeish, A.
Winnifrith, T., P. Murray and K.W.
Gransden, eds. Aspects of the Epic.
C. Martindale, 617(TLS):13Jul84-789
Winnington-Ingram, R.P. Sophocles.*
G.M. Kirkwood, 122:Oct83-350
Winnington-Ingram, R.P. Studies in
Aeschylus.
M. Griffith, 617(TLS):10Feb84-134
Winslow, G.R. Triage and Justice.
A. Lynch, 154:Dec83-754
P. Singer, 185:Oct83-142
Winston, K.I. - see Fuller, L.L.
Winston, R. Thomas Mann: The Making of an
Artist 1875-1911.*
W. Phillips, 473(PR):1/1983-145
Winter, H. - see Pepys, S.
Winter, R. and B. Carr, eds. Beethoven,
Performers, and Critics.*
R. Kramer, 308:Fall83-299
Winternitz, E. Leonardo da Vinci as a
Musician.*
J. Chater, 415:Oct83-617
J. Couchman, 414(MusQ):Fall83-599
C. Gould, 39:Oct83-354
M. Kemp, 317:Summer83-312
Wintle, J. Paradise for Hire.
J. Mellors, 362:26Apr84-31
Winton, J. Convoy.
I. McGeoch, 617(TLS):9Mar84-244
Wippermann, W. Faschismustheorien.
U-K. Ketelsen, 221(GQ):Mar83-351
Wiredu, K. Philosophy and African Cul-
ture.*
J. Teichman, 518:Jan83-60
Wirsig, K.H. Gleebs of Wizagon.
J.K. Kealy, 102(CanL):Winter82-160
"Wisden Cricketers' Almanack." (121st
year) (J. Woodcock, ed)
A.L. Le Quesne, 617(TLS):4May84-493
Wise, D. The Children's Game.
P. Taubman, 441:8Jan84-18
Wiseman, C. The Upper Hand.*
P.K. Smith, 102(CanL):Summer83-138
Wiseman, J., ed. Studies in the Antiqui-
ties of Stobi. (Vol 2)
C. Foss, 122:Jan83-91
Wiser, W. The Crazy Years.*
A. Field, 617(TLS):10Feb84-148
Wisse, F. The Profile Method for Classify-
ing and Evaluating Manuscript Evidence.
D. Yates, 124:Nov-Dec83-135
Wistrand, E. The Policy of Brutus the
Tyrannicide.*
J-C. Richard, 555:Vol57fasc2-358
de Wit, W., ed. The Amsterdam School.
I.B. Whyte, 617(TLS):17Aug84-922
Witemeyer, H. George Eliot and the Visual
Arts.*
B.G. Hornback, 301(JEGP):Jan83-136
Withers, C.W.J. Gaelic in Scotland 1698-
1981.
W. Gillies, 617(TLS):11May84-527

Withey, L. Dearest Friend.*
  E.F. Crane, 9(AlaR):Jan83-63
Withrington, D.J., ed. Shetland and the
  Outside World 1469-1969.
  J. Hunter, 617(TLS):6Jan84-18
Witte, H.A. Symboliek van de aarde bij de
  Yoruba.
  J. Povey, 2(AfrA):Feb83-88
Wittenberg, J.B. Faulkner.*
  D. Hewitt, 447(N&Q):Apr82-191
Wittgenstein, L. Leçons et conversations
  [suivi de] La conférence sur l'éthique.
  Remarques sur le "Rameau d'or" de Frazer
  [suivi de] Bouveresse, J. L'animal céré-
  moniel.
  M-A. Lescourret, 98:Oct83-764
Wittgenstein, L. Remarks on Frazer's
  "Golden Bough."
  I.C. Jarvie, 488:Mar83-117
Wittgenstein, L. Wittgenstein's Lectures,
  Cambridge 1932-1935. (from notes by A.
  Ambrose and M. Macdonald; A. Ambrose, ed)
  C. Imbert, 540(RIPh):Vol137fasc1/2-206
Wittkower, R. Allegory and the Migration
  of Symbols.
  C.H. Clough, 39:Jan83-67
Wittkowski, W., ed. Friedrich Schiller.
  J.D. Simons, 133:Band16Heft2/3-240
Wittkowski, W. - see Schiller, F.
Wittreich, J.A., Jr. Visionary Poetics.
  J.M.Q. Davies, 161(DUJ):Dec82-109
Wobbe, R.A. Graham Greene.*
  P. Miles, 354:Mar83-79
Wode, H. Learning a Second Language.
  K-M. Köpcke, 353:Vol20No1/2-147
Wohl, S. The Medical Industrial Complex.
  N.R. Kleinfield, 441:29Apr84-33
Wohlfart, G. Der Augenblick.
  R.A. Makkreel, 319:Oct84-497
Wojahn, D. Icehouse Lights.*
  J.D. McClatchy, 491:Dec83-179
Wojtyła, K. [Pope John Paul II] Collected
  Poems.
  A.C. Lupack, 497(PolR):Vol28No3-90
  639(VQR):Winter83-25
Woledge, B. La Syntaxe des substantifs
  chez Chrétien de Troyes.*
  N.L. Corbett, 545(RPh):May83-572
Wolf, B.J. Romantic Re-Vision.*
  A. Axelrod, 658(WinterW83-307
Wolf, C. Cassandra.
  M. Lefkowitz, 441:9Sep84-20
Wolf, C. A Model Childhood.*
  P. Lewis, 364:Jun83-95
Wolf, D., ed. The American Space.
  M.M. Hambourg, 617(TLS):20Jul84-821
Wolf, E. Europe and the People without
  History.
  I.K., 185:Oct83-164
Wolf, E.K. The Symphonies of Johann
  Stamitz.*
  F.K. Grave, 317:Summer83-322
  D. Patier, 537:Vol69No1-117
  R.W. Wade, 414(MusQ):Summer83-442
Wolf, L. and W. Hupka. Altfranzösisch.*
  P. Swiggers, 353:Vol20No1/2-157
Wolf, R. Das französische Roman um 1780.
  M. Delon, 535(RHL):May/Jun83-474
Wolf, U. Möglichkeit und Notwendigkeit
  bei Aristoteles und heute.
  G. Seel, 53(AGP):Band65Heft1-81
Wolfe, B.D. Revolution and Reality.*
  J.W. Strong, 529(QQ):Spring83-216

Wolfe, C. Murder at La Marimba.
  N. Callendar, 441:1Apr84-27
Wolfe, C.K. Kentucky Country.
  C.S. Guthrie, 650(WF):Oct83-300
Wolfe, K.M. The Churches and the British
  Broadcasting Corporation 1922-1956.
  P. Johnson, 362:14Jun84-21
  J. Whale, 617(TLS):13Jul84-787
Wolfe, P. Laden Choirs.
  W.J. Scheick, 659(ConL):Fall84-375
Wolfe, T. The Autobiography of an Ameri-
  can Novelist.* (L. Field, ed)
  F. Hobson, 578:Spring84-118
Wolfe, T. The Purple Decades.*
  J.L. Hopkins, 364:Jun83-90
  R. Weber, 639(VQR):Summer83-548
Wolfe, T. Welcome To Our City.* (R.S.
  Kennedy, ed)
  F. Hobson, 578:Spring84-118
  J.L. Idol, Jr., 580(SCR):Fall83-133
Wolfe, T. and A. Bernstein. My Other Lone-
  liness.* (S. Stutman, ed)
  J.L. Idol, Jr., 580(SCR):Spring84-144
Wolfe, T. and E. Nowell. Beyond Love and
  Loyalty.* (R.S. Kennedy, ed)
  J.L. Idol, Jr., 580(SCR):Spring84-144
Wolff, C. Aërometriae Elementa.
  J. Ecole, 192(EP):Jan-Mar83-115
Wolff, C. B.v.S. Sittenlehre widerleget
  von den berühmten Weltweisen unserer
  Zeit Herrn Christian Wolf.
  J. Ecole, 192(EP):Jan-Mar83-116
Wolff, C. and others. The Bach Family.*
  L. Salter, 415:Dec83-748
Wolff, D. The Real World.
  G.S.S. Chandra, 436(NewL):Fall83-120
Wolff, E. Utopie und Humor.
  M. Knapp, 221(GQ):Nov83-690
Wolff, J. Aesthetics and the Sociology of
  Art.
  V. Kavolis, 290(JAAC):Winter83-222
  S. Mitchell, 59:Dec83-499
Wolff, J. The Social Production of Art.*
  S. Mitchell, 59:Dec83-499
Wolff, J.U. Formal Indonesian.
  J.V. Dreyfuss, 293(JASt):Feb83-465
Wolff, J.U. and S. Poedjosoedarmo. Com-
  municative Codes in Central Java.
  J.J. Errington, 350:Mar84-196
Wolff, R.A. Wie sagt man in Bayern.*
  U. Bichel, 685(ZDL):2/1983-252
Wolff, R.L. Nineteenth-Century Fiction.*
  (Vol 1)
  T. Hofmann, 78(BC):Autumn83-356
Wolff, R.L. Nineteenth-Century Fiction.
  (Vol 2)
  T. Hofmann, 78(BC):Autumn83-356
  W.E. Smith, 517(PBSA):Vol77No2-251
  J. Sutherland, 617(TLS):3Feb84-123
Wolff, T. In the Garden of the North
  American Martyrs.*
  G. Garrett, 569(SR):Winter83-112
Wölfflin, H. Heinrich Wölfflin 1864-1945.
  (J. Gantner, ed)
  H. Osborne, 89(BJA):Autumn83-366
Wolford, C.L. The Anger of Stephen Crane.
  T.A. Gullason, 395(MFS):Winter83-716
  G. Locklin, 573(SSF):Spring-Summer83-
  151
  J. Nagel, 26(ALR):Autumn83-315
  295(JML):Nov83-456

"'The Woolgatherers' Handspun Pattern
Book."
  P. Bach, 614:Winter84-25
Woollatt, R. Eastbound from Alberta.
  W. Latta, 137:Apr83-41
Woolmer, J.H. Malcolm Lowry.
  B.C. Bloomfield, 617(TLS):18May84-563
Woolnough, B. Black Magic.
  P. Smith, 617(TLS):13Jan84-35
Woolrich, C. The Fantastic Stories of
  Cornell Woolrich. (C.G. Waugh and M.H.
  Greenberg, eds)
  B.L. St. Armand, 573(SSF):Winter83-63
Woolrych, A. Commonwealth to Protectorate.
  I. Roots, 366:Autumn83-268
  P. Zagorin, 551(RenQ):Autumn83-448
Woolsey, G. The Letters of Gamel Woolsey
  to Llewelyn Powys, 1930-1939. (K. Hop-
  kins, ed)
  F. Day, 580(SCR):Spring84-143
Woolsey, G. The Weight of Hours.
  A. Haberer, 189(EA):Jul-Sep84-349
Wootton, D. Paolo Sarpi.
  F. Gilbert, 617(TLS):20Jan84-57
Woozley, A.D. Law and Obedience.*
  J. Dybikowski, 449:Mar83-105
  J. Sisson, 479(PhQ):Jan83-103
Wordsworth, W. The Borderers.* (R.
  Osborn, ed)
  L. Goldstein, 385(MQR):Summer84-455
Wordsworth, W. The Oxford Authors: Wil-
  liam Wordsworth. (S. Gill, ed)
  W.W. Robson, 617(TLS):26Oct84-1221
Wordsworth, W. Poems, in Two Volumes, and
  Other Poems, 1800-1807. (J. Curtis, ed)
  K. Johnston, 661(WC):Summer83-115
Wordsworth, W. Wordsworth's Literary Crit-
  icism. (N.C. Smith, with H. Mills, eds)
  W.W. Robson, 97(CQ):Vol 12No1-74
Wordsworth, W. and D. The Letters of Wil-
  liam and Dorothy Wordsworth.* (2nd ed)
  (Vol 5) (A.G. Hill, ed)
  M. Isnard, 189(EA):Jan-Mar83-86
  W.J.B. Owen, 541(RES):May83-227
Wordsworth, W. and D. The Letters of Wil-
  liam and Dorothy Wordsworth. (Vol 6,
  Pt 3) (2nd ed) (A.G. Hill, ed)
  B. Darlington, 661(WC):Summer83-117
Wordsworth, W. and M. The Love Letters of
  William and Mary Wordsworth.* (B. Dar-
  lington, ed)
  P. Magnuson, 651(WHR):Spring83-67
"The World Atlas of Architecture."
  P. Goldberger, 441:2Dec84-18
Wormald, F. and P.M. Giles. A Descriptive
  Catalogue of the Additional Illuminated
  Manuscripts in the Fitzwilliam Museum.*
  L.M.C. Randall, 39:Jun83-510
Wormald, P., D. Bullough and R. Collins,
  eds. Ideal and Reality in Frankish and
  Anglo-Saxon Society.
  K.F. Morrison, 617(TLS):25May84-572
Wormser, B. The White Words.*
  P. Mesic, 491:Feb84-302
  639(VQR):Autumn83-134
Wörner, H.J. Architektur des Frühklas-
  sizismus in Süddeutschland.
  H. Wischermann, 683:Band46Heft4-456
Woronoff, D. The Thermidorean Régime and
  the Directory 1794-1799.
  W. Scott, 617(TLS):3Aug84-873
Woronoff, J. Hong Kong.
  M.K. Chan, 293(JASt):May83-589

Worpole, K. Dockers and Detectives.
  D. Craig, 617(TLS):23Mar84-298
  A. Croft, 362:12Jan84-24
Worrall, N. Nikolai Gogol and Ivan Tur-
  genev.
  R. Freeborn, 575(SEER):Jul83-422
Worrell, D., ed. The Economy of Barbados,
  1946-1980.
  R. Farley, 263(RIB):Vol33No2-271
Worth, G.J. Dickensian Melodrama.*
  R. Bennett, 541(RES):May83-236
  K. Tetzeli von Rosador, 38:Band101
  Heft1/2-284
Worth, K. The Irish Drama of Europe from
  Yeats to Beckett.*
  K. Tetzeli von Rosador, 72:Band220
  Heft1-177
Worth, K. Oscar Wilde.
  K. Beckson, 617(TLS):20Jul84-823
Wortham, T., with others - see Howells,
  W.D.
Worthen, J. - see Lawrence, D.H.
Wortman, M.L. Government and Society in
  Central America, 1680-1840.
  J.B. Warren, 263:Vol33No1-52
Wortman, W.A. A Guide to Serial Bibliogra-
  phies for Modern Literature.
  P. Coustillas, 189(EA):Jul-Sep84-314
Wouters, A. The Grammatical Papyri From
  Graeco-Roman Egypt.*
  P. Swiggers, 350:Sep84-658
Woytek, E. T. Maccius Plautus, "Persa."
  P. Flobert, 555:Vol157fasc2-328
  H.D. Jocelyn, 123:Vol33No2-194
Woźnicki, A.N. Journey to the Unknown.
  G.T. Kapolka, 497(PolR):Vol28No2-118
Wray, H. and H. Conroy, eds. Japan
  Examined.
  R.H. Mitchell, 407(MN):Autumn83-344
Wrede, H. Consecratio in formam deorum.
  J.A. North, 313:Vol73-169
Wreen, M.J. and D.M. Callen - see Beards-
  ley, M.C.
Wreggitt, A. Riding to Nicola Country.
  D. Daymond, 102(CanL):Summer83-140
Wren, M.K. Wake Up, Darlin' Corey.
  N. Callendar, 441:15Apr84-26
Wright, A. Literature of Crisis, 1910-22.
  A. Wright, 617(TLS):5Oct84-1125
Wright, A. Anthony Trollope.
  J. Adlard, 617(TLS):13Jan84-28
Wright, A.M. The Formal Principle in the
  Novel.
  W.R. Goetz, 651(WHR):Autumn83-274
  M. Rapisarda, 395(MFS):Summer83-362
Wright, B. and T. Mellors - see Fromentin,
  E. and P. Bataillard
Wright, B.A. - see Milton, J.
Wright, C. Country Music.
  P. Stitt, 219(GaR):Summer83-428
Wright, C. Music at the Court of Burgundy,
  1364-1419.
  N. Bridgman, 537:Vol69No2-230
Wright, C. The Other Side of the River.
  S. Burris, 344:Summer84-127
  D. Kalstone, 441:1Jul84-14
Wright, C. Rembrandt: Self-Portraits.
  90:Nov83-708
Wright, C. Wittgenstein on the Founda-
  tions of Mathematics.*
  M.D. Giaquinto, 307:Oct82-112

Wynar, L.R., with P. Kleeberger. Slavic
Ethnic Libraries, Museums and Archives
in the United States.*
R.H. Leibman, 292(JAF):Apr-Jun83-237
A.C. Lupack, 497(PolR):Vol28No2-120
Wyndham, F. and D. Melly - see Rhys, J.
Wynne, J. Crime Wave.
J.R.B., 148:Spring83-94
Wynot, E.D., Jr. Warsaw between the World
Wars.
M.B. Biskupski, 550(RusR):Oct83-453
639(VQR):Autumn83-122
Wyrwa, T. La Pensée politique polonaise a
l'époque de l'humanisme et de la Renais-
sance.*
J. Kosicka, 497(PolR):Vol28No2-105
Wysocki, B.A. Nad rzeką Ebro.
A.S. Cankardas, 497(PolR):Vol28No1-111
Wyss, D. Beziehung und Gestalt. Mitteil-
ung und Antwort.
H. Reinhardt, 489(PJGG):Band90Heft1-
216
Wyss, D. Zwischen Logos und Antilogos.
E.K. Ledermann, 323:Jan83-107
H. Reinhardt, 489(PJGG):Band90Heft1-
216
Wytrzens, G. Eine russische dichterische
Gestaltung der Sage vom Hamelner Ratten-
fänger.
G.S. Smith, 575(SEER):Apr83-313

Xanthakis-Karamanos, G. Studies in Fourth-
century Tragedy.*
A.F. Garvie, 123:Vol33No1-12
Xenakis, I. Musiques formelles.
B. Schiffer, 607:Mar83-25
Xianzu, T. - see under Tang Xianzu

Yacowar, M. Loser Take All.
S. Feldman, 106:Fall83-353
Yaguello, M. Alice au pays du langage.
F. Helgorsky, 209(FM):Jan83-58
Yahuda, M. Towards the End of Isola-
tionism.
D.S.G. Goodman, 617(TLS):18May84-554
Yakut, A. Sprache der Familie.
F.L. Tarallo, 355(LSoc):Mar83-146
Yallop, D.A. In God's Name.
M. Davie, 617(TLS):7Sep84-993
P. Hofmann, 441:8Jul84-32
Yamada, C., ed. Japonisme in Art.
H. Adams, 54:Sep83-495
Yamada, K., ed and trans. Gateless Gate.
B.M. Wilson, 485(PE&W):Jan83-101
Yamamoto, M. Betty-San.
J. Domini, 441:1Jan84-14
Yamamura, K., ed. Policy and Trade Issues
of the Japanese Economy.
Inoue Munemichi, 285(JapQ):Oct-Dec83-
429
Yamanouchi, H. The Search for Authentic-
ity in Modern Japanese Literature.
M.U. Docherty, 447(N&Q):Jun82-280
M.G. Ryan, 318(JAOS):Jul-Sep82-579
Yandell, C.M. - see de Tyard, P.
Yaney, G. The Urge to Mobilize.*
639(VQR):Spring83-52
Yang Jiang. Six Chapters From My Life
"Downunder."
J. Shapiro, 441:25Nov84-14

Yang, P.F-M. Chinese Dialectology.
W.H. Baxter 3d, 293(JASt):Nov82-158
Yang, W.L.Y. and C.P. Adkins, eds. Criti-
cal Essays on Chinese Fiction.
V.B. Cass, 293(JASt):May83-651
Yang, W.L.Y., P. Li and N.K. Mao. Clas-
sical Chinese Fiction.
Liu Ts'un-yan, 116:Jul82-295
Yang, W.L.Y. and N.K. Mao, eds. Modern
Chinese Fiction.
P.G. Pickowicz, 293(JASt):May83-652
"The Yankee Magazine Cookbook."
W. and C. Cowen, 639(VQR):Spring83-66
Yapp, B. Birds in Medieval Manuscripts.
B. Scott, 39:Feb83-152
Yardley, H.O. The Chinese Black Chamber.
H. Goodman, 441:4Mar84-23
Yarwood, E. Vsevolod Garshin.*
P. Varnai, 558(RLJ):Fall83-230
Yasinskaya, I. Revolutionary Textile
Design.
M. Sonday, 614:Spring84-27
Yasuoka Shotaro. A View by the Sea.
A.H. Chambers, 441:7Oct84-28
Yates, D. Descriptive Inventories of
Manuscripts Microfilmed for the Hill
Monastic Manuscript Library, Austrian
Libraries. (Vol 1)
E. Simon, 589:Jan83-252
Yates, F.A. Lull and Bruno. (Vol 1)
B.T. Moran, 551(RenQ):Autumn83-399
Yates, F.A. Renaissance and Reform: The
Italian Contribution.
F. Gilbert, 617(TLS):20Jan84-57
Yates, J.M. Fugue Brancusi.
H. Enrico, 648(WCR):Oct83-53
Yates, R. Liars in Love.*
G. Garrett, 569(SR):Winter83-112
Yates, R. Young Hearts Crying.
A. Broyard, 441:28Oct84-3
Yates, T.E. A College Remembered.
H.E.W. Turner, 161(DUJ):Jun83-149
Yates, W.E. Tradition in the German Son-
net.
K. Weissenberger, 221(GQ):Nov83-633
Yatim, O.M. Chinese Islamic Wares in the
Collection of Muzium Negara.
Fong Peng-Khuan, 60:Jan-Feb83-138
Yeager, R.F., ed. John Gower Materials.
P. Gradon, 447(N&Q):Aug82-357
"The Yearbook of English Studies."* (Vol
9) (G.K. Hunter and C.J. Rawson, with J.
Mezciems, eds)
M. Meisel, 610:Winter81/82-59
"The Yearbook of English Studies." (Vol
12) (G.K. Hunter and C.J. Rawson, eds)
G.G. Colomb, 402(MLR):Oct83-885
"Yearbook of German-American Studies, 16."
(J.A. Burzle, ed)
H. Froeschle, 564:Sep83-231
Yearley, L.H. The Ideas of Newman.
W. Myers, 569(SR):Spring83-275
"The Year's Work in Modern Language
Studies."* (Vol 41, 1979) (G. Price
and D.A. Wells, eds)
O. Klapp, 547(RF):Band95Heft1/2-134
Y.M., 545(RPh):Nov82-317
"The Year's Work in Modern Language
Studies." (Vol 42, 1980) (G. Price
and D.A. Wells, eds)
O. Klapp, 547(RF):Band95Heft1/2-134
F. Pierce, 86(BHS):Apr83-137

Zeldis, C. A Forbidden Love.
    F. Schumer, 441:29Jan84-22
    M. Skakun, 390:Dec83-56
Zell, H.M., C. Bundy and V. Coulon. A New
  Reader's Guide to African Literature.
  (2nd ed)
    C. Hope, 617(TLS):6Apr84-379
Zeller, K. Pädagogik und Drama.*
    R.J. Alexander, 406:Fall83-334
Zeller, L. In the Country of the Anti-
  podes.
    T. Konyves, 137:Nov82-18
Zellers, M. 1984 Fielding's Caribbean.
  1984 Fielding's Economy Caribbean.
  Caribbean, the Inn Way.
    B.F. Carruthers, 37:Nov-Dec83-62
Zeman, H., ed. Die Österreichische Lit-
  eratur.
    J. Müller, 680(ZDP):Band102Heft2-289
Zenzinger, P. My Muse is British.
    D. Strauss, 588(SSL):Vol 18-291
Zepeda, O. When It Rains.
    R. Evans, 649(WAL):Feb84-368
Zéphir, J. Néo-féminisme de Simone de
  Beauvoir.
    A.D. Ketchum, 207(FR):May84-889
Zernack, K. - see Amburger, E.
von Zesen, P. Sämtliche Werke. (Vol 1,
  Pt 1) (F. van Ingen, ed)
    R.E. Schade, 133:Band16Heft1-66
    P. Skrine, 402(MLR):Jan83-227
Zetzel, J.E.G. Latin Textual Criticism in
  Antiquity.
    J.W. Halporn, 121(CJ):Feb/Mar84-267
Zewen, L. and others. The Great Wall.
    W.N., 102(CanL):Winter82-176
Zgórniak, M. Sytuacja militarna Europy
  1938r.
    R. Woytak, 497(PolR):Vol28No2-120
Zguta, R. Russian Minstrels.
    S. Beckwith, 187:Sep84-570
Zhadova, L.A. Malevich.*
    P. Overy, 592:Jan-Feb83-61
Zhang Geng and others. Zhongguo Xiqu tong-
  shi (A General History of Chinese Drama).
  (Vols Shang and Zhong)
    K.C. Leung, 116:Jul82-273
Zhongshu, W. - see under Wang Zhongshu
Ziegler, H. and C. Bigsby, eds. The
  Radical Imagination and the Liberal
  Tradition.
    J-M. Rabaté, 189(EA):Apr-Sep83-343
    295(JML):Nov83-416
Ziegler, K. - see Cicero
Zieroth, D. Mid-River.*
    L.R. Ricou, 102(CanL):Summer83-118
Ziff, L. Literary Democracy.*
    E.S. Fussell, 591(SIR):Spring83-146
    P. Shaw, 569(SR):Spring83-299
    M.R. Stern, 587(SAF):Spring83-120
    A.M. Woodlief, 577(SHR):Fall83-375
Zilli, L. - see du Ryer, P.
Zilliacus, H. and others. Fifty Oxyrhyn-
  chus Papyri.*
    E. Boswinkel, 394:Vol36fasc3/4-452
Zillig, W. Bewerten.
    B.J. Koekkoek, 221(GQ):May83-490
Zima, P.V. L'Ambivalence romanesque.
    G.R. Kaiser, 52:Band17Heft2-220
Zimmer, R.K. James Shirley.
    B.J. McMullin, 447(N&Q):Feb82-78
    J. Robertson, 161(DUJ):Jun83-128

Zimmerman, B.K. Biofuture.
    G. Kolata, 441:15Jul84-17
Zimmerman, F.B. Henry Purcell 1659-1695.
  (2nd ed)
    A.J.G.H., 617(TLS):23Mar84-319
Zimmermann, E. La Liberté et le destin
  dans le théâtre de Jean Racine.
    M. Danahy, 210(FrF):Sep83-276
Zimmermann, E. Elizabeth Zimmermann's
  Knitting Workshop.
    P. Bach, 614:Fall84-15
Zimmermann, F.W. - see al-Farabi
Zimmermann, M., ed. Die Sterzinger Miszel-
  laneen-Handschrift.
    F. Goldin, 589:Jul83-858
    A. Robertshaw, 402(MLR):Oct83-965
Zimmermann, P. - see Duchamp, M.
Zimmermann, R.C. Das Weltbild des jungen
  Goethe.* (Vol 2)
    E. Waniek, 221(GQ):Jan83-138
Zinberg, N.E. Drug, Set, and Setting.
    S.M. Wolfe, 441:16Sep84-31
Zindel, P. When a Darkness Falls.
    R. Smith, 441:19Feb84-22
Zinner, H. Die Lösung.
    H. Herting, 654(WB):5/1982-152
Zinoviev, A. The Reality of Communism.
    S. Hook, 617(TLS):6Apr84-365
Zinsser, W. Willie and Dwike.
    R.P. Brickner, 441:15Jul84-14
    442(NY):3Sep84-95
Ziolkowski, T. The Classical German Elegy
  1795-1950.*
    R. Dove, 402(MLR):Jan83-237
Ziolkowski, T. Varieties of Literary
  Thematics.
    A.K. Thorlby, 617(TLS):20Apr84-434
Zipes, J. Breaking the Magic Spell.*
    R.B. Bottigheimer, 196:Band24Heft3/4-
      339
    H. Poser, 406:Summer83-201
Zipes, J. The Trials and Tribulations of
  Little Red Riding Hood.
    G.A. De Candido, 441:6May84-27
Zippel, G. - see Valla, L.
Zlotchew, C.W. - see Sorrentino, F.
Zlotkowski, E.A. Heinrich Heines Reise-
  bilder.*
    R.C. Holub, 406:Winter83-445
Zlotowitz, B.M. The Septuagint Transla-
  tion of the Hebrew Terms in Relation
  to God in the Book of Jeremiah.
    W.L. Holladay, 318(JAOS):Oct-Dec82-662
Žmegač, V., ed. Deutsche Literatur der
  Jahrhundertwende.*
    I. Diersen, 654(WB):6/1982-171
Žmegač, V., Z. Škreb and L. Sekulić. Ge-
  schichte der deutschen Literatur von den
  Anfängen bis zur Gegenwart.
    D.F. Stout, 221(GQ):Nov83-627
Zohn, H. - see Kraus, K.
Zola, É. Correspondance.* (Vol 1) (B.H.
  Bakker, ed)
    J.H. Matthews, 593:Fall83-244
Zola, É. Correspondance.* (Vol 2) (B.H.
  Bakker, ed)
    J. Allard, 627(UTQ):Summer83-461
    J.H. Matthews, 593:Fall83-244
Zola, É. Correspondance.* (Vol 3) (B.H.
  Bakker, with C. Becker, eds)
    J. Allard, 627(UTQ):Summer83-461
    C.A. Burns, 402(MLR):Oct83-929
                                            [continued]

Zola, É. Correspondance. (Vol 3) [continuing]
  M.G. Lerner, 356(LR):Aug83-244
  J.H. Matthews, 593:Fall83-244
  P. Walker, 207(FR):Mar84-561
Zola, É. Correspondance. (Vol 4) (B.H. Bakker, ed)
  F.W.J. Hemmings, 617(TLS):29Jun84-730
Zola, É. The Earth. (D. Parmée, ed and trans)
  R. Lethbridge, 208(FS):Apr83-236
Zola, É. La Fortune des Rougon. La Curée. Au Bonheur des dames. L'Argent. (H. Mitterand, ed of all)
  R. Lethbridge, 208(FS):Apr83-235
Zola, É. La Terre. (H. Mitterand, ed)
  R. Lethbridge, 208(FS):Jan83-95
Zolla, E., ed. L'Esotismo nella Letteratura Anglo-americana. (Vol 3)
  R.A., 189(EA):Apr-Jun84-239
Zorc, R.D.P. The Bisayan Dialects of the Philippines.
  H.P. McKaughan, 205(ForL):Apr82-270
  J.U. Wolff, 318(JAOS):Jan-Mar82-147
Zorraquino, M.A.M. - see under Martín Zorraquino, M.A.
Zorzetti, N. La pretesta e il teatro latino arcaico.
  H.D. Jocelyn, 123:Vol33No1-22
Zschorsch, G. Klappmesser.
  J. Adler, 617(TLS):9Mar84-239
Zuber, O., ed. The Languages of Theatre.
  A.G. White, 615(TJ):Oct82-414
Zubiri, X. Inteligencia sentiente.
  J. Muñoz Millanes, 400(MLN):Mar83-321
Zucchelli, B. Varro Logistoricus.*
  J-C. Richard, 555:Vol57fasc2-334
Zuckerman, E. The Day After World War III.
  L. Freedman, 441:19Aug84-14
  T. Powers, 61:Jun84-115
Zumthor, P. Parler du Moyen Age.
  N.J. Lacy, 188(ECr):Spring83-104
Zürcher, W. - see Demosthenes
Zurier, R. The American Firehouse.
  J. Maass, 576:May83-189
Zvelebil, K.V. The Irula (Ĕṛla) Language. (Pt 2)
  D.W. McAlpin, 318(JAOS):Oct-Dec82-678
Zviadadze, G. Dictionary of Contemporary American English.
  T.C. Frazer, 350:Dec84-989
Zwalf, W. Heritage of Tibet.
  R.A. Perry, 529(QQ):Autumn83-915
Zwass, A. Planwirtschaft im Wandel der Zeit. Money, Banking and Credit in the Soviet Union and Eastern Europe.
  M.C. Kaser, 575(SEER):Apr83-307
Zweig, P. Walt Whitman.
  Q. Anderson, 441:6May84-1
  H. Bloom, 453(NYRB):26Apr84-3
Zweig, S. Beware of Pity.
  P. Lewis, 565:Vol124No3-36
Zweig, S. Le Monde d'hier.
  L. Arénilla, 450(NRF):Mar83-140
Zweig, S. Montaigne. (rev by J-L. Baudet)
  A. Reix, 542:Oct-Dec83-463
Zwerin, M. Close Enough for Jazz.
  B. Morton, 617(TLS):3Feb84-118
Zwicky, F. Hostages.
  E. Webby, 381:Sep83-399

Zyla, W.T. and W. Aycock, eds. Ibero-American Letters in a Comparative Perspective.
  N.T. Francis, 552(REH):Oct83-432
Zytaruk, G.J. and J.T. Boulton - see Lawrence, D.H.

WITHDRAWAL